Mapping the Social Landscape

359
775

441
450

Mapping the Social Landscape

Readings in Sociology

Fifth Edition

SUSAN J. FERGUSON
Grinnell College

Boston   Burr Ridge, IL   Dubuque, IA   New York   San Francisco   St. Louis
Bangkok   Bogotá   Caracas   Kuala Lumpur   Lisbon   London   Madrid   Mexico City
Milan   Montreal   New Delhi   Santiago   Seoul   Singapore   Sydney   Taipei   Toronto

Higher Education

MAPPING THE SOCIAL LANDSCAPE, FIFTH EDITION
Published by McGraw-Hill, an imprint of The McGraw-Hill Companies, Inc., 1221 Avenue of
the Americas, New York, NY 10020.

1 2 3 4 5 6 7 8 9 0 DOC/DOC 0 9 8 7

ISBN: 978-0-07-352807-6
MHID: 0-07-352807-2

Editor-in-chief: *Emily Barrosse*
Publisher: *Frank Mortimer*
Sponsoring editor: *Gina Boedeker*
Developmental editor: *Kate Scheinman*
Marketing manager: *Lori DeShazo*
Senior designer: *Cassandra Chu*
Cover designer: *Bill Stanton*
Senior production supervisor: *Richard DeVitto*
Production service: *Vicki Moran*
Compositor: *ICC Macmillan Inc.*
Typeface: *Palatino*
Printing: *R. R. Donnelley & Sons*

Cover images: Bus: © Atlantide Phototravel/Corbis
Mom & son: © Alain Nogues/Corbis
Tai Chi: Edward Keating/The New York Times/Redux Pictures

Library of Congress Cataloging-in-Publication Data

Mapping the social landscape: readings in sociology / [edited by] Susan J. Ferguson.—5th ed.
      p. cm
   Includes bibliographical references.
      ISBN 978-0-07-352807-6 (softcover)
      1. Social institutions.   2. Socialization.   3. Equality.   4. Social change.   5. Sociology.
I. Ferguson, Susan J.
HM826.M36 2008
301—dc22   2006941053

www.mhhe.com

With love to my grandmother, Edna Catherine Clark, who always believed that an education would open the doors of the world to me. She was right.

Preface

As the title suggests, *Mapping the Social Landscape* is about exploration and discovery. It means taking a closer look at a complex, ever-changing social world in which locations, pathways, and boundaries are not fixed. Because sociology describes and explains our social surroundings, it enables us to understand this shifting landscape. Thus, sociology is about discovering society and discovering ourselves. The purpose of this anthology is to introduce the discipline of sociology and to convey the excitement and the challenge of the sociological enterprise.

Although a number of readers in introductory sociology are already available for students, I have yet to find one that exposes students to the broad diversity of scholarship, perspectives, and authorship that exists within the field of sociology. This diversity goes beyond recognizing gender, racial-ethnic, and social class differences to acknowledging a plurality of voices and views within the discipline. Like other anthologies, this one includes classic works by authors such as Karl Marx, Max Weber, C. Wright Mills, Kingsley Davis, and Wilbert Moore; in addition, however, I have drawn from a wide range of contemporary scholarship, some of which provides newer treatments of traditional concepts. This diversity of viewpoints and approaches should encourage students to evaluate and analyze the sociological ideas and research findings presented.

In addition, because I find it invaluable in my own teaching to use examples from personal experiences to enable students to see the connection between "private troubles and public issues," as C. Wright Mills phrased it, I have included in this collection a few personal narratives to help students comprehend how social forces affect individual lives. Thus, this anthology includes classic as well as contemporary writings, and the voices of other social scientists who render provocative sociological insights. The readings also exemplify functionalist, conflict, and symbolic interactionist perspectives and different types of research methodology. Each article is preceded by a brief headnote that sets the context within which the reader can seek to understand the sociological work. Thus, the selections communicate an enthusiasm for sociology while illustrating sociological concepts, theories, and methods.

During the past 30 years, sociology has benefited from a rich abundance of creative scholarship, but many of these original works have not been adequately presented in textbooks or readers. I believe an introductory anthology needs to reflect the new questions concerning research and theory within the discipline. Moreover, I find that students enjoy reading the actual words and research of sociologists. This anthology, therefore, includes many cutting-edge pieces of sociological scholarship and some very recent publications by recognized social analysts. Current issues are examined, including childhood school cliques, tourism in Hawaii, depression and identity, gangs, the tattoo subculture, working at McDonald's, the effects of globalization, racism in the United States, socialization in law school, poverty, sexual assault on college campuses, working in a slaughterhouse, military boot camps, teen suicide, the mommy tax, eating disorders, prison riots, and the political influence of corporate PACs. In essence, I have attempted, not to break new ground, but, rather, to compile a collection that provides a fresh, innovative look at the discipline of sociology.

Changes to the Fifth Edition

With this fifth edition, I maintain a balance of classical and contemporary readings. In addition to many of the classic pieces that appeared in the fourth edition, I have included some new classics including Andrew J. Cherlin's "The Deinstitutionalization of American Marriage" and Eduardo Bonilla-Silva's "'New Racism,' Color-Blind Racism, and the Future of Whiteness in America." Both of these newer classic pieces are wonderful "lead" articles for the sections they are in, and they lay the groundwork for enhanced sociological understanding. Other changes I have made to this fifth edition include the addition of 23 new selections of cutting-edge contemporary sociological research that illustrate analyses of timely social issues and the intersections between race, social class, and gender. These new selections examine single motherhood, street vendors in New York City, the culture of fear, the socialization of exotic dancers, social interaction in toy stores, the transmission of wealth, ambiguous gender identity, globalization and business, faith in American workplaces, male-dominated athletics and school culture, transracial adoption, the increase in social isolation, social class and parenting styles, the U.S. health care system, media violence and children, and the 1995 Chicago heat wave. Among these readings are some selections that I consider to be contemporary classics in that they provide an overview of the discipline of sociology or a specific content area. These readings include an essay by Joel Best on the sociology of gloom; a now classic work by George Ritzer on the McDonaldization of society; and an essay by Jonathan Kozol on racial segregation in American schools. Based on the reviewers' comments, I also have extensively revised the sections on gender, race, health and medicine, and social change. I think the students will find the newer pieces in these sections more accessible and interesting. Of course, for all of the readings, I have tried to choose selections that are compelling to students and demonstrate well the diversity within the discipline of sociology. Please note that I welcome feedback from professors and students on this edition of *Mapping the Social Landscape*. You can e-mail me at Grinnell College. My e-mail address is fergusos@grinnell.edu.

Supplemental Learning Materials

I have written an accompanying test bank that contains numerous examination and discussion questions for each reading. As the editor of this anthology, I developed these items with the goal of helping instructors test students' understanding of key concepts and themes. Instructors can access this password-protected test bank on the Web site that accompanies the fifth edition of *Mapping the Social Landscape* at www.mhhe.com/ferguson5. Student resources, including extensive discussion questions and self-quizzes, are available on the student side of the same Web site.

Acknowledgments

The completion of this book involved the support and labor of many people. I would like to begin by acknowledging my former sociology editor, Serina Beauparlant of Mayfield Publishing Company, who challenged me, almost 12 years ago, to take on this project. Much of Serina's vision is contained within the structure of this book. Over the years we have spent many hours on the telephone debating the strengths and weaknesses of various readings. Serina, if I am a clutch hitter, then you are the phenomenal batting coach. I could not have asked for a more thoughtful and attentive sociology editor. Thank you for initiating this project with me.

I also am indebted to the Grinnell College faculty secretaries, Karen Groves, Karla Landers, and Linda Price, for their time typing and copying portions of the manuscript. My student research assistants, Abigail Hagel and Madison Van Oort, also need to be commended for copying material, carrying innumerable pounds of books between my office and the library, or helping me to write questions and find websites for the supplemental learning materials. I am especially indebted to Grinnell College for its generous research support.

Over the past twelve years, over 72 sociologists have reviewed earlier drafts of the manuscript and provided me with valuable observations concerning the readings and teaching introductory sociology. First and foremost, I want to acknowledge the early insights of Agnes Riedmann, who suggested several key pieces in the first draft. I also appreciate the suggestions for selections made by Joan Ferrante, Annette Lareau, and Michael Messner.

My special thanks go to Arnold Arluke, Northeastern University; Joanne M. Badagliacco, University of Kentucky; Gary L. Brock, Southwest Missouri State University; Tom Gerschick, Illinois State University; Thomas B. Gold, University of California at Berkeley; Jack Harkins, College of DuPage; Paul Kamolnick, East Tennesse State University; Peter Kivisto, Augustana College; Fred Kniss, Loyola University; Diane E. Levy, University of North Carolina at Wilmington; Peter Meiksins, Cleveland State University; Roslyn Arlin Mickelson, University of North Carolina at Charlotte; and Carol Ray,

San Jose State University, for their feedback on the first edition of the manuscript. As a team of reviewers, your detailed comments were enormously helpful in the tightening and refining of the manuscript. Moreover, your voices reflect the rich and varied experiences with teaching introductory sociology.

For the second edition, I would like to thank the following team of reviewers: Angela Danzi, State University of New York at Farmingdale; Diane Diamond, State University of New York at Stony Brook; Yvonne Downs, State University of New York at Fredonia; Kay Forest, Northern Illinois University; Bob Granfield, University of Denver; Susan Greenwood, University of Maine; Kate Hausbeck, University of Nevada at Las Vegas; Arthur J. Jipson, Miami University; James Jones, Mississippi State University; Carolyn A Kapinus, Penn State University; J. Richard Kendrick, Jr., State University of New York at Cortland; M. Kris McIlwaine, University of Arizona; Kristy McNamara, Furman University; Tracy Ore, University of Illinois at Urbana; Denise Scott, State University of New York at Geneseo; Maynard Seider, Massachusetts College of Liberal Arts; Thomas Soltis, Westmoreland County Community College; Martha Thompson, Northeastern Illinois University; Huiying Wei-Arthus, Weber State University; Adam S. Weinberg, Colgate University; Amy S. Wharton, Washington State University; and John Zipp, University of Wisconsin at Milwaukee.

For the third edition, I would like to thank the following reviewers: Stephen Adair, Central Connecticut State University; Javier Auyero, State University of New York, Stony Brook; David K. Brown, University of Illinois at Urbana-Champaign; Kay B. Forest, Northern Illinois University; Angela J. Hattery, Wake Forest University; Karen Honeycutt, University of Michigan; Neal King, Belmont University; Judith N. Lasker, Lehigh University; Rosemary F. Powers, Eastern Oregon University; Melissa Riba, Michigan State University; Deirdre Royster, University of Massachusetts, Amherst; James T. Salt, Lane Community College; H. Lovell Smith, Loyola College in Maryland; and Thomas Soltis, Westmoreland County Community College.

For the fourth edition, I would like to thank the following reviewers: Kevin J. Delaney, Temple University; Patricia L. Gibbs, Foothill College; Rebecca Klatch, University of California, San Diego; David Rohall, University of New Hampshire; Patricia Shropshire, Michigan State University; Thomas Soltis, Westmoreland County Community College; Kevin A. Tholin, Indiana University, South Bend; and several anonymous reviewers. All of your comments were extremely helpful to me during the revision process.

For the fifth edition, I would like to thank the following reviewers:

Thomas Brignall III, Tennessee Tech University;

Kenneth Colburn, Butler University; Susan A. Dumais, Louisiana State University;

Colleen R. Greer, Bemidji State University;

Joseph A. Kotarba, University of Houston;

Heather Laube, University of Michigan, Flint;

Philip Manning, Cleveland State University;

David Schweingruber, Iowa State University;

and Mohammad H. Tamdgidi, University of Massachusetts, Boston.

Finally, at McGraw-Hill Companies, I would like to recognize the creative and patient efforts of several individuals, including Cassandra Chu, Marty Granahan, Dan Loch, Kate Scheinman, and Amy Shaffer. I also want to acknowledge the detailed work of the copy editor, Margaret Moore, the permissions editor, Frederick Courtright, and the production editor, Vicki Moran. Thank you all for whipping my manuscript into shape!

Contents

Part II   CULTURE   62

Part III   SOCIALIZATION   102

Part IV   GROUPS AND SOCIAL STRUCTURE   155

Part VII   SOCIAL INSTITUTIONS   407

RELIGION

HEALTH AND MEDICINE

EDUCATION

THE FAMILY

Part VIII   SOCIAL CHANGE 650

Tell me the landscape in which you live, and I will tell you who you are.

José Ortega y Gasset

PART I

The Sociological Perspective

1

THE PROMISE

C. WRIGHT MILLS

The initial three selections examine the sociological perspective. The first of these is written by C. Wright Mills (1916–1962), a former professor of sociology at Columbia University. During his brief academic career, Mills became one of the best known and most controversial sociologists. He was critical of the U.S. government and other social institutions where power was unfairly concentrated. He also believed that academics should be socially responsible and speak out against social injustice. The excerpt that follows is from Mills' acclaimed book *The Sociological Imagination*. Since its original publication in 1959, this text has been required reading for most introductory sociology students around the world. Mills' sociological imagination perspective not only compels the best sociological analyses but also enables the sociologist and the individual to distinguish between "personal troubles" and "public issues." By separating these phenomena, we can better comprehend the sources of and solutions to social problems.

Nowadays men often feel that their private lives are a series of traps. They sense that within their everyday worlds, they cannot overcome their troubles, and in this feeling, they are often quite correct: What ordinary men are directly aware of and what they try to do are bounded by the private orbits in which they live; their visions and their powers are limited to the close-up scenes of job, family, neighborhood; in other milieux, they move vicariously and remain spectators. And the more aware they become, however vaguely, of ambitions and of threats which transcend their immediate locales, the more trapped they seem to feel.

Underlying this sense of being trapped are seemingly impersonal changes in the very structure of continent-wide societies. The facts of

---

This article was written in 1959 before scholars were sensitive to gender inclusivity in language. The references to masculine pronouns and men are, therefore, generic to both males and females and should be read as such. Please note that I have left the author's original language in this selection and other readings.—*Editor* contemporary history are also facts about the success and the failure of individual men and women. When a society is industrialized, a peasant becomes a worker; a feudal lord is liquidated or becomes a businessman. When classes rise or fall, a man is employed or unemployed; when the rate of investment goes up or down, a man takes new heart or goes broke. When wars happen, an insurance salesman becomes a rocket launcher; a store clerk, a radar man; a wife lives alone; a child grows up without a father. Neither the life of an individual nor the history of a society can be understood without understanding both.

Yet men do not usually define the troubles they endure in terms of historical change and institutional contradiction. The well-being they enjoy, they do not usually impute to the big ups and downs of the societies in which they live. Seldom aware of the intricate connection between the patterns of their own lives and the course of world history, ordinary men do not usually know what this connection means for the kinds of men they are becoming and for the kinds of history making in which they might take part. They do not possess the quality of mind essential to grasp the interplay of man and society, of biography and history, of self and world. They cannot cope with their personal troubles in such ways as to control the structural transformations that usually lie behind them.

Surely it is no wonder. In what period have so many men been so totally exposed at so fast a pace to such earthquakes of change? That Americans have not known such catastrophic changes as have the men and women of other societies is due to historical facts that are now quickly becoming "merely history." The history that now affects every man is world history. Within this scene and this period, in the course of a single generation, one-sixth of mankind is transformed from all that is feudal and backward into all that is modern, advanced, and fearful. Political colonies are freed; new and less visible forms of imperialism installed. Revolutions occur; men feel the intimate grip of new kinds of authority. Totalitarian societies rise and are smashed to bits—or succeed fabulously. After two centuries of ascendancy, capitalism is shown up as only one way to make society into an industrial apparatus. After two centuries of hope, even formal democracy is restricted to a quite small portion of mankind. Everywhere in the underdeveloped world, ancient ways of life are broken up and vague expectations become urgent demands. Everywhere in the overdeveloped world, the means of authority and of violence become total in scope and bureaucratic in form. Humanity itself now lies before us, the super-nation at either pole concentrating its most coordinated and massive efforts upon the preparation of World War Three.

The very shaping of history now outpaces the ability of men to orient themselves in accordance with cherished values. And which values? Even when they do not panic, men often sense that older ways of feeling and thinking have collapsed and that newer beginnings are ambiguous to the point of moral stasis. Is it any wonder that ordinary men feel they cannot cope with the larger worlds with which they are so suddenly confronted?

That they cannot understand the meaning of their epoch for their own lives? That—in defense of selfhood—they become morally insensible, trying to remain altogether private men? Is it any wonder that they come to be possessed by a sense of the trap?

It is not only information that they need—in this Age of Fact, information often dominates their attention and overwhelms their capacities to assimilate it. It is not only the skills of reason that they need—although their struggles to acquire these often exhaust their limited moral energy.

What they need, and what they feel they need, is a quality of mind that will help them to use information and to develop reason in order to achieve lucid summations of what is going on in the world and of what may be happening within themselves. It is this quality, I am going to contend, that journalists and scholars, artists and publics, scientists and editors are coming to expect of what may be called the sociological imagination.

The sociological imagination enables its possessor to understand the larger historical scene in terms of its meaning for the inner life and the external career of a variety of individuals. It enables him to take into account how individuals, in the welter of their daily experience, often become falsely conscious of their social positions. Within that welter, the framework of modern society is sought, and within that framework the psychologies of a variety of men and women are formulated. By such means the personal uneasiness of individuals is focused upon explicit troubles and the indifference of publics is transformed into involvement with public issues.

The first fruit of this imagination—and the first lesson of the social science that embodies it—is the idea that the individual can understand his own experience and gauge his own fate only by locating himself within his period, that he can know his own chances in life only by becoming aware of those of all individuals in his circumstances. In many ways it is a terrible lesson; in many ways a magnificent one. We do not know the limits of man's capacities for supreme effort or willing degradation, for agony or glee, for pleasurable brutality or the sweetness of reason. But in our time we have come to know that the limits of "human nature" are frighteningly broad. We have come to know that every individual lives, from one generation to the next, in some society; that he lives out a biography, and that he lives it out within some historical sequence. By the fact of his living he contributes, however minutely, to the shaping of this society and to the course of its history, even as he is made by society and by its historical push and shove.

The sociological imagination enables us to grasp history and biography and the relations between the two within society. That is its task and its promise. To recognize this task and this promise is the mark of the classic social analyst. It is characteristic of Herbert Spencer—turgid, polysyllabic, comprehensive; of E. A. Ross—graceful, muckraking, upright; of Auguste Comte and Emile Durkheim; of the intricate and subtle Karl Mannheim. It is the quality of all that is intellectually excellent in Karl Marx; it is the clue to

Thorstein Veblen's brilliant and ironic insight, to Joseph Schumpeter's many-sided constructions of reality; it is the basis of the psychological sweep of W. E. H. Lecky no less than of the profundity and clarity of Max Weber. And it is the signal of what is best in contemporary studies of man and society.

No social study that does not come back to the problems of biography, of history and of their intersections within a society, has completed its intellectual journey. Whatever the specific problems of the classic social analysts, however limited or however broad the features of social reality they have examined, those who have been imaginatively aware of the promise of their work have consistently asked three sorts of questions:

1. What is the structure of this particular society as a whole? What are its essential components, and how are they related to one another? How does it differ from other varieties of social order? Within it, what is the meaning of any particular feature for its continuance and for its change?

2. Where does this society stand in human history? What are the mechanics by which it is changing? What is its place within and its meaning for the development of humanity as a whole? How does any particular feature we are examining affect, and how is it affected by, the historical period in which it moves? And this period—what are its essential features? How does it differ from other periods? What are its characteristic ways of history making?

3. What varieties of men and women now prevail in this society and in this period? And what varieties are coming to prevail? In what ways are they selected and formed, liberated and repressed, made sensitive and blunted? What kinds of "human nature" are revealed in the conduct and character we observe in this society in this period? And what is the meaning for "human nature" of each and every feature of the society we are examining?

Whether the point of interest is a great power state or a minor literary mood, a family, a prison, a creed—these are the kinds of questions the best social analysts have asked. They are the intellectual pivots of classic studies of man in society—and they are the questions inevitably raised by any mind possessing the sociological imagination. For that imagination is the capacity to shift from one perspective to another—from the political to the psychological; from examination of a single family to comparative assessment of the national budgets of the world; from the theological school to the military establishment; from considerations of an oil industry to studies of contemporary poetry. It is the capacity to range from the most impersonal and remote transformations to the most intimate features of the human self—and to see the relations between the two. Back of its use there is always the urge to know the social and historical meaning of the individual in the society and in the period in which he has his quality and his being.

That, in brief, is why it is by means of the sociological imagination that men now hope to grasp what is going on in the world, and to understand what is happening in themselves as minute points of the intersections of biography and history within society. In large part, contemporary man's self-conscious view of himself as at least an outsider, if not a permanent stranger, rests upon an absorbed realization of social relativity and of the transformative power of history. The sociological imagination is the most fruitful form of this self-consciousness. By its use men whose mentalities have swept only a series of limited orbits often come to feel as if suddenly awakened in a house with which they had only supposed themselves to be familiar. Correctly or incorrectly, they often come to feel that they can now provide themselves with adequate summations, cohesive assessments, comprehensive orientations. Older decisions that once appeared sound now seem to them products of a mind unaccountably dense. Their capacity for astonishment is made lively again. They acquire a new way of thinking, they experience a transvaluation of values: in a word, by their reflection and by their sensibility, they realize the cultural meaning of the social sciences.

Perhaps the most fruitful distinction with which the sociological imagination works is between "the personal troubles of milieu" and "the public issues of social structure." This distinction is an essential tool of the sociological imagination and a feature of all classic work in social science.

Troubles occur within the character of the individual and within the range of his immediate relations with others; they have to do with his self and with those limited areas of social life of which he is directly and personally aware. Accordingly, the statement and the resolution of troubles properly lie within the individual as a biographical entity and within the scope of his immediate milieu—the social setting that is directly open to his personal experience and to some extent his willful activity. A trouble is a private matter: Values cherished by an individual are felt by him to be threatened.

Issues have to do with matters that transcend these local environments of the individual and the range of his inner life. They have to do with the organization of many such milieux into the institutions of a historical society as a whole, with the ways in which various milieux overlap and interpenetrate to form the larger structure of social and historical life. An issue is a public matter: Some value cherished by publics is felt to be threatened. Often there is a debate about what that value really is and about what it is that really threatens it. This debate is often without focus if only because it is the very nature of an issue, unlike even widespread trouble, that it cannot very well be defined in terms of the immediate and everyday environments of ordinary men. An issue, in fact, often involves a crisis in institutional arrangements, and often too it involves what Marxists call "contradictions" or "antagonisms."

In these terms, consider unemployment. When, in a city of 100,000, only one man is unemployed, that is his personal trouble, and for its relief we properly look to the character of the man, his skills, and his immediate opportunities. But when in a nation of 50 million employees, 15 million men are unemployed, that is an issue, and we may not hope to find its solution within the range of opportunities open to any one individual. The very structure of opportunities has collapsed. Both the correct statement of the problem and the range of possible solutions require us to consider the economic and political institutions of the society, and not merely the personal situation and character of a scatter of individuals.

Consider war. The personal problem of war, when it occurs, may be how to survive it or how to die in it with honor; how to make money out of it; how to climb into the higher safety of the military apparatus; or how to contribute to the war's termination. In short, according to one's values, to find a set of milieux and within it to survive the war or make one's death in it meaningful. But the structural issues of war have to do with its causes; with what types of men it throws up into command; with its effects upon economic and political, family and religious institutions, with the unorganized irresponsibility of a world of nation-states.

Consider marriage. Inside a marriage a man and a woman may experience personal troubles, but when the divorce rate during the first four years of marriage is 250 out of every 1,000 attempts, this is an indication of a structural issue having to do with the institutions of marriage and the family and other institutions that bear upon them.

Or consider the metropolis—the horrible, beautiful, ugly, magnificent sprawl of the great city. For many upper-class people, the personal solution to "the problem of the city" is to have an apartment with a private garage under it in the heart of the city, and forty miles out, a house by Henry Hill, garden by Garrett Eckbo, on a hundred acres of private land. In these two controlled environments—with a small staff at each end and a private helicopter connection—most people could solve many of the problems of personal milieux caused by the facts of the city. But all this, however splendid, does not solve the public issues that the structural fact of the city poses. What should be done with this wonderful monstrosity? Break it all up into scattered units, combining residence and work? Refurbish it as it stands? Or, after evacuation, dynamite it and build new cities according to new plans in new places? What should those plans be? And who is to decide and to accomplish whatever choice is made? These are structural issues; to confront them and to solve them requires us to consider political and economic issues that affect innumerable milieux.

Insofar as an economy is so arranged that slumps occur, the problem of unemployment becomes incapable of personal solution. Insofar as war is inherent in the nation-state system and in the uneven industrialization of the world, the ordinary individual in his restricted milieu will be powerless—with or without psychiatric aid—to solve the troubles this system or lack of system imposes upon him. Insofar as the family as an institution turns women into darling little slaves and men into their chief providers and unweaned dependents, the problem of a satisfactory marriage remains incapable of purely private solution. Insofar as the overdeveloped megalopolis and the overdeveloped automobile are built-in features of the overdeveloped society, the issues of urban living will not be solved by personal ingenuity and private wealth.

What we experience in various and specific milieux, I have noted, is often caused by structural changes. Accordingly, to understand the changes of many personal milieux we are required to look beyond them. And the number and variety of such structural changes increase as the institutions within which we live become more embracing and more intricately connected with one another. To be aware of the idea of social structure and to use it with sensibility is to be capable of tracing such linkages among a great variety of milieux. To be able to do that is to possess the sociological imagination.

2

PROMISES I CAN KEEP
Why Poor Women
Put Motherhood before Marriage

KATHRYN EDIN • MARIA KEFALAS

This reading by Kathryn Edin and Maria Kefalas is excerpted from their critically acclaimed book *Promises I Can Keep: Why Poor Women Put Motherhood before Marriage* (2005). Edin, an associate professor of sociology at the University of Pennsylvania, and Kefalas, an assistant professor of sociology at Saint Joseph's University in Philadelphia, spent five years talking with low-income mothers about their lives and how they perceive marriage and family. This excerpt is an example of sociological research that employs Mills' sociological imagination and, specifically, his distinction between personal troubles and public issues and also the importance of social researchers using the lenses of both biography and history to understand social phenomena. As Edin and Kefalas illustrate, when a middle- or upper-class woman cannot have a child it is seen as a personal tragedy, but when groups of lower-income women are having children outside of marriage, their fertility becomes a matter of public concern. In order to explain adequately why this distinction occurs, Edin and Kefalas examine both the biographies and the larger social contexts of poor women who become single mothers.

In spring 2002, the cover of *Time* magazine featured a controversial new book that claimed to "tell the truth" to ambitious young women hoping to have children. The book, *Creating a Life: Professional Women and the Quest for Children,* was written by economist Sylvia Ann Hewlett to "break the silence" about age-related infertility. Most professional women believe that female fertility doesn't begin to decline until after age forty, but Hewlett claims they are tragically wrong. Shockingly, she reports, the actual age is twenty-seven, and because of their misperception, large numbers of high-achieving women are left involuntarily childless. Having a baby "was supposed to be the easy part, right?" quips the *Time* cover story. "Not like getting into Harvard. Not like making partner. The baby was to be Mother Nature's gift. Anyone can do it; high school dropouts stroll through the mall with their babies in a Snugli. What can be so hard. . . ?"[1]

Hewlett's *Creating a Life* portrays involuntary childlessness as a tragedy for successful women who have played by the rules for the way a professional woman's life should unfold: get a college diploma, get even more education, get established in a career, get married, get more solidly established in that career, and then have a baby. But achieving these goals takes time—apparently more time for some than the biological clock allows.

Creating a Life didn't just make the cover of *Time;* it received extensive coverage in most major newspapers, including a three-part series in the London *Times,* and was named one of the ten best books of the year by *Business Week.* Hewlett appeared on *60 Minutes, The Today Show, Saturday Night Live, NBC Nightly News,* and *Oprah.* All this attention implies a great deal of public sympathy for the affluent highflier who inadvertently misses her chance to become a mother.

Our [research] also describes a crisis of fertility—one that occurs among a different population for very different reasons, and that draws a very different reaction from the general public. For those middle-class women Hewlett spoke to, the tragedy was unintended childlessness following educational and professional success. For the low-income women we spoke to, the tragedy is unintended pregnancy and childbirth before a basic education has been completed, while they are still poor and unmarried. How ironic that so many "Mistresses of the Universe" (as *Time* calls them) make all the right moves yet find they cannot have children, while those at the bottom of the American class ladder seem to have more children than they know what to do with.[2] And the plight of these poor women tends to generate not pity but outrage.

In 1950 only one in twenty children was born to an unmarried mother. Now the rate is more than one in three.[3] Having a child while single is three times as common for the poor as for the affluent.[4] Half of poor women who give birth while unmarried have no high school diploma at the time, and nearly a third have not worked at all in the last year.[5] First-time unwed mothers are also quite young—twenty-one on average.[6] And the situations of the men that father their children are not much better. More than four in ten poor men who have a child outside of marriage have already been to prison or jail by the time the baby is born; nearly half lack a high school diploma, and a quarter have no job. Thus it is not surprising that almost half of them earned less than $10,000 in the year before the birth.[7]

But there is another, even more pressing, reason to worry about the growing number of single mothers. Just when new legal and social freedoms, technological advances, and economic opportunities have given American women immense control over when (and if) they marry and when (and if) they choose to bear a child, social scientists have come to a troubling conclusion: children seem to benefit when parents get married and stay that way. Though many single mothers are admirable parents, it remains true that, on average, children raised outside of marriage typically learn less in school, are more likely to have children while they are teens, are less likely to graduate from high school and enroll in college, and have more trouble finding jobs as adults.[8] About half of the disadvantage occurs simply because their families have less money. Part of it arises because those who become single parents are more likely to be disadvantaged in other ways. But even when these factors are taken into account, children of single parents are still at greater risk.[9]

It is no surprise, therefore, that many Americans believe a whole host of social ills can be traced to the lapse in judgment that a poor, unmarried woman shows when she bears a child she can't afford. The solution to these problems seems obvious to most Americans: these young women should wait to have children until they are older and more economically stable, and they should get married first. Policymakers have been campaigning against teen childbearing for decades, and the downturn has been profound.[10] But because marriage rates for those in the prime family-building years have declined even more rapidly, nonmarital childbearing has continued to increase. Public concern over the rise in nonmarital childbearing cannot be dismissed as mere moralistic finger-pointing, since it is indeed true that if more of these mothers married their children's fathers, fewer would be poor.

In response, the Bush Administration resolved to restore marriage among the poor. Ironically, this controversial new domestic policy initiative has found encouragement in the work of liberal social scientists. A new landmark study of unwed couples, the Fragile Families and Child Wellbeing Study,[11] surveyed unmarried parents shortly after their child's birth. The results show that, contrary to popular perception, poor women who have children while unmarried are usually romantically involved with the baby's father when the child is born, and four in ten even live with him. More surprising still, given the stereotypes most Americans hold about poor single mothers, the vast majority of poor, unmarried new parents say they plan to marry each other.[12] But the survey also shows that their chances for marriage or for staying together over the long term are slim. It seems that the child's birth is a "magic moment" in the lives of these parents. And it is at this magic moment that Bush's marriage initiatives aim to intervene.

The "marriage cure" for poverty that the Bush administration launched has infuriated many on the political left. The *Village Voice* exclaims, "It's as if Washington had, out of nowhere, turned into a giant wedding chapel with

Bush performing the nuptials." A left-leaning columnist for the *Atlanta Journal and Constitution* insists, "Many of us don't believe that the traditional family is the only way to raise a healthy child. . . . A growing number of us will 'just say no.' And no amount of law is going to change that." The *San Jose Mercury News* editorializes, "It's impossible to justify spending $1.5 billion on unproven marriage programs when there's not enough to pay for back-to-work *basics* like child care." And on the web, a *Women's eNews* headline reads, "Bush Marriage Initiative Robs Billions from the Needy." Yet, a *Washington Post* editorial recently chided liberals for their "reflexive hostility" to the "not-so-shocking idea that for poor mothers, getting married might in some cases do more good than harm." "Why not find out," they ask, "whether helping mothers—and fathers—tackle the challenging task of getting and staying married could help families find their way out of poverty?"[13]

Even those who support the political agenda with regard to marriage acknowledge that if it is to succeed, we need to know why childbearing and marriage have become so radically decoupled among the poor. All policy should be based on a sound understanding of the realities it seeks to address. Since these trends first became apparent, some of the best scholars in America have sought answers, using the best survey data social science has at its disposal. They suggest several intuitively appealing answers—the extraordinary rise in women's employment that presumably allows them to more easily live apart from men, the decline of marriageable men in disadvantaged groups, or the expansion of the welfare state. Even taken together, however, these explanations can account for only a small portion of the dramatic break between marriage and childrearing that has occurred. So the reasons remain largely a mystery—perhaps the biggest demographic mystery of the last half of the twentieth century.

What is striking about the body of social science evidence is how little of it is based on the perspectives and life experiences of the women who are its subjects. Survey data can, of course, teach us a great deal, but surveys, though they have meticulously tabulated the trend, have led us to a dead end when it comes to fully understanding the forces behind it. Social science currently tells us much more about what *doesn't* explain the trend than what *does*, and it tells us next to nothing about what will make marriage more likely among single mothers.[14]

We provide new ideas about the forces that may be driving the trend by looking at the problems of family formation through the eyes of 162 low-income single mothers living in eight economically marginal neighborhoods across Philadelphia and its poorest industrial suburb, Camden, New Jersey. Their stories offer a unique point of view on the troubling questions of why low-income, poorly educated young women have children they can't afford and why they don't marry. *Promises I Can Keep* follows the course of couple relationships from the earliest days of courtship through the tumultuous months of pregnancy and into the magic moment of birth and beyond. It shows us what poor mothers think marriage and motherhood mean, and tells us why they nearly always put motherhood first.

These stories suggest that solving the mystery will demand a thorough reevaluation of the social forces at work behind the retreat from marriage, a trend affecting the culture as a whole, though its effects look somewhat different for the middle class than for the poor. But while members of the middle class delay marriage, they delay childbearing even more.[15] The poor also delay marriage—or avoid it altogether—but they have not delayed having children.[16]

The growing rarity of marriage among the poor, particularly prior to childbirth, has led some observers to claim that marriage has lost its meaning in low-income communities. We spent five years talking in depth with women who populate some of America's poorest inner-city neighborhoods and, to our surprise, found astonishingly little evidence of the much-touted rejection of the institution of marriage among the poor. In fact, these mothers told us repeatedly that they revered marriage and hoped to be married themselves one day. Marriage was a dream that most still longed for, a luxury they hoped to indulge in someday when the time was right, but generally not something they saw happening in the near, or even the foreseeable, future. Most middle-class women in their early to mid-twenties, the average age of the mothers we spoke to, would no doubt say the same, but their attitudes about childbearing would contrast sharply with those of our respondents. While the poor women we interviewed saw marriage as a luxury, something they aspired to but feared they might never achieve, they judged children to be a necessity, an absolutely essential part of a young woman's life, the chief source of identity and meaning.

To most middle-class observers, depending on their philosophical take on things, a poor woman with children but no husband, diploma, or job is either a victim of her circumstances or undeniable proof that American society is coming apart at the seams. But in the social world inhabited by poor women, a baby born into such conditions represents an opportunity to prove one's worth. The real tragedy, these women insist, is a woman who's missed her chance to have children.

The Stories the Mothers Tell

Young women like Antonia Rodriguez, who grow up in the slums of Philadelphia's inner core, first meet the men destined to become the fathers of their children in all the usual places: on the front stoop, in the high school hallway, in the homes of relatives and friends. Romance brings poor youth together as it does their middle-class peers. But rather than "hooking up," carefully avoiding conception, or ending an unwanted pregnancy, inner-city girls often become mothers before they leave their teens. [Our research] tells of romantic relationships that proceed at lightning speed—where a man woos a woman with the line "I want to have a baby by you," and she views it as high praise; where birth control is quickly abandoned, if practiced at all; and where conception often occurs after less than a year together. Stories like

Antonia's reveal why children are so seldom conceived by explicit design, yet are rarely pure accident either.

Mahkiya Washington . . . illustrates how the news of a pregnancy can quickly put a fledgling romantic relationship into overdrive. How does the man who can do no wrong become the deadbeat who can do nothing right, even though his behavior may not change much at all? And how does he feel when his admiring girlfriend is transformed into the demanding woman who is about to become his baby's mother? The experiences of women like Mahkiya illustrate how an expectant mother uses pregnancy to test the strength of her bond with her man and take a measure of his moral worth. Can he "get himself together"—find a job, settle down, and become a family man—in time? What explosive confrontations result when he doesn't? Why do some men who once prodded their girlfriends toward pregnancy end up greeting the news with threats, denials, abandonment, and sometimes physical violence?

Yet the most remarkable part of the stories many mothers tell is of relational transformation at the "magic moment" of birth. Few couples escape some form of relational trauma during pregnancy, and for some the distress becomes extreme. So how does it happen that by the time the baby is ready to leave the hospital, most couples have reunited and committed themselves to staying together? The euphoria of the birth may suddenly resolve the tumultuousness of the previous nine months; even a father who has tried desperately to avoid impending fatherhood—by demanding that his girlfriend abort the baby or by claiming the child is not his, thus branding her as a "cheater" or "whore"—may feel a powerful bond with his newborn, so much so that he may vow to mend his ways. The mothers are all too eager to believe these promises.

Still, despite these young couples' new resolve to stay together, most relationships end long before the child enters preschool. . . . When we first meet Jen Burke, Rick, the father of her two-year-old son, has just proposed to her. Now, with a second baby on the way, he says he is ready for marriage. Surprisingly, when we run into Jen a couple of months later, Rick is no longer in the picture at all. What accounts for the high rate of relationship failure among couples like Jen and Rick? The lack of a job can cause strain, but it's seldom the relationship breaker. Sometimes, it's the man's unwillingness to "stay working" even when he can find a job—that was one of Jen's problems with Rick. Or he may blow his earnings on partying or stereo equipment. But most women point to larger problems than a lack of money, such as Rick's chronic womanizing. The stories these women tell uncover the real sources of relational ruin.

But what about the couples that stay together—why don't they marry? . . . We tell the story of Deena Vallas, who has had one nonmarital birth and is about to have another. She's in a stable relationship with the unborn child's father, a steady worker in a legitimate job who's off drugs, doesn't beat her or cheat on her, and eagerly plays daddy to her son, a child from a prior relationship. Yet there's no marriage. Is that a sign that marriage has no meaning in poor neighborhoods like hers? No. Her story doesn't indicate a disinterest in marriage; to the contrary, she believes her reluctance shows her deep reverence for marriage. So why does she feel she must avoid marriage for now?

Stories like Deena's show that the retreat from marriage among the poor flows out of a radical redefinition of what marriage means. In the 1950s childrearing was the primary function of marriage, but, as we show, these days the poor see its function very differently. A steady job and the ability to pay the rent on an apartment no longer automatically render a man marriageable. We investigate exactly what does.

Poor women often say they don't want to marry until they are "set" economically and established in a career. A young mother often fears marriage will mean a loss of control—she believes that saying "I do" will suddenly transform her man into an authoritarian head of the house who insists on making all the decisions, who thinks that he "owns" her. Having her own earnings and assets buys her some "say-so" power and some freedom from a man's attempts to control her behavior. After all, she insists, a woman with money of her own can credibly threaten to leave and take the children with her if he gets too far out of line. But this insistence on economic independence also reflects a much deeper fear: no matter how strong the relationship, somehow the marriage will go bad. Women who rely on a man's earnings, these mothers warn, are setting themselves up to be left with nothing if the relationship ends.

So does marriage merely represent a list of financial achievements? Not at all. The poor women we talked to insist it means lifelong commitment. In a surprising reversal of the middle-class norm, they believe it is better to have children outside of marriage than to marry unwisely only to get divorced later. One might dismiss these poor mothers' marriage aspirations as deep cynicism, candy-coated for social science researchers, yet demographers project that more than seven in ten will marry someone eventually. What moral code underlies the statement of one mother who said, "I don't believe in divorce—that's why none of the women in my family are married"? And what does it take to convince a young mother that her relationship is safe enough from the threat of divorce to risk marriage?

Dominique Watkins' story illustrates why poor young mothers seldom view an out-of-wedlock birth as a mark of personal failure, but instead see it as an act of valor. [Our research] reveals our mothers' remarkable confidence in their ability to parent their children well and describes the standards they hold themselves to. As we explain, it is possible for a poor woman to judge her mothering a success even when her child fails in school, gets pregnant as a teen, becomes addicted to drugs, or ends up in juvenile detention. The women whose stories we share believe the central tenet of good mothering can be summed up in two words—being there. This unique definition of good parenting allows mothers to take great pride in having enough Pampers to diaper an infant, in potty training a two-year-old and teaching her to eat with a spoon, in getting a grade-schooler to and from school safely, in satisfying the ravenous appetite of a growing teenager, and in keeping the light on to welcome a prodigal adolescent back home.

. . . Millie Acevedo, who, like many of her friends and neighbors, believes that having children young is a normal part of life, though she admits she and Carlos got started a year or two earlier than they should have. Millie's story helps to resolve a troubling contradiction raised in our earlier account: If the poor hold marriage to such a high standard, why don't they do the same for childbearing? Shouldn't they audition their male partners even more carefully for the father role than they do for the husband role? Millie's experiences show why the standards for prospective fathers appear to be so low. The answer is tangled up in these young women's initial high hopes regarding the men in their lives, and the supreme confidence they have in their ability to rise to the challenge of motherhood. The key to the mystery lies not only in what mothers believe they can do for their children, but in what they hope their children will do for them.

Through the tales of mothers like Millie we paint a portrait of the lives of these young women before pregnancy, a portrait that details the extreme loneliness, the struggles with parents and peers, the wild behavior, the depression and despair, the school failure, the drugs, and the general sense that life has spun completely out of control. Into this void comes a pregnancy and then a baby, bringing the purpose, the validation, the companionship, and the order that young women feel have been so sorely lacking. In some profound sense, these young women believe, a baby has the power to solve everything.

The redemptive stories our mothers tell speak to the primacy of the mothering role, how it can become virtually the only source of identity and meaning in a young woman's life. There is an odd logic to the statements mothers made when we asked them to imagine life without children: "I'd be dead or in jail," "I'd still be out partying," "I'd be messed up on drugs," or "I'd be nowhere at all." These mothers, we discovered, almost never see children as bringing them hardship; instead, they manage to credit virtually every bit of good in their lives to the fact they have children—they believe motherhood has "saved" them.

Eight Philadelphia Neighborhoods

As is the case for all Americans—regardless of their circumstances—people's beliefs about the meaning of marriage and children draw first from the family of origin. As children move into adolescence and adulthood, the hundreds of daily interactions they have both within and outside the family—with kin, neighbors, teachers, and peers—further shape their view of what "family" means. America's poor live in a wide array of communities, but since the 1970s, they have increasingly come to live in urban neighborhoods with people who are as disadvantaged as they are. It is these poor urban neighborhoods that have seen the most dramatic increases in single motherhood.[17]

The Philadelphia area, the setting for our story, has more than its fair share of such neighborhoods. . . . America's fifth-largest city entered the twenty-first century with almost a quarter of its citizens, and nearly a third of its children, living in poverty.[18] This is precisely why it was a perfect site for our research. Because of the high rates of poverty there, we found poor whites, blacks, and Latinos living in roughly similar circumstances. Though racial minorities often live in high-poverty neighborhoods, cities where whites live in the same circumstances are rare. The white urban poor usually live in mixed-income neighborhoods and thus have considerable advantages over the minority poor—better schools, better parks and recreational facilities, better jobs, safer streets, and so on. But in Philadelphia, the high poverty rates in several former white ethnic strongholds—those once-proud industrial villages—create a rare opportunity for students of race and inequality to study whites, Latinos, and African Americans whose social contexts are quite similar. This unique feature of our study may explain why we found the experiences and worldviews of these groups to be so similar, and why class, not race, is what drives much of our account.

We share the stories of the residents of eight hardscrabble neighborhoods across Philadelphia and its inner industrial suburbs: East Camden, Kensington, North Camden, North Central, PennsPort, South Camden, Strawberry Mansion, and West Kensington. . . . In each of these neighborhoods, we followed the tack we had taken in Camden and spent time talking to local business owners, representatives of grassroots neighborhood organizations and institutions, and private social services agencies to get some sense of the range of families who lived there. These contacts led us to an initial group of low-income single mothers of black, white, and Puerto Rican descent who were willing to share their lives with us. These mothers then introduced us to others in similar situations. We aimed for 50 to 60 mothers from each racial and ethnic group, and talked in depth with 162 mothers in all.

We limited our sample to mothers who had earned less than $16,000 in the past year, an amount about equal to the federal poverty line in those years. We wanted to capture both welfare-reliant mothers and mothers working at low-wage jobs. And because of the unusually strong economy at the time, women leaving welfare for employment were averaging $8 per hour in earnings, an annualized income of $16,000 for a full-time worker.[19] All of them lived in neighborhoods where at least 20 percent of the residents were poor. Each had at least one child under eighteen living at home, and though some had been married, all were now single, at least in the legal sense, although most did not live on their own or apart from male partners: only about three in ten maintained their own households. Nearly half were doubled up with relatives or friends, but a smaller yet significant number were living with men.[20] Some of these men were the fathers of at least one of their children, but others were boyfriends who had not yet fathered any children with the mother.

Mothers ranged in age from fifteen to fifty-six, but were twenty-five years old on average. Forty-five percent had no high school diploma, but

15 percent had earned a GED. A surprising number, nearly a third of the total, had participated in some kind of post–high school educational activities such as college, nurses- or teachers-aid training, or cosmetology school. Nearly three-quarters (73 percent) had borne their first child when they were still in their teens. Mothers under twenty-five had 1.6 children, while those twenty-five and older had 3.1 children on average. Almost half had collected cash welfare at some point in the past two years, and almost half were neither working nor in school when we met them. Forty percent held low-end service-sector jobs at the time, working as telemarketers, childcare workers, teacher's aids, nurse's aids, factory workers, cashiers, fast-food workers, waitresses, and the like.[21]

Aside from our informal interactions, we sat down with each mother for at least two in-depth conversations that we taped and transcribed. These focused exchanges typically lasted two to three hours and usually took place in the mother's own home, often around the kitchen table. When we could, we drove mothers to work or accompanied them on errands. Sometimes we were lucky enough to be invited to family gatherings such as birthday parties, christenings, sixth-grade graduation celebrations, and even a wedding or two.

Our goal was to give poor single mothers the opportunity to address the questions so many affluent Americans ask about them: namely, why they so seldom marry, and why they have children when they have to struggle so hard to support them. In the course of our conversations, we learned something of their life histories, including how they met their children's fathers, what happened in the relationship as they moved through pregnancy and birth, and where things stood for them at the present. We also learned much about how motherhood had affected their lives. Women openly, and often eagerly, shared life lessons they had learned about relationships, marriage, and children.

ENDNOTES

[1] Nancy Gibbs, "Making Time for a Baby," *Time,* April 15, 2002, 48–58.

[2] Only two in ten high school dropouts reach age twenty-five without having borne a child, almost always outside of marriage, and few are childless by age forty. Meanwhile, nearly 25 percent of middle-class women reach forty without having any children (Ellwood and Jencks 2001).

[3] *National Vital Statistics Reports,* 51, no. 11 (June 25, 2003): 3, table A.

[4] Ellwood and Jencks use education, not income, as a measure of socioeconomic status. The comparison referred to here as between the "poor" and "affluent" is between the least educated third and the most educated third of the educational distribution. See Ellwood and Jencks (2001).

[5] Unpublished figures from the Fragile Families and Child Wellbeing Study (McLanahan et al. 2003), calculated by Marcia Carlson. These figures are for all unmarried mothers in the survey sample (not just those with first births) who reported annual incomes below the federal poverty threshold, and their male partners.

[6] Wu, Bumpass, and Musick (2001).

[7] Unpublished figures from the Fragile Families and Child Wellbeing Study, calculated by Marcia Carlson. These figures are for all unmarried mothers in the survey sample (not just

those with first births) who reported annual incomes below the federal poverty threshold, and their male partners.

[8] McLanahan and Sandefur (1994).

[9] Parke (2003).

[10] Child Trends (2002).

[11] The Fragile Families and Child Wellbeing Study (McLanahan et al. 2003) is a longitudinal survey of roughly five thousand couples who had just had a child. About three-fourths of these couples were not married at the time of the birth. The survey, when weighted, is nationally representative of nonmarital births in cities of more than two hundred thousand people. Both parents were surveyed soon after the child's birth and again when their child reached ages twelve, thirty-six, and sixty months. Hereafter referred to as the Fragile Families Study.

[12] These unpublished figures, compiled by Marcia Carlson, are for mothers responding to the survey whose annual income was below the federal poverty line. For a description of the sample as a whole, see "Is Marriage a Viable Alternative for Fragile Families?" Fragile Families Research Brief 9 (Princeton, NJ: Center for Child Wellbeing, Princeton University, June 2002).

[13] Sharon Lerner, "Bush's Marriage Proposal," *Village Voice*, May 1–7, 2002; Diane Glass, "Do We Need Stronger Family Values?" *Atlanta Journal and Constitution*, July 31, 2003; "Quick Hit" (editorial), *San Jose Mercury News*, September 19, 2003; Elizabeth Bauchner, "Bush Marriage Initiative Robs Billions from the Needy," *Women's eNews*, September 10, 2003 (www.womensenews.org); "The Left's Marriage Problem," *Washington Post*, April 5, 2002, A22.

[14] Ellwood and Jencks (2001).

[15] Even those who marry may not remain so; more than 40 percent of first marriages now end in divorce, and subsequent marriages dissolve at an even higher rate (Bramlett and Mosher 2001).

[16] See U.S. Census Bureau (2002) and earlier reports, as well as Ellwood and Jencks (2001).

[17] Wilson (1987).

[18] Annie E. Casey Foundation (2001).

[19] The exact figures, collected at only two points in time, are $7.20 in 1998 and $8.60 in 2002. See Michalopolous et al. (2003). Note that not all of those who left welfare for work worked full time.

[20] Just over 7 percent of those doubled up with relatives or friends also had a boyfriend living with them. In total, 30 percent lived with a boyfriend and 22 percent with a boyfriend alone.

[21] All mothers' reported incomes were below the poverty line for a family of four, and all had at least one minor child living with them. All were currently single, but a relatively small number had been married.

REFERENCES

Annie E. Casey Foundation. 2001. *City Kids Count: Data on the Wellbeing of Children in Large Cities.* Baltimore, MD: Annie E. Casey Foundation.

Bramlett, Matthew D. and William T. Mosher. 2001. "First Marriage Dissolution, Divorce, and Remarriage: United States." *Advance Data from Vital and Health Statistics.* No. 323. Hyattsville, MD: National Center for Health Statistics.

Child Trends. 2002. "Facts at a Glance 2002: Annual Newsletter on Teen Pregnancy." No. 2002–50.

Ellwood, David T. and Christopher Jencks. 2001. "The Spread of Single-Parent Families in the United States since 1960." Cambridge, MA: John F. Kennedy School of Government, Harvard University.

McLanahan, Sara S., Irwin Garfinkel, Nancy Reichman, Julian Teitler, Marcia Carlson, and Christina Norland Audigier. 2003. *The Fragile Families and Child Wellbeing Study: Baseline National Report.* Princeton University.

McLanahan, Sara S. and Gary Sandefur. 1994. *Growing Up with a Single Parent: What Helps, What Hurts.* Cambridge, MA: Harvard University Press.

Michalopoulos, Charles, Kathryn Edin, Barbara Fink, Mirella Landriscina, Denise Polit, Judy Polyne, Lashawn Richburg-Hayes, David Seith, and Nandita Verma. 2003. *Welfare Reform in Philadelphia: Implementation, Effects, and Experiences of Poor Families and Neighborhoods.* New York: Manpower Demonstration Research Corporation.

Parke, Mary. 2003. "Are Married Parents Really Better for Children? What Research Says about the Effects of Family Structure on Child Well-Being." Policy Brief 3, Couples and Marriage Series. Washington, DC: Center for Law and Social Policy.

U.S. Census Bureau. 2002. "Children's Living Arrangements and Characteristics." Annual Demographic Supplement to the March 2002 Current Population Survey. Current Population Reports, Series P20–547. Washington, DC: U.S. Government Printing Office.

Wilson, William Julius. 1987. *The Truly Disadvantaged: The Inner City, the Underclass, and Public Policy.* Chicago: University of Chicago Press.

Wu, Lawrence L., Larry L. Bumpass, and Kelly Musick. 2001. "Historical and Life-Course Trajectories of Nonmarital Childbearing." Pp. 3–48 in *Out of Wedlock: Causes and Consequences of Nonmarital Fertility,* edited by Lawrence L. Wu and Barbara Wolfe. New York: Russell Sage Foundation.

3

AN INTERSECTION OF BIOGRAPHY AND HISTORY
My Intellectual Journey

MARY ROMERO

This selection by Mary Romero is another example of C. Wright Mills' sociological imagination. Romero is a professor in the School of Justice and Social Inquiry at Arizona State University, where she teaches sociology and Chicano studies. In this excerpt, Romero explains how biography and history influenced her investigation of domestic service work done by Chicanas. In particular, she describes her research process, which involved reinterpreting her own and others' domestic service experiences within the larger work history of Mexican Americans and the devaluation of housework. Thus, this selection is from the introduction to Romero's 1992 book, *Maid in the U.S.A.,* a study of domestic work and the social interactions between domestics and their employers.

When I was growing up many of the women whom I knew worked cleaning other people's houses. Domestic service was part of my taken-for-granted reality. Later, when I had my own place, I considered housework something you did before company came over. My first thought that domestic service and housework might be a serious research interest came as a result of a chance encounter with live-in domestics along the

U.S.–Mexican border. Before beginning a teaching position at the University of Texas at El Paso, I stayed with a colleague while apartment hunting. My colleague had a live-in domestic to assist with housecleaning and cooking. Asking around, I learned that live-in maids were common in El Paso, even among apartment and condominium dwellers. The hiring of maids from Mexico was so common that locals referred to Monday as the border patrol's day off because the agents ignored the women crossing the border to return to their employers' homes after their weekend off. The practice of hiring undocumented Mexican women as domestics, many of whom were no older than 15, seemed strange to me. It was this strangeness that raised the topic of domestic service as a question and made problematic what had previously been taken for granted.

I must admit that I was shocked at my colleague's treatment of the 16-year-old domestic whom I will call Juanita. Only recently hired, Juanita was still adjusting to her new environment. She was extremely shy, and her timidity was made even worse by constant flirting from her employer. As far as I could see, every attempt Juanita made to converse was met with teasing so that the conversation could never evolve into a serious discussion. Her employer's sexist, paternalistic banter effectively silenced the domestic, kept her constantly on guard, and made it impossible for her to feel comfortable at work. For instance, when she informed the employer of a leaky faucet, he shot her a look of disdain, making it clear that she was overstepping her boundaries. I observed other encounters that clearly served to remind Juanita of her subservient place in her employer's home.

Although Juanita was of the same age as my colleague's oldest daughter and but a few years older than his two sons, she was treated differently from the other teenagers in the house. She was expected to share her bedroom with the ironing board, sewing machine, and other spare-room types of objects.[1] More importantly, she was assumed to have different wants and needs. I witnessed the following revealing exchange. Juanita was poor. She had not brought toiletries with her from Mexico. Since she had not yet been paid, she had to depend on her employer for necessities. Yet instead of offering her a small advance in her pay so she could purchase the items herself and giving her a ride to the nearby supermarket to select her own toiletries, the employer handled Juanita's request for toothbrush, toothpaste, shampoo, soap, and the like in the following manner. In the presence of all the family and the houseguest, he made a list of the things she needed. Much teasing and joking accompanied the encounter. The employer shopped for her and purchased only generic brand items, which were a far cry from the brand-name products that filled the bathroom of his 16-year-old daughter. Juanita looked at the toothpaste, shampoo, and soap with confusion; she may never have seen generic products before, but she obviously knew that a distinction had been made.

One evening I walked into the kitchen as the employer's young sons were shouting orders at Juanita. They pointed to the dirty dishes on the table and pans in the sink and yelled "WASH!" "CLEAN!" Juanita stood frozen next to the kitchen door, angry and humiliated. Aware of possible repercussions for Juanita if I reprimanded my colleague's sons, I responded awkwardly by reallocating chores to everyone present. I announced that I would wash the dishes and the boys would clear the table. Juanita washed and dried dishes alongside me, and together we finished cleaning the kitchen. My colleague returned from his meeting to find us in the kitchen washing the last pan. The look on his face was more than enough to tell me that he was shocked to find his houseguest—and future colleague—washing dishes with the maid. His embarrassment at my behavior confirmed my suspicion that I had violated the normative expectations of class behavior within the home. He attempted to break the tension with a flirtatious and sexist remark to Juanita which served to excuse her from the kitchen and from any further discussion.

The conversation that followed revealed how my colleague chose to interpret my behavior. Immediately after Juanita's departure from the kitchen, he initiated a discussion about "Chicano radicals" and the Chicano movement. Although he was a foreign-born Latino, he expressed sympathy for *la causa*. Recalling the one Chicano graduate student he had known to obtain a Ph.D. in sociology, he gave several accounts of how the student's political behavior had disrupted the normal flow of university activity. Lowering his voice to a confidential whisper, he confessed to understanding why Marxist theory has become so popular among Chicano students. The tone of his comments and the examples that he chose made me realize that my "outrageous" behavior was explained, and thus excused, on the basis of my being one of those "Chicano radicals." He interpreted my washing dishes with his maid as a symbolic act; that is, I was affiliated with *los de abajo.*

My behavior had been comfortably defined without addressing the specific issue of maids. My colleague then further subsumed the topic under the rubric of "the servant problem" along the border. (His reaction was not unlike the attitude employers have displayed toward domestic service in the United States for the last hundred years.)[2] He began by providing me with chapter and verse about how he had aided Mexican women from Juarez by helping them cross the border and employing them in his home. He took further credit for introducing them to the appliances found in an American middle-class home. He shared several funny accounts about teaching country women from Mexico to use the vacuum cleaner, electric mixer, and microwave (remember the maid scene in the movie *El Norte*?) and implicitly blamed them for their inability to work comfortably around modern conveniences. For this "on-the-job training" and introduction to American culture, he complained, his generosity and goodwill had been rewarded by a high turnover rate. As his account continued, he assured me that most maids were simply working until they found a husband. In his experience they worked for a few months or less and then did not return to work on Monday morning after their first weekend off. Of course it never dawned on him that they may simply have found a job with better working conditions.

The following day, Juanita and I were alone in the house. As I mustered up my best Spanish, we shared information about our homes and families. After a few minutes of laughter about my simple sentence structure, Juanita lowered her head and in a sad, quiet voice told me how isolated and lonely she felt in this middle-class suburb literally within sight of Juarez. Her feelings were not the consequence of the work or of frustrations with modern appliances, nor did she complain about the absence of Mexican people in the neighborhood; her isolation and loneliness were in response to the norms and values surrounding domestic service. She described the situation quite clearly in expressing puzzlement over the social interactions she had with her employer's family: Why didn't her employer's children talk to her or include her in any of their activities when she wasn't working? Her reaction was not unlike that of Lillian Pettengill, who wrote about her two-year experience as a domestic in Philadelphia households at the turn of the century: "I feel my isolation alone in a big house full of people."[3]

Earlier in the day, Juanita had unsuccessfully tried to initiate a conversation with the 16-year-old daughter while she cleaned her room. She was of the same age as the daughter (who at that moment was in bed reading and watching TV because of menstrual cramps—a luxury the maid was not able to claim). She was rebuffed and ignored and felt that she became visible only when an order was given. Unable to live with this social isolation, she had already made up her mind not to return after her day off in Juarez. I observed the total impossibility of communication. The employer would never know why she left, and Juanita would not know that she would be considered simply another ungrateful Mexican whom he had tried to help.

After I returned to Denver, I thought a lot about the situations of Juanita and the other young undocumented Mexican women living in country club areas along the border. They worked long days in the intimacy of American middle-class homes but were starved for respect and positive social interaction. Curiously, the employers did not treat the domestics as "one of the family," nor did they consider themselves employers. Hiring a domestic was likely to be presented within the context of charity and good works; it was considered a matter of helping "these Mexican women" rather than recognized as a work issue.

I was bothered by my encounter along the border, not simply for the obvious humanitarian reasons, but because I too had once worked as a domestic, just as my mother, sister, relatives, and neighbors had. As a teenager, I cleaned houses with my mother on weekends and vacations. My own working experience as a domestic was limited because I had always been accompanied by my mother or sister instead of working alone. Since I was a day worker, my time in the employer's home was limited and I was able to return to my family and community each day. In Juanita's situation as a live-in domestic, there was no distinction between the time on and off work. I wondered whether domestic service had similarly affected my mother, sister, and neighbors. Had they too worked beyond the agreed-upon time? Did they have difficulty managing relationships with employers? I never worked alone and was spared the direct negotiations with employers. Instead, I cooperated with my mother or sister in completing the housecleaning as efficiently and quickly as possible.

I could not recall being yelled at by employers or their children, but I did remember anger, resentment, and the humiliation I had felt at kneeling to · scrub other people's toilets while they gave step-by-step cleaning instructions. I remember feeling uncomfortable around employers' children who never acknowledged my presence except to question where I had placed their belongings after I had picked them up off the floor to vacuum. After all, my experience was foreign to them; at the age of 14 I worked as a domestic while they ran off to swimming, tennis, and piano lessons. Unlike Juanita, I preferred to remain invisible as I moved around the employer's house cleaning. Much later, I learned that the invisibility of workers in domestic service is a common characteristic of the occupation. Ruth Schwartz Cowan has commented on the historical aspect of invisibility:

> The history of domestic service in the United States is a vast, unresolved puzzle, because the social role "servant" so frequently carries with it the unspoken adjective *invisible*. In diaries and letters, the "invisible" servant becomes visible only when she departs employment ("Mary left today"). In statistical series, she appears only when she is employed full-time, on a live-in basis; or when she is willing to confess the nature of her employment to a census taker, and (especially since the Second World War) there have frequently been good reasons for such confessions to go unmade.[4]

Although I remained invisible to most of the employers' family members, the mothers, curiously enough, seldom let me move around the house invisibly, dusting the woodwork and vacuuming carpets. Instead, I was subjected to constant supervision and condescending observations about "what a good little girl I was, helping my mother clean house." After I had moved and cleaned behind a hide-a-bed and Lazy-boy chair, vacuumed three floors including two sets of stairs, and carried the vacuum cleaner up and downstairs twice because "little Johnny" was napping when I was cleaning the bedrooms—I certainly didn't feel like a "little girl helping mother." I felt like a domestic worker!

There were employers who attempted to draw parallels between my adolescent experience and their teenagers' behavior: they'd point to the messy bedrooms and claim, "Well, you're a teenager, you understand clothes, books, papers, and records on the floor." Even at 14, I knew that being sloppy and not picking up after yourself was a privilege. I had two brothers and three sisters. I didn't have my own bedroom but shared a room with my sisters. Not one of us would think of leaving our panties on the floor for the others to pick up. I didn't bother to set such employers straight but continued to clean in silence, knowing that at the end of the day I would get cash and confident that I would soon be old enough to work elsewhere.

Many years later, while attending graduate school, I returned to domestic service as an "off-the-record" means to supplement my income. Graduate fellowships and teaching assistantships locked me into a fixed income that frequently was not enough to cover my expenses.[5] So once again I worked alongside my mother for seven hours as we cleaned two houses. I earned about 50 dollars for the day. Housecleaning is strenuous work, and I returned home exhausted from climbing up and down stairs, bending over, rubbing, and scrubbing.

Returning to domestic service as a graduate student was awkward. I tried to reduce the status inconsistency in my life by electing to work only in houses from which families were absent during the day. If someone appeared while I worked, I ignored their presence as they did mine. Since working arrangements had been previously negotiated by my mother, I had limited face-to-face interactions with employers. Most of the employers knew I was a graduate student, and fortunately, most seemed reluctant to ask me too many questions. Our mutual silence served as a way to deal with the status inconsistency of a housewife with a B.A. hiring an ABD to clean her house.

I came to El Paso with all of these experiences unquestioned in my memory. My presuppositions about domestic service were called into question only after observing the more obviously exploitative situation in the border town. I saw how vulnerable undocumented women employed as live-in domestics are and what little recourse they have to improve their situation, short of finding another job. Experiencing Juanita's shame and disgust at my colleague's sons' behavior brought back a flood of memories that eventually influenced me to study the paid housework that I had once taken for granted. I began to wonder professionally about the Chicanas employed as domestics that I had known throughout my own life: how vulnerable were they to exploitation, racism, and sexism? Did their day work status and U.S. citizenship provide protection against degradation and humiliation? How did Chicanas go about establishing a labor arrangement within a society that marked them as racial and cultural inferiors? How did they deal with racial slurs and sexist remarks within their employers' homes? How did Chicanas attempt to negotiate social interactions and informal labor arrangements with employers and their families?

An Exploratory Study

The Research Process

Intending to compare my findings with the research on U.S. minority women employed as domestics, I chose to limit my study to Chicanas, that is, women of Mexican descent born and raised in the United States. Although many women born in Mexico and living in the United States consider themselves Chicanas, my sample did not include women born outside the United States. My major concern in making this distinction was to avoid bringing into the analysis immigration issues that increase the vulnerability of the women employed as domestics. I wanted to keep conditions as constant as possible to make comparisons with the experiences Judith Rollins, Bonnie Thornton Dill, and Soraya Moore Coley report among African American women and with Evelyn Nakano Glenn's study of Japanese American women.[6] In order to duplicate similar residential and citizenship characteristics of these studies, I restricted my sample to Chicanas living in Denver whose families had migrated from rural areas of New Mexico and Colorado. All of the women interviewed were U.S. citizens and lived in Denver most of their adult lives.

I began the project by soliciting the cooperation of current and former domestics from my own family. I relied on domestics to provide entree into informal networks. These networks turned out to be particularly crucial in gaining access to an occupation that is so much a part of the underground economy. My mother, sister, and sister-in-law agreed to be interviewed and to provide names of relatives, friends, and neighbors. I also identified Chicana domestics in the community with the assistance of outreach workers employed by local churches and social service agencies. The snowball sampling was achieved by asking each interviewee to recommend other Chicana domestics as potential interviewees.

The women were extremely cautious about offering the names of friends and relatives. In most cases, they contacted the person first and only then gave me the name and telephone number. This actually turned out to be quite helpful. Potential interviewees had already heard about my study from someone who had been interviewed. They had a general idea of the questions I was going to ask and in some cases a little background information about who I was. However, on three occasions, I called women to ask for an interview and was confronted with resistance and shame. The women expressed embarrassment at being identified by their work—as a "housekeeper" or "cleaning lady." I responded by sharing my research interests in the occupation and in the relationship between work and family. I also shared my previous experience as a domestic.[7] One woman argued with me for 20 minutes about conducting research on an occupation that was low status, suggesting instead that I study Chicana lawyers or doctors, that is, "another occupation that presents our people in a more positive light." Another woman denied ever having worked as a domestic even though several women, including her sister-in-law, had given me her name as someone currently employed as a domestic.

The stigma of domestic service was a problem during the interviews as well. From the outset, it was very important for each woman to establish herself as someone more than a private household worker. Conducting nonstructured, free-flowing, and open-ended interviews allowed the women to establish multiple identities, particularly diffuse family and community roles.

The interviews were conducted in the women's homes, usually while sitting in the living room or at the dining room table with the radio or television on in the background. Although family members peeked in, for the most part there were few interruptions other than an occasional telephone call. From time to time, the women called to their husbands in the other room to ask the name of a street where they had once lived or the year the oldest son had been born in order to figure out when they had left and returned to work. The average interview lasted two hours, but I often stayed to visit and chat long after the interview was over. They told me about their church activities and plans to remodel the house and asked me for my opinion on current Chicano politics. Some spread out blankets, tablecloths, and pillow covers to exhibit their needlework. They showed me pictures of their children and grandchildren, giving me a walking tour of living rooms and bedrooms where wedding and high school portraits hung. As each one was identified, I learned more about their lives.

I conducted 25 open-ended interviews with Chicanas living and working in the greater Denver metropolitan area. The most visible Chicano communities in Denver are in the low-income neighborhood located in the downtown area or in one of two working-class neighborhoods in the northern and western areas of the city. I interviewed women from each of these communities. I asked them to discuss their overall work histories, with particular emphasis on their experiences as domestics. I probed for detailed information on domestic work, including strategies for finding employers, definitions of appropriate and inappropriate tasks, the negotiation of working conditions, ways of doing housework efficiently, and the pros and cons of domestic service. The accounts included descriptions of the domestics' relationships with white middle-class mistresses and revealed Chicanas' attitudes toward their employers' lifestyles.

All of the interviewees' families of orientation were from northern New Mexico or southern Colorado, where many of them had lived and worked on small farms. Some of the women had arrived in Denver as children with their parents, others as young brides, and still others as single women to join siblings and cousins in Denver's barrios. Several women recalled annual migrations to northern Colorado to pick sugar beets, prior to their permanent relocation to Denver. In some cases, the women's entire families of orientation had migrated to Denver; in others, parents and siblings had either remained behind or migrated to other cities. Many older women had migrated with their husbands after World War II, and several younger women interviewed had arrived at the same time, as children. Women who had migrated as single adults typically had done so in the last 10 or 15 years. Now they were married and permanently living in Denver. . . .

Historical Background

After the Mexican American War, Mexicans were given the option to maintain their Mexican citizenship and leave the country or become U.S. citizens. Many reluctantly chose the latter in order to keep their homes. Although the

Treaty of Guadalupe Hidalgo was supposed to guarantee land grant provisions to those who chose to remain in occupied territory, legal and illegal maneuvers were used to eliminate communal usage of land and natural resources. Between 1854 and 1930, an estimated 2,000,000 acres of private land and 1,700,000 acres of communal land were lost.[8] In the arid Southwest, small plots were insufficient to continue a subsistence-based farming economy, thus the members of the Hispano community were transformed from landowners to wage laborers. Enclosure of the common lands forced Mexicans from their former economic roles, "freed" Mexicans for wage labor, and established a racially stratified labor force in the Southwest.

As early as 1900, the Hispano farming and ranching communities of northern New Mexico and southern Colorado began to lose their population. A combination of push-pull factors conspired to force rural Hispanos off the land and attracted them to urban areas like Denver. Rural northern New Mexico and southern Colorado experienced drastic depopulation as adults left to find jobs. During the Depression, studies conducted in cooperation with the Works Progress Administration (WPA) noted the desperate situation:

> The Tewa Basin Study by the U.S. Department of Agriculture showed that in 11 Spanish-American villages containing 1,202 families, an average of 1,110 men went out of the villages to work for some part of each year prior to 1930. In 1934, only 157 men out of 1,202 families had found outside work.[9]

Migration in search of jobs became a way of life for many families. New Mexicans and southern Coloradans joined the migratory farm labor stream from Texas, California, and Mexico. World War II further depopulated the rural villages as people flocked to the cities in response to job openings in defense plants and related industries. Postwar migration from New Mexico was estimated to be one-fifth of the 1940 rural Chicano population.[10] This pattern continued in the following decades. For instance, Thomas Malone found that during the decade of the 1950s, only one of seven northern counties in New Mexico had not experienced a decrease in its former predominantly Spanish-speaking population.[11] By 1960, 61 percent of the population had been urbanized,[12] and between 1950 and 1960, an additional 24 percent left their rural communities.[13]

Perhaps because research on population movement among Chicanos has been so overwhelmingly concerned with emigration from Mexico, this type of internal population movement among Chicanos has not been well studied. What research is available has focused primarily on male workers and the relationship between urbanization and acculturation.[14] Chicanas have been either ignored or treated simply as family members—mothers, daughters, or wives, accompanying male relatives in search of work—rather than as wage earners in their own right. Nevertheless, for many women migration to an urban area made it necessary that they enter the labor market. Domestic service became a significant occupation in the experience.

Profile of Chicana Household Workers

Only the vaguest statistical data on Chicana private household workers are available; for the most part these workers remain a doubly hidden population. The reasons are themselves instructive. Domestic workers tend to be invisible because paid domestic work has not been one of the occupations recorded in social science surveys, and the U.S. Census Bureau uses a single code lumping together all private household workers, including launderers, cooks, house-keepers, child-care workers, cleaners, and servants. Even when statistics on domestics can be teased out of the census and labor data bases, they are marred by the common practice of underreporting work in the informal sector. Unlike some of the private household workers in the East, Chicana domestics are not unionized and remain outside the "counted" labor force. Many private household workers are not included in the statistics collected by the Department of Labor. The "job" involves an informal labor arrangement made between two people, and in many cases payment is simply a cash transaction that is never recorded with the Internal Revenue Service (IRS).

Governmental undercounting of Chicanos and Mexican immigrants in the United States further adds to the problem of determining the number of Chicanas and Mexicanas employed as private household workers. For many, domestic service is part of the underground economy, and employing undocumented workers is reported neither to the IRS nor to the Immigration and Naturalization Service (INS), thus making another source of statistical information unreliable. Chicanos continue to be an undercounted and obscure population. Problems with the categorization of domestics have been still further complicated by changing identifiers for the Mexican American population: Mexican, Spanish-speaking, Hispanic, Spanish-surnamed, and the like make it impossible to segment out the Chicano population.

The 25 Chicanas whom I interviewed included welfare recipients as well as working-class women, ranging in age from 29 to 68. Thirteen of the 25 women were between 29 and 45 years old. The remaining 12 were over 52 years old. All the women had children, and the older women also had grandchildren. The smallest family consisted of one child, and the largest family had seven children. The average was three children. All but one of the women had been married. Five of the women were single heads of households, two of them were divorced, and the other three were single, separated, or widowed. The married women were currently living with husbands employed in blue-collar positions, such as construction and factory work. At the time of the interview, the women who were single heads of households were financially supporting no more than two children.

Educational backgrounds ranged from no schooling to completion of high school. Six women had completed high school, and seven had no high school experience, including one who had never attended school at all. The remaining 12 had at least a sixth-grade education. Although the least educated were the older women, eight of the women under 42 had not completed high school. The youngest woman with less than an eighth-grade education was 53 years old. The 12 women over 50 averaged eight years of schooling. Three of the high school graduates were in their early thirties, two were in their early forties, and one was 57 years old. Although one woman preferred to be interviewed in Spanish, all the women spoke English.

Work experience as a private household worker ranged from five months to 30 years. Women 50 years and older had worked in the occupation from eight to 30 years, while four of the women between the ages of 33 and 39 had worked as domestics for 12 years. Half of the women had worked for more than 10 years as private household workers. Only three women had worked as domestics prior to marriage; each of these women had worked in live-in situations in rural areas in Colorado. Several years later, after marriage and children, they returned as day workers. All the other women, however, had turned to nonresidential day work in response to a financial crisis; in the majority of cases, it was their first job after marriage and having children. Some of the women remained domestics throughout their lives, but others moved in and out of domestic work. Women who returned to domestic service after having other types of jobs usually did so following a period of unemployment.

The work histories revealed that domestic service was only one of several low-paying, low-status jobs the women had held during their lives. They had been hired as waitresses, laundresses, janitors, farmworkers, nurse's aides, fast-food servers, cooks, dishwashers, receptionists, school aides, cashiers, baby-sitters, salesclerks, factory workers, and various types of line workers in poultry farms and car washes. Almost half of the women had worked as janitors in hospitals and office buildings or as hotel maids. About one-fourth of the women had held semiskilled and skilled positions such as beauticians, typists, and medical-record clerks. Six of the women had worked only as domestics.

Paid and Unpaid Domestic Work

In describing their daily routine activities, these Chicanas drew my attention to the interrelationship between paid and unpaid housework. As working women, Chicana private household workers face the "double day" or "second shift," but in their case both days consisted of the same types of tasks. Paid housework done for an employer was qualitatively different from housework done for their own families.

In the interviews, Chicanas described many complexities of domestic service. They explained how they used informal networks to find new employers for themselves and for relatives and friends. As they elaborated on the advantages and disadvantages of particular work arrangements and their reasons for refusing certain household tasks, I soon realized that these women not only knew a great deal about cleaning and maintaining homes, but they understood the influence of social relationships on household tasks. Analysis of the extensive planning and negotiation involved in the informal and underground arrangements of domestic service highlighted the significance of the social relationships surrounding housework.

Their work histories included detailed explanations of beginning, returning to, and continuing in domestic service. In the discussions, I began to understand the paradox of domestic service: On the one hand, cleaning houses is degrading and embarrassing; on the other, domestic service can be higher paying, more autonomous, and less dehumanizing than other low-status, low-skilled occupations. Previous jobs in the beet fields, fast-food restaurants, car washes, and turkey farms did not offer annual raises, vacations, or sick leave. Furthermore, these jobs forced employees to work long hours and to keep rigid time schedules, and they frequently occurred outside or in an unsafe work environment. Unlike the other options available, domestic service did have the potential for offering flexible work schedules and autonomy. In most cases, domestic service also paid much more. Although annual raises, vacation, and social security were not the norm for most Chicanas in domestic service, there remained the possibility that such benefits could be negotiated with employers. Furthermore, as former farmworkers, laundresses, and line workers, the women found freedom in domestic work from exposure to dangerous pesticides, poor ventilation, and other health risks. This paradox foreshadowed a critical theoretical issue, the importance of understanding the social process that constructs domestic service as a low-status occupation.

Stigma as a perceived occupational hazard of domestic service emerged during the initial contact and throughout most of the interviews. The stigma attached to domestic service punctuated the interviews. I knew that many women hid their paid household labor from the government, but I did not realize that this secrecy encompassed neighbors, friends, and even extended family members. Several women gave accounts that revealed their families' efforts to conceal their employment as domestics. Children frequently stated that their mothers "just did housework," which was ambiguous enough to define them as full-time homemakers and not necessarily as domestics.

Faced with limited job opportunities, Chicanas selected domestic service and actively sought to make the most of the situation. In comparison with other jobs they had held, domestic service usually paid more and offered greater flexibility in arranging the length of the workday and workweek. Although other jobs did not carry the stigma of servitude, workers were under constant supervision, and the work was similarly low status. Therefore, the women who chose domestic service over other low-paying, low-status jobs based their selection on the occupation that offered some possibility of control. Their challenge was to structure the work so as to reap the most benefits: pay, work hours, labor, and autonomy. Throughout the interviews, the women emphasized job flexibility as the major advantage of domestic service over previous jobs. Nonrigid work schedules allowed time to do their own housework and fulfill family obligations, such as caring for sick children or attending school functions. By stressing the benefits gained by doing day work, Chicanas diffused the low status in their work identities and emphasized their family and community identities. The ways in which they arranged both work and family revealed coping strategies used to deal with the stigma, and this drew me to analyze housework as a form of labor having both paid and unpaid manifestations.

The conventional social science separation of work and family is an analytical construct and is not found in the lived reality of Chicana domestics. Invariably the interviewees mixed and intertwined discussions of work and family. Moreover, the actual and practical relationships between work and family were explicit in their descriptions of daily activities: The reasons for seeking employment included the family's financial situation and the desire to raise its standard of living; earning extra money for the household was viewed as an extension of these women's roles as mothers and wives; arranging day work involved planning work hours around the children's school attendance, dentist and doctor appointments, and community and church activities; in some cases, young mothers even took their preschool-age children with them to work. The worlds of paid and unpaid housework were not disconnected in the lives of these women.

Attending to the importance of the relationship between paid and unpaid domestic work led me to ponder new questions about the dynamics of buying and selling household labor. How does housework differ when it is paid work? How does the housewife role change when part of her work is allocated to another woman? What is the range of employer–employee relationship in domestic service today? And is there a difference in the type of relationships developed by employed and unemployed women buying household labor?

The importance of attending to both paid and unpaid housework in researching domestic service became more apparent as I began presenting my research to academic audiences. When I read papers on the informal labor market or on family and community networks used to find work, some of my colleagues responded as women who employed domestics. Frequently, question-and-answer sessions turned into a defense of such practices as hiring undocumented workers, not filing income taxes, or gift giving in lieu of raises and benefits. Although I was aware that as working women, many academics employed someone to clean their houses, I was not prepared for scholars and feminists to respond to my scholarly work as housewives or employers. I was also surprised to discover that many of the maternalistic practices traditionally found in domestic service were common practices in their homes. The recurring responses made me realize that my feminist colleagues had never considered their relationships with the "cleaning woman" on the same plane as those with secretaries, waitresses, or janitors; that is, they thought of the former more or less in terms of the mistress–maid relationship. When, through my research, I pointed out the contradiction, many still had difficulty thinking of their homes—the haven from the cruel academic world—as someone's workplace. Their overwhelming feelings of discomfort, guilt, and resentment, which sometimes came out as hostility, alerted me to the fact that something more was going on. . . .

Domestic service must be studied because it raises a challenge to any feminist notion of "sisterhood." A growing number of employed middle- and upper-middle-class women escape the double-day syndrome by hiring poor women of color to do housework and child care. David Katzman underscored the class contradiction:

> Middle-class women, the employers, gained freedom from family roles and household chores and assumed or confirmed social status by the employment of a servant. . . . The greater liberty of these middle-class women, however, was achieved at the expense of working-class women, who, forced to work, assumed the tasks beneath, distasteful to, or too demanding for the family members.[15]

Housework is ascribed on the basis of gender, and it is further divided along class lines and, in most cases, by race and ethnicity. Domestic service accentuates the contradiction of race and class in feminism, with privileged women of one class using the labor of another woman to escape aspects of sexism.

ENDNOTES

[1] The conditions I observed in El Paso were not much different from those described by D. Thompson in her 1960 article, "Are Women Bad Employers of Other Women?" *Ladies' Home Journal:* "Quarters for domestic help are usually ill placed for quiet. Almost invariably they open from pantry or kitchen, so that if a member of the family goes to get a snack at night he wakes up the occupant. And the live-in maid has nowhere to receive a caller except in the kitchen or one [of] those tiny rooms." "As a general rule anything was good enough for a maid's room. It became a catchall for furniture discarded from other parts of the house. One room was a cubicle too small for a regular-sized bed." Cited in Linda Martin and Kerry Segrave, *The Servant Problem: Domestic Workers in North America* (Jefferson, NC: McFarland, 1985), p. 25.

[2] David Katzman addresses the "servant problem" in his historical study of domestic service, *Seven Days a Week: Women and Domestic Service in Industrializing America* (Chicago: University of Illinois Press, 1981). Defined by middle-class housewives, the problem includes both the shortage of servants available and the competency of women willing to enter domestic service. Employers' attitudes about domestics have been well documented in women's magazines. Katzman described the topic as "the bread and butter of women's magazines between the Civil War and World War I"; moreover, Martin and Segrave, *The Servant Problem,* illustrate the continuing presence of articles on the servant problem in women's magazines today.

[3] Lillian Pettengill's account *Toilers of the Home: The Record of a College Woman's Experience As a Domestic Servant* (New York: Doubleday, 1903) is based on two years of employment in Philadelphia households.

[4] Ruth Schwartz Cowan, *More Work for Mother: The Ironies of Household Technology from the Open Hearth to the Microwave* (New York: Basic Books, 1983), p. 228.

[5] Earning money as domestic workers to pay college expenses not covered by scholarships is not that uncommon among other women of color in the United States. Trudier Harris interviewed several African American women public school and university college teachers about their college-day experiences in domestic service. See *From Mammies to Militants: Domestics in Black American Literature* (Philadelphia: Temple University Press, 1982), pp. 5–6.

[6] Judith Rollins, *Between Women: Domestics and Their Employers* (Philadelphia: Temple University Press, 1985); Bonnie Thornton Dill, "Across the Boundaries of Race and Class: An Exploration of the Relationship between Work and Family among Black Female Domestic Servants" (Ph.D. dissertation, New York University, 1979): Judith Rollins, "'Making Your Job Good Yourself': Domestic Service and the Construction of Personal Dignity," in *Women and the Politics of Empowerment,* ed. Ann Bookman and Sandra Morgen (Philadelphia: Temple University Press, 1988), pp. 33–52; Soraya Moore Coley, "'And Still I Rise': An Exploratory Study of Contemporary Black Private Household Workers" (Ph.D. dissertation, Bryn Mawr College, 1981); Evelyn

Nakano Glenn, *Issei, Nisei, War Brides: Three Generations of Japanese American Women in Domestic Service* (Philadelphia: Temple University Press, 1986).

[7] In some cases, it was important to let women know that my own background had involved paid housework and that my mother and sister were currently employed full-time as private household workers. Sharing this information conveyed that my life had similarities to theirs and that I respected them. This sharing of information is similar to the concept of "reciprocity" (R. Wax, "Reciprocity in Field Work," in *Human Organization Research: Field Relationships and Techniques,* ed. R. N. Adams and J. J. Preiss [New York: Dorsey, 1960], pp. 90–98).

[8] Clark Knowlton, "Changing Spanish-American Villages of Northern New Mexico," *Sociology and Social Research* 53 (1969): 455–75.

[9] Nancie Gonzalez, *The Spanish-Americans of New Mexico* (Albuquerque: University of New Mexico Press, 1967), p. 123.

[10] William W. Winnie, "The Hispanic People of New Mexico" (Master's thesis, University of Florida, 1955).

[11] Thomas J. Malone, "Recent Demographic and Economic Changes in Northern New Mexico," *New Mexico Business* 17 (1964): 4–14.

[12] Donald N. Barrett and Julian Samora, *The Movement of Spanish Youth from Rural to Urban Settings* (Washington, DC: National Committee for Children and Youth, 1963).

[13] Clark Knowlton, "The Spanish Americans in New Mexico," *Sociology and Social Research* 45 (1961): 448–54.

[14] See Paul A. Walter, "The Spanish-Speaking Community in New Mexico," *Sociology and Social Research* 24 (1939): 150–57; Thomas Weaver, "Social Structure, Change and Conflict in a New Mexico Village" (Ph.D. dissertation, University of California, 1965); Florence R. Kluckhohn and Fred L. Stodtbeck, *Variations in Value Orientations* (Evanston, IL: Row, Peterson, 1961); Frank Moore, "San Jose, 1946: A Study in Urbanization" (Master's thesis, University of New Mexico, 1947); Donald N. Barrett and Julian Samora, *The Movement of Spanish Youth* (Washington, DC: National Committee for Children and Youth, 1963).

[15] David Katzman, *Seven Days a Week* (Chicago: University of Illinois Press, 1981), pp. 269–70.

SOCIAL RESEARCH

4

FINDING OUT HOW
THE SOCIAL WORLD WORKS

MICHAEL SCHWALBE

Most sociologists agree that the best way to learn about research is through hands-on experience gained by conducting a study. The research process, examined in the next three readings, often turns up new questions and challenges for the researcher. The first reading is by Michael Schwalbe, a professor of sociology at North Carolina State University, and is excerpted from his

1998 book, *The Sociologically Examined Life: Pieces of the Conversation.* In this selection, Schwalbe explains the advantages of utilizing systematic research to study the social world. Schwalbe also summarizes the kinds of questions sociologists often ask and argues that it is important to be "sociologically mindful" whenever addressing social research.

Without looking up any statistics, can you say whether there are more poor black people or poor white people in the United States? A common mistake, because blacks are often represented as being poor, is to say that there are more poor black people than poor white people. But blacks make up only about 12 percent of the U.S. population. And even though the rate of poverty is higher among blacks (about 30 percent) than among whites (about 15 percent), there are so many more white people in the United States that whites still make up the majority of those living in poverty. . . . A few facts and a bit of logic make this easy to figure out.

So logical deduction is one way to know things, or to find out the implications of what we know. Much of what we know comes straight from others. It is passed on to us by parents, teachers, friends, and so on. We can also know things from personal experience or observation, from systematic research, and from mystical revelation. It is possible, too, that some knowledge is instinctive, as, for example, when an infant "knows" that it should suck on whatever is put in its mouth.

It is interesting to think about where our knowledge comes from. What usually concerns us more, however, is how to be sure that our knowledge is valid and reliable. Each source of knowledge has limitations in these respects. Part of being sociologically mindful is being aware of these limitations.

Logical deduction, for instance, is a fine way to elaborate our knowledge—except that if our *premises* are wrong, then our conclusions will also be wrong; we will simply reason our way to further ignorance. One strength of logical deduction, however, is that others can check up on our assumptions and our reasoning, and thus correct us if we go astray.

Relying on what others tell us is necessary and is often a good way to learn, but how do we know that what others tell us is right? Surely you have had the experience of being told—by a parent, teacher, or mentor—something that later turned out to be wrong. Then there is the problem of deciding between different versions of the truth that come to us from sources that seem equally credible. How do we decide who is right?

Personal experience and observation are good sources of knowledge, except that it is easy to misjudge and overgeneralize from these sources. For example, your own observations might tell you that the sun revolves around the earth, or that all Lithuanians are slobs because both of the Lithuanians you've met in your life were a bit slobby, or that there is no ruling class in the United States because you've never seen it gathered in one place, or that crime is rising because you were just robbed. The problem in each case is not that you don't know what you've seen, but that what you've seen isn't enough to support the conclusion you reached. . . .

Advantages of Systematic Research

Careful research is perhaps the best way to create valid and reliable knowledge about the state of the social world and how it works. It is the best way for several reasons. First, by using standard, widely accepted means of finding things out, we can control personal biases. If we can do this, we are less likely to mistake what we would like to be true for what is really true.

Suppose, for example, I believe that democratic work organizations are better than authoritarian ones and would therefore like to believe that they are also more efficient. My bias would be to look only for evidence that supports my belief. But if I use a standard method of assessing efficiency, and use it carefully and fairly to compare democratic and authoritarian work organizations, I will have to accept whatever I find. My bias would thus be canceled out, or at least controlled.

Second, research can get us beyond personal experience and casual observation, because to re-*search* is to look beyond what is obvious to us from where we stand. It is to look for ideas and information that might challenge the common sense that gets us through daily life. It means considering the quality and correctness of knowledge created by others, even if we find their knowledge irritating. All this can be difficult, because our usual habit is to settle comfortably into believing that we already know what is right.

A third reason for doing research is that it lets us check up on each other. If we use methods that others agree are proper, they can look at our results and say, "Hmmm, yes, you did it right; these results must be correct." Or they can say, "Ah, you went astray here at this point, so your conclusions are not trustworthy." We can make the same judgments when others offer us knowledge they have created. In this way, by working together, we can do better at dispelling illusions and, in the long run, creating knowledge that is valid and reliable.

Perhaps you noticed that I had only good things to say about knowledge that comes from research. Does this mean that one should accept as true whatever is published in a scientific or scholarly journal? No. Knowledge from any source should be critically interrogated. Careful research is just a way to avoid problems that are common when knowledge is created in other ways. And if research is not done properly, it can yield as much foolishness as any other method.

The larger point here is that we should be mindful, to the extent we can, of where our own knowledge comes from. We can be mindful in this way by asking ourselves how we know what we claim to know. Is some piece of knowledge a result of logical deduction? (If so, have we reasoned correctly? How do we know that our premises are correct?) Is some piece of knowledge a hand-me-down from others? (If so, where did *their* knowledge come from?

How can we be sure it is correct?) Is some piece of knowledge a result of personal experience or observation? (If so, are we claiming to know more than our personal experience can warrant? Is it possible that we have observed only what we want to believe is true, or that our observations have been limited in some crucial way?)

The point of asking ourselves these questions is not to arrive at a paralyzing state of doubt about what we know, but to more wisely decide how much faith to put in what we know. If we can do this, we can open ourselves to new knowledge without fear of surrendering our minds to yet another fishy belief system. Being sociologically mindful, we can get a better view of what is coming at us by way of new knowledge and where it is coming from. We can also see what is worth catching.

The Kinds of Questions We Can Ask

All attempts to create knowledge are responses to questions, and knowledge must be created in a way that suits the question. For example, if you asked, "How much does this book weigh?" the proper way to get an answer is to weigh it. How many words does it contain? Count them. Will it fly like a boomerang? Give it the right kind of throw and observe the result. These are *empirical* questions, which means that they are answerable by measuring, counting, or looking to see what happens.

But suppose you asked, "Is the cover of this book beautiful?" What then? You could ask ten artists for their opinions. What if seven said it was ugly, two were ambivalent, and one thought it was beautiful? In this case no measuring stick will settle the matter, because you have asked an *aesthetic* question—a question about what is subjectively pleasing to the senses—and aesthetic questions are not answerable with data. We can try to say why something strikes us as ugly or beautiful, tasteful or crass, but no evidence or logic will prove us right and others wrong.

Here is another kind of question: Was it worthwhile for me to write this [article], considering that I might have been doing other useful things with my time? Again, this is not an empirical question, since there is no way to get an answer by measuring, counting, or observing. It is a *moral* question, since it calls for a judgment about what is right to do. I could say why it seemed to me a good thing to write this [article], but my reasons would be based on moral precepts and on my sense of how the future is likely to unfold. There is no data I can show, no standard analysis, to prove that my answer is right. All I can do is to offer reasonable arguments.

There are also questions of *interpretation*, the most simple of which is "What does this thing mean?" Such questions often arise when we confront works of art. We might look at a painting or read a novel and wonder what the writer or artist wanted us to understand. But any fact, object, gesture, phrase, or behavior—anything that has meaning—can raise a question of interpretation.

Sometimes we can get an answer by asking for clarification. Perhaps the writer or artist can tell us what s/he meant (although writers and artists can't always fully explain what their work means). Or perhaps there is expert opinion available to help us make sense of things. Other times there might be so much ambiguity that no clear interpretation can be nailed down. All anyone can do then is to give reasons to support the plausibility of a particular interpretation.

You can perhaps see now that research is better suited to answering some questions than others. It is a good way to answer empirical questions. It can also be useful for answering interpretive questions, because we can sometimes dig up evidence that supports the plausibility of an interpretation. And although it is wise to search for ideas and information to help guide our moral and aesthetic judgments, research will not tell us which judgments are correct.

It is good to be mindful of the kind of question we are facing. Sometimes we get into fruitless debates because we are not clear about this. There is no point, for example, in trading opinions about the correct answer to a simple empirical question. Are crime rates rising? Go to the library and look up the best answer you can find. If it is the answer to an empirical question that is in dispute, we should stop disputing and go get the answer.

Interpreting the Answers to Empirical Questions

Sometimes the answer to an empirical question can create a great deal of interpretive trouble. For example, to ask "What are the rates of poverty among blacks and whites living in the United States?" is to ask an empirical question. We can look up the answers because someone else (the U.S. Census Bureau) has already done the counting and the arithmetic. As I noted earlier, the poverty rate among blacks is about 30 percent and among whites it is about 15 percent (these figures fluctuate somewhat and can also vary depending on how poverty is defined). But what do these figures mean? How can we interpret them?

I once presented these figures during a discussion of racial inequality. The class suddenly got quiet. No one wanted to comment on the meaning of the percentages. When I pressed for some reaction, a white student said, "I think no one is talking because the figures are embarrassing." Did he mean that the figures were embarrassing because they pointed out a failure to overcome racial inequality? I wasn't sure, so I asked him to be more explicit. "The figures are embarrassing," he said with some hesitation, "to black students." I was baffled by this.

After further conversation, it became clear that the student who spoke about the figures being "embarrassing to black students" saw the figures as evidence of black inferiority. His presumption was that the poverty rate of a group was an indicator of the capability of people in that group. I saw the figures as evidence of racism and discrimination. In this case, the facts about poverty rates were clear, but they did not speak for themselves. The same facts lent themselves to nearly opposite interpretations.

To support my interpretation, I might have said that in the United States, millions of people, black and white, are poor because they can't find jobs that pay a decent wage, or they can't find jobs at all. Sometimes the jobs available in an area don't match people's skills. Or else the jobs disappear when employers move factories to foreign countries where they can pay workers less. And so people can end up poor, or very nearly poor, even though they are able and willing to work.

I might have added that the higher poverty rate among blacks is a result of factories being closed down in inner cities in the North, where a lot of the black population is concentrated. It's a result of schools that do not serve black children well. It's a result of discrimination in hiring and network advantages enjoyed by whites. In some cases, part of the problem is a lack of marketable skills, but that's because access to education and training is limited, not because people's natural abilities are limited.

I might have said all this—and probably did—but was it enough to establish my interpretation as correct? Although I am sure that my statement helped some people see why the white student's interpretation was wrong, others who preferred to hold onto that interpretation could point out, correctly, that I had not really *proven*—by anything I'd said or any evidence I'd shown—that blacks were not inferior to whites. All I had done was to suggest that "black inferiority" was not a plausible explanation—if other things were taken into account, if those other things were true, and if no significant counterevidence was being overlooked.

My interpretation was not, however, a matter of opinion. My interpretation was based on previously answered empirical questions. Have jobs disappeared in areas heavily populated by blacks? Do employers discriminate against blacks? Do whites enjoy network advantages when it comes to getting jobs? Do schools serve black kids as well as they serve white kids? Is there a lack of access to education and job training? With knowledge of the answers to these empirical questions, we can determine which interpretation of the poverty-rate figures is most likely to be correct. . . .

Mindful Skepticism

Once, during a discussion of the benefits of education, a black woman said she was outraged to learn that, on the average, a high-school diploma was likely to yield higher earnings (by mid-life) for a white man than a college degree was likely to yield for a black woman. When she said this, another student, a white male said, "I don't believe it. How can you possibly know that?" Before she could answer, I said, "She probably read the article that was assigned for today. If you look on page 34 in the text, you'll see a table that shows what she's referring to." He paged through his book and found the table. After studying it for a few moments, he harumphed and said, "Well, anybody can make up numbers."

As a teacher, I was irritated by this response, because it meant this: "No matter what information I am presented with, if it does not suit my prior beliefs, if it does not make me comfortable, I will discount it, so I can continue to believe what I want to believe." An attitude like this leaves little room for education to make a dent. I wondered why this student would bother to study anything at all, or read any books at all, if he was so intent on being unchanged.

And yet I could not say that his attitude was entirely foolish. Numbers are often cooked up to mislead us, and numbers can be wrong because of honest mistakes, so it is reasonable to be skeptical of numbers, whatever the source. Is there any way to tell which numbers are right? Yes, it can be done; it just requires training. Since most people do not have such training, however, it is understandable that they might say, "I can't tell what's right or wrong, so I'm going to treat all statistics as hogwash."

This is clearly not a mindful response to the situation. It is like saying, "I can't read, so I am going to treat all books as hogwash." It would be better to learn to read and to learn also what is necessary to distinguish the hog from the wash. This is hard but not impossible. What helps is being mindfully, rather than indiscriminately, skeptical of new information.

One of the difficulties in learning about the social world is that we must rely on information created and filtered by others. We can't check out everything for ourselves, even if we know how. This being the case, we must pay attention to how information (in the form of words or numbers) is created, by whom, for what purposes. We must ask, Who stands to benefit if this information is accepted as true? Being mindful in these ways puts us on alert against fraud, yet it does not cut us off from learning.

We should also seek alternative views, since this can help us see the limits of our own knowledge. A bit of conventional knowledge—that "Columbus discovered America," for instance—seems simple and true until an alternative is suggested: "Columbus launched a brutal invasion of an already populated continent." This is not just a different way to describe the same events, but a different way of seeing what those events were. If we try out this alternative view, we can look at what passes for conventional knowledge and see that it is, at the very least, contestable.

What is conventional and what is alternative depends, of course, on where you stand. A view that you consider alternative might seem conventional to someone else. Recognizing this relativity of perspectives is part of being sociologically mindful. But there is more to it. Being sociologically mindful, we can also see that these alternative perspectives create the possibility of understanding the world more fully, because they give us more angles from which to view it.

Perhaps by looking for and seriously considering alternative views—and there are always multiple alternatives—we will eventually get closer to a better version of the truth. That is something to aim for. In the meantime, it is wise to consider alternative views because doing so can help us see how competing versions of the truth are created. In this way we can learn more about how others see the world, how we have come to see the world, and what more we might see if we are willing to suffer a bit of uncertainty.

Partial Truth and Inevitable Uncertainty

The student who said, "Anyone can make up numbers," did not want to suffer uncertainty. Perhaps he was afraid that if he let go of what he already believed, he would end up lost, not knowing what to believe. He did not know how to be mindfully skeptical.

Part of what we fear is losing what we think is the truth. If we are sociologically mindful, however, we know that we never possess the absolute, complete truth. What we have is a head full of humanly-created images, representations, and accounts that seem to pretty well make sense of the world as we know it. Why not stand ready, as we see and experience more of the world, to invent or borrow new ways of making sense?

If we can admit that there is more to the world than we have yet seen or experienced—and more than we could see and experience in a lifetime—perhaps we can also say to ourselves, "In anticipation of learning more about the world, as I surely will do, I will treat my current beliefs as provisional and explore alternative ways of making sense of things, because one of these ways might come in handy some day."

To adopt this stance toward knowledge does not mean flitting from one belief to another. It is like the deliberate movement of wading upstream in a river. To move ahead you must take gentle steps, making sure of your footing before you shift your weight forward. You must stay flexible and lean into the current. If you rush or lose concentration, you will end up all wet. So you pay attention, moving mindfully when it makes sense to move.

Being sociologically mindful, we know that we never get to the whole truth about the social world. All the truths that we invent or borrow—all the images, representations, and accounts we come upon—are partial views of a whole that is unknowable because it is always changing in ways that run ahead of our ability to understand. We thus need not fear that new ideas and information will wrest the truth from us. They might, however, give us a larger, more complex, and unruly truth to contend with, and that can be unsettling.

For some people it is scary to think of never being sure of having it right. Imagining that one has it right, now and forever, is comforting. The problem, however, is that other people see things differently, and when conflicts arise, others will neither happily conform to the version of truth that comforts us nor lay down their knowledge to embrace ours. And so, if we want to understand and get along with others, we must be willing to seriously consider their perspectives and to tolerate the uncertainty that comes with this openness.

Perpetual Inquiry and Conversation

I have been recommending a mindful skepticism toward all knowledge—that which we already possess and that which strikes us as new and strange.

In this way we can avoid the dead ends of nihilism ("There is no truth. Anyone can make up numbers. You might as well believe what you want.") and fanaticism ("There is only one truth and my people know it! All other beliefs are false or insane!"). These are dead ends because they make conversation pointless and offer no hope of resolving conflict.

A mindful skepticism toward knowledge keeps us inquiring, observing, and trying to make better sense of things; it keeps us trying to create more accurate, complete, and useful representations; it keeps us open to new information; and it keeps us connected to others as we try to do all this. Conversation is both a means to this end and an end in itself—at least it is if we believe that it is better to try to understand others than to ignore or to hurt them. Be mindfully skeptical, then, of all knowledge, including that which I have offered in this [article]. After fair consideration, take and use what is helpful for making sense and for keeping the conversation going.

Curiosity, Care, and Hope

If you could live forever, would life get boring? Some people might say, "Yes, because it would be the same old thing, day after day, forever." But here is another possibility: Life would get more *interesting* because as one learned more about the world, one would see more complexities, more mysteries, more problems to be solved, and more things to be done. Why might some people see life as holding such great promise? I think it is because they are full of curiosity, care, and hope.

If there is no curiosity about the nature of things and how they work, then the world will seem like a drab backdrop against which life is endured until it is over. If there is no care about anything outside one's self or beyond one's time, then it will seem pointless to worry about things that don't matter for getting through the day. Without hope, it will seem pointless to invest much effort in analyzing the social world. So it seems that we need curiosity, care, and hope to spark a desire to pay attention to the social world, to try to understand it as it is, and to use this awareness to pursue change.

Sometimes the conditions of people's lives do not inspire much curiosity, care, or hope. There might be so much day-to-day hardship and sameness, and so few prospects for change, that people limit their attention to each day's tasks and fleeting amusements. Other people might be so comfortable that they too lose interest in critically examining the world beyond their cocoon of privilege. Under these conditions, people are not likely to develop much sociological mindfulness. Then again, perhaps the process can be turned around. Perhaps a lesson in mindfulness can spark curiosity, care, and hope.

Being mindful that the world is a complex and mysterious place, and that penetrating these mysteries is satisfying, ought to arouse our curiosity. Being mindful of how our actions affect others' experiences of joy and suffering ought to encourage feelings of care. And being mindful of how human action creates the world ought to give us hope that we can make the world a better place. Obviously these are expressions of my own wishes, yet I have tried to do more than put them forth as wishes.

I have tried to show how much there is to be curious about: the many connections, patterns, contingencies, appearances, and interdependencies that constitute the social world; all the ways that people try to solve problems together and end up creating cultural habits; the ways that some people create social arrangements to benefit themselves at the expense of others; and all the ways that people create the images, accounts, and representations that make up our knowledge of social reality. We could study these matters forever and always be learning something new.

I have also shown that sociological mindfulness gives us reasons for caring. The more we pay attention to and understand connections, interdependencies, and contingencies, the better we can see how *our* ways of thinking and acting affect *others'* chances for good lives. We can see, too, that what others think and do affects us as well. Being sociologically mindful helps us see how this is true in a way that goes beyond what is obvious in everyday life as we interact with others who are close to us.

And just as we care about the others who are close to us, we can, if we are sociologically mindful, come to care about the distant others whose lives are intertwined with ours. At the least, we can thus see new reasons for caring about the social arrangements that bind us to others, for better or worse.

Perhaps you are thinking, "What about hope? It seems that 'being sociologically mindful' just makes us aware of how messed up the social world is. How is *that* supposed to inspire hope?" Actually, mere awareness of problems—inequalities, exploitation, the suffering of others—is not supposed to inspire hope. It is supposed to inspire outrage and a desire to change things. Unfortunately, when awareness of problems is combined with feelings of powerlessness, the result is often despair.

Being sociologically mindful, however, we know that the social world is, for all its seeming solidity, a social construction. All the ideas, habits, arrangements, and so on that make up the social world are human creations. We know, too, that the social world keeps going as it does because of the beliefs people share and because of how they keep doing things together on an everyday basis. If we are mindful of all this, we can see that the problems that exist now need not exist forever; they are all within our power to overcome.

Of course it will not be easy, because many powerful people benefit from the arrangements that cause problems for so many others. There is also the problem of changing the arrangements that are devised to keep things from changing. Yet the possibility of change always exists, if only people can organize to make it happen, and that is a good reason for hope.

Mindfulness can get us out of the rut of despair by reminding us that we cannot change a society overnight by ourselves. It is silly to say, "I failed to bring about a revolution this week, even though I tried very hard. That proves it's hopeless. I guess I'll give up and just march along with everyone else." Yet many people fall into this kind of trap. The way out is through awareness that change requires working with others to challenge existing arrangements and to create new ones. We cannot do it alone.

There is no point in despairing because we cannot single-handedly change the world. Of course we can't. We can, however, try to find or organize others who recognize a need for change and are willing to work for it. It is amazing how being in community with others can help alleviate the despair that arises from failed dreams of heroism.

Sociological mindfulness also reminds us that we *can* change a small part of the social world single-handedly. If we treat others with more respect and compassion, if we refuse to participate in re-creating inequalities even in little ways, if we raise questions about official representations of reality, if we refuse to work in destructive industries, then we are making change. We do not have to join a group or organize a protest to make these kinds of changes. We can make them on our own, by deciding to live differently.

Perhaps our modest efforts will reverberate with others and inspire them to live differently. Or perhaps no one will notice, or they will notice but think we are strange. And so you might think, "If no one is going to notice that I am a superior moral being, then what is the point? Why bother to be different and risk ridicule?" That is one way to look at it. Being sociologically mindful, however, suggests a different thought: "I cannot be sure that *anything,* I do will change things for the better, yet I can be sure that if I do not at least *try,* then I will fail to do what I think is right and will be contributing to keeping things the same. Therefore I will opt to do what is right, whether much or little comes of it."

In the end, sociological mindfulness must be about more than studying how the social world works. It must also do more than inspire curiosity, care, and hope—although these we cannot do without. If it is to be worth practicing, sociological mindfulness must help us change ourselves and our ways of doing things together so that we can live more peacefully and productively with others, without exploitation, disrespect, and inequality. Sociological mindfulness is a way to see where we are and what needs to be done. It is a path to heartful membership in a conversation that ought to have no end.

RELATED READINGS

Kuhn, Thomas. 1970. *The Structure of Scientific Revolutions.* 2d ed. Chicago: University of Chicago Press.

Lofland, John and Lyn H. Lofland. 1995. *Analyzing Social Settings.* 3d ed. Belmont, CA: Wadsworth.

Maxwell, Nicholas. 1984. *From Knowledge to Wisdom.* New York: Basil Blackwell.

O'Hear, Anthony. 1989. *An Introduction to the Philosophy of Science.* New York: Oxford University Press.

Thomas, Jim. 1993. *Doing Critical Ethnography.* Newbury Park, CA: Sage.

Winch, Peter. 1958. *The Idea of a Social Science and Its Relations to Philosophy.* London: Routledge and Kegan Paul.

5

INTERPERSONAL DYNAMICS IN A SIMULATED PRISON

CRAIG HANEY • W. CURTIS BANKS
• PHILIP G. ZIMBARDO

Ethical questions concerning social research are a rather recent discussion in the history of social science. It was not until the 1960s and early 1970s that we began to question research protocols and the effects of social experiments on humans. This second reading in the social research section, by Craig Haney, W. Curtis Banks, and Philip G. Zimbardo, reviews the research methodology used in Zimbardo's famous prison study conducted in 1971. Zimbardo, a professor emeritus of psychology at Stanford University, was fascinated with the social dynamics of prisons, especially the social interaction that takes place between guards and prisoners. The selection below takes us inside the research world of the prison environment and reveals many ethical and logistical concerns about using social experiments to study human behavior.

Although we have passed through many periods of so-called prison "reform," in which physical conditions within prisons have improved and in which the rhetoric of rehabilitation has replaced the language of punitive incarceration, the social institution of prison has continued to fail. On purely pragmatic grounds, there is substantial evidence that prisons really neither "rehabilitate" nor act as a deterrent to future crime—in America, recidivism rates upwards of 75 percent speak quite decisively to these criteria. And, to perpetuate what is additionally an economic failure, American taxpayers alone must provide an expenditure for "corrections" of 1.5 billion dollars annually. On humanitarian grounds as well, prisons have failed: our mass media are increasingly filled with accounts of atrocities committed daily, man against man, in reaction to the penal system or in the name of it.

Attempts at explaining the deplorable condition of our penal system, and its dehumanizing effects upon prisoners and guards, characteristically focus upon what can be called the *dispositional hypothesis*. Rarely expressed explicitly, it is central to a prevalent nonconscious ideology: The state of the social institution of prison is due to the "nature" of the people who administrate it, or the "nature" of the people who populate it, or both. The dispositional

Craig Haney, W. Curtis Banks, and Philip G. Zimbardo, "Interpersonal Dynamics in a Simulated Prison" [abridged] from *International Journal of Criminology and Penology* 1 (1973): 69–97. Reprinted with the permission of Craig Haney.

hypothesis has been embraced by the proponents of the prison status quo (blaming violence on the criminal dispositions of prisoners), as well as by its critics (attributing brutality of guards and staff to their sadistic personality structures). The appealing simplicity of this proposition localizes the source of prison riots, recidivism, and corruption in these "bad seeds" and not in the conditions of the "prison soil." The system itself goes on essentially unchanged, its basic structure unexamined and unchallenged.

A critical evaluation of the dispositional hypothesis, however, cannot be made directly through observation in existing prison settings, since such naturalistic observation necessarily confounds the acute effects of the environment with the chronic characteristics of the inmate and guard populations. To partial out the situational effects of the prison environment per se from those attributable to a priori dispositions of its inhabitants requires a research strategy in which a "new" prison is constructed, comparable in its fundamental social-psychological milieu to existing prison systems but entirely populated by individuals who are undifferentiated in all essential dimensions from the rest of society.

Such was the approach taken in the present empirical study, namely, to create a prisonlike situation in which the guards and inmates were initially comparable and characterized as being "psychologically healthy," and then to observe the patterns of behavior which resulted and to record the cognitive, emotional, and attitudinal reactions that emerged.

No specific hypotheses were advanced other than the general one that assignment to the treatment of "guard" or "prisoner" would result in significantly different reactions on behavioral measures of interaction, emotional measures of mood state and pathology, and attitudes toward self, as well as other indices of coping and adaptation to this extreme situation.

Method

The effects of playing the role of "guard" or "prisoner" were studied in the context of an experimental simulation of a prison environment. The research design was a relatively simple one, involving as it did only a single treatment variable, the random assignment to either a "guard" or "prisoner" condition. These roles were enacted over an extended period of time (nearly one week) within an environment which had been physically constructed to closely resemble a prison. Central to the methodology of creating and maintaining the psychological state of imprisonment was the functional simulation of significant properties of "real prison life" (established through information from former inmates, correctional personnel, and texts).

Subjects

The 22 subjects who participated in the experiment were selected from an initial pool of 75 respondents who answered a newspaper ad asking for male volunteers to participate in a psychological study of "prison life," in return for payment of $15 per day. Those who responded to the notice completed an extensive questionnaire concerning their family background, physical and mental health history, prior experience, and attitudinal propensities with respect to any possible sources of psychopathology (including their involvements in crime). Each respondent who completed the background questionnaire was interviewed by one of two experimenters. Finally, the 24 subjects who were judged to be *most stable* (physically and mentally) were selected to participate in the study. On a random basis, half of the subjects were assigned the role of "guard," half were assigned to the role of "prisoner."

The subjects were normal, healthy males attending colleges throughout the United States who were in the Stanford [University] area during the summer. They were largely of middle-class background and Caucasians (with the exception of one Asian subject). Initially they were strangers to each other, a selection precaution taken to avoid the disruption of any preexisting friendship patterns and to mitigate against any transfer of previously established relationships or patterns of behavior into the experimental situation.

Procedure

Role Instructions   All subjects had been told that they would be randomly assigned either the guard or the prisoner role, and all had voluntarily agreed to play either role for $15 per day for up to two weeks. They signed a contract guaranteeing a minimally adequate diet, clothing, housing, and medical care, as well as the financial remuneration, in return for their stated "intention" of serving in the assigned role for the duration of the study.

It was made explicit in the contract that those assigned to be prisoners should expect to be under surveillance (have little or no privacy) and to have some of their basic civil rights suspended during their imprisonment. They were aware that physical abuse was explicitly prohibited. Subjects were given no other information about what to expect and no instructions about behavior "appropriate" for the prisoner role. Those actually assigned to this treatment were informed by phone to be available at their place of residence on a given Sunday, when we would start the experiment.

The subjects assigned to be guards attended an orientation meeting on the day prior to the induction of the prisoners. At this time they were introduced to the principal investigators, the "superintendent" of the prison (P.G.Z.) and an undergraduate research assistant who assumed the administrative role of "warden." They were told that we were attempting to simulate a prison environment within the limits imposed by pragmatic and ethical considerations. Their assigned task was to "maintain the reasonable degree of order within the prison necessary for its effective functioning," although the specifics of how this duty might be implemented were not explicitly detailed. To involve the subjects in their roles even before the first prisoner was incarcerated, the guards assisted in the final phases of completing the prison complex—putting the cots in the cells, posting signs on the walls, setting up the guards' quarters, and moving furniture, water coolers, and refrigerators.

The guards generally believed that we were interested primarily in studying the behavior of prisoners. Of course, we were also concerned with effects which enacting the role of guard in this environment would have on their behavior and subjective states. For this reason, they were given few explicit instructions on what it meant to be a guard and were left to "fill in" their own definitions of the role. A notable exception was the explicit and categorical prohibition against the use of physical punishment or aggression, which we emphasized from the outset of the study.

The prisoner subjects remained in the mock prison 24 hours a day for the duration of the study. Three were arbitrarily assigned to each of the three cells, and two others were on standby call at their homes. The guard subjects worked on three-man, eight-hour shifts, remaining in the prison environment only during their work shifts and going about their usual routines at other times. The one subject assigned to be a standby guard withdrew just before the simulation phase began. Final data analysis, then, is based on 11 prisoners and 10 guards.

Physical Aspects of the Prison   The prison was built in a 35-foot section of a basement corridor in the psychology building at Stanford University. It was partitioned by two fabricated walls, one of which was fitted with the only entrance door to the cell block; the other contained a small observation screen. Three small cells (6 × 9 feet) were made from converted laboratory rooms by replacing the usual doors with steel-barred doors painted black and removing all furniture. A cot (with mattress, sheet, and pillow) for each prisoner was the only furniture in the cells. A small closet across from the cells served as a solitary confinement facility; its dimensions were extremely small (2 × 2 × 7 feet), and it was unlit.

In addition, several rooms in an adjacent wing of the building were used as guards' quarters (to change in and out of uniform or for rest and relaxation), a bedroom for the "warden" and "superintendent," and an interview-testing room. Concealed video recording equipment was located in the testing room and behind the observation screen at one end of the "yard," where there was also sufficient space for several observers.

Uniforms   In order to promote feelings of anonymity in the subjects, each group was issued uniforms. For the guards, this consisted of plain khaki shirts and trousers, a whistle, a police nightstick (wooden baton), and reflecting sunglasses which made eye contact impossible. The prisoners' uniforms were loosely fitting muslin smocks with an identification number on front and back. A light chain and lock were placed around one ankle. On their feet they wore rubber sandals, and their hair was covered with a nylon stocking made into a cap. Each prisoner was also issued a toothbrush, soap, soapdish, towel, and bed linen. No personal belongings were allowed in the cells. The outfitting of both prisoners and guards in this manner served to enhance group identity and reduce individual uniqueness within the two groups.

Induction Process With the cooperation of the Palo Alto City Police Department, all of the subjects assigned to the prisoner treatment were unexpectedly "arrested" at their residences. A police officer charged them with either suspicion of burglary or armed robbery, advised them of their legal rights, handcuffed them, thoroughly searched them (often as curious neighbors looked on), and carried them off to the police station in the rear of the police car. At the station they went through the standard booking routines of being fingerprinted, having an identification file prepared, and then being placed in a detention cell. Subsequently, each prisoner was blindfolded and driven by one of the experimenters and a subject-guard to our mock prison. Throughout the entire arrest procedure, the police officers involved maintained a formal, serious attitude, avoiding answering any questions of clarification as to the relation of this "arrest" to the mock prison study.

Upon arrival at our experimental prison, each prisoner was stripped, sprayed with a delousing preparation (deodorant spray), and made to stand alone, naked, in the cell yard before being outfitted. After being given their uniforms and having an I.D. picture ("mug shot") taken, each prisoner was put in his cell.

Administrative Routine When all the cells were occupied, the warden greeted the prisoners and read them the rules of the institution (developed the previous day by the guards and the warden). They were to be memorized and to be followed. Prisoners were to be referred to only by the number of their uniforms, in a further effort to depersonalize them.

The prisoners were served three bland meals per day, were allowed three supervised toilet visits, and were given two hours daily for the privilege of reading or letter writing. Work assignments were issued for which the prisoners were to receive an hourly wage to constitute their $15 daily payment. Two visiting periods per week were scheduled, as were movie rights and exercise periods. Three times a day all prisoners were lined up for a "count" (one on each guard work-shift). The initial purpose of the count was to ascertain that all prisoners were present and to test them on their knowledge of the rules and of their I.D. numbers. The first perfunctory counts lasted only about 10 minutes, but on each successive day (or night) they were spontaneously increased in duration by the guards until some lasted several hours. Many of the preestablished features of administrative routine were modified or abandoned by the guards, and some privileges were forgotten by the staff over the course of study.

Data Collection: Dependent Measures

The exploratory nature of this investigation and the absence of specific hypotheses led us to adopt the strategy of surveying as many behavioral and psychological manifestations of the prison experience on the guards and the prisoners as was possible. The dependent measures were of two general types: (1) transactions between and within each group of subjects, recorded on video- and audiotape as well as directly observed, and (2) individual reactions on questionnaires, mood inventories, personality tests, daily guard shift reports, and postexperimental interviews.

Data collection was organized around the following sources:

1. *Videotaping*   Using the concealed video equipment, about 12 hours of recordings were made of daily, regularly occurring events such as the counts and meals, as well as unusual interactions such as a prisoner rebellion; visits from a priest, a lawyer, and parents; parole board meetings; and others.

2. *Audio recording*   Concealed microphones recorded over 30 hours of verbal interactions between guards and prisoners in the prison yard, as well as some within the cells and in the testing-interview room.

3. *Rating scales*   Mood adjective checklists and sociometric measures were administered on several occasions to assess emotional changes in affective state and interpersonal dynamics among the guard and prisoner groups.

4. *Individual difference scales*   Prior to the start of the simulation, all subjects had completed a series of paper-and-pencil personality tests selected to provide dispositional indicators of interpersonal behavior styles—the F scale of Authoritarian Personality (Adorno, Frenkel-Brunswik, Levinson, and Sanford 1950) and the Machiavellianism Scale (Christie and Geis 1970)—and to isolate areas of possible personality pathology through the newly developed Comrey Personality Scale (Comrey 1970).

5. *Personal observations*   The guards made daily reports of their observations after each shift, the experimenters kept informal diaries, and all subjects completed postexperimental questionnaires of their reactions to the experience about a month after the study was over.

Data Analysis: Video Recordings

Special analyses were required only of the video and audio material. The other data sources were analyzed following established scoring procedures. Since the present discussion is based primarily on the videotaped material, details of this analysis are outlined here.

There were 25 relatively discrete incidents identifiable on the tapes of prisoner–guard interactions. Each incident or scene was scored for the presence of nine behavioral (and verbal) categories by two judges who had not been involved with the simulation study. These categories were defined as follows:

- ▾ *Question*   All questions asked, requests for information or assistance (excluding rhetorical questions).
- ▾ *Command*   An order to commence or abstain from a specific behavior, directed to either individuals or groups. Also generalized orders; e.g., "Settle down."
- ▾ *Information*   A specific piece of information proffered by anyone, whether requested or not, dealing with any contingency of the simulation.
- ▾ *Individuating reference*   Positive: use of a person's real name, nickname, or allusion to special positive physical characteristics. Negative: use of

prison number, title, generalized "you," or reference to derogatory characteristic.

- ▾ *Threat* Verbal statement of contingent negative consequences of a wide variety; e.g., no meal, long count, pushups, lock-up in hole, no visitors.
- ▾ *Deprecation/insult* Use of obscenity, slander, malicious statement directed toward individuals or groups, e.g., "You lead a life of mendacity," "You guys are really stupid."
- ▾ *Resistance* Any physical resistance, usually prisoners to guards, such as holding onto beds, blocking doors, shoving guard or prisoner, taking off stocking caps, refusing to carry out orders.
- ▾ *Help* Person physically assisting another (excludes verbal statements of support); e.g., guard helping another to open door, prisoner helping another prisoner in cleanup duties.
- ▾ *Use of instruments* Use of any physical instrument to either intimidate, threaten, or achieve specific end; e.g., fire extinguisher, batons, whistles.

Results

The results of the present experiment support many commonly held conceptions of prison life and validate anecdotal evidence supplied by articulate exconvicts. The environment of arbitrary custody had great impact upon *the affective states* of both guards and prisoners as well as upon *the interpersonal processes* between and within those role-groups.

In general, guards and prisoners showed a marked decrease in positive affect or emotion, and their overall outlook became increasingly negative. As the experiment progressed, prisoners expressed intentions to do harm to others more frequently. For both prisoners and guards, self-evaluations were more deprecating as the experience of the prison environment became internalized.

Overt behavior was generally consistent with the subjective self-reports and affective expressions of the subjects. While guards and prisoners were essentially free to engage in any form of interaction (positive or negative, supportive or affrontive, etc.), the characteristic nature of their encounters tended to be negative, hostile, affrontive, and dehumanizing. Prisoners immediately adopted a generally passive style of responding, while guards assumed a very active initiative role in all interactions. Throughout the experiment, commands were the most frequent form of verbal behavior and, generally, verbal exchanges were strikingly impersonal, with few references to individual identity. Although it was clear to all subjects that the experimenters would not permit physical violence to take place, varieties of less direct aggressive behavior were observed frequently (especially on the part of guards). In fact, varieties of verbal affronts became the most frequent form of interpersonal contact between guards and prisoners.

The most dramatic evidence of the impact of the mock prison upon the participants was seen in the gross reactions of five prisoners who had to be released from the study because of extreme emotional depression, crying, rage, or acute anxiety. The pattern of symptoms was quite similar in four of the subjects and began as early as the second day of imprisonment. The fifth subject was released after being treated for a psychosomatic rash which covered portions of his body. Of the remaining prisoners, only two said they were unwilling to forfeit all the money they had earned in return for being "paroled" from the study. When the experiment was terminated prematurely after only six days, all the remaining prisoners were delighted by their unexpected good fortune; in contrast, most of the guards seemed to be distressed by the decision to stop the experiment. It appeared to us that the guards had become sufficiently involved in their roles so that they now enjoyed the extreme control and power they exercised and were reluctant to give it up. One guard, who did report being personally upset at the suffering of the prisoners, claimed to have considered asking to change his role to become one of them—but never did so. None of the guards ever failed to come to work on time for their shift, and indeed, on several occasions guards remained on duty voluntarily and uncomplainingly for extra hours—without additional pay.

The extreme reactions which emerged in both groups of subjects provide clear evidence of the power of the social forces operating in this pathological setting. There were, however, individual differences observed in *styles* of coping with this stressful experience, as well as varying degrees of success in adaptation to it. While all were somewhat adversely affected by it, half the prisoners did "endure" the oppressive atmosphere—at least in the sense that they remained until the study was completed. Not all of the guards resorted to the overt and inventive forms of hostility employed by others. Some guards were tough but fair ("played by the rules"), some went far beyond their roles to engage in cruelty and harassment, while a few were passive and rarely instigated any coercive control over the prisoners. It is important to emphasize, however, that at some time during the six days *all* guards participated in what could be characterized as sadistic treatment of prisoners. . . .

Representative Personal Statements

Much of the flavor and impact of this prison experience has been unavoidably lost in the relatively formal, objective analyses outlined in [other papers]. The following quotations taken from interviews, conversations, and questionnaires provide a more personal view of what it was like to be a prisoner or guard in the "Stanford County Prison" experiment.

GUARDS' COMMENTS

They [the prisoners] seemed to lose touch with the reality of the experiment—they took me so seriously.

I didn't interfere with any of the guards' actions. Usually if what they were doing bothered me, I would walk out and take another duty.

. . . looking back, I am impressed by how little I felt for them.

They [the prisoners] didn't see it as an experiment. It was real and they were fighting to keep their identity. But we were always there to show them just who was boss.

I was tired of seeing the prisoners in their rags and smelling the strong odors of their bodies that filled the cells. I watched them tear at each other, on orders given by us.

Acting authoritatively can be fun. Power can be a great pleasure.

During the inspection, I went to cell 2 to mess up a bed which the prisoner had made and he grabbed me, screaming that he had just made it, and he wasn't going to let me mess it up. He grabbed my throat, and although he was laughing I was pretty scared. I lashed out with my stick and hit him in the chin (although not very hard) and when I freed myself I became angry.

PRISONERS' COMMENTS

The way we were made to degrade ourselves really brought us down, and that's why we all sat docile toward the end of the experiment.

I realize now (after it's over) that no matter how together I thought I was inside my head, my prison behavior was often less under my control than I realized. No matter how open, friendly, and helpful I was with other prisoners I was still operating as an isolated, self-centered person, being rational rather than compassionate.

I began to feel I was losing my identity, that the person I call _____ , the person who volunteered to get me into this prison (because it was a prison to me, it still is a prison to me, I don't regard it as an experiment or a simulation . . .) was distant from me, was remote until finally I wasn't that person, I was 416. I was really my number and 416 was really going to have to decide what to do.

I learned that people can easily forget that others are human.

Debriefing Encounter Sessions

Because of the unexpectedly intense reactions (such as the above) generated by this mock prison experience, we decided to terminate the study at the end of six days rather than continue for the second week. Three separate encounter sessions were held, first for the prisoners, then for the guards, and finally for all participants together. Subjects and staff openly discussed their reactions, and strong feelings were expressed and shared. We analyzed the moral conflicts posed by this experience and used the debriefing sessions to make explicit alternative courses of action that would lead to more moral behavior in future comparable situations.

Follow-ups on each subject over the year following termination of the study revealed that the negative effects of participation had been temporary, while the personal gain to the subjects endured.

Conclusions and Discussion

It should be apparent that the elaborate procedures (and staging) employed by the experimenters to ensure a high degree of "mundane realism" in this mock prison contributed to its effective functional simulation of the psychological dynamics operating in "real" prisons. We observed empirical relationships in the simulated prison environment which were strikingly isomorphic to the internal relations of real prisons, corroborating many of the documented reports of what occurs behind prison walls. Most dramatic and distressing to us were the ease with which sadistic behavior could be elicited from individuals who were not "sadistic types" and the frequency with which acute emotional breakdowns could occur in persons selected precisely for their emotional stability.

Authors' Note: This research was funded by an ONR grant: N00014-67-A-0112-0041 to Professor Philip G. Zimbardo.

The ideas expressed in this paper are those of the authors and do not imply endorsement of ONR or any sponsoring agency. We wish to extend our thanks and appreciation for the contributions to this research by David Jaffe who served as "warden" and pretested some of the variables in the mock prison situation. In addition, Greg White provided invaluable assistance during the data reduction phase of this study. Many others (most notably Carolyn Burkhart, Susie Phillips, and Kathy Rosenfeld) helped at various stages of the experiment, with the construction of the prison, prisoner arrest, interviewing, testing, and data analysis—we extend our sincere thanks to each of these collaborators. Finally, we especially wish to thank Carlo Prescott, our prison consultant, whose personal experience gave us invaluable insights into the nature of imprisonment.

REFERENCES

Adorno, T. W., E. Frenkel-Brunswik, D. J. Levinson, and R. N. Sanford. 1950. *The Authoritarian Personality.* New York: Harper.

Christie, R., and F. L. Geis, eds. 1970. *Studies in Machiavellianism.* New York: Academic Press.

Comrey, A. L. 1970. *Comrey Personality Scales.* San Diego, CA: Educational and Industrial Testing Service.

6

SIDEWALK

MITCHELL DUNEIER

Social research is concerned with the definition and assessment of social phenomena. Many social phenomena in day-to-day interaction are taken for granted, such as riding on a city bus, the daily routine inside a beauty salon, and children playing on a playground. Social researchers enable us to get inside these diverse social worlds and discover what social forces are at work in creating social life. This selection from Mitchell Duneier's critically acclaimed ethnography, *Sidewalk* (1999), takes us inside the social world of street vendors in New York City. Duneier, a Distinguished Professor of Sociology at The Graduate Center of the City University of New York, conveys well the character and complexity of urban life. In this excerpt, Duneier discusses his research questions and the research process he utilized to study urban street vending.

Hakim Hasan is a book vendor and street intellectual at the busy intersection of Eighth Street, Greenwich Avenue, and the Avenue of the Americas—aka Sixth Avenue. He is a sturdy and stocky five-foot-seven African American, forty-two years old. In the winter, he wears Timberland boots, jeans, a hooded sweatshirt, a down vest, and a Banana Republic baseball cap.

One Thursday in February 1996, an African American man in his mid-thirties came up to Hakim's table and asked for a copy of Alice Walker's book *The Same River Twice,* about her experiences in turning her novel *The Color Purple* into a movie. Hakim was all sold out, but said he would get some more in stock soon.

"When you get some, you let me know," said the man, who worked delivering groceries.

"I'll let you know."

"Because, you see, not only that," said the man, "I've got a friend that loves to read."

"Male or female?" asked Hakim.

"Female. She's like this: when she gets a book in her hand, in another hour it's finished. In other words—like, with me, I'll read maybe . . . five chapters, then I'll put it down 'cause I gotta do something, then maybe I'll come back to it. But with her, she gets into it and goes through the whole book like that. Boom. And she puts it on the shelf and it's just like brand-new. Like, when it's her birthday or what-have-you, I buy her books, because that's one of the things that she likes. I bought the book *Waiting to Exhale* in paperback, right? Listen to this: when I approached her with the book, the movie was coming out and she said, 'You late! I been read that book!'"

Hakim laughed. "I think she had a point."

"I said, 'Better late than never.' I wish I read that book before I seen the movie. Now, you can tell me this, Hakim: is it the same thing in the paperback as the hardcover?"

"Yeah, it's just different print."

"Just different print? Okay. Well, when you get the other book by Alice Walker, you let me know."

The man made a motion to leave, but then he continued talking.

"Because, you see, what happens is that there are a lot of females . . . authors that are coming out that are making their voices heard. More so than ever black. Even Alice Walker says something about this. It goes deep, man."

"Yeah, I'm gonna read that book by Alice Walker," said Hakim. "I'm gonna read it today."

"Oh, you're gonna read it today?" the man asked, laughing.

"I just finished two books over the weekend. I read at least one book a week," said Hakim.

"I try to tell my son that," said the deliveryman. "If you read one book a week, man, you don't know how much knowledge you can get."

Hakim doesn't just name titles. He knows the contents. I have observed the range and depth of his erudition impress scholars, and have seen him show great patience with uneducated people who are struggling with basic ideas and don't know much about books. He might sit for hours without having a single customer step up to his table; other times the table becomes a social center where men and women debate into the night.

For two years, I lived around the corner from where Hakim sets up. Almost every day, whenever I had time to amble about on the block, I'd visit and listen to the conversations taking place at his table.

At first, Hakim sold what he called "black books," works exclusively by or about blacks. In later years, he became romantically involved with a Filipina book vendor named Alice, who carried used paperback classics and *New York Times* best-sellers, and they merged their vending tables. Now they are on their own again, working side by side. Alice is the only woman who works outside on Sixth Avenue every day, and she has practically raised her daughters and granddaughters there. Whereas Alice tends to be "about business," local residents, workers, and visitors come to Hakim to discuss topics of all kinds, from burning issues of the day to age-old questions.

Not long after we met, I asked Hakim how he saw his role.

"I'm a public character," he told me.

"A what?" I asked.

"Have you ever read Jane Jacobs' *The Death and Life of Great American Cities?*" he asked. "You'll find it in there."

I considered myself quite familiar with the book, a classic study of modern urban life published in 1961, and grounded in the author's observations of her own neighborhood, Greenwich Village. But I didn't recall the discussion of public characters. Nor did I realize that Hakim's insight would figure in a central way in the manner in which I would come to see the sidewalk life of this neighborhood. When I got home, I looked it up:

> The social structure of sidewalk life hangs partly on what can be called self-appointed public characters. A public character is anyone who is in frequent contact with a wide circle of people and who is sufficiently interested to make himself a public character. A public character need have no special talents or wisdom to fulfill his function—although he often does. He just needs to be present, and there needs to be enough of his counterparts. His main qualification is that he *is* public, that he talks to lots of different people. In this way, news travels that is of sidewalk interest.[1]

Jacobs had modeled her idea of the public character after the local shopkeepers with whom she and her Greenwich Village neighbors would leave their spare keys. These figures could be counted on to let her know if her children were getting out of hand on the street, or to call the police, if a strange-looking person was hanging around for too long: "Storekeepers and other small businessmen are typically strong proponents of peace and order," Jacobs explained. "They hate broken windows and holdups."[2] She also modeled the public character after persons like herself, who distributed petitions on local political issues to neighborhood stores, spreading local news in the process.

Although the idea is meaningful to anyone who has lived in an urban neighborhood where people do their errands on foot, Jacobs did not define her concept except to say, "A public character is anyone who is . . . sufficiently interested to make himself a public character." To clarify, we may consider her opening observation that the social structure "hangs partly" on the public characters. What Jacobs means is that the social context of the sidewalk is patterned in a particular way because of the presence of the public character: his or her actions have the effect of making street life safer, stabler, and more predictable. As she goes on to explain, this occurs because the public character has "eyes upon the street."

Following Jacobs, urban theorists have emphasized what city dwellers in pedestrian areas like Greenwich Village have always known: sidewalk life is crucial because the sidewalk is *the* site where a sense of mutual support must be felt *among strangers* if they are to go about their lives there together. Unlike most places in the United States, where people do their errands in cars, the people of Greenwich Village do many, if not most, of their errands by walking. The neighborhood's sidewalk life matters deeply to residents and visitors alike. Jacobs emphasized that social contact on the sidewalks must take place within a context of mutual respect for appropriate limits on interaction and intimacy. This made for interactive pleasantness, adding up to "an almost unconscious assumption of general street support when the chips are down."[3] The Village's "eyes upon the street," in Jacobs' famous dictum, indicated that residents and strangers were safe and consequently produced safety in fact.

———————

Greenwich Village looked very different forty years ago, when Jane Jacobs was writing her classic book. Much of the architecture remains, and many people still live the way Jacobs' descriptions suggest; but there is another, more marginal population on these streets: poor black men who make their lives on the Village sidewalks. The presence of such people today means that pedestrians handle their social boundaries *in situ*, whereas, in the past, racial segregation and well-policed skid-row areas kept the marginal at bay.

In this [excerpt], I will offer a framework for understanding the changes that have taken place on the sidewalk over the past four decades. In asking *why* the sidewalk life has changed in this affluent neighborhood, I provide the context and point of departure for my research. It has changed because the concentration of poverty in high poverty zones has produced social problems of a magnitude that cannot be contained by even the most extreme forms of social control and exclusion. Many people living and/or working on Sixth Avenue come from such neighborhoods. Some were among the first generation of crack users, and so were affected by the war on those who use the drug and the failure of prisons to help them prepare for life after released. Some, under new workfare rules, have lost their benefits when they refused to show up to work as "the Mayor's slave."

In asking *how* the sidewalk life works today, I begin by looking at the lives of the poor (mainly) black men who work and/or live on the sidewalks of an upper-middle-class neighborhood. Unlike Hakim, who has an apartment in New Jersey, magazine vendors like Ishmael Walker are without a home; the police throw their merchandise, vending tables, clothes, and family photos in the back of a garbage truck when they leave the block to relieve themselves. Mudrick Hayes and Joe Garbage "lay shit out" on the ground (merchandise retrieved from the trash) to earn their subsistence wages. Keith Johnson sits in his wheelchair by the door of the automated teller machine and panhandles.

How do these persons live in a moral order? How do they have the ingenuity to do so in the face of exclusion and stigmatization on the basis of race and class? How does the way they do so affront the sensibilities of the working and middle classes? How do their acts intersect with a city's mechanisms to regulate its public spaces?

The people making lives on Sixth Avenue depend on one another for social support. The group life upon which their survival is contingent is crucial to those who do not rely on religious institutions or social service agencies. For some of these people, the informal economic life is a substitute for illegal ways of supporting excessive drug use. For others, informal modes of self-help enable them to do things most citizens seek to achieve by working: to support families, others in their community, or themselves. For still others, the informal economy provides a forum where they can advise, mentor, and encourage one another to strive to live in accordance with standards of moral worth.

Yet the stories of these sidewalks cannot ultimately serve as sociological romance, celebrating how people on the streets "resist" the larger structures of society. The social order these relationships carve out of what seems to be pure chaos, powerful as its effects are, still cannot control many acts that affront the sensibilities of local residents and passersby. How can we comprehend types of behavior such as sidewalk sleeping, urinating in public, selling stolen goods, and entangling passersby in unwanted conversations? What factors engender and sustain such behavior? How can we understand the processes that lead many people to regard those who engage in such acts as "indecent"? How do the quantity and quality of their "indecency" make them different from conventional passersby?

One of the greatest strengths of firsthand observation is also its greatest weakness. Through a careful involvement in people's lives, we can get a fix on how their world works and how they see it. But the details can be misleading if they distract us from the forces that are less visible to the people we observe but which influence and sustain the behaviors.[4] How do economic, cultural, and political factors contribute to make these blocks a habitat—a place where poor people can weave together complementary elements to organize themselves for subsistence? And how do such forces contribute to bringing these men to the sidewalk in the first place?

I look at all these aspects of sidewalk life in a setting where government retrenchment on welfare is keenly felt, as is the approbation of influential business groups. When government does assume responsibility in the lives of people like these, it attempts to eradicate them from the streets or to shape their behavior. These "social controls"—e.g., cutting down on the space for vending or throwing vendors' belongings in the back of garbage trucks—are the intended and unintended results of what has become the most influential contemporary idea about deviance and criminality: the "broken windows" theory, which holds that minor signs of disorder lead to serious crime. What are the consequences of this theory, its assumptions, and the formal social controls to which it has led?

In trying to understand the sidewalk life, I refer to an area of about three city blocks. Here we can see the confluence of many forces: some global (deindustrialization), some national (stratification of race and class and gender), some local (restrictive and punitive policies toward street vendors). Here, also, are blocks which can be studied in light of Jane Jacobs' earlier account and which contain the kinds of social problems that have become iconic in representations of the city's "quality of life" crisis. My visits to some other New York neighborhoods[5] and some other American cities suggest that they, too, have tensions surrounding inequalities and cultural differences in dense pedestrian areas. Across the country, liberals have voted to elect moderate, "law and order" mayors, some of them Republican. Whereas disorderly-conduct statutes were once enough, anti-panhandling statutes have been passed in Seattle, Atlanta, Cincinnati, Dallas, Washington, D.C., San Francisco, Santa Barbara, Long Beach, Philadelphia, New Haven, Raleigh, and Baltimore.

Yet New York City and Greenwich Village are unique in a multitude of ways. I certainly cannot hope to account for life in the majority of places, which have not seen severe sidewalk tensions in dense pedestrian districts; even many places that *have* seen such tensions are different from Greenwich village.[6] Nor can I hope to show how the sidewalk works in low-income neighborhoods where the majority of tense sidewalk interactions occur among members of the same class or racial group. In the end, I must leave it to readers to test my observations against their own, and hope that the concepts I have developed to make sense of this neighborhood will prove useful in other venues.

I gained entrée to this social world when I became a browser and customer at Hakim's table in 1992. Through my relationship with him, I came to know others in the area. He introduced me to unhoused and formerly unhoused people who scavenge and sell on the street, as well as other vendors who compete with him for sidewalk space and access to customers. These relations then led me to panhandlers, some of whom also sometimes scavenge and vend.

Once I was in the network, contacts and introductions took place across the various spheres. Eventually, I worked as a general assistant—watching vendors' merchandise while they went on errands, buying up merchandise offered in their absence, assisting on scavenging missions through trash and recycling bins, and "going for coffee." Then I worked full-time as a magazine vendor and scavenger during the summer of 1996, again for three days a week during the summer of 1997 and during part of the fall of 1997. I also made daily visits to the blocks during the summer of 1998, often for hours at a time, and worked full-time as a vendor for two weeks in March 1999, when my research came to an end.

Although in race, class, and status I am very different from the men I write about, I was myself eventually treated by them as a fixture of the blocks, occasionally referred to as a "scholar" or "professor," which is my occupation. My designation was Mitch. This seemed to have a variety of changing meanings, including a naïve white man who could himself be exploited for "loans" of small change and dollar bills; a Jew who was going to make a lot of money off the stories of people working the streets; a white writer who was trying to "state the truth about what was going on." . . .

My continual presence as a vendor provided me with opportunities to observe life among the people working and/or living on the sidewalk, including their interactions with passersby. This enabled me to draw many of my conclusions about what happens on the sidewalk from incidents I myself witnessed, rather than deriving them from interviews. Often I simply asked questions while participating and observing.

Sometimes, when I wanted to understand how the local political system had shaped these blocks, I did my interviews at the offices of Business Improvement Districts, politicians, and influential attorneys. I also questioned police officers, pedestrians, local residents, and the like. I carried out more than twenty interviews with people working the sidewalk in which I explicitly asked them to tell me their "story." These sessions, held on street corners, in coffee shops, and on subway platforms, lasted between two and six hours. I paid the interviewees fifty dollars when their sessions were over, as compensation for time they could have spent selling or panhandling. Throughout the book, I try to be clear about the kind of research from which a quotation has been culled.

After I had been observing on the block for four years, Ovie Carter, an African American photojournalist who has been taking pictures of the inner city for three decades, agreed to take photographs to illustrate the things I was writing about. He visited the blocks year-round and came to know the people in the book intimately. Ovie's photographs helped me to see things that I had not noticed, so that my work has now been influenced by his.

After three years passed, I believed I had a strong sense of the kinds of events and conversations that were typical on the blocks. In the next two years of this research, my field methods evolved to the point where intense use was made of a tape recorder. The tape recorder was on throughout my days on the block, usually kept in a milk crate under my vending table. People working and/or living on the sidewalk became accustomed to the machine and, after being exposed to it over a period of weeks, came to talk in ways that I determined to be like the talk I had heard before. Since the machine was taping on a public street, I hoped that I was not violating any expectation of privacy if it picked up the words of people who couldn't efficiently be informed that it was on. I have since received permission to quote almost all the people who were taped without their knowledge. When names are used, they are real ones, and I do so with consent. In those few cases when this is not possible (such as incidents involving police officers whose speech was recorded by my microphone without their knowing it), I have not used names at all or have indicated that a name is false.

I am committed to the idea that the voices of the people on Sixth Avenue need to be heard. To that end, my goal has been to assure the reader that what appears between quotation marks is a reasonably reliable record of what was said. (Some quotes have been edited slightly to make them more concise.) When the best I could do was rely on my memory or notes, quotation marks are not used. I have come to believe that this is perhaps especially necessary when a scholar is writing about people who occupy race and class positions widely divergent from his or her own, for the inner meanings and logics embodied in language that is distinctive to those positions can easily be misunderstood and misrepresented if not accurately reproduced. Furthermore, the increasingly popular practice of creating composite characters, and combining events and quotations sometimes occurring months or years apart, is *not* employed here. No characters have been combined. No events have been reordered.

Some of the people on the street volunteered to "manage" the taping by themselves, leaving the tape recorder on while wearing it in their pocket or resting it on their table when I was away from the scene or out of town. Such acts demonstrated the desire of persons in [my research] to ask their own questions, have their own topics addressed and recognized, and enable me to hear some things that went on when I could not be present. Sometimes they used the machine to interview one another and gave me the tapes. . . . Given the knowledge Hakim had of both Jane Jacobs' work (which he inspired me to reread) and the life of these sidewalks, I asked him to respond to this [research]. He took time out of his daily grind as a vendor to write an afterword.

There was another way in which the vendors, scavengers, and panhandlers worked with me as collaborators. I invited some of them to classes to teach my students, in both Santa Barbara and Wisconsin. And I asked all of them to judge my own "theories" of the local scene when the book was complete, though always indicating that, while respecting their interpretations, I would not be bound by them. Throughout [my research], it is I who have selected the material presented, and I take responsibility for the interpretations that go along with that material. For twenty-one people who figure prominently on the blocks, I have now made a commitment to return the advance and a share of any royalties or other forms of income that the book might yield.

Like all observers, I have my subjectivities. I know that scrupulous adherence to rules of method will not lead necessarily to objective truth. I believe that what is most important is that I try to help the reader recognize the lens through which the reality is refracted. I have written a statement on method to that end, and throughout [my research] I endeavor to explain my procedures for selecting data and my own biases and uncertainties about the inferences I draw.

Fieldwork is presumed to require trust. But one never can know for certain that he or she has gained such trust, given the absence of any agreed-upon indicator of what "full" trust would look like. In this case, I think, some level of trust was shown by people's readiness to provide access to information, settings, and activities of the most intimate sort. They sometimes revealed illegal activities or actions which, if others knew of them, might result in violent retribution.

But . . . there were times when the trust I thought I had developed was nothing more than an illusion: deep suspicion lingered despite an appearance of trust. In some cases, perhaps it always will. Surely it takes more than goodwill to transcend distrust that comes out of a complex history. Though participant observers often remark on the rapport they achieve and how they are seen by the people they write about, in the end it is best to be humble about such things, because one never really knows.

ENDNOTES

[1] Jane Jacobs, *The Death and Life of Great American Cities* (New York: Vintage, 1961), p. 68.

[2] Ibid., p. 47.

[3] Ibid., p. 56.

[4] For an excellent statement, see Stephen Steinberg, "The Urban Villagers: Thirty Years Later," remarks prepared for a plenary session at meeting of the Eastern Sociology Society, Boston, March 25, 1993.

[5] For an excellent collection of ethnographies of the East Village, see Janet L. Abu-Lughod, *From Urban Village to "East Village": The Battle for New York's Lower East Side* (Cambridge: Blackwell, 1994); for an excellent ethnography of the political culture of Corona, with reference to quality-of-life discourse among working-class blacks in Queens, see Steven Gregory, *Black Corona: Race and the Politics of Place in an Urban Community* (Princeton. NJ: Princeton, University Press, 1988).

[6] For a comprehensive analysis, see Lyn H. Lofland, *The Public Realm* (Hawthorne, NY: Aldine De Gruyter, 1998).

PART II

Culture

7

THE CULTURE OF FEAR
Why Americans Are Afraid of the
Wrong Things

BARRY GLASSNER

Culture is defined as the shared ways of a human social group. This definition includes the ways of thinking, understanding, and feeling that have
been gained through common experience in social groups and are passed on
from one generation to another. Thus, culture reflects the social patterns of
thought, emotions, and practices that arise from social interaction within a
given society. In this reading, the first of four to explore culture, Barry
Glassner examines one aspect of American culture, which he labels *the culture of fear.* Glassner, a professor of sociology at Washington University in
St. Louis, raises interesting questions about our culture and the implications
of living in a culture of fear. This excerpt is taken from Glassner's 1999
award-winning book of the same name: *The Culture of Fear: Why Americans
Are Afraid of the Wrong Things.*

W hy are so many fears in the air, and so many of them unfounded?
Why, as crime rates plunged throughout the 1990s, did two-thirds
of Americans believe they were soaring? How did it come about
that by mid-decade 62 percent of us described ourselves as "truly desperate"
about crime—almost twice as many as in the late 1980s, when crime rates
were higher? Why, on a survey in 1997, when the crime rate had already
fallen for a half dozen consecutive years, did more than half of us disagree
with the statement "This country is finally beginning to make some progress
in solving the crime problem"?[1]

In the late 1990s the number of drug users had decreased by half compared to a decade earlier; almost two-thirds of high school seniors had never
used any illegal drugs, even marijuana. So why did a majority of adults rank
drug abuse as the greatest danger to America's youth? Why did nine out of

ten believe the drug problem is out of control, and only one in six believe the country was making progress?[2]

Give us a happy ending and we write a new disaster story. In the late 1990s the unemployment rate was below 5 percent for the first time in a quarter century. People who had been pounding the pavement for years could finally get work. Yet pundits warned of imminent economic disaster. They predicted inflation would take off, just as they had a few years earlier—also erroneously—when the unemployment rate dipped below 6 percent.[3]

We compound our worries beyond all reason. Life expectancy in the United States has doubled during the twentieth century. We are better able to cure and control diseases than any other civilization in history. Yet we hear that phenomenal numbers of us are dreadfully ill. In 1996 Bob Garfield, a magazine writer, reviewed articles about serious diseases published over the course of a year in the *Washington Post,* the *New York Times,* and *USA Today.* He learned that, in addition to 59 million Americans with heart disease, 53 million with migraines, 25 million with osteoporosis, 16 million with obesity, and 3 million with cancer, many Americans suffer from more obscure ailments such as temporomandibular joint disorders (10 million) and brain injuries (2 million). Adding up the estimates, Garfield determined that 543 million Americans are seriously sick—a shocking number in a nation of 266 million inhabitants. "Either as a society we are doomed, or someone is seriously double-dipping," he suggested.[4]

Garfield appears to have underestimated one category of patients: for psychiatric ailments his figure was 53 million. Yet when Jim Windolf, an editor of the *New York Observer,* collated estimates for maladies ranging from borderline personality disorder (10 million) and sex addiction (11 million) to less well-known conditions such as restless leg syndrome (12 million) he came up with a figure of 152 million. "But give the experts a little time," he advised. "With another new quantifiable disorder or two, everybody in the country will be officially nuts."[5]

Indeed, Windolf omitted from his estimates new-fashioned afflictions that have yet to make it into the *Diagnostic and Statistical Manual of Mental Disorders* of the American Psychiatric Association: ailments such as road rage, which afflicts more than half of Americans, according to a psychologist's testimony before a congressional hearing in 1997.[6] . . .

Killer Kids

When we are not worrying about deadly diseases we worry about homicidal strangers. Every few months for the past several years it seems we discover a new category of people to fear: government thugs in Waco, sadistic cops on Los Angeles freeways and in Brooklyn police stations, mass-murdering youths in small towns all over the country. A single anomalous event can provide us with multiple groups of people to fear. After the 1995 explosion at the federal building in Oklahoma City, first we panicked about Arabs.

"Knowing that the car bomb indicates Middle Eastern terrorists at work, it's safe to assume that their goal is to promote free-floating fear and a measure of anarchy, thereby disrupting American life," a *New York Post* editorial asserted. "Whatever we are doing to destroy Mideast terrorism, the chief terrorist threat against Americans, has not been working," wrote A. M. Rosenthal in the *New York Times.*[7]

When it turned out that the bombers were young white guys from middle America, two more groups instantly became spooky: right-wing radio talk show hosts who criticize the government—depicted by President Bill Clinton as "purveyors of hatred and division"—and members of militias. No group of disgruntled men was too ragtag not to warrant big, prophetic news stories.[8]...

The more things improve the more pessimistic we become. Violence-related deaths at the nation's schools dropped to a record low during the 1996–97 academic year (19 deaths out of 54 million children), and only one in ten public schools reported *any* serious crime. Yet *Time* and *U.S. News & World Report* both ran headlines in 1996 referring to "Teenage Time Bombs." In a nation of "Children Without Souls" (another *Time* headline that year), "America's beleaguered cities are about to be victimized by a paradigm shattering wave of ultraviolent, morally vacuous young people some call 'the superpredators,'" William Bennett, the former Secretary of Education, and John DiIulio, a criminologist, forecast in a book published in 1996.[9]

Instead of the arrival of superpredators, violence by urban youths continued to decline. So we went looking elsewhere for proof that heinous behavior by young people was "becoming increasingly more commonplace in America" (CNN). After a sixteen-year-old in Pearl, Mississippi, and a fourteen-year-old in West Paducah, Kentucky, went on shooting sprees in late 1997, killing five of their classmates and wounding twelve others, these isolated incidents were taken as evidence of "an epidemic of seemingly depraved adolescent murderers" (Geraldo Rivera). Three months later, in March 1998, all sense of proportion vanished after two boys ages eleven and thirteen killed four students and a teacher in Jonesboro, Arkansas. No longer, we learned in *Time,* was it "unusual for kids to get back at the world with live ammunition." When a child psychologist on NBC's "Today" show advised parents to reassure their children that shootings at schools are rare, reporter Ann Curry corrected him. "But this is the fourth case since October," she said.[10]

Over the next couple of months young people failed to accommodate the trend hawkers. None committed mass murder. Fear of killer kids remained very much in the air nonetheless. In stories on topics such as school safety and childhood trauma, reporters recapitulated the gory details of the killings. And the news media made a point of reporting every incident in which a child was caught at school with a gun or making a death threat. In May, when a fifteen-year-old in Springfield, Oregon, did open fire in a cafeteria filled with students, killing two and wounding twenty-three others, the event felt like a continuation of a "disturbing trend" (*New York Times*). The day after the shooting, on National Public Radio's "All Things Considered," the criminologist Vincent Schiraldi tried to explain that the recent string of incidents did not constitute a trend, that youth homicide rates had declined by 30 percent in recent years, and more than three times as many people were killed by lightning than by violence at schools. But the show's host, Robert Siegel, interrupted him. "You're saying these are just anomalous events?" he asked, audibly peeved. The criminologist reiterated that *anomalous* is precisely the right word to describe the events, and he called it "a grave mistake" to imagine otherwise. . . .

Roosevelt Was Wrong

We had better learn to doubt our inflated fears before they destroy us. Valid fears have their place; they cue us to danger. False and overdrawn fears only cause hardship. . . .

I do not contend, as did President Roosevelt in 1933, that "the only thing we have to fear is fear itself." My point is that we often fear the wrong things. In the 1990s middle-income and poorer Americans should have worried about unemployment insurance, which covered a smaller share of workers than twenty years earlier. Many of us have had friends or family out of work during economic downturns or as a result of corporate restructuring. Living in a nation with one of the largest income gaps of any industrialized country, where the bottom 40 percent of the population is worse off financially than their counterparts two decades earlier, we might also have worried about income inequality. Or poverty. During the mid- and late 1990s, 5 million elderly Americans had no food in their homes, more than 20 million people used emergency food programs each year, and one in five children lived in poverty—more than a quarter million of them homeless. All told, a larger proportion of Americans were poor than three decades earlier.[11]

One of the paradoxes of a culture of fear is that serious problems remain widely ignored even though they give rise to precisely the dangers that the populace most abhors. Poverty, for example, correlates strongly with child abuse, crime, and drug abuse. Income inequality is also associated with adverse outcomes for society as a whole. The larger the gap between rich and poor in a society, the higher its overall death rates from heart disease, cancer, and murder. Some social scientists argue that extreme inequality also threatens political stability in a nation such as the United States, where we think of ourselves not as "haves and have nots" but as "haves and will haves." "Unlike the citizens of most other nations, Americans have always been united less by a shared past than by the shared dreams of a better future. If we lose that common future," the Brandeis University economist Robert Reich has suggested, "we lose the glue that holds our nation together."[12]

The combination of extreme inequality and poverty can prove explosive. In an insightful article in *U.S. News & World Report* in 1997 about militia groups, reporters Mike Tharp and William Holstein noted that people's motivations for joining these groups are as much economic as ideological.

The journalists argued that the disappearance of military and blue-collar jobs, along with the decline of family farming, created the conditions under which a new breed of protest groups flourished. "What distinguishes these antigovernment groups from, say, traditional conservatives who mistrust government is that their anger is fueled by direct threats to their livelihood, and they carry guns," Tharp and Holstein wrote.[13]

That last phrase alludes to a danger that by any rational calculation deserves top billing on Americans' lists of fears. So gun crazed is this nation that Burger King had to order a Baltimore franchise to stop giving away coupons from a local sporting goods store for free boxes of bullets with the purchase of guns. We have more guns *stolen* from their owners—about 300,000 annually—than many countries have gun owners. In Great Britain, Australia, and Japan, where gun ownership is severely restricted, no more than a few dozen people are killed each year by handguns. In the United States, where private citizens own a quarter-billion guns, around 15,000 people are killed, 18,000 commit suicide, and another 1,500 die accidentally from firearms. American children are twelve times more [likely] to die from gun injuries than are youngsters in other industrialized nations.[14]

Yet even after tragedies that could not have occurred except for the availability of guns, their significance is either played down or missed altogether. Had the youngsters in the celebrated schoolyard shootings of 1997–98 not had access to guns, some or all of the people they killed would be alive today. Without their firepower those boys lacked the strength, courage, and skill to commit multiple murders. Nevertheless, newspapers ran editorials with titles such as "It's Not Guns, It's Killer Kids" (*Fort Worth Star-Telegram*) and "Guns Aren't the Problem"(*New York Post*), and journalists, politicians, and pundits blathered on endlessly about every imaginable cause of youthful rage, from "the psychology of violence in the South" to satanism to fights on "Jerry Springer" and simulated shooting in Nintendo games.[15]. . .

In Praise of Journalists

Any analysis of the culture of fear that ignored the news media would be patently incomplete, and of the several institutions most culpable for creating and sustaining scares the news media are arguably first among equals. They are also the most promising candidates for positive change. Yet, by the same token, critiques such as Stolberg's presage a crucial shortcoming in arguments that blame the media. Reporters not only spread fears, they also debunk them and criticize one another for spooking the public. A wide array of groups, including businesses, advocacy organizations, religious sects, and political parties, promote and profit from scares. News organizations are distinguished from other fear-mongering groups because they sometimes bite the scare that feeds them.

A group that raises money for research into a particular disease is not likely to negate concerns about that disease. A company that sells alarm systems is not about to call attention to the fact that crime is down. News organizations, on the other hand, periodically allay the very fears they arouse to lure audiences. Some newspapers that ran stories about child murderers, rather than treat every incident as evidence of a shocking trend, affirmed the opposite. After the schoolyard shooting in Kentucky the *New York Times* ran a sidebar alongside its feature story with the headline "Despite Recent Carnage, School Violence Is Not on Rise." Following the Jonesboro killings they ran a similar piece, this time on a recently released study showing the rarity of violent crimes in schools.[16]

Several major newspapers parted from the pack in other ways. *USA Today* and the *Washington Post,* for instance, made sure their readers knew that what should worry them is the availability of guns. *USA Today* ran news stories explaining that easy access to guns in homes accounted for increases in the number of juvenile arrests for homicide in rural areas during the 1990s. While other news outlets were respectfully quoting the mother of the thirteen-year-old Jonesboro shooter, who said she did not regret having encouraged her son to learn to fire a gun ("it's like anything else, there's some people that can drink a beer, and not become an alcoholic"), *USA Today* ran an op-ed piece proposing legal parameters for gun ownership akin to those for the use of alcohol and motor vehicles. And the paper published its own editorial in support of laws that require gun owners to lock their guns or keep them in locked containers. Adopted at that time by only fifteen states, the laws had reduced the number of deaths among children in those states by 23 percent.[17]

Morality and Marketing

Why do news organizations and their audiences find themselves drawn to one hazard rather than another? . . .

In the first half of the 1990s, U.S. cities spent at least $10 billion to purge asbestos from public schools, even though removing asbestos from buildings posed a greater health hazard than leaving it in place. At a time when about one-third of the nation's schools were in need of extensive repairs, the money might have been spent to renovate dilapidated buildings. But hazards posed by seeping asbestos are morally repugnant. A product that was supposed to protect children from fires might be giving them cancer. By directing our worries and dollars at asbestos, we express outrage at technology and industry run afoul.[18] . . .

Within public discourse fears proliferate through a process of exchange. It is from crosscurrents of scares and counterscares that the culture of fear swells ever larger. Even as feminists disparage large classes of men, they themselves are a staple of fear mongering by conservatives. To hear conservatives tell it, feminists are not only "anti-child and anti-family" (Arianna Huffington) but through women's studies programs on college campuses they have fomented an "anti-science and anti-reason movement" (Christina Hoff Sommers).[19]

Conservatives also like to spread fears about liberals, who respond in kind. Among other pet scares, they accuse liberals of creating "children without consciences" by keeping prayer out of schools—to which liberals rejoin with warnings that right-wing extremists intend to turn youngsters into Christian soldiers.[20]

Samuel Taylor Coleridge was right when he claimed, "In politics, what begins in fear usually ends up in folly." Political activists are more inclined, though, to heed an observation from Richard Nixon: "People react to fear, not love. They don't teach that in Sunday school, but it's true." That principle, which guided the late president's political strategy throughout his career, is the sine qua non of contemporary political campaigning. Marketers of products and services ranging from car alarms to TV news programs have taken it to heart as well.[21]

The short answer to why Americans harbor so many misbegotten fears is that immense power and money await those who tap into our moral insecurities and supply us with symbolic substitutes.

ENDNOTES

[1] Crime data here and throughout are from reports of the Bureau of Justice Statistics unless otherwise noted. Fear of crime: Esther Madriz, *Nothing Bad Happens to Good Girls* (Berkeley: University of California Press, 1997), ch. 1; Richard Morin, "As Crime Rate Falls, Fears Persist," *Washington Post* National Edition, 16 June 1997, p. 35; David Whitman, "Believing the Good News," *U.S. News & World Report*, 5 January 1998, pp. 45–46.

[2] Eva Bertram, Morris Blachman et al., *Drug War Politics* (Berkeley: University of California Press, 1996), p. 10; Mike Males, *Scapegoat Generation* (Monroe, ME: Common Courage Press, 1996), ch. 6; Karen Peterson, "Survey: Teen Drug Use Declines," *USA Today*, 19 June 1998, p. A6; Robert Blendon and John Young, "The Public and the War on Illicit Drugs," *Journal of the American Medical Association* 279 (18 March 1998): 827–32. In presenting these statistics and others I am aware of a seeming paradox: I criticize the abuse of statistics by fearmongering politicians, journalists, and others but hand down precise-sounding numbers myself. Yet to eschew all estimates because some are used inappropriately or do not withstand scrutiny would be as foolhardy as ignoring all medical advice because some doctors are quacks. Readers can be assured I have interrogated the statistics presented here as factual. As notes make clear, I have tried to rely on research that appears in peer-reviewed scholarly journals. Where this was not possible or sufficient, I traced numbers back to their sources, investigated the research methodology utilized to produce them, or conducted searches of the popular and scientific literature for critical commentaries and conflicting findings.

[3] Bob Herbert, "Bogeyman Economics," *New York Times*, 4 April 1997, p. A15; Doug Henwood, "Alarming Drop in Unemployment," *Extra*, September 1994, pp. 16–17, Christopher Shea, "Low Inflation and Low Unemployment Spur Economists to Debate 'Natural Rate' Theory," *Chronicle of Higher Education*, 24 October 1997, p. A13.

[4] Bob Garfield, "Maladies by the Millions," *USA Today*, 16 December 1996, p. A15.

[5] Jim Windolf, "A Nation of Nuts," *Wall Street Journal*, 22 October 1997, p. A22.

[6] Andrew Ferguson, "Road Rage," *Time*, 12 January 1998, pp. 64–68; Joe Sharkey, "You're Not Bad, You're Sick. It's in the Book," *New York Times*, 28 September 1997, pp. N1, 5.

[7] Jim Naureckas, "The Jihad That Wasn't," *Extra*, July 1995, pp. 6–10, 20 (contains quotes). See also Edward Said, "A Devil Theory of Islam," *Nation*, 12 August 1996, pp. 28–32.

[8] Lewis Lapham, "Seen but Not Heard," *Harper's*, July 1995, pp. 29–36 (contains Clinton quote). See also Robin Wright and Ronald Ostrow, "Illusion of Immunity Is Shattered," *Los Angeles Times*, 20 April 1995, pp. Al, 18; Jack Germond and Jules Witcover, "Making the Angry White Males Angrier," column syndicated by Tribune Media Services, May 1995; and articles by James Bennet and Michael Janofsky in the *New York Times*, May 1995.

9 Statistics from "Violence and Discipline Problems in U.S. Public Schools: 1996–97," National Center on Education Statistics, U.S. Department of Education, Washington, DC, March 1998; CNN, "Early Prime," 2 December 1997; and Tamar Lewin, "Despite Recent Carnage, School Violence Is Not on Rise," *New York Times*, 3 December 1997, p. A14. Headlines: *Time*, 15 January 1996; *U.S. News & World Report*, 25 March 1996; Margaret Carlson, "Children Without Souls," *Time*, 2 December 1996, p. 70; William J. Bennett, John J. DiIulio, and John Walters, *Body Count* (New York: Simon & Schuster, 1996).

10 CNN, "Talkback Live," 2 December 1997; CNN, "The Geraldo Rivera Show," 11 December 1997; Richard Lacayo, "Toward the Root of Evil," *Time*, 6 April 1998, pp. 38–39; NBC, "Today," 25 March 1998. See also Rick Bragg, "Forgiveness, After 3 Die in Shootings in Kentucky," *New York Times*, 3 December 1997, p. A14; Maureen Downey, "Kids and Violence," 28 March 1998, *Atlanta Journal and Constitution*, p. A12.

11 "The State of America's Children," report by the Children's Defense Fund, Washington, DC, March 1998; "Blocks to Their Future," report by the National Law Center on Homelessness and Poverty, Washington, DC, September 1997; reports released in 1998 from the National Center for Children in Poverty, Columbia University, New York; Douglas Massey, "The Age of Extremes," *Demography*, 33 (1996): 395–412; Trudy Lieberman, "Hunger in America," *Nation*, 30 March 1998, pp. 11–16; David Lynch, "Rich Poor World," *USA Today*, 20 September 1996, p. B1; Richard Wolf, "Good Economy Hasn't Helped the Poor," *USA Today*, 10 March 1998, p. A3; Robert Reich, "Broken Faith," *Nation*, 16 February 1998, pp. 11–17.

12 Inequality and mortality studies; Bruce Kennedy et al., "Income Distribution and Mortality," *British Medical Journal* 312 (1996): 1004–7; Ichiro Kawachi and Bruce Kennedy, "The Relationship of Income Inequality to Mortality," *Social Science and Medicine* 45 (1997): 1121–27. See also Barbara Chasin, *Inequality and Violence in the United States* (Atlantic Highlands, NJ: Humanities Press, 1997). Political stability: John Sloan, "The Reagan Presidency, Growing Inequality, and the American Dream," *Policy Studies Journal* 25 (1997): 371–86 (contains Reich quotes and "will haves" phrase). On both topics see also Philippe Bourgois, *In Search of Respect: Selling Crack in El Barrio* (Cambridge: Cambridge University Press, 1996); William J. Wilson, *When Work Disappears* (New York, Knopf, 1996); Richard Gelles, "Family Violence," *Annual Review of Sociology* 11 (1985): 347–67; Sheldon Danziger and Peter Gottschalk, *America Unequal* (Cambridge, MA: Harvard University Press, 1995); Claude Fischer et al. *Inequality by Design* (Princeton, NJ: Princeton University Press, 1996).

13 Mike Tharp and William Holstein, "Mainstreaming the Militia," *U.S. News & World Report*, 21 April 1997, pp. 24–37.

14 Burger King: "Notebooks," *New Republic*, 29 April 1996, p. 8. Statistics from the FBI's Uniform Crime Reports, Centers for Disease Control reports, and Timothy Egan, "Oregon Freeman Goes to Court," *New York Times*, 23 May 1998, pp. Al, 8.

15 Bill Thompson, "It's Not Guns, It's Killer Kids," *Fort Worth Star-Telegram*, 31 March 1998, p. 14; "Guns Aren't the Problem," *New York Post* 30 March 1998 (from *Post* Web site); "Arkansas Gov. Assails 'Culture of Violence,'" *Reuters*, 25 March 1998; Bo Emerson, "Violence Feeds 'Redneck,' Gun-Toting Image," *Atlanta Journal and Constitution*, 29 March 1998, p. A8; Nadya Labi, "The Hunter and the Choir Boy," *Time*, 6 April 1998, pp. 28–37; Lacayo, "Toward the Root of Evil."

16 Lewin, "More Victims and Less Sense"; Tamar Lewin, "Study Finds No Big Rise in Public-School Crimes," *New York Times*, 25 March 1998, p. A18.

17 "Licensing Can Protect," *USA Today*, 7 April 1998, p. A11; Jonathan Kellerman, "Few Surprises When It Comes to Violence," *USA Today*, 27 March 1998, p. A13; Gary Fields, "Juvenile Homicide Arrest Rate on Rise in Rural USA," *USA Today*, 26 March 1998, p. A11; Karen Peterson and Glenn O'Neal, "Society More Violent, So Are Its Children," *USA Today*, 25 March 1998, p. A3; Scott Bowles, "Armed, Alienated and Adolescent," *USA Today*, 26 March 1998, p. A9. Similar suggestions about guns appear in Jonathan Alter, "Harnessing the Hysteria," *Newsweek*, 6 April 1998, p. 27.

18 Mary Douglas and Aaron Wildavsky, *Risk and Culture* (Berkeley: University of California Press, 1982), see esp. pp. 6–9; Mary Douglas, *Risk and Blame* (London: Routledge, 1992). See also Mary Douglas, *Purity and Danger* (New York: Praeger, 1966). Asbestos and schools: Peter Cary, "The Asbestos Panic Attack," *U.S. News & World Report*, 20 February 1995, pp. 61–64; Children's Defense Fund, "State of America's Children."

19 CNN, "Crossfire," 27 August 1995 (contains Huffington quote); Ruth Conniff, "Warning: Feminism Is Hazardous to Your Health," *Progressive*, April 1997, pp. 33–36 (contains Sommers

quote). See also Susan Faludi, *Backlash* (New York: Crown, 1991); Deborah Rhode, "Media Images, Feminist Issues," *Signs* 20 (1995): 685–710; Paula Span, "Did Feminists Forget the Most Crucial Issues?" *Los Angeles Times*, 28 November 1996, p. E8.

[20] See Katha Pollitt, "Subject to Debate," *Nation*, 26 December 1994, p. 788, and 20 November 1995, p. 600.

[21] Henry Nelson Coleridge, ed., *Specimens of the Table Talk of the Late Samuel Taylor Coleridge* (London: J. Murray, 1935), entry for 5 October 1930. Nixon quote cited in William Safire, *Before the Fall* (New York: Doubleday, 1975), Prologue.

8

THE NEW TATTOO SUBCULTURE

ANNE M. VELLIQUETTE • JEFF B. MURRAY

In this selection, Anne Velliquette and Jeff Murray explore the social and symbolic meanings of body adornment in the "new" tattoo subculture. A *subculture* is defined as a system of values, attitudes, modes of behavior, and lifestyles of a social group that is distinct from, but related to, the dominant culture of society. In particular, this ethnographic study investigates what tattoos, as cultural objects, signify, for both the tattooist (the service provider) and the tattooee (the client). The reading also discusses *impression management* and other techniques used to control social interaction. Remember that at the time this article was written in the late 1990s, getting a tattoo was just beginning to become popular, whereas today, getting a tattoo is more commonplace.

In the past, what you were determined what you looked like. Today, what you choose to look like expresses who—or indeed what—you would like to be. The choice is yours.

—TED POLHEMUS

Humans are the only known species that deliberately alters its appearance through the customization of our bodies (Randall and Polhemus 1996). At the most basic level, we get up every morning and make decisions about what to wear. The customization of our bodies, however, goes far beyond the clothing we choose to wear as a "second skin" (Randall and Polhemus 1996:79). At the surface level, our skin can be tattooed, pierced, branded, scarred, and adorned with jewelry, cosmetics, and

---

Anne M. Velliquette and Jeff B. Murray, "The New Tattoo Subculture." Reprinted with the permission of Anne M. Velliquette and Jeff B. Murray.

various articles of clothing. Our hair can also be creatively modified and adorned. Beyond redefining our surface appearance, we can also alter the body's actual shape through techniques such as body building and plastic surgery. In all cultures, human beings spend time and effort customizing the body strictly for the sake of appearance (Randall and Polhemus 1996). This customization often involves not only time and energy, but pain and discomfort (Myers 1992; Randall and Polhemus 1996). This leads to an engaging question: Why do human beings of all cultures alter their natural inherited appearance?

In most societies, the likely reason for altering the body is that such alteration provides a vehicle for self-expression (Finkelstein 1991; Randall and Polhemus 1996; Velliquette, Murray, and Creyer 1998). Permanent as well as temporary forms of body adornment may signify a wide array of symbolic meanings. For example, permanent forms of body decoration (e.g., tattoos, piercings, and scarification) have been known to represent emblems of accomplishment, group membership, social status, personal identity, or a willingness to endure pain in order to please a lover (Bohannan 1988; Drewal 1988; Gathercole 1988; Gritton 1988; Sanders 1988; Velliquette et al. 1998). Temporary forms of body adornment also provide an invaluable means of self-expression. Our personal choice in clothing, hairstyle, body shape, and use of objects may display various identity features such as gender, status, values, interests, and a particular approach to life. Clearly, body adornment has become a way for human beings to present their desired self-image to others (Blumer 1969; Finkelstein 1991; Goffman 1959). Thus, understanding the way that individuals use nonverbal signs and symbols to construct, revise, and maintain symbolic meaning is important for the construction of self-identity.

Focusing on one type of body adornment, this article presents an ethnographic account of symbolic meaning as expressed by two segments of the *New Tattoo Subculture*,[1] the tattooist (the service provider) and the tattooee (the client). Although it is difficult to assess the number of people participating in the new tattoo subculture, it has been estimated that 12 to 20 million Americans have joined the ranks of the tattooed (Blouin 1996; Velliquette et al. 1998). This is not surprising given that in 1996, tattoo studios were among the top six growth businesses in the United States (American Business Information, Inc. 1996; Velliquette et al. 1998). During the 1990s, observers have also witnessed sharp increases in the sale of tattoo ink, books, magazines, videos, special clothing designed to show off the decorated body, and other tattoo-related odds and ends, as well as the expansion of tattoo associations and conventions, the growth of state regulations, and an increase in the number of advertisements featuring tattooed models and celebrities (Ball 1996; Blouin 1996; Krakow 1994; Peterson 1996).

Tattooing's recent popularity, as well as the increased interest in the tattoo as popular culture (e.g., Gap and Polo ads featuring tattoos, and a tattooed Barbie doll by Mattel), leads to some interesting research questions. What is it about the tattoo as a cultural object that draws people to participate in this subculture? In what ways is the tattoo used as a form of expression? What is involved in the experience of acquiring a tattoo? What transpires during the service interaction between the tattooist and tattooee? To address these questions, we begin with a brief discussion of the literature on tattooing as an art form, its rich history, and its cultural and subcultural roots. Next, we summarize the ethnographic method used for data collection. Following this summary, we offer an ethnographic account of the tattoo subculture in order to demonstrate the symbolic nature of the act of tattooing. We draw from our own experiences and observations (including fieldwork at two tattoo studios, a tattoo museum/archive, and a tattoo convention) to illustrate ways in which the tattoo is used as a form of expression. We also consider the process itself via interactions between tattooists and their clients. Finally, we consider emergent aspects of this research that may further illustrate what has been described as the New Tattoo Subculture.

Tattooing: Yesterday and Today

Tattoo is a word loaded with rich visual associations summoning images that range from circus sideshow freaks or tribal warriors to WWII sailors, the Holocaust, street gangs, criminals, or the more recent association of media stars and athletes (Velliquette et al. 1998). With such vivid associations spanning across decades, it becomes clear that tattoos have a long and fascinating history. . . . The practice of tattooing is one of the oldest art forms discovered by archaeologists (Ball 1996; Randall and Polhemus 1996). The word *tattoo* is derived from the Tahitian word *ta-tu* meaning "to strike." A *ta* was a sharp, jagged piece of antler or bone. Different types of bones, or *tas*, were used to create different designs by tapping or pushing ink, usually made from vegetable or fruit dyes, into the flesh (Ball 1996; Randall and Polhemus 1996). Because it is usually only the bones and not the skin of our distant ancestors that remain intact, it is impossible to determine just how old the tattoo really is. The oldest irrefutable evidence of tattooing entered the archaeological record only a few years ago, when the complete body of an Iceman was found frozen in a glacier in the Alps. Some 5,000 years old, this ancient hunter's body was adorned with 15 tattoos (Randall and Polhemus 1996). In order to appreciate the history of tattooing, one must appreciate its social logic and functions.

The social-symbolic role that tattoos have played in society varies a great deal, depending on factors such as historical period, geography, economic development, innovation, and cultural diffusion. In ancient societies, tattoos, as well as other forms of permanent body modification, were most commonly associated with permanency in one's life (e.g., gender and maturity), lifelong social connections (e.g., tribe membership), or a celebrated appearance style that showed considerable continuity through dozens of generations (Randall and Polhemus 1996; Sanders 1988). The permanency of the tattoo symbolized premodern society's need for social integration, order, and stability (Randall and Polhemus 1996). . . . The current trend in tattooing has been explained as serving a number of social-symbolic roles: as a mark of affiliation to express group commitment and belonging (e.g., the logo worn by Harley Davidson riders), as a mark of personal identity (e.g., a symbol that represents a unique personal experience), as a mark of resistance (e.g., a symbol that violates consumption codes), or as a mark of identity change (e.g., a symbol that emulates a media image) (Randall and Polhemus 1996; Sanders 1988; Velliquette et al. 1998).

The recent popular interest in tattoos, along with remarkable changes in the practices and styles of tattooing, has attracted a number of new artists, some of them classically trained at prestigious art institutes (e.g., the tattoo artist Jamie Summers; see Rubin 1988:256). The role the artist/tattooist plays becomes an important part of this "Tattoo Renaissance" (Rubin 1988:233). The tattooist engages in *impression management* to set the stage for an artistic service encounter. Erving Goffman (1959) argues that in everyday life, there is a clear understanding that first impressions are important and seldom overlooked. Those in service occupations have many motives for trying to control the impression they present during the service encounter. This process is called *impression management*. For example, the tattooist sets an artistic tone by impressing upon the client that her shop is a studio, that her work is art, and that her identity is an artist (Sanders 1989). Thus tattooists who view themselves as artists are continually engaged in legitimation talk in order to neutralize the stigma that has been historically associated with tattooing (Sanders 1989). As tattoo artists legitimize their work as art, it seems that they in turn decrease the stigma for the consumer. This increased recognition of tattooing as an art form has not only led to its development as a creative medium for some artists, it has also led to a new creative form of expression for the consumer (Rubin 1988; Velliquette et al. 1998). The consumer engages in experiential consumption, and through negotiated order with the artist, the consumer embarks upon a symbolic journey where the choice in artist, design, colors, and body location are all linked to the consumer's personal experiences and sense of identity (Sanders 1988).

In summary, a review of literature suggests two central a priori themes: *collective legitimization* and *self-identity*. These themes are not mutually exclusive, but rather are intertwined analytical categories that are useful for the framework of discovery. Further, to allow for a discussion of several aspects of interaction, several "sensitizing concepts" are introduced within each theme (Blumer 1969:147–48). . . .

Ethnographic Method and Setting

Tattooing is one topic that "demands a plunge into the waters, not a comfortable observer's beach chair at the side of the ocean" (Steward 1990:198). According to Blumer (1969) and Hebdige (1979), immersion in the field (or hovering close) produces some of the most compelling and evocative accounts of subculture and human interaction. Given the symbolic complexity associated with the artist–client interaction, the choice of design, and the act of becoming tattooed, we decided to use ethnographic interviews and participant observation as our primary data-gathering techniques.

We collected the majority of the text for this study over a six-month period in 1996. We returned to the field in 1997 for approximately two to three months in order to follow up on questions regarding support for both a priori and emerging themes grounded in the data. The text consists of over 400 pages of typed fieldnotes composed immediately after each participant observation in the everyday activities of two tattoo studios. Generally, we spent two to four hours at a time, at least once a week, in one of the studios, helping to maintain files of tattoo designs, working behind the front desk, sitting with customers as they were tattooed, assisting with some technical procedures, interviewing customers, and interviewing artists when they were not tattooing. . . . In addition to participating in the studios, we collected fieldnotes and took photographs at a 1996 national tattoo convention and two tattoo artwork museum gallery exhibitions. Further, in order to gain more historical appreciation, we traveled to the Tattoo Archive in Berkeley, California. The Tattoo Archive is a national museum of tattoo history and collectibles. We spent four days collecting relevant information and interviewing the curator.

Although the primary goal of ethnography is immersion in the lifeworlds and everyday experiences of a group of people, the researcher inevitably remains an outsider (Emerson, Fretz, and Shaw 1995). Since both "outsider" and "insider" perspectives are important in this type of research (Rubin 1988:11, n. 2), we decided to reinforce an insider's perspective by becoming tattooed. I (first author) chose a *cat* (ankle) for my first tattoo and a *butterfly* (lower front hip) for my second. . . . I carefully recorded the details of this experience in a private journal. These notes also became part of the text. . . .

Findings from the Field

As expected, we found support for many of the *collective legitimization* issues that had been discussed in previous literature on tattooing. For example, we found that tattooists often tried to convince their clients that tattooing is an art form and that "tattoos aren't just for bikers anymore" (fieldnotes January 31, 1996). The tattooists worked hard to legitimize their field of work by becoming certified, referring to themselves as artists, attending national tattoo conventions, showing their work at local art galleries, and studying other artists in the field. The artists often conversed about different tattoo artists' reputations in the field, often ranking them in terms of their favorites. . . . The artists also discussed how bored they get with customer-requested designs that do not allow them to use their creative, artistic talent. One artist referred to these simplistic, uncreative designs as "cartoon characters." This artist hated these simple designs because she felt "like a kid coloring in a coloring book. . . . Something you do when you're five years old" (fieldnotes April 15, 1997).

> The artist says to me, "The owner is tired of doing the small cartoon characters like the tazmanian devil. . . . She hates doing that shit. She is into the big pieces that she can really get creative with. . . . You know, custom work." (fieldnotes April 9, 1997)

We also found that the artists worked hard to impress upon their clients that their studios were clean and met all of the health department's regulations. Several neutralization tactics were employed by the artists to change the perceptions of those individuals who viewed tattooing as deviant and tattoo shops as dirty, underground holes where deviants hung out. The following passage represents an attempt to neutralize the tattooing experience:

> The male artist calls the Irish man back to the room and I stay to watch. The artist sits him down in the chair and shows him the needles that will be used. The artist tells him they are clean, new needles and that they are sealed in the bags. I ask the artist to repeat what he said and he says, "I like to let the customers see that the needles are new and sterile. I would want to see that if I were the customer." The artist then cuts open the sealed bags to get the needles out. (fieldnotes March 1, 1997)

The owners of the tattoo studios worked hard to legitimize their businesses further by creating a clinical atmosphere. For example, in the client rooms where tattooing took place, there were several glass jars on the counter filled with supplies (e.g., cotton, disposable razors, gauze), paper towels, antiseptic cleaning sprays, lotions, ointments, and tattooing equipment (e.g., guns, disposable ink trays, and ink). Some of the equipment was displayed on the wall (e.g., pliers and parts to the gun). There were also boxes of surgical gloves on the counter, a washing sink, and a hazardous waste container for disposal of needles and other infectious material. The room had an appearance similar to that of a doctor's office.

Although the tattoo artists employed these neutralization tactics, a certain amount of stigma remained, as viewed and expressed by a few informants. One informant described how he thought others would react to his tattoos in his profession: "I know it is not totally acceptable. I would catch crap if I ever showed up here in the future to teach with my tattoos hanging out. . . . They would lay down and die!" (fieldnotes April 17, 1997). Several customers stated that there are levels of social acceptance for various kinds of tattoos. One informant explained how the sun design she wanted on her hip was more socially acceptable than a skull and crossbones on a person's chest. To further illustrate the stigma associated with tattoos, we provide the following quoted passage:

> *I want to get it where I can cover it up. You know, so my mom won't see it. My mom hates tattoos. She lives in a place where she associates all tattoos with gang members.* (fieldnotes March 1, 1997)

As discussed in the literature, collective legitimization is a process of *impression management* (Goffman 1959). Early in the ethnography, it became apparent that, in many respects, tattooists are performers. We often observed tattooists putting on a public display of professionalism. For example, tattooists often impressed upon their clients that they were artistic, friendly, and most of all technically competent and sterile. The following passage is representative of this theme:

> The artist and I continue to talk and she tells me, "I was so nervous when I had to do my first tongue piercing." She then tells me she was shaking when she did it, which made the guy nervous. Then the artist said, "You really have to pretend like you know what the hell you are doing." (fieldnotes February 15, 1997)

Within the studio setting, we observed the tattooists spending their time in two different regions: the front stage and the back stage areas of the shop. In the front stage, "permanent cosmetic/tattoo artist" certificates were hung on the wall in the lobby. The walls in the lobby area were covered with photographs of tattoos given to previous clients: the best and most unique work made the "wall." The wall attracted customers who were entering the shop and added to the credibility of the artists. Also included in the front stage region were the rooms where clients became tattooed. In the front stage region, including both the lobby and the tattoo rooms, we often observed tattooists engaging in what Goffman (1959:80) refers to as "team performance."

> The artist is finishing a large, colorful, elaborate design with a horse, clouds, and moon on a woman's arm. The artist calls the other artist in to come and look at the work. The female artist says, "This design is a dual effort between me and _____." The male artist had done the outline the week before and now the female artist was adding color. They were both happy with the results of their work. They complimented one another's artistic work (telling each other how good they were) in front of the client. (fieldnotes March 1, 1997)

Another important concept related to impression management is emotion management. The artists often managed their emotions when in the presence of clients. The artists typically refrained from displaying disappointment, anger, disgust, or impatience when interacting with their customers.

> A guy came in looking for someone to quote him a price on some touch-up work. The owner asked him where he got the tattoo done and he replied, "By a friend of mine in Oklahoma City. He is a paraplegic and he does real good work. I just don't want to have to drive to OK City to have it touched up." After he left the owner said, "He thought that was a good tattoo?" She then said, "It was hard not to laugh!! You really have to control yourself from laughing in situations like that." (fieldnotes March 28, 1997)

The tattooists usually segregated their audiences by keeping conversations like this one within the circle of the other artists. However, a few instances were observed where this segregation did not take place and customers were allowed to hear backstage talk:

> The male artist assists this time on a tongue piercing. The owner talks to the male artist about piercing and tells him the first time she did a navel, she was extremely nervous. She says this in front of the customer as if he is not there. She then says, "The only way to really practice is to just get in there and do one." The customer then asks with a nervous tone of voice, "Is this your first one?" He says this with surprise and anxiety. She said, "Oh no, I have done many, I am just saying that this is really the only way to get used to it." The male artist then tells the guy (as if to calm him down), "Everything we are using on you is sterile." The guy sits still as the two artists pierce his tongue and the client's friend and I watch. (fieldnotes March 19, 1997)

In the tattoo studio, the artists attempted to gain and maintain control during the service encounter by *negotiating order* (Strauss and Corbin 1990). The artists claimed that the average client's lack of experience and knowledge necessitated the need for the artist to be in control at all times to ensure a successful interaction. . . .

As we observed, most negotiations appeared to go smoothly during artist–client interactions. A working consensus was usually achieved, because most clients seemed to realize the artist's role as the expert in the situation.

> The female customer then said, "It is not the pain I am worried about. . . . I just want to know where it will look best." The owner replies, "Well, ankles are a nice place because the skin is so smooth and tight there, so it is easier to tattoo a nice design on the ankle. The skin is stretched tight on the ankle unlike the spongy skin of the breast, stomach, back or hip area." The owner then also tells her that the "shoulders [back] make a nice canvas as well." The artist refers to the skin as canvas for the ink. . . . The girl continues to ask the owner for advice on colors, size, and location. (fieldnotes February 15, 1997)

It appeared to us that most interactions were controlled by the artists. It was discovered rather quickly that the customer is literally in the tattooist's hands.

> The artist didn't like the way she had drawn the leaf. She said she had kind of made a mistake when tattooing it. I asked her about making mistakes. She said, "It happens. . . . When you make a mistake, you just cover it up. The customer won't ever know." I thought about this and realized that the customer usually can't see what is going on up-close during the process and that they probably wouldn't know if a mistake had been made. (fieldnotes February 22, 1997)

Although most interactions and negotiations went smoothly, there were instances where this was not the case. The artists labeled the clients involved in the unsuccessful interactions as "bad clients" and the customers involved in the successful interactions as "good clients." The following passages provide examples of "bad clients" as defined by the artists:

> The owner explains, "This chick came in the other day for a navel piercing and she had the dirtiest belly button I had ever seen! It took me five minutes to pick all of the shit out of it! I thought about charging her extra just for that!" (fieldnotes April 9, 1997)

> The artist defines bad customers: "The ones where price is the most important thing. . . . The customers that will let you run with it and do whatever you want to, those are the great ones. . . . Unfortunately there aren't many of those. . . . Most people say, "I can only afford 50 dollars' worth." I sometimes give them a few free colors just to make it look better. . . . The whiny ones are bad too, when you step on your pedal and you're not even touching them and they are like, 'Ow! Quit!' you know. . . . You just feel like slapping them." (fieldnotes April 15, 1997)

It was very common for customers to bring friends with them for support during the tattooing procedure. The social support often helped the potential client with such decisions as choice of design, size, colors, and body location. Friends offered further support by engaging in conversation to keep the client's mind off the painful procedure. We also observed this type of conversational support between the artists and their clients. One artist described how she felt this conversational support was part of the job:

> *You get to talk to a lot of people. Sitting there with them for an hour or an hour and a half, you get to talking and make new friends. We're actually like bartenders you know, people cry on our shoulder. . . . You usually know their life story by the time they leave.* (fieldnotes April 15, 1997)

The second a priori theme identified in the literature reveals how tattoos are used to reinforce one's *self-identity.* We discovered that the use of tattoos to express one's inner self was probably the most commonly stated motivation for acquiring a tattoo. In this context, the tattoo becomes an extension of the person, symbolizing the person's narrative story. One informant described how becoming tattooed "is more of a reflection of who you think you are" (fieldnotes April 17, 1997). As one artist explained, "The tattoo is already there inside those who really want it, it is already a part of them, the tattoo artist just brings it out" (fieldnotes July 12, 1996). . . . One of the informants, who had acquired tattoos from 35 different artists, described his tattoos as a "scrapbook" symbolizing his life story:

> I asked him if there was one he favored or if any particular one had great meaning. He said, "They all do." He told me that he considers his tattoo art work "his personal scrapbook." Each and every tattoo reminds the informant of a person, place, time or period in his life. A personal scrapbook of one's life or self. (fieldnotes July 12, 1996)

During the ethnography, we discovered that customers choose tattoos to represent who they are in different ways. Some choose symbols for personal distinction, whereas others choose symbols for integration purposes. Both cases contributed to an expression of identity: the former case seemed to represent one's personal identity whereas the latter case represented one's social identity. One informant described how tattoos distinguish him from others in a crowd (and help create a sense of personal identity):

> *When you make the decision, "I'm going to be a person with a tattoo," you know you are different from most people. . . . Just the bottom line, standing in the line at Wal-Mart, I know I'm different. . . . It is fun being different, it is even more fun being more different.* (fieldnotes April 17, 1997)

Other examples from interviews in which the tattoo symbolized the owner's personal identity include a Mickey Mouse tattooed to the informant's arm because his grandfather called him "Mickey"; a butterfly tattooed to the client's hip symbolizing her given name; a rattlesnake design chosen in memory of being bitten and almost dying; a rose tattooed on the wrist for every child born and a butterfly tattooed on the ankle for every family member who had died; and a cat design that reflected a woman's long history of living with and loving cats. There were other instances where the design seemed to represent the client's social identity (integration):

> Back at the counter, a young man (30s) with an Irish accent comes in and asks to see the hog file. The owner asks him to clarify what kind of hog and he says, "You know, a razorback." Shortly after that remark he says, "I am not getting a hog because of THE Razorbacks basketball team, the hog is part of my family crest. It looks just like the razorback, only it's not running. . . . It is just standing there." I ask him where he is from and he says, "Dublin." He then tells me that every family name has a crest and that his has the hog in the design. (fieldnotes March 1, 1997)

Often the process of becoming tattooed could be explained as experiential consumption (Holbrook and Hirschman 1982), where the event was tied to a meaningful experience. The following passages are representative of this concept:

> The two girls who were best friends got matching tattoos on vacation in Mexico to bond their friendship. I ask her why the tribal piece and she says, "I don't know, we didn't really care what the design was. . . . We just wanted something simple . . . to represent our friendship." (fieldnotes April 15, 1997)

> A young woman comes in (WF 20) with her mother to get a tattoo of a moon and fairy. She tells me that she had drawn the design herself. This will be her fourth tattoo as she has gotten one every year for her birthday since she was 16 years old. (fieldnotes March 19, 1997)

As discovered in this ethnography, tattoos are consumed for many different reasons. Most informants agreed, however, that tattoos are a form of self-expression, a way to communicate to others some aspect of the wearer's self-identity. . . .

Discussion and Conclusions

The preceding review of literature and ethnographic account suggests some feasible answers to the research questions stated in the introduction: What is it about the tattoo as a cultural object that draws people to participate in the tattoo subculture? In what ways is the tattoo used as a form of expression? What is involved in the experience of acquiring a tattoo? What transpires during the service interaction between the tattooist and tattooee? The a priori and emergent themes suggest that there are many reasons why individuals are drawn to participate in the new tattoo subculture. A subculture "signifies a way of life of a group of people" and is "characterized by interaction, continuity, and outsider and insider definitions of distinctiveness" (Prus 1996:85). The tattoo subculture is no different in that the tattoo as a cultural object attracts people who want to express difference as well as integration. In this realm, the tattoo indicates the separate domains to which its wearers belong, while it expresses unity and connects otherwise diverse domains. For example, as we discovered in this ethnography, the tattoo was a common bond among all informants regardless of social class or background. Further, the tattoo was a form of distinction, separating the informants from the rest of society, or the non-tattooed.

Another reason that members are drawn to this subculture can be attributed to the phenomenon of certain objects becoming so firmly associated with an individual that they are understood as literal extensions of that individual's being. The tattoo as a cultural object is a "document that describes our past, an image that reflects our present, and a sign that calls us into the future" (Richardson 1989). Informants used tattoos to express symbolically the meanings they attached to themselves from past, present, and future perspectives. In other words, tattoos were used both to reflect one's past or current identity and to construct and revise one's future identity. Two of the most important themes used to represent this idea are *self-identity* and *simulated self*. Following the ideas presented under the self-identity theme, most informants used the tattoo to express the inner self, "to bring a little bit or a lot of their inner self out for others to see" (fieldnotes March 31, 1996). In this sense, tattoos were extensions of self-conceptions. In contrast, with the simulated self, informants believed that by adopting a symbol, they were changing their images and becoming someone different.

We conclude by stating that it is important and most "useful to examine subcultures by understanding the identities people achieve as participants, the activities deemed consequential in that context, the bonds participants develop with one another, and the sorts of commitments the people involved make with respect to the setting at hand" (Prus 1996:85). This study has achieved such a thorough examination of the new tattoo subculture. If the implications of the examples surveyed in this research can be summarized into a single idea, that idea would be the importance of cultural objects in constituting culture and human relations. Cultural artifacts, such as the tattoo, have properties and tendencies that in an era where material culture is rapidly increasing, deserve to be investigated in their own right.

ENDNOTE

[1] The modifier *New* signifies the recent expansion of popular interest in tattooing as a form of marking identity (Krakow 1994; Lautman 1994; Randall and Polhemus 1996; Velliquette et al. 1998).

REFERENCES

American Business Information, Inc. 1996. "1996 Business Changes Report." Omaha, NE: Marketing Research Division. Jeff Ferris, Project Manager.

Ball, Keith, ed. 1996. "Skin and Bones: Tools of the Trade." *Tattoo* 82 (June): 76–79.

Blouin, Melissa, ed. 1996. "Tattoo You: Health Experts Worried about Artful Trend." *Northwest Arkansas Times*, July 14, p. C4.

Blumer, Herbert. 1969. *Symbolic Interactionism: Perspective and Method*. Englewood Cliffs, NJ: Prentice-Hall.

Bohannan, Paul. 1988. "Beauty and Scarification amongst the Tiv." Pp. 77–82 in *Marks of Civilization*, edited by Arnold Rubin. Los Angeles: Museum of Cultural History.

Drewal, Henry John. 1988. "Beauty and Being: Aesthetics and Ontology in Yoruba Body Art." Pp. 83–96 in *Marks of Civilization*, edited by Arnold Rubin. Los Angeles: Museum of Cultural History.

Emerson, Robert M., Rachael I. Fretz, and Linda L. Shaw. 1995. *Writing Ethnographic Fieldnotes*. Chicago: University of Chicago Press.

Finkelstein, Joanne. 1991. *The Fashioned Self*. Philadelphia: Temple University Press.

Gathercole, Peter. 1988. "Contexts of Maori Moko." Pp. 171–78 in *Marks of Civilization*, edited by Arnold Rubin. Los Angeles: Museum of Cultural History.

Goffman, Erving. 1959. *The Presentation of Self in Everyday Life*. New York: Doubleday.

Gritton, Joy. 1988. "Labrets and Tattooing in Native Alaska." Pp. 181–90 in *Marks of Civilization*, edited by Arnold Rubin. Los Angeles: Museum of Cultural History.

Hebdige, Dick. 1979. *Subculture: The Meaning of Style*. New York: Routledge.

Holbrook, Morris B. and Elizabeth C. Hirschman. 1982. "The Experiential Aspects of Consumption: Consumer Fantasies, Feelings, and Fun." *Journal of Consumer Research* 9 (September): 132–40.

Krakow, Amy. 1994. *Total Tattoo Book*. New York: Warner Books.

Lautman, Victoria. 1994. *The New Tattoo*. New York, London, and Paris: Abbeville Press.

Myers, James. 1992. "Nonmainstream Body Modification: Genital Piercing, Branding, Burning, and Cutting." *Journal of Contemporary Ethnography* 21(3): 267–306.

Peterson, Andrea. 1996. "Parents Spur Laws against Tattoos for Kids." *Wall Street Journal*, September, pp. B1–B2.

Prus, Robert. 1996. *Symbolic Interaction and Ethnographic Research: Intersubjectivity and the Study of Human Lived Experience*. Albany: State University of New York Press.

Randall, Housk and Ted Polhemus. 1996. *The Customized Body*. London and New York: Serpent's Tail.

Richardson, Miles. 1989. "The Artifact as Abbreviated Act: A Social Interpretation of Material Culture." Pp. 172–78 in *The Meaning of Things*, edited by Ian Hodder. London: Unwin Hyman.

Rubin, Arnold. 1988. "The Tattoo Renaissance." Pp. 233–62 in *Marks of Civilization*, edited by Arnold Rubin. Los Angeles: Museum of Cultural History.

Sanders, Clinton R. 1988. "Drill and Frill: Client Choice, Client Typologies, and Interactional Control in Commercial Tattoo Settings." Pp. 219–33 in *Marks of Civilization*, edited by Arnold Rubin. Los Angeles: Museum of Cultural History.

———. 1989. "Organizational Constraints on Tattoo Images: A Sociological Analysis of Artistic Style." Pp. 232–41 in *The Meaning of Things*, edited by Ian Hodder. London: Unwin Hyman.

Steward, Samuel M. 1990. *Bad Boys and Tough Tattoos: A Social History of the Tattoo with Gangs, Sailors, and Street Corner Punks, 1950–1965*. New York: Harrington Park Press.

Strauss, Anselm and Juliet Corbin. 1990. *Basics of Qualitative Research: Grounded Theory Procedures and Techniques.* Beverly Hills, CA: Sage Publications.
Velliquette, Anne M., Jeff B. Murray, and Elizabeth H. Creyer. 1998. "The Tattoo Renaissance: An Ethnographic Account of Symbolic Consumer Behavior." *Advances in Consumer Research* 25:461–67.

9

THE RACIAL CONSTRUCTION OF ASIAN AMERICAN WOMEN AND MEN

YEN LE ESPIRITU

Sociologists are interested in how culture limits our free choice and shapes social interaction. Because each of us is born into a particular culture that has certain norms and values, our personal values and life expectations are profoundly influenced by our culture. For example, what are the values of American culture? Many scholars agree that dominant U.S. values are achievement, Judeo-Christian morals, material comfort, patriotism, and individualism. This selection by Yen Le Espiritu, taken from *Asian American Women and Men: Labor, Laws, and Love* (1997), examines how racial and gender stereotypes of the dominant culture influence our thinking about Asian Americans. Specifically, Espiritu, a professor of ethnic studies at the University of California, San Diego, finds that the cultural images of Asian Americans often contain sexual stereotypes, which are both racist and sexist, and that they reinforce racial, patriarchal, and social class domination.

The slit-eyed, bucktooth Jap thrusting his bayonet, thirsty for blood. The inscrutable, wily Chinese detective with his taped eyelids and wispy moustache. The childlike, indolent Filipino houseboy. Always giggling. Bowing and scraping. Eager to please, but untrustworthy. The sexless, hairless Asian male. The servile, oversexed Asian female. The Geisha. The sultry, sarong-clad, South Seas maiden. The serpentine, cunning Dragon Lady. Mysterious and evil, eager to please. Effeminate. Untrustworthy. Yellow Peril. Fortune Cookie Psychic. Savage. Dogeater. Invisible. Mute. Faceless peasants breeding too many children. Gooks. Passive Japanese Americans obediently marching off to "relocation camps" during the Second World War.

—JESSICA HAGEDORN (1993:XXII)

Focusing on the material lives of Asian Americans, . . . [earlier research explored] . . . how racist and gendered immigration policies and labor conditions have worked in tandem to keep Asian Americans in an assigned, subordinate place. But as is evident from the stereotypes listed above, besides structural discrimination, Asian American men and women have been subject to ideological assaults. Focusing on the ideological dimension of Asian American oppression, this [article] examines the cultural symbols—or what Patricia Hill Collins (1991) called "controlling images" (pp. 67–68)—generated by the dominant group to help justify the economic exploitation and social oppression of Asian American men and women over time. Writing on the objectification of black women, Collins (1991) observed that the exercise of political-economic domination by racial elites "always involves attempts to objectify the subordinate group" (p. 69). Transmitted through cultural institutions owned, controlled, or supported by various elites, these "controlling images" naturalize racism, sexism, and poverty by branding subordinate groups as alternatively inferior, threatening, or praiseworthy. These controlling images form part of a larger system of what Donald G. Baker (1983) referred to as "psychosocial dominance" (p. 37). Along with the threat and occasional use of violence, the psychosocial form of control conditions the subject minority to become the stereotype, to "live it, talk it, embrace it, measure group and individual worth in its terms, and believe it" (Chin and Chan 1972:66–67). In so doing, minority members reject their own individual and group identity and accept in its stead "a white supremacist complex that establishes the primacy of Euro-American cultural practices and social institutions" (Hamamoto 1994:2). But the objectification of Asian Americans as the exotic and inferior "other" has never been absolute. Asian Americans have always, but particularly since the 1960s, resisted race, class, and gender exploitation not only through political and economic struggles but also through cultural activism. My goal is to understand how the internalization and renunciation of these stereotypes have shaped sexual and gender politics within Asian America. In particular, I explore the conflicting politics of gender between Asian American men and women as they negotiate the difficult terrain of cultural nationalism—the construction of an antiassimilationist, native Asian American subject—and gender identities.

Yellow Peril, Charlie Chan, and Suzie Wong

A central aspect of racial exploitation centers on defining people of color as "the other" (Said 1979). The social construction of Asian American "otherness"—through such controlling images as the Yellow Peril, the model minority, the Dragon Lady, and the China Doll—is "the precondition for their cultural marginalization, political impotence, and psychic alienation from mainstream American society" (Hamamoto 1994:5). As indicated by these stereotypes, representations of gender and sexuality figure strongly in the articulation of racism. These racist stereotypes collapse gender and sexuality:

Asian men have been constructed as hypermasculine, in the image of the "Yellow Peril," but also as effeminate, in the image of the "model minority," and Asian women have been depicted as superfeminine, in the image of the "China Doll," but also as castrating, in the image of the "Dragon Lady" (Mullings 1994:279–80; Okihiro 1995). As Mary Ann Doane (1991) suggested, sexuality is "indissociable from the effects of polarization and differentiation, often linking them to structures of power and domination" (p. 217). In the Asian American case, the gendering of ethnicity—the process whereby white ideology assigns selected gender characteristics to various ethnic "others"— cast Asian American men and women as simultaneously masculine and feminine but also as neither masculine nor feminine. On the one hand, as part of the Yellow Peril, Asian American men and women have been depicted as a *masculine* threat that needs to be contained. On the other hand, both sexes have been skewed toward the female side: an indication of the group's marginalization in U.S. society and its role as the compliant "model minority" in contemporary U.S. cultural ideology. Although an apparent disjunction, both the feminization and masculinization of Asian men and women exist to define and confirm the white man's superiority (Kim 1990). . . .

The Racial Construction of Asian American Manhood

Like other men of color, Asian American men have been excluded from white-based cultural notions of the masculine. Whereas white men are depicted both as virile and as protectors of women, Asian men have been characterized both as asexual *and* as threats to white women. It is important to note the historical contexts of these seemingly divergent representations of Asian American manhood. The racist depictions of Asian men as "lascivious and predatory" were especially pronounced during the nativist movement against Asians at the turn of the century (Frankenberg 1993:75–76). The exclusion of Asian women from the United States and the subsequent establishment of bachelor societies eventually reversed the construction of Asian masculinity from "hypersexual" to "asexual" and even "homosexual." The contemporary model-minority stereotype further emasculates Asian American men as passive and malleable. Disseminated and perpetuated through the popular media, these stereotypes of the emasculated Asian male construct a reality in which social and economic discrimination against these men appears defensible. As an example, the desexualization of Asian men naturalized their inability to establish conjugal families in pre–World War II United States. Gliding over race-based exclusion laws that banned the immigration of most Asian women and antimiscegenation laws that prohibited men of color from marrying white women, these dual images of the eunuch and the rapist attributed the "womanless households" characteristic of prewar Asian America to Asian men's lack of sexual prowess and desirability.

A popular controlling image applied to Asian American men is that of the sinister Oriental—a brilliant, powerful villain who plots the destruction of Western civilization. Personified by the movie character of Dr. Fu Manchu, this Oriental mastermind combines Western science with Eastern magic and commands an army of devoted assassins (Hoppenstand 1983:178). Though ruthless, Fu Manchu lacks masculine heterosexual prowess (Wang 1988:19), thus privileging heterosexuality. Frank Chin and Jeffrey Chan (1972), in a critique of the desexualization of Asian men in Western culture, described how the Fu Manchu character undermines Chinese American virility:

> Dr. Fu, a man wearing a long dress, batting his eyelashes, surrounded by muscular black servants in loin cloths, and with his habit of caressingly touching white men on the leg, wrist, and face with his long fingernails is not so much a threat as he is a frivolous offense to white manhood. (P. 60)

In another critique that glorifies male aggression, Frank Chin (1972) contrasted the neuterlike characteristics assigned to Asian men to the sexually aggressive images associated with other men of color: "Unlike the white stereotype of the evil black stud, Indian rapist, Mexican macho, the evil of the evil Dr. Fu Manchu was not sexual, but homosexual" (p. 66). However, Chin failed to note that as a homosexual, Dr. Fu (and, by extension, Asian men) threatens and offends white masculinity—and therefore needs to be contained ideologically and destroyed physically.[1]

Whereas the evil Oriental stereotype marks Asian American men as the white man's enemy, the stereotype of the sexless Asian sidekick—Charlie Chan, the Chinese laundryman, the Filipino houseboy—depicts Asian men as devoted and impotent, eager to please. William Wu (1982) reported that the Chinese servant "is the most important single image of the Chinese immigrants" in American fiction about Chinese Americans between 1850 and 1940 (p. 60). More recently, such diverse television programs as *Bachelor Father* (1957–1962), *Bonanza* (1959–1973), *Star Trek* (1966–1969), and *Falcon Crest* (1981–1990) all featured the stock Chinese bachelor domestic who dispenses sage advice to his superiors in addition to performing traditional female functions within the household (Hamamoto 1994:7). By trapping Chinese men (and, by extension, Asian men) in the stereotypical "feminine" tasks of serving white men, American society erases the figure of the Asian "masculine" plantation worker in Hawaii or railroad construction worker in the western United States, thus perpetuating the myth of the androgynous and effeminate Asian man (Goellnicht 1992:198). This feminization, in turn, confines Asian immigrant men to the segment of the labor force that performs women's work.

The motion picture industry has been key in the construction of Asian men as sexual deviants. In a study of Asians in the U.S. motion pictures, Eugene Franklin Wong maintained that the movie industry filmically castrates Asian males to magnify the superior sexual status of white males (1978:27). As on-screen sexual rivals of whites, Asian males are neutralized, unable to sexually engage Asian women and prohibited from sexually engaging white women. By saving the white woman from sexual contact with the racial "other," the motion picture industry protects the Anglo-American, bourgeois male establishment from any challenges to its hegemony

(Marchetti 1993:218). At the other extreme, the industry has exploited one of the most potent aspects of the Yellow Peril discourses—the sexual danger of contact between the races—by concocting a sexually threatening portrayal of the licentious and aggressive Yellow Man lusting after the White Woman (Marchetti 1993:3). Heedful of the larger society's taboos against Asian male–white female sexual union, white male actors donning "yellowface"—instead of Asian male actors—are used in these "love scenes." Nevertheless, the message of the perverse and animalistic Asian male attacking helpless white women is clear (Wong 1978). Though depicting sexual aggression, this image of the rapist, like that of the eunuch, casts Asian men as sexually undesirable. As Wong (1978) succinctly stated, in Asian male–white female relations, "There can be rape, but there cannot be romance" (p. 25). Thus, Asian males yield to the sexual superiority of the white males who are permitted filmically to maintain their sexual dominance over both white women and women of color. A young Vietnamese American man describes the damaging effect of these stereotypes on his self-image:

> Every day I was forced to look into a mirror created by white society and its media. As a young Asian man, I shrank before white eyes. I wasn't tall, I wasn't fair, I wasn't muscular, and so on. Combine that with the enormous insecurities any pubescent teenager feels, and I have no difficulty in knowing now why I felt naked before a mass of white people. (Nguyen 1990:23)

White cultural and institutional racism against Asian males is also reflected in the motion picture industry's preoccupation with the death of Asians—a filmic solution to the threats of the Yellow Peril. In a perceptive analysis of Hollywood's view of Asians in films made from the 1930s to the 1960s, Tom Engelhardt (1976) described how Asians, like Native Americans, are seen by the movie industry as inhuman invaders, ripe for extermination. He argued that the theme of the nonhumanness of Asians prepares the audience to accept, without flinching, "the levelling and near-obliteration of three Asian areas in the course of three decades" (Engelhardt 1976:273). The industry's death theme, though applying to all Asians, is mainly focused on Asian males, with Asian females reserved for sexual purposes (Wong 1978:35). Especially in war films, Asian males, however advantageous their initial position, inevitably perish at the hands of the superior white males (Wong 1978:34).

The Racial Construction of Asian American Womanhood

Like Asian men, Asian women have been reduced to one-dimensional caricatures in Western representation. The condensation of Asian women's multiple differences into gross character types—mysterious, feminine, and nonwhite—obscures the social injustice of racial, class, and gender oppression (Marchetti 1993:71). Both Western film and literature promote dichotomous stereotypes of the Asian woman: She is either the cunning Dragon Lady or the servile Lotus Blossom Baby (Tong 1994:197). Though connoting two extremes, these stereotypes are interrelated: Both eroticize Asian women as exotic "others"—sensuous, promiscuous, but untrustworthy. Whereas American popular culture denies "manhood" to Asian men, it endows Asian women with an excess of "womanhood," sexualizing them but also impugning their sexuality. In this process, both sexism and racism have been blended together to produce the sexualization of white racism (Wong 1978:260). Linking the controlling images of Asian men and women, Elaine Kim (1990) suggested that Asian women are portrayed as sexual for the same reason that men are asexual: "Both exist to define the white man's virility and the white man's superiority" (p. 70).

As the racialized exotic "others," Asian American women do not fit the white-constructed notions of the feminine. Whereas white women have been depicted as chaste and dependable, Asian women have been represented as promiscuous and untrustworthy. In a mirror image of the evil Fu Manchu, the Asian woman was portrayed as the castrating Dragon Lady who, while puffing on her foot-long cigarette holder, could poison a man as easily as she could seduce him. "With her talon-like six-inch fingernails, her skin-tight satin dress slit to the thigh," the Dragon Lady is desirable, deceitful, and dangerous (Ling 1990:11). In the 1924 film *The Thief of Baghdad*, Anna May Wong, a pioneer Chinese American actress, played a handmaid who employed treachery to help an evil Mongol prince attempt to win the hand of the Princess of Baghdad (Tajima 1989:309). In so doing, Wong unwittingly popularized a common Dragon Lady social type: treacherous women who are partners in crime with men of their own kind. The publication of *Daughter of Fu Manchu* (1931) firmly entrenched the Dragon Lady image in white consciousness. Carrying on her father's work as the champion of Asian hegemony over the white race, Fah Lo Sue exhibited, in the words of American studies scholar William F. Wu, "exotic sensuality, sexual availability to a white man, and a treacherous nature" (cited in Tong 1994:197). A few years later, in 1934, Milton Caniff inserted into his adventure comic strip *Terry and the Pirates* another version of the Dragon Lady who "combines all the best features of past moustache twirlers with the lure of the handsome wench" (Hoppenstand 1983:178). As such, Caniff's Dragon Lady fuses the image of the evil male Oriental mastermind with that of the Oriental prostitute first introduced some 50 years earlier in the dime novels.

At the opposite end of the spectrum is the Lotus Blossom stereotype, reincarnated throughout the years as the China Doll, the Geisha Girl, the War Bride, or the Vietnamese prostitute—many of whom are the spoils of the last three wars fought in Asia (Tajima 1989:309). Demure, diminutive, and deferential, the Lotus Blossom Baby is "modest, tittering behind her delicate ivory hand, eyes downcast, always walking ten steps behind her man, and, best of all, devot[ing] body and soul to serving him" (Ling 1990:11). Interchangeable in appearance and name, these women have no voice; their "non-language" includes uninterpretable chattering, pidgin English, giggling, or silence (Tajima 1989). These stereotypes of Asian women as submissive and dainty sex objects not only have impeded women's economic mobility but also have fostered an enormous demand for X-rated films and pornographic materials featuring Asian women in bondage, for "Oriental" bathhouse workers in U.S. cities, and for Asian mail-order brides (Kim 1984:64).

Sexism, Racism, and Love

The racialization of Asian manhood and womanhood upholds white masculine hegemony. Cast as sexually available, Asian women become yet another possession of the white man. In motion pictures and network television programs, interracial sexuality, though rare, occurs principally between a white male and an Asian female. A combination of sexism and racism makes this form of miscegenation more acceptable: Race mixing between an Asian male and a white female would upset not only racial taboos but those that attend patriarchal authority as well (Hamamoto 1994:39). Whereas Asian men are depicted as either the threatening rapist or the impotent eunuch, white men are endowed with the masculine attributes with which to sexually attract the Asian women. Such popular television shows as *Gunsmoke* (1955–1975) and *How the West Was Won* (1978–1979) clearly articulate the theme of Asian female sexual possession by the white male. In these shows, only white males have the prerogative to cross racial boundaries and to choose freely from among women of color as sex partners. Within a system of racial and gender oppression, the sexual possession of women and men of color by white men becomes yet another means of enforcing unequal power relations (Hamamoto 1994:46).

The preference for white male–Asian female is also prevalent in contemporary television news broadcasting, most recently in the 1993–1995 pairing of Dan Rather and Connie Chung as co-anchors of the *CBS Evening News*. Today, virtually every major metropolitan market across the United States has at least one Asian American female newscaster (Hamamoto 1994:245). While female Asian American anchorpersons—Connie Chung, Tritia Toyota, Wendy Tokuda, and Emerald Yeh—are popular television news figures, there is a nearly total absence of Asian American men. Critics argue that this is so because the white male hiring establishment, and presumably the larger American public, feels more comfortable (i.e., less threatened) seeing a white male sitting next to a minority female at the anchor desk than the reverse. Stephen Tschida of WDBJ-TV (Roanoke, Virginia), one of only a handful of male Asian American television news anchors, was informed early in his career that he did not have the proper "look" to qualify for the anchorperson position. Other male broadcast news veterans have reported being passed over for younger, more beauteous, female Asian Americans (Hamamoto 1994:245). This gender imbalance sustains the construction of Asian American women as more successful, assimilated, attractive, and desirable than their male counterparts.

To win the love of white men, Asian women must reject not only Asian men but their entire culture. Many Hollywood narratives featuring romances between Anglo American men and Asian women follow the popular Pocahontas mythos: The Asian woman, out of devotion for her white

American lover, betrays her own people and commits herself to the dominant white culture by dying, longing for, or going to live with her white husband in his country. For example, in the various versions of *Miss Saigon,* the
contemporary version of *Madame Butterfly,* the tragic Vietnamese prostitute
eternally longs for the white boy soldier who has long abandoned her and
their son (Hagedorn 1993:xxii). These tales of interracial romance inevitably
have a tragic ending. The Asian partner usually dies, thus providing a cinematic resolution to the moral lapse of the Westerner. The Pocahontas paradigm can be read as a narrative of salvation; the Asian woman is saved either
spiritually or morally from the excesses of her own culture, just as she physically saves her Western lover from the moral degeneracy of her own people
(Marchetti 1993:218). For Asian women, who are marginalized not only by
gender but also by class, race, or ethnicity, the interracial romance narratives
promise "the American Dream of abundance, protection, individual choice,
and freedom from the strictures of a traditional society in the paternalistic
name of heterosexual romance" (Marchetti 1993:91). These narratives also
carry a covert political message, legitimizing a masculinized Anglo American rule over a submissive, feminized Asia. The motion picture *China Gate*
(1957) by Samuel Fuller and the network television program *The Lady from
Yesterday* (1985), for example, promote an image of Vietnam that legitimizes
American rule. Seduced by images of U.S. abundance, a feminized Vietnam
sacrifices herself for the possibility of future incorporation into America, the
land of individual freedom and economic opportunities. Thus, the interracial
tales function not only as a romantic defense of traditional female roles
within the patriarchy but also as a political justification of American hegemony in Asia (Marchetti 1993:108).

Fetishized as the embodiment of perfect womanhood and genuine exotic
femininity, Asian women are pitted against their more modern, emancipated
Western sisters (Tajima 1989). In two popular motion pictures, *Love Is a Many-
Splendored Thing* (1955) and *The World of Suzie Wong* (1960), the white women
remain independent and potentially threatening, whereas both Suyin and
Suzie give up their independence in the name of love. Thus, the white female
characters are cast as calculating, suffocating, and thoroughly undesirable,
whereas the Asian female characters are depicted as truly "feminine"—
passive, subservient, dependent, and domestic. Implicitly, these films warn
white women to embrace the socially constructed passive Asian beauty as
the feminine ideal if they want to attract and keep a man. In pitting white
women against Asian women, Hollywood affirms white male identity
against the threat of emerging feminism and the concomitant changes in gender relations (Marchetti 1993:115–16). As Robyn Wiegman (1991) observed,
the absorption of women of color into gender categories traditionally
reserved for white women is "part of a broader program of hegemonic
recuperation, a program that has as its main focus the reconstruction of white
masculine power" (p. 320). It is also important to note that as the racialized
exotic "other," Asian women do not replace but merely substitute for white
women, and thus will be readily dismissed once the "real" mistress returns.

The controlling images of Asian men and Asian women, exaggerated out of all proportion in Western representation, have created resentment and tension between Asian American men and women. Given this cultural milieu, many American-born Asians do not think of other Asians in sexual terms (Fung 1994:163). In particular, due to the persistent desexualization of the Asian male, many Asian females do not perceive their ethnic counterparts as desirable marriage partners (Hamamoto 1992:42). In so doing, these women unwittingly enforce the Eurocentric gender ideology that objectifies both sexes and racializes all Asians (see Collins 1990:185–86). In a column to *Asian Week*, a weekly Asian American newspaper, Daniel Yoon (1993) reported that at a recent dinner discussion hosted by the Asian American Students Association at his college, the Asian American women in the room proceeded, one after another, to describe how "Asian American men were too passive, too weak, too boring, too traditional, too abusive, too domineering, too ugly, too greasy, too short, too . . . Asian. Several described how they preferred white men, and how they never had and never would date an Asian man" (p. 16). Partly as a result of the racist constructions of Asian American womanhood and manhood and their acceptance by Asian Americans, intermarriage patterns are high, with Asian American women intermarrying at a much higher rate than Asian American men.[2] Moreover, Asian women involved in intermarriage have usually married white partners (Agbayani-Siewert and Revilla 1995:156; Min 1995:22; Nishi 1995:128). In part, these intermarriage patterns reflect the sexualization of white racism that constructs white men as the most desirable sexual partners, frowns on Asian male–white women relations, and fetishizes Asian women as the embodiment of perfect womanhood. Viewed in this light, the high rate of outmarriage for Asian American women is the "material outcome of an interlocking system of sexism and racism" (Hamamoto 1992:42).[3]

Cultural Resistance: Reconstructing Our Own Images

"One day/I going to write/about you," wrote Lois-Ann Yamanaka (1993) in "Empty Heart" (p. 548). And Asian Americans did write—"to inscribe our faces on the blank pages and screens of America's hegemonic culture" (Kim 1993:xii). As a result, Asian Americans' objectification as the exotic aliens who are different from, and other than, Euro-Americans has never been absolute. Within the confines of race, class, and gender oppression, Asian Americans have maintained independent self-definitions, challenging controlling images and replacing them with Asian American standpoints. The civil rights and ethnic studies movements of the late 1960s were training grounds for Asian American cultural workers and the development of oppositional projects. Grounded in the U.S. black power movement and in anticolonial struggles of Third World countries, Asian American antihegemonic projects have been unified by a common goal of articulating cultural resistance. Given the historical distortions and misrepresentations of Asian Americans in mainstream media, most cultural projects produced by Asian American men and women perform the important tasks of correcting histories, shaping legacies, creating new cultures, constructing a politics of resistance, and opening spaces for the forcibly excluded (Fung 1994:165; Kim 1993:xiii).

Fighting the exoticization of Asian Americans has been central in the ongoing work of cultural resistance. As discussed above, Asian Americans, however rooted in this country, are represented as recent transplants from Asia or as bearers of an exotic culture. . . . Asian American cultural workers simply do not accept the exotic, one-dimensional caricatures of themselves in U.S. mass media. . . . Asian American cultural projects also deconstruct the myth of the benevolent United States promised to women and men from Asia. . . . To reject the myth of a benevolent United States is also to refute ideological racism: the justification of inequalities through a set of controlling images that attribute physical and intellectual traits to racially defined groups (Hamamoto 1994:3). . . . Finally, Asian American cultural workers reject the narrative of salvation: the myth that Asian women (and a feminized Asia) are saved, through sexual relations with white men (and a masculinized United States), from the excesses of their own culture. Instead, they underscore the considerable potential for abuse in these inherently unequal relationships. . . .

Conclusion

Ideological representations of gender and sexuality are central in the exercise and maintenance of racial, patriarchal, and class domination. In the Asian American case, this ideological racism has taken seemingly contrasting forms: Asian men have been cast as both hypersexual and asexual, and Asian women have been rendered both superfeminine and masculine. Although in apparent disjunction, both forms exist to define, maintain, and justify white male supremacy. The racialization of Asian American manhood and womanhood underscores the interconnections of race, gender, and class. As categories of difference, race and gender relations do not parallel but intersect and confirm each other, and it is the complicity among these categories of difference that enables U.S. elites to justify and maintain their cultural, social, and economic power. Responding to the ideological assaults on their gender identities, Asian American cultural workers have engaged in a wide range of oppositional projects to defend Asian American manhood and womanhood. In the process, some have embraced a masculinist cultural nationalism, a stance that marginalizes Asian American women and their needs. Though sensitive to the emasculation of Asian American men, Asian American feminists have pointed out that Asian American nationalism insists on a fixed masculinist identity, thus obscuring gender differences. Though divergent, both the nationalist and feminist positions advance the dichotomous stance of man or woman, gender or race or class, without recognizing the complex relationality of these categories of oppression. It is only when Asian Americans recognize the intersections of race, gender, and class that we can transform the existing hierarchical structure.

ENDNOTES

[1]I thank Mary Romero for pointing this out to me.

[2]Filipino Americans provide an exception in that Filipino American men tend to intermarry as frequently as Filipina American women. This is partly so because they are more Americanized and have a relatively more egalitarian gender-role orientation than other Asian American men (Agbayani-Siewert and Revilla 1995:156).

[3]In recent years, Asian Americans' rising consciousness, coupled with their phenomenal growth in certain regions of the United States, has led to a significant increase in inter-Asian marriages (e.g., Chinese Americans to Korean Americans). In a comparative analysis of the 1980 and 1990 Decennial Census, Larry Hajimi Shinagawa and Gin Yong Pang [1993] found a dramatic decrease of interracial marriages and a significant rise of inter-Asian marriages. In California (where 39% of all Asian Pacific Americans reside), inter-Asian marriages increased from 21.1% in 1980 to 64% in 1990 of all intermarriages for Asian American husbands, and from 10.8% to 45% for Asian American wives during the same time period.

REFERENCES

Agbayani-Siewart, Pauline and Linda Revilla. 1995. "Filipino Americans." Pp. 134–68 in *Asian Americans: Contemporary Trends and Issues,* edited by P. G. Min. Thousand Oaks, CA: Sage.

Baker, Donald G. 1983. *Race, Ethnicity, and Power: A Comparative Study.* New York: Routledge.

Chin, Frank. 1972. "Confessions of the Chinatown Cowboy." *Bulletin of Concerned Asian Scholars* 4(3):66.

Chin, Frank and Jeffrey P. Chan. 1972. "Racist Love." Pp. 65–79 in *Seeing through Shuck,* edited by R. Kostelanetz. New York: Ballantine.

Collins, Patricia Hill. 1990. *Black Feminist Thought: Knowledge, Consciousness, and the Politics of Empowerment.* New York: Routledge.

Doane, Mary Ann. 1991. *Femme Fatales: Feminism, Film Theory, Psychoanalysis.* New York: Routledge.

Engelhardt, Tom. 1976. "Ambush at Kamikaze Pass." Pp. 270–79 in *Counterpoint: Perspectives on Asian America,* edited by E. Gee. Los Angeles: University of California at Los Angeles, Asian American Studies Center.

Frankenberg, Ruth. 1993. *White Women, Race Matters: The Social Construction of Whiteness.* Minneapolis: University of Minnesota Press.

Fung, R. 1994. "Seeing Yellow: Asian Identities in Film and Video." Pp. 161–71 in *The State of Asian America,* edited by K. Aguilar-San Juan. Boston: South End Press.

Goellnicht, D. C. 1992. "Tang Ao in America: Male Subject Positions in *China Men.*" Pp. 191–212 in *Reading the Literatures of Asian America,* edited by S. G. Lim and A. Ling. Philadelphia: Temple University Press.

Hagedorn, J. 1993. "Introduction: 'Role of Dead Man Requires Very Little Acting.'" Pp. xxi–xxx in *Charlie Chan Is Dead: An Anthology of Contemporary Asian American Fiction,* edited by J. Hagedorn. New York: Penguin.

Hamamoto, D. Y. 1992. "Kindred Spirits: The Contemporary Asian American Family on Television." *Amerasia Journal* 18(2):35–53.

———. 1994. *Monitored Peril: Asian Americans and the Politics of Representation.* Minneapolis: University of Minnesota Press.

Hoppenstand, G. 1983. "Yellow Devil Doctors and Opium Dens: A Survey of the Yellow Peril Stereotypes in Mass Media Entertainment." Pp. 171–85 in *The Popular Culture Reader,* edited by C. D. Geist and J. Nachbar. Bowling Green, OH: Bowling Green University Press.

Kim, E. 1984. "Asian American Writers: A Bibliographical Review." *American Studies International* 22:2.

———. 1990. "'Such Opposite Creatures': Men and Women in Asian American Literature." *Michigan Quarterly Review* 29:68–93.

———. 1993. "Preface." Pp. vii–xiv in *Charlie Chan Is Dead: An Anthology of Contemporary Asian American Fiction,* edited by J. Hagedorn. New York: Penguin.

Ling, A. 1990. *Between Worlds: Women Writers of Chinese Ancestry.* New York: Pergamon.

Marchetti, G. 1993. *Romance and the "Yellow Peril": Race, Sex, and Discursive Strategies in Hollywood Fiction.* Berkeley: University of California Press.

Min, P. G. 1995. "Korean Americans." Pp. 199–231 in *Asian Americans: Contemporary Trends and Issues,* edited by P. G. Min. Thousand Oaks, CA: Sage.

Mullings, L. 1994. "Images, Ideology, and Women of Color." Pp. 265–89 in *Women of Color in U.S. Society*, edited by M. B. Zinn and B. T. Dill. Philadelphia: Temple University Press.

Nguyen, V. 1990. "Growing Up in White America." *Asian Week*, December 7, p. 23.

Nishi, S. M. 1995. "Japanese Americans." Pp. 95–133 in *Asian Americans: Contemporary Trends and Issues*, edited by P. G. Min. Thousand Oaks, CA: Sage.

Okihiro, G. Y. 1995. "Reading Asian Bodies, Reading Anxieties." Paper presented at the University of California, San Diego Ethnic Studies Colloquium, La Jolla, CA. November.

Said, E. 1979. *Orientalism*. New York: Random House.

Shinagawa, Larry Hajimi and Gin Yong Pang. 1999. *Asian American Intermarriage*. Boston: Beacon Press.

Tajima, R. 1989. "Lotus Blossoms Don't Bleed: Images of Asian Women." Pp. 308–17 in *Making Waves: An Anthology of Writings by and about Asian American Women*, edited by Asian Women United of California. Boston: Beacon.

Tong, B. 1994. *Unsubmissive Women: Chinese Prostitutes in Nineteenth-Century San Francisco*. Norman: University of Oklahoma Press.

Wang, A. 1988. "Maxine Hong Kingston's Reclaiming of America: The Birthright of the Chinese American Male." *South Dakota Review* 26:18–29.

Wiegman, Robin. 1991. "Black Bodies/American Commodities: Gender, Race, and the Bourgeois Ideal in Contemporary Film." Pp. 308–28 in *Unspeakable Images: Ethnicity and the American Cinema*, edited by L. D. Friedman. Urbana: University of Illinois Press.

Wong, Eugene Franklin. 1978. *On Visual Media Racism: Asians in the American Motion Pictures*. New York: Arno.

Wu, William F. 1982. *The Yellow Peril: Chinese Americans in American Fiction, 1850–1940*. Hamden, CT: Archon.

Yamanaka, Lois-Ann. 1993. "Empty Heart." Pp. 544–50 in *Charlie Chan Is Dead: An Anthology of Contemporary Asian American Fiction*, edited by J. Hagedorn. New York: Penguin.

Yoon, D. D. 1993. "Asian American Male: Wimp or What?" *Asian Week*, November 26, p. 16.

10

LOVELY HULA HANDS
Corporate Tourism and the Prostitution of Hawaiian Culture

HAUNANI-KAY TRASK

Many U.S. racial-ethnic groups, including Native Americans, Latina/os and African Americans, have experienced cultural exploitation. Exploitation occurs when aspects of a subculture, such as its beliefs, rituals, and social customs, are commodified and marketed without the cultural group's permission. This selection by Haunani-Kay Trask explores the cultural commodification and exploitation of Hawaiian culture. Trask, a descendant from the Pi'ilani line of Maui and the Kahakumakaliua line of Kaua'i, is a

Haunani-Kay Trask, "Lovely Hula Hands: Corporate Tourism and the Prostitution of Hawaiian Culture" from *From a Native Daughter: Colonialism and Sovereignty in Hawai'i*. (Honolulu: University of Hawaii, 1999) Copyright © by Haunani-Kay Trask. Reprinted with the permission of the author.

professor of Hawaiian Studies at the University of Hawai'i at Manoa. In this excerpt, taken from her 1993 book, *From a Native Daughter: Colonialism and Sovereignty in Hawai'i*, Trask argues that several aspects of Polynesian and Hawaiian cultures, including their language, dress, and dance forms, have been marketed as products for the mass consumption of tourists.

I am certain that most, if not all, Americans have heard of Hawai'i and have wished, at some time in their lives, to visit my native land. But I doubt that the history of how Hawai'i came to be territorially incorporated, and economically, politically, and culturally subordinated to the United States is known to most Americans. Nor is it common knowledge that Hawaiians have been struggling for over 20 years to achieve a land base and some form of political sovereignty on the same level as American Indians. Finally, I would imagine that most Americans could not place Hawai'i or any other Pacific island on a map of the Pacific. But despite all this appalling ignorance, five million Americans will vacation in my homeland this year *and* the next, and so on into the foreseeable capitalist future. Such are the intended privileges of the so-called American standard of living: ignorance of, and yet power over, one's relations to native peoples.

Thanks to postwar American imperialism, the ideology that the United States has no overseas colonies and is, in fact, the champion of self-determination the world over holds no greater sway than in the United States itself. To most Americans, then, Hawai'i is *theirs:* to use, to take, and, above all, to fantasize about long after the experience.

Just five hours away by plane from California, Hawai'i is a thousand light-years away in fantasy. Mostly a state of mind, Hawai'i is the image of escape from the rawness and violence of daily American life. Hawai'i—the word, the vision, the sound in the mind—is the fragrance and feel of soft kindness. Above all, Hawai'i is "she," the Western image of the native "female" in her magical allure. And if luck prevails, some of "her" will rub off on you, the visitor.

This fictional Hawai'i comes out of the depths of Western sexual sickness which demands a dark, sin-free native for instant gratification between imperialist wars. The attraction of Hawai'i is stimulated by slick Hollywood movies, saccharine Andy Williams music, and the constant psychological deprivations of maniacal American life. Tourists flock to my native land for escape, but they are escaping into a state of mind while participating in the destruction of a host people in a native place.

To Hawaiians, daily life is neither soft nor kind. In fact, the political, economic, and cultural reality for most Hawaiians is hard, ugly, and cruel.

In Hawai'i, the destruction of our land and the prostitution of our culture are planned and executed by multinational corporations (both foreign-based and Hawai'i-based), by huge landowners (like the missionary-descended Castle and Cook—of Dole Pineapple fame—and others) and by collaborationist state and county governments. The ideological gloss that claims tourism to be our economic savior and the "natural" result of Hawaiian culture is manufactured by ad agencies (like the state-supported Hawai'i Visitors' Bureau) and tour companies (many of which are owned by the airlines), and spewed out to the public through complicitous cultural engines like film, television and radio, and the daily newspapers. As for the local labor unions, both rank and file and management clamor for more tourists while the construction industry lobbies incessantly for larger resorts. . . .

My use of the word *tourism* in the Hawai'i context refers to a mass-based, corporately controlled industry that is both vertically and horizontally integrated such that one multinational corporation owns an airline, the tour buses that transport tourists to the corporation-owned hotel where they eat in a corporation-owned restaurant, play golf and "experience" Hawai'i on corporation-owned recreation areas, and eventually consider buying a second home built on corporation land. Profits, in this case, are mostly repatriated back to the home country. In Hawai'i, these "home" countries are Japan, Taiwan, Hong Kong, Canada, Australia, and the United States. . . .

With this as a background on tourism, I want to move now into the area of cultural prostitution. "Prostitution" in this context refers to the entire institution which defines a woman (and by extension the "female") as an object of degraded and victimized sexual value for use and exchange through the medium of money. The "prostitute" is then a woman who sells her sexual capacities and is seen, thereby, to possess and reproduce them at will, that is, by her very "nature." The prostitute and the institution which creates and maintains her are, of course, of patriarchal origin. The pimp is the conduit of exchange, managing the commodity that is the prostitute while acting as the guard at the entry and exit gates, making sure the prostitute behaves as a prostitute by fulfilling her sexual–economic functions. The victims participate in their victimization with enormous ranges of feeling, including resistance and complicity, but the force and continuity of the institution are shaped by men.

There is much more to prostitution than my sketch reveals but this must suffice for I am interested in using the largest sense of this term as a metaphor in understanding what has happened to Hawaiian culture. My purpose is not to exact detail or fashion a model but to convey the utter degradation of our culture and our people under corporate tourism by employing "prostitution" as an analytic category.

Finally, I have chosen four areas of Hawaiian culture to examine: our homeland, or *one hānau* that is Hawai'i, our lands and fisheries, the outlying seas and the heavens; our language and dance; our familial relationships; and our women.

Nā Mea Hawai'i—Things Hawaiian

The *mo'ōlelo,* or history of Hawaiians, is to be found in our genealogies. From our great cosmogonic genealogy, the *Kumulipo,* derives the Hawaiian identity. The "essential lesson" of this genealogy is "the interrelatedness of the Hawaiian world, and the inseparability of its constituent parts." Thus, "the genealogy of the land, the gods, chiefs, and people intertwine one with the other, and with all aspects of the universe."[1]

In the *moʻolelo* of Papa and Wākea, earth-mother and sky-father, our islands are born: Hawaiʻi, Maui, Oʻahu, Kauaʻi, and Niʻihau. From their human offspring came the *taro* plant and from the taro came the Hawaiian people. The lessons of our genealogy are that human beings have a familial relationship to land and to the *taro*, our elder siblings or *kuaʻana*.

In Hawaiʻi, as in all of Polynesia, younger siblings must serve and honor elder siblings who, in turn, must feed and care for their younger siblings. Therefore, Hawaiians must cultivate and husband the land which will feed and provide for the Hawaiian people. This relationship of people to land is called *mālama ʻāina* or *aloha ʻāina*, care and love of the land.

When people and land work together harmoniously, the balance that results is called *pono*. In Hawaiian society, the *aliʻi* or chiefs were required to maintain order, abundance of food, and good government. The *makaʻāinana* or common people worked the land and fed the chiefs; the *aliʻi* organized production and appeased the gods.

Today, *mālama ʻāina* is called stewardship by some, although that word does not convey spiritual and genealogical connections. Nevertheless, to love and make the land flourish is a Hawaiian value. *ʻĀina*, one of the words for land, means *that which feeds*. *Kamaʻāina*, a term for native-born people, means *child of the land*. Thus is the Hawaiian relationship to land both familial and reciprocal.

Our deities are also of the land: Pele is our volcano, Kāne and Lono our fertile valleys and plains, Kanaloa our ocean and all that lives within it, and so on with the 40,000 and 400,000 gods of Hawaiʻi. Our whole universe, physical and metaphysical, is divine.

Within this world, the older people or *kūpuna* are to cherish those who are younger, the *moʻopuna*. Unstinting generosity is a value and of high status. Social connections between our people are through *aloha*, simply translated as love but carrying with it a profoundly Hawaiian sense that is, again, familial and genealogical. Hawaiians feel *aloha* for Hawaiʻi whence they come and for their Hawaiian kin upon whom they depend. It is nearly impossible to feel or practice *aloha* for something that is not familial. This is why we extend familial relations to those few non-natives whom we feel understand and can reciprocate our *aloha*. But *aloha* is freely given and freely returned; it is not and cannot be demanded, or commanded. Above all, *aloha* is a cultural feeling and practice that works among the people and between the people and their land.

The significance and meaning of *aloha* underscores the centrality of the Hawaiian language or *ʻōlelo* to the culture. *ʻŌlelo* means both language and tongue; *moʻolelo*, or history, is that which comes from the tongue, that is, a story. *Haole* or white people say we have oral history, but what we have are stories passed on through the generations. These are different from the *haole* sense of history. To Hawaiians in traditional society, language had tremendous power, thus the phrase, *i ka ʻōlelo ke ola; i ka ʻōlelo ka make*—in language is life, in language is death.

After nearly 2,000 years of speaking Hawaiian, our people suffered the near extinction of our language through its banning by the American-imposed government in 1896. In 1900, Hawaiʻi became a territory of the United States. All schools, government operations, and official transactions were thereafter conducted in English, despite the fact that most people, including non-natives, still spoke Hawaiian at the turn of the century.

Since 1970, *ʻōlelo Hawaiʻi*, or the Hawaiian language, has undergone a tremendous revival, including the rise of language immersion schools. The state of Hawaiʻi now has two official languages, Hawaiian and English, and the call for Hawaiian language speakers and teachers grows louder by the day.[2]

Along with the flowering of Hawaiian language has come a flowering of Hawaiian dance, especially in its ancient form, called *hula kahiko*. Dance academies, known as *hālau*, have proliferated throughout Hawaiʻi as have *kumu hula*, or dance masters, and formal competitions where all-night presentations continue for three or four days to throngs of appreciative listeners. Indeed, among Pacific Islanders, Hawaiian dance is considered one of the finest Polynesian art forms today.

Of course, the cultural revitalization that Hawaiians are now experiencing and transmitting to their children is as much a *repudiation* of colonization by so-called Western civilization in its American form as it is a *reclamation* of our past and our own ways of life. This is why cultural revitalization is often resisted and disparaged by anthropologists and others: they see very clearly that its political effect is de-colonization of the mind. Thus our rejection of the nuclear family as the basic unit of society and of individualism as the best form of human expression infuriates social workers, the churches, the legal system, and educators. Hawaiians continue to have allegedly "illegitimate" children, to *hānai* or adopt both children and adults outside of sanctioned Western legal concepts, to hold and use land and water in a collective form rather than a private property form, and to proscribe the notion and the value that one person should strive to surpass and therefore outshine all others.

All these Hawaiian values can be grouped under the idea of *ʻohana*, loosely translated as family, but more accurately imagined as a group of both closely and distantly related people who share nearly everything, from land and food to children and status. Sharing is central to this value since it prevents individual decline. Of course, poverty is not thereby avoided, it is only shared with everyone in the unit. The *ʻohana* works effectively when the *kuaʻana* relationship (elder sibling/younger sibling reciprocity) is practiced.

Finally, within the *ʻohana*, our women are considered the lifegivers of the nation, and are accorded the respect and honor this status conveys. Our young women, like our young people in general, are the *pua*, or flower of our *lāhui*, or our nation. The renowned beauty of our women, especially their sexual beauty, is not considered a commodity to be hoarded by fathers and brothers but an attribute of our people. Culturally, Hawaiians are very open and free about sexual relationships, although Christianity and organized religion have done much to damage these traditional sexual values.

With this understanding of what it means to be Hawaiian, I want to move now to the prostitution of our culture by tourism.

Hawai'i itself is the female object of degraded and victimized sexual value. Our *'āina,* or lands, are not any longer the source of food and shelter, but the source of money. Land is now called real estate, rather than our mother, *Papa.* The American relationship of people to land is that of exploiter to exploited. Beautiful areas, once sacred to my people, are now expensive resorts; shorelines where net fishing, seaweed gathering, and crabbing occurred are more and more the exclusive domain of recreational activities: sunbathing, windsurfing, jet skiing. Now, even access to beaches near hotels is strictly regulated or denied to the local public altogether.

The phrase *mālama 'āina*—to care for the land—is used by government officials to sell new projects and to convince the locals that hotels can be built with a concern for "ecology." Hotel historians, like hotel doctors, are stationed in-house to soothe the visitors' stay with the pablum of invented myths and tales of the "primitive."

High schools and hotels adopt each other and funnel teenagers through major resorts for guided tours from kitchens to gardens to honeymoon suites in preparation for postsecondary jobs in the lowest-paid industry in the state. In the meantime, tourist appreciation kits and movies are distributed through the state department of education to all elementary schools. One film, unashamedly titled "What's in It for Me?," was devised to convince locals that tourism is, as the newspapers never tire of saying, "the only game in town."

Of course, all this hype is necessary to hide the truth about tourism, the awful exploitative truth that the industry is the major cause of environmental degradation, low wages, land dispossession, and the highest cost of living in the United States.

While this propaganda is churned out to local residents, the commercialization of Hawaiian culture proceeds with calls for more sensitive marketing of our native values and practices. After all, a prostitute is only as good as her income-producing talents. These talents, in Hawaiian terms, are the *hula;* the generosity, or *aloha,* of our people; the *u'i* or youthful beauty of our women and men; and the continuing allure of our lands and waters, that is, of our place, Hawai'i.

The selling of these talents must produce income. And the function of tourism and the state of Hawai'i is to convert these attributes into profits.

The first requirement is the transformation of the product, or the cultural attribute, much as a woman must be transformed to look like a prostitute, that is, someone who is complicitous in her own commodification. Thus *hula* dancers wear clownlike make-up, don costumes from a mix of Polynesian cultures, and behave in a manner that is smutty and salacious rather than powerfully erotic. The distance between the smutty and the erotic is precisely the distance between Western culture and Hawaiian culture. In the hotel version of the *hula,* the sacredness of the dance has completely evaporated while the athleticism and sexual expression have been packaged like ornaments. The purpose is entertainment for profit rather than a joyful and truly Hawaiian celebration of human and divine nature.

But let us look at an example that is representative of literally hundreds of images that litter the pages of scores of tourist publications. From an Aloha Airlines booklet—shamelessly called the "Spirit of Aloha"—there is a characteristic portrayal of commodified *hula* dancers, one male and one female. The costuming of the female is more South Pacific—the Cook Islands and Tahiti—while that of the male is more Hawaiian. (He wears a Hawaiian loincloth called a *malo.*) The ad smugly asserts the hotel dinner service as a *lū'au,* a Hawaiian feast (which is misspelled) with a continuously open bar, lavish "island" buffet, and "thrilling" Polynesian revue. Needless to say, Hawaiians did not drink alcohol, eat "island" buffets, or participate in "thrilling" revues before the advent of white people in our islands.

But back to the advertisement. Lahaina, the location of the resort and once the capital of Hawai'i, is called "royal" because of its past association with our *ali'i,* or chiefs. Far from being royal today, Lahaina is sadly inundated by California yuppies, drug addicts, and valley girls.

The male figure in the background is muscular, partially clothed, and unsmiling. Apparently, he is supposed to convey an image of Polynesian sexuality that is both enticing and threatening. The white women in the audience can marvel at this physique and still remain safely distant. Like the black American male, this Polynesian man is a fantasy animal. He casts a slightly malevolent glance at our costumed maiden whose body posture and barely covered breasts contradict the innocent smile on her face.

Finally, the "wondrous allure" referred to in the ad applies to more than just the dancers in their performances; the physical beauty of Hawai'i "alive under the stars" is the larger reference.

In this little grotesquerie, the falseness and commercialism fairly scream out from the page. Our language, our dance, our young people, even our customs of eating are used to ensnare tourists. And the price is only a paltry $39.95, not much for two thousand years of culture. Of course, the hotel will rake in tens of thousands of dollars on just the *lū'au* alone. And our young couple will make a pittance.

The rest of the magazine, like most tourist propaganda, commodifies virtually every part of Hawai'i: mountains, beaches, coastlines, rivers, flowers, our volcano goddess, Pele, reefs and fish, rural Hawaiian communities, even Hawaiian activists.

The point, of course, is that everything in Hawai'i can be yours, that is, you the tourist, the non-native, the visitor. The place, the people, the culture, even our identity as a "native" people is for sale. Thus, the magazine, like the airline that prints it, is called *Aloha.* The use of this word in a capitalist context is so far removed from any Hawaiian cultural sense that it is, literally, meaningless.

Thus, Hawai'i, like a lovely woman, is there for the taking. Those with only a little money get a brief encounter; those with a lot of money, like the Japanese, get more. The state and counties will give tax breaks, build infrastructure, and have the governor personally welcome tourists to ensure they keep coming. Just as the pimp regulates prices and guards the commodity of the prostitute, so the state bargains with developers for access to Hawaiian land and culture. Who builds the biggest resorts to attract the most affluent tourists gets the best deal: more hotel rooms, golf courses, and restaurants approved. Permits are fast-tracked, height and density limits are suspended, new groundwater sources are miraculously found.

Hawaiians, meanwhile, have little choice in all this. We can fill up the unemployment lines, enter the military, work in the tourist industry, or leave Hawai'i. Increasingly, Hawaiians are leaving, not by choice but out of economic necessity.

Our people who work in the industry—dancers, waiters, singers, valets, gardeners, housekeepers, bartenders, and even a few managers—make between $10,000 and $25,000 a year, an impossible salary for a family in Hawai'i. Psychologically, our young people have begun to think of tourism as the only employment opportunity, trapped as they are by the lack of alternatives. For our young women, modeling is a "cleaner" job when compared to waiting on tables, or dancing in a weekly revue, but modeling feeds on tourism and the commodification of Hawaiian women. In the end, the entire employment scene is shaped by tourism.

Despite their exploitation, Hawaiians' participation in tourism raises the problem of complicity. Because wages are so low and advancement so rare, whatever complicity exists is secondary to the economic hopelessness that drives Hawaiians into the industry. Refusing to contribute to the commercialization of one's culture becomes a peripheral concern when unemployment looms.

Of course, many Hawaiians do not see tourism as part of their colonization. Thus tourism is viewed as providing jobs, not as a form of cultural prostitution. Even those who have some glimmer of critical consciousness don't generally agree that the tourist industry prostitutes Hawaiian culture. To me, this is a measure of the depth of our mental oppression: We can't understand our own cultural degradation because we are living it. As colonized people, we are colonized to the extent that we are unaware of our oppression. When awareness begins, then so too does de-colonization. Judging by the growing resistance to new hotels, to geothermal energy and manganese nodule mining which would supplement the tourist industry, and to increases in the sheer number of tourists, I would say that de-colonization has begun, but we have many more stages to negotiate on our path to sovereignty.

My brief excursion into the prostitution of Hawaiian culture has done no more than give an overview. Now that you have heard a native view, let me just leave this thought behind. If you are thinking of visiting my homeland, please don't. We don't want or need any more tourists, and we certainly don't like them. If you want to help our cause, pass this message on to your friends.

ENDNOTES

Author's Note: "Lovely Hula Hands" is the title of a famous and very saccharine song written by a *haole* who fell in love with Hawai'i in the pre-statehood era. It embodies the worst romanticized views of *hula* dancers and Hawaiian culture in general.

[1] Lilikalā Kameʻeleihiwa, *Native Land and Foreign Desires* (Honolulu: Bishop Museum Press, 1992), p. 2.

[2] See Larry Kimura, 1983. "Native Hawaiian Culture," in *Native Hawaiians Study Commission Report,* Vol. 1 (Washington, DC: U.S. Department of the Interior), pp. 173–97.

PART III
Socialization

11

"NIGHT TO HIS DAY"
The Social Construction of Gender

JUDITH LORBER

In this and the following three selections, we examine socialization, the process of learning cultural values and norms. *Socialization* refers to those social processes through which an individual becomes integrated into a social group by learning the group's culture and his or her roles in that group. It is largely through this process that an individual's concept of self is formed. Thus, socialization teaches us the cultural norms, values, and skills necessary to survive in society. Socialization also enables us to form social identities and an awareness about ourselves as individuals. The following reading by Judith Lorber, a professor emerita of sociology and women's studies at Brooklyn College and the Graduate School, City University of New York, is taken from her comprehensive study *Paradoxes of Gender* (1993). Here, Lorber examines socialization and how we learn our gender identities following birth.

[Gethenians] do not see each other as men or women. This is almost impossible for our imagination to accept. What is the first question we ask about a newborn baby?

—URSULA K. LE GUIN

Talking about gender for most people is the equivalent of fish talking about water. Gender is so much the routine ground of everyday activities that questioning its taken-for-granted assumptions and presuppositions is like thinking about whether the sun will come up.[1] Gender is so pervasive that in our society we assume it is bred into our genes. Most people find it hard to believe that gender is constantly created and re-created out of human interaction, out of social life, and is the texture and order of that social life. Yet gender, like culture, is a human production that depends on everyone constantly "doing gender" (West and Zimmerman 1987).

And everyone "does gender" without thinking about it. Today, on the subway, I saw a well-dressed man with a year-old child in a stroller. Yesterday, on a bus, I saw a man with a tiny baby in a carrier on his chest. Seeing men taking care of small children in public is increasingly common—at least in New York City. But both men were quite obviously stared at—and smiled at, approvingly. Everyone was doing gender—the men who were changing the role of fathers and the other passengers, who were applauding them silently. But there was more gendering going on that probably fewer people noticed. The baby was wearing a white crocheted cap and white clothes. You couldn't tell if it was a boy or a girl. The child in the stroller was wearing a dark blue T-shirt and dark print pants. As they started to leave the train, the father put a Yankee baseball cap on the child's head. Ah, a boy, I thought. Then I noticed the gleam of tiny earrings in the child's ears, and as they got off, I saw the little flowered sneakers and lace-trimmed socks. Not a boy after all. Gender done.

Gender is such a familiar part of daily life that it usually takes a deliberate disruption of our expectations of how women and men are supposed to act to pay attention to how it is produced. Gender signs and signals are so ubiquitous that we usually fail to note them—unless they are missing or ambiguous. Then we are uncomfortable until we have successfully placed the other person in a gender status; otherwise, we feel socially dislocated. In our society, in addition to man and woman, the status can be *transvestite* (a person who dresses in opposite-gender clothes) and *transsexual* (a person who has had sex-change surgery). Transvestites and transsexuals carefully construct their gender status by dressing, speaking, walking, gesturing in the ways prescribed for women or men—whichever they want to be taken for—and so does any "normal" person.

For the individual, gender construction starts with assignment to a sex category on the basis of what the genitalia look like at birth.[2] Then babies are dressed or adorned in a way that displays the category because parents don't want to be constantly asked whether their baby is a girl or a boy. A sex category becomes a gender status through naming, dress, and the use of other gender markers. Once a child's gender is evident, others treat those in one gender differently from those in the other, and the children respond to the different treatment by feeling different and behaving differently. As soon as they can talk, they start to refer to themselves as members of their gender. Sex doesn't come into play again until puberty, but by that time, sexual feelings and desires and practices have been shaped by gendered norms and expectations. Adolescent boys and girls approach and avoid each other in an elaborately scripted and gendered mating dance. Parenting is gendered, with different expectations for mothers and for fathers, and people of different genders work at different kinds of jobs. The work adults do as mothers and fathers and as low-level workers and high-level bosses, shapes women's and men's life experiences, and these experiences produce different feelings, consciousness, relationships, skills—ways of being that we call feminine or masculine.[3] All of these processes constitute the social construction of gender.

Gendered roles change—today fathers are taking care of little children, girls and boys are wearing unisex clothing and getting the same education, women and men are working at the same jobs. Although many traditional social groups are quite strict about maintaining gender differences, in other social groups they seem to be blurring. Then why the one-year-old's earrings? Why is it still so important to mark a child as a girl or a boy, to make sure she is not taken for a boy or he for a girl? What would happen if they were? They would, quite literally, have changed places in their social world.

To explain why gendering is done from birth, constantly and by every-one, we have to look not only at the way individuals experience gender but at gender as a social institution. As a social institution, gender is one of the major ways that human beings organize their lives. Human society depends on a predictable division of labor, a designated allocation of scarce goods, as-signed responsibility for children and others who cannot care for themselves, common values and their systematic transmission to new members, legiti-mate leadership, music, art, stories, games, and other symbolic productions. One way of choosing people for the different tasks of society is on the basis of their talents, motivations, and competence—their demonstrated achievements. The other way is on the basis of gender, race, ethnicity— ascribed membership in a category of people. Although societies vary in the extent to which they use one or the other of these ways of allocating people to work and to carry out other responsibilities, every society uses gender and age grades. Every society classifies people as "girl and boy children," "girls and boys ready to be married," and "fully adult women and men," con-structs similarities among them and differences between them, and assigns them to different roles and responsibilities. Personality characteristics, feel-ings, motivations, and ambitions flow from these different life experiences so that the members of these different groups become different kinds of people. The process of gendering and its outcome are legitimated by religion, law, science, and the society's entire set of values. . . .

Western society's values legitimate gendering by claiming that it all comes from physiology—female and male procreative differences. But gen-der and sex are not equivalent, and gender as a social construction does not flow automatically from genitalia and reproductive organs, the main physio-logical differences of females and males. In the construction of ascribed social statuses, physiological differences such as sex, stage of development, color of skin, and size are crude markers. They are not the source of the social sta-tuses of gender, age grade, and race. Social statuses are carefully constructed through prescribed processes of teaching, learning, emulation, and enforce-ment. Whatever genes, hormones, and biological evolution contribute to human social institutions is materially as well as qualitatively transformed by social practices. Every social institution has a material base, but culture and social practices transform that base into something with qualita-tively different patterns and constraints. The economy is much more than producing food and goods and distributing them to eaters and users; family and kinship are not the equivalent of having sex and procreating; morals and religions cannot be equated with the fears and ecstasies of the brain; language goes far beyond the sounds produced by tongue and larynx. No one eats "money" or "credit"; the concepts of "god" and "angels" are the subjects of theological disquisitions; not only words but objects, such as their flag, "speak" to the citizens of a country.

Similarly, gender cannot be equated with biological and physiological differences between human females and males. The building blocks of gender are *socially constructed statuses*. Western societies have only two genders, "man" and "woman." Some societies have three genders—men, women, and *berdaches* or *hijras* or *xaniths*. Berdaches, hijras, and xaniths are biological males who behave, dress, work, and are treated in most respects as social women; they are therefore not men, nor are they female women; they are, in our language, "male women."[4] There are African and American Indian societies that have a gender status called *manly hearted women*—biological females who work, marry, and parent as men; their social status is "female men" (Amadiume 1987; Blackwood 1984). They do not have to behave or dress as men to have the social responsibilities and prerogatives of husbands and fathers; what makes them men is enough wealth to buy a wife.

Modern Western societies' *transsexuals* and *transvestites* are the nearest equivalent of these crossover genders, but they are not institutionalized as third genders (Bolin 1987). Transsexuals are biological males and females who have sex-change operations to alter their genitalia. They do so in order to bring their physical anatomy in congruence with the way they want to live and with their own sense of gender identity. They do not become a third gender; they change genders. Transvestites are males who live as women and females who live as men but do not intend to have sex-change surgery. Their dress, appearance, and mannerisms fall within the range of what is expected from members of the opposite gender, so that they "pass." They also change genders, sometimes temporarily, some for most of their lives. Transvestite women have fought in wars as men soldiers as recently as the nineteenth century; some married women, and others went back to being women and married men once the war was over.[5] Some were discovered when their wounds were treated; others not until they died. In order to work as a jazz musician, a man's occupation, Billy Tipton, a woman, lived most of her life as a man. She died at 74, leaving a wife and three adopted sons for whom she was husband and father, and musicians with whom she had played and traveled, for whom she was "one of the boys" (*New York Times* 1989).[6] There have been many other such occurrences of women passing as men to do more prestigious or lucrative men's work (Matthaei 1982:192–93).[7]

Genders, therefore, are not attached to a biological substratum. Gender boundaries are breachable, and individual and socially organized shifts from one gender to another call attention to "cultural, social, or aesthetic dissonances" (Garber 1992:16). These odd or deviant or third genders show us what we ordinarily take for granted—that people have to learn to be women and men. Men who cross-dress for performances or for pleasure often learn from women's magazines how to "do femininity" convincingly (Garber 1992:41–51). Because transvestism is direct evidence of how gender is constructed, Marjorie Garber (1992) claims it has "extraordinary power . . . to disrupt, expose, and challenge, putting in question the very notion of the 'original' and of stable identity" (p. 16).

Gender Bending

It is difficult to see how gender is constructed because we take it for granted that it's all biology, or hormones, or human nature. The differences between women and men seem to be self-evident, and we think they would occur no matter what society did. But in actuality, human females and males are physiologically more similar in appearance than are the two sexes of many species of animals and are more alike than different in traits and behavior (Epstein 1988). Without the deliberate use of gendered clothing, hairstyles, jewelry, and cosmetics, women and men would look far more alike.[8] Even societies that do not cover women's breasts have gender-identifying clothing, scarification, jewelry, and hairstyles.

The ease with which many transvestite women pass as men and transvestite men as women is corroborated by the common gender misidentification in Westernized societies of people in jeans, T-shirts, and sneakers. Men with long hair may be addressed as "miss," and women with short hair are often taken for men unless they offset the potential ambiguity with deliberate gender markers (Devor 1987, 1989). Jan Morris, in *Conundrum*, an autobiographical account of events just before and just after a sex-change operation, described how easy it was to shift back and forth from being a man to being a woman when testing how it would feel to change gender status. During this time, Morris (1975) still had a penis and wore more or less unisex clothing; the context alone made the man and the woman:

> Sometimes the arena of my ambivalence was uncomfortably small. At the Travellers' Club, for example, I was obviously known as a man of sorts—women were only allowed on the premises at all during a few hours of the day, and even then were hidden away as far as possible in lesser rooms or alcoves. But I had another club, only a few hundred yards away, where I was known only as a woman, and often I went directly from one to the other, imperceptibly changing roles on the way— "Cheerio, sir," the porter would say at one club, and "Hello, madam," the porter would greet me at the other. (P. 132)

Gender shifts are actually a common phenomenon in public roles as well. Queen Elizabeth II of England bore children, but when she went to Saudi Arabia on a state visit, she was considered an honorary man so that she could confer and dine with the men who were heads of a state that forbids unrelated men and women to have face-to-unveiled face contact. In contemporary Egypt, lower-class women who run restaurants or shops dress in men's clothing and engage in unfeminine aggressive behavior, and middle-class educated women of professional or managerial status can take positions of authority (Rugh 1986:131). In these situations, there is an important status change: These women are treated by the others in the situation as if they are men. From their own point of view, they are still women. From the social perspective, however, they are men.[9]

In many cultures, gender bending is prevalent in theater or dance—the Japanese kabuki are men actors who play both women and men; in Shakespeare's theater company, there were no actresses—Juliet and Lady Macbeth were played by boys. Shakespeare's comedies are full of witty comments on gender shifts. Women characters frequently masquerade as young men, and other women characters fall in love with them; the boys playing these masquerading women, meanwhile, are acting out pining for the love of men characters.[10] . . .

But despite the ease with which gender boundaries can be traversed in work, in social relationships, and in cultural productions, gender statuses remain. Transvestites and transsexuals do not challenge the social construction of gender. Their goal is to be feminine women and masculine men (Kando 1973). Those who do not want to change their anatomy but do want to change their gender behavior fare less well in establishing their social identity. . . .

Paradoxically, then, bending gender rules and passing between genders does not erode but rather preserves gender boundaries. In societies with only two genders, the gender dichotomy is not disturbed by transvestites, because others feel that a transvestite is only transitorily ambiguous—is "really a man or woman underneath." After sex-change surgery, transsexuals end up in a conventional gender status—a "man" or a "woman" with the appropriate genitals (Eichler 1989). When women dress as men for business reasons, they are indicating that in that situation, they want to be treated the way men are treated; when they dress as women, they want to be treated as women:

> By their male dress, female entrepreneurs signal their desire to suspend the expectations of accepted feminine conduct without losing respect and reputation. By wearing what is "unattractive" they signify that they are not intending to display their physical charms while engaging in public activity. Their loud, aggressive banter contrasts with the modest demeanor that attracts men. . . . Overt signalling of a suspension of the rules preserves normal conduct from eroding expectations. (Rugh 1986:131)

For Individuals, Gender Means Sameness

Although the possible combinations of genitalia, body shapes, clothing, mannerisms, sexuality, and roles could produce infinite varieties in human beings, the social institution of gender depends on the production and maintenance of a limited number of gender statuses and of making the members of these statuses similar to each other. Individuals are born sexed but not gendered, and they have to be taught to be masculine or feminine.[11] As Simone de Beauvoir said: "One is not born, but rather becomes, a woman . . . ; it is civilization as a whole that produces this creature . . . which is described as feminine" ([1949] 1953:267).

Children learn to walk, talk, and gesture the way their social group says girls and boys should. Ray Birdwhistell (1970:39–46), in his analysis of body motion as human communication, calls these learned gender displays *tertiary* sex characteristics and argues that they are needed to distinguish genders because humans are a weakly dimorphic species—their only sex markers are genitalia. Clothing, paradoxically, often hides the sex but displays the gender.

In early childhood, humans develop gendered personality structures and sexual orientations through their interactions with parents of the same and opposite gender. As adolescents, they conduct their sexual behavior according to gendered scripts. Schools, parents, peers, and the mass media guide young people into gendered work and family roles. As adults, they take on a gendered social status in their society's stratification system. Gender is thus both ascribed and achieved (West and Zimmerman 1987).

The case of the male child who was gender-reassigned and raised as a girl after a botched circumcision destroyed his penis, who then chose to become a boy when he became a teenager, seems to clinch the argument that biology trumps socialization (Colapinto 2000). Money and Ehrhardt (1972) claimed that this case was a natural experiment in whether you could raise a male as a girl because the child in question had an identical twin, who was being raised as a boy. But this case can be read as the rejection of a devalued gender status as much as it can the inevitable emergence of bodily and psychological hard-wiring.

The child chose to reject the reassigned sex status on reaching puberty, when hormones and further genital surgery were prescribed by doctors to create additional feminization. According to the original account of the case, the mother said early on that her gender-reassigned daughter was a tomboy (Money and Ehrhardt 1972:118–23). But the mother had also been a tomboy, and she acknowledged that the behavior she was imposing on her daughter was more restrictive than what she demanded of her son. Femininity never had any appeal for "Joan." Colapinto (1997:68) quotes Joan's identical twin brother as saying, "'When I say there was nothing feminine about Joan,' Kevin laughs, 'I mean there was *nothing* feminine. She walked like a guy. She talked about guy things, didn't give a crap about cleaning house, getting married, wearing makeup. . . . We both wanted to play with guys, build forts and have snowball fights and play army.'" Enrolled in Girl Scouts, Joan was miserable. "I remember making daisy chains and thinking, 'If this is the most exciting thing in Girl Scouts, forget it,' John says. 'I kept thinking of the fun stuff my brother was doing in Cubs.'"

Is this rejection of conventional "girl things" the result of internal masculinization or the gender resistance of a rebellious child? Being a man is a preferred status in many societies, so it is not surprising for those with ambiguous genitalia to prefer that gender identity (Herdt and Davidson 1988). More research needs to be done on the life histories of intersexed adolescents and adults in today's less gender-fixed climate to see to what extent they have chosen to go against their sex assignment as infants and how their lives compare to transsexuals who opt to have genital surgery to change their sex.

People go along with the imposition of gender norms because the weight of morality as well as immediate social pressure enforces them. Consider how many instructions for properly gendered behavior are packed into this mother's admonition to her daughter: "This is how to hem a dress when you see the hem coming down and so to prevent yourself from looking like the slut I know you are so bent on becoming" (Kincaid 1978).

Gender norms are inscribed in the way people move, gesture, and even eat. In one African society, men were supposed to eat with their "whole mouth, wholeheartedly, and not, like women, just with the lips, that is halfheartedly, with reservation and restraint" (Bourdieu [1980] 1990:70). Men and women in this society learned to walk in ways that proclaimed their different positions in the society:

> The manly man . . . stands up straight into the face of the person he approaches, or wishes to welcome. Ever on the alert, because ever threatened, he misses nothing of what happens around him. . . . Conversely, a well brought-up woman . . . is expected to walk with a slight stoop, avoiding every misplaced movement of her body, her head or her arms, looking down, keeping her eyes on the spot where she will next put her foot, especially if she happens to have to walk past the men's assembly. (P. 70)

Many cultures go beyond clothing, gestures, and demeanor in gendering children. They inscribe gender directly into bodies. In traditional Chinese society, mothers bound their daughters' feet into three-inch stumps to enhance their sexual attractiveness. Jewish fathers circumcise their infant sons to show their covenant with God. Women in African societies remove the clitoris of prepubescent girls, scrape their labia, and make the lips grow together to preserve their chastity and ensure their marriageability. In Western societies, women augment their breast size with silicone and reconstruct their faces with cosmetic surgery to conform to cultural ideals of feminine beauty. . . .

Most parents create a gendered world for their newborn by naming, birth announcements, and dress. Children's relationships with same-gendered and different-gendered caretakers structure their self-identifications and personalities. Through cognitive development, children extract and apply to their own actions the appropriate behavior for those who belong in their own gender, as well as race, religion, ethnic group, and social class, rejecting what is not appropriate. If their social categories are highly valued, they value themselves highly; if their social categories are low status, they lose self-esteem (Chodorow 1974). Many feminist parents who want to raise androgynous children soon lose their children to the pull of gendered norms (Gordon 1990:87–90). My son attended a carefully nonsexist elementary school, which didn't even have girls' and boys' bathrooms. When he was seven or eight years old, I attended a class play about "squares" and "circles" and their need for each other and noticed that all the girl squares and circles wore makeup, but none of the boy squares and circles did. I asked the teacher about it after the play, and she said, "Bobby said he was not going to wear makeup, and he is a powerful child, so none of the boys would either." In a long discussion about conformity, my son confronted me with the question of who the conformists were, the boys who followed their leader or the girls who listened to the woman teacher. In actuality, they both were, because they both followed same-gender leaders and acted in gender-appropriate ways. (Actors may wear makeup, but real boys don't.)

For human beings there is no essential femaleness and maleness, femininity or masculinity, womanhood or manhood, but once gender is ascribed, the social order constructs and holds individuals to strongly gendered norms and expectations. Individuals may vary on many of the components of gender and may shift genders temporarily or permanently, but they must fit into the limited number of gender statuses their society recognizes. In the process, they re-create their society's version of women and men: "If we do gender appropriately, we simultaneously sustain, reproduce, and render legitimate the institutional arrangements. . . . If we fail to do gender appropriately, we as individuals—not the institutional arrangements—may be called to account (for our character, motives, and predispositions)" (West and Zimmerman 1987:146).

The gendered practices of everyday life reproduce a society's view of how women and men should act (Bourdieu [1980] 1990). Gendered social arrangements are justified by religion and cultural productions and backed by law, but the most powerful means of sustaining the moral hegemony of the dominant gender ideology is that the process is made invisible; any possible alternatives are virtually unthinkable (Foucault 1972; Gramsci 1971).[12]

For Society, Gender Means Difference

The pervasiveness of gender as a way of structuring social life demands that gender statuses be clearly differentiated. Varied talents, sexual preferences, identities, personalities, interests, and ways of interacting fragment the individual's bodily and social experiences. Nonetheless, these are organized in Western cultures into two and only two socially and legally recognized gender statuses, "man" and "woman."[13] In the social construction of gender, it does not matter what men and women actually do; it does not even matter if they do exactly the same thing. The social institution of gender insists only that what they do is *perceived* as different.

If men and women are doing the same tasks, they are usually spatially segregated to maintain gender separation, and often the tasks are given different job titles as well, such as executive secretary and administrative assistant (Reskin 1988). If the differences between women and men begin to blur, society's "sameness taboo" goes into action (Rubin 1975:178). At a rock and roll dance at West Point in 1976, the year women were admitted to the prestigious military academy for the first time, the school's administrators "were reportedly perturbed by the sight of mirror-image couples dancing in short hair and dress gray trousers," and a rule was established that women cadets could dance at these events only if they wore skirts (Barkalow and Raab 1990:53).[14] Women recruits in the U.S. Marine Corps are required to wear makeup—at a minimum, lipstick and eye shadow—and they have to take classes in makeup, hair care, poise, and etiquette. This feminization is part of a deliberate policy of making them clearly distinguishable from men Marines. Christine Williams (1989) quotes a 25-year-old woman drill instructor as saying: "A lot of the recruits who come here don't wear makeup; they're tomboyish or athletic. A lot of them have the preconceived idea that going into the military means they can still be a tomboy. They don't realize that you are a *Woman* Marine" (pp. 76–77).[15]

If gender differences were genetic, physiological, or hormonal, gender bending and gender ambiguity would occur only in hermaphrodites, who are born with chromosomes and genitalia that are not clearly female or male. Since gender differences are socially constructed, all men and all women can enact the behavior of the other, because they know the other's social script: "'Man' and 'woman' are at once empty and overflowing categories. Empty because they have no ultimate, transcendental meaning. Overflowing because even when they appear to be fixed, they still contain within them alternative, denied, or suppressed definitions" (Scott 1988:49). Nonetheless, though individuals may be able to shift gender statuses, the gender boundaries have to hold, or the whole gendered social order will come crashing down.

Paradoxically, it is the social importance of gender statuses and their external markers—clothing, mannerisms, and spatial segregation—that makes gender bending or gender crossing possible—or even necessary. The social viability of differentiated gender statuses produces the need or desire to shift statuses. Without gender differentiation, transvestism and transsexuality would be meaningless. You couldn't dress in the opposite gender's clothing if all clothing were unisex. There would be no need to reconstruct genitalia to match identity if interests and lifestyles were not gendered. There would be no need for women to pass as men to do certain kinds of work if jobs were not typed as "women's work" and "men's work." Women would not have to dress as men in public life in order to give orders or aggressively bargain with customers.

Gender boundaries are preserved when transsexuals create congruous autobiographies of always having felt like what they are now. The transvestite's story also "recuperates social and sexual norms" (Garber 1992:69). In the transvestite's normalized narrative, he or she "is 'compelled' by social and economic forces to disguise himself or herself in order to get a job, escape repression, or gain artistic or political 'freedom'" (Garber 1992:70). The "true identity," when revealed, causes amazement over how easily and success-fully the person passed as a member of the opposite gender, not a suspicion that gender itself is something of a put-on.

ENDNOTES

[1] Gender is, in Erving Goffman's (1983) words, an aspect of *Felicity's Condition:* "any arrange-ment which leads us to judge an individual's . . . acts not to be a manifestation of strangeness. Behind Felicity's Condition is our sense of what it is to be sane" (p. 27). Also see Bem 1993; Frye 1983:17–40; Goffman 1977.

[2] In cases of ambiguity in countries with modern medicine, surgery is usually performed to make the genitalia more clearly male or female.

[3] See J. Butler 1990 for an analysis of how doing gender *is* gender identity.

[4] On the hijras of India, see Nanda 1990; on the xaniths of Oman, Wikan 1982:168–86; on the American Indian berdaches, W. L. Williams 1986. Other societies that have similar institution-alized third-gender men are the Koniag of Alaska, the Tanala of Madagascar, the Mesakin of Nuba, and the Chukchee of Siberia (Wikan 1982:170).

[5] Durova 1989; Freeman and Bond 1992; Wheelwright 1989.

[6] Gender segregation of work in popular music still has not changed very much, according to Groce and Cooper 1990, despite considerable androgyny in some very popular figures. See Garber 1992 on the androgyny. She discusses Tipton on pp. 67–70.

[7] In the nineteenth century, not only did these women get men's wages, but they also "had male privileges and could do all manner of things other women could not: open a bank ac-count, write checks, own property, go anywhere unaccompanied, vote in elections" (Faderman 1991:44).

[8] When unisex clothing and men wearing long hair came into vogue in the United States in the mid-1960s, beards and mustaches for men also came into style again as gender identifications.

[9] For other accounts of women being treated as men in Islamic countries, as well as accounts of women and men cross-dressing in these countries, see Garber 1992:304–52.

[10] Dollimore 1986; Garber 1992:32–40; Greenblatt 1987:66–93; Howard 1988. For Renaissance accounts of sexual relations with women and men of ambiguous sex, see Lacqueur 1990: 134–39. For modern accounts of women passing as men that other women find sexually at-tractive, see Devor 1989:136–37; Wheelwright 1989:53–59.

[11] For an account of how a potential man-to-woman transsexual learned to be feminine, see Garfinkel 1967:116–85, 285–88. For a gloss on this account that points out how, throughout his encounters with Agnes, Garfinkel failed to see how he himself was constructing his own mas-culinity, see Rogers 1992.

[12] The concepts of moral hegemony, the effects of everyday activities (praxis) on thought and personality, and the necessity of consciousness of these processes before political change can occur are all based on Marx's analysis of class relations.

[13] Other societies recognize more than two categories, but usually no more than three or four (Jacobs and Roberts 1989).

[14] Carol Barkalow's book has a photograph of 11 first-year West Pointers in a math class, who are dressed in regulation pants, shirts, and sweaters, with short haircuts. The caption challenges the reader to locate the only woman in the room.

[15] The taboo on males and females looking alike reflects the U.S. military's homophobia (Bérubé 1989). If you can't tell those with a penis from those with a vagina, how are you going to deter-mine whether their sexual interest is heterosexual or homosexual unless you watch them hav-ing sexual relations?

REFERENCES

Amadiume, Ifi. 1987. *Male Daughters, Female Husbands: Gender and Sex in an African Society.* London: Zed Books.
Barkalow, Carol, with Andrea Raab. 1990. *In the Men's House.* New York: Poseidon Press.
Beauvoir, Simone de. [1949] 1953. *The Second Sex,* translated by H. M. Parshley. New York: Knopf.

Bem, Sandra Lipsitz. 1993. *The Lenses of Gender: Transforming the Debate on Sexual Inequality.* New Haven, CT: Yale University Press.

Bérubé, Allan. 1989. "Marching to a Different Drummer: Gay and Lesbian GIs in World War II." In *Hidden from History: Reclaiming the Gay and Lesbian Past,* edited by Martin Bauml Duberman, Martha Vicinus, and George Chauncey Jr. New York: New American Library.

Birdwhistell, Ray L. 1970. *Kinesics and Context: Essays on Body Motion Communication.* Philadelphia: University of Pennsylvania Press.

Blackwood, Evelyn. 1984. "Sexuality and Gender in Certain Native American Tribes: The Case of Cross-Gender Females." *Signs* 10:27–42.

Bolin, Anne. 1987. "Transsexualism and the Limits of Traditional Analysis." *American Behavior Scientist* 31:41–65.

Bourdieu, Pierre. [1980] 1990. *The Logic of Practice.* Stanford, CA: Stanford University Press.

Butler, Judith. 1990. *Gender Trouble: Feminism and the Subversion of Identity.* New York: Routledge.

Chodorow, Nancy. 1974. "Family Structure and Feminine Personality." In *Woman, Culture and Society,* edited by Michelle Zimbalist Rosaldo and Louise Lamphere. Stanford, CA: Stanford University Press.

Colapinto, John. 1997. "The True Story of John/Joan." *Rolling Stone,* December 11, pp. 54–97.

———. 2000. *As Nature Made Him: The Boy Who Was Raised as a Girl.* New York: HarperCollins.

Devor, Holly. 1987. "Gender Blending Females: Women and Sometimes Men." *American Behavior Scientist* 31:12–40.

———. 1989. *Gender Blending: Confronting the Limits of Duality.* Bloomington: University of Indiana Press.

Dollimore, Jonathan. 1986. "Subjectivity, Sexuality, and Transgression: The Jacobean Connection." *Renaissance Drama,* n.s. 17:53–81.

Durova, Nadezhda. 1989. *The Cavalry Maiden: Journals of a Russian Officer in the Napoleonic Wars,* translated by Mary Fleming Zirin. Bloomington: Indiana University Press.

Eichler, Margrit. 1989. "Sex Change Operations: The Last Bulwark of the Double Standard." In *Feminist Frontiers II,* edited by Laurel Richardson and Verta Taylor. New York: Random House.

Epstein, C. F. 1988. *Deceptive Distinctions: Sex, Gender and the Social Order.* New Haven, CT: Yale University Press.

Faderman, Lillian. 1991. *Odd Girls and Twilight Lovers: A History of Lesbian Life in Twentieth-Century America.* New York: Columbia University Press.

Foucault, Michel. 1972. *The Archeology of Knowledge and the Discourse on Language,* translated by A. M. Sheridan Smith. New York: Pantheon.

Freeman, Lucy and Alma Halbert Bond. 1992. *America's First Woman Warrior: The Courage of Deborah Sampson.* New York: Paragon.

Frye, Marilyn. 1983. *The Politics of Reality: Essays in Feminist Theory.* Trumansburg, NY: Crossing Press.

Garber, Marjorie. 1992. *Vested Interests: Cross-Dressing and Cultural Anxiety.* New York: Routledge.

Garfinkel, Harold. 1967. *Studies in Ethnomethodology.* Englewood Cliffs, NJ: Prentice-Hall.

Goffman, Erving. 1977. "The Arrangement between the Sexes." *Theory and Society* 4:301–33.

———. 1983. "Felicity's Condition." *American Journal of Sociology* 89:1–53.

Gordon, Tuula. 1990. *Feminist Mothers.* New York: New York University Press.

Gramsci, Antonio. 1971. *Selections from the Prison Notebooks,* translated and edited by Quintin Hoare and Geoffrey Nowell Smith. New York: International Publishers.

Greenblatt, Stephen. 1987. *Shakespearean Negotiations: The Circulation of Social Energy in Renaissance England.* Berkeley: University of California Press.

Groce, Stephen B. and Margaret Cooper. 1990. "Just Me and the Boys? Women in Local-Level Rock and Roll." *Gender & Society* 4:220–29.

Herdt, Gilbert and Julian Davidson. 1988. "The Sambia 'Turnim-Man': Sociocultural and Clinical Aspects of Gender Formation in Male Pseudohermaphrodites with 5α-Reductase Deficiency in Papua, New Guinea." *Archives of Sexual Behavior* 17:33–56.

Howard, Jean E. 1988. "Crossdressing, the Theater, and Gender Struggle in Early Modern England." *Shakespeare Quarterly* 39:418–41.

Jacobs, Sue-Ellen and Christine Roberts. 1989. "Sex, Sexuality, Gender, and Gender Variance." In *Gender and Anthropology,* edited by Sandra Morgen. Washington, DC: American Anthropological Association.

Kando, Thomas. 1973. *Sex Change: The Achievement of Gender Identity among Feminized Transsexuals.* Springfield, IL: Charles C. Thomas.

Kincaid, Jamaica. 1978. "Girl." *The New Yorker,* June 26.

Lacqueur, Thomas. 1990. *Making Sex: Body and Gender from the Greeks to Freud.* Cambridge, MA: Harvard University Press.

Lorber, Judith. 2001. "Feminist Theories of the Body." Pp. 214–15 in *Gender Inequality: Feminist Theories and Politics,* 2d ed., Los Angeles: Roxbury.

Matthaei, Julie A. 1982. *An Economic History of Woman's Work in America.* New York: Schocken.

Money, John and Anke A. Ehrhardt. 1972. *Man and Woman, Boy and Girl.* Baltimore, MD: Johns Hopkins University Press.

Morris, Jan. 1975. *Conundrum.* New York: Signet.

Nanda, Serena. 1990. *Neither Man nor Woman: The Hijras of India.* Belmont, CA: Wadsworth.

New York Times. 1989. "Musician's Death at 74 Reveals He Was a Woman." February 2.

Reskin, Barbara F. 1988. "Bringing the Men Back In: Sex Differentiation and the Devaluation of Women's Work." *Gender & Society* 2:58–81.

Rogers, Mary R. 1992. "They Were All Passing: Agnes, Garfinkel, and Company." *Gender & Society* 6:169–91.

Rubin, Gayle. 1975. "The Traffic in Women: Notes on the Political Economy of Sex." In *Toward an Anthropology of Women,* edited by Rayna Rapp Reiter. New York: Monthly Review Press.

Rugh, Andrea B. 1986. *Reveal and Conceal: Dress in Contemporary Egypt.* Syracuse, NY: Syracuse University Press.

Scott, Joan Wallach. 1988. *Gender and the Politics of History.* New York: Columbia University Press.

West, Candace and Don Zimmerman. 1987. "Doing Gender." *Gender & Society* 1:125–51.

Wheelwright, Julie. 1989. *Amazons and Military Maids: Women Who Cross-Dressed in Pursuit of Life, Liberty and Happiness.* London: Pandora Press.

Wikan, Unni. 1982. *Behind the Veil in Arabia: Women in Oman.* Baltimore, MD: Johns Hopkins University Press.

Williams, Christine L. 1989. *Gender Differences at Work: Women and Men in Nontraditional Occupations.* Berkeley: University of California Press.

Williams, Walter L. 1986. *The Spirit and the Flesh: Sexual Diversity in American Indian Culture.* Boston: Beacon Press.

12

MAKING IT BY FAKING IT
Working-Class Students in an Elite Academic Environment

ROBERT GRANFIELD

An important point about socialization is that societal values, identities, and social roles are learned, *not* instinctual. We have to learn the social norms and behaviors our society expects from us. We also learn or are socialized into different identities—our gender identity, our racial-ethnic identity, and our social class identity—among several others. In this reading, published in

Robert Granfield, "Making It by Faking It: Working-Class Students in an Elite Academic Environment" from *Journal of Contemporary Ethnography* (formerly *Urban Life*) 20, no. 3 (October 1991): 331–51. Copyright © 1991 by Sage Publications, Inc. Reprinted with the permission of Sage Publications, Inc.

1991, Robert Granfield examines how the working-class identities of some law students are challenged during their years at elite law schools. Law students experience an intense period of professional socialization during their graduate-school years that not only teaches them their occupation, but also changes their values, identities, and social roles. Granfield, an associate professor of sociology at the University of Buffalo, argues that this intense socialization has consequences not only for the individual students but also for the legal profession.

Research on stigma has generated significant insights into the complex relationship between self and society. The legacy of Goffman's (1963) seminal work on the subject can be found in studies on alcoholism, mental illness, homosexuality, physical deformities, and juvenile delinquency. Even the literature on gender and racial inequality has benefited from an emphasis on stigma. Goffman's attention to the social processes of devaluation and the emerging self-concepts of discredited individuals not only created research opportunities for generations of sociologists but contributed to a humanistic ideology that viewed stigma assignment and its effects as unjust.

One of the most vibrant research programs that emerged from Goffman's classic work has been in the area of stigma management. A host of conceptual terms have been employed to describe the process through which discreditable individuals control information about themselves so as to manage their social identity. Concepts such as passing, deviance disavowal, accounts, disclaimers, and covering have often been used in analyzing accommodations and adjustments to deviance, as Pfuhl's (1986) review shows. These tactics, while offering rewards associated with being seen as normal, frequently contribute to psychological stress. Possessing what Goffman (1963:5) referred to as "undesired differentness" often has significant consequences for one's personal identity as well as for available life chances. . . .

In this article, I focus on class stigma by examining a group of highly successful, upwardly mobile, working-class students who gained admission to a prestigious Ivy League law school in the East. While upward mobility from the working class occurs far less often within elite branches of the legal profession (Heinz and Laumann 1982; Smigel 1969) or corporate management (Useem and Karabel 1986), a certain amount of this type of mobility does take place. Working-class aspirants to the social elite, however, must accumulate cultural capital (Bourdieu and Passeron 1990; Cookson and Persell 1985) before they are able to transcend their status boundaries.

First, this article examines the ways in which working-class students experience a sense of differentness and marginality within the law school's elite environment. Next, I explore how these students react to their emerging class stigma by managing information about their backgrounds. I then demonstrate that the management strategies contribute to identity ambivalence and consider the secondary forms of adjustment students use to resolve this tension. Finally, I discuss why an analysis of social class can benefit from the insights forged by Goffman's work on stigma.

Setting and Methodology

The data analyzed for this article were collected as part of a much larger project associated with law school socialization (Granfield 1989). The subjects consist of students attending a prestigious, national law school in the eastern part of the United States. The school has had a long reputation of training lawyers who have become partners in major Wall Street law firms, Supreme Court judges, United States presidents and other politicians, heads of foundations, and . . . [have assumed many] other eminent leadership positions. Throughout the school's history, it has drawn mostly on the talents of high-status males. It was not until the second half of the twentieth century that women, minorities, and members of the lower classes were allowed admission into this esteemed institution (Abel 1989).

Most of the students attending the university at the time the study was being conducted were white and middle class.[1] The overwhelming majority are the sons and daughters of the professional-managerial class. Over 70 percent of those returning questionnaires had Ivy League or other highly prestigious educational credentials. As one would expect, fewer working-class students possessed such credentials.

A triangulated research design (Fielding and Fielding 1986) was used to collect the data. The first phase consisted of extensive fieldwork at the law school from 1985 to 1988, during which time I became a "peripheral member" (Adler and Adler 1987) in selected student groups. My activities while in the field consisted of attending classes with students, participating in their Moot Court[2] preparations, studying with students on campus, and at times, in their apartments, lunching with them, becoming involved in student demonstrations over job recruiting and faculty hiring, attending extracurricular lectures presented on campus, and participating in orientation exercises for first-year students. Throughout the entire fieldwork phase, I assumed both overt and covert roles. During the observation periods in classrooms, I recorded teacher–student interactions that occurred.

To supplement these observations, I conducted in-depth interviews with 103 law students at various stages in their training. Both personal interviews and small-group interviews with three or four students were recorded. The interviews lasted approximately two hours each and sought to identify the lived process through which law students experience legal training.

Finally, I administered a survey to 50 percent of the 1,540 students attending the law school. The survey examined their backgrounds, motives for attending law school, subjective perceptions of personal change, expectations about future practice, and evaluations of various substantive areas of practice. Over half (391) of the questionnaires were returned—a high rate of response for a survey of six pages requiring approximately 30 minutes of the respondent's time.

For this article, a subset of working-class students was selected for extensive analysis. Of the 103 students interviewed for the larger study, 23 came from working-class backgrounds, none of these from either the labor aristocracy or the unstable sectors of the working class. Typical parental occupations include postal worker, house painter, factory worker, fireman, dock worker, and carpenter. Many of these students were interviewed several times during their law school career. Many of the students selected for interviews were identified through questionnaires, while others were selected through the process of snowball sampling (Chadwick, Bahr, and Albrecht 1984).

Feeling Out of Place

Working-class students entered this elite educational institution with a great deal of class pride. This sense of class pride is reflected in the fact that a significantly larger proportion of working-class students reported entering law school for the purposes of contributing to social change than their non-working-class counterparts (see Granfield and Koenig 1990). That these students entered law school with the desire to help the downtrodden suggests that they identified with their working-class kin. In fact, students often credited their class background as being a motivating factor in their decision to pursue a career in social justice. One third-year student, whose father worked as a postal worker, recalled her parental influence:

> I wanted a career in social justice. It seemed to me to be a good value for someone who wanted to leave this world a little better than they found it. My parents raised me with a sense that there are right things and wrong things and that maybe you ought to try to do some right things with your life.

A second-year student said that he was influenced by the oppressive experiences that his father endured as a factory laborer. Coming to law school to pursue a career in a labor union, this student explained, "I was affected by my father, who had a job as a machinist. My father believes that corporations have no decency. I would term it differently, but we're talking about the same thing." Identifying with their working-class heritage produced not only a sense of pride but a system of values and ideals that greatly influenced their initial career objectives.

However, identification with the working class began to diminish soon after these students entered law school. Not long after arriving, most working-class students encountered an entirely new moral career. Although initially proud of their accomplishments, they soon came to define themselves as different and their backgrounds a burden. Lacking the appropriate cultural capital (Bourdieu 1984) associated with their more privileged counterparts, working-class students began to experience a crisis in competency. Phrases such as "the first semester makes you feel extremely incompetent," "the first year is like eating humble pie," and "I felt very small, powerless, and dumb" were almost universal among these working-class students. Some students felt embarrassed by their difficulty in using the elaborated speech codes (Bernstein 1977) associated with the middle class. One working-class woman said that she was very aware of using "proper" English, adding that "it makes me self-conscious when I use the wrong word or tense. I feel that if I had grown up in the middle class, I wouldn't have lapses. I have difficulty expressing thoughts while most other people here don't."

The recognition of their apparent differentness is perhaps best noted by examining the students' perception of stress associated with the first year of studies. Incoming working-class students reported significantly higher levels of personal stress than did their counterparts with more elite backgrounds. Much of this anxiety came from fears of academic inadequacy. Despite generally excellent college grades and their success in gaining admission to a nationally ranked law school, these students often worried that they did not measure up to the school's high standards. Nearly 62 percent of the first-year working-class students reported experiencing excessive grade pressure, compared to only 35 percent of those students from higher social class backgrounds.

In the words of Sennett and Cobb (1973), this lack of confidence is a "hidden injury of class," a psychological burden that working-class students experienced as they came to acquire the "identity beliefs" associated with middle-class society. While most students experience some degree of uncertainty and competency crisis during their first year, working-class students face the additional pressure of being cultural outsiders. Lacking manners of speech, attire, values, and experiences associated with their more privileged counterparts, even the most capable working-class student felt out of place:

> I had a real problem my first year because law and legal education are based on upper-middle-class values. The class debates had to do with profit maximization, law and economics, atomistic individualism. I remember in class we were talking about landlords' responsibility to maintain decent housing in rental apartments. Some people were saying that there were good reasons not to do this. Well, I think that's bullshit because I grew up with people who lived in apartments with rats, leaks, and roaches. I feel really different because I didn't grow up in suburbia.

Another student, a third-year working-class woman, felt marginalized because even her teachers assumed class homogeneity:

> I get sensitive about what professors have to say in class. I remember in a business class the professor seemed to assume that we all had fathers that worked in business and that we all understood about family investments. He said, "You're all pretty much familiar with this because of your family background." I remember thinking, doesn't he think there's any people in this law school who come from a working-class background?

Such experiences contributed to a student's sense of living in an alien world. The social distance these students experienced early in their law school career produced considerable discomfort.

This discomfort grew more intense as they became increasingly immersed into this new elite world. Within a short span of time, these students began to experience a credential gap vis-à-vis other students who possessed more prestigious academic credentials. A first-year male student who attended a state school in the Midwest explained:

> *I'm not like most people here. I didn't go to prestigious schools. I'm a bit of a minority here because of that. When I got here I was really intimidated by the fact of how many Yale and Harvard people there were here.*

At times, working-class law students were even embarrassed by their spouse's lower status. One first-year student described how her husband's credential gap caused her some anxiety:

> *People would ask me what my husband did and I would say he works for Radio Shack. People would be surprised. That was hard. Lately, we haven't done as much with [law school] people.*

Thus, students sometimes pruned contacts that would potentially result in stigma disclosure. In general, then, as working-class students progressed through law school, they began to adopt a view of themselves as different. The recognition of this difference subsequently led them to develop techniques of adjusting to their perceived secondary status.

Faking It

The management of identity has critical strategic importance not only for group affiliation and acceptance but for life chances. Stigma limits one's opportunities to participate in social life as a complete citizen, particularly so for those possessing gender or racial stigmas. However, because of the visibility of these stigmas, a person's adjustment to second-class citizenship is accomplished typically through either role engulfment in which a person accepts a spoiled identity (Schur 1971) or through direct confrontation where assignment of secondary status is itself challenged (Schur 1980). Rarely are these groups able to employ the concealment tactics typical among those groups whose stigma is not overtly visible.

Unlike gender or racial stigma, however, individuals often adjust to class stigma by learning to conceal their uniqueness. The practice of concealing one's class background, for instance, is not unusual. Certainly, members of the elite frequently learn that it is in "bad taste" to flaunt their privileged background and that it is more gracious to conceal their eminent social status (Baltzell 1958). Similarly, individuals who experience downward mobility often attempt to maintain their predecline image by concealing loss of status. Camouflaging unemployment in the world of management by using such terms as "consultant" and by doctoring résumés are ways that downwardly mobile executives "cover" their spoiled status (Newman 1988). Concealing one's social class circumstances and the stigma that may be associated with it assist individuals in dealing with any rejection and ostracism that may be forthcoming were the person's actual status known.

Initially, students who took pride in having accomplished upward mobility openly displayed a working-class presentation of self. Many went out of their way to maintain this presentation. One first-year student who grew up in a labor union family in New York explained that "I have consciously maintained my working-class image. I wear work shirts or old flannel shirts and blue jeans every day." During his first year, this student flaunted his working-class background, frequently also donning an old army jacket, hiking boots, and a wool hat. Identifying himself as part of the "proletarian left," he tried to remain isolated from what he referred to as the "elitist" law school community.

This attempt to remain situated in the working class, however, not only separated these students from the entire law school community but alienated them from groups that shared their ideological convictions. While much of the clothing worn by non-working-class students suggests resistance to being identified as a member of the elite, working-class students become increasingly aware of their differentness. Although these students identify with the working class, others, despite their appearance, possess traits and lifestyles that are often associated with more privileged groups (see Lurie 1983; Stone 1970). One first-year woman who described herself as "radical" complained that the other law school radicals were really "a bunch of upper-class white men." Subsequently, working-class students must disengage from their backgrounds if they desire to escape feeling discredited.

Working-class students disengaged from their previous identity by concealing their class backgrounds. Just as deviants seek to manage their identity by "passing" as nondeviants (Goffman 1963), these working-class law students often adopted identities that were associated with the more elite social classes.[3] Concealment allowed students to better participate in the culture of eminence that exists within the law school and reap available rewards.

This concealment meant, for instance, that students needed to acquire new dress codes. As Stone (1970) illustrated, appearance signifies identity and exercises a regulatory function over the responses of others. Such cultural codes pertaining to appearance often are used to exclude individuals from elite social positions (Bourdieu 1984; Jackell 1988; Lamont and Lareau 1988). Although working-class students lacked the cultural capital of higher social classes, they began to realize that they could successfully mimic their more privileged counterparts. Like undistinguished prep school students (Cookson and Persell 1985), working-class law students learned how to behave in an upper-class world, including how to dress for a new audience whose favorable appraisal they must cultivate. One second-year male discussed this process:

> *I remember going to buy suits here. I went to Brooks Brothers for two reasons. One, I don't own a suit. My father owns one suit, and it's not that good. Second,*

relationship to members of less privileged social classes. Seconda adjustments were therefore critical in helping students mitigate the lence they experienced over their own success and subsequent se from the working class.

Resolving Ambivalence

Although accommodation strategies were typical throughout the entire student body,[6] working-class students at this law school were more likely to employ particular types of strategies to help manage their identity. Students sought to manage their ambivalence by remaining "ideologically" distanced from the very social class their elite law school credential had facilitated alignment with. Many of these students became deliberate role models, unreservedly immersing themselves in higher social classes for that specific purpose. Such adjustments might be thought of as political since they were intended to directly challenge the domination of social elites. A black working-class student described how his actions would benefit the less fortunate:

> I get slammed for being a corporate tool. People feel that I have sold out. I'm irritated by that. For years, blacks have been treated as slaves, sharecroppers, or porters. So I think that whether I want to be a partner at Cravath or to be an NAACP defense attorney, either of these positions are politically correct. We need black people with money and power. I think that I can make significant contributions to black causes.

For many students who experienced ambivalence, working in elite law firms was seen as the best way to help those they left behind. Other students redefined the value of large corporate law firms for the opportunities that such positions offered in contributing to social change. One third-year student suggested:

> I used to think that social change would come about by being an activist. That's why I originally wanted to do public interest law. But you really can't accomplish much by doing this. The hiring partner at [a major New York law firm] convinced me that this is the only way to get things done. He served as the under secretary of state in the [former president's] administration. He made sense when he told me that if I wanted to contribute to social change I had to become an important person.

Students became less convinced that directly serving the less-privileged social classes would effectively resolve the problems that concerned them. A third-year student explained how disenchanted she had become with public interest law:

> I used to think that you could do good things for people. . . . I don't think that anymore. I'm no longer troubled by the idea of being a corporate lawyer as

> I think it's important to look good. A lot of my friends went to Brooks Brothers, and I feel it's worth it to do it right and not to have another hurdle to walk in and have the wrong thing on. It's all a big play act. . . . During my first year, I had no luck with interviews. I was in my own little world when I came here. I wished I had paid more attention to the dressing habits of second- and third-year students.

Being in their own "working-class world" forced these students to begin recognizing the importance of different interpersonal skills. A second-year woman commented that

> I have really begun to see the value of having good social skills. I think that is one of the ways that law firms weed out people. In order to get jobs you have to have those social skills. I'm real conscious of that when I go out on interviews now.

The recognition among working-class students that they were able to imitate upper-class students increasingly encouraged them to conceal their backgrounds. One second-year student, whose father worked as a house painter, boasted of his mastery of "passing":

> I generally don't tell people what my father does or what my mother does. I notice that I'm different, but it's not something other people here notice because I can fake it. They don't notice that I come from a blue-collar background.

Paying attention to the impression that one presents becomes extremely important for the upwardly mobile working-class student.

These students were sometimes assisted in their performances by professional career counselors employed by the law school. These professionals gave students instructions on how to present themselves as full-fledged members of this elite community. Students were taught that unless they downplayed their social class background, the most lucrative opportunities would be denied them. A third-year woman from a working-class area in Boston recalled learning this new norm of presentation:

> I'm sort of proud that I'm from South Boston and come from a working-class background. During my second year, however, I wasn't having much luck with my first interviews. I went to talk with my adviser about how to change my résumé a bit or how to present myself better. I told my adviser that on the interviews I was presenting myself as a slightly unusual person with a different background. We talked about that, and he told me that it probably wasn't a good idea to present myself as being a little unusual. I decided that he was right and began to play up that I was just like them. After that, the interviews and offers began rolling in. I began to realize that they [interviewers] really like people who are like themselves.

Recognizing that job recruiters seek homogeneity is an important lesson that upwardly mobile working-class students must learn if they are to gain admission into high status and financially rewarding occupations.[4] Kanter

(1977) demonstrated, for instance, that managers come to reward those who resemble themselves. More recently, Jackell (1988) documented how the failure of managers to "fit in" resulted in suspicion and subsequent exclusion from advancement. Fitting in is particularly important in prestigious law firms which tend to resemble the high-status clients they represent (Abel 1989). During interviews, however, working-class law students faced a distinct disadvantage, as the interviewers who actively pursued new recruits rarely posed questions about the student's knowledge of law.[5] Most seemed intent on finding students who fit into the law firm's corporate structure. The entire recruitment process itself, from the initial interview to "fly out," represents ceremonial affirmation of these students' elite status in which they need only demonstrate their "social" competence. Working-class students typically found such interactions stressful. One third-year student explained her experiences:

> They [the recruiters] didn't test my knowledge of law. They were interested in finding out what kind of person I was and what my background was. I tried to avoid talking about that and instead stressed the kind of work I was interested in. I think that most firms want a person who they can mold, that fits into their firm.

Some of the most successful working-class students enjoyed the accolades bestowed on them because of their hard work and natural abilities. In speaking of her success, a third-year student on law review said that when she entered law school, it never occurred to her that she would clerk for the Supreme Court and then work for a major Wall Street law firm, adding that "once you begin doing well and move up the ladder and gain a whole new set of peers, then you begin to think about the possibilities." However, such success comes at a price, particularly for working-class students of color. Although having achieved success, many of these students continued to feel like outsiders. One such student, a third-year black male, reflected on what he considered the unfortunate aspects of affirmative action programs:

> I have mixed feelings about the law review because of its affirmative action policies. On the one hand, I think it's good that minorities are represented on the law review. On the other hand, there's a real stigma attached to it. Before law school, I achieved by my own abilities. On law review, I don't feel I get respect. I find myself working very hard and getting no respect. Other students don't work as hard. I spend a lot of time at the review because I don't want to turn in a bad assignment. I don't want them [other law review members] to think that I don't have what it takes.

Students who perceived themselves as outsiders frequently overcompensated for their failings because they felt judged by the "master status" associated with their social identity. This reaction to class stigma is typical among working-class students in educational institutions. In addition to developing their educational skills, working-class students are confronted with learning social skills as well. This makes succeeding particularly difficult for these

students and is a task fraught with the fear of being discovered as tent (Sennett and Cobb 1973).

Ambivalence

Despite their maneuvers, these working-class students had difficulty scending their previous identity. The attempt by these students to m. their stigma resulted in what Goffman (1963:107) termed "identity am. lence." Working-class students who sought to exit their class backgro could neither embrace their group nor let it go. This ambivalence is o felt by working-class individuals who attain upward mobility into professional–managerial class (Steinitz and Solomon 1986). Many experier the "stranger in paradise" syndrome, in which working-class individuals fe like virtual outsiders in middle-class occupations (Ryan and Sackrey 1984 Such experiences frequently lead to considerable identity conflict among work ing-class individuals who attempt to align themselves with the middle class.

The working-class law students in my sample typically experienced identity conflicts on their upward climb. Not only did they feel deceptive in their adjustment strategies, but many felt the additional burden of believing they had "sold out" their own class and were letting their group down. Like other stigmatized individuals who gain acceptance among dominant groups (Goffman 1963), these students often felt they were letting down their own group by representing elite interests. One third-year female student ruefully explained:

> My brother keeps asking me whether I'm a Republican yet. He thought that after I finished law school I would go to work to help people, not work for one of those firms that do business. In a way, he's my conscience. Maybe he's right. I've got a conflict with what I'm doing. I came from the working class and wanted to do public interest law. I have decided not to do that. It's been a difficult decision for me. I'm not completely comfortable about working at a large firm.

Another student, who grew up on welfare, expressed similar reservations about his impending career in law:

> I'm not real happy about going to a large firm. I make lots of apologies. I'm still upset about the fact that my clients are real wealthy people, and it's not clear as to what the social utility of that will be.

Like the previous example, this student experienced a form of self-alienation as a result of his identity ambivalence. Students often experience a sense of guilt as they transcend their working-class backgrounds. Such guilt, however, needs to be abated if these students are to successfully adjust to their new reference group and reduce the status conflict they experience. For these working-class students, making the primary adjustment to upward mobility required strategies of accommodation in personal attitudes regarding their

opposed to a public interest one. I'm still concerned about social problems like poverty or poor housing, but I'm not sure that being a public interest attorney is the way to resolve those things. The needs of the people that public interest lawyers serve are just beyond what I can do as an attorney. I think I can do more good for people if I commit myself to working with community groups or activities in the bar during my spare time.

The offering of such accounts helps students resolve the contradiction they experience by choosing a large law firm practice, as does the practical planning to use one's spare time (e.g., to do community activities). Unfortunately, given the structure of contemporary large law firms, spare time is a rarity (Nelson 1988; Spangler 1986). Adopting these new definitions regarding the pursuit of effective social change means that working-class students need not feel penitent over their upward mobility. Such strategies, of course, are attractive, as they suggest that the student is becoming elite not solely because he or she is striving for personal reward and success but as a means to best pursue the noble ideals of public service and social activism.

A more drastic accommodation involved avoidance of those who reminded working-class students of their social obligations toward helping the less fortunate. Just associating with individuals whose career path was geared toward helping the downtrodden caused considerable uneasiness in working-class students who had decided to enter large law firms. One third-year student said that he had begun to avoid law students who had retained their commitment to work with the poor:

It's taken for granted here that you can work for a large firm and still be a good person. The people who don't reinforce that message make me uncomfortable now. Frankly, that's why I'm not hanging out with the public interest people. They remind me of my own guilt.

In some cases, avoidance turned into open hostility. Another third-year student described how she now saw other students who remained committed to their ideals of helping the less fortunate: "They're so single-minded at times and I think a little naive. They've really pushed me away from wanting to do public interest work as a full-time occupation." Condemning her condemners helped this student neutralize the guilt she felt over working for a corporate law firm.

Conclusion

Upwardly mobile working-class students in this study, as well as in others, interpret and experience their social class from the perspective of stigma. However, since the stigma of being a member of the lower classes is thought to be just, upwardly mobile working-class students frequently construct identities in which they seek to escape the taint associated with their affiliation. Overcoming this stigma is therefore considered an individual rather than a collective effort. As was demonstrated in this study, such efforts often involve managing one's identity in the ways that Goffman outlined. Research that explores identity struggles as they relate to class could offer further extensions of Goffman's comments on stigma. Such research also has potential value in contributing to our understanding of working-class movements in the United States. Indeed, exploring the experience of class from the perspective of stigma and its management could offer great insight into the social psychology of working-class disempowerment.

ENDNOTES

Author's Note: Partial funding for this research was provided by the Woodrow Wilson Foundation.

[1] The following are the percentage distributions of social class background on the random sample of questionnaire returnees I collected for the larger project: upper class (2.8), upper-middle (44.6), middle (30.0), lower-middle (8.0), working (13.1), and lower (0.5).

[2] This is a first-year exercise in which students select a case to argue in front of a three-person panel consisting of a law professor, a third-year student, and an invited guest from the legal community. First-year students prepare their cases for several months in advance before formally presenting their oral argument.

[3] Similar findings were reported by Domhoff and Zweigenhaft (1991) in which they described the experiences of black students who were enrolled in elite prep schools as a result of affirmative action.

[4] Students are actively pursued. During the 1987 recruitment seasons at the law school, an average of 44 recruiters from commercial law firms conducted interviews with students each day. This represents nearly one law firm for each law student eligible to interview. In most cases, law firms are looking to hire more than one student.

[5] A study of hiring policies among large law firms found that "personal characteristics" ranked second among the criteria for selecting new lawyers (see Buller and Beck-Dudley 1990).

[6] Many students are confronted with identity conflicts that stem from the separation of personal values from professional roles. This is felt most among those students who entered law school with social activist ideals (for further discussion of this, see Granfield 1986, 1989, 1992).

REFERENCES

Abel, R. 1989. *American Lawyers.* New York: Oxford University Press.

Adler, P. and P. Adler. 1987. *Membership Roles in Field Research.* Newbury Park, CA: Sage.

Baltzell, E. D. 1958. *Philadelphia Gentlemen.* New York: Free Press.

Bernstein, B. 1977. *Class Codes and Control.* Vol. 3, *Towards a Theory of Educational Transmission.* London: Routledge & Kegan Paul.

Bourdieu, P. 1984. *Distinction: A Social Critique of the Judgment of Taste.* Cambridge, MA: Harvard University Press.

Bourdieu, P. and J. C. Passeron. 1990. *Reproduction in Education, Society and Culture.* London: Routledge & Kegan Paul.

Buller, P. and C. Beck-Dudley. 1990. "Performance, Policies and Personnel." *American Bar Association Journal* 76:94.

Chadwick, B., H. Bahr, and S. Albrecht. 1984. *Social Science Research Methods.* Englewood Cliffs, NJ: Prentice-Hall.

Cookson, P. and C. Persell. 1985. *Preparing for Power: America's Elite Boarding Schools.* New York: Basic Books.

Domhoff, G. W. and R. Zweigenhaft. 1991. *Blacks in the White Establishment: A Study of Race and Class in America.* New Haven, CT: Yale University Press.

Fielding, N. and J. Fielding. 1986. *Linking Data.* Beverly Hills, CA: Sage.

Goffman, E. 1963. *Stigma: Notes on the Management of Spoiled Identity.* Englewood Cliffs, NJ: Prentice-Hall.

Granfield, R. 1986. "Legal Education As Corporate Ideology: Student Adjustment to the Law School Experience." *Sociological Forum* 1:514–23.

———. 1989. "Making the Elite Lawyer: Culture and Ideology in Legal Education." Ph.D. dissertation, Northeastern University, Boston.

———. 1992. *Making Elite Lawyers.* New York: Routledge, Chapman & Hall.

Granfield, R. and T. Koenig. 1990. "From Activism to Pro Bono: The Redirection of Working Class Altruism at Harvard Law School." *Critical Sociology* 17:57–80.

Heinz, J. and E. Laumann. 1982. *Chicago Lawyers: The Social Structure of the Bar.* New York: Russell Sage.

Jackell, R. 1988. *Moral Mazes: The World of the Corporate Manager.* New York: Oxford University Press.

Kanter, R. 1977. *Men and Women of the Corporation.* New York: Basic Books.

Lamont, M. and A. Lareau. 1988. "Cultural Capital: Allusions, Gaps and Glissandos in Recent Theoretical Development." *Sociological Theory* 6:153–68.

Lurie, A. 1983. *The Language of Clothes.* New York: Vintage.

Nelson, R. 1988. *Partners with Power: The Social Transformation of the Large Law Firm.* Berkeley: University of California Press.

Newman, K. 1988. *Falling from Grace: The Experience of Downward Mobility in the American Middle Class.* New York: Free Press.

Pfuhl, E. 1986. *The Deviance Process.* Belmont, CA: Wadsworth.

Ryan, J. and C. Sackrey. 1984. *Strangers in Paradise: Academics from the Working Class.* Boston: South End Press.

Schur, E. 1971. *Labeling Deviant Behavior.* New York: Harper & Row.

———. 1980. *The Politics of Deviance.* Englewood Cliffs, NJ: Prentice-Hall.

Sennett, R. and R. Cobb. 1973. *The Hidden Injuries of Class.* New York: Random House.

Smigel, E. 1969. *The Wall Street Lawyer.* Bloomington: Indiana University Press.

Spangler, E. 1986. *Lawyers for Hire: Salaried Professionals at Work.* New Haven, CT: Yale University Press.

Steinitz, V. and E. Solomon. 1986. *Starting Out: Class and Community in the Lives of Working Class Youth.* Philadelphia: Temple University Press.

Stone, G. 1970. "Appearance and the Self." Pp. 394–414 in *Social Psychology through Symbolic Interaction,* edited by G. Stone and H. Farberman. New York: Wiley.

Useem, M. and J. Karabel. 1986. "Paths to Corporate Management." *American Sociological Review* 51:184–200.

13

LEARNING TO STRIP
The Socialization Experiences of Exotic Dancers

JACQUELINE LEWIS

Learning an occupation is a common form of adult socialization. Occupational socialization occurs during formal education, during job training, and during time spent on the job. Every profession has a set of values that it wants its colleagues to embrace. For example, to become a doctor one needs to learn the skills and knowledge of practicing medicine as well as the

Jacqueline Lewis, "Learning to Strip: The Socialization Experiences of Exotic Dancers" from *Canadian Journal of Human Sexuality* 7, no. 1 (1998): 51–56. Copyright © 1998. Reprinted with the permission of SIECCAN.

attitudes and values of the medical profession. Medical students experience an intense period of professional socialization during the years, almost a decade, they spend in medical school and residency. The previous reading on law students is another example of professional socialization. This selection by Jacqueline Lewis, an associate professor of sociology at the University of Windsor, Ontario, Canada, illustrates the occupational socialization experiences of exotic dancers.

Introduction

Entering any new job or social role requires a process of socialization where the individual acquires the necessary values, attitudes, interests, skills and knowledge in order to be competent at her/his job. As with any new job or social role, becoming an exotic dancer requires a process of socialization. For exotic dancers, achieving job competence involves getting accustomed to working in a sex-related occupation, and the practice of taking their clothes off in public for money. In addition, in order to be a successful exotic dancer, women must also learn how to manipulate clientele and to rationalize such behavior and their involvement in a deviant occupation.[1] For some dancers, the socialization process is partially anticipatory in nature, although dancers reported that most of their socialization occurred once they had made their decision to dance and found themselves actually working in the strip club environment. In this [reading], I explore the factors influencing entry into exotic dancing, the socialization experiences of exotic dancers and the process of obtaining job competence.

Background

Since the late 1960s, exotic dancing and the experiences of exotic dancers have been the focus of academic inquiry. The relevance of some of the available literature to the present study is, however, limited by the focus of the articles. Within this literature on exotic dancers, only the articles by Boles and Garbin (1974, 1974c), Carey, Peterson, and Sharpe (1974), Dressel and Petersen (1982), McCaghy and Skipper (1972), Prus and Styllianoss (1980), Skipper and McCaghy (1971), and Thompson and Harred (1992) address the socialization experiences of dancers in any detail. Dressel and Petersen's (1982b) focus on the socialization of male exotic dancers makes their work of limited applicability to the present study.

Although much of this research was conducted over [25 to 30] years ago, some of it remains relevant to the work reported here. For example, [some works listed above] provide an historical point of comparison that indicates some consistency between past and current research findings on the occupational socialization of exotic dancers.

The literature on occupational socialization of exotic dancers emphasizes two basic themes: (1) the factors that influence entry into dancing; and (2) anticipatory and on-the-job socialization experiences. Two types of models have been advanced to explain entry into exotic dancing: (1) career contingency models and (2) conversion models. In some research reports, these models are used on their own, and in others they are used in combination. Although a variety of singular and combined models have been used to explain entry into exotic dancing, there are several common factors that are identified across the studies: (1) knowledge and accessibility of an opportunity structure that makes exotic dancing an occupational alternative; (2) an awareness of the economic rewards associated with being an exotic dancer; (3) a recruitment process involving personal networks; and (4) financial need or a need for employment.

With respect to the anticipatory and on-the-job socialization experiences of dancers (Boles and Garbin 1974c; Dressel and Petersen 1982; Thompson and Harred 1992), early research found that most female dancers had either professional training in dance, music or theatre, had been previously employed in the entertainment industry, or received extensive training in stripping prior to dancing before an audience (Boles and Garbin 1974c; McCaghy and Skipper 1972; Prus and Styllianoss 1980). However, despite their advanced (anticipatory) preparation, a large part of the occupational socialization dancers experienced occurred through informal channels after they had entered the occupation. Through observing and interacting with other subcultural members, dancers learned the tricks of the trade, such as how to interact with customers for profit; manage their deviant lifestyle; and be successful at their job (Boles and Garbin 1974c; Dressel and Petersen 1982; McCaghy and Skipper 1972; Thompson and Harred 1992).

Method

This study used a combination of field observations inside strip clubs and interviews with exotic dancers and other club staff to identify issues associated with the work and careers of exotic dancers. Observations were conducted at clubs in several cities in southern Ontario. Observational data were collected primarily to supplement interview data and to assist us in describing the work environment of exotic dancers including physical setting; contacts between those present in the club (employees and clients); and the atmosphere of different clubs.

Thirty semi-structured, in-depth interviews were conducted with female exotic dancers, club staff and key informants. Participants were recruited either by the research team during field trips to the clubs or by dancers who had participated in the study. Each interview was audiotaped and took place in a location chosen by the respondent (e.g., respondent's home, a research team member's office, a private space at a strip club, a local coffee shop). Interviews lasted anywhere from one to three hours, with the majority taking approximately one and a half hours. All interviews were conducted informally to allow participants to freely express themselves and to allow for exploration of new or unanticipated topics that arose in the interview.

The interviews explored each woman's work history, her perception of her future in the occupation, a description of her work, the various forms of interaction engaged in with clients, use of drugs and alcohol, current sexual practices, perception of risk for HIV and other STDs associated with dancing, sexual health-maintaining strategies, factors influencing risk and ability to maintain sexual health, and the presence and/or possibility of a community among exotic dancers. Interviews with other club employees were designed to tap their experiences in, and impressions of, club-related activities.

As interviews were collected and transcribed, it became increasingly apparent that there was a variety of recurrent themes that ran throughout the interviews (e.g., motivations for entry, socialization process, health and safety concerns, relationships between club employees, impact of dancing on dancers' lives, etc.). Coding categories were developed to fit with these emerging themes. . . . As noted by Glaser and Straus (1967), "[. . .] in discovering theory, one generates conceptual categories or their properties from evidence; then the evidence from which the category emerged is used to illustrate the concept" (p. 23). The quotes that appear in this [reading] were selected as examples of the responses provided by the women interviewed that fit the various conceptual categories that emerged during data analysis.

Becoming an Exotic Dancer

Unlike other more conventional occupations with formally structured socialization programs, the socialization experiences of the women we spoke with were informal in nature. Dancers reported that they acquired the requisite skills for the job through informal socialization processes that either (1) were anticipatory in nature, occurring prior to dancing; and/or (2) occurred on-the-job, once they were employed to dance in a strip club.

Anticipatory Socialization

Early studies of female exotic dancers (see Boles and Garbin 1974b; McCaghy and Skipper 1972) found that most dancers had fairly broad anticipatory socialization experiences, having been previously employed in an entertainment-related job, having some type of professional training in dance, music or theatre, or having an agent who helped prepare them for the career of exotic dancing. In this study, we, however, found little indication of the latter two types of anticipatory socialization experiences.

Although one woman had a background in drama, she talked about how it actually did little to prepare her for the job:

> *I thought you know, O.K. being in Drama, ya, I'm kind of a freer person, whatever. But, like, actually taking off your clothes—nothing, nothing prepares you*

for it. Nothing. Seconds before I went up to go dance [for the first time], I'm thinking, oh my God, I can't do this, I can't do this. I can't do this. Then my music started playing and I'm like, I guess I have to now. And you know, your stomach's all in knots and you just do it. There's no way to describe it. You just do it.

Even the few women who indicated that they began dancing with the help of an agent talked about how they received little job preparation. For example, one woman said:

I responded to an ad in the local paper and there was a number and you phoned the number and then you met with this guy and he made you sign a contract and then he kind of talked to you about what goes on. There was no training. Then he just took me to the bar later that evening and that was it.

Although the experiences dancers reported during their interviews varied, the women we spoke with who reported engaging in anticipatory socialization, talked about spending time in strip clubs before deciding to dance. In recalling their entry into exotic dancing, some of the dancers we interviewed spoke of being curious about dancing, and wanting to find out if it was something they could do. These women reported that they sussed out and gained familiarity with dancing by going out to strip clubs on their own and talking to dancers or by going out to the clubs with friends who hung out at or worked in strip clubs.

So, I read some more about it. I read a couple of books on the sex industry and strippers in particular and burlesque dancers. Um, and then I visited a lot of the clubs and tried to talk to the dancers about how they got interested in it and how they get paid and what the job entails. They were pretty open to talking to me about it. . . . and she's like, I'm not really just waitressing, I'm dancing too. And I'm like, "Wow, oh, how much money are you making doing that?" And she's like, "Well, really good and you know if you want to help make your daughter's life better, why don't you come with me one night?" And I'm like, "Oh, man, I don't know if I could do that, you know." I got real scared and everything, but we set a date for the next Friday.

The other women who had anticipatory socialization experiences reported experiencing a more gradual drift into dancing (Matza 1990).[2] Instead of purposefully going to strip clubs and talking to people in the industry with the intention of sussing it out, these women drifted into dancing through associations they had with people in the industry or by working as a waitress in one of the clubs.

I didn't start out dancing. First I was a waitress. Eventually, I quit waitressing and I went and started dancing at a strip club.

I waitressed for about a year at the Maverick, and then I started to dance. I've been dancing for 7 years, just over 7 years.

I used to date this guy and some of his friends worked in the clubs, so we could go and hang out. He used to try to get me to try it [dancing], but I wouldn't. But, once we broke up, I decided to try it. . . .

According to Ritzer and Walczak (1986), "[. . .] deviant occupational skills may be learned through involvement in different but related occupations or through nonoccupational activities" (p. 144). Through hanging out with people associated with the industry or by working in a strip club in some other capacity, these women experienced a form of anticipatory socialization that enabled them to view dancing as a viable job option. As noted by Matza (1990), "some learning is truly a discovery [for the individual], for until they have experimented with the forbidden, [. . . they] are largely unaware that infraction is feasible behavior" (p. 184).

A lot of my friends and a lot of the group that I used to hang around with while I was waitressing were uh, we were all in the same circles with the guys from a strip club for women and uh, the two clubs were connected, and so they kept saying "try it" and, you know, "go to this bar, start there" and that's just how I ended up there.

I lived with a guy when I was at [high] school. . . . We moved right into the city, downtown Toronto and he was hanging out with strippers. . . . And I used to threaten him, you know, if you keep hanging out with these girls, I'm gonna become one. And I did.

I used to waitress at a saloon and then I was hanging out with some of the girls and then dating guys from a dance club for women, heaven forbid, and it just went from there, I guess that's how I got into dancing. . . .

The experiences of the women who drifted into dancing can be viewed as a form of recruitment or conversion process whereby the individual is gradually introduced/exposed to the inner world of a new role or career and gives up one view of that role, or one world view, for another (see Becker 1964; Lofland and Stark 1965; Prus and Sharper 1977). According to Lofland and Stark (1965), the reinforcement and encouragement made available through intensive interaction with subgroup members is necessary if the recruit is to experience a complete conversion process.

Regardless of how they began their process of occupational socialization, in providing themselves with time to think things through, and to learn to identify with the norms, values and beliefs of the dancing subculture prior to entering it, these women were engaging in a form of role rehearsal and anticipatory socialization. Such efforts provided them with the opportunity to prepare themselves for the eventual reality of their new status, thereby easing the difficulties associated with the transition. Through engaging in anticipatory socialization, the women interviewed became accustomed to the strip club environment and the idea of taking their clothes off in public for money, thereby facilitating their entry into dancing.

On-the-Job Socialization

Similar to the socialization experiences of individuals in other occupations, novice dancers learn through interaction and observation while on-the-job. Since exotic dancers, however, have little, if any, formal training, learning through observation and interaction is crucial for attaining job competence (see Sanders 1974). Although some of this learning may be anticipatory in nature and occur prior to the initial dancing experience, it takes some time and experience to move from being a novice dancer to a seasoned pro. Since there is no formal certification structure, peers play an important role in this transformation process. During this period, novices can continue to acquire knowledge from those around them about how to be successful at their job. Experienced strip club staff can therefore play an important role in the socialization process of the novice dancer. As one woman noted:

> *You learn as you go. Other people in the club give you advice. And, you know, you gradually learn about how to make more money and who to talk to and that kind of stuff as you go.*

Through talking to and receiving advice about the job from other staff members, novice dancers learn how to handle situations that may arise while working in the club, and how to dance for profit.

> *The DJ at the first club I danced at was very good. On my first night he was like, "don't worry about it. . . . You know, just go up there and do your thing and you know, don't worry about it." And the other girls were kind of supportive, like, "Oh, you'll get used to it, it's not that bad after a while." You know, some of them kind of take you under their wing and sort of show you the ropes so to speak. . . .*

> *I learned a lot just watching the other women. Some of them had been dancing for a while and they were really good at handling customers when they tried to break the rules.*

Other dancers play a particularly important role in the socialization process. As the following quotes illustrate, novices can learn how to dress, dance and interact with customers for profit, through observing and interacting with dancers more experienced than themselves.

> *Most of the dancers are really nice, like, they're really understanding. They knew, you know, I hadn't danced for very long. Everybody was offering me advice. There were a few that were kind of like, stay away from me and I'll stay away from you sort of thing.*

> *I get ideas for my show from watching, you know, the ones that have been doing this [dancing] for a while. . . . There were these three other dancers there that were amazing. Like, they couldn't have helped me more. . . . I'd only been dancing for about a week and you know, they were offering me advice left, right and center. And you know, they were just so nice. They couldn't be more helpful.*

One woman explained how a friend of hers, who was an experienced dancer, helped teach her how to table dance.

> [Talking about her first table dance] So, she comes up beside me and the next thing I know, both our tops are off and she's like all rubbing close to me and I'm like going, "Oh my God." I never thought of her that way before, you know. Cuz we've always just been friends, you know. So, it was kind of a funny experience. But, he [the customer] ended up spending like a hundred dollars on songs. So, I'm thinking, hey, this is great, you know. I mean, this is awesome. I've got money to come home with, you know, it wasn't a wasted night. I thought, O.K., I can deal with this a couple nights a week.

She went on to describe how her friend, along with a few other dancers, also helped her with her first stage performance:

> The only thing that was really scary after my first night in the club was the stage, because I had never been on a stage before, and I'm thinking, "Oh my God, I don't have big breasts, I'm not like toned and tanned and blonde" or whatever. So, my friend's like, "Well, we can do like the dance that we did with that guy. We should do a dance on stage together." And, I'm like, "But I'm not gay and I'm not going to be able to make them think that I am." She's like, "Well, don't worry, just follow my lead [. . .]." . . . And then after doing that a few times I decided that, you know, I wanted to try it on my own. So I did, and I didn't like it as much because, you know, you sort of feel really centered out. But eventually I got used to it and I was able to do it, you know. Now I've got the hang of it.

Rationalizing Participation in a Deviant Occupation

Since exotic dancing is viewed as a deviant occupation in our society, if novice dancers are to retain a valued sense of self, they must learn ways to justify their involvement in the strip club subculture. According to Sykes and Matza (1957), in order to deviate people must have access to a set of rationalizations or neutralizations that allow them to reduce the guilt they feel about violating social norms. Neutralization makes norm violations "morally feasible since it serves to obliterate, or put out of mind, the dereliction implicit in it" (Matza 1990:182).

During interviews with dancers, it became apparent that dancers typically rely on several "techniques of neutralization" (Sykes and Matza 1957) to justify their involvement in deviant behavior. Similar to Thompson and Harred's (1992) research on topless dancers, we found that the dancers we interviewed tended to rely primarily on three of Sykes and Matza's (1957) techniques of neutralization.

They denied injury or harm:

> Ya well, we pretend [that they like the customers], but what do they really expect. Do they really think we are there because we like them, that we like to dance

for men—no. And really, who are we hurting? We may take their money, and although sometimes it may be a lot, but, they are adults, they should know better. And besides, it's just money.

They condemned the condemners:

People may judge us and say that dancing is bad, but they seem to forget who it is we are dancing for—doctors, lawyers, sports figures. If it wasn't for them there would be no dancing—so maybe the focus is on the wrong people [the dancers rather than the customers].

As soon as you tell people you dance, it's "Oh." It's a totally different idea of what kind of person you are, or however you are is a put on. I just think what is the big deal. We are all the same here.

So I take my clothes off for a living. Doesn't make you any different. You all go there smoking dope and drinking beer anyway so. . . .

And they appealed to higher loyalties:[3]

Well, they say that you're not supposed to show your body to lustful men and that that's a sin. . . . But, the other way I looked at it was, I have a daughter who is two years old and the government really doesn't give you enough to survive, so I had to do something. And I figured that if it's a sin to take off your clothes and it's a sin to let your child starve, definitely, I would take care of the second one, and it's probably more normal. . . .

In addition to using some of Sykes and Matza's (1957) techniques of neutralization to justify their involvement in exotic dancing, we found that dancers used the technique of normalization. As the following quote illustrates, some women attempted to justify or neutralize their involvement in exotic dancing by refuting the deviancy associated with it.

And I looked at the salaries these people were making and it was, you know, a thousand dollars a night, some nights, and it was really, really substantially helping with their tuition. And these were people working on Master's degrees and Doctorates and all kinds of things and I thought, "Wow, if they can do this, hey, maybe I can."

Despite the deviancy associated with being an exotic dancer and the negative aspects of the job, most of the women we spoke with seemed to be able to rationalize or justify their involvement in exotic dancing. In summarizing the use of justifications by exotic dancers, one woman said:

You can justify it because you bring home money and at the end of the night that feels great. You don't reflect on, you know, how you were degraded, the leering and the other bad stuff. You know, you don't think about it because you've got a big wad of money in your hand.

In other words, the major incentive for entering dancing, money,[4] is also used as the main justification or rationale for continuing to do it. As with Hong and Duff's (1977) study of taxi-dancers, the neutralization techniques or rationalizations used by exotic dancers to downplay the norm-violating nature of their behavior, soothe guilt feelings, and cope with the unpleasant aspects of their jobs, were learned during the informal socialization processes that occur on-the-job.

Putting on a Show

Beyond acquiring the courage to take off one's clothes in public and learning how to justify one's actions, obtaining competence as an exotic dancer also requires learning to be good at the job. In order to become a successful exotic dancer, the novice dancer must learn how to put on a good show or performance. As with any successful performer, dancers need to learn how to use impression management skills to create an illusion that will allow them to control/manipulate their audience in order to achieve some specified goal, in this case the acquisition of money. In their interviews, the women talked about how their job required they put on a skillful performance that would lure men in and get them to spend their money on dancers.

> *A dance is not just dancing, it is the way you present yourself, the way you talk to the customer, the way you introduce yourself. If you gonna have a smile, right away it's gonna be easy [to make money].*

> *Just turn the guys on, make them think that we are like, you know, licking each other [when performing with another woman]. But we weren't, it's all show. I mean, you don't have to do anything, you know, that's real. You just have to make it look real. So, you know, you would lift up the girl's leg, put your head down, you know, pretend that you're like, oh, you know, that kind of stuff. You know, like men are kind of stupid, so they buy it, right. . . .*

As dancers reported in their interviews, learning how to control or manipulate an audience is acquired through observation and interaction with subcultural members within the club setting.

> *I was really glad I waitressed before dancing. I got to overhear a lot of the conversations between the dancers and the customers. It was that way that I figured out how to operate and ways to play the men for their money.*

> *Some of the girls that have been dancing a while here were really nice to me. They gave me advice on how to keep the guys interested so they will buy several table dances in a row.*

Skill development, improvement, and job competence more generally were affirmed by coworkers through praise, and by customers through applause, requests for table dances, the development of a regular clientele, and increased take-home pay.

Typology of Dancers

Although the women interviewed reported that they experienced a process of adjustment in becoming a dancer, this process differed somewhat according to the type of dancer each woman could be classified as. Based on the interview data collected, there appear to be two types of dancers: the career dancer and the goal-oriented dancer. Both types of dancers report money as the primary motivating factor for entry into dancing; however, they differ in the types of future they envision for themselves. Despite the fact that most of the women we spoke with told us that they never intended on making dancing a career, some ended up staying in the industry for many years, essentially making it one. Other women reported that they entered the world of dancing with the expectation that dancing would be their career for a while. Whether they intended on making dancing a career or not, the career dancers we spoke with tended to possess limited skill training and education. As a result, they saw dancing as an employment opportunity that enabled them to make a decent living that would otherwise be unavailable to them through other channels.

> *This is a career for me, it's seventeen years. I don't want to stop this now. And besides, what other job could I get where I can earn this kind of money.*

> *There really are no jobs for women like me who have little education. At least none where I could make this much money. . . .*

> *I've been a stripper for 7 years, what else am I gonna be able to do? You know, even if I try I'm always gonna be a dancer, I'm always gonna be labelled. I make good money, so why go work for minimum wage?*

In contrast with the career dancer, the goal-oriented dancer enters dancing with a specific goal in mind.

> *I don't look at it like a career so it's kind of like a means to an end. You know how you put yourself on a program, like a five-year program. Get in there and make a whack of cash and then go on to something else. Like that can't be the only thing that I want to do for the rest of my life.*

> *There's aspects of the job I like, I mean, I do like some of the girls that work there, some of the bar staff. You know, they're fun to be around at work. And the guys, if they're nice, I can, you know, have had some good conversations. But, I do not like taking my clothes off you know? And I don't want to make this a career. It is a means to an end.*

Some dancers report being motivated to enter dancing in order to make the money they needed to get or stay out of debt. . . .

> *The bills kept coming in and coming in and I couldn't keep my head above water and everybody was threatening to take me to court and I had all these debts and I just, I needed money fast. So, I thought I could dance for a bit until I got on top of things.*

I don't want to do it, but you have to, I have to do it, I don't have a choice. I have a car payment, I have to pay my rent, I can't not do it.

Nothing else will pay my bills. So that's it.

One specific group of goal-oriented dancers are the students. These women report that for them dancing is a short-term job that pays well and that can fit in with their class schedule.

It's ideal when you're going to school because you just make your own schedules. When I have exam week I don't go at all. So, it fits in with school. So, I guess, I mean, I don't think I would work [as a dancer] once I finish school, unless I couldn't find a job or something. . . .

The commonality among goal-oriented dancers is that dancing is seen as a short-term thing, a means to an end, once the end is achieved (e.g., they graduate from university, pay off their debts, etc.), the plan is to leave dancing. It is important to note though, that although many goal-oriented dancers reported planning on leaving, some spoke of difficulties exiting once they got used to the money they could earn.

It's kinda hard once you get used to the money to leave [dancing]. I mean, like, I always said I would leave when I got out of debt, but the money draws you back.

I've wanted out for so many years now and just didn't know how. You get so trapped in there and I didn't know what to do or what I could do.

I started dancing to help pay off the mortgage on my house and get rid of some debts. I thought it was a one shot deal, but I seem to fall back on it whenever I need money.

The type of dancer one identifies as has implications for the socialization experiences of dancers. Women who see dancing as a career, rather than as a temporary job, tend to be more inclined to get involved in the "dancer life," develop relationships with other dancers and club employees, and become immersed in the strip club subculture. As a result, they are likely to experience a more complete socialization process than goal-oriented dancers. Goal-oriented dancers, in contrast, tend to limit their ties to others in the business. As the following quotes illustrate, they try to keep dancing and their private lives separate.

I don't hang out with other dancers. When I leave here I go back to my other life.

Although I try to be friendly to everyone here [at the club] I stick to myself as much as possible and when I leave [work], I try to leave it and everybody associated with it behind.

The implication of keeping the two aspects of their lives separate is that goal-oriented dancers have to contend with the stigma associated with dancing on their own and, as a result, often live very closeted/secretive lives.

I work really hard at keeping this [dancing] a secret from my family. It is hard cuz I still live at home with my parents. So, I keep my costumes in the trunk of my car and I make sure I am the only one with a key.

And I went home to visit and my mom's like, "So, how's your summer going?" And she's asking me all these questions and I had to lie and say that I was working for a security company. I hate it [lying], cuz my mom and I just started to get really close again and here I was suddenly back to the way I was when I was a teenager, the lying and you know, staying out all hours of the night and all this stuff, and you know, it hurt to lie to her. . . .

It's really hard because, you know, you're lying to your parents. Well, I am, and I'm close to my family. And I was lying to my friends and to my boyfriend at the time.

Without a community of supportive others, these women have limited access to competing definitions of reality and are therefore more likely to feel some sort of guilt and shame for choosing to dance. Since it is through interacting with other subcultural members that people learn rationalizations for their behavior, these women are likely to have limited access to the techniques of neutralization used by other dancers that are important for the maintenance of a positive sense of self.

Limitations of the Dancer's Socialization Process

Although both career and goal-oriented dancers felt they were able to experience successful occupational socialization that enabled them to achieve competence as exotic dancers, most of the women interviewed talked about how the socialization process inadequately prepared them for some of the realities of the life of an exotic dancer. A Stripper's Handbook (1997), a booklet written by several dancers in the Toronto region, nicely illustrates the benefits and limitations of learning about exotic dancing through informal channels. Although the booklet contains helpful information and advice about the job (e.g., where to get a license, how much a license costs, how to save money on costumes, stage show rules, DJ fees, fines, freelancing vs. working on schedule, etc.), it also glosses over some of the negative effects the job can have on women's lives (e.g., relationship problems, inhibition of heterosexual desire, etc.). The tendency to overlook the negative is typical of the advice women reported being given by subcultural members, especially the women with limited ties to the subculture.

When discussing the limitations of their socialization experiences, the women we spoke with reported having little knowledge of, and therefore being unprepared for the impact of, dancing on their private lives. The area of impact most often mentioned was relationships. In terms of relationships, women spoke of the difficulties of having and sustaining heterosexual relationships with males outside of the industry. For some women, relationship difficulties were tied to the problems men they date tend to have with their occupation (see Prus and Styllianoss 1980):

> *I'd suggest to any girl that ever dances, unless your boyfriend's a male dancer, don't date someone when you're stripping. Most guys say they can handle it. They can't and then they start coming into clubs and causing bull shit.*

> *My ex didn't like it. It wasn't because he didn't trust me, he just didn't like the whole idea. He didn't want me dancing not because he was jealous or anything, just because I think he knows it's stressful and it's just not good for you psychologically. . . . My current boyfriend, he dances at a gay bar so he knows what it's all about.*

Other women report that the difficulty of developing or sustaining heterosexual relationships was tied to the nature of their job (i.e., they usually work at night, in a bar, in a job that requires them be around and constantly interacting with customers, many of whom they don't like).

> *Relationshipwise it's very hard. I think it's hard for someone to take a dancer seriously, it takes a certain type of guy that can, look beyond that and ah, if I'm involved I have a really hard time doing my job. If I'm single I'm better with my job. It's hard to meet people cuz I work nights all the time. When I was working full time I was there a good 5 nights a week. On my night off I don't want to go to a bar or anything, I'm in one every day, so you never get a chance to meet people. It's pretty much taboo to date someone you meet at work, cuz you don't know who they are outside of there and they've been giving you money to strip in front of them all night, and they are like, "Ooh yeah, I want to take you on a date." And you are thinking, "Yeah, sure you do. For what, why?" So that's hard. And it's hard if you have a boyfriend, it's hard for them to deal with it. . . .*

Despite the difficulties exotic dancers confront in terms of developing and sustaining relationships, some of the women interviewed expressed an interest/desire to have a stable intimate heterosexual relationship. Others, however, talked about being disinterested in men.

> *I'm kind of sick of, you know the men and, I just, I've always been a, you know, a big chested person. So, I always gotten the yee-haw's and stuff walking down the street and I just kinda had it after a while, you know?*

> *I hate to be looked at. I don't like to be looked at by men. I don't like men very much.*

One solution identified by dancers to the relationship difficulties and inhibited heterosexual desire dancers experience, is pursuing relationships with other women. According to the women we interviewed, it is not uncommon for female exotic dancers to develop lesbian relationships, either because of a disinterest in heterosexual relationships stemming from dancing or because relationships with women are just easier to develop and sustain while they are working as exotic dancers (see Carey et al. 1974; McCaghy and Skipper 1969; Prus and Styllianoss 1980).

> *I think a lot of girls end up bi. . . . I think it's convenient because it's easier to go out with another dancer, another girl than go out with a guy. You know what I mean? They understand your likes and a lot of guys that date dancers are assholes. So why deal with the hassle of going out? Why not just date a girl? I would have [dated women] if I met a nice girl.*

> *It's a lot easier to date a girl than to bother with going out. But I just happened to meet Paul who dances as well and fits into my lifestyle. But, if I wouldn't have met him I probably would date women. But I just never, I just never met any girl that I had enough in common with. A lot of the girls are [lesbian]. But a lot of people stereotype you. You know what I mean?*

As noted by McCaghy and Skipper (1969), three conditions associated with the occupation are supportive of same sex relationships: "(1) isolation from affective social relationships; (2) unsatisfactory relationships with males; and (3) an opportunity structure allowing a wide range of sexual behavior" (p. 266).

Conclusion

As other studies of exotic dancers have found, there are various factors influencing occupational entry into exotic dancing. This study provides support for a combined career contingency/conversion model. According to this model, four factors influence entry into the exotic dancing: (1) knowledge and accessibility of an opportunity structure that makes exotic dancing an occupational alternative; (2) an awareness of the economic rewards associated with being an exotic dancer; (3) a recruitment process involving personal networks; and (4) financial need or a need for employment. For the women interviewed, these factors played a significant role in their anticipatory socialization process and their movement in the direction of exotic dancing.

Although similar to earlier studies of exotic dancers (this study found evidence of a combined career contingency/conversion model for entry into exotic dancing), there were also some differences between the findings of this study and that of previous research in the area. For example, contrary to earlier studies, we found little indication of dancers' having pre-job formal socialization experiences that involved professional training in entertainment-related fields, prior to entering dancing. This difference, however, may be tied to the evolution of stripping. Over the past [35] years or so, stripping has gone from a form of theatre or burlesque stage show, where complete nudity was rare and touching was prohibited, to the more raunchy table and lap dances performed today that often involve complete nudity, and sometimes physical and sexual contact between the dancer and the customer.

Despite some different findings in terms of the anticipatory socialization experiences of dancers, similar to other research in the area, we found that once the decision to dance was made and they were employed as dancers, the women we interviewed continued to experience a socialization process through interacting with and observing other subcultural members. The on-the-job, informal occupational socialization the women reported experiencing enabled them to achieve job competence, even in a deviant occupation.

As social learning theories of deviance suggest, although most of us learn the norms and values of society, some of us also learn techniques for committing deviance and the specific motives, drives, rationalizations, and attitudes that allow us to neutralize our violation of normative codes. The socialization experiences of dancers fit with this framework. Learning occurs through observing and interacting with strip club employees, especially more experienced dancers. Through such observations and interactions, novice dancers learn techniques for rationalizing their involvement in the occupation, a process which enables them to stay in the job and succeed, while retaining a valued sense of self.

Although exotic dancers can experience socialization processes that result in job competence, their occupational socialization often inadequately prepares them for the potential impact of their job on their lives outside of the club. The most often mentioned area of concern was intimate relationships, due to the difficulties exotic dancers reported on developing and sustaining heterosexual relationships and desire.

ENDNOTES

[1] According to Ritzer and Walczak (1986), "an occupation will be treated as deviant if it meets one or more of the following criteria: (1) it is illegal; (2) one or more of the central activities of the occupation is a violation of nonlegalized norms and values; and (3) the culture, lifestyle, or setting associated with the occupation is popularly presumed to involve rule-breaking behavior" (p. 374).

[2] According to Matza (1990), "drift is motion guided gently by underlying influences. The guidance is gentle and not constraining. The drift may be initiated or deflected by events so numerous as to defy codification. But underlying influences are operative nonetheless in that they make initiation to . . . [deviant behaviour] more probable, and they reduce the chances that an event will deflect the drifter from his [/her deviant] . . . path. Drift is a gradual process of movement, unperceived by the actor, in which the first stage may be accidental or unpredictable" (p. 29).

[3] Appeal to higher loyalties involves rationalizing deviant behavior by couching it within an altruistic framework.

[4] Although money is part of the motivation for anyone seeking employment, for dancers, it was the amount of money that could be earned dancing, compared with the amount that could be earned in more legitimate jobs, that motivated them to try dancing.

REFERENCES

Becker, Gary S. 1964. *Human Capital*. New York: Columbia University Press.

Boles, Jacqueline M. and A. P. Garbin. 1974a. "The Strip Club and Stripper-Customer Patterns of Interaction." *Sociology and Social Research* 58:136–44.

———. 1974b. "The Choice of Stripping for a Living: An Empirical and Theoretical Explanation." *Sociology of Work and Occupations* 1:110–23.

———. 1974c. "Stripping for a Living: An Occupational Study of the Night Club Stripper." Pp. 312–35 in *Deviant Behavior: Occupational and Organizational Bases*, edited by C. D. Bryant. Chicago: Rand McNally.

Carey, S. H., R. A. Peterson, and L. K. Sharpe. 1974. "A Study of Recruitment and Socialization into Two Deviant Female Occupations." *Sociological Symposium* 8:11–24.

Dressel, P. L. and D. M. Peterson. 1982. "Becoming a Male Stripper: Recruitment, Socialization and Ideological Development." *Work and Occupations* 9:387–406.

Glaser, B. G. and A. K. Straus. 1967. *The Discovery of Grounded Theory: Strategy for Qualitative Research*. Chicago: Aldine Publishing Company.

Hong, L. K. and R. W. Duff. 1977. "Becoming a Taxi-Dancer: The Significance of Neutralization in a Semi-Deviant Occupation." *Sociology of Work and Occupations* 4:327–42.

Lofland, J. and R. Stark. 1965. "Becoming a World-Saver: A Theory of Conversion to a Deviant Perspective." *American Sociological Association* 30:862–75.

Matza, David. 1990. *Delinquency and Drift*. New York: Transaction Books.

McCaghy, C. H. and J. K. Skipper. 1969. "Lesbian Behavior as an Adaptation to the Occupation of Stripping." *Social Problems* 17:262–70.

———. 1972. "Stripping: Anatomy of a Deviant Life Style." Pp. 362–73 in *Life Styles: Diversity in American Society*, edited by S. D. Feldman and G. W. Thielbar. Boston: Little, Brown.

Prus, R. C. and C. R. D. Sharper. 1977. *Road Hustler: The Career Contingencies of Professional Card and Dice Hustlers*. Toronto: Lexington Books.

Prus, R. C. and I. Styllianoss. 1980. *Hookers, Rounders, and Desk Clerks: The Social Organization of the Hotel Community*. Toronto: Gage Publishing Limited.

Ritzer, George and David Walczak. 1986. *Working: Conflict and Change*. Englewood Cliffs, NJ: Prentice Hall.

Sanders, C. R. 1974. "Psyching out the Crowd: Folk Performers and Their Audiences." *Urban Life and Culture* 3:264–82.

Skipper, J. K. and C. H. McCaghy. 1971. "Stripteasing: A Sex-Oriented Occupation." Pp. 275–296 in *Studies in the Sociology of Sex*, edited by James M. Henslin. New York: Appleton-Century-Crofts.

Sykes, G. M. and D. Matza. 1957. "Techniques of Neutralization: A Theory of Delinquency." *American Sociological Review* 22:664–70.

Thompson, W. E. and J. L. Harred. 1992. "Topless Dancers: Managing Stigma in a Deviant Occupation." *Deviant Behavior* 13:291–311.

14

ANYBODY'S SON WILL DO

GWYNNE DYER

An important point about socialization is that if culture is learned, it also can be unlearned. Sociologists call this process *resocialization*. This situation occurs when an individual gives up one way of life and one set of values for another. Examples of resocialization include the experience of new immigrants, of a person changing careers, of someone joining a feminist consciousness-raising group, or of an individual undergoing a religious conversion, such as a woman entering a convent to become a nun or a person being initiated into a cult. The following reading by journalist Gwynne Dyer is from his 1985 book, *War: Past, Present, and Future.* Here, Dyer focuses on the intense resocialization civilians experience during military basic training.

You think about it and you know you're going to have to kill but you don't understand the implications of that, because in the society in which you've lived murder is the most heinous of crimes . . . and you are in a situation in which it's turned the other way round. . . . When you do actually kill someone the experience, my experience, was one of revulsion and disgust. . . .

I was utterly terrified—petrified—but I knew there had to be a Japanese sniper in a small fishing shack near the shore. He was firing in the other direction at Marines in another battalion, but I knew as soon as he picked off the people there—there was a window on our side—that he would start picking us off. And there was nobody else to go . . . and so I ran towards the shack and broke in and found myself in an empty room. . . .

There was a door which meant there was another room and the sniper was in that—and I just broke that down. I was just absolutely gripped by the fear that this man would expect me and would shoot me. But as it turned out he was in a sniper harness and he couldn't turn around fast enough. He was entangled in the harness so I shot him with a .45, and I felt remorse and shame. I can remember whispering foolishly, "I'm sorry" and then just throwing up. . . . I threw up all over myself. It was a betrayal of what I'd been taught since a child.

—WILLIAM MANCHESTER

Yet he did kill the Japanese soldier, just as he had been trained to—the revulsion only came afterward. And even after Manchester knew what it was like to kill another human being, a young man like himself, he went on trying to kill his "enemies" until the war was over. Like all the other tens of millions of soldiers who had been taught from infancy that killing was wrong, and had then been sent off to kill for their countries, he was almost helpless to disobey, for he had fallen into the hands of an institution so powerful and so subtle that it could quickly reverse the moral training of a lifetime.

The whole vast edifice of the military institution rests on its ability to obtain obedience from its members even unto death—and the killing of others. It has enormous powers of compulsion at its command, of course, but all authority must be based ultimately on consent. The task of extracting that consent from its members has probably grown harder in recent times, for the gulf between the military and the civilian worlds has undoubtedly widened: Civilians no longer perceive the threat of violent death as an everyday hazard of existence, and the categories of people whom it is not morally permissible to kill have broadened to include (in peacetime) the entire human race. Yet the armed forces of every country can still take almost any young male civilian and turn him into a soldier with all the right reflexes and attitudes in only a few weeks. Their recruits usually have no more than twenty years' experience of the world, most of it as children, while the armies have had all of history to practice and perfect their techniques.

> Just think of how the soldier is treated. While still a child he is shut up in the barracks. During his training he is always being knocked about. If he makes the least mistake he is beaten, a burning blow on his body, another on his eye, perhaps his head is laid open with a wound. He is battered and bruised with flogging. On the march . . . they hang heavy loads round his neck like that of an ass.
>
> —EGYPTIAN, CIRCA. 1500 B.C.[1]

> The moment I talk to the new conscripts about the homeland I strike a land mine. So I kept quiet. Instead, I try to make soldiers of them. I give them hell from morning to sunset. They begin to curse me, curse the army, curse the state. Then they begin to curse together, and become a truly cohesive group, a unit, a fighting unit.
>
> —ISRAELI, CIRCA. A.D. 1970[2]

All soldiers belong to the same profession, no matter what country they serve, and it makes them different from everybody else. They have to be different, for their job is ultimately about killing and dying, and those things are not a natural vocation for any human being. Yet all soldiers are born civilians. The method for turning young men into soldiers—people who kill other people and expose themselves to death—is basic training. It's essentially the same all over the world, and it always has been, because young men everywhere are pretty much alike.

Human beings are fairly malleable, especially when they are young, and in every young man there are attitudes for any army to work with: the inherited values and postures, more or less dimly recalled, of the tribal warriors who were once the model for every young boy to emulate. Civilization did not involve a sudden clean break in the way people behave, but merely the progressive distortion and redirection of all the ways in which people in the old tribal societies used to behave, and modern definitions of maleness still contain a great deal of the old warrior ethic. The anarchic machismo of the primitive warrior is not what modern armies really need in their soldiers, but it does provide them with promising raw material for the transformation they must work in their recruits.

Just how this transformation is wrought varies from time to time and from country to country. In totally militarized societies—ancient Sparta, the samurai class of medieval Japan, the areas controlled by organizations like the Eritrean People's Liberation Front today—it begins at puberty or before, when the young boy is immersed in a disciplined society in which only the military values are allowed to penetrate. In more sophisticated modern societies, the process is briefer and more concentrated, and the way it works is much more visible. It is, essentially, a conversion process in an almost religious sense—and as in all conversion phenomena, the emotions are far more important than the specific ideas. . . .

Armies know this. It is their business to get men to fight, and they have had a long time to work out the best way of doing it. All of them pay lip service to the symbols and slogans of their political masters, though the amount of time they must devote to this activity varies from country to country. . . . Nor should it be thought that the armies are hypocritical—most of their members really do believe in their particular national symbols and slogans. But their secret is that they know these are not the things that sustain men in combat.

What really enables men to fight is their own self-respect, and a special kind of love that has nothing to do with sex or idealism. Very few men have died in battle, when the moment actually arrived, for the United States of America or for the sacred cause of Communism, or even for their homes and families; if they had any choice in the matter at all, they chose to die for each other and for their own vision of themselves. . . .

The way armies produce this sense of brotherhood in a peacetime environment is basic training: a feat of psychological manipulation on the grand scale which has been so consistently successful and so universal that we fail to notice it as remarkable. In countries where the army must extract its recruits in their late teens, whether voluntarily or by conscription, from a civilian environment that does not share the military values, basic training involves a brief but intense period of indoctrination whose purpose is not really to teach the recruits basic military skills, but rather to change their values and their loyalties. "I guess you could say we brainwash them a little bit," admitted a U.S. Marine drill instructor, "but you know they're good people."

The duration and intensity of basic training, and even its major emphases, depend on what kind of society the recruits are coming from, and on what sort of military organization they are going to. It is obviously quicker to train men from a martial culture than from one in which the dominant values are civilian and commercial, and easier to deal with volunteers than with reluctant conscripts. Conscripts are not always unwilling, however; there are many instances in which the army is popular for economic reasons. . . .

It's easier if you catch them young. You can train older men to be soldiers; it's done in every major war. But you can never get them to believe that they like it, which is the major reason armies try to get their recruits before they are 20. There are other reasons too, of course, like the physical fitness, lack of dependents, and economic dispensability of teenagers, that make armies prefer them, but the most important qualities teenagers bring to basic training are enthusiasm and naiveté. Many of them actively want the discipline and the closely structured environment that the armed forces will provide, so there is no need for the recruiters to deceive the kids about what will happen to them after they join.

> *There is discipline. There is drill. . . . When you are relying on your mates and they are relying on you, there's no room for slackness or sloppiness. If you're not prepared to accept the rules, you're better off where you are.*
> —BRITISH ARMY RECRUITING ADVERTISEMENT, 1976

> *People are not born soldiers, they become soldiers. . . . And it should not begin at the moment a new recruit is enlisted into the ranks, but rather much earlier, at the time of the first signs of maturity, during the time of adolescent dreams.*
> —*RED STAR* (SOVIET ARMY NEWSPAPER), 1973

Young civilians who have volunteered and have been accepted by the Marine Corps arrive at Parris Island, the Corps's East Coast facility for basic training, in a state of considerable excitement and apprehension: Most are aware that they are about to undergo an extraordinary and very difficult experience. But they do not make their own way to the base; rather, they trickle in to Charleston airport on various flights throughout the day on which their training platoon is due to form, and are held there, in a state of suppressed but mounting nervous tension, until late in the evening. When the buses finally come to carry them the 76 miles to Parris Island, it is often after midnight—and this is not an administrative oversight. The shock treatment they are about to receive will work most efficiently if they are worn out and somewhat disoriented when they arrive.

The basic training organization is a machine, processing several thousand young men every month, and every facet and gear of it has been designed with the sole purpose of turning civilians into Marines as efficiently as possible. Provided it can have total control over their bodies and their environment for approximately three months, it can practically guarantee converts. Parris Island provides that controlled environment, and the recruits do not set foot outside it again until they graduate as Marine privates 11 weeks later.

> *They're allowed to call home, so long as it doesn't get out of hand—every three weeks or so they can call home and make sure everything's all right, if they haven't gotten a letter or there's a particular set of circumstances. If it's a case of an emergency call coming in, then they're allowed to accept that call; if not, one of my staff will take the message. . . .*
>
> *In some cases I'll get calls from parents who haven't quite gotten adjusted to the idea that their son had cut the strings—and in a lot of cases that's what they're doing. The military provides them with an opportunity to leave home but they're still in a rather secure environment.*
>
> —CAPTAIN BRASSINGTON, USMC

For the young recruits, basic training is the closest thing their society can offer to a formal rite of passage, and the institution probably stands in an unbroken line of descent from the lengthy ordeals by which young males in precivilized groups were initiated into the adult community of warriors. But in civilized societies it is a highly functional institution whose product is not anarchic warriors, but trained soldiers.

Basic training is not really about teaching people skills; it's about changing them so that they can do things they wouldn't have dreamt of otherwise. It works by applying enormous physical and mental pressure to men who have been isolated from their normal civilian environment and placed in one where the only right way to think and behave is the way the Marine Corps wants them to. The key word the men who run the machine use to describe this process is *motivation.*

> *I can motivate a recruit and in third phase, if I tell him to jump off the third deck, he'll jump off the third deck. Like I said before, it's a captive audience and I can train that guy; I can get him to do anything I want him to do. . . . They're good kids and they're out to do the right thing. We get some bad kids, but you know, we weed those out. But as far as motivation—here, we can motivate them to do anything you want, in recruit training.*
>
> —USMC DRILL INSTRUCTOR, PARRIS ISLAND

The first three days the raw recruits spend at Parris Island are actually relatively easy, though they are hustled and shouted at continuously. It is during this time that they are documented and inoculated, receive uniforms, and learn the basic orders of drill that will enable young Americans (who are not very accustomed to this aspect of life) to do everything simultaneously in large groups. But the most important thing that happens in "forming" is the surrender of the recruits' own clothes, their hair—all the physical evidence of their individual civilian identities.

During a period of only 72 hours, in which they are allowed little sleep, recruits lay aside their former lives in a series of hasty rituals (like being shaven to the scalp) whose symbolic significance is quite clear to them even though they are quite deliberately given absolutely no time for reflection, or any hint that they might have the option of turning back from their commitment. The men in charge of them know how delicate a tightrope they are walking, though, because at this stage the recruits are still newly caught civilians who have not yet made their ultimate inward submission to the discipline of the Corps.

Forming Day One makes me nervous. You've got a whole new mob of recruits, you know, 60 or 70 depending, and they don't know anything. You don't know what kind of a reaction you're going to get from the stress you're going to lay on them, and it just worries me the first day. . . .

Things could happen, I'm not going to lie to you. Something might happen. A recruit might decide he doesn't want any part of this stuff and maybe take a poke at you or something like that. In a situation like that it's going to be a spur-of-the-moment thing and that worries me.

—USMC Drill Instructor

But it rarely happens. The frantic bustle of forming is designed to give the recruit no time to think about resisting what is happening to him. And so the recruits emerge from their initiation into the system, stripped of their civilian clothes, shorn of their hair, and deprived of whatever confidence in their own identity they may previously have had as 18-year-olds, like so many blanks ready to have the Marine identity impressed upon them.

The first stage in any conversion process is the destruction of an individual's former beliefs and confidence, and his reduction to a position of helplessness and need. It isn't really as drastic as all that, of course, for three days cannot cancel out 18 years; the inner thoughts and the basic character are not erased. But the recruits have already learned that the only acceptable behavior is to repress any unorthodox thoughts and to mimic the character the Marine Corps wants. Nor are they, on the whole, reluctant to do so, for they *want* to be Marines. From the moment they arrive at Parris Island, the vague notion that has been passed down for a thousand generations that masculinity means being a warrior becomes an explicit article of faith, relentlessly preached: To be a man means to be a Marine.

There are very few 18-year-old boys who do not have highly romanticized ideas of what it means to be a man, so the Marine Corps has plenty of buttons to push. And it starts pushing them on the first day of real training: The officer in charge of the formation appears before them for the first time, in full dress uniform with medals, and tells them how to become men.

The United States Marine Corps has 205 years of illustrious history to speak for itself. You have made the most important decision in your life . . . by signing your name, your life, your pledge to the Government of the United States, and even more importantly, to the United States Marine Corps—a brotherhood, an elite unit. In 10.3 weeks you are going to become a member of that history, those traditions, this organization—if you have what it takes. . . .

All of you want to do that by virtue of your signing your name as a man. The Marine Corps says that we build men. Well, I'll go a little bit further. We develop the tools that you have—and everybody has those tools to a certain extent right now. We're going to give you the blueprints, and we are going to show you how to build a Marine. You've got to build a Marine—you understand?

—Captain Pingree, USMC

The recruits, gazing at him in awe and adoration, shout in unison, "Yes, sir!" just as they have been taught. They do it willingly, because they are volunteers—but even conscripts tend to have the romantic fervor of volunteers if they are only 18 years old. Basic training, whatever its hardships, is a quick way to become a man among men, with an undeniable status, and beyond the initial consent to undergo it, it doesn't even require any decisions.

I had just dropped out of high school and I wasn't doing much on the street except hanging out, as most teenagers would be doing. So they gave me an opportunity—a recruiter picked me up, gave me a good line, and said that I could make it in the Marines, that I have a future ahead of me. And since I was living with my parents, I figured that I could start my own life here and grow up a little.

—USMC Recruit, 1982

I like the hand-to-hand combat and . . . things like that. It's a little rough going on me, and since I have a small frame I would like to become deadly, as I would put it. I like to have them words, especially the way they've been teaching me here.

—USMC Recruit (from Brooklyn), Parris Island, 1982

The training, when it starts, seems impossibly demanding physically for most of the recruits—and then it gets harder week by week. There is a constant barrage of abuse and insults aimed at the recruits, with the deliberate purpose of breaking down their pride and so destroying their ability to resist the transformation of values and attitudes that the Corps intends them to undergo. At the same time, the demands for constant alertness and for instant obedience are continuously stepped up, and the standards by which the dress and behavior of the recruits are judged become steadily more unforgiving. But it is all carefully calculated by the men who run the machine, who think and talk in terms of the stress they are placing on the recruits: "We take so many c.c.'s of stress and we administer it to each man—they should be a little bit scared and they should be unsure, but they're adjusting." The aim is to keep the training arduous but just within most of the recruits' capability to withstand. One of the most striking achievements of the drill instructors is to create and maintain the illusion that basic training is an extraordinary challenge, one that will set those who graduate apart from others, when in fact almost everyone can succeed.

There has been some preliminary weeding out of potential recruits even before they begin basic training, to eliminate the obviously unsuitable minority, and some people do "fail" basic training and get sent home, at least in peacetime. The standards of acceptable performance in the U.S. armed forces, for example, tend to rise and fall in inverse proportion to the number and quality of recruits available to fill the forces to the authorized manpower levels. (In 1980, about 15% of Marine recruits did not graduate from basic training.) But there are very few young men who cannot be turned into passable soldiers if the forces are willing to invest enough effort in it.

Not even physical violence is necessary to effect the transformation, though it has been used by most armies at most times.

> *It's not what it was 15 years ago down here. The Marine Corps still occupies the position of a tool which the society uses when it feels like that is a resort that they have to fall to. Our society changes as all societies do, and our society felt that through enlightened training methods we could still produce the same product—and when you examine it, they're right. . . . Our 100 c.c.'s of stress is really all we need, not two gallons of it, which is what used to be. . . . In some cases with some of the younger drill instructors it was more an initiation than it was an acute test, and so we introduced extra officers and we select our drill instructors to "fine-tune" it.*
>
> —Captain Brassington, USMC

There is, indeed, a good deal of fine-tuning in the roles that the men in charge of training any specific group of recruits assume. At the simplest level, there is a sort of "good cop–bad cop" manipulation of recruits' attitudes toward those applying the stress. The three younger drill instructors with a particular serial are quite close to them in age and unremittingly harsh in their demands for ever higher performance, but the senior drill instructor, a man almost old enough to be their father, plays a more benevolent and understanding part and is available for individual counseling. And generally offstage, but always looming in the background, is the company commander, an impossibly austere and almost godlike personage.

At least these are the images conveyed to the recruits, although of course all these men cooperate closely with an identical goal in view. It works: In the end they become not just role models and authority figures, but the focus of the recruits' developing loyalty to the organization.

> *I imagine there's some fear, especially in the beginning, because they don't know what to expect. . . . I think they hate you at first, at least for a week or two, but it turns to respect. . . . They're seeking discipline, they're seeking someone to take charge, 'cause at home they never got it. . . . They're looking to be told what to do and then someone is standing there enforcing what they tell them to do, and*

it's kind of like the father-and-son game, all the way through. They form a fatherly image of the DI whether they want to or not.

—SERGEANT CARRINGTON, USMC

Just the sheer physical exercise, administered in massive doses, soon has recruits feeling stronger and more competent than ever before. Inspections, often several times daily, quickly build up their ability to wear the uniform and carry themselves like real Marines, which is a considerable source of pride. The inspections also help to set up the pattern in the recruits of un-questioning submission to military authority: Standing stock-still, staring straight ahead, while somebody else examines you closely for faults is about as extreme a ritual act of submission as you can make with your clothes on.

But they are not submitting themselves merely to the abusive sergeant making unpleasant remarks about the hair in their nostrils. All around them are deliberate reminders—the flags and insignia displayed on parade, the military music, the marching formations and drill instructors' cadenced calls—of the idealized organization, the "brotherhood" to which they will be admitted as full members if they submit and conform. Nowhere in the armed forces are the military courtesies so elaborately observed, the staffs' uniforms so immaculate (some DIs change several times a day), and the ritual aspects of military life so highly visible as on a basic training establishment.

Even the seeming inanity of close-order drill has a practical role in the conversion process. It has been over a century since mass formations of men were of any use on the battlefield, but every army in the world still drills its troops, especially during basic training, because marching in formation, with every man moving his body in the same way at the same moment, is a direct physical way of learning two things a soldier must believe: that orders have to be obeyed automatically and instantly, and that you are no longer an indi-vidual, but part of a group.

The recruits' total identification with the other members of their unit is the most important lesson of all, and everything possible is done to foster it. They spend almost every waking moment together—a recruit alone is an anomaly to be looked into at once—and during most of that time they are en-during shared hardships. They also undergo collective punishments, often for the misdeed or omission of a single individual (talking in the ranks, a bed not swept under during barracks inspection), which is a highly effective way of suppressing any tendencies toward individualism. And, of course, the DIs place relentless emphasis on competition with other "serials" in training: There may be something infinitely pathetic to outsiders about a marching group of anonymous recruits chanting, "Lift your heads and hold them high, 3313 is a-passin' by," but it doesn't seem like that to the men in the ranks.

Nothing is quite so effective in building up a group's morale and soli-darity, though, as a steady diet of small triumphs. Quite early in basic train-ing, the recruits begin to do things that seem, at first sight, quite dangerous: descend by ropes from 50-foot towers, cross yawning gaps hand-over-hand on high wires (known as the Slide for Life, of course), and the like. The common denominator is that these activities are daunting but not really dangerous: The ropes will prevent anyone from falling to his death off the rappelling tower, and there is a pond of just the right depth—deep enough to cushion a falling man, but not deep enough that he is likely to drown—under the Slide for Life. The goal is not to kill recruits, but to build up their confidence as individuals and as a group by allowing them to overcome apparently frightening obstacles.

> *You have an enemy here at Parris Island. The enemy that you're going to have at Parris Island is in every one of us. It's in the form of cowardice. The most rewarding experience you're going to have in recruit training is standing on line every evening, and you'll be able to look into each other's eyes, and you'll be able to say to each other with your eyes: "By God, we've made it one more day! We've defeated the coward."*
>
> —Captain Pingree, USMC

> *Number on deck, sir, 45 . . . highly motivated, truly dedicated, rompin', stompin', bloodthirsty, kill-crazy United States Marine Corps recruits, SIR!*
>
> —Marine Chant, Parris Island, 1982

If somebody does fail a particular test, he tends to be alone, for the hurdles are deliberately set low enough that most recruits can clear them if they try. In any large group of people there is usually a goat: someone whose intelligence or manner or lack of physical stamina marks him for failure and contempt. The competent drill instructor, without deliberately setting up this unfortunate individual for disgrace, will use his failure to strengthen the solidarity and confidence of the rest. When one hapless young man fell off the Slide for Life into the pond, for example, his drill instructor shouted the usual invective—"Well, get out of the water. Don't contaminate it all day"—and then delivered the payoff line: "Go back and change your clothes. You're useless to your unit now."

"Useless to your unit" is the key phrase, and all the recruits know that what it means is "useless *in battle.*" The Marine drill instructors at Parris Island know exactly what they are doing to the recruits, and why. They are not rear-echelon people filling comfortable jobs, but the most dedicated and intelligent NCOs [non-commissioned officers] the Marine Corps can find; even now, many of them have combat experience. The Corps has a clear-eyed understanding of precisely what it is training its recruits for—combat—and it ensures that those who do the training keep that objective constantly in sight.

The DIs [drill instructors] stress the recruits, feed them their daily ration of synthetic triumphs over apparent obstacles, and bear in mind all the time that the goal is to instill the foundations for the instinctive, selfless reactions and the fierce group loyalty that is what the recruits will need if they ever see combat. They are arch-manipulators, fully conscious of it, and utterly unashamed. These kids have signed up as Marines, and they could well see combat; this is the way they have to think if they want to live.

I've seen guys come to Vietnam from all over. They were all sorts of people that had been scared—some of them had been scared all their life and still scared. Some of them had been a country boy, city boys—you know, all different kinds of people— but when they got in combat they all reacted the same—99 percent of them reacted the same. . . . A lot of it is training here at Parris Island, but the other part of it is survival. They know if they don't conform—conform I call it, but if they don't react in the same way other people are reacting, they won't survive. That's just it. You know, if you don't react together, then nobody survives.

—USMC Drill Instructor, Parris Island, 1982

When I went to boot camp and did individual combat training, they said if you walk into an ambush what you want to do is just do a right face—you just turn right or left, whichever way the fire is coming from, and assault. I said, "Man, that's crazy. I'd never do anything like that. It's stupid." . . .

The first time we came under fire, on Hill 1044 in Operation Beauty Canyon in Laos, we did it automatically. Just like you look at your watch to see what time it is. We done a right face, assaulted the hill—a fortified position with concrete bunkers emplaced, machine guns, automatic weapons—and we took it. And we killed—I'd estimate probably 35 North Vietnamese soldiers in the assault, and we only lost three killed. I think it was about two or three, and about eight or ten wounded. . . .

But you know, what they teach you, it doesn't faze you until it comes down to the time to use it, but it's in the back of your head, like, What do you do when you come to a stop sign? It's in the back of your head, and you react automatically.

—USMC Sergeant, 1982

Combat is the ultimate reality that Marines—or any other soldiers, under any flag—have to deal with. Physical fitness, weapons training, battle drills, are all indispensable elements of basic training, and it is absolutely essential that the recruits learn the attitudes of group loyalty and interdependency which will be their sole hope of survival and success in combat. The training inculcates or fosters all of those things, and even by the halfway point in the 11-week course, the recruits are generally responding with enthusiasm to their tasks. . . .

In basic training establishments, . . . the malleability is all one way: in the direction of submission to military authority and the internalization of military values. What a place like Parris Island produces when it is successful, as it usually is, is a soldier who will kill because that is his job.

ENDNOTES

[1]Leonard Cottrell, *The Warrior Pharaohs* (London: Evans Brothers, 1968).
[2]Samuel Rolbart, *The Israeli Soldier* (New York: A. S. Barnes, 1970), p. 206.

PART IV
Groups and Social Structure

15

PEER POWER
Clique Dynamics among School Children

PATRICIA A. ADLER • PETER ADLER

The following four selections explore groups and social structure. The basic components of social structure are the roles and social statuses of individuals. Over the course of a lifetime, people occupy numerous statuses and roles. A *status* is a social position an individual holds within a group or a social system. A *role* is a set of expectations about the behavior assigned to a particular social status. Each role helps to define the nature of interaction with others and contributes to social organization by creating patterns of interpersonal and group relationships. Because we modify social roles more than we do our social statuses, roles are the dynamic aspect of social status. In the first reading, Patricia Adler, a professor of sociology at the University of Colorado at Boulder, and Peter Adler, a professor of sociology at the University of Denver, investigate the social roles and social statuses children hold in social cliques. Of particular interest to the Adlers is how social hierarchies are formed and how power is distributed among the friendship groups of third- to sixth-grade students.

A dominate feature of children's lives is the clique structure that organizes their social world. The fabric of their relationships with others, their levels and types of activity, their participation in friendships, and their feelings about themselves are tied to their involvement in, around, or outside the cliques organizing their social landscape. Cliques are, at their base, friendship circles, whose members tend to identify each other as mutually connected.[1] Yet they are more than that; cliques have a hierarchical structure, being dominated by leaders, and are exclusive in nature, so that not all individuals who desire membership are accepted. They function as bodies of power within grades, incorporating the most popular individuals, offering the most exciting social lives, and commanding the most interest and attention from classmates (Eder and Parker 1987). As such, they represent a vibrant component of the preadolescent experience, mobilizing powerful forces that produce important effects on individuals.[2] . . .

In this [reading] we look at these dynamics and their association, at the way clique leaders generate and maintain their power and authority (leadership, power/dominance), and at what it is that influences followers to comply so readily with clique leaders' demands (submission). These interactional dynamics are not intended to apply to all children's friendship groups, only those (populated by one-quarter to one-half of the children) that embody the exclusive and stratified character of cliques.

Techniques of Inclusion

The critical way that cliques maintained exclusivity was through careful membership screening. Not static entities, cliques irregularly shifted and evolved their membership, as individuals moved away or were ejected from the group and others took their place. In addition, cliques were characterized by frequent group activities designed to foster some individuals' inclusion (while excluding others). Cliques had embedded, although often unarticulated, modes for considering and accepting (or rejecting) potential new members. These modes were linked to the critical power of leaders in making vital group decisions. Leaders derived power through their popularity and then used it to influence membership and social stratification within the group. This stratification manifested itself in tiers and subgroups within cliques composed of people who were hierarchically ranked into levels of leaders, followers, and wannabes. Cliques embodied systems of dominance, whereby individuals with more status and power exerted control over others' lives.

Recruitment

. . . Potential members could be brought to the group by established members who had met and liked them. The leaders then decided whether these individuals would be granted a probationary period of acceptance during which they could be informally evaluated. If the members liked them, the newcomers would be allowed to remain in the friendship circle, but if they rejected them, they would be forced to leave.

Tiffany, a popular, dominant girl, reflected on the boundary maintenance she and her best friend Diane, two clique leaders, had exercised in fifth grade:

Q: Who defines the boundaries of who's in or who's out?

Tiffany: *Probably the leader. If one person might like them, they might introduce them, but if one or two people didn't like them, then they'd start to get everyone up. Like in fifth grade, there was Dawn Bolton and she was new. And the girls in her class that were in our clique liked her, but Diane and I didn't like her, so we kicked her out. So then she went to the other clique, the Emily clique.*

Timing was critical to recruitment. The beginning of the year, when classes were being reconstructed and people formed new social configurations, was the major time when cliques considered additions. Once these alliances were set, cliques tended to close their boundaries once again and stick to socializing primarily within the group. Kara, a fifth-grade girl, offered her view: *"In the fall, right after school starts, when everyone's lining up and checking each other out, is when people move up, but not during the school year. You can move down during the school year, if people decide they don't like you, but not up."* . . .

Most individuals felt that invitation to membership in the popular clique represented an irresistible offer. They repeatedly asserted that the popular group could get anybody they wanted to join them. One of the strategies used was to try to select new desirables and go after them. This usually meant separating the people from their established friends. Melody, an unpopular fourth-grade girl, described her efforts to hold on to her best friend who was being targeted for recruitment by the popular clique:

> *She was saying that they were really nice and stuff. I was really worried. If she joined their group, she would have to leave me. She was over there, and she told me that they were making fun of me, and she kind of sat there and went along with it. So I kind of got mad at her for doing that. "Why didn't you stick up for me?" She said, "Because they wouldn't like me anymore."*

Melody subsequently lost her friend to the clique.

When clique members wooed someone to join them, they usually showed only the better side of their behavior. It was not until they had the new person firmly committed to the group that the shifts in behavior associated with leaders' dominance and status stratification activities began. Diane recalled her inclusion into the popular clique and its aftermath:

> *In fifth grade I came into a new class and I knew nobody. None of my friends from the year before were in my class. So I get to school, a week late, and Tiffany comes up to me and she was like, 'Hi Diane, how are you? Where were you? You look so pretty.' And I was like, wow, she's so nice. And she was being so nice for like two weeks, kiss-ass major. And then she started pulling her bitch moves. Maybe it was for a month that she was nice. And so then she had clawed me into her clique and her group, and so she won me over that way, but then she was a bitch to me once I was inside it, and I couldn't get out because I had no other friends. 'Cause I'd gone in there and already been accepted into the popular clique, so everyone else in the class didn't like me, so I had nowhere else to go.*

Eder (1985) also notes that popular girls are often disliked by unpopular people because of their exclusive and elitist manner (as befits their status).

Application

A second way for individuals to gain initial membership into a clique occurred through their actively seeking entry (Blau 1964). . . . According to Rick, a fifth-grade boy who was in the popular clique but not a central member, application for clique entry was more easily accomplished by individuals than groups. He described the way individuals found routes into cliques:

> *It can happen any way. Just you get respected by someone, you do something nice, they start to like you, you start doing stuff with them. It's like you just kind of follow another person who is in the clique back to the clique, and he says, "Could this person play?" So you kind of go out with the clique for a while and you start doing stuff with them, and then they almost like invite you in. And then soon after, like a week or so, you're actually in. It all depends. . . . But you can't bring your whole group with you, if you have one. You have to leave them behind and just go in on your own.*

Successful membership applicants often experienced a flurry of immediate popularity. Because their entry required clique leaders' approval, they gained associational status.

Friendship Realignment

Status and power in a clique were related to stratification, and people who remained more closely tied to the leaders were more popular. Individuals who wanted to be included in the clique's inner echelons often had to work regularly to maintain or improve their position.

Like initial entry, this was sometimes accomplished by people striving on their own for upward mobility. In fourth grade, Danny was brought into the clique by Mark, a longtime member, who went out of his way to befriend him. After joining the clique, however, Danny soon abandoned Mark when Brad, the clique leader, took an interest in him. Mark discussed the feelings of hurt and abandonment this experience left him with:

> *I felt really bad, because I made friends with him when nobody knew him and nobody liked him, and I put all my friends to the side for him, and I brought him into the group, and then he dumped me. He was my friend first, but then Brad wanted him. . . . He moved up and left me behind, like I wasn't good enough anymore.*

The hierarchical structure of cliques, and the shifts in position and relationships within them, caused friendship loyalties within these groups to be less reliable than they might have been in other groups. People looked toward those above them and were more susceptible to being wooed into friendship with individuals more popular than they. When courted by a higher-up, they could easily drop their less popular friends.

Cliques' stratification hierarchies might motivate lower-echelon members to seek greater inclusion by propelling themselves toward the elite inner circles, but membership in these circles was dynamic, requiring active effort to sustain. More popular individuals had to put repeated effort into their friendship alignments as well, to maintain their central positions relative to people just below them, who might rise up and gain in group esteem. Efforts to protect themselves from the potential incursions of others took several forms, among them co-optation, position maintenance, follower realignment, and membership challenge, only some of which draw upon inclusionary dynamics.

Follower realignment involved the perception that other clique members were gaining in popularity and status and might challenge leaders' position. But instead of trying to hold them in place (position maintenance) or exclude them from the group (membership challenge), leaders shifted their base of support; they incorporated lesser but still loyal members into their activities, thereby replacing problematic supporters with new ones. . . .

Co-optation involved leaders diminishing others' threats to their position by drawing them into their orbit, increasing their loyalty, and diminishing their independence. Clique members gaining in popularity were sometimes given special attention. At the same time, leaders might try to cut out their rivals' independent base of support from other friends.

Darla, a fourth grader, had occupied a second-tier leadership position with Kristy, her best friend. She explained what happened when Denise, the clique leader, came in and tore their formerly long-standing friendship apart:

> Me and Kristy used to be best friends, but she [Denise] hated that. 'Cause even though she was the leader, we were popular and we got all the boys. She didn't want us to be friends at all. But me and Kristy were, like, getting to be a threat to her, so Denise came in the picture and tore me and Kristy apart, so we weren't even friends. She made Kristy make totally fun of me and stuff. And they were so mean to me. . . .

. . . Hence, friendship realignment involved clique members' abandoning previous friendships or plowing through existing ones in order to assert themselves into relationships with those in central positions. These actions were all geared toward improving instigators' positions and thus their inclusion. Their outcome, whether anticipated or not, was often the separation of people and the destruction of their relationships.

Ingratiation

Currying favor with people in the group, like previous inclusionary endeavors, can be directed either upward (supplication) or downward (manipulation). Addressing the former, Dodge et al. (1983) note that children often begin their attempts at entry into groups with low-risk tactics; they first try to become accepted by more peripheral members, and only later do they direct their gaze and inclusion attempts toward those with higher status. The children we observed did this as well, making friendly overtures toward clique followers and hoping to be drawn by them into the center.

The more predominant behavior among group members, however, involved currying favor with the leader to enhance their popularity and attain greater respect from other group members. One way they did this was by imitating the style and interests of the group leader. Marcus and Adam, two fifth-grade boys, described the way borderline people would fawn on their clique and its leader to try to gain inclusion:

> Marcus: *Some people would just follow us around and say, "Oh yeah, whatever he says, yeah, whatever his favorite kind of music is, is my favorite kind of music."*

Adam: *They're probably in a position where they want to be more **in** because if they like what we like, then they think more people will probably respect them. Because if some people in the clique think this person likes their favorite group, say it's REM, or whatever, so it's say Bud's [the clique leader's], this person must know what we like in music and what's good and what's not, so let's tell him that he can come up and join us after school and do something.*

Fawning on more popular people not only was done by outsiders and peripherals but was common practice among regular clique members, even those with high standing. Darla, the second-tier fourth-grade girl mentioned earlier, described how, in fear, she used to follow the clique leader and parrot her opinions:

I was never mean to the people in my grade because I thought Denise might like them and then I'd be screwed. Because there were some people that I hated that she liked and I acted like I loved them, and so I would just be mean to the younger kids, and if she would even say, "Oh she's nice," I'd say, "Oh yeah, she's really nice!"

Clique members, then, had to stay abreast of the leader's shifting tastes and whims if they were to maintain status and position in the group. Part of their membership work involved a regular awareness of the leader's fads and fashions, so that they could accurately align their actions and opinions with the current trends in a timely manner. (See also Eder and Sanford 1986.)

Besides outsiders supplicate to insiders and insiders supplicate to those of higher standing, individuals at the top had to think about the effects of their actions on their standing with those below them. While leaders did not have to explicitly imitate the style and taste of their followers, they did have to act in a way that held their adulation and loyalty. This began with people at the top making sure that those directly below them remained firmly placed where they could count on them. Any defection, especially by the more popular people in a clique, could seriously threaten their standing.

Leaders often employed manipulation to hold the attention and loyalty of clique members.[3] Another manipulative technique involved acting different ways toward different people. Rick recalled how Brad, the clique leader in fifth grade, used this strategy to maintain his position of centrality: *"Brad would always say that Trevor is so annoying. 'He is such an idiot, a stupid baby,' and everyone would say, 'Yeah, he is so annoying. We don't like him.' So they would all be mean to him. And then later in the day, Brad would go over and play with Trevor and say that everyone else didn't like him, but that he did. That's how Brad maintained control over Trevor."* Brad employed similar techniques of manipulation to ensure that all the members of his clique were similarly tied to him. Like many leaders, he would shift his primary attention among the different clique members, so that everyone experienced the power and status associated with his favor. Then, when they were out of favor, his followers felt relatively deprived and strove to regain their privileged status. This ensured their loyalty and compliance.

To a lesser degree, clique members curried friendship with outsiders. Although they did not accept them into the group, they sometimes included them in activities and tried to influence their opinions. While the leaders had their in-group followers, lower-status clique members, if they cultivated them well, could look to outsiders for respect, admiration, and imitation. This attitude and behavior were not universal, however; some popular cliques were so disdainful and mean to outsiders that nonmembers hated them. Diane, Tiffany, and Darla, three popular girls who had gone to two different elementary schools, reflected on how the grade school cliques to which they had belonged displayed opposing relationships with individuals of lesser status:

> Darla: *We hated it if the dorks didn't like us and want us to be with them. 'Cause then we weren't the popularest ones 'cause we always had to have them look up to us, and when they wouldn't look up to us, we would be nice to them.*
>
> Diane: *The medium people always hated us.*
>
> Tiffany: *They hated us royally, and we hated them back whenever they started.*
>
> Darla: *Sometimes we acted like we didn't care, but it bothered me.*
>
> Tiffany: *We always won, so it didn't matter.*

Thus, while there were notable exceptions (see Eder 1985), many popular clique members strove to ingratiate themselves with people less popular than they, from time to time, to ensure that their dominance and adulation extended beyond their own boundaries, throughout the grade.

Techniques of Exclusion

Although inclusionary techniques reinforced individuals' popularity and prestige while maintaining the group's exclusivity and stratification, they failed to contribute to other, essential, clique features such as cohesion and integration, the management of in-group and out-group relationships, and submission to clique leadership. These features are rooted, along with further sources of domination and power, in cliques' exclusionary dynamics.

Out-Group Subjugation

When they were not being nice to try to keep outsiders from straying too far from their realm of influence, clique members predominantly subjected outsiders to exclusion and rejection.[4] They found sport in picking on these lower-status individuals. As one clique follower remarked, "*One of the main things is to keep picking on unpopular kids because it's just fun to do.*" Eder (1991) notes that this kind of ridicule, where the targets are excluded and not enjoined to participate in the laughter, contrasts with teasing, where friends make fun of each other in a more lighthearted manner but permit the targets to remain included in the group by also jokingly making fun of themselves. Diane, a clique leader in fourth grade, described the way she acted toward outsiders: *"Me and my friends would be mean to the people outside of our clique. Like, Eleanor Dawson, she would always try to be friends with us, and we would be like, 'Get away, ugly.'"*

Interactionally sophisticated clique members not only treated outsiders badly but managed to turn others in the clique against them. Parker and Gottman (1989) observe that one of the ways people do this is through gossip. Diane recalled the way she turned all the members of her class, boys as well as girls, against an outsider:

> *I was always mean to people outside my group like Crystal, and Sally Jones; they both moved schools. . . . I had this gummy bear necklace, with pearls around it and gummy bears. She [Crystal] came up to me one day and pulled my necklace off. I'm like, "It was my favorite necklace," and I got all of my friends, and all the guys even in the class, to revolt against her. No one liked her. That's why she moved schools, because she tore my gummy bear necklace off and everyone hated her. They were like, "That was mean. She didn't deserve that. We hate you."*

Turning people against an outsider served to solidify the group and to assert the power of the strong over the vulnerability of the weak. Other classmates tended to side with the dominant people over the subordinates, not only because they admired their prestige but also because they respected and feared the power of the strong.

Insiders' ultimate manipulation in leading the group to pick on outsiders involved instigating the bullying and causing others to take the blame. Davey, the fifth-grade clique follower mentioned earlier, described, with some mystery and awe, the skilled maneuvering of Joe, his clique leader: *"He'd start a fight and then he would get everyone in it, 'cause everyone followed him, and then he would get out of it so he wouldn't get in trouble."*

Q: How'd he do that?

Davey: *One time he went up to this kid Morgan, who nobody liked, and said, "Come on Morgan, you want to talk about it?" and started kicking him, and then everyone else started doing it. Joe stopped and started watching, and then some parapro[fessional] came over and said, "What's going on here?" And then everyone got in trouble except for him.*

Q: Why did he pick on Morgan?

Davey: *'Cause he couldn't do anything about it, 'cause he was a nerd.*

Getting picked on instilled outsiders with fear, grinding them down to accept their inferior status and discouraging them from rallying together to challenge the power hierarchy.[5] In a confrontation between a clique member and an outsider, most people sided with the clique member. They knew that clique members banded together against outsiders, and that they could easily become the next target of attack if they challenged them. Clique members picked on outsiders with little worry about confrontation or repercussion. They also knew that their victims would never carry the tale to teachers or administrators (as they might against other targets; see Sluckin 1981) for fear of reprisal. As Mike, a fifth-grade clique follower, observed, *"They know if they tell on you, then you'll 'beat them up,' and so they won't tell on you, they just kind of take it in, walk away."*

In-Group Subjugation

Picking on people within the clique's confines was another way to exert dominance. More central clique members commonly harassed and were mean to those with weaker standing.[6] Many of the same factors prompting the ill treatment of outsiders motivated high-level insiders to pick on less powerful insiders. Rick, a fifth-grade clique follower, articulated the systematic organization of downward harassment:

> *Basically the people who are the most popular, their life outside in the playground is picking on other people who aren't as popular, but are in the group. But the people just want to be more popular so they stay in the group, they just kind of stick with it, get made fun of, take it. . . . They come back everyday, you do more ridicule, more ridicule, more ridicule, and they just keep taking it because they want to be more popular, and they actually like you but you don't like them. That goes on a lot, that's the main thing in the group. You make fun of someone, you get more popular, because insults is what they like, they like insults.*

The finger of ridicule could be pointed at any individual but the leader. It might be a person who did something worthy of insult, it might be someone who the clique leader felt had become an interpersonal threat, or it might be someone singled out for no apparent reason (see Eder 1991). Darla, the second-tier fourth grader discussed earlier, described the ridicule she encountered and her feelings of mortification when the clique leader derided her hair:

> *Like I remember, she embarrassed me so bad one day. Oh my God, I wanted to kill her! We were in music class and we were standing there and she goes, "Ew! what's all that shit in your hair?" in front of the whole class. I was so embarrassed, 'cause, I guess I had dandruff or something.[7]*

Often, derision against insiders followed a pattern, where leaders started a trend and everyone followed it. This intensified the sting of the mockery by compounding it with multiple force. Rick analogized the way people in cliques behaved to the links on a chain:

> *Like it's a chain reaction, you get in a fight with the main person, then the person right under him will not like you, and the person under him won't like you, and et cetera, and the whole group will take turns against you. A few people will*

still like you because they will do their own thing, but most people will do what the person in front of them says to do, so it would be like a chain reaction. It's like a chain; one chain turns, and the other chain has to turn with them or else it will tangle.

Compliance

Going along with the derisive behavior of leaders or other high-status clique members could entail either active or passive participation. Active participation occurred when instigators enticed other clique members to pick on their friends. For example, leaders would often come up with the idea of placing phony phone calls to others and would persuade their followers to do the dirty work. They might start the phone call and then place followers on the line to finish it, or they might pressure others to make the entire call, thus keeping one step distant from becoming implicated, should the victim's parents complain.

Passive participation involved going along when leaders were mean and manipulative, as when Trevor submissively acquiesced in Brad's scheme to convince Larry that Rick had stolen his money. Trevor knew that Brad was hiding the money the whole time, but he watched while Brad whipped Larry into a frenzy, pressing him to deride Rick, destroy Rick's room and possessions, and threaten to expose Rick's alleged theft to others. It was only when Rick's mother came home, interrupting the bedlam, that she uncovered the money and stopped Larry's onslaught. The following day at school, Brad and Trevor could scarcely contain their glee. As noted earlier, Rick was demolished by the incident and cast out by the clique; Trevor was elevated to the status of Brad's best friend by his co-conspiracy in the scheme.

Many clique members relished the opportunity to go along with such exclusive activities, welcoming the feelings of privilege, power, and inclusion. Others were just thankful that they weren't the targets. This was especially true of new members, who, as Sanford and Eder (1984) describe, often feel unsure about their standing in a group. Marcus and Adam, two fifth-grade clique followers introduced earlier, expressed their different feelings about such participation:

Q: What was it like when someone in your group got picked on?

Marcus: *If it was someone I didn't like or who had picked on me before, then I liked it. It made me feel good.*

Adam: *I didn't really enjoy it. It made me feel better if they weren't picking on me. But you can't do too much about it, so you sort of get used to it.*

Like outsiders, clique members knew that complaining to persons in authority did them no good. Quite the reverse, such resistance tactics made their situation worse, as did showing their vulnerabilities to the aggressors.[8] Kara, a popular fifth-grade girl, explained why such declarations had the opposite effect from that intended: "*Because we knew what bugged them, so we could use it against them. And we just did it to pester 'em, aggravate 'em, make us feel better about ourselves. Just to be shitty."*

When people saw their friends in tenuous situations, they often reacted in a passive manner. Popular people who got in fights with other popular people might be able to count on some of their followers for support, but most people could not command such loyalty. Jeff, a fifth-grade boy, explained why people went along with hurtful behavior:

It's a real risk if you want to try to stick up for someone because you could get rejected from the group or whatever. Some people do, and nothing happens because they're so high up that other people listen to them. But most people would just find themselves in the same boat. And we've all been there before, so we know what that's like.

Clique members thus went along with picking on their friends, even though they knew it hurt, because they were afraid (see also Best 1983). They became accustomed to living within a social world where the power dynamics could be hurtful, and accepted it.

Stigmatization

Beyond individual incidents of derision, clique insiders were often made the focus of stigmatization for longer periods of time. Unlike outsiders who commanded less enduring interest, clique members were much more involved in picking on their friends, whose discomfort more readily held their attention. Rick noted that the duration of this negative attention was highly variable: *"Usually at certain times, it's just a certain person you will pick on all the time, if they do something wrong. I've been picked on for a month at a time, or a week, or a day, or just a couple of minutes, and then they will just come to respect you again."* When people became the focus of stigmatization, as happened to Rick, they were rejected by all their friends. The entire clique rejoiced in celebrating their disempowerment. They would be made to feel alone whenever possible. Their former friends might join hands and walk past them through the play yard at recess, physically demonstrating their union and the discarded individual's aloneness.

Worse than being ignored was being taunted. Taunts ranged from verbal insults to put-downs to singsong chants. Anyone who could create a taunt was favored with attention and imitated by everyone (see Fine 1981). Even outsiders, who would not normally be privileged to pick on a clique member, were able to elevate themselves by joining in on such taunting (see Sanford and Eder 1984).

The ultimate degradation was physical. Although girls generally held themselves to verbal humiliation of their members, the culture of masculinity gave credence to boys' injuring each other (Eder and Parker 1987; Oswald et al. 1987; Thorne 1993). Fights would occasionally break out in which boys were punched in the ribs or stomach, kicked, or given black eyes. When this happened at school, adults were quick to intervene. But after hours or on the school bus, boys could be hurt. Physical abuse was also heaped on people's homes or possessions. People spit on each other or others' books or toys, threw eggs at their family's cars, and smashed pumpkins in front of their house.

Expulsion

While most people returned to a state of acceptance following a period of severe derision (see Sluckin 1981 for strategies children use to help attain this end), this was not always the case. Some people became permanently excommunicated from the clique. Others could be cast out directly, without undergoing a transitional phase of relative exclusion. Clique members from any stratum of the group could suffer such a fate, although it was more common among people with lower status.

When Davey, mentioned earlier, was in sixth grade, he described how expulsion could occur as a natural result of the hierarchical ranking, where a person at the bottom rung of the system of popularity was pushed off. He described the ordinary dynamics of clique behavior:

Q: How do clique members decide who they are going to insult that day?

Davey: *It's just basically everyone making fun of everyone. The small people making fun of smaller people, the big people making fun of the small people. Nobody is really making fun of people bigger than them because they can get rejected, because then they can say, "Oh yes, he did this and that, this and that, and we shouldn't like him anymore." And everybody else says, "Yeah, yeah, yeah," 'cause all the lower people like him, but all the higher people don't. So the lowercase people just follow the highercase people. If one person is doing something wrong, then they will say, "Oh yeah, get out, good-bye."*

Being cast out could result either from a severely irritating infraction or from individuals standing up for their rights against the dominant leaders. Sometimes expulsion occurred as a result of breakups between friends or friendship realignments leading to membership challenges (mentioned earlier), where higher-status people carried the group with them and turned their former friends into outcasts. . . .

On much rarer occasions, high-status clique members or even leaders could be cast out of the group (see Best 1983). One sixth-grade clique leader, Tiffany, was deposed by her former lieutenants for a continued pattern of petulance and self-indulgent manipulations:

Q: Who kicked you out?

Tiffany: *Robin and Tanya. They accepted Heidi into their clique, and they got rid of me. They were friends with her. I remember it happened in one blowup in the cafeteria. I asked for pizza and I thought I wasn't getting enough attention anymore, so I was pissed and in a bitchy mood all the time and stuff, and so I asked them for some, so she [Robin] said like, "Wait, hold on, Heidi is*

*taking a bite," or something, and I got so mad I said, "Give the whole fuckin'
thing to Heidi," and something like that, and they got so sick of me right then,
and they said like, "Fuck you."*

When clique members get kicked out of the group, they leave an established circle of friends and often seek to make new ones. Some people have a relatively easy time making what Davies (1982) calls "contingency friends" (temporary replacements for their more popular friends), and, according to one fifth-grade teacher, they are "hot items" for the unpopular crowd. . . .

Many cast-outs found new friendships harder to establish, however. They went through a period where they kept to themselves, feeling rejected, stigmatized, and cut off from their former social circle and status. Because of their previous behavior and their relations with other classmates, they had trouble being accepted by unpopular kids. Others had developed minimum acceptability thresholds for friends when they were in the popular crowd, and had difficulty stooping to befriend unpopular kids. When Mark was ejected from his clique in fifth grade, he explained why he was unsuccessful in making friends with the unpopular people: *"Because there was nobody out there I liked. I just didn't like anybody. And I think they didn't like me because when I was in the popular group we'd make fun of everyone, I guess, so they didn't want to be around me, because I had been too mean to them in the past."*

Occasionally, rejects from the popular clique had trouble making friends among the remainder of the class due to the interference of their former friends. If clique members got angry at one of their friends and cast him or her out, they might want to make sure that nobody else befriended that individual. By soliciting friendship with people outside the clique, they could influence outsiders' behavior, causing their outcast to fall beyond the middle crowd to the status of pariah, or loner. Darla explained why and how people carried out such manipulations:

Q: Have you ever seen anyone cast out?

Darla: *Sure, like, you just make fun of them. If they don't get accepted to the medium group, if they see you like, "Fuck, she's such a dork," and like you really don't want them to have any friends, so you go to the medium group, and you're like, "Why are you hanging out with THAT loser, she's SUCH a dork, we HATE her," and then you be nice to them so they'll get rid of her so she'll be such a dork. I've done that just so she'll be such a nerd that no one will like her. You're just getting back at them. And then they will get rid of her just 'cause you said to, so then, you've done your way with them. If you want something, you'll get it.*

People who were cast out of their group often kept to themselves, staying in from the playground at recess and coming home after school alone. They took the bus to school, went to class, did what they had to do, but didn't have friends. Their feelings about themselves changed, and this was often reflected in the way they dressed and carried themselves. Being ejected from the clique thus represented the ultimate form of exclusion, carrying with it severe consequences for individuals' social lives, appearance, and identity.

The techniques of inclusion and exclusion represent the means by which the behavioral dynamics of cliques are forged. As such, they offer the basis for a generic model of clique functioning that interweaves these processes with the essential clique features of exclusivity, power and dominance, status stratification, cohesion and integration, popularity, submission, and in-group and out-group relations. . . .

These two dynamics work hand in hand. The inclusionary dynamic is central to cliques' foundation of attraction. Cliques' boundary maintenance makes them exclusive. They can recruit the individuals they want, wooing them from competing friendships, and reject the supplications of others they evaluate as unworthy. The popularity of their membership (with leaders to lend status and followers to lend power) strengthens their position at the center of activity. Upheavals and friendship realignments within cliques keep the hierarchical alignment of prestige and influence fluid, giving those successful at maneuvering toward and staying near the top the greatest esteem among their peers. The systematic upward ingratiation of individuals toward the leading members, and leading members' ability to easily ingratiate themselves downward with others, thereby securing the favors they desire, enhance the attractiveness of inclusion in the clique.

The exclusionary dynamic is central to cliques' bases of cohesion. Clique members solidify together in disparaging outsiders, learning that those in the in-group can freely demean out-group members, only to have their targets return for renewed chances at acceptance. They learn sensitivity toward changes in group boundaries, acting one way toward insiders and another way toward outsiders. This lesson manifests itself not only at the group's outer edges but within the clique, as individuals move in and out of relative favor and have to position themselves carefully to avoid the stigma of association with the disfavored. They learn the hierarchy of group positions and the perquisites of respect and influence that go with those roles, submitting to the dominance of clique leaders in order to earn a share of their reflected status and position. The periodic minicyclings of exclusion serve to manipulate followers into dependence and subservience, at the same time enhancing leaders' centrality and authority. The ultimate sanction of expulsion represents a dramatic example of the effects of exclusion, weakening or bringing down potential rivals from positions of power while herding other group members into cohesion. The dynamic of inclusion lures members into cliques, while the dynamic of exclusion keeps them there.[9]

ENDNOTES

[1]See Hallinan (1979), Hubbell (1965), Peay (1974), and Varenne (1982) for a discussion of cliques' sociometric characteristics.

[2]They are primary groups, offering individuals the opportunity to select close friendships of their own choosing (Elkin and Handel 1989), to learn about society, to practice their behavior,

and to evolve their selves and identities. Autonomous from the world of adults (Fine 1981), they are often forged in opposition to adult values (Elkin and Handel 1989), with a culture of resistance to adult standards (Corsaro 1985). They thus encompass a robust form of children's peer culture that is both unique in its own right yet at the same time a staging ground for future adult behavior.

[3]Oswald, Krappmann, Chowdhuri, and von Salisch (1987) note that one way children assert superiority over others and indebt them with loyalty is to offer them "help," either materially or socially.

[4]Hogg and Abrams (1988) find that denigrating out-group members enhances a group's solidarity and improves the group status of people participating in such denigration. This tendency is particularly strong where two groups perceive themselves to be in conflict or competition.

[5]Eder and Sanford (1986) and Merten (1994) note the same tendency among adolescent peer groups in middle school.

[6]Eder (1991) also notes that when insiders pick on other members of their clique, this can have good-natured overtones, indicating that they like them.

[7]Eder and Sanford (1986) and Eder and Parker (1987) discuss the importance of physical appearance, particularly hair, in adhering to group norms and maintaining popularity.

[8]Merten (1994, 1996) discusses the dilemma faced by children who are picked on, who would like to report the problem to a teacher but cannot do so out of fear that the teacher's intervention would incur the wrath of others. He notes the consequences for one boy whose mother complained to other parents about the way their children treated her son: when these others came to school the next day, they ridiculed the boy even more, taunting and deriding him for being a tattletale.

[9]Bigelow, Tesson, and Lewko (1996) also note this "Lord of the Flies" phenomenon.

REFERENCES

Best, Raphaela. 1983. *We've All Got Scars*. Bloomington: Indiana University Press.

Bigelow, Brian J., Geoffrey Tesson, and John H. Lewko. 1996. *Learning the Rules*. New York: Guilford Press.

Blau, Peter M. 1964. *Exchange and Power in Social Life*. New York: Wiley.

Corsaro, William A. 1985. *Friendship and Peer Culture in the Early Years*. Norwood, NJ: Ablex.

Davies, Bronwyn. 1982. *Life in the Classroom and Playground: The Accounts of Primary School Children*. London: Routledge and Kegan Paul.

Dodge, Kenneth A., David C. Schlundt, Iris Schocken, and Judy D. Delugach. 1983. "Social Competence and Children's Sociometric Status: The Role of Peer Group Entry Strategies." *Merrill-Palmer Quarterly* 29:309–36.

Eder, Donna. 1985. "The Cycle of Popularity: Interpersonal Relations among Female Adolescents." *Sociology of Education* 58:154–65.

———. 1991. "The Role of Teasing in Adolescent Peer Group Culture." Pp. 181–97 in *Sociological Studies of Child Development*, vol. 1, edited by P. A. Adler and P. Adler. Greenwich, CT: JAI Press.

Eder, Donna and Stephen Parker. 1987. "The Cultural Production and Reproduction of Gender: The Effect of Extracurricular Activities on Peer-Group Culture." *Sociology of Education* 60:200–213.

Eder, Donna and Stephanie Sanford. 1986. "The Development and Maintenance of Interactional Norms among Early Adolescents." Pp. 283–300 in *Sociological Studies of Child Development*, vol. 1, edited by P. A. Adler and P. Adler. Greenwich, CT: JAI Press.

Elkin, Frederick and Gerald Handel. 1989. *The Child and Society*. 5th ed. New York: Random House.

Fine, Gary Alan. 1981. "Friends, Impression Management, and Preadolescent Behavior." Pp. 29–52 in *The Development of Children's Friendships*, edited by S. Asher and J. Gottman. New York: Cambridge University Press.

Hallinan, Maureen. 1979. "Structural Effects on Children's Friendships and Cliques." *Social Psychology Quarterly* 42:43–54.

Hogg, Michael A. and Dominic Abrams. 1988. *Social Identifications*. New York: Routledge.

Hubbell, Charles H. 1965. "An Input-Output Approach to Clique Identification." *Sociometry* 28:377–99.

Merten, Don E. 1994. "The Cultural Context of Aggression: The Transition to Junior High School." *Anthropology and Education Quarterly* 25:29–43.

———. 1996. "Visibility and Vulnerability: Responses to Rejection by Nonaggressive Junior High School Boys." *Journal of Early Adolescence* 16:5–26.

Oswald, Hans, Lothar Krappmann, Irene Chowdhuri, and Maria von Salisch. 1987. "Gaps and Bridges: Interactions between Girls and Boys in Elementary School." Pp. 205–23 in *Sociological Studies of Child Development*, vol. 1, edited by P. A. Adler and P. Adler. Greenwich, CT: JAI Press.

Parker, Jeffrey G. and John M. Gottman. 1989. "Social and Emotional Development in a Relational Context." Pp. 95–131 in *Peer Relationships in Child Development*, edited by T. J. Berndt and G. W. Ladd. New York: Wiley.

Peay, Edmund R. 1974. "Hierarchical Clique Structures." *Sociometry* 37:54–65.

Sanford, Stephanie and Donna Eder. 1984. "Adolescent Humor during Peer Interaction." *Social Psychology Quarterly* 47:235–43.

Sluckin, Andy. 1981. *Growing Up in the Playground*. London: Routledge and Kegan Paul.

Thorne, Barrie. 1993. *Gender Play*. New Brunswick, NJ: Rutgers University Press.

Varenne, Herve. 1982. "Jocks and Freaks: The Symbolic Structure of the Expression of Social Interaction among American Senior High School Students." Pp. 210–35 in *Doing the Ethnography of Schooling*, edited by G. Spindler. New York: Holt, Rinehart, and Winston.

16

GANG BUSINESS
Making Ends Meet

MARTÍN SÁNCHEZ JANKOWSKI

This selection by Martín Sánchez Jankowski is excerpted from his book *Islands in the Street: Gangs and American Urban Society* (1991). Sánchez Jankowski, a professor of sociology at the University of California at Berkeley, studies the *primary group* of social gangs that exist in urban settings across the United States. Examples of other primary groups are families, friendship cliques, sororities and fraternities, neighborhood coffee klatches, and small work groups. Thus, primary groups emerge when people live or work closely together. As this reading by Sánchez Jankowski shows, gangs are similar to other primary groups in that they are small, intimate, and informal. Sánchez Jankowski also argues that, contrary to the stereotype of gang culture, gangs have some social values that are similar to those of other American groups, including a work ethic and an entrepreneurial spirit.

Cunning and deceit will serve a man better than force to rise from a base condition to great fortune.

—NICCOLÒ MACHIAVELLI, THE DISCOURSES (1517?)

I f there is one theme that dominates most studies of gangs, it is that gangs are collectives of individuals who are social parasites, and that they are parasitic not only because they lack the skills to be productive members of society but, more important, because they lack the values, particularly the work ethic, that would guide them to be productive members of society.[1] However, one of the most striking factors I observed was how much the entrepreneurial spirit, which most Americans believe is the core of their productive culture, was a driving force in the worldview and behavior of gang members.[2] If entrepreneurial spirit denotes the desire to organize and manage business interests toward some end that results in the accumulation of capital, broadly defined, nearly all the gang members that I studied possessed, in varying degrees, five attributes that are either entrepreneurial in character or that reinforce entrepreneurial behavior.

The first of these entrepreneurial attitudes is competitiveness. Most gang members I spoke with expressed a strong sense of self-competence and a drive to compete with others. They believed in themselves as capable of achieving some level of economic success and saw competition as part of human nature and an opportunity to prove one's self-worth. This belief in oneself often took on a dogmatic character, especially for those individuals who had lost in some form of economic competition. The losers always had ready excuses that placed the blame on something other than their own personal inadequacy, thereby artificially reinforcing their feelings of competence in the face of defeat.[3]

Gang members' sense of competitiveness also reflected their general worldview that life operates under Social Darwinist principles. In the economic realm, they believed there is no ethical code that regulates business ventures, and this attitude exempted them from moral constraints on individual economic-oriented action.[4] The views of Danny provide a good example of this Social Darwinist outlook. Danny was a 20-year-old Irish gang member from Boston:

> I don't worry about whether something is fair or not when I'm making a business deal. There is nothing fair or unfair, you just go about your business of trying to make a buck, and if someone feels you took advantage of him, he has only himself to blame. If someone took advantage of me, I wouldn't sit around bellyaching about it, I'd just go and try to get some of my money back. One just has to ask around here [the neighborhood] and you'd find that nobody expects that every time you're going to make a business deal, that it will be fair—you know, that the other guy is not going to be fair, hell, he is trying to make money, not trying to be fair. This is the way those big business assholes operate too! The whole thing [the system] operates this way. . . .

The second entrepreneurial attribute I observed is the desire and drive to accumulate money and material possessions. Karl Marx, of course, described this desire as the "profit motive" and attributed it primarily to the bourgeoisie.[5] There is a profit-motive element to the entrepreneurial values of gang members, but it differs significantly from Marx's analysis of the desire to accumulate material and capital for their own sake, largely divorced from the desire to improve one's material condition. Nor is gang members' ambition to accumulate material possessions related to a need for achievement, which the psychologist David McClelland identifies as more central to entrepreneurial behavior in certain individuals than the profit motive per se.[6] Rather, the entrepreneurial activity of gang members is predicated on their more basic understanding of what money can buy.[7] The ambition to accumulate capital and material possessions is related, in its initial stages (which can last for a considerable number of years), to the desire to improve the comfort of everyday living and the quality of leisure time.

This desire, of course, is shared by most people who live in low-income neighborhoods. Some of them resign themselves to the belief that they will never be able to secure their desires. Others attempt to improve their life situation by using various "incremental approaches," such as working in those jobs that are made available to them and saving their money, or attempting to learn higher-level occupational skills. In contrast, the entrepreneurs of low-income neighborhoods, especially those in gangs, attempt to improve their lives by becoming involved in a business venture, or a series of ventures, that has the potential to create large changes in their own or their family's socioeconomic condition.

The third attribute of entrepreneurial behavior prevalent in gangs is status-seeking. Mirroring the dominant values of the larger society, most gang members attempt to achieve some form of status with the acquisition of possessions. However, most of them cannot attain a high degree of status by accumulation alone. To merit high status among peers and in the community, gang members must try, although most will be unsuccessful, to accumulate a large number of possessions and be willing to share them. Once gang members have accumulated sufficient material possessions to provide themselves with a relative level of comfort or leisure above the minimal, they begin to seek the increase in status that generosity affords. (For philanthropic purposes, accumulating cash is preferable to accumulating possessions, because the more money one has, the more flexibility one has in giving away possessions.)

The fourth entrepreneurial attribute one finds among gang members is the ability to plan. Gang members spend an impressive amount of time planning activities that will bring them fortune and fame, or, at least, plenty of spending money in the short term. At their grandest, these plans have the character of dreams, but as the accounts of renowned business tycoons show, having big dreams has always been a hallmark of entrepreneurial endeavors.[8] At the other end of the spectrum are short-range plans (also called small scams) that members try to pull on one another, usually to secure a loan. . . .

Gang members also engage in intermediary and long-range planning. A typical intermediary plan might concern modest efforts to steal some type of merchandise from warehouses, homes, or businesses. Because most of the sites they select are equipped with security systems, a more elaborate plan involving more time is needed than is the case for those internal gang scams just described. Long-range planning and organization, sometimes quite elaborate, are, as other studies have reported, at times executed with remarkable precision.[9]

Finally, the fifth entrepreneurial attribute common among gang members is the ability to undertake risks. Generally, young gang members (nine to fifteen years of age) do not understand risk as part of a risk-reward calculus, and for this age group, risk-taking is nearly always pursued for itself, as an element of what Thrasher calls the "sport motive,"[10] the desire to test oneself. As gang members get older, they gradually develop a more sophisticated understanding of risk-taking, realizing that a certain amount of risk is necessary to secure desired goals. Now they attempt to calculate the risk factors involved for nearly every venture, measuring the risk to their physical well-being, money, and freedom. Just like mainstream businessmen, they discover that risk tends to increase proportionally to the level of innovation undertaken to secure a particular financial objective. Most of these older gang members are willing to assume risks commensurate with the subjective "value" of their designated target, but they will not assume risks just for the sake of risk-taking. . . .

Economic Activity: Accumulating

With a few exceptions, nearly all the literature on gangs focuses on their economic delinquency.[11] This is a very misleading picture, however, for although gangs operate primarily in illegal markets, they also are involved in legal markets. Of the 37 gangs observed in the present study, 27 generated some percentage of their revenues through legitimate business activity. It is true that gangs do more of their business activity in the illegal markets, but none of them wants to be exclusively active in these markets.[12]

In the illegal market, gangs concentrate their economic activities primarily in goods, services, and recreation. In the area of goods, gangs have been heavily involved in accumulating and selling drugs, liquor, and various stolen products such as guns, auto parts, and assorted electronic equipment. These goods are sometimes bought and sold with the gang acting as the wholesaler and/or retailer. At other times, the gang actually produces the goods it sells. For example, while most gangs buy drugs or alcohol and retail them, a few gangs manufacture and market homemade drugs and moonshine liquor. Two gangs (one African American and one Irish) in this study had purchased stills and sold their moonshine to people on the street, most of whom were derelicts, and to high school kids too young to buy liquor legally.[13] Three other gangs (two Puerto Rican and one Dominican) made a moonshine liquor from fermented fruit and sold it almost exclusively to teenagers. Both types of moonshine were very high in alcohol, always above one hundred proof. While sales of this liquor were not of the magnitude to create fortunes, these projects were quite surprisingly capable of generating substantial amounts of revenue.

The biggest money-maker and the one product nearly every gang tries to market is illegal drugs.[14] The position of the gang within the illegal drug market varies among gangs and between cities. In New York, the size of the gang and how long it has been in existence have a great deal to do with whether it will have access to drug suppliers. The older and larger gangs are able to buy drugs from suppliers and act as wholesalers to pushers. They shun acting as pushers (the lowest level of drug sales) themselves because there are greater risks and little, if any, commensurate increase in profit. In addition, because heroin use is forbidden within most gangs, the gang leaders prefer to establish attitudes oriented to the sale rather than the consumption of drugs within the organization. In the past, when the supply was controlled by the Italian Mafia, it was difficult for gangs to gain access to the quantity of drug supplies necessary to make a profit marketing them. In the past ten years, though, the Mafia has given way (in terms of drug supply) to African American, Puerto Rican, and Mexican syndicates.[15] In addition, with the increased popularity of cocaine in New York, the African American, Puerto Rican, and Dominican syndicates' connections to Latin American sources of cocaine supply rival, and in many cases surpass, those of Mafia figures.[16] With better access to supplies, gangs in New York have been able to establish a business attitude toward drugs and to capitalize on the opportunities that drugs now afford them.

Some gangs have developed alternative sources of supply. They do so in two ways. Some, particularly the Chicano gangs, have sought out pharmacies where an employee can be paid off to steal pills for the gang to sell on the street.[17] Other gangs, particularly in New York, but also some in Los Angeles, have established "drug mills" to produce synthetic drugs such as LSD (or, more recently, crack cocaine) for sale on the street. The more sophisticated drug mills, which are controlled by various organized crime families, manufacture a whole line of drugs for sale, including cut heroin, but gangs are almost never involved in them. Those gangs that have established a production facility for generating drugs, no matter how crude it may be, generate sizable sums of money. Whether a gang is able to establish a sophisticated production and distribution system for drug sales depends on the sophistication of the gang organization and the amount of capital available for start-up purposes.

Stolen guns are another popular and profitable product. Gangs sometimes steal guns and then redistribute them, but most often they buy them from wholesale gun peddlers and then resell them. Sometimes the gangs will buy up a small number of shotguns and then cut the barrel and stock down to about 13 to 15 inches in length and then sell them as "easily concealable." A prospective buyer can get whatever gun he wants if he is willing to pay the going price. In the present study, the Irish gangs have been, commercially speaking, the most involved with guns, often moving relatively large shipments, ranging from sawed-off shotguns to fully automatic rifles and pistols of the most sophisticated types.[18] It was reported that these guns were being moved, with the help of the Irish social clubs, to the Catholics of Northern

Ireland for their struggle with the Protestants there. No matter what the destination, rather large sums of money were paid to the Irish gangs for their efforts in acquiring the weapons or in helping move them. Although all the gangs studied were involved in the sale of illegal guns, illegal gun sales constituted a larger proportion of the economic activities of Irish gangs than they did for the others.

Gangs in all three cities were also involved in the selling of car parts. All the parts sold were stolen, some stolen to fill special orders from customers and others stolen and reworked in members' home garages into customized parts for resale. Business was briskest in Los Angeles, where there is a large market, especially among the low-rider clientele, for customized auto parts.[19] The amount of money made from stolen auto parts varies according to the area, whether or not the gang has an agent to whom to sell the parts, and the types of parts sold. On the whole, revenues from stolen auto parts are not nearly as high as those from selling illegal drugs, guns, or liquor, and so less time is devoted by gangs to this activity.

Gangs' business activities also include a number of services, the three most common being protection, demolition (usually arson), and indirect participation in prostitution. Protection is the most common service, both because there is a demand for it in the low-income areas in which gangs operate and because the gangs find it the easiest service to deliver, since it requires little in the way of resources or training. Gangs offer both personal and business protection. Nearly all the gangs had developed a fee schedule according to the type of protection desired. Most, but certainly not all, of the protection services offered by the gangs in this study involved extortion. Usually the gang would go into a store and ask the owner if he felt he needed protection from being robbed. Since it was clear what was being suggested, the owner usually said yes and asked how much it would cost him. When dealing with naive owners, those who did not speak English very well or did not know American ghetto customs, or with owners who flatly resisted their services, the gang would take time to educate or persuade them to retain its services. In the case of the immigrants (most of whom were Asian or Near Eastern), the gang members would begin by explaining the situation, but usually such owners did not understand, and so the gang would demonstrate its point by sending members into the store to steal. Another tactic was to pay a dope addict to go in and rob the store. After such an incident occurred, the gang would return and ask the owner if he now needed protection. If he refused, the tactics were repeated, and almost all the owners were finally convinced. However, for those owners who understood and resisted from the start, more aggressive tactics were used, such as destruction of their premises or harassment of patrons. More often than not, continued pressure brought the desired result. However, it should be noted that in the vast majority of cases, no coercion was needed, because store owners in high-crime areas were, more often than not, happy to receive protection. As one owner said to me: "I would need to hire a protection company anyway, and frankly the gang provides much more protection than they could ever do."

Gangs also offer their services as enforcers to clients who need punishment administered to a third party. Small-time hustlers or loan sharks, for example, hired some gangs to administer physical coercion to borrowers delinquent in their repayments. More recently one gang offered and apparently was hired by a foreign government to undertake terrorist attacks against the government and people of the United States.[20] Although that was an extreme case, nearly all gangs seek enforcement contracts because the fee is usually high, few resources have to be committed, and relatively little in the way of planning (compared to other projects) is needed.

The permanent elimination of or damage to property is another service gangs offer. This more often than not involves arson, and the buildings hit are commonly dilapidated. The gangs' clients are either landlords who want to torch the building to get the insurance money or residents who are so frustrated by the landlord's unwillingness to provide the most basic services that they ask the gang to retaliate. In both cases, there is usually much preliminary discussion of the project within the gang. These service jobs require a good deal of discussion and planning because there is the potential to hurt someone living in the building or to create enormous hardship if people have no alternative place to live, and the gang will do almost anything to avoid injuring people in its community. The gangs of New York have had the most business along these lines, particularly in the South Bronx, but arson is a service offered in Detroit, Chicago, and Philadelphia as well. As one gang leader from the Bronx said:

> You just don't bomb or torch any building that someone wants down. You got to find out who lives there, if they got another place to go, if they would be for takin' out the building and if they'd be OK with the folks [law enforcement authorities]. Then you got to get organized to get everybody out and sometimes that ain't many people and sometimes it is. If there is lots of people in the building, we'd just pass [refuse] on the job. . . . Now if we can work all these things out, we take the job and we deliver either a skeleton [outer walls are standing, but nothing else] or a cremation [just ashes].

Many potential clients know that a gang will refuse to burn down a building in its neighborhood if some type of harm will come to residents of its community, and so they contract with a gang from another area to do the job. Such incidents always ignite a war not only between the affected gangs but also between the communities. Take the example of the Hornets, a gang from one borough in New York that had contracted to set on fire a building in another borough. Although no one was killed in the fire, a few people were slightly burned, and of course everyone who lived in the building became homeless. At the request of a number of residents, the Vandals, a gang from the affected area, began to investigate and found out who had contracted to torch the building and which gang had been responsible. Then, at the request of an overwhelming majority of the community, the Vandals retaliated by burning down a building in the culprit gang's community. Hipper, a 20-year-old member of the Vandals, said:

We got to protect our community, they depend on us and they want us to do something so this [the burning of an apartment building in the neighborhood] don't happen again. . . . We be torchin' one of their buildings. I hope this don't hurt anybody, but if we don't do this, they be back hurting the people in our community and we definitely don't be letting that happen!

This is an excellent example of the bond that exists between the community and the gang. There is the understanding, then, among the community that the gang is a resource that can be counted on, particularly in situations where some form of force is necessary. Likewise, the gang knows that its legitimacy and existence are tied to being integrated in and responsible to community needs.

Prostitution is one illegal service in which gangs do not, for the most part, become directly involved. Gangs will accept the job of protecting pimps and their women for a fee (15, or 40 percent, of the gangs in this study had), and in this way they become indirectly associated with the prostitution business. Yet they generally avoid direct involvement because they feel protective of the females in their communities, and their organizations are wary of being accused by neighborhood residents of exposing female members of the community to the dangers associated with prostitution.

The last type of illegal economic activity in which all of the gangs in the present study were involved has to do with providing recreation. Some gangs establish numbers games in their neighborhoods. One New York gang had rented what had been a small Chinese food take-out place and was running numbers from the back where the kitchen had once been. (When I first observed the place, I thought it was a Chinese take-out and even proposed we get some quick food from it, which met with much laughter from the members of the gang I was with.) This gang became so successful that it opened up two other numbers establishments. One had been a pizza place (and was made to look as though it still served pizza slices); the other was a small variety store, which still functioned in that capacity, but also housed the numbers game in the back rooms.

Setting up gambling rooms is another aspect of the recreation business. Eleven of the gangs (or 30 percent) rented small storefronts, bought tables and chairs, and ran poker and/or domino games. The gang would assume the role of the "house," receiving a commission for each game played. Some of the gangs bought slot machines and placed them in their gambling rooms. Five (or 14 percent) of the gangs had as many as fifteen machines available for use.

Finally, ten gangs (27 percent), primarily those with Latino members, rented old buildings and converted them to accommodate cockfights. The gang would charge each cock owner a fee for entering his bird and an entrance fee for each patron. All of these ventures could, at various times, generate significant amounts of capital. The exact amount would depend on how often they were closed by the police and how well the gang managed the competition in its marketplace.

Turning to the legal economic activities undertaken by gangs, I observed that two ran "mom and pop" stores that sold groceries, candy, and soft drinks. Three gangs had taken over abandoned apartment buildings, renovated them, and rented them very cheaply—not simply because the accommodations were rather stark, but also because the gang wanted to help the less fortunate members of its community. The gangs also used these buildings to house members who had nowhere else to live. Undertaken and governed by social as much as economic concerns, these apartment ventures did not generate much income.

Interestingly, the finances of these legal activities were quite tenuous. The gangs that operated small grocery stores experienced periodic failures during which the stores had to be closed until enough money could be acquired (from other sources) to either pay the increased rent, rebuild shelf stock, or make necessary repairs. For those gangs who operated apartment buildings, in every case observed, the absence of a deed to the building or the land forced the gang to relinquish its holdings to either the city or a new landlord who wanted to build some new structure. Though there was a plentiful supply of abandoned buildings, most gangs lost interest in the renovation-and-rental business because such projects always created a crisis in their capital flow, which in turn precipitated internal bickering and conflict.

Other legal economic activities undertaken by the gangs I studied were automobile and motorcycle repair shops, car parts (quasi junkyards), fruit stands, and hair shops (both barber and styling). However, most of these ventures contributed only very modest revenues to the gangs' treasuries. Furthermore, the gang leadership had difficulty keeping most of the legal economic activities functioning because the rank and file were, by and large, not terribly enthusiastic about such activities. Rank-and-file resistance to most of these activities was of three sorts: members did not want to commit regularly scheduled time to any specific ongoing operation; members felt that the legal activities involved considerable overhead costs that lowered the profit rate; and members calculated that the time required to realize a large profit was far too long when compared to illegal economic activity. Thus, when such projects were promoted by the gang leadership and undertaken by the rank and file, they were done under the rubric of community service aid projects. The comments of Pin, a 19-year-old African American gang member from New York, are representative of this general position on legal economic activity:

> No, I don't go for those deals where we [the gang] run some kind of hotel out of an old building or run some repair shop or something like that. When you do that you can't make no money, or if you do make something it so small and takes so long to get it that it's just a waste of our [the gang's] money. But when the leadership brings it up as a possibility, well, sometimes I vote for it because I figure you got to help the community, many of them [people in the community] say they sort of depend on our help in one way or another, so I always say this is one way to help the community and me and the brothers go along with it. But everybody knows you can't make no money on shit like this.

ENDNOTES

[1] Nearly all studies of gangs incorporate this theme into their analysis. One of the exceptions is Cloward and Ohlin, *Delinquency and Opportunity*, which argues that many delinquents have the same values as other members of American society. However, even Cloward and Ohlin incorporate some of the conventional argument by accepting the premise that gang members' skills to compete in the larger society have been retarded by a lack of opportunity.

[2] See Charles Sabel, *Work and Politics* (Cambridge: Cambridge University Press, 1987), pp. 1–30, on the importance of worldviews in affecting the behavior of individuals in industrial organizations and politics.

[3] David Matza mentions a comparable tendency among delinquents to deny guilt associated with wrongdoing when he discusses the delinquent's belief that he is nearly always the victim of a "bum rap" (see Matza, *Delinquency and Drift* [New Brunswick, NJ: Transaction Books], pp. 108–10).

[4] I use the term *economic oriented action* the way Weber does: "Action will be said to be 'economical oriented' so far as, according to its subjective meaning, it is concerned with the satisfaction of a desire for 'utilities' *(Nutzleistung)*" (Weber, *Economy and Society* 1:63).

[5] See Karl Marx, *The Economic and Philosophical Manuscripts of 1844*, 4th rev. ed. (Moscow: Progress Publishers, 1974), p. 38.

[6] See David C. McClelland, *The Achieving Society* (New York: Free Press, 1961), pp. 233–37.

[7] See Lee Rainwater, *What Money Buys: Inequality and the Social Meanings of Income* (New York: Basic Books, 1974). Also see Richard P. Coleman and Lee Rainwater, *Social Standing in America: New Dimensions of Class* (New York: Basic Books, 1978), pp. 29–45.

[8] See the accounts of successful entrepreneurs from poor families who dreamed of grandeur and became America's most renowned business tycoons in Matthew Josephson, *The Robber Barons: The Great American Capitalists, 1861–1901* (New York: Harcourt, Brace & World, 1962), especially the chapter titled "What Young Men Dream," pp. 32–49.

[9] See Thrasher, *The Gang*, p. 86.

[10] Ibid., p. 86.

[11] Both the theoretical and empirical literature focus on the gang's criminal activity. For theoretical discussions, see Kornhauser, *Social Sources of Delinquency*, pp. 51–61. For empirical studies, see nearly all of the classic and contemporary work on gangs. A sample of this literature would include Thrasher, *The Gang*; Herman Schwendinger and Julia Schwendinger, *Adolescent Subcultures and Delinquency* (New York: Praeger, 1985); Cloward and Ohlin, *Delinquency and Opportunity*; Cohen, *Delinquent Boys*. Two exceptions are Horowitz, *Honor and the American Dream*, and Vigil, *Barrio Gangs*.

[12] There are two factors that have encouraged gangs to be more active in illegal markets. First, gangs, like organized crime syndicates, attempt to become active in many economic activities that are legal. However, because so much of the legal market is controlled by groups that have established themselves in strategic positions (because they entered that market a considerable time in the past), gangs have found it difficult at best to successfully penetrate many legal markets. Further, there are financial incentives that have encouraged gangs to operate in the illegal market. These include the fact that costs are relatively low, and while personal risk (in terms of being incarcerated and/or physically hurt) is rather high, high demand along with high risk can produce greater profit margins. Despite the fact that these two factors have encouraged gangs to be more active in the illegal market, it is important to emphasize that nearly all the gangs studied attempted to, and many did, conduct business in the legal market as well.

[13] The Schwendingers indicate that "youthful tastes regulate the flow of goods and services in the [adolescent] market" and gangs do take advantage of these tastes. See Schwendinger and Schwendinger, *Adolescent Subcultures and Delinquency*, p. 286.

[14] See Fagan, "Social Organization of Drug Use and Drug Dealing among Urban Gangs," pp. 633–67; and Jerome H. Skolnick, *Forum: The Social Structure of Street Drug Dealing* (Sacramento: Bureau of Criminal Statistics/Office of the Attorney General, 1989).

[15] See Francis A. J. Ianni, *Black Mafia: Ethnic Succession in Organized Crime* (New York: Simon & Schuster, 1974). Also see Moore, *Homeboys*, pp. 86–92, 114–16.

[16]See Peter Lupsha and K. Schlegel, "The Political Economy of Drug Trafficking: The Herrera Organization (Mexico and the United States)" (paper presented at the Latin American Studies Association, Philadelphia, 1979).

[17]This paying off of employees for drug supplies began, according to Joan Moore, in Los Angeles in the 1940s and 1950s (see Moore, *Homeboys*, pp. 78–82).

[18]These gangs can procure fully automatic M-16s, Ingrams, and Uzzis.

[19]Low riders are people, nearly all of whom are of Mexican descent, who drive customized older automobiles (1950s and 1960s models are preferred), one of the characteristics being that the springs for each wheel are cut away so that the car rides very low to the ground. Some of these cars have hydraulic systems that can be inflated at the flip of a switch so that the car can ride low to the ground at one moment and at the normal level the next. For a discussion of the importance of customized automobiles in Los Angeles, especially among Chicano youth, see Schwendinger and Schwendinger, *Adolescent Subcultures and Delinquency*, pp. 234–45.

[20]The El Rukn gang in Chicago was indicted and convicted of contracting with the Libyan government to carry out terrorist acts within the United States. See *Chicago Tribune*, November 3, 4, 6, 7, 1987.

REFERENCES

Cloward, Richard A. and Lloyd B. Ohlin. 1960. *Delinquency and Opportunity: A Theory of Delinquent Gangs.* New York: Free Press.

Cohen, Albert K. 1955. *Delinquent Boys: The Culture of the Gang.* Glencoe, IL: Free Press.

Coleman, Richard P. and Lee Rainwater. 1978. *Social Standing in America: New Dimensions of Class.* New York: Basic Books.

Fagan, Jeffery. 1989. "The Social Organization of Drug Use and Drug Dealing among Urban Gangs." *Criminology* 27, no. 4 (November): 633–70.

Horowitz, Ruth. 1983. *Honor and the American Dream: Culture and Identity in a Chicano Community.* New Brunswick: Rutgers University Press.

Ianni, Francis, A. J. 1974. *Black Mafia: Ethnic Succession in Organized Crime.* New York: Simon & Schuster.

Josephson, Matthew. 1962. *The Robber Barons: The Great American Capitalists, 1861–1901.* New York: Harcourt, Brace & World.

Kornhauser, Ruth Rosner. 1978. *Social Sources of Delinquency: An Appraisal of Analytic Models.* Chicago: University of Chicago Press.

Lupsha, Peter and K. Schlegel. 1979. "The Political Economy of Drug Trafficking: The Herrera Organization (Mexico and the United States)." Paper presented at a meeting of the Latin American Studies Association, Philadelphia.

McClelland, David C. 1961. *The Achieving Society.* New York: Free Press.

Marx, Karl. 1974. *The Economic and Philosophical Manuscripts of 1844.* 4th rev. ed. Moscow: Progress Publishers.

Matza, David. 1990. *Delinquency and Drift.* New Brunswick, NJ: Transaction Books.

Moore, Joan W. 1978. *Homeboys: Gangs, Drugs, and Prisons in the Barrios of Los Angeles.* Philadelphia: Temple University Press.

Rainwater, Lee. 1970. *Behind Ghetto Walls: Black Family Life in a Federal Slum.* Chicago: Aldine Press.

———. 1974. *What Money Buys: Inequality and the Social Meanings of Income.* New York: Basic Books.

Thrasher, Frederic. 1928. *The Gang: A Study of 1303 Gangs in Chicago.* Chicago: University of Chicago Press.

Vigil, James Diego. 1988. *Barrio Gangs: Street Life and Identity in Southern California.* Austin: University of Texas Press.

Weber, Max. 1978. *Economy and Society: An Outline of Interpretive Sociology.* Edited by Guenther Roth and Claus Wittich. Berkeley: University of California Press.

17

SHOPPING AS SYMBOLIC INTERACTION
Race, Class, and Gender
in the Toy Store

CHRISTINE L. WILLIAMS

This reading by Christine Williams, a professor of sociology at the University of Texas at Austin, is taken from Williams' 2006 book, *Inside Toyland: Working, Shopping, and Social Inequality.* As part of her research on the social organization of toy stores, Williams worked as an employee in two toy stores, where she examined the social relationships and social interaction between clerks and customers. Thus, this excerpt illustrates well the social interaction found in secondary relationships. *Secondary relationships* tend to be temporal, less intimate, and more formal than primary relationships. Moreover, secondary relationships are often utilitarian in that they serve some function. Williams discovered that these secondary relationships also reflect and reproduce social inequalities based on race, gender, and social class.

Erving Goffman (1967, 1977) claimed that face-to-face public encounters with strangers typically rely on ritualized scripts to make them go smoothly. In service work, this insight has been transformed into a maxim. Visit McDonald's and you are likely to encounter the "six steps of counter service" (Leidner 1993), beginning with the question "May I take your order please?" and until recently ending with "Do you want to super-size that?" Usually, this scripted server–customer interaction comes off without a hitch. When it does not, the result is often conflict. If customers linger too long over their food order or request some special item not on the menu, they will likely face disapproval, mostly from the customers behind them. Workers who refuse to say their lines will likely be fired.

This approach to understanding service work has been enormously popular and fruitful, especially in the gender literature where the "doing gender" approach (West and Zimmerman 1987), which was influenced by Goffman's theory, has become practically hegemonic. I would argue, however, that Goffman's perspective is limited for reasons that Herbert Blumer (1969) identified years ago. The meanings of these rituals are not self-evident. It is only through a process of symbolic interaction among active, creative, knowledgeable participants that the meanings and consequences of these rituals emerge. This [reading] focuses on the rituals of toy shopping. But it also examines the ongoing innovations, negotiations, and reinterpretations of shopping from the perspective of salesclerks.

I was employed for three months, a total of more than 300 hours, in two large stores that were parts of national chains. One of these stores, which I call Toy Warehouse (all store names have been changed for this [reading]), was a "big box" toy store located in a low-income redevelopment zone. I was one of four white women who worked on the staff of about seventy; most of my coworkers were African American women and men. The other store, which I call Diamond Toys, was in an urban, upscale shopping district that catered to high-income shoppers and tourists. At that store, most of the workers were white; only three African Americans (all women) worked on the staff of about seventy. Latina/os and Asian Americans also worked at these stores, making up about 20 percent of the workforce. This [reading] examines interactions between clerks and customers and discusses the relevance of symbolic interactionism for understanding labor processes.

The [reading] first describes the "rules" governing salesclerks in their interactions with customers at the two toy stores. These "official" rules are formulated by the corporations that own the toy store chains. Second, the [reading] discusses the "ropes," the informal rules that employees devise and follow to ensure order and preserve their self-respect in their interactions with customers. I argue that both the "rules" and the "ropes" take into account the race, gender, and class characteristics of the clerk and the customer. Finally, the [reading] discusses what happens when these formal and informal rules are not followed and interactions break down into conflict. Whether an interaction can be repaired depends on race, class, and gender: because different groups have different resources to draw on to assert their will in the toy store, the resolution of any particular conflict is shaped by social inequality and the creative efforts of the individuals involved.

The Rules: Corporate Culture in Toy Stores

Today, nearly every large store in a specialty area offers the same goods. Because of this, corporations attempt to develop specific "themes" to distinguish themselves from their competitors (Michman and Mazze 2001). Their goal is to entertain as they sell. Thus, toy stores, like other specialty stores, now sell a "mood" in addition to Barbies and Big Wheels.

The corporation that owned the Toy Warehouse wanted its stores to create a fun, family-oriented atmosphere. Sales workers were expected to demonstrate a high degree of spirited enthusiasm. We were required to hand out balloons and stickers to children and sing to them on their birthdays. The name badge I wore proclaimed that I had been "delighting guests since 2001." Like all new employees, I was required on my first morning shift to hula-hoop in front of the staff. All clerks were required to form a gauntlet around the front door when the store opened and applaud the customers as they entered the store, much to their bewilderment.

In giant retail stores, corporate culture is usually communicated to new hires through perfunctory training sessions that last no more than one day. At the Toy Warehouse, our training consisted of watching nine 20-minute videotapes on everything from handling returns to selling the new Game Boy. One videotape showed executives, on stage at a corporate event, leading store directors in group singing and rousing cheers.

Whereas the Toy Warehouse aspired to present an image as an exciting playground for children and their families, Diamond Toys portrayed itself as a high-end specialty store oriented toward meeting the needs of discriminating adult shoppers. The store aimed to flatter the sophisticated tastes of the elite or those who would like to be elite. The very set-up of the store encouraged this aura. Diamond Toys resembled a fancy department store, not a warehouse. A door attendant out front greeted customers. Inside were lavish displays of giant toys with mechanical moving parts. A theme song played in a continuous loop, making me at times feel trapped inside a ride at Disneyland. The store also seemed to have the theme park effect on the many adults and children who stood in awe and marveled at the displays.

We did not have to watch videos during our training at Diamond Toys. Instead, we were issued an employee handbook. The personnel manager, Leslie, took the three new hires to a seminar room and read the entire 30-page document to us. We were invited to interrupt the presentation at any time to ask questions.

Much was said about the dress code. We were required to wear the company-issued maroon polo shirt tucked into belted chino slacks or skirt. Belts had to be black, tan, cordovan, or brown. No outside stitching or pockets were allowed, as this conveyed the look of jeans, which were forbidden. Leslie showed us where the ironing board and iron were kept "just in case" we needed them. We were allowed only two earrings per ear and a single nose stud. No visible tattoos and no unconventional hair color were allowed.

The corporate instruction we received as salesclerks was summed up in the "Five Is of Customer Service." These were: initiate, inquire, inform, include, and into the register. We were told we must initiate contact within thirty seconds with each customer who wandered into our section. The corporation offered some suggestions on the best ways to do this: we might invite them to play with a toy, comment on some article of their clothing ("That's a great Bulls sweatshirt!"), or mention some little known fact about the merchandise ("Did you realize that $99 stuffed animal is 100 percent washable?"). After a successful initiation, we were instructed to try to determine the customer's needs with open-ended questions or remarks, such as "Tell me about the kind of party you are planning." At the "inform" stage we were to match the customer's needs with product features (about which we never received instruction), and at the "include" stage we were to recommend accessories to complement the main purchase (e.g., doll clothes to go with dolls). Our goal was to sell a minimum of two UPTs (units per transaction). We received a printout three times per shift showing us how we were doing.

Thus, the corporate board of Diamond Toys imagined a sales staff of Jeeves-like butlers. Correspondingly, their ideal customer was a member of the bourgeoisie in need of professional consultation on his or her purchases. Oddly, this customer was never shown in the instructional materials. There were no people in the toy catalogs, either; the focus was always on the "special" merchandise we offered.

The Toy Warehouse, on the other hand, was quite explicit about what its ideal customer looks like: she was a middle-class white mother. Several of the videos featured this woman and demonstrated the ways we were supposed to serve her. She usually knew what she wanted (a Game Boy, for instance), but she might need to be told that it required game cartridges, batteries, and a light worm. She did not like to be kept waiting, so we were supposed to work quickly to accommodate her (no lingering over party decorations). My manager, Olive, urged me to treat every woman in the store as if she were my mother. Mothers made the purchasing decisions, she said, so they got the special treatment. Olive said that the average child has $20,000 spent on toys for them before they are eighteen, and the Toy Warehouse wanted to be the place where most of that money was spent.

Advertising displayed in the Toy Warehouse was directed to middle-class families. The store "sponsored" National Day for Children, for example. This was celebrated by posting signs that read "National Day for Children" and putting out a stack of leaflets on a card table that gave "10 reasons to celebrate your child!" Also offered were a college savings plan (which put a small percentage of any purchase in a special account for college tuition), a parenting newsletter, and a summer camp program at which children could be dropped off for a two-hour activity on weekday mornings.

The "child" imagined by the Toy Warehouse's corporate office was thus middle-class and college-bound, from a traditional family where the mother did not work for pay but did all the shopping. Children were expected to have their own ideas about what they want. The store sold "gift cards" to give to children for their birthdays and special occasions. The equivalent of gift certificates, these were little plastic cards that look like credit cards. They were packaged in greeting-card envelopes with a space to write in the child's name and the dollar amount of the gift. At Diamond Toys, in contrast, children were much less central to the marketing agenda. Although they were the intended consumers of most of the merchandise, they were treated more as pampered and coddled pets than as willing and engaged buyers. At Diamond Toys, adults were our primary focus; it was to them that we directed our expert knowledge and solicitous attention. Leslie told us that people came to our store and were willing to pay more because we were "the ultimate toy experts." (In contrast, the Toy Warehouse considered kids to be the ultimate toy experts.) At Diamond Toys, we did not strive to make the shopping experience fun for families; rather, the mood we aspired to set was one of careful and quiet deliberation to assist adults in making a suitable purchase.

How did these corporate expectations play out in practice? In the most obvious sense, they selected for different kinds of customers. Shoppers at the Toy Warehouse represented all levels of the stratification system. I would often marvel at how our "guests" (as we were required to call them) were from every racial-ethnic group and every social class. Rich women with huge diamond rings shopped next to very poor families who were shabbily dressed. Recent immigrants from Africa, India, and Central America were also there, some in traditional clothes. Diamond Toys attracted a more upper-class clientele. It was like a gated community for rich whites. Although the doors opened onto diverse and chaotic urban streets, only the wealthy or the tourist class entered.

But what impact did the corporate rules have on actual interactions between clerks and customers? Retail workers were expected to conform to the corporate culture, but they often developed their own rules for dealing with customers that sometimes clashed with that agenda. I call those rules "the ropes."

The "Ropes": Shop Floor Culture

New hires learned the ropes from observing experienced workers on the shopping floor. One of the first lessons I learned at the Toy Warehouse was that middle-class white women shoppers got whatever they wanted. I suppose that as a middle-class white woman myself, I should have felt empowered by this knowledge. Instead, I have come to understand this preferential treatment as a result of race and class privilege.

Most of the customers at both stores were women. At the Toy Warehouse we were told that women make 90 percent of the purchase decisions, so we were to treat women deferentially. Olive told me that the store abides by the "$19,800 rule." If a customer wanted to return merchandise and it was questionable whether we should take the return (because it had been broken or worn out by the customer, or because the customer had lost the receipt), we should err on the side of the customer. The company was willing to take a $200 loss because doing so might please the customer so much that she would return to the store and spend the rest of the $20,000 on each of her children.

But in my experience, only the white women got this kind of treatment. Not surprisingly, many developed a sense of entitlement and threw fits when they were not accommodated. The following occurred at the Toy Warehouse.

> A white woman in her fifties came into the store to pick up a bike that she had ordered two days previously. She had paid for the bike to be assembled and ready for her to pick up that day. She waited for almost a half hour as we scoured the back room for the bike. We couldn't find it. The woman was getting madder and madder as she waited. There were some other bikes like it that were in boxes and the bike guys offered to assemble one for her but that would have required another wait, so she yelled,

"To hell with it, give me my money back, and I will never ever come to this store again!" She demanded to talk to the manager. Olive tried to appease her by offering her a $25 gift certificate, but she refused and yelled about how terrible we all are. After she left the store Olive called the whole staff up to the service desk and chewed us out. Losing this customer was a really big deal to Olive. (author's field notes)

Middle-class white women had a reputation at the store of being overly demanding and abusive. Susan, a thirty-five-year-old Latina, agreed with my observation that rich white women were the most demanding customers; she said they always demanded to see the manager and they always got mollified. In contrast, African American and Latina/o customers hardly ever complained. If they did complain, she said, they would not get any satisfaction.

Susan's remarks illustrate some of the elaborate stereotypes that service-desk workers used in the course of their daily transactions. Immediate assumptions were made about customers based on their race, gender, and apparent social class; workers responded to customers using these cues. Middle-class white women were the most privileged customers, so not surprisingly, many developed a sense of entitlement. One of the most eye-opening examples of white women's sense of entitlement that I witnessed in the Toy Warehouse was their refusal to check their bags at the counter. Stealing was a big problem in the store, so customers were required to leave all large bags and backpacks at the service desk. A large sign indicating this policy was posted on the store's entrance. The vast majority of customers carrying bags immediately approached the desk to comply with the rule. The exception was white women, who almost universally ignored the sign. When challenged, they would argue, and we would have to insist so as not to appear to be unfair to the other people. I guiltily recognized myself in their behavior. Since then, I always turn over my bag.

White women developed a sense of entitlement because in most instances they got what they wanted. Members of other groups who wanted to return used merchandise, or who needed special consideration, rarely were accommodated. The week before the bike incident, I was working at a cash register that broke down in the middle of a credit card transaction. A middle-class black woman in her forties was buying in-line skates for her ten-year-old daughter. The receipt came out of the register but not the slip for her to sign, so I had to call a manager. Olive came over and explained that the customer needed to go to another register and repeat the transaction, but the customer refused because the sale seemed to go through all right and she did not want to be charged twice. She had to wait over an hour to get this situation resolved, and she was not offered any compensation. She did not yell or make a scene; she acted stoically through the long wait for a resolution. I felt sorry for her. I went over to the service desk to tell a couple of my fellow workers there what was happening, and I said they should just give her the stuff and let her go. My fellow workers thought that was the funniest thing they had ever heard. I asked, "What about Olive's $19,800 rule?" but they just laughed at me. Celeste said, "I want Christine to be the manager, she just lets the customers have whatever they want!

It has been well documented that African Americans suffer discrimination in public places, including stores (Feagin and Sikes 1995). They report that they are followed by security personnel, treated harshly by attendants, and flatly refused service. The flip side of this discrimination is the privilege experienced by middle-class whites. This privilege is not recognized precisely because it is so customary. Whites expect first-rate service; when it is not forthcoming, some feel victimized, even discriminated against. This was especially apparent in the Toy Warehouse, where most of the sales people were black. I noticed that when white women customers were subjected to long waits in line or if they received what they perceived as uncaring attention, they would often sigh loudly, roll their eyes, and try to make eye contact with other whites, looking for a sign of recognition that the service they were receiving was inferior and unfair.

Just as white customers are treated with more respect, so are white service workers, especially by white customers. At the Toy Warehouse, where I was one of only four white women workers, I noticed that shoppers frequently assumed that I was in charge. . . .

In addition . . ., customers at both stores frequently assumed that I was an expert on childhood. This is not an altogether irrational assumption. I was working in a toy store, and I suppose that I looked like a mother with personal experience of children's toys. But I did not have children, and I knew virtually nothing about toys or children's popular culture before I took these jobs. And I was not alone in this. It is important to realize that workers being paid $7.50 an hour do not necessarily have any expertise regarding the merchandise they are selling. We received no training whatsoever. Any advice we gave we literally made up.

At the Toy Warehouse, most customers did not expect elaborate advice from the salesclerks. Anyone who has ever shopped in a big-box store has probably observed workers trying to avoid customers as if they were playing a game of hide-and-seek. Customers have to make a special effort to find a clerk if they need advice. Crossing the floor I would often look down to avoid eye contact with customers either because I was dealing with a previous request or I was trying to make it to the break room for my fifteen-minute rest. Any time we spent interacting with a customer was deducted from our break.

Sometimes worker resistance to customers at the Toy Warehouse was more blatant. In addition to avoidance, we would sometimes perform our role half-heartedly, tell a customer we did not carry a particular toy (even if we did), or palm off a demanding customer on a new or especially eager employee. In the break room we constantly made fun of customers' stupidity and congratulated each other on our ability to control disgusting and hostile shoppers. We also made an art out of ignoring requests.

In contrast, avoiding or ignoring customers was taboo at Diamond Toys. Although we complained about customers in the break room, we never expressed our disdain publicly. At Diamond Toys, our job was to cater to customers. It was not unusual to spend fifteen to twenty minutes assisting a single customer. Customers asked me such questions as "What are going to be the hot toys for one-year-olds this Christmas?" and "What one toy would you recommend for two sisters, aged five and nine?" One mother asked me to help pick out a $58 quartz watch for her seven-year-old son. A personal shopper phoned in and asked me to describe the three Britney Spears dolls we carried, help her pick the "nicest" one, and then arrange to ship it to her employer's niece. Customers also asked detailed questions about how the toys were meant to work, and they were especially curious about comparing the merits of the various educational toys we offered (for example, I was asked to compare the relative merits of the "Baby Mozart" and the "Baby Bach"). . . .

The culture of the stores also reflected race and class dynamics. Diamond Toys embodied whiteness both physically and symbolically; the Toy Warehouse embodied a more diverse, creative, and flamboyant style. This was reflected in our uniforms. The dress code was strictly enforced at Diamond Toys, much to the chagrin of my younger coworkers, who especially hated the belted and tucked-in look. Some tried to subvert it by wearing their pants low on their hips, but this was a minor alteration. I personally thought the uniforms were hideous. I was completely taken aback once when a customer complimented me on how I looked. I was on a ladder retrieving a doll stroller from the valence, and a middle-aged white woman looked up, smiling, and said, "Your uniforms look so nice and comfortable!"

The dress code at Diamond Toys was not unlike the one that many area school districts had recently imposed on elementary and middle-school children, which probably explains my younger coworkers' disdain for them. But why do customers like them? Edward Morris (2005), who has written about school uniforms in minority schools, has argued that a "tucked in shirt" signifies whiteness, middle-class respectability, and a professional demeanor, especially for the middle-class teachers who enforce the dress code. (To the kids, the uniforms evoked prison garb comparisons.) This analysis matches my experience at Diamond Toys, where our uniforms seemed to reassure customers that we were professionals who knew what we were talking about.

At the Toy Warehouse we wore bright orange vests over matching company-issued camp shirts, giving us the look of warehouse attendants. The bright colors were intended, no doubt, to make us easy to spot on the floor. We were allowed to wear black jeans to work. Most of the young men wore fashionable low riders that hung below their underwear and dragged on the floor. The young women wore super skin-tight hip huggers. Because it was summer, we were also given the option to wear shorts. A coworker named Socorro told me that she was not planning to take advantage of that because people did not need to see the tattoos on her calves. Most of my other coworkers were only too eager to show off their art, as they called it. The younger ones had multiple piercings, including tongue studs. Careful attention was also paid to hairstyles—the more outrageous and intricate the better. Most men and women wore very elaborate and intricate hair designs incorporating dyeing, shaving, sculpting, braiding, and extensions.

White customers at the Toy Warehouse seemed frequently unnerved by their interactions with the clerks in the store. I recall one time when a white woman customer stopped my coworker Gail to ask for a gift suggestion for a ten-year-old boy. Gail, who was swiftly walking across the floor to deal with another customer's request, practically shouted at her, "Don't ask me about no boys; I got girls, not sons!" and then she took off. The white woman looked startled at the response. What she did not know was that Gail found a coworker who had sons to answer the woman's question. The caring, efficiency, and sense of humor of my coworkers at the Toy Warehouse often went unnoticed by white customers.

Realizing that white customers in particular treated them with disrespect and even disdain, my African American coworkers developed interactional skills to minimize their involvement with them. I noticed at the service desk that the black women who worked there did not smile or act concerned when customers came up for complaints or returns. They did their work well and efficiently, but they did not exude a sense that they really cared. Rather, they looked suspicious, or bored, or resigned, or even a little miffed. Over time I learned that this attitude of ennui or suspicion was cultivated as a way to garner respect for the work. It was saying, "This isn't my problem, it's your problem, but I will see what can be done to fix it." If workers were more enthusiastic and it turned out the problem could not be fixed, they would look incompetent, which was the assumption that too many white customers were willing to make of black women. So those workers made it appear that the problem was insurmountable and when they did resolve it (which was most of the time), they garnered a little bit of respect. But it was at the cost of appearing unfriendly, so the store received negative customer-service evaluations.

With experience, I developed my own set of facial gestures and attitudes to manage customers. At the cash register, I learned to look cheerful, unless there was a void and I had to wait for a manager to respond to a page, in which case I became expressionless and looked off to the distance, like a computer in shut-down mode. If I acted impatient, I learned, the customers would become impatient. At the service desk, where customers returned or exchanged merchandise, I learned to act like a student. To get a refund, customers had to explain what the problem was. I found that the best technique to do this work effectively was to bow my head a little, but raise my eyebrows and look into the eyes of the customer. No smiling and no frowning. This made me look a little skeptical, but also subservient. It also made me look stupid. I had to listen to the stories but not act as if I cared or was interested and then efficiently process the request. If they requested something that was against store policy, I just had to report that, without sounding apologetic or giving the impression that the rule was wrong. "That's just the rule, it's store policy, no exceptions." If they argued, I would call a manager.

This kind of affectless performance kept customers under control and less likely to be insulting or to make a scene.

Manipulating customers through self-presentation constitutes an informal "feeling rule" (Hochschild 1983). These techniques for displaying affect were developed by workers to manage and minimize difficult customer interactions. I call them informal rules because management would have preferred that we always conveyed serious concern and solicitude, but workers at the Toy Warehouse knew that would only spell trouble. Moreover, the informal rules were sensitive to race and gender dynamics in a way that management rules could not be. The fact is that different groups had to use different means to assert themselves and their interests, and the stratification of the jobs at the store meant that we all had different levels of formal and informal power to resolve situations. White men had the most institutionalized power and authority in the stores. The store directors in both places where I worked were white men who could and did trump any decision made by managers or sales associates. Sales associates had severely limited options for resolving disputes, owing in large part to surveillance mechanisms intended to keep us from stealing. But maintaining control was also dependent on the race and gender of both workers and customers.

Interaction Breakdown: Social Control in the Toy Store

It may seem incongruous to talk about power and control in the context of toy shopping. But customers frequently misbehave in stores. In addition to seeing customers throwing fits at the service desk, every day I witnessed customers ripping open packages, hiding garbage, spilling soft drinks, and generally making a mess of the store.

As a middle-aged white woman, I could exercise some control over the extremes of this bad behavior. I could stand nearby, for example, and the customers might notice me and guiltily try to stuff the toy back into the box or replace the dozen toys they had pulled off the shelf. We were not allowed to confront customers, even if we suspected them of stealing or destroying the merchandise, but we were expected to develop subtle ways to control them. I could not do this as well as my male coworkers could, but I was definitely more respected (and feared) than my women coworkers who were African American, Asian American, and Latina.

One example of this involved two of my African American coworkers at the Toy Warehouse. One night, the store had officially closed but I was still at my register. I saw Selma, an African American woman in her late forties, and told her that there were still people in the store shopping. She went to clear them out, saying, "We're closed, you must leave now, the registers are closing down!" I walked over to the service desk to close out my register and I saw Selma and Doris, the night manager (an African American woman in her fifties), escorting some white people out. Later, when I was being audited in the manager's office, Selma came in very upset because the woman she and

Doris escorted out spat out her chewing gum at Selma. Doris and Selma were appalled. Doris had said to them, "That is really disgusting, how could you do that?" And the woman said to Doris, "What is your name?"—as if she intended to report her. This angered Selma so much that she said, "If you take her name, take mine too," and showed her name tag. Selma told the woman that she was never invited back to this store. Selma was very distressed. She knew she could be fired for what she said. I sensed it was doubly humiliating to have to be concerned that she would be punished for talking back to a white woman who spat at her.

I did not have too much trouble controlling white women. The customers that I had the hardest time controlling were men. Men were outnumbered by women in both stores. At the Toy Warehouse, I saw them mostly on the weekends, which seemed to be the most popular time for fathers to come in with their children. At Diamond Toys, I observed men tourists shopping with their families, businessmen buying small gifts for their children back home, and during the Christmas season, men buying high-end toys for their wives. In general men seemed to be annoyed to be in the stores, and they sometimes acted annoyed with me, especially when unaccompanied by women. One white man at the Toy Warehouse tossed his shopping list at me when I was working at the service desk. He expected me to assemble the items for him or to get someone else to do it. Some men were just mean. On two occasions, men demanded to use my telephone, against which there were strict rules. I said they were not allowed to use it, and they just reached over the counter and did it anyway. I was terrified that my manager would walk by and yell at me, maybe even fire me. On another occasion at Diamond Toys, a business professor in town for a conference was upset because a Barney sippy cup he wanted to buy was missing its price tag and I could not find it listed in the store inventory. He made me call over the store director and subjected both of us to a critique of store operations, which he threatened to submit for publication to a business journal unless we sold him the sippy cup.

The sense of entitlement I observed in these men customers was different from that which I observed in white women. Perhaps the expectation that shopping was "women's work" made these men feel entitled to make me do their shopping for them or reorganize the store to make it more convenient for them. To assert masculinity while engaging in this otherwise feminine activity seemed to require them to disrupt the routinized clerk–customer relationship.

In an extreme manifestation of this shopping masculinity, on three occasions (all at the Toy Warehouse), men threw things in my direction. Once a male customer threw a toy that struck me on the head. The customer was a young African American, maybe thirty years old. . . . [He] was yelling at Jack [the store manager], using swear words. "Fuck this shit, I don't give a damn!" Jack was trying to calm him down, "Please do not use that language, sir, this is a toy store." The customer was so angry that he threw the toy on the counter, accidentally dislodging the phone, which came flying toward me, hitting me on the left side of my face and neck. I shrieked as I fell to the floor, and I thought I might cry. Jack said to Leticia, "Call the police *now.*" The man started to walk toward the exit, but first he said loudly, "If I don't get a cash refund, my kids won't eat tonight," and he left the store (without his toy). . . .

Jack was not the only one who threatened to call the police when black men customers became angry in the store. I noticed that this particular strategy for control was also used by the African American women supervisors and manager at the Toy Warehouse.

African American shoppers sometimes resisted what they apparently perceived as discriminatory treatment, which is in keeping with the long tradition of black protest against racism in stores (Cohen 2003; Weems 1998). Some black customers were quick to speak out if they felt subjected to unfair or unequal treatment, including one who accused me of racism for not helping another black customer (I was not sure that she accepted my explanation). The rules of shopping are subject to constant negotiation and rewriting.

Conclusion

As a nation of consumers, we spend a great deal of our time in stores interacting with sales workers. In this [reading], I have tried to make a case for paying attention to these interactions as sites for the reproduction of social inequality.

In particular, I have argued that how we shop is shaped by and bolsters race, class, and gender inequalities. I have emphasized three dimensions of this process. First, corporations script the customer–server interaction in ways that are designed to appeal to a particular kind of customer. The fun, child-centered Toy Warehouse was designed to appeal to middle-class white women. The sophisticated and discriminating Diamond Toys was designed to appeal to an upper-class clientele. These rules influenced who entered the stores as customers and also shaped the hiring practices in the two stores. The Toy Warehouse was a dazzling mix of customers catered to by a staff of mostly African American workers, whereas Diamond Toys hired mainly whites to serve a mostly white, well-to-do clientele.

Second, actual interactions between clerks and customers stray from these ideal rituals in ways that take into account the social inequalities of race, class, and gender. Both clerks and customers drew on elaborate stereotypes in crafting their working and shopping practices. White customers received preferential treatment, and many developed a sense of entitlement because of this. Similarly, white workers were treated with more deference and respect, particularly by white shoppers. African American and Latina/o workers developed elaborate strategies to protect their self-respect in the face of this white privilege.

Third, when interactions break down, the ability to repair them depends on how the characteristics of the customer and the worker are interpreted. As a white woman I had a different repertoire of control strategies than my African American women coworkers. They had to reckon with racist as well as sexist assumptions from irate white customers, whereas most of my difficulties were due to customer sexism. White men had more power in the stores, but they seemed to have difficulty managing and controlling black customers, in particular, black men. Control is an achievement that must be negotiated anew with each service interaction.

Herbert Blumer (1969) wrote that people act toward things on the basis of the meanings that they give to them, and further, that those meanings arise in the course of interactions. The meanings of race, class, and gender are not given in the rituals handed down by management, nor are they brought into the store ready-made by the clerks and customers possessing these discrete demographic characteristics. Rather, they derive their meaning and significance through interactions that are the creative products of interpretive acts by individuals.

The theory of symbolic interactionism is useful for understanding race, class, and gender on the shopping floor. Moreover, in my view, this is a hopeful approach to analyzing the reproduction of inequalities: there is nothing inevitable about the ways that shopping interactions proceed on a daily basis. Because they are symbolically created, they can be recreated to lessen the social inequalities that they currently reproduce.

Author's Note: This article is drawn from a chapter in my book, *Inside Toyland: Working, Shopping, and Social Inequality* (University of California Press, 2006). Many thanks to Sherryl Kleinman for inviting me to deliver the Distinguished Lecture to the Society for the Study of Symbolic Interaction (SSSI). I am also grateful to Jessica Fields, and to the other members of SSSI who attended the talk and gave me valuable feedback. And thanks especially to editor Simon Gottschalk for his patience and support.

REFERENCES

Blumer, Herbert. 1969. *Symbolic Interactionism.* Berkeley: University of California Press.

Cohen, Lizabeth. 2003. A *Consumers' Republic: The Politics of Mass Consumption in Postwar America.* New York: Knopf.

Feagin, Joe and Melvin Sikes. 1995. *Living with Racism: The Black Middle Class Experience.* New York: Beacon.

Goffman, Erving. 1967. *Interaction Ritual: Essays on Face to Face Behavior.* Garden City, NY: Anchor.

———. 1977. "The Arrangement between the Sexes." *Theory and Society* 4:301–31.

Hochschild, Arlie. 1983. *The Managed Heart.* Berkeley: University of California Press.

Leidner, Robin. 1993. *Fast Food, Fast Talk: Service Work and the Routinization of Everyday Life.* Berkeley: University of California Press.

Michman, Ronald D. and Edward M. Mazze. 2001. *Specialty Retailers—Marketing Triumphs and Blunders.* Westport, CT: Quorum.

Morris, Edward. 2005. *An Unexpected Minority: White Kids in an Urban School.* New Brunswick, NJ: Rutgers University Press.

Weems, Robert E. 1998. *Desegregating the Dollar: African American Consumerism in the Twentieth Century.* New York: New York University Press.

West, Candace and Don Zimmerman. 1987. "Doing Gender." *Gender & Society* 1:125–51.

18

DESCENT INTO MADNESS
The New Mexico State Prison Riot

MARK COLVIN

Prisons are another type of social structure often studied by sociologists. This selection by Mark Colvin, a professor of sociology in the Department of Justice Studies at Kent State University, is written as the introduction to the 1997 book *Descent into Madness: An Inmate's Experience of the New Mexico State Prison Riot* by Mike Rolland. Colvin was hired by New Mexico's Office of the Attorney General to help with the investigation into the events and causes of the 1980 riot at the Penitentiary of New Mexico. In the excerpt that follows, Colvin provides important insights into the history and social structure of the prison and how the breakdown in that social structure enabled violence and disorganization to occur.

The riot at the Penitentiary of New Mexico (PNM) on February 2 and 3, 1980, is without parallel for its violence, destruction, and disorganization. During the 36 hours of the riot, 33 inmates were killed by other inmates; many of the victims were tortured and mutilated. (A 34th inmate died several months later from injuries he received during the riot.) As many as 200 inmates were severely injured from beatings, stabbings, and rapes. Many more suffered less serious injuries. In addition, scores of inmates were treated for overdoses of drugs taken from the prison's pharmacy during the riot. That more inmates did not die can be attributed to the dedicated work of medical personnel and emergency crews who treated the injured and transported them to local hospitals. In fact, many inmates were later surprised to learn of riot survivors whom they thought had certainly died during the event.

Seven of the 12 correctional officers who were taken hostage were beaten, stabbed, or sodomized. None of the hostages were killed. Some of the guard hostages were protected by small groups of inmates during the riot. A few hostages were even assisted in leaving the prison during the riot by sympathetic inmates.

Correctional officers and many more inmates would have certainly died in the riot had it not been for heroic efforts of some prisoners who risked their lives to save others from harm. Indeed, this prison riot brought out not only the evil potential of human beings (upon which we tend to focus after such an event) but also the potential for virtue. We are quick to condemn the evil acts and use these as an excuse to label all prisoners as "animals." But to do so is to ignore the acts of kindness and courage displayed by many inmates; to ignore the fact that the overwhelming majority of inmates only wanted to escape the mayhem, the violence, and the fear; and to ignore the essential humanity of the great majority of the people we lock up in prisons. Focusing on the evil acts of those few prisoners who engaged in them also distracts us from the evil of a taxpayer-supported prison system that produces events like the New Mexico State Prison riot.

The riot caused $20 million in physical damage to the institution. Fires were started throughout the prison, and water flooded the prison water mains. More than $200 million in riot-related expenses were incurred by the state for medical, police, fire, and national guard response, lawsuits for injuries and wrongful death, transportation of inmates to federal and other state prison systems, prosecutions of crimes committed during the riot, and official investigations of the events and causes of the riot.

The official investigation of the riot was headed by then-Attorney General of New Mexico Jeff Bingaman. I was hired by the Attorney General as a principal researcher for the riot investigation. In that role, I, along with the riot investigation team, conducted more than 300 in-depth interviews with former and then-current prisoners, correctional officers, and corrections officials in an attempt to reconstruct the events of the riot and understand its long-term causes and effects. The riot investigation presented its findings and conclusions in a two-part report (Office of the Attorney General 1980a,b). More recently, I published a book that presents a detailed social and organizational history of the Penitentiary of New Mexico State Prison leading up to this riot (Colvin 1992). . . .

In this introduction, I hope to provide the reader with a context for understanding . . . the New Mexico State Prison riot. It is important to understand the history of this prison, since it was not always a violent and disorderly institution. It was only in the three to four years preceding the riot that the prison had moved toward becoming the type of violent and disorganized organization that could produce an event as brutal as the 1980 riot. . . .

Background of the Riot

The 1980 New Mexico State Prison riot stands in stark contrast to the 1971 Attica prison riot. At Attica, after a few hours of chaos and destruction in which three inmates were killed by other inmates, inmate leaders were able to take command of rioting inmates and turn the event into an organized protest about prison conditions; after that point, no other deaths occurred until state authorities violently retook the prison, killing 29 inmates and 10 guard hostages in the process (Wicker 1975). At New Mexico, inmate leaders, to the extent that there were any, were unable to organize inmates or stop the inmate-on-inmate violence. All inmates were killed by other inmates. No one was killed when state authorities retook the prison. The disorganization of the riot and the inmate-on-inmate killings, and the brutality of many of these killings, are what distinguish the New Mexico State Prison riot.

As stated, the Penitentiary of New Mexico (PNM) was not always a violent, disorganized prison. In fact, on July 14, 1976, inmates at this prison staged a well-organized, peaceful protest of prison conditions. In the previous six months, a new prison administration had begun dismantling prison programs and reducing inmate privileges. The curtailment of programs and special privileges soon led to an open confrontation between the new prison administration and inmates. Prisoners organized a massive sit-down strike in which nearly 800 of the prison's 912 inmates refused to leave their living quarters for work or meals. The level of participation in this 1976 strike demonstrated a high degree of solidarity and cooperation among inmates. There was no violence among inmates during this event. (In fact, no inmate had been killed by another inmate at this prison since before 1970.) The prison administration's response to this June 1976 inmate strike inaugurated a new era in staff and inmate relations and in relations among inmates. It was a new era characterized by coercion and violence.

The strike was broken by the staff with violence. Housing units were teargassed and many inmates were forced to run a gauntlet of prison staff members who were armed with ax handles (Office of the Attorney General 1980b; Colvin 1992). Leaders of the strike were identified and segregated or transferred out of state. The stable inmate leadership, which had been the impetus for inmate social cohesion, was thus systematically eliminated. The prison staff, after this point, began to rely increasingly on coercion to maintain control of the institution. The "hole," which had been closed since 1968, was reopened and used frequently; the number of inmates in disciplinary segregation grew substantially (from less than 5 percent of the inmate population before June 1976 to as much as 25 percent of the inmate population after June 1976).

As this crackdown on organized inmate activity continued at the prison, the corrections department was undergoing rapid and confusing organizational changes. Turnover in the state's top corrections post occurred repeatedly, with five different heads of the corrections department between 1975 and 1980. A similar turnover in the warden's position took place, with five penitentiary wardens between 1975 and 1980. This administrative confusion resulted in inconsistent policy directives from the top of the organization and in the emergency of a middle-level clique of administrators who were virtually unaccountable to anyone in authority. This clique of administrators, by the middle of 1978, had been left to run the prison in any fashion they saw fit.

Under this middle-level clique, there were growing inconsistencies in both security procedures and discipline of inmates. Some shift supervisors followed very closely the proper security procedures; others did not follow them at all. Lax security had long been a problem at PNM, but the tendency toward inconsistency in security operations worsened after 1978 when various shift supervisors ran the prison at their own discretion. Similar problems of inconsistency in discipline were also evident. Some shift captains would enforce rules, at times inappropriately placing inmates in the "hole" for minor violations, while other shift captains would fail to punish some major violations of rules. Consistency in operation and a set routine provides stability for an institution. At PNM, it was difficult for inmates to calculate which behaviors would be punished or when they would be punished. Inmates were thus kept off balance.

This inconsistency by the prison staff was often interpreted by inmates as blatant harassment. In some cases, correctional officers, including some lieutenants and captains, were caught up in a game of mutual harassment with inmates. The game proceeded through interactions in which an officer would verbally humiliate an inmate and the inmate would respond in kind. Often this led to confrontations in which the inmate was led off to disciplinary segregation. The minority of prison officers who engaged in these activities poisoned relations between the staff and inmates and created enormous hostility.

As the middle-level administrators gained dominance after 1978, a new coercive "snitch system" emerged. This system had its roots in the aftermath of the June 1976 inmate strike when staff members attempted to identify the strike leaders. Inmates were threatened with disciplinary lockup if they did not identify strike participants and leaders. By 1978, these tactics had become a key aspect of the institution's inmate control system. Since inmates were not forthcoming with voluntary information, many members of the correctional staff began soliciting information through threats and promises. Inmates were promised early parole consideration, protection, and transfer to minimum-security institutions. They were also threatened with being locked up in disciplinary segregation or, in other cases, were refused protective custody if they did not inform. Another coercive tactic was to intimidate an inmate by threatening to "hang a snitch jacket" on him. This tactic, which involved the threat of labeling an inmate a "snitch" (or informant) was used to solicit information, gain control over an inmate, and, in some instances, retaliate against an inmate.

This came to be known as the "snitch game." The "snitch game" had the effect of breaking apart any sense of inmate solidarity. As the official report (Office of the Attorney General 1980b:24–25) on the riot maintained:

> The "snitch game" . . . create[d] suspicion and antagonism among inmates. "You can't even trust your old friends," was a sentiment voiced by several inmates. Inmate opinions of "snitches" included this often-repeated characterization, "It's just like in a war. You're all on the same side. It's us (inmates) against them (guards). And it's the same mentality. If you cross to the other side, you're no more, no less than a traitor and a spy." In the late '70s, correctional staff's increased use of the "snitch game" for information promoted enmity among inmates. In fact, some

prison staff attempted to use the hatred which the snitch game created in the inmate society as a means of controlling inmates. In order to coerce particular information from an inmate, some staff members threatened to tell other inmates that he was a snitch. The inmate would usually capitulate, knowing the consequences of wearing a "snitch jacket." The consequences could be severe. First, snitches became more easily identifiable because a few guards were reckless or careless about protecting the identify of inmates who provided information. . . . Inmates also knew that the prison increasingly used Cellblock 4 as a place to house and to protect "snitches" after they were "used up." Second, inmates and staff attributed some of the increase in violence during the late '70s to the motivation for revenge against "snitches." This vengeful violence reached its horrible climax in the 1980 riot.

Some inmates labeled as "snitches" may not have been informants at all. Correctional officers discussed with Attorney General investigators the labeling of inmates as "snitches" as a coercive tactic (quoted in Colvin 1992:154).

> Correctional Officer: *If I was a guard and he was an inmate and I didn't like him, I'd punch him around and say, "Hey, man, let's put a snitch jacket on this guy." And another inmate come up behind me and I'd say, "Hey man, this dude dropped a dime on this guy over here." They'll put a "jacket" on you and life expectancy with a "jacket" on you isn't too long. And that's what [gives names of several PNM administrators, captains, and lieutenants] all of them would do. If they didn't like you, they'd put a jacket on you, plain and simple. . . . I caught [name of correctional officer] lying about another inmate to four or five inmates and the other inmates turned around and looked at him and said, "We'll take care of this."*
>
> Interviewer: What was the purpose of doing this?
>
> Correctional Officer: *To get even . . . If I was to walk up to an inmate and just started kicking the hell out of him, I would have a lawsuit on me, but what goes on behind closed doors, only the inmates know.*

Whether an inmate had actually been an informant or not, the label of "snitch" could have deadly consequences, a fact that was used to intimidate inmates and create friction among prisoners. After inmate solidarity displayed during the June 1976 strike moved the prison administration to smash inmate organization and leadership, the inmate society became more fragmented and violent. From 1969 through July 1976 there were no killings at PNM, no prison officers were attacked, and inmate fights and sexual assaults were rare. From August 1976 to January 1980, six inmates were killed by other inmates, several attacks on prison officers occurred, and fighting among inmates became routine. And sexual assaults, by the late 1970s, had become so routine that there was "at least one reported case a day [and] 10 to 15 more nonreported cases daily" (*Albuquerque Journal*, 9/16/79:B1).

The administration's tactics for breaking up inmate solidarity led to a series of changes within the inmate society that spawned violence and disorder. As inmate groups broke down into small, self-protective cliques, forces within the inmate society that formerly were capable of holding back disorder and violence among inmates diminished. The lack of inmate leaders in the late 1970s meant that new inmates entering PNM were no longer under the restraints of an established order among inmates. Inmates could no longer socialize new arrivals to the increasingly unstable environment. Some of the new inmates directly challenged the power and control exercised by older inmates who had not already been removed by the administration.

While many observers relate the growing inmate violence to newly arriving inmates, it does not appear that the violent behavior was being imported from outside. Rather, new inmates, as never before, were entering a disorganized social situation with undefined roles and lack of leadership. As they confronted, and were confronted by, this increasingly chaotic situation, many of the new inmates resorted to violence. That the violence was not imported from outside is supported by data on inmates' convictions. In 1970, 45 percent of all crimes for which New Mexico prisoners were convicted were violent crimes. By 1975, the figure had dropped to 38 percent, and by 1979 it was 33 percent (Department of Corrections 1971, 1976, 1980). Also, a profile of PNM inmates compiled in 1977 (when the inmate violence began increasing dramatically) by consultants for the New Mexico Corrections Master Plan indicated that in comparison to national averages, PNM inmates were relatively nonviolent and unsophisticated in the criminal activity that led to their convictions (Governor's Council on Criminal Justice Planning 1978).

Rather than importing the violence, inmates were becoming more violent in reaction to a prison social structure that elicited such a response. With a paucity of inmate leaders to guide and ease the transition to prison life for younger inmates, these new inmates were left to their own devices to deal with the fear of assault. By 1978, the fear of being assaulted, especially of being sexually attacked, had become a prevalent feature of inmate life, especially for younger inmates. These new inmates were faced with a deadly dilemma that increasingly set the tone of inmate relations in the late 1970s. The fear created by violent confrontations, or by the mere anticipation of them, produced inmates who either submitted to the exploitation of other inmates (became "punks"), sought protection from officials (became "snitches"), or fought (to prove themselves as "good people" to other inmates by developing a reputation as violent). Most inmates agreed that the only rational choice when faced with the irrational confrontation of a sexual assault was to fight viciously and develop a reputation as someone who others "did not mess with." The other choices, submission or official protection, would lead to a prison experience of perpetual victimization.

In the late 1970s, confrontational situations among inmates sharply increased, forcing more inmates into the deadly dilemma of choosing a course

of action against assaults. Some submitted and were marked as punks or homosexuals. This submission did not label them necessarily as sexual deviants
but, more importantly, as "morally weak" individuals who would not stand
up for themselves. Inmates who chose to seek protective custody, who in the
inmates' vocabulary "pc'd up," were also seen as "weak" inmates who could
not withstand the pressures of prison life. Added to being marked as weak
was the stigma of being a snitch, since it was widely believed among inmates
(though by no means always true) that protective custody was a payoff for
informing. For "regular" inmates who were "on line" standing up for themselves in the daily battles with other inmates and the prison staff, an inmate
who gives in to pressure from other inmates by not standing up for himself,
and then gives in to pressure from the administration by informing, was
truly a person of "weak moral character." A snitch label (whether deserved
or not) thus implies the weakest of inmates who were so low as to sell out
their fellow inmates because of fear and intimidation. These inmates were
allowing both other inmates *and* the administration to humiliate them.
Succumbing to other people's attempts at humiliation is the worst possible
fate for a convict (Abbott 1981). Fear of humiliation drove much of the violence
in the inmate society. Violent confrontations were events in which inmates'
characters ("weak" or "strong") were being tested. They were also situations
in which reputations for violence were being built.

Developing a reputation for violence became a full-time activity as a
growing number of inmates were confronted by the prison's deadly dilemma. As inmates vied for violent reputations, the number of confrontational
incidents between inmates increased. This competition for violent reputations accelerated the cycle of confrontations and produced a growing number of both violence-prone inmates and those who were perceived as weak.
Under these circumstances, the struggle involved in relegating inmates to
the roles of victims or victimizers became a monotonous, horrifying, daily
occurrence.

The violence led to further fragmentation of the inmate society. Inmates
increasingly formed into small cliques for self-protection. These cliques did
not constitute the types of gang structures witnessed in other prisons (Irwin
1980; Jacobs 1977). For the most part, these cliques were very loosely organized groupings that provided inmates small, often temporary, "ecological
niches" (Hagel-Seymour 1988) relatively free from the violence of the prison.

Some inmate groups began to emerge as influential in 1978. The ACLU
lawsuit against PNM (*Duran v. Apodaca*) gave a few Chicano inmates a limited leadership role within some inmate factions. These inmates were
directly involved in negotiations for settlement of the lawsuit. But this leadership role was diminishing by late 1979 as the negotiations in the lawsuit
bogged down because of disagreements among state officials over issues involved in the lawsuit. Inmates, generally, began to perceive little gain from
the lawsuit and the inmates involved in it began to lose influence.

Other inmate cliques gained power by 1978 because of their violent reputations. In 1976 and 1977, Anglo convicts were very disorganized and were

regularly attacked by Chicano inmates. Then, some strong Anglo cliques began to surface in 1977. One of the more notorious cliques was associated with three Anglo inmates who, on April 16, 1978, beat another Anglo inmate to death with a baseball bat for allegedly being a snitch. This clique emerged as an important power that struggled with other inmate cliques for dominance.

The inmates caught up in the competition for dominance and violent reputations composed PNM's hardcore cliques. While the total number of inmates involved in these hardcore cliques was about 150 of the more than 1,000 inmates in the prison, their behavior and disruptiveness set the tone for inmate social relations. In stark contrast to the early 1970s, when inmate leaders helped keep the lid on violence among inmates, inmate leadership, to the extent that it existed at all, fell by 1979 to these small, hardcore cliques of inmates who actively engaged in violence and disruption. These hardcore cliques, produced inadvertently by the administration's coercive tactics used to break up inmate solidarity, were leading the inmate society toward an implosion of violence. Inmate solidarity had indeed been eliminated by 1980. But the administration's control of the prison was now more precarious than ever. Their coercive tactics, including use of the "snitch game," produced a fragmented inmate society that promoted inmate-on-inmate violence. The riot that exploded at 1:40 A.M. on February 2, 1980, would reflect this fragmented inmate society and the coercive tactics of control that produced an inmate society.

Overview of the 1980 Riot at the Penitentiary of New Mexico

There were a number of forewarnings that a major disturbance was imminent, yet no decisive actions were taken. Forewarnings included a mix of rumors and intelligence, none of which could be confirmed. Officials had no way to distinguish reliable from unreliable information, a legacy of the coercive snitch system which often resulted in inmates telling officials anything (whether true or not) to escape punishment or receive protection. As it turned out, among the many rumors was one specific bit of information, concerning a possible hostage-taking, that was an accurate forewarning.

Shortly after midnight, on February 2, 1980, the evening and morning shifts completed a count of inmates in the institution, which held 1,157 inmates that night, including 34 in a modular unit outside the main penitentiary building. All inmates were accounted for at the time of the count. About 1 A.M., two groups composed of four correctional officers each began a routine check of all cellhouses and dormitories in the south wing of the prison. At 1:40 A.M., one group, which included the shift captain, entered Dorm E-2, the upstairs dormitory in the E-wing.

Inmates in Dorm E-2 had been drinking "home brew" made of yeast and raisins smuggled in from the prison's kitchen. The inmates, sometime between 12:30 A.M. and 1:15 A.M., had hastily agreed upon a plan to jump the guards during their routine check of the dorm. It was not clear whether the plan included an attempt to exit the dormitory. Hostages would be taken in the dormitory; and if the entry door could be successfully jumped, additional hostages would be taken in the south wing of the prison. Beyond the plan to take some guards hostage, the inmates had no idea of what they would do next.

At 1:40 A.M., the dormitory door and the three officers who had just entered Dorm E-2 were jumped simultaneously. Inmates quickly overpowered the officer at the door and the other officers inside the dormitory. The guard at the door had the keys to other dormitories. Four hostages were then under the control of these inmates, who now had access to the main corridor.

At 1:45 A.M., inmates from Dorm E-2 jumped the officer outside Dorm F-2, seized the keys he held to other dormitories, and captured two other guards who were just entering Dorm F-2. A third guard, who had just entered the dorm, ran into the dayroom at the opposite end of the dorm; he was protected by some sympathetic Dorm F-2 inmates, who later helped him escape the prison. Total hostages were now eight, including the protected guard in the Dorm F-2 dayroom.

By 1:50 A.M., hundreds of inmates were milling around the main corridor in the south wing of the prison. At 1:57 A.M., two guards leaving the officers' mess hall, located in the central area of the institution, saw inmates beating and dragging a naked man (later identified as a hostage guard) up the south corridor toward the grill that separated the south wing from the central area of the prison. They also noticed that this corridor grill, contrary to prison policy, was open. Inmates were about to come through the opened grill. The two guards then raced north up the main corridor, passing the control center and entering the north wing of the prison, closing the corridor grill to the north wing behind them. Soon, scores of inmates were in front of the control center, which was separated from the rioters by what was supposed to be "shatterproof" glass. Inmates used a metal-canister fire extinguisher, pulled from the wall in the main corridor, to break the control center glass. The control center officers ran toward the front entrance of the prison and to the safety of the Tower 1 gatehouse. The inmates entered the control center through the smashed window and trashed its interior, sending keys flying in all directions from the key pegboards.

By 2:02 A.M., inmates had gained access to the north wing and to the administration wing, since the grills to these areas were opened electronically from the control center. It took the inmates time to find keys to specific cellblocks since keys were scattered by those inmates who first breached the control center, which indicates the unplanned nature of the takeover. But by 3 A.M., inmates had found the key to the disciplinary unit, Cellblock 3. Here they captured three more correctional officers, bringing the total to 11 hostages. (By this point, two guards had hidden themselves in the crawl space in the basement of Cellblock 5, where they remained undetected by rioters throughout the riot. And the hospital technician locked himself and seven inmate-patients into the upstairs floor of the Hospital Unit, where they also remained undetected until the riot was over.)

The first inmate killings during the riot occurred in Cellblock 3 at about 3:15 A.M. An inmate, shouting in Spanish, "No era yo. No lo hice." ("It wasn't me. I didn't do it.") was beaten, tortured, and mutilated. This inmate was assumed to have informed on other inmates who were also locked in the disciplinary unit. Another inmate, who was mentally disturbed and apparently had kept other Cellblock 3 inmates awake at night with his screams, was shot in the head at close range with a canister fired from a teargas launcher taken from the control center.

At about the same time, another group of inmates had found keys to the prison pharmacy, located on the first floor of the Hospital Unit. The pharmacy contained narcotics, barbiturates, and sedatives, which were ingested in massive doses by inmates throughout the riot.

Other inmates in the early morning hours of the first day of the riot found keys to the basement area of the prison, below the kitchen. Here they retrieved an acetylene blowtorch that was used at about 3:15 A.M. to open the far south corridor grill, leading to the Educational Unit and Dorm D-1, which contained the twelfth (and last) guard to be taken hostage. This blowtorch was later taken to the other end of the prison to open the far north corridor grill and Cellblock 5. Cellblock 5 was vacant due to renovation. But construction crews had left in the Cellhouse 2 additional acetylene torches. Later, these blowtorches would be used to open Cellblock 4, the Protective Custody unit.

The period between 3 A.M. and 7 A.M. was characterized by chaos, infighting, and violence. There was no leadership throughout the riot. Inmates' actions were completely uncoordinated. Some inmates were setting fires in the administrative offices, others in the Psychological Unit. At certain points, inmates manning walkie-talkies radioed for firefighting crews to come into the prison; when firefighters approached the prison they were driven back by other inmates who threw debris at them. Other inmates were fighting, forming into groups for self-protection, or hiding in fear.

While all these uncoordinated activities and fighting were going on during the early hours of the riot, a few inmates who had been released from Cellblock 3 and Cellhouse 6 discussed organizing the riot into a protest against the administration. These inmates included those involved in the ACLU lawsuit (*Duran v. Apodaca*). They managed in the early hours of the riot to get control of the three hostages captured in Cellblock 3. However, they were able to gain control of only one of the other nine hostages. The other hostages were being held by various groups in the south wing of the institution. A few were held by sympathetic inmates who protected them. The shift captain was moved frequently and may have been under the control of different groups throughout the riot, some of whom beat him mercilessly, others of whom tended to his wounds and protected him. Unlike the three hostages who were captured in Cellblock 3, who were treated relatively well for the remainder of the riot, many of the hostages held in the south wing of the prison were beaten, stabbed, and sodomized.

The Cellblock 3 and Cellhouse 6 inmates who were attempting to organize the riot into a protest had little influence on the behavior of the rioting inmates. One inmate, who identified himself as a leader in this attempt to turn the riot into a protest, said:

> *There were a few of us in here that were trying to freeze that [inmate-to-inmate violence] because it was wrong, it was dead wrong. Three hours after the riot started there was no stopping it. But there were a few of us that were saying, "Hey, if you want to burn it down, burn it down or tear it up or whatever you want, but quit killing people and don't turn this thing against ourselves. If you got to fight somebody now, fight the Man, fight the administration."*

(Quoted in Colvin 1992:183–84)

But his and the other inmates' efforts to turn the riot into a protest were futile.

As fights began to break out in the south wing of the prison, injuries to inmates and killings began to increase. Many of the deaths that occurred in the south wing were the result of fights between small groups of inmates and between individuals. Fights over hostages held in the south wing occurred. Many inmates, perceived as weak or defenseless, were attacked and raped; those offering resistance were beaten severely, a few were killed. Some assaults in the south wing appeared to be random. Inmates suffered injuries when they were hacked with meat cleavers, stabbed, or hit with pipes for no reasons apparent to the victims. A few of the killings in the south wing also appear to have been random. Of the 33 killings during the riot, 17 occurred in the south wing, many in the early morning hours of the first day. Of the approximately 400 injuries and rapes, the vast majority also occurred in the south wing.

More inmates would have been killed had Dorm E-1 been entered by the rioters. This semi-protection unit's inmates successfully fought off attempts by rioters to enter this dorm. A sympathetic inmate, who had some friends in the unit, tossed a three-foot long wrench through a hole in the wire mesh above the dorm entrance. This inmate was immediately jumped by other inmates in the main corridor who had observed this action; he was beaten to death. But because he had tossed them this heavy wrench the Dorm E-1 inmates were able to knock bars out of a window at the rear of the dormitory and make it to the perimeter fence and surrender to authorities for safety. Up to 80 inmates housed in the semi-protection unit were saved by this inmate's action.

The most horrific killings of the riot occurred in the north wing of the penitentiary, specifically in Cellblock 4, the Protective Custody unit. By 7 A.M., small groups of inmates entered Cellblock 4 after burning through its entrance grills with blowtorches. As these inmates entered the cellblock, they began shouting the names of intended victims. As rioting inmates operated the control panels that gang locked and unlocked cell doors, many Cellblock 4 inmates were able to leave their cells, blend in with the rioters, and escape the carnage. Other Cellblock 4 inmates were not so fortunate. On tiers where inmates had jammed the locks to their cell grills, the gang locking and un-locking mechanisms would not operate. These inmates were trapped in their cells. Using blowtorches, rioting inmates cut through the bars of entrance grills to the individual cells containing inmates. As the intended victims suf-fered through the agonizing wait while their cells were entered, they were taunted and told in vivid detail exactly how they would be tortured and killed.

These protective custody inmates were apparently killed by four or five small groups, containing three to five inmates each. The groups appeared to have acted independently in choosing victims. Inmates were tortured, stabbed, mutilated, burned, bludgeoned, hanged, and thrown off upper-tier catwalks into the basement. One Cellblock 4 inmate, a 36-year-old African American, was killed and decapitated. Whether this occurred in the cell-block or elsewhere in the prison could not be established by investigators. His head was reportedly placed on a pole, paraded through the main corri-dor, and shown to the guards captured in Cellblock 3. This inmate's body was later deposited outside the prison's front entrance with the head stuffed between the legs. Another inmate, while reportedly still alive, had a steel rod hammered completely through his head. One inmate victim was drenched with glue and set on fire. Other atrocities were also reported to investigators.

There was an apparent competition between the groups in both the quantity and "quality" of their killings. There does not appear to have been any motive, such as personal revenge, to account for these killings. No par-ticular inmate killer among the suspects, for example, had apparently been "snitched off" by any of the victims. In fact, only a few of the inmates killed in Cellblock 4 were later identified by staff and inmates as suspected infor-mants. These inmate victims were viewed as "weak" inmates and thus vul-nerable targets of violence, whose deaths would not be avenged by other in-mates. The fact that the victims were trapped in protective isolation not only increased the killers' sense of total domination but demonstrated the killers' "superiority" since they outsmarted the state authorities who were charged with protecting these inmate victims. In addition, a group dynamic of prov-ing one's commitment to deviance was amplified in Cellblock 4 since small groups of inmates were competing for images as dominatingly "awesome" deviants. (See Jack Katz [1988] for a discussion of the dynamics involved in cold-blooded killings.) Each group felt compelled to outdo the other in its acts of violence. These brutal acts marked their victims as "morally weak" and their perpetrators as "morally superior" in the upside-down world that the inmate society had become. Inmates involved in these killings could count on gaining reputations as the most violent and feared inmates in the prison.

Most of the Cellblock 4 killings were apparently over by 10 A.M. on the first morning of the riot. More inmates would have undoubtedly died had they not been able to escape Cellblock 4. Besides those inmates who left their cells and escaped the protective custody unit when it was opened, other inmates living in this unit were rescued by sympathetic inmates. Some individual inmates entered Cellblock 4, found specific inmate friends, and sneaked them out of the unit. One contingent of about 20 African American inmates from Cellhouse 6 converged on Cellblock 4 about 7:30 A.M. to rescue one of their leaders, a Black Muslim minister, who had been locked in the protection unit. Upon his release, the Muslim minister told his followers to get as many protective custody inmates out of Cellblock 4 as possible. This group saved many of the intended victims (Anglo, Hispanic, and African American) from certain death. They brought these inmates to Cellhouse 6 where they combined forces for self-protection. At about noon, on the first day of the riot, they were able to fight their way to Dorm E-1 and leave the prison through the rear window that had been broken open earlier.

By noon on the first day, many inmates had managed to find routes from which to exit the prison and surrender to authorities who controlled the perimeter fence. By 5 P.M., more than 350 inmates had left the prison. They would continue to stream out of the prison for the rest of the riot. By 1 P.M. on the second (and final) day of the riot, only 100 of the prison's 1,157 inmates remained inside.

The final morning of the riot saw the setting of more fires, an increasingly larger stream of inmates leaving the prison to surrender to authorities, inmates being rushed to hospitals for injuries and pharmacy-drug overdoses, and bodies of inmates being deposited in the yard in front of the prison. Intermittent negotiations between state authorities and some prisoners continued and seemed to reach a climax by the final morning of the riot.

Throughout the riot, sporadic attempts at negotiating the release of hostages were made by state authorities. Negotiations were complicated by the fact that more than one group controlled hostages, and some of these groups had no interest in negotiating release. Three hostages were released at different times either in anticipation of or in response to talking to the news media. At one point, an NBC cameraman entered the prison's entrance lobby and recorded inmates' grievances. The lobby was filled with smoke as inmates presented their grievances about poor food, nepotism, harassment, overcrowding, idleness, inadequate recreation facilities, and arbitrary discipline practices by the administration. At another point, two inmates met with two news reporters just outside the entrance of the prison building. Beyond the release of these three hostages, however, negotiations with inmates had very little to do with the release of hostages or ending the riot.

Two hostages managed, with the help of sympathetic inmates, to leave the prison disguised as inmates. Other hostages were released by inmates because these inmates feared these hostages might die from injuries, which they thought would provoke an immediate retaking of the prison. One other hostage was released after an apparent agreement emerged from negotiations.

At about 8:30 A.M. on February 3, the second (and last) day of the riot, three Hispanic inmates (Lonnie Duran, Vincent Candelaria, and Kendrick

Duran), who were among the few inmates attempting, unsuccessfully, to organize the riot into a protest over prison conditions, ironed out an agreement for ending the riot with prison authorities during a meeting in the gatehouse beneath Tower 1. The agreement had five points: (1) no retaliation against rioting inmates; (2) segregation policies be reviewed; (3) inmates be permitted to meet with the press; (4) no double-bunking of inmates in Cellblock 3; and (5) inmates be given water hoses to douse fires inside the prison. The Durans and Candelaria returned to the prison to seek approval from other inmates. They re-emerged from the prison shortly before noon for continued negotiations. By noon, only two hostages remained in the prison.

The final hour of negotiations leading up to the end of the riot was witnessed by reporter Peter Katel who later, with co-author Michael Serrill, gave the following account:

> The two Durans and Candelaria emerged from the prison and announced that they had approval from other inmates to sign the agreement negotiated [earlier that morning]. . . . Then negotiations became more complicated. Other inmates joined the Durans and Candelaria at the negotiating table. They haggled over exactly how the agreement was to be implemented by prison officials. . . . Officials were particularly worried about the presence of three new inmates, William Jack Stephens, Michael Colby and Michael Price, at the negotiations. Colby and Stephens escaped on Dec. 9 and were recaptured. . . . In 1978, they, together with Price, beat another inmate to death with baseball bats. . . . Their commitment to a peaceful resolution of the riot was considered dubious. Later, they were identified as prime suspects in some of the [riot] killings. . . . At about 12:30 P.M., Colby, Stephens and other inmates rejoined the talks and started making new demands. . . . [Deputy Corrections Director Felix] Rodriguez says that at this point he began to worry that the Durans and Candelaria were losing control. He also began to wonder whether the majority of inmates inside were really aware of and had agreed to the five rather mild demands. (Serrill and Katel 1980:21)

Rodriguez, fearing that Colby and Stephens were gaining control of the situation, made a deal with them. He promised to transport them immediately to another prison out of state and told them to go back inside the prison to get their belongings. As soon as Colby and Stephens left, Rodriguez ordered Vincent Candelaria and Lonnie and Kendrick Duran (the inmates with whom he had been negotiating) to get the remaining two hostages, who were now seated blindfolded on the grass outside the main entrance. A few minutes later, at about 1:30 P.M., these last hostages were brought to Rodriguez. Immediately, police, National Guardsmen, and prison employees rushed the prison to retake it from the approximately 100 inmates still within. Authorities encountered no resistance from inmates during the retaking of the prison. No shots were fired. The riot was over.

Summary

The 1980 riot was a dramatic and explosive episode in a continuing pattern of disorder that had its roots several years earlier. Two things stand out as characteristics of the 1980 riot at PNM: the almost total lack of organization by inmates and the inmate-to-inmate violence that punctuated the event. The extreme violence was caused by a small number of inmates who belonged to some particularly violent inmate cliques. The emergence of these violent inmate cliques was largely an organizational phenomenon. They had their origin in the 1976 shift in tactics of inmate control, when measures, including the coercive snitch system, were used to undermine inmate solidarity. As inmate solidarity disintegrated, young prisoners began entering a social situation that elicited violence from a growing number of inmates. These social dynamics came together in the early morning hours of February 2, 1980, to produce the most horrific prison riot in history.

REFERENCES

Abbott, Jack Henry. 1981. *In the Belly of the Beast.* New York: Vintage.
Albuquerque Journal. 1979. "Prison Sexual Brutality Changes Inmate." September 16, sec. B, p. 1.
Colvin, Mark. 1992. *The Penitentiary in Crisis: From Accommodation to Riot in New Mexico.* Albany, NY: SUNY Press.
Department of Corrections. 1980. *Annual Report.* Santa Fe, NM: State of New Mexico.
———. 1976. *Annual Report.* Santa Fe, NM: State of New Mexico.
———. 1971. *Annual Report.* Santa Fe, NM: State of New Mexico.
Governor's Council on Criminal Justice Planning. 1978. "Technical Report 6: Inmate Profile." *Sourcebook for New Mexico Corrections Planning.* Santa Fe, NM: State of New Mexico.
Hagel-Seymour, John. 1988. "Environmental Sanctuaries for Susceptible Prisoners." Pp. 267–84 in *The Pains of Imprisonment,* edited by Robert Johnson and Hans Toch. Prospect Hills, IL: Waveland Press.
Irwin, John. 1980. *Prisons in Turmoil.* Boston, MA: Little, Brown.
Jacobs, James B. 1977. *Stateville: The Penitentiary in Mass Society.* Chicago, IL: University of Chicago Press.
Katz, Jack. 1988. *Seductions of Crime.* New York: Basic Books.
Office of the Attorney General. 1980a. *Report of the Attorney General on the February 2 and 3, 1980 Riot at the Penitentiary of New Mexico, Part I.* Santa Fe, NM: State of New Mexico.
———. 1980b. *Report of the Attorney General on the February 2 and 3 Riot at the Penitentiary of New Mexico, Part II.* Santa Fe, NM: State of New Mexico.
Serrill, Michael S. and Peter Katel. 1980. "New Mexico: The Anatomy of a Riot." *Corrections Magazine* 6 (April): 6–24.
Wicker, Tom. 1975. *A Time to Die.* New York: Ballantine.

PART V

Deviance, Crime, and Social Control

19

ON BEING SANE IN INSANE PLACES

DAVID L. ROSENHAN

Sociologists have a long-standing interest in the study of social deviance, which is explored in the next four readings. *Deviance* is the recognized violation of social norms. As norms cover a wide range of human behavior, deviant acts are plentiful in any given society. Moreover, whether a person is labeled deviant depends on how others perceive, define, and respond to that person's behavior. In this selection, originally published in 1973, David L. Rosenhan explores the social deviance of mental illness and the consequences of labeling people "sane" or "insane." Rosenhan is currently professor emeritus of psychology and law at Stanford University.

I f sanity and insanity exist . . . how shall we know them? The question is neither capricious nor itself insane. However much we may be personally convinced that we can tell the normal from the abnormal, the evidence is simply not compelling. It is commonplace, for example, to read about murder trials wherein eminent psychiatrists for the defense are contradicted by equally eminent psychiatrists for the prosecution on the matter of the defendant's sanity. More generally, there is a great deal of conflicting data on the reliability, utility, and meaning of such terms as *sanity, insanity, mental illness,* and *schizophrenia.*[1] Finally, as early as 1934, Benedict suggested that normality and abnormality are not universal.[2] What is viewed as normal in one culture may be seen as quite aberrant in another. Thus, notions of normality and abnormality may not be quite as accurate as people believe they are.

To raise questions regarding normality and abnormality is in no way to question the fact that some behaviors are deviant or odd. Murder is deviant. So, too, are hallucinations. Nor does raising such questions deny the existence of the personal anguish that is often associated with "mental illness." Anxiety and depression exist. Psychological suffering exists. But normality and abnormality, sanity and insanity, and the diagnoses that flow from them may be less substantive than many believe them to be.

At its heart, the question of whether the sane can be distinguished from the insane (and whether degrees of insanity can be distinguished from each other) is a simple matter: Do the salient characteristics that lead to diagnoses reside in the patients themselves or in the environments and contexts in which observers find them? From Bleuler, through Kretchmer, through the formulations of the recently revised [1968] *Diagnostic and Statistical Manual* of the American Psychiatric Association, the belief has been strong that patients present symptoms, that those symptoms can be categorized, and, implicitly, that the sane are distinguishable from the insane. More recently, however, this belief has been questioned. Based in part on theoretical and anthropological considerations, but also on philosophical, legal, and therapeutic ones, the view has grown that psychological categorization of mental illness is useless at best and downright harmful, misleading, and pejorative at worst. Psychiatric diagnoses, in this view, are in the minds of the observers and are not valid summaries of characteristics displayed by the observed.[3, 4, 5]

Gains can be made in deciding which of these is more nearly accurate by getting normal people (that is, people who do not have, and have never suffered, symptoms of serious psychiatric disorders) admitted to psychiatric hospitals and then determining whether they were discovered to be sane and, if so, how. If the sanity of such pseudopatients were always detected, there would be *prima facie* evidence that a sane individual can be distinguished from the insane context in which he is found. Normality (and presumably abnormality) is distinct enough that it can be recognized wherever it occurs, for it is carried within the person. If, on the other hand, the sanity of the pseudopatients were never discovered, serious difficulties would arise for those who support traditional modes of psychiatric diagnosis. Given that the hospital staff was not incompetent, that the pseudopatient had been behaving as sanely as he had been outside of the hospital, and that it had never been previously suggested that he belonged in a psychiatric hospital, such an unlikely outcome would support the view that psychiatric diagnosis betrays little about the patient but much about the environment in which an observer finds him.

This article describes such an experiment. Eight sane people gained secret admission to twelve different hospitals.[6] Their diagnostic experiences constitute the data of the first part of this article; the remainder is devoted to a description of their experiences in psychiatric institutions. Too few psychiatrists and psychologists, even those who have worked in such hospitals, know what the experience is like. They rarely talk about it with former patients, perhaps because they distrust information coming from the previously insane. Those who have worked in psychiatric hospitals are likely to have adapted so thoroughly to the settings that they are insensitive to the impact of that experience. And while there have been occasional reports of researchers who submitted themselves to psychiatric hospitalization,[7] these researchers have commonly remained in the hospitals for short periods of time, often with the knowledge of the hospital staff. It is difficult to know the extent to which they were treated like patients or like research colleagues. Nevertheless, their reports about the inside of the psychiatric hospital have been valuable. This article extends those efforts.

Pseudopatients and Their Settings

The eight pseudopatients were a varied group. One was a psychology graduate student in his 20s. The remaining seven were older and "established." Among them were three psychologists, a pediatrician, a psychiatrist, a painter, and a housewife. Three pseudopatients were women, five were men. All of them employed pseudonyms, lest their alleged diagnoses embarrass them later. Those who were in mental health professions alleged another occupation in order to avoid the special attentions that might be accorded by staff, as a matter of courtesy or caution, to ailing colleagues.[8] With the exception of myself (I was the first pseudopatient and my presence was known to the hospital administrator and chief psychologist and, so far as I can tell, to them alone), the presence of pseudopatients and the nature of the research program were not known to the hospital staffs.[9]

The settings were similarly varied. In order to generalize the findings, admission into a variety of hospitals was sought. The 12 hospitals in the sample were located in five different states on the East and West coasts. Some were old and shabby, some were quite new. Some were research-oriented, others not. Some had good staff-patient ratios, others were quite understaffed. Only one was a strictly private hospital. All of the others were supported by state or federal funds or, in one instance, by university funds.

After calling the hospital for an appointment, the pseudopatient arrived at the admissions office complaining that he had been hearing voices. Asked what the voices said, he replied that they were often unclear, but as far as he could tell they said "empty," "hollow," and "thud." The voices were unfamiliar and were of the same sex as the pseudopatient. The choice of these symptoms was occasioned by their apparent similarity to existential symptoms. Such symptoms are alleged to arise from painful concerns about the perceived meaninglessness of one's life. It is as if the hallucinating person were saying, "My life is empty and hollow." The choice of these symptoms was also determined by the *absence* of a single report of existential psychoses in the literature.

Beyond alleging the symptoms and falsifying name, vocation, and employment, no further alterations of person, history, or circumstances were made. The significant events of the pseudopatient's life history were presented as they had actually occurred. Relationships with parents and siblings, with spouse and children, with people at work and in school, consistent with the aforementioned exceptions, were described as they were or had been. Frustrations and upsets were described along with joys and satisfactions. These facts are important to remember. If anything, they strongly biased the subsequent results in favor of detecting sanity, since none of their histories or current behaviors were seriously pathological in any way.

Immediately upon admission to the psychiatric ward, the pseudopatient ceased simulating *any* symptoms of abnormality. In some cases, there was a brief period of mild nervousness and anxiety, since none of the pseudo-patients really believed that they would be admitted so easily. Indeed, their shared fear was that they would be immediately exposed as frauds and greatly embarrassed. Moreover, many of them had never visited a psychiatric ward; even those who had, nevertheless had some genuine fears about what might happen to them. Their nervousness, then, was quite appropriate to the nov-elty of the hospital setting, and it abated rapidly.

Apart from that short-lived nervousness, the pseudopatient behaved on the ward as he "normally" behaved. The pseudopatient spoke to patients and staff as he might ordinarily. Because there is uncommonly little to do on a psy-chiatric ward, he attempted to engage others in conversation. When asked by the staff how he was feeling, he indicated that he was fine, that he no longer ex-perienced symptoms. He responded to instructions from attendants, to calls for medication (which was not swallowed), and to dining-hall instructions. Beyond such activities as were available to him on the admissions ward, he spent his time writing down his observations about the ward, its patients, and the staff. Initially these notes were written "secretly," but as it soon be-came clear that no one much cared, they were subsequently written on stan-dard tablets of paper in such public places as the dayroom. No secret was made of these activities.

The pseudopatient, very much as a true psychiatric patient, entered a hospital with no foreknowledge of when he would be discharged. Each was told that he would have to get out by his own devices, essentially by convinc-ing the staff that he was sane. The psychological stresses associated with hos-pitalization were considerable, and all but one of the pseudopatients desired to be discharged almost immediately after being admitted. They were, there-fore, motivated not only to behave sanely, but to be paragons of coopera-tion. That their behavior was in no way disruptive is confirmed by nursing reports, which have been obtained on most of the patients. These reports uni-formly indicate that the patients were "friendly," "cooperative," and "exhib-ited no abnormal indications."

The Normal Are Not Detectably Sane

Despite their public "show" of sanity, the pseudopatients were never de-tected. Admitted, except in one case, with a diagnosis of schizophrenia,[10] each was discharged with a diagnosis of schizophrenia "in remission." The label "in remission" should in no way be dismissed as a formality, for at no time during any hospitalization had any question been raised about any pseudo-patient's simulation. Nor are there any indications in the hospital records that the pseudopatient's status was suspect. Rather, the evidence is strong that, once labeled schizophrenic, the pseudopatient was stuck with that label. If the pseudopatient was to be discharged, he must naturally be "in remission"; but he was not sane, nor, in the institution's view, had he ever been sane.

The uniform failure to recognize sanity cannot be attributed to the quality of the hospitals, for, although there were considerable variations among them, several are considered excellent. Nor can it be alleged that there was simply not enough time to observe the pseudopatients. Length of hospitalization ranged from 7 to 52 days, with an average of 19 days. The pseudopatients were not, in fact, carefully observed, but this failure clearly speaks more to the traditions within psychiatric hospitals than to lack of opportunity.

Finally, it cannot be said that the failure to recognize the pseudopatients' sanity was due to the fact that they were not behaving sanely. While there was clearly some tension present in all of them, their daily visitors could detect no serious behavioral consequences—nor, indeed, could other patients. It was quite common for the patients to "detect" the pseudopatients' sanity. During the first three hospitalizations, when accurate counts were kept, 35 of a total of 118 patients on the admissions ward voiced their suspicions, some vigorously. "You're not crazy. You're a journalist, or a professor [referring to the continual note-taking]. You're checking up on the hospital." While most of the patients were reassured by the pseudopatient's insistence that he had been sick before he came in but was fine now, some continued to believe that the pseudopatient was sane throughout his hospitalization.[11] The fact that the patients often recognized normality when staff did not raises important questions.

Failure to detect sanity during the course of hospitalization may be due to the fact that physicians operate with a strong bias toward what statisticians call the type 2 error.[12] This is to say that physicians are more inclined to call a healthy person sick (a false positive, type 2) than a sick person healthy (a false negative, type 1). The reasons for this are not hard to find: It is clearly more dangerous to misdiagnose illness than health. Better to err on the side of caution, to suspect illness even among the healthy.

But what holds for medicine does not hold equally well for psychiatry. Medical illnesses, while unfortunate, are not commonly pejorative. Psychiatric diagnoses, on the contrary, carry with them personal, legal, and social stigmas.[13] It was therefore important to see whether the tendency toward diagnosing the sane insane could be reversed. The following experiment was arranged at a research and teaching hospital whose staff had heard these findings but doubted that such an error could occur in their hospital. The staff was informed that at some time during the following three months, one or more pseudopatients would attempt to be admitted into the psychiatric hospital. Each staff member was asked to rate each patient who presented himself at admissions or on the ward according to the likelihood that the patient was a pseudopatient. A 10-point scale was used, with a 1 and 2 reflecting high confidence that the patient was a pseudopatient.

Judgments were obtained on 193 patients who were admitted for psychiatric treatment. All staff who had had sustained contact with or primary responsibility for the patient—attendants, nurses, psychiatrists, physicians, and psychologists—were asked to make judgments. Forty-one patients were alleged, with high confidence, to be pseudopatients by at least one member of the staff. Twenty-three were considered suspect by at least one psychiatrist. Nineteen were suspected by one psychiatrist and one other staff member. Actually, no genuine pseudopatient (at least from my group) presented himself during this period.

The experiment is instructive. It indicates that the tendency to designate sane people as insane can be reversed when the stakes (in this case, prestige and diagnostic acumen) are high. But what can be said of the 19 people who were suspected of being "sane" by one psychiatrist and another staff member? Were these people truly "sane," or was it rather the case that in the course of avoiding the type 2 error the staff tended to make more errors of the first sort—calling the crazy "sane"? There is no way of knowing. But one thing is certain: Any diagnostic process that lends itself so readily to massive errors of this sort cannot be a very reliable one.

The Stickiness of Psychodiagnostic Labels

Beyond the tendency to call the healthy sick—a tendency that accounts better for diagnostic behavior on admission than it does for such behavior after a lengthy period of exposure—the data speak to the massive role of labeling in psychiatric assessment. Having once been labeled schizophrenic, there is nothing the pseudopatient can do to overcome the tag. The tag profoundly colors others' perceptions of him and his behavior.

From one viewpoint, these data are hardly surprising, for it has long been known that elements are given meaning by the context in which they occur. Gestalt psychology made this point vigorously, and Asch[14] demonstrated that there are "central" personality traits (such as "warm" versus "cold") which are so powerful that they markedly color the meaning of other information in forming an impression of a given personality.[15] "Insane," "schizophrenic," "manic-depressive," and "crazy" are probably among the most powerful of such central traits. Once a person is designated abnormal, all of his other behaviors and characteristics are colored by that label. Indeed, that label is so powerful that many of the pseudopatients' normal behaviors were overlooked entirely or profoundly misinterpreted. Some examples may clarify this issue.

Earlier I indicated that there were no changes in the pseudopatient's personal history and current status beyond those of name, employment, and, where necessary, vocation. Otherwise, a veridical description of personal history and circumstances was offered. Those circumstances were not psychotic. How were they made consonant with the diagnosis of psychosis? Or were those diagnoses modified in such a way as to bring them into accord with the circumstances of the pseudopatient's life, as described by him?

As far as I can determine, diagnoses were in no way affected by the relative health of the circumstances of a pseudopatient's life. Rather, the reverse occurred: The perception of his circumstances was shaped entirely by the diagnosis. A clear example of such translation is found in the case of a pseudopatient who had had a close relationship with his mother but was rather remote from his father during his early childhood. During adolescence and beyond, however, his father became a close friend, while his relationship with his mother cooled. His present relationship with his wife was characteristically close and warm. Apart from occasional angry exchanges, friction was minimal. The children had rarely been spanked. Surely there is nothing especially pathological about such a history. Indeed, many readers may see a similar pattern in their own experiences, with no markedly deleterious consequences. Observe, however, how such a history was translated in the psychopathological context, this from the case summary prepared after the patient was discharged.

> This white 39-year-old male . . . manifests a long history of considerable ambivalence in close relationships, which begins in early childhood. A warm relationship with his mother cools during adolescence. A distant relationship to his father is described as becoming very intense. Affective stability is absent. His attempts to control emotionality with his wife and children are punctuated by angry outbursts and, in the case of the children, spankings. And while he says that he has several good friends, one senses considerable ambivalence embedded in those relationships also.

The facts of the case were unintentionally distorted by the staff to achieve consistency with a popular theory of the dynamics of schizophrenic reaction.[16] Nothing of an ambivalent nature had been described in relations with parents, spouse, or friends. To the extent that ambivalence could be inferred, it was probably not greater than is found in all human relationships. It is true the pseudopatient's relationships with his parents changed over time, but in the ordinary context that would hardly be remarkable—indeed, it might very well be expected. Clearly, the meaning ascribed to his verbalizations (that is, ambivalence, affective instability) was determined by the diagnosis: schizophrenia. An entirely different meaning would have been ascribed if it were known that the man was "normal."

All pseudopatients took extensive notes publicly. Under ordinary circumstances, such behavior would have raised questions in the minds of observers, as, in fact, it did among patients. Indeed, it seemed so certain that the notes would elicit suspicion that elaborate precautions were taken to remove them from the ward each day. But the precautions proved needless. The closest any staff member came to questioning these notes occurred when one pseudopatient asked his physician what kind of medication he was receiving and began to write down the response. "You needn't write it," he was told gently. "If you have trouble remembering, just ask me again."

If no questions were asked of the pseudopatients, how was their writing interpreted? Nursing records for three patients indicate that the writing was seen as an aspect of their pathological behavior. "Patient engages in writing behavior" was the daily nursing comment on one of the pseudopatients who was never questioned about his writing. Given that the patient is in the hospital, he must be psychologically disturbed. And given that he is disturbed, continuous writing must be a behavioral manifestation of that disturbance, perhaps a subset of the compulsive behaviors that are sometimes correlated with schizophrenia.

One tacit characteristic of psychiatric diagnosis is that it locates the sources of aberration within the individual and only rarely within the complex of stimuli that surrounds him. Consequently, behaviors that are stimulated by the environment are commonly misattributed to the patient's disorder. For example, one kindly nurse found a pseudopatient pacing the long hospital corridors. "Nervous, Mr. X?" she asked. "No, bored," he said.

The notes kept by pseudopatients are full of patient behaviors that were misinterpreted by well-intentioned staff. Often enough, a patient would go "berserk" because he had, wittingly or unwittingly, been mistreated by, say, an attendant. A nurse coming upon the scene would rarely inquire even cursorily into the environmental stimuli of the patient's behavior. Rather, she assumed that his upset derived from his pathology, not from his present interactions with other staff members. Occasionally, the staff might assume that the patient's family (especially when they had recently visited) or other patients had stimulated the outburst. But never were the staff found to assume that one of themselves or the structure of the hospital had anything to do with a patient's behavior. One psychiatrist pointed to a group of patients who were sitting outside the cafeteria entrance half an hour before lunchtime. To a group of young residents he indicated that such behavior was characteristic of the oral-acquisitive nature of the syndrome. It seemed not to occur to him that there were very few things to anticipate in the psychiatric hospital besides eating.

A psychiatric label has a life and an influence of its own. Once the impression has been formed that the patient is schizophrenic, the expectation is that he will continue to be schizophrenic. When a sufficient amount of time has passed, during which the patient has done nothing bizarre, he is considered to be in remission and available for discharge. But the label endures beyond discharge, with the unconfirmed expectation that he will behave as a schizophrenic again. Such labels, conferred by mental health professionals, are as influential on the patient as they are on his relatives and friends, and it should not surprise anyone that the diagnosis acts on all of them as a self-fulfilling prophecy. Eventually, the patient himself accepts the diagnosis, with all of its surplus meanings and expectations, and behaves accordingly.[17]

The inferences to be made from these matters are quite simple. Much as Zigler and Phillips have demonstrated that there is enormous overlap in the symptoms presented by patients who have been variously diagnosed,[18] so there is enormous overlap in the behaviors of the sane and the insane. The sane are not "sane" all of the time. We lose our tempers "for no good reason." We are occasionally depressed or anxious, again for no good reason. And we may find it difficult to get along with one or another person—again for no reason that we can specify. Similarly, the insane are not always insane.

Indeed, it was the impression of the pseudopatients while living with them that they were sane for long periods of time—that the bizarre behaviors upon which their diagnoses were allegedly predicated constituted only a small fraction of their total behavior. If it makes no sense to label ourselves permanently depressed on the basis of an occasional depression, then it takes evidence that is presently available to label all patients insane or schizophrenic on the basis of bizarre behaviors or cognitions. It seems more useful, as Mischel[19] has pointed out, to limit our discussions to *behaviors*, the stimuli that provoke them, and their correlates.

It is not known why powerful impressions of personality traits, such as "crazy" or "insane," arise. Conceivably, when the origins of and stimuli that give rise to a behavior are remote or unknown, or when the behavior strikes us as immutable, trait labels regarding the *behavior* arise. When, on the other hand, the origins and stimuli are known and available, discourse is limited to the behavior itself. Thus, I may hallucinate because I am sleeping, or I may hallucinate because I have ingested a peculiar drug. These are termed sleep-induced hallucinations, or dreams, and drug-induced hallucinations, respectively. But when the stimuli to my hallucinations are unknown, that is called craziness, or schizophrenia—as if that inference were somehow as illuminating as the others.

The Consequences of Labeling and Depersonalization

Whenever the ratio of what is known to what needs to be known approaches zero, we tend to invent "knowledge" and assume that we understand more than we actually do. We seem unable to acknowledge that we simply don't know. The needs for diagnosis and remediation of behavioral and emotional problems are enormous. But rather than acknowledge that we are just embarking on understanding, we continue to label patients "schizophrenic," "manic-depressive," and "insane," as if in those words we had captured the essence of understanding. The facts of the matter are that we have known for a long time that diagnoses are often not useful or reliable, but we have nevertheless continued to use them. We now know that we cannot distinguish insanity from sanity. It is depressing to consider how that information will be used.

Not merely depressing, but frightening. How many people, one wonders, are sane but not recognized as such in our psychiatric institutions? How many have been needlessly stripped of their privileges of citizenship, from the right to vote and drive to that of handling their own accounts? How many have feigned insanity in order to avoid the criminal consequences of their behavior, and conversely, how many would rather stand trial than live interminably in a psychiatric hospital—but are wrongly thought to be mentally ill? How many have been stigmatized by well-intentioned, but nevertheless erroneous, diagnoses? On the last point, recall again that a "type 2 error" in psychiatric diagnosis does not have the same consequences it does in medical diagnosis. A diagnosis of cancer that has been found to be in error is cause for celebration. But psychiatric diagnoses are rarely found to be in error. The label sticks, a mark of inadequacy forever.

ENDNOTES

[1] P. Ash, *Journal of Abnormal and Social Psychology* 44 (1949): 272; A. T. Beck, *American Journal of Psychiatry* 119 (1962): 210; A. T. Boisen, *Psychiatry* 2 (1938): 233; J. Kreitman, *Journal of Mental Science* 107 (1961): 876; N. Kreitman, P. Sainsbury, J. Morrisey, J. Towers, and J. Scrivener, *Journal of Mental Science* 107 (1961): 887; H. O. Schmitt and C. P. Fonda, *Journal of Abnormal Social Psychology* 52 (1956): 262; W. Seeman, *Journal of Nervous Mental Disorders* 118 (1953): 541. For analysis of these artifacts and summaries of the disputes, see J. Zubin, *Annual Review of Psychology* 18 (1967): 373; L. Phillips and J. G. Draguns, *Annual Review of Psychology* 22 (1971): 447.

[2] R. Benedict, *Journal of General Psychology* 10 (1934): 59.

[3] See in this regard Howard Becker, *Outsiders: Studies in the Sociology of Deviance* (New York: Free Press, 1963); B. M. Braginsky, D. D. Braginsky, and K. Ring, *Methods of Madness: The Mental Hospital As a Last Resort* (New York: Holt, Rinehart and Winston, 1969); G. M. Crocetti and P. V. Lemkau, *American Sociological Review* 30 (1965): 577; Erving Goffman, *Behavior in Public Places* (New York: Free Press, 1964); R. D. Laing, *The Divided Self: A Study of Sanity and Madness* (Chicago: Quadrangle, 1960); D. L. Phillips, *American Sociological Review* 28 (1963): 963; T. R. Sarbin, *Psychology Today* 6 (1972): 18; E. Schur, *American Journal of Sociology* 75 (1969): 309; Thomas Szasz, *The Myth of Mental Illness: Foundations of a Theory of Mental Illness* (New York: Hoeber Harper, 1963). For a critique of some of these views, see W. R. Gave, *American Sociological Review* 35 (1970): 873.

[4] Erving Goffman, *Asylums* (Garden City, NY: Doubleday, 1961).

[5] T. J. Scheff, *Being Mentally Ill: A Sociological Theory* (Chicago: Aldine, 1966).

[6] Data from a ninth pseudopatient are not incorporated in this report because, although his sanity went undetected, he falsified aspects of his personal history, including his marital status and parental relationships. His experimental behaviors therefore were not identical to those of the other pseudopatients.

[7] A. Barry, *Bellevue Is a State of Mind* (New York: Harcourt Brace Jovanovich, 1971); I. Belknap, *Human Problems of a State Mental Hospital* (New York: McGraw-Hill, 1956); W. Caudill, F. C. Redlich, H. R. Gilmore, and E. B. Brody, *American Journal of Orthopsychiatry* 22 (1952): 314; A. R. Goldman, R. H. Bohr, and T. A. Steinberg, *Professional Psychology* 1 (1970): 427; *Roche Report* 1, no. 13 (1971): 8.

[8] Beyond the personal difficulties that the pseudopatient is likely to experience in the hospital, there are legal and social ones that, combined, require considerable attention before entry. For example, once admitted to a psychiatric institution, it is difficult, if not impossible, to be discharged on short notice, state law to the contrary notwithstanding. I was not sensitive to these difficulties at the outset of the project, nor to the personal and situational emergencies that can arise, but later a writ of habeas corpus was prepared for each of the entering pseudopatients and an attorney was kept "on call" during every hospitalization. I am grateful to John Kaplan and Robert Bartels for legal advice and assistance in these matters.

[9] However distasteful such concealment is, it was a necessary first step to examining these questions. Without concealment, there would have been no way to know how valid these experiences were; nor was there any way of knowing whether whatever detections occurred were a tribute to the diagnostic acumen of the staff or to the hospital's rumor network. Obviously, since my concerns are general ones that cut across individual hospitals and staffs, I have respected their anonymity and have eliminated clues that might lead to their identification.

[10] Interestingly, of the 12 admissions, 11 were diagnosed as schizophrenic and one, with the identical symptomatology, as manic-depressive psychosis. This diagnosis has a more favorable prognosis, and it was given by the only private hospital in our sample. On the relations between social class and psychiatric diagnosis, see A. B. Hollinghead and F. C. Redlich, *Social Class and Mental Illness: A Community Study* (New York: Wiley, 1958).

[11] It is possible, of course, that patients have quite broad latitudes in diagnosis and therefore are inclined to call many people sane, even those whose behavior is patently aberrant. However, although we have no hard data on this matter, it was our distinct impression that this was not

the case. In many instances, patients not only singled us out for attention, but came to imitate our behaviors and styles.

[12] Scheff, *Being Mentally Ill.*

[13] J. Cumming and E. Cumming, *Community Mental Health* 1 (1965): 135; A. Farina and K. Ring, *Journal of Abnormal Psychology* 40 (1965): 47; H. E. Freeman and O. G. Simmons, *The Mental Patient Comes Home* (New York: Wiley, 1963); W. J. Johannsen, *Mental Hygiene* 53 (1969): 218; A. S. Linsky, *Social Psychology* 5 (1970): 166.

[14] S. E. Asch, *Abnormal Social Psychology* 41 (1946): 258; S. E. Asch, *Social Psychology* (New York: Prentice-Hall, 1952).

[15] See also I. N. Mensch and J. Wishner, *Journal of Personality* 16 (1947): 188; J. Wishner, *Psychological Review* 67 (1960): 96; J. S. Bruner and K. R. Tagiuri in *Handbook of Social Psychology,* vol. 2, ed. G. Lindzey (Cambridge, MA: Addison-Wesley, 1954), pp. 634–54; J. S. Bruner, D. Shapiro, and R. Tagiuri in *Person Perception and Interpersonal Behavior,* ed. R. Tagiuri and L. Petrullo (Stanford, CA: Stanford University Press, 1958), pp. 277–88.

[16] For an example of a similar self-fulfilling prophecy, in this instance dealing with the "central" trait of intelligence, see R. Rosenthal and L. Jacobson, *Pygmalion in the Classroom* (New York: Holt, Rinehart and Winston, 1968).

[17] Scheff, *Being Mentally Ill.*

[18] E. Zigler and L. Phillips, *Journal of Abnormal and Social Psychology* 63 (1961): 69. See also R. K. Freudenberg and J. P. Robertson, *A.M.A. Archives of Neurological Psychiatry* 76 (1956): 14.

[19] W. Mischel, *Personality and Assessment* (New York: Wiley, 1968).

20

ANOREXIA NERVOSA AND BULIMIA
The Development of Deviant Identities

PENELOPE A. MCLORG • DIANE E. TAUB

Symbolic interactionists claim that deviance is relative depending on the situation and who is perceiving the act of deviance. Thus, according to *labeling theory,* people label certain acts as deviant and others as normal. This reading by Penelope McLorg and Diane Taub further illustrates this subjective process of deviance identification. In the reading below, originally published in 1987, McLorg and Taub employ labeling theory to explain how eating disorders have become defined as deviant behaviors and how some young women acquire deviant identities by modifying their self-concepts to conform to the societal labels of a person with an eating disorder. Penelope McLorg is director of the Gerontology Program and assistant professor of Anthropology and Diane Taub is professor and chair of Sociology at Indiana University–Purdue University, Fort Wayne.

Introduction

Current appearance norms stipulate thinness for women and muscularity for men; these expectations, like any norms, entail rewards for compliance and negative sanctions for violations. Fear of being overweight—of being visually deviant—has led to a striving for thinness, especially among women. In the extreme, this avoidance of overweight engenders eating disorders, which themselves constitute deviance. Anorexia nervosa, or purposeful starvation, embodies visual as well as behavioral deviation; bulimia, binge-eating followed by vomiting and/or laxative abuse, is primarily behaviorally deviant.

Besides a fear of fatness, anorexics and bulimics exhibit distorted body images. In anorexia nervosa, a 20–25 percent loss of initial body weight occurs, resulting from self-starvation alone or in combination with excessive exercising, occasional binge-eating, vomiting and/or laxative abuse. Bulimia denotes cyclical (daily, weekly, for example) binge-eating followed by vomiting or laxative abuse; weight is normal or close to normal (Humphries, Wrobel, and Weigert 1982). Common physical manifestations of these eating disorders include menstrual cessation or irregularities and electrolyte imbalances; among behavioral traits are depression, obsessions/compulsions, and anxiety (Russell 1979; Thompson and Schwartz 1982).

Increasingly prevalent in the past two decades, anorexia nervosa and bulimia have emerged as major health and social problems. Termed an epidemic on college campuses (Brody, as quoted in Schur 1984:76), bulimia affects 13 percent of college students (Halmi, Falk, and Schwartz 1981). Less prevalent, anorexia nervosa was diagnosed in 0.6 percent of students utilizing a university health center (Stangler and Printz 1980). However, the overall mortality rate of anorexia nervosa is 6 percent (Schwartz and Thompson 1981) to 20 percent (Humphries et al. 1982); bulimia appears to be less life-threatening (Russell 1979).

Particularly affecting certain demographic groups, eating disorders are most prevalent among young, white, affluent (upper-middle to upper class) women in modern, industrialized countries (Crisp 1977; Willi and Grossman 1983). Combining all of these risk factors (female sex, youth, high socio-economic status, and residence in an industrialized country), prevalence of anorexia nervosa in upper-class English girls' schools is reported at 1 in 100 (Crisp, Palmer, and Kalucy 1976). The age of onset for anorexia nervosa is bimodal at 14.5 and 18 years (Humphries et al. 1982); the most frequent age of onset for bulimia is 18 (Russell 1979).

Eating disorders have primarily been studied from psychological and medical perspectives.[1] Theories of etiology have generally fallen into three categories: the ego psychological (involving an impaired child–maternal environment); the family systems (implicating enmeshed, rigid families); and the endocrinological (involving a precipitating hormonal defect). Although relatively ignored in previous studies, the sociocultural components of anorexia nervosa and bulimia (the slimness norm and its agents of reinforcement, such as role models) have been postulated as accounting for the recent, dramatic increases in these disorders (Boskind-White 1985; Schwartz, Thompson, and Johnson 1982).[2]

Medical and psychological approaches to anorexia nervosa and bulimia obscure the social facets of the disorders and neglect the individuals' own definitions of their situations. Among the social processes involved in the development of an eating disorder is the sequence of conforming behavior, primary deviance, and secondary deviance. Societal reaction is the critical mediator affecting the movement through the deviant career (Becker 1973). Within a framework of labeling theory, this study focuses on the emergence of anorexic and bulimic identities, as well as on the consequences of being career deviants.

Methodology

Sampling and Procedures

Most research on eating disorders has utilized clinical subjects or nonclinical respondents completing questionnaires. Such studies can be criticized for simply counting and describing behaviors and/or neglecting the social construction of the disorders. Moreover, the work of clinicians is often limited by therapeutic orientation. Previous research may also have included individuals who were not in therapy on their own volition and who resisted admitting that they had an eating disorder.

Past studies thus disregard the intersubjective meanings respondents attach to their behavior and emphasize researchers' criteria for definition as anorexic or bulimic. In order to supplement these sampling and procedural designs, the present study utilizes participant observation of a group of self-defined anorexics and bulimics.[3] As the individuals had acknowledged their eating disorders, frank discussion and disclosure were facilitated.

Data are derived from a self-help group, BANISH, Bulimics/Anorexics in Self-Help, which met at a university in an urban center of the mid-South. Founded by one of the researchers (D.E.T.), BANISH was advertised in local newspapers as offering a group experience for individuals who were anorexic or bulimic. Despite the local advertisements, the campus location of the meeting may have selectively encouraged university students to attend. Nonetheless, in view of the modal age of onset and socioeconomic status of individuals with eating disorders, college students have been considered target populations (Crisp et al. 1976; Halmi et al. 1981).

The group's weekly two-hour meetings were observed for two years. During the course of this study, 30 individuals attended at least one of the meetings. Attendance at meetings was varied: Ten individuals came nearly every Sunday; five attended approximately twice a month; and the remaining 15 participated once a month or less frequently, often when their eating problems were "more severe" or "bizarre." The modal number of members at meetings was 12. The diversity in attendance was to be expected in self-help groups of anorexics and bulimics:

> Most people's involvement will not be forever or even a long time. Most people get the support they need and drop out. Some take the time to help others after they themselves have been helped but even they may withdraw after a time. It is a natural and in many cases *necessary* process (emphasis in original). (American Anorexia and Bulimia Association 1983)

Modeled after Alcoholics Anonymous, BANISH allowed participants to discuss their backgrounds and experiences with others who empathized. For many members, the group constituted their only source of help; these respondents were reluctant to contact health professionals because of shame, embarrassment, or financial difficulties.

In addition to field notes from group meetings, records of other encounters with all members were maintained. Participants visited the office of one of the researchers (D.E.T.), called both researchers by phone, and invited them to their homes or out for a cup of coffee. Such interaction facilitated genuine communication and mutual trust. Even among the 15 individuals who did not attend the meetings regularly, contact was maintained with 10 members on a monthly basis.

Supplementing field notes were informal interviews with 15 group members, lasting from two to four hours. Because they appeared to represent more extensive experience with eating disorders, these interviewees were chosen to amplify their comments about the labeling process, made during group meetings. Conducted near the end of the two-year observation period, the interviews focused on what the respondents thought antedated and maintained their eating disorders. In addition, participants described others' reactions to their behaviors as well as their own interpretations of these reactions. To protect the confidentiality of individuals quoted in the study, pseudonyms are employed.

Description of Members

The demographic composite of the sample typifies what has been found in other studies (Crisp 1977; Fox and James 1976; Herzog 1982; Schlesier-Stropp 1984). Group members' ages ranged from 19 to 36, with the modal age being 21. The respondents were white, and all but one were female. The sole male and three of the females were anorexic; the remaining females were bulimic.[4]

Primarily composed of college students, the group included four nonstudents, three of whom had college degrees. Nearly all members derived from upper-middle- or lower-upper-class households. Eighteen students and two nonstudents were never married and uninvolved in serious relationships; two nonstudents were married (one with two children); two students were divorced (one with two children); and six students were involved in serious relationships. The duration of eating disorders ranged from 3 to 15 years.

Conforming Behavior

In the backgrounds of most anorexics and bulimics, dieting figures prominently, beginning in the teen years (Crisp 1977; Johnson, Stuckey, Lewis, and Schwartz 1982; Lacey, Coker, and Birtchnell 1986). As dieters, these individuals are conformist in their adherence to the cultural norms emphasizing thinness (Garner, Garfinkel, Schwartz, and Thompson 1980; Schwartz, Thompson, and Johnson 1982). In our society, slim bodies are regarded as the most worthy and attractive; overweight is viewed as physically and morally unhealthy—"obscene," "lazy," "slothful," and "gluttonous" (DeJong 1980; Ritenbaugh 1982; Schwartz et al. 1982).

Among the agents of socialization promoting the slimness norm is advertising. Female models in newspaper, magazine, and television advertisements are uniformly slender. In addition, product names and slogans exploit the thin orientation; examples include "Ultra Slim Lipstick," "Miller Lite," and "Virginia Slims." While retaining pressures toward thinness, an Ayds commercial attempts a compromise for those wanting to savor food: "Ayds . . . so you can taste, chew, and enjoy, while you lose weight." Appealing particularly to women, a nationwide fast-food restaurant chain offers low-calorie selections, so individuals can have a "license to eat." In the latter two examples, the notion of enjoying food is combined with the message to be slim. Food and restaurant advertisements overall convey the pleasures of eating, whereas advertisements for other products, such as fashions and diet aids, reinforce the idea that fatness is undesirable.

Emphasis on being slim affects everyone in our culture, but it influences women especially because of society's traditional emphasis on women's appearance. The slimness norm and its concomitant narrow beauty standards exacerbate the objectification of women (Schur 1984). Women view themselves as visual entities and recognize that conforming to appearance expectations and "becoming attractive object[s] [are] role obligation[s]" (Laws, as quoted in Schur 1984:66). Demonstrating the beauty motivation behind dieting, a Nielson survey indicated that of the 56 percent of all women aged 24 to 54 who dieted during the previous year, 76 percent did so for cosmetic, rather than health, reasons (Schwartz et al. 1982). For most female group members, dieting was viewed as a means of gaining attractiveness and appeal to the opposite sex. The male respondent, as well, indicated that "when I was fat, girls didn't look at me, but when I got thinner, I was suddenly popular."

In addition to responding to the specter of obesity, individuals who develop anorexia nervosa and bulimia are conformist in their strong commitment to other conventional norms and goals. They consistently excel at school and work (Bruch 1981; Humphries et al. 1982; Russell 1979), maintaining high aspirations in both areas (Lacey et al. 1986; Theander 1970).

Group members generally completed college-preparatory courses in high school, aware from an early age that they would strive for a college degree. Also, in college as well as high school, respondents joined honor societies and academic clubs.

Moreover, pre-anorexics and -bulimics display notable conventionality as "model children" (Humphries et al. 1982:199), "the pride and joy" of their parents (Bruch 1981:215), accommodating themselves to the wishes of others. Parents of these individuals emphasize conformity and value achievement (Bruch 1981). Respondents felt that perfect or near-perfect grades were expected of them; however, good grades were not rewarded by parents, because "A's" were common for these children. In addition, their parents suppressed conflicts, to preserve the image of the "all-American family" (Humphries et al. 1982). Group members reported that they seldom, if ever, heard their parents argue or raise their voices.

Also conformist in their affective ties, individuals who develop anorexia nervosa and bulimia are strongly, even excessively, attached to their parents. Respondents' families appeared close-knit, demonstrating palpable emotional ties. Several group members, for example, reported habitually calling home at prescribed times, whether or not they had any news. Such families have been termed "enmeshed" and "overprotective," displaying intense interaction and concern for members' welfare (Minuchin, Rosman, and Baker 1978; Selvini-Palazzoli 1978). These qualities could be viewed as marked conformity to the norm of familial closeness.[5]

Another element of notable conformity in the family milieu of pre-anorexics and -bulimics concerns eating, body weight and shape, and exercising (Humphries et al. 1982; Kalucy, Crisp, and Harding 1977). Respondents reported their fathers' preoccupation with exercising and their mothers' engrossment in food preparation. When group members dieted and lost weight, they received an extraordinary amount of approval. Among the family, body size became a matter of "friendly rivalry." One bulimic informant recalled that she, her mother, and her coed sister all strived to wear a size 5, regardless of their heights and body frames. Subsequent to this study, the researchers learned that both the mother and sister had become bulimic.

As pre-anorexics and -bulimics, group members thus exhibited marked conformity to cultural norms of thinness, achievement, compliance, and parental attachment. Their families reinforced their conformity by adherence to norms of family closeness and weight and body shape consciousness.

Primary Deviance

Even with familial encouragement, respondents, like nearly all dieters (Chernin 1981), failed to maintain their lowered weights. Many cited their lack of willpower to eat only restricted foods. For the emerging anorexics and bulimics, extremes such as purposeful starvation or binging accompanied by vomiting and/or laxative abuse appeared as "obvious solutions" to the problem of retaining weight loss. Associated with these behaviors was a regained feeling of control in lives that had been disrupted by a major crisis. Group members' extreme weight-loss efforts operated as coping mechanisms for entering college, leaving home, or feeling rejected by the opposite sex.

The primary inducement for both eating adaptations was the drive for slimness. With slimness came more self-respect and a feeling of superiority over "unsuccessful dieters." Brian, for example, experienced a "power trip" upon consistent weight loss through starvation. Binges allowed the purging respondents to cope with stress through eating while maintaining a slim appearance. As former strict dieters, Teresa and Jennifer used binging and purging as an alternative to the constant self-denial of starvation. Acknowledging their parents' desires for them to be slim, most respondents still felt it was a conscious choice on their part to continue extreme weight-loss efforts. Being thin became the "most important thing" in their lives—their "greatest ambition."

In explaining the development of an anorexic or bulimic identity, Lemert's (1951, 1967) concept of primary deviance is salient. Primary deviance refers to a transitory period of norm violations which do not affect an individual's self-concept or performance of social roles. Although respondents were exhibiting anorexic or bulimic behavior, they did not consider themselves to be anorexic or bulimic.

At first, anorexics' significant others complimented their weight loss, expounding on their new "sleekness" and "good looks." Branch and Eurman (1980) also found anorexics' families and friends describing them as "well groomed," "neat," "fashionable," and "victorious" (p. 631). Not until the respondents approached emaciation did some parents or friends become concerned and withdraw their praise. Significant others also became increasingly aware of the anorexics' compulsive exercising, preoccupation with food preparation (but not consumption), and ritualistic eating patterns (such as cutting food into minute pieces and eating only certain foods at prescribed times).

For bulimics, friends or family members began to question how the respondents could eat such large amounts of food (often in excess of 10,000 calories a day) and stay slim. Significant others also noticed calluses across the bulimics' hands, which were caused by repeated inducement of vomiting. Several bulimics were "caught in the act," bent over commodes. Generally, friends and family required substantial evidence before believing that the respondents' binging or purging was no longer sporadic.

Secondary Deviance

Heightened awareness of group members' eating behavior ultimately led others to label the respondents "anorexic" or "bulimic." Respondents differed in their histories of being labeled and accepting the labels. Generally

first termed anorexic by friends, family, or medical personnel, the anorexics initially vigorously denied the label. They felt they were not "anorexic
enough," not skinny enough; Robin did not regard herself as having the
"skeletal" appearance she associated with anorexia nervosa. These group
members found it difficult to differentiate between socially approved
modes of weight loss—eating less and exercising more—and the extremes
of those behaviors. In fact, many of their activities—cheerleading, modeling, gymnastics, aerobics—reinforced their pursuit of thinness. Like other
anorexics, Chris felt she was being "ultra-healthy," with "total control"
over her body.

For several respondents, admitting they were anorexic followed the realization that their lives were disrupted by their eating disorder. Anorexics'
inflexible eating patterns unsettled family meals and holiday gatherings.
Their regimented lifestyle of compulsively scheduled activities—exercising,
school, and meals—precluded any spontaneous social interactions. Realization of their adverse behaviors preceded the anorexics' acknowledgment of
their subnormal body weight and size.

Contrasting with anorexics, the binge/purgers, when confronted, more
readily admitted that they were bulimic and that their means of weight
loss was "abnormal." Teresa, for example, knew "very well" that her bulimic behavior was "wrong and unhealthy," although "worth the physical
risks." While the bulimics initially maintained that their purging was only a
temporary weight-loss method, they eventually realized that their disorder
represented a "loss of control." Although these respondents regretted the
self-indulgence, "shame," and "wasted time," they acknowledged their
growing dependence on binging and purging for weight management and
stress regulation.

The application of anorexic or bulimic labels precipitated secondary
deviance, wherein group members internalized these identities. Secondary
deviance refers to norm violations which are a response to society's labeling:
"Secondary deviation . . . becomes a means of social defense, attack or adaptation to the overt and covert problems created by the societal reaction to
primary deviance" (Lemert 1967:17). In contrast to primary deviance, secondary deviance is generally prolonged, alters the individual's self-concept,
and affects the performance of his/her social roles.

As secondary deviants, respondents felt that their disorders "gave a purpose" to their lives. Nicole resisted attaining a normal weight because it was
not "her"—she accepted her anorexic weight as her "true" weight. For Teresa,
bulimia became a "companion"; and Julie felt "every aspect of her life," including time management and social activities, was affected by her bulimia.
Group members' eating disorders became the salient element of their self-
concepts so that they related to familiar people and new acquaintances as
anorexics or bulimics. For example, respondents regularly compared their
body shapes and sizes with those of others. They also became sensitized to
comments about their appearance, whether or not the remarks were made by
someone aware of their eating disorder.

With their behavior increasingly attuned to their eating disorders, group members exhibited role engulfment (Schur 1971). Through accepting anorexic or bulimic identities, individuals centered activities around their deviant role, downgrading other social roles. Their obligations as students, family members, and friends became subordinate to their eating and exercising rituals. Socializing, for example, was gradually curtailed because it interfered with compulsive exercising, binging, or purging.

Labeled anorexic or bulimic, respondents were ascribed a new status with a different set of role expectations. Regardless of other positions the individuals occupied, their deviant status, or master status (Becker 1973; Hughes 1958), was identified before all others. Among group members, Nicole, who was known as the "school's brain," became known as the "school's anorexic." No longer viewed as conforming model individuals, some respondents were termed "starving waifs" or "pigs."

Because of their identities as deviants, anorexics' and bulimics' interactions with others were altered. Group members' eating habits were scrutinized by friends and family and used as a "catchall" for everything negative that happened to them. Respondents felt self-conscious around individuals who knew of their disorders; for example, Robin imagined people "watching and whispering" behind her. In addition, group members believed others expected them to "act" anorexic or bulimic. Friends of some anorexic group members never offered them food or drink, assuming continued disinterest on the respondents' part. While being hospitalized, Denise felt she had to prove to others she was not still vomiting, by keeping her bathroom door open. Other bulimics, who lived in dormitories, were hesitant to use the restroom for normal purposes lest several friends be huddling at the door, listening for vomiting. In general, individuals interacted with the respondents largely on the basis of their eating disorder; in doing so, they reinforced anorexic and bulimic behaviors.

Bulimic respondents, whose weight-loss behavior was not generally detectable from their appearance, tried earnestly to hide their bulimia by binging and purging in secret. Their main purpose in concealment was to avoid the negative consequences of being known as a bulimic. For these individuals, bulimia connoted a "cop-out": Like "weak anorexics," bulimics pursued thinness but yielded to urges to eat. Respondents felt other people regarded bulimia as "gross" and had little sympathy for the sufferer. To avoid these stigmas or "spoiled identities," the bulimics shrouded their behaviors.

Distinguishing types of stigma, Goffman (1963) describes discredited (visible) stigmas and discreditable (invisible) stigmas. Bulimics, whose weight was approximately normal or even slightly elevated, harbored discreditable stigmas. Anorexics, on the other hand, suffered both discreditable and discredited stigmas—the latter due to their emaciated appearance. Certain anorexics were more reconciled than the bulimics to their stigmas: For Brian, the "stigma of anorexia was better than being fat." Common to the stigmatized individuals was an inability to interact spontaneously with others. Respondents were constantly on guard against topics of eating and body size.

Both anorexics and bulimics were held responsible by others for their behavior and presumed able to "get out of it if they tried." Many anorexics reported being told to "just eat more," while bulimics were enjoined to simply "stop eating so much." Such appeals were made without regard for the complexities of the problem. Ostracized by certain friends and family members, anorexics and bulimics felt increasingly isolated. For respondents, the self-help group presented a nonthreatening forum for discussing their disorders. Here, they found mutual understanding, empathy, and support. Many participants viewed BANISH as a haven from stigmatization by "others."

Group members, as secondary deviants, thus endured negative consequences, such as stigmatization, from being labeled. As they internalized the labels anorexic or bulimic, individuals' self-concepts were significantly influenced. When others interacted with the respondents on the basis of their eating disorders, anorexic or bulimic identities were encouraged. Moreover, group members' efforts to counteract the deviant labels were thwarted by their master status.

Discussion

Previous research on eating disorders has dwelt almost exclusively on medical and psychological facets. Although necessary for a comprehensive understanding of anorexia nervosa and bulimia, these approaches neglect the social processes involved. The phenomena of eating disorders transcend concrete disease entities and clinical diagnoses. Multifaceted and complex, anorexia nervosa and bulimia require a holistic research design, in which sociological insights must be included.

A limitation of medical and psychiatric studies, in particular, is researchers' use of a priori criteria in establishing salient variables. Rather than utilizing predetermined standards of inclusion, the present study allows respondents to construct their own reality. Concomitant to this innovative approach to eating disorders is the selection of a sample of self-admitted anorexics and bulimics. Individuals' perceptions of what it means to become anorexic or bulimic are explored. Although based on a small sample, findings can be used to guide researchers in other settings.

With only 5 to 10 percent of reported cases appearing in males (Crisp 1977; Stangler and Printz 1980), eating disorders are primarily a women's aberrance. The deviance of anorexia nervosa and bulimia is rooted in the visual objectification of women and attendant slimness norm. Indeed, purposeful starvation and binging and purging reinforce the notion that "a society gets the deviance it deserves" (Schur 1979:71). As noted (Schur 1984), the sociology of deviance has generally bypassed systematic studies of women's norm violations. Like male deviants, females endure label applications, internalizations, and fulfillments.

The social processes involved in developing anorexic or bulimic identities comprise the sequence of conforming behavior, primary deviance, and secondary deviance. With a background of exceptional adherence to conventional norms, especially the striving for thinness, respondents subsequently exhibit the primary deviance of starving or binging and purging. Societal reaction to these behaviors leads to secondary deviance, wherein respondents' self-concepts and master statuses become anorexic or bulimic. Within this framework of labeling theory, the persistence of eating disorders, as well as the effects of stigmatization, are elucidated.

Although during the course of this research some respondents alleviated their symptoms through psychiatric help or hospital treatment programs, no one was labeled "cured." An anorexic is considered recovered when weight is normal for two years; a bulimic is termed recovered after being symptom-free for one and one-half years (American Anorexia and Bulimia Association Newsletter 1985). Thus deviance disavowal (Schur 1971), or efforts after normalization to counteract deviant labels, remains a topic for future exploration.

ENDNOTES

[1] Although instructive, an integration of the medical, psychological, and sociocultural perspectives on eating disorders is beyond the scope of this paper.

[2] Exceptions to the neglect of sociocultural factors are discussions of sex-role socialization in the development of eating disorders. Anorexics' girlish appearance has been interpreted as a rejection of femininity and womanhood (Bruch 1981; Orbach 1979, 1985). In contrast, bulimics have been characterized as overconforming to traditional female sex roles (Boskind-Lodahl 1976).

[3] Although a group experience for self-defined bulimics has been reported (Boskind-Lodahl 1976), the researcher, from the outset, focused on Gestalt and behaviorist techniques within a feminist orientation.

[4] One explanation for fewer anorexics than bulimics in the sample is that, in the general population, anorexics are outnumbered by bulimics at 8 or 10 to 1 (Lawson, as reprinted in American Anorexia and Bulimia Association Newsletter 1985:1). The proportion of bulimics to anorexics in the sample is 6.5 to 1. In addition, compared to bulimics, anorexics may be less likely to attend a self-help group as they have a greater tendency to deny the existence of an eating problem (Humphries et al. 1982). However, the four anorexics in the present study were among the members who attended the meetings most often.

[5] Interactions in the families of anorexics and bulimics might seem deviant in being inordinately close. However, in the larger societal context, the family members epitomize the norms of family cohesiveness. Perhaps unusual in their occurrence, these families are still within the realm of conformity. Humphries and colleagues (1982) refer to the "highly enmeshed and protective" family as part of the "idealized family myth" (p. 202).

REFERENCES

American Anorexia/Bulimia Association. 1983, April. Correspondence.
American Anorexia/Bulimia Association Newsletter. 1985. 8(3).
Becker, Howard S. 1973. *Outsiders*. New York: Free Press.
Boskind-Lodahl, Marlene. 1976. "Cinderella's Stepsisters: A Feminist Perspective on Anorexia Nervosa and Bulimia." *Signs, Journal of Women in Culture and Society* 2:342–56.
Boskind-White, Marlene. 1985. "Bulimarexia: A Sociocultural Perspective." Pp. 113–26 in *Theory and Treatment of Anorexia Nervosa and Bulimia: Biomedical, Sociocultural and Psychological Perspectives*, edited by S. W. Emmett. New York: Brunner/Mazel.
Branch, C. H. Hardin and Linda J. Eurman. 1980. "Social Attitudes toward Patients with Anorexia Nervosa." *American Journal of Psychiatry* 137:631–32.
Bruch, Hilda. 1981. "Developmental Considerations of Anorexia Nervosa and Obesity." *Canadian Journal of Psychiatry* 26:212–16.
Chernin, Kim. 1981. *The Obsession: Reflections on the Tyranny of Slenderness*. New York: Harper & Row.

Crisp, A. H. 1977. "The Prevalence of Anorexia Nervosa and Some of Its Associations in the General Population." *Advances in Psychosomatic Medicine* 9:38–47.

Crisp, A. H., R. L. Palmer, and R. S. Kalucy. 1976. "How Common Is Anorexia Nervosa? A Prevalence Study." *British Journal of Psychiatry* 128:549–54.

DeJong, William. 1980. "The Stigma of Obesity: The Consequences of Naive Assumptions Concerning the Causes of Physical Deviance." *Journal of Health and Social Behavior* 21:75–87.

Fox, K. C. and N. McI. James. 1976. "Anorexia Nervosa: A Study of 44 Strictly Defined Cases." *New Zealand Medical Journal* 84:309–12.

Garner, David M., Paul E. Garfinkel, Donald Schwartz, and Michael Thompson. 1980. "Cultural Expectations of Thinness in Women." *Psychological Reports* 47:483–91.

Goffman, Erving. 1963. *Stigma.* Englewood Cliffs, NJ: Prentice-Hall.

Halmi, Katherine A., James R. Falk, and Estelle Schwartz. 1981. "Binge-Eating and Vomiting: A Survey of a College Population." *Psychological Medicine* 11:697–706.

Herzog, David B. 1982. "Bulimia: The Secretive Syndrome." *Psychosomatics* 23:481–83.

Hughes, Everett C. 1958. *Men and Their Work.* New York: Free Press.

Humphries, Laurie L., Sylvia Wrobel, and H. Thomas Wiegert. 1982. "Anorexia Nervosa." *American Family Physician* 26:199–204.

Johnson, Craig L., Marilyn K. Stuckey, Linda D. Lewis, and Donald M. Schwartz. 1982. "Bulimia: A Descriptive Survey of 316 Cases." *International Journal of Eating Disorders* 2(1):3–16.

Kalucy, R. S., A. H. Crisp, and Britta Harding. 1977. "A Study of 56 Families with Anorexia Nervosa." *British Journal of Medical Psychology* 50:381–95.

Lacey, Hubert J., Sian Coker, and S. A. Birtchnell. 1986. "Bulimia: Factors Associated with Its Etiology and Maintenance." *International Journal of Eating Disorders* 5:475–87.

Lemert, Edwin M. 1951. *Social Pathology.* New York: McGraw-Hill.

———. 1967. *Human Deviance, Social Problems and Social Control.* Englewood Cliffs, NJ: Prentice-Hall.

Minuchin, Salvador, Bernice L. Rosman, and Lester Baker. 1978. *Psychosomatic Families: Anorexia Nervosa in Context.* Cambridge, MA: Harvard University Press.

Orbach, Susie. 1979. *Fat Is a Feminist Issue.* New York: Berkeley.

———. 1985. "Visibility/Invisibility: Social Considerations in Anorexia Nervosa—a Feminist Perspective." Pp. 127–38 in *Theory and Treatment of Anorexia Nervosa and Bulimia: Biomedical, Sociocultural and Psychological Perspectives,* edited by S. W. Emmett. New York: Brunner/Mazel.

Ritenbaugh, Cheryl. 1982. "Obesity As a Culture-Bound Syndrome." *Culture, Medicine and Psychiatry* 6:347–61.

Russell, Gerald. 1979. "Bulimia Nervosa: An Ominous Variant of Anorexia Nervosa." *Psychological Medicine* 9:429–48.

Schlesier-Stropp, Barbara. 1984. "Bulimia: A Review of the Literature." *Psychological Bulletin* 95:247–57.

Schur, Edwin M. 1971. *Labeling Deviant Behavior.* New York: Harper & Row.

———. 1979. *Interpreting Deviance: A Sociological Introduction.* New York: Harper & Row.

———. 1984. *Labeling Women Deviant: Gender, Stigma, and Social Control.* New York: Random House.

Schwartz, Donald M. and Michael G. Thompson. 1981. "Do Anorectics Get Well? Current Research and Future Needs." *American Journal of Psychiatry* 138:319–23.

Schwartz, Donald M., Michael G. Thompson, and Craig L. Johnson. 1982. "Anorexia Nervosa and Bulimia: The Socio-Cultural Context." *International Journal of Eating Disorders* 1(3):20–36.

Selvini-Palazzoli, Mara. 1978. *Self-Starvation: From Individual to Family Therapy in the Treatment of Anorexia Nervosa.* New York: Jason Aronson.

Stangler, Ronnie S. and Adolph M. Printz. 1980. "DSM-III: Psychiatric Diagnosis in a University Population." *American Journal of Psychiatry* 137:937–40.

Theander, Sten. 1970. "Anorexia Nervosa." *Acta Psychiatrica Scandinavica Supplement* 214:24–31.

Thompson, Michael G. and Donald M. Schwartz. 1982. "Life Adjustment of Women with Anorexia Nervosa and Anorexic-like Behavior." *International Journal of Eating Disorders* 1(2):47–60.

Willi, Jurg and Samuel Grossman. 1983. "Epidemiology of Anorexia Nervosa in a Defined Region of Switzerland." *American Journal of Psychiatry* 140:564–67.

21

IN SEARCH OF RESPECT
Selling Crack in El Barrio

PHILIPPE BOURGOIS

One type of social deviance, according to sociologists, is crime. If deviance is the violation of a social norm, then a *crime* is the violation of social norms that have been made into laws. One type of crime that sociologists have long studied is illegal drug use. Why do segments of the population use and abuse illegal drugs? How can we explain the growing underground economy of illegal drugs? In this selection, taken from *In Search of Respect: Selling Crack in El Barrio* (1995), Philippe Bourgois takes us inside the crack economy in East Harlem, New York City. Bourgois, professor and chair of anthropology at the San Francisco Urban Institute, spent three and a half years living in "El Barrio," where he came to know the residents and their day-to-day struggles for economic survival. Bourgois' ethnographic account of life and social marginalization in this inner-city neighborhood reveals that many social factors lead people to deal illegal drugs and that other social barriers prevent them from reentering the legal economy.

I was forced into crack against my will. When I first moved to East Harlem—"El Barrio"—as a newlywed in the spring of 1985, I was looking for an inexpensive New York City apartment from which I could write about the experience of poverty and ethnic segregation in the heart of one of the most expensive cities in the world. I was interested in the political economy of inner-city street culture. I wanted to probe the Achilles' heel of the richest industrialized nation in the world by documenting how it imposes racial segregation and economic marginalization on so many of its Latino/a and African American citizens.

My original subject was the entire underground (untaxed) economy, from curbside car repairing and baby-sitting to unlicensed off-track betting and drug dealing. I had never even heard of crack when I first arrived in the neighborhood—no one knew about this particular substance yet, because this brittle compound of cocaine and baking soda processed into efficiently smokable pellets was not yet available as a mass-marketed product. By the end of the year, however, most of my friends, neighbors and acquaintances had been swept into the multibillion-dollar crack cyclone: selling it, smoking it, fretting over it. I followed them, and I watched the murder rate in the projects opposite my crumbling tenement apartment spiral into one of the highest in Manhattan.

But this essay is not about crack, or drugs, per se. Substance abuse in the inner city is merely a symptom—and a vivid symbol—of deeper dynamics of social marginalization and alienation. Of course, on an immediately visible personal level, addiction and substance abuse are among the most immediate, brutal facts shaping daily life on the street. Most important, however, the two dozen street dealers and their families that I befriended were not interested in talking primarily about drugs. On the contrary, they wanted me to learn all about their daily struggles for subsistence and dignity at the poverty line.

Through the 1980s and 1990s, slightly more than one in three families in El Barrio have received public assistance. Female heads of these impoverished households have to supplement their meager checks in order to keep their children alive. Many are mothers who make extra money by babysitting their neighbors' children, or by housekeeping for a paying boarder. Others may bartend at one of the half-dozen social clubs and after-hours dancing spots scattered throughout the neighborhood. Some work "off the books" in their living rooms as seamstresses for garment contractors. Finally, many also find themselves obliged to establish amorous relationships with men who are willing to make cash contributions to their household expenses.

Male income-generating strategies in the underground economy are more publicly visible. Some men repair cars on the curb; others wait on stoops for unlicensed construction subcontractors to pick them up for fly-by-night demolition jobs or window renovation projects. Many sell "numbers"—the street's version of off-track betting. The most visible cohorts hawk "nickels and dimes" of one illegal drug or another. They are part of the most robust, multibillion-dollar sector of the booming underground economy. Cocaine and crack, in particular during the mid-1980s and through the early 1990s, followed by heroin in the mid-1990s, have become the fastest-growing—if not the only—equal-opportunity employers of men in Harlem. Retail drug sales easily outcompete other income-generating opportunities, whether legal or illegal.

Why should these young men and women take the subway to work minimum-wage jobs—or even double-minimum-wage jobs—in downtown offices when they can usually earn more, at least in the short run, by selling drugs on the street corner in front of their apartment or schoolyard? In fact, I am always surprised that so many inner-city men and women remain in the legal economy and work nine-to-five plus overtime, barely making ends meet. According to the 1990 Census of East Harlem, 48 percent of all males and 35 percent of females over 16 were employed in officially reported jobs, compared with a citywide average of 64 percent for men and 49 percent for women. In the census tracts surrounding my apartment, 53 percent of all men over 16 years of age (1,923 out of 3,647) and 28 percent of all women over 16 (1,307 out of 4,626) were working legally in officially censused jobs. An additional 17 percent of the civilian labor force was unemployed but actively looking for work, compared with 16 percent for El Barrio as a whole, and 9 percent for all of New York City.

"If I Was Working Legal . . ."

Street dealers tend to brag to outsiders and to themselves about how much money they make each night. In fact, their income is almost never as consistently high as they report it to be. Most street sellers, like my friend Primo (who, along with other friends and co-workers, allowed me to tape hundreds of hours of conversation with him over five years), are paid on a piece-rate commission basis. When converted into an hourly wage, this is often a relatively paltry sum. According to my calculations, the workers in the Game Room crackhouse, for example, averaged slightly less than double the legal minimum wage—between seven and eight dollars an hour. There were plenty of exceptional nights, however, when they made up to ten times minimum wage—and these are the nights they remember when they reminisce. They forget about all the other shifts when they were unable to work because of police raids, and they certainly do not count as forfeited working hours the nights they spent in jail.

This was brought home to me symbolically one night as Primo and his co-worker Caesar were shutting down the Game Room. Caesar unscrewed the fuses in the electrical box to disconnect the video games. Primo had finished stashing the leftover bundles of crack vials inside a hollowed-out live electrical socket and was counting the night's thick wad of receipts. I was struck by how thin the handful of bills was that he separated out and folded neatly into his personal billfold. Primo and Caesar then eagerly lowered the iron riot gates over the Game Room's windows and snapped shut the heavy Yale padlocks. They were moving with the smooth, hurried gestures of workers preparing to go home after an honest day's hard labor. Marveling at the universality in the body language of workers rushing at closing time, I felt an urge to compare the wages paid by this alternative economy. I grabbed Primo's wallet out of his back pocket, carefully giving a wide berth to the fatter wad in his front pocket that represented Ray's share of the night's income—and that could cost Primo his life if it were waylaid. Unexpectedly, I pulled out fifteen dollars' worth of food stamps along with two $20 bills. After an embarrassed giggle, Primo stammered that his mother had added him to her food-stamp allotment.

> Primo: *I gave my girl, Maria, half of it. I said, "Here take it, use it if you need it for whatever." And then the other half I still got it in my wallet for emergencies.*
>
> *Like that, we always got a couple of dollars here and there, to survive with. Because tonight, straight cash, I only got garbage. Forty dollars! Do you believe that?*

At the same time that wages can be relatively low in the crack economy, working conditions are often inferior to those in the legal economy. Aside from the obvious dangers of being shot, or of going to prison, the physical work space of most crackhouses is usually unpleasant. The infrastructure of the Game Room, for example, was much worse than that of any legal retail outfit in East Harlem: There was no bathroom, no running water, no telephone, no heat in the winter and no air conditioning in the summer. Primo occasionally complained:

> *Everything that you see here* [sweeping his arm at the scratched and dented video games, the walls with peeling paint, the floor slippery with litter, the filthy windows pasted over with ripped movie posters] *is fucked up. It sucks, man* [pointing at the red 40-watt bare bulb hanging from an exposed fixture in the middle of the room and exuding a sickly twilight].

Indeed, the only furnishings besides the video games were a few grimy milk crates and bent aluminum stools. Worse yet, a smell of urine and vomit usually permeated the locale. For a few months Primo was able to maintain a rudimentary sound system, but it was eventually beaten to a pulp during one of Caesar's drunken rages. Of course, the deficient infrastructure was only one part of the depressing working conditions.

> Primo: *Plus I don't like to see people fucked up* [handing over three vials to a nervously pacing customer]. *This is fucked-up shit. I don't like this crack dealing. Word up.*
>
> [gunshots in the distance] *Hear that?*

In private, especially in the last few years of my residence, Primo admitted that he wanted to go back to the legal economy.

> Primo: *I just fuck up the money here. I rather be legal.*
>
> Philippe: *But you wouldn't be the head man on the block with so many girlfriends.*
>
> Primo: *I might have women on my dick right now but I would be much cooler if I was working legal. I wouldn't be drinking and the coke wouldn't be there every night.*
>
> *Plus if I was working legally I would have women on my dick too, because I would have money.*
>
> Philippe: *But you make more money here than you could ever make working legit.*
>
> Primo: *O.K. So you want the money but you really don't want to do the job.*
>
> *I really hate it, man. Hate it! I hate the people! I hate the environment! I hate the whole shit, man! But it's like you get caught up with it. You do it, and you say, "Ay, fuck it today!" Another day, another dollar.* [pointing at an emaciated customer who was just entering] *But I don't really, really think that I would have hoped that I can say I'm gonna be richer one day. I can't say that. I think about it, but I'm just living day to day.*

If I was working legal, I wouldn't be hanging out so much. I wouldn't be treating you. [pointing to the 16-ounce can of Colt 45 in my hand] *In a job, you know, my environment would change . . . totally. 'Cause I'd have different friends. Right after work I'd go out with a co-worker, for lunch, for dinner. After work I may go home; I'm too tired for hanging out—I know I gotta work tomorrow.*

After working a legal job, I'm pretty sure I'd be good.

Burned in the FIRE Economy

The problem is that Primo's good intentions do not lead anywhere when the only legal jobs he can compete for fail to provide him with a livable wage. None of the crack dealers were explicitly conscious of the links between their limited options in the legal economy, their addiction to drugs, and their dependence on the crack economy for economic survival and personal dignity. Nevertheless, all of Primo's colleagues and employees told stories of rejecting what they considered to be intolerable working conditions at entry-level jobs.

Most entered the legal labor market at exceptionally young ages. By the time they were 12, they were bagging and delivering groceries at the supermarket for tips, stocking beer off the books in local bodegas, or running errands. Before reaching 21, however, virtually none had fulfilled their early childhood dreams of finding stable, well-paid legal work.

The problem is structural: From the 1950s through the 1980s, second-generation inner-city Puerto Ricans were trapped in the most vulnerable niche of a factory-based economy that was rapidly being replaced by service industries. Between 1950 and 1990, the proportion of factory jobs in New York City decreased approximately threefold at the same time that service-sector jobs doubled. The Department of City Planning calculates that more than 800,000 industrial jobs were lost from the 1960s through the early 1990s, while the total number of jobs in all categories remained more or less constant at 3.5 million.

Few scholars have noted the cultural dislocations of the new service economy. These cultural clashes have been most pronounced in the office-work service jobs that have multiplied because of the dramatic expansion of the finance, insurance and real estate (FIRE) sector in New York City. Service work in professional offices is the most dynamic place for ambitious inner-city youths to find entry-level jobs if they aspire to upward mobility. Employment as mailroom clerks, photocopiers, and messengers in the high-rise office corridors of the financial district propels many into a wrenching cultural confrontation with the upper-middle-class white world. Obedience to the norms of high-rise, office-corridor culture is in direct contradiction to street culture's definitions of personal dignity, especially for males who are socialized not to accept public subordination.

Most of the dealers have not completely withdrawn from the legal economy. On the contrary—they are precariously perched on its edge. Their poverty remains their only constant as they alternate between street-level crack dealing and just-above-minimum-wage legal employment. The working-class jobs they manage to find are objectively recognized to be among the least desirable in U.S. society; hence the following list of just a few of the jobs held by some of the Game Room regulars during the years I knew them: unlicensed asbestos remover, home attendant, street-corner flier distributor, deep-fat fry cook, and night-shift security guard on the violent ward at the municipal hospital for the criminally insane.

The stable factory-worker incomes that might have allowed Caesar and Primo to support families have largely disappeared from the inner city. Perhaps if their social network had not been confined to the weakest sector of manufacturing in a period of rapid job loss, their teenage working-class dreams might have stabilized them long enough to enable them to adapt to the restructuring of the local economy. Instead, they find themselves propelled headlong into an explosive confrontation between their sense of cultural dignity versus the humiliating interpersonal subordination of service work.

Workers like Caesar and Primo appear inarticulate to their professional supervisors when they try to imitate the language of power in the workplace; they stumble pathetically over the enunciation of unfamiliar words. They cannot decipher the hastily scribbled instructions—rife with mysterious abbreviations—that are left for them by harried office managers on diminutive Post-its. The "common sense" of white-collar work is foreign to them; they do not, for example, understand the logic in filing triplicate copies of memos or for postdating invoices. When they attempt to improvise or show initiative, they fail miserably and instead appear inefficient—or even hostile—for failing to follow "clearly specified" instructions.

In the high-rise office buildings of midtown Manhattan or Wall Street, newly employed inner-city high school dropouts suddenly realize they look like idiotic buffoons to the men and women for whom they work. But people like Primo and Caesar have not passively accepted their structural victimization. On the contrary, by embroiling themselves in the underground economy and proudly embracing street culture, they are seeking an alternative to their social marginalization. In the process, on a daily level, they become the actual agents administering their own destruction and their community's suffering.

Both Primo and Caesar experienced deep humiliation and insecurity in their attempts to penetrate the foreign, hostile world of high-rise office corridors. Primo had bitter memories of being the mailroom clerk and errand boy at a now-defunct professional trade magazine. The only time he explicitly admitted to having experienced racism was when he described how he was treated at that particular work setting.

> Primo: *I had a prejudiced boss. . . . When she was talking to people she would say, "He's illiterate," as if I was really that stupid that I couldn't understand what she was talking about.*

So what I did one day—you see they had this big dictionary right there on the desk, a big heavy motherfucker—so what I just did was open up the dictionary, and I just looked up the word, "illiterate." And that's when I saw what she was calling me.

So she's saying that I'm stupid or something. I'm stupid! [pointing to himself with both thumbs and making a hulking face] *"She doesn't know shit."*

In contrast, in the underground economy Primo never had to risk this kind of threat to his self-worth.

Primo: *Ray would never disrespect me that way; he wouldn't tell me that because he's illiterate too, plus I've got more education than him. I almost got a G.E.D.*

The contemporary street sensitivity to being dissed immediately emerges in these memories of office humiliation. The machismo of street culture exacerbates the sense of insult experienced by men because the majority of office supervisors at the entry level are women. In the lowest recesses of New York City's FIRE sector, tens of thousands of messengers, photocopy machine operators, and security guards serving the Fortune 500 companies are brusquely ordered about by young white executives—often female—who sometimes make bimonthly salaries superior to their underlings' yearly wages. The extraordinary wealth of Manhattan's financial district exacerbates the sense of sexist-racist insult associated with performing just-above-minimum-wage labor.

"I Don't Even Got a Dress Shirt"

Several months earlier, I had watched Primo drop out of a "motivational training" employment program in the basement of his mother's housing project, run by former heroin addicts who had just received a multimillion-dollar private sector grant for their innovative approach to training the "unemployable." Primo felt profoundly disrespected by the program, and he focused his discontent on the humiliation he faced because of his inappropriate wardrobe. The fundamental philosophy of such motivational job-training programs is that "these people have an attitude problem." They take a boot-camp approach to their unemployed clients, ripping their self-esteem apart during the first week in order to build them back up with an epiphanic realization that they want to find jobs as security guards, messengers, and data-input clerks in just-above-minimum-wage service-sector positions. The program's highest success rate had been with middle-aged African American women who wanted to terminate their relationship to welfare once their children leave home.

I originally had a "bad attitude" toward the premise of psychologically motivating and manipulating people to accept boring, poorly paid jobs. At the same time, however, the violence and self-destruction I was witnessing at the Game Room were convincing me that it is better to be exploited at work than to be outside the legal labor market. In any case, I persuaded

Primo and a half-dozen of his Game Room associates to sign up for the program. Even Caesar was tempted to join.

None of the crack dealers lasted for more than three sessions. Primo was the first to drop out, after the first day. For several weeks he avoided talking about the experience. I repeatedly pressed him to explain why he "just didn't show up" at the sessions. Only after repeated badgering on my part did he finally express the deep sense of shame and vulnerability he experienced whenever he attempted to venture into the legal labor market.

> Philippe: *Yo, Primo, listen to me. I worry that there's something taking place that you're not aware of, in terms of yourself. Like the coke that you be sniffing all the time; it's like every night.*
>
> Primo: *What do you mean?*
>
> Philippe: *Like not showing up at the job training. You say it's just procrastination, but I'm scared it's something deeper that you're not dealing with. Like wanting to be partying all night, and sniffing. Maybe that's why you never went back.*
>
> Primo: *The truth though—listen, Felipe—my biggest worry was the dress code, 'cause my gear is limited. I don't even got a dress shirt, I only got one pair of shoes, and you can't wear sneakers at that program. They wear ties too—don't they? Well, I ain't even got ties—I only got the one you lent me.*
>
>   *I would've been there three weeks in the same gear. T-shirt and jeans.* Estoy jodido como un bón! *[I'm all fucked up like a bum!]*
>
> Philippe: *What the fuck kinda bullshit excuse are you talking about? Don't tell me you were thinking that shit. No one notices how people are dressed.*
>
> Primo: *Yo, Felipe, this is for real! Listen to me! I was thinking about that shit hard. Hell yeah!*
>
>   *Hell yes they would notice, because I would notice if somebody's wearing a fucked-up tie and shirt.*
>
>   *I don't want to be in a program all* abochornado *[bumlike]. I probably won't even concentrate, getting dissed, like . . . and being looked at like a sucker. Dirty jeans . . . or like old jeans, because I would have to wear jeans, 'cause I only got one slack. Word though! I only got two dress shirts and one of them is missing buttons.*
>
>   *I didn't want to tell you about that because it's like a poor excuse, but that was the only shit I was really thinking about. At the time I just said, "Well, I just don't show up."*
>
>   *And Felipe, I'm a stupid [very] skinny nigga'. So I have to be careful how I dress, otherwise people will think I be on the stem* [a crack addict who smokes out of a glass-stem pipe].
>
> Philippe: [nervously] *Oh shit. I'm even skinnier than you. People must think I'm a total drug addict.*
>
> Primo: *Don't worry. You're white.*

Obviously, the problem is deeper than not having enough money to buy straight-world clothes. Racism and the other subtle badges of symbolic power are expressed through wardrobes and body language. Ultimately, Primo's biggest problem was that he had no idea of what clothes might be appropriate in the professional, service sector context. Like Caesar, he feared he might appear to be a buffoon on parade on the days when he was trying to dress up. He admitted that the precipitating factor in his decision not to go back to the job training program was when he overheard someone accusing Candy of "looking tacky" after she proudly inaugurated her new fancy clothes at the first class. As a matter of fact, Primo had thought she had looked elegant in her skintight, yellow jumpsuit when she came over to his apartment to display her new outfit proudly to him and his mother before going to class.

Isolating oneself in inner-city street culture removes any danger of having to face the humiliations Candy, Caesar, or Primo inevitably confront when they venture out of their social circle to try to find legal employment. . . .

Conclusion

Ooh, Felipe! You make us sound like such sensitive crack dealers.
                    —CAESAR [COMMENTING ON THE MANUSCRIPT]

There is no panacea for the suffering and self-destruction of the protagonists in these pages. Solutions to inner-city poverty and substance abuse framed in terms of public policy often appear naive or hopelessly idealistic. Given the dimensions of structural oppression in the United States, it is atheoretical to expect isolated policy initiatives, or even short-term political reforms, to remedy the plight of the poor in U.S. urban centers in the short or medium term. Racism and class segregation in the United States are shaped in too complex a mesh of political-economic structural forces, historical legacies, cultural imperatives, and individual actions to be susceptible to simple solutions.

There are also the inevitable limits of political feasibility. For a number of complicated historical and ideological reasons, the United States simply lacks the political will to address poverty in any concerted manner. Nevertheless, I hope my presentation of the experience of social marginalization in El Barrio, as seen through the struggles for dignity and survival of Ray's crack dealers and their families, contributes on a concrete practical level to calling attention to the tragedy of persistent poverty and racial segregation in the urban United States. I cannot resign myself to the terrible irony that the richest industrialized nation on earth, and the greatest world power in history, confines so many of its citizens to poverty and to prison. . . .

The increasing material and political powerlessness of the working poor in the United States needs to become a central concern. The concentration of poverty, substance abuse, and criminality within inner-city enclaves such as East Harlem is the product of state policy and free market forces that have inscribed spatially the rising levels of social inequality discussed earlier. More subtly, this urban decay expresses itself in the growing polarization around street culture in North America, giving rise to what some observers call a "crisis in U.S. race relations." Middle-class society and its elites increasingly have been able to disassociate themselves from the ethnically distinct, urban-based working poor and unemployed who inhabit the inner city. Budget cuts and fiscal austerity have accelerated the trend toward public sector breakdown in impoverished urban neighborhoods, while services improve, or at least stay the same, in Anglo-dominated, wealthy suburban communities.

The psychological-reductionist and cultural-essentialist analyses of social marginalization that pass for common sense in the United States frame solutions to racism and poverty around short-term interventions that target the "bad attitude" of individuals. The biggest sociological unit for most poverty policy intervention, for example, is the nuclear family. Job training programs emphasize attitude and personal empowerment. Seminars designed to promote multicultural sensitivity are fashionable in both public and private sector institutions. While these initiatives are not harmful, and might even help superficially on the margins, it is the institutionalized expression of racism—America's de facto apartheid and inner-city public sector breakdown—that government policy and private sector philanthropy need to address if anything is ever to change significantly in the long run.

In other words, to draw on a classic metaphor from sports, the United States needs to level its playing field. Concretely, this means that the garbage needs to be picked up, schools have to teach, and laws must be enforced, as effectively in Latino/a, African American, Asian, and Native American communities as they are in white, middle-class suburbs. There is nothing particularly complicated or subtle about remedying the unequal provision of public funds and services across class and ethnic lines. Hundreds of short-term policy and legal reforms immediately jump to mind: from tax reform—namely, taxing the home mortgages of the upper middle class and exempting the federal and state transfer benefits of the poor—to streamlining access to social welfare benefits and democratizing educational institutions—namely, universal affordable health care coverage, free day care, equalizing per capita funding for schools and universities, and so on.

One message the crack dealers communicated clearly to me is that they are not driven solely by simple economic exigency. Like most humans on earth, in addition to material subsistence, they are also searching for dignity and fulfillment. In the Puerto Rican context, this incorporates cultural definitions of *respeto* built around a personal concern for autonomy, self-assertion, and community within constantly changing social hierarchies of statuses based on kinship, age, and gender. Complex cultural and social dimensions that extend far beyond material and logistical requirements have to be addressed by poverty policies if the socially marginal in the United States are ever going to be able to demand, and earn, the respect that mainstream society needs to share with them for its own good. Specifically, this means evaluating how public policy initiatives and the more impersonal political economy forces of the larger society interact with rapidly changing cultural definitions of gender and family. Women, children, and the elderly constitute most of the poor in the United States. Public policy intervention consequently should prioritize the needs of women and children instead of marginalizing them. Most important, poor women should not be forced to seek desperate alliances with men in order to stay sheltered, fed, clothed, and healthy. Current welfare policy explicitly encourages mothers to seek men with unreported illegal income. . . .

The painful symptoms of inner-city apartheid will continue to produce record numbers of substance abusers, violent criminals, and emotionally disabled and angry youths if nothing is done to reverse the trends in the United States, since the late 1960s, around rising relative poverty rates and escalating ethnic and class segregation.

Given the bleak perspectives for policy reform at the federal level, on the one hand, or for political mobilization in the U.S. inner city, on the other, my most immediate goal in this research is to humanize the public enemies of the United States without sanitizing or glamorizing them. In documenting the depths of personal pain that are inherent to the experience of persistent poverty and institutional racism, I hope to contribute to our understanding of the fundamental processes and dynamics of oppression in the United States. More subtly, I also want to place drug dealers and street-level criminals into their rightful position within the mainstream of U.S. society. They are not "exotic others" operating in an irrational netherworld. On the contrary, they are "made in America." Highly motivated, ambitious inner-city youths have been attracted to the rapidly expanding, multibillion-dollar drug economy during the 1980s and 1990s precisely because they believe in Horatio Alger's version of the American Dream.

Like most other people in the United States, drug dealers and street criminals are scrambling to obtain their piece of the pie as fast as possible. In fact, in their pursuit of success they are even following the minute details of the classical Yankee model for upward mobility. They are aggressively pursuing careers as private entrepreneurs; they take risks, work hard, and pray for good luck. They are the ultimate rugged individualists braving an unpredictable frontier where fortune, fame, and destruction are all just around the corner, and where the enemy is ruthlessly hunted down and shot. In the specifically Puerto Rican context, resistance to mainstream society's domination and pride in street culture identity resonates with a reinvented vision of the defiant *jíbaro* who refused to succumb to elite society's denigration under Spanish and U.S. colonialism. The hyper-urban reconstruction of a hip-hop version of the rural *jíbaro* represents the triumph of a newly constituted Puerto Rican cultural assertion among the most marginalized members of the Puerto Rican diaspora. The tragedy is that the material base for this determined search for cultural respect is confined to the street economy.

At the same time, there is nothing exotically Puerto Rican about the triumphs and failures of the protagonists of this study. On the contrary, "mainstream America" should be able to see itself in the characters presented on these pages and recognize the linkages. The inner city represents the United States' greatest domestic failing, hanging like a Damocles sword over the larger society. Ironically, the only force preventing this suspended sword from falling is that drug dealers, addicts, and street criminals internalize their rage and desperation. They direct their brutality against themselves and their immediate community rather than against their structural oppressors. From a comparative perspective, and in a historical context, the painful and prolonged self-destruction of people like Primo, Caesar, Candy, and their children is cruel and unnecessary. There is no technocratic solution. Any long-term paths out of the quagmire will have to address the structural and political economic roots, as well as the ideological and cultural roots, of social marginalization. The first step out of the impasse, however, requires a fundamental ethical and political reevaluation of basic socioeconomic models and human values.

22

FRATERNITIES AND COLLEGIATE RAPE CULTURE
Why Are Some Fraternities More Dangerous Places for Women?

A. AYRES BOSWELL • JOAN Z. SPADE

Conflict theory suggests that, in our society, who and what the label "deviant" is placed on is based primarily on relative power. Those who have more authority and control define what is "normal" and what is deviant. Moreover, conflict theorists argue that social norms, including laws, generally reflect the interests of the rich and powerful. Thus, historically, we have property laws to protect against the theft of property of the landowning classes and domestic laws that protect the status of men, as patriarchs, within the family. This reading by A. Ayres Boswell and Joan Z. Spade, originally published in 1996, exemplifies this process, in which the privileged attempt to socially construct deviance and crime to their advantage. In particular, Boswell and Spade analyze the social contexts of and gendered relations in male fraternities that contribute to the high incidence of violence against women on many college campuses. Joan Z. Spade is a professor of sociology at the State University of New York, Brockport.

D ate rape and acquaintance rape on college campuses are topics of concern to both researchers and college administrators. Some estimate that 60 to 80 percent of rapes are date or acquaintance rape (Koss, Dinero, Seibel, and Cox 1988). Further, 1 out of 4 college women say they were raped or experienced an attempted rape, and 1 out of 12 college men say they forced a woman to have sexual intercourse against her will (Koss, Gidycz, and Wisniewski 1985).

Although considerable attention focuses on the incidence of rape, we know relatively little about the context or the *rape culture* surrounding date and acquaintance rape. Rape culture is a set of values and beliefs that provide an environment conducive to rape (Buchwald, Fletcher, and Roth 1993; Herman 1984). The term applies to a generic culture surrounding and promoting rape, not the specific settings in which rape is likely to occur. We believe that the specific settings also are important in defining relationships between men and women.

Some have argued that fraternities are places where rape is likely to occur on college campuses (Martin and Hummer 1989; O'Sullivan 1993; Sanday 1990) and that the students most likely to accept rape myths and be more sexually aggressive are more likely to live in fraternities and sororities, consume higher doses of alcohol and drugs, and place a higher value on social life at college (Gwartney-Gibbs and Stockard 1989; Kalof and Cargill 1991). Others suggest that sexual aggression is learned in settings such as fraternities and is not part of predispositions or preexisting attitudes (Boeringer, Shehan, and Akers 1991). To prevent further incidences of rape on college campuses, we need to understand what it is about fraternities in particular and college life in general that may contribute to the maintenance of a rape culture on college campuses.

Our approach is to identify the social contexts that link fraternities to campus rape and promote a rape culture. Instead of assuming that all fraternities provide an environment conducive to rape, we compare the interactions of men and women at fraternities identified on campus as being especially *dangerous* places for women, where the likelihood of rape is high, to those seen as *safer* places, where the perceived probability of rape occurring is lower. Prior to collecting data for our study, we found that most women students identified some fraternities as having more sexually aggressive members and a higher probability of rape. These women also considered other fraternities as relatively safe houses, where a woman could go and get drunk if she wanted to and feel secure that the fraternity men would not take advantage of her. We compared parties at houses identified as high-risk and low-risk houses as well as at two local bars frequented by college students.

Our analysis provides an opportunity to examine situations and contexts that hinder or facilitate positive social relations between undergraduate men and women.

The abusive attitudes toward women that some fraternities perpetuate exist within a general culture where rape is intertwined in traditional gender scripts. Men are viewed as initiators of sex and women as either passive partners or active resisters, preventing men from touching their bodies (LaPlante, McCormick, and Brannigan 1980). Rape culture is based on the assumptions that men are aggressive and dominant whereas women are passive and acquiescent (Buchwald, Fletcher, and Roth 1993; Herman 1984). What occurs on college campuses is an extension of the portrayal of domination and aggression of men over women that exemplifies the double standard of sexual behavior in U.S. society (Barthel 1988; Kimmel 1993).

Sexually active men are positively reinforced by being referred to as "studs," whereas women who are sexually active or report enjoying sex are derogatorily labeled as "sluts" (Herman 1984; O'Sullivan 1993). These gender scripts are embodied in rape myths and stereotypes such as "She really wanted it; she just said no because she didn't want me to think she was a bad girl" (Burke, Stets, and Pirog-Good 1989; Jenkins and Dambrot 1987; Lisak and Roth 1988; Malamuth 1986; Muehlenhard and Linton 1987; Peterson and Franzese 1987). Because men's sexuality is seen as more natural, acceptable, and uncontrollable than women's sexuality, many men and women excuse acquaintance rape by affirming that men cannot control their natural urges (Miller and Marshall 1987).

Whereas some researchers explain these attitudes toward sexuality and rape using an individual or a psychological interpretation, we argue that rape has a social basis, one in which both men and women create and recreate masculine and feminine identities and relations. Based on the assumption that rape is part of the social construction of gender, we examine how men and women "do gender" on a college campus (West and Zimmerman 1987). We focus on fraternities because they have been identified as settings that encourage rape (Sanday 1990). By comparing fraternities that are viewed by women as places where there is a high risk of rape to those where women believe there is a low risk of rape as well as two local commercial bars, we seek to identify characteristics that make some social settings more likely places for the occurrence of rape.

Results

The Settings

Fraternity Parties   We observed several differences in the quality of the interaction of men and women at parties at high-risk fraternities compared to those at low-risk houses. A typical party at a low-risk house included an equal number of women and men. The social atmosphere was friendly, with considerable interaction between women and men. Men and women danced in groups and in couples, with many of the couples kissing and displaying affection toward each other. Brothers explained that, because many of the men in these houses had girlfriends, it was normal to see couples kissing on the dance floor. Coed groups engaged in conversations at many of these houses, with women and men engaging in friendly exchanges, giving the impression that they knew each other well. Almost no cursing and yelling was observed at parties in low-risk houses; when pushing occurred, the participants apologized. Respect for women extended to the women's bathrooms, which were clean and well supplied.

At high-risk houses, parties typically had skewed gender ratios, sometimes involving more men and other times involving more women. Gender segregation also was evident at these parties, with the men on one side of a room or in the bar drinking while women gathered in another area. Men treated women differently in the high-risk houses. The women's bathrooms in the high-risk houses were filthy, including clogged toilets and vomit in the sinks. When a brother was told of the mess in the bathroom at a high-risk house, he replied, "Good, maybe some of these beer wenches will leave so there will be more beer for us."

Men attending parties at high-risk houses treated women less respectfully, engaging in jokes, conversations, and behaviors that degraded women. Men made a display of assessing women's bodies and rated them with thumbs up or thumbs down for the other men in the sight of the women. One man attending a party at a high-risk fraternity said to another, "Did you know that this week is Women's Awareness Week? I guess that means we get to abuse them more this week." Men behaved more crudely at parties at high-risk houses. At one party, a brother dropped his pants, including his underwear, while dancing in front of several women. Another brother slid across the dance floor completely naked.

The atmosphere at parties in high-risk fraternities was less friendly overall. With the exception of greetings, men and women rarely smiled or laughed and spoke to each other less often than was the case at parties in low-risk houses. The few one-on-one conversations between women and men appeared to be strictly flirtatious (lots of eye contact, touching, and very close talking). It was rare to see a group of men and women together talking. Men were openly hostile, which made the high-risk parties seem almost threatening at times. For example, there was a lot of touching, pushing, profanity, and name calling, some done by women.

Students at parties at the high-risk houses seemed self-conscious and aware of the presence of members of the opposite sex, an awareness that was sexually charged. Dancing early in the evening was usually between women. Close to midnight, the sex ratio began to balance out with the arrival of more men or more women. Couples began to dance together but in a sexual way (close dancing with lots of pelvic thrusts). Men tried to pick up women using lines such as "Want to see my fish tank?" and "Let's go upstairs so that we can talk; I can't hear what you're saying in here."

Although many of the same people who attended high-risk parties also attended low-risk parties, their behavior changed as they moved from setting to setting. Group norms differed across contexts as well. At a party that was held jointly at a low-risk house with a high-risk fraternity, the ambience was that of a party at a high-risk fraternity with heavier drinking, less dancing, and fewer conversations between women and men. The men from both high- and low-risk fraternities were very aggressive; a fight broke out, and there was pushing and shoving on the dance floor and in general.

As others have found, fraternity brothers at high-risk houses on this campus told about routinely discussing their sexual exploits at breakfast the morning after parties and sometimes at house meetings (cf. Martin and Hummer 1989; O'Sullivan 1993; Sanday 1990). During these sessions, the brothers we interviewed said that men bragged about what they did the night before with stories of sexual conquests often told by the same men, usually sophomores. The women involved in these exploits were women they did not know or knew but did not respect, or *faceless victims*. Men usually treated girlfriends with respect and did not talk about them in these storytelling sessions. Men from low-risk houses, however, did not describe similar sessions in their houses.

The Bar Scene   The bar atmosphere and social context differed from those of fraternity parties. The music was not as loud, and both bars had places to sit and have conversations. At all fraternity parties, it was difficult to maintain conversations with loud music playing and no place to sit. The volume of music at parties at high-risk fraternities was even louder than it was at low-risk houses, making it virtually impossible to have conversations. In general, students in the local bars behaved in the same way that students did at parties in low-risk houses with conversations typical, most occurring between men and women.

The first bar, frequented by older students, had live entertainment every night of the week. Some nights were more crowded than others, and the atmosphere was friendly, relaxed, and conducive to conversation. People laughed and smiled and behaved politely toward each other. The ratio of men to women was fairly equal, with students congregating in mostly coed groups. Conversation flowed freely and people listened to each other.

Although the women and men at the first bar also were at parties at low- and high-risk fraternities, their behavior at the bar included none of the blatant sexual or intoxicated behaviors observed at some of these parties. As the evenings wore on, the number of one-on-one conversations between men and women increased and conversations shifted from small talk to topics such as war and AIDS. Conversations did not revolve around picking up another person, and most people left the bar with same-sex friends or in coed groups.

The second bar was less popular with older students. Younger students, often under the legal drinking age, went there to drink, sometimes after leaving campus parties. This bar was much smaller and usually not as crowded as the first bar. The atmosphere was more mellow and relaxed than it was at the fraternity parties. People went there to hang out and talk to each other.

On a couple of occasions, however, the atmosphere at the second bar became similar to that of a party at a high-risk fraternity. As the number of people in the bar increased, they removed chairs and tables, leaving no place to sit and talk. The music also was turned up louder, drowning out conversation. With no place to dance or sit, most people stood around but could not maintain conversations because of the noise and crowds. Interactions between women and men consisted mostly of flirting. Alcohol consumption also was greater than it was on the less crowded nights, and the number of visibly drunk people increased. The more people drank, the more conversation and socializing broke down. The only differences between this setting and that of a party at a high-risk house were that brothers no longer controlled the territory and bedrooms were not available upstairs.

Gender Relations

Relations between women and men are shaped by the contexts in which they meet and interact. As is the case on other college campuses, *hooking up* has replaced dating on this campus, and fraternities are places where many students hook up. Hooking up is a loosely applied term on college campuses that had different meanings for men and women on this campus.

Most men defined hooking up similarly. One man said it was something that happens

> *when you're really drunk and meet up with a woman you sort of know, or possibly don't know at all and don't care about. You go home with her with the intention of getting as much sexual, physical pleasure as she'll give you, which can range anywhere from kissing to intercourse, without any strings attached.*

The exception to this rule is when men hook up with women they admire. Men said they are less likely to press for sexual activity with someone they know and like because they want the relationship to continue and be based on respect.

Women's version of hooking up differed. Women said they hook up only with men they cared about and described hooking up as kissing and petting but not sexual intercourse. Many women said that hooking up was disappointing because they wanted longer-term relationships. First-year women students realized quickly that hook-ups were usually one-night stands with no strings attached, but many continued to hook up because they had few opportunities to develop relationships with men on campus. One first-year woman said that *"70 percent of hook-ups never talk again and try to avoid one another; 26 percent may actually hear from them or talk to them again, and 4 percent may actually go on a date, which can lead to a relationship."* Another first-year woman said, *"It was fun in the beginning. You get a lot of attention and kiss a lot of boys and think this is what college is about, but it gets tiresome fast."*

Whereas first-year women get tired of the hook-up scene early on, many men do not become bored with it until their junior or senior year. As one upperclassman said, *"The whole game of hooking up became really meaningless and tiresome for me during my second semester of my sophomore year, but most of my friends didn't get bored with it until the following year."*

In contrast to hooking up, students also described monogamous relationships with steady partners. Some type of commitment was expected, but most people did not anticipate marriage. The term *seeing each other* was applied when people were sexually involved but free to date other people. This type of relationship involved less commitment than did one of boyfriend/ girlfriend but was not considered to be a hook-up.

The general consensus of women and men interviewed on this campus was that the Greek system, called "the hill," set the scene for gender relations. The predominance of Greek membership and subsequent living arrangements segregated men and women. During the week, little interaction occurred between women and men after their first year in college because students in fraternities or sororities live and dine in separate quarters. In addition, many non-Greek upper-class students move off campus into apartments. Therefore, students see each other in classes or in the library, but there is no place where students can just hang out together.

Both men and women said that fraternities dominate campus social life, a situation that everyone felt limited opportunities for meaningful interactions. One senior Greek man said,

> *This environment is horrible and so unhealthy for good male and female relationships and interactions to occur. It is so segregated and male dominated. . . . It is our party, with our rules and our beer. We are allowing these women and other men to come to our party. Men can feel superior in their domain.*

Comments from a senior woman reinforced his views: *"Men are dominant; they are the kings of the campus. It is their environment that they allow us to enter; therefore, we have to abide by their rules."* A junior woman described fraternity parties as

> *good for meeting acquaintances but almost impossible to really get to know anyone. The environment is so superficial, probably because there are so many social cliques due to the Greek system. Also, the music is too loud and the people are too drunk to attempt to have a real conversation, anyway.*

Some students claim that fraternities even control the dating relationships of their members. One senior woman said, *"Guys dictate how dating occurs on this campus, whether it's cool, who it's with, how much time can be spent with the girlfriend and with the brothers."* Couples either left campus for an evening or hung out separately with their own same-gender friends at fraternity parties, finally getting together with each other at about 2 A.M. Couples rarely went together to fraternity parties. Some men felt that a girlfriend was just a replacement for a hook-up. According to one junior man, *"Basically a girlfriend is someone you go to at 2 A.M. after you've hung out with the guys. She is the sexual outlet that the guys can't provide you with."*

Some fraternity brothers pressure each other to limit their time with and commitment to their girlfriends. One senior man said, *"The hill [fraternities] and girlfriends don't mix."* A brother described a constant battle between girlfriends and brothers over who the guy is going out with for the night, with the brothers usually winning. Brothers teased men with girlfriends with remarks such as "whipped" or "where's the ball and chain?" A brother from a high-risk house said that few brothers at his house had girlfriends; some did, but it was uncommon. One man said that from the minute he was a pledge he knew he would probably never have a girlfriend on this campus because *"it was just not the norm in my house. No one has girlfriends; the guys have too much fun with [each other]."*

The pressure on men to limit their commitment to girlfriends, however, was not true of all fraternities or of all men on campus. Couples attended low-risk fraternity parties together, and men in the low-risk houses went out on dates more often. A man in one low-risk house said that about 70 percent of the members of his house were involved in relationships with women, including the pledges (who were sophomores).

Treatment of Women

Not all men held negative attitudes toward women that are typical of a rape culture, and not all social contexts promoted the negative treatment of women. When men were asked whether they treated the women on campus with respect, the most common response was "On an individual basis, yes, but when you have a group of men together, no." Men said that, when together in groups with other men, they sensed a pressure to be disrespectful toward women. A first-year man's perception of the treatment of women was that *"they are treated with more respect to their faces, but behind closed doors, with a group of men present, respect for women is not an issue."* One senior man stated, *"In general, college-aged men don't treat women their age with respect because 90 percent of them think of women as merely a means to sex."* Women reinforced this perception. A first-year woman stated, *"Men here are more interested in hooking up and drinking beer than they are in getting to know women as real people."* Another woman said, *"Men here use and abuse women."*

Characteristic of rape culture, a double standard of sexual behavior for men versus women was prevalent on this campus. As one Greek senior man stated, *"Women who sleep around are sluts and get bad reputations; men who do are champions and get a pat on the back from their brothers."* Women also supported a double standard for sexual behavior by criticizing sexually active women. A first-year woman spoke out against women who are sexually active: *"I think some girls here make it difficult for the men to respect women as a whole."*

One concrete example of demeaning sexually active women on this campus is the "walk of shame." Fraternity brothers come out on the porches of their houses the night after parties and heckle women walking by. It is assumed that these women spent the night at fraternity houses and that the men they were with did not care enough about them to drive them home. Although sororities now reside in former fraternity houses, this practice continues and sometimes the victims of hecklings are sorority women on their way to study in the library.

A junior man in a high-risk fraternity described another ritual of disrespect toward women called "chatter." When an unknown woman sleeps over at the house, the brothers yell degrading remarks out the window at her as she leaves the next morning such as "Fuck that bitch" and "Who is that slut?" He said that sometimes brothers harass the brothers whose girlfriends stay over instead of heckling those women.

Fraternity men most often mistreated women they did not know personally. Men and women alike reported incidents in which brothers observed other brothers having sex with unknown women or women they knew only casually. A sophomore woman's experience exemplifies this anonymous state: *"I don't mind if 10 guys were watching or it was videotaped. That's expected on this campus. It's the fact that he didn't apologize or even offer to drive me home that really upset me."* Descriptions of sexual encounters involved the satisfaction of men by nameless women. A brother in a high-risk fraternity described a similar occurrence:

> *A brother of mine was hooking up upstairs with an unattractive woman who had been pursuing him all night. He told some brothers to go outside the window and watch. Well, one thing led to another and they were almost completely naked when the woman noticed the brothers outside. She was then unwilling to go any further, so the brother went outside and yelled at the other brothers and then closed the shades. I don't know if he scored or not, because the woman was pretty upset. But he did win the award for hooking up with the ugliest chick that weekend.*

Attitudes toward Rape

The sexually charged environment of college campuses raises many questions about cultures that facilitate the rape of women. How women and men define their sexual behavior is important legally as well as interpersonally. We asked students how they defined rape and had them compare it to the following legal definition: the perpetration of an act of sexual intercourse with a female against her will and consent, whether her will is overcome by force or fear resulting from the threat of force, or by drugs or intoxicants; or when, because of mental deficiency, she is incapable of exercising rational judgment. (Brownmiller 1975:368)

When presented with this legal definition, most women interviewed recognized it as well as the complexities involved in applying it. A first-year woman said, *"If a girl is drunk and the guy knows it and the girl says, 'Yes, I want to have sex,' and they do, that is still rape because the girl can't make a conscious, rational decision under the influence of alcohol."* Some women disagreed.

Another first-year woman stated, *"I don't think it is fair that the guy gets blamed when both people involved are drunk."*

The typical definition men gave for rape was "when a guy jumps out of the bushes and forces himself sexually onto a girl." When asked what date rape was, the most common answer was "when one person has sex with another person who did not consent." Many men said, however, that "date rape is when a woman wakes up the next morning and regrets having sex." Some men said that date rape was too gray an area to define. *"Consent is a fine line,"* said a Greek senior man student. For the most part, the men we spoke with argued that rape did not occur on this campus. One Greek sophomore man said, *"I think it is ridiculous that someone here would rape someone."* A first-year man stated, *"I have a problem with the word rape. It sounds so criminal, and we are not criminals; we are sane people."*

Whether aware of the legal definitions of rape, most men resisted the idea that a woman who is intoxicated is unable to consent to sex. A Greek junior man said, *"Men should not be responsible for women's drunkenness."* One first-year man said, *"If that is the legal definition of rape, then it happens all the time on this campus."* A senior man said, *"I don't care whether alcohol is involved or not; that is not rape. Rapists are people that have something seriously wrong with them."* A first-year man even claimed that when women get drunk, they invite sex. He said, *"Girls get so drunk here and then come on to us. What are we supposed to do? We are only human."*

Discussion and Conclusion

These findings describe the physical and normative aspects of one college campus as they relate to attitudes about and relations between men and women. Our findings suggest that an explanation emphasizing rape culture also must focus on those characteristics of the social setting that play a role in defining heterosexual relationships on college campuses (Kalof and Cargill 1991). The degradation of women as portrayed in rape culture was not found in all fraternities on this campus. Both group norms and individual behavior changed as students went from one place to another. Although individual men are the ones who rape, we found that some settings are more likely places for rape than are others. Our findings suggest that rape cannot be seen only as an isolated act and blamed on individual behavior and proclivities, whether it be alcohol consumption or attitudes. We also must consider characteristics of the settings that promote the behaviors that reinforce a rape culture.

Relations between women and men at parties in low-risk fraternities varied considerably from those in high-risk houses. Peer pressure and situational norms influenced women as well as men. Although many men in high- and low-risk houses shared similar views and attitudes about the Greek system, women on this campus, and date rape, their behaviors at fraternity parties were quite different.

Women who are at highest risk of rape are women whom fraternity brothers did not know. These women are faceless victims, nameless acquaintances—not friends. Men said their responsibility to such persons and the level of guilt they feel later if the hook-ups end in sexual intercourse are much lower if they hook up with women they do not know. In high-risk houses, brothers treated women as subordinates and kept them at a distance. Men in high-risk houses actively discouraged ongoing heterosexual relationships, routinely degraded women, and participated more fully in the hook-up scene; thus, the probability that women would become faceless victims was higher in these houses. The flirtatious nature of the parties indicated that women go to these parties looking for available men, but finding boyfriends or relationships was difficult at parties in high-risk houses. However, in the low-risk houses, where more men had long-term relationships, the women were not strangers and were less likely to become faceless victims.

The social scene on this campus, and on most others, offers women and men few other options to socialize. Although there may be no such thing as a completely safe fraternity party for women, parties at low-risk houses and commercial bars encouraged men and women to get to know each other better and decreased the probability that women would become faceless victims. Although both men and women found the social scene on this campus demeaning, neither demanded different settings for socializing, and attendance at fraternity parties is a common form of entertainment.

These findings suggest that a more conducive environment for conversation can promote more positive interactions between men and women. Simple changes would provide the opportunity for men and women to interact in meaningful ways such as adding places to sit and lowering the volume of music at fraternity parties or having parties in neutral locations, where men are not in control. The typical party room in fraternity houses includes a place to dance but not to sit and talk. The music often is loud, making it difficult, if not impossible, to carry on conversations; however, there were more conversations at the low-risk parties, where there also was more respect shown toward women. Although the number of brothers who had steady girlfriends in the low-risk houses as compared to those in the high-risk houses may explain the differences, we found that commercial bars also provided a context for interaction between men and women. At the bars, students sat and talked and conversations between men and women flowed freely, resulting in deep discussions and fewer hook-ups.

Alcohol consumption was a major focus of social events here and intensified attitudes and orientations of a rape culture. Although pressure to drink was evident at all fraternity parties and at both bars, drinking dominated high-risk fraternity parties, at which nonalcoholic beverages usually were not available and people chugged beers and became visibly drunk. A rape culture is strengthened by rules that permit alcohol only at fraternity parties. Under this system, men control the parties and dominate the men as well as the women who attend. As college administrators crack down on fraternities and alcohol on campus, however, the same behaviors and norms may transfer to other places such as parties in apartments or private homes where administrators have much less control. At commercial bars, interaction and socialization with others were as important as drinking, with the exception of the nights when the bar frequented by under-class students became crowded. Although one solution is to offer nonalcoholic social activities, such events receive little support on this campus. Either these alternative events lacked the prestige of the fraternity parties or the alcohol was seen as necessary to unwind, or both.

In many ways, the fraternities on this campus determined the settings in which men and women interacted. As others before us have found, pressures for conformity to the norms and values exist at both high-risk and low-risk houses (Kalof and Cargill 1991; Martin and Hummer 1989; Sanday 1990). The desire to be accepted is not unique to this campus or the Greek system (Holland and Eisenhart 1990; Horowitz 1988; Moffat 1989). The degree of conformity required by Greeks may be greater than that required in most social groups, with considerable pressure to adopt and maintain the image of their houses. The fraternity system intensifies the "groupthink syndrome" (Janis 1972) by solidifying the identity of the in-group and creating an us/them atmosphere. Within the fraternity culture, brothers are highly regarded and women are viewed as outsiders. For men in high-risk fraternities, women threatened their brotherhood; therefore, brothers discouraged relationships and harassed those who treated women as equals or with respect. The pressure to be one of the guys and hang out with the guys strengthens a rape culture on college campus by demeaning women and encouraging the segregation of men and women.

Students on this campus were aware of the contexts in which they operated and the choices available to them. They recognized that, in their interactions, they created differences between men and women that are not natural, essential, or biological (West and Zimmerman 1987). Not all men and women accepted the demeaning treatment of women, but they continued to participate in behaviors that supported aspects of a rape culture. Many women participated in the hook-up scene even after they had been humiliated and hurt because they had few other means of initiating contact with men on campus. Men and women alike played out this scene, recognizing its injustices in many cases but being unable to change the course of their behaviors.

Although this research provides some clues to gender relations on college campuses, it raises many questions. Why do men and women participate in activities that support a rape culture when they see its injustices? What would happen if alcohol were not controlled by groups of men who admit that they disrespect women when they get together? What can be done to give men and women on college campuses more opportunities to interact responsibly and get to know each other better? These questions should be studied on other campuses with a focus on the social settings in which the incidence of rape and the attitudes that support a rape culture exist. Fraternities are social contexts that may or may not foster a rape culture.

Our findings indicate that a rape culture exists in some fraternities, especially those we identified as high-risk houses. College administrators are responding to this situation by providing counseling and educational programs that increase awareness of date rape, including campaigns such as "No means no." These strategies are important in changing attitudes, values, and behaviors; however, changing individuals is not enough. The structure of campus life and the impact of that structure on gender relations on campus are highly determinative. To eliminate campus rape culture, student leaders and administrators must examine the situations in which women and men meet and restructure these settings to provide opportunities for respectful interaction. Change may not require abolishing fraternities; rather, it may require promoting settings that facilitate positive gender relations.

REFERENCES

Barthel, D. 1988. *Putting on Appearances: Gender and Advertising.* Philadelphia: Temple University Press.

Boeringer, S. B., C. L. Shehan, and R. L. Akers. 1991. "Social Contexts and Social Learning in Sexual Coercion and Aggression: Assessing the Contribution of Fraternity Membership." *Family Relations* 40:58–64.

Brownmiller, S. 1975. *Against Our Will: Men, Women and Rape.* New York: Simon & Schuster.

Buchwald, E., P. R. Fletcher, and M. Roth, eds. 1993. *Transforming a Rape Culture.* Minneapolis, MN: Milkweed Editions.

Burke, P., J. E. Stets, and M. A. Pirog-Good. 1989. "Gender Identity, Self-Esteem, Physical Abuse and Sexual Abuse in Dating Relationships." In *Violence in Dating Relationships: Emerging Social Issues,* edited by M. A. Pirog-Good and J. E. Stets. New York: Praeger.

Gwartney-Gibbs, P. and J. Stockard. 1989. "Courtship Aggression and Mixed-Sex Peer Groups." In *Violence in Dating Relationships: Emerging Social Issues,* edited by M. A. Pirog-Good and J. E. Stets. New York: Praeger.

Herman, D. 1984. "The Rape Culture." In *Women: A Feminist Perspective,* edited by J. Freeman. Mountain View, CA: Mayfield.

Holland, D. C. and M. A. Eisenhart. 1990. *Educated in Romance: Women, Achievement, and College Culture.* Chicago: University of Chicago Press.

Horowitz, H. I. 1988. *Campus Life: Undergraduate Cultures from the End of the 18th Century to the Present.* Chicago: University of Chicago Press.

Janis, I. L. 1972. *Victims of Groupthink.* Boston: Houghton Mifflin.

Jenkins, M. J. and F. H. Dambrot. 1987. "The Attribution of Date Rape: Observer's Attitudes and Sexual Experiences and the Dating Situation." *Journal of Applied Social Psychology* 17:875–95.

Kalof, I. and T. Cargill. 1991. "Fraternity and Sorority Membership and Gender Dominance Attitudes." *Sex Roles* 25:417–23.

Kimmel, M. S. 1993. "Clarence, William, Iron Mike, Tailhook, Senator Packwood, Spur Posse, Magic . . . and Us. In *Transforming a Rape Culture,* edited by E. Buchwald, P. R. Fletcher, and M. Roth. Minneapolis, MN: Milkweed Editions.

Koss, M. P., T. E. Dinero, C. A. Seibel, and S. L. Cox. 1988. "Stranger and Acquaintance Rape: Are There Differences in the Victim's Experience?" *Psychology of Women Quarterly* 12:1–24.

Koss, M. P., C. A. Gidycz, and N. Wisniewski. 1985. "The Scope of Rape: Incidence and Prevalence of Sexual Aggression and Victimization in a National Sample of Higher Education Students." *Journal of Consulting and Clinical Psychology* 55:162–70.

LaPlante, M. N., N. McCormick, and G. G. Brannigan. 1980. "Living the Sexual Script: College Students' Views of Influence in Sexual Encounters." *Journal of Sex Research* 16:338–55.

Lisak, D. and S. Roth. 1988. "Motivational Factors in Nonincarcerated Sexually Aggressive Men." *Journal of Personality and Social Psychology* 55:795–802.

Malamuth, N. 1986. "Predictors of Naturalistic Sexual Aggression." *Journal of Personality and Social Psychology* 50:953–62.

Martin, P. Y. and R. Hummer. 1989. "Fraternities and Rape on Campus." *Gender & Society* 3:457–73.

Miller, B. and J. C. Marshall. 1987. "Coercive Sex on the University Campus." *Journal of College Student Personnel* 28:38–47.

Moffat, M. 1989. *Coming of Age in New Jersey: College Life in American Culture.* New Brunswick, NJ: Rutgers University Press.

Muehlenhard, C. L. and M. A. Linton. 1987. "Data Rape and Sexual Aggression in Dating Situations: Incidence and Risk Factors." *Journal of Counseling Psychology* 34:186–96.

O'Sullivan, C. 1993. "Fraternities and the Rape Culture." In *Transforming a Rape Culture,* edited by E. Buchwald, P. R. Fletcher, and M. Roth. Minneapolis, MN: Milkweed Editions.

Peterson, S. A. and B. Franzese. 1987. "Correlates of College Men's Sexual Abuse of Women." *Journal of College Student Personnel* 28:223–28.

Sanday, P. R. 1990. *Fraternity Gang Rape: Sex, Brotherhood, and Privilege on Campus.* New York: New York University Press.

West, C. and D. Zimmerman. 1987. "Doing Gender." *Gender & Society* 1:125–51.

PART VI

Social Inequality

SOCIAL CLASS

23

SOME PRINCIPLES OF STRATIFICATION

KINGSLEY DAVIS • WILBERT E. MOORE
WITH A RESPONSE BY MELVIN TUMIN

In the following four selections, we investigate social inequality that results from social class membership. Social class refers to categories of people who share common economic interests in a stratification system. The first selection is a classic piece excerpted from a 1945 article by sociologists Kingsley Davis and Wilbert E. Moore. Davis and Moore argue that not only are all societies stratified, but that stratification is a functional necessity. Davis and Moore also argue that stratification occurs because some social positions are more important to the social system than others, and as such, social positions are valued and rewarded differently. In 1953, sociologist Melvin Tumin published a response to Davis and Moore's classic article, which suggests that social stratification may be dysfunctional for society.

Starting from the proposition that no society is "classless," or unstratified, an effort is made to explain, in functional terms, the universal necessity which calls forth stratification in any social system. Next, an attempt is made to explain the roughly uniform distribution of prestige as between the major types of positions in every society. Since, however, there occur between one society and another great differences in the degree and kind of stratification, some attention is also given to the varieties of social inequality and the variable factors that give rise to them. . . .

Throughout, it will be necessary to keep in mind one thing—namely, that the discussion relates to the system of positions, not to the individuals occupying those positions. It is one thing to ask why different positions carry different degrees of prestige, and quite another to ask how certain individuals get into those positions. Although, as the argument will try to show, both

---

Kingsley Davis and Wilbert E. Moore, "Some Principles of Stratification" from *American Sociological Review* 10, no. 2 (April 1945): 242–244.

questions are related, it is essential to keep them separate in our thinking. Most of the literature on stratification has tried to answer the second question (particularly with regard to the ease or difficulty of mobility between strata) without tackling the first. The first question, however, is logically prior and, in the case of any particular individual or group, factually prior.

The Functional Necessity of Stratification

Curiously, however, the main functional necessity explaining the universal presence of stratification is precisely the requirement faced by any society of placing and motivating individuals in the social structure. As a functioning mechanism a society must somehow distribute its members in social positions and induce them to perform the duties of these positions. It must thus concern itself with motivation at two different levels: to instill in the proper individuals the desire to fill certain positions, and, once in these positions, the desire to perform the duties attached to them. Even though the social order may be relatively static in form, there is a continuous process of metabolism as new individuals are born into it, shift with age, and die off. Their absorption into the positional system must somehow be arranged and motivated. This is true whether the system is competitive or noncompetitive. A competitive system gives greater importance to the motivation to achieve positions, whereas a noncompetitive system gives perhaps greater importance to the motivation to perform the duties of the positions; but in any system both types of motivation are required.

If the duties associated with the various positions were all equally pleasant to the human organism, all equally important to societal survival, and all equally in need of the same ability or talent, it would make no difference who got into which positions, and the problem of social placement would be greatly reduced. But actually it does make a great deal of difference who gets into which positions, not only because some positions are inherently more agreeable than others, but also because some require special talents or training and some are functionally more important than others. Also, it is essential that the duties of the positions be performed with the diligence that their importance requires. Inevitably, then, a society must have, first, some kind of rewards that it can use as inducements, and, second, some way of distributing these rewards differentially according to positions. The rewards and their distribution become a part of the social order, and thus give rise to stratification.

One may ask what kind of rewards a society has at its disposal in distributing its personnel and securing essential services. It has, first of all, the things that contribute to sustenance and comfort. It has, second, the things that contribute to humor and diversion. And it has, finally, the things that contribute to self-respect and ego expansion. The last, because of the peculiarly social character of the self, is largely a function of the opinion of others, but it nonetheless ranks in importance with the first two. In any social system all three kinds of rewards must be dispensed differentially according to positions.

In a sense the rewards are "built into" the position. They consist in the "rights" associated with the position, plus what may be called its accompaniments or perquisites. Often the rights, and sometimes the accompaniments, are functionally related to the duties of the position. (Rights as viewed by the incumbent are usually duties as viewed by other members of the community.) However, there may be a host of subsidiary rights and perquisites that are not essential to the function of the position and have only an indirect and symbolic connection with its duties, but which still may be of considerable importance in inducing people to seek the positions and fulfill the essential duties.

If the rights and perquisites of different positions in a society must be unequal, then the society must be stratified, because that is precisely what stratification means. Social inequality is thus an unconsciously evolved device by which societies insure that the most important positions are conscientiously filled by the most qualified persons. Hence every society, no matter how simple or complex, must differentiate persons in terms of both prestige and esteem, and must therefore possess a certain amount of institutionalized inequality.

It does not follow that the amount or type of inequality need be the same in all societies. This is largely a function of factors that will be discussed presently.

The Two Determinants of Positional Rank

Granting the general function that inequality subserves, one can specify the two factors that determine the relative rank of different positions. In general those positions convey the best reward, and hence have the highest rank, which (a) have the greatest importance for the society and (b) require the greatest training or talent. The first factor concerns function and is a matter of relative significance; the second concerns means and is a matter of scarcity.

Differential Functional Importance

Actually a society does not need to reward positions in proportion to their functional importance. It merely needs to give sufficient reward to them to ensure that they will be filled competently. In other words, it must see that less essential positions do not compete successfully with more essential ones. If a position is easily filled, it need not be heavily rewarded, even though important. On the other hand, if it is important but hard to fill, the reward must be high enough to get it filled anyway. Functional importance is therefore a necessary but not a sufficient cause of high rank being assigned to a position.[1]

Differential Scarcity of Personnel

Practically all positions, no matter how acquired, require some form of skill or capacity for performance. This is implicit in the very notion of position, which implies that the incumbent must, by virtue of his incumbency, accomplish certain things.

There are, ultimately, only two ways in which a person's qualifications come about: through inherent capacity or through training. Obviously, in concrete activities both are always necessary, but from a practical standpoint the scarcity may lie primarily in one or the other, as well as in both. Some positions require innate talents of such high degree that the persons who fill them are bound to be rare. In many cases, however, talent is fairly abundant in the population but the training process is so long, costly, and elaborate that relatively few can qualify. Modern medicine, for example, is within the mental capacity of most individuals, but a medical education is so burdensome and expensive that virtually none would undertake it if the position of the M.D. did not carry a reward commensurate with the sacrifice.

If the talents required for a position are abundant and the training easy, the method of acquiring the position may have little to do with its duties. There may be, in fact, a virtually accidental relationship. But if the skills required are scarce by reason of the rarity of talent or the costliness of training, the position, if functionally important, must have an attractive power that will draw the necessary skills in competition with other positions. This means, in effect, that the position must be high in the social scale—must command great prestige, high salary, ample leisure, and the like.

How Variations Are to Be Understood

Insofar as there is a difference between one system of stratification and another, it is attributable to whatever factors affect the two determinants of differential reward—namely, functional importance and scarcity of personnel. Positions important in one society may not be important in another, because the conditions faced by the societies, or their degree of internal development, may be different. The same conditions, in turn, may affect the question of scarcity; for in some societies the stage of development, or the external situation, may wholly obviate the necessity of certain kinds of skill or talent. Any particular system of stratification, then, can be understood as a product of the special conditions affecting the two aforementioned grounds of differential reward.

Critical Response by Melvin Tumin

The fact of social inequality in human society is marked by its ubiquity and its antiquity. Every known society, past and present, distributes its scarce and demanded goods and services unequally. And there are attached to the positions which command unequal amounts of such goods and services certain highly morally-toned evaluations of their importance for the society.

The ubiquity and the antiquity of such inequality have given rise to the assumption that there must be something both inevitable and positively functional about such social arrangements. . . . Clearly, the truth or falsity of such an assumption is a strategic question for any general theory of social organization. It is therefore most curious that the basic premises and implications of the assumption have only been most casually explored by American sociologists. . . .

Let us take [the Davis and Moore] propositions and examine them *seriatim.*

(1) *Certain positions in any society are more functionally important than others and require special skills for their performance.*

The key term here is "functionally important." The functionalist theory of social organization is by no means clear and explicit about this term. The minimum common referent is to something known as the "survival value" of a social structure. This concept immediately involves a number of perplexing questions. Among these are (a) the issue of minimum versus maximum survival, and the possible empirical referents which can be given to those terms; (b) whether such a proposition is a useless tautology since any *status quo* at any given moment is nothing more and nothing less than everything present in the *status quo.* In these terms, all acts and structures must be judged positively functional in that they constitute essential portions of the *status quo;* (c) what kind of calculus of functionality exists which will enable us, at this point in our development, to add and subtract long- and short-range consequences, with their mixed qualities, and arrive at some summative judgment regarding the rating an act or structure should receive on a scale of greater or lesser functionality? At best, we tend to make primarily intuitive judgments. Often enough, these judgments involve the use of value-laden criteria, or, at least, criteria which are chosen in preference to others not for any sociologically systematic reasons but by reason of certain implicit value preferences. . . .

A generalized theory of social stratification must recognize that the prevailing system of inducements and rewards is only one of many variants in the whole range of possible systems of motivation which, at least theoretically, are capable of working in human society. It is quite conceivable, of course, that a system of norms could be institutionalized in which the idea of threatened withdrawal of services, except under the most extreme circumstances, would be considered as absolute moral anathema. In such a case, the whole notion of relative functionality, as advanced by Davis and Moore, would have to be radically revised.

(2) *Only a limited number of individuals in any society have the talents which can be trained into the skills appropriate to these positions (i.e., the more functionally important positions).*

The truth of this proposition depends at least in part on the truth of proposition 1 above. It is, therefore, subject to all the limitations indicated above. But for the moment, let us assume the validity of the first proposition and concentrate on the question of the rarity of appropriate talent.

If all that is meant is that in every society there is a *range* of talent, and that some members of any society are by nature more talented than others, no sensible contradiction can be offered, but a question must be raised here regarding the amount of sound knowledge present in any society concerning the presence of talent in the population.

For, in every society there is some demonstrable ignorance regarding the amount of talent present in the population. *And the more rigidly stratified a society is, the less chance does that society have of discovering any new facts about the talents of its members.* Smoothly working and stable systems of stratification, wherever found, tend to build in obstacles to the further exploration of the range of available talent. This is especially true in those societies where the opportunity to discover talent in any one generation varies with the differential resources of the parent generation. Where, for instance, access to education depends upon the wealth of one's parents, and where wealth is differentially distributed, large segments of the population are likely to be deprived of the chance even to *discover* what are their talents.

Whether or not differential rewards and opportunities are functional in any one generation, it is clear that if those differentials are allowed to be socially inherited by the next generation, then the stratification system is specifically dysfunctional for the discovery of talents in the next generation. In this fashion, systems of social stratification tend to limit the chances available to maximize the efficiency of discovery, recruitment and training of "functionally important talent."

. . . In this context, it may be asserted that there is some noticeable tendency for elites to restrict further access to their privileged positions, once they have sufficient power to enforce such restrictions. This is especially true in a culture where it is possible for an elite to contrive a high demand and a proportionately higher reward for its work by restricting the numbers of the elite available to do the work. The recruitment and training of doctors in modern United States is at least partly a case in point. . . .

(3) *The conversion of talents into skills involves a training period during which sacrifices of one kind or another are made by those undergoing the training.*

Davis and Moore introduce here a concept, "sacrifice," which comes closer than any of the rest of their vocabulary of analysis to being a direct reflection of the rationalizations, offered by the more fortunate members of a society, of the rightness of their occupancy of privileged positions. It is the least critically thought-out concept in the repertoire, and can also be shown to be least supported by the actual facts.

In our present society, for example, what are the sacrifices which talented persons undergo in the training period? The possibly serious losses involve the surrender of earning power and the cost of the training. The latter is generally borne by the parents of the talented youth undergoing training, and not by the trainees themselves. But this cost tends to be paid out of income which the parents were able to earn generally by virtue of *their* privileged positions in the hierarchy of stratification. That is to say, the parents' ability to pay for the training of their children is part of the differential *reward* they, the parents, received for their privileged positions in the society. And to charge this sum up against sacrifices made by the youth is falsely to perpetuate a bill or a debt already paid by the society to the parents. . . .

What tends to be completely overlooked, in addition, are the psychic and spiritual rewards which are available to the elite trainees by comparison with their age peers in the labor force. There is, first, the much higher prestige enjoyed by the college student and the professional-school student as compared with persons in shops and offices. There is, second, the extremely highly valued privilege of having greater opportunity for self-development. There is, third, all the psychic gain involved in being allowed to delay the assumption of adult responsibilities such as earning a living and supporting a family. There is, fourth, the access to leisure and freedom of a kind not likely to be experienced by the persons already at work.

If these are never taken into account as rewards of the training period it is not because they are not concretely present, but because the emphasis in American concepts of reward is almost exclusively placed on the material returns of positions. The emphases on enjoyment, entertainment, ego enhancement, prestige and esteem are introduced only when the differentials in these which accrue to the skilled positions need to be justified. If these other rewards were taken into account, it would be much more difficult to demonstrate that the training period, as presently operative, is really sacrificial. Indeed, it might turn out to be the case that even at this point in their careers, the elite trainees were being differentially rewarded relative to their age peers in the labor force. . . .

(4) *In order to induce the talented persons to undergo these sacrifices and acquire the training, their future positions must carry an inducement value in the form of differential, i.e., privileged and disproportionate access to the scarce and desired rewards which the society has to offer.*

Let us assume, for the purposes of the discussion, that the training period is sacrificial and the talent is rare in every conceivable human society. There is still the basic problem as to whether the allocation of differential rewards in scarce and desired goods and services is the only or the most efficient way of recruiting the appropriate talent to these positions.

For there are a number of alternative motivational schemes whose efficiency and adequacy ought at least to be considered in this context. What can be said, for instance, on behalf of the motivation which De Man called "joy in work," Veblen termed "instinct for workmanship" and which we latterly have come to identify as "intrinsic work satisfaction"? Or, to what extent could the motivation of "social duty" be institutionalized in such a fashion that self-interest and social interest come closely to coincide? Or, how much prospective confidence can be placed in the possibilities of institutionalizing "social service" as a widespread motivation for seeking one's appropriate position and fulfilling it conscientiously?

Are not these types of motivations, we may ask, likely to prove most appropriate for precisely the "most functionally important positions"? Especially in a mass industrial society, where the vast majority of positions become standardized and routinized, it is the skilled jobs which are likely to retain most of the quality of "intrinsic job satisfaction" and be most readily identifiable as socially serviceable. Is it indeed impossible then to build these motivations into the socialization pattern to which we expose our talented youth? . . .

(5) *These scarce and desired goods consist of rights and perquisites attached to, or built into, the positions and can be classified into those things which contribute to (a) sustenance and comfort; (b) humor and diversion; (c) self-respect and ego expansion.*

(6) *This differential access to the basic rewards of the society has as a consequence the differentiation of the prestige and esteem which various strata acquire. This may be said, along with the rights and perquisites, to constitute institutionalized social inequality, i.e., stratification.*

With the classification of the rewards offered by Davis and Moore there need be little argument. Some question must be raised, however, as to whether any reward system, built into a general stratification system, must allocate equal amounts of all three types of reward in order to function effectively, or whether one type of reward may be emphasized to the virtual neglect of others. This raises the further question regarding which type of emphasis is likely to prove most effective as a differential inducer. Nothing in the known facts about human motivation impels us to favor one type of reward over the other, or to insist that all three types of reward must be built into the positions in comparable amounts if the position is to have an inducement value.

It is well known, of course, that societies differ considerably in the kinds of rewards they emphasize in their efforts to maintain a reasonable balance between responsibility and reward. There are, for instance, numerous societies in which the conspicuous display of differential economic advantage is considered extremely bad taste. In short, our present knowledge commends to us the possibility of considerable plasticity in the way in which different types of rewards can be structured into a functioning society. This is to say, it cannot yet be demonstrated that it is *unavoidable* that differential prestige and esteem shall accrue to positions which command differential rewards in power and property.

What does seem to be unavoidable is that differential prestige shall be given to those in any society who conform to the normative order as against those who deviate from that order in a way judged immoral and detrimental. On the assumption that the continuity of a society depends on the continuity and stability of its normative order, some such distinction between conformists and deviants seems inescapable.

It also seems to be unavoidable that in any society, no matter how literate its tradition, the older, wiser, and more experienced individuals who are charged with the enculturation and socialization of the young must have more power than the young, on the assumption that the task of effective socialization demands such differential power.

But this differentiation in prestige between the conformist and the deviant is by no means the same distinction as that between strata of individuals each of which operates *within* the normative order, and is composed of adults. . . .

(7) *Therefore, social inequality among different strata in the amounts of scarce and desired goods, and the amounts of prestige and esteem which they receive, is both positively functional and inevitable in any society.*

If the objections which have heretofore been raised are taken as reasonable, then it may be stated that the only items which any society *must* distribute unequally are the power and property necessary for the performance of different tasks. If such differential power and property are viewed by all as commensurate with the differential responsibilities, and if they are culturally defined as *resources* and not as rewards, then no differentials in prestige and esteem need follow.

Historically, the evidence seems to be that every time power and property are distributed unequally, no matter what the cultural definition, prestige and esteem differentiations have tended to result as well. Historically, however, no systematic effort has ever been made, under propitious circumstances, to develop the tradition that each man is as socially worthy as all other men so long as he performs his appropriate tasks conscientiously. While such a tradition seems utterly utopian, no known facts in psychological or social science have yet demonstrated its impossibility or its dysfunctionality for the continuity of a society. The achievement of a full institutionalization of such a tradition seems far too remote to contemplate. Some successive approximations at such a tradition, however, are not out of the range of prospective social innovation.

What, then, of the "positive functionality" of social stratification? Are there other, negative, functions of institutionalized social inequality which can be identified, if only tentatively? Some such dysfunctions of stratification have already been suggested in the body of this [reading]. Along with others they may now be stated, in the form of provisional assertions, as follows:

1. Social stratification systems function to limit the possibility of discovery of the full range of talent available in a society. This results from the fact of unequal access to appropriate motivation, channels of recruitment, and centers of training.

2. In foreshortening the range of available talent, social stratification systems function to set limits upon the possibility of expanding the productive resources of the society, at least relative to what might be the case under conditions of greater equality of opportunity.

3. Social stratification systems function to provide the elite with the political power necessary to procure acceptance and dominance of an ideology which rationalizes the *status quo*, whatever it may be, as "logical," "natural" and "morally right." In this manner, social stratification systems function as essentially conservative influences in the societies in which they are found.

4. Social stratification systems function to distribute favorable self-images unequally throughout a population. To the extent that such favorable self-images are requisite to the development of the creative potential inherent in men, to that extent stratification systems function to limit the development of this creative potential.

5. To the extent that inequalities in social rewards cannot be made fully acceptable to the less privileged in a society, social stratification systems function to encourage hostility, suspicion, and distrust among the various segments of a society and thus to limit the possibilities of extensive social integration.

6. To the extent that the sense of significant membership in a society depends on one's place on the prestige ladder of the society, social stratification systems function to distribute unequally the sense of significant membership in the population.

7. To the extent that loyalty to a society depends on a sense of significant membership in the society, social stratification systems function to distribute loyalty unequally in the population.

8. To the extent that participation and apathy depend upon the sense of significant membership in the society, social stratification systems function to distribute the motivation to participate unequally in a population.

Each of the eight foregoing propositions contains implicit hypotheses regarding the consequences of unequal distribution of rewards in a society in accordance with some notion of the functional importance of various positions. These are empirical hypotheses, subject to test. They are offered here only as exemplary of the kinds of consequences of social stratification which are not often taken into account in dealing with the problem. They should also serve to reinforce the doubt that social inequality is a device which is uniformly functional for the role of guaranteeing that the most important tasks in a society will be performed conscientiously by the most competent persons.

The obviously mixed character of the functions of social inequality should come as no surprise to anyone. If sociology is sophisticated in any sense, it is certainly with regard to its awareness of the mixed nature of any social arrangement, when the observer takes into account long- as well as short-range consequences and latent as well as manifest dimensions.

ENDNOTE

[1]Unfortunately, functional importance is difficult to establish. To use the position's prestige to establish it, as is often unconsciously done, constitutes circular reasoning from our point of view. There are, however, two independent clues: (a) the degree to which a position is functionally unique, there being no other positions that can perform the same function satisfactorily; and (b) the degree to which other positions are dependent on the one in question. Both clues are best exemplified in organized systems of positions built around one major function. Thus in most complex societies the religious, political, economic, and educational functions are handled by distinct structures not easily interchangeable. In addition, each structure possesses many different positions, some clearly dependent on, if not subordinate to, others. In sum, when an institutional nucleus becomes differentiated around one main function, and at the same time organizes a large portion of the population into its relationships, *key* positions in it are of the highest functional importance. The absence of such specialization does not prove functional unimportance, for the whole society may be relatively unspecialized; but it is safe to assume that the more important functions receive the first and clearest structural differentiation.

24
_____

WHO RULES AMERICA?
The Corporate Community and the Upper Class

G. WILLIAM DOMHOFF

Sociologists utilize various indicators to measure social class. For example, *socioeconomic status* (SES) is calculated using income, educational attainment, and occupational status. Sociologists also employ subjective indicators of social class, such as attitudes and values, class identification, and consumption patterns. This selection is by G. William Domhoff, a professor emeritus of psychology at the University of California, Santa Cruz, and it is taken from his 1998 book, *Who Rules America? Power and Politics in the Year 2000.* Using both objective and subjective indicators of social class status, Domhoff finds that in addition to wealth, the upper class shares a distinctive lifestyle through participation in various social institutions. Domhoff argues not only that there is a cohesive upper class in the United States, but also that the upper class has a disproportionate share of power through its control over economic and political decision making in this country.

Most Americans do not like the idea that there are social classes. Classes imply that people have relatively fixed stations in life. They fly in the face of beliefs about equality of opportunity and seem to ignore the evidence of upward social mobility. Even more, Americans tend to deny that social classes are based in wealth and occupational roles but then belie that denial through a fascination with rags-to-riches stories and the trappings of wealth. . . .

If there is an American upper class, it must exist not merely as a collection of families who feel comfortable with each other and tend to exclude outsiders from their social activities. It must exist as a set of interrelated social institutions. That is, there must be patterned ways of organizing the lives of its members from infancy to old age that create a relatively unique style of life, and there must be mechanisms for socializing both the younger generation and new adult members who have risen from lower social levels. If the class is a reality, the names and faces may change somewhat over the years, but the social institutions that underlie the upper class must persist with remarkably little change over several generations. This emphasis on the institutionalized nature of the upper class, which reflects a long-standing empirical tradition in studies of it, is compatible with the theoretical focus of the "new institutionalists" within sociology and political science.

Four different types of empirical studies establish the existence of an interrelated set of social institutions, organizations, and social activities. They are historical case studies, quantitative studies of biographical directories, open-ended surveys of knowledgeable observers, and interview studies with members of the upper-middle and upper classes. . . .

Prepping for Power

From infancy through young adulthood, members of the upper class receive a distinctive education. This education begins early in life in preschools that frequently are attached to a neighborhood church of high social status. Schooling continues during the elementary years at a local private school called a day school. During the adolescent years the student may remain at day school, but there is a strong chance that at least one or two years will be spent away from home at a boarding school in a quiet rural setting. Higher education will take place at one of a small number of heavily endowed private colleges and universities. Large and well-known Ivy League schools in the East and Stanford in the West head the list, followed by smaller Ivy League schools in the East and a handful of other small private schools in other parts of the country. Although some upper-class children may attend public high school if they live in a secluded suburban setting, or go to a state university if there is one of great esteem and tradition in their home state, the system of formal schooling is so insulated that many upper-class students never see the inside of a public school in all their years of education.

This separate educational system is important evidence for the distinctiveness of the mentality and lifestyle that exists within the upper class because schools play a large role in transmitting the class structure to their students. Surveying and summarizing a great many studies on schools in general, sociologist Randall Collins concludes: "Schools primarily teach vocabulary and inflection, styles of dress, aesthetic tastes, values and manners."[1] His statement takes on greater significance for studies of the upper class when it is added that only 1 percent of American teenagers attend independent private high schools of an upper-class nature.[2]

The training of upper-class children is not restricted to the formal school setting, however. Special classes, and even tutors, are a regular part of their extracurricular education. This informal education usually begins with dancing classes in the elementary years, which are seen as important for learning proper manners and the social graces. Tutoring in a foreign language may begin in the elementary years, and there are often lessons in horseback riding and music as well. The teen years find the children of the upper class in summer camps or on special travel tours, broadening their perspectives and polishing their social skills.

The linchpins in the upper-class educational system are the dozens of boarding schools founded in the last half of the nineteenth and the early part of the twentieth centuries. Baltzell concludes that these schools became "surrogate families" that played a major role "in creating an upper-class subculture on almost a national scale in America."[3] The role of boarding schools in providing connections to other upper-class social institutions is also important. As one informant explained to Ostrander in her interview study of upper-class women: "Where I went to boarding school, there were girls from all over the country, so I know people from all over. It's helpful when you move to a new city and want to get invited into the local social club."[4]

It is within these few hundred schools that are consciously modeled after their older and more austere British counterparts that a distinctive style of life is inculcated through such traditions as the initiatory hazing of beginning students, the wearing of school blazers or ties, compulsory attendance at chapel services, and participation in esoteric sports such as squash and crew. Even a different terminology is adopted to distinguish these schools from public schools. The principal is a headmaster or rector, the teachers are sometimes called masters, and the students are in forms, not grades. Great emphasis is placed on the building of "character." The role of the school in preparing the future leaders of America is emphasized through the speeches of the headmaster and the frequent mention of successful alumni. Thus, boarding schools are in many ways the kind of highly effective socializing agent that sociologist Erving Goffman calls "total institutions," isolating their members from the outside world and providing them with a set of routines and traditions that encompass most of their waking hours.[5] The end result is a feeling of separateness and superiority that comes from having survived a rigorous education. As a retired business leader told one of my research assistants: "At school we were made to feel somewhat better [than other people] because of our class. That existed, and I've always disliked it intensely. Unfortunately, I'm afraid some of these things rub off on one."[6]

Almost all graduates of private secondary schools go on to college, and almost all do so at prestigious universities. Graduates of the New England boarding schools, for example, historically found themselves at one of four large Ivy League universities: Harvard, Yale, Princeton, and Columbia. . . . Now many upper-class students attend a select handful of smaller private liberal arts colleges, most of which are in the East, but there are a few in the South and West as well.

Graduates of private schools outside of New England most frequently attend a prominent state university in their area, but a significant minority go to Eastern Ivy League and top private universities in other parts of the country. . . . A majority of private-school graduates pursue careers in business, finance, or corporate law. For example, a classification of the occupations of a sample of the graduates of four private schools—St. Mark's, Groton, Hotchkiss, and Andover—showed that the most frequent occupation for all but the Andover graduates was some facet of finance and banking. Others became presidents of medium-size businesses or were partners in large corporate law firms. A small handful went to work as executives for major national corporations.[7] . . .

Although finance, business, and law are the most typical occupations of upper-class males, there is no absence of physicians, architects, museum officials, and other professional occupations. This fact is demonstrated most systematically in Baltzell's study of Philadelphia: 39 percent of the Philadelphia architects and physicians listed in *Who's Who* for the early 1940s were also listed in the *Social Register,* as were 35 percent of the museum officials. These figures are close to the 51 percent for lawyers and the 42 percent for businessmen, although they are far below the 75 percent for bankers—clearly the most prestigious profession in Philadelphia at that time.[8] . . .

From kindergarten through college, then, schooling is very different for members of the upper class and it teaches them to be distinctive in many ways. In a country where education is highly valued and nearly everyone attends public schools, this private system benefits primarily members of the upper class and provides one of the foundations for the old-boy and old-girl networks that will be with them throughout their lives.

Social Clubs

Just as private schools are a pervasive feature in the lives of upper-class children, so, too, are private social clubs a major point of orientation in the lives of upper-class adults. These clubs also play a role in differentiating members of the upper class from other members of society. According to Baltzell, "the club serves to place the adult members of society and their families within the social hierarchy." He quotes with approval the suggestion by historian Crane Brinton that the club "may perhaps be regarded as taking the place of those extensions of the family, such as the clan and the brotherhood, which have disappeared from advanced societies."[9] Conclusions similar to Baltzell's resulted from an interview study in Kansas City: "Ultimately, say upper-class Kansas Citians, social standing in their world reduces to one issue: where does an individual or family rank on the scale of private club memberships and informal cliques?"[10]

The clubs of the upper class are many and varied, ranging from family-oriented country clubs and downtown men's and women's clubs to highly specialized clubs for yacht owners, gardening enthusiasts, and fox hunters. Many families have memberships in several different types of clubs, but the days when most of the men by themselves were in a half dozen or more clubs faded before World War II. Downtown men's clubs originally were places for having lunch and dinner, and occasionally for attending an evening performance or a weekend party. But as upper-class families deserted the city for large suburban estates, a new kind of club, the country club, gradually took over some of these functions. The downtown club became almost entirely a luncheon club, a site to hold meetings, or a place to relax on a free afternoon. The country club, by contrast, became a haven for all members of the family.

It offered social and sporting activities ranging from dances, parties, and banquets to golf, swimming, and tennis. Special group dinners were often arranged for all members on Thursday night—the traditional maid's night off across the United States.

Sporting activities are the basis for most of the specialized clubs of the upper class. The most visible are the yachting and sailing clubs, followed by the clubs for lawn tennis or squash. The most exotic are the several dozen fox hunting clubs. They have their primary strongholds in rolling countrysides from southern Pennsylvania down into Virginia, but they exist in other parts of the country as well. Riding to hounds in scarlet jackets and black boots, members of the upper class sustain over 130 hunts under the banner of the Masters of Fox Hounds Association. The intricate rituals and grand feasts accompanying the event, including the Blessing of the Hounds by an Episcopal bishop in the Eastern hunts, go back to the eighteenth century in the United States.[11]

Initiation fees, annual dues, and expenses vary from a few thousand dollars in downtown clubs to tens of thousands of dollars in some country clubs, but money is not the primary barrier in gaining membership to a club. Each club has a very rigorous screening process before accepting new members. Most require nomination by one or more active members, letters of recommendation from three to six members, and interviews with at least some members of the membership committee. Names of prospective members are sometimes posted in the clubhouse, so all members have an opportunity to make their feelings known to the membership committee. Negative votes by two or three members of what is typically a ten- to twenty-person committee often are enough to deny admission to the candidate. The carefulness with which new members are selected extends to a guarding of club membership lists, which are usually available only to club members. Older membership lists are sometimes given to libraries by members or their surviving spouses, but for most clubs there are no membership lists in the public domain.

Not every club member is an enthusiastic participant in the life of the club. Some belong out of tradition or a feeling of social necessity. One woman told Ostrander the following about her country club: "We don't feel we should withdraw our support even though we don't go much." Others mentioned a feeling of social pressure: "I've only been to [the club] once this year. I'm really a loner, but I feel I have to go and be pleasant even though I don't want to." Another volunteered: "I think half the members go because they like it and half because they think it's a social necessity."[12]

People of the upper class often belong to clubs in several cities, creating a nationwide pattern of overlapping memberships. These overlaps provide evidence for social cohesion within the upper class. An indication of the nature and extent of this overlapping is revealed by sociologist Philip Bonacich's study of membership lists for twenty clubs in several major cities across the country, including the Links in New York, the Century Association in New York, the Duquesne in Pittsburgh, the Chicago in Chicago, the Pacific Union in San Francisco, and the California in Los Angeles. Using his own original clustering technique based on Boolean algebra, his study revealed there was sufficient overlap among eighteen of the twenty clubs to form three regional groupings and a fourth group that provided a bridge between the two largest regional groups. The several dozen men who were in three or more of the clubs—most of them very wealthy people who also sat on several corporate boards—were especially important in creating the overall pattern. At the same time, the fact that these clubs often have from 1,000 to 2,000 members makes the percentage of overlap within this small number of clubs relatively small, ranging from as high as 20 to 30 percent between clubs in the same city to as low as 1 or 2 percent in clubs at opposite ends of the country.[13]

The overlap of this club network with corporate boards of directors provides evidence for the intertwining of the upper class and corporate community. In one study, the club memberships of the chairs and outside directors of the twenty largest industrial corporations were counted. The overlaps with upper-class clubs in general were ubiquitous, but the concentration of directors in a few clubs was especially notable. At least one director from twelve of the twenty corporations was a member of the Links Club, which Baltzell calls "the New York rendezvous of the national corporate establishment."[14] Seven of General Electric's directors were members, as were four from Chrysler, four from Westinghouse, three from IBM, and two from U.S. Steel. In addition to the Links, several other clubs had directors from four or more corporations. A study I did using membership lists from eleven prestigious clubs in different parts of the country confirmed and extended these findings. A majority of the top twenty-five corporations in every major sector of the economy had directors in at least one of these clubs, and several had many more. . . .

There seems to be a great deal of truth to the earlier-cited suggestion by Crane Brinton that clubs may function within the upper class the way that the clan or brotherhood does in tribal societies. With their restrictive membership policies, initiatory rituals, private ceremonials, and great emphasis on tradition, clubs carry on the heritage of primitive secret societies. They create among their members an attitude of prideful exclusiveness that contributes greatly to an in-group feeling and a sense of fraternity within the upper class.

In concluding this discussion of . . . [social clubs and] the intersection of the upper class and corporate community, it needs to be stressed that the [social club] is not a place of power. No conspiracies are hatched there, nor anywhere else. Instead, it is a place where powerful people relax, make new acquaintances, and enjoy themselves. It is primarily a place of social bonding. The main sociological function of . . . [social] clubs is stated by sociologist Thomas Powell, based on his own interview study of members in upper-class clubs:

> The clubs are a repository of the values held by the upper-level prestige groups in the community and are a means by which these values are transferred to the business environment. The clubs are places in which the beliefs, problems, and values of the industrial organization are

discussed and related to the other elements in the larger community. Clubs, therefore, are not only effective vehicles of informal communication, but also valuable centers where views are presented, ideas are modified, and new ideas emerge. Those in the interview sample were appreciative of this asset; in addition, they considered the club as a valuable place to combine social and business contacts.[15]

The Female Half of the Upper Class

During the late nineteenth and early twentieth centuries, women of the upper class carved out their own distinct roles within the context of male domination in business, finance, and law. They went to separate private schools, founded their own social clubs, and belonged to their own volunteer associations. As young women and party goers, they set the fashions for society. As older women and activists, they took charge of the nonprofit social welfare and cultural institutions of the society, serving as fund-raisers, philanthropists, and directors in a manner parallel to what their male counterparts did in business and politics. To prepare themselves for their leadership roles, in 1901 they created the Junior League to provide internships, role models, mutual support, and training in the management of meetings.

Due to the general social changes of the 1960s—and in particular the revival of the feminist movement—the socialization of wealthy young women has changed somewhat in recent decades. Many private schools are now coeducational. Their women graduates are encouraged to go to major four-year colleges rather than finishing schools. Women of the upper class are more likely to have careers; there are already two or three examples of women who have risen to the top of their family's business. They are also more likely to serve on corporate boards. Still, due to its emphasis on tradition, there may be even less gender equality in the upper class than there is in the professional stratum; it is not clear how much more equality will be attained.

The female half of the upper class has been studied by several sociologists. Their work provides an important window into the upper class and class consciousness in general as well as a portrait of the socialization of well-born women. But before focusing on their work, it is worthwhile to examine one unique institution of the upper class that has not changed very much in its long history—the debutante party that announces a young woman's coming of age and eligibility for marriage. It contains general lessons on class consciousness and the difficulties of maintaining traditional socializing institutions in a time of social unrest.

The Debutante Season

The debutante season is a series of parties, teas, and dances that culminates in one or more grand balls. It announces the arrival of young women of the upper class into adult society with the utmost of formality and elegance. These highly expensive rituals—in which great attention is lavished on every detail of the food, decorations, and entertainment—have a long history in the upper class. They made their first appearance in Philadelphia in 1748 and Charleston, South Carolina, in 1762, and they vary only slightly from city to city across the country. They are a central focus of the Christmas social season just about everywhere, but in some cities debutante balls are held in the spring as well.

Dozens of people are involved in planning the private parties that most debutantes have before the grand ball. Parents, with the help of upper-class women who work as social secretaries and social consultants, spend many hours with dress designers, caterers, florists, decorators, bandleaders, and champagne importers, deciding on just the right motif for their daughter's coming out. Most parties probably cost between $25,000 and $75,000, but sometimes the occasion is so extraordinary that it draws newspaper attention. Henry Ford II spent $250,000 on a debutante party for one of his daughters, hiring a Paris designer to redo the Country Club of Detroit in an eighteenth-century chateau motif and flying in 2 million magnolia boughs from Mississippi to cover the walls of the corridor leading to the reception room. A Texas oil and real estate family chartered a commercial jet airliner for a party that began in Dallas and ended with an all-night visit to the clubs in the French Quarter of New Orleans.[16]

The debutante balls themselves are usually sponsored by local social clubs. Sometimes there is an organization whose primary purpose is the selection of debutantes and the staging of the ball, such as the Saint Cecelia Society in Charleston, South Carolina, or the Allegro Club in Houston, Texas. Adding to the solemnity of the occasion, the selection of the season's debutantes is often made by the most prominent upper-class males in the city, often through such secret societies as the Veiled Prophet in St. Louis or the Mardi Gras krewes in New Orleans.

Proceeds from the balls are usually given to a prominent local charity sponsored by members of the upper class. "Doing something for charity makes the participants feel better about spending," explains Mrs. Stephen Van Rensselear Strong, a social press agent in New York and herself a member of the upper class.[17] It also makes at least part of the expense of the occasion tax deductible.

Evidence for the great traditional importance attached to the debut is to be found in the comments Ostrander received from women who thought the whole process unimportant but made their daughters go through it anyhow: "I think it's passé, and I don't care about it, but it's just something that's done," explained one woman. Another commented: "Her father wanted her to do it. We do have a family image to maintain. It was important to the grandparents, and I felt it was an obligation to her family to do it." When people begin to talk about doing something out of tradition or to uphold an image, Ostrander suggests, then the unspoken rules that dictate class-oriented behavior are being revealed through ritual behavior.[18]

Despite the great importance placed on the debut by upper-class parents, the debutante season came into considerable disfavor among young women as the social upheavals of the late 1960s and early 1970s reached their climax. This decline reveals that the reproduction of the upper class as a social class is an effort that must be made with each new generation. Although enough young women participated to keep the tradition alive, a significant minority refused to participate, which led to the cancellation of some balls and the curtailment of many others. Stories appeared on the women's pages across the country telling of debutantes who thought the whole process was "silly" or that the money should be given to a good cause. By 1973, however, the situation began to change again, and by the mid-1970s things were back to normal.[19]

The decline of the debutante season and its subsequent resurgence in times of domestic tranquility reveal very clearly that one of its latent functions is to help perpetuate the upper class from generation to generation. When the underlying values of the class were questioned by a few of its younger members, the institution went into decline. Attitudes toward such social institutions as the debutante ball are one indicator of whether adult members of the upper class have succeeded in insulating their children from the rest of society.

The Role of Volunteer

The most informative and intimate look at the adult lives of traditional upper-class women is provided in three different interview and observation studies, one on the East Coast, one in the Midwest, and one on the West Coast. They reveal the women to be both powerful and subservient, playing decision-making roles in numerous cultural and civic organizations but also accepting traditional roles at home vis-à-vis their husbands and children. By asking the women to describe a typical day and to explain which activities were most important to them, sociologists Arlene Daniels, Margot McLeod, and Susan Ostrander found that the role of community volunteer is a central preoccupation of upper-class women, having significance as a family tradition and as an opportunity to fulfill an obligation to the community. One elderly woman involved for several decades in both the arts and human services told Ostrander: "If you're privileged, you have a certain responsibility. This was part of my upbringing; it's a tradition, a pattern of life that my brothers and sisters do too."[20]

This volunteer role is institutionalized in the training programs and activities of a variety of service organizations, especially the Junior League, which is meant for women between 20 and 40 years of age, including some upwardly mobile professional women. "Volunteerism is crucial and the Junior League is the quintessence of volunteer work," said one woman. "Everything the League does improves the situation but doesn't rock the boat. It fits into existing institutions."[21]

Quite unexpectedly, Ostrander found that many of the women serving as volunteers, fund-raisers, and board members for charitable and civic organizations viewed their work as a protection of the American way of life against the further encroachment of government into areas of social welfare. Some even saw themselves as bulwarks against socialism. "There must always be people to do volunteer work," one said. "If you have a society where no one is willing, then you may as well have communism where it's all done by the government." Another commented: "It would mean that the government would take over, and it would all be regimented. If there are no volunteers, we would live in a completely managed society which is quite the opposite to our history of freedom." Another equated government support with social-ism: "You'd have to go into government funds. That's socialism. The more we can keep independent and under private control, the better it is."[22]

Despite this emphasis on volunteer work, the women placed high value on family life. They arranged their schedules to be home when children came home from school (thirty of the thirty-eight in Ostrander's study had three or more children), and they emphasized that their primary concern was to provide a good home for their husbands. Several wanted to have greater decision-making power over their inherited wealth, but almost all wanted to take on the traditional roles of wife and mother, at least until their children were grown.

In recent years, thanks to the pressures on corporations from the women's movement, upper-class women have expanded their roles to in-clude corporate directorships. A study of women in the corporate commu-nity by former sociologist Beth Ghiloni, now a corporate executive, found that 26 percent of all women directors had upper-class backgrounds, a figure very similar to overall findings for samples of predominantly male directors. The figure was even higher, about 71 percent, for the one-fifth of directors who described themselves as volunteers before joining corporate boards. Many of these women told Ghiloni that their contacts with male corporate leaders on the boards of women's colleges and cultural organizations led to their selection as corporate directors.[23]

Women of the upper class are in a paradoxical position. They are subor-dinate to male members of their class, but they nonetheless exercise impor-tant class power in some institutional arenas. They may or may not be fully satisfied with their ambiguous power status, but they bring an upper-class, antigovernment perspective to their exercise of power. There is thus class solidarity between men and women toward the rest of society. Commenting on the complex role of upper-class women, feminist scholar Catherine Stimson draws the following stark picture: "First they must do to class what gender has done to their work—render it invisible. Next, they must maintain the same class structure they have struggled to veil."[24]

Marriage and Family Continuity

The institution of marriage is as important in the upper class as it is in any level of American society, and it does not differ greatly from other levels in its patterns and rituals. Only the exclusive site of the occasion and the lavishness of the reception distinguish upper-class marriages. The prevailing wisdom within the upper class is that children should marry someone of their own social class. The women interviewed by Ostrander, for example, felt that marriage was difficult enough without differences in "interests" and "background," which seemed to be the code words for class in discussions of marriage. Marriages outside the class were seen as likely to end in divorce.[25]

The original purpose of the debutante season was to introduce the highly sheltered young women of the upper class to eligible marriage partners. It was an attempt to corral what Baltzell calls "the democratic whims of romantic love," which "often play havoc with class solidarity."[26] But the day when the debut could play such a role was long past, even by the 1940s. The function of directing romantic love into acceptable channels was taken over by fraternities and sororities, singles-only clubs, and exclusive summer resorts.

However, in spite of parental concerns and institutionalized efforts to provide proper marriage partners, some upper-class people marry members of the upper-middle and middle classes. Although there are no completely satisfactory studies, and none that are very recent, what information is available suggests that members of the upper class are no more likely to marry within their class than people of other social levels. The most frequently cited evidence on upper-class marriage patterns appears as part of biographical studies of prominent families. Though these studies demonstrate that a great many marriages take place within the class—and often between scions of very large fortunes—they also show that some marriages are to sons and daughters of middle-class professionals and managers. No systematic conclusions can be drawn from these examples.

Wedding announcements that appear in major newspapers provide another source of evidence on this question. In a study covering prominent wedding stories on the society pages on Sundays in June for two different years one decade apart, it was found that 70 percent of the grooms and 84 percent of the brides had attended a private secondary school. Two-thirds of the weddings involved at least one participant who was listed in the *Social Register,* with both bride and groom listed in the *Social Register* in 24 percent of the cases.[27] However, those who marry far below their station may be less likely to have wedding announcements prominently displayed, so such studies must be interpreted with caution.

A study that used the *Social Register* as its starting point may be indicative of rates of intermarriage within the upper class, but it is very limited in its scope and therefore can only be considered suggestive. It began with a compilation of all the marriages listed in the Philadelphia *Social Register* for 1940 and 1960. Since the decision to list these announcements may be a voluntary one, a check of the marriage announcements in the *Philadelphia Bulletin* for those years was made to see if there were any marriages involving listees in the *Social Register* that had not been included, but none was found. One in every three marriages for 1940 and one in five for 1961 involved partners who were both listed in the *Social Register.* When private-school attendance and social club membership as well as the *Social Register* were used as evidence for upper-class standing, the rate of intermarriage averaged 50 percent for the two years. This figure is very similar to that for other social levels.[28]

The general picture for social class and marriage in the United States is suggested in a statistical study of neighborhoods and marriage patterns in the San Francisco area. Its results are very similar to those of the Philadelphia study using the *Social Register.* Of eighty grooms randomly selected from the highest-level neighborhoods, court records showed that 51 percent married brides of a comparable level. The rest married women from middle-level neighborhoods; only one or two married women from lower-level residential areas. Conversely, 63 percent of eighty-one grooms from the lowest-level neighborhoods married women from comparable areas, with under 3 percent having brides from even the lower end of the group of top neighborhoods. Completing the picture, most of the eighty-two men from middle-level areas married women from the same types of neighborhoods, but about 10 percent married into higher-level neighborhoods. Patterns of intermarriage, then, suggest both stability and some upward mobility through marriage into the upper class.[29]

Turning now to the continuity of the upper class, there is evidence that it is very great from generation to generation. This finding conflicts with the oft-repeated folk wisdom that there is a large turnover at the top of the American social ladder. Once in the upper class, families tend to stay there even as they are joined in each generation by new families and by middle-class brides and grooms who marry into their families. One study demonstrating this point began with a list of twelve families who were among the top wealthholders in Detroit for 1860, 1892, and 1902. After demonstrating their high social standing as well as their wealth, it traced their Detroit-based descendants to 1970. Nine of the twelve families still had members in the Detroit upper class; members from six of the families were directors of top corporations in the city. The study cast light on some of the reasons why the continuity is not even greater. One of the top wealthholders of 1860 had only one child, who in turn had no children. Another family dropped out of sight after the six children of the original 1860 wealthholder's only child went to court to divide the dwindling estate of $250,000 into six equal parts. A third family persisted into a fourth generation of four great-granddaughters, all of whom married outside of Detroit.[30] . . .

Tracing the families of the steel executives into the twentieth century, John Ingham determined that most were listed in the *Social Register,* were members of the most exclusive social clubs, lived in expensive neighborhoods, and sent their children to Ivy League universities. He concludes that "there has been more continuity than change among the business elites and upper classes in America," and he contrasts his results with the claims made by several generations of impressionistic historians that there has been a decline of aristocracy, the rise of a new plutocracy, or a passing of the old order.[31] . . .

It seems likely, then, that the American upper class is a mixture of old and new members. There is both continuity and social mobility, with the newer members being assimilated into the lifestyle of the class through participation in the schools, clubs, and other social institutions described [here]. There may be some tensions between those newly arrived and those of established status—as novelists and journalists love to point out—but what they have in common soon outweighs their differences.[32]

ENDNOTES

[1] Randall Collins, "Functional and Conflict Theories of Educational Stratification," *American Sociological Review* 36 (1971): 1010.

[2] "Private Schools Search for a New Role," *National Observer* (August 26, 1968), p. 5. For an excellent account of major boarding schools, see Peter Cookson and Caroline Hodges Persell, *Preparing for Power: America's Elite Boarding Schools* (New York: Basic Books, 1985).

[3] E. Digby Baltzell, *Philadelphia Gentlemen: The Making of a National Upper Class* (Glencoe, IL: Free Press, 1958), p. 339.

[4] Susan Ostrander, *Women of the Upper Class* (Philadelphia: Temple University Press, 1984), p. 85.

[5] Erving Goffman, *Asylums* (Chicago: Aldine, 1961).

[6] Interview conducted for G. William Domhoff by research assistant Deborah Samuels, February 1975; see also Gary Tamkins, "Being Special: A Study of the Upper Class" (Ph.D. Dissertation, Northwestern University, 1974).

[7] Steven Levine, "The Rise of the American Boarding Schools" (Senior Honors Thesis, Harvard University, 1975), pp. 128–30.

[8] Baltzell, *Philadelphia Gentlemen*, pp. 51–65.

[9] Baltzell, *Philadelphia Gentlemen*, p. 373.

[10] Richard P. Coleman and Lee Rainwater, *Social Standing in America* (New York: Basic Books, 1978), p. 144.

[11] Sophy Burnham, *The Landed Gentry* (New York: G. P. Putnam's Sons, 1978).

[12] Ostrander, *Women of the Upper Class*, p. 104.

[13] Philip Bonacich and G. William Domhoff, "Latent Classes and Group Membership," *Social Networks* 3 (1981).

[14] G. William Domhoff, *Who Rules America?* (Englewood Cliffs, NJ: Prentice-Hall, 1967), p. 26; E. Digby Baltzell, *The Protestant Establishment*, op. cit., p. 371.

[15] Thomas Powell, *Race, Religion, and the Promotion of the American Executive* (Columbus: Ohio State University Press, 1969), p. 50.

[16] Gay Pauley, "Coming-Out Party: It's Back in Style," *Los Angeles Times*, March 13, 1977, section 4, p. 22; "Debs Put Party on Jet," *San Francisco Chronicle*, December 18, 1965, p. 2.

[17] Pauley, "Coming-Out Party."

[18] Ostrander, "Upper-Class Women: Class Consciousness As Conduct and Meaning," *Women of the Upper Class*, pp. 93–94; Ostrander, *Women of the Upper Class*, pp. 89–90.

[19] "The Debut Tradition: A Subjective View of What It's All About," *New Orleans Times-Picayune*, August 29, 1976, section 4, p. 13; Tia Gidnick, "On Being 18 in '78: Deb Balls Back in Fashion," *Los Angeles Times*, November 24, 1978, part 4, p. 1; Virginia Lee Warren, "Many Young Socialites Want Simpler Debutante Party, or None," *New York Times*, July 2, 1972, p. 34; Mary Lou Loper, "The Society Ball: Tradition in an Era of Change," *Los Angeles Times*, October 28, 1973, part 4, p. 1.

[20] Ostrander, *Women of the Upper Class*, pp. 128–29. For three other fine accounts of the volunteer work of upper-class women, see Arlene Daniels, *Invisible Careers* (Chicago: University of Chicago Press, 1988); Margot MacLeod, "Influential Women Volunteers" (paper presented to the meetings of the American Sociological Association, San Antonio, August 1984); and Margot MacLeod, "Older Generation, Younger Generation: Transition in Women Volunteers' Lives" (unpublished manuscript, 1987). For women's involvement in philanthropy and on the boards of nonprofit organizations, see Teresa Odendahl, *Charity Begins at Home: Generosity and*

Self-Interest among the Philanthropic Elite (New York: Basic Books, 1990), and Teresa Odendahl and Michael O'Neill, eds., *Women and Power in the Nonprofit Sector* (San Francisco: Jossey-Bass, 1994). For in-depth interviews of both women and men philanthropists, see Francie Ostrower, *Why the Wealthy Give: The Culture of Elite Philanthropy* (Princeton, NJ: Princeton University Press, 1995).

[21] Ostrander, *Women of the Upper Class*, pp. 113, 115.

[22] Ostrander, "Upper-Class Women," p. 84; Ostrander, *Women of the Upper Class*, pp. 132–37.

[23] Beth Ghiloni, "New Women of Power" (Ph.D. Dissertation, University of California, Santa Cruz, 1986), pp. 122, 159.

[24] Daniels, *Invisible Careers*, p. x.

[25] Ostrander, *Women of the Upper Class*, pp. 85–88.

[26] Baltzell, *Philadelphia Gentlemen*, p. 26.

[27] Paul M. Blumberg and P. W. Paul, "Continuities and Discontinuities in Upper-Class Marriages," *Journal of Marriage and the Family*, vol. 37, no. 1 (February 1975): 63–77; David L. Hatch and Mary A. Hatch, "Criteria of Social Status As Derived from Marriage Announcements in the *New York Times*," *American Sociological Review* 12 (August 1947): 396–403.

[28] Lawrence Rosen and Robert R. Bell, "Mate Selection in the Upper Class," *Sociological Quarterly* 7 (Spring 1966): 157–66. I supplemented the original study by adding the information on schools and clubs.

[29] Robert C. Tryon, "Identification of Social Areas by Cluster Analysis: A General Method with an Application to the San Francisco Bay Area," *University of California Publications in Psychology* 8 (1955); Robert C. Tryon, "Predicting Group Differences in Cluster Analysis: The Social Areas Problem," *Multivariate Behavioral Research* 2 (1967): 453–75.

[30] T. D. Schuby, "Class Power, Kinship, and Social Cohesion: A Case Study of a Local Elite," *Sociological Focus* 8, no. 3 (August 1975): 243–55; Donald Davis, "The Price of Conspicuous Production: The Detroit Elite and the Automobile Industry, 1900–1933," *Journal of Social History* 16 (1982): 21–46.

[31] John Ingham, *The Iron Barons* (Westport, CT: Greenwood Press, 1978), pp. 230–31. For the continuity of a more general sample of wealthy families, see Michael Allen, *The Founding Fortunes* (New York: Truman Talley Books, 1987).

[32] For further evidence of the assimilation of new members into the upper class, see the study of the social affiliations and attitudes of the successful Jewish business owners who become part of the upper class by Richard L. Zweigenhaft and G. William Domhoff, *Jews in the Protestant Establishment* (New York: Praeger, 1982).

25

THE HIDDEN COST OF BEING AFRICAN AMERICAN
How Wealth Perpetuates Inequality

THOMAS M. SHAPIRO

As G. William Domhoff argues in the previous selection, social classes do exist in America, and social class distinctions can be observed through a variety of objective and subjective indicators. To understand social class relationships fully, however, sociologists must also examine racial-ethnic differences in the indicators of socioeconomic status. For example, data show persistent wealth discrepancies between whites and African Americans with similar achievements and credentials. Sociologist Thomas M. Shapiro examines this racial inequality in wealth in his book *The Hidden Cost of Being African American: How Wealth Perpetuates Inequality* (2004). In the excerpt that follows, Shapiro, the Pokross Professor of Law and Social Policy at Brandeis University, analyzes the differences in assets and wealth in four families.

Vivian and Kathryn

There's nothin' I can do about it. . . . Maybe I might meet a millionaire or somethin', you know, but I doubt that very seriously. I wish that I wasn't in a lot of debt, though, because I had got out of debt, and now I'm back in debt.

Vivian Arrora, 40 years old, is the struggling single mother of a young teenage son, Lamar, and 4-year-old twin girls, Bria and Brittany. Vivian, who is African American, grew up in Watts, which is one of the poorest sections of Los Angeles and where about one in every three families falls below the government's poverty line. Several moves have inched her family away from this poverty-stricken black community toward more middle-class West L.A. She tells me she has been attacked and raped several times. With tenacity and determination, she has bootstrapped her family and, as she says, "branched further west, out of a gang-infested area, a drug area." She dreams of owning a house in "peaceful" and middle-class Culver City.

"After I gave birth to the twins, I was just ready to go to work because just receiving AFDC [welfare] just wasn't the thing to do," Vivian begins,

---

"and all my life I've been receiving AFDC." She took vocational classes at a technical school because she "wanted to learn how to do the computer." She completed the program and earned her certificate, acquiring substantial student loans along the way.

The next step was to find a job. "I was out lookin' for a job, and it seemed like nobody wanted to hire me and I got kind of discouraged, and I just kept lookin', I just kept lookin'." A friend then suggested going to a temporary agency.

> *We went to the temp agency on a Wednesday. It was raining, and we just kept on. We kept on going, and the rain didn't stop us. . . . I went in on a Wednesday, and they called me that Thursday and told me to start work that Monday. And I've been working ever since. And I'm like: Am I really, really ready to go to work? Mentally? But once I started, I just, I've been on a roll ever since.*

All this occurred two years before we talked. Vivian worked as a temp for a year and then was hired by the county to work full-time, with some medical benefits, processing adoption papers. She is proud of having worked herself off AFDC, declaring. "I'm worth more than 700 dollars a month. I'm worth more than that!" But this clerical work does not pay much—a tad under $20,000 per year, which is about $500 above the official poverty line for her family of four. She may be a poster girl for welfare reform because she successfully transitioned off welfare, but she has joined the swelling ranks of the working poor.

Vivian's job is very important because it provides skills, habits, stability, and self-worth that she said had not existed before, but she still is very concerned about crime and safety where they live and wants to move into a better place, even own her own home someday. Working hard and bootstrapping her family off welfare has neither lifted her out of poverty nor put the American Dream within her reach. I asked her how she found the neighborhood and apartment where she is living now; her answer reminds us of the fragile and precarious living situations of those without safety nets. She was forced out of her last place with 30 days' notice, and the family just

> *landed right here. This is not where I really wanted to be, but I was tired when I was looking because I was working full-time, and by the time I got off it was too late to go look, you know, to be out at night, in there with the kids, nobody to baby-sit, so I have to come home and cook. It's just me. I don't really like the surroundings. I don't like the traffic over here either. Sometimes when I come home I see a lot of guys, they hang out down here at the corner.*

She would like to buy a home in a safer neighborhood for Lamar and the twin girls. It would be the next step up on her mobility ladder because it would solidify her present stability and provide improved services for her family and better schools for her children. She faces serious obstacles. She has lots of debt and ruined credit. She does not seem to have the resources or capabilities to work out of her debt trap, at least not on poverty-level wages. Nonetheless, she is thinking about buying a home through a funding program that requires education, training, and clearing her credit. She wonders how she can find the time to do all this while working full-time, because it would mean finding costly day care for Bria and Brittany.

A modest, even small, amount of assets, together with day care provision, would make a huge difference in securing a better future for this resolute full-time working woman and stabilizing this family's mobility up from poverty. For example, if she had assets put aside, Vivian could acquire job skills and training, and these enhanced skills in turn might well lead to a better-paying job. In the view of mortgage lenders, difficulty in getting out of debt reveals a high credit risk, so if she could get out of debt, she would be in a better position to consider seriously buying a home. Vivian's story gives us glimpses of the kind of life that so many others like her live. Her struggles anchor a starting point regarding some broader asset themes of this [reading]. Poverty is not merely the lack of adequate income for daily needs and survival; for the Arrora family it means difficulties around community, housing, crime and safety, debt, environment, child care, and schools. While it is no doubt true that there are some people whom no amount of assets could help, because of handicaps or inclination, given how far she has taken the family already, I firmly believe that Vivian Arrora's family is poised for mobility and self-reliance. Lack of assets holds her back.

Kathryn MacDonald, like Vivian, is in her 40s and earning a salary close to the poverty line. She too is a single mother, but her life struggle tells a very different story. Kathryn works about 30 hours a week as a freelance contractor in publishing, earning approximately $16,000 a year. Her boyfriend left her just before her son, Evan, was born and she has raised him alone. She prefers to work part-time so she can spend part of her day with Evan, who she says has attention deficit disorder. According to her this was a major reason why she moved from New Jersey to St. Louis in 1995.

Kathryn and Evan MacDonald live in Florissant, a traditionally working-class and middle-income community in north St. Louis County. Kathryn worked at a large publishing house in Manhattan before moving. She grew weary of the city's frantic work pace, expensive New Jersey housing, and spending so much time away from her son, so they moved. Now Kathryn does the same work in her St. Louis home that she used to do in a Manhattan skyscraper, matching Library of Congress book subject headings to subject titles for publishers. Freelancing half-time at home allows her to spend much more time with Evan and to watch over his educational and social development. She also enjoys the freedom and autonomy of working at home. Kathryn earns a lot less than when she worked full-time in New York, but she is far happier with her life now, even if her earnings only amount to poverty wages. She likes the community and schools, which are largely white.

Kathryn clearly is pleased that things have worked out so well.

We're in a good neighborhood. My son can go out to play and I don't have to worry about what he's going to get into or who he is going to be encountering. I don't have to worry about him being abducted. . . . I don't have to worry too much about drive-by shootings. I don't have to worry that something terrible is going to happen to him just because he was out on the street.

Kathryn is especially pleased with Evan's school situation. Evan is smart, just a notch below getting into gifted programs, and the system has special programs for bright kids like him. The school also has understanding and knowledgeable teachers working in small-group settings who can help him overcome his ADD.

Normally, $16,000 does not afford a great deal more than what Kathryn calls "life support," much less the kinds of services and opportunities available in middle-class communities. What makes Kathryn's life so different from Vivian Arrora's? How is she able to live on essentially poverty wages and yet plan for a future that looks to have better prospects? How is she able to live in a place that is safe for herself and Evan? How is Kathryn able to find a school where Evan can thrive? It is not as simple as that one is white and the other is black. The answer is transformative assets.

For one thing, Kathryn is free of debt. Her brother has been sending $100 a month for several years to help her out with Evan's educational and day care expenses. She lost a job several years ago, when Evan was 2, but was able to move in with her father for five years. She has no school loans because her family paid her college bills. Even today, unlike the average American, she does not owe any credit card debt.

But her financial stability goes far beyond just lack of debt, Kathryn explains. She has inherited money from her family.

I have the proceeds from my father's estate, and also my grandmother. I don't even pretend to understand this—my cousin the lawyer handles all this—but if her estate gets to a certain size, she is liable for more estate taxes, so every so often he has to disburse some of that money.

Kathryn tells us that she has already inherited about $125,000, of which about $90,000 remains, and will inherit another $80,000 when her 94-year-old grandmother passes away. "That could be when I buy a house. That could be what pushes me over the top. With that plus with the mortgage I could get, I could get something decent." She hopes to buy a home with her new boyfriend, who will not be able to contribute much because he pays alimony to a first wife.

When her father died, "the first thing I did was take some money out, and we took a vacation." When another chunk of money came from her grandmother's estate, she and Evan took off to a family wedding in Alaska. She dips into the inheritance every few months as bills mount up, especially when her quarterly estimated income tax is due. She is looking into magnet schools and even private schooling for Evan, in case the local public schools cannot continue to meet his special needs and provide an environment in which he can thrive.

If Kathryn MacDonald did not have assets, one might think of her in an entirely different light, and many questions might arise. For instance: What is she doing to better herself? Why is she not working full-time? Why are her ambitions so low? If she were black, the questions might have a harsher tone, and we can imagine the social condemnation and scorn this single mom might face. Although one might question some of Kathryn's choices, her story is an example of how financial inheritance can provide advantages and a head start in life. Maybe even more important for Kathryn MacDonald, assets supply an anchor for her family's middle-class status and identity that her work and income cannot.

Vivian Arrora's and Kathryn MacDonald's stories provide a concrete starting point for considering how racial inequality is passed from one generation to the next. In many ways they are so alike; yet in many other ways their lives are so different. Vivian's legacy is growing up black in a welfare family in Watts and becoming a single mother herself. She is the first in her family to go to college. The big issues for her are work, debt and bad credit, finding time for the kids, the fear of violence, drugs, and gangs, and figuring out a way to buy a home in a stable and safer community. Hers is a remarkable success story, but her mobility from welfare to working poor may have reached its own limit. Her children go to weak urban schools where getting ahead is a difficult task accomplished only by a few. Lamar, Bria, and Brittany will inherit America's lack of commitment to equal education for all.

Kathryn's situation, if not her accomplishments, is very different. She does not worry about drugs, violence, and gangs, the adequacy of the public schools, or finding time to spend with her child. Her upper-middle-class inheritance includes a debt-free present, a substantial amount of assets, and palpable prospects of inheriting considerably more in the near future. Her inheritance, one could argue, includes class standing that sustains her comfortable and respectable middle-class situation. In looking at these legacies and inheritances, we begin to see that family assets are more than mere money; they also provide a pathway for handing down racial legacies from generation to generation.

Finally, Vivian's greatest dream is to own a home in a safe place with decent schools for her kids. As far as I can tell, this is not likely to happen, unless she actually meets and marries her millionaire—or unless a bold and imaginative policy helps to make her hard work pay off. Kathryn's dream home most likely will become a reality after her grandmother passes away. The lives and opportunities of their children already are being acted out upon different stages, and the gulf between Evan and Lamar is likely to widen further. What the two boys make of their lives from these different starting points will be their own doing, but let us not delude ourselves that Kathryn and Evan and Vivian, Lamar, and the twins share even remotely similar opportunities.

The Ackerman Family

This is a step up from our starter home. We looked at the city, and the bottom line was we weren't happy with the schools. We wanted to be in a public school in the county. The benefits. The tax benefit; the ownership and not having a neighbor right on your next wall; privacy. We didn't end up here, we chose to be here. We were definitely trying to buy our life house.

Chris and Peter Ackerman and their three children are middle-class residents of south suburban St. Louis. Chris is a plant accounting manager, and Peter is a technical service manager; together their incomes top $80,000. Through "working and saving, working and saving" they have built their net worth to more than $100,000. As is true for most American families, their largest pool of wealth is their home equity, accounting for about $67,000 of their assets. They also own about $60,000 in various retirement programs, which, as they note, carry heavy tax and withdrawal penalties if used before retirement.

In our conversation, Chris and Peter express a keen sense of economic security and the firm belief that their children have a bright future: Because they both work for a large organization that promises to pay college tuition for long-standing employees, they will not have to dip into their assets or take out loans for college. Like most Americans, they believe their assets put them right in the middle of the wealth distribution, but when I tell them they own more than most Americans, Chris remarks, "Good."

Because these college graduates come from middle-class families, are not burdened with student loans, and are good credit risks, they were able to get a mortgage for a classic starter home. Peter's parents helped with the down payment, which allowed them to buy in the community of their choosing. As with many families, the increased property value in their starter home provided a sizable portion of the down payment when they moved up to their present suburban home.

It was a pivotal moment for them, as it is for many American families. With three children reaching school age, the Ackermans' space, community, and schooling needs were changing and growing. The flexibility families with assets have at these times sorts them and their children onto different life trajectories from those without assets. Chris begins explaining how they approached these important issues.

I had cousins growing up in the city, and—this is my own blood, but basically they turned out really trashy. Their friends were trashy. [I] did not even want sometimes to bring my own children around my cousins, because their lifestyles were different, their values were different. Things that were important to us were not important to them.

Peter talks about those things that were important to them.

It seemed like the areas we could afford in the city, the neighborhoods were different. One street would be really nice, clean-kept houses, and two streets over there would be boarded-up houses or just really trashy houses. And we just thought, the mix of the group and then all of these people going to the same school, it did not fit with what we wanted for our family. . . .

Peter and Chris bought a home in a suburban part of St. Louis where nearly everybody owns a home built since the 1950s and families have similar incomes, in the $60,000 to $80,000 range. The community they chose is almost all white; less than one percent of blacks and Hispanics live in their zip code. When I ask about the diversity of their community, Peter explains:

It is unfortunate that it is bound by race too. As far as I am concerned, that has nothing to do with it [lack of diversity]. I think it's economic because it's the same issue we dealt with when we lived in the city. It didn't matter if our neighbors were white or black, as long as they had the same standards we had.

The Ackermans' assets—help with the down payment, no college loans, and especially the equity built up from their starter home—along with stable jobs and high-quality benefits allow them to own a home in the suburban community of their choice, one up to their "standards," and to select the kind of schools they want for their kids. Most middle-class families with school-age children face similar school, community, and space issues. Of all the options available to Peter and Chris Ackerman, they chose a segregated suburb and segregated schools. . . .

"Worlds Away"

Elizabeth Wainwright Cummings works part-time as an accountant; her husband teaches in the same city schools that drove the Ackermans to the suburbs. Their incomes do not cover their expenses, which include a mortgage on a large, historic home, day care for 4-year-old Anna, and exclusive schooling and private tutoring for 9-year-old Alexander. Their incomes are supplemented by $30,000 a year in interest from an inheritance, and her parents are paying the private school bills. She explains that the family money goes way, way back—it is money her father inherited—and it will last a long time. She already has inherited about $350,000, with "more than a million dollars sitting there with my name on it." Their home is in a suburban school district that she feels is not strong. This didn't matter, she explains, because "we knew we weren't using the school district." Her comment is a good example of a privatized notion of citizenship: Since she can use ample family wealth for her own benefit, she does not have to worry about or invest in the public infrastructure that would help everyone.

Although "once we are inside our house, we love it," she is wary of her largely middle-class neighborhood, because not all the homes look like hers and some of her neighbors are still at early points in their careers. Elizabeth is planning to move to an upper-class neighborhood that fits her class identity better and where she is more comfortable with the neighbors. As she puts it, she has her "eye on this area really close to our house but *worlds* away."

Perhaps because she comes from a family that has handed down money for generations, Elizabeth is conscious of how wealth confers privileges and advantages. At the end of our conversation, I say that I have just one last, big, complex question: How do you feel that wealth has impacted your life?

> *No question about it. I mean, if my parents hadn't had the money to send my kids to [the private] Hills School, we couldn't have considered it. We would have had to really do belt tightening, and financial aid, and many more loans, more mortgages. It would have been very difficult and a real strain on us, especially with two. And we probably would have felt like we just couldn't swing it as a family. So, I don't know, I would have had to have gone out and gotten a job that would pay enough to justify two kids in private school. With that, it would have meant not being able to mother them as much myself. Or my husband having to change work, and all the soul-searching that would have meant for him. It's unimaginable. I can't envision a path that we would have been able to so comfortably just sail on over to Hills School. And, yeah, [we would have had to] go through a lot of heart-wrenching decisions about Alexander [school and tutors]. But they never had to do with money. None of these decisions have had to do with money. I can't imagine it being any other way.*

The world that Elizabeth has trouble imagining includes difficulty paying a mortgage out of earnings, working full-time, working at a job you may not like, public school, family budgeting and making choices, and worrying about money issues. The world she cannot imagine is reality for most Americans. The Cummings family is a possibly excessive but nonetheless illustrative example of how a reservoir of wealth and expected inheritance opens the door to all opportunities and can make dreams come true more easily.

Families and Safety Nets

Let us ask a question of the four families we have met thus far that penetrates further the ways in which assets matter. What if these families lost their jobs? Vivian Arrora has nothing to fall back on and might well find herself back on welfare or worse. The consequences for Kathryn and Evan MacDonald, on the other hand, would be less catastrophic. She could sustain her present lifestyle for several years while progressively drawing more money from her inherited assets. Soon, however, if they were not replenished from other expected inheritances, she would need to tap her assets for everyday living. Without a full-time or higher-paying job, she would have to postpone becoming a homeowner. The Ackermans' financial assets provide a resource cushion that can absorb economic shocks and personal misfortune. They could survive on their nest egg for some time, but it would mean scaling back the lifestyle they treasure—fewer vacations, giving up their boat—and even then they could not endure a prolonged absence of income. More important, their resources secure a desired status for them and educational opportunities for their children. The wealthy Cummings family probably would not notice the financial impact for a long time because the interest on Elizabeth's inheritance alone gives them more money than Vivian Arrora earns working a full-time job.

The stories of these four families introduce themes that I will weave throughout [this reading]. I want to use the cases just presented to expand the idea of transformative assets. Wealth is critical to a family's class standing, social status, whether they own or rent housing, the kind of community they live in, and the quality of their children's schools. Based upon a thorough familiarity with the textured lives of the families we interviewed, I suggest that it is possible to distinguish whether a family's current position and life trajectory is based upon earnings and achievements, or wealth and family legacies, or some combination. The notion of transformative assets is most trenchant for our purposes when the financial resources that make current status possible are inherited in some fashion. In the families we have heard about already, Kathryn MacDonald provides the clearest example of the power of inherited assets to transform her current position far beyond what she earns. The Cummings family illustrates the old-fashioned and better-understood notion of very wealthy families handing down resources. The Ackerman case is not so clear-cut. They enjoyed a head start because their families paid the college bills, and they received family financial assistance on their first home. At the same time, the Ackermans' assets also represent the fruits of savings and investments based upon their earned achievements in the workplace. Vivian Arrora works as hard as anyone in these four families—and has the least to show for it. Lack of assets, much less family money, caps her family's mobility.

These four accounts highlight the role that assets—or lack of them—plays in a family's quest for well-being and promoting opportunities for their children. When asked to name the primary benefit of money, 87 percent of affluent baby boomers in one survey answered, "It enables you to give advantages to your children."

American families are in the process of passing along a $9 trillion legacy from one generation to the next. This is a lot of money, but it is distributed very unevenly. Most whites do not inherit considerable wealth; an even smaller percentage of African Americans benefit. Hand in hand with this money, I submit, what is really being handed down from generation to generation is the profound legacy of reproducing racial inequality. This legacy will be difficult to discern because the language of family heritage hides it from our political consciousness. Mainstream sociological theory sees differences in jobs, skills, and education as the primary causes of inequality, and substantial wealth transfers embarrass this theory. The classical sociologist Emilé Durkheim, for example, predicted that family inheritances would decline over time in favor of giving to charitable and nonprofit organizations, but studies examining actual bequests invalidate this prediction.[1] Andrew Carnegie's belief that giving relatives money only makes them lazy (a belief he put into action) may correspond with this perspective, but the empirical evidence tells a different story. In 1989 charitable bequests constituted less than 10 percent of proceeds of estates valued over $600,000 in the United States.[2] Even Karl Marx was more concerned with production and the circulation of money than with property and family legacies.

The Asset Perspective

A core part of my argument is that wealth, as distinct from income, offers the key to understanding racial stratification. Thus a wealth perspective provides a fresh way to examine the "playing field." Indeed, I believe that this perspective challenges a standard part of the American credo—that similar accomplishments result in roughly equal rewards—which needs serious reexamination. First, however, I need to outline this wealth perspective and why I believe it is so important.

By wealth I mean the total value of things families own minus their debts. Income, on the other hand, includes earnings from work, interest and dividends, pensions, and transfer payments. The distinction between wealth and income is significant because one signifies ownership and control of resources and the other represents salary or its replacement. However, the difference between the two is often muddled in the public mind, and only recently have the social sciences begun to treat wealth as an intrinsically important indicator of family well-being that is quite different from income. Another perspective on advantage and disadvantage emerges when wealth is used as an indicator of racial inequality. Wealth represents a more permanent capacity to secure advantages in both the short and long term, and it is transferred across generations. Income data is collected regularly, and vast stores of it exist. In contrast, wealth data has not been collected systematically, and issues such as how to value a home, how to view home equity, whether retirement plans should be counted, and how to value a business make it harder to measure.

Wealth has been a neglected dimension of the social sciences' concern with the economic and social status of Americans in general and racial minorities in particular. We have been much more comfortable describing and analyzing occupational, educational, and income inequality than examining the economic foundation of a capitalist society, "private property." When wealth surveys became available in the mid-1980s, journalists and social scientists began to pay more attention to the issue of wealth. The growing concentration of wealth at the top and the growing racial wealth gap have become important public policy issues that undergird many political debates but, unfortunately, not many policy discussions.[3]

Social scientists typically analyze racial inequality as imbalances in the distribution of power, economic resources, and opportunities. Most research on racial inequality has focused on the economic dimension. This economic component has emphasized jobs and wages. Until very recently, the social sciences and the policy arena neglected the effect of wealth disparity and inheritance on the differing opportunities and well-being of white and black families. We are suggesting that wealth motivates much of what Americans do, grounds their life chances, and provides enduring advantages and disadvantages across generations. Wealth ownership is the single dimension on which whites and blacks are most persistently unequal.[4]

Our understanding of racial inequality comes typically from data on income. Primarily this represents earnings from work, but it also includes social assistance and pensions. Income is a tidy and valuable gauge of present inequality. Indeed, a very strong case can be made that reducing racial discrimination in the workplace has resulted in narrowing the *hourly wage gap* between whites and racial minorities.[5] Reducing discrimination in jobs, promotion, and pay is an effective way to narrow racial inequality. The average American family uses income for food, shelter, clothing, and other necessities. Wealth is different, and I argue that it is used differently than income. Wealth is what families own, a storehouse of resources. Wealth signifies a command over financial resources that when combined with income can produce the opportunity to secure the "good life" in whatever form is needed—education, business, training, justice, health, comfort, and so on. In this sense wealth is a special form of money not usually used to purchase milk and shoes or other life necessities. More often it is used to create opportunities, secure a desired stature and standard of living, or pass class status along to one's children. It is obvious that the positions of two families with the same income but widely different wealth assets are not identical, and it is time for us to take this into account in public policy. . . .

I have made much of the distinction between income and wealth, but this would only be an academic distinction if the two were highly correlated, that is, if a family's income were a reliable predictor of its wealth, and if savings were the primary source of wealth accumulation. If this were the case, we could continue to tell the income story as a sort of proxy for all resources, as we have in the past. If they are not powerfully correlated, however, fusing them prevents us from addressing an important basis of racial inequality, the increasing concentration of wealth, and public policies that mitigate the consequences of such inequalities. Sociologist Lisa Keister's *Wealth in America* reviews this issue and concludes that the correlation between income and wealth is weak. This suggests that, according to Keister, "studies that focus solely on income miss a large part of the story of advantage and disadvantage in America."[6]

Because wealth sometimes represents inequalities from the past, it not only is a measure of differences in contemporary resources but also suggests inequalities that will play out in the future. Looking at racial inequality through wealth changes our conception of its nature and magnitude and of whether it is declining or increasing. Most recent analyses have concluded that continuing racial inequality primarily results from disparities in educational achievement and jobs. Sociologist Christopher Jencks, for instance, argues that improving educational performance for African Americans would be the biggest step toward racial equality. William Julius Wilson has consistently maintained in several books that advances in the workplace are the linchpin of racial equality. The asset perspective does not neglect the importance of these powerful insights. I maintain, however, that exclusively focusing on contemporary class-based factors like jobs and education disregards the currency of the historical legacy of African Americans. A focus on wealth sheds light on both historical and contemporary impacts not only of class but also of race. Income is an indicator of the current status of racial inequality; I argue that an examination of wealth discloses the consequences of the racial patterning of opportunities.

The legacy of the American dilemma of democracy and race continues to haunt the American scene. The dynamics of race and class intertwine in a way that becomes more clearly explicable upon examining how families use private wealth to expand their chances and—just as important—how lack of assets dampens aspirations. Americans highly value two cherished but contradictory notions: equal opportunity and a family's ability to pass along advantages to their children. By focusing on assets rather than exclusively on income, we can unravel this legacy and examine how it affects racial inequality.

In summary, I argue that we have been seriously underestimating racial inequality by focusing primarily on workplace and income and that an examination of wealth is an indispensable part of understanding inequality. Tragically, policies based solely in the workplace that seek to narrow differences will fail to close the breach. Taken together, however, asset and labor market approaches open new windows of possibility. . . .

ENDNOTES

[1]Robert K. Miller Jr. and Stephen J. McNamee, "The Inheritance of Wealth in America," in *Inheritance and Wealth in America,* edited by Robert K. Miller, Jr. and Stephen J. McNamee (New York and London: Plenum Press, 1998).

[2]Barry Johnson and Martha Eller, "Federal Taxation of Inheritance and Wealth Transfers," in *Inheritance and Wealth in America,* edited by Robert K. Miller, Jr. and Stephen J. McNamee (New York and London: Plenum Press, 1998).

[3]An emerging body of work and policy initiatives takes up this challenge. I have in mind here the work of Dalton Conley, *Being Black, Living in the Red* (Berkeley: University of California Press, 1999); Lisa Keister, *Wealth in America* (New York: Cambridge University Press, 2000); and Edward N. Wolff, *Top Heavy* (New York: New Press, 2000).

[4]See the work of Conley, Keister, Wolff, and Oliver and Shapiro, *Black Wealth/White Wealth: A New Perspective on Racial Inequality* (New York: Routledge, 1995).

[5]Strong evidence for a narrowing black–white hourly wage gap is found in David Card and Thomas Lemieux, "Changing Wage Structure and Black–White Wage Differentials," *American Economic Review* 84, no. 2 (1994): 29–33; and discussed in Joseph Altonji and Rebecca Blank, "Race and Gender in the Labor Market," in *Handbook of Labor Economics,* vol. 3, edited by Orley Ashenfelter and David Card (Amsterdam: Elsevier, 1999). In contrast, the annual earnings gap results from number of hours worked, job status, working at a second job, and self-employment. See Barry Bluestone and Mary Huff Stevenson, *The Boston Renaissance: Race, Space, and Economic Change in an American Metropolis* (New York: Russell Sage Foundation, 2000).

[6]Keister 2000:10. Indeed, when asset income is not included, the correlation between income and net worth is only .26.

26

NICKEL-AND-DIMED
On (Not) Getting By in America

BARBARA EHRENREICH

As the previous reading by Shapiro demonstrated, the American Dream and accumulation of wealth have been difficult to obtain for African Americans. They have also been impossible goals for the working poor. Instead, many working-class people struggle to meet the economic requirements of every-day survival. In the excerpt below, Barbara Ehrenreich describes what it is like to try to work and survive on the wages most unskilled workers receive in America. Ehrenreich began her field research in 1998 to find out whether welfare reform's back-to-work programs really have the ability to lift poor women out of poverty and provide them a future in the labor market. The results of Ehrenreich's research are published in her 2001 book, *Nickel and Dimed: On (Not) Getting By in America.*

At the beginning of June 1998 I leave behind everything that normally soothes the ego and sustains the body—home, career, companion, reputation, ATM card—for a plunge into the low-wage workforce. There, I become another, occupationally much diminished "Barbara Ehrenreich"—depicted on job-application forms as a divorced homemaker whose sole work experience consists of housekeeping in a few private homes. I am terrified, at the beginning, of being unmasked for what I am: a middle-class journalist setting out to explore the world that welfare mothers are entering, at the rate of approximately 50,000 a month, as welfare reform kicks in. Happily, though, my fears turn out to be entirely unwarranted: during a month of poverty and toil, my name goes unnoticed and for the most part unuttered. In this parallel universe where my father never got out of the mines and I never got through college, I am "baby," "honey," "blondie," and, most commonly, "girl."

My first task is to find a place to live. I figure that if I can earn $7 an hour—which, from the want ads, seems doable—I can afford to spend $500 on rent, or maybe, with severe economies, $600. In the Key West area, where I live, this pretty much confines me to flophouses and trailer homes—like the one, a pleasing fifteen-minute drive from town, that has no air-conditioning, no screens, no fans, no television, and, by way of diversion, only the challenge of evading the landlord's Doberman pinscher. The big problem with this place, though, is the rent, which at $675 a month is well beyond my reach. All right, Key West is expensive. But so is New York City, or the Bay Area, or Jackson Hole, or Telluride, or Boston, or any other place where tourists and the wealthy compete for living space with the people who clean their toilets and fry their hash browns.[1] Still, it is a shock to realize that "trailer trash" has become, for me, a demographic category to aspire to.

So I decide to make the common trade-off between affordability and convenience, and go for a $500-a-month efficiency thirty miles up a two-lane highway from the employment opportunities of Key West, meaning forty-five minutes if there's no road construction and I don't get caught behind some sun-dazed Canadian tourists. I hate the drive, along a roadside studded with white crosses commemorating the more effective head-on collisions, but it's a sweet little place—a cabin, more or less, set in the swampy back yard of the converted mobile home where my landlord, an affable TV repairman, lives with his bartender girlfriend. Anthropologically speaking, a bustling trailer park would be preferable, but here I have a gleaming white floor and a firm mattress, and the few resident bugs are easily vanquished.

Besides, I am not doing this for the anthropology. My aim is nothing so mistily subjective as to "experience poverty" or find out how it "really feels" to be a long-term low-wage worker. I've had enough unchosen encounters with poverty and the world of low-wage work to know it's not a place you want to visit for touristic purposes; it just smells too much like fear. And with all my real-life assets—bank account, IRA, health insurance, multiroom home—waiting indulgently in the background, I am, of course, thoroughly insulated from the terrors that afflict the genuinely poor.

No, this is a purely objective, scientific sort of mission. The humanitarian rationale for welfare reform—as opposed to the more punitive and stingy impulses that may actually have motivated it—is that work will lift poor women out of poverty while simultaneously inflating their self-esteem and hence their future value in the labor market. Thus, whatever the hassles involved in finding child care, transportation, etc., the transition from welfare to work will end happily, in greater prosperity for all. Now there are many problems with this comforting prediction, such as the fact that the economy will inevitably undergo a downturn, eliminating many jobs. Even without a downturn, the influx of a million former welfare recipients into the low-wage labor market could depress wages by as much as 11.9 percent, according to the Economic Policy Institute (EPI) in Washington, D.C.

But is it really possible to make a living on the kinds of jobs currently available to unskilled people? Mathematically, the answer is no, as can be shown by taking $6 to $7 an hour, perhaps subtracting a dollar or two an hour for child care, multiplying by 160 hours a month, and comparing the result to the prevailing rents. According to the National Coalition for the Homeless, for example, in 1998 it took, on average nationwide, an hourly wage of $8.89 to afford a one-bedroom apartment, and the Preamble Center for Public Policy estimates that the odds against a typical welfare recipient's landing a job at such a "living wage" are about 97 to 1. If these numbers are right, low-wage work is not a solution to poverty and possibly not even to homelessness.

It may seem excessive to put this proposition to an experimental test. As certain family members keep unhelpfully reminding me, the viability of low-wage work could be tested, after a fashion, without ever leaving my study. I could just pay myself $7 an hour for eight hours a day, charge myself for room and board, and total up the numbers after a month. Why leave the people and work that I love? But I am an experimental scientist by training. In that business, you don't just sit at a desk and theorize; you plunge into the everyday chaos of nature, where surprises lurk in the most mundane measurements. Maybe, when I got into it, I would discover some hidden economies in the world of the low-wage worker. After all, if 30 percent of the workforce toils for less than $8 an hour, according to the EPI, they may have found some tricks as yet unknown to me. Maybe—who knows?—I would even be able to detect in myself the bracing psychological effects of getting out of the house, as promised by the welfare wonks at places like the Heritage Foundation. Or, on the other hand, maybe there would be unexpected costs—physical, mental, or financial—to throw off all my calculations. Ideally, I should do this with two small children in tow, that being the welfare average, but mine are grown and no one is willing to lend me theirs for a month-long vacation in penury. So this is not the perfect experiment, just a test of the best possible case: an unencumbered woman, smart and even strong, attempting to live more or less off the land.

On the morning of my first full day of job searching, I take a red pen to the want ads, which are auspiciously numerous. Everyone in Key West's booming "hospitality industry" seems to be looking for someone like me—trainable, flexible, and with suitably humble expectations as to pay. . . .

Most of the big hotels run ads almost continually, just to build a supply of applicants to replace the current workers as they drift away or are fired, so finding a job is just a matter of being at the right place at the right time and flexible enough to take whatever is being offered that day. This finally happens to me at one of the big discount hotel chains, where I go, as usual, for housekeeping and am sent, instead, to try out as a waitress at the attached "family restaurant," a dismal spot with a counter and about thirty tables that looks out on a parking garage and features such tempting fare as "Polish [sic] sausage and BBQ sauce" on 95-degree days. Phillip, the dapper young West Indian who introduces himself as the manager, interviews me with about as much enthusiasm as if he were a clerk processing me for Medicare, the principal questions being what shifts can I work and when can I start. I mutter something about being woefully out of practice as a waitress, but he's already on to the uniform: I'm to show up tomorrow wearing black slacks and black shoes; he'll provide the rust-colored polo shirt with HEARTHSIDE embroidered on it, though I might want to wear my own shirt to get to work, ha ha. At the word "tomorrow," something between fear and indignation rises in my chest. I want to say, "Thank you for your time, sir, but this is just an experiment, you know, not my actual life."

So begins my career at the Hearthside, I shall call it, one small profit center within a global discount hotel chain, where for two weeks I work from 2:00 till 10:00 P.M. for $2.43 an hour plus tips.[2] In some futile bid for gentility, the management has barred employees from using the front door, so my first day I enter through the kitchen, where a red-faced man with shoulder-length blond hair is throwing frozen steaks against the wall and yelling, "Fuck this shit!" "That's just Jack," explains Gail, the wiry middle-aged waitress who is assigned to train me. "He's on the rag again"—a condition occasioned, in this instance, by the fact that the cook on the morning shift had forgotten to thaw out the steaks. For the next eight hours, I run after the agile Gail, absorbing bits of instruction along with fragments of personal tragedy. All food must be trayed, and the reason she's so tired today is that she woke up in a cold sweat thinking of her boyfriend, who killed himself recently in an upstate prison. No refills on lemonade. And the reason he was in prison is that a few DUIs caught up with him, that's all, could have happened to anyone. Carry the creamers to the table in a monkey bowl, never in your hand. And after he was gone she spent several months living in her truck, peeing in a plastic pee bottle and reading by candlelight at night, but you can't live in a truck in the summer, since you need to have the windows down, which means anything can get in, from mosquitoes on up.

At least Gail puts to rest any fears I had of appearing overqualified. From the first day on, I find that of all the things I have left behind, such as home and identity, what I miss the most is competence. Not that I have ever felt utterly competent in the writing business, in which one day's success augurs nothing at all for the next. But in my writing life, I at least have some notion of procedure: do the research, make the outline, rough out a draft, etc. As a server, though I am beset by requests like bees: more iced tea here, ketchup over there, a to-go box for table fourteen, and where are the high chairs, anyway? Of the twenty-seven tables, up to six are usually mine at any time, though on slow afternoons or if Gail is off, I sometimes have the whole place to myself. There is the touch-screen computer-ordering system to master, which is, I suppose, meant to minimize server-cook contact, but in practice requires constant verbal fine-tuning: "That's gravy on the mashed, okay? None on the meatloaf," and so forth—while the cook scowls as if I were inventing these refinements just to torment him. Plus, something I had forgotten in the years since I was eighteen: about a third of a server's job is "side work" that's invisible to customers—sweeping, scrubbing, slicing, refilling, and restocking. If it isn't all done, every little bit of it, you're going to face the 6:00 P.M. dinner rush defenseless and probably go down in flames. I screw up dozens of times at the beginning, sustained in my shame entirely by Gail's support—"It's okay, baby, everyone does that sometime"—because, to my total surprise and despite the scientific detachment I am doing my best to maintain, I care. . . .

On my first Friday at the Hearthside there is a "mandatory meeting for all restaurant employees," which I attend, eager for insight into our overall marketing strategy and the niche (your basic Ohio cuisine with a tropical twist?) we aim to inhabit. But there is no "we" at this meeting. Phillip, our top manager except for an occasional "consultant" sent out by corporate headquarters, opens it with a sneer: "The break room—it's disgusting. Butts in the ashtrays, newspapers lying around, crumbs." This windowless little room, which also houses the time clock for the entire hotel, is where we stash our bags and civilian clothes and take our half-hour meal breaks. But a break room is not a right, he tells us. It can be taken away. We should also know that the lockers in the break room and whatever is in them can be searched at any time. Then comes gossip; there has been gossip; gossip (which seems to mean employees talking among themselves) must stop. Off-duty employees are henceforth barred from eating at the restaurant, because "other servers gather around them and gossip." When Phillip has exhausted his agenda of rebukes, Joan complains about the condition of the ladies' room and I throw in my two bits about the vacuum cleaner. But I don't see any backup coming from my fellow servers, each of whom has subsided into her own personal funk; Gail, my role model, stares sorrowfully at a point six inches from her nose. The meeting ends when Andy, one of the cooks, gets up, muttering about breaking up his day off for this almighty bullshit.

Just four days later we are suddenly summoned into the kitchen at 3:30 P.M., even though there are live tables on the floor. We all—about ten of us—stand around Phillip, who announces grimly that there has been a report of some "drug activity" on the night shift and that, as a result, we are now to be a "drug-free" workplace, meaning that all new hires will be tested, as will possibly current employees on a random basis. I am glad that this part of the kitchen is so dark, because I find myself blushing as hard as if I had been caught toking up in the ladies' room myself: I haven't been treated this way—lined up in the corridor, threatened with locker searches, peppered with carelessly aimed accusations—since junior high school. Back on the floor, Joan cracks, "Next they'll be telling us we can't have sex on the job." When I ask Stu what happened to inspire the crackdown, he just mutters about "management decisions" and takes the opportunity to upbraid Gail and me for being too generous with the rolls. From now on there's to be only one per customer, and it goes out with the dinner, not with the salad. He's also been riding the cooks, prompting Andy to come out of the kitchen and observe—with the serenity of a man whose customary implement is a butcher knife—that "Stu has a death wish today."

The other problem, in addition to the less-than-nurturing management style, is that this job shows no sign of being financially viable. You might imagine, from a comfortable distance, that people who live, year in and year out, on $6 to $10 an hour have discovered some survival stratagems unknown to the middle class. But no. It's not hard to get my co-workers to talk about their living situations, because housing, in almost every case, is the principal source of disruption in their lives, the first thing they fill you in on when they arrive for their shifts. After a week, I have compiled the following survey:

- ▾ Gail is sharing a room in a well-known downtown flophouse for which she and a roommate pay about $250 a week. Her roommate, a male friend, has begun hitting on her, driving her nuts, but the rent would be impossible alone.
- ▾ Claude, the Haitian cook, is desperate to get out of the two-room apartment he shares with his girlfriend and two other, unrelated, people. As far as I can determine, the other Haitian men (most of whom only speak Creole) live in similarly crowded situations.
- ▾ Annette, a twenty-year-old server who is six months pregnant and has been abandoned by her boyfriend, lives with her mother, a postal clerk.
- ▾ Marianne and her boyfriend are paying $170 a week for a one-person trailer.
- ▾ Jack, who is, at $10 an hour, the wealthiest of us, lives in the trailer he owns, paying only the $400-a-month lot fee.
- ▾ The other white cook, Andy, lives on his dry-docked boat, which, as far as I can tell from his loving descriptions, can't be more than twenty feet long. He offers to take me out on it, once it's repaired, but the offer comes with inquiries as to my marital status, so I do not follow up on it.
- ▾ Tina and her husband are paying $60 a night for a double room in a Days Inn. This is because they have no car and the Days Inn is within walking distance of the Hearthside. When Marianne, one of the breakfast servers, is tossed out of her trailer for subletting (which is against the trailer-park rules), she leaves her boyfriend and moves in with Tina and her husband.
- ▾ Joan, who had fooled me with her numerous and tasteful outfits (hostesses wear their own clothes), lives in a van she parks behind a shopping center at night and showers in Tina's motel room. The clothes are from thrift shops.[3]

It strikes me, in my middle-class solipsism, that there is gross improvidence in some of these arrangements. When Gail and I are wrapping silverware in napkins—the only task for which we are permitted to sit—she tells me she is thinking of escaping from her roommate by moving into the Days Inn herself. I am astounded: How can she even think of paying between $40 and $60 a day? But if I was afraid of sounding like a social worker, I come out just sounding like a fool. She squints at me in disbelief, "And where am I supposed to get a month's rent and a month's deposit for an apartment?" I'd been feeling pretty smug about my $500 efficiency, but of course it was made possible only by the $1,300 I had allotted myself for start-up costs when I began my low-wage life: $1,000 for the first month's rent and deposit, $100 for initial groceries and cash in my pocket, $200 stuffed away for emergencies. In poverty, as in certain propositions in physics, starting conditions are everything.

There are no secret economies that nourish the poor; on the contrary, there are a host of special costs. If you can't put up the two months' rent you need to secure an apartment, you end up paying through the nose for a room by the week. If you have only a room, with a hot plate at best, you can't save by cooking up huge lentil stews that can be frozen for the week ahead. You eat fast food, or the hot dogs and styrofoam cups of soup that can be microwaved in a convenience store. If you have no money for health insurance—and the Hearthside's niggardly plan kicks in only after three months—you go without routine care or prescription drugs and end up paying the price. Gail, for example, was fine until she ran out of money for estrogen pills. She is supposed to be on the company plan by now, but they claim to have lost her application form and need to begin the paperwork all over again. So she spends $9 per migraine pill to control the headaches she wouldn't have, she insists, if her estrogen supplements were covered. Similarly, Marianne's boyfriend lost his job as a roofer because he missed so much time after getting a cut on his foot for which he couldn't afford the prescribed antibiotic.

My own situation, when I sit down to assess it after two weeks of work, would not be much better if this were my actual life. The seductive thing about waitressing is that you don't have to wait for payday to feel a few bills in your pocket, and my tips usually cover meals and gas, plus something left over to stuff into the kitchen drawer I use as a bank. But as the tourist business slows in the summer heat, I sometimes leave work with only $20 in tips (the gross is higher, but servers share about 15 percent of their tips with the busboys and bartenders). With wages included, this amounts to about the minimum wage of $5.15 an hour. Although the sum in the drawer is piling up, at the present rate of accumulation it will be more than a hundred dollars short of my rent when the end of the month comes around. Nor can I see any expenses to cut. True, I haven't gone the lentil-stew route yet, but that's because I don't have a large cooking pot, pot holders, or a ladle to stir with (which cost about $30 at Kmart, less at thrift stores), not to mention onions, carrots, and the indispensable bay leaf. I do make my lunch almost every day—usually some slow-burning, high-protein combo like frozen chicken patties with melted cheese on top and canned pinto beans on the side. Dinner is at the Hearthside, which offers its employees a choice of BLT, fish sandwich, or hamburger for only $2. The burger lasts longest, especially if it's heaped with gut-puckering jalapenos, but by midnight my stomach is growling again.

So unless I want to start using my car as a residence, I have to find a second, or alternative, job. I call all the hotels where I filled out housekeeping applications weeks ago—the Hyatt, Holiday Inn, Econo Lodge, Hojo's, Best Western, plus a half dozen or so locally run guesthouses. Nothing. Then I start making the rounds again, wasting whole mornings waiting for some assistant manager to show up, even dipping into places so creepy that the front-desk clerk greets you from behind bulletproof glass and sells pints of liquor over the counter. But either someone has exposed my real-life housekeeping habits—which are, shall we say, mellow—or I am at the wrong end of some infallible ethnic equation: most, but by no means all, of the working house-keepers I see on my job searches are African Americans, Spanish-speaking, or immigrants from the Central European post-Communist world, whereas servers are almost invariably white and monolingually English-speaking. When I finally get a positive response, I have been identified once again as server material. Jerry's, which is part of a well-known national family restaurant chain and physically attached here to another budget hotel chain, is ready to use me at once. The prospect is both exciting and terrifying, because, with about the same number of tables and counter seats, Jerry's attracts three or four times the volume of customers as the gloomy old Hearthside. . . .

I start out with the beautiful, heroic idea of handling the two jobs at once, and for two days I almost do it: the breakfast/lunch shift at Jerry's, which goes till 2:00, arriving at the Hearthside at 2:10, and attempting to hold out until 10:00. In the ten minutes between jobs, I pick up a spicy chicken sandwich at the Wendy's drive-through window, gobble it down in the car, and change from khaki slacks to black, from Hawaiian to rust polo. There is a problem, though. When during the 3:00 to 4:00 P.M. dead time I finally sit down to wrap silver, my flesh seems to bond to the seat. I try to refuel with a purloined cup of soup, as I've seen Gail and Joan do dozens of times, but a manager catches me and hisses "No eating!" though there's not a customer around to be offended by the sight of food making contact with a server's lips. So I tell Gail I'm going to quit, and she hugs me and says she might just follow me to Jerry's herself.

But the chances of this are minuscule. She has left the flophouse and her annoying roommate and is back to living in her beat-up old truck. But guess what? She reports to me excitedly later that evening: Phillip has given her permission to park overnight in the hotel parking lot, as long as she keeps out of sight, and the parking lot should be totally safe, since it's patrolled by a hotel security guard! With the Hearthside offering benefits like that, how could anyone think of leaving? . . .

Management at Jerry's is generally calmer and more "professional" than at the Hearthside, with two exceptions. One is Joy, a plump, blowsy woman in her early thirties, who once kindly devoted several minutes to instructing me in the correct one-handed method of carrying trays but whose moods change disconcertingly from shift to shift and even within one. Then there's B.J., a.k.a. B.J.-the-bitch, whose contribution is to stand by the kitchen counter and yell, "Nita, your order's up, move it!" or, "Barbara, didn't you see you've got another table out there? Come on, girl!" Among other things, she is hated for having replaced the whipped-cream squirt cans with big plastic whipped-cream-filled baggies that have to be squeezed with both hands—because, reportedly, she saw or thought she saw employees trying to inhale the propellant gas from the squirt cans, in the hope that it might be nitrous oxide. On my third night, she pulls me aside abruptly and brings her face so close that it looks as if she's planning to butt me with her forehead.

But instead of saying, "You're fired," she says, "You're doing fine." The only trouble is I'm spending time chatting with customers: "That's how they're getting you." Furthermore I am letting them "run me," which means harassment by sequential demands: you bring the ketchup and they decide they want extra Thousand Island; you bring that and they announce they now need a side of fries; and so on into distraction. Finally she tells me not to take her wrong. She tries to say things in a nice way, but you get into a mode, you know, because everything has to move so fast. . . .[4]

I make the decision to move closer to Key West. First, because of the drive. Second and third, also because of the drive: gas is eating up $4 to $5 a day, and although Jerry's is as high-volume as you can get, the tips average only 10 percent, and not just for a newbie like me. Between the base pay of $2.15 an hour and the obligation to share tips with the busboys and dishwashers, we're averaging only about $7.50 an hour. Then there is the $30 I had to spend on the regulation tan slacks worn by Jerry's servers—a setback it could take weeks to absorb. (I had combed the town's two downscale department stores hoping for something cheaper but decided in the end that these marked-down Dockers, originally $49, were more likely to survive a daily washing.) Of my fellow servers, everyone who lacks a working husband or boyfriend seems to have a second job: Nita does something at a computer eight hours a day; another welds. Without the forty-five-minute commute, I can picture myself working two jobs and having the time to shower between them.

So I take the $500 deposit I have coming from my landlord, the $400 I have earned toward the next month's rent, plus the $200 reserved for emergencies, and use the $1,100 to pay the rent and deposit on trailer number 46 in the Overseas Trailer Park, a mile from the cluster of budget hotels that constitute Key West's version of an industrial park. Number 46 is about eight feet in width and shaped like a barbell inside, with a narrow region—because of the sink and the stove—separating the bedroom from what might optimistically be called the "living" area, with its two-person table and half-sized couch. The bathroom is so small my knees rub against the shower stall when I sit on the toilet, and you can't just leap out of the bed; you have to climb down to the foot of it in order to find a patch of floor space to stand on. Outside, I am within a few yards of a liquor store, a bar that advertises "free beer tomorrow," a convenience store, and a Burger King—but no supermarket or, alas, laundromat. By reputation, the Overseas Park is a nest of crime and crack, and I am hoping at least for some vibrant, multicultural street life. But desolation rules night and day, except for a thin stream of pedestrian traffic heading for their jobs at the Sheraton or 7-Eleven. There are not exactly people here but what amounts to canned labor, being preserved from the heat between shifts.

In line with my reduced living conditions, a new form of ugliness arises at Jerry's. First we are confronted—via an announcement on the computers through which we input orders—with the new rule that the hotel bar is henceforth off-limits to restaurant employees. The culprit, I learn through the grapevine, is the ultra-efficient gal who trained me—another trailer-home dweller and a mother of three. Something had set her off one morning, so she slipped out for a nip and returned to the floor impaired. This mostly hurts Ellen, whose habit it is to free her hair from its rubber band and drop by the bar for a couple of Zins before heading home at the end of the shift, but all of us feel the chill. Then the next day, when I go for straws, for the first time I find the dry-storage room locked. Ted, the portly assistant manager who opens it for me, explains that he caught one of the dishwashers attempting to steal something, and, unfortunately, the miscreant will be with us until a replacement can be found—hence the locked door. I neglect to ask what he had been trying to steal, but Ted tells me who he is—the kid with the buzz cut and the earring. You know, he's back there right now.

I wish I could say I rushed back and confronted George to get his side of the story. I wish I could say I stood up to Ted and insisted that George be given a translator and allowed to defend himself, or announced that I'd find a lawyer who'd handle the case pro bono. The mystery to me is that there's not much worth stealing in the dry-storage room, at least not in any fence-able quantity: "Is Gyorgi here, and am having 200—maybe 250—ketchup packets. What do you say?" My guess is that he had taken—if he had taken anything at all—some Saltines or a can of cherry-pie mix, and that the motive for taking it was hunger.

So why didn't I intervene? Certainly not because I was held back by the kind of moral paralysis that can pass as journalistic objectivity. On the contrary, something new—something loathsome and servile—had infected me, along with the kitchen odors that I could still sniff on my bra when I finally undressed at night. In real life I am moderately brave, but plenty of brave people shed their courage in concentration camps, and maybe something similar goes on in the infinitely more congenial milieu of the low-wage American workplace. Maybe, in a month or two more at Jerry's, I might have regained my crusading spirit. Then again, in a month or two I might have turned into a different person altogether—say, the kind of person who would have turned George in.

But this is not something I am slated to find out. When my month-long plunge into poverty is almost over, I finally land my dream job—housekeeping. I do this by walking into the personnel office of the only place I figure I might have some credibility, the hotel attached to Jerry's, and confiding urgently that I have to have a second job if I am to pay my rent and, no, it couldn't be front-desk clerk. "All right," the personnel lady fairly spits, "so it's housekeeping," and she marches me back to meet Maria, the house-keeping manager, a tiny, frenetic Hispanic woman who greets me as "babe" and hands me a pamphlet emphasizing the need for a positive attitude. The hours are nine in the morning till whenever, the pay is $6.10 an hour, and there's one week of vacation a year. I don't have to ask about health insurance once I meet Carlotta, the middle-aged African American woman who will be training me. Carla, as she tells me to call her, is missing all of her top front teeth.

On that first day of housekeeping and last day of my entire project—although I don't yet know it's the last—Carla is in a foul mood. We have been given nineteen rooms to clean, most of them "checkouts," as opposed to "stay-overs," that require the whole enchilada of bed-stripping, vacuuming, and bathroom-scrubbing. When one of the rooms that had been listed as a stay-over turns out to be a checkout, Carla calls Maria to complain, but of course to no avail. "So make up the motherfucker," Carla orders me, and I do the beds while she sloshes around the bathroom. For four hours without a break I strip and remake beds, taking about four and a half minutes per queen-sized bed, which I could get down to three if there were any reason to. We try to avoid vacuuming by picking up the larger specks by hand, but often there is nothing to do but drag the monstrous vacuum cleaner—it weighs about thirty pounds—off our cart and try to wrestle it around the floor. Sometimes Carla hands me the squirt bottle of "BAM" (an acronym for something that begins, ominously, with "butyric"; the rest has been worn off the label) and lets me do the bathrooms. No service ethic challenges me here to new heights of performance. I just concentrate on removing the pubic hairs from the bathtubs, or at least the dark ones that I can see. . . .

When I request permission to leave at about 3:30, another housekeeper warns me that no one has so far succeeded in combining housekeeping at the hotel with serving at Jerry's: "Some kid did it once for five days, and you're no kid." With that helpful information in mind, I rush back to number 46, down four Advils (the name brand this time), shower, stooping to fit into the stall, and attempt to compose myself for the oncoming shift. So much for what Marx termed the "reproduction of labor power," meaning the things a worker has to do just so she'll be ready to work again. The only unforeseen obstacle to the smooth transition from job to job is that my tan Jerry's slacks, which had looked reasonably clean by 40-watt bulb last night when I hand-washed my Hawaiian shirt, prove by daylight to be mottled with ketchup and ranch-dressing stains. I spend most of my hour-long break between jobs attempting to remove the edible portions with a sponge and then drying the slacks over the hood of my car in the sun.

I can do this two-job thing, is my theory, if I can drink enough caffeine and avoid getting distracted by George's ever more obvious suffering.[5] The first few days after being caught he seemed not to understand the trouble he was in, and our chirpy little conversations had continued. But the last couple of shifts he's been listless and unshaven, and tonight he looks like the ghost we all know him to be, with dark half-moons hanging from his eyes. At one point, when I am briefly immobilized by the task of filling little paper cups with sour cream for baked potatoes, he comes over and looks as if he'd like to explore the limits of our shared vocabulary, but I am called to the floor for a table. I resolve to give him all my tips that night and to hell with the experiment in low-wage money management. At eight, Ellen and I grab a snack together standing at the mephitic end of the kitchen counter, but I can only manage two or three mozzarella sticks and lunch had been a mere handful of McNuggets. I am not tired at all, I assure myself, though it may be that there is simply no more "I" left to do the tiredness monitoring. What I would see, if I were more alert to the situation, is that the forces of destruction are already massing against me. There is only one cook on duty, a young man named Jesus ("Hay-Sue," that is) and he is new to the job. And there is Joy, who shows up to take over in the middle of the shift, wearing high heels and a long, clingy white dress and fuming as if she'd just been stood up in some cocktail bar.

Then it comes, the perfect storm. Four of my tables fill up at once. Four tables is nothing for me now, but only so long as they are obligingly staggered. As I bev table 27, tables 25, 28, and 24 are watching enviously. As I bev 25, 24 glowers because their bevs haven't even been ordered. Twenty-eight is four yuppyish types, meaning everything on the side and agonizing instructions as to the chicken Caesars. Twenty-five is a middle-aged black couple, who complain, with some justice, that the iced tea isn't fresh and the tabletop is sticky. But table 24 is the meteorological event of the century: ten British tourists who seem to have made the decision to absorb the American experience entirely by mouth. Here everyone has at least two drinks—iced tea and milk shake, Michelob and water (with lemon slice, please)—and a huge promiscuous orgy of breakfast specials, mozz sticks, chicken strips, quesadillas, burgers with cheese and without, sides of hash browns with cheddar, with onions, with gravy, seasoned fries, plain fries, banana splits. Poor Jesus! Poor me! Because when I arrive with their first tray of food—after three prior trips just to refill bevs—Princess Di refuses to eat her chicken strips with her pancake-and-sausage special, since, as she now reveals, the strips were meant to be an appetizer. Maybe the others would have accepted their meals, but Di, who is deep into her third Michelob, insists that everything else go back while they work on their "starters." Meanwhile, the yuppies are waving me down for more decaf and the black couple looks ready to summon the NAACP.

Much of what happened next is lost in the fog of war. Jesus starts going under. The little printer on the counter in front of him is spewing out orders faster than he can rip them off, much less produce the meals. Even the invincible Ellen is ashen from stress. I bring table 24 their reheated main courses, which they immediately reject as either too cold or fossilized by the microwave. When I return to the kitchen with their trays (three trays in three trips), Joy confronts me with arms akimbo: "What is this?" She means the food—the plates of rejected pancakes, hash browns in assorted flavors, toasts, burgers, sausages, eggs. "Uh, scrambled with cheddar," I try, "and that's . . ." "NO," she screams in my face. "Is it a traditional, a super-scramble, an eye-opener?" I pretend to study my check for a clue, but entropy has been up to its tricks, not only on the plates but in my head, and I have to admit that the original order is beyond reconstruction. "You don't know an eye-opener from a traditional?" she demands in outrage. All I know, in fact, is that my legs have lost interest in the current venture and have announced their intention to fold. I am saved by a yuppie (mercifully not one of mine) who chooses this moment to charge into the kitchen to bellow that his food is twenty-five minutes late. Joy screams at him to get the hell out of her kitchen, please, and then turns on Jesus in a fury, hurling an empty tray across the room for emphasis.

I leave. I don't walk out; I just leave. I don't finish my side work or pick up my credit-card tips, if any, at the cash register or, of course, ask Joy's permission to go. And the surprising thing is that you can walk out without permission, that the door opens, that the thick tropical night air parts to let me pass, that my car is still parked where I left it. There is no vindication in this exit, no fuck-you surge of relief, just an overwhelming, dank sense of failure pressing down on me and the entire parking lot. I had gone into this venture in the spirit of science, to test a mathematical proposition, but somewhere along the line, in the tunnel vision imposed by long shifts and relentless concentration, it became a test of myself, and clearly I have failed. Not only had I flamed out as a housekeeper/server, I had even forgotten to give George my tips, and, for reasons perhaps best known to hardworking, generous people like Gail and Ellen, this hurts. I don't cry, but I am in a position to realize, for the first time in many years, that the tear ducts are still there, and still capable of doing their job.

When I moved out of the trailer park, I gave the key to number 46 to Gail and arranged for my deposit to be transferred to her. She told me that Joan is still living in her van and that Stu had been fired from the Hearthside. I never found out what happened to George.

In one month, I had earned approximately $1,040 and spent $517 on food, gas, toiletries, laundry, phone, and utilities. If I had remained in my $500 efficiency, I would have been able to pay the rent and have $22 left over (which is $78 less than the cash I had in my pocket at the start of the month). During this time I bought no clothing except for the required slacks and no prescription drugs or medical care (I did finally buy some vitamin B to compensate for the lack of vegetables in my diet). Perhaps I could have saved a little on food if I had gotten to a supermarket more often, instead of convenience stores, but it should be noted that I lost almost four pounds in four weeks, on a diet weighted heavily toward burgers and fries.

How former welfare recipients and single mothers will (and do) survive in the low-wage workforce, I cannot imagine. Maybe they will figure out how to condense their lives—including child-raising, laundry, romance, and meals—into the couple of hours between full-time jobs. Maybe they will take up residence in their vehicles, if they have one. All I know is that I couldn't hold two jobs and I couldn't make enough money to live on with one. And I had advantages unthinkable to many of the long-term poor—health, stamina, a working car, and no children to care for and support. Certainly nothing in my experience contradicts the conclusion of Kathryn Edin and Laura Lein, in their [1997] book *Making Ends Meet: How Single Mothers Survive Welfare and Low-Wage Work,* that low-wage work actually involves more hardship and deprivation than life at the mercy of the welfare state. In the coming months and years, economic conditions for the working poor are bound to worsen, even without the almost inevitable recession. As mentioned earlier, the influx of former welfare recipients into the low-skilled workforce will have a depressing effect on both wages and the number of jobs available. A general economic downturn will only enhance these effects, and the working poor will of course be facing it without the slight, but nonetheless often saving, protection of welfare as a backup.

The thinking behind welfare reform was that even the humblest jobs are morally uplifting and psychologically buoying. In reality they are likely to be fraught with insult and stress. But I did discover one redeeming feature of the most abject low-wage work—the camaraderie of people who are, in almost all cases, far too smart and funny and caring for the work they do and the wages they're paid. The hope, of course, is that someday these people will come to know what they're worth, and take appropriate action.

ENDNOTES

[1] According to the Department of Housing and Urban Development, the "fair-market rent" for an efficiency is $551 here in Monroe County, Florida. A comparable rent in the five boroughs of New York City is $704; in San Francisco, $713; and in the heart of Silicon Valley, $808. The fair-market rent for an area is defined as the amount that would be needed to pay rent plus utilities for "privately owned, decent, safe, and sanitary rental housing of a modest (non-luxury) nature with suitable amenities."

[2] According to the Fair Labor Standards Act, employers are not required to pay "tipped employees," such as restaurant servers, more than $2.13 an hour in direct wages. However, if the sum of tips plus $2.13 an hour falls below the minimum wage, or $5.15 an hour, the employer is required to make up the difference. This fact was not mentioned by managers or otherwise publicized at either of the restaurants where I worked.

[3] I could find no statistics on the number of employed people living in cars or vans, but according to the National Coalition for the Homeless' 1997 report "Myths and Facts about Homelessness," nearly one in five homeless people (in twenty-nine cities across the nation) is employed in a full- or part-time job.

[4] In *Workers in a Lean World: Unions in the International Economy* (Verso, 1997), Kim Moody cites studies finding an increase in stress-related workplace injuries and illness between the mid-1980s and the early 1990s. He argues that rising stress levels reflect a new system of "management by stress," in which workers in a variety of industries are being squeezed to extract maximum productivity, to the detriment of their health.

[5] In 1996, the number of persons holding two or more jobs averaged 7.8 million, or 6.2 percent of the workforce. It was about the same rate for men and for women (6.1 versus 6.2), though the kinds of jobs differ by gender. About two-thirds of multiple jobholders work one job full-time and the other part-time. Only a heroic minority—4 percent of men and 2 percent of women—work two full-time jobs simultaneously. (From John F. Stinson Jr., "New Data on Multiple Jobholding Available from the CPS," in the *Monthly Labor Review*, March 1997.)

GENDER

27

GENDER AS STRUCTURE

BARBARA RISMAN

Gender stratification, examined in the next four selections, refers to those social systems in which socioeconomic resources and political power are distributed on the basis of one's sex and gender. In any social system, we can measure the gendered distribution of resources and rewards to see whether men or women have a higher social status. Objective indices of gender inequality include income, educational attainment, wealth, occupational status, mortality rates, and access to social institutions. In the selection that follows, Barbara Risman, a professor of sociology at North Carolina State University, examines four theories that attempt to explain why gender stratification exists.

There are three distinct theoretical traditions that help us to understand sex and gender, and a fourth is now taking shape. The first tradition focuses on gendered selves, whether sex differences are biological or social in origin. The second tradition . . . focuses on how the social structure (as opposed to biology or individual learning) creates gendered behavior. The third tradition . . . emphasizes contextual issues and how doing gender re-creates inequality during interaction. The fourth, multilevel approach treats gender itself as built in to social life via socialization, interaction, and institutional organization. This new perspective integrates the previous ones; it is formed on the assumption that each viewpoint sheds different light on the same question. . . .

Gendered Selves

There are numerous theoretical perspectives within this tradition, but all share the assumption that maleness and femaleness are, or become, properties of individuals. . . . Research questions in this tradition focus on the development of sex differences and their relative importance for behavior. . . .

Sociobiologists have argued that such behaviors as male aggressiveness and female nurturance result from natural selection. Biosociologists stress

---

the infant care skills in which females appear to excel. Their perspective has been criticized for its ethnocentrism and its selective use of biological species as evidence. . . .

More recent biosocial theories have posited complex interactions between environment and biological predispositions, with attention to explaining intrasex differences. This new version of biosociology may eventually help to identify the biological parameters that, in interaction with environmental stimuli, affect human behavior. . . .

Sex-role theory suggests that early childhood socialization is an influential determinant of later behavior, and research has focused on how societies create feminine women and masculine men. There is an impressive variety of sex-role explanations for gender-differentiated behavior in families. Perhaps the most commonly accepted explanation is reinforcement theory (e.g., Bandura and Walters 1963, Mischel 1966, and Weitzman 1979). Reinforcement theory suggests, for example, that girls develop nurturant personalities because they are given praise and attention for their interest in dolls and babies, and that boys develop competitive selves because they are positively reinforced for winning, whether at checkers or football. Although much literature suggests that the socialization experiences of boys and girls continue to differ dramatically, it is clearly the case that most girls raised in the 1990s have received ambiguous gender socialization: they have been taught to desire domesticity (dolls remain a popular toy for girls), as well as to pursue careers. For generations, African American girls have been socialized for both motherhood and paid work (Collins 1990).

Nancy Chodorow's (1978, 1989) feminist psychoanalytic analysis approach has also been influential, particularly in feminist scholarship. Chodorow develops an object-relations psychoanalytic perspective to explain how gendered personalities develop as a result of exclusively female mothering. . . . Chodorow notices . . . that mothers are responsible for young children almost universally. She argues that mothers relate to their boy and girl infants differently, fusing identities with their daughters while relating to their sons as separate and distinct. As a result, according to this feminist version of psychoanalysis, girls develop selves based on connectedness and relationships while boys develop selves based on independence and autonomy. In addition, boys must reject their first love-object (mother) in order to adopt masculinity, and they do this by rejecting and devaluing what is feminine in themselves and in society. Thus, we get nurturant women and independent men in a society dominated by men and which values independence. Many feminist studies have incorporated this psychoanalytic view of gender as an underlying assumption (Keller 1985; L. Rubin 1982; Williams 1989). . . .

Other feminist theorists, such as Ruddick (1989, 1992) and Aptheker (1989), build on the notion that the constant nature of mothering creates a certain kind of thinking, what Ruddick calls "maternal thinking." The logic of this argument does not depend on a psychoanalytic framework, but it implicitly uses one: through nurturing their children, women develop psychological frameworks that value peace and justice. Therefore, if women (or men who mothered children) were powerful political actors, governments would use more peaceful conflict resolution strategies and value social justice more highly.

All individualist theories, including sex-role socialization and psychoanalytic thought, posit that by adulthood most men and women have developed very different personalities. Women have become nurturant, person oriented, and child centered. Men have become competitive and work oriented. According to individualist theorists, there are limits to flexibility. Intensely held emotions, values, and inclinations developed during childhood coalesce into a person's self-identity. Although these theorists do not deny that social structures influence family patterns, nor that notions of gender meaning are always evolving . . . they focus on how culturally determined family patterns and sex-role socialization create gendered selves, which then provide the motivations for individuals to fill their socially appropriate roles.

Historically, sex-role theorists have assumed that men and women behave differently because gender resides primarily in personality. This approach has several serious conceptual weaknesses. . . . First, such theories usually presume behavioral continuity throughout the life course. In fact, women socialized for nurturance are capable of competitive and aggressive behavior, and men raised without any expectation of taking on primary responsibility can "mother" when they need to (Bielby and Bielby 1984; Gerson 1985, 1993; Risman 1987). Another weakness of these individualist-oriented theories is their oversocialized conception of human behavior—that once we know how an individual has been raised, the training is contained primarily inside his or her head (cf. Wrong 1961). Such theories might suggest, for example, that women do not revolt and are not necessarily unhappy with their subordinate status because they have been so well trained for femininity. . . .

This overdependence on internalization of culture and socialization leads to the most serious problem with sex-role theory: its depoliticization of gender inequality. Although sex-role socialization and revisionist psychoanalytic theorists often have explicitly feminist goals, their focus on sex differences has legitimated a dualistic conception of gender that relies on a reified male/female dichotomy. The very notion of comparing all men to all women without regard for diversity within groups presumes that gender is primarily about individual differences between biological males and biological females, downplaying the role of interactional expectations and the social structure.

The sex-role socialization theory is an application of a normative role theory for human behavior. It assumes that social stability is motivated primarily by beliefs and values acquired during socialization. Individuals are assumed to use whatever resources are available to realize these values and to maintain their identities. As Stokes and Hewitt (1976) have argued, socialization cannot serve as the fundamental link between culture and action. Indeed, studies of intergenerational shifts in values suggest that economic and political conditions produce beliefs, attitudes, and preferences for action that overcome those acquired during childhood (Inglehart 1977, 1981; Lesthaeghe 1980). We cannot assume that internalization of norms—through psychoanalytic processes or sex-role socialization—is the primary means by which society organizes human conduct. . . .

Structure vs. Personality

The overreliance on gendered selves as the primary explanation for sexual stratification led many feminist sociologists—myself included—to argue that what appear to be sex differences are really, in Epstein's terms, "deceptive distinctions" (Epstein 1988; Kanter 1977; Risman and Schwartz 1989). Although empirically documented sex differences do occur, structuralists like me have argued that men and women behave differently because they fill different positions in institutional settings, work organizations, or families. That is, the previous structural perspectives on gender assume that work and family structures create empirically distinct male and female behavior. . . . Within this perspective, men and women in the same structural slots are expected to behave identically. Epstein's (1988) voluminous review of the multidisciplinary research on gender and sex differences is perhaps the strongest and most explicit support for a social-structural explanation of gendered behavior. She suggests that there are perhaps no empirically documented differences that can be traced to the predispositions of males and females. Instead, the deceptive differences reflect women's lack of opportunity in a male-dominated society.

Gender relations in the labor force have received far more of this sort of structural analysis than have gender relations in intimate settings. Kanter's classic work *Men and Women of the Corporation* (1977) introduced this kind of structural perspective on gender in the workplace. Kanter showed that when women had access to powerful mentors, interactions with people like themselves, and the possibility for upward mobility, they behaved like others—regardless of sex—with similar advantages. These social network variables could explain success at work far better than could assumptions of masculine versus feminine work styles. Women were less often successful because they were more often blocked from network advantages, not because they feared success or had never developed competitive strategies. Men who lacked such opportunities did not advance, and they behaved with stereotypical feminine work styles. Kanter argued persuasively that structural system properties better explain sex differences in workplace behavior than does sex-role socialization. . . .

The application of a structural perspective to gender within personal relationships has been less frequent. . . . In a series of studies (Risman 1986, 1987, 1988), I tested whether apparent sex differences in parenting styles are better attributed to sex-role socialization or to the structural contingencies of adult life. The question I asked was "Can men mother?" The answer is yes, but only if they do not have women to do it for them. The lack of sex-role socialization for nurturance did not inhibit the development of male mothering when structural contingencies demanded it. This is an important part of the story, but not all of it. . . .

While applications of structural perspectives both to workplaces and to intimate relationships have furthered the sociological understanding of gender, there is a fundamental flaw in the logic of these arguments. . . .

Several studies (Williams 1992; Yoder 1991; Zimmer 1988) found that Kanter's hypotheses about the explanatory power of social structural variables such as relative numbers, access to mentors, and upward mobility are not, in fact, gender neutral. That is, Kanter's hypotheses are supported empirically only when societally devalued groups enter traditionally white male work environments. When white males enter traditionally female work environments, they do not hit the glass ceiling, they ride glass elevators. Reskin (1988) has suggested that we have so accepted these "structural" arguments that we sometimes forget that sexism itself stratifies our labor force. Evidence similarly points to continued existence of gendered behavior in family settings. Hertz reported that in her 1986 study of couples in which husbands and wives held equivalent, high-status corporate jobs and brought similar resources to their marriages, the wives continued to shoulder more responsibility for family work (even if that means hiring and supervising help). Despite the importance of structural variables in explaining behavior in families, the sex category itself remains a powerful predictor of who does what kind of family work (Brines 1994; South and Spitz 1994). Gender stratification remains even when other structural aspects of work or of family life are divorced from sex category. The interactionist theory discussed below helps us to understand why.

Doing Gender

This approach to gender was best articulated by West and Zimmerman in their 1987 article "Doing Gender." . . . West and Zimmerman suggest that once a person is labeled a member of a sex category, she or he is morally accountable for behaving as persons in that category do. That is, the person is expected to "do gender"; the ease of interaction depends on it. One of the groundbreaking aspects in this argument is that doing gender implies legitimating inequality. The authors suggest that, by definition, what is female in a patriarchal society is devalued. Within this theoretical framework, the very belief that biological males and females are essentially different (apart from their reproductive capabilities) exists to justify male dominance.

The tradition of doing gender has been well accepted in feminist sociology (West and Zimmerman's article was cited in journals more than one hundred times by 1995). West and Zimmerman articulated an insight whose time had come—that gender is not what we are but something that we do. Psychologists Deaux and Major (1990) . . . argue that interactional contexts take priority over individual traits and personality differences; others' expectations create the self-fulfilling prophecies that lead all of us to do gender. . . . They suggest that actual behavior depends on the interaction of participants' self-definitions, the expectations of others, and the cultural expectations attached to the context itself. I agree. The weakness in the doing-gender approach is that it undertheorizes the pervasiveness of gender inequality in organizations and gendered identities.

Although gender is always present in our interaction, it is not present only in interaction. We must have a theoretical link from material constraints to what we do now, to who we think we are. I suggest that the doing-gender perspective is incomplete because it slights the institutional level of analysis and the links among institutional gender stratification, situational expectations, and gendered selves.

West and Fenstermaker (1995) have extended the argument from doing gender to "doing difference." They suggest that just as we create inequality when we create gender during interaction, so we create race and class inequalities when we interact in daily life. Race does not generally hold the biologically based assumption of dichotomy (as sex category does), yet in American society we constantly use race categories to guide our interactional encounters. This extension of theoretical ideas from gender to the analysis of inequalities is perhaps the most important direction gender theorizing has taken in the past decade. . . .

Gender as Social Structure

The sex-differences literature, the doing-gender contextual analyses, and the structural perspectives are not necessarily incompatible, although I, as well as others, have portrayed them as alternatives (e.g., Epstein 1988, Ferree 1990, Kanter 1977, Risman 1987, Risman and Schwartz 1989). . . . My view of gender as a social structure incorporates each level of analysis. . . .

Lorber (1994) argues that gender is an entity in and of itself that establishes patterns of expectations for individuals, orders social processes of everyday life, and is built into all other major social organizations of society. She goes further, however, to argue that gender difference is *primarily* a means to justify sexual stratification. Gender is so ubiquitous because unless we see difference, we cannot justify inequality. Lorber provides much cross-cultural, literary, and scientific evidence to show that gender difference is socially constructed and yet is universally used to justify stratification. She writes that "the continuing purpose of gender as a modern social institution is to construct women as a group to be subordinate to men as a group" (p. 33).

I build on this notion that gender is an entity in and of itself and has consequences at every level of analysis. And I share the concern that the very creation of difference is the foundation on which inequality rests. In my view, it is most useful to conceptualize gender as a structure that has consequences for every aspect of society. . . .

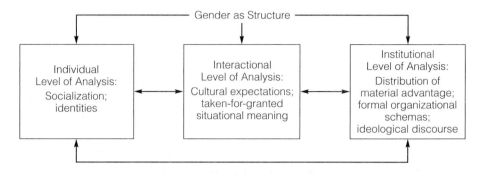

FIGURE 1   Gender as Structure.

Gender itself must be considered a structural property of society. It is not manifested just in our personalities, our cultural rules, or other institutions. Gender is deeply embedded as a basis for stratification, differentiating opportunities and constraints. This differentiation has consequences on three levels: (1) at the individual level, for the development of gendered selves; (2) at the interactional level, for men and women face different expectations even when they fill the identical structural position; and (3) at the institutional level, for rarely will women and men be given identical positions. Differentiation at the institutional level is based on explicit regulations or laws regarding resource distribution, whether resources be defined as access to opportunities or actual material goods. (See Figure 1 for a schematic summary of the argument thus far.)

While the *gender structure* clearly affects selves, cultural rules, and institutions, far too much explanatory power is presumed to rest in the motivation of gendered selves. We live in a very individualistic society that teaches us to make our own choices and take responsibility for our own actions. What this has meant for theories about gender is that a tremendous amount of energy is spent on trying to understand why women and men "choose" to devote their life energies to such different enterprises. The distinctly sociological contribution to the explanation hasn't had enough attention: even when individual women and men do *not* desire to live gendered lives or to support male dominance, they often find themselves compelled to do so by the logic of gendered choices. That is, interactional pressures and institutional design create gender and the resultant inequality, even in the absence of individual desires. . . .

Choices often assumed to be based on personalities and individual preferences (e.g., consequences of the gender structure at the individual level) are better understood as social constructions based on institutionally constrained opportunities and the limited availability of nongendered cognitive images. . . .

Even if individuals are capable of change and wish to eradicate male dominance from their personal lives, the influence of gendered institutions and interactional contexts persists. These contexts are organized by

gender stratification at the institutional level, which includes the distribution of material resources organized by gender, the ways by which formal organizations and institutions themselves are gendered, and gendered ideological discourse. For example, in a society in which girls are not taught to read, we could never find a young woman who would be considered a potential international leader. Nor would men denied access to jobs with "family wages" be seen by middle-class American women as good catches for husbands.

At this moment in American society, cultural rules and cognitive images that operate at the interactional level are particularly important in the persistence of gender stratification in families. It is not that sex-role socialization or early childhood experience is trivial; gender structure creates gendered selves. But, at this point in history, sex-role socialization itself is ambivalent. In addition, it is clear that even women with feminist worldviews and substantial incomes are constrained by gender structures.

In spite of the removal of some gender discrimination in both law and organizations, gender stratification remains. That is, formal access to opportunities may be gender neutral, yet equality of results may not ensue. Therefore, neither the individual-level explanations nor those based solely on institutional discrimination can explain continued gender stratification in families. Instead, the cognitive images to which we must respond during interaction are the engines that drive continued gender stratification when individuals desire egalitarian relationships and the law allows them (cf. Ridgeway 1997). . . .

The social structure clearly constrains gendered action even as it makes it possible. Wives, even those who have no motivation to provide domestic service to their husbands, are constrained to do so by social expectations. A husband who has a disheveled appearance reflects poorly on his wife's domestic abilities (in real life as well as in "ring around the collar" commercials). A wife will be sanctioned by friends and family for keeping a cluttered and dusty home; a husband will not be. Husbands' behaviors are constrained as well. A husband who is content with a relatively low-wage, low-stress occupation may be pressured (by his wife, among others) to provide more for his family. Few wives, however, are pressured into higher-stress, higher-wage occupations by their families. The expectations we face during ongoing interaction often push us to behave as others want us to (Heiss 1981).

Cultural images within marriage also make gendered action possible. Husbands are not free to work long hours in order to climb the career ladder or increase income unless they are superordinate partners in a system in which wives provide them the "leisure" (i.e., freedom from responsibility for self-care or family care) to do so. Some married women may leave jobs they dislike because the position of domestic wife is open to them. A husband and father unable to keep a job has few other options for gaining self-esteem and identity.

Individuals often act in a structurally patterned fashion, without much thought. Routine is taken for granted even when the action re-creates the inequitable social structure. A woman may choose to change her name upon marriage simply because it seems easier. (Some women may not even know they are making a choice, as name change is so routine in their social circle.) Yet by changing her name a woman implicitly supports and re-creates a reflective definition of wifehood. She does gender. Similarly, when a woman assents to her children carrying her husband's surname (even when she herself has retained her own), she is re-creating a patrilineal system by which family identity is traced primarily through the male line. In both these examples, a couple's intention may be to create a nuclear family identity and to avoid the awkwardness of hyphenated names for children. Whatever the intention, the structure has constrained the possible choices available to them. Their purposive actions may provide them with both the desired consequences (one family name) *and* the unintended consequence of re-creating a gender structure based on reflective female identity and patrilineal family names.

REFERENCES

Aptheker, Bettina. 1989. *Tapestries of Life: Women's Work, Women's Consciousness, and the Meaning of Daily Experience.* Amherst: University of Massachusetts Press.

Bandura, Albert and Richard H. Walters. 1963. *Social Learning and Personality.* New York: Holt, Rinehart and Winston.

Bielby, Denise D. and William T Bielby. 1984. "Work Commitment and Sex-Role Attitudes." *American Sociological Review* 49:234–47.

Brines, Julie. 1994. "Economic Dependency and the Division of Labor." *American Journal of Sociology* 100(3):652–88.

Chodorow, Nancy. 1978. *The Reproduction of Mothering.* Berkeley: University of California Press.

———. 1989. *Feminism and Psychoanalytic Theory.* New Haven, CT: Yale University Press.

Collins, Patricia Hill. 1990. *Black Feminist Thought: Knowledge, Consciousness, and the Politics of Empowerment.* Boston: Unwin, Hyman.

Deaux, Kay and Brenda Major. 1990. "A Social–Psychological Model of Gender." In *Theoretical Perspectives on Sexual Difference*, edited by Deborah Rhode. New Haven, CT: Yale University Press.

Epstein, Cynthia Fuchs. 1988. *Deceptive Distinctions: Sex, Gender, and the Social Order.* New Haven, CT: Yale University Press.

Ferree, Myra Marx. 1990. "Beyond Separate Spheres: Feminism and Family Research." *Journal of Marriage and the Family* 53(4):866–84.

Gerson, Kathleen. 1985. *Hard Choices.* Berkeley: University of California Press.

———. 1993. *No Man's Land.* New York: Basic Books.

Heiss, Jerold. 1981. "Social Rules." In *Social Psychology: Sociological Perspectives*, edited by Morris Rosenberg and Ralph H. Turner. New York: Basic Books.

Hertz, Rosanna. 1986. *More Equal Than Others: Women and Men in Dual-Career Marriages.* Berkeley: University of California Press.

Inglehart, Ronald. 1977. *The Silent Revolution: Changing Values and Political Styles among Western Publics.* Princeton, NJ: Princeton University Press.

———. 1981. "Post-Materialism in an Environment of Insecurity." *American Political Science Review* 75:880–900.

Kanter, Rosabeth. 1977. *Men and Women of the Corporation.* New York: Harper and Row.

Keller, Evelyn Fox. 1985. *Reflections on Gender and Science.* New Haven, CT: Yale University Press.

Lesthaeghe, Ron. 1980. "On the Social Control of Human Reproduction." *Population and Development Review* 4:427–548.

Lorber, Judith. 1994. *Paradoxes of Gender.* New Haven, CT: Yale University Press.

Mischel, Walter. 1966. "A Social Learning View of Sex Differences in Behavior." Pp. 56–81 in *The Development of Sex Differences*, edited by Eleanor Maccoby. Stanford, CA: Stanford University Press.

Reskin, Barbara. 1988. "Bringing the Men Back In: Sex Differentiation and the Devaluation of Women's Work." *Gender and Society* 2:58–81.

Ridgeway, Cecilia. 1997. "Interaction and the Conservation of Gender Inequality: Con Employment." *American Sociological Review* 62:218–35.

Risman, Barbara. 1986. "Can Men 'Mother'?: Life as a Single Father." *Family Relations 3*

———. 1987. "Intimate Relationships from a Microstructural Perspective: Mothering Men." *Gender and Society* 1:6–32.

———. 1988. "Just the Two of Us: Parent–Child Relationships in Single Parent Homes." *Journal of Marriage and the Family* 50:1049–62.

Risman, Barbara and Pepper Schwartz. 1989. *Gender in Intimate Relationships.* Belmont, CA: Wadsworth.

Rubin, Lillian. 1982. *Intimate Strangers.* New York: Harper and Row.

Ruddick, Sara. 1989. *Maternal Thinking.* Boston: Beacon Press.

———. 1992. "Thinking About Fathers." In *Rethinking the Family: Some Feminist Questions,* edited by Barrie Thorne. Boston: Northeastern University Press.

South, Scott J. and Glenna Spitz. 1994. "Housework in Marital and Nonmarital Households." *American Sociological Review* 59:327–47.

Stokes, Randall and John Hewitt. 1976. "Aligning Actions." *American Sociological Review* 41:838–49.

Weitzman, Lenore Jacqueline. 1979. *Sex Role Socialization: A Focus on Women.* Palo Alto, CA: Mayfield.

West, Candace and Sarah Fenstermaker. 1995. "Doing Difference." *Gender and Society* 9:8–37.

West, Candace and Don H. Zimmerman. 1987. "Doing Gender." *Gender and Society* 1(2):125–51.

Williams, Christine. 1989. *Gender Differences at Work.* Berkeley: University of California Press.

———. 1992. "The Glass Escalator: Hidden Advantages for Men in the 'Female' Professions." *Social Problems* 39:253–67.

Wrong, Dennis H. 1961. "The Oversocialized Conception of Man in Modern Sociology." *American Sociological Review* 26:183–93.

Yoder, Janice. 1991. "Rethinking Tokenism: Looking Beyond Numbers." *Social Problems* 5:178–92.

Zimmer, Lynn. 1988. "Tokenism and Women in the Workplace: The Limits of Gender-Neutral Theory." *Social Problems* 35:64–77.

28

WHAT IT MEANS TO BE GENDERED ME
Life on the Boundaries of a
Dichotomous Gender System

BETSY LUCAL

Sociologists argue that individuals learn gender roles and gender stereotyping through socialization. Gender role socialization often reinforces gender inequality because men and women are expected to fulfill different and often opposite family and occupational roles. What are the implications of living in a gender system that recognizes "two and only two" genders?

Betsy Lucal, "What It Means to Be Gendered Me: Life on the Boundaries of a Dichotomous Gender System" from *Gender & Society* 13, no. 6 (1999). Copyright © 1999 by Sociologists for Women in Society. Reprinted with the permission of Sage Publications, Inc.

What about individuals whose gender displays are more ambiguous? In this excerpt, Betsy Lucal, an associate professor of sociology at Indiana University, South Bend, uses her biography to examine the social construction of gender and the implications of *gender bending* for gender identity and social interaction.

I understood the concept of "doing gender" (West and Zimmerman 1987) long before I became a sociologist. I have been living with the consequences of inappropriate "gender display" (Goffman 1976; West and Zimmerman 1987) for as long as I can remember.

My daily experiences are a testament to the rigidity of gender in our society, to the real implications of "two and only two" when it comes to sex and gender categories (Garfinkel 1967; Kessler and McKenna 1978). Each day, I experience the consequences that our gender system has for my identity and interactions. I am a woman who has been called "Sir" so many times that I no longer even hesitate to assume that it is being directed at me. I am a woman whose use of public restrooms regularly causes reactions ranging from confused stares to confrontations over what a man is doing in the women's room. I regularly enact a variety of practices either to minimize the need for others to know my gender or to deal with their misattributions.

I am the embodiment of Lorber's (1994) ostensibly paradoxical assertion that the "gender bending" I engage in actually might serve to preserve and perpetuate gender categories. As a feminist who sees gender rebellion as a significant part of her contribution to the dismantling of sexism, I find this possibility disheartening.

In this [reading], I examine how my experiences both support and contradict Lorber's (1994) argument using my own experiences to illustrate and reflect on the social construction of gender. My analysis offers a discussion of the consequences of gender for people who do not follow the rules as well as an examination of the possible implications of the existence of people like me for the gender system itself. Ultimately, I show how life on the boundaries of gender affects me and how my life, and the lives of others who make similar decisions about their participation in the gender system, has the potential to subvert gender.

Because this [reading] analyzes my experiences as a woman who often is mistaken for a man, my focus is on the social construction of gender for women. My assumption is that, given the gendered nature of the gendering process itself, men's experiences of this phenomenon might well be different from women's.

The Social Construction of Gender

It is now widely accepted that gender is a social construction, that sex and gender are distinct, and that gender is something all of us "do." This conceptualization of gender can be traced to Garfinkel's (1967) ethnomethodological study of "Agnes."[1] In this analysis, Garfinkel examined the issues facing a male who wished to pass as, and eventually become, a woman. Unlike individuals who perform gender in culturally expected ways, Agnes could not take her gender for granted and always was in danger of failing to pass as a woman (Zimmerman 1992).

This approach was extended by Kessler and McKenna (1978) and codified in the classic "Doing Gender" by West and Zimmerman (1987). The social constructionist approach has been developed most notably by Lorber (1994, 1996). Similar theoretical strains have developed outside of sociology, such as work by Butler (1990) and Weston (1996). Taken as a whole, this work provides a number of insights into the social processes of gender, showing how gender(ing) is, in fact, a process.

We apply gender labels for a variety of reasons; for example, an individual's gender cues our interactions with her or him. Successful social relations require all participants to present, monitor, and interpret gender displays (Martin 1998; West and Zimmerman 1987). We have, according to Lorber, "no social place for a person who is neither woman nor man" (1994:96); that is, we do not know how to interact with such a person. There is, for example, no way of addressing such a person that does not rely on making an assumption about the person's gender ("Sir" or "Ma'am"). In this context, gender is "omnirelevant" (West and Zimmerman 1987). Also, given the sometimes fractious nature of interactions between men and women, it might be particularly important for women to know the gender of the strangers they encounter; do the women need to be wary, or can they relax (Devor 1989)?

According to Kessler and McKenna (1978), each time we encounter a new person, we make a gender attribution. In most cases, this is not difficult. We learn how to read people's genders by learning which traits culturally signify each gender and by learning rules that enable us to classify individuals with a wide range of gender presentations into two and only two gender categories. As Weston observed, "Gendered traits are called attributes for a reason: People attribute traits to others. No one possesses them. Traits are the product of evaluation" (1996:21). The fact that most people use the same traits and rules in presenting genders makes it easier for us to attribute genders to them.

We also assume that we can place each individual into one of two mutually exclusive categories in this binary system. As Bem (1993) notes, we have a polarized view of gender; there are two groups that are seen as polar opposites. Although there is "no rule for deciding 'male' or 'female' that will always work" and no attributes "that always and without exception are true of only one gender" (Kessler and McKenna 1978:158, 1), we operate under the assumption that there are such rules and attributes. . . .

Patriarchal constructs of gender also devalue the marked category. Devor (1989) found that the women she calls "gender blenders" assumed that femininity was less desirable than masculinity; their gender blending sometimes was a product of their shame about being women. This assumption affects not only our perceptions of other people but also individuals' senses of their own gendered selves.

Not only do we rely on our social skills in attributing genders to others, but we also use our skills to present our own genders to them. The roots of this understanding of how gender operates lie in Goffman's (1959) analysis of the "presentation of self in everyday life," elaborated later in his work on "gender display" (Goffman 1976). From this perspective, gender is a performance, "a stylized repetition of acts" (Butler 1990:140, emphasis removed). Gender display refers to "conventionalized portrayals" of social correlates of gender (Goffman 1976). These displays are culturally established sets of behaviors, appearances, mannerisms, and other cues that we have learned to associate with members of a particular gender.

In determining the gender of each person we encounter and in presenting our genders to others, we rely extensively on these gender displays. Our bodies and their adornments provide us with "texts" for reading a person's gender (Bordo 1993). As Lorber noted, "Without the deliberate use of gendered clothing, hairstyles, jewelry, and cosmetics, women and men would look far more alike" (1994:18–19). Myhre summarized the markers of femininity as "having longish hair; wearing makeup, skirts, jewelry, and high heels; walking with a wiggle; having little or no observable body hair; and being in general soft, rounded (but not too rounded), and sweet-smelling" (1995:135). (Note that these descriptions comprise a Western conceptualization of gender.) Devor identified "mannerisms, language, facial expressions, dress, and a lack of feminine adornment" (1989:x) as factors that contribute to women being mistaken for men. . . .

But these processes also mean that a person who fails to establish a gendered appearance that corresponds to the person's gender faces challenges to her or his identity and status. First, the gender nonconformist must find a way in which to construct an identity in a society that denies her or him any legitimacy (Bem 1993). A person is likely to want to define herself or himself as "normal" in the face of cultural evidence to the contrary. Second, the individual also must deal with other people's challenges to identity and status—deciding how to respond, what such reactions to their appearance mean, and so forth.

Because our appearances, mannerisms, and so forth constantly are being read as part of our gender display, we do gender whether we intend to or not. For example, a woman athlete, particularly one participating in a nonfeminine sport such as basketball, might deliberately keep her hair long to show that, despite actions that suggest otherwise, she is a "real" (i.e., feminine) woman. But we also do gender in less conscious ways such as when a man takes up more space when sitting than a woman does. In fact, in a society so clearly organized around gender, as ours is, there is no way in which to not do gender (Lorber 1994).

Given our cultural rules for identifying gender (i.e., that there are only two and that masculinity is assumed in the absence of evidence to the contrary), a person who does not do gender appropriately is placed not into a third category but rather into the one with which her or his gender display seems most closely to fit; that is, if a man appears to be a woman, then he will be categorized as "woman," not as something else. Even if a person does not want to do gender or would like to do a gender other than the two recognized by our society, other people will, in effect, do gender for that person by placing her or him in one and only one of the two available categories. We cannot escape doing gender or, more specifically, doing one of two genders. (There are exceptions in limited contexts such as people doing "drag" [Butler 1990; Lorber 1994].)

People who follow the norms of gender can take their genders for granted. Kessler and McKenna asserted, "Few people besides transsexuals think of their gender as anything other than 'naturally' obvious"; they believe that the risks of not being taken for the gender intended "are minimal for nontranssexuals" (1978:126). However, such an assertion overlooks the experiences of people such as those women Devor (1989) calls "gender blenders" and those people Lorber (1994) refers to as "gender benders." As West and Zimmerman (1987) pointed out, we all are held accountable for, and might be called on to account for, our genders.

People who, for whatever reasons, do not adhere to the rules, risk gender misattribution and any interactional consequences that might result from this misidentification. What are the consequences of misattribution for social interaction? When must misattribution be minimized? What will one do to minimize such mistakes? In this article, I explore these and related questions using my biography.

For me, the social processes and structures of gender mean that, in the context of our culture, my appearance will be read as masculine. Given the common conflation of sex and gender, I will be assumed to be a male. Because of the two-and-only-two genders rule, I will be classified, perhaps more often than not, as a man—not as an atypical woman, not as a genderless person. I must be one gender or the other. I cannot be neither, nor can I be both. This norm has a variety of mundane and serious consequences for my everyday existence. Like Myhre (1995), I have found that the choice not to participate in femininity is not one made frivolously.

My experiences as a woman who does not do femininity illustrate a paradox of our two-and-only-two gender system. Lorber argued that "bending gender rules and passing between genders does not erode but rather preserves gender boundaries" (1994:21). Although people who engage in these behaviors and appearances do "demonstrate the social constructedness of sex, sexuality, and gender" (Lorber 1994:96), they do not actually disrupt gender. Devor made a similar point: "When gender blending females refused to mark themselves by publicly displaying sufficient femininity to be recognized as women, they were in no way challenging patriarchal gender assumptions" (1989:142). As the following discussion shows, I have found that my own experiences both support and challenge this argument. Before detailing these experiences, I explain my use of my self as data.

My Self As Data

This analysis is based on my experiences as a person whose appearance and gender/sex are not, in the eyes of many people, congruent. How did my experiences become my data? I began my research "unwittingly" (Krieger 1991). This [reading] is a product of "opportunistic research" in that I am using my "unique biography, life experiences, and/or situational familiarity to understand and explain social life" (Riemer 1988:121; see also Riemer 1977). It is an analysis of "unplanned personal experience," that is, experiences that were not part of a research project but instead are part of my daily encounters (Reinharz 1992). . . .

It also is useful, I think, to consider my analysis an application of Mills' (1959) "sociological imagination." Mills (1959) and Berger (1963) wrote about the importance of seeing the general in the particular. This means that general social patterns can be discerned in the behaviors of particular individuals. In this [reading], I am examining portions of my biography, situated in U.S. society during the 1990s, to understand the "personal troubles" my gender produces in the context of a two-and-only-two gender system. I am not attempting to generalize my experiences; rather, I am trying to use them to examine and reflect on the processes and structure of gender in our society.

Because my analysis is based on my memories and perceptions of events, it is limited by my ability to recall events and by my interpretation of those events. However, I am not claiming that my experiences provide the truth about gender and how it works. I am claiming that the biography of a person who lives on the margins of our gender system can provide theoretical insights into the processes and social structure of gender. Therefore, after describing my experiences, I examine how they illustrate and extend, as well as contradict, other work on the social construction of gender.

Gendered Me

Each day, I negotiate the boundaries of gender. Each day, I face the possibility that someone will attribute the "wrong" gender to me based on my physical appearance.

I am six feet tall and large-boned. I have had short hair for most of my life. For the past several years, I have worn a crew cut or flat top. I do not shave or otherwise remove hair from my body (e.g., no eyebrow plucking). I do not wear dresses, skirts, high heels, or makeup. My only jewelry is a class ring, a "men's" watch (my wrists are too large for a "women's" watch), two small earrings (gold hoops, both in my left ear), and (occasionally) a necklace. I wear jeans or shorts, T-shirts, sweaters, polo/golf shirts, button-down collar shirts, and tennis shoes or boots. The jeans are "women's" (I do have hips) but do not look particularly "feminine." The rest of the outer garments are from men's departments. I prefer baggy clothes, so the fact that I have "womanly" breasts often is not obvious (I do not wear a bra). Sometimes, I wear a baseball cap or some other type of hat. I also am white and relatively young (30 years old).[2]

My gender display—what others interpret as my presented identity—regularly leads to the misattribution of my gender. An incongruity exists between my gender self-identity and the gender that others perceive. In my encounters with people I do not know, I sometimes conclude, based on our interactions, that they think I am a man. This does not mean that other people do not think I am a man, just that I have no way of knowing what they think without interacting with them.

Living with It

I have no illusions or delusions about my appearance. I know that my appearance is likely to be read as "masculine" (and male) and that how I see myself is socially irrelevant. Given our two-and-only-two gender structure, I must live with the consequences of my appearance. These consequences fall into two categories: issues of identity and issues of interaction.

My most common experience is being called "Sir" or being referred to by some other masculine linguistic marker (e.g., "he," "man"). This has happened for years, for as long as I can remember, when having encounters with people I do not know.[3] Once, in fact, the same worker at a fast-food restaurant called me "Ma'am" when she took my order and "Sir" when she gave it to me.

Using my credit cards sometimes is a challenge. Some clerks subtly indicate their disbelief, looking from the card to me and back at the card and checking my signature carefully. Others challenge my use of the card, asking whose it is or demanding identification. One cashier asked to see my driver's license and then asked me whether I was the son of the cardholder. Another clerk told me that my signature on the receipt "had better match" the one on the card. Presumably, this was her way of letting me know that she was not convinced it was my credit card.

My identity as a woman also is called into question when I try to use women-only spaces. Encounters in public restrooms are an adventure. I have been told countless times that "This is the ladies' room." Other women say nothing to me, but their stares and conversations with others let me know what they think. I will hear them say, for example, "There was a man in there." I also get stares when I enter a locker room. However, it seems that women are less concerned about my presence there, perhaps because, given that it is a space for changing clothes, showering, and so forth, they will be able to make sure that I am really a woman. Dressing rooms in department stores also are problematic spaces. I remember shopping with my sister once and being offered a chair outside the room when I began to accompany her into the dressing room. . . .

Being perceived as a man has made me privy to male–male interactional styles of which most women are not aware. I found out, quite by accident, that many men greet, or acknowledge, people (mostly other men) who make eye contact with them with a single nod. For example, I found that when I walked down the halls of my brother's all-male dormitory making eye contact, men nodded their greetings at me. Oddly enough, these same men did not greet my brother; I had to tell him about making eye contact and nodding as a greeting ritual. Apparently, in this case I was doing masculinity better than he was!

I also believe that I am treated differently, for example, in auto parts stores (staffed almost exclusively by men in most cases) because of the assumption that I am a man. Workers there assume that I know what I need and that my questions are legitimate requests for information. I suspect that I am treated more fairly than a feminine-appearing woman would be. I have not been able to test this proposition. However, Devor's participants did report "being treated more respectfully" (1989:132) in such situations.

There is, however, a negative side to being assumed to be a man by other men. Once, a friend and I were driving in her car when a man failed to stop at an intersection and nearly crashed into us. As we drove away, I mouthed "stop sign" to him. When we both stopped our cars at the next intersection, he got out of his car and came up to the passenger side of the car, where I was sitting. He yelled obscenities at us and pounded and spit on the car window. Luckily, the windows were closed. I do not think he would have done that if he thought I was a woman. This was the first time I realized that one of the implications of being seen as a man was that I might be called on to defend myself from physical aggression from other men who felt challenged by me. This was a sobering and somewhat frightening thought.

Recently, I was verbally accosted by an older man who did not like where I had parked my car. As I walked down the street to work, he shouted that I should park at the university rather than on a side street nearby. I responded that it was a public street and that I could park there if I chose. He continued to yell, but the only thing I caught was the last part of what he said: "Your tires are going to get cut!" Based on my appearance that day—I was dressed casually and carrying a backpack, and I had my hat on backward—I believe he thought that I was a young male student rather than a female professor. I do not think he would have yelled at a person he thought to be a woman—and perhaps especially not a woman professor.

Given the presumption of heterosexuality that is part of our system of gender, my interactions with women who assume that I am a man also can be viewed from that perspective. For example, once my brother and I were shopping when we were "hit on" by two young women. The encounter ended before I realized what had happened. It was only when we walked away that I told him that I was pretty certain that they had thought both of us were men. A more common experience is realizing that when I am seen in public with one of my women friends, we are likely to be read as a heterosexual dyad. It is likely that if I were to walk through a shopping mall holding hands with a woman, no one would look twice, not because of their open-mindedness toward lesbian couples but rather because of their assumption that I was the male half of a straight couple. Recently, when walking through a mall with a friend and her infant, my observations of others' responses to us led me to believe that many of them assumed that we were a family on an outing, that is, that I was her partner and the father of the child.

Dealing with It

Although I now accept that being mistaken for a man will be a part of my life so long as I choose not to participate in femininity, there have been times when I consciously have tried to appear more feminine. I did this for a while when I was an undergraduate and again recently when I was on the academic job market. The first time, I let my hair grow nearly down to my shoulders and had it permed. I also grew long fingernails and wore nail polish. Much to my chagrin, even then one of my professors, who did not know my name, insistently referred to me in his kinship examples as "the son." Perhaps my first act on the way to my current stance was to point out to this man, politely and after class, that I was a woman.

More recently, I again let my hair grow out for several months, although I did not alter other aspects of my appearance. Once my hair was about two and a half inches long (from its original quarter inch), I realized, based on my encounters with strangers, that I had more or less passed back into the category of "woman." Then, when I returned to wearing a flat top, people again responded to me as if I were a man.

Because of my appearance, much of my negotiation of interactions with strangers involves attempts to anticipate their reactions to me. I need to assess whether they will be likely to assume that I am a man and whether that actually matters in the context of our encounters. Many times, my gender really is irrelevant, and it is just annoying to be misidentified. Other times, particularly when my appearance is coupled with something that identifies me by name (e.g., a check or credit card) without a photo, I might need to do something to ensure that my identity is not questioned. As a result of my experiences, I have developed some techniques to deal with gender misattribution.

In general, in unfamiliar public places, I avoid using the restroom because I know that it is a place where there is a high likelihood of misattribution and where misattribution is socially important. If I must use a public restroom, I try to make myself look as nonthreatening as possible. I do not wear a hat, and I try to rearrange my clothing to make my breasts more obvious. Here, I am trying to use my secondary sex characteristics to make my gender more obvious rather than the usual use of gender to make sex obvious. While in the restroom, I never make eye contact, and I get in and out as quickly as possible. Going in with a woman friend also is helpful; her presence legitimizes my own. People are less likely to think I am entering a space where I do not belong when I am with someone who looks like she does belong.[4]

To those women who verbally challenge my presence in the restroom, I reply, "I know," usually in an annoyed tone. When they stare or talk about me to the women they are with, I simply get out as quickly as possible. In general, I do not wait for someone I am with because there is too much chance of an unpleasant encounter.

I stopped trying on clothes before purchasing them a few years ago because my presence in the changing areas was met with stares and whispers. Exceptions are stores where the dressing rooms are completely private, where there are individual stalls rather than a room with stalls separated by curtains, or where business is slow and no one else is trying on clothes. If I am trying on a garment clearly intended for a woman, then I usually can do so without hassle. I guess the attendants assume that I must be a woman if I have, for example, a women's bathing suit in my hand. But usually, I think it is easier for me to try the clothes on at home and return them, if necessary, rather than risk creating a scene. Similarly, when I am with another woman who is trying on clothes, I just wait outside.

My strategy with credit cards and checks is to anticipate wariness on a clerk's part. When I sense that there is some doubt or when they challenge me, I say, "It's my card." I generally respond courteously to requests for photo ID, realizing that these might be routine checks because of concerns about increasingly widespread fraud. . . .

Another strategy I have been experimenting with is wearing nail polish in the dark bright colors currently fashionable. I try to do this when I travel by plane. Given more stringent travel regulations, one always must present a photo ID. But my experiences have shown that my driver's license is not necessarily convincing. Nail polish might be. I also flash my polished nails when I enter airport restrooms, hoping that they will provide a clue that I am indeed in the right place.

There are other cases in which the issues are less those of identity than of all the norms of interaction that, in our society, are gendered. My most common response to misattribution actually is to appear to ignore it, that is, to go on with the interaction as if nothing out of the ordinary has happened. Unless I feel that there is a good reason to establish my correct gender, I assume the identity others impose on me for the sake of smooth interaction. For example, if someone is selling me a movie ticket, then there is no reason to make sure that the person has accurately discerned my gender. Similarly, if it is clear that the person using "Sir" is talking to me, then I simply respond as appropriate. I accept the designation because it is irrelevant to the situation. It takes enough effort to be alert for misattributions and to decide which of them matter; responding to each one would take more energy than it is worth.

Sometimes, if our interaction involves conversation, my first verbal response is enough to let the other person know that I am actually a woman and not a man. My voice apparently is "feminine" enough to shift people's attributions to the other category. I know when this has happened by the apologies that usually accompany the mistake. I usually respond to the apologies by saying something like "No problem" and/or "It happens all the time." Sometimes, a misattributor will offer an account for the mistake, for example, saying that it was my hair or that they were not being very observant.

These experiences with gender and misattribution provide some theoretical insights into contemporary Western understandings of gender and into the social structure of gender in contemporary society. Although there are a number of ways in which my experiences confirm the work of others, there also are some ways in which my experiences suggest other interpretations and conclusions.

What Does It Mean?

Gender is pervasive in our society. I cannot choose not to participate in it. Even if I try not to do gender, other people will do it for me. That is, given our two-and-only-two rule, they must attribute one of two genders to me. Still, although I cannot choose not to participate in gender, I can choose not to participate in femininity (as I have), at least with respect to physical appearance.

That is where the problems begin. Without the decorations of femininity, I do not look like a woman. That is, I do not look like what many people's commonsense understanding of gender tells them a woman looks like. How I see myself, even how I might wish others would see me, is socially irrelevant. It is the gender that I *appear* to be (my "perceived gender") that is most relevant to my social identity and interactions with others. The major consequence of this fact is that I must be continually aware of which gender I "give off" as well as which gender I "give" (Goffman 1959).

Because my gender self-identity is "not displayed obviously, immediately, and consistently" (Devor 1989:58), I am somewhat of a failure in social terms with respect to gender. Causing people to be uncertain or wrong about one's gender is a violation of taken-for-granted rules that leads to embarrassment and discomfort; it means that something has gone wrong with the interaction (Garfinkel 1967; Kessler and McKenna 1978). This means that my nonresponse to misattribution is the more socially appropriate response; I am allowing others to maintain face (Goffman 1959:1967). By not calling attention to their mistakes, I uphold their images of themselves as competent social actors. I also maintain my own image as competent by letting them assume that I am the gender I appear to them to be.

But I still have discreditable status; I carry a stigma (Goffman 1963). Because I have failed to participate appropriately in the creation of meaning with respect to gender (Devor 1989), I can be called on to account for my appearance. If discredited, I show myself to be an incompetent social actor. I am the one not following the rules, and I will pay the price for not providing people with the appropriate cues for placing me in the gender category to which I really belong.

I do think that it is, in many cases, safer to be read as a man than as some sort of deviant woman. "Man" is an acceptable category; it fits properly into people's gender worldview. Passing as a man often is the "path of least resistance" (Devor 1989; Johnson 1997). For example, in situations where gender does not matter, letting people take me as a man is easier than correcting them.

Conversely, as Butler noted, "We regularly punish those who fail to do their gender right" (1990:140). Feinberg maintained, "Masculine girls and women face terrible condemnation and brutality—including sexual violence—for crossing the boundary of what is 'acceptable' female expression" (1996:114). People are more likely to harass me when they perceive me to be a woman who looks like a man. For example, when a group of teenagers realized that I was not a man because one of their mothers identified me correctly, they began to make derogatory comments when I passed them. One asked, for example, "Does she have a penis?"

Because of the assumption that a "masculine" woman is a lesbian, there is the risk of homophobic reactions (Gardner 1995; Lucal 1997). Perhaps surprisingly, I find that I am much more likely to be taken for a man than for a lesbian, at least based on my interactions with people and their reactions to me. This might be because people are less likely to reveal that they have taken me for a lesbian because it is less relevant to an encounter or because they believe this would be unacceptable. But I think it is more likely a product of the strength of our two-and-only-two system. I give enough masculine cues that I am seen not as a deviant woman but rather as a man, at least in most cases. The problem seems not to be that people are uncertain about my gender, which might lead them to conclude that I was a lesbian once they realized I was a woman. Rather, I seem to fit easily into a gender category—just not the one with which I identify. . . .

Boundaries and margins are an important component of both my experiences of gender and our theoretical understanding of gendering processes. I am, in effect, both woman and not-woman. As a woman who often is a social man but who also is a woman living in a patriarchal society, I am in a unique position to see and act. I sometimes receive privileges usually limited to men, and I sometimes am oppressed by my status as a deviant woman. I am, in a sense, an outsider-within (Collins 1991). Positioned on the boundaries of gender categories, I have developed a consciousness that I hope will prove transformative (Anzaldua 1987).

In fact, one of the reasons why I decided to continue my nonparticipation in femininity was that my sociological training suggested that this could be one of my contributions to the eventual dismantling of patriarchal gender constructs. It would be my way of making the personal political. I accepted being taken for a man as the price I would pay to help subvert patriarchy. I believed that all of the inconveniences I was enduring meant that I actually was doing something to bring down the gender structures that entangled all of us.

Then, I read Lorber's (1994) *Paradoxes of Gender* and found out, much to my dismay, that I might not actually be challenging gender after all. Because of the way in which doing gender works in our two-and-only-two system, gender displays are simply read as evidence of one of the two categories. Therefore, gender bending, blending, and passing between the categories do not question the categories themselves. If one's social gender and personal (true) gender do not correspond, then this is irrelevant unless someone notices the lack of congruence.

This reality brings me to a paradox of my experiences. First, not only do others assume that I am one gender or the other, but I also insist that I *really am* a member of one of the two gender categories. That is, I am female; I self-identify as a woman. I do not claim to be some other gender or to have no gender at all. I simply place myself in the wrong category according to stereotypes and cultural standards; the gender I present, or that some people perceive me to be presenting, is inconsistent with the gender with which I identify myself as well as with the gender I could be "proven" to be. Socially, I display the wrong gender; personally, I identify as the proper gender.

Second, although I ultimately would like to see the destruction of our current gender structure, I am not to the point of personally abandoning gender. Right now, I do not want people to see me as genderless as much as I want them to see me as a woman. That is, I would like to expand the category of "woman" to include people like me. I, too, am deeply embedded in our gender system, even though I do not play by many of its rules. For me, as for most people in our society, gender is a substantial part of my personal identity (Howard and Hollander 1997). Socially, the problem is that I do not present a gender display that is consistently read as feminine. In fact, I consciously do not participate in the trappings of femininity. However, I do identify myself as a woman, not as a man or as someone outside of the two-and-only-two categories.

Yet, I do believe, as Lorber (1994) does, that the purpose of gender, as it currently is constructed, is to oppress women. Lorber analyzed gender as a "process of creating distinguishable social statuses for the assignment of rights and responsibilities" that ends up putting women in a devalued and oppressed position (1994:32). As Martin put it, "Bodies that clearly delineate gender status facilitate the maintenance of the gender hierarchy" (1998:495).

For society, gender means difference (Lorber 1994). The erosion of the boundaries would problematize that structure. Therefore, for gender to operate as it currently does, the category "woman" *cannot* be expanded to include people like me. The maintenance of the gender structure is dependent on the creation of a few categories that are mutually exclusive, the members of which are as different as possible (Lorber 1994). It is the clarity of the boundaries between the categories that allows gender to be used to assign rights and responsibilities as well as resources and rewards.

It is that part of gender—what it is used for—that is most problematic. Indeed, is it not *patriarchal*—or, even more specifically, *heteropatriarchal*—constructions of gender that are actually the problem? It is not the differences between men and women, or the categories themselves, so much as the meanings ascribed to the categories and, even more important, the hierarchical

gender under patriarchy that is the problem (Johnson 1997). There-
n rebelling not against my femaleness or even my womanhood;
I am protesting contemporary constructions of femininity and, at
rectly, masculinity under patriarchy. We do not, in fact, know what
gender would look like if it were not constructed around heterosexuality in
the context of patriarchy.

Although it is possible that the end of patriarchy would mean the end of
gender, it is at least conceivable that something like what we now call gender
could exist in a postpatriarchal future. The two-and-only-two categorization
might well disappear, there being no hierarchy for it to justify. But I do not
think that we should make the assumption that gender and patriarchy are
synonymous. . . .

. . . In a . . . book, *The Gender Knot*, Johnson (1997) argued that when it
comes to gender and patriarchy, most of us follow the paths of least resistance; we "go along to get along," allowing our actions to be shaped by the
gender system. Collectively, our actions help patriarchy maintain and perpetuate a system of oppression and privilege. Thus, by withdrawing our
support from this system by choosing paths of greater resistance, we can
start to chip away at it. Many people participate in gender because they cannot imagine any alternatives. In my classroom, and in my interactions and
encounters with strangers, my presence can make it difficult for people not to
see that there *are* other paths. In other words, following from West and
Zimmerman (1987), I can subvert gender by doing it differently.

For example, I think it is true that my existence does not have an effect on
strangers who assume that I am a man and never learn otherwise. For them,
I do uphold the two-and-only-two system. But there are other cases in which
my existence can have an effect. For example, when people initially take me
for a man but then find out that I actually am a woman, at least for that moment, the naturalness of gender may be called into question. In these cases,
my presence can provoke a "category crisis" (Garber 1992:16) because it challenges the sex/gender binary system.

The subversive potential of my gender might be strongest in my classrooms. When I teach about the sociology of gender, my students can see me
as the embodiment of the social construction of gender. Not all of my students have transformative experiences as a result of taking a course with me;
there is the chance that some of them see me as a "freak" or as an exception.
Still, after listening to stories about my experiences with gender and reading
literature on the subject, many students begin to see how and why gender is
a social product. I can disentangle sex, gender, and sexuality in the contemporary United States for them. Students can begin to see the connection between biographical experiences and the structure of society. As one of my
students noted, I clearly live the material I am teaching. If that helps me to
get my point across, then perhaps I am subverting the binary gender system
after all. Although my gendered presence and my way of doing gender
might make others—and sometimes even me—uncomfortable, no one ever
said that dismantling patriarchy was going to be easy.

Author's Note: "I thank the journal's reviewers, my writing group (Linda Chen, Louise Collins, April Lidinsky, Margarete Myers, Monica Tetzlaff, and Becky Torstrick), Heather Bulan, and Linda Fritschner for their helpful comments on earlier versions of this article.

ENDNOTES

[1] Ethnomethodology has been described as "the study of commonsense practical reasoning" (Collins 1988:274). It examines how people make sense of their everyday experiences. Ethnomethodology is particularly useful in studying gender because it helps to uncover the assumptions on which our understandings of sex and gender are based.

[2] I obviously have left much out by not examining my gendered experiences in the context of race, age, class, sexuality, region, and so forth. Such a project clearly is more complex. As Weston pointed out, gender presentations are complicated by other statuses of their presenters: "What it takes to kick a person over into another gendered category can differ with race, class, religion, and time" (1996:168). Furthermore, I am well aware that my whiteness allows me to assume that my experiences are simply a product of gender (see, e.g., hooks 1981; Lucal 1996; Spelman 1988; West and Fenstermaker 1995). For now, suffice it to say that it is my privileged position on some of these axes and my more disadvantaged position on others that combine to delineate my overall experience.

[3] In fact, such experiences are not always limited to encounters with strangers. My grandmother, who does not see me often, twice has mistaken me for either my brother-in-law or some unknown man.

[4] I also have noticed that there are certain types of restrooms in which I will not be verbally challenged; the higher the social status of the place, the less likely I will be harassed. For example, when I go to the theater, I might get stared at, but my presence never has been challenged.

REFERENCES

Anzaldua, G. 1987. *Borderlands/La Frontera*. San Francisco: Aunt Lute Books.
Bem, S. L. 1993. *The Lenses of Gender*. New Haven, CT: Yale University Press.
Berger, P. 1963. *Invitation to Sociology*. New York: Anchor.
Bordo, S. 1993. *Unbearable Weight*. Berkeley: University of California Press.
Butler, J. 1990. *Gender Trouble*. New York: Routledge.
Collins, P. H. 1991. *Black Feminist Thought*. New York: Routledge.
Collins, R. 1988. *Theoretical Sociology*. San Diego: Harcourt Brace Jovanovich.
Devor, H. 1989. *Gender Blending: Confronting the Limits of Duality*. Bloomington: Indiana University Press.
Feinberg, L. 1996. *Transgender Warriors*. Boston: Beacon.
Garber, M. 1992. *Vested Interests: Cross-Dressing and Cultural Anxiety*. New York: HarperPerennial.
Gardner, C. B. 1995. *Passing By: Gender and Public Harassment*. Berkeley: University of California.
Garfinkel, H. 1967. *Studies in Ethnomethodology*. Englewood Cliffs, NJ: Prentice Hall.
Goffman, E. 1959. *The Presentation of Self in Everyday Life*. Garden City, NY: Doubleday.
———. 1963. *Stigma*. Englewood Cliffs, NJ: Prentice Hall.
———. 1976. "Gender Display." *Studies in the Anthropology of Visual Communication* 3:69–77.
hooks, b. 1981. *Ain't I a Woman: Black Women and Feminism*. Boston: South End Press.
Howard, J. A. and J. Hollander. 1997. *Gendered Situations, Gendered Selves*. Thousand Oaks, CA: Sage.
Johnson, A. G. 1997. *The Gender Knot: Unraveling Our Patriarchal Legacy*. Philadelphia: Temple University Press.
Kessler, S. J. and W. McKenna. 1978. *Gender: An Ethnomethodological Approach*. New York: John Wiley.
Krieger, S. 1991. *Social Science and the Self*. New Brunswick, NJ: Rutgers University Press.
Lorber, J. 1994. *Paradoxes of Gender*. New Haven, CT: Yale University Press.
———. 1996. "Beyond the Binaries: Depolarizing the Categories of Sex, Sexuality, and Gender." *Sociological Inquiry* 66:143–59.
Lucal, B. 1996. "Oppression and Privilege: Toward a Relational Conceptualization of Race." *Teaching Sociology* 24:245–55.

———. 1997. "'Hey, This Is the Ladies' Room!': Gender Misattribution and Public Harassment." *Perspectives on Social Problems* 9:43–57.

Martin, K. A. 1998. "Becoming a Gendered Body: Practices of Preschools." *American Sociological Review* 63:494–511.

Mills, C. W. 1959. *The Sociological Imagination*. London: Oxford University Press.

Myhre, J. R. M. 1995. "One Bad Hair Day Too Many, or the Hairstory of an Androgynous Young Feminist." In *Listen Up: Voices from the Next Feminist Generation*, edited by B. Findlen. Seattle, WA: Seal Press.

Reinharz, S. 1992. *Feminist Methods in Social Research*. New York: Oxford University Press.

Riemer, J. W. 1977. "Varieties of Opportunistic Research." *Urban Life* 5:467–77.

———. 1988. "Work and Self" in *Personal Sociology*, edited by P. C. Higgins and J. M. Johnson. New York: Praeger.

Spelman, E. V. 1988. *Inessential Woman: Problems of Exclusion in Feminist Thought*. Boston: Beacon.

West, C. and S. Fenstermaker. 1995. "Doing Difference." *Gender & Society* 9:8–37.

West, C. and D. H. Zimmerman. 1987. Doing gender. *Gender & Society* 1:125–51.

Weston, K. 1996. *Render Me, Gender Me*. New York: Columbia University Press.

Zimmerman, D. H. 1992. "They Were All Doing Gender, but They Weren't All Passing: Comment on Rogers." *Gender & Society* 6:192–98.

29

OUR GUYS/GOOD GUYS
Playing with High School Privilege and Power

NANCY LESKO

Few social institutions mold the social environment as faithfully as schools do. The institution of education reinforces social inequality by teaching the dominant culture's values and biases. The following reading by Nancy Lesko, a professor of education at Columbia University, examines how the social institution of education has replicated social hierarchies that perpetuate gender inequality. In particular, Lesko investigates how competitive high school athletics *masculinize* schools and create gender bias that affects school discipline, management, and curricula. This excerpt is taken from Lesko's critically acclaimed book, *Act Your Age! A Cultural Construction of Adolescence* (2001).

The faces of the [football] players were young, but the perfection of their equipment, the gleaming shoes and helmets and the immaculate pants and jersies, the solemn ritual that was attached to almost everything, made them seem like boys going off to fight a war for the benefit of someone else, unwitting sacrifices to a strange and powerful god.[1]

T he Super Bowl has become *the* cultural event of American life, one of many indications that sports, especially the more violent ones like football, have become like a religion or a nationalist ideology to which everyone bows. Sports seem to unite the races, social classes, and the political left and right as well. Although women may watch the Super Bowl in growing numbers, football idolizes that other thing that women can never have—muscle mass. Sports events like the Super Bowl are filled with military language at the same time that football imagery has become the "root metaphor of American political discourse." George Bush dubbed the 1992 Gulf War his "Super Bowl." The potent mix of football, political order, war, and scripted emotion, which was starkly and regularly paraded during the Persian Gulf action against Saddam Hussein, grounds this examination of athletics in secondary school (Jansen and Sabo 1994:3; Nadelhaft 1993:27).

The most popular and highest status boys are in the "athletic clique" of high schools. Athletic programs demand huge slices of school budgets, and coaches can be gods with a capability of making or ruining a school and its community. Despite these undisputed facts, little attention has been given to the significance and effects of competitive athletics and their brand of masculinity within contemporary discussions of teaching, schooling, and school reform. That is, sports in schools, especially in high schools, have generally been treated as a separate sphere—extracurricular, court- or field-based. This [reading] seeks to understand male-dominated athletics as a systemic "logic of practice" and to map their influences on school culture, teaching, curricula, and our ideas of successful teenagers.

I utilize the personal narratives of one coach-in-training who was a football star in high school to help map the circulation of football-politics-war perspectives and how they impact the social relations of youth and teachers from the gridiron to the classroom. I examine the competitive relationships of playing football and the implications of schools becoming "level playing fields"; the privilege and power conferred on male athletes, and the implications of these masculinized, stratified, gridiron social relations for high school curricula and teaching. Thus I am in pursuit of the rewards that await successful school team members; the ways that the logic of competitive athletics affects school discipline, management, and curricula; and how team loyalties and values sustain an intolerance of "outcasts," those who do not meet the criteria of successful athletes, the "winners."

Since studies of teenagers are usually stocked with stories of problems, risks, and crises, I devote this [reading] to the "good guys"—the idealized stars of secondary schools, those young men who garner positive media attention and enhance school histories and local real estate values. These boys often conform to the successful kid image: "attractive, well groomed articulate, and doing well in school or in some enterprise, like sports" (Lefkowitz

1997:65). In examining the successes and problems of school athletics, I keep
my eye on those outside the athletic circle as well, those kids who do not
meet the standards for appearance, success, and social presence. I want to consider the athletes in relation to the less prestigious students. This [reading]
looks at the *winners*. . . . [and] begins with the understanding that competitive
athletics *masculinize* schools, by which I mean that schools support and
highlight the processes and persons who represent particular masculine interests, traits, and attitudes. British scholars have described a new wave of male
dominance amid school change, which they term a *remasculinizing* of schools
and school management. A particular version of masculinity—"competitive,
point-scoring, overconfident, sporting, career and status conscious"—has
come to dominate school management, writes Lynn Davies. . . .

In the United States, the remasculinizing of schools includes a number of
features: the spread of competitive sports; higher standards through increased
testing; a more rigorous curriculum; zero-tolerance policies; and redoubled
efforts in math, science, and technology. This [reading] pursues themes that
might be imagined as circulating among these high stakes testing and other
changes—a logic of competition and an absence of compassion for people
with different abilities and/or critical perspectives. This analysis also examines variations in schools' promotion of all students' learning. I am trying to
understand an attitude that seems based in schools but is also more broadly
operative in domestic and international political realms.

Positioning Football, Masculinity, and the Gulf War

My interviews with Woody Rockne,[2] the subject of this [reading], were part
of a larger study of a secondary teacher education program.[3] They began in
August of 1993, slightly more than a year after the Persian Gulf War ended.
The emotional tenor of his narratives, coupled with the alleged efficiency
and rationality of his life, sounded familiar. For me, Woody's stories echoed
the mix of irrationality and reason surrounding the U.S. invasion of Iraq during the Gulf War. I felt a similarity between the plot and emotional pitch of
this preservice teacher's life stories and the popular response to the attack on
Saddam Hussein by George Bush. . . .

This re-presentation of Woody's stories of playing football, coaching, and
preparing to teach within the context of the Gulf War's nationalistic aggression begins with the need to view the following topics as linked: (1) sports
and war, (2) sports and nationalism, (3) football as nationalist spectacle, and
(4) the militarization of civilian life through "permanent war." The latter
part of the [reading] examines the individual and classroom dimensions of
these sports-war-masculinity connections that are so powerfully fueled in
secondary school sports. My broader concern is the impact of these sports
and masculinity connections on expectations for all adolescents. . . .

The football spectacle as the model of "socially dominant life" (DeBord
1977:2–3) will be explored on the individual level with Woody's stories of his
football career, his disciplined body, and the social relations of playing and

coaching football. I investigate Woody's narratives of football as parables for a successful teenage career and as policy statements for how young people should act and how society should be organized—as on a playing field. If we are encouraged to imagine schools as "level playing fields" and teachers as "coaches," we need to look more closely at the assumptions about adolescent social relations carried in those images. Woody's life history will help us specify the social relations of football and coaching before examining their implications for teaching.

Woody's Disciplined Body

Woody was a white, middle-class, 20-year-old junior in college, dividing his coursework among physical education, history, and secondary education, when he narrated his own adolescence. Unlike the adolescents he characterized as "trying to become as adult as possible as quickly as possible" or those he described as reactors to stimuli without self-determination, Woody presented himself as always fully rational and purposeful:

> I knew, probably from day three in the womb, I was going to play football. . . . My parents swear on my baby book that the first two words I ever put together were my high school, Holy Cross. They swear that ever since day one, it was just football and that was it. That's all I wanted.

Although he described many of his teenaged friends as confused and acting on whims, Woody portrayed himself as masterful, reasoning, and autonomous.

> I never did anything because I had to do it. . . . I did what I thought was right. . . . 99 percent of the time. It wasn't like, "Well, I'm in high school now and if I want to be a big, big star, I'm going to play football and get As and Bs." Na, I just lived my life how I was going to do it. . . . Did I succumb to peer pressure? No, I never did . . . other than like styles or clothes . . . I was just, you know, I think I should do this. It would be right if I did this.

Woody's story portrayed a boy-man[4] who knew exactly what he wanted; he wanted, like other adolescent males, to be an athlete, for boys are judged according to their ability in competitive sports (Messner 1992:24). He pursued his goal single-mindedly except for his eight-month "James Dean" period, which he described with relish:

> I guess my teen years did not start until I was 16, when I got a car. . . . I was driving fast and getting into all kinds of trouble. . . . I was running around with some guys that were a little older than me and they were a lot crazier than I was. . . . After they graduated, [and entered the Marines] I went back and refound myself. . . . The only thing that mattered to me, after the rebel period, was playing football and getting grades, because I had been recruited to play ball by Notre Dame, so I was just kind of straight and narrow. . . . I just kind of wanted to be a football player, go to work, come home, and coach my little brother is all I really wanted.

Except for the lapse of eight months, strategically positioned between the end of one football season and the beginning of the next, Woody never was an adolescent, if an adolescent is rebellious, confused, and prone to be influenced by others. He was purposive and focused, and his life was an orderly progression toward football stardom and academic achievement. He did not *learn* rationality; his orderly development was naturally occurring. Woody's narratives indicated that he had strength of will—"one of the distinguishing marks of the proper male ideal as opposed to so-called weak and womanly men," (Mosse 1996:100) a popular male attribute with turn-of-the-twentieth-century boyologists, too. . . .

When Woody talked about his coaching experiences, he admitted that he found it difficult to work with kids who were not like himself. The "lackadaisical athlete" reminded him of his middle brother, an irritant, who barely made it to practice on time. As a coach, he ran lackadaisical team members to death, which did not accomplish much but rid him "of the problems of having to deal with them."

In these excerpts, Woody portrayed several aspects of ideal masculinity that begins in adolescence: rational, purposive, disciplined, and focused. Woody and his younger brother remained self-determining, except for Woody's short "rebel" period. As we track these rational, disciplined, self-determining men into competitive sports, additional aspects of the social world governed by football are clarified. Woody's rational, purposive, focused "citizen" believes he has earned his privilege, believes that his is the standard for all other team members (and citizens), and rebukes suggestions of pluralistic diversity.

Producing Woody's Privileged Position

In this section, I trace some connections between sports and the establishment of a sense of privilege, the belief that one is superior and deserves special treatment. The limitations of regular people drop away for superior athletes as they receive adulation from fans, families, and the media; the "pain principle" mandates that they give until it hurts (and beyond), conferring a sense of superior will and courage. The ability to take pain is part of the embodiment of masculine privilege that distinguishes strong men from weak others.

Privilege

In both Woody's narratives and other sociological studies, success in sports creates a sense of privilege that involves specific material rewards, status, and an exemption from ordinary routines. In Odessa, Texas, the football coach began each new season by telling his players, "You guys are a very special breed" (Bissinger 1990:24). Sociologist Don Sabo recalled the pull toward high school football in very specific terms: "Winning at sports meant winning friends and carving a place for myself within the male pecking order" (Sabo 1994:83). Girls were part of the bounty won by athletes, as

Woody explicitly described: "Our football coach used to always say: 'If you guys win this sectional or if you win this big game, there's going to be girls waiting for you when you get back.'"

Having been deemed special, athletes come to believe that they are "supposed to win—every game" and they count on other entitlements as well. Both Bissinger's report on West Texas and Lefkowitz's account of athletes in New Jersy demonstrate how successful athletes assumed they were above the law. Woody's sense of superiority was also produced through a private school education:

> *I competed in Catholic leagues, but then I played football and baseball in the city leagues and . . . the kids I played with, I always thought they had no manners, I was more adult acting than they were. . . .* **I just always had an idea in my head that they were lollygagging around all the time while I had to sit and study and learn. Our grade scale was higher, so we definitely thought we were smarter when we graduated.** [Emphasis added]

Woody's sense of superiority is a phenomenon widely chronicled in scholarship on masculinity and sports, but I am emphasizing its impacts on all young men and young women, when sports stars rule.

Don Sabo connects the privileges of competitive athletics with domination of women and other men. It is a hierarchical system in which men dominate women and a minority of men dominate other men: "The inter-male dominance hierarchy exploits the majority of those it beckons to climb its heights. Patriarchy's mythos of heroism and its morality of power-worship implant visions of masculine excellence and ecstasy in the minds of the boys who ultimately will defend its inequities and ridicule its victims" (1994:86). The social relations of sports create a small group of privileged young men who dominate women and lower-status men, which they learn in their teens.

The Pain Principle

High status athletes must embrace pain; facing pain with courage distinguishes strong men from weak others. Football, of course, is especially brutal. In a recent survey of retired football players, 78 percent reported that they suffer physical disabilities related directly to football, and 66 percent believed that having played football will negatively affect their life spans (Messner 1992:62). "Boys are taught that to endure pain is courageous, to survive pain is manly." Reflecting on his own football career, Sabo writes:

> I learned to be an animal. Coaches took notice of animals. Animals made first team. Being an animal meant being fanatically aggressive and ruthlessly competitive. If I saw an arm in front of me, I trampled it. Whenever blood was spilled, I nodded approval. The coaches taught me to "punish the other man," and to secretly see my opponents' broken bones as little victories within the bigger struggle. (1994:84–86)

The path to privilege and domination was via becoming an animal. Masculinity draws vigor from animality, a theme that connects contemporary sports with G. Stanley Hall and Theodore Roosevelt.[5] If men are to dominate they must draw upon the primitive, animal energy that competitive sports offers.

Male athletes learn to view their bodies as instruments and thus, while dependent upon their bodies, athletes may also be alienated from them. Bodies may become merely tools or a machine to be utilized. Physical and emotional pain are nuisances to be ignored or minimized, often through the use of alcohol or other drugs. Coming to see the body as an instrument often accompanies violence expressed toward others and ultimately toward oneself (Messner 1992:62).

Athletes who reject the pain principle become pariahs among their teammates, coaches, and fans. Michael Messner tells the story of Bill S., who injured his knee before the state football championship game:

> I was hurt. I couldn't play, and I got a lot of flack from everybody. The coach said, Are you faking it? And I was in the whirlpool and a teammate said "You fucking pussy." That hurt more than the injury. Later, people told me it was my fault that we lost . . . not just other players and coaches, but people in the whole town. It hurt, it just really hurt. (1992:72)

Players with suspicious injuries receive the silent treatment, which often makes them frantic to play: "They will plead with the team physician to shoot them up so they can play. The player will totally disregard the risk of permanent injury" (Messner 1992:74).

Painkillers are an illegal but necessary part of the brutal culture of professional football. As National Football League (NFL) medical staffs try to contain the use of prescribed painkillers, players trade tickets or locker room passes to pharmaceutical sales representatives for drugs. Playing in pain is typical in the NFL, since the sport consists of 300-pound guys smashing into one another. Painkillers are a necessity, according to New York Giants quarterback Dave Brown, because "No one cares about how hurt you are. The coach doesn't care, the fans don't care and the media doesn't care. They just want you to play."[6]

The pain principle causes young men and boys to place efficiency and the goals of the team as priorities and to ignore personal hurts and injuries. In language that often appears in media stories about domestic violence and murder, men become adept at channeling the feelings that boil up inside them into a "rage which is directed at opponents and enemies" (Sabo 1994:86).

Woody's stories of playing high school football exemplified these themes: the stifling of personal pain; the prioritizing of the team, efficiency, and doing one's best; the trivializing of others' hurts and pains; and the channeling of feelings toward opponents and those who did not subscribe to the same principles that he did. Woody enumerated his injuries as a separated shoulder, a fracture in his left hand, a torn-up ankle, and, of course, his major knee injury:

> When I was a freshman, I got hit by a kid who is the middle linebacker for the University of Illinois now. I actually went unconscious, the only time I've ever been blacked out, and my knee cap was laying on the inside of my leg when they woke me up.

Woody elaborated on playing through the pain, a story that resembled innumerable ones reported by sports sociologists and journalists:[7]

> *I played sometimes in so much pain I didn't know if I could make it through the game. I mean my knee would act up in the middle of the game, and I'd come off the sidelines and tell the coach, "I don't know if I can go anymore." He'd say, "You've got to go. You have to do it." It's just that . . . I always watched ball players get hurt all the time. I mean, I remember when I was little, my dad always wanted me to play regardless. . . . [N]one of us are quitters. They [his parents] never wanted to see anybody quit if you started something. . . . I've always lived by that and always tried to do that as much as I could, play as hard as I could for however long. . . .*

The pain principle has an additional implication for social relations off the field. Violent sports support male dominance, not only through exclusion of women but also through the association of males and maleness with sanctioned use of aggression, force, and violence. Thus modern sports help to naturalize the equation of maleness with physical power and to place those values at the center of secondary school life. . . .

Weak Others

My interviews with Woody occasionally moved to educational and public policy, and he invariably emphasized hard work within an assumed meritocracy.

> *I always had to work for whatever I got, so I think everyone should have to do that. . . . No one's going to get anything for free. I don't believe in the free stuff, and I don't care how much you have to work for everything, I won't give grades. I won't give playing time. . . . I've had parents come up to me and holler that my kid's not playing enough. Well, he's not good enough, you know. I'm sorry, he's not, and maybe if he practiced or whatever. I mean, I'm not going to just give anybody anything.*

Woody's backing for "the level playing field" image of schooling and social policy became emotionally charged when I queried him on youth rights issues. Woody advocated the prohibition of rights, such as voting, marriage, and so on for persons under 21 years of age: "These kids are so immature, they have no clue of what's going on. . . . You just end up with too many problems." If parents are abusive or neglectful, should a young person be able to instigate a termination of their parents' rights, I asked. Without knowing much about the high profile 1992 case in which "Gregory K." wanted to legally replace his biological parents with more responsible parents of his choosing, Woody wondered whether Gregory K. was just a *whiner*:

> *How was his father abusive? What did his dad do? Holler at him? Well, you're a little girl, kid—not little girl, but you know what I mean—little baby. I'm sorry you're a little baby, but things happen. You're going to get yelled at in your life.*

Woody adeptly retreated from his gendered denigration of the whining, and made his derogation age-based instead, calling Gregory K. a baby. Woody proceeded to portray teenagers as apt to make up stories about things that happened to them. On a rhetorical roll, he asserted that "35 to 40 percent of date rape is a farce." He was convinced that it was a combination of teenagers lying about what had happened or whining over trivial occurrences. In this way he trivialized both child abuse and date rape, saying that many of these kids were either wimps or liars. Thus Woody demeaned those who failed to endure pain courageously and silently, and identified all "outsiders" as lacking control of their passions (Mosse 1985:134). Being tough and macho, the core of competitive, sporting masculinity, became a central criterion for good citizens beyond the playing field—people who complained were seen as wimps and their protests were not taken seriously. . . .

Against Multiculturalism

The rage of a white male just beyond adolescence deprived of his privilege surfaced when Woody discussed his experience with the required course on multicultural education (Weis 1993). Woody had filed a formal complaint for reverse discrimination against the African American woman instructor.

> *I seriously think that she is the worst teacher that I ever had because everything that she did was to degrade white males. White males were the downfall of everything. White males cause abortion. White males cause black kids not to get educations. White males cause Chinese kids to be, you know, come over here on boats from Bangkok and be sick. You know, the last time, I checked, I never chartered a group of aliens over here and I never caused a black kid to not get an education.*

The focus of the course on racism in schools and society was intolerable for Woody, who reached his limit one day and recalled giving an "I'm mad as hell" speech:

> *I said, "Look, I'm sorry if I have offended anyone for being a White male, but you know this is ridiculous. I'm really pissed, so I'm just going to leave now" and [I] walked out of class. This was in fact during one of our panel discussions. . . . I just got up and left for lieu of later, you know, causing myself to be an ass. . . . In all honesty I was really disappointed with this university at that time.*

In these statements, Woody took the position of the beleaguered white male who was held responsible for all the nation's shortcomings. He deflected the criticism by saying that he personally never did any of those things. Woody concluded that he had never been prejudiced and rejected ideas that emphasized past patterns of race relations: *"Everything that occurred in that class was prejudged on past racial tendencies, and . . . I don't want that [racial, ethnic, or class discrimination] to occur in anything I've ever done or will do."*

I can only describe Woody's response to the multicultural education class as *rage;* and his rage led to contesting his grade and the instructor's approach to the course. That is, he challenged her authority to grade him and her legitimacy in teaching about racism. Given Woody's descriptions of good teachers and his expertise in exerting control over classroom dynamics, pacing, and topics, it is small wonder that he reacted so strongly to the multicultural course. Not only were the social dynamics, topics, and perspectives beyond his control, but his usual privileged position (as clown, as articulate student, as high status student) was diminished. Indeed, his usual position of dominance in classroom dynamics was a topic of the multicultural course, for such patterns perpetuated certain students' achievement.

Although Woody occasionally critiqued high school history courses for presenting a sanitized version of the past, we can expect that his curriculum will remain Eurocentric and dominated by the study of the accomplishments of white men and that his classroom will similarly be dominated by young men who are skilled at athletics and verbal repartee and demand a disproportionate amount of the teacher's time and attention. His appropriation of the traditional image of social studies coach/teacher combined with the ultimate control of a science fiction Terminator offered a contemporary remasculinized coach and teacher, who alternated between entertaining, giving lecture notes, playing the dozens, and putting students in their places.

Remasculinizing Secondary Schools

> Woody: *Let's put it this way. I'm not going into education because I want to teach children.*

Gendered school change—coded as upward mobility; academic rigor; the importance of math, science, and technology; and moral standards—can be viewed as part of a broad remasculinizing of schools, into which Woody fits nicely. When this competitive, point-scoring sense of privilege is established in schools, it will combine with the epistemology of the bunker to hunt down spoilers: critics of athletics, of the academic canon, and of male-centered school practices.[8] When coaches become school administrators, it is nearly impossible for them to see the combination of privilege and violence to others that schools typically enact.

The problems of hypermasculinity in athletics and in gendered violence have begun to receive some national attention as a social problem, no longer completely dismissed as "boys being boys." Nevertheless, given the mounting scholarship on gendered violence and athletics (Katz 1995; Miedzian 1991; Stein 1995), schools have a long way to go in seeing, understanding, and changing the hypermasculinity that is often synonymous with being a successful teenage boy. This [reading] has traced Woody's youthful enchantment with football and how this enmeshment of a teenage boy and sports grounds his orientation toward teaching and coaching the next generation. He remains the athlete-boy as he plans to become the coach-man. His evocative story of boyhood to manhood enacts the early twentieth-century reformers' vision and beliefs on raising courageous, strong-willed leaders. Woody's life accords perfectly with the boyologists' scientific character-building program.

Utilizing critiques of competitive athletics and explorations of the hegemonic masculinity of sports, I have emphasized the social relations produced in football spectacles, with their scripted emotions and linkages with nationalism and war. The hierarchy through unity of competitive athletics, its violence, loyalty, and emphasis on winning are principles that would seem quite distant from classroom life. However, using one preservice teacher's life-history narratives, I began to track the circulation of disciplined bodies, the pain principle, and privilege across fields and classrooms. Woody's ideas about teaching were in part rooted in its unimportance, while coaching counted. Through flashbacks and imaginary forwards, Woody figured himself as a domineering teacher, a boy-man who moved between jokes and serious history, between being the most popular and the most feared teacher. These teaching fantasies gave preeminence in the classroom to those with Woody's characteristics: athletic, joking, articulate, competitive, and masculine. Woody eschewed all student-centered teaching and acknowledged an impatience with all but the best and the brightest.

Education conceptualized as a game open to all players repudiates multicultural education, at least any version that contains a serious examination of structural racism and sexism in schools. Woody's view of the classroom as a level playing field glossed the educational process as an athletic event, with the imputation of fairness and justice; everyone was equal to compete. This perspective, combined with his violent rejection of the existence of racism or sexism (those people just need to stop whining) and the failure to see his own privilege, kept Woody-as-teacher/coach within practices that will connect with the male athletes. The social relations of the gridiron are smoothly embraced within a teacher-centered, level-playing-field approach that is staunchly against affirmative action and antiracist policies and practices. In these social relations, persons who do not hold the same values and physical prowess will be labeled weak or whining and will be dismissed. The hierarchy within the alleged unity of the "team" perspective will prevail in classrooms and curriculum. The emphases on team loyalty, playing by the rules, energetic participation, and self-determination contain strong links to the boyologists' ideas and practices. These values and the practices in which they are imbedded are difficult to question; they are so familiar that few question what and how they teach. The familiarity must be created over and over, of course, but the long tradition begun by turn-of-the-century boy reformers around the inherent value of team sports for the individual, the team, the school, and the nation remains strong.

Competitiveness, aggressive masculinity, dominance, and privilege are key players on and off the football field. If educators and taxpayers accept the inevitability of high status athletics in secondary schools, it is questionable whether the problems of hegemonic masculinity, school management, and hierarchical social relations in the classroom can be raised, much less changed. Woody's narratives raise disturbing questions about "athletic discourse" and its logic of practice in schools.

ENDNOTES

[1]Bissinger (1990:II).

[2]Participants in this study chose their own pseudonyms, and the football influence on Woody's choice is evident. All proper nouns, such as the name of Woody's high school, are also pseudonyms.

[3]The research project occurred over the academic year 1993–1994 in a midwestern university. A research assistant and I interviewed four undergraduate preservice teachers across two semesters while they were enrolled in teacher education courses, specifically educational psychology and multicultural education. We conducted both group and individual interviews to understand the participants' experiences in secondary schools, in their families, and in college, as well as their expectations for teaching.

[4]In using the descriptor "boy-man," I draw on Jeal's (1990) biography of Baden-Powell, the founder of the worldwide Boy Scout Movement.

[5]The direct exploitation of animality (savagery) for Western male domination has a long history in the United States. Gail Bederman (1995) directly links psychologist G. Stanley Hall and Theodore Roosevelt with this turn-of-the-century association between developing masculinity and promoting civilization by using animal or primitive energy. These primitive energies were gathered by being in nature, by hunting, by competitive games, and through righteous wars.

[6]Cited in Freeman (1997:22). Freeman adds that many players face drug withdrawal rigors at the end of each season.

[7]The pain principle and its collective making and remaking are an example of what Connell (1995) calls body-reflexive practices, which are an important dimension of masculinity.

[8]Professor Linda Bensel-Meyers blew the whistle on unethical academic practices to keep athletes at the University of Tennessee eligible, and she has become a pariah. Meanwhile, two national groups of faculty, the Drake Group and the Rutgers 1000, have called big-time college athletics a corrupting influence on universities (Lipsyte 2000).

REFERENCES

Bederman, G. 1995. *Manliness and Civilization: A Cultural History of Gender and Race in the United States, 1880–1917.* Chicago: University of Chicago Press.

Bissinger, H. G. 1990. *Friday Night Lights: A Town, a Team, a Dream.* New York: HarperCollins.

Connell, R. W. 1995. *Masculinities.* Berkeley: University of California Press.

Davies, Lynn. 1992. "School Power Cultures under Economic Constraint." *Educational Review* 43(2):127–136.

DeBord, G. 1977. *The Society of the Spectacle.* Detroit: Red and Black Press.

Freeman, M. 1997. "Painkillers and Addiction Are Prevalent in N.F.L." *New York Times,* April 13, pp. 19, 22.

Jansen, S. C., and D. Sabo. 1994. "The Sport/War Metaphor: Hegemonic Masculinity, the Persian Gulf War, and the New World Order." *Sociology of Sport Journal* II:1–17.

Jeal, T. 1990. *The Boy-Man: The Life of Lord Baden-Powell.* New York: Morrow.

Katz, M. 1995. *Improving Poor People: The Welfare State, the "Underclass" and Urban Schools as History.* Princeton, NJ: Princeton University Press.

Lefkowitz, B. 1997. *Our Guys: The Glen Ridge Rape and the Secret Life of the Perfect Suburb.* Berkeley: University of California Press.

Lipsyte, R. 2000. "What Happens after the Whistle Blows?" *New York Times,* July 20, pp. D 1–D2.

Messner, M. A. 1992. *Power at Play: Sports and the Problem of Masculinity.* Boston: Beacon Press.

Miedzian, M. 1991. *Boys Will Be Boys: Breaking the Link between Masculinity and Violence.* New York: Anchor Books.

Mosse, G. L. 1985. *Nationalism and Sexuality: Middle Class Morality and Sexual Norms in Modern Europe.* Madison: University of Wisconsin Press.

———. 1996. *The Image of Man: The Creation of Modern Masculinity.* New York: Oxford University Press.

Nadelhaft, M. 1993. "Metawar: Sports and the Persian Gulf War." *Journal of American Culture* 16(4):25–33.

Sabo, D. 1994. "Pigskin, Patriarchy and Pain." Pp. 82–88 in *Sex, Violence and Power in Sports: Rethinking Masculinity,* edited by M. A. Messner and D. Sabo. Freedom, CA: Cross Press.

Stein, N. 1995. "Sexual Harassment in School: The Public Performance of Gendered Violence." *Harvard Educational Review* 65(2):145–62.

Weis, L. 1993. "White Male Working-Class Youth: An Exploration of Relative Privilege and Loss." Pp. 237–58 in *Beyond Silenced Voices: Class, Race, and Gender in United States Schools,* edited by L. Weis and M. Fine. Albany: State University of New York Press.

30

WORKING AT BAZOOMS
The Intersection of Power, Gender, and Sexuality

MEIKA LOE

Gender inequality has enormous consequences for women, men, and society. Gender inequality reinforces and perpetuates *sexism,* which is prejudice and discrimination against a person on the basis of his or her sex. The costs and consequences of sexism are extensive and include the wage gap, the feminization of poverty, high rates of female victimization as a result of male violence, and psychological and physical health problems in both women and men. This selection was written by Meika Loe, an assistant professor of sociology, anthropology, and women's studies at Colgate University, when Loe was an undergraduate. The award-winning study excerpted here utilizes in-depth interviews and participant observation to reveal how gender and sexuality affect one workplace culture.

T his [reading] is an investigation into power, gender, and sexuality in the workplace. This research is based on six months of participant observation and interviews at a restaurant I will call "Bazooms."[1] Bazooms is an establishment that has been described both as "a family restaurant" and as "a titillating sports bar."[2] The name of this restaurant, according to the menu, is a euphemism for "what brings a gleam into men's eyes everywhere besides beer and chicken wings and an occasional winning football team." Breasts, then, form the concept behind the name.

The purpose of this [reading] is to examine the dynamics of power, gender, and sexuality as they operate in Bazooms workplace. This is a setting in which gender roles, sexuality, and job-based power dynamics are all being constructed and reconstructed through customer, management, and waitress

Meika Loe, "Working at Bazooms: The Intersection of Power, Gender, and Sexuality" from *Sociological Inquiry* 66, no. 4 (November 1996): 399–421. Reprinted with the permission of Blackwell.

interactions. The first half of the [reading] describes how power, gender, and sexuality shape, and are concurrently shaped by, Bazooms' management and customers. The second half deals specifically with how Bazooms waitresses attempt to reshape these dynamics and to find strategies for managing the meaning and operation of gender, power, and sexuality. By using Bazooms waitresses as examples, I hope to show that women are not merely "objectified victims" of sexualized workplaces, but are also active architects of gender, power, and sexuality in such settings.

The Bazooms Workplace Environment

Bazooms is the fastest-growing restaurant chain in the nation. . . .

When I applied for a job at Bazooms in the winter of 1994, the first thing I was told was "The 'Bazooms girl' is what this restaurant revolves around; she is a food server, bartender, hostess, table busser, promo girl, and more." At the job interview I was shown a picture of a busty blonde in a tight top and short shorts leaning seductively over a plateful of buffalo wings and was asked if I would be comfortable wearing the Bazooms uniform. Then I was told that the managers try to make the job "fun," by supplying the "girls" with "toys" like hula hoops to play with in between orders. Finally, I was asked to sign Bazooms' official sexual harassment policy form, which explicitly states: "In a work atmosphere based upon sex appeal, joking and innuendo are commonplace."

Sixty "lucky" women were chosen to be "Bazooms girls" out of about eight hundred applications. Most of the "new hires" were local college students, ranging in age from eighteen to twenty-eight years, and as I found out later, more than several were mothers. The hiring process was extremely competitive owing to the fact that Bazooms hired minors and inexperienced waitresses. Also, everyone had been told that working at Bazooms could be quite lucrative. The general "Bazooms girl type" seemed to be white, thin, with blonde or brown hair, although there were several black, Chicana, and Asian American women in the bunch.[3] We all went through full-time training together (which included appearance training, menu workshops, song learning, alcohol and food service licensing, and reviewing the employee manual), and eventually were placed in a new location opened in Southern California.

Women work at Bazooms for a variety of reasons. No one in management ever asked me why I was applying, and I never told them, but the fact is that I applied for a position as a Bazooms girl because I wanted to know more about how the women who worked there experienced and responded to a highly sexualized workplace. I worked there for six months, during which I "became the phenomenon" (Mehan and Wood 1975).[4]

During my six months of participant observation and interviews with coworkers, I explained that I was interviewing people in my place of work as part of a class research project.[5] I made no attempt to construct a random sample of Bazooms girls to interview; rather, I interviewed those whom I felt closest to, and worked regularly with, and who I thought would feel comfortable responding honestly to my questions. The waitresses I interviewed for the most part were very committed to their jobs. Some were upset with their conditions of employment, and their voices may stand out for the reader. But I should emphasize that others, whose voices may not attract notice, expressed general contentment with the job. In the pages that follow I will present their views and my observations about the ways in which power, gender, and sexuality are constructed and negotiated in the sexualized workplace of a Bazooms restaurant.

Job-Based Power

Formal Power

Gender and power at Bazooms are reflected in its management structure. In this restaurant, four men manage more than 100 employees working various shifts: 60 Bazooms girls and 40 kitchen guys. In addition, both the franchise owners and the founders are all male. This is not rare. According to Catherine MacKinnon (1980:60), countless studies have shown that "women are overwhelmingly in positions that other people manage, supervise, or administer. Even in 'women's jobs' the managers are men." As in most workplace environments, formal authority and power are concentrated in management positions at Bazooms. In everything from scheduling to paychecks, floor assignments, and breaks, managers have the last word. In this way, Bazooms girls are placed in a subordinate position. This is not an unusual finding. MacKinnon contends that as "low-prestige" workers, women are often placed in positions of dependence upon men for economic security, hiring, retention, and advancement.

In these dependent situations, a woman's job is literally on the line all the time. One waitress whom I interviewed described management procedures for getting a worker fired at a Colorado Bazooms as follows:

> *All of a sudden, we would have menu tests and we were told that if we missed too many we would be fired. Now, I know I missed about twenty. These girls they wanted to fire missed less than that, I'm sure. They were fired right away because they missed some . . . but they didn't say a thing to me. Or, if they really wanted to get rid of certain people, they would put up one schedule, then put a different copy up with different hours (the "real" one) after the girls left. The girls wouldn't know, so they were fired for not showing up to their shifts.*

Disciplinary action based upon "company rules" is one of management's most common exertions of power. Before every shift, managers hold "jump start" which, in theory, is supposed to motivate the workers to "get out there and have fun." Instead, it becomes an ideal time for management to assert authority. Each waitress is quickly checked for uniform cleanliness, "natural" yet "styled" hair, make-up, and so forth. Then the group is counseled on "proper" Bazooms girl behavior and attitude. Sometimes "pop quizzes" are given to each woman, with questions about proper Bazooms girl service and responsibilities. At other times, lectures are given reiterating rules that have been ignored or broken earlier in the week. The practice of "jump start," at the beginning of each shift, operates in a way that makes power relations explicit. Lori was simply told at jump start in front of fifteen others: "That necklace doesn't work," leaving her feeling hurt, confused, and uncomfortable.[6] Contrary to its name, jump start usually does little to build morale. At another jump start, Janine was told to take her hair down:

> *I felt like I was going to cry. I spent all of this time and effort putting it into a French twist, all pretty and styled and they tell me to take it down. The rest of the night I felt so self-conscious, I did a really bad job on the floor.*

In short, male management's right to exercise veto power over each worker's appearance, attitude, and so forth reflects gendered power relations at Bazooms.

Informal Power

Besides having the ultimate say in formal matters such as scheduling, hiring, and firing, male managers sustain dominance at Bazooms in other, more subtle, ways. Eleanor LaPointe (1992:382) identifies a number of "interactional techniques" often used by men to sustain dominance and maintain the inferior status of women. At Bazooms such power was exercised by the use of derogatory terms of address, disciplinary actions, direct orders, threats, general avoidance of waitresses' concerns, cynicism, and even humiliation. For instance, the fact that female employees between the ages of eighteen and thirty are called girls by Bazooms managers and customers alike is an example of such an "interactional technique" used to sustain dominance. Everyone knows that the managers (all men in their twenties and thirties) are not to be called boys (neither are the "kitchen guys" to be called boys). Yet, by seeing and addressing the "low-status" employees as girls (based upon the "Bazooms girl" concept), one can retain dominance as a manager or customer (since waitresses are referred to by all as Bazooms girls) and maintain the subordinate status of female employees. Humiliating comments during the work shift about personal appearance (such as those that Lori and Janine received) from managers is another example of an interactional technique causing Bazooms girls to feel that they aren't respected or that they are treated poorly. In the words of one (Trina), "*[The management] has no respect for any of us waitresses. No respect.*"

Gender

It has already been established that Bazooms is a "gendered workplace," where, according to MacKinnon (1980), women "tend to be employed in occupations that are considered 'for women,' to be men's subordinates on the job and to be paid less than men both on the average and for the same work." . . . The notion of "women's work" is based upon the gendered division of labor, in which women occupy roles that are seen as "natural." Besides taking on "female" tasks, in the sex-typed workplace it is commonly known that a woman at work must "act like a woman." This may mean embodying "traditionally female" behavior and roles, besides dressing or behaving "feminine."[7] Women's work, to Paules, involves "job tasks which center around traditionally female duties: serving, waiting, smiling, flattering; and emphasize putatively female qualities: patience, sociability, submissiveness" (1991:170).

Behavior Rules

Management codes and guidelines shape gendered identities in work environments. At Bazooms, women work as "girls." According to one Bazooms manager, "What differentiates us from every other restaurant in the marketplace are the Bazooms girls. That's the reason that there's a Bazooms concept, that's the reason that we're successful." . . .

The following are Bazooms girl guidelines selected from the employee handbook:

- ▾ Wholesome-looking, All American cheerleading types (the kind you would be proud to take home to mother). Prom-like appearance.
- ▾ Hair should always be styled. The girls are always "on stage" and should be camera ready at all times.
- ▾ Make-up needs to be worn. It should not be excessive, and at the same time it needs to highlight her natural features.
- ▾ Always smiling, extremely friendly and courteous.
- ▾ Always should appear to be having a great time.
- ▾ Extremely attentive to all customers. . . .

Simultaneously she is "the girl next door," the "cheerleader," the "actress" (always camera-ready), the "good daughter" (attentive, subservient), the "prom queen," and the shining, happy personality. One waitress said matter-of-factly, *"It's like they [managers] have an ideal image in their heads of us"* (Katy). With all of these demands placed upon her, the Bazooms girl is constantly in the process of learning how to adapt to the company's expectations, and acting out her gender (according to men's rules).

Appearance Rules

It is clear from these guidelines that the "Bazooms girl" role embodies what are seen as traditionally "feminine" (in this case, many "girlish") qualities. One way gender is symbolized is through uniform style, which, according to LaPointe (1992), "incorporates a gendered meaning into the work" (p. 382).[8] The uniforms, short shorts, and choice of tight tank top, crop, or tight T-shirt, may be part of the popular "beach theme," which Bazooms likes to accentuate, but it carries gendered meaning as well. Few men, if any, work in what is considered a "neighborhood restaurant" wearing a size too small dolphin shorts and a shirt showing off his midriff and chest.[9] But for a woman this is "beach wear," revealing her truly feminine characteristics.

Barbara Reskin and Patricia Roos (1987:9) argue that the "sexual division of labor is grounded in stereotypes of innate sex differences in traits and abilities, and maintained by gender-role socialization and various social control mechanisms." . . . The director of training at Bazooms advised new hires to *"look like you are going on a date. You were chosen because you all are pretty. But I say makeup makes everyone look better. Push-up bras make everyone look better. And we all want to look our best."* These "feminine ideals" not only define "the perfect" Bazooms girl, but are used by management to constantly reify femininity in the workplace through the dissemination of "rules" and the use of discipline to uphold these rules. In this way, through interaction, not only power relations but gender roles are constantly being defined and redefined in the workplace.

Emotional Labor

The gendered workplace demands more than manipulation of behavior and appearance. Arlie Hochschild's (1979) ethnography of flight attendants introduces another type of labor that is common in female-dominated occupations, which she dubs "emotional labor." Emotional labor requires one to *induce or suppress feeling* in order to sustain an outward countenance that produces the desired state of mind in others (Hochschild 1983:7). Thus, emotion workers must always "display" an image that is determined by management, and "over time 'display' comes to assume a certain relation to feeling" (p. 90). Hochschild found that emotion workers, over time, may become estranged from their true feelings, which are ignored, disguised, or created in order to achieve a desired image.[10]

Hochschild's notion of "display" and manipulation of feeling can be found at Bazooms, especially among the female employees. According to management, the Bazooms girl, when on the floor, is expected to "perform as if [she] is on stage." This means embodying a specific image, sustaining an outward countenance, and behaving in specific ways. One manager with whom I spoke put it this way:

> Well, after working eight years I can pretty much tell who will be perfect for the job and who won't. [By looking at them?] Well, by talking with them and seeing what type of personality they have. You know, they must be performers as Bazooms girls. Nobody can be bubbly that long, but when you're working you put on an act.

As Greta Paules (1991:160) put it, "By furnishing the waitress with a script, a costume, and a backdrop of a servant, the restaurant is encouraging her to become absorbed in her role—to engage in deep acting." . . .

The corporate image that Bazooms projects of happy, sexy, eager-to-serve workers is what sells. What became clear to me on one of my first days on the job was that emotional labor is demanded not only by management, but by customers as well. For instance, one afternoon I approached a table full of marines without a smile or a "Can I help you?" look on my face. Their first words to me were, "You look pissed." I felt I had to make excuses for what I realized was poor emotion management on my part.

Deference is a large portion of emotion work, according to Hochschild. "Ritualized deference is always involved when one is in a subordinate position" (Reskin and Roos 1987:8). Clearly, in the service industry, employees (the majority women) are expected to have been trained in "niceness" from an early age (Girls are made of sugar and spice and everything nice). So "working as women" (or girls) naturally assumes that "a friendly and courteous manner" will be incorporated into the job. During training at Bazooms, new hires were instructed to "kill them [rude customers] with kindness and class." In other words, suppress any desire to yell or lecture rude customers, and instead, defer to the old maxim "the customer always is right," and treat them only with kindness. In this case, emotion work entails being at the service of others to the point of devaluing oneself and one's own emotions. Because of their subordination and vulnerable positioning, women become easy targets of verbal abuse, and of others' (managers', customers', even colleagues') displaced feelings. When kindness is not effective enough in handling rude customers, Bazooms asks their waitresses to defer to the management. "Problems" are then handled by the men, who must also manage their emotions, but they are more allowed to wield anger, since they have been socialized to express "negative" emotions from an early age (Hochschild 1983:163).

In a gendered workplace, one cannot ignore the gender roles that employees are expected to enact. At Bazooms, sex-typed behavior, appearance, and emotion management are all part of the Bazooms girl concept. This concept is commodified and sold, producing pressures from management (who see the Bazooms girl as the secret to their success) and customers (who come expecting happy and smiling, sexy "girls") on waitresses to perfectly embody the Bazooms girl image.

The Sexualized Workplace

It is beyond my—my mental capacity to understand how anyone could walk into a [Bazooms] restaurant and apply for a job and look at the sign and look at the—the concept and look at the uniform and not understand that female sex appeal is an essential ingredient in the concept.

—MR. McNEIL, MANAGER OF BAZOOMS, MINNESOTA

At the turn of the century Emma Goldman suggested, "Nowhere is woman treated according to the merit of her work but rather as a sex. . . . She must assert herself as a personality, not as a sex commodity" (1870:7, 12). Close to a century later, Catherine MacKinnon (1980) related a similar point in her book

Sexual Harassment of Working Women: "Most women perform the jobs they do because of their gender, with the element of sexuality pervasively explicit" (p. 60). According to Goldman, MacKinnon, and other feminist theorists, women not only work "as women" but as *sexualized* women.

Bazooms makes no secret about sexuality as a part of its key to success. The employee manual states in its sexual harassment policy that employees should be aware that they are employed in an establishment "based upon female sex appeal." As Mr. McNeil pointed out, everything right down to the waitresses' uniforms and the name of the restaurant connotes sex appeal. The slang term *bazooms* is usually used in the context of male desire and breast fetishism; it is a term that treats one part of the female body as an object of sexual desire. Tanya, director of training for Bazooms, answered a new hire's question about the term *bazooms* in this way:

> So what if [Bazooms] means "tits." That doesn't offend me. It's all in fun . . . just six guys in Florida trying to be goofy. They used to want us to hide the fact that it means breasts. But now we figure, Why be ashamed of it? You girls should never be ashamed of where you work. And if anyone asks you what it means, you just say, "Whatever you want it to mean.

Why is female sex appeal such a great marketing success? Probably because it appeals to male fantasy. Customers (roughly eighty-five percent male at my workplace) buy into the commodified Bazooms girl, which they hear about everywhere. Since "no publicity is bad publicity" to Bazooms, Bazooms girls have been highlighted in popular magazines such as *Playboy*. In a leading national business magazine, Bazooms is described as a place with "food, folks, and fun, and a little bit of sex appeal." In fact, according to this magazine, the idea for Bazooms came from a Florida football player/contractor in 1983 who wanted "a mildly profitable excuse for swilling beer and ogling blondes." Thus, Bazooms is premised on women's bodies and their presence in male fantasies. This premise can be seen and heard constantly in the restaurant. Pages from the Bazooms girl calendar (similar to the *Sports Illustrated Swimsuit Calendar* but with "actual Bazooms girls" wearing Bazooms merchandise and bikinis) are posted in the men's bathroom. . . .

Comments that customers made to me reflect the "titillating" nature of Bazooms, and the expectations they have about what the waitresses symbolize. One man said he didn't want to embarrass himself, but he thought that I was "too wholesome" to work at Bazooms. Answering my question about why he didn't think I fit in, he whispered to me, "You are not slutty enough." Another male customer called me over to remark, "I've been watching you all night and I think you have to be the most innocent-looking girl here. This means that you must have a wild side and I like that." Both of these comments encapsulate this male fantasy of the virgin/whore. I was obviously too much "virgin" for both of them, but the second man made up for this by fantasizing that I had a "wild side" (the "whore" was simply latent or hidden away).

Further comments and behaviors reflected the sexualized expectations of customers. I asked one man who looked interested in buying a shirt, "Can I show you something?" pointing to the merchandise counter. The customer responded, "I'll tell you what I want to see . . ." and tossed a dollar my way. Another customer commented to me, "I will leave here dreaming about either the food or the women. I think it will be the women." In these limited exchanges with customers, it is clear that male fantasy is an explicit part of the Bazooms experience.

It is in this sexually charged workplace catering to male fantasy that "masculine culture" emerges. A major newspaper describes Bazooms as "a lot of men's idea of big fun." With women (Bazooms girls) "acting out" feminine roles (pet, mother, sex object), men (customers) perform as well. At Bazooms, customers perform masculinity rituals, often in groups. One might encounter groups of male customers engaging in a number of masculine "acts." These generally include flirting with waitresses and vying for their attention, joking about body parts and other publicly taboo subjects, challenging each other in the area of alcohol consumption, setting each other up with waitresses, making requests for hula-hooping, and so on. For example, comments such as, "You give good head," can be heard among groups of males when a waitress is pouring beer. One man asked, "Why don't you wear the low-cut tank top?" while another said, "My friend wants to meet that girl over there. Can you get her to come over?" . . .

Socialized through interaction with customers, Bazooms girls learn to "manage feeling" in order to keep the customers as happy as possible. "The masculinity rituals [in the bar] would not be effective without the cooperation of the waitress. She has learned to respond demurely to taunts, invitations, and physical invasions of her personal space. . . . The cultural expectations are clear: she should remain dependent and passive" (Spradley and Mann 1975:133). In this way, gendered sexual identities, expectations, and roles are shaped through customer interaction. As the "audience, marginal participant, and sex object," the Bazooms girl is there to "enhance" masculine culture (add to the eroticism by playing out visual and interactive elements of male fantasy) and at the same time, enjoy the attention she gets as "the object" (p. 133).

The fact that Bazooms is male-identified is well illustrated by the feelings of intimidation experienced by female customers. The most common question asked by a female customer upon entering the restaurant is "Am I the only woman in here?" Although there are between six and fourteen Bazooms girls within the restaurant at any given time, the "men's club" atmosphere is quite obvious. . . .

Sexual Harassment and "Sex Joking"

. . . In her study of sex in the workplace, Gutek (1985:144) found that of a random national sample of 827 "traditionally employed women . . . 75% said that sexual jokes and comments were common in their places of work."

Similarly, Spradley and Mann (1975:95) found joking to be a powerful force in the work environment they studied. The "joking relationship" was essential to establishing the "masculine atmosphere" of Bradys' Bar, "centering on insults made in jest, direct references to sexual behavior, comments about anatomical features with sexual meanings, and to related topics normally taboo for conversations between men and women."

I observed numerous examples of this sort of sexual harassment/"sex joking" at Bazooms. Comments made by customers such as "You give good head," or "Your lips would be so nice to kiss," or "I wish I were in the shower with all of you," are not common at Bazooms, but they also are not taboo. I was warned by one Bazooms girl when I went to apply for the job: "You do have to put up with a lot of shit."

A national business magazine reports that "appropriate activities among [Bazooms] customers include winking, leering, nudging and smirking." According to Bazooms girl Sheri, there's something about the Bazooms environment that permits behaviors one wouldn't find at another restaurant. *"What makes it different is that Bazooms customers are a little more open because of the atmosphere. They [customers] are a lot more forward—instead of waiting a couple of times to establish themselves as regulars until they attempt to ask you something."* Trina also pointed out other ways in which Bazooms customers are anything but subtle in the Bazooms environment:"

> *It's really rare to be harassed at other places. But the kissing noises, referring to your body parts in any way, "hey-babying" and wiggin out [at Bazooms] . . . It's not worth my pride. Looks I don't consider sexual harassment because you can look all you want but once someone says something that offends you, that is pushing it.*

What a sexually permissive environment allows for is room for degrading comments, sexist behaviors, and "insults made in jest." As a consequence, women working at Bazooms reported feelings of hurt, embarrassment, and humiliation. . . .

Kanja felt embarrassed and upset about behavior that occurred at Bazooms:

> *The worst experience was when this rock station was in the restaurant and they were asking me and another Bazooms girl about which actresses had real or fake boobs. The last question was whether I had real or fake boobs. I just sat there silent, I was so upset. And then they started asking bra sizes at one of the tables. That just makes me so mad.*

In restaurants subtle yet pervasive forms of sex joking and sexual harassment are used as social distancing techniques that reinforce a waitress's vulnerable position and maintain her inferiority (LaPointe 1992:388; MacKinnon 1980:60). The joking relationship is asymmetrical; so, while women may "marginally participate," they must be careful not to say things that would appear coarse or crude. Thus, insults operate mostly one-way, initiated and followed up on by men (Spradley and Mann 1975:97).

Some Bazooms girls mentioned that they wished they knew how to "manage" better when it came to uncomfortable comments, sex joking, and innuendo. . . .

Part of the job responsibilities of the Bazooms girl is to be able to "put up with shit." In Katy's case, she realizes that she has to learn a lot in terms of dealing with customers' sexual comments (being the "conversational cheerleader") and not letting herself be bothered by them. Hochschild's emotion management takes the form of "sex-joking or harassment management" in this case. While Bazooms' management espouses an open-door policy for all workers, Bazooms girl Jeni describes management's ideal Bazooms girl:

> *What they want is the ones who can deal with people and shit and don't complain. They don't want you there if you are going to stick up for yourself.*

Gutek found that women working in female-dominated occupations (i.e., "traditionally female jobs") are less likely to report and view sexual harassment as a problem, because it is "part of the job" (1985:136). The idea that sexual harassment is part of the job at Bazooms came up constantly in subtle ways during my interviews. The fact that these women expected to have to learn to deal with sex joking and sexist behaviors from customers or managers is a commentary on what women are willing to put up with in the nineties workplace. . . . Bazooms' sexual harassment policy states specifically: "Sexual harassment does not refer to occasional compliments of a socially acceptable nature. It does not refer to mutually acceptable joking or teasing. It refers to behavior which is unwelcome, that is personally offensive, that debilitates morale, and that, therefore, interferes with work effectiveness" (Bazooms Employee Handbook).

The part that managers play in the "elimination" of sexual harassment at Bazooms has been criticized severely in sexual discrimination and harassment lawsuits in at least three states. A leading law journal charged recently that Bazooms' managers are breaking their own sexual harassment policies, and "promoting misogyny and inflicting it on their own employees and inviting the public to come in and inflict it on the employees." Ex-Bazooms girls point to one of Bazooms' most popular merchandise items—the Bazooms girl calendar—as an example of corporate misogyny. The calendar contains jokes referring to the stupidity of Bazooms girls, with the months out of order "because the Bazooms girls put it together." Media accounts say that managers defend these degrading comments as "humor, like Polish jokes." Degrading signs are posted at some Bazooms restaurants like the one in South Carolina where your receipt reads: "Caution: Blondes thinking."

Agency

What is missing so far in this analysis is women's responses to these dynamics. There is no question that by following workplace rules of dress and demeanor, Bazooms girls were participants in the interplay of power, gender, and sexuality in the Bazooms workplace. Some waitresses dressed and behaved in ways that emphasized their sexuality and encouraged male patrons' attention—strategies that were seen to result in bigger tips. The financial bottom line no doubt underlay most Bazooms girls' calculations about the trade-off between sometimes demeaning dress and behavior expectations and the wages and tips they could expect to receive. There were limits, however, to how much unwelcome attention or harassment the waitresses would tolerate. When these limits were reached, Bazooms girls resisted and manipulated their gendered and sexualized workplace role in a variety of ways. . . .

At Bazooms, waitresses work within and against the constraints imposed by these factors in at least three ways: (1) They attempt to undermine or otherwise challenge the power structure, (2) they manipulate gender to preserve self-image, and (3) they both co-opt and counteract sexualized identities.

Undermining and Challenging the Power Structure

At Bazooms, formal power can be undermined by informal means. Challenges to the established power structure at Bazooms mainly take the form of gossip. Waitresses often expressed negative sentiments and shared complaints about management's constant exercise of authority.[11] During any given shift, one may overhear comments made by waitresses such as, "*They always pick out the bad instead of rewarding or encouraging us on the good stuff*" (Lori), or "*You know we aren't respected at all*" (Trina), or "*I've never been in a restaurant where the workers are so badly treated*" (Kelly), or "*They are on a total power trip. Especially since they are in control of a lot of girls, and because they are men, they are taking that authority a bit too far*" (Teri). Thus, by coming together and sharing grievances, gossip can be a form of resistance.

In some cases at Bazooms, waitresses have been known to challenge managers directly on their policies. One waitress, after being denied a break for eight hours, let one of the managers know how she was feeling. "*I was so mad I was pretty much crying and he said 'Get in the office. What's wrong with you?' I said 'You know, you have no respect for any of us waitresses.' He said, 'You know, I should just send you home for good.' Then I shut up*" (Trina). This was a clear use of the interactional technique of threatening a waitress with the loss of her job to sustain the established power structure at Bazooms (classical management dominance and waitress subordination). In Trina's case, a boundary was set by management that could not be crossed unless she was willing to sacrifice her job. She "vented" backstage, by saying to me:

> If it comes down to it and [the manager] tries to get me fired, I will fight it. I've never been late, I'm a hard worker, and I bust my ass. I'm professional and I'm always dressed when I walk in. I'll take them. There are plenty of girls who will back me up on how the management treats us.

Another waitress became defensive and upset when she was told that her hair wasn't styled enough. In talking back, this waitress challenged authority and used informal power to get her way. (The manager on that particular day decided it was not worth arguing about and let her keep her hair the way it was.) In both of these cases, established power boundaries were consciously tested by management and waitress alike.

It is clear that even after indirect and direct challenges to the established power hierarchy by waitresses, management retains its ultimate power over workers. Direct challenges to authority generally are squelched, as reflected in Teri's statement, *"You can't talk back or you will get fired or written up. It's a power play."* Bazooms wouldn't be Bazooms without the established power hierarchy (males on top). Nonetheless it is important to note that the women who work at Bazooms do not simply accept these power relations. They struggle to create solidarity and actively resist the passivity management wants from them.

Gender-Based Strategies

Just as waitresses attempt to resist the power structure at Bazooms, they also resist and manipulate gender roles to fit their needs. As one would expect, not all of the women hired at Bazooms were comfortable with the Bazooms girl role they were supposed to embody on the job. Much of the controversy about taking a job at Bazooms centers around the uniforms. About half of my interviewees described initial nervousness and insecurity about the uniforms. But at the time of most of the interviews (two to three months after the interviewees had started work), these thoughts had changed.

> At first it was hard wearing the uniform. But after a couple of weeks I got used to it, since everyone else is wearing one and its the same as wearing sweats. What is wrong is that I've heard managers tell girls at this store to get smaller shorts. They didn't let me have a medium shirt, and they said my Colorado Bazooms shirt was too big and I couldn't wear it. That is wrong.

> The only thing I hate about the Bazooms uniform is that they tie the knots [on the back of the tank top] so tight that I can't breathe. And the nylons, they are always running and I have to buy new ones. They tried to get me to wear XX small shorts and I minded that. They made me try it on and I'm, like, "I'm not wearing this!" But the X small isn't bad. . . .

Each waitress went through a socializing process that often began with feeling nervous, even opposing the uniform. Waitresses then went through a period of adjustment based upon the fact that each wore the same thing as her coworkers did. Thus, as the definition of *normal* was revised, the nervous comments and complaints tended to subside. Yet, not everyone wears the same thing in the same ways. As their comments suggest, waitresses make choices about what to wear, and how to wear their outfits. The women made these choices based upon how comfortable they felt with the Bazooms girl image and their calculations about the financial utility of various style choices. Choices about whether to show cleavage, to wear a T-shirt (seen as more conservative by not highlighting the breasts) or a tank, to hike up the shorts, and so forth are also examples of negotiating the Bazooms girl's sexualized image. In other words, through manipulation of uniforms, these women manipulated the Bazooms girl concept to fit their own self-images and goals. . . .

But dress codes aren't the only thing that waitresses actively negotiate. Along with the dress codes come other pressures associated with "female-ness," especially in terms of appearance. [Trina] stated that appearance-based insecurities often became obsessions:

> *A lot of the girls are obsessed with the way they look. I know with our society looks are so important. I care about how I look. And there's not one girl in there who isn't really pretty. But I walk in there and people are talking about losing weight and stuff. It's too much based upon looks. I tell them "I can tell you how to lose fat, and I can do it if I want, but I like eating what I eat. . . .*

By being aware of pressures to be thin and pretty, and counseling [her] coworkers on resisting these pressures, Trina [was] actively redefining gender ideals in the workplace.

Counteracting and Co-opting Sexual Identities

Women who dress to get attention, to show off their bodies, to look or feel "sexy" in our society, often end up getting labeled "whore," or "slut," and may be seen as "asking for it." Many of the Bazooms waitresses were concerned that their provocative outfits would force them into one of these sexualized roles. In response to a sexual slogan printed on the back of every T-shirt and tank, one Bazooms girl stated, *"My hair covers the slogan, and we're not those kind of girls anyway."* Nonetheless, Bazooms girls are associated with "those kind of girls," that is, sex workers or prostitutes working in a sexually charged environment where sex appeal is part of the product commodified and sold in the marketplace to men. The girls I worked with became aware of these associations early on, and they spent much time sharing and reacting to these negative associations. One waitress was in the bathroom and overheard two customers comment to each other: "You'd better use the seat covers." "We don't know who these girls have been with." This she shared with the other waitresses, one of whom commented:

> *[Professional football players] come in here and think they are 'the ones,' that we'll do anything for them." According to one waitress, "One football player said, 'I'm just gonna make my rounds in this restaurant and get to all of them.' Well, [we] are not that stupid. Some may jump at the chance but [we] don't like being put down like that.*

Some of the women who work at Bazooms attempt to counteract these negative associations. One Bazooms girl remarked, *"We need to educate men. Just because you are wearing this uniform doesn't mean that you are asking for anything, doesn't mean that you want anything more than a job."* Several Bazooms girls made a point of telling customers that they were college students, or mothers, waitressing in order to save up money for education or family expenses. In this way the "girls" challenge the Bazooms girl (ditzy, sexual pawn) image most customers have and try to make the role more personal and respectable by sharing their own stories.

Some of the women, on the other hand, do not resist the negative associations but use them to achieve their own ends. In co-opting the "bad girl" role, some hope to appeal to customers by using sex appeal to their advantage, hoping to get bigger tips (or more attention) this way. To Katy, "learning to deal with people more sexually" is to be able to control the situation in order to avoid embarrassment. Although it is harder to get people to admit to using the sexualized image for their own ends, once in a while stories fly among customers and waitresses about "what some [Bazooms] girls will do for money." Playing up the sexualized Bazooms girl role can be a serious money-making strategy.

> I've seen girls hula-hoop and get money thrown at them. Then they lean over and give the cleavage shot to the men. And at the downtown store the girls do things with pitchers of beer to make it look like a wet T-shirt contest. These things just do not work for me at all.

> I don't get real into it and flirty. Some [of the girls] are flirty and that's part of their personality. But I'm not sure of the kind of treatment they get. I'm nice and I give them good service without anything else.

There appears to be a split among these women: those who try to resist the Bazooms girl role, downplaying the sexualized, flirty image, and those who co-opt it, embellishing it as their own. One employee rejects the company's expectation; another turns it to her own ends. While all of the waitresses knew of women who have co-opted this sexualized role, the attached stigma means that few will admit to doing it themselves. Lori came the closest, saying she didn't mind the attention.

Negotiation of Sexuality and Sexual Harassment

There are times when the Bazooms game goes too far. What may be fun and games to one woman may be sexual harassment to another. Responses to crudeness or to offensive comments or actions by customers take many different forms at Bazooms. Katy says that when customers deal "sexually" with her, "*I just get so embarrassed and walk away. But if they said something that offended me, I'd just go to the managers. I wouldn't even hesitate.*" Trina concurs, saying, "*We don't have to put up with jack. I won't take [offensive remarks]. It's not worth my pride. I give customers the gnarliest looks.*" Kristy's response to offensive remarks is different: "I usually just laugh and walk away." As illustrated in these differing instances, women are responding in varied ways to the sexualized nature of the job, and to offensiveness from customers. . . .

Harassment is taken for granted as part of the job at Bazooms. By defining abuse as part of the job, waitresses can continue to work without necessarily internalizing or accepting the daily hassles and degradations as aspects of their self-definitions or sense of self-worth (LaPointe 1992:391). In other words, if women enter into a waitressing job expecting crude remarks, degrading uniforms, and unnecessary management-based power plays, they may prepare themselves for the worst by setting personal boundaries, with conditions attached.

The waitress (Christine) who had her "butt grabbed" made a decision to deal with the harassment in a way that she thought would bring a higher tip. And it did. Another waitress, Twayla, made a decision to react quite differently in a similar circumstance. "I turned right around and told him, 'You will not do these things to me.'" These two women weighed personal priorities and dealt with similar sexual behavior in different ways. Christine decided to allow a man to cross a particular boundary—but for a price, turning the incident to her advantage. Twayla made clear her boundary would not be crossed. . . .

For others, self-esteem is more undermined than affirmed by the sexualization of the workplace, and the tips are not worth the price. *"Bazooms is kind of degrading sometimes,"* says Trina. *"[Customers] refer to us as if we are stupid. It's hard to explain, the way they talk . . . they are talking down to us."* Of course, contempt sometimes goes the other way. Trina goes on to add that the waitresses don't respect the customers either. *"I think the waitresses kind of look down on the men. Because all of them—it's like they are dirty old men."*

Conclusion

Bazooms is a good deal more than a "family" restaurant or a place where men can "swill beer and ogle blondes." It is a theater in which dramas of power, gender, and sexuality are played out. Within this drama, women play an explicitly subordinate role. As MacKinnon, LaPointe, Reskin and Roos, and Hochschild point out, their behaviors are severely constrained by the realities of employment in the service sector. Women are hired to put on a specific performance, and at Bazooms they are constrained by the formal script that Bazooms encourages its employees to follow. Furthermore, women are limited greatly by the assumptions men make about the appropriate and desirable place for women, especially in a sexually charged atmosphere. In the Bazooms environment, it is easy to classify these women as objects.

Yet, women are also actively shaping their own experiences at Bazooms. The constraints on their actions are severe, but within them women struggle to retain their self-esteem, exercise power, and affirm the identities they value. . . .

Bazooms girls are not helpless performers. They are women struggling to find ways to alter their roles, rewrite the script, and refashion the nature of the drama. . . . Women sometimes also turn the play to their own advantage, finding opportunities to increase tips, support their kids, and even find some affirmation of self worth.

In sum, the waitress is not a passive casualty of the hardships of her work. Within the structure of the job, she has developed an arsenal of often subtle but undeniably effective tactics to moderate the exploitive elements of her occupation and secure attention to her own needs (Paules 1991:171). Few people passively watch their lives go by. The notion of agency suggests that workers in all fields, regardless of their formal options, actively take at least some control of their own destinies. In the voices of Trina, Katy, Christine, and others we can hear women responding to their circumstances and asserting themselves as agents within the Bazooms drama.

ENDNOTES

[1] For reasons of confidentiality, all names used in this paper have been changed. Identifying traits (of this establishment) have been removed and identifying references are not included. This [research] was cleared through the University of California Human Subjects Committee as a student project.

[2] Bazooms' management likes to characterize their establishment as catering to families, probably in order to counter the sexy, bachelor-pad reputation that the local media assign to the establishment.

[3] Interestingly, only about half of the chosen group would be considered "busty" by society's standards.

[4] This falls under the category of opportunistic research or "auto-ethnography," in which the researcher becomes a participant in the setting so as not to alter the flow of interaction unnaturally, as well as to immerse oneself and grasp the depth of the subjectively lived experience (Denzin and Lincoln 1994).

[5] I am aware that covert research has come under significant attack from social scientists. The issue seems to be that of disguise: misrepresentation of self in order to enter a new or forbidden domain, and deliberate misrepresentation of the character of research one is engaged in (Denzin and Lincoln 1994). These issues do not apply to my project, since I did not disguise myself in any way in order to get "in" at Bazooms. The management did not ask why I was applying and I therefore did not volunteer the information. Furthermore, I was up front with my subjects about "doing a school project," upon interviewing them. Finally, with names and identities changed throughout, I cannot see this report inflicting harm in any way. All quotes (from waitresses) are based upon recorded interviews.

[6] Greta Paules (1991) notes that "the common interdiction in service dress codes against conspicuous jewelry may serve the same purpose as medieval decrees forbidding low-ranking employees to wear gold. In each case those of subordinate status are prohibited from assuming symbols of wealth or status that might obscure their position and blur class lines" (p. 134).

[7] Statistics from the U.S. Department of Labor, Bureau of Labor Statistics, 1984, show that the service industry was made up of sixty percent female workers (Reskin and Hartmann 1986:22).

[8] LaPointe argues that requiring employees to wear degrading uniforms emphasizes their "low status" and distinguishes them from their superiors.

[9] Recent news coverage did report that, based upon a four-year investigation, Bazooms is being charged $22 million by the Equal Employment Opportunity Commission for sex discrimination in hiring. Yet, amid recent controversy over the EEOC's decision, Bazooms Company took out full-page ads in major national newspapers to insist that men do not belong as servers at Bazooms. Each ad featured a picture of a brawny man ludicrously dressed in a Bazooms girl uniform.

[10] It must be mentioned that, like women, males are also often required to do "emotional labor" in the workplace. Nonetheless, as Hochschild points out, females hold the majority of responsibility for emotion work. According to Hochschild:

> With the growth of large organizations calling for skills in personal relations, the womanly art of status enhancement and the emotion work that it requires has been made more public, more systematized, more standardized. It is performed by mostly middle-class women in largely public-contact jobs. Jobs involving emotional labor comprise over a third of all jobs. But they form only a quarter of all jobs that men do, and over half of all the jobs that women do (1983:171).

[11] It is important to add that some of the waitresses believe "management is just doing their job," and don't complain.

REFERENCES

Denzin, N. K. and Y. S. Lincoln. 1994. *Handbook of Qualitative Research*. Thousand Oaks, CA: Sage.

Goldman, Emma. 1970. *The Traffic in Women*. Ojai, CA: Times Change Press.

Gutek, Barbara. 1985. *Sex and the Workplace*. San Francisco: Jossey-Bass.

Hochschild. Arlie. 1979. "Emotion Work, Feeling Rules, and Social Structure." *American Journal of Sociology* 85(3):551–72.

———. 1983. *The Managed Heart*. Berkeley. University of California Press.

LaPointe, Eleanor. 1992. "Relationships with Waitresses: Gendered Social Distance in Restaurant Hierarchies." *Qualitative Sociology* 15(4):377–93.

MacKinnon, Catherine. 1980. "Women's Work," and "Sexual Harassment Cases." Pp. 59–66 and 111–13 in *Sexuality in Organizations*, edited by D. A. Neugarten and J. M. Shafritz. Oak Park, IL: Moore Publishing.

Paules, Greta. 1991. *Dishing It Out: Power and Resistance among Waitresses in a New Jersey Restaurant*. Philadelphia: Temple University Press.

Reskin, B. F. and P. A. Roos. 1987. "Status Hierarchies and Sex Segregation." Pp. 3–22 in *Ingredients for Women's Employment Policy*. New York: State University of New York Press.

Spradley, James P. and Brenda J. Mann. 1975. *The Cocktail Waitress, Woman's Work in a Man's World*. New York: Wiley.

RACE AND ETHNICITY

31

"NEW RACISM," COLOR-BLIND RACISM, AND THE FUTURE OF WHITENESS IN AMERICA

EDUARDO BONILLA-SILVA

Race and ethnicity are the topics explored in the next four selections. *Race* is a creation of culture that reflects social distinctions and power. To say that race is a social construction, however, does not mean that race is not real. Many people believe in the existence of discrete biological categories and treat people differently based on their perceptions of race. The first reading, by Eduardo Bonilla-Silva, a sociology professor at Duke University, examines current racial relationships and racial inequality in the United States. In particular, Bonilla-Silva investigates what he calls the *new racism* and the *Latin-Americanization of race* in the United States.

In most postmodern writing, whiteness is regarded as an identity, a performance, a mere cultural construct or [it] is framed as a moral problem. In sharp contrast, we [believe] the idea that whiteness is the foundational category of "white supremacy" (Mills 1997). *Whiteness, then, in all of its manifestations, is embodied racial power.* Whether expressed in militant (e.g., the Klan) or tranquil fashion (e.g., most members of the white middle class) and whether actors deemed "white" are cognizant of it, *whiteness is the visible uniform of the dominant racial group.* Therefore all actors socially regarded as "white"—and, as I shall argue later, as "near white"—receive systemic privileges by virtue of wearing the white—or virtually white—outfit, whereas those regarded as nonwhite are denied those privileges.[1] This explains, for instance, why "not-yet-white" ethnic immigrants (Roediger 2002) historically strove to become white as well as why immigrants of color always attempt to distance themselves from dark identities (blackness) when they enter the United States' racial polity (Bonilla-Silva 1997; Bonilla-Silva and Lewis 1999).

. . . [Scholars] have addressed various aspects of whiteness as embodied racial power (e.g., whiteness in neighborhoods, whiteness by class, whiteness among biracials, whiteness in certain professions, whiteness among Latinos, etc.). In this [reading] I attempt to explain how whiteness survives in a country that proclaims to be "beyond race" and to forecast how whiteness will play out in the twenty-first century. First, I discuss the nature of the "new racism"—the racial structure (specific set of social arrangements and practices that produce and reproduce a racial order) that replaced Jim Crow in the 1960s and 1970s. I follow this with a description of the basic contours of "color-blind racism," or the racial ideology that bonds the "new racism." After explaining the structural and ideological context for whiteness in post–civil rights America, I suggest in the next section that whiteness will undergo a major transformation in the twenty-first century and become Latin America–like. I conclude . . . with an analysis of the political implications of the "new racism," color-blind racism, and the Latin-Americanization of whiteness and offer various strategies to challenge them.

Now You See it, Now You Don't: Post–Civil Rights White Supremacy

Although whites' common sense on racial matters ("We used to have a lot of racism, but things are so much better today!") is not totally without foundation (e.g., traditional forms of racial discrimination and exclusion as well as Jim Crow–based racist beliefs have decreased in significance), it is ultimately false. A number of researchers have documented the manifold subtle yet systematic ways in which racial privilege is reproduced in the United States (Feagin 2000; R. C. Smith 1995). I have labeled this new, kinder and gentler, white supremacy as the "new racism" and have argued that it is the main force behind contemporary racial inequality (Bonilla-Silva 2001; Bonilla-Silva and Lewis 1999).

Although the "new racism" seems to be racism lite, it is as effective as slavery and Jim Crow in maintaining the racial status quo. The central elements of this new structure are: (1) the increasingly *covert* nature of racial discourse and practices; (2) the avoidance of racial terminology and the ever-growing claim by whites that they experience "reverse racism"; (3) the invisibility of most mechanisms to reproduce racial inequality; (4) the incorporation of "safe minorities" (e.g., Clarence Thomas, Condoleezza Rice, or Colin Powell) to signify the nonracialism of the polity; and (5) the rearticulation of some racial practices characteristic of the Jim Crow period of race relations. In what follows, I explain why this "new racism" emerged and succinctly, because of space constraints, discuss how it operates in the area of social interaction (for a full discussion on how it works in other areas, see Bonilla-Silva 2001).

Why a "New Racism"?

Systems of racial domination, which I have labeled elsewhere as "racialized social systems" (Bonilla-Silva 1997, 2001; Bonilla-Silva and Lewis, 1999), are not static. Much like capitalism and patriarchy, they change due to external and internal pressures. The racial apartheid that blacks and other people of color experienced in the United States from the 1860s until the 1960s was predicated on (1) keeping them in rural areas, mostly in the South; (2) maintaining them as agricultural workers; and (3) excluding them from the political process. However, as people of color successfully challenged their socioeconomic position by migrating initially from rural areas to urban areas in the South and later to the North and West, by pushing themselves by whatever means necessary into nonagricultural occupations (Tuttle 1970), and by developing political organizations and movements such as Garveyism, the NAACP, CORE, La Raza Unida Party, Brown Berets, and SNCC (Payne 1995; Montejano 1987), the infrastructure of apartheid began to crumble.

Among the external factors leading to the abolition of the Jim Crow racial order, the most significant were the participation of people of color in World Wars I and II, which patently underscored the contradiction between fighting for freedom abroad and lacking it at home; the Cold War, which made it a necessity to eliminate overt discrimination at home in order to sell the United States as the champion of democracy; and a number of judicial decisions, legislative acts, and presidential decrees that have transpired since the forties.

These demographic, social, political, and economic factors and the actions of various racial minority groups made change almost inevitable. But ripe conditions are not enough to change any structural order. Hence the racial order had to be directly challenged if it was going to be effectively transformed. That was the role fulfilled by the civil rights movement and the other forms of mass protest by blacks that took place in the sixties and seventies (Payne 1995). Organized and spontaneous challenges (e.g., the over three-hundred racial riots in the 1960s) were the catalysts that brought down Jim Crow white supremacy.

"New Racism" in Social Interaction

Despite the real progress that the abolition of most of the formal, overt, and humiliating practices associated with Jim Crow represented, this did not mean the end of practices to reproduce racial hierarchy. Instead, new racism practices have replaced Jim Crow ones in all areas of life. In terms of social interaction among the races in neighborhoods, schools, stores, and other areas, whites and minorities (but blacks in particular) have very limited and regimented interactions.

Yet the way in which racial inequality is reproduced in this area is vastly different from how it was reproduced in the past. For instance, residential segregation today, which is almost as high as it was forty years ago (Lewis Mumford Center 2001; Yinger 1995), is no longer accomplished through clearly discriminatory practices, such as real-estate agents employing outright refusal or subterfuge to avoid renting or selling to minority customers, federal government redlining policies, antiminority insurance and lending practices, and racially restrictive covenants on housing deeds (Massey and Denton 1993). In contrast, in the face of equal housing laws and other civil rights legislation, covert behaviors and strategies have largely replaced Jim Crow practices and have maintained the same outcome—separate communities. For example, housing audits indicate that blacks are denied available housing from 35 percent to 75 percent of the time, depending on the city in question (Smith 1995; Yinger 1995). These housing studies have shown that, when paired with similar white counterparts, minorities are likely to be shown fewer apartments, be quoted higher rents, or offered worse conditions, and be steered to specific neighborhoods (Galster 1990a, 1990b; Turner, Struyk, and Yinger 1991).

In the realm of everyday life, several recent works have attempted to examine the experiences blacks have with discrimination (S. Collins 1997; Feagin and Sikes 1994). In his interviews of middle-class blacks who have supposedly "made it," Ellis Cose ([1993] 1995) repeatedly discovered a sense among these "successful blacks" that they were being continually blocked and constrained (see also Hochschild 1995). Cose cites the cases of a trade association vice president who is kept in charge of "minority affairs," a law partner always viewed as a *"black* litigator," a prominent journalist who is demoted for pointing out how race affects news reporting, and a law professor at Georgetown who is embarrassed by Harvard in a recruitment effort (Cose [1993] 1995, Chap. 1). The same pattern was evident in Sharon Collins' work in the Chicago area).

In 1981 Howard Schuman and his colleagues replicated a 1950 study of restaurants in New York's Upper East Side and found a substantial amount of discrimination remained (Schuman et al. 1983). Similar to the housing audits the discrimination was of a subtle nature. Lawrence Otis-Graham reports in his book *Member of the Club* (1995) that in ten of New York's best restaurants he and his friends visited, they were stared at, mistaken for restaurant workers, seated in terrible spots, and buffered so as to avoid proximity to whites in most of them. He reports that they were treated reasonably well in only two of the ten restaurants. The suits recently filed against Denny's, Shoney's, and the International House of Pancakes suggest that discrimination in restaurants is experienced by blacks of *all* class backgrounds (Feagin and Sikes 1994).

The existence of everyday discrimination is also confirmed by existing survey data. For instance, one study found that 38 percent of blacks report discrimination as a result of being unfairly fired or denied a promotion, 37 percent report harassment by the police, and 32 percent report not being hired for a job (Forman, Williams, and Jackson 1997). Similar to other studies, the rates of discrimination reported by blacks on any single item were quite modest (see also Bobo and Suh 2000; Sigelman and Welch 1991). However, a shift to the question of how many blacks have experienced at least one form of discrimination in their lifetime provides some intriguing results (they were asked about six different types): 70 percent of blacks report experiencing at least one form of major discrimination in their lifetime (Forman, Williams, and Jackson 1997). Students of color on predominantly white college campuses have also reported extensive patterns of daily discrimination (Feagin, Vera and Imani 1996).

Joe Feagin and Melvin Sikes (1994) also document the dense network of discriminatory practices confronted by middle-class blacks in everyday life. Although they correctly point out that blacks face discriminatory practices that range from overt and violent to covert and gentle, the latter seem to be prevalent. In public spaces the discriminatory behavior described by black interviewees included poor service, special requirements applied only to them, surveillance in stores, being ignored at retail stores selling expensive commodities, receiving the worst accommodations in restaurants or hotels, being constantly confused with menial workers, along with the usual but seemingly less frequent epithets and overtly racist behavior (see chapter 2 in Feagin and Sikes 1994).

Moreover, many of these patterns experienced by middle–income blacks are more apparent only because they have at least secured access to previously inaccessible social space. For low-income racial minorities, these kinds of experiences with daily discrimination are perhaps less rampant because they are, for the most part, physically excluded from white environs (neighborhoods, board meetings, classrooms, etc.; however, see my arguments about light-skinned Latinos and many Asians below). For example, in a study of families in several different school communities, low-income Latino families reported very little racial discrimination because they had contact primarily with other low-income Latinos in their neighborhoods and in the workplace. Discrimination was most apparent in those moments when these parents had to interact with large public institutions, where they reported rampant disrespect and disregard if not explicit racism (Fine and Weis 1998). Tyrone Forman and colleagues also found a similar pattern in their study of African Americans in the Detroit metropolitan area. That is, blacks who have attended college or received a college degree report experiencing more discrimination than those who have not (Forman, Williams, and Jackson 1997).

This almost invisible racial structure maintains the "wages of whiteness" (Du Bois [1920] 1969) at the social, economic, political, and even psychological levels. By hiding their racial motif, new racism practices have become the present-day Trojan horse of white power.

Color-Blind Racism: How Whites Justify Contemporary Racial Inequality

If Jim Crow's racial structure has been replaced by a "new racism," what happened to Jim Crow racial ideology? What happened to beliefs about minorities' mental, moral, and intellectual inferiority?—to the idea that "it is the [black's] own fault that he is a lower-caste . . . a lower-class man" or the assertion that blacks lack initiative, are shiftless, and have no sense of time; in short, what happened to the basic claim that minorities (but again, blacks in particular) are subhuman? (Dollard 1949:372). Social analysts of all stripes agree that most whites no longer subscribe to these tenets in a traditional, straightforward fashion. However, this does not mean the "end of racism," as a few conservative commentators have suggested (D'Souza 1995; Thernstrom and Thernstrom 1997). Instead, a new powerful racial ideology[2] has emerged that combines elements of liberalism with culturally based antiminority views to justify the contemporary racial order: color-blind racism. Yet this new ideology is a curious one. Although it engages, as all such ideologies do, in "blaming the victim," it does so in a very indirect "now you see it, now you don't" style that matches perfectly the character of the "new racism." In this section, I discuss briefly its central frames with examples drawn from in-depth interviews conducted as part of the 1997 Survey of College Students' Social Attitudes and the 1998 Detroit Area Study (DAS henceforth)[3] and from the material presented by [other authors] (for a full discussion of all the features of this ideology, see Bonilla-Silva 2003).

The Frames of Color-Blind Racism

Color-blind racism has four central frames, namely, *abstract liberalism, naturalization, cultural racism,* and *minimization of racism*. I illustrate here the first two frames and explain how whites use them to defend and, ultimately, justify contemporary racial inequality.

Abstract Liberalism: Unmasking Reasonable Racism When minorities were slaves, contract laborers, or *"braceros,"* the principles of liberalism and humanism were not extended to them. Today whites believe minorities are part of the body-politic but extend the ideas associated with liberalism in an *abstract* and *decontextualized* manner ("I am all for equal opportunity, that's why I oppose affirmative action") that ends up rationalizing racially unfair situations. An archetypal example of how whites use this frame to oppose racial fairness is Sue, a college student in a southern university. When asked if minority students should be provided unique opportunities to be admitted into universities, Sue stated:

I don't think that they should be provided with unique opportunities. I think that they should have the same opportunities as everyone else. You know, it's up to them to meet the standards and whatever that's required for entrance into universities or whatever. I don't think that just because they're a minority that they should, you know, not meet the requirements, you know.

Sue, like most whites in contemporary America, ignores the effects of past and contemporary discrimination on the social, economic, and educational status of minorities. Therefore, by supporting equal opportunity for everyone without a concern for the savage racial inequalities between whites and minorities, her stance safeguards white privilege.

Naturalization: Decoding the Meaning of "That's the Way It Is"   A frame that has not yet been brought to the fore by social scientists is whites' naturalization of race-related matters. Whites invoke this frame mostly when discussing school or neighborhood matters to explain the limited contact between whites and minorities and to justify whites' preference for whites as significant others. The word ("natural") or the phrase "that's the way it is" is often interjected to normalize events or actions that could otherwise be interpreted as racially motivated (residential segregation) or racist (preference for whites as friends and partners). For instance, Bill, a manager in a manufacturing firm, explained the limited level of school integration as follows:

Bill: *I don't think it's anybody's fault. Because people tend to group with their own people. Whether it's white or black or upper-middle-class or lower-class or, you know, upper-class, you know, Asians. People tend to group with their own. Doesn't mean if a black person moves into your neighborhood, they shouldn't go to your school. They should and you should mix and welcome them and everything else, but you can't force people together. If people want to be together, they should intermix more.*

Interviewer: *OK. So the lack of mixing is really just kind of an individual lack of desire?*

Bill: *Well, individuals, it's just the way it is. You know, people group together for lots of different reasons: social, religious. Just as animals in the wild, you know. Elephants group together, cheetahs group together. You bus a cheetah into an elephant herd because they should mix? You can't force that [laughs].*

Bill's crude, unflattering, and unfitting metaphor comparing racial segregation to the separation of species, however, is not the only way of using the naturalization frame. Many whites naturalize in a gentler fashion. For instance, Steve and Jan Hadley . . . explain their lack of racial mix in their neighborhood and in the schools their children attended as follows:

Steve: *No, I mean, it, it just happened. So, um.*

Jan: *No, it's just, it's based on the churches, you know, the four churches that own the school and—*

> Steve: *Yeah, and, they, they're from the south county also so, and there just are, there aren't many blacks.*
>
> Jan: *Unless they are part of the bussing program, and you will find that in the public school system, but not in the private sector. So. And that's, I mean, that's not a problem as far as I'm—see, we have black friends, but it just happens to work out that way.*

Despite whites' belief that residential and school segregation, friendship, and attraction are natural, raceless occurrences, social scientists have documented how racial considerations affect all these issues. For example, residential segregation is created by white buyers searching for white neighborhoods and aided by Realtors, bankers, and sellers. As white neighborhoods develop, white schools follow—an outcome that further contributes to the process of racial isolation. Socialized in a "white habitus" (Bonilla-Silva 2003) and influenced by our Eurocentric culture, it is no wonder whites interpret their racialized choices for white significant others as "natural." All these "choices" are the "natural" consequences of a white socialization process.

Although this frame seems to contradict the color-blind script, it is in fact used to deflate charges of racism. If someone argues that whites go to school, live with, befriend, and date other whites, whites can say "It's a natural thing" and that all groups do it. Hence something that presumably everybody does "naturally" is something that is "beyond race."

The Latin-Americanization of Whiteness in the United States

What will be the cartography of whiteness in twenty-first-century America? Who will be "white" and who will be "nonwhite"? Will the traditional (albeit always somewhat porous) lines of whiteness and nonwhiteness remain or will they be reconfigured? In what follows I suggest that whiteness will shed its traditional garb and slip into Latin American–like clothes. Specifically, I argue that the United States will develop a triracial system with "whites" at the top, an intermediary group of "honorary whites"—similar to the coloreds in South Africa—and a nonwhite group or the "collective black" at the bottom (see Figure 1). In addition, as is the case in Latin America and the Caribbean, I expect the color logic of white supremacy to become more salient. "Shade discrimination" (Kinsbrunner 1996), or preference for people who are light-skinned, will become a more important factor in all kinds of social transactions.

There are multiple reasons why I posit that whiteness will become Latin-Americanized. The most basic one is demographic-political in nature. The white population, which has always been a numerical majority in the country—with a few notable exceptions during some historical junctures in some regions—is decreasing in size and by the middle of this century may have become a numerical minority. This rapid darkening of America is

"Whites"

Whites
New whites (Russians, Albanians, etc.)
Assimilated light-skinned Latinos
Some multiracials
Assimilated (urban) Native Americans
A few Asian-origin people

"Honorary Whites"

Light-skinned Latinos
Japanese Americans
Korean Americans
Asian Indians
Chinese Americans
Middle Eastern Americans
Most multiracials

"Collective Black"

Filipinos
Vietnamese
Hmong
Laotians
Dark-skinned Latinos
Blacks
New West Indian and African immigrants
Reservation-bound Native Americans

FIGURE 1   Preliminary Map of Triracial System in the United States.*

creating a situation similar to that of many Latin American and Caribbean countries in the sixteenth and seventeenth centuries (e.g., Puerto Rico, Cuba, and Venezuela), or of South American countries such as Argentina, Chile, and Uruguay in the late eighteenth and early nineteenth centuries. In both historical periods, white elites realized their countries were becoming majority nonwhite and devised a number of strategies (unsuccessful in the former and successful in the latter) to whiten their population and preserve racial power (Helg 1990). Although whitening the population through immigration or by classifying many newcomers as white (Gans 1999; Warren and Twine 1997) is a possible solution to the new American dilemma, a more plausible one is to create an intermediate racial group to buffer racial conflict, allow some newcomers into the white racial strata, and incorporate most immigrants of color into a new bottom strata.

---

*This is a heuristic rather than an analytical device. Hence not all groups are included and the position of a few groups may change.

Even though Latin-Americanization will not fully materialize for several more decades, many social trends that correspond to the emerging stratification order are already evident. For example, the standing of the groups in Figure 1 in terms of income, education, wealth, occupations, and even social prestige largely follows the expected patterns. Hence in general terms, whites have higher income, education, and better occupations than "honorary whites," who in turn have a higher standing than members of the collective black in all those areas.

If these groups develop significant status differences, those differences should be reflected in their consciousness. Specifically, if my Latin-Americanization thesis is accurate, whites should be making distinctions among "honorary whites" and the "collective black" (exhibiting a more positive outlook toward "honorary whites" than toward members of the "collective black"). Similarly, "honorary whites" should exhibit attitudes toward the "collective black" similar to those of whites (see them as "inferior," etc.). Finally, members of the "collective black" should exhibit a less coherent and more disarticulated racial consciousness than in the past,[4] as is the case of the subordinated caste in Latin America and the Caribbean (Hanchard 1994; Twine 1998).

Although assessing some of these matters is very problematic as few data sets include information on skin tone, the available data are very suggestive as they mostly fit my Latin-Americanization thesis. For example, various surveys on Latinos confirm that they tend to self-identify as "white." However, the proportion varies tremendously by groups in a manner that is congruent with my expectations. Whereas over 75 percent of Cubans, Argentines, Chileans, and Venezuelans identify as white, fewer than 45 percent of dark-skinned or Indian-looking Latinos such as Puerto Ricans, Salvadorans, and Dominicans do so (Rodriguez 2000). In line with this finding, data from the Latino National Political Survey reveal that Mexicans and Puerto Ricans—two groups primarily composed of people who will belong to the "collective black"—are more likely than Cubans—a group that will mostly be comprised of "honorary whites"—to be sympathetic toward blacks. More significantly, the degree of closeness toward blacks *was greater* among those Latinos who self-identify as black while those who self-identify as white who were more sympathetic toward whites and Asians (Forman, Martinez, and Bonilla-Silva unpublished).

Various studies have documented that Asians tend to hold antiblack and anti-Latino attitudes. For instance, Lawrence Bobo and associates (1995) found that Chinese residents of Los Angeles expressed negative racial attitudes toward blacks. One Chinese resident stated: "Blacks in general seem to be overly lazy" and another asserted: "Blacks have a definite attitude problem" (Bobo et al. 1995:78; see also Bobo and Johnson 2000). Studies of Korean shopkeepers in various locales have found that over 70 percent of them hold antiblack attitudes (Min 1996; Weitzer 1997; Yoon 1997). In a more recent study of Asians (Chinese, Koreans, and Japanese) in Los Angeles (Bobo and Johnson 2000), Asians were more likely than even whites to hold antiblack and anti-Latino views. In line with this finding and with my thesis, they held more positive views about whites than about Latinos and blacks. Not surprisingly, as the racial attitudes of whites and Asians are converging, their views on racial policies are too. For example in a recent poll in California, 78 percent of blacks and 66 percent of Latinos supported maintaining affirmative action, but only 27 percent of whites and 49 percent of Asians did so (Hajnal and Baldassare 2001). Similarly, as the views of Asians and whites converge, their political allegiances may too. The same recent study in California found that Latinos and blacks register mostly as Democrats, while Asians lean slightly toward the Democratic Party and whites split their party allegiances.

If groups develop status differences and translate them to their consciousness they should also show signs of behavioral and associational patterns consistent with their new position. Whites should exhibit a clear preference for associating with "honorary whites" and vice versa. "Honorary whites" should not favor mingling with members of the "collective black" but members of the "collective black" should favor associating with members who are higher in the racial order. The rates of interracial marriage (the bulk of it is with whites) tend to fit the Latin-Americanization expectations. Whereas 93 percent of whites and blacks marry within-group, 70 percent of Latinos and Asians do so and only 33 percent of Native Americans marry Native Americans (Moran 2001:103). More significantly, when one disentangles the generic terms "Asians" and "Latinos," the data fit the Latin-Americanization thesis even more closely. For example, among Latinos, the groups that potentially include more members of the "honorary white" category, such as Cubans, Mexicans, Central Americans, and South Americans, have higher rates of intermarriage than the groups that have more individuals belonging to the "collective black" category, such as Puerto Ricans and Dominicans (Gilbertson, Kitzpatrick, and Yang 1996). Although interpreting the Asian-American outmarriage patterns is very complex (groups such as Filipinos and Vietnamese have higher-than-expected rates in part due to the Vietnam War and the military bases in the Philippines), it is worth pointing out that the highest outmarriage rate belongs to Japanese Americans and Chinese (the Asian overclass) (Kitano and Daniels 1995) and the lowest to Southeast Asians.

Data on racial assimilation through marriage ("whitening") show that the children of Asian–white and Latino–white unions are more likely to be classified as white than the children of black–white unions. Hence, whereas only 22 percent of the children of black fathers and white mothers are classified as white, the children of similar unions between whites and Asians are twice as likely to be classified as white (Waters 1997). For Latinos, the data fit my thesis even closer, as Latinos of Cuban, Mexican, and South American origin have high rates of exogamy compared to Puerto Ricans and Dominicans (Gilbertson et al. 1996). This may reflect the fact that these latter groups have far more dark-skinned members, which would limit their chances for outmarriage in a highly racialized marriage market.

Repercussions of Latin-Americanization for the Future of Whiteness in America

With some trepidation, given the data limitations I have pointed out, I suggest that the Latin-Americanization of race relations in the United States is already under way. If this is the case, what will be the repercussions for whiteness? First, the category white, which has always been fluid, as evidenced by the fact that over the last two hundred years it has incorporated "ethnic" groups such as Irish, Jews, Italians, Polish, Greeks, and so on, will undergo a major transformation. The white category will *darken* and include unexpected company as a segment of the "multiracial" community joins its ranks (Rockquemore 2002, 2003). "Whites" will also include assimilated light-skinned Latinos (Barry Alvarez, the football coach at the University of Wisconsin, Lauro Cavazos, former secretary of education under Reagan, etc.), some well-to-do assimilated Asians, and maybe even a few "blacks" who "marry up" (Ward Connelly, Tiger Woods, etc.).

Second, Latin-Americanization will force a reshuffling of *all* ethnic identities. Certain "ethnic" claims may dissipate (or, in some cases, decline in significance) as mobility will increasingly be seen as based on (1) whiteness or near-whiteness and (2) intermarriage with whites (this seems to be the case among many Japanese-Americans, particularly those who have intermarried). This dissipation of ethnicity will not be limited to "honorary whites," as members of the "collective black" strata strive to position themselves higher on the new racial totem pole based on degrees of proximity or closeness to whiteness. Will Vietnamese, Filipinos, and other members of the Asian underclass coalesce with blacks and dark-skinned Latinos, or will they try to distance themselves from them and struggle to emphasize their "Americanness"?

Third, whiteness will have a new ally in near-whiteness. "Honorary whites" will do the bulk of the dirty work to preserve white supremacy as they will think their fate is tied to whites. Two incidents reported by Norman Matloff in an op-ed piece in the *San Francisco Chronicle* (1997) are examples of things to come:

> In the newsletter of the Oakland chapter of the Organization of Chinese Americans, editor Peter Eng opined: "Chinese Americans will need to separate and distance ourselves from other ethnic immigrant groups" and suggested that Latino immigration was a burden to society.

> Elaine Kim, a Korean American UC Berkeley professor, has written that a major Latino organization suggested to her [actually to Korean community activist Bong-Huan Kim—added by Matloff] that Asians and Latinos work together against blacks in an Oakland redistricting proposal. And an Asian/Latino coalition is suing Oakland, claiming it awards too many city contracts to black-owned firms.

Lastly, the space for contesting whiteness and white supremacy will be drastically reduced, as is the case all over Latin America. As the mantra of "We are all Americans" becomes part of the fabric of the United States, traditional racial politics will become harder to maintain. Activists trying to organize in the future around the "we" versus "them" dynamic will be declared "racist" and accused of trying to divide the "long and hard-fought national unity."

How to Fight Whiteness and White Supremacy in the Twenty-First Century

How can we organize to fight a racial structure that is almost invisible, an ideology that denies being racial, and a whiteness that will be stretched out and be seemingly "inclusive"? In what follows, I outline a political strategy to fight the three heads of postmodern white supremacy in the United States.

The first head of contemporary white supremacy is the "new racism." I argued that because post-1960s racial practices tend to be covert, subtle, institutional, and apparently nonracial, white privilege is maintained in a "now you see it, now you don't fashion." Furthermore, because systemic advantage is less dependent on virulent actions by individual actors,[5] the average white person does not see "racism" or is less likely than ever to understand minorities' complaints. Instead, whites believe the passage of civil rights legislation leveled the playing field and thus regard any talk about racism as an "excuse" used by minorities to avoid dealing with the real problems in their communities. The filler for whites' racial narratives comes from the second head of postmodern white supremacy, color-blind racism or the dominant post–civil rights racial ideology.

I have suggested elsewhere that the task for progressive social scientists and activists fighting contemporary white supremacy and color-blind racism is to unmask the racial character of many of these practices and accompanying beliefs; to make visible what remains invisible (Bonilla-Silva 2001). To this effect, we can follow the lead of the Department of Housing and Urban Development, which has developed the audit strategy of sending out testers evenly matched on all characteristics except race to investigate claims of housing discrimination. This strategy can be used by researchers and activists alike in a variety of venues: banks, retail stores, jobs, and so on.

Another strategy that may prove useful is to do undercover work on racial affairs. Investigative news shows such as *Prime Time, 20/20,* and others have used this technique quite successfully to document discrimination. Lawrence Otis-Graham used this strategy for gathering data for his book *Member of the Club* (1995). Otis-Graham, who is a black lawyer, worked at a private golf club as a waiter and showed that elite whites talk about race in an old-fashioned manner when they are in the comfort of their (almost) all-white environments. We can use this technique in an even more effective manner if white progressives do the undercover work.

Yet uncovering these new racism practices and documenting the whiteness of color blindness, as important as this is, will not lead to a major change unless we can organize a new civil rights movement. The task at hand is to demand what whites do not want to give us: *equality of results.* Equal opportunity is not equal if the groups in competition do not have similar foundations (e.g., levels of income, education, etc.) and if some groups still suffer from discrimination. This new movement should demand proportional representation in everything. If blacks and Latinos represent 25 percent of the nation, that should be their proportion among lawyers, doctors, and engineers as well as among people in the nations' prisons. How to achieve this (reparations, affirmative action, a Marshall-like program?) is a matter to be fought and discussed by this new civil rights movement (for details, see Bonilla-Silva 2001).

I have left the last head for the end—the Latin-Americanization of whiteness—because I believe this will be the hardest one to slay. Why? Because if whiteness becomes Latin American–like, then race will disappear from the social radar, and contesting racial issues will be an extremely difficult thing to do (How can we fight something that is not *socially* accepted as real?) That said, my point is that race relations will become Latin American–*like*, not *exactly like* in Latin America. Hence, for example, the black–white fracture will remain in place, albeit in a changed format. Similarly, the deep racism experienced by dark-skinned Latinos will also form part of the future. Lastly, the discrimination that Asian Americans have experienced will not dissipate totally in years to come.

Therein lies the weakness of the emerging triracial order and the possibilities for challenging Latin American–like whiteness. Members of the "collective black" must be the backbone of the new civil rights movement as they are the ones who will remain literally "at the bottom of the well." However, if they want to be successful, they must wage, in coalition with progressive Asian and Latino organizations, a concerted effort to politicize the segments I label "honorary whites" and make them aware of the *honorary* character of their status. Dr. Moses Seenarine (1999), professor and a South Asian–Indian organizer recently put it:

> As long as a particular minority community continue to exclude others, they themselves will be excluded. As long as one group discriminates and are prejudiced to those who are poorer or "blacker" than themselves and their communities, they continue to reinforce and maintain the system of white racism. It is of no use of Indo-Caribbeans trying to distance themselves from Africans, or for South Asians distancing themselves from Indo-Caribbeans and Africans, because ultimately, these groups are all considered "black" by the dominant whites. Instead of excluding others, all "Indian-looking" peoples should build alliances with each other, and with African, Latino and other minority groups, to prevent racism in all of our communities.

This is the way out of the new quandary. We need to short-circuit the belief in near-whiteness as the solution to status differences and create a coalition of all "people of color" and their white allies. If the Latin American model of race prevails and "pigmentocracy" crystallizes, we will all scramble for the meager wages that near-whiteness will provide to all who are willing to play the "we are all American" game.

ENDNOTES

[1]Although the profitability of whiteness varies by class and gender (e.g., elite white men earn more than poor white women), *all* actors socially designated as "white" receive a better deal—more social, economic, political, and psychological benefits—than their nonwhite equivalents. Hence, poor white men do better than poor black men, poor white women [do better] than poor black women, and so on.

[2]By racial ideology I mean the racially based frameworks used by actors to explain and justify (dominant race) or challenge (subordinate races) the racial status quo. I have suggested that it can be operationalized as comprised of frames, style, and racial stories (see Bonilla-Silva 2001, 2003). In this [reading] I discuss only its frames.

[3]I was the principal investigator in these two projects. For details on these projects, see Bonilla-Silva and Forman (2000) and Bonilla-Silva (2001).

[4]This new disarticulated consciousness will reflect (1) the effects of a triracial order, which blunts the "us" versus "them" racial dynamic; and (2) the fact that members of the "collective black" can expect some real degree of racial (and class) mobility through association and marriage with lighter-skinned people.

[5]Most whites, unlike during slavery and Jim Crow, need not take direct action for "keeping minorities in their place." By just following the post-1960s white script (i.e., living in white neighborhoods, sending their children to white schools, and associating primarily with whites), they help produce the geopolitical and cultural conditions needed for white supremacy.

REFERENCES

Bobo, Lawrence and Devon Johnson. 2000. "Racial Attitudes in a Prismatic Metropolis: Mapping Identity, Stereotypes, Competition, and Views on Affirmative Action." Pp. 81–166 in *Prismatic Metropolis: Inequality in Los Angeles,* edited by Lawrence Bobo, Melvin Oliver, James Johnson Jr., and Abel Valenzuela Jr. New York: Russell Sage Foundation.

Bobo, Lawrence and Susan Suh. 2000. "Surveying Racial Discrimination: Analyses from a Multiethnic Labor Market." Pp. 523–60 in *Prismatic Metropolis: Inequality in Los Angeles,* edited by Lawrence Bobo, Melvin Oliver, James Johnson Jr., and Abel Valenzuela Jr. New York: Russell Sage Foundation.

Bobo, Lawrence, Camille Zubrinksy, James Johnson Jr., and Melvin Oliver. 1995. "Work Orientation, Job Discrimination, and Ethnicity." *Research in the Sociology of Work* 5:45–85.

Bonilla-Silva, Eduardo. 1997. "Rethinking Racism: Toward a Structural Interpretation." *American Sociological Review* 62:465–80.

———. 2001. *White Supremacy and Racism in the Post–Civil Rights Era.* Boulder, CO: Lynne Riemmer.

———. 2003. *Racism without Racists: Color Blind Racism and the Persistence of Racial Inequality in the United States.* Boulder, CO: Rowman and Littlefield.

Bonilla-Silva, Eduardo and Tyrone A. Forman. 2000. "'I Am Not a Racist But . . .': Mapping White College Students' Racial Ideology in the USA." *Discourse and Society* 11:50–85.

Bonilla-Silva, Eduardo and Amanda Lewis. 1999. "The New Racism: Toward an Analysis of the U.S. Racial Structure, 1960–1990." In *Race, Ethnicity and Nationality in the United States: Toward the Twenty-First Century,* edited by Paul Wong. Boulder, CO: Westview.

Collins, Sharon. 1997. *Black Corporate Executives: The Making and Breaking of the Black Middle Class.* Philadelphia: Temple University Press.

Cose, Ellis. [1993] 1995. *The Rage of a Privileged Class.* New York: HarperCollins.

Dollard, John. 1949. *Caste and Class in a Southern Town.* New York: Harper.

D'Souza, Dinesh. 1995. *The End of Racism.* New York: Free Press.

Du Bois, W. E. B. [1920] 1969. *Darkwater.* New York: Schocken.

Feagin, Joe R. 2000. *Racist America: Roots, Current Realities, and Future Reparations.* New York: Routledge.

Feagin, Joe R. and Melvin P. Sikes. 1994. *Living with Racism: The Black Middle-Class Experience.* Boston: Beacon.

Feagin, Joe R., Hernán Vera, and Nikitah Imani. 1996. *The Agony of Education: Black Students at White Colleges and Universities.* New York: Routledge.

Fine, Michelle and Lois Weis. 1998. *The Unknown City.* Boston: Beacon.

Forman, Tyrone, David Williams, and James Jackson. 1997. "Race, Place, and Discrimination." *Perspectives on Social Problems* 9:231–61.

Forman, Tyrone A., Gloria Martinez, and Eduardo Bonilla-Silva. Unpublished. "Latinos' Perceptions of Blacks and Asians: Testing the Immigrant Hypothesis."

Galster, George C. 1990a. "Racial Steering by Real Estate Agents: Mechanisms and Motives." *The Review of Black Political Economy* 18 (Spring): 39–61.

———. 1990b. "Racial Steering in Urban Housing Markets: A Review of the Audit Evidence." *Review of Black Political Economy* 48(3):105–29.

Gans, Herbert. 1999. "The Possibility of a New Racial Hierarchy in the Twenty-First-Century United States." Pp. 371–90 in *The Cultural Territories of Race*, edited by Michelle Lamont. Chicago: University of Chicago Press.

Gilbertson, Greta, Joseph P. Kitzpatrick, and Lijun Yang. 1996. "Hispanic Outmarriage in New York City: New Evidence from 1991." *International Migration Review* 30:445–50.

Hajnal, Zoltan and Mark Baldassare. 2001. *Finding Common Ground: Racial and Ethnic Attitudes in California*. San Francisco: Public Policy Institute of California.

Hanchard, Michael G. 1994. *Orpheus and Power*. Princeton, NJ: Princeton University Press.

Helg, Aline. 1990. "Race in Argentina and Cuba, 1880–1930: Theory, Policies, and Popular Reaction." Pp. 37–61 in *The Idea of Race in Latin America, 1870–1940*, edited by Richard Graham. Austin: University of Texas Press.

Hochschild, Jennifer. 1995. *Facing Up to the American Dream: Race, Class and the Soul of the Nation*. Princeton, NJ: Princeton University Press.

Kinsbrunner, Jay. 1996. *Not of Pure Blood: The Free People of Color and Racial Prejudice in Nineteenth-Century Puerto Rico*. Durham, NC: Duke University Press.

Kitano, Harry H. L. and Roger Daniels. 1995. *Asian Americans: Emerging Minorities*. Upper Saddle River, NJ: Prentice Hall.

Lewis Mumford Center. 2001. "Ethnic Diversity Grows, Neighborhood Integration Lags Behind." Report by Lewis Mumford Center. Albany, NY: University at Albany. Available from http://mumford1.dyndns.org/cen2000/WholePop/WPreport/MumfordReport.pdf.

Massey, Douglas S. and Nancy A. Denton: 1993. *American Apartheid: Segregation and the Making of the Underclass*. Cambridge, MA: Harvard University Press.

Matloff, Norman. 1997. "Asians" Blacks, and Intolerance. *San Francisco Chronicle*, May 20.

Mills, Charles. 1997. *The Racial Contract*. Ithaca, NY: Cornell University Press.

Min, Pyong Gap. 1996. *Caught in the Middle: Korean Communities in New York and Los Angeles*. Berkeley: University of California Press.

Montejano, David. 1987. *Anglos and Mexicans in the Making of Texas, 1836–1986*. Austin: University of Texas Press.

Moran, Rachel. 2001. *Interracial Intimacy*. Chicago: University of Chicago Press.

Otis-Graham, L. 1995. *Member of the Club: Reflections on Life in a Racially Polarized World*. New York: HarperCollins.

Payne, Charles. 1995. *I've Got the Light of Freedom*. Berkeley: University of California Press.

Rockquemore, Kerry Ann. 2002. "Negotiating the Color Line: The Gendered Process of Racial Identity Construction among Black/White Biracial Women." *Gender and Society* 16:485–503.

———. 2003. "Socially Embedded Identities: Theories, Typologies, and Processes of Racial Identity among Biracials." *The Sociological Quarterly* 43:335–56.

Rodriguez, Clara. 2000. *Changing Race: Latinos, the Census, and the History of Ethnicity in the United States*. New York: New York University Press.

Roediger, David R. 2002. *Colored White: Transcending the Racial Past*. Berkeley: University of California Press.

Schuman, H., E. Singer, R. Donovan, and C. Sellitz. 1983. "Discriminatory Behavior in New York Restaurants." *Social Indicators Research* 13:69–83.

Seenarine, Moses. 1999. "South Asians and Indo-Caribbeans Confronting Racism in the U.S." *Cricket International.*

Sigelman, Lee and Susan Welch. 1991. *Black Americans' Views of Racial Inequality*. New York: Cambridge University Press.

Smith, Robert Charles. 1995. *Racism in the Post–Civil Rights Era*. Albany: State University of New York Press.

Thernstrom, Stephen and Abigail Thernstrom. 1997. *America in Black and White: One Nation, Indivisible*. New York: Simon and Schuster.

Turner, Margery A., Raymond Struyk, and John Yinger. 1991. *The Housing Discrimination Study*. Washington, DC: The Urban Institute.

Tuttle, William M., Jr. 1970. *Race Riot: Chicago in the Red Summer of 1919*. New York: Atheneum.

Twine, France Winddance. 1998. *Racism in a Racial Democracy: The Maintenance of White Supremacy in Brazil*. New Brunswick, NJ: Rutgers University Press.

Warren, Jonathan and France Winddance Twine. 1997. "White Americans, the New Minority? Non-Blacks and the Ever-Expanding Boundaries of Whiteness." *Journal of Black Studies* 28:200–18.

Waters, Mary C. 1997. "Prepared Testimony of Professor Mary C. Waters, Department of Sociology, Harvard University." House Committee on Government Reform and Oversight, Subcommittee on Government Management, Information, and Technology. Washington, DC: Federal News Service.

Weitzer, Ronald. 1997. "Racial Prejudice among Korean Merchants in African-American Neighborhoods." *The Sociological Quarterly* 38:587–606.

Yinger, J. Milton. 1995. *Closed Doors: Opportunities Lost: The Continuing Costs of Housing Discrimination.* New York: Russell Sage.

Yoon, In-jin. 1997. *On My Own: Korean Business and Race Relations in America.* Chicago: University of Chicago Press.

32

BEYOND BLACK AND WHITE
Remaking Race in America

JENNIFER LEE • FRANK D. BEAN • KATHY SLOANE

Sociologists are concerned not only with how race and ethnicity are defined but also with the consequences of those distinctions. One important aspect in the social construction of race and ethnicity is how the U.S. government defines and measures both of these concepts. Until the 1990s, many government documents simply measured race as "white, black, or other." Think how difficult it would be to answer this question on racial identification if one had a parent who was African American and another parent who was Latina/o. Thus, in 2000, the U.S. Census began allowing Americans to identify more than one racial group on the U.S. Census forms. In the selection that follows, Jennifer Lee, an associate professor of sociology at the University of California at Irvine, and Frank D. Bean, a professor of sociology at the University of California, examine the consequences of this measurement change and the growing numbers of multiracial people in the United States.

Starting with the 2000 census, Americans could officially label themselves and their children as members of more than one race. Nearly 7 million Americans, 2.4 percent of the nation's population, were recorded as being multiracial. This option and these numbers signal a profound loosening of the rigid racial and ethnic boundaries that have so long divided the country.

The immigration patterns behind these changes also point to potentially important realignments in America's color lines.

How might a black father and a white mother fill out official government documents, like U.S. Census forms, requiring them to designate the race of their child? Before 2000, such an intermarried couple had no alternative but to list their child as either black or white. Similarly, a child born to a white father and an Asian mother had to be listed as either Asian or white, but not Asian and white. Not any more. Americans can now officially identify themselves and their children as black and white, or white and Asian. Indeed, respondents can now choose a combination of up to six different categories of races, including "Other." The 2000 Census reported one in every forty Americans was registered as belonging to two or more racial groups. Many sociologists think this ratio could soar to one in five Americans by the year 2050.

Why does this checking of additional boxes matter? For one thing, how people report themselves racially provides information needed to implement and enforce important legislation, such as the Voting Rights Act. The Department of Justice uses the statistics to identify places where substantial minority populations exist and may be subject to disenfranchisement. For another, the counts document social and economic disparities among racial groups in America. Countries like France that do not collect data on race cannot verify the existence and effects of racial discrimination even when other evidence suggests such discrimination is a major problem. These data also signal the official recognition and hence the influence of groups that define themselves on the basis of common national origin, skin color, or ancestry. Americans of Pacific Islander origin, for example, recently asked to be separately classified. On the other hand, critics worry that official data on race perpetuate rather than eliminate racial identities and divisions. A ballot initiative being circulated in California, for example, would largely ban the state's collection of racial information.

But the new opportunity to mark more than one race is also important because it indicates that people can now officially recognize the mixing of racial backgrounds in American society. If the United States was once thought of as a black-and-white society, this is certainly no longer so. Continued immigration from Latin America and Asia, the rise in intermarriage over the past 30 years, and the formal recognition of the multiracial population are moving America far beyond black and white. Yet, while America's increasing diversity implies that racial divisions may be weakening, it does not mean that race has become irrelevant. Instead, new kinds of color lines may be emerging. For now, however, the rearrangement seems to leave African Americans facing a new black–nonblack, instead of the old black–white, racial divide.

Why There Are More Multiracial Americans

The growth of the multiracial population is a result both of increasing intermarriage between whites and nonwhites and of peoples' increasing willingness to report their multiracial backgrounds. The number of racial intermarriages in the United States grew from 150,000 in 1960 to 1.6 million in 1990—a tenfold increase over three decades. It is still the exception rather than the rule for whites and blacks in this country, however. Just 6 percent of whites and 10 percent of blacks marry someone of a different race. By contrast, more than one-quarter of all native-born Asians and Latinos marry someone of a different race. (For this discussion, we will speak of Latinos as if they were a "race," although government forms count Hispanic background separately, so that people who say they are Latino can report themselves as belonging to any racial group, such as white, black, or Asian.) Even more striking is that two of every five young Latinos and two of every three young Asians born in the United States marry someone of a different race, and the majority marry whites. Asians and Latinos—many of whom are either immigrants or the children of immigrants—are three times as likely to marry whites as blacks are to marry whites.

Coinciding with the rise in intermarriage has been the growth of a new immigrant stream from Latin America and Asia. Today, immigrants and their children total more than 60 million people, approximately 22 percent of the U.S. population. The increase in immigration from non-European countries over the past 35 years has converted the United States from a largely white and black society into one that is comprised of numerous racial and ethnic groups. This, plus increasing intermarriage, and the increasing willingness of Americans to call themselves multiracial has changed the way race is measured in America.

The Origin of "Mark One or More Races"

Since its inception in 1790, the decennial U.S. Census has determined taxation, the numbers of representatives from each state, and the boundaries of Congressional districts. And it has always counted the U.S. population by race. The way that race is measured and even the racial categories themselves, however, have changed considerably. For example, in 1850, the Census added the category "mulatto," and in 1890, it added the categories "quadroon" and "octoroon" in an effort to more precisely measure the representation of black mixtures in the population. ("Mulatto" refers to people of mixed black and white "blood," "quadroon" to people with one-fourth black blood, and "octoroon" to those with one-eighth black blood). However, "quadroon" and "octoroon" were promptly removed in 1900 because they caused countless statistical inaccuracies. The Census Board determined that the "mulatto" category provided clearer data on the U.S. population with mixed blood, but eventually dropped this category in 1930. By that time, the law of the country, with the census following suit, had adopted the "one-drop rule" of hypodescent (by which all persons with any trace of black ancestry were labeled racially black) as an appropriate criterion by which to attempt to measure race. Importantly, census enumerators classified the people they interviewed by race.

In the 1960s, racial categories came under scrutiny once again, and the Civil Rights Movement prompted one of the most significant changes in the political context and purpose of racial categorization. The argument spread that Americans should be able to mark their own race to identify themselves and their children rather than leaving this to enumerators. Some politicians and experts asserted that the racial categories should more accurately reflect America's diversity and lobbied for new categories, distinguishing among categories of whites, and substituting the term "ethnic" in place of "race." Changes in the 1970 Census reflected some of these currents, with self-identification replacing enumerator identification in order to satisfy public sentiments. By the mid-1970s, groups wanting to be recognized as racial minorities organized advisory committees to seek official statistical representation so that they could participate in federal programs designed to assist racial "minorities." These advisory committees lobbied for the adoption of five racial categories—white, black, Asian, Native American, and other—by the Census and all federal agencies. In 1980, the Census categories changed yet again, this time including the category of Hispanic origin separately from race, and modifying one of the racial categories to Asian–Pacific Islander.

During the early 1990s, new advocacy groups arose with a different agenda. These groups criticized the government standards for not accurately reflecting the diversity in the country brought about by increases in immigration and interracial marriage. In particular, advocates from groups such as the Association for Multi-Ethnic Americans (AMEA) and Project RACE (Reclassify All Children Equally) lobbied the Census Bureau to adopt a "multiracial" category. Advocates argued that it was an affront to force them or their children into a single racial category. Furthermore, they argued that forced mono-racial identification was inaccurate because it denies the existence of interracial marriages, and is ultimately discriminatory. A year later, in 1994, the Office of Management and Budget (OMB), which managed this issue, acknowledged that the racial categories were of decreasing value and considered an alternate strategy: allowing respondents to identify with as many races as they wished. While the spokespeople for the multiracial movement were not entirely satisfied with this option, they conceded that it was an improvement over forced mono-racial identification.

Not everyone favored adding a multiracial category or allowing Americans to mark more than one race. Civil rights groups—and in particular, black civil rights groups such as the NAACP—strongly objected. They feared that those who would otherwise be counted as black or Hispanic would now choose to identify as multiracial and, depending on how such persons were counted, diminish their official counts. This, in turn, could undermine enforcement of the Voting Rights Act and potentially reduce the size and effectiveness of government programs aimed at helping minorities.

On October 30, 1997, the Census Bureau announced its final decision that all persons would have the option to identify with two or more races, starting with the 2000 Census and extending to all federal data systems by the year 2003. The racial options on the 2000 Census included "White," "Black," "Asian," "Native Hawaiian or Other Pacific Islander," "American Indian and Alaska Native," and "Other." While "Latino" or "Hispanic" was not a racial category on the 2000 Census, OMB mandated two distinct questions: one on race and a second asking whether a person is "Spanish/Hispanic/Latino." Because those who classify themselves as "Spanish/Hispanic/Latino" can be of any race, the Census asks both questions in order to identify the Latino population in the United States.

The Census Bureau's decision to allow Americans to "mark one or more races" is a landmark change in the way the U.S. government collects data on race. Perhaps even more importantly, it gives official status and recognition to individuals who see themselves or their children as having mixed racial heritage—an acknowledgement that speaks volumes about how far the country has come since the days when the "one-drop rule" enjoyed legal legitimacy. Moreover, such changes may mean that old racial divides are beginning to fade. Multiracial reporting, however, has not been equally distributed across all racial and ethnic groups. Rather, those who choose to mark two or more races are distinctive.

Who Are the Multiracials?

As we noted, in 2000, 6.8 million people, or 2.4 percent of the population, were reported as multiracial. While these figures may not appear large, a recent National Academy of Science study estimated that the multiracial population could rise to 21 percent by the year 2050 because of rising intermarriage, when as many as 35 percent of Asians and 45 percent of Hispanics could claim a multiracial background. Of the multiracial population in 2000, 93 percent reported two races, 6 percent reported three races, and 1 percent reported four or more races.

As Table 1 illustrates, the groups with high percentages of multiracial persons include "Native Hawaiian or Other Pacific Islander," "American Indian and Alaska Native," "Other," and "Asian." The categories with the lowest proportion of persons who claim a multiracial background are "White" and "Black."

The proportion of blacks who identify as multiracial is quite small, accounting for just 4.2 percent of the total black population. These figures stand in sharp contrast to those among American Indian/Alaska Natives and Native Hawaiian or other Pacific Islanders, who have the highest percentage of multiracials as a proportion of their populations at 36.4 and 44.8 percent, respectively. The particular combinations are of interest. Among those identified as black, Asian, or Latino, 2 percent, 7 percent, and 5 percent, respectively, also claim a white identity. Among Asians, the Asian–white multiracial combination is about three and a half times more likely to occur, and among Latinos, the Latino–white combination is more than two and a half times more likely to occur, as the black–white combination occurs among

TABLE 1   Multiracial Identification by Race: People Recorded as One Race Who Are Also Recorded as One or More Other Races

	Racial Identification (millions)	Multiracial Identification (millions)	Percent Multiracial
White	216.5	5.1	2.3%
Black	36.2	1.5	4.2
Asian	11.7	1.4	12.4
Other	18.4	3.0	16.4
American Indian and Alaska Native	3.9	1.4	36.4
Native Hawaiian or Other Pacific Islander	0.7	0.3	44.8

Source: U.S. Census 2000.

blacks. Why this is so is particularly perplexing when we consider that the Census Bureau has estimated that at least three-quarters of black Americans have some white ancestry and thus could claim a multiracial identity on this basis alone.

The tendency of black Americans not to report multiracial identifications undoubtedly owes in part to the legacy of slavery, lasting discrimination, and both the legal and de facto invocation of the "one-drop rule." For no other racial or ethnic group in the United States does the one-drop rule limit identity choices and options. Recent sociological studies find that about 50 percent of American Indian–white and Asian–white intermarried couples report a white racial identity for their children. In a study of multiracial Hispanic students, we found that 44 percent chose a Hispanic identity. Without the imposition of the "one-drop rule" that historically imposed a black racial identity on multiracial black Americans, multiracial Asians, Latinos, and American Indians appear to have much more leeway to choose among different racial options.

In addition, because a significant proportion of Latinos and Asians in the United States are either immigrants or the children of immigrants, their understanding of race, racial boundaries, and the black–white color divide is shaped by a different set of circumstances than those of African Americans. Most importantly, Latinos' and Asians' experiences are not rooted in the same legacy of slavery with its systematic and persistent patterns of legal and institutional discrimination and inequality through which the tenacious black-white divide was formed and cemented. For these reasons, racial and ethnic boundaries appear more fluid for the newest immigrants than for native-born blacks, providing multiracial Asians and Latinos more racial options than their black counterparts.

Remaking Race and Redrawing the Color Line

What do current trends and patterns in immigration, intermarriage, and multiracial identification tell us about the remaking of race in America? It appears that increases in intermarriage and the growth of the multiracial population reflect a blending of races and the shifting of color lines. Because interracial marriage and multiracial identification indicate a reduction in social distance and racial prejudice, these phenomena provide evidence of loosening racial boundaries. At first glance, these patterns offer an optimistic portrait of the weakening of color lines. For instance, interracial marriage was illegal in 16 states as recently as 1967, but today, about 13 percent of American marriages involve persons of different races. If we go back even further to 1880, the rates of intermarriage among Asians and Latinos in this country were close to zero, but now, more than a quarter of all native-born Asians and Latinos marry someone of a different racial background, mostly whites.

Yet, upon closer examination, we find that patterns of intermarriage and multiracial identification are not similar across all groups. Not only are Latinos and Asians more likely to intermarry than blacks, they are also more likely to report a multiracial identification. These different rates suggest that while racial boundaries may be fading, they are not disappearing at the same pace for all groups.

What is crucial here is how we interpret the intermarriage and multiracial identification rates for Latinos and Asians. If we consider Latinos and Asians as discriminated-against racial minorities, closer to blacks than whites in their social disadvantages, then their high levels of multiracial identification suggest that racial border lines might be fading for all nonwhite groups. Latinos and Asians look more, however, like immigrant groups whose disadvantages derive from their not having had time to join the economic mainstream, but who soon will. Their high levels of intermarriage and multiracial reporting therefore signal an experience and trajectory different from that of blacks. Their situations do not necessarily indicate that similar assimilation can be expected among blacks.

Based on the patterns of intermarriage and multiracial identification noted above, the color line appears less rigid for Latinos and Asians than blacks. Asians and Latinos have high rates of intermarriage and multiracial reporting because they were not and are not treated as blacks have been. While the color line may also be shifting for blacks, this shift is occurring more slowly, leaving Asians and Latinos socially nearer to whites. Much of America's racial history has revolved around who was white and who was not; the next phase may revolve instead around who is black and who is not.

The emergence of a black–nonblack divide in a context where diversity is increasing and other racial and ethnic boundaries are diminishing represents a good news–bad news outcome for America. That a white–nonwhite color line does not seem to be enduring is the good news. But that newer nonwhite immigrant groups appear to be jumping ahead of African Americans in a hierarchy still divided by race is the bad news. Based on immigration, inter-marriage, and multiracial identification, it appears that Latinos and Asians are closer to whites than to blacks, and consequently may be participants in a new color line that continues to disadvantage blacks.

As a final matter, one might ask: What does all of this imply for the future of measuring race in the census? Critics of racial labels argue that if racial and ethnic boundaries are loosening, we should abandon the use of racial categories in the census altogether and learn to get along without them in our policy making. They argue that if racial labels could be elimi-nated, racial discrimination itself would be eradicated. However, in the United States today, because the practice of discrimination based on physi-cal characteristics such as skin color continues to persist, at least for African Americans, eradicating racial labels would simply put us in a position where we know less about the disadvantages experienced by blacks and can do less about it.

RECOMMENDED RESOURCES

Bean, Frank D. and Gillian Stevens. 2003. *America's Newcomers and the Dynamics of Diversity.* New York: Russell Sage Foundation. This book explores the significance of immigration for America, including its implications for loosening racial and ethnic boundaries.

Davis, F. James. 1991. *Who Is Black? One Nation's Definition.* University Park: Pennsylvania State University Press. Davis details the history of the "one-drop rule" in the United States.

Gerstle, Gary. 1991. "Liberty, Coercion, and the Making of Americans." In *The Handbook of International Migration,* edited by Charles Hirschman, Philip Kasinitz, and Josh DeWind. New York: Russell Sage Foundation. A history of racial categories and how they have changed.

Loewen, James. 1971. *The Mississippi Chinese: Between Black and White.* Cambridge, MA: Harvard University Press. Loewen shows how Chinese immigrants changed their racial classification from almost black to almost white.

Nobles, Melissa. 2000. *Shades of Citizenship: Race and the Census in Modern Politics.* Stanford, CA: Stanford University Press. A history of racial categories in the Census in the United States.

Perlmann, Joel and Mary C. Waters, eds. 2002. *The New Race Question: How the Census Counts Multiracial Individuals.* New York: Russell Sage Foundation. This anthology examines the his-tory of racial enumeration, the likely effects of the Census change in the race question, and possible policy implications for the future.

Qian, Zhenchao. 1997. "Breaking the Racial Barriers: Variations in Interracial Marriage between 1980 and 1990." *Demography* 34(2):263–76. This study illustrates the growing trends in interra-cial marriage.

Waters, Mary C. 2000. "Multiple Ethnicities and Identity in the United States." In *We Are a People: Narrative and Multiplicity in Constructing Identity,* edited by Paul Spikard and W. Jeffrey Burroughs. Philadelphia: Temple University Press. Waters examines the different ways inter-racial couples identify their children.

33

AT A SLAUGHTERHOUSE, SOME THINGS NEVER DIE

CHARLIE LeDUFF

Racism is any prejudice or discrimination against an individual or a group based on their race, ethnicity, or some other perceived difference. The following reading by Charlie LeDuff, a reporter for the *New York Times*, takes us inside one workplace site to examine the everyday reality of racial interactions among one group of employees. In the slaughterhouse in Tar Heel, North Carolina, racism occurs on many levels, including racial stereotyping, verbal harassment, and even the threat of physical violence and death. The employers also effectively use racist strategies, such as enforcing a racial hierarchy among workers and exploiting racial tensions among their workers, to maintain an economic advantage and social control over their employees.

Tar Heel, North Carolina

It must have been 1 o'clock. That's when the white man usually comes out of his glass office and stands on the scaffolding above the factory floor. He stood with his palms on the rails, his elbows out. He looked like a tower guard up there or a border patrol agent. He stood with his head cocked.

One o'clock means it is getting near the end of the workday. Quota has to be met and the workload doubles. The conveyor belt always overflows with meat around 1 o'clock. So the workers double their pace, hacking pork from shoulder bones with a driven single-mindedness. They stare blankly, like mules in wooden blinders, as the butchered slabs pass by.

It is called the picnic line: eighteen workers lined up on both sides of a belt, carving meat from bone. Up to 16 million shoulders a year come down that line here at the Smithfield Packing Company, the largest pork production plant in the world. That works out to about 32,000 a shift, sixty-three a minute, one every seventeen seconds for each worker for eight and a half hours a day. The first time you stare down at that belt you know your body is going to give in way before the machine ever will.

On this day the boss saw something he didn't like. He climbed down and approached the picnic line from behind. He leaned into the ear of a broad-shouldered black man. He had been riding him all day, and the day before. The boss bawled him out good this time, but no one heard what was said.

The roar of the machinery was too ferocious for that. Still, everyone knew what was expected. They worked harder.

The white man stood and watched for the next two hours as the blacks worked in their groups and the Mexicans in theirs. He stood there with his head cocked.

At shift change the black man walked away, hosed himself down and turned in his knives. Then he let go. He threatened to murder the boss. He promised to quit. He said he was losing his mind, which made for good comedy since he was standing near a conveyor chain of severed hogs' heads, their mouths yoked open.

"Who that cracker think he is?" the black man wanted to know. There were enough hogs, he said, "not to worry about no fleck of meat being left on the bone. Keep treating me like a Mexican and I'll beat him."

The boss walked by just then and the black man lowered his head.

Who Gets the Dirty Jobs

The first thing you learn in the hog plant is the value of a sharp knife. The second thing you learn is that you don't want to work with a knife. Finally you learn that not everyone has to work with a knife. Whites, blacks, American Indians, and Mexicans, they all have their separate stations.

The few whites on the payroll tend to be mechanics or supervisors. As for the Indians, a handful are supervisors; others tend to get clean menial jobs like warehouse work. With few exceptions, that leaves the blacks and Mexicans with the dirty jobs at the factory, one of the only places within a fifty-mile radius in this muddy corner of North Carolina where a person might make more than $8 an hour.

While Smithfield's profits nearly doubled in the past year, wages have remained flat. So a lot of Americans here have quit and a lot of Mexicans have been hired to take their places. But more than management, the workers see one another as the problem, and they see the competition in skin tones.

The locker rooms are self-segregated and so is the cafeteria. The enmity spills out into the towns. The races generally keep to themselves. Along Interstate 95 there are four tumbledown bars, one for each color: white, black, red, and brown.

Language is also a divider. There are English and Spanish lines at the Social Security office and in the waiting rooms of the county health clinics. This means different groups don't really understand one another and tend to be suspicious of what they do know.

You begin to understand these things the minute you apply for the job.

Blood and Burnout

"Treat the meat like you going to eat it yourself," the hiring manager told the thirty applicants, most of them down on their luck and hungry for work. The Smithfield plant will take just about any man or woman with a pulse and a sparkling urine sample, with few questions asked. This reporter was hired using his own name and acknowledged that he was currently employed, but was not asked where and did not say.

Slaughtering swine is repetitive, brutish work, so grueling that three weeks on the factory floor leave no doubt in your mind about why the turnover is 100 percent. Five thousand quit and five thousand are hired every year. You hear people say, They don't kill pigs in the plant, they kill people. So desperate is the company for workers, its recruiters comb the streets of New York's immigrant communities, personnel staff members say, and word of mouth has reached Mexico and beyond.

The company even procures criminals. Several at the morning orientation were inmates on work release in green uniforms, bused in from the county prison.

The new workers were given a safety speech and tax papers, shown a promotional video and informed that there was enough methane, ammonia, and chlorine at the plant to kill every living thing here in Bladen County. Of the thirty new employees, the black women were assigned to the chitterlings room, where they would scrape feces and worms from intestines. The black men were sent to the butchering floor. Two free white men and the Indian were given jobs making boxes. This reporter declined a box job and ended up with most of the Mexicans, doing knife work, cutting sides of pork into smaller and smaller products.

Standing in the hiring hall that morning, two women chatted in Spanish about their pregnancies. A young black man had heard enough. His small town the next county over was crowded with Mexicans. They just started showing up three years ago—drawn to rural Robeson County by the plant—and never left. They stood in groups on the street corners, and the young black man never knew what they were saying. They took the jobs and did them for less. Some had houses in Mexico, while he lived in a trailer with his mother.

Now here he was, trying for the only job around, and he had to listen to Spanish, had to compete with peasants. The world was going to hell.

"This is America and I want to start hearing some English, now!" he screamed.

One of the women told him where to stick his head and listen for the echo. "Then you'll hear some English," she said.

An old white man with a face as pinched and lined as a pot roast complained, "The tacos are worse than the niggers," and the Indian leaned against the wall and laughed. In the doorway, the prisoners shifted from foot to foot, watching the spectacle unfold from behind a cloud of cigarette smoke.

The hiring manager came out of his office and broke it up just before things degenerated into a brawl. Then he handed out the employment stubs. "I don't want no problems," he warned. He told them to report to the plant on Monday morning to collect their carving knives.

$7.70 an Hour, Pain All Day

Monday. The mist rose from the swamps and by 4:45 A.M. thousands of head-lamps snaked along the old country roads. Cars carried people from the back-woods, from the single and double-wide trailers, from the cinder-block houses and wooden shacks: whites from Lumberton and Elizabethtown; blacks from Fairmont and Fayetteville; Indians from Pembroke; the Mexicans from Red Springs and St. Pauls.

They converge at the Smithfield plant, a 973,000-square-foot leviathan of pipe and steel near the Cape Fear River. The factory towers over the tobacco and cotton fields, surrounded by pine trees and a few of the old whitewashed plantation houses. Built seven years ago, it is by far the biggest employer in this region, seventy-five miles west of the Atlantic and ninety miles south of the booming Research Triangle around Chapel Hill.

The workers filed in, their faces stiffened by sleep and the cold, like saucers of milk gone hard. They punched the clock at 5 A.M., waiting for the knives to be handed out, the chlorine freshly applied by the cleaning crew burning their eyes and throats. Nobody spoke.

The hallway was a river of brown-skinned Mexicans. The six prisoners who were starting that day looked confused.

"What the hell's going on?" the only white inmate, Billy Harwood, asked an older black worker named Wade Baker.

"Oh," Baker said, seeing that the prisoner was talking about the Mexicans. "I see you been away for a while."

Billy Harwood had been away—nearly seven years, for writing phony payroll checks from the family pizza business to buy crack. He was Rip Van Winkle standing there. Everywhere he looked there were Mexicans. What he didn't know was that one out of three newborns at the nearby Robeson County health clinic was a Latino; that the county's Roman Catholic church had a special Sunday Mass for Mexicans said by a Honduran priest; that the schools needed Spanish speakers to teach English.

With less than a month to go on his sentence, Harwood took the pork job to save a few dollars. The word in jail was that the job was a cakewalk for a white man.

But this wasn't looking like any cakewalk. He wasn't going to get a box-ing job like a lot of other whites. Apparently inmates were on the bottom rung, just like Mexicans.

Billy Harwood and the other prisoners were put on the picnic line. Knife work pays $7.70 an hour to start. It is money unimaginable in Mexico, where the average wage is $4 a day. But the American money comes at a price. The work burns your muscles and dulls your mind. Staring down into the meat for hours strains your neck. After thousands of cuts a day your fingers no longer open freely. Standing in the damp 42-degree air causes your knees to lock, your nose to run, your teeth to throb.

The whistle blows at three, you get home by four, pour peroxide on your nicks by five. You take pills for your pains and stand in a hot shower trying to wash it all away. You hurt. And by eight o'clock you're in bed, exhausted, thinking of work.

The convict said he felt cheated. He wasn't supposed to be doing Mexican work. After his second day he was already talking of quitting. "Man, this can't be for real," he said, rubbing his wrists as if they'd been in handcuffs. "This job's for an ass. They treat you like an animal."

He just might have quit after the third day had it not been for Mercedes Fernández, a Mexican. He took a place next to her by the conveyor belt. She smiled at him, showed him how to make incisions. That was the extent of his on-the-job training. He was peep-eyed, missing a tooth and squat from the starchy prison food, but he acted as if this tiny woman had taken a fancy to him. In truth, she was more fascinated than infatuated, she later confided. In her year at the plant, he was the first white person she had ever worked with.

The other workers noticed her helping the white man, so unusual was it for a Mexican and a white to work shoulder to shoulder, to try to talk or even to make eye contact.

As for blacks, she avoided them. She was scared of them. "Blacks don't want to work," Fernández said when the new batch of prisoners came to work on the line. "They're lazy."

Everything about the factory cuts people off from one another. If it's not the language barrier, it's the noise—the hammering of compressors, the screeching of pulleys, the grinding of the lines. You can hardly make your voice heard. To get another's attention on the cut line, you bang the butt of your knife on the steel railings, or you lob a chunk of meat. Fernández would sometimes throw a piece of shoulder at a friend across the conveyor and wave good morning.

The Kill Floor

The kill floor sets the pace of the work, and for those jobs they pick strong men and pay a top wage, as high as $12 an hour. If the men fail to make quota, plenty of others are willing to try. It is mostly the blacks who work the kill floor, the stone-hearted jobs that pay more and appear out of bounds for all but a few Mexicans. Plant workers gave various reasons for this: the Mexicans are too small; they don't like blood; they don't like heavy lifting; or just plain "We built this country and we ain't going to hand them everything," as one black man put it.

Kill-floor work is hot, quick, and bloody. The hog is herded in from the stockyard, then stunned with an electric gun. It is lifted onto a conveyor belt, dazed but not dead, and passed to a waiting group of men wearing blood-stained smocks and blank faces. They slit the neck, shackle the hind legs and watch a machine lift the carcass into the air, letting its life flow out in a purple gush, into a steaming collection trough.

The carcass is run through a scalding bath, trolleyed over the factory floor, and then dumped onto a table with all the force of a quarter-ton water balloon. In the misty-red room, men slit along its hind tendons and skewer the beast with hooks. It is again lifted and shot across the room on a pulley and bar, where it hangs with hundreds of others as if in some kind of horrific dry-cleaning shop. It is then pulled through a wall of flames and met on the other side by more black men who, stripped to the waist beneath their smocks, scrape away any straggling bristles.

The place reeks of sweat and scared animal, steam and blood. Nothing is wasted from these beasts, not the plasma, not the glands, not the bones. Everything is used, and the kill men, repeating slaughterhouse lore, say that even the squeal is sold.

The carcasses sit in the freezer overnight and are then rolled out to the cut floor. The cut floor is opposite to the kill floor in nearly every way. The workers are mostly brown—Mexicans—not black; the lighting yellow, not red. The vapor comes from cold breath, not hot water. It is here that the hog is quartered. The pieces are parceled out and sent along the disassembly lines to be cut into ribs, hams, bellies, loins, and chops.

People on the cut lines work with a mindless fury. There is tremendous pressure to keep the conveyor belts moving, to pack orders, to put bacon and ham and sausage on the public's breakfast table. There is no clock, no window, no fragment of the world outside. Everything is pork. If the line fails to keep pace, the kill men must slow down, backing up the slaughter. The boxing line will have little to do, costing the company payroll hours. The blacks who kill will become angry with the Mexicans who cut, who in turn will become angry with the white superintendents who push them.

10,000 Unwelcome Mexicans

The Mexicans never push back. They cannot. Some have legitimate work papers, but more, like Mercedes Fernández, do not.

Even worse, Fernández was several thousand dollars in debt to the smugglers who had sneaked her and her family into the United States and owed a thousand more for the authentic-looking birth certificate and Social Security card that are needed to get hired. She and her husband, Armando, expected to be in debt for years. They had mouths to feed back home.

The Mexicans are so frightened about being singled out that they do not even tell one another their real names. They have their given names, their work-paper names, and "Hey you," as their American supervisors call them. In the telling of their stories, Mercedes and Armando Fernández insisted that their real names be used, to protect their identities. It was their work names they did not want used, names bought in a back alley in Barstow, Texas.

Rarely are the newcomers welcomed with open arms. Long before the Mexicans arrived, Robeson County, one of the poorest in North Carolina, was an uneasy racial mix. In the 1990 census, of the 100,000 people living in Robeson, nearly 40 percent were Lumbee Indian, 35 percent white, and 25 percent black. Until a dozen years ago the county schools were de facto segregated, and no person of color held any meaningful county job from sheriff to court clerk to judge.

At one point in 1988, two armed Indian men occupied the local newspaper office, taking hostages and demanding that the sheriff's department be investigated for corruption and its treatment of minorities. A prominent Indian lawyer, Julian Pierce, was killed that same year, and the suspect turned up dead in a broom closet before he could be charged. The hierarchy of power was summed up on a plaque that hangs in the courthouse commemorating the dead of World War I. It lists the veterans by color: "white" on top, "Indian" in the middle, and "colored" on the bottom.

That hierarchy mirrors the pecking order at the hog plant. The Lumbees—who have fought their way up in the county apparatus and have built their own construction businesses—are fond of saying they are too smart to work in the factory. And the few who do work there seem to end up with the cleaner jobs.

But as reds and blacks began to make progress in the 1990s—for the first time an Indian sheriff was elected, and a black man is now the public defender—the Latinos began arriving. The United States Census Bureau estimated that one thousand Latinos were living in Robeson County in 1999. People only laugh at that number.

"A thousand? Hell, there's more than that in the Wal-Mart on a Saturday afternoon," said Bill Smith, director of county health services. He and other officials guess that there are at least 10,000 Latinos in Robeson, most having arrived since 1997.

"When they built that factory in Bladen, they promised a trickle-down effect," Smith said. "But the money ain't trickling down this way. Bladen got the money and Robeson got the social problems."

In Robeson there is the strain on public resources. There is the substandard housing. There is the violence. In 1999 twenty-seven killings were committed in Robeson, mostly in the countryside, giving it a higher murder rate than Detroit or Newark. Three Mexicans were robbed and killed that fall. Latinos have also been the victims of highway stickups.

In the yellow-walled break room at the plant, Mexicans talked among themselves about their three slain men, about the midnight visitors with obscured faces and guns, men who knew that the illegal workers used mattresses rather than banks. Mercedes Fernández, like many Mexicans, would not venture out at night. "Blacks have a problem," she said. "They live in the past. They are angry about slavery, so instead of working, they steal from us."

She and her husband never lingered in the parking lot at shift change. That is when the anger of a long day comes seeping out. Cars get kicked and faces slapped over parking spots or fender benders. The traffic is a serpent. Cars jockey for a spot in line to make the quarter-mile crawl along the plant's one-lane exit road to the highway. Usually no one will let you in. A lot of the scuffling is between black and Mexican. . . .

Living It, Hating It

Billy Harwood had been working at the plant ten days when he was released from the Robeson County Correctional Facility. He stood at the prison gates in his work clothes with his belongings in a plastic bag, waiting. A friend dropped him at the Salvation Army shelter, but he decided it was too much like prison. Full of black people. No leaving after 10 P.M. No smoking indoors. "What you doing here, white boy?" they asked him.

He fumbled with a cigarette outside the shelter. He wanted to quit the plant. The work stinks, he said, "but at least I ain't a nigger. I'll find other work soon. I'm a white man." He had hopes of landing a roofing job through a friend. The way he saw it, white society looks out for itself.

On the cut line he worked slowly and allowed Mercedes Fernández and the others to pick up his slack. He would cut only the left shoulders; it was easier on his hands. Sometimes it would be three minutes before a left shoulder came down the line. When he did cut, he didn't clean the bone; he left chunks of meat on it.

Fernández was disappointed by her first experience with a white person. After a week she tried to avoid standing by Billy Harwood. She decided it wasn't just the blacks who were lazy, she said.

Even so, the supervisor came by one morning, took a look at one of Harwood's badly cut shoulders and threw it at Fernández, blaming her. He said obscene things about her family. She didn't understand exactly what he said, but it scared her. She couldn't wipe the tears from her eyes because her gloves were covered with greasy shreds of swine. The other cutters kept their heads down, embarrassed.

Her life was falling apart. She and her husband both worked the cut floor. They never saw their daughter. They were twenty-six but rarely made love anymore. All they wanted was to save enough money to put plumbing in their house in Mexico and start a business there. They come from the town of Tehuacán, in a rural area about 150 miles southeast of Mexico City. His mother owns a bar there and a home but gives nothing to them. Mother must look out for her old age.

"We came here to work so we have a chance to grow old in Mexico," Fernández said one evening while cooking pork and potatoes. Now they were into a smuggler for thousands. Her hands swelled into claws in the evenings and stung while she worked. She felt trapped. But she kept at it for the money, for the $9.60 an hour. The smuggler still had to be paid.

They explained their story this way: The coyote drove her and her family from Barstow a year ago and left them in Robeson. They knew no one. They did not even know they were in the state of North Carolina. They found shelter in a trailer park that had once been exclusively black but was rapidly filling with Mexicans. There was a lot of drug dealing there and a lot of tension. One evening, Armando Fernández said, he asked a black neighbor to move his business inside and the man pulled a pistol on him.

"I hate the blacks," he said in Spanish, sitting in the break room not ten feet from Wade Baker and his black friends. Billy Harwood was sitting two tables away with the whites and Indians.

After the gun incident, Armando Fernández packed up his family and moved out into the country, to a prefabricated number sitting on a brick foundation off in the woods alone. Their only contact with people is through the satellite dish. Except for the coyote. The coyote knows where they live and comes for his money every other month.

Their five-year-old daughter has no playmates in the back country and few at school. That is the way her parents want it. "We don't want her to be American," her mother said.

"We Need a Union"

The steel bars holding a row of hogs gave way as a woman stood below them. Hog after hog fell around her with a sickening thud, knocking her senseless, the connecting bars barely missing her face. As co-workers rushed to help the woman, the supervisor spun his hands in the air, a signal to keep working. Wade Baker saw this and shook his head in disgust. Nothing stops the disassembly lines.

"We need a union," he said later in the break room. It was payday and he stared at his check: $288. He spoke softly to the black workers sitting near him. Everyone is convinced that talk of a union will get you fired. After two years at the factory, Baker makes slightly more than $9 an hour toting meat away from the cut line, slightly less than $20,000 a year, 45 cents an hour less than Mercedes Fernández.

"I don't want to get racial about the Mexicans," he whispered to the black workers. "But they're dragging down the pay. It's pure economics. They say Americans don't want to do the job. That ain't exactly true. We don't want to do it for $8. Pay $15 and we'll do it."

These men knew that in the late seventies, when the meat-packing industry was centered in northern cities like Chicago and Omaha, people had a union getting them $18 an hour. But by the mid-eighties, to cut costs, many of the packing houses had moved to small towns where they could pay a lower, nonunion wage.

The black men sitting around the table also felt sure that the Mexicans pay almost nothing in income tax, claiming eight, nine even ten exemptions. The men believed that the illegal workers should be rooted out of the factory. "It's all about money," Baker said.

His co-workers shook their heads. "A plantation with a roof on it," one said.

For their part, many of the Mexicans in Tar Heel fear that a union would place their illegal status under scrutiny and force them out. The United Food and Commercial Workers Union last tried organizing the plant in 1997, but the idea was voted down nearly two to one.

One reason Americans refused to vote for the union was because it refuses to take a stand on illegal laborers. Another reason was the intimidation. When workers arrived at the plant the morning of the vote, they were met by Bladen County deputy sheriffs in riot gear. "Nigger Lover" had been scrawled on the union trailer.

Five years ago the work force at the plant was 50 percent black, 20 percent white and Indian, and 30 percent Latino, according to union statistics. Company officials say those numbers are about the same today. But from inside the plant, the breakdown appears to be more like 60 percent Latino, 30 percent black, 10 percent white and red.

Sherri Buffkin, a white woman and the former director of purchasing who testified before the National Labor Relations Board in an unfair-labor-practice suit brought by the union in 1998, said in an interview that the company assigns workers by race. She also said that management had kept lists of union sympathizers during the '97 election, firing blacks and replacing them with Latinos. "I know because I fired at least fifteen of them myself," she said.

The company denies those accusations. Michael H. Cole, a lawyer for Smithfield who would respond to questions about the company's labor practices only in writing, said that jobs at the Tar Heel plant were awarded through a bidding process and not assigned by race. The company also denies ever having kept lists of union sympathizers or singled out blacks to be fired.

The hog business is important to North Carolina. It is a multibillion-dollar-a-year industry in the state, with nearly two pigs for every one of its 7.5 million people. And Smithfield Foods, a publicly traded company based in Smithfield, Virginia, has become the No. 1 producer and processor of pork in the world. It slaughters more than 20 percent of the nation's swine, more than 19 million animals a year.

The company, which has acquired a network of factory farms and slaughterhouses, worries federal agriculture officials and legislators, who see it siphoning business from smaller farmers. And environmentalists contend that Smithfield's operations contaminate local water supplies. (The Environmental Protection Agency fined the company $12.6 million in 1996 after its processing plants in Virginia discharged pollutants into the Pagan River.) The chairman and chief executive, Joseph W. Luter III, declined to be interviewed.

Smithfield's employment practices have not been so closely scrutinized. And so every year, more Mexicans get hired. "An illegal alien isn't going to complain all that much," said Ed Tomlinson, acting supervisor of the Immigration and Naturalization Service Bureau in Charlotte.

But the company says it does not knowingly hire illegal aliens. Smithfield's lawyer, Cole, said all new employees must present papers showing that they can legally work in the United States. "If any employee's documentation appears to be genuine and to belong to the person presenting it," he said in his written response, "Smithfield is required by law to take it at face value."

The naturalization service—which has only eighteen agents in North Carolina—has not investigated Smithfield because no one has filed a complaint, Ed Tomlinson said. "There are more jobs than people," he said, "and a lot of Americans will do the dirty work for a while and then return to their couches and eat bonbons and watch Oprah."

34

OUT OF SORTS
Adoption and (Un)Desirable Children

KATHERIN M. FLOWER KIM

In this reading, Katherin M. Flower Kim presents her findings of how race and racism influence the adoption decisions of white parents in the United States. Kim, a postdoctorate student in the Department of Sociology at the University of Minnesota, interviewed 73 adoptive parents in central New York in the late 1990s. Kim investigates the ways parents in her study came to construct, sort, and talk about Asian children in general, and children from Korea in particular, as desirable for adoption and African American and Latino children as undesirable. This reading illustrates well several of the concepts related to race and racial inequality introduced in the Bonilla-Silva article, Reading 31.

Adoption has become an increasingly important and common path for forming a family with children, and it illustrates the importance adopters place on having a family that includes children. Yet adoption is not simply a case of adopting any child. Differential rates of adoption for different groups of children as well as categories of "waiting children" reflect the ways some children are considered more desirable than other children and helps explain why some children are more likely to be adopted, and adopted more quickly, than are other children. I draw on interview data collected during 1997–1999 from 43 mothers and 30 of their husbands in Central City, a pseudonym for a city in central New York, who adopted children from Korea in the 1980s and 1990s, to investigate the sorting, and in many instances ranking, of children throughout the adoption process. All but one of the participants identified themselves as white.[1] While their comments indicated that a range of factors contributed to parental perceptions and talk about (un)desirable children, this reading is principally concerned with exploring and analyzing the ways race shaped American parents' thinking and discourse about who was more or less desirable as a potential family member. More specifically, I use parents' descriptions of assembling their families to explore and highlight how they came to explain the desirability of children from Korea and the undesirability of African American children.

A key aspect of understanding constructions of desirable children and parental preferences for certain children is clarifying who the adopters are, particularly in terms of race. More specifically, the majority of parents who adopt through formal, legal channels[2] were, and continue to be, whites who experience fertility problems (May 1995; Roberts 1997). As Elaine Tyler May (1995:11) noted,

> "Barren" is a term laden with historical weight. It carries negative meanings: unproductive, sterile, bare, empty, stark, deficient, lacking, wanting, destitute, devoid. It is the opposite of fertile, lavish, abounding, productive. . . . Until the mid-nineteenth century, men were believed to be fertile if they were not impotent, so "barren" women carried the blame if a married couple did not have children. The term, like the condition, suggested moral and spiritual failure, and the words like "blame," "fault" and "guilt" have been attached to childlessness ever since.

From this perspective, the desire for white children was connected to the potential for parents, especially women, to avoid the social stigma of infertility.[3] Racial matching policies were, however, not only about avoiding the social stigma of infertility. Rather, preferences and policies regarding racial matching were also about supporting social norms related to race relations. More to the point, given the tension and polarization between U.S. whites and racial-ethnic minorities (especially those between whites and blacks), adopting white children and avoiding other children was not just about masking infertility; it was also a way of managing race relations and racism. Thus, the social location and characteristics of the majority of formal–legal adopters (i.e., whites), in conjunction with the sociohistorical context, offers a more complete explanation of why white infants were more desirable (and therefore adopted) and other infants and children were considered undesirable and subsequently not adopted.

Following World War II, a number of social changes occurred in the United States, which had important ramifications for adoption policies and practices, especially in relation to the availability of healthy, white infants. Factors, such as postwar affluence as well as changes in the age, education, and occupation of "birth" parents and adoption applicants, impacted adoption trends (Carp 2002). In addition, two of the most commonly cited shifts in socio-cultural norms influencing adoption in the United States are the availability of contraception and abortion as well as an increased acceptance of out-of-wedlock births (Luker 1996; May 1995; Solinger 1992). These changes drastically decreased the number of healthy, white infants available for adoption, creating an atmosphere of scarcity for "desirable" children. The imbalance in formal legal adoption between the adopters (white middle/upper class) and the desirable child (a healthy, white infant) was such that by the 1970s a "healthy white baby" was a request deemed unrealistic by social workers (Melosh 2002:162). In light of the "context of scarcity" some parents looked for alternatives to a healthy, white infant. One alternative was to reconstruct the desirable child to include non-white children as acceptable and pursue transracial adoption. Two options for transracial adoption were racial-ethnic minority children in the United States or children born outside the United States.

Healthy, but . . .

In my interviews, most parents pointed out that a notable and unique aspect of the adoption process was the opportunity to make specific choices about the children they would adopt. In various ways, they could sort potential family members as more or less desirable by indicating what types of children they were willing to adopt.[4] As such, notions of "choices" and "choosing" were central to parents' adoption narratives and practices,[5] and parents and adoption agencies expressed a range of feelings and practices regulating the choices parents could or could not make. Most adoptive parents initially indicated resistance, or at least ambivalence, to indicating preferences for certain characteristics of children. As if given a script, the majority of parents in my sample responded to the question "When thinking about adopting a child, what was important to you?" by noting they wanted only *a healthy* child. The consistency of the response was not entirely surprising given available cultural discourses and norms that emphasize the idea of wanting a healthy child.

Parents' responses indicated that when they expressed a desire for a healthy child, part of their wish did, in fact, translate into the literal physical health of the child. For instance, Paula, a mother of two adopted children, described taking the information provided by the adoption agency to the pediatrician to interpret the child's health. She noted,

> *Part of the issue was we certainly wanted and wished [for] a child who was in good health, and what do we know, we were sent these things that were both vague or unfamiliar to us, birth weights and heights and we had no sense of how to see if that meant anything, so I think one thing we did do was go to our pediatrician with the information we had. . . .*

Her response was typical of other adoptive parents' remarks as others noted seeking advice from a physician to evaluate the health status of the child.

Thus, parents' descriptions of their search for healthy children were remarkably similar. In general, they began their search for healthy children by exploring domestic adoptions. One mother, Erin, offered,

> *We looked at domestic . . . and we thought we'd talked with just about everybody in town and we were really discouraged because [my husband] was already thirty-nine and I was thirty-six and we thought [pause] you know if we have to wait ten years, that's too, we're too old. So we were really discouraged about it.*

Notably, although parents talked about pursuing "domestic adoption," they generally pursued only one specific type of domestic adoption. For most parents, "domestic" adoptions were understood and coded almost exclusively as the search for healthy, *white* infants. One clue to decoding parents' particular understanding of domestic adoption was the time frames they cited. More specifically, the waiting time this mother and others in my sample cited was, in fact, only reflective of the waiting time for healthy, white infants in the United States. Other children in the United States were more readily available and did not have an extensive waiting time. For instance, in my interview with Amy, she described her experience with domestic adoption, and at one point in the interview, I attempted to clarify who was included in her domestic adoption search by asking her if she and her husband had investigated children other than healthy, white infants. She responded, "*. . . but as far as other nationalities here [in the United States], I don't think that even occurred to us, come to think of it.*" Amy's comments reinforced the idea that adoption was not about adopting <u>any</u> child and illustrated how some children were not included in domestic adoption searches. Importantly, rather than address the issue in terms of race, Amy took up the question of nonwhite children in terms of nationalities. While it is possible that she might not have understood my question, my strong sense is that answering it using the term "nationalities" may have allowed her to verbally maneuver through contested terrain. Furthermore, Amy does not make a distinction between the health status of children from other "nationalities" (likely coded as racial-ethnic minorities) here in the United States. Instead, the undesirability of children from "other nationalities here" was not necessarily linked to their health status. Rather, their "nationality" appeared to trump their health status, as well as their age. "Nationality" was used by parents as a primary factor for sorting children as undesirable.

Amy's report of not having children from "other nationalities" in the United States on her list of potentially adoptable children was not an isolated response. Although Amy was unique in invoking a language of "nationality," the claim that it did not occur to her to consider nonwhite children was shared by half of the participants. That it did not even occur to 50 percent of the participants to consider adopting children of color was a powerful statement about how race privilege operated, since one way privilege works is to socially buffer those in privileged positions from having to be aware of or consider minorities. In addition, it illustrated strong support for the contention that even when faced with the desire to have "healthy" children (and with the knowledge that there are children more readily available for adoption in the United States), some children were not considered desirable as potential family members because of their race-ethnicity or their nationality.[6]

On many occasions, getting informants to be specific and direct about their view on racial preference was difficult because rather than specifically articulating or addressing race, parents used language that was racially coded. As Amy's comments demonstrated, for example, one way to talk about race without specifying it was to substitute "nationalities," or as discussed earlier, parents frequently used "healthy child" and "domestic adoptions" to signal the search for healthy, white infants. The language choices were likely due to convention as well as more conscious efforts to avoid the appearance of racism. Regardless, parents traded on common assumptions about who were perceived as desirable children for adoption and with what characteristics.

In fact, all but two parents—of the 73 parents in my sample—talked about domestic adoptions almost exclusively in terms of white children, as evidenced by the extensive wait times they cited. Thus, by not specifying and articulating whiteness and still finding an interpretive community that understood what was meant without being explicit about the racialized dimensions, whiteness was, in a very real sense, so normative as to be taken for granted. While some may discount this point, I think it was precisely the subtlety of the racial codes and the ability of whiteness to remain hidden and taken for granted that was so powerful. For example, in the following excerpt, Donna talked about the advice she received from an adoption agency. Consider the way Donna and the adoption agency used the term "American." She said,

> *We had gone to [the adoption agency] for an American adoption. . . . But I hate to say this, but it was true, [the agency], they said, don't even try for them because they're hard to get. . . . the waiting list [was] as long as it would take for an American child.*

In this case, both the agency and parents had a common understanding of "American child." Her description regarding difficulties of getting an "American child" and her focus on the waiting list indicated that the agency and the parents understood the search for an "American child" as the search for a healthy, white infant.

In another example that illustrated the narrow way "American" was used, Linda stated,

> *Well, we were married for several years and um, unable to have children, and we finally decided that we would adopt. [Pause] So we started with um, like every other person, I guess, thinking about adopting an American baby. You know, so we started off with [the adoption agency], and um, . . . so we knew [this adoption agency] did adoption, so we went to a meeting, [pause] and um, to adopt an American baby, at that point it was like a 7-year wait, they just, I think, [were]*

not readily available. So we thought well, this is not going to do, because we were not terribly young at that point, um, [pause]. So we decided that we could go with a foreign adoption.

This mother considered it normative to start with an American baby. Yet, similar to other parents, as revealed by the extensive waiting period (7 years), it was normative for this mother to investigate only certain American children (i.e., whites), since other American children (i.e., racial-ethnic minorities) were, in fact, more readily available and did not necessarily have the extensive waiting period.

In contrast to those who were vague or used coded racial language, some parents were quite clear in verbalizing their unwillingness to consider adopting a child who was African American. In sharing her recollection of the adoption process, Marlene brought up her distress about the possibility of not being able to adopt a child.

> K: *And so, . . . in pursuing avenues for adoption, how did you make that transition?*
>
> M: *Um, oh boy, all I remember is for me it was very traumatic because, I was afraid that we wouldn't be able to [adopt]. Um. . . . If we wanted a Black or Hispanic, if we wanted a Black or Hispanic child, [we could adopt] which we did not, so, we ruled that out.*

Marlene was fairly definitive about not wanting a Black or Hispanic child. She did not expand her explanation and specify that she would not accept a Black or Hispanic child who was not healthy. Instead, race (for Hispanics and Blacks) became a master status of children waiting to be adopted, and they were, quite literally, sorted out of the adoption process by white parents.

In the following selection, Molly, a mother of one adopted boy and one genetically related daughter, clearly illustrated the desire for a healthy baby, but not a healthy African American baby. Her account highlighted the way some children were not able to shed the stigma associated with their racial status. She stated,

> *We wanted a healthy baby, we just wanted a healthy baby and um, . . . We had thought briefly about an African American baby . . . and I had some reservations about that also because I thought we would grow up right next to a culture that I don't always like very well. You know, and so that would be real strange if he felt like he had to act like, you know, one of the boys from the hood. That would be hard for us.*

Molly's statement was important because it offered clues about why race was a salient factor influencing the desirability of a child for some white parents. I read Molly's explanation for not wanting an African American baby as a comment on the way race (understood as socially created) was frequently used as a proxy for cultural practices. In this case, race had a specific meaning for Molly. "African American" was understood as a set of distinct (gendered) cultural practices, i.e., acting like a "boy from the hood." Thus, it was not simply resistance to adopting an "African American" child as such, but resistance to adopting what "African American" was presumed to mean and signify culturally. From Molly's perspective, African American cultural practices were oppositional to and incompatible with white cultural practices as indicated by her statement "That would be hard for us." Some parents, like Molly, seemed to believe that racial culture was so powerful that their child would participate in it, regardless of how the family might socialize the child. Thus, the connection between race and presumed cultural practices was so strong that for some parents, it did not appear to make a difference whether the African American child was adopted as an "*infant.*" Parents' comments indicated that socialization could not erase the propensity for oppositional racial and cultural practices.

There are different ways to think about and situate her comments. On the one hand, it is possible that the resistance to adopting African American children (including healthy infants) was because Molly and other parents who shared similar perspectives, were aware of and sensitive to larger structures of racism. For instance, although she did not cite the NABSW's (National Association of Black Social Workers') position on transracial adoption (read as whites adopting Black children), she might have been aware of their statement. It is also possible that she (and others) anticipated ways that race would influence her child's behavior. That is, in the face of oppression and a society structured by and through racism, the family is only one agent of socialization and perhaps they felt truly unprepared and unequipped to deal with it.

Yet her statements also revealed a personal ambivalence—for Molly, adopting an African American meant engaging and confronting a culture that she "didn't always like very well." Her feelings concerning African Americans were focused on particular aspects of African American culture and reflected common stereotypes of "hood culture." Molly and other prospective parents relied on negative racial stereotypes (and therefore, incomplete and inaccurate information) throughout the decision-making process. From this framework, her sentiments were likely magnified when she considered that this child (read: bad boy from the hood) would be in the intimate and daily setting of her family.

In contrast to Molly and Marlene, who illustrated how race activated a wholesale rejection of some African American children, another respondent, Rachel, noted that an African American baby was not desirable unless the option was no baby. The following is an excerpt from the beginning of our conversation.

K: *Did you know where you wanted to adopt from?*

R: *Well, we probably didn't, you know, think that far ahead, you know, we were, um* [pause] *the way you mean it started for Korean?*

K: *Yes.*

R: *Well, okay, plain and simple in my mind, um* [pause] *if you waited for, . . .
so, hey, you know, so I think anything, we probably didn't want to go* [pause]
I, [pause] *I don't, I shouldn't say didn't, we wanted a baby, I was going to say
didn't want an African American, but you know, we didn't really, we didn't
really have to, ah, I mean versus no baby, I mean, I know we would have, but
I'm just saying, because my son's godfather is African American, so we don't
have anything against it, but, we're just saying, I'm white. . . .*

Both the format and content of Rachel's comments are instructive for a number of reasons. First, her explanation of how she came to adopt from Korea focused on her standpoint on adopting African American children. Rachel's feelings about adopting African American children were strong enough that even without direct probing (and even though we had just met and started the interview) she still shared information that is commonly considered taboo. In addition, her comments illustrated the ways hierarchies of racial desirability were constructed as well as how unstable these notions of desirability were. More specifically, the possibility of *not* having a child was able to transform Rachel's opinion about race. Although Rachel initially had reservations about adopting an African American child, an African American child would be desirable if it was the only way to have a family with children. As she described her feelings, Rachel indicated that they may not be popular or acceptable to say. I read her pauses and self interruptions (i.e., "um") as underscoring the difficulties of being honest about and articulating such sentiments, and thus raised larger issues about what the available and acceptable ways to talk about these feelings were. For instance, offering statements like "we don't have anything against it" is a common rhetorical strategy used in deflecting perceptions of racist attitudes. Noting that the godfather of one of their children is African American also may be perceived as a way to socially buffer against accusations of being a racist. These strategies perhaps serve as a method of contemporary racial etiquette (Collins 1998; Park 1950) thus making it seem more acceptable to have these feelings, or at least make it feel safer to express these feelings.

One of the two families who talked about being open to the possibility of adopting an African American child reported that it would present problems with their extended family. One mother, Becca, recalled phoning her mother after they received news that she and her husband were matched with a child and shared her experience of telling her mother. She stated,

So *[my husband and I] decided to tell our parents, so, we called up all excited
that we were gonna be adopting, and [my mother] said after a dead silence, "Is
the baby Black?" Interesting reaction.* [Pause] *And we said, "No," and [my
mother] said, "That's fine."*

In this mother's adoption experience, the issue of race dominated the interaction with her biological family. For the soon-to-be grandmother, race was framed as a binary: Black and not Black. Knowing the child was not Black appeared to be sufficient for accepting the child.

International: Why Korea?

> *It was quick, it was easy, and they were Oriental, I mean that seemed like a nice thing. . . .*

In deciding that "domestic" adoptions were not a viable option (because of the lengthy waiting period for healthy, white infants coupled with resistance to adopting African American children (whether or not they were healthy infants) or other special needs children, parents shifted their attention to intercountry adoptions. Historically, Korea has been an important sending country of children for adoption, and during the 1980s, it was by far, the largest sending country. Yet, Korea has never been the sole country available to parents. Given the choices for intercountry adoption, why were children from Korea perceived and sorted as desirable?

A range of pragmatic factors influenced parental decisions to adopt from Korea. Since each sending country, as well as each adoption agency, constructed (un)desirable parents differently, participants said that Korea was an attractive country to adopt from because they met the eligibility requirements and were considered desirable parents. In addition, Korea met many of the other factors parents felt were important. Adopting a healthy infant was possible in a short period of time, it was generally convenient (e.g., parents were not required to travel to Korea), and parents felt that when adopting from Korea they were working with a well-established program.

Moreover, while all of these aspects were relevant to parents, as the quotation that opens this section states, unlike sentiments parents expressed about Black children, the racial status of a child from Korea was seen as a "nice thing." While some parents initially indicated ambivalence or trepidation about adopting a child from Korea, each of the parents came to view children from Korea as desirable. One way of explaining this change is that some contemporary stereotypes of Asians make Asian children seem more compatible with white, middle-class culture. For example, stereotypes of Asians as the model minority (Kibria 2002; Min 1995) or as "Honorary Whites" (Bonilla-Silva 2004; Tuan 1998) likely promote Asians, especially Asian females, as less oppositional and more compatible to whites than other racial-ethnic minorities.

In fact, most parents expressed fairly positive attitudes about the racial status and characteristics of children adopted from Korea. Kara, for example, did not recall investigating countries other than Korea. She shared,

> *. . . we never really looked at others, no, um, there, you know, there was something about the Asian culture, I don't know what it is, you know. I hate to sound hoaky but um, there's something that, I don't know. [Pause] I remember one time [my husband] and I went out to dinner and we saw this family, mother, father and ah, a little Korean girl, she was only about 10 and we were just watching, and we just like couldn't take our eyes off her, you know? And we didn't want to stare but, you know, it's just, it just gave us a good feeling.*

Thus, Kara felt positively about Asian culture, and seeing another Korean child before she adopted gave her a good feeling about Korean features.

Molly also expressed enthusiasm regarding the physical characteristics of children adopted from Korea. After describing a meeting with a social worker who worked with Korean adoptions, Molly emphatically stated,

> *So you know, [my husband and I said], "Oh, the babies are beautiful!" We saw the babies and they had pictures of all these little toddlers, and they were so pretty.*

Amy echoed Molly's positive sentiments. At one point in our conversation, I asked her to expand on the process of adopting from Korea.

> K: *So how did you come up with Korea?*
>
> A: *Well, you know, that's a good question. My husband, I think [pause] thought of that idea because he thinks Asian people are beautiful, and they are beautiful . . . so he, I think he came up with that. He was kind of drawn to that.*

In Amy's and Molly's opinions, Asian babies were physically attractive, and thus, one nice thing about adopting children from Korea was the appeal of their physical characteristics.

In contrast to the examples above, Lois, a mother of an adopted son and daughter (both from Korea) noted that it was not necessarily anything about the racial status of Asians in particular that she was attracted to. Unlike Amy and Molly, Lois did not focus on the beauty of Asian babies. Rather, for her, there came a point where having a baby that physically resembled them in terms of race became secondary. She stated,

> *[We] had contacted our attorney, actually, um, [pause] who had done a lot of adoptions and asked him, you know, what avenue, which avenues he thought would be best. And he sort of [pause] told us about a few different things, because at this point we also were looking at a time frame where we didn't want to wait another 7 years, [pause] it wasn't important to us, to, to have [pause] um, [pause] a, you know, [pause] Caucasian baby that looks similar to us, or, or whatever, so [pause] so I contacted all these different agencies and asked them to send some information.*

Lois' comments were instructive because they suggested that whiteness was pivotal to her decision-making process. Similar to other respondents, it was only in the face of a substantial wait time for healthy, white infants that the idea of having a baby that looks similar (i.e., racial matching) became less important for her.

While Lois' description indicated that it was "not important" to have a Caucasian baby, her description of the adoption process still points to an important tension. As previously discussed, there were children available in the United States who did not have an extended waiting period (i.e., Black and Latino infants). Yet, Black children and infants of color who were more readily available would not look like them, especially in terms of racial matching.

Although I do not have specific evidence from this mother, one interpretation might be that even though it was not important to have a baby that looked similar, it was important that the child not look *too different*. More specifically, while Asian children might not provide an exact match, Asians might signal an acceptable amount of racial-ethnic difference. Additionally, the racial-ethnic differences may be perceived as compatible (and perhaps complementary to) whiteness, especially within a framework of viewing Asians as "Honorary Whites." For instance, in an ironic twist, at different moments, some parents noted that they thought their adoptive kids looked like them. For example, Shelby described telling others about the physical features she felt were similar between her and her son. She stated, *"What we used to say to people when [my son came], and we still do, 'I think he has my straight hair and his father's brown eyes.' So we tell him he looks like us too."* These cases may suggest that it is not just the racial status of Asians that is considered a "nice thing," but that parents needed to feel like they could make connections with their children about how similar they look. For instance, Holly pointed out that her daughters initiated comments about the physical similarities. She recalled her daughters saying, *"Mommy, aren't we starting to look more like you?"* Another mother, Ellen, commenting on her age and the fact that she was starting to color her hair and consequently every month it was a different color, noted how much she liked her daughter's hair. She stated, *"I have always strived to have the same color as [my daughter]. I want to have the same color hair as her."* While talking about physical similarities between parents and children is not exclusive to families who adopt, such conversations do take on particular significance in adoption, especially in the context of race and racial dynamics. In light of racism, white parents adopting children from Korea might be understood as a way of avoiding direct engagement with racial dynamics that feel oppositional and, instead, engaging with parts that feel more comfortable. As illustrated by this mother's comments, in some cases, it may be more than merely comfort—it could be envy and admiration for certain characteristics like her daughter's hair.[7]

Discussion

This reading explored the ways adoptive parents used various characteristics to sort children as desirable or undesirable. While parents generally began their explanations by framing their responses such that having a healthy child was paramount, health was not necessarily the most important characteristic that shaped decisions about who parents would adopt. Instead, other factors, most notably, race, appeared to be significant, although at times it remained "unmarked" or racially coded. For Asians, specifically those from Korea, racial stereotypes appeared to act as a resource, which allowed them to be sorted as desirable potential family members in transracial adoptions. Conversely, for African Americans, race became their master status and, as signaled by the title of this piece, they were quite literally sorted out of the adoption process. As such, my data on adoption indicate support for Bonilla-Silva's (2004) contention that a system of tri-racialization is at work in the United States.

Studying adoption in general, and transracial, intercountry adoptions in particular, is sociologically relevant for a number of reasons. For one, written within constructions of racial desirability are constructions of undesirability. As such, racial-ethnic hierarchies (and at times binaries) are produced in which the desirable and the preferable child is understood and constructed in direct relation to the undesirable child (i.e., knowing who and what is desirable offers clues about what is undesirable and vice versa).

Additionally, interpretations and constructions of racial and gender desirability are, in large part, contingent upon and reflective of the preferences of the adopters. While parents' preferences for certain children might be framed as matters of individual choice and personal taste, focusing on their choices as merely individual preferences or private decisions, leaves issues of larger social structures, such as racism and white privilege, unchallenged.[8] It is critical to realize that individual choices and preferences are inextricably linked and indeed embedded in broader social, cultural, and historical contexts—families and adoption do not occur outside of or independent from other sociohistorical forces. Thus, in terms of racial-ethnic preferences, parental decisions and inclinations for whites and Asians, and an avoidance of adopting Blacks and Latinos, can (and should) be understood within larger sociohistorical contexts and processes. In short, the issues, questions, and struggles adoptive parents described are significant not only because of the constructions of desirability themselves (i.e., which children are perceived as adoptable and which children are actually (not) adopted) but given historical and current social inequalities, these issues also contribute to our understanding of the ways privilege, especially parents' racial privilege, operates and, at certain moments, perpetuates social inequalities.

Finally, while one way of interpreting parents' accounts and standpoints is to view parents who would not adopt (or who showed hesitancy toward adopting) Black and Latino children as racist, those who were willing to adopt children of color as not racist, such a binary is weak and much too simplistic. Indeed, it is more complicated and complex than this statement. Certainly, those who (more openly) expressed hostility and ambivalence toward adopting Black children reflected and perpetuated racist ideologies. But those who were willing to adopt nonwhites also operated and were embedded in sociohistorical forces that were deeply implicated in racist ideologies and practices. Thus, openness to adopting a racial-ethnic minority, and a Black child in particular, does not mean adoptive parents have not absorbed and subscribed to other pieces of racism in the culture.

ENDNOTES

[1]The one exception to this was a father who identified himself as second-generation Chinese.

[2]I highlight the "formal legal" aspect of this process in an effort to address common assumptions and misperceptions that African Americans do not adopt or do not want to adopt. It is

important to note that alternatives to the formal legal channels have been established and utilized by African Americans but have not been recognized as legitimate adoptions by the legal system. Often labeled "kinship adoptions" (Hill 1977; Stack 1974), these have been an important and integral part of African American family life, especially in light of persistent structural challenges (such as poverty) and oppression. In addition, current scholarship indicates that African Americans are just as likely to adopt as whites. One way to interpret the lack of parity in adoptions, then, is to revisit Joyce Ladner's (1977) assertion: "The fact that adoption agencies do not carry out a brisk business in placing children in black homes should not be used as documentation for the myth that blacks do not adopt. It is probably more reasonable to examine the effectiveness of agencies in locating and recruiting black adoptive parents" (p. 68). Part of a larger research project could indeed expand on this idea.

[3]Racial matching also allowed parents a degree of freedom in "hiding" the adoption from their child. In fact, until recently, concealing adoptions from children was not uncommon and was even advocated by some parents and professionals. For further discussion of secrecy and disclosure issues, see Grotevant and McRoy 1997; Carp 1998; and Baran, Reuben, and Sorosky 1997.

[4]In some cases, adoptive parents were required to choose or reject the actual children.

[5]The attention to the ways parents who adopt make "choices" often obscures and/or ignores the range of choices that parents who have genetically related children make as well, e.g., who their partners or spouses are (their race-ethnicity, body type, etc.).

[6]Moreover, this highlights an important tension, since Amy's family, as well as that of others in this study, included children adopted from Korea. Her description revealed a common pattern—attention to other nationalities was directed toward Korea, not "other nationalities here," in the United States.

[7]Significantly, given cultural scripts, it is difficult to imagine substituting African American in this situation.

[8]As I write this conclusion, there is a small movement trying to bring awareness to the disparity in adoption fees for babies of different races. One U.S. ad campaign has a picture of three infants, one white, one Black, and one who is a racial-ethnic minority with skin coloring in between the white and Black infants. Across each of the infants is their "value"—the white child has $35,000, the Black child has $4,000, and the child with the skin coloring in between the white and Black infants says $10,000.

WORKS CITED

Baran, Annette, P. Reuben, and A. Sorosky. 1997. "Open Adoption." *Social Work* 21(2):97–100.

Bonilla-Silva, Eduardo. 2004. "From Bi-Racial to Tri-Racial: Towards a New System of Racial Stratification in the USA." *Ethnic and Racial Studies* 27(6):931–50.

Carp, Wayne E., ed. 1998. *Family Matters: Secrecy and Disclosure in the History of Adoption.* Cambridge: Harvard University Press.

———, ed. 2002. *Adoption in America: Historical Perspectives.* Ann Arbor: University of Michigan Press.

Collins, Patricia Hill. 1998. *Fighting Words: Black Women and the Search for Justice.* Minneapolis: University of Minnesota Press.

Grotevant, Harold and R. McRoy. 1997. "The Minnesota/Texas Adoption Research Project: Implications of Openness in Adoption for Development and Relationship." *Applied Developmental Science* 1(4):168–87.

Hill, Robert. 1977. *Informal Adoption among Black Families.* Washington, DC: National Urban League Research Department.

Kibria, Nazli. 2002. *Becoming Asian American: Second-Generation Chinese and Korean American Identities.* Baltimore: Johns Hopkins University Press.

Ladner, Joyce. 1977. *Mixed Families: Adopting across Racial Boundaries.* New York: Anchor Press/Doubleday.

Luker, Kristin. 1996. *Dubious Conceptions: The Politics of Teenage Pregnancy.* Cambridge: Harvard University Press.

May, Elaine Tyler. 1995. *Barren in the Promised Land: Childless Americans and the Pursuit of Happiness.* Boston: Harvard University Press.

Melosh, Barbara. 2002. *Strangers and Kin: The American Way of Adoption.* Cambridge: Harvard University Press.

Min, Pyong Gap. 1995. "Major Issues Relating to Asian American Experiences." In *Asian Americans: Contemporary Trends and Issues (1st ed.),* edited by Pyong Gap Min. Thousand Oaks: Sage.

Park, Robert. 1950. *Race and Culture.* Glencoe: Free Press.

Roberts, Dorothy. 1997. *Killing the Black Body: Race, Reproduction and the Meaning of Liberty.* New York: Pantheon.

Solinger, Rickie. 1992. "Race and 'Value': Black and White Illegitimate Babies, in the U.S., 1945–1965." In *Unequal Sisters: A Multicultural Reader in U.S. Women's History,* edited by Vicki L. Ruiz and Ellen Carol Dubois. New York: Routledge.

———. 1992. *Wake Up Little Susie: Single Pregnancy and Race before Roe v. Wade.* New York: Routledge.

Stack, Carol. 1974. *All Our Kin.* New York: Basic Books.

Tuan, Mia. 1998. *Forever Foreigners or Honorary Whites? The Asian Ethnic Experience Today.* New Brunswick, NJ: Rutgers University Press.

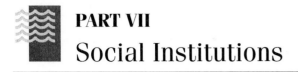

PART VII

POWER AND POLITICS

35

THE POWER ELITE

C. WRIGHT MILLS

Who really governs in the United States? In this selection, sociologist C. Wright Mills argues that the most important decisions in this country are made by a cohesive "power elite." This *power elite* consists of the top leaders in three areas: The corporate elite is made up of the executives from large companies; the military elite is the senior officers; and the small political elite includes the president and top officials in the executive and legislative branches. According to Mills' argument, these elite officials all know each other and act in unison when critical decisions must be made. This selection, originally published in 1956, is the first of three addressing power and politics.

The powers of ordinary men are circumscribed by the everyday worlds in which they live, yet even in these rounds of job, family, and neighborhood, they often seem driven by forces they can neither understand nor govern. "Great changes" are beyond their control, but affect their conduct and outlook nonetheless. The very framework of modern society confines them to projects not their own, but from every side, such changes now press upon the men and women of the mass society, who accordingly feel that they are without purpose in an epoch in which they are without power.

But not all men are in this sense ordinary. As the means of information and of power are centralized, some men come to occupy positions in American society from which they can look down upon, so to speak, and by their decisions mightily affect, the everyday worlds of ordinary men and women. They are not made by their jobs; they set up and break down jobs for thousands of others; they are not confined by simple family responsibilities; they can escape. They may live in many hotels and houses, but they are bound by no one community. They need not merely "meet the demands of the day and hour"; in some part, they create these demands and cause others to meet them. Whether or not they profess their power, their technical and political experience of it far transcends that of the underlying population. What Jacob Burckhardt [a German historian, 1818–1897] said of "great men," most Americans might well say of their elite: "They are all that we are not."

The power elite is composed of men whose positions enable them to transcend the ordinary environments of ordinary men and women; they are in positions to make decisions having major consequences. Whether they do or do not make such decisions is less important than the fact that they do occupy such pivotal positions: Their failure to act, their failure to make decisions, is itself an act that is often of greater consequence than the decisions they do make. For they are in command of the major hierarchies and organizations of modern society. They rule the big corporations. They run the machinery of the state and claim its prerogatives. They direct the military establishment. They occupy the strategic command posts of the social structure, in which are now centered the effective means of the power and the wealth and the celebrity which they enjoy.

The power elite are not solitary rulers. Advisers and consultants, spokesmen and opinion makers are often the captains of their higher thought and decision. Immediately below the elite are the professional politicians of the middle levels of power, in the Congress and in the pressure groups, as well as among the new and old upper classes of town and city and region. Mingling with them, in curious ways which we shall explore, are those professional celebrities who live by being continually displayed but are never, so long as they remain celebrities, displayed enough. If such celebrities are not at the head of any dominating hierarchy, they do often have the power to distract the attention of the public or afford sensations to the masses, or, more directly, to gain the ear of those who do occupy positions of direct power. More or less unattached, as critics of morality and technicians of power, as spokesmen of God and creators of mass sensibility, such celebrities and consultants are part of the immediate scene in which the drama of the elite is enacted. But that drama itself is centered in the command posts of the major institutional hierarchies.

The truth about the nature and the power of the elite is not some secret which men of affairs know but will not tell. Such men hold quite various theories about their own roles in the sequence of event and decision. Often they are uncertain about their roles, and even more often they allow their fears and their hopes to affect their assessment of their own power. No matter how great their actual power, they tend to be less acutely aware of it than of the resistances of others to its use. Moreover, most American men of affairs have learned well the rhetoric of public relations, in some cases even to the point of using it when they are alone, and thus coming to believe it. The personal awareness of the actors is only one of the several sources one must examine in order to understand the higher circles. Yet many who believe that there is no elite, or at any rate none of any consequence, rest their argument upon what men of affairs believe about themselves, or at least assert in public.

There is, however, another view: Those who feel, even if vaguely, that a compact and powerful elite of great importance does now prevail in America often base that feeling upon the historical trend of our time. They have felt, for example, the domination of the military event, and from this they infer that generals and admirals, as well as other men of decision influenced by them, must be enormously powerful. They hear that the Congress has again abdicated to a handful of men decisions clearly related to the issue of war or peace. They know that the bomb was dropped over Japan in the name of the United States of America, although they were at no time consulted about the matter. They feel that they live in a time of big decisions; they know that they are not making any. Accordingly, as they consider the present as history, they infer that at its center, making decisions or failing to make them, there must be an elite of power.

On the one hand, those who share this feeling about big historical events assume that there is an elite and that its power is great. On the other hand, those who listen carefully to the reports of men apparently involved in the great decisions often do not believe that there is an elite whose powers are of decisive consequence.

Both views must be taken into account, but neither is adequate. The way to understand the power of the American elite lies neither solely in recognizing the historic scale of events nor in accepting the personal awareness reported by men of apparent decision. Behind such men and behind the events of history, linking the two, are the major institutions of modern society. These hierarchies of state and corporation and army constitute the means of power; as such they are now of a consequence not before equaled in human history—and at their summits, there are now those command posts of modern society which offer us the sociological key to an understanding of the role of the higher circles in America.

Within American society, major national power now resides in the economic, the political, and the military domains. Other institutions seem off to the side of modern history, and, on occasion, duly subordinated to these. No family is as directly powerful in national affairs as any major corporation; no church is as directly powerful in the external biographies of young men in America today as the military establishment; no college is as powerful in the shaping of momentous events as the National Security Council. Religious, educational, and family institutions are not autonomous centers of national power; on the contrary, these decentralized areas are increasingly shaped by the big three, in which developments of decisive and immediate consequence now occur.

Families and churches and schools adapt to modern life; governments and armies and corporations shape it; and, as they do so, they turn these lesser institutions into means for their ends. Religious institutions provide chaplains to the armed forces where they are used as a means of increasing the effectiveness of its morale to kill. Schools select and train men for their jobs in corporations and their specialized tasks in the armed forces. The extended family has, of course, long been broken up by the industrial revolution, and now the son and the father are removed from the family, by compulsion if need be, whenever the army of the state sends out the call. And the symbols of all these lesser institutions are used to legitimate the power and the decisions of the big three.

The life-fate of the modern individual depends not only upon the family into which he was born or which he enters by marriage, but increasingly upon the corporation in which he spends the most alert hours of his best years; not only upon the school where he is educated as a child and adolescent, but also upon the state which touches him throughout his life; not only upon the church in which on occasion he hears the word of God, but also upon the army in which he is disciplined.

If the centralized state could not rely upon the inculcation of nationalist loyalties in public and private schools, its leaders would promptly seek to modify the decentralized educational system. If the bankruptcy rate among the top 500 corporations were as high as the general divorce rate among the 37 million married couples, there would be economic catastrophe on an international scale. If members of armies gave to them no more of their lives than do believers to the churches to which they belong, there would be a military crisis.

Within each of the big three, the typical institutional unit has become enlarged, has become administrative, and, in the power of its decisions, has become centralized. Behind these developments there is a fabulous technology, for as institutions, they have incorporated this technology and guide it, even as it shapes and paces their developments.

The economy—once a great scatter of small productive units in autonomous balance—has become dominated by two or three hundred giant corporations, administratively and politically interrelated, which together hold the keys to economic decisions.

The political order, once a decentralized set of several dozen states with a weak spinal cord, has become a centralized, executive establishment which has taken up into itself many powers previously scattered, and now enters into each and every cranny of the social structure.

The military order, once a slim establishment in a context of distrust fed by state militia, has become the largest and most expensive feature of government, and, although well-versed in smiling public relations, now has all the grim and clumsy efficiency of a sprawling bureaucratic domain.

In each of these institutional areas, the means of power at the disposal of decision makers have increased enormously; their central executive powers have been enhanced; within each of them modern administrative routines have been elaborated and tightened up.

As each of these domains becomes enlarged and centralized, the consequences of its activities become greater, and its traffic with the others increases. The decisions of a handful of corporations bear upon military and political as well as upon economic developments around the world. The decisions of the military establishment rest upon and grievously affect political life as well as the very level of economic activity. The decisions made within the political domain determine economic activities and military programs. There is no longer, on the one hand, an economy, and, on the other hand, a political order containing a military establishment unimportant to politics and to money making. There is a political economy linked, in a thousand ways, with military institutions and decisions. On each side of the world-split running through central Europe and around the Asiatic rimlands, there is an ever-increasing interlocking of economic, military, and political structures. If there is government intervention in the corporate economy, so is there corporate intervention in the governmental process. In the structural sense, this triangle of power is the source of the interlocking directorate that is most important for the historical structure of the present.

The fact of the interlocking is clearly revealed at each of the points of crisis of modern capitalist society—slump, war, and boom. In each, men of decision are led to an awareness of the interdependence of the major institutional orders. In the nineteenth century, when the scale of all institutions was smaller, their liberal integration was achieved in the automatic economy, by an autonomous play of market forces, and in the automatic political domain, by the bargain and the vote. It was then assumed that out of the imbalance and friction that followed the limited decisions then possible a new equilibrium would in due course emerge. That can no longer be assumed, and it is not assumed by the men at the top of each of the three dominant hierarchies.

For given the scope of their consequences, decisions—and indecisions—in any one of these ramify into the others, and hence top decisions tend either to become coordinated or to lead to a commanding indecision. It has not always been like this. When numerous small entrepreneurs made up the economy, for example, many of them could fail and the consequences still remain local; political and military authorities did not intervene. But now, given political expectations and military commitments, can they afford to allow key units of the private corporate economy to break down in slump? Increasingly, they do intervene in economic affairs, and as they do so, the controlling decisions in each order are inspected by agents of the other two, and economic, military, and political structures are interlocked.

At the pinnacle of each of the three enlarged and centralized domains, there have arisen those higher circles which make up the economic, the political, and the military elites. At the top of the economy, among the corporate rich, there are the chief executives; at the top of the political order, the members of the political directorate; at the top of the military establishment, the elite of soldier-statesmen clustered in and around the Joint Chiefs of Staff and the upper echelon. As each of these domains has coincided with the others, as decisions tend to become total in their consequence, the leading men in each of the three domains of power—the warlords, the corporation chieftains, the political directorate—tend to come together, to form the power elite of America.

The higher circles in and around these command posts are often thought of in terms of what their members possess: They have a greater share than other people of the things and experiences that are most highly valued. From this point of view, the elite are simply those who have the most of what there is to have, which is generally held to include money, power, and prestige—as well as all the ways of life to which these lead. But the elite are not simply those who have the most, for they could not "have the most" were it not for their positions in the great institutions. For such institutions are the necessary bases of power, of wealth, and of prestige, and at the same time, the chief means of exercising power, of acquiring and retaining wealth, and of cashing in the higher claims for prestige.

By the powerful we mean, of course, those who are able to realize their will, even if others resist it. No one, accordingly, can be truly powerful unless he has access to the command of major institutions, for it is over these institutional means of power that the truly powerful are, in the first instance, powerful. Higher politicians and key officials of government command such institutional power; so do admirals and generals, and so do the major owners and executives of the larger corporations. Not all power, it is true, is anchored in and exercised by means of such institutions, but only within and through them can power be more or less continuous and important.

Wealth also is acquired and held in and through institutions. The pyramid of wealth cannot be understood merely in terms of the very rich; for the great inheriting families, as we shall see, are now supplemented by the corporate institutions of modern society: Every one of the very rich families has been and is closely connected—always legally and frequently managerially as well—with one of the multimillion-dollar corporations.

The modern corporation is the prime source of wealth, but, in latter-day capitalism, the political apparatus also opens and closes many avenues to wealth. The amount as well as the source of income, the power over consumer's goods as well as over productive capital, are determined by position within the political economy. If our interest in the very rich goes beyond their lavish or their miserly consumption, we must examine their relations to modern forms of corporate property as well as to the state; for such relations now determine the chances of men to secure big property and to receive high income.

Great prestige increasingly follows the major institutional units of the social structure. It is obvious that prestige depends, often quite decisively, upon access to the publicity machines that are now a central and normal feature of all the big institutions of modern America. Moreover, one feature of these hierarchies of corporation, state, and military establishment is that their top positions are increasingly interchangeable. One result of this is the accumulative nature of prestige. Claims for prestige, for example, may be initially based on military roles, then expressed in and augmented by an educational institution run by corporate executives, and cashed in, finally, in the political order, where, for General Eisenhower and those he represents, power and prestige finally meet at the very peak. Like wealth and power, prestige tends to be cumulative: The more of it you have, the more you can get. These values also tend to be translatable into one another: The wealthy find it easier than the poor to gain power; those with status find it easier than those without it to control opportunities for wealth.

If we took the one hundred most powerful men in America, the one hundred wealthiest, and the one hundred most celebrated away from the institutional positions they now occupy, away from their resources of men and women and money, away from the media of mass communication that are now focused upon them—then they would be powerless and poor and uncelebrated. For power is not of a man. Wealth does not center in the person of the wealthy. Celebrity is not inherent in any personality. To be celebrated, to be wealthy, to have power requires access to major institutions, for the institutional positions men occupy determine in large part their chances to have and to hold these valued experiences.

The people of the higher circles may also be conceived as members of a top social stratum, as a set of groups whose members know one another, see one another socially and at business, and so, in making decisions, take one another into account. The elite, according to this conception, feel themselves to be, and are felt by others to be, the inner circle of "the upper social classes." They form a more or less compact social and psychological entity; they have become self-conscious members of a social class. People are either accepted into this class or they are not, and there is a qualitative split, rather than merely a numerical scale, separating them from those who are not elite. They are more or less aware of themselves as a social class, and they behave toward one another differently from the way they do toward members of other classes. They accept one another, understand one another, marry one another, tend to work and to think if not together at least alike.

Now, we do not want by our definition to prejudge whether the elite of the command posts are conscious members of such a socially recognized class, or whether considerable proportions of the elite derive from such a clear and distinct class. These are matters to be investigated. Yet in order to be able to recognize what we intend to investigate, we must note something that all biographies and memoirs of the wealthy and the powerful and the eminent make clear: No matter what else they may be, the people of these higher circles are involved in a set of overlapping "crowds" and intricately connected "cliques." There is a kind of mutual attraction among those who "sit on the same terrace"—although this often becomes clear to them, as well as to others, only at the point at which they feel the need to draw the line; only when, in their common defense, they come to understand what they have in common, and so close their ranks against outsiders.

The idea of such a ruling stratum implies that most of its members have similar social origins, that throughout their lives they maintain a network of informal connections, and that to some degree there is an interchangeability of position between the various hierarchies of money and power and celebrity. We must, of course, note at once that if such an elite stratum does exist, its social visibility and its form, for very solid historical reasons, are quite different from those of the noble cousinhoods that once ruled various European nations.

That American society has never passed through a feudal epoch is of decisive importance to the nature of the American elite, as well as to American society as a historic whole. For it means that no nobility or aristocracy, established before the capitalist era, has stood in tense opposition to the higher bourgeoisie. It means that this bourgeoisie has monopolized not only wealth but prestige and power as well. It means that no set of noble families has commanded the top positions and monopolized the values that are generally held in high esteem; and certainly that no set has done so explicitly by inherited right. It means that no high church dignitaries or court nobilities, no entrenched landlords with honorific accouterments, no monopolists of high army posts have opposed the enriched bourgeoisie and in the name of birth and prerogative successfully resisted its self-making.

But this does *not* mean that there are no upper strata in the United States. That they emerged from a "middle class" that had no recognized aristocratic superiors does not mean they remained middle class when enormous increases in wealth made their own superiority possible. Their origins and their newness may have made the upper strata less visible in America than elsewhere. But in America today there are in fact tiers and ranges of wealth and power of which people in the middle and lower ranks know very little and may not even dream. There are families who, in their well-being, are quite insulated from the economic jolts and lurches felt by the merely prosperous and those farther down the scale. There are also men of power who in quite small groups make decisions of enormous consequence for the underlying population.

36

DOLLARS AND VOTES
How Business Campaign
Contributions Subvert Democracy

DAN CLAWSON • ALAN NEUSTADTL • MARK WELLER

Sociological research supports the thesis that a power elite exists in this country. A point of debate is the degree of interconnection among the three groups—the corporate, military, and political elite. Nonetheless, current social research still indicates that power is concentrated among a few social groups and institutions, as shown in a 1998 study discussed in this selection by sociologists Dan Clawson, Alan Neustadtl, and Mark Weller. After investigating 309 corporate political action committees (PACs), the authors conclude that PACs, which represent corporate interests, ensure that the concerns of Big Business are heard on Capitol Hill.

The Money Primary

Imagine the November election is just a few weeks away, and your friend Sally Robeson is seriously considering running for Congress two years from now. This year the incumbent in your district, E. Chauncey DeWitt III, will (again!) be reelected by a substantial margin, but you and Sally hate Chauncey's positions on the issues and are convinced that with the right campaign he can be beaten. Sally is capable, articulate, well informed, respected in the community, politically and socially connected, charming, good at talking to many kinds of people, and highly telegenic. She has invited you and several other politically active friends to meet with her immediately after the election to determine what she would need to do to become a viable candidate.

The meeting that takes place covers a host of topics: What are the key issues? On which of these are Sally's stands popular, and on which unpopular? What attacks, and from what quarters, will be launched against her? What individuals or groups can she count on for support? How, why, and where is the incumbent vulnerable? But lurking in the background is the question that cannot be ignored: *Can Sally (with the help of her friends and backers) raise enough money to be a contender?*

This is the *money primary, the first, and, in many instances, the most important round of the contest.* It eliminates more candidates than any other hurdle. Because it eliminates them so early and so quietly, its impact is often unobserved. To make it through, candidates don't have to come in first, but they do need to raise enough money to be credible contenders. Although having the most money is no guarantee of victory, candidates who don't do well in the money primary are no longer serious contenders. Certainly, plenty of well-funded candidates lose—Michael Huffington spent $25 million of his own money in an unsuccessful 1994 race for the Senate. But in order to be viable, a candidate needs to raise a substantial minimum.

How much is needed? If Sally hopes to win, rather than just put up a good fight, she, you, and the rest of her supporters will need to raise staggering amounts. (At least they are staggering from the perspective of most Americans; Ross Perot, Steve Forbes, or Michael Huffington may view the matter differently.) In order to accumulate the *average* amount for major-party congressional candidates in the general election, you will collectively need to raise $4,800 next week. And the week after. And *every* week for the next two years.

But even that is not enough. The average amount includes many candidates who were never "serious"; that is, they didn't raise enough to have a realistic hope of winning. If you and your friends want to raise the average amount spent by a *winning* candidate for the House, you'll have to come up with $6,730 next week and every single week until the election, two years away.

Well, you say, your candidate is hardly average. She is stronger, smarter, more politically appealing, and more viable than the "average" challenger. You think she can win even if she doesn't raise $6,730 a week. Let's use past experience—the results of the 1996 elections—to consider the likelihood of winning for challengers, based on how much money they raised. In 1996 more than 360 House incumbents were running for reelection; only 23 of them were beaten by their challengers. The average successful challenger spent $1,045,361—that is, he or she raised an average of over $10,000 every week for two years. What were the chances of winning without big money? Only one winning challenger spent less than $500,000, 12 spent between a half-a-million and a million dollars, and 10 spent more than a million dollars. Furthermore, 13 of the 23 winning challengers outspent the incumbent. A House challenger who can't raise at least a half-million dollars doesn't have a one percent chance of winning; the key primary is the money primary. The *Boston Globe* reported that "House candidates who headed into the final three weeks with the most in combined spending and cash on hand won 93 percent of the time."[1] What about that one low-spending winner? She is Carolyn Cheeks Kilpatrick, who won election by beating an incumbent in the primary and then having a walkover in the general election; the district, in Detroit, is the fourth poorest in the nation and consistently votes more than 80 percent Democratic. Although Kilpatrick spent only $174,457, few other districts make possible a similar election strategy.

In the Senate, even more money is needed. Suppose your candidate were going to run for the Senate, and started fundraising immediately after an election, giving her six years to prepare for the next election. How much money would she need to raise each and every week for those *six* years? The average winning Senate candidate raised approximately $15,000 per week.

For presidential candidates, the stakes are, of course, much higher: "The prevailing view is that for a politician to be considered legitimate, he or she must collect at least $20 million by the first of January 2000."[2] Presumably any candidate who does not do so is "illegitimate" and does not belong in the race. . . .

Coming up with the money is a major hassle; even for incumbents, it requires constant effort. *National Journal*, probably the single most authoritative source on the Washington scene, reports that "there is widespread agreement that the congressional money chase has become an unending marathon, as wearying to participants as it is disturbing to spectators," and quoted an aide to a Democratic senator as observing, "During hearings of Senate committees, you can watch senators go to phone booths in the committee rooms to dial for dollars." Just a few years ago—in 1990, the date of this statement—soliciting funds from federal property, whether Congress or the White House, was routine, openly discussed, and not regarded as problematic. The activity had always been technically illegal, but only in 1997 did it become an issue, with President Clinton and (especially) Vice President Gore singled out as if they were the only offenders. . . .

Not only is it necessary to raise lots of money; it is important—for both incumbents and challengers—to raise it early. Senator Rudy Boschwitz, Republican of Minnesota, was clear about this as a strategy. He spent $6 million getting reelected in 1984 and had raised $1.5 million of it by the beginning of the year, effectively discouraging the most promising Democratic challengers. After the election he wrote, and typed up himself, a secret evaluation of his campaign strategy:

> "Nobody in politics (except me!) likes to raise money, so I thought the best way of discouraging the toughest opponents from running was to have a few dollars in the sock. I believe it worked. . . . From all forms of fundraising I raised $6 million plus and got 3 or 4 (maybe even 5) stories and cartoons that irked me," he said. "In retrospect, I'm glad I had the money."[3]

Similarly, in March 1996 Bill Paxon, chair of the House Republican campaign committee, said, "We've been pounding on members to raise more money by the filing deadline; if they show a good balance, that could ward off opponents."[4]

The Contributors' Perspective

Candidates need money, lots of it, if they are to have any chance of winning. The obvious next question, and in some sense the focus of [our research], is who gives, why, and what they expect for it.

Contributions are made for many different reasons. The candidate's family and friends chip in out of loyalty and affection. Others contribute because they are asked to do so by someone who has done favors for them. People give because they agree with the candidate's stand on the issues, either on a broad ideological basis or on a specific issue. Sometimes these donations are portrayed as a form of voting—people show that they care by putting their money where their mouth is, anyone can contribute, and the money raised reflects the wishes of the people. Even for these contributions, however, if voting with dollars replaces voting at the ballot box, then the votes will be very unequally distributed: the top 1 percent of the population by wealth will have more "votes" than the bottom 90 percent of the population. In the 1996 elections, less than one-fourth of one percent of the population gave contributions of $200 or more to a federal candidate.[5] PACs and large contributors provide most of the money, however; small contributors accounted for under one-third of candidate receipts.[6]

It is not just that contributions come from the well-to-do. Most contributors have a direct material interest in what the government does or does not do. Their contributions, most of them made directly or indirectly by business, provide certain people a form of leverage and "access" not available to the rest of us. The chair of the political action committee at one of the twenty-five largest manufacturing companies in the United States explained to us why his corporation has a PAC:

> The PAC gives you access. It makes you a player. These congressmen, in particular, are constantly fundraising. Their elections are very expensive, and getting increasingly expensive each year. So they have an ongoing need for funds.
>
> It profits us in a sense to be able to provide some funds because in the provision of it you get to know people, you help them out. There's no real quid pro quo. There is nobody whose vote you can count on, not with the kind of money we are talking about here. But the PAC gives you access. Puts you in the game.
>
> You know, some congressman has got X number of ergs of energy and here's a person or a company who wants to come see him and give him a thousand dollars, and here's another one who wants to just stop by and say hello. And he only has time to see one. Which one? So the PAC's an attention getter.

So-called soft money, where the amount of the contribution is unlimited, might appear to be an exception: Isn't $100,000 enough to buy a guaranteed outcome? We will argue that it is *not*, at least not in any simple and straightforward way. PAC contributions are primarily for members of Congress; they are for comparatively small amounts, but enough to gain access to individual members of Congress. The individual member, however, has limited power. Soft money donations are best thought of as a way of gaining access to the president, top party leaders, and the executive branch. These individuals are more powerful than ordinary members of Congress, so access to them comes at a higher price. That privileged access is invaluable, but, as we will try to show, it does not—and is not expected to—*guarantee* a quid pro quo. The following example illustrates how corporations benefit from this "access" and how they use it to manipulate the system.

Why Does the Air Stink?

Everybody wants clean air. Who could oppose it? "I spent seven years of my life trying to stop the Clean Air Act," explained the vice president of a major corporation that is a heavy-duty polluter. Nonetheless, he was perfectly willing to make campaign contributions to members who voted for the act:

> How a person votes on the final piece of legislation often is not representative of what they have done. Somebody will do a lot of things during the process. How many guys voted against the Clean Air Act? But during the process some of them were very sympathetic to some of our concerns.

In the world of Congress and political action committees things, are not always what they seem. Members of Congress all want to vote for clean air, but they also want to get campaign contributions from corporations, and they want to pass a law that business will accept as "reasonable." The compromise solution is to gut the bill by crafting dozens of loopholes. These are inserted in private meetings or in subcommittee hearings that don't get much (if any) attention in the press. Then the public vote on the final bill can be nearly unanimous. Members of Congress can reassure both their constituents and their corporate contributors: constituents, that they voted for the final bill; corporations, that they helped weaken it in private. [Our research] analyzes how this happens; clean air, and especially the Clean Air Act of 1990, can serve as an introduction to the kind of process we try to expose.

The public strongly supports clean air and is unimpressed when corporate officials and apologists trot out their normal arguments—"corporations are already doing all they reasonably can to improve environmental quality," "we need to balance the costs against the benefits," "people will lose their jobs if we make controls any stricter." The original Clean Air Act was passed in 1970, revised in 1977, and not revised again until 1990. Although the initial goal was to have us breathing clean air by 1975, the deadline has been repeatedly extended—and the 1990 legislation provides a new set of deadlines to be reached sometime in the distant future.

Corporations control the production process unless the government specifically intervenes. Therefore, any delay in government action leaves corporations free to do as they choose; business often prefers a weak, ineffective, and unenforceable law. The laws have not only been slow to come, but corporations have also fought to delay or subvert implementation. The 1970 law ordered the Environmental Protection Agency (EPA) to regulate the hundreds of poisonous chemicals that are emitted by corporations, but, as William Greider notes, "In twenty years of stalling, dodging, and fighting off court orders, the EPA has managed to issue regulatory standards for a total of seven toxics."[7]

Corporations have done exceptionally well politically, given the problem they face: The interests of business are diametrically opposed to those of the public. Clean-air laws and amendments have been few and far between, enforcement is ineffective, and the penalties minimal. On the one hand, corporations *have* had to pay *billions* for cleanups; on the other, the costs to date are a small fraction of what would be needed to actually clean up the environment.

This corporate struggle for the right to pollute has taken place on many fronts. The most visible is public relations: the Chemical Manufacturers Association took out a two-page Earth Day ad in the *Washington Post* to demonstrate its concern; coincidentally, the names of many of the corporate signers of this ad appear on the EPA's list of high-risk producers.[8] Another front is expert studies that delay action while more information is gathered. The federally funded National Acid Precipitation Assessment Program took ten years and $600 million to figure out whether acid rain was in fact a problem. Both business and the Reagan administration argued that nothing should be done until the study was completed.[9] Ultimately, the study was discredited: The "summary of findings" minimized the impact of acid rain, even though this did not accurately represent the expert research in the report. But the key site of struggle was Congress. For years, corporations successfully defeated legislation. In 1987 utility companies were offered a compromise bill on acid rain, but they "were very adamant that they had beat the thing since 1981 and they could always beat it," according to Representative Edward Madigan

(Republican–Illinois).[10] The utilities beat back all efforts at reform through the 1980s, but their intransigence probably hurt them when revisions finally came to be made.

The stage was set for a revision of the Clean Air Act when George Bush, "the environmental president," was elected, and George Mitchell, a strong supporter of environmentalism, became the Senate majority leader. But what sort of clean air bill would it be? "What we wanted," said Richard Ayres, head of the environmentalists' Clean Air Coalition, "is a health based standard—one-in-1-million cancer risk," a standard that would require corporations to clean up their plants until the cancer risk from their operations was reduced to 1 in a million. "The Senate bill still has the requirement," Ayres said, "but there are forty pages of extensions and exceptions and qualifications and loopholes that largely render the health standard a nullity."[11] Greider reports, for example, "According to the EPA, there are now twenty-six coke ovens that pose a cancer risk greater than 1 in 1000 and six where the risk is greater than 1 in 100. Yet the new clean-air bill will give the steel industry another thirty years to deal with the problem."[12]

This change from what the bill was supposed to do to what it did do came about through what corporate executives like to call the "access" process. The principal aim of most corporate campaign contributions is to help corporate executives gain "access" to key members of Congress and their staffs. In these meetings, corporate executives (and corporate PAC money) work to persuade the member of Congress to accept a predesigned loophole that will sound innocent but effectively undercut the stated intention of the bill. Representative John D. Dingell (Democrat–Michigan), who was chair of the House committee, is a strong industry supporter; one of the people we interviewed called him "the point man for the Business Roundtable on clean air." Representative Henry A. Waxman (Democrat–California), chair of the subcommittee, is an environmentalist. Observers had expected a confrontation and contested votes on the floor of the Congress.

The problem for corporations was that, as one Republican staff aide said, "If any bill has the blessing of Waxman and the environmental groups, unless it is totally in outer space, who's going to vote against it?"[13] But corporations successfully minimized public votes. Somehow, Waxman was persuaded to make behind-the-scenes compromises with Dingell so members, during an election year, didn't have to side publicly with business against the environment. Often the access process leads to loopholes that protect a single corporation, but for "clean" air most of the special deals targeted not specific companies but entire industries. The initial bill, for example, required cars to be able to use carefully specified, cleaner fuels. But the auto industry wanted the rules loosened, and Congress eventually incorporated a variant of a formula suggested by the head of General Motors' fuels and lubricants department.

Nor did corporations stop fighting even after they gutted the bill through amendments. Business pressed the EPA for favorable regulations to implement the law: "The cost of this legislation could vary dramatically, depending on how EPA interprets it," said William D. Fay, vice president of the National Coal Association, who headed the hilariously misnamed Clean Air Working Group, an industry coalition that fought to weaken the legislation.[14] As one EPA aide working on acid rain regulations reported, "We're having a hard time getting our work done because of the number of phone calls we're getting" from corporations and their lawyers.

Corporations trying to get federal regulators to adopt the "right" regulations don't rely exclusively on the cogency of their arguments. They often exert pressure on a member of Congress to intervene for them at the EPA or other agency. Senators and representatives regularly intervene on behalf of constituents and contributors by doing everything from straightening out a social security problem to asking a regulatory agency to explain why it is pressuring a company. This process—like campaign finance—usually follows rules of etiquette. In addressing a regulatory agency, the senator does not say: "Lay off my campaign contributors or I'll cut your budget." One standard phrasing for letters asks regulators to resolve the problem "as quickly as possible within applicable rules and regulations."[15] No matter how mild and careful the inquiry, the agency receiving the request is certain to give it extra attention; only after careful consideration will they refuse to make any accommodation.

Soft money—unregulated megabuck contributions—also shaped what happened to air quality. Archer Daniels Midland argued that increased use of ethanol would reduce pollution from gasoline; coincidentally, ADM controls a majority of the ethanol market. To reinforce its arguments, in the 1992 election ADM gave $90,000 to Democrats and $600,000 to Republicans, the latter supplemented with an additional $200,000 as an individual contribution from the company head, Dwayne Andreas. Many environmentalists were skeptical about ethanol's value in a clean-air strategy, but President Bush issued regulations promoting wider use of ethanol; we presume he was impressed by the force of ADM's 800,000 Republican arguments. Bob Dole, the 1996 Republican presidential candidate, helped pass and defend special breaks for the ethanol industry; he not only appreciated ADM's Republican contributions, but presumably approved of the more than $1 million they gave to the American Red Cross during the period when it was headed by his wife, Elizabeth Dole.[16] What about the post-1994 Republican-controlled Congress, defenders of the free market and opponents of government giveaways? Were they ready to end this subsidy program, cracking down on corporate welfare as they did on people welfare? Not a chance. In 1997, the Republican chair of the House Ways and Means Committee actually attempted to eliminate the special tax breaks for ethanol. Needless to say, he was immediately put in his place by other members of the Republican leadership, including Speaker Newt Gingrich and most of the Senate, with the subsidy locked in place for years to come,[17] in spite of a General Accounting Office report that "found that the ethanol subsidy justifies none of its political boasts."[18] The Center for Responsive Politics calculated that ADM, its executives and PAC, made more than $1 million in campaign contributions of various types; the only thing that had changed was that in 1996, with a Democratic president, this money was "divided more or less evenly between Republicans and Democrats."[19]

The disparity in power between business and environmentalists looms large during the legislative process, but it is enormous afterward. When the Clean Air Act passed, corporations and industry groups offered positions, typically with large pay increases, to congressional staff members who wrote the law. The former congressional staff members who now work for corporations both know how to evade the law and can persuasively claim to EPA that they know what Congress intended. Environmental organizations pay substantially less than Congress and can't afford large staffs. They are seldom able to become involved in the details of the administrative process or to influence implementation and enforcement.[20]

Having pushed Congress and the Environmental Protection Agency to allow as much pollution as possible, business then went to the Quayle council for rules allowing even more pollution. Vice President J. Danforth Quayle's council, technically known as the "Council on Competitiveness," was created by President Bush specifically to help reduce regulations on business. Quayle told the *Boston Globe* "that his council has an 'open door' to business groups and that he has a bias against regulations."[21] During the Bush administration, this council reviewed, and could override, all regulations, including those by the EPA setting the limits at which a chemical was subject to regulation. The council also recommended that corporations be allowed to increase their polluting emissions if a state did not object within seven days of the proposed increase. Corporations thus have multiple opportunities to win. If they lose in Congress, they can win at the regulatory agency; if they lose there, they can try again at the Quayle council (or later equivalent). If they lose there, they can try to reduce the money available to enforce regulations, or tie the issue up in the courts, or plan on accepting a minimal fine.

The operation of the Quayle council would probably have received little publicity, but reporters discovered that the executive director of the council, Allan Hubbard, had a clear conflict of interest. Hubbard chaired the biweekly White House meetings on the Clean Air Act. He owned half of World Wide Chemical, received an average of more than $1 million a year in profits from it while directing the Quayle council, and continued to attend quarterly stockholder meetings. According to the *Boston Globe*, "Records on file with the Indianapolis Air Pollution Control Board show that World Wide Chemical emitted 17,000 to 19,000 pounds of chemicals into the air" in 1991.[22] At that time, the company did "not have the permit required to release the emissions," was "putting out nearly four times the allowable emissions without a permit, and could be subject to a $2,500-a-day penalty" according to David Jordan, director of the Indianapolis Air Pollution Board.[23]

This does not, however, mean that business always gets exactly what it wants. In 1997, the Environmental Protection Agency proposed tough new rules for soot and smog. Business fought hard to weaken or eliminate the rules: hiring experts (from pro-business think tanks) to attack the scientific studies supporting the regulations and putting a raft of lobbyists ("many of them former congressional staffers," the *Washington Post* reported[24]) to work securing the signatures of 250 members of Congress questioning the standards. But the late 1990s version of these industry mobilizations adds a new twist—creating a pseudo-grassroots campaign. For example, business, operating under a suitably disguised name (Foundation for Clean Air Progress), paid for television ads telling farmers that the EPA rules would prohibit them from plowing on dry windy days, with other ads predicting the EPA rules "would lead to forced carpooling or bans on outdoor barbecues—claims the EPA dismisses as ridiculous."[25] Along with the ads, industry worked to mobilize local politicians and business executives in what business groups called a "grass tops" campaign.

Despite a massive industry campaign, EPA head Carol Browner remained firm, and President Clinton was persuaded to go along. Of course, industry immediately began working on ways to undercut the regulations with congressional loopholes and exceptions—but business had suffered a defeat, and proponents of clean air (that is, most of the rest of us) had won at least a temporary and partial victory. And who leads the struggles to overturn or uphold these regulations? Just as before, Dingell and Waxman; Republicans "are skittish about challenging" the rules publicly, "so they gladly defer to Dingell as their surrogate."[26] Dingell's forces have more than 130 cosponsors (about one-third of them Democrats) for a bill to, in effect, override the EPA standards.

In business–government relations, most attention becomes focused on instances of scandal. The real issue, however, is not one or another scandal or conflict of interest, but rather the *system* of business–government relations, and especially of campaign finance, that offers business so many opportunities to craft loopholes, undermine regulations, and subvert enforcement. Still worse, many of these actions take place beyond public scrutiny. . . . [Our research] focuses on business and the way it uses money and power to subvert the democratic process. . . .

What Is Power?

Our analysis is based on an understanding of power that differs from that usually articulated by both business and politicians. The corporate PAC directors we interviewed insisted that they have no power.

> *If you were to ask me what kind of access and influence do we have, being roughly the 150th largest PAC, I would have to tell you that on the basis of our money we have zero. . . . If you look at the level of our contributions, we know we're not going to buy anybody's vote, we're not going to rent anybody, or whatever the clichés have been over the years. We know that.*

The executives who expressed these views clearly meant these words sincerely. Their statements are based on roughly the same understanding of "power" that is current within political science, which is also the way the term was defined by Max Weber, the classical sociological theorist. Power, in this common conception, is the ability to make someone do something against their will. If that is what power means, then corporations rarely have any in relation to members of Congress, nor does soft money give the donor power over presidents. As one senior vice president said to us: "You certainly aren't going to be able to buy anybody for $500 or $1,000 or $10,000—it's a joke." . . . In this regard we agree with the corporate officials we interviewed: A corporation is not in a position to say to a member of Congress, "Either you vote for this bill or we will defeat your bid for reelection." Rarely do they even say: "You vote for this bill or you won't get any money from us."

The definition of power as the ability to make someone do something against their will is what Steven Lukes calls a "one-dimensional" view of power.[27] A two-dimensional view recognizes the existence of nondecisions: A potential issue never gets articulated or, if articulated by someone somewhere, never receives serious consideration. For example, in 1989 and 1990 one of the major political battles, and a focus of great effort by corporate PACs, was the Clean Air Act. Yet twenty or thirty years earlier, before the rise of the environmental movement, pollution was a nonissue: it simply was not considered, although its effects were, in retrospect, of great importance. In one of the Sherlock Holmes stories, the key clue is that the dog didn't bark.[28] A two-dimensional view of power makes the same point: The most important clue in some situation may be that no one noticed power was exercised—because there was no overt conflict.

Even this model of power is too restrictive, however, because it still focuses on discrete decisions and nondecisions. Tom Wartenberg . . . argues, instead, for a "field theory" of power that analyzes social power as a force similar to a magnetic field. A magnetic field alters the motion of objects susceptible to magnetism. Similarly, the mere presence of a powerful social agent alters the social space for others and causes them to orient themselves toward the powerful agent.[29] For example, one of the executives we interviewed took it for granted that "if we go see the congressman who represents [a city where the company has a major plant], where 10,000 of our employees are also his constituents, we don't need a PAC to go see him." The corporation is so important in that area that the member has to orient himself in relation to the corporation and its concerns. In a different sense, the very act of accepting a campaign contribution changes the way a member relates to a PAC, creating a sense of obligation, a need to reciprocate. The PAC contribution has altered the member's social space, his or her awareness of the company and wish to help it, even if no explicit commitments have been made.

Business Is Different

Power, we would argue, is not just the ability to force someone to do something against their will; it is most effective (and least recognized) when it shapes the field of action. Moreover, business's vast resources, influence on the economy, and general legitimacy place it on a different footing from other campaign contributors. Every day, a member of Congress accepts a $1,000 donation from a corporate PAC, goes to a committee hearing, proposes "minor" changes in a bill's wording, and has those changes accepted without discussion or examination. The changes "clarify" the language of the bill, legalizing higher levels of pollution for a specific pollutant, or exempting the company from some tax. The media do not report this change and no one speaks against it. . . .

Even groups with great social legitimacy encounter more opposition and controversy than business faces for proposals that are virtually without public support. One example is the contrast between the largely unopposed commitment of tens or hundreds of billions of dollars for the savings and loan bailout, compared to the sharp debate, close votes, and defeats for the rights of men and women to take *unpaid* parental leaves. The classic term for something noncontroversial that everyone must support is "a motherhood issue," and while it costs little to guarantee every woman the right to an *un*paid parental leave, this measure nonetheless generated intense scrutiny and controversy—going down to defeat under President Bush, passing under President Clinton, and then again becoming a focus of attack after the 1994 Republican takeover of Congress. Few indeed are the people publicly prepared to defend pollution or tax evasion. Nonetheless, business is routinely able to win pollution exemptions and tax loopholes. Although cumulatively some vague awareness of these provisions may trouble people, most are allowed individually to pass without scrutiny. *No* analysis of corporate political activity makes sense unless it begins with a recognition of this absolutely vital point. The PAC is a vital element of corporate power, but it does not operate by itself. The PAC donation is always backed by the wider power and influence of business.

Corporations are unlike other "special interest" groups not only because business has far more resources, but also because of its acceptance and legitimacy. When people feel that "the system" is screwing them, they tend to blame politicians, the government, the media—but rarely business. In terms of campaign finance, while much of the public is outraged at the way money influences elections and public policy, the issue is almost always posed in terms of politicians, what they do or don't do. This is part of a pervasive double standard that largely exempts business from criticism. We, however, believe it is vital to scrutinize business as well. . . .

The Limits to Business Power

We have argued that power is more than winning an open conflict and that business is different from other groups because its pervasive influence on our society shapes the social space for all other actors. These two arguments, however, are joined with a third: a recognition—in fact an insistence—on the limits to business power. Though we stress the power of business, business does not feel powerful. As one executive said to us:

> I really wish that our PAC in particular, and our lobbyists, had the influence that is generally perceived by the general population. If you see it written in the press, and you talk to people, they tell you about all that influence that you've got, and frankly I think that's far overplayed, as far as the influence goes. Certainly you can get access to a candidate, and certainly you can get your position known; but as far as influencing that decision, the only way you influence it is by the providing of information.

Executives believe that corporations are constantly under attack, primarily because government simply doesn't understand that business is crucial to everything the society does, but can easily be crippled by well-intentioned but unrealistic government policies. A widespread view among the people we interviewed is, "Far and away the vast majority of things that we do are literally to protect ourselves from public policy that is poorly crafted and nonresponsive to the needs and realities and circumstances of our company." These misguided policies, they feel, can come from many sources: labor unions, environmentalists, the pressure of unrealistic public interest groups, the government's constant need for money or the weight of its oppressive bureaucracy. Therefore, simply to stay even requires a pervasive effort. If attention slips for even a minute, an onerous regulation will be imposed or a precious resource taken away. To some extent such a view is an obvious consequence of the position of the people we interviewed: If business could be sure of always winning, the government relations unit (and thus the jobs of its members) would be unnecessary; if it is easy to win, PAC directors deserve little credit for company victories and much blame for defeats. But evidently the corporation agrees with them, since it devotes significant resources to political action of many kinds, including the awareness and involvement of top officials. Chief executive officers and members of the board of directors repeatedly express similar views. . . .

. . . Once upon a time, perhaps, business could simply make its wishes known and receive what it wanted; today, corporations must form PACs, give soft money, actively lobby, make their case to the public, run advocacy ads, and engage in a whole range of costly and degrading activities that they wish were unnecessary. From the outside, we are impressed with their high success rates over a wide range of issues and with the absence of a credible challenge to the general authority of business. From the inside, corporations are impressed with the serious consequences of their occasional losses and with the unremitting effort needed to maintain their privileged position.

ENDNOTES

[1] *Boston Globe,* November 8, 1996, p. A26.
[2] *New York Times,* September 3, 1997, p. A18.

[3]Boschwitz, quoted in Brooks Jackson, *Honest Graft: Big Money and the American Political Process* (New York: Knopf, 1988), pp. 251–52. Emphasis in book. (Obviously, the secret memo didn't stay secret.) Boschwitz's 1990 strategy backfired. He discouraged the most "promising" Democratic candidates, but Paul Wellstone—a true long shot by all accounts—beat him, despite Boschwitz's 4 to 1 spending advantage. In the 1996 rematch between the two candidates, Wellstone outspent Boschwitz and won handily.

[4]Quoted in Elizabeth Drew, *Whatever It Takes: The Real Struggle for Political Power in America* (New York: Viking, 1997), pp. 19–20.

[5]David Donnelly, Janice Fine, and Ellen S. Miller, "Going Public," *Boston Review,* April–May 1997. Larry Makinson, "The Big Picture: Money Follows Power Shift on Capitol Hill" (Washington, DC: Center for Responsive Politics, 1997, www.crp.org).

[6]www.fec.gov.

[7]William Greider, "Whitewash: Is Congress Conning Us on Clean Air?" *Rolling Stone,* June 14, 1990, p. 40.

[8]Greider, "Whitewash," p. 40.

[9]Margaret E. Kriz, "Dunning the Midwest," *National Journal,* April 14, 1990, p. 895.

[10]Kriz, "Dunning the Midwest," p. 895.

[11]Quoted in Greider, "Whitewash," p. 40.

[12]Greider, "Whitewash," p. 41.

[13]Margaret E. Kriz, "Politics at the Pump," *National Journal,* June 2, 1990, p. 1328.

[14]Why can't industry just come out and name its groups "Polluters for Profit" or the "Coalition for Acid Rain Preservation" (CARP)? All quotes in this paragraph are from Carol Matlack, "It's Round Two in Clean Air Fight," *National Journal,* January 26, 1991, p. 226.

[15]*Washington Post,* January 16, 1991, p. A17.

[16]*New York Times,* April 16, 1996, p. A16.

[17]*New York Times,* June 22, 1997, p. 17.

[18]*Wall Street Journal,* June 6, 1997.

[19]*New York Times,* June 22, 1997, p. 17.

[20]Matlack, "It's Round Two," p. 227.

[21]*Boston Globe,* November 21, 1991, p. 17.

[22]*Boston Globe,* November 21, 1991, p. 17.

[23]*Boston Globe,* November 20, 1991, p. 4.

[24]*Washington Post,* June 17, 1997, p. A1.

[25]*Washington Post,* June 17, 1997, p. A1.

[26]Richard E. Cohen, "Two Dems Are on Familiar Battlefield," *National Journal,* September 6, 1997, p. 1742.

[27]Steven Lukes, *Power: A Radical View* (New York: Macmillan, 1974).

[28]Theodore J. Eismeier and Philip H. Pollock III, "The Retreat from Partisanship: Why the Dog Didn't Bark in the 1984 Election." In *Business Strategy and Public Policy,* edited by Alfred A. Marcus, Allen M. Kaufman, and David R. Beam (Westport, CT: Quorum Books, 1987), pp. 137–47.

[29]Thomas Wartenberg, *The Forms of Power: From Domination to Transformation* (Philadelphia: Temple University Press, 1990), p. 74.

37
_____

ONE WORLD UNDER BUSINESS

CHARLES DERBER

C. Wright Mills' notion of the *power elite* can be seen in many social contexts in the United States, including the recent political and economic maneuvering related to terrorism, homeland security, the war in Iraq, and the aftermath of Hurricane Katrina. The following reading by Charles Derber, a professor of sociology at Boston College, examines the complicated relationship between governments and global companies. Derber reveals a global power elite as transnational companies dominate government agendas and expand their business into larger global financial markets. This excerpt is taken from Derber's critically acclaimed book, *People Before Profit: The New Globalization in an Age of Terror, Big Money, and Economic Crisis* (2002).

Democracy is a word all public men use and none understand.

—George Bernard Shaw

Globalization enthrones three intertwined institutions. The first are the global financial markets and transnational companies at the heart of the world economy. The second are national governments that are business-oriented regimes linked to each other in economic and military alliances led by the United States. The third are rising "global governments" such as the World Trade Organization, the International Monetary Fund, and the World Bank, also strongly led from the White House. These three power centers increasingly operate as a system. The new sovereign is not an individual such as George Bush or Rupert Murdoch, or a single organization like the U.S. government or the World Trade Organization. Instead, global power lies in the system itself and the new corporate elites who seek to manage it.

This new world system can be called a *global corpocracy*. By joining the words *corporation* and *democracy*, this appellation perfectly evokes a corporate-driven system that celebrates the idea of democracy more than any earlier global order. It's true that globalization has helped bring free elections to many nations. But it comes with a price tag that ultimately subverts the people's voice, especially that of the global poor, in the economic and social decisions that matter. The crisis of globalization and a sure recipe for violence is the contradiction between the rhetoric of democracy and the realities of corpocracy.[1]

The commanding role of business has become the key element of the new system. This partly reflects the astonishing new size and global reach of transnational corporations, the largest being virtually world empires in their own right, with their own global rules and private armies. The biggest global corporations are each far larger than most countries in the world. General Motors' annual sales are larger than the gross domestic product of Denmark. Wal-Mart is bigger than Poland. Ford is larger than South Africa, and Daimler Chrysler is bigger than Greece. Philip Morris' sales are greater than the GDPs of 148 countries.[2]

Of the hundred biggest economies in the world—counting both corporations and countries—fifty-one are global corporations. The top ten alone in terms of sale—GM, Wal-Mart, Ford, Exxon Mobil, DaimlerChrysler, Toyota, GE, Royal Dutch/Shell, IBM, and BP Amoco—are each larger than about 140 of the 190 nations in the world. The top five corporations are each bigger than 182 of 190 countries.[3]

Corpocracy globally joins these giant transnational companies and governments in an entangled and unequal partnership. In a robust democracy, there is a firewall between government and business. The firewall ensures that people rather than business control the government and make the rules. It is legitimate for business and government to communicate, but they should not be in bed together. The wall acts as a checks-and-balance system that limits the power of both and keeps business from taking over.

In corpocracy, the story line is different. The firewall between big business and government is chipped away, flooding money into government and eroding popular control. The American example of Enron, which for many years paid thousands of dollars to the highest-ranking Washington officials of both parties, symbolizes the corrupting new ties. Business and government forge an intimate relationship, both within the nation-state and the larger world order. In the new system, government still wields formal sovereign authority, but sovereign power has actually been transferred to a partnership increasingly dominated in times of peace by the business sector.

The business and government partners maintain separate identities but also join to create a new system. Business increasingly wields more influence, but there are serious power struggles. In times of war, as occurred after September 11, military and political leaders reassert their own claims to dominance.

The incestuous melding of business and constitutional government makes governments look and act more like corporations and corporations look and act more like governments. Governments act to protect profits, and corporations speak the language of social responsibility and democracy. Business takes on the planning and rule-making roles of government, and government becomes increasingly about money. The global firewall seems nearly as obsolete as the Berlin Wall. This must change. In order for globalization to become a truly democratizing force, it must acknowledge and reconstruct the relation between business and government to ensure popular control.

The new union of global business with U.S.-led constitutional democracies and "world government" is a breathtaking development. Unlike any prior world system, it creates the aura of a new global constitutionalism. Business now speaks a global language of transparency and accountability, and its leaders call for a more democratic world. Many see hope in the rise of a more lawful commercial world and the practice of global corporate responsibility. But the increasingly incestuous ties between global companies and the governments charged with regulating them undermine the prospects for global democracy. Corporate social responsibility cannot replace government as a basis for law or a way to ensure that business serves public needs. And the new marriage of business and government undermines the hope that people can rely on the political system to serve their needs.

In the past, global business waltzed with dictators in Latin America and sheikdoms in the Middle East who used brute force to stabilize their nations and protect lucrative business deals. After September 11, Western governments and business continued alliances with repressive regimes that deliver valuable goods, such as oil, and strategic military assets. But the legitimacy of globalization and global business rests on a shift toward a less repressive system of political sponsorship and ever closer ties to governments that are increasingly unified by markets, U.S.-led alliances, and a common commitment to elections. The shift toward formal democracy legitimates globalization while veiling the antidemocratic collusion between business and government that it represents.

Wrapping business in the arms of constitutional democracy began in the United States more than a century ago. Optimists subscribing to the mystique see globalization as the spread of American-style liberal democracy around the world. The American Constitution will, in this view, become the basis of a unifying democracy in nations everywhere and in the WTO and the other emerging global governments. The presumption is that government regulation and corporate responsibility will combine to humanize the rising global capitalist order, a deeply misleading conception of the meaning of both regulation and responsibility in a corporate-driven system.

After the attack on the World Trade Center, much is up for grabs. Globalization seems newly threatened, and the ties of global business with many governments around the world will be reorganized according to new military and security imperatives. The U.S. government and military leaders will take more overt command, and business will depend on new political and military alignments dictated from Washington. But whatever the future holds, global business has established its global authority in a way that no terrorist can undo. Giant corporations are everywhere, and the magic of their logos has captured the world's imagination. It is becoming impossible to find a person on the planet who hasn't heard of Nike or been enchanted by a Disney cartoon. I recently saw a picture of a shoeless boy in rural Africa who had scratched the Nike swoosh logo onto his bare foot. The Beatles once got into trouble by saying they were more famous than Jesus.

Corporations can now truthfully claim that more people have heard of them than most of the worlds' political leaders.

—————

The truth behind globalization is that business, whether national or global, simply can't survive or wield its great power over all of us without government. Part of what government delivers is military stability, a huge issue after September 11. But economic and political intervention by government is essential to ensuring stability, profit, and the very survival of business—in peace as well as war. We all learn that the last thing business wants is an intimate affair with government. Both national and global corporations portray government as a burden and themselves as swimming or sinking on their own. This is a key tenet of the globalization mystique: that business and the markets run themselves and leave governments in the hands of the people rather than seeking to take them over for their own ends.

While this idea is at the heart of the new global mystique, it has always been mostly rhetoric. From the historical origins of the corporation in seventeenth-century Britain to its development in the United States after the Civil War, the corporation has long been intimate with government. The nature of the intimacy has changed over the centuries, but the importance of it to business—and its danger for democracy—has always existed.[4] . . .

The enormous role that government has to play in creating the property rights and a constitutional framework that business requires is obvious today in a country like Russia. The Russian government has thus far created neither a sustainable framework of enforceable property rights and national regulation nor transparency in the financial system and a functioning tax system. This has made it difficult for a viable corporate structure and market system to emerge, endangering the rise of a successful Russian national corporation and the prospects of global business taking root there.

In Africa, Asia, and Latin America, there are many weak or crumbling governments barely able to provide order of any kind. This creates major obstacles for companies who need functioning governments to deliver stability, resources, and commercial protections. Anarchism is anathema to business, and corporations will work hard to establish protective governments everywhere, increasingly democratic in form, but often corrupt and tyrannical in practice.

The corporation is inherently a political creature, and the free-market order itself is a government-based system. The idea of free markets, a core tenet of the globalization mystique, obscures the reality that markets are always constructed by governments and can survive only with multiple forms of government intervention and public subsidy. There can be no market without state power establishing, regulating, and militarily defending property and no corporations without state charters and governments managing and stabilizing the economic and social order. And all market systems rest on abundant forms of "corporate welfare" involving not just tax breaks and subsidies, but expenditure on education, infrastructure, and research and development without which the economy would collapse. Most important, the government stands as the ultimate guarantor that contracts will be enforced and laws against fraud upheld so that people's trust in the market remains secure.[5]

The 2002 outbreak of what Senator Joseph Lieberman called "Enron-itis" makes clear just how important that role is today. U.S. and global markets were severely rattled as people worried that their Dow or Nasdaq portfolios might never be safe. How many other Enrons and WorldComs might be betraying them through deception, "creative accounting," and shredding of documents? The U.S. Congress and President Bush immediately responded to ensure the public that government would do everything necessary to restore trust. Bush declared in his 2002 State of the Union message that government must intervene to create "stricter accounting standards and tougher disclosure requirements." In other words, even the most zealous defender of the free market understood that government activism is essential to the survival of the market itself.

This was true of national capitalism before globalization, and it is the essential truth of the new world system that globalization is creating. Global companies are now looking to create and control the political system at the world level that earlier corporations found in both state and national governments. This requires a system of economic stabilization international law and the beginnings of a constitution for the world economy, backed up by military enforcement power. In recent decades, the United States provided the global economic management and political and military sponsorship that business needs. But globalization is leading toward a world government that is likely to gain greater autonomy from the United States over time. It will be harnessed to global business and more concerned with profits than people, a direct contradiction to the globalization mystique's message about a win-win world.

————————

The global business groom dominates the ruling marriage I call corpocracy, but he is very dependent on his government brides. He needs government to manage and stabilize the system, keep order, and sustain the democratic image on which the globalization mystique rests. He has confidence that he can remake his government partners in his corporate image and harness them to his mission. But the power struggle is never entirely predictable and this makes global business nervous. He gets even more nervous in periods of war, which potentially threaten his reach abroad and his safety at home.

The events of September 11 point to this vulnerability. Hundreds of powerful financial companies were devastated by the attacks on the Twin Towers, and corporations everywhere are facing new crises that could bankrupt them. Violence has threatened their very identity as global players. Within weeks of the New York attacks, thousands of Western apparel and electronic companies had withdrawn from Pakistan, Bangladesh, and other nations in Asia, war zones deemed too unsafe even as new security challenges loomed at home. The new military climate will intensify business dependency on government and may dangerously expose the illusion of the free-market religion that sustains both global business and globalization itself. Global business, though, will survive September 11 and remains, even in an era of war, the dominant and unifying force of our time. It is itself a partnership of two huge institutions: global financial markets and global corporations. Together, they control more wealth than any institution in history and create a network that increasingly unites all of us, whatever our culture or religion.[6]

Global financial markets are best seen as the brain—and global corporations as the muscle—of global business. The financial markets are something like an electronic cortex sending out billions of buy and sell orders from millions of investors. Meanwhile, the global companies race to make sure they understand and comply with the message the markets are sending. When the corporate muscle acts against the will of the financial brain, the markets will starve it of its oxygen—that is, global capital.

Globalization is often associated with direct corporate foreign investment creating jobs. But the mushrooming of the global financial markets is the more eye-opening development. By 1997, more than *$1.5 trillion* in such foreign-exchange transactions took place every day. Analysts have noted that "only one to two percent of these transactions are related to trade or foreign direct investment. The remainder is for speculation or short-term investments that are subject to rapid flight when investors' perceptions change." Between 1980 and 1995, the value of world merchandise trade increased 400 percent, while the value of the world stock exchanges increased 970 percent and foreign-exchange transactions 2,100 percent. The amount of money exchanged globally *each day* "is more than the total value of world trade in goods and services each quarter."[7]

The rising power of the global financial markets is a leading theme of nearly all commentators on globalization. Thomas Friedman calls the global markets "the Electronic Horde" and celebrates them as the centerpiece of globalization. He recognizes, though, that they put nations into a "Golden Straitjacket," eroding national sovereignty. "As your country puts on the Golden Straitjacket, two things tend to happen: your economy grows and your politics shrink." Your "political choices," Friedman summarizes, "get reduced to Pepsi or Coke." But he believes that this loss of control is acceptable because the markets are forcing nations to make rational choices promoting growth that they can't or won't do on their own. These include "making the private sector the primary engine . . . shrinking the size of its state bureaucracy . . . eliminating and lowering tariffs . . . privatizing state-owned industries . . . eliminating government corruption, subsidies, and kickbacks . . . opening its banking and telecommunications system to private ownership and competition."[8]

Some of these virtues are real, but the notion that such critical national policies should be imposed by investors is hardly a democratic idea. Decisions about size of government, financial regulation, and the role of the market are at the heart of democracy. Take them away, and you really *are* electing leaders just to decide whether they prefer Pepsi or Coke. Friedman accepts such a drastic assault on democracy because he takes on faith the economic theories that markets allocate money most efficiently and maximize efficiency and growth. But what if countries do not view economic growth as their highest priority? What if preserving their antipoverty programs or democracy itself is more important to them? And what if, as the Argentine debacle, the traumatic setbacks in Thailand and other Southeast Asian nations, and America's own post-Enron crisis suggest, leaving it all to the markets does not promote sustainable growth?

Beyond the fundamental concern about democracy, there are other serious issues. The mushrooming of global exchanges in currency, derivatives, and other short-term investments represents an effort by investors to exploit new global rules permitting vast sums of money to be invested and withdrawn at lightning speed without national controls. This was not part of the original globalization system or the concept of trade developed by American and British planners after World War II. They worried that speculators or other short-term investors, whether finance firms or rich individuals, could exploit such freedom for enormous profits while destabilizing whole nations and regions of the world. They created initially a strongly regulated trade regime, with special protections for national banks and financial systems to prevent such possibilities.

The new freedom of money to race anywhere creates enormous dynamism as well as frightening instability. The Clinton administration led an aggressive financial deregulation campaign in the 1990s through the International Monetary Fund and the World Trade Organization. Globalization leaders overturned long-standing restrictions by governments that limited foreign ownership of their banks, deregulated currency exchanges, and eliminated restrictions on how quickly money could be withdrawn by foreign investors. Most analysts now believe that such deregulation helped give rise to the catastrophic Asian financial meltdown in 1998 that devastated Thailand, Malaysia, Indonesia, and South Korea. In late 1997, when short-term investors precipitously withdrew huge sums, they helped bankrupt these Southeast Asian economies that had reconstructed themselves around the large foreign sums originally loaned and invested. The same chaotic pattern hit Mexico in 1994 and Russia and Brazil in 1998.[9]

The liberalization of financial markets has helped globalize the unstable, "irrational exuberance" of stock markets described by Federal Bank chief Alan Greenspan, and also helped produce a cesspool of unsupervised global "hot money." As one analyst argues, "International financial transactions are carried out in a realm that is close to anarchy. Numerous committees and organizations attempt to coordinate domestic regulatory policies and negotiate international standards but they have no enforcement powers. The Cayman Islands and Bermuda offer not only beautiful beaches but also harbors that are safe from most financial regulation and international agreements."

U.S. leaders have led the charge for deregulation of the world's financial system for many reasons, including the dazzling financial opportunities it offers for U.S. and other global financial companies. Once opened financially, the ability of these countries to develop their own economic models or regional economies independent of American influence erodes substantially. This is viewed by U.S. leaders as another core benefit. But after the Enron scandal, in which the giant Texan company created thousands of such offshore havens to conceal its financial dealings and debts, Americans can newly appreciate the dangers of redefining free trade and globalization itself as the creation of a deregulated and often anarchistic global financial order.[10]

There are now more than 45,000 corporations worldwide, with 300,000 affiliates. But the top 200 global companies, including such giants as General Motors, Shell, Citigroup, Sony, AOL Time Warner, Exxon Mobil, Siemens, Mitsubishi, and Microsoft, dominate the world economy and are the heart of global business. The majority are headquartered in the United States (82), Japan (41), and Germany (20), with many of the rest in other European countries, but they all have branches and contractors in nations everywhere. Their profits exploded 224 percent between 1983 and 1997, a far faster rate than the 144 percent growth in the world economy as a whole during the same period. Their sales are bigger than the combined economies of 180 of the 190 countries of the world, and eighteen times the combined income of the world's 1.2 billion poorest people.[11]

The sales of the top 200 account for more than 25 percent of the entire output of the world economy (global GDP), and thus the entire world economy is increasingly a proprietary production of a few giant firms. The top 200 hold 90 percent of the world's patents; grow, refine, and sell much of the world's food; supply the oil that runs our cars and heats our homes; operate the global media and entertainment companies that reach billions of people; and create most of the world's software and manufacture the computers it runs on. They build the airplanes and cars we travel in, make most of our clothes, provide most of the world's banking and financial services, and increasingly dominate services from health care to financial services to retailing. Finally the top 200 produce nearly all the weapons that cram the arsenals of nations everywhere.[12]

It sounds almost old hat to say that the globalizing of business produces these huge wealth monopolies. But it is integrating and controlling the world more profoundly than ever before. This is happening through a corporate version of the process that my sociological colleague, Diane Vaughan, calls "uncoupling" in her study of divorce. Globalization is the process of corporations (and financial markets) uncoupling from the nation-state in a strategy to accumulate astonishing wealth as well as unify the world. It is something different than simply choosing to operate in many different countries, which corporations have always done. And it is also not quite the same thing as divorce, because the corporation remains legally tied to its old partner while in effect marrying a new set of partners.[13]

This new corporate uncoupling is *not* from national government. As is obvious after September 11, when the airlines and insurance companies in the United States rushed to Washington for bailouts, global companies are snuggling ever closer to national governments. Corporate uncoupling is from the nation itself, and it involves abandonment of loyalty to any particular nation's interests or those of its citizens, even as ties to the nation's government may intensify. This endangers the well-being of insecure middle classes and the poor in every country.

Uncoupling is a strategy to further corporatize all aspects of life in *every* nation by freeing companies from responsibility to any particular country. By claiming loyalty to all countries equally, and moving from national monogamy to a kind of global polygamy, corporate uncoupling actually binds nations to corporations in a far deeper way and turns both national government and social life everywhere into an expression of global corporate values. Corporate uncoupling, in this sense, is a "denationalization" of business but a far more intimate coupling of corporations and global social life. It integrates the world politically as well as economically, begins to build a worldwide business civilization, and is the foundation of the "denationalizing" of sovereignty and the weakening of democratic states.

The authoritative chronicler of corporate denationalization is Leslie Sklair, a British sociologist. Just as Vaughan interviewed couples who were divorcing, Sklair went directly to the companies (about 80 of the global top 500) to talk to executives. Almost all of the executives he interviewed in the 1990s described themselves as going through a profound shift. Their companies had long operated with subsidiaries in foreign countries. But in Sklair's words, they saw themselves now as global citizens and no longer as "national companies with units abroad." This is a sign of a total, revolutionary shift in their identities and loyalties.[14]

As early as the 1970s, the chairman of Dow Chemical painted a graphic picture of where the new corporation was going. "I have long dreamed of buying an island owned by no nation and of establishing the World Headquarters of the Dow Chemical Company on truly neutral ground of such an island beholden to no nation." GE's famed former leader Jack Welch has been quoted as saying he thought the corporation should be headquartered on a barge floating free in the ocean, free of national identity and moral obligations to any nation and empowered to speak for the world as a whole.[15]

Such uncoupling is far from consummated, and it should not be viewed as conspiratorial or nefarious. It also should not be overestimated. Global companies remain dependent on their home countries for economic subsidies, and they also rely on favorable trade and other political and military policies essential to their global business prospects. Moreover, while uncoupling can be part and parcel of the "race to the bottom," a strategy for pitting vulnerable workers and states against each other, some of the most highly uncoupled companies, such as Unilever, which is based in the Netherlands, have also created highly developed global codes of conduct and model forms of global "corporate citizenship." There is no simple relation between the social responsiveness of the corporation and its degree of uncoupling. Foreign companies can bring higher standards of performance to nations where the norm has been abysmally poor. As with globalization generally, the problem is not uncoupling per se, nor the integration of global operations, but the lack of global accountability systems and of worldwide countervailing power to limit abuse and provide checks and balances to global business. . . .

Globalization is creating a vast new system of global partnerships that looks like a global octopus. As individual companies globalize, they need to merge with or partner with hundreds of allies in other countries to lock in unfamiliar markets, secure adequate capital for playing on a planetary field, and monopolize market share. States and companies must unite into coalitions in order to succeed on the new global playing field. You can't win the game, whether economic or military, without a global team operating under loose common command. This is novel for countries in a world of sacred national sovereignty, and it is even stranger in an economy based on the god of competition. Global coalitions of companies do not eliminate competition, but they undermine any traditional notions of free markets by turning the two or three dominant players in every global industry into kissing cousins with huge new power to influence the markets and all of us with lives bound up in them. . . .

The alliance system also bridges different industries. In the Gilded Age, John D. Rockefeller, J. P. Morgan, and Andrew Carnegie sat on each other's corporate boards and ultimately merged steel, banking, railroads, and oil to create an American octopus integrating the whole national economy. Today, most of the global top 200 are partnering feverishly, not only with thousands of subsidiaries and contractors, but also with many other top 200 firms within and across industries. In the auto industry, GM and Toyota are hopping into bed with each other on numerous new projects following their initial joint venture of the Nummi plant in California. Chrysler is negotiating with Mitsubishi to engineer all its small cars. In big oil, Texaco and Royal Dutch/Shell have long been partners in refining and marketing, while Texaco is marrying Chevron to catch up with Exxon Mobil. The truth is that all the biggest auto, energy, media, computer, financial, and other global oligopolies are already partnered with nearly all their competitors in nearly every global industry. . . .

The globalization of the alliance system leads inexorably toward the creation of a transnational financial and corporate elite. The corporate leaders all over the world are now a small, closely knit club. They are not a conspiracy of tycoons running the world from smoke-filled secret dens. They do not share the same cultural values, religion, or view of foreign policy. But they are increasingly intertwined in transnational political and lobbying associations as well as joint business ventures. The creation of a genuinely global, corporate-dominated governing elite uncoupled from nationality not only in its membership but its institutions, cultural sensibilities, and business strategy would be truly unprecedented. No earlier world system has created anything like it. It would be the most impressive achievement of globalization and the most alarming, because it would concentrate global power in the hands of the few and thus doom democracy.

In the United States, workers and citizens spent a century building unions and civic groups that balanced the power of business elites with countervailing forces and kept Washington from being a pure handmaiden of business. But in much of the world there have never been unions or civic associations that are counterweights to business. Globalization has allowed business to unravel much of the power of unions and community groups in the First World by exiting to union-free Third World environments without any history of civil society or democracy.[16]

As global business uses exit threats to gain influence over First World unions and governments, it has an even easier job yoking Third World governments to its cause. Many such governments, even those with the formalities of elections, have never been accountable to their own people. Easily seduced by the money and jobs that global companies can dangle in front of them, they have become increasingly hostage to the global financial markets and institutions, such as the International Monetary Fund, that control credit and their ability to survive in the world economy.

The question then is this: Who can protect the people in either First or Third World nations when their governments are in a race to seduce and please the global giants that bring money and jobs? Many corporations champion self-regulation and "corporate responsibility" initiatives that have brought higher standards to some nations than ever existed in domestic businesses. These are important developments and should not be dismissed as pure public relations, although they often are.

But such self-policing is not enough. Even when well-intentioned, it leaves it up to the businesses themselves to define responsibility, and it offers outsiders no public means of verifying information and claims of good business conduct. The monitoring and disclosure arrangements presented by Nike and Reebok have helped create improvements in global factories, but public-interest groups have uncovered a long string of broken promises that are the inevitable product of a system lacking public transparency and accountability, as Enron proved in the United States itself.

It took countervailing power by new American unions and progressive community groups to finally tame the robber barons, end sweatshop conditions, and begin to recapture government for the people in the Progressive Era and New Deal years. But countervailing power in the world seems vanishingly small compared to that in the United States following the Gilded Age. Building global democracy is going to require organizing unions for Samima and billions of workers like her. And it will take a wider coalition of global civic groups that can create worldwide, citizen-based power and build a New Deal for the world.[17]

Global business is itself a work in progress, far from fully consolidating global unity or power. As the liability suits against Enron and the antitrust suit against Microsoft demonstrate, giant corporations are far from omnipotent in their own home countries, let alone in the world at large. The erosion of countervailing power is something quite different than the capture of absolute power, and corporations are far from accomplishing that end in the United States or the rest of the world. To consummate that power, global corporations need to further build the global octopus and its political capabilities and overcome huge political and cultural differences across the world. We are seeing a rapid proliferation of new corporate partnerships and transnational, politically oriented business associations spanning the Atlantic and the Pacific. But the International Chamber of Commerce and all such rising global business associations have not demonstrated yet the ability to create a new basis for enduring control and remain vulnerable to new movements for democracy and human rights.

Global business needs to legitimate its already immense worldwide power and authority as the will of the people. This leads to the presentation of the corporation as a new global citizen and the corporate system itself as a new kind of socially responsible democracy.

The "democracy of the market" has become the phrase of the day. The concept goes something like this. The will of the market is nothing but millions of consumers and investors democratically voting their preferences. When you participate in the market, you are exercising a kind of global citizenship. And your market vote may be even more important than the one you make in your local polling booth. This idea of market democracy is seductive. It is based on the reality that the consumer's choice of a brand or the investor's purchase of a specific company's stock does represent a kind of vote in the world economy. Consumers and investors are emotionally invested in this kind of choice or vote. And it has some impact, when combined with the choice of millions of other consumers and investors, on the economy and larger society. When I talk to my own students, they tell me they feel powerless to affect government, but they perk up because at least they can still choose what brand of coffee to buy or boycott.[18]

Corpocracy depends on people accepting the view that market choice is a meaningful democratic exercise. As people become more disenchanted with government, believing that their vote in the polling booth makes no difference because of the dominance of special interests (mostly large corporations), they will become rebels against the system—unless, of course, they feel they have another way of exercising their voice. Market democracy, our choice as consumers or investors, provides this sense of empowerment. But while it can make us feel good, it is something different than democracy. Market democracy is based on the principle of one dollar, one vote. Real democracy is one person, one vote. One dollar, one vote, is the logic of the market, but it is the opposite of the equal representation of all citizens that democracy is about. As a sovereign principle, one dollar, one vote, is inherently undemocratic, and it ensures a growing gap between the rich and poor because it gives the rich far more political representation.

Choosing what brand of sneaker to buy, the kind of vote market democracy offers, is not like electing a president, and it cannot create the accountability of the government to the will of the people. For that to occur, both national government and global government will have to abandon their servile marriage to business and start serving ordinary people.

ENDNOTES

[1] Robert Monks has used the term *corpocracy* in a different way, to describe corporations that have become unaccountable even to their own shareholders. . . . See Robert Monks, "Growing Corporate Governance: From George Ill to George Bush," in *The Legitimate Corporation,* edited by Brenda Sutton (Cambridge, MA: Basil Blackwell, 1993), pp. 165–77.

[2] See Sarah Anderson and John Cavanagh, *The Top 200: The Rise of Corporate Power* (Washington, DC: Institute for Policy Studies, 2000). I have constructed these data from *Fortune,* "The World's Largest Corporations," July 24, 2000.

[3] Ibid.

[4] Scott Bowman, *The Modern Corporation and American Political Thought* (University Park: Pennsylvania State Press), 1996.

[5] See Derber, *Corporation Nation* (New York: St. Martin's Griffin), 1998, especially Chapter 8 for a detailed discussion of the dependency of the corporation and all markets on public expenditures and government intervention.

[6] For further discussion of the illusion, see Derber, *Corporation Nation,* ibid.

[7] Sara Anderson and John Cavanagh with Thea Lee, *Field Guide to the Global Economy* (New York: New Press, 2000), pp. 16, 33. This is an invaluable and easily accessible guide to the way the global economy works. The last quote is drawn from Walden Bello, Nicola Bullard, and Kamal Malhotra, *Global Finance* (Dhaka: University Press in association with Zed Books, London, 2000), p. 5.

[8] Thomas Friedman, *The Lexus and the Olive Tree.* (New York: Farrar Straus & Giroux), 1999, pp. 105, 107.

[9] Bello et al., *Global Finance.* Op. cit.

[10] Ibid.

[11] Anderson and Cavanagh, *The Top 200.* See also Anderson and Cavanagh, *Field Guide to the Global Economy.*

[12] See Josh Karliner, *The Corporate Planet* (Sierra Club Books, 1997). See also David Korten, *When Corporations Rule the World,* 2nd ed. (San Francisco: Berrett Kohler, 2001).

[13] Diane Vaughan, *Uncoupling* (New York: Vintage, 1990).

[14] Leslie Sklair, *The Trans-National Capitalist Class.* (Oxford: Blackwell, 2001), p. 75. This issue is explored richly throughout Sklair's work.

[15] Ibid., p. 50.

[16] See also Derber, *Corporation Nation,* chapter 2.

[17] Ibid.

[18] This is the theme of Thomas Frank's *One Market under God* (New York: Anchor, 2001).

MASS MEDIA

38

MEDIA UNLIMITED
How the Torrent of Images and Sounds Overwhelms Our Lives

TODD GITLIN

This selection by Todd Gitlin is the first of three readings to examine the institution of the mass media. Gitlin, a professor of culture, journalism, and sociology at New York University, has researched the mass media for a number of years. His book *Media Unlimited: How the Torrent of Images and Sounds
Overwhelms Our Lives* (2001) examines not only how American mass media
defines and dominates culture in the United States, but also how it defies national boundaries and overwhelms other cultures in the world. The excerpt
below describes the global spread of American mass media and the effects it
has on other cultures.

Everywhere, the media flow defies national boundaries. This is one of its
obvious, but at the same time amazing, features. A global torrent is not,
of course, the master metaphor to which we have grown accustomed.
We're more accustomed to Marshall McLuhan's *global village*. Those who resort to this metaphor casually often forget that if the world is a global village,
some live in mansions on the hill, others in huts. Some dispatch images
and sounds around town at the touch of a button; others collect them at the
touch of *their* buttons. Yet McLuhan's image reveals an indispensable half-
truth. If there is a village, it speaks American. It wears jeans, drinks Coke,
eats at the golden arches, walks on swooshed shoes, plays electric guitars,
recognizes Mickey Mouse, James Dean, E.T., Bart Simpson, R2-D2, and
Pamela Anderson.

At the entrance to the champagne cellar of Piper-Heidsieck in Reims, in
eastern France, a plaque declares that the cellar was dedicated by Marie
Antoinette. The tour is narrated in six languages, and at the end you walk
back upstairs into a museum featuring photographs of famous people drinking champagne. And who are they? Perhaps members of today's royal houses,
presidents or prime ministers, economic titans or Nobel Prize winners? Of

course not. They are movie stars, almost all of them American—Marilyn Monroe to Clint Eastwood. The symmetry of the exhibition is obvious, the premise unmistakable: Hollywood stars, champions of consumption, are the royalty of this century, more popular by far than poor doomed Marie.

Hollywood is the global cultural capital—capital in both senses. The United States presides over a sort of World Bank of styles and symbols, an International Cultural Fund of images, sounds, and celebrities. The goods may be distributed by American-, Canadian-, European-, Japanese-, or Australian-owned multinational corporations, but their styles, themes, and images do not detectably change when a new board of directors takes over. Entertainment is one of America's top exports. In 1999, in fact, film, television, music, radio, advertising, print publishing, and computer software together *were* the top export, almost $80 billion worth, and while software alone accounted for $50 billion of the total, some of that category also qualifies as entertainment—video games and pornography, for example.[1] Hardly anyone is exempt from the force of American images and sounds. French resentment of Mickey Mouse, Bruce Willis, and the rest of American civilization is well known. Less well known, and rarely acknowledged by the French, is the fact that *Terminator 2* sold 5 million tickets in France during the month it opened—with no submachine guns at the heads of the customers. The same culture minister, Jack Lang, who in 1982 achieved a moment of predictable notoriety in the United States for declaring that *Dallas* amounted to cultural imperialism, also conferred France's highest honor in the arts on Elizabeth Taylor and Sylvester Stallone. The point is not hypocrisy pure and simple but something deeper, something obscured by a single-minded emphasis on American power: dependency. American popular culture is the nemesis that hundreds of millions—perhaps billions—of people love, and love to hate. The antagonism and the dependency are inseparable, for the media flood—essentially American in its origin, but virtually unlimited in its reach—represents, like it or not, a common imagination.

How shall we understand the Hong Kong T-shirt that says "I Feel Coke"? Or the little Japanese girl who asks an American visitor in all innocence, "Is there really a Disneyland in America?" (She knows the one in Tokyo.) Or the experience of a German television reporter sent to Siberia to film indigenous life, who after flying out of Moscow and then traveling for days by boat, bus, and jeep, arrives near the Arctic Sea where live a tribe of Tungusians known to ethnologists for their bearskin rituals. In the community store sits a grandfather with his grandchild on his knee. Grandfather is dressed in traditional Tungusian clothing. Grandson has on his head a reversed baseball cap.[2]

American popular culture is the closest approximation today to a global lingua franca, drawing the urban and young in particular into a common cultural zone where they share some dreams of freedom, wealth, comfort, innocence, and power—and perhaps most of all, youth as a state of mind. In general, despite the rhetoric of "identity," young people do not live in monocultures. They are not monocular. They are both local and cosmopolitan. Cultural bilingualism is routine. Just as their "cultures" are neither hard-wired nor uniform, so there is no simple way in which they are "Americanized," though there are American tags on their experience—low-cost links to status and fun.[3] Everywhere, fun lovers, efficiency seekers, Americaphiles, and Americaphobes alike pass through the portals of Disney and the arches of McDonald's wearing Levi's jeans and Gap jackets. Mickey Mouse and Donald Duck, John Wayne, Marilyn Monroe, James Dean, Bob Dylan, Michael Jackson, Madonna, Clint Eastwood, Bruce Willis, the multicolor chorus of Coca-Cola, and the next flavor of the month or the universe are the icons of a curious sort of one-world sensibility, a global semiculture. America's bid for global unification surpasses in reach that of the Romans, the British, the Catholic Church, or Islam; though without either an army or a God, it requires less. The Tungusian boy with the reversed cap on his head does not automatically think of it as "American," let alone sides with the U.S. Army.

The misleadingly easy answer to the question of how American images and sounds became omnipresent is: American imperialism. But the images are not even faintly force-fed by American corporate, political, or military power. The empire strikes from inside the spectator as well as from outside. This is a conundrum that deserves to be approached with respect if we are to grasp the fact that Mickey Mouse and Coke are everywhere recognized and often enough *enjoyed*. In the peculiar unification at work throughout the world, there is surely a supply side, but there is not only a supply side. Some things are true even if multinational corporations claim so: there is demand.

What do American icons and styles mean to those who are not American? We can only imagine—but let us try. What young people graced with disposable income encounter in American television shows, movies, soft drinks, theme parks, and American-labeled (though not American-manufactured) running shoes, T-shirts, baggy pants, ragged jeans, and so on, is a way of being in the world, the experience of a flow of ready feelings and sensations bobbing up, disposable, dissolving, segueing to the next and the next after that—all in all, the kinetic feel that I have tried to describe in [my research]. It is a quality of immediacy and casualness not so different from what Americans desire. But what the young experience in the video-game arcade or the music megastore is more than the flux of sensation. They flirt with a loose sort of social membership that requires little but a momentary (and monetary) surrender. Sampling American goods, images, and sounds, they affiliate with an empire of informality. Consuming a commodity, wearing a slogan or a logo, you affiliate with disaffiliation. You make a limited-liability connection, a virtual one. You borrow some of the effervescence that is supposed to emanate from this American staple, and hope to be recognized as one of the elect. When you wear the Israeli version that spells *Coca-Cola* in Hebrew, you express some worldwide connection with unknown peers, or a sense of irony, or both—in any event, a marker of membership. In a world of ubiquitous images, of easy mobility and casual tourism, you get to feel not only local or national but global—without locking yourself in a box so confining as to deserve the name "identity."

We are seeing on a world scale the familiar infectious rhythm of modernity. The money economy extends its reach, bringing with it a calculating mentality. Even in the poor countries it stirs the same hunger for private feeling, the same taste for disposable labels and sensations on demand, the same attention to fashion, the new and the now, that cropped up earlier in the West. Income beckons; income rewards. The taste for the marketed spectacle and the media-soaked way of life spreads. The culture consumer may not like the American goods in particular but still acquires a taste for the media's speed, formulas, and frivolity. Indeed, the lightness of American-sponsored "identity" is central to its appeal. It imposes few burdens. Attachments and affiliations coexist, overlap, melt together, form, and re-form.

Marketers, like nationalists and fundamentalists, promote "identities," but for most people, the mélange is the message. Traditional bonds bend under pressure from imports. Media from beyond help you have your "roots" and eat them, too. You can watch Mexican television in the morning and American in the afternoon, or graze between Kurdish and English. You can consolidate family ties with joint visits to Disney World—making Orlando, Florida, the major tourist destination in the United States, and the Tokyo and Marne-la-Vallée spin-offs massive attractions in Japan and France. You can attach to your parents, or children, by playing oldie music and exchanging sports statistics. You plunge back into the media flux, looking for—what? Excitement? Some low-cost variation on known themes? Some next new thing? You don't know just what, but you will when you see it—or if not, you'll change channels. . . .

The Supply Side

About the outward thrust of the American culture industry there is no mystery. The mainspring is the classic drive to expand markets. In the latter half of the 1980s, with worldwide deregulation, export sales increased from 30 percent to 40 percent of Hollywood's total revenue for television and film. Since then, the percentages have stabilized.[4] In 2000, total foreign revenues for all film and video revenue streams averaged 37 percent—for theatrical releases, 51 percent; for television, 41 percent; and for video, 27 percent.[5]

Exporters benefit from the economies of scale afforded by serial production. American industrialists have long excelled at efficiencies, first anticipating and later developing the standardized production techniques of Henry Ford's assembly line. Early in the nineteenth century, minstrel shows were already being assembled from standardized components.[6] Such efficiencies were later applied to burlesque, melodrama, vaudeville, radio soap opera, comic books, genre literature, musical comedy, and Hollywood studio productions. Cultural formula is not unique to the United States, but Americans were particularly adept at mass-producing it, using centralized management to organize road shows and coordinate local replicas.

If the American culture industry has long depended on foreign markets, foreign markets now also depend on American formulas: Westerns, action heroes, rock music, hip-hop. Globalized distribution expedites imitation. The

American way generates proven results. Little imagination is required to understand why global entertainment conglomerates copy proven recipes or why theater owners outside the United States (many of whom are themselves American) want to screen them, even if they exaggerate the degree to which formula guarantees success. In a business freighted with uncertainty, the easiest decision is to copy. Individuals making careers also want to increase their odds of success. . . .

American industrial advantages have been especially potent in movies and television, where mass promotion is linked to mass production, and language and local traditions are not as significant as in popular music. Compared with European rivals, Hollywood has the tremendous advantage of starting with a huge domestic market. Once the movie or TV show is made, each additional copy is cheap—by local standards, often ridiculously cheap. In the early 1980s, Danish television could lease a one-hour episode of *Dallas* for the cost of producing a single original *minute* of Danish drama. In television exports, Brazilian and Mexican soap operas rival American products; the Japanese remain dominant in the production and distribution of video games; and it is not inconceivable that other export powerhouses will develop. Still, for the moment, American exports predominate.

The Demand Side

But the supply-side argument won't suffice to explain global cultural dominance. American popular culture is not uniquely formulaic or transportable. . . . Moreover, availability is not popularity. No one forced Danes to watch *Dallas,* however cheaply purchased. In fact, when a new television entertainment chief took charge in 1981–82 and proceeded to cancel the show, thirty thousand protest letters poured in, and hundreds of Danes (mostly women, many rural) demonstrated in Copenhagen.[7] When the chief's superiors told him he had better rethink his decision, he passed a sleepless night, bowed, and reversed himself. The dominance of American popular culture is a soft dominance—a collaboration. In the words of media analyst James Monaco, "American movies and TV are popular because they're *popular.*"[8]

That popularity has much to do with the fusion of market-mindedness and cultural diversity. The United States has the advantages of a polyglot, multirooted (or rather, uprooted) society that celebrates its compound nature and common virtues (and sins) with remarkable energy. Popular culture, by the time it ships from American shores, has already been "pretested" on a heterogeneous public—a huge internal market with variegated tastes. American popular culture is, after all, the rambunctious child of Europe and Africa. Our popular music and dance derive from the descendants of African slaves, among others. Our comic sense derives principally from the English, East European Jews, and, again, African Americans, with growing Hispanic infusions. Our stories come from everywhere; consider Ralph Waldo Ellison's *Invisible Man,* inspired jointly by Dostoyevsky, African American folktales, and jazz. American culture is spongy, or in James Monaco's happy term, *promiscuous*. He adds, "American culture simply doesn't exist without its African and European progenitors, and despite occasional outbursts of 'Americanism' it continues to accept almost any input."[9]

To expand in the United States, popular culture had a clear avenue. It did not have to squeeze up against an aristocratic model, there being no wealthy landowning class to nourish one except in the plantation South—and there, slaves were the population that produced the most influential popular culture. Outside the South, from the early nineteenth century on, the market enjoyed prestige; it was no dishonor to produce culture for popular purposes. Ecclesiastical rivals were relatively weak. From the early years of the Republic, American culture was driven by a single overriding purpose: to entertain the common man and woman. . . .

It is to America's advantage as well that commercial work emerges from Hollywood, New York, and Nashville in the principal world language. Thanks to the British Empire-cum-Commonwealth, English is the second most commonly spoken native language in the world, and the most international. . . . English is spoken and read as a second language more commonly than any other. Increasingly, the English that is taught and learned, the language in demand, is American, not British. It is the language of business and has acquired the cachet of international media. Of the major world languages, English is the most compressed; partly because of its Anglo-Saxon origins, the English version of any text is almost always shorter than translations in other languages. English is grammatically simple. American English in particular is pungent, informal, absorptive, evolving, precise when called upon to be precise, transferable between written and verbal forms, lacking in sharp distinctions between "high" and "low" forms, and all in all, well adapted for slogans, headlines, comic strips, song lyrics, jingles, slang, dubbing, and other standard features of popular culture. English is, in a word, the most torrential language.[10]

Moreover, the American language of images is even more accessible than the American language of words. The global popularity of Hollywood product often depends less on the spoken word, even when kept elementary (non-English-speakers everywhere could understand Arnold Schwarzenegger without difficulty), than on crackling edits, bright smiles, the camera tracking and swooping, the cars crashing off cliffs or smashing into other cars, the asteroids plunging dramatically toward earth. In action movies, as in the Westerns that preceded them, speech is a secondary mode of expression. European competitors cannot make this claim, though Hong Kong can.

It is also an export advantage that "American" popular culture is frequently not so American at all. "Hollywood" is an export platform that happens to be located on the Pacific coast of the United States but uses capital, hires personnel, and depicts sites from many countries. Disney casually borrows mythologies from Britain, Germany, France, Italy, Denmark, China, colonial America, the Old Testament, anywhere. Any myth can get the Disney treatment: simplified, smoothed down, prettified. Pavilions as emblems of foreign countries, sites as replicas of sites, *Fantasia, Pinocchio, Song of the South,*

Pocahontas, Mulan—Disney takes material where it can, as long as it comes out Disney's industrialized fun.

Moreover, to sustain market advantages, the Hollywood multinationals, ever thirsting for novelty, eagerly import, process, and export styles and practitioners from abroad. Consider, among directors, Alfred Hitchcock, Charlie Chaplin, Douglas Sirk, Michael Curtiz, Billy Wilder, Otto Preminger, Ridley Scott, Peter Weir, Bruce Beresford, Paul Verhoeven, John Woo, Ang Lee. . . . Consider, among stars, Greta Garbo, Ingrid Bergman, Cary Grant, Anthony Quinn, Sean Connery, Arnold Schwarzenegger, Jean-Claude Van Damme, Mel Gibson, Hugh Grant, Jackie Chan, Kate Winslet, Michelle Yeoh, Chow Yun-Fat, Catherine Zeta-Jones, Antonio Banderas, Penelope Cruz. Hollywood is the global magnet—and (to mix metaphors) the acid bath into which, often enough, talent dissolves. Even the locales come from everywhere, or nowhere. It is striking how many blockbusters take place in outer space (the *Star Wars, Alien,* and *Star Trek* series), in the prenational past (the *Jurassic Park* series), in the postnational future (the *Planet of the Apes* series, the two *Terminator* films, *The Matrix*), at sea (*Titanic, The Perfect Storm*—the latter also directed by a German, Wolfgang Petersen), or on an extended hop-skip-and-jump around the world (the James Bond series, *Mission: Impossible*). . . .

No matter. Of Americanized popular culture, nothing more or less is asked but that it be *interesting,* a portal into the pleasure dome. . . .

So the disrespectful, lavish, energetic American torrent flows on and on, appealing to ideals of action and self-reinvention, extending the comforts of recognition to the uprooted. In a world of unease and uprooting, the American images, sounds, and stories overlap nations and global diasporas. Cultivating and nourishing desires, unifying but flexible, everywhere they leave behind deposits of what can only be called a civilization—not an ideology, or a system of belief, but something less resistible, a way of life soaked in feeling, seeming to absorb with equal conviction traces of every idea or, for that matter, the absence of all ideas. It has a clear field. In this time, one-world ideologies are decidedly flimsy. With socialism largely discredited, and each world religion checked by the others, the way of life with the greatest allure turns out to be this globalizing civilization of saturation and speed that enshrines individuals, links freedom to taste, tickles the senses. How odd, but inescapable, that insofar as there are unifying symbols today, they should be the undemanding ones—not the cross, the crescent, or the flag, let alone the hammer and sickle, but Coke and Mickey Mouse.

At least for now.

An End to Culture?

I have been arguing that American culture is a complex collaboration between venal, efficient suppliers and receptive, fickle consumers. The suppliers were already well understood by Alexis de Tocqueville, with his emphasis on efficiency and convenience; the consumers by Georg Simmel, with his emphasis on the hunger for feeling and the taste for the transitory. The suppliers built a machine for delivering cultural goods; the consumers acquired a taste for them. What was true when commercial American culture poured across the country in the twentieth century remains true as it pours through the world today. The preeminence of America's styles and themes is not rule from on high. To take it that way is to misunderstand its soft power.

What I have been calling the demand side is not necessarily clamor or hunger. It is more a compound of interest, liking, tolerance—and enthusiasm. There are fanatics who talk and write feverishly about the *Star Wars* movies, auctioning and purchasing rare merchandise, going so far as to take a day off from work to buy a movie ticket to see the debut of the *trailer* for Episode I, *The Phantom Menace;* there is the wider circle of millions who look forward less passionately to the next installment; and an even wider one of more or less curious, possibly halfhearted customers keeping up with their crowds. The multiplex is filled with American films because the United States was first to produce a culture of comfort and convenience whose popularity was its primary reason for being. All in all, American popular culture is popular because (and to the extent that) its sleek, fast, fleeting styles of entertainment—its commitment to entertainment—dovetail with modern displacement and desire. . . .

There is no going back to the forest clan or the village. There is no repealing the technologies that spray images on our walls, graft stories onto our screens, sing songs into our headphones. There is no diversion from the seduction and clamor, the convenience and irritation of media. There is no avoiding the spread of American-style pop—its coupling of irreverence and brutality; its love of the road and its degradation of the word; its light rock and heavy metal. This amalgam flows through the world for worse and for better, inviting, in unknowable proportions, immigration, emulation, and revulsion. Where the flow goes, there follows a fear that American marketing exudes a uniform "McWorld" —and brings, in its wake, with dialectical certainty, destructive "Jihads." [11]

Yet for all the fear of standardization, American pop does not erase all the vernacular alternatives, all the local forms in which artists and writers give forth their styles and stories. The emergence of a global semiculture coexists with local sensibilities. It does not simply replace them. As the Norwegian media theorist Helge Rønning suggests, it's plausible to suppose that globalized, largely American pop has become, or is in the process of becoming, almost everyone's second culture. . . .

As for the media as a whole, what could stop the flood but a catastrophic breakdown of civilization? (In Steven Spielberg's *A.I.,* not even global warming and the total immersion of Manhattan wipe out the media.) Why would the beat not go on? Too much desire and too much convenience converge in the nonstop spectacle; too much of the human desire to play, to test and perfect oneself, to feel, to feel good, to feel with others, to feel conveniently; too much of the desire for sensory pleasure, for a refuge from calculation, for a flight from life, or from death, or from both. The media have been gathering force for centuries. Why should their songs and stories cease to generate enthusiasm and anxiety, production and consumption, celebrity and irony, fandom and boredom, criticism and jamming, paranoia and secession? Why would a society in which people have the time to indulge their fancies this way repeal these options? The media will sweep down, their flow continuous and widening, bearing banalities and mysteries, achievements and potentials, strangeness and disappointments— this would appear to be our complex fate.

I am not proposing that anyone cease trying to launch better work. Surely there will be—there *deserve* to be—fights over who gets to harness media power, over censorship, over improving contents and broadening access. Conservatives will want today's colossal controllers to keep control but clean up the sewage. Liberals will want new tributaries to flow and to bend the stream in their preferred directions. Techno-utopians will agree with the liberal law professor who writes of digital online sharing: "The result will be more music, poetry, photography, and journalism available to a far wider audience. . . . For those who worry about the cultural, economic and political power of the global media companies, the dreamed-of revolution is at hand. . . . It is we, not they, who are about to enter the promised land."[12] But these apparently different ideas share an ideal: more media, more of the time.

I cannot pretend to offer a definitive balance sheet on our odd form of life immersed in images, sounds, and stories. Nor can I suggest a ten-point program for revitalization or a list of preferable activities. I have tried to confront the media as a whole, to reconceive their onrushing immensity, and to explain how they became central to our civilization. To fans, critics, paranoids, exhibitionists, ironists, and the rest, to reformers of all stripes, I would propose taking some time to step back, forgoing the fantasies of electronic perfection, leaving behind the trend-spotting gurus and pundits who purport to interpret for us the hottest and latest. I propose that we stop—and imagine the whole phenomenon freshly, taking the media seriously not as a cornucopia of wondrous gadgets or a collection of social problems, but as a central condition of an entire way of life. Perhaps if we step away from the ripples of the moment, the week, or the season, and contemplate the torrent in its entirety, we will know what we want to do about it besides change channels.

ENDNOTES

[1] Economists Incorporated for the International Intellectual Property Alliance, Executive Summary, 2000_SIWEK_EXEC.pdf. Thanks to Siva Vaidhyanathan for his discerning analysis of these statistics.

[2] This story is told by Berndt Ostendorf in "What Makes American Popular Culture So Popular? A View from Europe" (Odense, Denmark: Oasis, 2000).

[3] I benefited from a discussion about the overuse of the term *culture* with Kevin Robins, March 2, 2001.

[4] National Technical Information Service, *Globalization of the Mass Media* (Washington, DC: Department of Commerce, 1993), pp. 1–2, cited in Edward S. Herman and Robert W. McChesney, *The Global Media: The New Missionaries of Corporate Capitalism* (London: Cassell, 1997), p. 39.

[5] Calculated from *Schroder's International Media and Entertainment Report 2000*, p. 37. Courtesy of David Lieberman, media business editor of *USA Today.*

[6] Ostendorf, "What Makes American Popular Culture So Popular?" pp. 16–18, 47.

[7] Personal communications, Henrik Christiansen, former chief of entertainment for Danish television (and previously head of news), September 1998.

[8] "Images and Sounds as Cultural Commodities," p. 231, from an article I clipped a long time ago but without noting from which magazine I'd clipped it.

[9] Ibid., p. 231.

[10] Jeremy Tunstall, *Media Are American: Anglo-American Media in the World* (New York: Columbia University Press, 1977).

[11] The most impressive articulation of this position in recent years is Benjamin Barber, *Jihad vs. McWorld* (New York: Times Books, 1995). But see the critique by Fareed Zakaria, *New Republic,* January 22, 1996, pp. 27 ff.

[12] Eben Moglen, "Liberation Musicology," *Nation,* March 12, 2001, p. 6.

39

MEDIA MAGIC
Making Class Invisible

GREGORY MANTSIOS

This second selection on the institution of the mass media is by Gregory Mantsios, who works in the Center for Worker Education at Queen's College, New York. Mantsios argues that the mass media is a powerful institution not only because it is the most influential in molding public consciousness but because the ownership and control of the mass media is highly concentrated. Think of the AOL-Time Warner merger in recent years as one example of a media giant. In addition to owning networks, publishing houses, newspapers, and so on, AOL-Time Warner also owns the CNN news affiliate. This concentration of ownership ensures little diversity in the messages that the media promotes. For example, one way the mass media shapes culture and public opinion is in the portrayals of social class. In the excerpt below, Mantsios examines the portrayals of social class in American media.

O f the various social and cultural forces in our society, the mass media is arguably the most influential in molding public consciousness. Americans spend an average twenty-eight hours per week watching television. They also spend an undetermined number of hours reading periodicals, listening to the radio, and going to the movies. Unlike other cultural

Gregory Mantsios, "Media Magic: Making Class Invisible" from *Race, Class, and Gender in the United States, Sixth Edition,* edited by Paula Rothenberg. Reprinted with the permission of the author.

and socializing institutions, ownership and control of the mass media are highly concentrated. Twenty-three corporations own more than one-half of all the daily newspapers, magazines, movie studios, and radio and television outlets in the United States.[1] The number of media companies is shrinking and their control of the industry is expanding. And a relatively small number of media outlets is producing and packaging the majority of news and entertainment programs. For the most part, our media is national in nature and single-minded (profit-oriented) in purpose. This media plays a key role in defining our cultural tastes, helping us locate ourselves in history, establishing our national identity, and ascertaining the range of national and social possibilities. In this essay, we will examine the way the mass media shapes how people think about each other and about the nature of our society.

The United States is the most highly stratified society in the industrialized world. Class distinctions operate in virtually every aspect of our lives, determining the nature of our work, the quality of our schooling, and the health and safety of our loved ones. Yet remarkably, we, as a nation, retain illusions about living in an egalitarian society. We maintain these illusions, in large part, because the media hides gross inequities from public view. In those instances when inequities are revealed, we are provided with messages that obscure the nature of class realities and blame the victims of class-dominated society for their own plight. Let's briefly examine what the news media, in particular, tells us about class.

About the Poor

The news media provides meager coverage of poor people and poverty. The coverage it does provide is often distorted and misleading.

The Poor Do Not Exist

For the most part, the news media ignores the poor. Unnoticed are forty million poor people in the nation—a number that equals the entire population of Maine, Vermont, New Hampshire, Connecticut, Rhode Island, New Jersey, and New York combined. Perhaps even more alarming is that the rate of poverty is increasing twice as fast as the population growth in the United States. Ordinarily, even a calamity of much smaller proportion (e.g., flooding in the Midwest) would garner a great deal of coverage and hype from a media usually eager to declare a crisis, yet less than one in five hundred articles in the *New York Times* and one in one thousand articles listed in the *Reader's Guide to Periodic Literature* are on poverty. With remarkably little attention to them, the poor and their problems are hidden from most Americans.

When the media does turn its attention to the poor, it offers a series of contradictory messages and portrayals.

The Poor Are Faceless

Each year the Census Bureau releases a new report on poverty in our society and its results are duly reported in the media. At best, however, this coverage emphasizes annual fluctuations (showing how the numbers differ from previous years) and ongoing debates over the validity of the numbers (some argue the number should be lower, most that the number should be higher). Coverage like this desensitizes us to the poor by reducing poverty to a number. It ignores the human tragedy of poverty—the suffering, indignities, and misery endured by millions of children and adults. Instead, the poor become statistics rather than people.

The Poor Are Undeserving

When the media does put a face on the poor, it is not likely to be a pretty one. The media will provide us with sensational stories about welfare cheats, drug addicts, and greedy panhandlers (almost always urban and black). Compare these images and the emotions evoked by them with the media's treatment of middle-class (usually white) "tax evaders," celebrities who have a "chemical dependency," or wealthy businesspeople who use unscrupulous means to "make a profit." While the behavior of the more affluent offenders is considered an "impropriety" and a deviation from the norm, the behavior of the poor is considered repugnant, indicative of the poor in general, and worthy of our indignation and resentment.

The Poor Are an Eyesore

When the media does cover the poor, they are often presented through the eyes of the middle class. For example, sometimes the media includes a story about community resistance to a homeless shelter or storekeeper annoyance with panhandlers. Rather than focusing on the plight of the poor, these stories are about middle-class opposition to the poor. Such stories tell us that the poor are an inconvenience and an irritation.

The Poor Have Only Themselves to Blame

In another example of media coverage, we are told that the poor live in a personal and cultural cycle of poverty that hopelessly imprisons them. They routinely center on the black urban population and focus on perceived personality or cultural traits that doom the poor. While the women in these stories typically exhibit an "attitude" that leads to trouble or a promiscuity that leads to single motherhood, the men possess a need for immediate gratification that leads to drug abuse or an unquenchable greed that leads to the pursuit of fast money. The images that are seared into our mind are sexist, racist, and classist. Census figures reveal that most of the poor are white not black or Hispanic, that they live in rural or suburban areas not urban centers, and hold jobs at least part of the year.[2] Yet, in a fashion that is often framed in an understanding and sympathetic tone, we are told that the poor have inflicted poverty on themselves.

The Poor Are Down on Their Luck

During the Christmas season, the news media sometimes provides us with accounts of poor individuals or families (usually white) who are down on their luck. These stories are often linked to stories about soup kitchens or other charitable activities and sometimes call for charitable contributions. These "Yule time" stories are as much about the affluent as they are about the poor: they tell us that the affluent in our society are a kind, understanding, giving people—which we are not.[3] The series of unfortunate circumstances that have led to impoverishment are presumed to be a temporary condition that will improve with time and a change in luck.

Despite appearances, the messages provided by the media are not entirely disparate. With each variation, the media informs us what poverty is not (i.e., systemic and indicative of American society) by informing us what it is. The media tells us that poverty is either an aberration of the American way of life (it doesn't exist, it's just another number, it's unfortunate but temporary) or an end product of the poor themselves (they are a nuisance, do not deserve better, and have brought their predicament upon themselves).

By suggesting that the poor have brought poverty upon themselves, the media is engaging in what William Ryan has called "blaming the victim."[4] The media identifies in what ways the poor are different as a consequence of deprivation, then defines those differences as the cause of poverty itself. Whether blatantly hostile or cloaked in sympathy, the message is that there is something fundamentally wrong with the victims—their hormones, psychological makeup, family environment, community, race, or some combination of these—that accounts for their plight and their failure to lift themselves out of poverty.

But poverty in the United States is systemic. It is a direct result of economic and political policies that deprive people of jobs, adequate wages, or legitimate support. It is neither natural nor inevitable: there is enough wealth in our nation to eliminate poverty if we chose to redistribute existing wealth or income. The plight of the poor is reason enough to make the elimination of poverty the nation's first priority. But poverty also impacts dramatically on the nonpoor. It has a dampening effect on wages in general (by maintaining a reserve army of unemployed and underemployed anxious for any job at any wage) and breeds crime and violence (by maintaining conditions that invite private gain by illegal means and rebellion-like behavior, not entirely unlike the urban riots of the 1960s). Given the extent of poverty in the nation and the impact it has on us all, the media must spin considerable magic to keep the poor and the issue of poverty and its root causes out of the public consciousness.

About Everyone Else

Both the broadcast and the print news media strive to develop a strong sense of "we-ness" in their audience. They seek to speak to and for an audience that is both affluent and like-minded. The media's solidarity with affluence, that is, with the middle and upper class, varies little from one medium to another. Benjamin DeMott points out, for example, that the *New York Times* understands affluence to be intelligence, taste, public spirit, responsibility, and a readiness to rule and "conceives itself as spokesperson for a readership awash in these qualities."[5] Of course, the flip side to creating a sense of "we," or "us," is establishing a perception of the "other." The other relates back to the faceless, amoral, undeserving, and inferior "underclass." Thus, the world according to the news media is divided between the "underclass" and everyone else. Again the messages are often contradictory.

The Wealthy Are Us

Much of the information provided to us by the news media focuses attention on the concerns of a very wealthy and privileged class of people. Although the concerns of a small fraction of the populace, they are presented as though they were the concerns of everyone. For example, while relatively few people actually own stock, the news media devotes an inordinate amount of broadcast time and print space to business news and stock market quotations. Not only do business reports cater to a particular narrow clientele, so do the fashion pages (with $2,000 dresses), wedding announcements, and the obituaries. Even weather and sports news often have a class bias. An all-news radio station in New York City, for example, provides regular national ski reports. International news, trade agreements, and domestic policies issues are also reported in terms of their impact on business climate and the business community. Besides being of practical value to the wealthy, such coverage has considerable ideological value. Its message: the concerns of the wealthy are the concerns of us all.

The Wealthy (as a Class) Do Not Exist

While preoccupied with the concerns of the wealthy, the media fails to notice the way in which the rich as a class of people create and shape domestic and foreign policy. Presented as an aggregate of individuals, the wealthy appear without special interests, interconnections, or unity in purpose. Out of public view are the class interests of the wealthy, the interlocking business links, the concerted actions to preserve their class privileges and business interests (by running for public office, supporting political candidates, lobbying, etc.). Corporate lobbying is ignored, taken for granted, or assumed to be in the public interest. (Compare this with the media's portrayal of the "strong arm of labor" in attempting to defeat trade legislation that is harmful to the interests of working people.) It is estimated that two-thirds of the U.S. Senate is composed of millionaires.[6] Having such a preponderance of millionaires in the Senate, however, is perceived to be neither unusual nor anti-democratic; these millionaire senators are assumed to be serving "our" collective interests in governing.

The Wealthy Are Fascinating and Benevolent

The broadcast and print media regularly provide hype for individuals who have achieved "super" success. These stories are usually about celebrities and superstars from the sports and entertainment world. Society pages and gossip columns serve to keep the social elite informed of each others' doings, allow the rest of us to gawk at their excesses, and help to keep the American dream alive. The print media is also fond of feature stories on corporate empire builders. These stories provide an occasional "insider's" view of the private and corporate life of industrialists by suggesting a rags-to-riches account of corporate success. These stories tell us that corporate success is a series of smart moves, shrewd acquisitions, timely mergers, and well thought out executive suite shuffles. By painting the upper class in a positive light, innocent of any wrongdoing (labor leaders and union organizations usually get the opposite treatment), the media assures us that wealth and power are benevolent. One person's capital accumulation is presumed to be good for all. The elite, then, are portrayed as investment wizards, people of special talent and skill, whom even their victims (workers and consumers) can admire.

The Wealthy Include a Few Bad Apples

On rare occasions, the media will mock selected individuals for their personality flaws. Real estate investor Donald Trump and New York Yankees owner George Steinbrenner, for example, are admonished by the media for deliberately seeking publicity (a very un–upper class thing to do); hotel owner Leona Helmsley was caricatured for her personal cruelties; and junk-bond broker Michael Milkin was condemned because he had the audacity to rob the rich. Michael Parenti points out that by treating business wrongdoings as isolated deviations from the socially beneficial system of "responsible capitalism," the media overlooks the features of the system that produce such abuses and the regularity with which they occur. Rather than portraying them as predictable and frequent outcomes of corporate power and the business system, the media treats abuses as if they were isolated and atypical. Presented as an occasional aberration, these incidents serve not to challenge, but to legitimate, the system.[7]

The Middle Class Is Us

By ignoring the poor and blurring the lines between the working people and the upper class, the news media creates a universal middle class. From this perspective, the size of one's income becomes largely irrelevant: what matters is that most of "us" share an intellectual and moral superiority over the disadvantaged. As *Time* magazine once concluded, "Middle America is a state of mind."[8] "We are all middle class," we are told, "and we all share the same concerns": job security, inflation, tax burdens, world peace, the cost of food and housing, health care, clean air and water, and the safety of our streets. While the concerns of the wealthy are quite distinct from those of the middle class (e.g., the wealthy worry about investments, not jobs), the media convinces us that "we [the affluent] are all in this together."

The Middle Class Is a Victim

For the media, "we" the affluent not only stand apart from the "other"—the poor, the working class, the minorities, and their problems—"we" are also victimized by the poor (who drive up the costs of maintaining the welfare rolls), minorities (who commit crimes against us), and by workers (who are greedy and drive companies out and prices up). Ignored are the subsidies to the rich, the crimes of corporate America, and the policies that wreak havoc on the economic well-being of middle America. Media magic convinces us to fear, more than anything else, being victimized by those less affluent than ourselves.

The Middle Class Is Not a Working Class

The news media clearly distinguishes the middle class (employees) from the working class (i.e., blue-collar workers) who are portrayed, at best, as irrelevant, outmoded, and a dying breed. Furthermore, the media will tell us that the hardships faced by blue-collar workers are inevitable (due to progress), a result of bad luck (chance circumstances in a particular industry), or a product of their own doing (they priced themselves out of a job). Given the media's presentation of reality, it is hard to believe that manual, supervised, unskilled, and semiskilled workers actually represent more than 50 percent of the adult working population.[9] The working class, instead, is relegated by the media to "the other."

In short, the news media either lionizes the wealthy or treats their interests and those of the middle class as one in the same. But the upper class and the middle class do not share the same interests or worries. Members of the upper class worry about stock dividends (not employment), they profit from inflation and global militarism, their children attend exclusive private schools, they eat and live in a royal fashion, they call on (or are called upon by) personal physicians, they have few consumer problems, they can escape whenever they want from environmental pollution, and they live on streets and travel to other areas under the protection of private police forces.[10]

The wealthy are not only a class with distinct lifestyles and interests, they are a ruling class. They receive a disproportionate share of the country's yearly income, own a disproportionate amount of the country's wealth, and contribute a disproportionate number of their members to governmental bodies and decision-making groups—all traits that William Domhoff, in his classic work *Who Rules America?*, defined as characteristic of a governing class.[11]

This governing class maintains and manages our political and economic structures in such a way that these structures continue to yield an amazing proportion of our wealth to a minuscule upper class. While the media is not above referring to ruling classes in other countries (we hear, for example,

references to Japan's ruling elite),[12] its treatment of the news proceeds as though there were no such ruling class in the United States.

Furthermore, the news media inverts reality so that those who are working class and middle class learn to fear, resent, and blame those below, rather than those above, them in the class structure. We learn to resent welfare, which accounts for only two cents out of every dollar in the federal budget (approximately $10 billion) and provides financial relief for the needy,[13] but learn little about the $11 billion the federal government spends on individuals with incomes in excess of $1,000,000 (not needy),[14] or the $17 billion in farm subsidies, or the $214 billion (twenty times the cost of welfare) in interest payments to financial institutions.

Middle-class whites learn to fear African Americans and Latinos, but most violent crime occurs within poor and minority communities and is neither interracial[15] nor interclass. As horrid as such crime is, it should not mask the destruction and violence perpetrated by corporate America. In spite of the fact that 14,000 innocent people are killed on the job each year, 100,000 die prematurely, 400,000 become seriously ill, and 6 million are injured from work-related accidents and diseases, most Americans fear government regulation more than they do unsafe working conditions.

Through the media, middle-class—and even working class—Americans learn to blame blue-collar workers and their unions for declining purchasing power and economic security. But while workers who managed to keep their jobs and their unions struggled to keep up with inflation, the top 1 percent of American families saw their average incomes soar 80 percent in the last decade.[16] Much of the wealth at the top was accumulated as stockholders and corporate executives moved their companies abroad to employ cheaper labor (56 cents per hour in El Salvador) and avoid paying taxes in the United States. Corporate America is a world made up of ruthless bosses, massive layoffs, favoritism and nepotism, health and safety violations, pension plan losses, union busting, tax evasions, unfair competition, and price gouging, as well as fast-buck deals, financial speculation, and corporate wheeling and dealing that serve the interests of the corporate elite, but are generally wasteful and destructive to workers and the economy in general.

It is no wonder Americans cannot think straight about class. The mass media is neither objective, balanced, independent, nor neutral. Those who own and direct the mass media are themselves part of the upper class, and neither they nor the ruling class in general have to conspire to manipulate public opinion. Their interest is in preserving the status quo, and their view of society as fair and equitable comes naturally to them. But their ideology dominates our society and justifies what is in reality a perverse social order—one that perpetuates unprecedented elite privilege and power on the one hand and widespread deprivation on the other. A mass media that did not have its own class interests in preserving the status quo would acknowledge that inordinate wealth and power undermines democracy and that a "free market" economy can ravage a people and their communities.

ENDNOTES

[1] Martin Lee and Norman Solomon, *Unreliable Sources* (New York: Lyle Stuart, 1990), p. 71. See also Ben Bagdikian, *The Media Monopoly* (Boston: Beacon Press, 1990).

[2] Department of Commerce, Bureau of the Census, "Poverty in the United States: 1992," *Current Population Reports, Consumer Income,* Series P60–185, pp. xi, xv.

[3] American households with incomes of less than $10,000 give an average of 5.5 percent of their earnings to charity or to a religious organization, while those making more than $100,000 a year give only 2.9 percent. After changes in the 1986 tax code reduced the benefits of charitable giving, taxpayers earning $500,000 or more slashed their average donation by nearly one-third. Furthermore, many of these acts of benevolence do not help the needy. Rather than provide funding to social service agencies that aid the poor, the voluntary contributions of the wealthy go to places and institutions that entertain, inspire, cure, or educate wealthy Americans—art museums, opera houses, theaters, orchestras, ballet companies, private hospitals, and elite universities. (Robert Reich, "Secession of the Successful," *New York Times Magazine,* February 17, 1991, p. 43.)

[4] William Ryan, *Blaming the Victim* (New York: Vintage, 1971).

[5] Benjamin DeMott, *The Imperial Middle* (New York: William Morrow, 1990), p. 123.

[6] Fred Barnes, "The Zillionaires Club," *The New Republic,* January 29, 1990, p. 24.

[7] Michael Parenti, *Inventing Reality* (New York: St. Martin's Press, 1986), p. 109.

[8] *Time,* January 5, 1979, p. 10.

[9] Vincent Navarro, "The Middle Class—A Useful Myth," *The Nation,* March 23, 1992, p. 1.

[10] Charles Anderson, *The Political Economy of Social Class* (Englewood Cliffs, NJ: Prentice Hall, 1974), p. 137. The number of private security guards in the United States now exceeds the number of public police officers. (Robert Reich, "Secession of the Successful," *New York Times Magazine,* February 17, 1991, p. 42.)

[11] William Domhoff, *Who Rules America?* (Englewood Cliffs, NJ: Prentice Hall, 1967), p. 5.

[12] Lee and Solomon, *Unreliable Sources,* p. 179.

[13] A total of $20 billion is spent on welfare when you include all state funding. But the average state funding also comes to only two cents per state dollar.

[14] *Newsweek,* August 10, 1992, p. 57.

[15] In 92 percent of the murders nationwide, the assailant and the victim are of the same race (46 percent are white/white, 46 percent are black/black), 5.6 percent are black on white, and 2.4 percent are white on black. (FBI and Bureau of Justice Statistics, 1985–1986, quoted in Raymond S. Franklin, *Shadows of Race and Class* [Minneapolis: University of Minnesota Press, 1991], p. 108.)

[16] *Business Week,* June 8, 1992, p. 86.

40
———

IT'S NOT THE MEDIA
The Truth about Pop Culture's Influence on Children

KAREN STERNHEIMER

One interesting area of research on the mass media is the effects media has on people, especially children. Karen Sternheimer, a sociologist at the University of Southern California, is particularly interested in how the media affects children. Her book *It's Not the Media: The Truth about Pop Culture's Influence on Children* (2003) is excerpted here. In this selection, Sternheimer addresses four fallacies of media violence and the effects it has on children.

April 20, 1999: I remember that Tuesday morning clearly. I was working at home, exhausted after teaching a Monday night class. When I turned on the television I knew that something horrible had happened because news programs had gone into crisis mode, with the "breaking news" banner underlining each station's coverage. There had been a shooting at a high school in Littleton, Colorado.

While the shooting at Columbine High School was discussed in context with other high-profile school shootings of the 1990s, it was clear that this one was different. The casualties were greater, the school larger and more affluent. Nonstop coverage ensued—I joined the news event as cameras were stationed at an off-site location where parents eagerly awaited the arrival of kids bused to safety. Parents hugged children, classmates held onto each other sobbing while telling reporters what it was like inside. As several students described crouching under tables in the library, I imagined myself in my own high school library, a place I went nearly every day after lunch for a little bit of quiet. I began to feel relieved that my high school days were long past. High school was hard enough without worrying about being shot.

Once the initial shock of the shootings ended, the commentators appeared to try to explain how something like this could happen. It didn't take long before pundits invoked the popular culture rationale. What music did the killers listen to? Why did they wear those trench coats? Wasn't the scene eerily reminiscent of the 1995 movie *The Basketball Diaries,* where Leonardo DiCaprio opens fire on his classmates and teacher and is met by the applause of his buddies? Did they learn to make bombs on the Internet? They sure seemed to play lots of violent video games where they could take virtual target practice at their classmates. The commentary appeared to point to mounting evidence: the media were guilty, and the public has had enough. Columbine seemed to tell us that violent media could create tragedy, as we had long suspected.

[My research] is not about the Columbine High School shooting, but the incident serves as a powerful example of American anxieties about our media culture and our fear of what it may have "done to" children in the years leading up to and following the tragedy. Although the Columbine killers were in their teens, the word "child" is frequently used to encompass all minors to heighten the sense of young people's vulnerability to media culture. Throughout [my work] I try to be clear about which age group I'm talking about, but keep in mind that others aren't. My intent . . . is to take a step back and think about exactly why it is that we fear the effects of popular culture. As we will see, a great deal of our concern about media and media's potential effects on kids has more to do with uncertainty about the future and the changing landscape of childhood. In addition to considering why we are concerned about the impact of popular culture, I also explore why many researchers and politicians encourage us to remain afraid of media culture. . . .

Four Fallacies of Media-Violence Effects

. . . Historically, psychologists have focused the bulk of the research about media and violence on individual "effects" that have been used to draw conclusions on a sociological level. Adding sociological analysis gives us information about the larger context. We will see that from a sociological perspective media violence is important, but not in the way we tend to think it is. It cannot help us explain real violence well, but it can help us understand American culture and why stories of conflict and violent resolution so often reoccur.

Media violence has become a scapegoat, onto which we lay blame a host of social problems. Sociologist Todd Gitlin describes how "the indiscriminate fear of television in particular displaces justifiable fears of actual dangers— dangers of which television . . . provides some disturbing glimpses."[1] Concerns about media and violence rest on several flawed, yet taken-for-granted assumptions about both media and violence. These beliefs appear to be obvious in emotional arguments about "protecting" children. So while these are not the only problems with blaming media, this [reading] will address four central assumptions:

1. As media culture has expanded, children have become more violent.
2. Children are prone to imitate media violence with deadly results.
3. Real violence and media violence have the same meaning.
4. Research proves media violence is a major contributor to social problems.

As someone who has been accused of only challenging the media–violence connection because I am secretly funded by the entertainment industry (which I can assure you I am not), I can attest we are entering hostile and emotional territory.[2] This [reading] demonstrates where these assumptions come from and why they are misplaced.

Assumption #1: As Media Culture Has Expanded, Children Have Become More Violent

You won't get an argument from me on the first part of this assumption—media culture has expanded exponentially over the last few decades. The low cost of production of the microchip has made a wide variety of new media technologies like video games and computers available to a large number of consumers, and we have been buying billions of dollars worth of these products. Traditional media like television have expanded from a handful of channels to hundreds. Our involvement with media culture has grown to the degree that media use has become an integral part of everyday life. There is so much content out there that we cannot know about or control, so we can never be fully sure what children may come in contact with. This fear of the unknown underscores the anxiety about harmful effects. Is violent media imagery, a small portion of a vast media culture, poisoning the minds and affecting the behavior of countless children, as an August 2001 *Kansas City Star* article warns?[3] The fear seems real and echoes in newsprint across the country.

Perhaps an article in the *Pittsburgh Post-Gazette* comes closest to mirroring popular sentiment and exposing three fears that are indicative of anxiety about change. Titled "Media, Single Parents Blamed for Spurt in Teen Violence," the article combines anxieties about shifts in family structure and the expansion of media culture with adults' fear of youth by falsely stating that kids are now more violent at earlier and earlier ages.[4] This certainly reflects a common perception, but its premise is fundamentally flawed: as media culture has expanded, young people have become *less* violent. During the 1990s arrest rates for violent offenses (like murder, rape, and aggravated assault) among fifteen- to seventeen-year-olds fell steadily, just as they did for people fourteen and under.[5] Those with the highest arrest rates now and in the past are adults. Fifteen- to seventeen-year-olds only outdo adults in burglary and theft, but these rates have been falling for the past twenty-five years. In fact, theft arrest rates for fifteen- to seventeen-year-olds have declined by 27 percent since 1976 and the rates for those fourteen and under have declined 41 percent, while the arrest rate for adults has increased.[6] Yet we seldom hear public outcry about the declining morals of adults—this complaint is reserved for youth. . . .

So why do we seem to think that kids are now more violent than ever? A Berkeley Media Studies Group report found that half of news stories about youth were about violence and that more than two-thirds of violence stories focused on youth.[7] We think kids are committing the lion's share of violence because they comprise a large proportion of crime news. The reality is that adults commit most crime, but a much smaller percentage of these stories make news. The voices of reason that remind the public that youth crime decreased in the 1990s are often met with emotional anecdotes that draw attention away from dry statistics. A 2000 Discovery Channel "town meeting" called "Why Are We Violent" demonstrates this well. The program, described as a "wake-up call" for parents, warned that violence is everywhere, and their kids could be the next victims. Host Forrest Sawyer presented statistics indicating crime had dropped but downplayed them as only "part of the story." The bulk of the program relied on emotional accounts of experiences participants had with violence. There was no mention of violence committed by adults, the most likely perpetrators of violence against children. Kids serve as our scapegoat, blamed for threatening the rest of us, when, if anything, kids are more likely to be the victims of adult violence.

But how do we explain the young people who do commit violence? Can violent media help us here? Broad patterns of violence do not match media use as much as they mirror poverty rates. Take the city of Los Angeles, where I live, as an example. We see violent crime rates are higher in lower-income areas relative to the population. The most dramatic example is demonstrated by homicide patterns. For example, the Seventy-Seventh Street division (near the flashpoint of the 1992 civil unrest) reported 12 percent of the city's homicides in 1999, yet comprised less than 5 percent of the city's total population. Conversely, the West Los Angeles area (which includes affluent neighborhoods such as Brentwood and Bel-Air) reported less than 1 percent of the city's homicides but accounted for nearly 6 percent of the total population. If media culture were a major indicator, wouldn't the children of the wealthy, who have greater access to the Internet, video games, and other visual media, be at greater risk for becoming violent? The numbers don't bear out because violence patterns do not match media use.

Violence can be linked with a variety of issues, the most important one being poverty. Criminologist E. Britt Patterson examined dozens of studies of crime and poverty and found that communities with extreme poverty, a sense of bleakness, and neighborhood disorganization and disintegration were most likely to support higher levels of violence.[8] Violence may be an act committed by an individual, but violence is also a sociological, not just an individual, phenomenon. To fear media violence we would have to believe that violence has its origins mostly in individual psychological functioning and thus that any kid could snap from playing too many video games. Ongoing sociological research has identified other risk factors that are based on environment: poverty, substance use, overly authoritarian or lax parenting, delinquent peers, neighborhood violence, and weak ties to one's family or community.[9] If we are really interested in confronting youth violence, these are the issues that must be addressed first. Media violence is something worth looking at, but not the primary cause of actual violence.

What about the kids who aren't from poor neighborhoods and who come from supportive environments? When middle-class white youths commit acts of violence, we seem to be at a loss for explanations beyond media violence. These young people often live in safe communities, enjoy many material privileges, and attend well-funded schools. Opportunities are plentiful. What else could it be, if not media?

For starters, incidents in these communities are rare but extremely well publicized. These stories are dramatic and emotional and thus great ratings-boosters. School shootings or mere threats of school shootings are often not just local stories but make national news. Public concern about violence swells when suburban white kids are involved. Violence is not "supposed" to happen there. Central-city violence doesn't raise nearly the same attention or public outcry to ban violent media. We seem to come up empty when looking for explanations of why affluent young white boys, for example, would plot to blow up their school. We rarely look beyond the media for our explanations, but the social contexts are important here too. Even well-funded suburban schools can become overgrown, impersonal institutions where young people easily fall through the cracks and feel alienated. Sociologists Wayne Wooden and Randy Blazak suggest that the banality and boredom of suburban life can create overarching feelings of meaninglessness within young people, that perhaps they find their parents' struggles to obtain material wealth empty and are not motivated by the desire for money enough to conform.[10] It is too risky to criticize the American Dream—the house in the suburbs, homogeneity, a Starbucks at every corner—because ultimately that requires many of us to look in the mirror. It is easier to look at the TV for the answer.

The truth is there is no epidemic of white suburban violence, but isolated and tragic examples have gained a lot of attention. Between 1980 and 1999 the homicide arrest rate for whites aged ten to seventeen fell 41 percent.[11] In 1999 there was 1.1 arrest for every 100,000 white kids—hardly an epidemic. Fearing media enables adults to condemn youth culture and erroneously blame young people for crimes they don't commit.

Assumption #2: Children Are Prone to Imitate Media Violence with Deadly Results

Blaming a perceived crime wave on media seems reasonable when we read examples in the news about eerie parallels between a real-life crime and entertainment. *Natural Born Killers, The Basketball Diaries, South Park*, and *Jerry Springer* have all been blamed for inspiring violence.[12] Reporting on similarities from these movies does make for a dramatic story and good ratings, but too often journalists do not dig deep enough to tell us the context of the incident. By leaving out the non-media details, news reports make it is easy for us to believe that the movies made them do it. . . .

. . . Let's consider cases that [involved actual violence], which on the surface seem to be proof that some kids are copycat killers. In the summer of

1999, a twelve-year-old boy named Lionel Tate beat and killed six-year-old Tiffany Eunick, the daughter of a family friend in Pembroke Pines, Florida. Claiming he was imitating wrestling moves he had seen on television, Lionel's defense attorney attempted to prove that Lionel did not know what he was doing would hurt Tiffany. He argued that Lionel should not be held criminally responsible for what he called a tragic accident. The jury didn't buy this defense, finding that the severity of the girl's injuries was inconsistent with the wrestling claim. Nonetheless, the news media ran with the wrestling alibi. Headlines shouted "Wrestle Slay-Boy Faces Life," "Boy, 14, Gets Life in TV Wrestling Death," and "Young Killer Wrestles Again in Broward Jail."[13] This case served to reawaken fears that media violence, particularly as seen in wrestling, is dangerous because kids allegedly don't understand that real violence can cause real injuries. Cases like this one are used to justify claims that kids may imitate media violence without recognizing the real consequences.

Lionel's defense attorney capitalized on this fear by stating that "Lionel had fallen into the trap so many youngsters fall into."[14] But many youngsters don't fall into this "trap" and neither did Lionel. Lionel Tate was not an average twelve-year-old boy; the warning signs were certainly present before that fateful summer evening. Most news reports focused on the alleged wrestling connection without exploring Lionel's troubled background. He was described by a former teacher as "almost out of control," prone to acting out, disruptive, and seeking attention.[15]

Evidence from the case also belies the claim that Lionel and Tiffany were just playing, particularly the more than thirty-five serious injuries that Tiffany sustained, including a fractured skull and massive internal damage. These injuries were not found to be consistent with play wrestling as the defense claimed. The prosecutor pointed out that Lionel did not tell investigators he was imitating wrestling moves initially; instead, he said they were playing tag but changed his story to wrestling weeks later. Although his defense attorney claimed Lionel didn't realize someone could really get hurt while wrestling, Lionel admitted that he knew television wrestling was "fake."[16]

This story would probably not have made national news if Lionel's lawyers had not invoked the wrestling defense, but the publicity surrounding the case ultimately reveals a double tragedy: Tiffany's death and Lionel's trial as an "adult" and subsequent sentence of life in prison. We as a society promote the idea that children are too naïve to know the difference between media violence and real violence, but we are also quick to apply adult punishment. Completely lost in the discussion surrounding this case is our repeated failure as a society to treat children like Lionel *before* violent behavior escalates, to recognize the warning signs before it is too late.

The imitation hypothesis suggests that violence in media puts kids like Lionel over the edge, the proverbial straw that breaks the camel's back, but this enables us to divert our attention from the seriousness of other risk factors. . . .

The biggest problem with the imitation hypothesis is that it suggests that we focus on media instead of the other 99 percent of the pieces of the violence puzzle. When a lack of other evidence is provided in news accounts, it appears as though media violence is the most compelling explanatory factor. It is certainly likely that young people who are prone to become violent are also drawn toward violent entertainment, just as funny kids may be drawn to comedies. But children whose actions parallel media violence come with a host of other more important risk factors. We blame media violence to deflect blame away from adult failings—not simply the failure of parents but our society's failure to create effective programs and solutions to help troubled young people.

Assumption #3: Real Violence and Media Violence Have the Same Meaning

. . . It is a mistake to presume media representations of violence and real violence have the same meaning for audiences. Consider the following three scenarios:

1. Wile E. Coyote drops an anvil on Road Runner's head, who keeps on running;
2. A body is found on *Law and Order* (or your favorite police show);
3. A shooting at a party leaves one person dead and another near death after waiting thirty minutes for an ambulance.

Are all three situations examples of violence? Unlike the first two incidents, the third was real. All three incidents have vastly different contexts, and thus different meanings. The first two are fantasies in which no real injuries occurred, yet are more likely to be the subject of public concerns about violence. Ironically, because the third incident received no media attention, its details, and those of incidents like it, are all but ignored in discussions of violence. Also ignored is the context in which the real shooting occurred; it was sparked by gang rivalries which stem from neighborhood tensions, poverty, lack of opportunity, and racial inequality. The fear of media violence is founded on the assumption that young people do not recognize a difference between media violence and real violence. Ironically, adults themselves seem to have problems distinguishing between the two.

Media violence is frequently conflated with actual violence in public discourse, as one is used to explain the other. It is adults who seem to confuse the two. For instance, the *Milwaukee Journal Sentinel* reported on a local school district that created a program to deal with bullying.[17] Yet media violence was a prominent part of the article, which failed to take into account the factors that create bullying situations in schools. Adults seem to have difficulty separating media representations from actual physical harm. Media violence is described as analogous to tobacco, a "smoking gun" endangering children.[18] This is probably because many middle-class white adults who fear media have had little exposure to violence other than through media representations.

I discovered the difference a few years ago as a researcher studying juvenile homicides. We combed through police investigation files looking for details about the incidents while carefully avoiding crime scene and coroner's photographs to avoid becoming emotionally overwhelmed. One morning while looking through a case file the book accidentally fell open to the page with the crime scene photos. I saw a young man slumped over the steering wheel of his car. He had a gunshot wound to his forehead, a small red circle. His eyes were open. I felt a wrenching feeling in my stomach, a feeling I have never felt before and have fortunately never felt since. At that point I realized that regardless of the hundreds, if not thousands, of violent acts I had seen in movies and television, none could come close to this. I had never seen the horrific simplicity of a wound like that one, never seen the true absence of expression in a person's face. No actor has ever been able to truly "do death" right, I realized. It became clear that I knew nothing about violence, thankfully. Yes, I have read the research, but that knowledge was just academic; this was real.

This is not to say that violent media do not create real emotional responses. Good storytelling can create sadness and fear, and depending on the context violence can even be humorous (as in *The Three Stooges*). Media violence may elicit no emotional response—but this does not necessarily mean someone is "desensitized" or uncaring. It may mean that a script was mediocre and that the audience doesn't care about its characters. But it could be because media violence is not real and most of us, even children, know it. Sociologist Todd Gitlin calls media violence a way of getting "safe thrills."[19] Viewing media violence is a way of dealing with the most frightening aspect of life in a safe setting, like riding a roller-coaster while knowing that you will get out and walk away in a few minutes.

Nonetheless, many people, fueled by media reports of studies that seem to be very compelling, fear that kids can't really distinguish between real violence and media violence. An unpublished study of eight children made news across the United States and Canada. "Kids may say they know the difference between real violence and the kind they see on television and video, but new research shows their brains don't," announced Montreal's *Gazette*.[20] This research, conducted by John Murray, a developmental psychologist at Kansas State University, involved MRIs of eight children, aged eight to thirteen. As the kids watched an eighteen-minute fight scene from *Rocky IV*, their brains showed activity in areas that are commonly activated in response to threats and emotional arousal. This should come as no surprise, since entertainment often elicits emotional response; if film and television had no emotional payoff, why would people watch?

But the press took this small study as proof of what we already think we know: that kids can't tell the difference between fantasy and reality. A *Kansas City Star* reporter described this as "a frightening new insight," and the study's author stated the children "were treating *Rocky IV* violence as real violence."[21] And while Yale psychologist Dorothy Singer warned that the size of the study was too small to draw any solid conclusions, she also said that the study is "very important."[22]

If a small study challenged the conventional media violence wisdom, you can bet that it would have been roundly dismissed as anecdotal. But instead, this study was treated as another piece to the puzzle, and clearly made the news because of its dramatic elements: a popular movie, medical technology, and children viewing violence. In any case, there are big problems with the interpretation offered by the study's author. First, this study actually discredits the idea of desensitization. The children's brains clearly showed some sort of emotional reaction to the violence they saw. They were not "emotionally deadened," as we are often told to fear. But kids can't win either way within the media-violence fear, since feeling "too little" or "too much" are both interpreted as proof that media violence is harmful to children.

Second, by insisting that children are completely different from adults we ignore the likelihood that adult brains would likely react in much the same way. Yet somehow by virtue of children being children, their *brains* can know things that *they* don't. Do an MRI on adults while they watch pornography and their brains will probably show arousal. Does that mean the person would think that he or she just had *actual* sex? The neurological reaction would probably be extremely similar, if not identical, but we can't read brain waves and infer meaning. That's what makes humans human: the ability to create meaning from our experiences. And adults are not the only ones capable of making sense of their lives.

Professor Murray's comments imply that researchers can "read" children's minds and find things that the kids themselves cannot, a rather troubling presumption. Violence has meanings that cannot simply be measured in brain waves, MRIs, or CAT scans. No matter what these high-tech tools may tell researchers, experiencing real violence is fundamentally different from experiencing media violence. It is adults, not kids, who seem to have trouble grasping this idea. Somehow lost in the fear of media violence is an understanding of how actual violence is experienced. . . .

Violence exists within specific social contexts; people make meaning of both real violence and media violence in the context of their lives. It is clear . . . that neighborhood violence and poverty are important factors necessary to understand the meanings these young people give to media violence. Other contexts would certainly be different, but focusing on media violence means real-life circumstances are often overlooked.

Watching media violence is obviously different from experiencing actual violence, yet public discourse has somehow melded the two together. Clearly media violence can be interpreted in many ways: as frightening, as cathartic, as funny, or absurd. We can't make assumptions about meaning no matter what the age of the audience.

We also need to acknowledge the meaning of violence in American media and American culture. It's too easy to say that media only reflect society or that producers are just giving the public what it wants, but certainly to some extent this is true. Violence is dramatic, a simple cinematic tool and easy to sell to domestic and overseas markets, since action-adventure movies present few translation problems for overseas distributors. But in truth, violence and aggression are very central facets of American society. Aggressive personalities tend to thrive in capitalism: risk-takers, people who are not afraid to "go for it," are highly prized within business culture. We celebrate sports heroes for being aggressive, not passive. The best hits of the day make the football highlights on ESPN, and winning means "decimating" and "destroying" in broadcast lingo.

We also value violence, or its softer-sounding equivalent, "the use of force," to resolve conflict. On local, national, and international levels violence is largely considered acceptable. Whether this is right or wrong is the subject for [another discussion], but the truth is that in the United States the social order has traditionally been created and maintained through violence. We can't honestly address media violence until we recognize that, in part, our media culture is violent because as a society we are.

Assumption #4: Research Conclusively Demonstrates the Link between Media and Violent Behavior

We engage in collective denial when we continually focus on the media as main sources of American violence. The frequency of news reports of research that allegedly demonstrates this connection helps us ignore the real social problems in the United States. Headlines imply that researchers have indeed found a preponderance of evidence to legitimate focus on media violence. Consider these headlines:

> "Survey Connects Graphic TV Fare, Child Behavior" (*Boston Globe*)
> "Cutting Back on Kids' TV Use May Reduce Aggressive Acts" (*Denver Post*)
> "Doctors Link Kids' Violence to Media" (*Arizona Republic*)
> "Study Ties Aggression to Violence in Games" (*USA Today*)

The media violence connection seems very real, with studies and experts to verify the alleged danger in story after story. Too often studies reported in the popular press provide no critical scrutiny and fail to challenge conceptual problems. In our sound-bite society, news tends to contain very little analysis or criticism of any kind.

The *Los Angeles Times* ran a story called "In a Wired World, TV Still Has Grip on Kids.[23] The article provided the reader the impression that research provided overwhelming evidence of negative media effects: only three sentences out of a thousand-plus words offered any refuting information. Just two quoted experts argued against the conventional wisdom, while six offered favorable comments. Several studies' claims drew no challenge, in spite of serious shortcomings.

For example, researchers considered responses to a "hostility questionnaire" or children's "aggressive" play as evidence that media violence can lead to real-life violence. But aggression is not the same as violence, although in some cases it may be a precursor to violence. Nor it is clear that these "effects" are anything but immediate. We know that aggression in itself is not necessarily a pathological condition; in fact, we all have aggression that we need to learn to deal with. Second, several of the studies use correlation statistics as proof of causation. Correlation indicates the existence of relationships, but cannot measure cause and effect. Reporters may not recognize this, but have the responsibility to present the ideas of those who question such claims.

This pattern repeats in story after story. A *Denver Post* article described a 1999 study that claimed that limiting TV and video use reduced children's aggression.[24] The story prefaced the report by stating that "numerous studies have indicated a connection between exposure to violence and aggressive behavior in children," thus making this new report appear part of a large body of convincing evidence. The only "challenge" to this study came from psychologist James Garbarino, who noted that the real causes of violence are complex, although his list of factors began with "television, video games, and movies." He did cite guns, child abuse, and economic inequality as important factors, but the story failed to address any of these other problems.

The reporter doesn't mention the study's other shortcomings. First is the assumption that the television and videos kids watch contain violence at all. The statement we hear all the time in various forms—"the typical American child will be exposed to 200,000 acts of violence on television by age eighteen"—is based on the estimated time kids spend watching television, but tells us nothing about what they have actually watched.[25] Second, in these studies, aggression in play serves as a proxy for violence. But there is a big difference between playing "aggressively" and committing acts of violence. Author Gerard Jones points out that play is a powerful way by which kids can deal with feelings of fear.[26] Thus, watching the Power Rangers and then play-fighting is not necessarily an indicator of violence; it is part of how children fantasize about being powerful without ever intending to harm anyone. Finally, the researchers presumed that reducing television and video use explained changes in behavior, when in fact aggression and violence are complex responses to specific circumstances created by a variety of environmental factors. Nonetheless, the study's author stated that "if you . . . reduce their exposure to media you'll see a reduction in aggressive behavior."

A spring 2003 study claiming to have long-term evidence that children who watch television violence become violent adults even made news the week that American troops entered Iraq. This study is unique in that it tracked 329 respondents for fifteen years, but it contains several serious shortcomings that prevent us from concluding that television creates violence later in life.[27] First, the study measures aggression, not violence. Aggression is broadly defined by researchers, who constructed an "aggression composite" that includes such antisocial behavior as having angry thoughts, talking rudely to or about others, and having moving violations on one's driving record. Violence is a big jump from getting lots of speeding tickets. But beyond this composite, the connection between television viewing and physical aggression for males, perhaps the most interesting measure, is relatively weak. Television viewing explains only 3 percent of what led to physical aggression in the men studied.[28] Although some subjects did report getting into physical altercations, fewer than 10 of the 329 participants had ever been convicted of a crime, too small of a sample to make any predictions about serious violent offenders.

By focusing so heavily on media violence, both researchers and news accounts divert attention from the factors we know to be associated with violence. Both also downplay the serious limitations of traditional media-effects research. A *Boston Globe* article conceded that a great deal of "evidence" is anecdotal, stating that "the real link between televised sex and violence and actual behavior has been difficult to prove," but only after seven paragraphs about the "growing concern of mental health specialists."[29] In spite of news reports about the "tremendous problem" of media violence allegedly demonstrated by "classic studies" and "sweeping new" research, as the *Boston Globe* and *Los Angeles Times* reported, this body of research contains leaps in logic, questionable methods, and exaggerated findings.[30]

There is a preponderance of evidence, but not the result of "thirty years of research and more than 1000 studies," as the St. Louis *Post-Dispatch* described, but the fact that Americans spend so much time, energy, and money researching this loaded question instead of researching violence itself.[31] If youth violence is really the issue of importance here, we should start by studying violence, before studying media. But media culture is on trial, not violence. These studies are smoke screens that enable us to continue along the media trail while disregarding actual violence patterns. . . .

Whenever critics challenge the results of media-effects research authors tend to respond with arrogance, hostility, and occasionally personal insults. The spirit of debate is all but absent. Within the scientific method, researchers are supposed to continually consider the possibility that they are wrong. But within this field dissenters are not just researchers with different findings; they are regarded as heretics. If this is indeed an open-and-shut question, as its proponents argue, why do media-effects researchers get so nasty with their critics?

Perhaps science itself is in question—good science is supposed to encourage, not suppress, debate. Ideally the scientific community shares ideas not to intimidate dissent or boost egos, but to improve scholarship. Instead, media-violence research has created a sort of intellectual totalitarianism, where researchers only listen to people who agree with them.

The media-violence story, the research, and its emotional baggage make open debate next to impossible. Those who fear media violence police the boundaries of this dogma to avoid challenging their intuitive belief that popular culture is dangerous. But taste and influence are two very different things: media researchers are often media critics in disguise. There's nothing wrong with media criticism—we could probably use more of it—but when media criticism takes the place of understanding the roots of violence, we have a problem. Dissent is dismissed as Hollywood propaganda, reinforced when the press quotes a studio executive to "balance" a story on media's alleged danger.

Media violence enables American discussion about violence to avoid the tough questions about actual violence: Why is it so closely associated with poverty? How can we provide families with resources to cope in violent communities? By focusing so much energy on media violence, we avoid our responsibility to pressure politicians to create policies that address these difficult issues. To hear that "Washington (is) again taking on Hollywood" may feel good to the public and make it appear as though lawmakers are onto something, but real violence remains off the agenda.[32] This tactic appeals to many middle-class constituents whose experience with violence is often limited. Economically disadvantaged people are most likely to experience real violence, but least likely to appear on politicians' radar. A national focus on media rather than real violence draws on existing fears and reinforces the view that popular culture, not public policy, leads to violence.

Violence in media reminds us that we cannot control what children know about. But unfortunately many children are exposed to real violence, not only in their communities, but sometimes in their own homes. We should not deny this and use the illusion of childhood (as always carefree until the media gets to them) to shield ourselves from this reality. The concern about media and violence is not just a fear for children, but a fear *of* children. We often deal with this fear by calling for stricter controls of other people's children, both by the state and by parents. These "solutions" fail to address the real problems.

ENDNOTES

[1] Todd Gitlin, *Media Unlimited: How the Torrent of Images and Sounds Overwhelms Our Lives* (New York: Metropolitan Books, 2001), p. 145.

[2] After publishing an op-ed (Karen Sternheimer, "Blaming Television and Movies Is Easy and Wrong," *Los Angeles Times*, February 4, 2001, p. M5), I received e-mails that presumed that my work must be funded by the entertainment industry, which it is not.

[3] Jim Sullinger, "Forum Examines Media Violence," *Kansas City Star*, August 26, 2001, p. B5.

[4] Jennifer Blanton, "Media, Single Parents Blamed for Spurt in Teen Violence," *Pittsburgh Post-Gazette*, August 2, 2001, p. A1.

[5] Federal Bureau of Investigation, Violence Index, *Uniform Crime Reports for the United States, 1999* (Washington, DC: U.S. Department of Justice, 2000).

[6] Federal Bureau of Investigation, Property Index, *Uniform Crime Reports for the United States, 1999* (Washington, DC: U.S. Department of Justice, 2000).

[7] Lori Dorfman et al., "Youth and Violence on Local Television News in California," *American Journal of Public Health* 87 (1997): 1311–16.

[8] E. Britt Patterson, "Poverty, Income Inequality and Community Crime Rates," in *Juvenile Delinquency: Historical, Theoretical and Societal Reactions to Youth*, 2d ed., edited by Paul M. Sharp and Barry W. Hancock (Upper Saddle River, NJ: Prentice Hall, 1998), pp. 135–50.

[9] Rosie Mestel, "Triggers of Violence Still Elusive," *Los Angeles Times*, March 7, 2001, p. A1.

[10] Wayne Wooden and Randy Blazak, *Renegade Kids, Suburban Outlaws: From Youth Culture to Delinquency*, 2d ed. (Belmont, CA: Wadsworth, 2001).

[11] Federal Bureau of Investigation, *Uniform Crime Reports for the United States, 1980–1999* (Washington, DC: U.S. Department of Justice, 2000).

[12] Mediascope, "Copycat Crimes," http://www.mediascope.org/pubs/ibriefs/cc.htm.

[13] Caroline J. Keough, "Young Killer Wrestles Again in Broward Jail," *Miami Herald*, February 17, 2001, p. A1. Michael Browning et al., "Boy, 14, Gets Life in TV Wrestling Death," *Chicago*

Sun-Times, March 10, 2001, p. A1. "Wrestle Slay-Boy Faces Life," *Daily News,* January 26, 2001, p. 34.

[14] "13-Year-Old Convicted of First-Degree Murder," *Atlanta Journal and Constitution,* January 26, 2001, p. 1B.

[15] Caroline Keough, "Teen Killer Described as Lonely, Pouty, Disruptive," *Miami Herald,* February 5, 2001, p. A1.

[16] "Murder Defendant, 13, Claims He Was Imitating Pro Wrestlers on TV," *Los Angeles Times,* January 14, 2001, p. A24. Later in media interviews, Lionel said that Tiffany was lying down on the stairs and he accidentally crushed her when he came bounding down the steps.

[17] Scott Williams, "Schools Address Bullying Issue," *Milwaukee Journal Sentinel,* March 25, 2001, p. 1Z.

[18] Carol J. Smith, Letter to the editor, *Los Angeles Times,* September 17, 2000, sec. M.

[19] Todd Gitlin, *Media Unlimited: How the Torrent of Images and Sounds Overwhelms Our Lives* (New York: Metropolitan Books, 2001), p. 92.

[20] Chris Zdeb, "Violent TV Affects Kids' Brains Just as Real Trauma Does," *The Gazette,* June 5, 2001, p. C5.

[21] Jim Sullinger, "Forum Examines Media Violence," *Kansas City Star,* August 29, 2001, p. B5.

[22] Marilyn Elias, "Beaten Unconsciously: Violent Images May Alter Kids' Brain Activity, Spark Hostility," *USA Today,* April 19, 2001, p. 8D.

[23] Rosie Mestel, "In a Wired World, TV Still Has Grip on Kids," *Los Angeles Times,* September 18, 2000, p. F1. The same article also appeared in Montreal's *Gazette* as "The Great Debate: Experts Disagree over the Extent of the Effects of Media Violence on Children" on September 30, 2000.

[24] Susan FitzGerald, "Cutting Back on Kids' TV Use May Reduce Aggressive Acts," *Denver Post,* January 15, 2001, p. A2.

[25] Ibid., p. A2.

[26] See Gerard Jones, *Killing Monsters: Why Children Need Fantasy, Super Heroes, and Make-Believe Violence* (New York: Basic Books, 2002).

[27] L. Rowell Huesman et al., "Longitudinal Relations between Children's Exposure to TV Violence and Their Aggressive and Violent Behavior in Young Adulthood: 1977–1992," *Developmental Psychology* 39, no. 2 (2003): 201–21. Kids who regularly watched shows like *Starsky and Hutch, The Six Million Dollar Man,* and *Road Runner* cartoons in 1977 were regarded as high-violence viewers.

[28] Based on $r = .17$.

[29] Richard Saltus, "Survey Connects Graphic TV Fare, Child Behavior," *Boston Globe,* March 21, 2001, p. A1.

[30] Mestel, op. cit., p. F1; Saltus, op. cit. p. A1.

[31] "A Poisonous Pleasure," editorial, St. Louis *Post-Dispatch,* July 30, 2000, p. B2. Psychologist Jonathan Freedman suggests that the claim of one thousand studies is inflated and that there have been more like 200 studies conducted. Jonathan L. Freedman, *Media Violence and Its Effect on Aggression* (Toronto: University of Toronto Press, 2002), p. 24.

[32] Megan Garvey, "Washington Again Taking on Hollywood," *Los Angeles Times,* June 2, 2001, p. A1.

41

MANIFESTO OF THE COMMUNIST PARTY

KARL MARX • FRIEDRICH ENGELS

The economy and work are the focus of the next three readings. The first selection in this group is an excerpt from the classic "Manifesto of the Communist Party," written by Karl Marx and Friedrich Engels in 1848. Students often are surprised to discover the currency of many of the topics discussed by Marx (1818–1883) and Engels (1820–1895). Specifically, Marx and Engels foresaw the rise of global capitalism. They also accurately described exploitive industrial conditions and the oppositional interests of workers and capitalists. Even though Marx and Engels are criticized for not foreseeing the rise of other social agents (such as the middle class, the government, and unions) in mediating the conflict between capitalists and workers, their theory of class struggle and revolution is still provocative and a source for worldwide social change.

The history of all hitherto existing society is the history of class struggles.

Freeman and slave, patrician and plebeian, lord and serf, guild-master and journeyman, in a word, oppressor and oppressed, stood in constant opposition to one another, carried on an uninterrupted, now hidden, now open fight, a fight that each time ended, either in a revolutionary reconstitution of society at large, or in the common ruin of the contending classes.

In the earlier epochs of history, we find almost everywhere a complicated arrangement of society into various orders, a manifold gradation of social rank. In ancient Rome we have patricians, knights, plebeians, slaves; in the Middle Ages, feudal lords, vassals, guild-masters, journeymen, apprentices, serfs; in almost all of these classes, again, subordinate gradations.

The modern bourgeois society that has sprouted from the ruins of feudal society has not done away with class antagonisms. It has but established new classes, new conditions of oppression, new forms of struggle in place of the old ones.

Our epoch, the epoch of the bourgeoisie, possesses, however, this distinctive feature: It has simplified the class antagonisms. Society as a whole is more

Karl Marx and Friedrich Engels, "The Manifesto of the Communist Party," translated by Friedrich Engels (1888).

and more splitting up into two great hostile camps, into two great classes directly facing each other: Bourgeoisie and Proletariat.

From the serfs of the Middle Ages sprang the chartered burghers of the earliest towns. From these burgesses the first elements of the bourgeoisie were developed.

The discovery of America, the rounding of the Cape, opened up fresh ground for the rising bourgeoisie. The East-Indian and Chinese markets, the colonization of America, trade with the colonies, the increase in the means of exchange and in commodities generally, gave to commerce, to navigation, to industry, an impulse never before known, and thereby, to the revolutionary element in the tottering feudal society, a rapid development.

The feudal system of industry, under which industrial production was monopolized by closed guilds, now no longer sufficed for the growing wants of the new markets. The manufacturing system took its place. The guild-masters were pushed on one side by the manufacturing middle class; division of labour between the different corporate guilds vanished in the face of division of labour in each single workshop.

Meantime the markets kept ever growing, the demand ever rising. Even manufacture no longer sufficed. Thereupon, steam and machinery revolutionized industrial production. The place of manufacture was taken by the giant, Modern Industry, the place of the industrial middle class, by industrial millionaires, the leaders of whole industrial armies, the modern bourgeois.

Modern industry has established the world-market, for which the discovery of America paved the way. This market has given an immense development to commerce, to navigation, to communication by land. This development has, in its turn, reacted on the extension of industry; and in proportion as industry, commerce, navigation, railways extended, in the same proportion the bourgeoisie developed, increased its capital, and pushed into the background every class handed down from the Middle Ages.

We see, therefore, how the modern bourgeoisie is itself the product of a long course of development, of a series of revolutions in the modes of production and of exchange.

Each step in the development of the bourgeoisie was accompanied by a corresponding political advance of that class. An oppressed class under the sway of the feudal nobility, an armed and self-governing association in the mediaeval commune; here independent urban republic (as in Italy and Germany), there taxable "third estate" of the monarchy (as in France), afterwards, in the period of manufacture proper, serving either the semi-feudal or the absolute monarchy as a counterpoise against the nobility, and, in fact, corner-stone of the great monarchies in general, the bourgeoisie has at last, since the establishment of Modern Industry and of the world-market, conquered for itself, in the modern representative State, exclusive political sway. The execution of the modern State is but a committee for managing the common affairs of the whole bourgeoisie.

The bourgeoisie, historically, has played a most revolutionary part.

The bourgeoisie, wherever it has got the upper hand, has put an end to all feudal, patriarchal, idyllic relations. It has pitilessly torn asunder the motley feudal ties that bound man to his "natural superiors," and has left remaining no other nexus between man and man than naked self-interest, than callous "cash payment." It has drowned the most heavenly ecstasies of religious fervor, of chivalrous enthusiasm, of philistine sentimentalism, in the icy water of egotistical calculation. It has resolved personal worth into exchange value and, in place of the numberless indefeasible chartered freedoms, has set up that single, unconscionable freedom—Free Trade. In one word, for exploitation, veiled by religious and political illusions, it has substituted naked, shameless, direct, brutal exploitation.

The bourgeoisie has stripped of its halo every occupation hitherto honored and looked up to with reverent awe. It has converted the physician, the lawyer, the priest, the poet, the man of science, into its paid wage-labourers.

The bourgeoisie has torn away from the family its sentimental veil, and has reduced the family relation to a mere money relation.

The bourgeoisie has disclosed how it came to pass that the brutal display of vigor in the Middle Ages, which Reactionists so much admire, found its fitting complement in the most slothful indolence. It has been the first to show what man's activity can bring about. It has accomplished wonders far surpassing Egyptian pyramids, Roman aqueducts, and Gothic cathedrals; it has conducted expeditions that put in the shade all former Exoduses of nations and crusades.

The bourgeoisie cannot exist without constantly revolutionizing the instruments of production, and thereby the relations of production, and with them the whole relations of society. Conservation of the old modes of production in unaltered form, was, on the contrary, the first condition of existence for all earlier industrial classes. Constant revolutionizing of production, uninterrupted disturbance of all social conditions, everlasting uncertainty and agitation distinguish the bourgeois epoch from all earlier ones. All fixed, fast-frozen relations, with their train of ancient and venerable prejudices and opinions, are swept away, all new-formed ones become antiquated before they can ossify. All that is solid melts into air, all that is holy is profaned, and man is at last compelled to face with sober senses, his real conditions of life, and his relations with his kind.

The need of a constantly expanding market for its products chases the bourgeoisie over the whole surface of the globe. It must nestle everywhere, settle everywhere, establish connections everywhere.

The bourgeoisie has through its exploitation of the world-market given a cosmopolitan character to production and consumption in every country. To the great chagrin of Reactionists, it has drawn from under the feet of industry the national ground on which it stood. All old-established national industries have been destroyed or are daily being destroyed. They are dislodged by new industries, whose introduction becomes a life and death question for all civilized nations, by industries that no longer work up indigenous raw material, but raw material drawn from the remotest zones; industries whose products are consumed, not only at home, but in every quarter of the globe. In place of the old wants, satisfied by the productions of the country, we find new wants, requiring for their satisfaction the products of distant lands and climes. In place of the old local and national seclusion and self-sufficiency, we have intercourse in every direction, universal inter-dependence of nations. And as in material, so also in intellectual production. The intellectual creations of individual nations become common property. National one-sidedness and narrow-mindedness become more and more impossible, and from the numerous national and local literatures, there arises a world literature.

The bourgeoisie, by the rapid improvement of all instruments of production, by the immensely facilitated means of communication, draws all, even the most barbarian, nations into civilization. The cheap prices of its commodities are the heavy artillery with which it batters down all Chinese walls, with which it forces the barbarians' intensely obstinate hatred of foreigners to capitulate. It compels all nations, on pain of extinction, to adopt the bourgeois mode of production; it compels them to introduce what it calls civilization into their midst, *i.e.*, to become bourgeois themselves. In one word, it creates a world after its own image.

The bourgeoisie has subjected the country to the rule of the towns. It has created enormous cities, has greatly increased the urban population as compared with the rural, and has thus rescued a considerable part of the population from the idiocy of rural life. Just as it has made the country dependent on the towns, so it has made barbarian and semi-barbarian countries dependent on the civilized ones, nations of peasants on nations of bourgeois, the East on the West.

The bourgeoisie keeps more and more doing away with the scattered state of the population, of the means of production, and of property. It has agglomerated population, centralized means of production, and has concentrated property in a few hands. The necessary consequence of this was political centralization. Independent, or but loosely connected provinces, with separate interests, laws, governments and systems of taxation, became lumped together into one nation, with one government, one code of laws, one national class-interest, one frontier and one customs-tariff.

The bourgeoisie, during its rule of scarce one hundred years, has created more massive and more colossal productive forces than have all preceding generations together. Subjection of Nature's forces to man, machinery, application of chemistry to industry and agriculture, steam-navigation, railways, electric telegraphs, clearing of whole continents for cultivation, canalization of rivers, whole populations conjured out of the ground—what earlier century had even a presentiment that such productive forces slumbered in the lap of social labour?

We see then: the means of production and of exchange, on whose foundation the bourgeoisie built itself up, were generated in feudal society. At a certain stage in the development of these means of production and of exchange, the conditions under which feudal society produced and exchanged, the feudal organization of agriculture and manufacturing industry, in one word, the feudal relations of property became no longer compatible with the already developed productive forces; they became so many fetters. They had to be burst asunder; they were burst asunder.

Into their place stepped free competition, accompanied by a social and political constitution adapted to it, and by the economical and political sway of the bourgeois class.

A similar movement is going on before our own eyes. Modern bourgeois society with its relations of production, of exchange and of property, a society that has conjured up such gigantic means of production and of exchange, is like the sorcerer, who is no longer able to control the powers of the nether world whom he has called up by his spells. For many a decade past the history of industry and commerce is but the history of the revolt of modern productive forces against modern conditions of production, against the property relations that are the conditions for the existence of the bourgeoisie and of its rule. It is enough to mention the commercial crises that by their periodical return put on its trial, each time more threateningly, the existence of the entire bourgeois society. In these crises a great part not only of the existing products, but also of the previously created productive forces, are periodically destroyed. In these crises there breaks out an epidemic that, in all earlier epochs, would have seemed an absurdity—the epidemic of overproduction. Society suddenly finds itself put back into a state of momentary barbarism; it appears as if a famine, a universal war of devastation had cut off the supply of every means of subsistence; industry and commerce seem to be destroyed; and why? Because there is too much civilization, too much means of subsistence, too much industry, too much commerce. The productive forces at the disposal of society no longer tend to further the development of the conditions of bourgeois property; on the contrary, they have become too powerful for these conditions, by which they are fettered, and so soon as they overcome these fetters, they bring disorder into the whole of bourgeois society, endanger the existence of bourgeois property. The conditions of bourgeois society are too narrow to comprise the wealth created by them. And how does the bourgeoisie get over these crises? On the one hand, by enforced destruction of a mass of productive forces; on the other, by the conquest of new markets, and by the more thorough exploitation of the old ones. That is to say, by paving the way for more extensive and more destructive crises, and by diminishing the means whereby crises are prevented.

The weapons with which the bourgeoisie felled feudalism to the ground are now turned against the bourgeoisie itself.

But not only has the bourgeoisie forged the weapons that bring death to itself; it has also called into existence the men who are to wield those weapons—the modern working class—the proletarians.

In proportion as the bourgeoisie, *i.e.,* capital, is developed, in the same proportion is the proletariat, the modern working class, developed—a class of labourers, who live only so long as they find work and who find work only so long as their labour increases capital. These labourers, who must sell themselves piece-meal, are a commodity, like every other article of commerce, and are consequently exposed to all the vicissitudes of competition, to all the fluctuations of the market.

Owing to the extensive use of machinery and to division of labour, the work of the proletarians has lost all individual character and, consequently, all charm for the workman. He becomes an appendage of the machine, and it is only the most simple, most monotonous, and most easily acquired knack that is required of him. Hence, the cost of production of a workman is restricted, almost entirely, to the means of subsistence that he requires for his maintenance and for the propagation of his race. But the price of a commodity, and therefore also of labour, is equal to its cost of production. In proportion, therefore, as the repulsiveness of the work increases, the wage decreases. Nay more, in proportion as the use of machinery and division of labour increases, in the same proportion the burden of toil also increases, whether by prolongation of the working hours, by increase of the work exacted in a given time, or by increased speed of the machinery, etc.

Modern industry has converted the little workshop of the patriarchal master into the great factory of the industrial capitalist. Masses of labourers, crowded into the factory, are organised like soldiers. As privates of the industrial army they are placed under the command of a perfect hierarchy of officers and sergeants. Not only are they slaves of the bourgeois class and of the bourgeois State; they are daily and hourly enslaved by the machine, by the over-looker, and, above all, by the individual bourgeois manufacturer himself. The more openly this despotism proclaims gain to be its end and aim, the more petty, the more hateful and the more embittering it is.

The less the skill and exertion of strength implied in manual labour, in other words, the more modern industry becomes developed, the more is the labour of men superseded by that of women. Differences of age and sex have no longer any distinctive social validity for the working class. All are instruments of labour, more or less expensive to use, according to their age and sex.

No sooner is the exploitation of the labourer by the manufacturer, so far, at an end, that he receives his wages in cash, than he is set upon by the other portions of the bourgeoisie, the landlord, the shopkeeper, the pawnbroker, etc.

42
_____

OVER THE COUNTER
McDonald's

ROBIN LEIDNER

Robin Leidner's 1993 case study, "Over the Counter: McDonald's," takes us inside one employment organization and reveals what it is like to work there. Leidner, an associate professor of sociology at the University of Pennsylvania, shows how McDonald's employees are intensively socialized. She also illustrates how the work is reduced to simple steps, and therefore routinized, so that managers and owners can maintain the most control over their product and over their employees. This process of increased routinization in the workplace has a long history in industrialization, especially within factory work. Many social analysts, including Karl Marx (1818–1883), have argued that the routinization of work leads to workers' feeling alienated from their products and from their sense of self.

O rganizations have many ways of obtaining the cooperation of participants, ranging from persuasion and enticement to force and curtailment of options. All organizations "hope to make people want to do what the organization needs done" (Biggart 1989:128), but when they cannot count on success in manipulating people's desires they can do their best to compel people to act in the organization's interests.

Organizations choose strategies that rely on socialization and social control in varying mixtures that are determined by the aims of the organization, the constraints set by the organizational environment and the nature of the work, and the interests and resources of the parties involved. In service-providing organizations, upper-level management must concern itself with the wishes and behavior of service recipients and various groups of workers.[1] For each group, service organizations try to find the most effective and least costly ways to get people to act in the organizations' interests, proffering various carrots and sticks, making efforts to win hearts and minds, closing off choices.

Organizations that routinize work exert control primarily by closing off choices. There is much room for variation, however, in what aspects of the work organizations will choose to routinize, how they go about it, and how much freedom of decision making remains. Moreover, even when routines radically constrain choice, organizations still must socialize participants and set up systems of incentives and disincentives to ensure the compliance of workers and customers.

. . . McDonald's . . . take[s] routinization to extremes . . . includ[ing] predetermination of action and transformation of character. . . . McDonald's stresses minute specification of procedures, eliminating most decision making for most workers, although it does make some efforts to standardize operations by transforming the characters of its store-level managers. . . .

This . . . [selection] show[s] how the compan[y's] approaches to routinizing the work of those who interact with customers depend largely on the predictability of service recipients' behavior, which in turn depends on the kinds of resources the organizations have available to channel consumer behavior. . . . At McDonald's . . . the routines sharply limit the workers' autonomy without giving them much leverage over customers.

McDonald's

No one ever walks into a McDonald's and asks, "So, what's good today?" except satirically. The heart of McDonald's success is its uniformity and predictability. Not only is the food supposed to taste the same every day everywhere in the world, but McDonald's promises that every meal will be served quickly, courteously, and with a smile. Delivering on that promise over 20 million times a day in 54 countries is the company's colossal challenge (*McDonald's Annual Report* 1990:2). Its strategy for meeting that challenge draws on scientific management's most basic tenets: Find the One Best Way to do every task and see that the work is conducted accordingly.[2]

To ensure that all McDonald's restaurants serve products of uniform quality, the company uses centralized planning, centrally designed training programs, centrally approved and supervised suppliers, automated machinery and other specially designed equipment, meticulous specifications, and systematic inspections. To provide its customers with a uniformly pleasant "McDonald's experience," the company also tries to mass produce friendliness, deference, diligence, and good cheer through a variety of socialization and social control techniques. Despite sneers from those who equate uniformity with mediocrity, the success of McDonald's has been spectacular.

McFacts

By far the world's largest fast-food company, McDonald's has over 11,800 stores worldwide (*McDonald's Annual Report* 1990:1), and its 1990 international sales surpassed those of its three largest competitors combined (Berg 1991 sec. 3:6).[3] In the United States, consumer familiarity with McDonald's is virtually universal: The company estimates that 95 percent of U.S. consumers eat at a McDonald's at least once a year (Koepp 1987:58). McDonald's 1990 profits were $802.3 million, the third highest profits of any retailing company in the world (*Fortune* 1991:179). At a time when the ability of many U.S. businesses to compete on the world market is in question, McDonald's continues to expand around the globe—most recently to Morocco—everywhere remaking consumer demand in its own image.

As politicians, union leaders, and others concerned with the effects of the shift to a service economy are quick to point out, McDonald's is a major employer. McDonald's restaurants in the United States employ about half a million people (Bertagnoli 1989:33), including one out of 15 first-time job seekers (Wildavsky 1989:30). The company claims that 7 percent of all current U.S. workers have worked for McDonald's at some time (Koepp 1987:59). Not only has McDonald's directly influenced the lives of millions of workers, but its impact has also been extended by the efforts of many kinds of organizations, especially in the service sector, to imitate the organizational features they see as central to McDonald's success. . . .

The relentless standardization and infinite replication that inspire both horror and admiration are the legacy of Ray Kroc, a salesman who got into the hamburger business in 1954, when he was 52 years old, and created a worldwide phenomenon.[4] His inspiration was a phenomenally successful hamburger stand owned by the McDonald brothers of San Bernardino, California. He believed that their success could be reproduced consistently through carefully controlled franchises, and his hamburger business succeeded on an unprecedented scale. The basic idea was to serve a very few items of strictly uniform quality at low prices. Over the years, the menu has expanded somewhat and prices have risen, but the emphasis on strict, detailed standardization has never varied. . . .

Enforcement of McDonald's standards has been made easier over the years by the introduction of highly specialized equipment. Every company-owned store in the United States now has an "in-store processor," a computer system that calculates yields and food costs, keeps track of inventory and cash, schedules labor, and breaks down sales by time of day, product, and worker (*McDonald's Annual Report* 1989:29). In today's McDonald's, lights and buzzers tell workers exactly when to turn burgers or take fries out of the fat, and technologically advanced cash registers, linked to the computer system, do much of the thinking for window workers. Specially designed ketchup dispensers squirt exactly the right amount of ketchup on each burger in the approved flower pattern. The french-fry scoops let workers fill a bag and set it down in one continuous motion and help them gauge the proper serving size.

The extreme standardization of McDonald's products, and its workers, is closely tied to its marketing. The company advertises on a massive scale—in 1989, McDonald's spent $1.1 billion systemwide on advertising and promotions (*McDonald's Annual Report* 1989:32). In fact, McDonald's is the single most advertised brand in the world (*Advertising Age* 1990:6).[5] The national advertising assures the public that it will find high standards of quality, service, and cleanliness at every McDonald's store. The intent of the strict quality-control standards applied to every aspect of running a McDonald's outlet, from proper cleaning of the bathrooms to making sure the hamburgers are served hot, is to help franchise owners keep the promises made in the company's advertising.[6]

The image of McDonald's outlets promoted in the company's advertising is one of fun, wholesomeness, and family orientation. Kroc was particularly concerned that his stores not become teenage hangouts, since that would discourage families' patronage. To minimize their attractiveness to teenage loiterers, McDonald's stores do not have jukeboxes, video games, or even telephones. Kroc initially decided not to hire young women to work behind McDonald's counters for the same reason: "They attracted the wrong kind of boys" (Boas and Chain 1976:19).

You Deserve a Break Today: Conditions of Employment

Although McDonald's does not want teenagers to hang out on its premises, it certainly does want them to work in the stores. Almost half of its U.S. employees are under 20 years old (Wildavsky 1989:30). In recent years, as the McDonald's chain has grown faster than the supply of teenagers, the company has also tried to attract senior citizens and housewives as workers. What people in these groups have in common is a preference or need for part-time work, and therefore a dearth of alternative employment options. Because of this lack of good alternatives, and because they may have other means of support for themselves and their dependents, many people in these groups are willing to accept jobs that provide less than subsistence wages.

Traditionally, McDonald's has paid most of its employees the minimum wage, although labor shortages have now forced wages up in some parts of the country, raising the average hourly pay of crew people to $4.60 by 1989 (Gibson and Johnson 1989:B1). Benefits such as health insurance and sick days are entirely lacking for crew people at most franchises. In fact, when the topic of employee benefits was introduced in a class lecture at McDonald's management training center, it turned out to refer to crew meetings, individual work-evaluation sessions, and similar programs to make McDonald's management seem accessible and fair.

The lack of more tangible benefits is linked to the organization of employment at McDonald's as part-time work. According to the manager of the franchise I studied, all McDonald's hourly employees are officially part-time workers, in that no one is guaranteed a full work week. The company's labor practices are designed to make workers bear the costs of uncertainty based on fluctuation in demand. McDonald's places great emphasis on having no more crew people at work at any time than are required by customer flow at that period, as measured in half-hour increments. Most workers therefore have fluctuating schedules, and they are expected to be flexible about working late or leaving early depending on the volume of business.

Not surprisingly, McDonald's employee-turnover rates are extremely high. Turnover averaged 153 percent in 1984, and 205 percent in 1985 (training center lecture). These high rates are partly attributable to the large percentage of teenage workers, many of whom took the job with the intention of working for only a short time. However, the limited job rewards, both financial and personal, of working at McDonald's are certainly crucial contributing factors.

Some argue that the conditions of employment at McDonald's are unproblematic to the workers who take them. If we assume that most McDonald's workers are teenagers who are in school and are not responsible for supporting themselves or others, then many of the features of McDonald's work do not seem so bad. Fringe benefits and employment security are relatively unimportant to them, and the limited and irregular hours of work may actually be attractive (see Greenberger and Steinberg 1986). These arguments are less persuasive when applied to other McDonald's employees, such as mothers of young children, and retirees, although those workers might similarly appreciate the part-time hours, and access to other forms of income and benefits could make McDonald's employment conditions acceptable, if not desirable. Employment security would not be important to the many people who choose to work at McDonald's as a stopgap or for a limited period.[7] Many of the workers at the franchise I studied had taken their jobs with the intention of holding them only temporarily, and many were being supported by their parents. However, other workers there were trying to support themselves and their dependents on earnings from McDonald's, sometimes in combination with other low-paying jobs. . . .

McDonald's wants both managers and workers to dedicate themselves to the values summed up in its three-letter corporate credo, "QSC." Quality, service, and cleanliness are the ends that the company's thousands of rules and specifications are intended to achieve. Kroc promised his customers QSC,[8] and he believed firmly that if, at every level of the organization, McDonald's workers were committed to providing higher-quality food, speedier service, and cleaner surroundings than the competition, the success of the enterprise was assured. McDonald's extraordinarily elaborate training programs are designed both to teach McDonald's procedures and standards and to instill and enforce corporate values.

Kroc approached his business with a zeal and dedication that even he regarded as religious: "I've often said that *I believe in God, family, and McDonald's—and in the office that order is reversed*" (Kroc with Anderson 1977:124 [emphasis in original]). Throughout the organization, Kroc is still frequently quoted and held up as a model, and nowhere is his ongoing influence more apparent than at Hamburger University.

Taking Hamburgers Seriously: Training Managers

McDonald's main management training facility is located on 80 beautifully landscaped acres in Oak Brook, Illinois, a suburb of Chicago. Its name, Hamburger University, captures the thoroughness and intensity with which McDonald's approaches management training, and it also suggests the comic possibilities of immersion in McDonald's corporate world.[9] The company tries to produce managers "with ketchup in their veins," a common McDonald's phrase for people who love their work, take pride in it, and are extraordinarily hardworking, competitive, and loyal to McDonald's. A line I heard frequently at Hamburger U. was "We take hamburgers very seriously here." Nothing I saw called this fixity of purpose into doubt.

Ensuring uniformity of service and products in its far-flung empire is a major challenge for McDonald's. In each McDonald's store, in regional training centers, and at Hamburger University, crew people, managers, and franchisees learn that there is a McDonald's way to handle virtually every detail of the business and that doing things differently means doing things wrong. Training begins in the stores, where crew people are instructed using materials provided by the corporation and where managers prepare for more advanced training. Management trainees and managers seeking promotion work with their store managers to learn materials in manuals and workbooks provided by the corporation. When they have completed the manual for the appropriate level, they are eligible for courses taught in regional training centers and at Hamburger University: the Basic Operations Course, the Intermediate Operations Course, the Applied Equipment Course, and, finally, the Advanced Operations Course, taught only at Hamburger University. Altogether, the full training program requires approximately six hundred to one thousand hours of work. It is required of everyone who wishes to own a McDonald's store, and it is strongly recommended for all store managers. By the time trainees get to Hamburger University for the Advanced Operations Course, they have already put in considerable time working in a McDonald's store—two to three and a half years, on average—and have acquired much detailed knowledge about McDonald's workings.

Hamburger University sometimes offers special programs and seminars in addition to the regular training courses. For example, a group of McDonald's office workers attended Hamburger University during my visit; a training manager told me that they had been brought in to get "a little shot of ketchup and mustard."[10]

The zeal and competence of franchisees and managers are of special concern to McDonald's, since they are the people responsible for daily enforcement of corporate standards. Their training therefore focuses as much on building commitment and motivation as on extending knowledge of company procedures. In teaching management skills, McDonald's also works on the personalities of its managers, encouraging both rigid adherence to routines and, somewhat paradoxically, personal flexibility. Flexibility is presented as a virtue both because the company wants to minimize resistance to adopting McDonald's ways of doing things and to frequent revision of procedures, and because managers must provide whatever responsiveness to special circumstances the system has, since crew people are allowed virtually no discretion. Hamburger University therefore provides a large dose of personal-growth cheerleading along with more prosaic skills training. . . .

The curriculum of the Advanced Operating Course includes inculcation with pride in McDonald's. Sessions are devoted to McDonald's history and McDonald's dedication to ever-improving QSC. Lectures are sprinkled with statistics attesting to McDonald's phenomenal success. Students hear the story of Ray Kroc's rise to wealth and prominence, based on his strength of character and willingness to work hard, and are assigned his autobiography, *Grinding It Out* (Kroc with Anderson 1977). Kroc is quoted frequently in lectures, and students are encouraged to model themselves on him. They are told repeatedly that they have all proven themselves "winners" by getting as far as they have at McDonald's. The theme throughout is "We're the best in the world, we know exactly what we're doing, but our success depends on the best efforts of every one of you."[11]

About 3,500 students from all over the world attend classes at Hamburger University each year, most of them taking the Advanced Operations Course (Rosenthal 1989). Those who complete the course receive diplomas proclaiming them Doctors of Hamburgerology. As late as 1978 or 1979, a training manager told me, most classes included only one or two women, but women now comprise 40–60 percent of the students, and women and minorities now make up 54 percent of McDonald's franchisees (Bertagnoli 1989:33). In my homeroom, however, the proportion of women was much smaller, and there was just a handful of minority students.

The course lasts two weeks and is extremely rigorous. Class time is about evenly divided between work in the labs and lectures on store operations and personnel management. In the labs, trainees learn the mechanics of ensuring that McDonald's food is of consistent quality and its stores in good working order. They learn to check the equipment and maintain it properly so that fries cook at precisely the right temperature, shakes are mixed to just the right consistency, and ice cubes are uniform. "Taste of Quality" labs reinforce McDonald's standards for food quality. For instance, in a Condiments Lab, trainees are taught exactly how to store vegetables and sauces, what the shelf lives of these products are, and how they should look and taste. Samples of "McDonald's quality" Big Mac Special Sauce are contrasted with samples that have been left too long unrefrigerated and should be discarded. The importance of serving only food that meets McDonald's standards is constantly emphasized and, a trainer pointed out, "McDonald's has standards for everything, down to the width of the pickle slices." . . .

The training at Hamburger University combines a sense of fun with dead seriousness about keeping McDonald's on top in the hamburger business through relentless quality control and effective management of workers and customers. It is up to the owners and managers of individual McDonald's stores to make that happen. . . .

Learning the Job

As a manager at Hamburger University explained to me, the crew training process is how McDonald's standardization is maintained, how the company ensures that Big Macs are the same everywhere in the world. The McDonald's central administration supplies franchisees with videotapes and other materials for use in training workers to meet the company's exacting specifications. The company produces a separate videotape for each job in the store, and it encourages franchisees to keep their tape libraries up-to-date as product specifications change. The Hamburger University professor who taught the Advanced Operating Course session on training said that, to keep current, franchisees should be buying 10 or 12 tapes a year. For each work station in the store, McDonald's also has a "Station Operation Checklist" (SOC), a short but highly detailed job description that lays out exactly how the job should be done: how much ketchup and mustard go on each kind of hamburger, in what sequence the products customers order are to be gathered, what arm motion is to be used in salting a batch of fries, and so on. . . .

The Routine

McDonald's had routinized the work of its crews so thoroughly that decision making had practically been eliminated from the jobs. As one window worker told me, "They've tried to break it down so that it's almost idiot-proof." Most of the workers agreed that there was little call for them to use their own judgment on the job, since there were rules about everything. If an unusual problem arose, the workers were supposed to turn it over to a manager.

Many of the noninteractive parts of the window workers' job had been made idiot-proof through automation.[12] The soda machines, for example, automatically dispensed the proper amount of beverage for regular, medium, and large cups. Computerized cash registers performed a variety of functions handled elsewhere by human waitresses, waiters, and cashiers, making some kinds of skill and knowledge unnecessary. As a customer gave an order, the window worker simply pressed the cash register button labeled with the name of the selected product. There was no need to write the orders down, because the buttons lit up to indicate which products had been selected. Nor was there any need to remember prices, because the prices were programmed into the machines. Like most new cash registers, these added the tax automatically and told workers how much change customers were owed, so the window crew did not need to know how to do those calculations. The cash registers also helped regulate some of the crew's interactive work by reminding them to try to increase the size of each sale. For example, when a customer ordered a Big Mac, large fries, and a regular Coke, the cash register buttons for cookies, hot apple pies, ice cream cones, and ice cream sundaes would light up, prompting the worker to suggest dessert. It took some skill to operate the relatively complicated cash register, as my difficulties during my first work shift made clear, but this organizationally specific skill could soon be acquired on the job.

In addition to doing much of the workers' thinking for them, the computerized cash registers made it possible for managers to monitor the crew members' work and the store's inventory very closely.[13] For example, if the number of Quarter Pounder with Cheese boxes gone did not match the number of Quarter Pounders with Cheese sold or accounted for as waste, managers might suspect that workers were giving away or taking food. Managers could easily tell which workers had brought in the most money during a given interval and who was doing the best job of persuading customers to buy a particular item. The computerized system could also complicate what would otherwise have been simple customer requests, however. For example, when a man who had not realized the benefit of ordering his son's food as a Happy Meal came back to the counter to ask whether his little boy could have one of the plastic beach pails the Happy Meals were served in, I had to ask a manager what to do, since fulfilling the request would produce a discrepancy between the inventory and the receipts.[14] Sometimes the extreme systematization can induce rather than prevent idiocy, as when a window worker says she cannot serve a cup of coffee that is half decaffeinated and half regular because she would not know how to ring up the sale.[15]

The interactive part of window work is routinized through the Six Steps of Window Service and also through rules aimed at standardizing attitudes and demeanors as well as words and actions. The window workers were taught that they represented McDonald's to the public and that their attitudes were therefore an important component of service quality. Crew people could be reprimanded for not smiling, and often were. The window workers were supposed to be cheerful and polite at all times, but they were also told to be themselves while on the job. McDonald's does not want its workers to seem like robots, so part of the emotion work asked of the window crew is that they act naturally. "Being yourself" in this situation meant behaving in a way that did not seem stilted. Although workers had some latitude to go beyond the script, the short, highly schematic routine obviously did not allow much room for genuine self-expression.

Workers were not the only ones constrained by McDonald's routines, of course. The cooperation of service recipients was crucial to the smooth functioning of the operation. In many kinds of interactive service work . . . constructing the compliance of service recipients is an important part of the service worker's job. The routines such workers use may be designed to maximize the control each worker has over customers. McDonald's window workers' routines were not intended to give them much leverage over customers' behavior, however. The window workers interacted only with people who had already decided to do business with McDonald's and who therefore did not need to be persuaded to take part in the service interaction. Furthermore, almost all customers were familiar enough with McDonald's routines to know how they were expected to behave. For instance, I never saw a customer who did not know that she or he was supposed to come up to the counter rather than sit down and wait to be served. This customer training was accomplished through advertising, spatial design, customer experience, and the example of other customers, making it unnecessary for the window crew to put much effort into getting customers to fit into their work routines.[16]

McDonald's ubiquitous advertising trains consumers at the same time that it tries to attract them to McDonald's. Television commercials demonstrate how the service system is supposed to work and familiarize customers with new products. Additional cues about expected customer behavior are provided by the design of the restaurants. For example, the entrances usually lead to the service counter, not to the dining area, making it unlikely that customers will fail to realize that they should get in line, and the placement of waste cans makes clear that customers are expected to throw out their own trash. Most important, the majority of customers have had years of experience with McDonald's, as well as with other fast-food restaurants that have similar arrangements. The company estimates that the average customer visits a McDonald's 20 times a year (Koepp 1987:58), and it is not uncommon for a customer to come in several times per week. For many customers, then, ordering at McDonald's is as routine an interaction as it is for the window worker. Indeed, because employee turnover is so high, steady customers may be more familiar with the work routines than the workers serving them are. Customers who are new to McDonald's can take their cue from more experienced customers.[17]

Not surprisingly, then, most customers at the McDonald's I studied knew what was expected of them and tried to play their part well. They sorted themselves into lines and gazed up at the menu boards while waiting to be served. They usually gave their orders in the conventional sequence: burgers or other entrees, french fries or other side orders, drinks, and desserts. Hurried customers with savvy might order an item "only if it's in the bin," that is, ready to be served. Many customers prepared carefully so that they could give their orders promptly when they got to the counter. This preparation sometimes became apparent when a worker interrupted to ask, "What kind of dressing?" or "Cream and sugar?", flustering customers who could not deliver their orders as planned.

McDonald's routines, like those of other interactive service businesses, depend on the predictability of customers, but these businesses must not grind to a halt if customers are not completely cooperative. Some types of deviations from standard customer behavior are so common that they become routine themselves, and these can be handled through subroutines (Stinchcombe 1990:39). McDonald's routines work most efficiently when all customers accept their products exactly as they are usually prepared; indeed, the whole business is based on this premise. Since, however, some people give special instructions for customized products, such as "no onions," the routine allows for these exceptions.[18] At the franchise I studied, workers could key the special requests into their cash registers, which automatically printed out "grill slips" with the instructions for the grill workers to follow. Under this system, the customer making the special order had to wait for it to be prepared, but the smooth flow of service for other customers was not interrupted. Another type of routine difficulty was customer dissatisfaction with food quality. Whenever a customer had a complaint about the food—cold fries, dried-out burger—window workers were authorized to supply a new product immediately without consulting a supervisor.[19]

These two kinds of difficulties—special orders and complaints about food—were the only irregularities window workers were authorized to handle. The subroutines increased the flexibility of the service system, but they did not increase the workers' discretion, since procedures were in place for dealing with both situations. All other kinds of demands fell outside the window crew's purview. If they were faced with a dispute about money, an extraordinary request, or a furious customer, workers were instructed to call a manager; the crew had no authority to handle such problems.

Given the almost complete regimentation of tasks and preemption of decision making, does McDonald's need the flexibility and thoughtfulness of human workers? As the declining supply of teenagers and legislated increases in the minimum wage drive up labor costs, it is not surprising that McDonald's is experimenting with electronic replacements. So far, the only robot in use handles behind-the-scenes work rather than customer interactions. ARCH (Automated Restaurant Crew Helper) works in a Minnesota McDonald's where it does all the frying and lets workers know when to prepare sandwich buns, when supplies are running low, and when fries are no longer fresh enough to sell. Other McDonald's stores (along with Arby's and Burger King units) are experimenting with a touch-screen computer system that lets customers order their meals themselves, further curtailing the role of the window worker. Although it requires increased customer socialization and cooperation, early reports are that the system cuts service time by 30 seconds and increases sales per window worker 10–20 percent (Chaudhry 1989:F61).

Overview

McDonald's pioneered the routinization of interactive service work and remains an exemplar of extreme standardization. Innovation is not discouraged at McDonald's; the company favors experimentation, at least among managers and franchisees. Ironically, though, "the object is to look for new, innovative ways to create an experience that is exactly the same no matter what McDonald's you walk into, no matter where it is in the world" (Rosenthal 1989:12). Thus, when someone in the field comes up with a good idea—and such McDonald's success stories as the Egg McMuffin and the Big Mac were store-level inspirations (Koepp 1987:60)—the corporation experiments, tests, and refines the idea and finally implements it in a uniform way systemwide. One distinctive feature of McDonald's-style routinization is that there, to a great extent, uniformity is a goal in itself. . . .

McDonald's . . . does promise uniform products and consistent service, and to provide them the company has broken down virtually every task required to run a store into detailed routines with clear instructions and standards. For those routines to run smoothly, conditions must be relatively predictable, so McDonald's tries to control as many contingencies as possible, including the attitudes and behavior of workers, managers, and customers. The company uses a wide array of socialization and control techniques to ensure that these people are familiar with McDonald's procedures and willing to comply with them.

Most McDonald's work is organized as low-paying, low-status, part-time jobs that give workers little autonomy. Almost every decision about how to do crew people's tasks has been made in advance by the corporation, and many of the decisions have been built into the stores' technology. Why use human workers at all, if not to take advantage of the human capacity to respond to circumstances flexibly? McDonald's does want to provide at least a simulacrum of the human attributes of warmth, friendliness, and recognition. For that reason, not only workers' movements but also their words, demeanor, and attitudes are subject to managerial control.

Although predictability is McDonald's hallmark, not all factors can be controlled by management. One of the most serious irregularities that store management must deal with is fluctuation in the flow of customers, both expected and unexpected. Since personnel costs are the most manipulable variable affecting a store's profitability, managers want to match labor power to consumer demand as exactly as possible. They do so by paying all crew people by the hour, giving them highly irregular hours based on expected sales—sometimes including split shifts—and sending workers home early or keeping them late as conditions require. In other words, the costs of uneven demand are shifted to workers whenever possible. Since most McDonald's crew people cannot count on working a particular number of hours at precisely scheduled times, it is hard for them to make plans based on how much money they will earn or exactly what times they will be free. Workers are pressured to be flexible in order to maximize the organization's own flexibility in staffing levels. In contrast, of course, flexibility in the work process itself is minimized.

Routinization has not made the crew people's work easy. Their jobs, although highly structured and repetitive, are often demanding and stressful. Under these working conditions, the organization's limited commitment to workers, as reflected in job security, wages, and benefits, makes the task of maintaining worker motivation and discipline even more challenging. A variety of factors, many orchestrated by the corporation, keeps McDonald's crew people hard at work despite the limited rewards. Socialization into McDonald's norms, extremely close supervision (both human and electronic), individual and group incentives, peer pressure, and pressure from customers all play their part in getting workers to do things the McDonald's way.

Because franchisees and store-level managers are responsible for enforcing standardization throughout the McDonald's system, their socialization includes a more intensive focus on building commitment to and pride in the organization than does crew training. In fact, it is the corporate attempt at transforming these higher-level McDonald's people by making them more loyal, confident, flexible, and sensitive to others, as well as more knowledge-able about company procedures, that makes the extreme rigidity of the crew training workable. The crew people do not have to be trusted with decision-making authority, because all unusual problems are referred to managers. Their more extensive training gives them the knowledge and attitudes to make the kinds of decisions the corporation would approve. . . . In addition to thorough socialization, McDonald's managers and franchisees are sub-jected to close corporate oversight. Every aspect of their stores' operations is rated by corporate staff, and they are sanctioned accordingly.

Despite elaborate socialization and social controls, McDonald's stores do not, of course, carry out every corporate directive exactly as recommended. In the store I studied, managers did not always provide their workers with the mandated support and encouragement, crew trainers did not always fol-low the four-step training system, and window workers did not always carry out the Six Steps of Window Service with the required eye contact and smile. There were many kinds of pressures to deviate from corporate standards. Nonetheless, the benefits of standardization should not be underestimated. As every Durkheimian knows, clear rules and shared standards provide sup-port and coherence as well as constraint. Although some aspects of the routines did strike the participants as overly constraining, undignified, or silly, the approved routines largely worked. In all of these examples of devi-ation, the routines would have produced more efficient and pleasant service, and those that apply to management and training would have benefited workers as well as customers.

Obtaining the cooperation of workers and managers is not enough to ensure the smooth functioning of McDonald's relatively inflexible routines. Customers must be routinized as well. Not only do customers have to un-derstand the service routine and accept the limited range of choices the com-pany offers, they also must be willing to do some kinds of work that are done for them in conventional restaurants, including carrying food to the table and throwing out their trash. Experience, advertising, the example set by other customers, and clear environmental cues familiarize customers with McDonald's routines, and most want to cooperate in order to speed service. For these reasons, McDonald's interactive service workers do not have to di-rect most customers, and window workers' routines are therefore not de-signed to give them power over customers.

ENDNOTES

[1] Suppliers, competitors, and other parties outside of the organization are also relevant actors, but organizational efforts to control their behavior will not be considered here (see Prus 1989).

[2] The 1990s may bring unprecedented changes to McDonald's. Although its overseas business continues to thrive, domestic sales have been declining. To overcome the challenges to profitability presented by the economic recession, lower-priced competitors, and changes in consumer tastes, CEO Michael Quinlan has instituted experimental changes in the menu, in pricing strategy, and even in the degree of flexibility granted to franchisees (see *Advertising Age* 1991; Berg 1991; *McDonald's Annual Report* 1990; Therrien 1991).

[3] McDonald's restaurants are generally referred to as "stores" by McDonald's staff. The company's share of the domestic fast-food market has declined from 18.7 percent in 1985 to 16.6 percent in 1990 (Therrien 1991).

[4] Information about McDonald's history comes primarily from Boas and Chain 1976; Kroc with Anderson 1977; Love 1986; Luxenberg 1985; and McDonald's training materials. Reiter's (1991) description of Burger King reveals numerous parallels in the operation of the two companies, although Burger King, unlike McDonald's, is a subsidiary of a multinational conglomerate.

[5] In addition to paid advertising, McDonald's bolsters its public image with promotional and philanthropic activities such as an All-American High School Basketball Game, essay contests and scholarship programs for black and Hispanic students, and Ronald McDonald Houses where outpatient children and their families and the parents of hospitalized children can stay at minimal cost.

[6] Conversely, details of the routines are designed with marketing in mind. The bags that hold the regular-size portions of french fries are shorter than the french fries are, so that when workers fill them with their regulation french-fry scoops, the servings seem generous, overflowing the packaging. The names of the serving sizes also are intended to give customers the impression that they are getting a lot for their money: French fries come in regular and large sizes, sodas in regular, medium, and large cups. I was quickly corrected during a work shift when I inadvertently referred to an order for a "small" drink.

[7] Some commentators fall into the trap of assuming that workers' preferences are determinative of working conditions, a mistake they do not make when discussing higher-status workers such as faculty who must rely on a string of temporary appointments.

[8] Actually, Kroc usually spoke of QSCV—quality, service, cleanliness, and value (see Kroc with Anderson 1977)—but QSC was the term used in most McDonald's training and motivational materials at the time of my research. The company cannot enforce "value" because antitrust restrictions prevent McDonald's from dictating prices to its franchisees (Love 1986:145). Nevertheless, recent materials return to the original four-part pledge of QSC & V (see, e.g., *McDonald's Annual Report* 1989:i).

[9] Branches of Hamburger University now operate in London, Munich, and Tokyo (*McDonald's Annual Report* 1989:28). Burger King University is similar in many respects (Reiter 1991).

[10] The effort to involve corporate employees in the central mission of the organization extends beyond such special programs. McDonald's prides itself on keeping its corporate focus firmly on store-level operations, and it wants all its employees to have a clear idea of what it takes to make a McDonald's restaurant work. Therefore, all McDonald's employees, from attorneys to data-entry clerks, spend time working in a McDonald's restaurant.

[11] Biggart (1989:143–47) shows that both adulation of a charismatic founder and repeated characterization of participants as winners are common in direct-sales organizations. Like McDonald's, such organizations face the problem of motivating people who are widely dispersed geographically and who are not corporate employees.

[12] The in-store processors similarly affected managers' work. A disaffected McDonald's manager told Garson, "There is no such thing as a McDonald's manager. The computer manages the store" (Garson 1988:39).

[13] Garson (1988) provides an extended discussion of this point.

[14] The manager gave him the pail but had to ring it up on the machine as if he had given away a whole Happy Meal.

[15] Thanks to Charles Bosk for this story.

[16] Mills (1986) elaborates on "customer socialization." Environmental design as a factor in service provision is discussed by Wener (1985) and Normann (1984).

[17] The importance of customer socialization becomes apparent when people with very different consumer experiences are introduced to a service system. When the first McDonald's opened in the Soviet Union in 1990, Moscow's citizens did not find the system immediately comprehensible. They had to be persuaded to get on the shortest lines at the counter, since they had learned from experience that desirable goods were available only where there are long lines (Goldman 1990).

[18] Burger King's "Have it your way" campaign virtually forced McDonald's to allow such customized service.

[19] The defective food or its container was put into a special waste bin. Each shift, one worker or manager had the unenviable task of counting the items in the waste bin so that the inventory could be reconciled with the cash intake.

REFERENCES

Advertising Age. 1990. "Adman of the Decade: McDonald's Fred Turner: Making All the Right Moves," January 1, p. 6.

———. 1991. "100 Leading National Advertisers: McDonald's," September 25, pp. 49–50.

Berg, Eric N. 1991. "An American Icon Wrestles with a Troubled Future." *New York Times,* May 12, sec. 3, pp. 1, 6.

Bertagnoli, Lisa. 1989. "McDonald's: Company of the Quarter Century." *Restaurants and Institutions,* July 10, pp. 32–60.

Biggart, Nicole Woolsey. 1989. *Charismatic Capitalism: Direct Selling Organizations in America.* Chicago: University of Chicago Press. Pp. 128, 143–47.

Boas, Max and Steve Chain. 1976. *Big Mac: The Unauthorized Story of McDonald's.* New York: New American Library. P. 19.

Chaudhry, Rajan. 1989. "Burger Giants Singed by Battle." *Nation's Restaurant News,* August 7, p. F61.

"Fortune Global Service 500: The 50 Largest Retailing Companies." 1991. *Fortune,* August 26, p. 179.

Garson, Barbara. 1988. *The Electronic Sweatshop: How Computers Are Transforming the Office of the Future into the Factory of the Past.* New York: Simon and Schuster. P. 39.

Gibson, Richard and Robert Johnson. 1989. "Big Mac Plots Strategy to Regain Sizzle." *Wall Street Journal,* September 29, p. B1.

Goldman, Marshall. 1990. Presentation at colloquium on Reforming the Soviet Economy, University of Pennsylvania, May 17.

Greenberger, Ellen and Laurence Steinberg. 1986. *When Teenagers Work: The Psychological and Social Costs of Adolescent Employment.* New York: Basic Books.

Koepp, Stephen. 1987. "Big Mac Strikes Back." *Time,* April 13, p. 60.

Kroc, Ray with Robert Anderson. 1977. *Grinding It Out: The Making of McDonald's.* Chicago: Contemporary Books. P. 124.

Love, John F. 1986. *McDonald's: Behind the Arches.* New York: Bantam Books. P. 145.

Luxenberg, Stan. 1985. *Roadside Empires: How the Chains Franchised America.* New York: Viking.

McDonald's Annual Report. 1989. Oak Brook, Illinois. Pp. i, 28, 29, 32.

———. 1990. Oak Brook, Illinois. Pp. 1–2.

Mills, Peter K. 1986. *Managing Service Industries: Organizational Practices in a Post-Industrial Economy.* Cambridge, MA: Ballinger.

Normann, Richard. 1984. *Service Management: Strategy and Leadership in Service Businesses.* Chichester, England: Wiley.

Prus, Robert. 1989. *Pursuing Customers: An Ethnography of Marketing Activities.* Newbury Park, CA: Sage.

Reiter, Ester. 1991. *Making Fast Food: From the Frying Pan into the Fryer.* Montreal: McGill-Queen's University Press.

Rosenthal, Herman M. 1989. "Inside Big Mac's World." *Newsday,* June 4, p. 12.

Stinchcombe, Arthur L. 1990. *Information and Organizations.* Berkeley: University of California Press. P. 39.

Therrien, Lois. 1991. "McRisky." *Business Week,* October 21, pp. 114–22.

Wener, Richard E. 1985. "The Environmental Psychology of Service Encounters." Pp. 101–12 in *The Service Encounter: Managing Employee/Customer Interaction in Service Businesses,* edited by John A. Czepiel, Michael R. Solomon, and Carol F. Surprenant. Lexington, MA: Lexington Books.

Wildavsky, Ben. 1989. "McJobs: Inside America's Largest Youth Training Program." *Policy Review* 49:30–37.

43

————————

THE TIME BIND
When Work Becomes
Home and Home Becomes Work

ARLIE RUSSELL HOCHSCHILD

What are the relationships between work life and family life? How do individuals negotiate the role demands of both social institutions? Arlie Russell Hochschild, a professor of sociology at the University of California at Berkeley, investigates these questions in her three-year study of a large corporation, which she calls "Amerco." Hochschild interviewed 130 employees, including middle and upper management, clerks and factory workers, most of whom were working parents. Hochschild also talked with human resource specialists, psychologists, child-care workers, and homemakers who were married to Amerco employees. In this selection, adapted from her book *The Time Bind: When Work Becomes Home and Home Becomes Work* (1997), Hochschild discusses her findings about the changing relationship between work life and home life for many working parents.

It's 7:40 A.M. when Cassie Bell, 4, arrives at the Spotted Deer Child-Care Center, her hair half-combed, a blanket in one hand, a fudge bar in the other. "I'm late," her mother, Gwen, a sturdy young woman whose short-cropped hair frames a pleasant face, explains to the child-care worker in charge. "Cassie wanted the fudge bar so bad, I gave it to her," she adds apologetically.

"*Pleeese,* can't you take me with you?" Cassie pleads.

"You know I can't take you to work," Gwen replies in a tone that suggests that she has been expecting this request. Cassie's shoulders droop. But she has struck a hard bargain—the morning fudge bar—aware of her mother's anxiety about the long day that lies ahead at the center. As Gwen explains later, she continually feels that she owes Cassie more time than she gives her—she has a "time debt."

Arriving at her office just before 8, Gwen finds on her desk a cup of coffee in her personal mug, milk no sugar (exactly as she likes it), prepared by a co-worker who managed to get in ahead of her. As the assistant to the head of public relations at a company I will call Amerco, Gwen has to handle responses to any reports that may appear about the company in the press—a challenging job, but one that gives her satisfaction. As she prepares for her first meeting of the day, she misses her daughter, but she also feels relief; there's a lot to get done at Amerco.

Gwen used to work a straight eight-hour day. But over the last three years, her workday has gradually stretched to eight and a half or nine hours, not counting the e-mail messages and faxes she answers from home. She complains about her hours to her co-workers and listens to their complaints—but she loves her job. Gwen picks up Cassie at 5:45 and gives her a long, affectionate hug.

At home, Gwen's husband, John, a computer programmer, plays with their daughter while Gwen prepares dinner. To protect the dinner "hour"— 8:00–8:30—Gwen checks that the phone machine is on, hears the phone ring during dinner but resists the urge to answer. After Cassie's bath, Gwen and Cassie have "quality time," or "Q.T.," as John affectionately calls it. Half an hour later, at 9:30, Gwen tucks Cassie into bed.

There are, in a sense, two Bell households: the rushed family they actually are and the relaxed family they imagine they might be if only they had time. Gwen and John complain that they are in a time bind. What they say they want seems so modest—time to throw a ball, to read to Cassie, to witness the small dramas of her development, not to speak of having a little fun and romance themselves. Yet even these modest wishes seem strangely out of reach. Before going to bed, Gwen has to e-mail messages to her colleagues in preparation for the next day's meeting; John goes to bed early, exhausted— he's out the door by 7 every morning.

Nationwide, many working parents are in the same boat. More mothers of small children than ever now work outside the home. In 1993, 56 percent of women with children between 6 and 17 worked outside the home full time year-round; 43 percent of women with children 6 and under did the same. Meanwhile, fathers of small children are not cutting back hours of work to help out at home. If anything, they have increased their hours at work. According to a 1993 national survey conducted by the Families and Work Institute in New York, American men average 48.8 hours of work a week, and women 41.7 hours, including overtime and commuting. All in all, more women are on the economic train, and for many—men and women alike— that train is going faster.

But Amerco has "family-friendly" policies. If your division head and supervisor agree, you can work part time, share a job with another worker, work some hours at home, take parental leave or use "flex time." But hardly anyone uses these policies. In seven years, only two Amerco fathers have taken formal parental leave. Fewer than 1 percent have taken advantage of the opportunity to work part time. Of all such policies, only flex time—which rearranges but does not shorten work time—has had a significant number of takers (perhaps a third of working parents at Amerco).

Forgoing family-friendly policies is not exclusive to Amerco workers. A 1991 study of 188 companies conducted by the Families and Work Institute found that while a majority offered part-time shifts, fewer than 5 percent of employees made use of them. Thirty-five percent offered "flex place"—work from home—and fewer than 3 percent of their employees took advantage of it. And an earlier Bureau of Labor Statistics survey asked workers whether they preferred a shorter workweek, a longer one or their present schedule. About 62 percent preferred their present schedule; 28 percent would have preferred longer hours. Fewer than 10 percent said they wanted a cut in hours.

Still, I found it hard to believe that people didn't protest their long hours at work. So I contacted Bright Horizons, a company that runs 136 company-based child-care centers associated with corporations, hospitals and Federal agencies in 25 states. Bright Horizons allowed me to add questions to a questionnaire they sent out to 3,000 parents whose children attended the centers. The respondents, mainly middle-class parents in their early 30s, largely confirmed the picture I'd found at Amerco. A third of fathers and a fifth of mothers described themselves as "workaholic," and 1 out of 3 said their partners were.

To be sure, some parents have tried to shorten their hours. Twenty-one percent of the nation's women voluntarily work part time, as do 7 percent of men. A number of others make under-the-table arrangements that don't show up on surveys. But while working parents say they need more time at home, the main story of their lives does not center on a struggle to get it. Why? Given the hours parents are working these days, why aren't they taking advantage of an opportunity to reduce their time at work?

The most widely held explanation is that working parents cannot afford to work shorter hours. Certainly this is true for many. But if money is the whole explanation, why would it be that at places like Amerco, the best-paid employees—upper-level managers and professionals—were the least interested in part-time work or job sharing, while clerical workers who earned less were more interested?

Similarly, if money were the answer, we would expect poorer new mothers to return to work more quickly after giving birth than rich mothers. But among working women nationwide, well-to-do new mothers are not much more likely to stay home after 13 weeks with a new baby than low-income new mothers. When asked what they look for in a job, only a third of respondents in a recent study said salary came first. Money is important, but by itself, money does not explain why many people don't want to cut back hours at work.

A second explanation goes that workers don't dare ask for time off because they are afraid it would make them vulnerable to layoffs. With recent downsizings at many large corporations, and with well-paying, secure jobs being replaced by lower-paying, insecure ones, it occurred to me that perhaps employees are "working scared." But when I asked Amerco employees whether they worked long hours for fear of getting on a layoff list, virtually everyone said no. Even among a particularly vulnerable group—factory workers who were laid off in the downturn of the early 1980s and were later rehired—most did not cite fear for their jobs as the only, or main, reason they worked overtime. For unionized workers, layoffs are assigned by seniority, and for nonunionized workers, layoffs are usually related to the profitability of the division a person works in, not to an individual work schedule.

Were workers uninformed about the company's family-friendly policies? No. Some even mentioned that they were proud to work for a company that offered such enlightened policies. Were rigid middle managers standing in the way of workers using these policies? Sometimes. But when I compared Amerco employees who worked for flexible managers with those who worked for rigid managers, I found that the flexible managers reported only a few more applicants than the rigid ones. The evidence, however counter-intuitive, pointed to a paradox: workers at the company I studied weren't protesting the time bind. They were accommodating to it.

Why? I did not anticipate the conclusion I found myself coming to: namely, that work has become a form of "home" and home has become "work." The worlds of home and work have not begun to blur, as the conventional wisdom goes, but to reverse places. We are used to thinking that home is where most people feel the most appreciated, the most truly "themselves," the most secure, the most relaxed. We are used to thinking that work is where most people feel like "just a number" or "a cog in a machine." It is where they have to be "on," have to "act," where they are least secure and most harried.

But new management techniques so pervasive in corporate life have helped transform the workplace into a more appreciative, personal sort of social world. Meanwhile, at home the divorce rate has risen, and the emotional demands have become more baffling and complex. In addition to teething, tantrums and the normal developments of growing children, the needs of elderly parents are creating more tasks for the modern family—as are the blending, unblending, reblending of new stepparents, stepchildren, exes and former in-laws.

This idea began to dawn on me during one of my first interviews with an Amerco worker. Linda Avery, a friendly, 38-year-old mother, is a shift supervisor at an Amerco plant. When I meet her in the factory's coffee-break room over a couple of Cokes, she is wearing blue jeans and a pink jersey, her hair pulled back in a long, blond ponytail. Linda's husband, Bill, is a technician in the same plant. By working different shifts, they manage to share the care of their 2-year-old son and Linda's 16-year-old daughter from a previous marriage. "Bill works the 7 A.M. to 3 P.M. shift while I watch the baby," she explains. "Then I work the 3 P.M. to 11 P.M. shift and he watches the baby. My daughter works at Walgreen's after school."

Linda is working overtime, and so I begin by asking whether Amerco required the overtime or whether she volunteered for it. "Oh, I put in for it," she replies. I ask her whether, if finances and company policy permitted, she'd be interested in cutting back on the overtime. She takes off her safety glasses, rubs her face and, without answering my question, explains: "I get home, and the minute I turn the key, my daughter is right there. Granted, she needs somebody to talk to about her day. . . . The baby is still up. He should have been in bed two hours ago, and that upsets me. The dishes are piled in the sink. My daughter comes right up to the door and complains about anything her stepfather said or did, and she wants to talk about her job. My husband is in the other room hollering to my daughter, 'Tracy, I don't ever get any time to talk to your mother, because you're always monopolizing her time before I even get a chance!' They all come at me at once."

Linda's description of the urgency of demands and the unarbitrated quarrels that await her homecoming contrast with her account of arriving at her job as a shift supervisor: "I usually come to work early, just to get away from the house. When I arrive, people are there waiting. We sit, we talk, we joke. I let them know what's going on, who has to be where, what changes I've made for the shift that day. We sit and chitchat for 5 or 10 minutes. There's laughing, joking, fun."

For Linda, home has come to feel like work and work has come to feel a bit like home. Indeed, she feels she can get relief from the "work" of being at home only by going to the "home" of work. Why has her life at home come to seem like this? Linda explains it this way: "My husband's a great help watching our baby. But as far as doing housework or even taking the baby when I'm at home, no. He figures he works five days a week; he's not going to come home and clean. But he doesn't stop to think that I work seven days a week. Why should I have to come home and do the housework without help from anybody else? My husband and I have been through this over and over again. Even if he would just pick up from the kitchen table and stack the dishes for me, that would make a big difference. He does nothing. On his weekends off, he goes fishing. If I want any time off, I have to get a sitter. He'll help out if I'm not here, but the minute I am, all the work at home is mine."

With a light laugh, she continues: "So I take a lot of overtime. The more I get out of the house, the better I am. It's a terrible thing to say, but that's the way I feel."

When Bill feels the need for time off, to relax, to have fun, to feel free, he climbs in his truck and takes his free time without his family. Largely in response, Linda grabs what she also calls "free time"—at work. Neither Linda nor Bill Avery wants more time together at home, not as things are arranged now.

How do Linda and Bill Avery fit into the broader picture of American family and work life? Current research suggests that however hectic their lives, women who do paid work feel less depressed, think better of themselves and are more satisfied than women who stay at home. One study reported that women who work outside the home feel more valued at home than housewives do. Meanwhile, work is where many women feel like "good mothers." As Linda reflects: "I'm a good mom at home, but I'm a better mom at work. At home, I get into fights with Tracy. I want her to apply to a junior college, but she's not interested. At work, I think I'm better at seeing the other person's point of view."

Many workers feel more confident they could "get the job done" at work than at home. One study found that only 59 percent of workers feel their "performance" in the family is "good or unusually good," while 86 percent rank their performance on the job this way.

Forces at work and at home are simultaneously reinforcing this "reversal." This lure of work has been enhanced in recent years by the rise of company cultural engineering—in particular, the shift from Frederick Taylor's principles of scientific management to the Total Quality principles originally set out by W. Edwards Deming. Under the influence of a Taylorist world view, the manager's job was to coerce the worker's mind and body, not to appeal to the worker's heart. The Taylorized worker was de-skilled, replaceable and cheap, and as a consequence felt bored, demeaned and unappreciated.

Using modern participative management techniques, many companies now train workers to make their own work decisions, and then set before their newly "empowered" employees moral as well as financial incentives. At Amerco, the Total Quality worker is invited to feel recognized for job accomplishments. Amerco regularly strengthens the familylike ties of co-workers by holding "recognition ceremonies" honoring particular workers or self-managed production teams. Amerco employees speak of "belonging to the Amerco family," and proudly wear their "Total Quality" pins or "High Performance Team" T-shirts, symbols of their loyalty to the company and of its loyalty to them.

The company occasionally decorates a section of the factory and serves refreshments. The production teams, too, have regular get-togethers. In a New Age recasting of an old business slogan—"The Customer Is Always Right"—Amerco proposes that its workers "Value the Internal Customer." This means: Be as polite and considerate to co-workers inside the company as you would be to customers outside it. How many recognition ceremonies for competent performance are being offered at home? Who is valuing the internal customer there?

Amerco also tries to take on the role of a helpful relative with regard to employee problems at work and at home. The education-and-training division offers employees free courses (on company time) in "Dealing With Anger," "How to Give and Accept Criticism," "How to Cope With Difficult People."

At home, of course, people seldom receive anything like this much help on issues basic to family life. There, no courses are being offered on "Dealing With Your Child's Disappointment in You" or "How to Treat Your Spouse Like an Internal Customer."

If Total Quality calls for "re-skilling" the worker in an "enriched" job environment, technological developments have long been de-skilling parents at home. Over the centuries, store-bought goods have replaced homespun cloth, homemade soap and home-baked foods. Day care for children, retirement homes for the elderly, even psychotherapy are, in a way, commercial substitutes for jobs that a mother once did at home. Even family-generated entertainment has, to some extent, been replaced by television, video games and the VCR. I sometimes watched Amerco families sitting together after their dinners, mute but cozy, watching sitcoms in which television mothers, fathers and children related in an animated way to one another while the viewing family engaged in relational loafing.

The one "skill" still required of family members is the hardest one of all—the emotional work of forging, deepening or repairing family relationships. It takes time to develop this skill, and even then things can go awry. Family ties are complicated. People get hurt. Yet as broken homes become more common—and as the sense of belonging to a geographical community grows less and less secure in an age of mobility—the corporate world has created a sense of "neighborhood," of "feminine culture," of family at work. Life at work can be insecure; the company can fire workers. But workers aren't so secure at home, either. Many employees have been working for Amerco for 20 years but are on their second or third marriages or relationships. The shifting balance between these two "divorce rates" may be the most powerful reason why tired parents flee a world of unresolved quarrels and unwashed laundry for the orderliness, harmony and managed cheer of work. People are getting their "pink slips" at home.

Amerco workers have not only turned their offices into "home" and their homes into workplaces; many have also begun to "Taylorize" time at home, where families are succumbing to a cult of efficiency previously associated mainly with the office and factory. Meanwhile, work time, with its ever longer hours, has become more hospitable to sociability—periods of talking with friends on e-mail, patching up quarrels, gossiping. Within the long workday of many Amerco employees are great hidden pockets of inefficiency while, in the far smaller number of waking weekday hours at home, they are, despite themselves, forced to act increasingly time-conscious and efficient.

The Averys respond to their time bind at home by trying to value and protect "quality time." A concept unknown to their parents and grandparents, "quality time" has become a powerful symbol of the struggle against the growing pressures at home. It reflects the extent to which modern parents feel the flow of time to be running against them. The premise behind "quality time" is that the time we devote to relationships can somehow be separated from ordinary time. Relationships go on during quantity time, of course, but then we are only passively, not actively, wholeheartedly, specializing in our emotional ties. We aren't "on." Quality time at home becomes like an office appointment. You don't want to be caught "goofing off around the water cooler" when you are "at work."

Quality time holds out the hope that scheduling intense periods of togetherness can compensate for an overall loss of time in such a way that a relationship will suffer no loss of quality. But this is just another way of transferring the cult of efficiency from office to home. We must now get our relationships in good repair in less time. Instead of nine hours a day with a child, we declare ourselves capable of getting "the same result" with one intensely focused hour.

Parents now more commonly speak of time as if it is a threatened form of personal capital they have no choice but to manage and invest. What's new here is the spread into the home of a financial manager's attitude toward time. Working parents at Amerco owe what they think of as time debts at home. This is because they are, in a sense, inadvertently "Taylorizing" the house—speeding up the pace of home life as Taylor once tried to "scientifically" speed up the pace of factory life.

Advertisers of products aimed at women have recognized that this new reality provides an opportunity to sell products, and have turned the very pressure that threatens to explode the home into a positive attribute. Take, for example, an ad promoting Instant Quaker Oatmeal: it shows a smiling mother ready for the office in her square-shouldered suit, hugging her happy son. A caption reads: "Nicky is a very picky eater. With Instant Quaker Oatmeal, I can give him a terrific hot breakfast in just 90 seconds. And I don't have to spend any time coaxing him to eat it!" Here, the modern mother seems to have absorbed the lessons of Frederick Taylor as she presses for efficiency at home because she is in a hurry to get to work.

Part of modern parenthood seems to include coping with the resistance of real children who are not so eager to get their cereal so fast. Some parents try desperately not to appease their children with special gifts or smooth-talking promises about the future. But when time is scarce, even the best parents find themselves passing a system-wide familial speed-up along to the most vulnerable workers on the line. Parents are then obliged to try to control the damage done by a reversal of worlds. They monitor mealtime, homework time, bedtime, trying to cut out "wasted" time.

In response, children often protest the pace, the deadlines, the grand irrationality of "efficient" family life. Children dawdle. They refuse to leave places when it's time to leave. They insist on leaving places when it's not time to leave. Surely, this is part of the usual stop-and-go of childhood itself, but perhaps, too, it is the plea of children for more family time and more control over what time there is. This only adds to the feeling that life at home has become hard work.

Instead of trying to arrange shorter or more flexible work schedules, Amerco parents often avoid confronting the reality of the time bind. Some minimize their ideas about how much care a child, a partner or they themselves "really need." They make do with less time, less attention, less understanding and less support at home than they once imagined possible. They *emotionally downsize* life. In essence, they deny the needs of family members, and they themselves become emotional ascetics. If they once "needed" time with each other, they are now increasingly "fine" without it.

Another way that working parents try to evade the time bind is to buy themselves out of it—an approach that puts women in particular at the heart of a contradiction. Like men, women absorb the work-family speed-up far more than they resist it; but unlike men, they still shoulder most of the workload at home. And women still represent in people's minds the heart and soul of family life. They're the ones—especially women of the urban middle and upper-middle classes—who feel most acutely the need to save time, who are the most tempted by the new "time saving" goods and services—and who wind up feeling the most guilty about it. For example, Playgroup Connections, a Washington-area business started by a former executive recruiter, matches playmates to one another. One mother hired the service to find her child a French-speaking playmate.

In several cities, children home alone can call a number for "Grandma, Please!" and reach an adult who has the time to talk with them, sing to them or help them with their homework. An ad for Kindercare Learning Centers, a for-profit child-care chain, pitches its appeal this way: "You want your child to be active, tolerant, smart, loved, emotionally stable, self-aware, artistic and get a two-hour nap. Anything else?" It goes on to note that Kindercare accepts children 6 weeks to 12 years old and provides a number to call for the Kindercare nearest you. Another typical service organizes children's birthday parties, making out invitations ("sure hope you can come") and providing party favors, entertainment, a decorated cake and balloons. Creative Memories is a service that puts ancestral photos into family albums for you.

An overwhelming majority of the working mothers I spoke with recoiled from the idea of buying themselves out of parental duties. A bought birthday party was "too impersonal," a 90-second breakfast "too fast." Yet a surprising amount of lunchtime conversation between female friends at Amerco was devoted to expressing complex, conflicting feelings about the lure of trading time for one service or another. The temptation to order flash-frozen dinners or to call a local number for a homework helper did not come up because such services had not yet appeared at Spotted Deer Child-Care Center. But many women dwelled on the question of how to decide where a mother's job began and ended, especially with regard to baby-sitters and television. One mother said to another in the breakroom of an Amerco plant: "Damon doesn't settle down until 10 at night, so he hates me to wake him up in the morning and I hate to do it. He's cranky. He pulls the covers up. I put on cartoons. That way, I can dress him and he doesn't object. I don't like to use TV that way. It's like a drug. But I do it."

The other mother countered: "Well, Todd is up before we are, so that's not a problem. It's after dinner, when I feel like watching a little television, that I feel guilty, because he gets too much TV at the sitter's."

As task after task falls into the realm of time-saving goods and services, questions arise about the moral meanings attached to doing or not doing such tasks. Is it being a good mother to bake a child's birthday cake (alone or together with one's partner)? Or can we gratefully save time by ordering it, and be good mothers by planning the party? Can we save more time by hiring a planning service, and be good mothers simply by watching our children have a good time? "Wouldn't that be nice!" one Amerco mother exclaimed. As the idea of the "good mother" retreats before the pressures of work and the expansion of motherly services, mothers are in fact continually reinventing themselves.

The final way working parents tried to evade the time bind was to develop what I call "potential selves." The potential selves that I discovered in my Amerco interviews were fantasy creations of time-poor parents who dreamed of living as time millionaires.

One man, a gifted 55-year-old engineer in research and development at Amerco, told how he had dreamed of taking his daughters on a camping trip in the Sierra Mountains: "I bought all the gear three years ago when they were 5 and 7, the tent, the sleeping bags, the air mattresses, the backpacks, the ponchos. I got a map of the area. I even got the freeze-dried food. Since then the kids and I have talked about it a lot, and gone over what we're going to do. They've been on me to do it for a long time. I feel bad about it. I keep putting it off, but we'll do it, I just don't know when."

Banished to garages and attics of many Amerco workers were expensive electric saws, cameras, skis and musical instruments, all bought with wages it took time to earn. These items were to their owners what Cassie's fudge bar was to her—a substitute for time, a talisman, a reminder of the potential self.

Obviously, not everyone, not even a majority of Americans, is making a home out of work and a workplace out of home. But in the working world, it is a growing reality, and one we need to face. Increasing numbers of women are discovering a great male secret—that work can be an escape from the pressures of home, pressures that the changing nature of work itself are only intensifying. Neither men nor women are going to take up "family-friendly" policies, whether corporate or governmental, as long as the current realities of work and home remain as they are. For a substantial number of time-bound parents, the stripped-down home and the neighborhood devoid of community are simply losing out to the pull of the workplace.

There are several broader, historical causes of this reversal of realms. The last 30 years have witnessed the rapid rise of women in the workplace. At the same time, job mobility has taken families farther from relatives who might lend a hand, and made it harder to make close friends of neighbors who could help out. Moreover, as women have acquired more education and have joined men at work, they have absorbed the views of an older, male-oriented work world, its views of a "real career," far more than men have taken up their share of the work at home. One reason women have changed more than men is that the world of "male" work seems more honorable and valuable than the "female" world of home and children.

So where do we go from here? There is surely no going back to the mythical 1950s family that confined women to the home. Most women don't wish to return to a full-time role at home—and couldn't afford it even if they did. But equally troubling is a workaholic culture that strands both men and women outside the home.

For a while now, scholars on work-family issues have pointed to Sweden, Norway and Denmark as better models of work-family balance. Today, for example, almost all Swedish fathers take two paid weeks off from work at the birth of their children, and about half of fathers and most mothers take additional "parental leave" during the child's first or second year. Research shows that men who take family leave when their children are very young are more likely to be involved with their children as they grow older. When I mentioned this Swedish record of paternity leave to a focus group of American male managers, one of them replied, "Right, we've already heard about Sweden." To this executive, paternity leave was a good idea not for the U.S. today, but for some "potential society" in another place and time.

Meanwhile, children are paying the price. In her book *When the Bough Breaks: The Cost of Neglecting Our Children,* the economist Sylvia Hewlett claims that "compared with the previous generation, young people today are more likely to underperform at school; commit suicide; need psychiatric help; suffer a severe eating disorder; bear a child out of wedlock; take drugs; be the victim of a violent crime." But we needn't dwell on sledgehammer problems like heroin or suicide to realize that children like those at Spotted Deer need more of our time. If other advanced nations with two-job families can give children the time they need, why can't we?

Author's Note: Over three years, I interviewed 130 respondents for a book. They spoke freely and allowed me to follow them through "typical" days, on the understanding that I would protect their anonymity. I have changed the names of the company and of those I interviewed, and altered certain identifying details. Their words appear here as they were spoken.—A.R.H.

RELIGION

44

THE PROTESTANT ETHIC AND THE SPIRIT OF CAPITALISM

MAX WEBER

The institution of religion is the topic of the following three selections. Sociologists have long studied how religion affects the social structure and the personal experience of individuals in society. Max Weber (1864–1920), for example, often placed the institution of religion at the center of his social analyses. Weber was particularly concerned with how changes in the institution of religion influenced changes in other social institutions, especially the economy. The selection excerpted here is from Weber's definitive and most famous study, *The Protestant Ethic and the Spirit of Capitalism* (1905). In his analysis of capitalism, Weber argues that the early Protestant worldviews of Calvinism and Puritanism were the primary factors in influencing the development of a capitalist economic system. Without the Protestant Reformation and a change in societal values toward rationality, capitalism would not have evolved as we know it today.

A product of modern European civilization, studying any problem of universal history, is bound to ask himself to what combination of circumstances the fact should be attributed that in Western civilization, and in Western civilization only, cultural phenomena have appeared which (as we like to think) lie in a line of development having *universal* significance and value. . . . All over the world there have been merchants, wholesale and retail, local and engaged in foreign trade. . . .

But in modern times the Occident has developed, in addition to this, a very different form of capitalism which has appeared nowhere else: the rational capitalistic organization of (formally) free labour. Only suggestions of it are found elsewhere. Even the organization of unfree labour reached a considerable degree of rationality only on plantations and to a very limited extent in the *Ergasteria* of antiquity. In the manors, manorial workshops, and domestic industries on estates with serf labour it was probably somewhat less developed. Even real domestic industries with free labour have definitely been proved to have existed in only a few isolated cases outside the Occident. . . .

Rational industrial organization, attuned to a regular market, and neither to political nor irrationally speculative opportunities for profit, is not, however, the only peculiarity of Western capitalism. The modern rational organization of the capitalistic enterprise would not have been possible without two other important factors in its development: the separation of business from the household, which completely dominates modern economic life, and closely connected with it, rational bookkeeping. . . .

Hence in a universal history of culture the central problem for us is not, in the last analysis, even from a purely economic view-point, the development of capitalistic activity as such, differing in different cultures only in form: the adventurer type, or capitalism in trade, war, politics, or administration as sources of gain. It is rather the origin of this sober bourgeois capitalism with its rational organization of free labour. Or in terms of cultural history, the problem is that of the origin of the Western bourgeois class and of its peculiarities, a problem which is certainly closely connected with that of the origin of the capitalistic organization of labour, but is not quite the same thing. For the bourgeois as a class existed prior to the development of the peculiar modern form of capitalism, though, it is true, only in the Western hemisphere.

Now the peculiar modern Western form of capitalism has been, at first sight, strongly influenced by the development of technical possibilities. Its rationality is today essentially dependent on the calculability of the most important technical factors. But this means fundamentally that it is dependent on the peculiarities of modern science, especially the natural sciences based on mathematics and exact and rational experiment. On the other hand, the development of these sciences and of the technique resting upon them now receives important stimulation from these capitalistic interests in its practical economic application. It is true that the origin of Western science cannot be attributed to such interests. Calculation, even with decimals, and algebra have been carried on in India, where the decimal system was invented. But it was only made use of by developing capitalism in the West, while in India it led to no modern arithmetic or book-keeping. Neither was the origin of mathematics and mechanics determined by capitalistic interests. But the *technical* utilization of scientific knowledge, so important for the living conditions of the mass of people, was certainly encouraged by economic considerations, which were extremely favourable to it in the Occident. But this encouragement was derived from the peculiarities of the social structure of the Occident. We must hence ask, from *what* parts of that structure was it derived, since not all of them have been of equal importance?

Among those of undoubted importance are the rational structures of law and of administration. For modern rational capitalism has need, not only of the technical means of production, but of a calculable legal system and of administration in terms of formal rules. Without it adventurous and speculative trading capitalism and all sorts of politically determined capitalisms are possible, but no rational enterprise under individual initiative, with fixed capital and certainty of calculations. Such a legal system and such administration have been available for economic activity in a comparative state of legal and formalistic perfection only in the Occident. We must hence inquire where that law came from. Among other circumstances, capitalistic interest have in turn undoubtedly also helped, but by no means alone nor even principally, to prepare the way for the predominance in law and administration of a class of jurists specially trained in rational law. But these interests did not themselves create that law. Quite different forces were at work in this development. And why did not the capitalistic interests do the same in China or India? Why did not the scientific, the artistic, the political, or the economic development there enter upon that path of rationalization which is peculiar to the Occident?

For in all the above cases it is a question of the specific and peculiar rationalism of Western culture. . . . It is hence our first concern to work out and to explain genetically the special peculiarity of Occidental rationalism, and within this field that of the modern Occidental form. Every such attempt at explanation must, recognizing the fundamental importance of the economic factor, above all take account of the economic conditions. But at the same time the opposite correlation must not be left out of consideration. For though the development of economic rationalism is partly dependent on rational technique and law, it is at the same time determined by the ability and disposition of men to adopt certain types of practical rational conduct. When these types have been obstructed by spiritual obstacles, the development of rational economic conduct has also met serious inner resistance. The magical and religious forces, and the ethical ideas of duty based upon them, have in the past always been among the most important formative influences on conduct. In the studies collected here we shall be concerned with these forces.

Two older essays have been placed at the beginning which attempt, at one important point, to approach the side of the problem which is generally most difficult to grasp: the influence of certain religious ideas on the development of an economic spirit, or the *ethos* of an economic system. In this case we are dealing with the connection of the spirit of modern economic life with the rational ethics of ascetic Protestantism. Thus we treat here only one side of the causal chain. . . .

. . . [T]hat side of English Puritanism which was derived from Calvinism gives the most consistent religious basis for the idea of the calling. . . . For the saints' everlasting rest is in the next world; on earth man must, to be certain of his state of grace, "do the works of him who sent him, as long as it is yet day." Not leisure and enjoyment, but only activity serves to increase the glory of God according to the definite manifestations of His will.

Waste of time is thus the first and in principle the deadliest of sins. The span of human life is infinitely short and precious to make sure of one's own election. Loss of time through sociability, idle talk, luxury, even more sleep than is necessary for health, six to at most eight hours, is worthy of absolute moral condemnation. It does not yet hold, with Franklin, that time is money, but the proposition is true in a certain spiritual sense. It is infinitely valuable because every hour lost is lost to labour for the glory of God. Thus inactive contemplation is also valueless, or even directly reprehensible if it is at the expense of one's daily work. . . .

[T]he same prescription is given for all sexual temptation as is used against religious doubts and a sense of moral unworthiness: "Work hard in your calling." But the most important thing was that even beyond that labour came to be considered in itself the end of life, ordained as such by God. St. Paul's "He who will not work shall not eat" holds unconditionally for everyone. Unwillingness to work is symptomatic of the lack of grace.

Here the difference from the mediæval viewpoint becomes quite evident. Thomas Aquinas also gave an interpretation of that statement of St. Paul. But for him labour is only necessary *naturali ratione* for the maintenance of individual and community. Where this end is achieved, the precept ceases to have any meaning. Moreover, it holds only for the race, not for every individual. It does not apply to anyone who can live without labour on his possessions, and of course contemplation, as a spiritual form of action in the Kingdom of God, takes precedence over the commandment in its literal sense. Moreover, for the popular theology of the time, the highest form of monastic productivity lay in the increase of the *Thesaurus eccleslic* through prayer and chant.

. . . For everyone without exception God's Providence has prepared a calling, which he should profess and in which he should labour. And this calling is not, as it was for the Lutheran, a fate to which he must submit and which he must make the best of, but God's commandment to the individual to work for the divine glory. This seemingly subtle difference had far-reaching psychological consequences, and became connected with a further development of the providential interpretation of the economic order which had begun in scholasticism.

It is true that the usefulness of a calling, and thus its favour in the sight of God, is measured primarily in moral terms, and thus in terms of the importance of the goods produced in it for the community. But a further, and, above all, in practice the most important, criterion is found in private profitableness. For if that God, whose hand the Puritan sees in all the occurrences of life, shows one of His elect a chance of profit, he must do it with a purpose. Hence the faithful Christian must follow the call by taking advantage of the opportunity. "If God show you a way in which you may lawfully get more than in another way (without wrong to your soul or to any other), if you refuse this, and choose the less gainful way, you cross one of the ends of your calling, and you refuse to be God's steward, and to accept His gifts and use them for Him when He requireth it: you may labour to be rich for God, though not for the flesh and sin.". . .

The superior indulgence of the *seigneur* and the parvenu ostentation of the *nouveau riche* are equally detestable to asceticism. But, on the other hand, it has the highest ethical appreciation of the sober, middle-class, self-made man. "God blesseth His trade" is a stock remark about those good men who had successfully followed the divine hints. The whole power of the God of the Old Testament, who rewards His people for their obedience in this life, necessarily exercised a similar influence on the Puritan who . . . compared his own state of grace with that of the heroes of the Bible. . . .

Although we cannot here enter upon a discussion of the influence of Puritanism in all . . . directions, we should call attention to the fact that the toleration of pleasure in cultural goods, which contributed to purely aesthetic or athletic enjoyment, certainly always ran up against one characteristic limitation: They must not cost anything. Man is only a trustee of the goods which have come to him through God's grace. He must, like the servant in the parable, give an account of every penny entrusted to him, and it is at least hazardous to spend any of it for a purpose which does not serve the glory of God but only one's own enjoyment. What person, who keeps his eyes open, has not met representatives of this viewpoint even in the present? The idea of a man's duty to his possessions, to which he subordinates himself as an obedient steward, or even as an acquisitive machine, bears with chilling weight on his life. The greater the possessions the heavier, if the ascetic attitude toward life stands the test, the feeling of responsibility for them, for holding them undiminished for the glory of God and increasing them by restless effort. The origin of this type of life also extends in certain roots, like so many aspects of the spirit of capitalism, back into the Middle Ages. But it was in the ethic of ascetic Protestantism that it first found a consistent ethical foundation. Its significance for the development of capitalism is obvious.

This worldly Protestant asceticism, as we may recapitulate up to this point, acted powerfully against the spontaneous enjoyment of possessions; it restricted consumption, especially of luxuries. On the other hand, it had the psychological effect of freeing the acquisition of goods from the inhibitions of traditionalistic ethics. It broke the bonds of the impulse of acquisition in that it not only legalized it, but (in the sense discussed) looked upon it as directly willed by God. . . .

As far as the influence of the Puritan outlook extended, under all circumstances—and this is, of course, much more important than the mere encouragement of capital accumulation—it favoured the development of a rational bourgeois economic life; it was the most important, and above all the only consistent influence in the development of that life. It stood at the cradle of the modern economic man.

To be sure, these Puritanical ideals tended to give way under excessive pressure from the temptations of wealth, as the Puritans themselves knew very well. With great regularity we find the most genuine adherents of Puritanism among the classes which were rising from a lowly status, the small bourgeois and farmers while the *beati possidentes,* even among Quakers, are often found tending to repudiate the old ideals. It was the same fate which again and again befell the predecessor of this worldly asceticism, the monastic asceticism of the Middle Ages. In the latter case, when rational economic activity had worked out its full effects by strict regulation of conduct and limitation of consumption, the wealth accumulated either succumbed directly to the nobility, as in the time before the Reformation, or monastic discipline threatened to break down, and one of the numerous reformations became necessary.

In fact the whole history of monasticism is in a certain sense the history of a continual struggle with the problem of the secularizing influence of wealth. The same is true on a grand scale of the worldly asceticism of Puritanism. The great revival of Methodism, which preceded the expansion of English industry toward the end of the eighteenth century, may well be compared with such a monastic reform. We may hence quote here a passage from John Wesley himself which might well serve as a motto for everything which has been said above. For it shows that the leaders of these ascetic movements understood the seemingly paradoxical relationships which we have here analysed perfectly well, and in the same sense that we have given them. He wrote:

> I fear, wherever riches have increased, the essence of religion has decreased in the same proportion. Therefore I do not see how it is possible, in the nature of things, for any revival of true religion to continue long. For religion must necessarily produce both industry and frugality, and these cannot but produce riches. But as riches increase, so will pride, anger, and love of the world in all its branches. How then is it possible that Methodism, that is, a religion of the heart, though it flourishes now as a green bay tree, should continue in this state? For the Methodists in every place grow diligent and frugal; consequently they increase in goods. Hence they proportionately increase in pride, in anger, in the desire of the flesh, the desire of the eyes, and the pride of life. So, although the form of religion remains, the spirit is swiftly vanishing away. Is there no way to prevent this—this continual decay of pure religion? We ought not to prevent people from being diligent and frugal; *we must exhort all Christians to gain all they can, and to save all they can; that is, in effect, to grow rich.*

As Wesley here says, the full economic effect of those great religious movements, whose significance for economic development lay above all in their ascetic educative influence, generally came only after the peak of the purely religious enthusiasm was past. Then the intensity of the search for the Kingdom of God commenced gradually to pass over into sober economic virtue; the religious roots died out slowly, giving way to utilitarian worldliness. Then, as Dowden puts it, as in *Robinson Crusoe,* the isolated economic man who carries on missionary activities on the side takes the place of the lonely spiritual search for the Kingdom of Heaven of Bunyan's pilgrim, hurrying through the market-place of Vanity. . . .

A specifically bourgeois economic ethic had grown up. With the consciousness of standing in the fullness of God's grace and being visibly blessed by Him, the bourgeois business man, as long as he remained within the bounds of formal correctness, as long as his moral conduct was spotless and the use to which he put his wealth was not objectionable, could follow his pecuniary interests as he would and feel that he was fulfilling a duty in doing so. The power of religious asceticism provided him in addition with sober, conscientious, and unusually industrious workmen, who clung to their work as to a life purpose willed by God.

Finally, it gave him the comforting assurance that the unequal distribution of the goods of this world was a special dispensation of Divine Providence, which in these differences, as in particular grace, pursued secret ends unknown to men. . . .

One of the fundamental elements of the spirit of modern capitalism, and not only of that but of all modern culture: Rational conduct on the basis of the idea of the calling, was born—that is what this discussion has sought to demonstrate—from the spirit of Christian asceticism. One has only to reread the passage from Franklin, quoted at the beginning of this essay, in order to see that the essential elements of the attitude which was there called the spirit of capitalism are the same as what we have just shown to be the content of the Puritan worldly asceticism, only without the religious basis, which by Franklin's time had died away. . . .

Since asceticism undertook to remodel the world and to work out its ideals in the world, material goods have gained an increasing and finally an inexorable power over the lives of men as at no previous period in history. Today the spirit of religious asceticism—whether finally, who knows?—has escaped from the cage. But victorious capitalism, since it rests on mechanical foundations, needs its support no longer. The rosy blush of its laughing heir, the Enlightenment, seems also to be irretrievably fading, and the idea of duty in one's calling prowls about in our lives like the ghost of dead religious beliefs. Where the fulfilment of the calling cannot directly be related to the highest spiritual and cultural values, or when, on the other hand, it need not be felt simply as economic compulsion, the individual generally abandons the attempt to justify it at all. In the field of its highest development, in the United States, the pursuit of wealth, stripped of its religious and ethical meaning, tends to become associated with purely mundane passions, which often actually give it the character of sport.

No one knows who will live in this cage in the future, or whether at the end of this tremendous development entirely new prophets will arise, or there will be a great rebirth of old ideas and ideals, or, if neither, mechanized petrification, embellished with a sort of convulsive self-importance. For of the last stage of this cultural development, it might well be truly said: "Specialists without spirit, sensualists without heart; this nullity imagines that it has attained a level of civilization never before achieved."

But this brings us to the world of judgments of value and of faith, with which this purely historical discussion need not be burdened. . . .

Here we have only attempted to trace the fact and the direction of its influence to their motives in one, though a very important point. But it would also further be necessary to investigate how Protestant Asceticism was in turn influenced in its development and its character by the totality of social conditions, especially economic. The modern man is in general, even with the best will, unable to give religious ideas a significance for culture and national character which they deserve. But it is, of course, not my aim to substitute for a one-sided materialistic an equally one-sided spiritualistic causal interpretation of culture and of history. Each is equally possible, but each, if it does not serve as the preparation, but as the conclusion of an investigation, accomplishes equally little in the interest of historical truth.

45

ABIDING FAITH

MARK CHAVES

Sociologists who study the institution of religion are documenting the changes occurring within this social institution. One current debate is whether religiosity is growing in the United States or if it is declining due to increasing secularization. In this reading, Mark Chaves, a professor of sociology at the University of Arizona, investigates this controversy and finds that contrary to popular opinion, Americans have not become more secular, but are as religious as ever. Chaves argues that organized religion occupies less of Americans' time and exerts less influence on society as a whole than it did in the past.

Mark Chaves and Dianne Hagaman, "Abiding Faith" from *Contexts* 1, no. 2 (Summer 2002): 19–26. Copyright © 2002 by American Sociological Association. Reprinted with permission.

God is dead—or God is taking over. Depending on the headlines of the day, soothsayers pronounce the end of religion or the ascendancy of religious extremists. What is really going on?

Taking stock of religion is almost as old as religion itself. Tracking religious trends is difficult, however, when religion means so many different things. Should we look at belief in the supernatural? Frequency of formal religious worship? The role of faith in major life decisions? The power of individual religious movements? These different dimensions of religion can change in different ways. Whether religion is declining or not depends on the definition of religion and what signifies a decline.

Perhaps the most basic manifestation of religious observance is piety: individual belief and participation in formal religious worship. Recent research on trends in American piety supports neither simple secularization nor staunch religious resilience in the face of modern life. Instead, Americans seem to believe as much but practice less.

Religious Belief

Conventional Judeo-Christian religious belief remains very high in the United States, and little evidence suggests it has declined in recent decades. Gallup polls and other surveys show that more than 90 percent of Americans believe in a higher power, and more than 60 percent are certain that God exists. Approximately 80 percent believe in miracles and in life after death, 70 percent believe in heaven, and 60 percent believe in hell. Far fewer Americans—from two in three in 1963 to one in three today—believe the Bible is the literal Word of God. The number who say the Bible is either the inerrant or the inspired Word of God is still impressively high, however—four of every five.

Religious faith in the United States is more broad than deep, and it has been for as long as it has been tracked. Of Americans who say the Bible is either the actual or the inspired Word of God, only half can name the first book in the Bible and only one-third can say who preached the Sermon on the Mount. More than 90 percent believe in a higher power, but only one-third say they rely more on that power than on themselves in overcoming adversity. People who claim to be born-again or evangelical Christians are no less likely than others to believe in ideas foreign to traditional Christianity, such as reincarnation (20 percent of all Americans), channeling (17 percent), or astrology (26 percent), and they are no less likely to have visited a fortune teller (16 percent).

Despite the superficiality of belief among many, the percentage of Americans expressing religious faith is still remarkably high. How should we understand this persistent religious belief? High levels of religious belief in the United States seem to show that, contrary to widespread expectations of many scholars, industrialization, urbanization, bureaucratization, advances in science and other developments associated with modern life do not automatically undermine religious belief. In part this is because modernization does not immunize people against the human experiences that inspire religious sentiment. As anthropologist Mary Douglas points out, scientific advances do not make us less likely to feel awe and wonder when we ponder the universe and its workings. For example, our feelings of deference to physicians, owing to their experience and somewhat mysterious scientific knowledge, may not be so different from the way other people feel about traditional healers—even if the outcomes of treatment are indeed different. Likewise, bureaucracy does not demystify our world—on the contrary, it may make us feel more helpless and confused in the face of powers beyond our control. When confronted with large and complex bureaucracies, modern people may not feel any more in control of the world around them than a South Pacific Islander confronted with the prospect of deep-sea fishing for shark. Modern people still turn to religion in part because certain experiences—anthropologist Clifford Geertz emphasizes bafflement, pain, and moral dilemmas— remain part of the human condition.

That condition cannot, however, completely explain the persistence of religious belief. It is clearly possible to respond in nonreligious ways to these universal human experiences, and many people do, suggesting that religiosity is a feature of some responses to these experiences, not an automatic consequence of the experiences themselves. From this perspective, attempting to explain religion's persistence by the persistence of bafflement, pain and moral paradox sidesteps a key question: Why do so many people continue to respond to these experiences by turning to religion?

Another, more sociological explanation of the persistence of religious belief emphasizes the fact that religion—like language and ethnicity—is one of the main ways of delineating group boundaries and collective identities. As long as who we are and how we differ from others remains a salient organizing principle for social movements and institutions, religion can be expected to thrive. Indeed, this identity-marking aspect of religion may also explain why religious belief often seems more broad than deep. If affirming that the Bible is the inerrant Word of God serves in part to identify oneself as part of the community of Bible-believing Christians, it is not so important to know in much detail what the Bible actually says.

The modern world is not inherently inhospitable to religious belief, and many kinds of belief have not declined at all over the past several decades. Certain aspects of modernity, however, do seem to reduce levels of religious observance. In a recent study of 65 countries, Ronald Inglehart and Wayne Baker find that people in industrialized and wealthy nations are typically less religious than others. That said, among advanced industrial democracies the United States still stands out for its relatively high level of religious belief. When asked to rate the importance of God in their lives on a scale of 1 to 10, 50 percent of Americans say "10," far higher than the 28 percent in Canada, 26 percent in Spain, 21 percent in Australia, 16 percent in Great Britain and Germany, and 10 percent in France. Among advanced industrial democracies, only Ireland, at 40 percent, approaches the U.S. level of religious conviction.

Religious Participation

Cross-national comparisons also show that Americans participate in organized religion more often than do people in other affluent nations. In the
United States, 55 percent of those who are asked say they attend religious
services at least once a month, compared with 40 percent in Canada, 38 percent in Spain, 25 percent in Australia, Great Britain, and West Germany, and
17 percent in France.

The trends over time, however, are murkier. Roger Finke and Rodney
Stark have argued that religious participation has increased over the course
of American history. This claim is based mainly on increasing rates of church
membership. In 1789 only 10 percent of Americans belonged to churches,
with church membership rising to 22 percent in 1890 and reaching 50 to
60 percent in the 1950s. Today, about two-thirds of Americans say they are
members of a church or a synagogue. These rising figures should not, however, be taken at face value, because churches have become less exclusive
clubs than they were earlier in our history. Fewer people attend religious
services today than claim formal membership in religious congregations, but
the opposite was true in earlier times. The long-term trend in religious participation is difficult to discern.

Although we have much more evidence about recent trends in religious
participation, it still is difficult to say definitively whether religious-service
attendance—the main way Americans participate collectively in religion—
has declined or remained stable in recent decades. The available evidence is
conflicting. Surveys using the traditional approach of asking people directly
about their attendance mainly show stability over time, confirming the consensus that attendance has not declined much.

New evidence, however, points toward decline. Drawing on time-use
records, which ask individuals to report everything they do on a given day,
Stanley Presser and Linda Stinson find that weekly religious-service attendance has declined over the past 30 years from about 40 percent in 1965 to
about 25 percent in 1994. Sandra Hofferth and John Sandberg also find a decline in church attendance reported in children's time-use diaries. Time-use
studies mitigate the over-reporting of religious-service attendance that
occurs when people are asked directly whether or not they attend. Also,
these time-use studies find the same lower attendance rates found by researchers who count the number of people who actually show up at church
rather than take them at their word when they say they attend.

Additional evidence of declining activity comes from political scientist
Robert Putnam's book on civic engagement in the United States, *Bowling
Alone*. Combining survey data from five different sources, Putnam finds
some decline in religious participation. Perhaps more important, because of
the context they provide, are Putnam's findings about a range of civic and
voluntary association activities that are closely related to religious participation. Virtually every type of civic engagement declined in the last third of the
20th century: voting, attending political, public, and club meetings, serving

as officer or committee member in local clubs and organizations, belonging to national organizations, belonging to unions, playing sports and working on community projects. If religious participation has indeed remained constant, it would be virtually the only type of civic engagement that has not declined in recent decades. Nor did the events of September 11, 2001, alter attendance patterns. If there was a spike in religious service attendance immediately following September 11, it was short-lived.

Overall, the following picture emerges from recent research: since the 1960s, Americans have engaged less frequently in religious activities, but they have continued to believe just as much in the supernatural and to be just as interested in spirituality. This pattern characterizes many other countries around the world as well. Inglehart and Baker's data suggest that American trends are similar to those in other advanced industrialized societies: declining religious activities, stability in religious belief, and increasing interest in the meaning and purpose of life.

Important differences among subgroups remain nonetheless. Blacks are more religiously active than whites, and women are more active than men. There is little reason to think, however, that the recent declines in participation vary among subgroups.

New forms of religious participation are not replacing attendance at weekend worship services. When churchgoers are asked what day they attended a service, only 3 percent mention a day other than Sunday. Perhaps more telling, when those who say they did not attend a religious service in the past week are asked if they participated in some other type of religious event or meeting, such as a prayer or Bible study group, only 2 percent say yes (although 21 percent of non-attendees say they watched religious television or listened to religious radio). The vast majority of religious activity in the United States takes place at weekend religious services. If other forms of religious activity have increased, they have not displaced traditional weekend attendance.

Overall, the current knowledge of individual piety in the United States does not conform to expectations that modernity is fundamentally hostile to religion. Many conventional religious beliefs remain popular, showing no sign of decline. That said, research on individual piety neither points to stability on every dimension nor implies that social changes associated with modernity leave religious belief and practice unimpaired. The evidence supports neither a simple version of secularization nor a wholesale rejection of secularization. Moreover, focusing on levels of religious piety diverts attention from what may be more important: the social significance of religion.

Of course, when many people are religiously active, religion can have more social influence. A society like the United States, with more than 300,000 religious congregations, presents opportunities for political mobilization that do not exist in societies where religion is a less prominent part of society. Witness the Civil Rights movement, the Religious Right and other causes that mix religion and politics. Nonetheless, religion in the United States, as in most other advanced societies, is organizationally separate from (even if occasionally overlapping) government, the economy and other parts of civil society. This limits a religion's capacity to change the world, even if it converts millions.

The social significance of religious belief and participation depends on the institutional settings in which they occur. This is why the religious movements of our day with the greatest potential for increasing religion's influence are not those that simply seek new converts or spur belief and practice, no matter how successful they may be. The movements with the greatest such potential are those that seek to expand religion's authority or influence in other domains. In some parts of the contemporary world, this has meant religious leaders seeking and sometimes achieving the power to veto legislation, dictate university curricula, exclude girls from schooling and women from working in certain jobs, and determine the kinds of art or literature offered to the public. In the United States, the most significant contemporary movement to expand religious influence probably is the effort to shape school curricula concerning evolution and creationism. Wherever they occur, when such movements succeed they change the meaning and significance of religious piety. Efforts like these reflect and shape the abiding role of religion in a society in ways that go beyond the percentages of people who believe in God, pray, or attend religious services.

RECOMMENDED RESOURCES

Chaves, Mark. 1994. "Secularization as Declining Religious Authority." *Social Forces* 72:749–74.

Gallup, George Jr. and D. Michael Lindsay. 1999. *Surveying the Religious Landscape.* Harrisburg, PA: Morehouse Publishing.

Hofferth, Sandra L. and John F. Sandberg. 2001. "Children at the Millennium: Where Have We Come From, Where Are We Going?" In *Advances in Life Course Research,* edited by T. Owens and S. Hofferth. New York: Elsevier Science. Also available at www.ethno.isr.umich.edu/06papers/html/.

Inglehart, Ronald and Wayne E. Baker. 2000. "Modernization, Cultural Change, and the Persistence of Traditional Values." *American Sociological Review* 65:19–51.

Presser, Stanley and Linda Stinson. 1998. "Data Collection Mode and Social Desirability Bias in Self-Reported Religious Attendance." *American Sociological Review* 63:134–45.

Putnam, Robert. 2000. "Religious Participation." In *Bowling Alone: The Collapse and Revival of American Community.* New York: Simon and Schuster.

46
_____

FAITH AT WORK

RUSSELL SHORTO

In the tradition of Max Weber (see Reading 44), who examined how the institution of religion influenced changes in the economy, this excerpt by Russell Shorto similarly investigates this relationship. In the United States, a growing number of evangelical and fundamentalist Christians are starting businesses they designate to be "Christian" workplaces. Many of these people identify themselves as *marketplace Christians* who operate their businesses as they think the Bible would tell them to. In this selection, Shorto, an author and contributing writer at the *New York Times Magazine,* interviews the people involved in running a Christian bank.

C huck Ripka is a moneylender—that is to say, a mortgage banker—and his institution, the Riverview Community Bank in Otsego, Minnesota, is a way station for Christ. When he's not approving mortgages, or rather especially when he is, Ripka lays his hands on customers and colleagues, bows his head and prays: "Lord, I pray that you will bring Matt and Jaimie the best buyer for their house so that they have the money to purchase the new home they feel called to. And I pray, Lord, that you grant me the wisdom to give them the best advice to meet their financial needs."

The bank is F.D.I.C. approved. It has a drop ceiling and fluorescent lighting. Current yield on a 30-year mortgage is 5.75 percent. The view out Ripka's office window is of an Embers chain restaurant. Yet for all the modern normalcy, the sensibility that permeates the place comes straight out of the first century A.D., when Christianity was not a churchbound institution but an ecstatic Jewish cult traveling humanity's byways.

The bank opened 18 months ago as a "Christian financial institution," with a Bible buried in the foundation and the words "In God We Trust" engraved in the cornerstone. In that time, deposits have jumped from $5 million to more than $75 million. The phone rings; it's a woman from Minneapolis who has $1.5 million in savings and wants to transfer it here. "I heard about the Christian bank," she tells Ripka, "and I said, 'That's where I want my money.'" Because of people like her, Riverview is one of the fastest growing start-up banks in the state, and if you ask Ripka, who is a vice president, or his boss, the bank president, Duane Kropuenske, whose office wall features a large color print of two businessmen with Christ, or Gloria

Oshima, a teller who prays with customers at the drive-up window, all will explain the bank's success in the same way. Jesus Christ has blessed them because they are obedient to his will. Jesus told them to take his word out of the church and bring it to where people interact: the marketplace.

Chuck Ripka says he sometimes slips and says to people, "Come on over to the church—I mean the bank." He's not literally a man of the cloth, but in the parlance of the initiated, he is a marketplace pastor, one node of a sprawling, vigorous faith-at-work movement. An auto-parts manufacturer in downtown Philadelphia. An advertising agency in Fort Lauderdale. An Ohio prison. A Colorado Springs dental office. A career-counseling firm in Portland, Oregon. The Curves chain of fitness centers. American Express, Intel. The Centers for Disease Control and Prevention. The I.R.S. The Pentagon. The White House. Thousands of businesses and other entities, from one-man operations to global corporations to divisions of the federal government, have made room for Christianity on the job, and in some cases have oriented themselves completely around Christian precepts. Well-established Christian groups, including the Billy Graham Evangelistic Association and the Promise Keepers, are putting money and support behind the movement. There are faith-at-work newsletters and blogs and books with titles like "God@Work," "Believers in Business" and "Loving Monday."

The idea is that Christians have for too long practiced their faith on Sundays and left it behind during the workweek, that there is a moral vacuum in the modern workplace, which leads to backstabbing careerism, empty routines for employees and C.E.O.'s who push for profits at the expense of society, the environment and their fellow human beings. No less a figure than the Rev. Billy Graham has predicted that "one of the next great moves of God is going to be through believers in the workplace." To listen to marketplace pastors, you would think churches were almost passé; for them work is the place, and Jesus is the antidote to both cubicle boredom and Enron-style malfeasance.

Os Hillman, a former golf professional and advertising executive in Georgia, is an unofficial leader of the movement. "We teach men and women to see their work as not just where they collect a check, but actually as their calling in life," he says. "We teach them to see what the Bible says about work, to see the spiritual value of their work." Through two organizations, the International Coalition of Workplace Ministries and Marketplace Leaders, Hillman and his wife, Angie, offer workshops, publish books and organize conferences. More than 900 "workplace ministries" are listed in I.C.W.M.'s member directory, and Hillman's faith-at-work e-mail devotional—which features stories noting that Jesus and the apostles all had jobs and that most of the parables in the New Testament have workplace settings—goes out to 80,000 subscribers daily.

Of course, Christianity isn't the only spiritual force in the workplace. There is an overarching faith-at-work movement afoot. Some companies are paying for, or at least allowing, workplace meditation sessions and Talmudic-study groups and shamanistic-healing retreats for employees. But this remains an overwhelmingly Christian nation. According to the Gallup polling organization (which itself fits into the subject of this article, as George Gallup Jr. is an evangelical Christian who has called his work "a kind of ministry"), 42 percent of Americans consider themselves evangelical or born again, and the aggressiveness with which some evangelicals are asserting their faith on the job suggests that the movement's impact, for better or worse, is going to come from them.

Most mainline Christian denominations have been slow to embrace the movement. Church leaders either haven't recognized it as significant or have determined that since it takes place outside the walls of their institutions, it is by definition not of concern to them. But some pastors are out in front of their leaders: they have left their churches to become workplace–ministry consultants or have landed jobs as "corporate chaplains," spiritual counselors hired by companies as a perk for employees. Rich Marshall, who is now a consultant, was a pastor in San Jose, Calif., for 25 years. "I realized what I was preaching in my pulpit wasn't helping people in their work lives," he says. "Now I'm on the road, speaking to businesspeople about integrating faith and work."

Looked at in light of some recent trends, there is a certain logic in all of this. First came the withering of the mainline Christian denominations and the proliferation of new, breakaway churches. Then consumerism took hold: today, many serious Christians are transient, switching churches and theologies again and again to suit their changing needs. With traditional institutions fragmenting and many people both hungry for spiritual guidance and spending more time at work than ever, it was perhaps inevitable that the job site would become a kind of new church.

When it comes to writing about religion, objectivity is a false god. In the interest of full disclosure, I would like to state here that my own orientation is secular but that I also believe that all religions have more or less equal dollops of spiritual truth in them, which become corrupted by personal and cultural dross. This puts me at a certain distance from most of the people in this article. For one thing, all the marketplace Christians I encountered were firmly of the belief that Christian truth is the only truth and that part of their duty as Christians is to save the unsaved.

My task, then, was to try to understand a phenomenon that has, from my perspective, an inherent conflict in it. One of the movement's objectives is to give Christians an opportunity to "out" themselves on the job, to let them express who they are, freely and without feeling persecuted. Few would argue with such a goal: it suits an open society. And if it increases productivity and keeps C.E.O.'s from turning into reptiles, all the better.

Then again, the idea of corporations dominated by a particular religious faith has a hint of oppressiveness, a "Taliban Inc." aspect. As it is, Christian holidays are the only official religious holidays in 99 percent of American workplaces surveyed by the Tanenbaum Center for Interreligious Understanding. Religious-discrimination complaints to the Equal Employment

Opportunity Commission have increased 84 percent since 1992 and 30 percent since 2000. Georgette Bennett, the director of the Tanenbaum Center, attributes the rise in part to the influx of workers from Asian and African countries and an overall aging of the largely Christian homegrown workforce, leading to a clash of traditions. "Added to that is the way in which religion has entered the public square and been politicized," she says.

Some friction may come from the insistence of marketplace Christians on seeing offices and factories as arenas for evangelism. Converting others, after all, is what being an evangelical Christian is all about. One tenet listed in the Riverview Community Bank's first annual report is to "use the bank's Christian principles to expand Christianity." If that wasn't clear enough, Ripka put it in even starker terms for me: "We use the bank as a front to do full-time ministry." Ken Beaudry, a marketplace pastor whose heating-oil company is just down the road from the Riverview bank, takes the same view. "It's all about understanding that your business has a cause," he says. "It's about recognizing that we exist as a company not just to make profits, but to change society. And our employees are on board with that."

On-the-job evangelism extends far beyond Ripka's community. In 2001, Angie Tracey, an employee at the Centers for Disease Control, organized what she calls a "comprehensive workplace ministry," among the first officially sanctioned employee religious groups within the federal government. She says that many colleagues have been "saved" at her group's Bible studies and other gatherings on government property, and she describes the federal agency's not-yet-saved employees as "fertile ground." Her program has spread rapidly within the C.D.C., and employees at other divisions of the federal government—the Census Bureau, the General Services Administration, the Office of Personnel Management—have contacted her about bringing the Word into their workplaces, too.

To explore this movement, I felt I needed a guide. Of all the marketplace pastors I spoke with, Ripka stood out at once in the intensity of his faith, his commitment to using his workplace as a vehicle for spreading it and his openness—his purity, if you will. There was also a modest personal connection between us; we are the same age and both grew up Catholic. After several telephone conversations, we made a kind of pact. He would welcome me into his bank and his home and would open up to me his world so that I might better understand why he and others think the faith-at-work movement is part of the next phase of Christianity.

And what would Ripka get in return? "The Lord told me you would call, Russell," he said in our first conversation. Through me, he would get a chance to spread the Word.

So, the first thing to know about Chuck Ripka is that he says Jesus talks to him—actually speaks to him, calling him "Chuck." Ripka is 45, a father of five and grandfather of two who has been married to his high-school sweetheart for 25 years. He has a compact build and pinprick eyes; he talks in a soft, rapid monotone. He once fasted for 40 days and 40 nights, just as Jesus did in the wilderness. He says he has performed more than 60 faith healings in the bank and has "saved" another 60 people on bank premises. Knowing him at first only via telephone, and listening to his talk of visions and voices and Satan and ecstatic healings, I began to think of him as potentially unbalanced. Yet on meeting him, I quickly discovered that he is a pillar of his community. The mayor stopped by his office for a chat while I was there. The chief of police and the superintendent of schools see him for prayer. He occasionally gives spiritual counseling to Carl Pohlad, the owner of the Minnesota Twins. Ripka runs a quarterly faith-in-the-workplace lunch, which attracts up to 260 area businesspeople. Many Christian business owners and residents say they consider him to be not only a community leader and an expert in small-business loans but also a conduit of the divine, a genuine holy man. . . .

[Ripka] worked odd jobs after high school and was born again when he was 21, during an Amway meeting. Shortly after, Jesus began talking to him. "I used to assume that all Christians heard God the way I do," he said. "But I realized over time that a lot of people don't hear, or they don't recognize, his voice. They think, 'Are these my thoughts or God's?'

Like many marketplace Christians, the Ripkas have an individualistic theology. Though they currently belong to a Christian and Missionary Alliance church—an evangelical subdivision that holds, among other things, that the second coming of Jesus Christ is imminent—they have changed churches often, and for periods of time have belonged to no church. One of Chuck's refrains is that he's no theologian: he can't rattle off scriptural citations to suit every situation. So while quite a few people look to him as a spiritual leader, his own faith is based not on a denomination's core doctrine so much as on inner voices and convictions.

An individual reliance on the voice of God is part of the increasingly free-form nature of charismatic and evangelical Christianity in America. It jibes with the tradition's ultimate goal—a personal relationship with Jesus Christ—but many evangelical leaders worry that it's dangerously subjective. "Pat Robertson is the one who uses it most: 'God told it to me,'" says Michael Cromartie, the director of the Evangelicals in Civic Life program of the Ethics and Public Policy Center, a conservative research center. "I think theologically that's unfounded." Nonetheless, it seems fairly common among marketplace pastors. Don Couchman, a dentist in Colorado who has made his dental practice a workplace ministry, related a story not long ago about how in the middle of performing a root canal, the Lord spoke to him and told him to go on a pilgrimage to Argentina. I interrupted to ask how he knew it was the Lord. "The sheep know the shepherd's voice," he said. (Some workplace Bible-study groups, including those at the Riverview bank, feature training in how to distinguish between God's voice and random thoughts.)

Ripka had his marketplace epiphany 20 years ago when he was a salesman at Levitz furniture in downtown St. Paul. "From out of the blue the Lord said to me, 'Chuck, one day you're going to pray with a customer,'" Ripka said. "Then several months later, I saw a man standing in the store looking at beds, and the Lord said, 'This is the one.' The man started to walk toward me, and I felt nervous and I said, 'Lord, I need your help.' The gentleman started to talk to me, and soon he was telling me he was divorced and his wife had custody of their children. Then he said: 'Why am I telling you this? I came in to buy a mattress.' I told him that three months before, the Lord told me someone would come in and we would pray together. So we did. And then something really important happened. The man bought a mattress. The Lord said, 'Chuck, I wanted to show you how to talk to people about me at work, and I wanted to prove to you that you would be able to do that and prosper.'"

It took some time, but when the Lord spoke next on the topic, he was very specific. "The Lord told me in 2000 that Duane Kropuenske and I were supposed to begin a new bank," Ripka said. Ripka worked for Kropuenske and his wife, Patsy, at a bank in the 90's. When the couple were considering opening a new one, they wanted to found it on Christian principles. "One day Duane came to me and said, 'The Lord told me I should talk to Chuck Ripka,'" Patsy Kropuenske says. When her husband got in touch with Ripka, Ripka was already expecting the call. Plans for Christianizing the bank expanded as they developed the project, with the three principals believing more every day that they were doing God's work.

As with all bankers, Ripka and the Kropuenskes care a lot about money, but they see it as a token of God's favor rather than a thing in itself. "The Lord spoke to me again on the day we opened," Ripka said. "He told me: 'Chuck, if you do all the things I want you to do, I promise I'll take care of the bottom line. I'm going to cause such a rate of growth, the secular world is going to take notice.' And that is happening."

————

One of the most striking things about the Riverview Community Bank is its location. This isn't exactly the Bible Belt. We are 30 miles northwest of Minneapolis, that bastion of Minnesota's secular-liberal tradition. The adjoining communities of Otsego and Elk River lie on either shore of a lazy bend in the Mississippi, a smaller mirror image of the Twin Cities to the south. This is big-sky country, a landscape of wide prairies and cornfield sunsets, but change is all around. Much that was farmland just a few years ago is now bustling exurbia, where brand-new Targets and OfficeMaxes and Applebees sit like boxy packages on the horizon. Few residents commute to Minneapolis or St. Paul; few seem even to venture there. They have their own culture, which is fast evolving, and religion is part of the change. The Minnesota stereotype of Garrison Keillor's Lake Wobegon—the pinched, resourceful, left-leaning Lutheran who eschews emotion—is becoming less common. There is more charismatic and evangelical expression in the state than ever before.

"I was born and raised here, and of course we were Lutherans," Patsy Kropuenske says. "Confessing your faith vocally—that wasn't our style. There's been a cultural change, and I feel it's something that's needed, with the way the world is going today. With all the terrorism and fear, people need guidance." She and her husband had long been serious about their faith: Duane sends $50 a month to support the televangelist Robert Schuller's

"Hour of Power" program and has a shelf of American eagle statuettes in his office to show for it. But when Chuck and Kathi Ripka healed Patsy's debilitating back pain in the bank, the day before it opened—laying their hands on her and praying—the healing demonstrated to her the kind of power Christ would bring to the bank, and she became more open in her faith.

As you drive along Route 101, heading here from Minneapolis, the bank is visible from three-quarters of a mile away: a massive temple-like structure of red stone blocks. Step inside, and you are softly assaulted by muted tones, wall-to-wall carpeting and curvilinear faux-wood desks—standard-issue bank décor. Spend some time, and you begin to soak up an atmosphere of, well, peace. It is a very calm, orderly place, governed by Christian principles from the ground up. Many marketplace pastors say they try to be fair and aboveboard with customers and competitors alike and will even refer business to a competitor they know can do a better job of meeting a client's needs. At the Riverview bank, Ripka says, they make a special point of arranging loans for "ethnic" churches in the Twin Cities, which typically have a hard time getting banks to approve them. And when customers are behind on payments, he says, Riverview will "give more grace" than the typical bank.

The atmosphere of calm extends to the bank's 42 employees, who seem strikingly contented. Most are Christians, meaning not merely that they were raised in a Christian household but that their faith is overt. "I've been in the banking business for 15 years, but this is my first Christian bank," says Shelly Nemerov, the operations officer, and laughs. "I was a Christian before, but I didn't have a relationship with God. Here, I've gone from saying I'm a Christian to actually being a Christian." She handles returned checks and overdrafts, and at some point, under the Riverview influence, she had a Christian epiphany about her work: "You hear constant problems—'I'm out of work,' 'My husband left me'—and I used to think. Yeah, I've heard it all before. Then it hit me: these people need help. So now I say: 'What can I help you do? Can I teach you how to balance an account or how to manage your money?' And I'll say, 'I think we should pray over this.'"

Praying with customers is one thing Riverview has become known for. Gloria Oshima, a teller, was hired because of her previous experience at the nearby First National Bank of Elk River, but her faith, which she describes as "bold," was also apparent in the job interview: "When Gloria came applying for a job, I had a vision of her praying with customers," Ripka says. Referring to the bank's drive-up window, Oshima says: "The Holy Spirit speaks to me when certain people drive up. A young lady pulled up one day. I looked at her, and she had tears in her eyes. I said: 'Are you O.K.? Would you mind if I prayed for you?' She said O.K. I said, 'Inside the bank, or right here?' She said, 'This is fine here.' So we prayed. I asked the Lord to remove the hurts within her and bless her day. She came again later, into the lobby this time, and she said, 'I'm doing so good, and I just wanted to thank you for your prayers.'"

Considering that many bank customers—those seeking loans, say, or involved in bankruptcy—are at a vulnerable moment in their lives, some may see this as preying on the weak. But the people at Riverview say they are only doing their jobs—their *real* jobs. They seem to have realized that they are in a unique position not only to offer comfort to people who are going through difficult times but also to zoom in on lost souls. Nemerov says that none of the bankrupt or overdrawn customers she has offered to pray with have ever said no, and she is confident she knows why: "Their hearts are already broken down and ready for it."

Well, all right, this is strange-sounding stuff. To someone unfamiliar with marketplace Christianity, the questions pile up. Is this legal? Aren't there separation-of-church-and-state issues here somewhere? What about discrimination?

As it happens, thanks to the value American law places on religious expression, proselytizing on the job is perfectly legal, even in a government workplace, even when it's the boss who is doing the pushing. If the legal aspects of the Christian-workplace phenomenon seem bewildering, it may be because, while the United States has always been a deeply religious nation, until recently it has also been fairly resolute about keeping faith out of the public sphere. Thomas Jefferson's famous metaphor of a wall of separation between church and state has long been a part of the national psyche. The historical reasons for erecting that wall are worth restating. The European experience of the 16th and 17th centuries, the effects of which carried over into the 18th, was of state-sponsored religious warfare, of populations decimated and minorities oppressed in the name of one branch of Christianity or another. Part of the genius and daring of the framers of the American system was in their decision to break with the European tradition of establishing a national church, in their conviction that religion was too combustible a material to be fused with political power.

You might think that recent religion-inspired violence would result in a renewed conviction to keep religion out of the public sphere, yet just the opposite has been happening. A major response in this country to Islamic terrorism has been a rippling of Christian muscle. In the post-9/11 universe, Christians have become more aggressive in pushing a religious agenda on social issues ranging from gay marriage to stem-cell research. "The whole war on terror has made evangelicals more politically engaged," says Michael Cromartie of the Ethics and Public Policy Center.

The workplace-ministry phenomenon, too, seems to have gained momentum since 9/11, but it is also part of the broad trend that began in the 80s with the rise of the Moral Majority and continued at the national political level with the emergence of the Christian Coalition. Many workplace ministries have received legal advice from the public-interest law firm the American Center for Law and Justice, which was founded in 1990 by Pat Robertson "to undo the damage done by almost a century of liberal thinking and activism." In 1990, there were about 50 coalitions of workplace ministries, according to Os Hillman's research; today there are thousands of businesses that, in the words of yet another consortium of workplace ministries, the

American Chamber of Christians in Business, have "Jesus Christ as our chairman of the board." And as with the Riverview Community Bank, they aren't restricted to the Bible Belt. Rich Marshall, a marketplace-ministry consultant and the author of "God @ Work," crisscrosses the country giving seminars on the topic. The week I spoke to him he was going to be in Los Angeles, El Paso and Rutland, Vt. Two years ago, Don Thomas, a Christian business executive in San Francisco, started looking for like-minded businesses in his famously liberal area with whom his company might ally and says he received "an overwhelming response." There are now 43 organizations in the Bay Area Coalition of Workplace Ministries.

The laws governing religion in the workplace are technically fairly clear, but in practice they can be nearly impossible to enforce. While proselytizing is legal, what is forbidden is religious harassment, the creation of a hostile work environment or using religion as a basis for hiring, raises or promotions. Businesses like the Riverview Community Bank are acutely aware of this. Ask Duane Kropuenske about a Christian litmus test for employees and he practically recites chapter and verse from the Civil Rights Act of 1964, which laid down the law on a wide variety of discrimination. "I have stressed when I hire people that it's based on their qualifications, and we have no intent to pressure them into any kind of religious experience," he says. They might choose to join one of the bank's Bible-study groups or pray with Chuck Ripka, but "it's not going to have any involvement with their next raise or promotion or that type of thing."

When I asked Ripka if a Jew or Muslim had ever applied for a job at the bank, his choice of language was a bit odd: "We don't really have that in our community at this point." But his response highlights some of the realities that govern many marketplace ministries. The population of the Otsego–Elk River area is well over 90 percent white and Christian, according to Stephanie Klinzing, the mayor of Elk River (who is herself a charismatic Catholic and an enthusiastic supporter of the bank and other Christian businesses in the community). Besides that, why would a Jew or Muslim or Hindu apply for a job at a business that is known throughout the area to the flamboyantly Christian? So there is a certain self-selecting aspect to a business that wears its faith on its sleeve.

Then, too, Ripka added that in its hiring the bank pays no mind to employees' religious backgrounds, and for a reason quite beyond mere legality. "It doesn't matter where they are in their walk," he said. "In the job interview, I sit down and explain to them that we're doing God's work at our bank. We don't say, 'You have to do this'"—meaning become as devout as some in the bank are—"but we say it's something that will probably happen." What you are isn't important, because they hope to make you into something new.

It doesn't always work. I spoke with one employee of the bank, who asked that her name not be used, and she told me that while she had been raised Catholic, she did not consider herself part of the bank's Christian culture. "You will never find me going into Chuck's office to pray," she said. On the other hand, she said that the bank was a "wonderful" place to work because "here the people are all nice—it's a healthy environment." Another employee, a young man who until recently worked at a competing bank, also said that while he hasn't given his soul to Jesus, he liked the wholesome atmosphere of Riverview, and that the only downside was having to put up with his former colleagues teasing him about his bosses making him say his prayers before bed.

There's a matter of competing rights in all of this. When you apply for a loan, or walk into a grocery store, or take your seat on an airplane, do you have a right to expect a secular atmosphere, uncontaminated by religiosity? Or is the greater right that of the company's owners to express their faith? For a long time, Alaska Airlines has included a prayer card with in-flight meals, a practice that was instituted by a former executive. "It has received mixed reviews, some people liking it and others writing to tell us they don't appreciate it," a spokesman for the airline says. No one has taken the airline to court over it, and in a case of the bottom line trumping all, the prayer cards have largely vanished as in-flight meals have. But the salient point is that under United States law, freedom of religious expression trumps many other rights.

A related factor is the surprisingly vague status of the workplace in the eyes of the law. You might think that the establishment clause of the First Amendment forbids religious expression in a federal workplace, but in 1997, President Clinton issued guidelines creating a broad area of religious freedom for federal employees, including the right to evangelize, while forbidding government endorsement of a religion. Curiously, the situation regarding corporations is less clear. Is a bank—or a restaurant or a factory or a corporate headquarters—in the public or the private realm? "The separation of church and state is as firmly established as any doctrine can be, but the separation of corporation and state is not nearly as well defined," says Alan Wolfe, director of the Boisi Center for Religion and American Public Life at Boston College. "An issue like the role of religion in the workplace is fuzzy because we've never defined the public nature of a corporation. And I think many corporations themselves have been confused about how to deal with it."

Beginning in the 90's, many large corporations were sued by employees who claimed discrimination in hiring and promotions because of race, gender or sexual orientation. In the aftermath, as a vehicle for handling diversity issues, some corporations formed or formalized employee "affinity groups"—complete with by-laws and objectives—that could meet on company property, often during the lunch hour, and would be given a small budget from the corporation. Some companies included religious groups in their roster of affinity groups; others balked—apparently confused about how to deal with religion.

"Employers thought if they allowed religious expression in the workplace, they would get in trouble legally," says Jay Sekulow, the chief counsel for the American Center for Law and Justice. "It was a knee-jerk response. But the tide has turned, and it's a much more receptive environment today." Not everyone is on board, though. General Motors is involved in a lawsuit right now brought by an employee who has demanded the right to form a Christian group under G.M.'s affinity-group program. Coca-Cola, as part of the settlement of a $192 million racial-discrimination suit brought by employees, agreed to establish affinity groups, but religious groups are not among them. There is a Christian group operating within the company, which the workplace–ministry leader Os Hillman points out as an example of the acceptance the movement has won at big corporations, but Coca-Cola begs to differ. "The Christian group here is almost an underground group, and they're certainly not company sanctioned," says Racquel White, a Coca-Cola spokeswoman. "We don't sanction political or religious groups. What happened was, a number of employee groups popped up after our discrimination suit. They're not supposed to be doing it. Our preference is to stay out of these types of stories. Frankly, we'd rather not even talk to you about it."

That kind of corporate thinking seems to be on the way out, however. "The large corporations tend to be agnostic, not only with respect to religion but everything," Alan Wolfe says. "They don't want to offend anybody who is a potential market. They tend to think of themselves as in the public sphere and to institute policies according to their perception of political correctness." . . .

But as Christianity moves into a broader arena, directly confronting some of the social mores that an open, secular society is built on, it presents a new challenge. A question that will probably be asked as the movement grows is: This is legal, but is it right? Protecting religion and religious expression is one hallmark of American society. Another is protecting minorities. And there is probably no more insidious form of bullying than religion.

It's possible, though, that the point will become moot. While marketplace Christianity has the law on its side—as well as America's deep arid historic regard for religious faith—other forces may work against it. Alan Wolfe says he thinks the phenomenon has a natural limit. Evangelicals and other Christians who are charged to spread the Word in secular society, he argues, face becoming contaminated by that society. Unlike fundamentalists, who withdraw from the secular culture, they engage it, using pop music, books, television and now the workplace to spread their message. But as you do that, the message becomes swamped by the might of the broader culture. Wolfe points to the Coors beer company as an example. "They used to be known as an evangelical company—never mind the fact that they were selling beer in the first place, a product that used to be considered a sin—but as they grew, that spiritual purity changed. Today their television advertisements are almost pornographic." The challenge, Wolfe says, is for the workplace ministries to keep their faith pure as they expand. As if on cue, the same day I spoke to Wolfe, Chuck Ripka called to tell me that the Riverview bank was expanding, adding its first branch in the town of Anoka, 10 miles away.

HEALTH AND MEDICINE

47

THE U.S. HEALTH CARE SYSTEM
On a Road to Nowhere?

JONATHAN OBERLANDER

Medical sociology is one of the largest and fastest growing sub-specialties within the discipline of sociology. Medical sociologists are concerned with all aspects of the social institution of medicine, including the socialization of doctors, the social construction of health and illness, and the social structure of hospitals and the health care system. The following three readings illustrate different perspectives within the field of medical sociology, beginning with an article by Jonathan Oberlander, an associate professor of political science at the University of North Carolina at Chapel Hill. In this selection, Oberlander critically examines the current state of the U.S. health care system and the future outlook for health care reform.

The health care system in the United States remains a "paradox of excess and deprivation."[1] The United States spends more on medical services than any other nation, and U.S. physicians earn more than their counterparts in Canada, Europe, and Japan. An extraordinary amount of money—as much as $300 billion annually—goes to pay just for the system's administrative costs.[2] Americans with insurance have access to the latest in sophisticated medical technology and innovative medical procedures; rates of diffusion for many medical technologies, such as magnetic resonance imaging, are higher in the United States than in other countries.[3] Indeed, the availability of these resources is so widespread that some analysts believe that well-insured Americans receive too many medical services.

At the same time, millions of Americans receive too little medical care. Over 40 million (and counting) Americans do not have health insurance, which makes the United States the only industrial democracy in the world with a substantial uninsured population. Even those with health insurance may be underinsured, lacking both coverage for key services and adequate financial protection against the costs of medical care.

The 1990s was a decade of great expectations in U.S. health policy—expectations that ultimately were not met. Health reform efforts in both the public and private sectors failed to resolve the major problems in American medical care. In 1993, President Bill Clinton proposed a government-sponsored system of universal health insurance, but despite initial optimism about its political prospects, the bill failed in Congress. After the defeat of the Clinton plan, the private market emerged as the engine of health care reform. The U.S. health insurance system moved toward "managed care" arrangements, with rising enrollment in health maintenance organizations (HMOs) and the growth of for-profit health plans. Proponents touted market-based reform as a solution to health care cost inflation and an opportunity to enhance both quality of care and patient choice. However, by decade's end a widespread backlash against managed care had developed, initial success in controlling costs had abated, and managed care's appeal as the latest magic bullet in American health policy was waning.

What is the state of the U.S. health care system after a decade of turbulence? What political dynamics are driving health policy? And what is the outlook for health care reform? This [reading] introduces readers to issues in American health policy and reviews the contemporary politics and future prospects of health care reform. In particular I focus on the persistent problem of the uninsured, efforts at cost control and incremental reform, and the rise and fall of managed care.

Little Progress for the Uninsured

The U.S. health care system is often erroneously labeled a private health care system. In fact, the United States has a mixed system of public and private insurance, though the word "system" connotes much more organization, rationale, and logic than is actually at work. Most working-age Americans receive health insurance through their employers (Table 1).[4] This private insurance is voluntary in the sense that companies are not required by law to provide health coverage, though employer-based insurance is subsidized by

TABLE 1   Sources of Health Insurance Coverage in the United States, 2002

Type of Coverage	Population Covered, %*
Any private plan	69.6
Employer-based plan	61.3
Government plan	25.7
Medicare	13.4
Medicaid	11.6
Military plan	3.5
None	15.2

*Total is not 100%, because some people have multiple sources of insurance.
Source: Source of data is U.S. Census Bureau.

federal tax policies (employers' premium contributions are tax exempt) at an annual cost to the government of over $100 billion in foregone revenues.[5] Medicare, a federal government program, provides health insurance to virtually all Americans over 65 years of age, as well as to persons with disabilities and end-stage renal disease. Medicaid, a jointly funded federal–state program, pays for medical services for low-income Americans (though it covers only about 40% of the poor), including seniors who spend down their incomes and assets to a level that qualifies them for Medicaid-funded nursing home care. In between those covered by this hodgepodge of private and public plans, however, lies a substantial population without any health insurance at all.

In 2003, 45 million Americans—15.6% of the population—lacked health insurance.[6] About 80% of the uninsured are workers or live in families with workers. They typically have low-wage jobs or work in small businesses in which the employer does not offer health insurance or, if it is offered, they cannot afford to purchase it. However, a growing share of the uninsured population is employed by large firms, a trend explained primarily by the decline in manufacturing jobs and reduced rates of unionization; companies such as Wal-Mart, the largest private employer in the United States, employ eligibility restrictions and long waiting periods on insurance coverage for part-time workers. The uninsured are also disproportionately of low income. In 2002, one-third of the poor were uninsured and nearly two-thirds of the uninsured had incomes less than 200% of the federal poverty line, or $29,000 for a family of 3.[7] A substantially higher percentage of black (20%) and Hispanic (32%) than white (14%) Americans were uninsured in 2002.[8]

Many Americans mistakenly believe that the uninsured obtain adequate medical care from hospital emergency rooms and other charity sources. Studies have consistently found, however, that the uninsured receive much less medical care than insured Americans.[9] Nearly 25% of uninsured children and 40% of uninsured adults have no regular source of medical care. The uninsured are much more likely to delay or forgo needed treatment, have their conditions diagnosed at a later stage, and be admitted to hospitals for avoidable conditions; overall, the uninsured use 50% fewer medical services than those with private insurance.[10] The Institute of Medicine estimates that 18,000 uninsured Americans die each year prematurely due to a lack of access to proper medical care.[11] Moreover, inadequate insurance coverage carries with it financial as well as medical risks: the costs of medical treatment are a leading cause of bankruptcy in the United States.[12] Indeed, about half of all bankruptcies in the United States "involve a medical reason or large medical debt."[13]

The number of uninsured Americans has climbed steadily upward since the 1980s. . . . During much of the 1990s the United States enjoyed ideal conditions for an expansion of health insurance. The economy went through an unprecedented era of sustained growth, the rates of general inflation and unemployment were both exceptionally low, and health care inflation moderated. Still, from 1990 to 1999 the number of uninsured Americans increased by nearly 8 million.

That even these favorable circumstances did not generate any significant expansion of health insurance was disquieting. It also revealed the limits of the market and the voluntary health insurance system, left to their own devices, to solve or even substantially ameliorate the problem of the uninsured. Nor did it bode well for the future when the inevitable economic downturn would come and pressure the employment-based health insurance system. Indeed, economic growth slowed in 2000, and in 2001 in the aftermath of the September 11 attacks, the United States entered a recession with substantially higher rates of unemployment. The predictable result of job loss was a sharp increase in the ranks of the uninsured: in 2002, the number of uninsured Americans rose by 2.4 million, the biggest one-year increase in America's uninsured population since 1992.[14]

In coming years, a reenergized economy could well slow the rate of growth in the uninsured population, but it will not reverse the long-term trend. For the foreseeable future, the number of uninsured Americans is likely to continue to grow absent government action.

The Politics of Health Insurance

National health insurance periodically emerged on the U.S. political agenda during the 20th century and occasionally was tantalizingly close to enactment. The most recent failure came in 1994, with the defeat of the Health Security Act, sponsored by President Bill Clinton (and drafted under the guidance of his wife, Hillary Rodham Clinton). President Clinton proposed to achieve universal coverage in the United States by mandating that all employers provide private health insurance to their employees and by giving small businesses and unemployed Americans subsidies with which to purchase insurance. However, the Clinton plan triggered fierce opposition from the insurance industry (which disliked the proposed limits on their profits and regulation of behaviors, such as experience rating, that enabled them to charge higher premiums for sick patients), the business community (which criticized the employer mandate), ideological conservatives who saw the plan as an unwarranted nationalization of the health care system), and large segments of the public (who were anxious about the plan's emphasis on moving patients into HMOs). Confronted with this opposition, and despite Democratic Party majorities in both the House of Representatives and Senate, the Clinton health plan—along with all other compromise proposals—was defeated. The American Medical Association, which initially endorsed and then waffled on the idea of universal coverage, did not play a prominent role in the 1993–1994 debate, a sign of its deteriorating influence on U.S. health politics.

One legacy of the Clinton plan's failure was caution regarding health policy. Most politicians took the lesson of the plan's demise to be that comprehensive reform was not politically feasible. Consequently, from 1994 to 2003 talk of attaining universal coverage all but disappeared from the political landscape. Neither of the two major parties' presidential candidates in the 2000 election, Al Gore and George W. Bush, offered plans that would cover all or even most of the uninsured. Nor did any legislation for universal coverage that had a serious chance of passing emanate from Congress during this decade. One of the only organized advocacy groups for the uninsured, Families USA, even toned down its calls for universal coverage in favor of more modest policy goals. . . .

It is clear, then, that the most relevant fact about U.S. health politics is not that 15% of the population is uninsured but that 85% of Americans are insured. Those who are insured are generally satisfied with their own medical care, even if they think poorly of the system as a whole; consequently, they are not a reliable constituency for change. Indeed, any reform that threatens to alter the medical care arrangements of the well insured is likely to provoke public opposition. The formidable constituency—led by the insurance industry—against reform is mobilized, wealthy, and politically influential. Meanwhile, the uninsured are disproportionately low-income, unorganized, and apparently politically expendable. As the Clinton plan vividly demonstrated, the political benefits to a president and legislators willing to take on a $2 trillion health care industry that literally profits from the status quo and opposes reform are uncertain, but the political costs are certain to be high. The result is that universal coverage remains an elusive reform in the United States, and the uninsured continue to live in an "aura of invisibility."[15]

Incremental Reforms

In the aftermath of the Clinton plan's defeat, there was little appetite for comprehensive reforms that would assure universal coverage. One consequence was resort to a familiar foundation of American political life: federalism. By virtue of federal inaction, states became the locus for health care reform, as Oregon, Vermont, and Tennessee, among others, implemented ambitious reforms to expand access to health insurance.[16] Focused largely on extending coverage to low-income children and adults, these reforms represented a political success story when contrasted with the deadlock over health policy in Washington, D.C. However, while some states achieved noteworthy reductions in their uninsured rate, no state came close to attaining universal coverage; initial aspirations for coverage gains and cost savings were often not met, and economic troubles and budgetary shortfalls created pressures that threatened the sustainability of much-heralded state programs like the Oregon Health Plan and Tenncare. In 2002, none of the aforementioned reform-minded states had uninsured rates lower than 9%.[17] There appeared to be very real limits, then, to the potential of state-led health reform to cope with the uninsured problem.

At the federal level, incrementalism was in vogue. In 1996 Congress adopted the Health Insurance Portability and Accountability Act (HIPAA), which was designed to limit preexisting condition exclusion periods and make it easier for workers losing group coverage to purchase health insurance on the individual market. However, the law's insurance market reforms did not address the affordability of individual market health policies, limiting its impact on the uninsured. In 1997, Congress enacted the State Children's Health Insurance Program (SCHIP), which targeted children who lived in families with incomes below 200% of the federal poverty line but who were not eligible for Medicaid. By 2003, 4 million children were enrolled in SCHIP (funded through a federal block grant to the states), and the program helped reduce the percentage of uninsured low-income children by one-third between 1997 and 2002. However, faced with severe budget shortfalls, following the 2001 recession some states instituted enrollment freezes and waiting lists for children applying for SCHIP, potentially "undermin[ing] further progress toward reducing this number."[18] . . .

Yet the era of moderate medical care inflation that made inattention to cost control comfortable in the mid-1990s has ended. Absent cost control, incremental reforms may become self-defeating: higher rates of medical care inflation could lead to growing numbers of uninsured persons and higher than expected program costs, making expansion of insurance coverage less affordable, more politically problematic, and ultimately undercutting prior incremental gains in coverage. Higher costs for medical care would also increase the gap between the size of tax credits and the price of health insurance.

The Rise of Managed Care

U.S. medical care has long been the most expensive in the world, thanks to higher prices and provider incomes, greater administrative costs, and more extensive use of some costly medical procedures and technologies than other nations.[19] The defeat of comprehensive health reform in 1994 did not obviate the pressures to control health spending; rather, it shifted the engine of control to the private sector. Employers looking to hold down their medical bills embraced managed care and, in a staggeringly short time, managed care became the norm in U.S. health insurance. By 2000, 92% of persons with employer-sponsored insurance were enrolled in a managed care plan.[20] Managed care also spread to public programs for the poor, elderly, and disabled—Medicare and Medicaid—though enrollment of elderly Medicare beneficiaries in such plans was far lower than for the employer-sponsored population.

"Managed care" came to refer to a wide range of health plans and practices that departed from the traditional American model of insurance. In the traditional model, insured patients chose their physician; physicians treated patients with absolute clinical autonomy; insurers generally paid physicians whatever they billed on a fee-for-service basis; and employers paid premiums for their workers to private insurers, footing the bill regardless of the cost. Managed care altered all of these arrangements. As a consequence of not having national health insurance, cost control in the United States focused more on setting limits on the individual medical encounter ("managing care") than on establishing budgetary limits for the entire health care sector.

The rise of managed care brought about four major changes in U.S. medical care. First was the substantial decline in traditional insurance arrangements, which allowed unfettered access to physicians and unregulated delivery of medical care. The proportion of Americans with employer-sponsored indemnity coverage declined from 95% in 1978 to 14% by 1998.[21] This drop was accompanied by an increase in enrollment in a wide variety of managed-care insurance programs, including HMOs, preferred provider organizations (PPOs), and point of service plans (POs). Not only did HMOs grow in enrollment—from 36.5 million in 1990 to 58.2 million in 1995—but they also changed substantially in form. In particular, there was rapid growth in for-profit HMOs as well as network and individual-practice association (IPA) models that contracted with providers; in contrast group or staff-model HMOs (such as Kaiser Permanente) owned their facilities, and physicians worked exclusively for them. Yet, while they continued to be regarded as the symbol of managed care, the growth of HMOs stalled in the late 1990s, and by 2003, PPOs covered more than twice as many Americans (54%) with employer-provided insurance than HMOs (24%).[22]

Second, patients in managed care received full coverage for services only if they chose a physician within the plan's network. In the case of HMOs, patients generally received no coverage if they saw an out-of-network provider. In some plans, patients had to go through a gatekeeper, typically a primary care physician, to obtain a specialty referral. The corollary was that many insurers no longer contracted with all physicians in a community. Rather, they selectively contracted with a limited number of doctors, negotiating price discounts in exchange for guaranteed patient volume and excluding high-cost providers.

Third, physicians' decisions were regularly subject to external review by insurance plans. Indeed, U.S. physicians probably experienced more intrusion into their clinical lives than physicians anywhere in the industrialized world, an ironic development given that the American Medical Association long opposed national health insurance as a threat to clinical autonomy.[23] Under utilization review arrangements, physicians had to seek permission from the patient's insurance company for admission to a hospital, diagnostic tests, or medical procedures. Utilization review and physician profiling also occurred after treatment, with the goal of identifying "inappropriate" or "excessive" care according to the insurer's standards. Proponents of managed care argued that these practices could not only control costs but also enhance quality of care—for instance, by assuring adherence to evidence-based medicine and eliminating medically unnecessary services.

Fourth, insurers no longer gave physicians a blank check; instead, they dictated not only what doctors were paid but also how they were paid. This led to the widespread adoption of predetermined fee schedules for physician payment by managed care plans, which sought discounts from "normal" fees. HMOs also adopted capitated payment, often focusing on primary care providers. Under capitated payment, physicians received a set amount for each patient enrolled in their practice, regardless of that patient's actual use of services. The stated aim was to avoid the financial incentive for overtreatment inherent in fee-for-service payment. Another important change in payment arrangements was the introduction of bonuses and other incentives for physicians to meet targets in providing care. Frequently these incentives were aimed at ensuring that physicians held down costs in a capitated environment; for instance, bonuses were provided to physicians whose rate of admission to hospital for their patient pool was lower than the insurer's target. Along with capitation, these arrangements put the incomes of many physicians at substantial risk.[24]

The Impact of Managed Care on Costs and Quality

After the spread of managed care in the early 1990s, health care spending in the United States slowed. From 1993 to 1998, the share of gross domestic product (GDP) devoted to national health spending declined from 13.7% to 13.5%, and premiums for employer-sponsored health insurance actually grew more slowly than per capita GDP.[25] From 1994 to 1997, per capita medical care spending rose by an annual average of 2.4%. In historical terms, this was a period of remarkable restraint in U.S. medical spending, though the United States continued to spend far more on medical care than any other nation. . .

Evidence for the impact of managed care on the quality of care during the 1990s was mixed. Most studies found little difference in quality of care between traditional insurers and managed care plans, though there was some evidence of worse outcomes for chronically ill seniors in HMOs.[26] In addition, higher rates of managed care plans' market penetration were associated with physicians providing lower rates of charity and uncompensated care to uninsured patients.

That quality of medical care in many cases did not deteriorate, despite reduced volume and intensity of services, suggested that the previous standard of "unmanaged" care incorporated significant amounts of unnecessary services. However, these findings also cast doubt on the premise that managed care was improving quality through practice guidelines, preventive care, primary care, disease management, integrated delivery systems, and other strategies. Too often, these strategies existed more as marketing labels than as workable or proven innovations, though that did not stop them from being aggressively promoted outside the United States, often to receptive audiences overseas looking for new levers to control costs and improve quality and consumer service. Yet managed care plans in the United States had not consistently implemented these practices, and market competition did not result in significant quality improvements. Instead, plans focused on managing costs, a decision reinforced by employers, who were much more likely to select insurance on the basis of price than on the basis of quality.

The End of Managed Care?

Regardless of the evidence, there was strong sentiment among both physicians and patients that managed care was harming quality of care. Consequently, a backlash against managed care emerged, culminating in a push to enact patients' bills of rights and other laws that regulated the behavior of managed care plans. In the 1990s, the 50 U.S. states adopted 900 such laws, including reforms that established procedures for appealing health plan decisions, assured coverage of emergency room visits, banned "gag clauses" that prevented physicians from discussing treatment options, and guaranteed access to specialists.[27] These laws were popular with legislators precisely because they served to reassure the voting public that something was being done about HMO abuses, though the effectiveness of many of these provisions was uncertain. The issue also drew national political attention in the late 1990s, but Congress deadlocked over competing versions of a Patient's Bill of Rights and failed to pass a bill.

Legislative activity, however, was not the only source or sign of growing disenchantment with managed care. By the end of the 1990s, managed care plans, in reaction to patient and doctor complaints, were loosening many of their restrictions on health care utilization, such as gatekeeping requirements, and broadening previously restricted physician and hospital networks.[28] The decline in HMO enrollment and shift to looser insurance arrangements like PPOs was another indication of dissatisfaction with managed care's constraints on access to medical care. PPOS were commonly regarded by analysts as an insurance model "particularly incapable of managing quality or cost,[29] and arguably had more in common with traditional insurance than they did with HMOs. Employers, who had triggered the managed care revolution, also retreated from their embrace of HMOs and aim of managing workers' medical experiences, partly in response to tight labor market conditions that advantaged workers. Thus the vision of managed care ushering in a new world in American medical care, a system of integrated health plans based on capitation, managed competition, and quality innovation had been, at best, deferred; others saw it as having collapsed altogether.[30]

The cause of managed care's deteriorating ability to hold down costs was again debated, with some analysts blaming the politically inspired managed care backlash or providers' success in consolidating to gain market power and economic leverage over health plans. Others argued managed care's ability to slow health spending always had been exaggerated and that it did little to stem the most important long-term factor in rising costs: development and diffusion of costly medical technology. Nor did managed care do much, critics argued, to curtail the prohibitive administrative costs of American medicine. In any case, as managed care lost its capacity to control costs, the willingness of key constituencies to tolerate its limitations, which has been tenuous even at its apex, evaporated.

By 2001 managed care's future appeared sufficiently bleak that one prominent analyst declared the "end of managed care."[31] This may well be a premature declaration—despite the backlash, the U.S. health care system has not gone back to what it was before. HMOs continue to be a significant presence in U.S. health insurance and many managed care practices remain prevalent. Indeed, interest in some forms of care management still appears to be growing. There is ongoing development, for instance, of quality initiatives that manage the care of chronically ill patients. And rising levels of medical care spending and insurance premiums could lead to a resurgence of managed care–style cost controls, perhaps under a politically more palatable label such as "enhanced care." To be sure, though, the confidence that managed care can swiftly cure the ills of American medicine which characterized the early 1990s has been lost.

Conclusion

After a decade of much anticipated changes and largely failed efforts at health reform, the United States appears to be no closer to solving the problems of cost control and access that have characterized its health care system for the past three decades. The number of uninsured is once again marching ever upward, and after the experiment with managed care and market competition, health care spending is again climbing at a steep rate. Where does health reform in the United States go from here?

The market is already moving past managed care onto the next supposed magic bullet: consumer-driven health care. Under this rubric a variety of trends are touted, including the proliferation of web-based medical information and Internet technology that allows employees to tailor their own custom-made health benefits packages and provider networks.[32] Consumer-driven health care also refers to health insurance arrangements that combine high-deductible catastrophic coverage with medical or health savings accounts to pay for "routine" expenditures. While such arrangements have potential appeal for healthy and wealthy patients (as well as employers looking to limit their annual health care bill to a defined contribution), they will not help high-cost, chronically ill patients who desire more health security and could be hit hard financially by higher deductibles. As a result, if consumer-driven plans spread in employer-provided insurance, the American health insurance system could further segment on the basis of health risk.[33]

Another market trend (often grouped under the same banner of consumerism) is rising patient cost-sharing in the form of increases in employees' share of premiums, as well as higher deductibles and larger copayments that may vary according to patients' choice of hospitals or physicians from tiered (differentially priced) networks of medical care providers.[34] The focus on increasing cost sharing (known as "buying down" coverage) represents a tool for employers looking to limit their bill for rising insurance premiums, as well as a shift away from HMOs' earlier efforts to limit financial barriers to primary care. While increasing patient cost-sharing may not constrain overall inflation in medical care, it nonetheless appeals to companies as an effective form of cost shifting that moves the burden of rising health costs onto employees.

Consumer-driven health care is thus the magic bullet *du jour* in U.S. health policy, but it still comprises a minority of the insurance market, and its ultimate impact and staying power are difficult to predict. After all, "revolutionary" changes in health care that were once much anticipated have, in retrospect, looked more like ill-fated fads. The future direction of market-led changes in the health system is consequently uncertain. We can, though, based on the history of American health care predict three dynamics with a high degree of confidence: first, issues of cost control will dominate the agenda for U.S. employers; second, there will be ongoing innovations in insurance products and experimentation with payment mechanisms that promise to address these problems; and third, these innovations will not resolve the cost issue and may exacerbate other problems (such as inequalities in access to health insurance).

In the political arena, there is now renewed interest—driven by the familiar combination of rising costs, eroding access, and economic insecurity—in health reform proposals that expand insurance coverage. . . .

Yet despite these possibilities it is not clear that health reform will move beyond (if it can get there) the limited steps of incrementalism, which would leave much of the uninsured population untouched and fall far short of universal coverage. Prospects for systemwide cost controls in the United States are even more remote. Although rising prescription drug prices may continue to draw political attention, there is currently little enthusiasm in the American polity for the type of global budget constraints that other nations' health systems employ.

Time and again over the last century, reformers have discovered new reasons why the enactment of universal coverage is imminent, only to be bitterly disappointed when reform turned out to be a mirage. The resilience of the status quo in American health policy should never be underestimated. The more things change in U.S. health policy, the more they seem to stay the same.

ENDNOTES

Author's Note: The author gratefully acknowledges the support of the Greenwall Foundation and Larry Churchill for his invaluable comments. I would also like to thank Kathy Griggs for her assistance in preparing this essay. The original essay has been revised for this edition.

[1] Enthoven, A. and R. A. Kronick. 1989. "Consumer Choice Plan for the 1990s." *New England Journal of Medicine* 320:29.

[2] Woolhandler, S., T. Campbell, and D. U. Himmelstein. 2003. "Costs of Health Care Administration in the United States and Canada." *New England Journal of Medicine* 349:768–75.

[3] Rublee, D. 1994. "Medical Technology in Canada, Germany and the United States." *Health Affairs* (Millwood) 13:113–17.

[4] U.S. Census Bureau. 2003. *Health Insurance Coverage 2002*. Washington, DC: The Bureau.

[5] Burman, L. E., C. E. Uccello, L. Wheaton, et al. 2003. *Tax Subsidies for Private Health Insurance*. Washington, DC: Urban Institute. Retrieved June 8, 2004 (http://www.urban.org/urlprint.cfm?ID=843).

[6] U.S. Census Bureau. 2003. *Health Insurance 2002*. Washington, DC: The Bureau.

[7] Kaiser Commission on Medicaid and Uninsured. 2003. *Health Insurance Coverage in America*. Washington, DC: Kaiser Family Foundation.

[8] U.S. Census Bureau. 2003. *Health Insurance Coverage 2002*. Washington, DC: The Bureau.

[9] Ayanian, J. Z., J. S. Weissman, E. D. Schneider, J. A. Ginsburg, and A. M. Zaslavsky. 2000: "Unmet Health Needs of Uninsured Adults in the United States." *JAMA* 284:2061–69.

[10] Kaiser Commission on Medicaid and the Uninsured. 2001. *The Uninsured and Their Access to Health Care*. Washington, DC: Kaiser Family Foundation.

[11] Institute of Medicine. 2002. *Care without Coverage: Too Little, Too Late*. Washington, DC: National Academy Press.

[12] Crenshaw, A. 2000. "Study Cites Medical Bills for Many Bankruptcies." *Washington Post*, April 25, sec. E, p. 1.

[13] Himmelstein, D. and S. Woodhandler. 2001. *Bleeding the Patient: The Consequences of Corporate Health Care*. Monroe, ME: Common Courage Press. Pp. 24–25.

[14] Kaiser Commission on Medicaid and the Uninsured. 2003. *Health Insurance Coverage in America*. Washington, DC: Kaiser Family Foundation. P. 3.

[15] Grumbach, K. 2000. "Insuring the Uninsured: Time to End the Aura of Invisibility." *JAMA* 284:214–16.

[16] Leichter, H. M., ed. 1997. *Health Policy Reform in America: Innovations from the State*. 2nd ed. Armonk, NY: M. E. Sharpe.

[17] U.S. Census Bureau. 2003. *Health Insurance Coverage 2002*. Washington, DC: The Bureau.

[18] Kaiser Commission on Medicaid and the Uninsured. 2003. *Out in the Cold: Enrollment Freezes in Six State Children's Health Insurance Programs Withhold Coverage from Eligible Children*. Washington, DC: Kaiser Family Foundation. P. 1.

[19] Anderson, G. F., J. Hurst, P. S. Hussey, and M. Jee-Hughes. 2000. "Health Spending and Outcomes: Trends in OECD Countries, 1960–1998." *Health Affairs* (Millwood) 19:150–57.

[20] Gabel, J. R., L. Levitt, J. Pickreign, H. Whitmore, E. Holve, S. Hawkins, et al. 2000. "Job-Based Health Insurance in 2000: Premiums Rise Sharply While Coverage Grows." *Health Affairs* (Millwood) 19(5):144–51.

[21] Gabel, J. R., P. B. Ginsburg, H. H. Whitmore, and J. D. Pickreign. 2000. "Withering on the Vine: The Decline of Indemnity Health Insurance." *Health Affairs* (Millwood) 19(5):152–57.

[22] Kaiser Family Foundation. *Employer Health Benefits, 2003 Annual Survey Chart Pack*. Menlo Park, CA. P. 9.

[23] Starr, P. 1982. *The Social Transformation of American Medicine*. New York: Basic.

[24] Bodenheimer, T. 1999. "Physicians and the Changing Medical Marketplace." *New England Journal of Medicine* 340:585–88.

[25] Levit, K., C. Cowan, H. Lazenby, A. Sensening, P. McDonnell, J. Stiller, et al. 2000. "Health Spending in 1998: Signals of Change." *Health Affairs* (Millwood) 19:124–32.

[26] Miller, R. H. and H. S. Luft 1997. "Does Managed Care Lead to Better or Worse Quality of Care?" *Health Affairs* (Millwood) 16:7–25.

[27] Cauchi, R. 1999. "Managed Care: Where Do We Go From Here?" National Conference of State Legislatures. Retrieved June 8, 2004 (http://www.ncsl.org/programs/pubs/399mancare.htm).

[28] Robinson, J. C. 2001. "The End of Managed Care." *JAMA* 285:2622–28.

[29] Enthoven, A. C. 2003. "Market Forces and Efficient Health Care Systems." *Health Affairs* (Millwood) 23:25.

[30] Nichols, L. M., P. B. Ginsburg, R. A. Berenson, et al. 2004. "Are Market Forces Strong Enough to Deliver Efficient Health Care Systems? Confidence Is Waning." *Health Affairs* (Millwood) 23:13, 16.

[31] Robinson, J. C. 2001. "The End of Managed Care." *JAMA* 285:2622–28.

[32] Gabel, J., A. T. Lo Sasso, and T. Rice. 2002. "Consumer-Driven Health Plans: Are They More Than Talk Now?" *Health Affairs* Web Exclusive. Retrieved June 8, 2004 (http://content. healthaffairs.org/cgi/content/full/hlthaff.w2.395V1/DC1).

[33] Fuchs, V. R. 2002. "What's Ahead for Health Insurance in the United States?" *New England Journal of Medicine* 346:1822–24.

[34] Regopoulos, L. E. and S. Trude. 2004. "Employers Shift Rising Health Care Costs to Workers: No Long-Term Solution in Sight." Issue Brief 83. Washington, DC: Center for Studying Health System Change. Retrieved June 8, 2004 (http://www.hschange.org/CONTENT/677).

48

DYING ALONE
The Social Production of Urban Isolation

ERIC KLINENBERG

One important aspect of medical sociology is the study of social inequalities caused by the distribution and treatment of certain diseases. That is to say, how do *morbidity* (sickness) and *mortality* (death) vary between people of different races, genders, and social class backgrounds? This excerpt is taken from Eric Klinenberg's award-winning book *Heat Wave: A Social Autopsy of Disaster in Chicago* (2002). In this selection, Klinenberg, an associate professor of sociology at New York University, examines how age, poverty, and urban isolation led to an excess of deaths among the elderly during the July 1995 Chicago heat wave.

There is a file marked "Heat Deaths" in the recesses of the Cook County morgue. The folder holds hundreds of hastily scribbled death reports authored by city police officers in July 1995 as they investigated cases of mortality during the most proportionately deadly heat wave in recorded American history.[1] Over 700 Chicago residents in excess of the norm died during the week of 13th to 20th of July (Whitman et al. 1997),[2] and the following samples of the official reports hint at the conditions in which the police discovered the decedents.

Male, age 65, black, July 16, 1995:

R/Os [responding officers] discovered the door to apt. locked from the inside by means of door chain. No response to any knocks or calls. R/Os . . . gained entry by cutting chain. R/Os discovered victim lying on his back in rear bedroom on the floor. [Neighbor] last spoke with victim on 13 July 95. Residents had not seen victim recently. Victim was in full rigor mortis. R/Os unable to locate the whereabouts of victim's relatives . . .

Female, age 73, white, July 17, 1995:

A recluse for 10 yrs, never left apartment, found today by son, apparently DOA. Conditions in apartment when R/Os arrived thermostat was registering over 90 degrees F. with no air circulation except for windows opened by son [after death]. Possible heat-related death. Had a known heart problem 10 yrs ago but never completed medication or treatment . . .

Male, age 54, white, July 16, 1995:

R/O learned . . . that victim had been dead for quite a while. . . . Unable to contact any next of kin. Victim's room was uncomfortably warm. Victim was diabetic, doctor unk. Victim has daughter . . . last name unk. Victim hadn't seen her in years. . . . Body removed to C.C.M. [Cook County Morgue].

Male, age 79, black, July 19, 1995:

Victim did not respond to phone calls or knocks on victim's door since Sunday, 16 July 95. Victim was known as quiet, to himself and, at times, not to answer the door. X is landlord to victim and does not have any information to any relatives to victim. . . . Chain was on door. R/O was able to see victim on sofa with flies on victim and a very strong odor decay (decompose). R/O cut chain, per permission of [landlord], called M.E. [medical examiner] who authorized removal. . . . No known relatives at this time.

These accounts rarely say enough about a victim's death to fill a page, yet the words used to describe the deceased—"recluse," "to himself," "no known relatives"—and the conditions in which they were found—"chain was on door," "no air circulation," "flies on victim," "decompose"—are brutally succinct testaments to forms of abandonment, withdrawal, fear, and isolation that proved more extensive than anyone in Chicago had realized, and more dangerous than anyone had imagined. "During the summer heat wave of 1995 in Chicago," the authors of the most thorough epidemiological study of the disaster explained, "anything that facilitated social contact, even membership in a social club or owning a pet was associated with a decreased risk of death" (Semenza et al. 1996: 90). Chicago residents who lacked social ties and did not leave their homes regularly died disproportionately during the catastrophe.

Three questions motivate this article. First, why did so many Chicagoans *die alone* during the heat wave? Second, to expand this question, why do so many Chicagoans, particularly older residents, *live alone* with limited social contacts and weak support during normal times? What accounts for the social production of isolation? Third, what social and psychological processes organize and animate the experiential make-up of aging alone? How can we understand the lives and deaths of the literally isolated?

Dying Alone

If "bowling alone," the social trend reported by Robert Putnam and mined for significance by social critics and politicians of all persuasions (Putnam 1995), is a sign of a weakening American civil society, dying alone—a fate few Americans can confidently elude—carries even more powerful social and symbolic meaning. For while in advanced societies the normative "good death" takes place at home, it is even more crucial that the process of dying is collective, shared by the dying person and his or her community of family and friends.[3] When someone dies alone and at home, the death is a powerful symbol of social abandonment and failure. The community to which the deceased belonged, whether familial, friendship-based, or political, is likely to suffer from stigma or shame as a consequence, one which it must overcome with redemptive narratives and rituals that reaffirm the bonds among the living (Seale 1995).

The issues of aging and dying alone are hardly limited to Chicago. In Milwaukee, where a similar proportion of city residents died during the 1995 heat wave (U.S. Centers for Disease Control and Prevention 1996), 27 percent of the decedents, roughly 75 percent of whom were over 60, were found alone more than one day after the estimated time of death (Nashold et al., n.d.). Most older people in Western societies, and particularly in the United States, place great value on their independence, a characteristic of sufficient cultural and psychological importance that people for whom independence is objectively dangerous are often willing to risk its consequences in order to remain self-sufficient. The number of older people living alone is rising almost everywhere in the world, making it one of the major demographic trends of the contemporary period. According to the U.S. Census Bureau, the total number of people living alone in the United States rose from 10.9 million in 1970 to 23.6 million in 1994 (Wuthnow 1998); and . . . the proportions of American households inhabited by only one person and of elderly people living alone have soared since the 1950s. Dramatic as these figures are, they are certain to rise even higher in the coming decades as societies everywhere age.

Ethnographers have done little to document the daily routines and practices of people living alone,[4] but a study in the *New England Journal of Medicine* (Gurley et al. 1996) suggests that their solitary condition leaves them vulnerable in emergency situations and times of illness. Researchers in San Francisco, a city about one-quarter the size of Chicago, reported that in a 12-week period emergency medical workers found 367 people who lived alone and were discovered in their apartments either incapacitated or, in a quarter of the cases, dead. The victims, as in the Chicago heat wave, were disproportionately old, white and African American, with older black men most over-represented. Many of them, the researchers reported, suffered tremendously while they waited to be discovered in their homes, suffering that could have been reduced by earlier intervention but was exacerbated by the victims' isolation (Gurley et al. 1996).

In this [reading] I examine the lived experiences of isolated Chicago residents, placing them in the context of the changing demography and ecology of the city and paying special attention to the ways in which migration patterns, increasing life spans and changes in urban social morphology have altered the structural conditions of social and support networks. I also consider the impact of the spreading *culture of fear* that has transformed the nature of social life and community organization as well as the physical and political structure of cities. To illustrate how city residents experience these conditions and depict how they impact on the social life of the city, I return to the streets and neighborhoods of Chicago, drawing upon ethnographic research to flesh out the haunting spectre of dying alone in the great metropolis. Although we cannot speak with those who perished during the heat wave, we can look closely at the conditions in which they died and then follow up by examining the experiences of people in similar conditions today. Thus my focus moves outward from the heat wave to the years immediately following when I conducted fieldwork alongside seniors living alone in Chicago.

It is important to make distinctions between *living alone, being isolated, being reclusive,* and *being lonely.* I define alone as residing without other people in a household; being isolated as having limited social ties; being reclusive as largely confining oneself to the household; and being lonely as the subjective state of feeling alone.[5] Most people who live alone, seniors included, are neither lonely nor deprived of social contacts.[6] This is significant because seniors who are embedded in active social networks tend to have better health and greater longevity than those who are relatively isolated. Being isolated or reclusive, then, is more consequential than simply living alone. But older people who live alone are more likely than seniors who live with others to be depressed, isolated, impoverished, fearful of crime, and removed from proximate sources of support.[7] Moreover, seniors who live alone are especially vulnerable to traumatic outcomes during episodes of acute crisis because there is no one to help recognize emerging problems, provide immediate care, or activate support networks. . . .

What social conditions produce isolation? And how can we understand the lived experience of isolation itself? The heat wave mortality patterns pointed to places in the city where isolation proved to be especially dangerous and suggested sites where similarly situated isolates who survived the disaster but remained alone and vulnerable to the problems stemming from reclusiveness were concentrated. In addition, the disaster illuminated a set of demographic, cultural and political conditions that are associated with isolation, forming the broader social context in which social isolation emerges.

There are four key social conditions that contribute to the production of literal and extreme social isolation: first, the aging of the urban population, particularly the increases in the population of African American, Latino and Asian seniors; second, the fear of crime stemming from the violence and perceived violence of everyday life—in extreme forms this fear can result in the retreat from public life altogether and the creation of urban burrows, "safe houses" where the alone and the afraid protect themselves from a social world in which they no longer feel secure; third, the degradation and fortification of public spaces in poor urban areas and specific residential facilities (such as senior public housing units and some single-room-occupancy hotels); fourth, the transformation in the nature of state social services and support systems such as health care, public or subsidized housing, and home energy subsidies. The interaction of these conditions with poverty and the daily deprivations it entails renders poor seniors who live alone vulnerable to a variety of dangers whose consequences can be severe. . . .

"The Closest I've Come to Death"

The first of the conditions producing extreme urban isolation and its experiential correlates is the general aging of American society and the willingness of seniors to live alone. For cities there are three specific pre-disposing factors: first, the rise in the number of seniors living alone, often after outliving their social contacts and seeing their children migrate to the suburbs or other regions of the country altering their neighborhood populations so that they feel culturally or linguistically differentiated; second, the rapid increase in the population of "very old" seniors, 85 and above, who are more likely to be both alone and frail, sick, and unable or unwilling to enter into a public world in which they often feel vulnerable and who are, in fact, an historically new group, older than all previous cohorts and subjected to a distinct set of physical constraints; and third, the increase in the population of black and Latino seniors, who are more likely than their white counterparts to live in poverty and be at risk of the related forms of vulnerability, including illness and inadequate access to health care (Ford et al. 1992; Lawlor et al. 1993). There is a fourth implication for metropolitan areas (as distinct from central cities) which is the growth of the elderly population in the suburban ring which in general lacks the appropriate housing stock and support systems for aged and aging residents.

By 1990, one-third of Chicago's elderly population, roughly 110,000 seniors, lived alone. When a group of researchers from the Heartland Center on Aging, Disability and Long Term Care at Indiana University surveyed Chicago seniors in 1989 and 1990, they found that 48 percent of Chicagoans over 65, and 35 percent of suburbanites over 65, reported having no family members available to assist them (Fleming-Moran et al. 1991).

Pauline Jankowitz is one of the recluses I got to know during my fieldwork in Chicago.[8] Her story helps to illustrate some of the fundamental features of life alone and afraid in the city. I first met Pauline on her 85th birthday, when I was assigned to befriend her for a day by the local office of an international organization that supports seniors living alone by linking them up with volunteers who are willing to become "friends" and inviting them to the organization's center for a birthday party, Christmas, and a Thanksgiving dinner every year. A stranger before the day began, I became her closest companion for the milestone occasion when I picked her up at the uptown apartment where she had lived for 30 years.

Pauline and I had spoken on the phone the previous day and she was expecting me when I arrived late in the morning. She lived on a quiet residential street dominated by the small, three- and four-flat apartment buildings common in Chicago. The neighborhood, a key site of departure and arrival for suburbanizing and new urban migrants, had changed dramatically in the time she had lived there, and her block had shifted from a predominately white ethnic area in which Pauline was a typical resident to a mixed street with a sizable Asian and increasingly Mexican population. Uptown remained home to her, but she was less comfortable in it because the neighbors, whom she was eager to praise for their responsibility and good character, were no longer familiar to her. "They are good people," she explained, "but I just don't know them." Her situation is similar to that of thousands of Chicago residents and millions of seniors across the country who have *aged in place* while the environment around them changes.

The major sources of her discomfort were her physical infirmities which grew worse as she aged, a bladder problem that left her incontinent and a weak leg that required her to walk with a crutch and drastistically reduced her mobility, and her real terror of crime, which she heard about daily on the radio and television shows that she likes. "Chicago is just a shooting gallery," she told me, "and I am a moving target because I walk so slowly." Acutely aware of her vulnerability, Pauline reorganized her life to limit her exposure to the threats outside, bunkering herself in a third-floor apartment (in a building with no elevator) that she had trouble reaching because of the stairs, but which "is much safer than the first floor. . . . If I were on the first floor I'd be even more vulnerable to a break-in." With a home-care support worker, meals-on-wheels, and a publicly subsidized helper visiting weekly to do her grocery shopping and help with errands, Pauline has few reasons to leave home. "I go out of my apartment about six times a year," she told me, and three of them are for celebrations sponsored by the support organization.

It is, I would learn, a challenge for service providers and volunteers to help even the seniors with whom they have contact. Pauline and I made it to the birthday celebration after a difficult and painful trip down her stairway, during which we had to turn around and return to the apartment so that she could address "a problem" that she experienced on the stairs. Pauline's grimaces and sighs betrayed the depth of the pain the walk had inflicted, but she was so excited to be going out, and going to her party, that she urged me to get us to the center quickly.

During one visit, Pauline, who knew that I was studying the 1995 heat wave, told me that she wanted to tell me her story. "It was," she said softly, "the closest I've come to death." She has one air conditioner in her apartment which gets especially hot during the summer because it is on the third floor. But the machine "is old and it doesn't work too well," which left her place uncomfortably, if not dangerously warm during the disaster. A friend had told her that it was important for her to go outside if she was too hot indoors, so she woke up very early ("it's safer then") on what would become the hottest day of the heat wave and walked towards the local store to buy cherries ("my favorite fruit, but I rarely get fresh food so they're a real treat for me") and cool down in the air conditioned space. "I was so exhausted by the time I got down the stairs that I wanted to go straight back up again," she recounted, "but instead I walked to the corner and took the bus a few blocks to the store. When I got there I could barely move. I had to lean on the shopping cart to keep myself up." But the cool air revived her and she got a bag of cherries and returned home on the bus.

"Climbing the stairs was almost impossible," she remembers. "I was hot and sweaty and so tired." Pauline called a friend as soon as she made it into her place and as they spoke she began to feel her hands going numb and swelling, a sensation that quickly extended into other parts of her body, alarming her that something was wrong. "I asked my friend to stay on the line but I put the phone down and lied down." Several minutes later, her friend still on the line but the receiver on the floor, Pauline got up, soaked her head in water, directed a fan toward her bed, lay down, and placed a number of wet towels on her body and face. Remembering that she had left her friend waiting, Pauline got up, picked up the phone to report that she was feeling better and to thank her buddy for waiting before she hung up. Finally, she lay down again to cool off and rest in earnest. Before long she had fully recovered.

"Now," she ended her story, "I have a special way to beat the heat. You're going to laugh, but I like to go on a Caribbean cruise," which she does alone and, as she does nearly everything else, without leaving her home.

> I get several wash cloths and dip them in cold water. I then place them over my eyes so that I can't see. I lie down and set the fan directly on me. The wet towels and the wind from the fan give a cool breeze, and I imagine myself on a cruise around the islands. I do this whenever it's hot, and you'd be surprised at how nice it is. My friends know about my cruises too. So when they call me on hot

days they all say, "Hi Pauline, how was your trip?" We laugh about it, but it keeps me alive.

Social ecological conditions stemming from migration patterns and the widespread abandonment of urban regions have created new barriers to collective life and social support, particularly for the elderly. In *When Work Disappears* William Julius Wilson noted the significance of depopulation in poor black neighborhoods for both formal and informal social controls (1996:44–45). Most scholars who have analyzed urban social support systems have focused on provision for children, but the changing demographics of the city suggest that it is increasingly important to consider how these systems work for older neighborhood residents as well. The problems are not exclusive to black and Latino communities. Since the 1950s, many white ethnic groups have experienced a sweeping suburbanization that has undercut the morphological basis for cross-generational support, leaving thousands of white seniors estranged in neighborhoods that their families and friends had left behind, out of reach during times of need but also during everyday life. . . . These patterns are becoming more prevalent in Latino and African American communities as they join the suburban exodus, leaving behind older and poorer people for whom the loss of proximity to family and friends will be compounded by the relatively high rates of poverty and illness in America's so-called minority groups.

In addition to the fraying lines of social support from families experiencing generational rifts due to migration, the changing nature of friendship networks has also undermined the morphological basis of mutual assistance. For decades, community scholars have shown that many communities are no longer place-based, but organized instead around common interests and values. Advanced technology, including the telephone and the Internet, ease the process of establishing connections with people in disparate places and therefore increase the probability that new social networks will develop without much regard for spatial proximity. Yet, as much research has established, certain forms of social assistance, particularly emergency care and frequent visitation, are more likely when members of a network are physically close to one another. Indeed, after the heat wave, epidemiologists found that older Chicagoans who had died during the disaster were less likely than those who survived to have had friends in the city (Semenza et al. 1996:86). Spatial distance, in other words, imposes real barriers to social support for friends as well as family. Proximity is a life and death matter for some people, particularly for the elderly who suffer from limited mobility.

"I'll Talk through the Door"

Although old age, illness and spatial separation from her family and friends established the grounding for Pauline Jankowitz's condition, her isolation became particularly extreme because of her abiding fear of being victimized by crime. Pauline's perception of her own extreme vulnerability heightens her fear, but her concerns are in fact typical of city dwellers throughout the United States at a time when a veritable culture of fear and a powerful cultural industry based on crime have come to influence much of the organizational, institutional and political activity within the country as well as the thought and action of Americans in their everyday lives. By the late 1990s, fear of crime has taken on a paradoxical role in American urban life, on the one hand pushing people to dissociate from their neighbors and extend their social distance from strangers, and on the other hand becoming one of the organizing principles of new collective projects, such as neighborhood watch groups and community policing programs. Regardless of the form it takes, "coping with crime," as Wesley Skogan and Michael Maxfield put it in the title of their book (1981), has become a way of life for Americans in general and for residents of notably violent cities such as Chicago.

Throughout Chicago and especially in the most violent areas, city residents have reorganized their daily routines and behaviors in order to minimize their exposure to crime in an increasingly Hobbesian universe, scheming around the clock to avoid driving, parking or walking on the wrong streets or in the wrong neighborhoods, seeing the wrong people, and visiting the wrong establishments and public places. In Chicago, as in most other American cities, "wrong" in this context is associated with blacks in general and young men in particular, especially now that the massive dragnet cast by the drug warrior state has captured so many young blacks and labeled them as permanent public enemies (Wacquant 2001). Yet doing fieldwork in even the most objectively dangerous streets of Chicago makes it clear that the common depiction of city residents, and particularly those who live in poor and violent areas, as constantly paranoid and so acutely concerned about proximate threats that they can hardly move, is a gross misrepresentation of how fear is managed and experienced. "It's caution, not fear, that guides me," Eugene Richards, a senior citizen living in North Lawndale explained to me during a discussion of managing danger in the area. Eugene will walk a few blocks during the day, but he refuses to go more than four blocks without a car. Alice Nelson, a woman in her 70s who lives in the Little Village, walks during the day and carries small bags of groceries with her. "But I won't go out at night," she told me. "And if someone comes to the door I won't open it. I'll talk through the door because you never know. . . ."[9]

Preying on the elderly, who are presumed to be more vulnerable and easier to dupe, is a standard and recurrent practice of neighborhood deviants and legitimate corporations, mail-order businesses, and salespersons alike. Several of my informants said that turning strangers away at the door was part of their regular routine, and complained that they felt besieged by the combination of local hoodlums who paid them special attention around the beginning of the month when social security checks were delivered as well as outsiders who tried to visit or call and convince them to spend their scarce dollars. In the United States, where guns are easy to obtain and levels of gun-related violence are among the highest in the world, roughly one-quarter of households are touched by crime each year, and about one-half of the population will be victimized by a violent crime in their lifetime (Miethe 1995). The nature of the association between fear and vulnerability is enigmatic because it is impossible to establish that the lower levels of victimization are not at least partially attributable to fear which causes people to avoid potentially dangerous situations and, in the most extreme cases, pushes people to become recluses, "prisoners of their own fear," as one social worker I shadowed calls them. Nonetheless, many scholars of crime have argued that fear of crime is irrational because of the often-cited finding that the elderly and women, who are the least likely to be victimized, are the most fearful of crime. Yet ethnographic observation and more fine-grained surveys of fear can show what grounds these concerns. . . .

In interviews and casual conversations conducted during my fieldwork, Chicago seniors provided their own explanations for the fear that so many criminologists and city officials seem unable to understand. Many of the seniors I got to know said that although they knew that they were unlikely to be robbed or attacked, their heightened concern about victimization stemmed from their knowledge that if they were victimized, the consequences, particularly of violent crime, would be devastating in ways that they would not be for younger people. At the economic level, seniors living on fixed and limited incomes feared that a robbery or burglary could leave them without sufficient resources to pay for such basic needs as food, medication, rent or energy. In Chicago, where hunger, undermedication, homelessness, displacement and energy deprivation are not uncommon among seniors, these are not unfounded concerns. At the physical level, seniors, for whom awareness of bodily frailty is one of the defining conditions of life, are afraid that a violent attack could result in permanent disabilities, crippling and even death. The elderly make it clear that their fears of crime are directly related to their concerns about the difficulty of recovering from crime and that their sensitivities to danger were rational from their points of view.

Dead Space

A cause and consequence of this culture of fear is the degradation and fortification of urban public spaces in which city dwellers circulate. The loss of viable public space is the third condition that gives rise to literal social isolation undermining the social morphological foundations of collective social life and so giving rise to sweeping insecurity in everyday urban life. The real and perceived violence of the city has pushed Chicago residents to remake the sociospatial environment in which they live.[10] In Chicago the degradation of public space has been most rampant in the city's hyperghettos, where the flight of business, the retrenchment of state supports, the out-migration of middle-class residents, the rise of public drug markets, and the concentration of violent crime and victimization have radically reduced the viability of public spaces (Wacquant 1994). Despite the real decreases in crime that

Chicago experienced in the mid-1990s, the overall crime rate in Chicago is falling at a slower pace than in all of the other major American cities. According to the Chicago Community Policing Evaluation Consortium, a major research project directed by Wesley Skogan at Northwestern University, "the largest declines [in crime] have occurred in the highest-crime parts of the city," and "the greatest decline in gun-related crime has occurred in African-American neighborhoods" (Chicago Community Policing Evaluation Consortium 1997:6–8). Nonetheless the levels of violent crime concentrated in poor black areas of the city remain comparatively high, making it difficult for residents to feel safe in the streets. . . .

But the conditions of insecurity are hardly confined to the Chicago ghettos, and constant exposure to images and information about violence in the city has instilled genuine fear in communities throughout the city. Moreover, the depacification of daily life that is concentrated in the city's ghettos has emerged on a smaller scale in other parts of Chicago, affecting a broad set of buildings, blocks, and collective housing facilities as well as neighborhood clusters. Several studies have documented the erosion of the sociospatial infrastructure for public life in low-income barrios and ghettos; therefore I will focus here on showing the ways in which spatial degradation and public crime have fostered reclusiveness in settings, such as senior public housing units, where many of the heat wave deaths occurred.

In the four years leading up to the heat wave conditions in the city's senior public housing facilities bucked all of Chicago's crime trends. Residents of these special units experienced a soaring violent crime rate even as the overall crime levels in the Chicago Housing Authority (CHA) family projects and the rest of the city declined, forcing many residents to give up not only the public parks and streets that once supported their neighborhoods, but the public areas within their own apartment buildings as well. In the 1990s the CHA opened its 58 senior buildings, which house about 100,000 residents and are dispersed throughout the city although generally located in safer areas than the family public housing complexes, to people with disabilities as well as to the elderly. The 1990 Americans with Disabilities Act made people with substance abuse problems eligible for social security insurance and the CHA welcomed them into senior housing units as well. Unfortunately this act of accommodation has proven disastrous for senior residents and the communities they had once established within their buildings: the mix of low-income substance abusers, many of whom continue to engage in crime to finance their habits, and low-income seniors, many of whom keep everything they own, savings included, in their tiny apartments, creates a perfect formula for disaster in the social life of the housing complex.

In March of 1995, just a few months before the heat wave, the Chicago Housing Authority reported that from 1991 to 1994 the number of Part I crimes (in which the U.S. Justice Department includes homicide, criminal sexual assault, serious assault, robbery, burglary, theft and violent theft) committed and reported within CHA housing increased by over 50 percent. "The elderly in public housing," a group of CHA tenants and advisers called the

Building Organization and Leadership Development (BOLD) group reported, "are more vulnerable than seniors in assisted or private housing in that they are being victimized in many cases by their neighbors." Moreover, BOLD showed that thefts, forcible entry, armed robbery, "and other crimes of violence are substantially higher in those developments housing a large percentage of non-elderly disabled. . . . The reality appears to be that disabled youth are victimizing seniors" (BOLD 1995).

Elderly residents of senior buildings throughout the city now voice the same complaint: they feel trapped in their rooms, afraid that if they leave they might be attacked or have their apartment robbed, and the most afraid refuse to use the ground-floor common rooms unless security workers are there. The fortification of public space that contributes to isolation all over the city is exacerbated here. Most residents, to be sure, do manage to get out of their units, but they have to limit themselves to secure public areas, elevators and halls. . . .

Concern about the proximity of younger residents and their associates who are using or peddling drugs is ubiquitous in Chicago's senior housing complexes. During an interview in her home, one woman, a resident of a CHA building on the near west side, expressed remorse that a formerly pleasant and popular patio on the top floor had been vandalized and looted by younger residents and their friends. The group had first taken the space over and made it their hangout spot, then decided to take some of the furniture and even the fire extinguishers for themselves. Some older residents, she explained to me, did not want to make a big deal out of the problem because they worried that their young neighbors would learn who had informed security and then retaliate. The fear of young people and the demonization of drug users common in contemporary American society rendered the situation more difficult, as many building residents presumed that the younger residents would cause trouble and were scared to approach them. Ultimately, the seniors have been unable to fix up the area or win it back. "Now," she sighed, "no one uses that space. It's just empty, dead."

"I Never Have Enough Time to See Them"

The current array of programs and services is insufficient to provide primary goods such as adequate housing, transportation, energy assistance, reliable health care and medication for the elderly poor, leaving private agencies and numerous charities to address gaps that they have no means to fill. Local welfare state agencies in American cities historically have lacked the resources necessary to meet the needs of impoverished and insecure residents, but in the 1990s the rise of entrepreneurial state programs that required more active shopping services from consumerist citizens created additional difficulties for the most isolated and vulnerable city residents. Studies of Chicago's programs for the poor elderly had warned officials about the dangers of residents falling through gaps in the withering safety net. After conducting a major study of Chicago's support programs and emergency services, social service scholar Sharon Keigher concluded that "city agencies are not equipped to intervene substantially with older persons who do not ask for help, who have no family, or who do not go to senior centers and congregate at meal sites. Yet, increasingly these persons—who tend to be very old, poor and living alone—are in need of multiple services" (Keigher 1991:12). Published as both an official city report (in 1987) and a scholarly book (in 1991), Keigher's findings were known to city agencies responsible for serving vulnerable seniors long before the heat wave. But the city government lacked both the resources and the political priorities necessary to respond to them sufficiently, and its agencies were poorly prepared for assisting needy seniors in either the heat disaster of 1995 or the struggles they take on regularly.

Government policies and procedures that limited the capacity of residents to enter programs and obtain resources they need is the fourth condition that produces literal isolation. These changes have been disproportionately destructive for the city's most impoverished residents, who have had to struggle to secure the basic resources and services necessary for survival that a more generous welfare state would provide. In a political context where private organizations provide most of the human services to elderly city residents, research must shift from state agencies and agents to include the private offices and employees through which local governments reach their constituents. Spending time alongside social workers and home care providers for Chicago seniors, it became clear that the city's incapacity to reach isolated, sick or otherwise vulnerable seniors during the heat wave was by no means an anomaly created by the unusual environmental conditions. Underservice for Chicago's poor elderly is a structural certainty and everyday norm in an era where political pressures for state entrepreneurialism have grown hand-in-hand with social pressures for isolation. Embedded in a competitive market for gaining city contracts which provides perverse incentives for agencies to underestimate the costs of services and overestimate their capacity to provide them, the agencies and private organizations I observed had bargained themselves into responsibilities that they could not possibly meet. "Most entrepreneurial governments promote *competition* between service providers," David Osborne and Ted Gaebler wrote in *Reinventing Government* (Osborne and Gaebler 1992:19), but competition undermines the working conditions of human service providers if it fosters efficiency but compromises the time and human resources necessary to provide quality care. "My seniors love to see me," Mandy Evers, an African American woman in her late 20s who was on her fourth year working as a case manager, told me. "The problem is I never have enough time to get to them."

Stacy Geer, a seasoned advocate of Chicago seniors who spent much of the 1990s helping the elderly secure basic goods such as housing and energy, insists that the political mismatch between more entrepreneurial service

systems and isolated seniors contributed to the vulnerability of Chicago seniors during the heat wave. "The capacity of service delivery programs is realized fully only by the seniors who are most active in seeking them out, who are connected to their family, church, neighbors, or someone who helps them get the things they need." In some circumstances, the aging process can hinder seniors who have been healthy and financially secure for most of their lives. Geer continues, "As seniors become more frail their networks break down. As their needs increase, they have less ability to meet them. The people who are hooked into the Department on Aging, the AARP, the senior clubs at the churches, they are part of that word of mouth network and they hear. I know, just from doing organizing in the senior community, that you run into the same people, and the same are active in a number of organizations."[11] Seniors who are marginalized at the first, structural level of social networks and government programs are then doubly excluded at the second, conjunctural level of service delivery because they do not always know of—let alone know how to activate—networks of support. Those who are out of the loop in their daily life are more likely to remain so when there is a crisis. This certainly happened during the heat wave, when relatively active and informed seniors used official cooling centers set up by the city while the more inactive and isolated elderly stayed home.

During the 1990s, however, not even the best-connected city residents knew where to appeal if they needed assistance securing the most basic of primary goods: home, energy and water. In Chicago, the combination of cuts to the budget for the federally-sponsored Low Income Home Energy Assistance Program (LIHEAP) and a market-model managerial strategy for punishing consumers who are delinquent on their bills has placed the poor elderly in a permanent energy crisis. Facing escalating energy costs (even before prices soared in 2000), declining government subsidies and fixed incomes, seniors throughout the city express great concern about the cost of their utilities bills and take pains to keep their fees down.[12]

Poor seniors I got to know understood that they would face unaffordable utilities costs in the summer if they used air conditioners. Epidemiologists estimate that "more than 50 percent of the deaths related to the heat wave could have been prevented if each home had had a working air conditioner," arguing that surely this would be an effective public health strategy (Semenza et al. 1996:87). Yet the elderly who regularly struggle to make ends meet explain that they could not use air conditioners even if they owned them because activating the units would push their energy bills to unmanageable levels. But their energy crisis was pressing even during moderate temperatures. The most impoverished seniors I visited kept their lights off during the day, letting the television, their most consistent source of companionship, illuminate their rooms. Fear of losing their energy altogether if they failed to pay the bills has relegated these seniors to regular and fundamental forms of insecurity and duress. Yet their daily crisis goes largely unnoticed.

The Formula for Disaster

The four conditions highlighted here impose serious difficulties for all seniors. But they are particularly devastating for the elderly poor who cannot buy their way out of them by purchasing more secure housing in safer areas, visiting or paying for distant family members to visit, by obtaining private health insurance supplements or by using more expensive and safe transportation such as taxis to get out of the house or the neighborhood. Each one of the key conditions described in this article contributes to the production of the forms of isolation that proved so deadly during the heat wave and that continue to undermine the health and safety of countless older Chicagoans. But in many cases Chicago residents are subjected to all of the conditions together, and the combination creates a formula for disaster that makes extreme social, physical and psychological suffering a feature of everyday life. If aging alone, the culture of fear, the degradation and fortification of public space, and the reduction of redistributive and supportive state programs continue at their current pace, more seniors will retreat to their "safe houses," abandoning a society that has all but abandoned them. Collectively producing the conditions for literal isolation, we have made dying alone a fittingly tragic end.

ENDNOTES

Author's Note: The National Science Foundation Graduate Research Fellowship, the Jacob Javits Fellowship, and a grant from the Berkeley Humanities Division helped to support research for this project. This publication was also supported in part by a grant from the Individual Project Fellowship Program of the Open Society Institute. Thanks go to Loïc Wacquant, Mike Rogin, Jack Katz, Nancy Scheper-Hughes, Kim DaCosta, Dan Dohan, Paul Willis and Caitlin Zaloom for incisive comments on earlier drafts.

[1] For a synthetic sociological account of the conditions that helped produce the historic mortality rates, see Klinenberg (1999); for an epidemiological account, see Semenza et al. (1996).

[2] Roughly 70 Chicagoans died on a typical July day during the 1990s. "Excess deaths" measures the variance from the expected death rate. In assessing heat wave mortality, forensic scientists prefer the excess death measure to the heat-related death measure, which is based on the number of deaths examined and recorded by investigators, because many deaths during heat waves go unexamined or are not properly attributed to the heat (Shen et al. 1998).

[3] Sherwin Nuland is among the more recent writers to discuss the modern version of the *ars moriendi*. Describing a man dying of AIDS, Nuland writes, "During his terminal weeks in the hospital, Kent was never alone. Whatever help they could or could not provide him at the final hours, there is no question that the constant presence of his friends eased him beyond what might have been achieved by the nursing staff, no matter the attentiveness of their care" (Nuland 1993:196).

[4] There is, of course, a brighter side to the extension of the life span, which is itself a sign of significant social and scientific progress. Aging alone, as Robert Coles and Arlie Hochschild have argued, can be a rich personal and social experience, albeit one filled with challenges. In *The Unexpected Community*, Hochschild documents the active social lives of a group of Bay Area seniors who, as she emphatically stated, "were not isolated and not lonely" but instead "were part of a community I did not expect to find" (Hochschild 1973:xiv), one that worked together to solve the problem of loneliness that proves so troublesome for the elderly. . . . She wrote, "The most important point I am trying to make in this book concerns the people it does not discuss—the isolated. Merrill Court was an unexpected community, an exception. Living in ordinary apartments and houses, in shabby downtown hotels, sitting in parks and eating in

cheap restaurants, are old people in various degrees and sorts of isolation" (Hochschild 1973:137). Hochschild leaves it to others to render the social worlds of the isolated as explicit as she makes the world in Merrill Court.

[5] This conception of social isolation breaks from both sociological definitions of the term, which generally refer to relations between groups rather than people, and from conventional gerontological definitions of isolation, which define isolation as being single or living alone. . . . Gibson lists four types of loneliness: "physical aloneness," "loneliness as a state of mind," "the feeling of isolation due to a personal characteristic," and "solitude" (Gibson 2004:4–6).

[6] See Gibson (2000) for a review of studies showing that most seniors who live alone are not lonely.

[7] Thompson and Krause find that not only do people who live alone report more fear of crime than those who live with others, but also that "the greater sense of security among those who live with others appears to permeate beyond the home because they report less fear of crime than their counterparts" (1998:356).

[8] All personal names of Chicago residents have been changed.

[9] Yet, as Alex Kotlowitz and teenage journalists LeAlan Jones and Lloyd Newman have shown in their accounts of growing up in Chicago's West and South Side housing projects, even young residents of the most violent urban areas are subjected to so much brutality, death and suffering that they have learned from their infancy how to organize their daily routines around the temporal and seasonal variations of the criminal economy (Jones et al. 1997; Kotlowitz 1991). . . .

[10] In 1995 Chicago ranked 6th in robbery and 5th in aggravated assaults among all United States cities with a population of over 350,000; in 1998 the city was the national leader in homicide, with the annual figure of 698 exceeding New York City's by about 100 even though Chicago is roughly one-third as populous; and throughout the 1990s its violent crime rate decreased much more slowly than any of the eight largest American cities (New York City, Los Angeles, Chicago, Houston, Philadelphia, Phoenix, San Diego, Dallas).

[11] Internal pressures within state agencies and advocacy organizations push social workers and organizers to reward the most entrepreneurial clients with special attention. Overwhelmed with problem cases and operating in an environment where agencies must show successful outcome measures to garner resources from external funders who expect tangible results, the social workers I observed engaged in what Lipsky called "creaming," the practice of favoring and working intensively on the cases of people "who seem likely to succeed in terms of bureaucratic success criteria" (Lipsky 1980:107).

[12] While the average Illinois family spends roughly 6 percent of its income on heat-related utilities during winter months, for low-income families the costs constitute nearly 35 percent (Pearson 1995).

REFERENCES

BOLD. 1995. "Bold Group Endorses CHAPS Police Unit." Report by the Building Organization and Leadership Development Group, Chicago.

Chicago Community Policing Evaluation Consortium. 1997. "Community Policing in Chicago, Year Four: An Interim Report." Report by the Chicago Community Policing Evaluation Consortium.

Fleming-Moran, Millicent, T. Kenworthy-Bennett, and Karen Harlow. 1991. "Illinois State Needs Assessment Survey of Elders Aged 55 and Over. Report from the Heartland Center on Aging, Disability and Long Term Care, School of Public Health and Environmental Affairs, Indiana University and the National Center for Senior Living, South Bend, IN.

Ford, Amasa, Marie Haug, Paul Jones, and Steven Folmar. 1992. "New Cohorts of Urban Elders: Are They in Trouble?" *Journal of Gerontology* 47:S297–S303.

Gibson, Hamilton. 2000. *Loneliness in Later Life.* New York: St. Martin's Press.

Gurley, Jan, Nancy Lum, Merle Sande, Bernard Lo, and Mitchell Katz. 1996. "Persons Found in Their Homes Helpless or Dead." *New England Journal of Medicine* 334:1710–16.

Hochschild, Arlie Russell. 1973. *The Unexpected Community: Portrait of an Old-Age Subculture.* Berkeley: University of California Press.

Jones, LeAlan and Lloyd Newman with David Isay. 1997. *Our America: Life and Death on the South Side of Chicago.* New York: Washington Square Press.

Keigher, Sharon. 1987. "The City's Responsibility for the Homeless Elderly of Chicago." Report by the Chicago Department of Aging and Disability.

Klinenberg, Eric. 1999. "Denaturalizing Disaster: A Social Autopsy of the 1995 Chicago Heat Wave." *Theory and Society* 28:239–95.

Kotlowitz, Alex. 1991. *There Are No Children Here: The Story of Two Boys Growing Up in the Other America.* New York: Anchor Books.

Lawlor, Edward, Gunnar Almgren, and Mary Gomberg. 1993. "Aging in Chicago? Demography." Report, Chicago Community Trust.

Lipsky, Michael. 1980. *Street-Level Bureaucracy: Dilemmas of the Individual in Public Services.* New York: Russell Sage.

Miethe, Terance. 1995. "Fear and Withdrawal." *The Annals of the American Academy* 539:14–29.

Nashold, Raymond, Jeffrey Jentzen, Patrick Remington, and Peggy Peterson. (n.d.). "Excessive Heat Deaths, Wisconsin, June 20–August 19, 1995." Unpublished Manuscript.

Nuland, Sherwin. 1993. *How We Die: Reflections on Life's Final Chapter.* New York: Vintage.

Osborne, David and Ted Gaebler. 1992. *Reinventing Government: How the Entrepreneurial Spirit Is Transforming the Public Sector.* New York: Plume.

Pearson, Rick. 1995. "Funding to Help Poor Pay Heating Bills Evaporating." *Chicago Tribune*, July 20, Metro, p. 2.

Putnam, Robert. 1995. "Bowling Alone: America's Declining Social Capital." *Democracy* 6:65–78.

Seale, Clive. 1995. "Dying Alone." *Sociology of Health and Illness* 17:376–92.

Semenza, Jan, Carol Rubin, Kenneth Falter, Joel Selanikio, W. Dana Flanders, Holly Howe, and John Wilhelm. 1996. "Heat-Related Deaths during the July 1995 Heat Wave in Chicago." *The New England Journal of Medicine* 335:84–90.

Shen, Tiefu, Holly Howe, Celan Alo, and Ronald Moolenaar. 1998. "Toward a Broader Definition of Heat-Related Death: Comparison of Mortality Estimates from Medical Examiners' Classification with Those from Total Death Differentials during the July 1995 Chicago Heat Wave." *The American Journal of Forensic Medicine and Pathology* 19:113–18.

Skogan, Wesley and Michael Maxfield. 1981. *Coping with Crime: Individual and Neighborhood Reactions.* Newbury Park, CA: Sage.

Thompson, Emily and Neil Krause. 1998. "Living Alone and Neighborhood Characteristics as Predictors of Social Support in Later Life." *Journal of Gerontology* 53B(6):S354–S364.

U.S. Centers for Disease Control and Prevention. 1996. "Heat-Related Mortality—Milwaukee, Wisconsin, July 1995." *Morbidity and Mortality Weekly Report* 45:505–7.

Wacquant, Loïc. 1994. "The New Urban Color Line: The State and Fate of the Ghetto in Post-Fordist America." In *Social Theory and the Politics of Identity*, edited by Craig Calhoun. Oxford: Basil Blackwell.

———. 2001. "Deadly Symbiosis: When Ghetto and Prison Meet and Mesh." *Punishment and Society* 3(1):95–134.

Whitman, Steven, Glenn Good, Edmund Donoghue, Nanette Benbow, Wenyuan Shou, and Shanxuan Mou. 1997. "Mortality in Chicago Attributed to the July 1995 Heat Wave." *American Journal of Public Health* 87:1515–18.

Wilson, William Julius. 1996. *When Work Disappears: The World of the New Urban Poor.* New York: Alfred Knopf.

Wuthnow, Robert. 1998. *Loose Connections: Joining Together in America's Fragmented Communities.* Cambridge, MA: Harvard University Press.

49
_____

ILLNESS AND IDENTITY

DAVID A. KARP

How should a society treat the mentally ill? For decades, sociologists have researched this question concerning the treatment of the mentally ill, resulting in such classic studies as Erving Goffman's *Asylums* (1961) and David L. Rosenhan's "On Being Sane in Insane Places" (Reading 19). Today, the deinstitutionalization movement has meant that fewer mentally ill people are hospitalized; instead, they are more likely to be treated with psychotropic drugs on an outpatient basis. The patient's experience of mental illness is the focus of this reading, taken from David Karp's award-winning book, *Speaking of Sadness: Depression, Disconnection, and the Meanings of Illness* (1996). Here, Karp, a professor of sociology at Boston College, examines how clinically depressed people experience and interpret their illnesses and their altered senses of self.

You know, I was a mental patient. That was my identity. . . . Depression is very private. Then all of a sudden it becomes public and I was a mental patient. . . . It's no longer just my own pain. I am a mental patient. I am a depressive. I am a depressive (said slowly and with intensity). This is my identity. I can't separate myself from that. When people know me they'll have to know about my psychiatric history, because that's who I am.

—FEMALE GRADUATE STUDENT, AGED 24

At the time we spoke, Karen, whose words open this chapter, had been doing well for more than two years, but described being badly frightened by a recent two-week period during which the all-too-familiar feelings of depression had begun to reappear. Aside from the terror she felt at the prospect of becoming sick, Karen realized that if depression returned, it would mean recasting her identity yet again. After two years with nothing but the "normal" ups and downs of life, she had started to feel that it might be possible to leave behind the mental patient identity she earlier thought she never could shed. By the time of our interview, only her family and a few old friends knew of her several hospitalizations. Her current roommates thought of her simply as Karen, one of about eight students in the large house they shared. She told me, "No one in my life right now knows . . . I'm so eager to talk to you about it [in this interview] because I can't talk about it with people." I said, "It must be hurtful not to be able to talk about so critical a part of your biography," and Karen responded, "Yes, but I don't want to test it with people. . . . [If I told them] they might not say anything, but their perception of me would change."

Karen was willing to be interviewed because I was one of those who knew about her history with depression. Years previously, while taking one of my undergraduate courses, she had confided that she was having a terrible time completing her course work. After much tentative discussion, the word *depression* finally entered the conversation. She seemed embarrassed by the admission until I opened my desk drawer and showed her a bottle of pills *I* was taking for depression. With this, we began to trade depression experiences and thereby formed the kind of bond felt by those who go through a common difficulty. As her undergraduate years passed, Karen came to my office periodically and during these visits we often spoke about depression. Our shared identity as depressed persons blurred the age and status distinctions that otherwise might have prevented our friendship. . . .

Like nearly everyone whom I talked with, Karen could pinpoint the beginning of her depression career. Although she described a "home filled with feelings of sadness" for as long as she could remember, it was, she said, "the beginning of the ninth grade that touched off . . . ten years of depression." She elaborated with the observation, "I was always sad or upset, but I was so busy and social [that the feelings were muted]. You know, things were not doing so well at home, but at school no one knew how much of a hellhole I lived in." She described a home life that was fairly stable until her father became ill when she was a sixth grader. "When he came back from the hospital," she said, "he was very different, unstable [and] extremely violent." Till then Karen had been able to keep the misery of her home life apart from her school world, which served as a refuge. By the ninth grade, however, she "could no longer keep the two worlds separate" and in both places the same intrusive questions, feelings, and ruminations colonized her mind. Now she didn't feel safe anywhere in the world and had these relentless thoughts: "I'm miserable. [There is] such a feeling of emptiness. What the hell am I doing? What is my life all about? What is the point?" "And that," she said, "basically started it."

In the ninth grade Karen had no word for the "it" that had started. When I asked whether she recognized her pain as depression then, she replied, "Did I say this was depression [then]? Did I know [what it was]? It was pain, but I don't think I would have called it depression. I think I would have called it *my* pain." There was another factor that contributed to the anonymity of her misery and kept her pain from having a name—Karen was determined to keep her torment hidden. She said, "I lived with that for . . . a couple of years, from the ninth grade until the eleventh grade. [I lived] with that feeling. . . . But it was all very private. I kept it quiet. It was something inside. I didn't really talk about it. I might have talked about it with some of my friends, but no one understood."

During this time, though, a subtle transformation was taking place in her thinking about "it." Previously, Karen felt that her pain came exclusively from her difficulties at home, but by the eleventh grade she was beginning to suspect that its locus might be elsewhere. She told me, "My family life might have been hell, but it was always, 'Oh [I feel this way] because my father is crazy. It's because of something outside of me.' But it was the first time I'm feeling awful about myself." By the eleventh grade Karen's new consciousness was that there was something really wrong with *her*. Now, her feelings about the pain took a critical turn when she began to say to herself, "I can't live like this. I will not survive. I will not be here. I can't live with the pain. If I have to live with the pain I will eventually kill myself." Despite such a shift in thinking, Karen still succeeded in keeping things private until she experienced a very public crisis. It was, moreover, a "crash" that she understood as a major "turning point" in her identity. Here's what she said:

> *My whole family life just fell apart. There was no anchor. There was no anchor. . . . [Now] I was able to label it and say it was depression when I crashed in the eleventh grade and was hospitalized. You know, in ninth grade I told you about an experience where I was conscious of feeling pain, or whatever, but no one else knew about it. . . . It is sort of like what my life is like now. I couldn't tell people about it. How can you tell people about it? What do you say? . . .*

Then the interview turned to a lengthy discussion about psychiatric hospitals, doctors, and power—all of it negative. She expressed hostility toward doctors who wanted her to "open up" and toward institutional rules that seemed authoritarian and arbitrary. She said, "Psychiatrists and mental health workers have the power to decide when you are going to leave, if you're going to leave, if you can go out on a pass, if you're good, if you're not good." This first hospitalization (eventually there would be four) also started a long history with medications of all sorts. When I asked whether she was treated with medications she replied, "Yup, always medication. That's the big thing. . . . Oh my God, I've had so many. . . . I don't think they really affected me that much. By the time I left I was doing okay. Did I have these problems solved? No, [but] I had an added one. Now I felt crazy." I used Karen's observation about "feeling crazy" as a cue for asking if she had a disease. I said, "Did you now think of yourself as having an illness in the medical sense?" and her answer reflected the ambivalence and confusion I would later routinely hear when I asked this same question of others.

> *I think of it less as an illness and more something that society defines. That's part of it, but then, it is physical. Doesn't that make it an illness? That's a question I ask myself a lot. Depression is a special case because everyone gets depressed. . . . I think that I define it as not an illness. It's a condition. When I hear the term illness I think of sickness. . . . [but] the term mental illness seems to me to be very negative, maybe because I connect it with hospitalization. . . .*

Before it ended, my interview with Karen covered other difficult emotional terrain, including a major suicide attempt, additional periods of hospitalization, stays in halfway houses, a traumatic college experience, failed relationships with therapists, job interviews that required lies about health history, and a personal spiritual transformation. As indicated at the outset, things had gotten better by the time of our interview and Karen believed she was pretty much past her problem with depression. She told me, "A couple of years ago, three years ago, four years ago, I would feel a need to tell people about it because I still felt depressed, because I still felt mentally ill. But now I no longer see myself in that way. I'm other things. I'm Karen the grad student. I'm Karen the one who loves to garden, the one who's interested in a lot of things. I'm not just Karen the mentally ill person." Still, such optimism about being past depression was sometimes distressingly eroded by periods of bad feelings and the ever-present edge of fear that "it" might return in its full-blown, most grotesque form. . . .

A Career View of the Depression Experience

As in many areas of social life, the notion of career seems an extremely useful, sensitizing concept. In his voluminous and influential writings on work, Everett Hughes showed the value of conceptualizing career as "the moving perspective in which the person sees his life as a whole and interprets the meanings of his various attitudes, actions, and the things which happen to him."[1] Hughes' definition directs attention to the subjective aspects of the career process and the ways in which people attach evaluative meanings to the typical sequence of movements constituting their career path. Here I shall be concerned with describing the career features associated with an especially ambiguous illness—depression.

Hughes' definition also suggests that each stage,[2] juncture, or moment in a career requires a redefinition of self. The depression experience is a heuristically valuable instance for studying the intersection of careers and identities. The following data analysis illustrates that much of the depression career is caught up with assessing self, redefining self, reinterpreting past selves, and attempting to construct a future self that will "work" better. Although all careers require periodic reassessments of self, illness careers are especially characterized by critical "turning points" in identity. In his discussion of identity transformations, Anselm Strauss[3] comments on the intersection of career and identity turning points:

> In transformations of identities a person becomes something other than he or she once was. Such shifts necessitate new evaluations of self and others, of events, acts, and objects. . . . Transformation of perception is irreversible; once having changed there is no going back. One can look back, but evaluate only from the new status. . . . Certain critical incidences occur to force a person to recognize that "I am not the same as I

was, as I used to be." These critical incidents constitute turning points in the onward movement of persons' careers.

. . . While there is considerable variation in the timing of events, all the respondents in this study described a process remarkably similar to the one implicit in Karen's account. Every person I interviewed moved through these identity turning points in their view of themselves and their problem with depression:

1. A period of *inchoate feelings* during which they lacked the vocabulary to label their experience as depression.
2. A phase during which they conclude that *something is really wrong with me.*
3. A *crisis stage* that thrusts them into a world of therapeutic experts.
4. A stage of *coming to grips with an illness identity* during which they theorize about the cause(s) for their difficulty and evaluate the prospects for getting beyond depression.

Each of these career moments assumes and requires redefinitions of self.

Inchoate Feelings

. . . The ages of respondents in this study range from the early twenties to the middle sixties. All these people described a period of time during which they had no vocabulary for naming their problem. Many traced feelings of emotional discomfort to ages as young as three or four, although they could not associate their feelings with something called "depression" until years later. It was typical for respondents to go for long periods of time feeling different, uncomfortable, marginal, ill-at-ease, scared, and in pain without attaching the notion of depression to their situations. A sampling of comments indicating an inchoate, obscure experience includes these:

> *Well, I knew I was different from other children. I should say that from a very early age it felt like I had this darkness about me. Sort of shadow of myself. And I always had the sense that it wasn't going to go away so easily. And it was like my battle. . . . [female travel agent, aged 41]*

> *An awareness that was more intellectual was apparent to me about my sophomore year in high school, when I'd wake up depressed and drag myself to school. . . . I didn't know that's what it was. I just knew that I had an awful hard time getting out of bed and a hard time making my bed and a hard time, you know, getting myself to school. . . . I kind of just had the feeling that something wasn't right. . . . [It was] just like a constant knot in my stomach. But I didn't think that that was anxiety. I just thought I wasn't feeling good, you know (laughing). [unemployed disabled female, aged 39]*

> *If I think about it, I really can't pinpoint a moment [when I was aware that I was depressed]. . . . [male professor, aged 48]*

Most of those reporting bad feelings from an early age could not conclude that something was "abnormal" because they had no baseline of normalcy for comparison. As might be expected, several respondents in this sample came from what they now describe as severely dysfunctional family circumstances, often characterized by alcoholism and both physical and emotional abuse. These individuals described feeling unsafe at home and often devised strategies to spend as much time as they could elsewhere. . . .

For most respondents the phase of inchoate feelings was the longest in the eventual unfolding of their illness consciousness. Particularly salient in terms of personal identity is the fact that initial definitions of their problem centered on the "structural conditions" of their lives instead of on the structure of their selves. The focus of interpretation was on the situation rather than on the self. Their emerging definition was that escape from the situation would make things right. Over and again individuals recounted fantasies of escape from their families and often from the community in which they grew up. However, initially at least, they felt trapped without a clear notion of how the situation might change.

> I remember from like five, starting to subtract five from eighteen, to see how many years I have left before I could get out [of the house]. So, I would say the overwhelming feeling was that I felt powerless. I felt a lot of things early. And I felt that I was stuck in this house and these people controlled me, and there wasn't anything I could do about it, and I was stuck there. So I just started my little chart at about four and a half or five, counting when I could get out. [female baker, aged 41]

. . . A decisive juncture in the evolution of a "sickness" self-definition occurs when the circumstances individuals perceive as troubling their lives change, but mood problems persist. The persistence of problems in the absence of the putative cause requires a redefinition of what is wrong. A huge cognitive shift occurs when people come to see that the problem may be internal instead of situational; when they conclude that something is likely wrong with *them* in a manner that transcends their immediate situation.

Something Is Really Wrong with Me

In 1977, Robert Emerson and Sheldon Messinger published a paper entitled "The Micro-Politics of Trouble"[4] that analyzes the regular processes through which individuals come to see a personal difficulty as sufficiently troublesome a problem that something ought to be done about it. The materials offered in this [reading] affirm the general process they describe. The process begins with a state of affairs initially "experienced as difficult, unpleasant, or unendurable."[5] At first, sufferers try an informal remedy, which sometimes works. If it doesn't, they seek another remedy. The decision that a consequential problem exists warranting a formal remedy typically follows a "recurring cycle of trouble, remedy, failure, more trouble, and a new remedy, until the trouble stops or the troubled person forsakes further efforts."[6] Here, then, is their description of the transformation from vague, inchoate feelings to a clearer sense that one is sufficiently troubled to seek a remedy.

> Problems originate with the recognition that something is wrong and must be remedied. Trouble, in these terms, involves both definitional and remedial components. . . . On first apprehension troubles often involve little more than vague unease. . . . An understanding of the problem's dimensions may only begin to emerge as the troubled person thinks about them, discusses the matter with others, and begins to implement remedial strategies.[7]

Despite the difficulties they have in naming their feelings as a problem, all of the respondents eventually conclude that something is *really wrong with them*. To be sure, many used identical phrases in describing their situations. The phrases "something was really wrong with me" and "I felt that I could no longer live like this" were repeated over and over. Respondents commented in nearly identical ways on the heightened feeling that "something is really wrong with me."

> *When it really became apparent that I was just a mess was in January of 1989. I made the decision really quickly at the end of 1988 to go to school at [names a four-year college] and live with my father and my stepmother and commute. And I packed up all my stuff in my car and went. I was miserable. I cried every day. Every single day I cried. I think I went to two classes [at the new school] and lasted there only a month. I was absolutely miserable. There was a lot of different factors that were involved with it [but] I just didn't feel right. There was something wrong with me, you know. [unemployed female, aged 23]*

> *I guess it's the fall of '90 when I had done the family therapy. I felt great about that. I was back at Harvard. My work was going okay. I loved myself. I loved my husband. Everything was great. [But] I wanted to die. I had no pleasure in anything. What finally got me [was that] I looked at the trees turning and I didn't care. I couldn't believe it. I'd be looking at this big flaming maple and I'd look at it and I'd think, "There it is, it's a maple tree. It's bright orange and red." And nothing in me was touched. At that point I went back to my therapist and said, "There's something really wrong here." [female software quality control manager, aged 31]*

. . . These quotes suggest a fundamental transformation in perception and identity at this point in the evolution of a depression consciousness. Respondents now located the source of their problem as somewhere within their bodies and minds, as deep within themselves. Such a belief implies a problematic identity far more basic and immutable than those associated with social statuses. If, for example, someone has a disliked occupational identity, the possibilities for occupational change exist. If the occupational identity becomes onerous enough, it is possible to quit a job. Similarly, without minimizing the difficulties of change, we can choose to become single if married, to change from one religion to another, and, these days, even to change our sex if the motivation is great enough. However, to see oneself as somehow internally flawed poses substantially greater problems for identity change or remediation because one's whole personhood is implicated. Getting rid of a sick self poses far greater problems than dropping certain social statuses. The important point here is that the rejection of situational theories for bad feelings is a critical identity turning point. Full acceptance that one has a damaged self requires acknowledgment that "I am not the same as I was, as I used to be."

Another important dimension of the career process that becomes apparent at this point is the issue of whether to keep the problem private or to make it public, especially to family and friends. The private/public distinction was a dominant theme in respondents' talk throughout the history of their experience with depression. The question of being private or public is, of course, central to one's developing self-identification. As Peter Berger and Hansfried Kellner[8] point out in describing the "social construction of marriage" and Diane Vaughan[9] indicates in analyzing the process of "uncoupling" from a relationship, the moment a new status becomes public is a definitive one in solidifying a person's new identity. In the cases of both creating and disengaging from relationships, people are normally very careful not to make public announcements until they are certain they are ready to adopt new statuses and identities. The significance attached to public announcements of even modest shifts in life style is indicated by the considerable thought people sometimes give to making public such relatively benign decisions as going on diets or quitting cigarettes.

Decisions about "going public" are, of course, greatly magnified when the information to be imparted is negative and, in the case of emotional problems, potentially stigmatizing. As Emerson and Messinger note, the search for a remedy necessarily involves sharing information with others. Still, at this early juncture of dealing with bad feelings, most respondents elected to keep silent about their pain. . . .

Whether or not they made their feelings public, this second phase of their illness career involved the recognition that they possessed a self that was working badly in *every* situation. Although everyone continued to identify the kinds of *social* situations that had caused their bad feelings in the past and precipitated them in the present, the qualitative change at this juncture was in the locus of attention from external to internal causes. At this point, respondents were struggling to live their lives in the face of debilitating pain. This stage ended, however, when efforts to control things became impossible.

At some point, everyone interviewed experienced a crisis of some sort. For the majority (29) the crisis meant hospitalization. At the point of crisis, whatever their wishes might have been, they could not prevent their situation from becoming public knowledge to family, friends, and co-workers. Whether they were hospitalized or not, everyone reached a point where they felt obliged to rely on psychiatric experts to deal with their difficulty. Receiving an "official" diagnosis of depression and consequent treatment with medications greatly accelerated the need to redefine their past, present, and future in illness terms. The crisis solidified the emerging consciousness that the problem was within themselves. More than that, it was now a problem beyond their own efforts to control.

Crisis

Nearly everyone could pinpoint the precise time, situation, or set of events that moved them from the recognition that something was wrong to the realization that they were desperately sick. They could often remember in vivid detail the moment when things absolutely got out of hand.

> *So I went to law school in the fall. I was at Columbia and in the best of times Columbia is a depressing place. I mean, it's a shithole. And you know, I was pretty messed up when I got there. . . . I remember Columbia was a nightmare. . . . So, I was getting to the point where I was paranoid about going to class and so someone talked to the dean and said, "Hey, you've got to do something about this guy, he's off the deep edge." [male administrator, aged 54]*

> *I think the significant moment was when I got stage fright in high school. There were earlier moments when I felt something was wrong. I can remember feeling real dizzy when I was on the stage in the 8th grade. But the significant moment was in high school and I was seized by just pure terror. And the fear was so horrible that I couldn't tell it to anybody. I couldn't share it. It was something beyond my ability to communicate. It was so horrible that no one could understand it. [male professor, aged 66]*

. . . At the crisis point, people fully enter a therapeutic world of hospitals, mental health experts, and medications. For many, entrance into this world is simultaneous with first receiving the "official" diagnosis of depression.[10] It is difficult to overstate the critical importance of official diagnoses and labeling. The point of diagnosis was a double-edged benchmark in the illness career. On the one hand, knowing that you "have" something that doctors regard as a specific illness imposes definitional boundaries onto an array of behaviors and feelings that previously had no name. Acquiring a clear conception of what one has and having a label to attach to confounding feelings and behaviors was especially significant to those who had gone for years without being able to name their situation. To be diagnosed also suggests the possibility that the condition can be treated and that one's suffering can be diminished. At the same time, being a "depressive" places one in the devalued category of those with mental illness. On the negative side, respondents made comments like these:

> *I kept going to doctor after doctor, getting like all these new terms put on me. . . . My family was dysfunctional and I was an alcoholic with an eating disorder and bulimia and depression and it was just all these labels. "Oh my God!" [unemployed female, aged 22]*

> *My father went to his allergy doctor who referred us to a guy who turned out to be a reasonable psychiatrist. I'll never forget. He said, "Your daughter is*

clinically depressed." I remember sitting in his office. He saw us on a Saturday like at six o'clock. He did us a favor. And I remember I just sat there. It was a sort of darkened office. It was the first time I ever cried in front of anybody. [female social worker, aged 38]

And on the liberating side:

They gave me a blood test that measures the level of something in the blood, in the brain. And they pronounced me, they said, "Mr. Smith [a pseudonym], you're depressed." And I said, "Thank God," you know. I wasn't as batty as I thought. It was like the cat was out of the bag. You know? It was a break-through. . . . [Before that] depression wasn't in my vocabulary. . . . It was the beginning of being able to sort out a lifetime of feelings, events . . . my entire life. It was the chance for a new beginning. [male salesman, aged 30]

. . . It is impossible to consider the kinds of profound identity changes occasioned by any mental illness without paying special attention to the experience of hospitalization. It is one thing to deal alone with the demons of depression, or to privately see a psychiatrist for the problem, but once a person "shuts down" altogether and seeks asylum or is involuntarily "committed," he or she adds an institutional piece to their biography that is indelible. . . .

A few interviewees described the hospital as truly an asylum that provided relief and allowed them to "crash." Being hospitalized enabled them to give up the struggle of trying to appear and act normally. One person, in fact, described the hospital as a "wonderful place" where "I was taken care of, totally taken care of." Another was relieved "to go somewhere where I won't do anything to myself, where I can get in touch with this." Someone else explained, "I was glad to be there, definitely. It was a break from everything." Sometimes people were glad to be hospitalized since it provided dramatic and definitive evidence that something was really wrong with them when family and friends had been dismissing their complaints. More usual, though, were the responses like that of the person who said that "the experience of hospitalization was devastating to me" and the several who reported that being hospitalized made them feel like "damaged goods."

Of all the tough things associated with depression, nothing would frighten me more than hospitalization. . . .

Many of the 29 people who spoke of their time in hospitals spontaneously acknowledged the extraordinary impact of the experience on the way they thought about themselves. Sometimes they were themselves shocked that they had landed in a hospital. Several mentioned that hospitalization caused them to confront for the first time just how sick they were.

I remember being put onto the floor that was probably for the worst people of the sickness, because it was one of those floors where everything was really locked up. So I guess I was in pretty bad shape. [male administrator, aged 54]

So I went to [names hospital] and I remember praying that I would get out. To me it seemed at the time as if the door would close—it was a secure facility—and

I would never leave. I know I'm a basket case at this point. . . . The experience of having that severe depression, going to the hospital, and most of all being given shock treatments. . . . It made me feel . . . like damaged goods, impaired in some way that I was just not normal. It did make me feel impaired. [male professor, part-time, aged 48]

Among the identity-related comments about the hospitalization experience, one set of observations, although made by only a few individuals, caught my attention. Once in the hospital these persons surveyed their environment, both the oppressive physical character of the place and the sad shape of their fellow "inmates," many of whom seemed to them destined for an institutionalized life. However awful their condition, these respondents made a distinction between their trouble and patients who were overtly psychotic. Unlike those unfortunates, they had a choice to make, as they saw it. Either they would capitulate completely to their depression and possibly, therefore, to a life in the mental health system or they would do whatever necessary to leave the hospital as quickly as possible.

Giving up completely did have some appealing features. Full surrender meant relief from an exhausting battle and absolution from personal responsibility. One woman said,

I saw these people going back and forth [in and out of the hospital] for their whole lives [and] that I could be one [of them]. If I went in that direction, it somehow absolved me from responsibility. And I teetered on the edge for a long time. It involved a conscious decision . . . [about whether] I'm going to become a [permanent] part of the system because it's safe and where I belong. . . .

—————

. . . It should be noted that one outstanding uniformity in the interviews was the initially strong negative reaction people had to taking drugs. One person was "leery of it" and others variously described the idea of going on medications as "revolting," "certainly not my first choice," and "embarrassing." Others elaborated on the recommendation that they begin drug therapy in ways similar to the nurse who said: "I didn't want to be told that I had something that was going to affect the rest of my life and that could only be solved by taking pills. And there was sort of a rebellion in that: 'No, I'm not like that. I don't need you and your pills.'". . . [Respondents] held the shared feeling that taking drugs was yet another distressing indication of the severity of a problem they could not control by themselves. The concurrent events of crisis, hospitalization, and beginning a drug regimen worked synergistically to concretize and dramatize respondents' status as patients with an illness that required ongoing treatment by therapeutic experts.

Coming to Grips with an Illness Identity

Whether people are hospitalized or not, involvement with psychiatric experts and medications is the transition point to a number of simultaneous processes, all with implications for the reformulation of identity. They are

(1) reconstructing and reinterpreting one's past in terms of current experiences, (2) looking for causes for one's situation, (3) constructing new theories about the nature of depression, and (4) establishing modes of coping behavior. All of these activities require judgments about the appropriate metaphors for describing one's situation. Especially critical to ongoing identity construction is whether respondents approve of illness metaphors for describing their experience. A few individuals were willing clearly to define their condition as a mental illness:

> *I know I have a mental illness. I'm beginning to feel that. [But] actually, there is a real relief in that. It's a sense of "Whew! Okay, I don't have to masquerade." I mean, sure I'll masquerade with work, because, listen, I've got to get the bread and butter on the table. But I don't have to masquerade in other ways. . . . It's sort of like mentally ill people in some ways . . . are my people. There is a fair amount of really chronically mentally ill people at [names hospital where she works]. They're all on heavy-duty meds and I figure like "I know what it's like for you." I mean, I can imagine what it's like. I know some of that pain. I'm sure I don't know all of it, because, you know, I'm not that bad off, but there is sort of a sense like they could understand me and I could understand them in something that's really, really painful. [female physical therapist, aged 42]*

. . . Most, however, wanted simultaneously to embrace the definition of their problem as biochemical in nature while rejecting the notion that they suffer from a "mental" illness.

> *I don't see it as an illness. To me, it seems like part of myself that evolved, part of my personality. And, I mean, it sounds crazy, but it is almost like a dual personality, the happy side of me and the sad side of me. . . . [female nanny, aged 22]*

Well, do you have an illness? What do you have?

> *I tend to think of it as a condition. I don't think of it so much as an illness, although it feels like an illness sometimes. I think it's an unintegrated dimension of myself that's taken [on] kind of a life of its own, that has its own power. . . . [unemployed female, aged 35]*

. . . Adopting the view that one is victimized by a biochemically sick self constitutes a comfortable "account" for a history of difficulties and failures and absolves one of reponsibility. On the negative side, however, acceptance of a victim role, while diminishing a sense of personal responsibility, is also enfeebling. To be a victim of biochemical forces beyond one's control gives force to others' definition of oneself as a helpless, passive object of injury. . . .

Respondents generally fall into two broad categories regarding their hopes that they can put depression behind them. First are those who view having depression as a life condition that they will never fully defeat, and second are those who believe either that they are now past the depression forever or that they can attain such a status. As might be expected, the two categories are generally formed by those who have experienced depression as an ongoing chronic thing, on the one hand, in contrast to those who have had periods of depression punctuated by wellness. The role of medications is interesting in establishing for some the idea that depression is something they can leave behind. Among the words that reappeared in comments about drugs was "miracle." Although, as noted, most of those interviewed at first took medication reluctantly, several reported that often for the first time in their lives they felt okay after a drug "kicked in." Generally, subjects were split between those who felt that while there was always the possibility of a recurrence, they essentially could get past depression and those who have surrendered to its inevitability and chronicity in their lives. The following comments summarize the two positions:

> *I've stopped thinking, "OK, I'm going to get over this depression. I'm going to finally, like, do this primal scream thing, or whatever. . . . [At one point] I did buy into [the idea] of the pursuit of happiness and the pursuit of fulfillment. I hate that word. And the mental health equivalent to finding fulfillment is to fill up the gaps inside of you and everything grows green. And that's what [psychiatry] is really striving for . . . and that's the standard life should be lived on. . . . But then I finally realized that well, maybe I'm in a desert. Maybe your landscape is green, but, you know, I'm in the Sahara and I've stopped trying to get out. . . . I'd rather cure it if I had my choice, but I don't think that is going to happen. My choice is to integrate it into my life. So, no, I don't see it going away. I just see myself becoming, you know, better able to cope with it, more graceful about it. [female mental health worker, aged 27]*

> *I would say that this particular period of my life is a period where I don't have the fear or feeling [that depression will recur]. That's why, for me at least, I'm more inclined now to take the depression as an aberration and to take me in my more expansive, expressive state as the norm. For me, maybe I'm deluding myself, the way I feel now, and it's been three years since the hospitalization and I take no medications of any kind, [is] that I may be out of the woods, so to speak. . . . At the moment I don't have a fear of recurrence, but I do remember having it. [male professor, part-time, aged 48]*

Unfortunately, the norm is for people to have repeated bouts with depression. In this regard, the process described here has a feedback-loop quality to it. Individuals move through a crisis with all its attendant identity-altering features, come to grips with the meaning of their experience by constructing theories about causation, and then sometimes reach the point where they feel they have gone beyond the depression experience. A new episode of depression, of course, casts doubt on all the previous interpretive work and requires people to once again move through a process of sense-making and identity construction. In this way, depression is like a virus that keeps mutating since each reliving of an experience, as the philosopher Edmund Husserl tells us, is a new experience. Chronically depressed people are constantly in the throes of an illness that is tragically familiar, but always new. As such, depression often involves a life centered on a nearly continuous process of construction, destruction, and reconstruction of identities in the face of repeated problems. . . .

ENDNOTES

[1] E. Hughes, *Men and Their Work* (New York: Free Press, 1958).

[2] Although the notion of "stage" is difficult to avoid, I want to suggest that in much social science literature the term conveys a determinism that I find unfortunate. Stages imply that, for whatever process being described, everyone must move through them in a predictably timed sequence. Hence, I often use the terms "moment," "benchmark," or "juncture" in the depression career to suggest a process that is more fluid than the stage idea.

[3] A. Strauss, "Turning Points in Identity," in *Social Interaction*, edited by C. Clark and H. Robboy, (New York: St. Martin's, 1992). The identity transitions described in the pages to follow bear an instructive resemblance to the idea of biographical "epiphanies" developed by Norman Denzin in a number of important books. See N. Denzin, *The Alcoholic Self* (Newbury Park, CA: Sage, 1987); N. Denzin, *Interpretive Interactionism* (Newbury Park, CA: Sage, 1989); N. Denzin, *Interpretive Biography* (Newbury Park, CA: Sage, 1989).

[4] R. Emerson and S. Messinger, "The Micro-Politics of Trouble," *Social Problems* 25 (1977): 121–33. For another formulation of the trouble idea, see the early work of Charlotte Schwartz. Schwartz's doctoral dissertation studied how 30 people who sought help at a university psychiatric service conceptualized their problem. Her interview data suggested that informants distinguished three mutually exclusive subjective states of trouble. She calls them *exigencies of living* (or momentary difficulties), *normal trouble* (ordinary trouble), and *special trouble* (serious problems). An elaboration of these categories can be found in her work entitled *Clients' Perspectives on Psychiatric Troubles in a College Setting* (unpublished doctoral dissertation, Brandeis University, 1976). See also her article with Merton Kahne entitled "The Social Construction of Trouble and Its Implications for Psychiatrists Working in College Settings," *Journal of the American College Health Association* 25 (February 1977): 194–97.

[5] R. Emerson and S. Messinger, op. cit., p. 122.

[6] Ibid.

[7] Ibid.

[8] P. Berger and H. Kellner, "Marriage and the Construction of Reality," *Diogenes* 46 (1964): 1–25.

[9] D. Vaughan, *Uncoupling: Turning Points in Intimate Relationships* (New York: Oxford, 1986).

[10] Social scientists have been critical of the meaning of psychiatric diagnoses and the processes through which they are established. For examples, see P. Brown, "Diagnostic Conflict and Contradiction in Psychiatry," *Journal of Health and Social Behavior* 28 (1987): 37–50 and M. Rosenberg, "A Symbolic Interactionist View of Psychosis," *Journal of Health and Social Behavior* 25 (1984): 289–302.

EDUCATION

50

CIVILIZE THEM WITH A STICK

MARY CROW DOG • RICHARD ERDOES

Few students are aware of our nation's policies toward Native Americans, which included the separation of Indian children from their families and cultures so that these children could be "civilized" into the dominant society. Consequently, beginning in 1879, thousands of Native American children were forced to leave the reservation to attend boarding schools, day schools, or schools in converted army posts. These total institutions used tactics similar to those used by the military to resocialize the young Native Americans. The peak period for Native American boarding schools was 1879–1930, but they continue, in some places, today. In the following selection, taken from *Lakota Woman* (1990), Mary Crow Dog and Richard Erdoes reveal how the institution of education can be an agent of social control whose purpose is to assimilate racial-ethnic populations, such as Native Americans, into the dominant culture. Crow Dog is a Native American activist and Erdoes is the ghostwriter of her autobiography.

. . . Gathered from the cabin, the wickiup, and the tepee,
partly by cajolery and partly by threats;
partly by bribery and partly by force,
they are induced to leave their kindred
to enter these schools and take upon themselves
the outward appearance of civilized life.

—ANNUAL REPORT OF THE DEPARTMENT OF INTERIOR, 1901

It is almost impossible to explain to a sympathetic white person what a typical old Indian boarding school was like; how it affected the Indian child suddenly dumped into it like a small creature from another world, helpless, defenseless, bewildered, trying desperately and instinctively to survive and sometimes not surviving at all. I think such children were like the victims of Nazi concentration camps trying to tell average, middle-class

Americans what their experience had been like. Even now, when these schools are much improved, when the buildings are new, all gleaming steel and glass, the food tolerable, the teachers well trained and well intentioned, even trained in child psychology—unfortunately the psychology of white children, which is different from ours—the shock to the child upon arrival is still tremendous. Some just seem to shrivel up, don't speak for days on end, and have an empty look in their eyes. I know of an 11-year-old on another reservation who hanged herself, and in our school, while I was there, a girl jumped out of the window, trying to kill herself to escape an unbearable situation. That first shock is always there.

Although the old tiyospaye has been destroyed, in the traditional Sioux families, especially in those where there is no drinking, the child is never left alone. It is always surrounded by relatives, carried around, enveloped in warmth. It is treated with the respect due to any human being, even a small one. It is seldom forced to do anything against its will, seldom screamed at, and never beaten. That much, at least, is left of the old family group among full-bloods. And then suddenly a bus or car arrives, full of strangers, usually white strangers, who yank the child out of the arms of those who love it, taking it screaming to the boarding school. The only word I can think of for what is done to these children is kidnapping.

Even now, in a good school, there is impersonality instead of close human contact; a sterile, cold atmosphere, an unfamiliar routine, language problems, and above all the maza-skan-skan, that damn clock—white man's time as opposed to Indian time, which is natural time. Like eating when you are hungry and sleeping when you are tired, not when that damn clock says you must. But I was not taken to one of the better, modern schools. I was taken to the old-fashioned mission school at St. Francis, run by the nuns and Catholic fathers, built sometime around the turn of the century and not improved a bit when I arrived, not improved as far as the buildings, the food, the teachers, or their methods were concerned.

In the old days, nature was our people's only school and they needed no other. Girls had their toy tipis and dolls, boys their toy bows and arrows. Both rode and swam and played the rough Indian games together. Kids watched their peers and elders and naturally grew from children into adults. Life in the tipi circle was harmonious—until the whiskey peddlers arrived with their wagons and barrels of "Injun whiskey." I often wished I could have grown up in the old, before-whiskey days.

Oddly enough, we owed our unspeakable boarding schools to the do-gooders, the white Indian-lovers. The schools were intended as an alternative to the outright extermination seriously advocated by generals Sherman and Sheridan, as well as by most settlers and prospectors overrunning our land. "You don't have to kill those poor benighted heathen," the do-gooders said, "in order to solve the Indian Problem. Just give us a chance to turn them into useful farmhands, laborers, and chambermaids who will break their backs for you at low wages." In that way the boarding schools were born. The kids were taken away from their villages and pueblos, in their blankets and moccasins, kept completely isolated from their families—sometimes for as long as ten years—suddenly coming back, their short hair slick with pomade, their necks raw from stiff, high collars, their thick jackets always short in the sleeves and pinching under the arms, their tight patent leather shoes giving them corns, the girls in starched white blouses and clumsy, high-buttoned boots—caricatures of white people. When they found out—and they found out quickly—that they were neither wanted by whites nor by Indians, they got good and drunk, many of them staying drunk for the rest of their lives. I still have a poster I found among my grandfather's stuff, given to him by the missionaries to tack up on his wall. It reads:

1. Let Jesus save you.
2. Come out of your blanket, cut your hair, and dress like a white man.
3. Have a Christian family with one wife for life only.
4. Live in a house like your white brother. Work hard and wash often.
5. Learn the value of a hard-earned dollar. Do not waste your money on giveaways. Be punctual.
6. Believe that property and wealth are signs of divine approval.
7. Keep away from saloons and strong spirits.
8. Speak the language of your white brother. Send your children to school to do likewise.
9. Go to church often and regularly.
10. Do not go to Indian dances or to the medicine men.

The people who were stuck upon "solving the Indian Problem" by making us into whites retreated from this position only step by step in the wake of Indian protests.

The mission school at St. Francis was a curse for our family for generations. My grandmother went there, then my mother, then my sisters and I. At one time or other, every one of us tried to run away. Grandma told me once about the bad times she had experienced at St. Francis. In those days they let students go home only for one week every year. Two days were used up for transportation, which meant spending just five days out of 365 with her family. And that was an improvement. Before grandma's time, on many reservations they did not let the students go home at all until they had finished school. Anybody who disobeyed the nuns was severely punished. The building in which my grandmother stayed had three floors, for girls only. Way up in the attic were little cells, about five by five by ten feet. One time she was in church and instead of praying she was playing jacks. As punishment they took her to one of those little cubicles where she stayed in darkness because the windows had been boarded up. They left her there for a whole week with only bread and water for nourishment. After she came out she promptly ran away, together with three other girls. They were found and brought back. The nuns stripped them naked and whipped them. They used a horse buggy whip on my grandmother. Then she was put back into the attic—for two weeks.

My mother had much the same experiences but never wanted to talk about them, and then there I was, in the same place. The school is now run by the BIA—the Bureau of Indian Affairs—but only since about 15 years ago. When I was there, during the 1960s, it was still run by the Church. The Jesuit fathers ran the boys' wing and the Sisters of the Sacred Heart ran us—with the help of the strap. Nothing had changed since my grandmother's days. I have been told recently that even in the '70s they were still beating children at that school. All I got out of school was being taught how to pray. I learned quickly that I would be beaten if I failed in my devotions or, God forbid, prayed the wrong way, especially prayed in Indian to Wakan Tanka, the Indian Creator.

The girls' wing was built like an F and was run like a penal institution. Every morning at five o'clock the sisters would come into our large dormitory to wake us up, and immediately we had to kneel down at the sides of our beds and recite the prayers. At six o'clock we were herded into the church for more of the same. I did not take kindly to the discipline and to marching by the clock, left-right, left-right. I was never one to like being forced to do something. I do something because I feel like doing it. I felt this way always, as far as I can remember, and my sister Barbara felt the same way. An old medicine man once told me: "Us Lakotas are not like dogs who can be trained, who can be beaten and keep on wagging their tails, licking the hand that whipped them. We are like cats, little cats, big cats, wildcats, bobcats, mountain lions. It doesn't matter what kind, but cats who can't be tamed, who scratch if you step on their tails." But I was only a kitten and my claws were still small.

Barbara was still in the school when I arrived and during my first year or two she could still protect me a little bit. When Barb was a seventh grader she ran away together with five other girls, early in the morning before sunrise. They brought them back in the evening. The girls had to wait for two hours in front of the mother superior's office. They were hungry and cold, frozen through. It was wintertime and they had been running the whole day without food, trying to make good their escape. The mother superior asked each girl, "Would you do this again?" She told them that as punishment they would not be allowed to visit home for a month and that she'd keep them busy on work details until the skin on their knees and elbows had worn off. At the end of her speech she told each girl, "Get up from this chair and lean over it." She then lifted the girls' skirts and pulled down their underpants. Not little girls either, but teenagers. She had a leather strap about a foot long and four inches wide fastened to a stick, and beat the girls, one after another, until they cried. Barb did not give her that satisfaction but just clenched her teeth. There was one girl, Barb told me, the nun kept on beating and beating until her arm got tired.

I did not escape my share of the strap. Once, when I was 13 years old, I refused to go to Mass. I did not want to go to church because I did not feel well. A nun grabbed me by the hair, dragged me upstairs, made me stoop over, pulled my dress up (we were not allowed at the time to wear jeans), pulled my panties down, and gave me what they called "swats"—25 swats with a board around which Scotch tape had been wound. She hurt me badly.

My classroom was right next to the principal's office and almost every day I could hear him swatting the boys. Beating was the common punishment for not doing one's homework, or for being late to school. It had such a bad effect upon me that I hated and mistrusted every white person on sight, because I met only one kind. It was not until much later that I met sincere white people I could relate to and be friends with. Racism breeds racism in reverse.

The routine at St. Francis was dreary. Six A.M., kneeling in church for an hour or so; seven o'clock, breakfast; eight o'clock, scrub the floor, peel spuds, make classes. We had to mop the dining room twice every day and scrub the tables. If you were caught taking a rest, doodling on the bench with a fingernail or knife, or just rapping, the nun would come up with a dish towel and just slap it across your face, saying, "You're not supposed to be talking, you're supposed to be working!" Monday mornings we had cornmeal mush, Tuesday oatmeal, Wednesday rice and raisins, Thursday cornflakes, and Friday all the leftovers mixed together or sometimes fish. Frequently the food had bugs or rocks in it. We were eating hot dogs that were weeks old, while the nuns were dining on ham, whipped potatoes, sweet peas, and cranberry sauce. In winter our dorm was icy cold while the nuns' rooms were always warm.

I have seen little girls arrive at the school, first graders, just fresh from home and totally unprepared for what awaited them, little girls with pretty braids, and the first thing the nuns did was chop their hair off and tie up what was left behind their ears. Next they would dump the children into tubs of alcohol, a sort of rubbing alcohol, "to get the germs off." Many of the nuns were German immigrants, some from Bavaria, so that we sometimes speculated whether Bavaria was some sort of Dracula country inhabited by monsters. For the sake of objectivity I ought to mention that two of the German fathers were great linguists and that the only Lakota-English dictionaries and grammars which are worth anything were put together by them.

At night some of the girls would huddle in bed together for comfort and reassurance. Then the nun in charge of the dorm would come in and say, "What are the two of you doing in bed together? I smell evil in this room. You girls are evil incarnate. You are sinning. You are going to hell and burn forever. You can act that way in the devil's frying pan." She would get them out of bed in the middle of the night, making them kneel and pray until morning. We had not the slightest idea what it was all about. At home we slept two and three in a bed for animal warmth and a feeling of security.

The nuns and the girls in the two top grades were constantly battling it out physically with fists, nails, and hair-pulling. I myself was growing from a kitten into an undersized cat. My claws were getting bigger and were itching for action. About 1969 or 1970 a strange young white girl appeared on the reservation. She looked about 18 or 20 years old. She was pretty and had long, blond hair down to her waist, patched jeans, boots, and a backpack. She was different from any other white person we had met before. I think her name was Wise. I do not know how she managed to overcome our reluctance and distrust, getting us into a corner, making us listen to her, asking us how we were treated. She told us that she was from New York. She was the first real hippie or Yippie we had come across. She told us of people called the Black Panthers, Young Lords, and Weathermen. She said, "Black people are getting it on. Indians are getting it on in St. Paul and California. How about you?" She also said, "Why don't you put out an underground paper, mimeograph it. It's easy. Tell it like it is. Let it all hang out." She spoke a strange lingo but we caught on fast.

Charlene Left Hand Bull and Gina One Star were two full-blood girls I used to hang out with. We did everything together. They were willing to join me in a Sioux uprising. We put together a newspaper which we called the *Red Panther*. In it we wrote how bad the school was, what kind of slop we had to eat—slimy, rotten, blackened potatoes for two weeks—the way we were beaten. I think I was the one who wrote the worst article about our principal of the moment, Father Keeler. I put all my anger and venom into it. I called him a goddam wasičun son of a bitch. I wrote that he knew nothing about Indians and should go back to where he came from, teaching white children whom he could relate to. I wrote that we knew which priests slept with which nuns and that all they ever could think about was filling their bellies and buying a new car. It was the kind of writing which foamed at the mouth, but which also lifted a great deal of weight from one's soul.

On Saint Patrick's Day, when everybody was at the big powwow, we distributed our newspapers. We put them on windshields and bulletin boards, in desks and pews, in dorms and toilets. But someone saw us and snitched on us. The shit hit the fan. The three of us were taken before a board meeting. Our parents, in my case my mother, had to come. They were told that ours was a most serious matter, the worst thing that had ever happened in the school's long history. One of the nuns told my mother, "Your daughter really needs to be talked to." "What's wrong with my daughter?" my mother asked. She was given one of our *Red Panther* newspapers. The nun pointed out its name to her and then my piece, waiting for mom's reaction. After a while she asked, "Well, what have you got to say to this? What do you think?"

My mother said, "Well, when I went to school here, some years back, I was treated a lot worse than these kids are. I really can't see how they can have any complaints, because we was treated a lot stricter. We could not even wear skirts halfway up our knees. These girls have it made. But you should forgive them because they are young. And it's supposed to be a free country, free speech and all that. I don't believe what they done is wrong." So all I got out of it was scrubbing six flights of stairs on my hands and knees, every day. And no boy-side privileges.

The boys and girls were still pretty much separated. The only time one could meet a member of the opposite sex was during free time, between 4 and 5:30, in the study hall or on benches or the volleyball court outside, and that was strictly supervised. One day Charlene and I went over to the boys' side. We were on the ball team and they had to let us practice. We played three extra minutes, only three minutes more than we were supposed to. Here was the nuns' opportunity for revenge. We got 25 swats. I told

Charlene, "We are getting too old to have our bare asses whipped that way. We are old enough to have babies. Enough of this shit. Next time we fight back." Charlene only said, "Hoka-hay!". . .

In a school like this there is always a lot of favoritism. At St. Francis it was strongly tinged with racism. Girls who were near-white, who came from what the nuns called "nice families," got preferential treatment. They waited on the faculty and got to eat ham or eggs and bacon in the morning. They got the easy jobs while the skins, who did not have the right kind of background—myself among them—always wound up in the laundry room sorting out 10-bushel baskets of dirty boys' socks every day. Or we wound up scrubbing the floors and doing all the dishes. The school therefore fostered fights and antagonism between whites and breeds, and between breeds and skins. At one time Charlene and I had to iron all the robes and vestments the priests wore when saying Mass. We had to fold them up and put them into a chest in the back of the church. In a corner, looking over our shoulders, was a statue of the crucified Savior, all bloody and beaten up. Charlene looked up and said, "Look at that poor Indian. The pigs sure worked him over." That was the closest I ever came to seeing Jesus.

I was held up as a bad example and didn't mind. I was old enough to have a boyfriend and promptly got one. At the school we had an hour and a half for ourselves. Between the boys' and the girls' wings were some benches where one could sit. My boyfriend and I used to go there just to hold hands and talk. The nuns were very uptight about any boy-girl stuff. They had an exaggerated fear of anything having even the faintest connection with sex. One day in religion class, an all-girl class, Sister Bernard singled me out for some remarks, pointing me out as a bad example, an example that should be shown. She said that I was too free with my body. That I was holding hands which meant that I was not a good example to follow. She also said that I wore unchaste dresses, skirts which were too short, too suggestive, shorter than regulations permitted, and for that I would be punished. She dressed me down before the whole class, carrying on and on about my unchastity. . . .

We got a new priest in English. During one of his first classes he asked one of the boys a certain question. The boy was shy. He spoke poor English, but he had the right answer. The priest told him, "You did not say it right. Correct yourself. Say it over again." The boy got flustered and stammered. He could hardly get out a word. But the priest kept after him: "Didn't you hear? I told you to do the whole thing over. Get it right this time." He kept on and on.

I stood up and said, "Father, don't be doing that. If you go into an Indian's home and try to talk Indian, they might laugh at you and say, 'Do it over correctly. Get it right this time!'"

He shouted at me, "Mary, you stay after class. Sit down right now!"

I stayed after class, until after the bell. He told me, "Get over here!" He grabbed me by the arm, pushing me against the blackboard, shouting, "Why are you always mocking us? You have no reason to do this."

I said, "Sure I do. You were making fun of him. You embarrassed him. He needs strengthening, not weakening. You hurt him. I did not hurt you."

He twisted my arm and pushed real hard. I turned around and hit him in the face, giving him a bloody nose. After that I ran out of the room, slamming the door behind me. He and I went to Sister Bernard's office. I told her, "Today I quit school. I'm not taking any more of this, none of this shit anymore. None of this treatment. Better give me my diploma. I can't waste any more time on you people."

Sister Bernard looked at me for a long, long time. She said, "All right, Mary Ellen, go home today. Come back in a few days and get your diploma." And that was that. Oddly enough, that priest turned out okay. He taught a class in grammar, orthography, composition, things like that. I think he wanted more respect in class. He was still young and unsure of himself. But I was in there too long. I didn't feel like hearing it. Later he became a good friend of the Indians, a personal friend of myself and my husband. He stood up for us during Wounded Knee and after. He stood up to his superiors, stuck his neck way out, became a real people's priest. He even learned our language. He died prematurely of cancer. It is not only the good Indians who die young, but the good whites, too. It is the timid ones who know how to take care of themselves who grow old. I am still grateful to that priest for what he did for us later and for the quarrel he picked with me—or did I pick it with him?—because it ended a situation which had become unendurable for me. The day of my fight with him was my last day in school.

51

STILL SEPARATE, STILL UNEQUAL
America's Educational Apartheid

JONATHAN KOZOL

One of the most important legal decisions of the twentieth century was the 1954 U.S. Supreme Court case *Brown v. Board of Education.* This case made it a federal crime for the institution of education to segregate children on the basis of race in public schools. The intent was to challenge racial and social class inequality that created inferior classrooms and curricula for many of our nation's children. In this selection, adapted from *The Shame*

Jonathan Kozol, "Still Separate, Still Unequal: America's Educational Apartheid" from *Harper's* (September 2005). Copyright © 2005 by Jonathan Kozol. Reprinted with the permission of the author.

of the Nation: The Restoration of Apartheid Schooling in America (2005), Jonathan Kozol examines current racial segregation in American schools 50 years after *Brown v. Board of Education.* Kozol, an award-winning writer, visited over 60 public schools and interviewed children, teachers, and administrators about the status of education.

Many Americans who live far from our major cities and who have no firsthand knowledge of the realities to be found in urban public schools seem to have the rather vague and general impression that the great extremes of racial isolation that were matters of grave national significance some thirty-five or forty years ago have gradually but steadily diminished in more recent years. The truth, unhappily, is that the trend, for well over a decade now, has been precisely the reverse. Schools that were already deeply segregated twenty-five or thirty years ago are no less segregated now, while thousands of other schools around the country that had been integrated either voluntarily or by the force of law have since been rapidly resegregating.

In Chicago, by the academic year 2002–2003, 87 percent of public-school enrollment was black or Hispanic; less than 10 percent of children in the schools were white. In Washington, D.C., 94 percent of children were black or Hispanic; less than 5 percent were white. In St. Louis, 82 percent of the student population were black or Hispanic; in Philadelphia and Cleveland, 79 percent; in Los Angeles, 84 percent; in Detroit, 96 percent; in Baltimore, 89 percent. In New York City, nearly three quarters of the students were black or Hispanic.

Even these statistics, as stark as they are, cannot begin to convey how deeply isolated children in the poorest and most segregated sections of these cities have become. In the typically colossal high schools of the Bronx, for instance, more than 90 percent of students (in most cases, more than 95 percent) are black or Hispanic. At John F. Kennedy High School in 2003, 93 percent of the enrollment of more than 4,000 students were black and Hispanic; only 3.5 percent of students at the school were white. At Harry S. Truman High School, black and Hispanic students represented 96 percent of the enrollment of 2,700 students; 2 percent were white. At Adlai Stevenson High School, which enrolls 3,400 students, blacks and Hispanics made up 97 percent of the student population; a mere eight-tenths of one percent were white.

A teacher at P.S. 65 in the South Bronx once pointed out to me one of the two white children I had ever seen there. His presence in her class was something of a wonderment to the teacher and to the other pupils. I asked how many white kids she had taught in the South Bronx in her career. "I've been at this school for eighteen years," she said. "This is the first white student I have ever taught."

———

One of the most disheartening experiences for those who grew up in the years when Martin Luther King Jr. and Thurgood Marshall were alive is to visit public schools today that bear their names, or names of other honored leaders of the integration struggles that produced the temporary progress that took place in the three decades after *Brown v. Board of Education,* and to find out how many of these schools are bastions of contemporary segregation. It is even more disheartening when schools like these are not in deeply segregated inner-city neighborhoods but in racially mixed areas where the integration of a public school would seem to be most natural and where, indeed, it takes a conscious effort on the part of parents or school officials in these districts to avoid the integration option that is often right at their front door.

In a Seattle neighborhood that I visited in 2002, for instance, where approximately half the families were Caucasian, 95 percent of students at the Thurgood Marshall Elementary School were black, Hispanic, Native American, or of Asian origin. An African American teacher at the school told me—not with bitterness but wistfully—of seeing clusters of white parents and their children each morning on the corner of a street close to the school, waiting for a bus that took the children to a predominantly white school. . . .

There is a well-known high school named for Martin Luther King Jr. in New York City. This school, which I've visited repeatedly in recent years, is located in an upper-middle-class white neighborhood, where it was built in the belief—or hope—that it would draw large numbers of white students by permitting them to walk to school, while only their black and Hispanic classmates would be asked to ride the bus or come by train. When the school was opened in 1975, less than a block from Lincoln Center in Manhattan, "it was seen," according to the *New York Times,* "as a promising effort to integrate white, black and Hispanic students in a thriving neighborhood that held one of the city's cultural gems." Even from the start, however, parents in the neighborhood showed great reluctance to permit their children to enroll at Martin Luther King, and, despite "its prime location and its name, which itself creates the highest of expectations," notes the *Times,* the school before long came to be a destination for black and Hispanic students who could not obtain admission into more successful schools. It stands today as one of the nation's most visible and problematic symbols of an expectation rapidly receding and a legacy substantially betrayed.

———

Perhaps most damaging to any serious effort to address racial segregation openly is the refusal of most of the major arbiters of culture in our northern cities to confront or even clearly name an obvious reality they would have castigated with a passionate determination in another section of the nation fifty years before—and which, moreover, they still castigate today in retrospective writings that assign it to a comfortably distant and allegedly concluded era of the past. There is, indeed, a seemingly agreed-upon convention in much of the media today not even to use an accurate descriptor like "racial segregation" in a narrative description of a segregated school. Linguistic sweeteners, semantic somersaults, and surrogate vocabularies are repeatedly employed. Schools in which as few as 3 or 4 percent of students may be white or Southeast Asian or of Middle Eastern origin, for instance—and where *every other child* in the building is black or Hispanic—are referred to as "diverse." Visitors to schools like these discover quickly the eviscerated meaning of the word, which is no longer a proper adjective but a euphemism for a plainer word that has apparently become unspeakable.

School systems themselves repeatedly employ this euphemism in describing the composition of their student populations. In a school I visited in the fall of 2004 in Kansas City, Missouri, for example, a document distributed to visitors reports that the school's curriculum "addresses the needs of children from diverse backgrounds." But as I went from class to class, I did not encounter any children who were white or Asian—or Hispanic, for that matter—and when I was later provided with precise statistics for the demographics of the school, I learned that 99.6 percent of students there were African American. In a similar document, the school board of another district, this one in New York State, referred to "the diversity" of its student population and "the rich variations of ethnic backgrounds." But when I looked at the racial numbers that the district had reported to the state, I learned that there were 2,800 black and Hispanic children in the system, 1 Asian child, and 3 whites. Words, in these cases, cease to have real meaning; or, rather, they mean the opposite of what they say.

High school students whom I talk with in deeply segregated neighborhoods and public schools seem far less circumspect than their elders and far more open in their willingness to confront these issues. "It's more like being hidden," said a fifteen-year-old girl named Isabel.[1] I met some years ago in Harlem, in attempting to explain to me the ways in which she and her classmates understood the racial segregation of their neighborhoods and schools. "It's as if you have been put in a garage where, if they don't have room for something but aren't sure if they should throw it out, they put it there where they don't need to think of it again."

I asked her if she thought America truly did not "have room" for her or other children of her race. "Think of it this way," said a sixteen-year-old girl sitting beside her. "If people in New York woke up one day and learned that we were gone, that we had simply died or left for somewhere else, how would they feel?"

"How do you think they'd feel?" I asked. "I think they'd be relieved," this very solemn girl replied.

———

Many educators make the argument today that given the demographics of large cities like New York and their suburban areas, our only realistic goal should be the nurturing of strong, empowered, and well-funded schools in segregated neighborhoods. Black school officials in these situations have sometimes conveyed to me a bitter and clear-sighted recognition that they're being asked, essentially, to mediate and render functional an uncontested separation between children of their race and children of white people living sometimes in a distant section of their town and sometimes in almost their own immediate communities. Implicit in this mediation is a willingness to set aside the promises of *Brown* and—though never stating this or even thinking of it clearly in these terms—to settle for the promise made more than a century ago in *Plessy v. Ferguson,* the 1896 Supreme Court ruling in which "separate but equal" was accepted as a tolerable rationale for the perpetuation of a dual system in American society.

Equality itself—equality alone—is now, it seems, the article of faith to which most of the principals of inner-city public schools subscribe. And some who are perhaps most realistic do not even dare to ask for, or expect, complete equality, which seems beyond the realm of probability for many years to come, but look instead for only a sufficiency of means—"adequacy" is the legal term most often used today—by which to win those practical and finite victories that appear to be within their reach. Higher standards, higher expectations, are repeatedly demanded of these urban principals, and of the teachers and students in their schools, but far lower standards—certainly in ethical respect—appear to be expected of the dominant society that isolates these children in unequal institutions.

———————

"Dear Mr. Kozol," wrote the eight-year-old, "we do not have the things you have. You have Clean things. We do not have. You have a clean bathroom. We do not have that. You have Parks and we do not have Parks. You have all the thing and we do not have all the thing. Can you help us?"

The letter, from a child named Alliyah, came in a fat envelope of twenty-seven letters from a class of third-grade children in the Bronx. Other letters that the students in Alliyah's classroom sent me registered some of the same complaints. "We don't have no gardens," "no Music or Art," and "no fun places to play," one child said. "Is there a way to fix this Problem?" Another noted a concern one hears from many children in such overcrowded schools: "We have a gym but it is for lining up. I think it is not fair." Yet another of Alliyah's classmates asked me, with a sweet misspelling, if I knew the way to make her school into a "good" school—"like the other kings have"—and ended with the hope that I would do my best to make it possible for "all the kings" to have good schools.

The letter that affected me the most, however, had been written by a child named Elizabeth. "It is not fair that other kids have a garden and new things. But we don't have that," said Elizabeth. "I wish that this school was the most beautiful school in the whole why world."

"The whole why world" stayed in my thoughts for days. When I later met Elizabeth, I brought her letter with me, thinking I might see whether, in reading it aloud, she'd change the "why" to "wide" or leave it as it was. My visit to her class, however, proved to be so pleasant, and the children seemed so eager to bombard me with their questions about where I lived, and why I lived there rather than in New York, and who I lived with, and how many dogs I had, and other interesting questions of that sort, that I decided not to interrupt the nice reception they had given me with questions about usages and spelling. I left "the whole why world" to float around unedited and unrevised in my mind. The letter itself soon found a resting place on the wall above my desk.

In the years before I met Elizabeth, I had visited many other schools in the South Bronx and in one northern district of the Bronx as well. I had made repeated visits to a high school where a stream of water flowed down one of the main stairwells on a rainy afternoon and where green fungus molds were growing in the office where the students went for counseling. A large blue barrel was positioned to collect rainwater coming through the ceiling. In one makeshift elementary school housed in a former skating rink next to a funeral establishment in yet another nearly all-black-and-Hispanic section of the Bronx, class size rose to thirty-four and more; four kindergarten classes and a sixth-grade class were packed into a single room that had no windows. The air was stifling in many rooms, and the children had no place for recess because there was no outdoor playground and no indoor gym.

In another elementary school, which had been built to hold 1,000 children but was packed to bursting with some 1,500, the principal poured out his feelings to me in a room in which a plastic garbage bag had been attached somehow to cover part of the collapsing ceiling. "This," he told me, pointing to the garbage bag, then gesturing around him at the other indications of decay and disrepair one sees in ghetto schools much like it elsewhere, "would not happen to white children." ← *racist*

Libraries, once one of the glories of the New York City school system, were either nonexistent or, at best, vestigial in large numbers of the elementary schools. Art and music programs had also for the most part disappeared. "When I began to teach in 1969," the principal of an elementary school in the South Bronx reported to me, "every school had a full-time licensed art and music teacher and librarian." During the subsequent decades, he recalled, "I saw all of that destroyed." *libraries + school physician removed*

School physicians also were removed from elementary schools during these years. In 1970, when substantial numbers of white children still attended New York City's public schools, 400 doctors had been present to address the health needs of the children. By 1993 the number of doctors had been cut to 23, most of them part-time—a cutback that affected most severely children in the city's poorest neighborhoods, where medical facilities were most deficient and health problems faced by children most extreme. Teachers told me of asthmatic children who came into class with chronic wheezing and who at any moment of the day might undergo more serious attacks, but in the schools I visited there were no doctors to attend to them.

In explaining these steep declines in services, political leaders in New York tended to point to shifting economic factors, like a serious budget crisis in the middle 1970s, rather than to the changing racial demographics of the student population. But the fact of economic ups and downs from year to year, or from one decade to the next, could not convincingly explain the permanent shortchanging of the city's students, which took place routinely in good economic times and bad. The bad times were seized upon politically to justify the cuts, and the money was never restored once the crisis years were past.

"If you close your eyes to the changing racial composition of the schools and look only at budget actions and political events," says Noreen Connell, the director of the nonprofit Educational Priorities Panel in New York, "you're missing the assumptions that are underlying these decisions." When minority parents ask for something better for their kids, she says, "the assumption is that these are parents who can be discounted. These are kids who just don't count—children we don't value."

This, then, is the accusation that Alliyah and her classmates send our way: "You have . . . We do not have." Are they right or are they wrong? Is this a case of naive and simplistic juvenile exaggeration? What does a third-grader know about these big-time questions of fairness and justice? Physical appearances apart, how in any case do you begin to measure something so diffuse and vast and seemingly abstract as having more, or having less, or not having at all?

Around the time I met Alliyah in the school year 1997–1998, New York's Board of Education spent about $8,000 yearly on the education of a third-grade child in a New York City public school. If you could have scooped Alliyah up out of the neighborhood where she was born and plunked her down in a fairly typical white suburb of New York, she would have received a public education worth about $12,000 a year. If you were to lift her up once more and set her down in one of the wealthiest white suburbs of New York, she would have received as much as $18,000 worth of public education every year and would likely have had a third-grade teacher paid approximately $30,000 more than her teacher in the Bronx was paid.

The dollars on both sides of the equation have increased since then, but the discrepancies between them have remained. The present per-pupil spending level in the New York City schools is $11,700, which may be compared with a per-pupil spending level in excess of $22,000 in the well-to-do suburban district of Manhasset, Long Island. The present New York City level is, indeed, almost exactly what Manhasset spent per pupil eighteen years ago, in 1987, when that sum of money bought a great deal more in services and salaries than it can buy today. In dollars adjusted for inflation, New York City has not yet caught up to where its wealthiest suburbs were a quarter-century ago.

Gross discrepancies in teacher salaries between the city and its affluent white suburbs have remained persistent as well. In 1997 the median salary for teachers in Alliyah's neighborhood was $43,000, as compared with $74,000 in suburban Rye, $77,000 in Manhasset, and $81,000 in the town of Scarsdale, which is only about eleven miles from Alliyah's school. Five years later, in 2002, salary scales for New York City's teachers rose to levels that approximated those within the lower-spending districts in the suburbs, but salary scales do not reflect the actual salaries that teachers typically receive, which are dependent upon years of service and advanced degrees. Salaries for first-year teachers in the city were higher than they'd been four years before, but the differences in median pay between the city and its upper-middle-income suburbs had remained extreme. The overall figure for New

York City in 2002–2003 was $53,000, while it had climbed to $87,000 in Manhasset and exceeded $95,000 in Scarsdale.

———

"There are expensive children and there are cheap children," writes Marina Warner, an essayist and novelist who has written many books for children, "just as there are expensive women and cheap women." The governmentally administered diminishment in value of the children of the poor begins even before the age of five or six, when they begin their years of formal education in the public schools. It starts during their infant and toddler years, when hundreds of thousands of children of the very poor in much of the United States are locked out of the opportunity for preschool education for no reason but the accident of birth and budgetary choices of the government, while children of the privileged are often given veritable feasts of rich developmental early education. . . .

There are remarkable exceptions to this pattern in some sections of the nation. In Milwaukee, for example, virtually every four-year-old is now enrolled in a preliminary kindergarten program, which amounts to a full year of preschool education, prior to a second kindergarten year for five-year-olds. More commonly in urban neighborhoods, large numbers of low-income children are denied these opportunities and come into their kindergarten year without the minimal social skills that children need in order to participate in class activities and without even such very modest early-learning skills as knowing how to hold a crayon or a pencil, identify perhaps a couple of shapes and colors, or recognize that printed pages go from left to right.

Three years later, in third grade, these children are introduced to what are known as "high-stakes tests," which in many urban systems now determine whether students can or cannot be promoted. Children who have been in programs like those offered by the "Baby Ivies" since the age of two have, by now, received the benefits of six or seven years of education, nearly twice as many as the children who have been denied these opportunities; yet all are required to take, and will be measured by, the same examinations. Which of these children will receive the highest scores? The ones who spent the years from two to four in lovely little Montessori programs and in other pastel-painted settings in which tender and attentive and well-trained instructors read to them from beautiful storybooks and introduced them very gently for the first time to the world of numbers and the shapes of letters, and the sizes and varieties of solid objects, and perhaps taught them to sort things into groups or to arrange them in a sequence, or to do those many other interesting things that early childhood specialists refer to as pre-numeracy skills? Or the ones who spent those years at home in front of a TV or sitting by the window of a slum apartment gazing down into the street? There is something deeply hypocritical about a society that holds an eight-year-old inner-city child "accountable" for her performance on a high-stakes standardized exam but does not hold the high officials of our government accountable for robbing her of what they gave their own kids six or seven years earlier.

———

Perhaps in order to deflect these recognitions, or to soften them somewhat, many people, even while they do not doubt the benefit of making very large investments in the education of their own children, somehow—paradoxical as it may seem—appear to be attracted to the argument that money may not really matter that much at all. No matter with what regularity such doubts about the worth of spending money on a child's education are advanced, it is obvious that those who have the money, and who spend it lavishly to benefit their own kids, do not do it for no reason. Yet shockingly large numbers of well-educated and sophisticated people whom I talk with nowadays dismiss such challenges with a surprising ease. "Is the answer really to throw money into these dysfunctional and failing schools?" I'm often asked. "Don't we have some better ways to make them 'work'?" The question is posed in a variety of forms. "Yes, of course, it's not a perfectly fair system as it stands. But money alone is surely not the sole response. The values of the parents and the kids themselves must have a role in this as well—you know, housing, health conditions, social factors." "Other factors"—a term of overall reprieve one often hears—"have got to be considered, too." These latter points are obviously true but always seem to have the odd effect of substituting things we know we cannot change in the short run for obvious solutions like cutting class size and constructing new school buildings or providing universal preschool that we actually could put in place right now if we were so inclined.

Frequently these arguments are posed as questions that do not invite an answer because the answer seems to be decided in advance. "Can you really buy your way to better education for these children?" "Do we know enough to be quite sure that we will see an actual return on the investment that we make?" "Is it even clear that this is the right starting point to get to where we'd like to go? It doesn't always seem to work, as I am sure that you already know," or similar questions that somehow assume I will agree with those who ask them.

Some people who ask these questions, although they live in wealthy districts where the schools are funded at high levels, don't even send their children to these public schools but choose instead to send them to expensive private day schools. At some of the well-known private prep schools in the New York City area, tuition and associated costs are typically more than $20,000 a year. During their children's teenage years, they sometimes send them off to very fine New England schools like Andover or Exeter or Groton, where tuition, boarding, and additional expenses rise to more than $30,000. Often a family has two teenage children in these schools at the same time, so they may be spending more than $60,000 on their children's education every year. Yet here I am one night, a guest within their home, and dinner has been served and we are having coffee now; and this entirely likable, and generally sensible, and beautifully refined and thoughtful person looks me in the eyes and asks me whether you can really buy your way to better education for the children of the poor.

As racial isolation deepens and the inequalities of education finance remain unabated and take on new and more innovative forms, the principals of many inner-city schools are making choices that few principals in public schools that serve white children in the mainstream of the nation ever need to contemplate. Many have been dedicating vast amounts of time and effort to create an architecture of adaptive strategies that promise incremental gains within the limits inequality allows.

New vocabularies of stentorian determination, new systems of incentive, and new modes of castigation, which are termed "rewards and sanctions," have emerged. Curriculum materials that are alleged to be aligned with governmentally established goals and standards and particularly suited to what are regarded as "the special needs and learning styles" of low-income urban children have been introduced. Relentless emphasis on raising test scores, rigid policies of nonpromotion and nongraduation, a new empiricism and the imposition of unusually detailed lists of named and numbered "outcomes" for each isolated parcel of instruction, an oftentimes fanatical insistence upon uniformity of teachers in their management of time, an openly conceded emulation of the rigorous approaches of the military and a frequent use of terminology that comes out of the world of industry and commerce—these are just a few of the familiar aspects of these new adaptive strategies.

Although generically described as "school reform," most of these practices and policies are targeted primarily at poor children of color; and although most educators speak of these agendas in broad language that sounds applicable to all, it is understood that they are valued chiefly as responses to perceived catastrophe in deeply segregated and unequal schools.

"If you do what I tell you to do, how I tell you to do it, when I tell you to do it, you'll get it right," said a determined South Bronx principal observed by a reporter for the *New York Times*. She was laying out a memorizing rule for math to an assembly of her students. "If you don't, you'll get it wrong." This is the voice, this is the tone, this is the rhythm and didactic certitude one hears today in inner-city schools that have embraced a pedagogy of direct command and absolute control. "Taking their inspiration from the ideas of B. F. Skinner ... ," says the *Times*, proponents of scripted rote-and-drill curricula articulate their aim as the establishment of "faultless communication" between "the teacher, who is the stimulus," and "the students, who respond."

The introduction of Skinnerian approaches (which are commonly employed in penal institutions and drug-rehabilitation programs), as a way of altering the attitudes and learning styles of black and Hispanic children, is provocative, and it has stirred some outcries from respected scholars. To actually go into a school where you know some of the children very, very well and see the way that these approaches can affect their daily lives and thinking processes is even more provocative.

On a chilly November day four years ago in the South Bronx, I entered P.S. 65, a school I had been visiting since 1993. There had been major changes since I'd been there last. Silent lunches had been instituted in the cafeteria, and on days when children misbehaved, silent recess had been introduced as well. On those days the students were obliged to sit in rows and maintain perfect silence on the floor of a small indoor room instead of going out to play. The words SUCCESS FOR ALL, the brand name of a scripted curriculum—better known by its acronym, SFA—were prominently posted at the top of the main stairway and, as I would later find, in almost every room. . . .

I entered the fourth grade of a teacher I will call Mr. Endicott, a man in his mid-thirties who had arrived here without training as a teacher, one of about a dozen teachers in the building who were sent into this school after a single summer of short-order preparation. Now in his second year, he had developed a considerable sense of confidence and held the class under a tight control. . . .

My attention was distracted by some whispering among the children sitting to the right of me. The teacher's response to this distraction was immediate: his arm shot out and up in a diagonal in front of him, his hand straight up, his fingers flat. The young co-teacher did this, too. When they saw their teachers do this, all the children in the classroom did it, too.

"Zero noise," the teacher said, but this instruction proved to be unneeded. The strange salute the class and teachers gave each other, which turned out to be one of a number of such silent signals teachers in the school were trained to use, and children to obey, had done the job of silencing the class.

"Active listening!" said Mr. Endicott. "Heads up! Tractor beams!" which meant, "Every eye on me." . . .

A well-educated man, Mr. Endicott later spoke to me about the form of classroom management that he was using as an adaptation from a model of industrial efficiency. "It's a kind of 'Taylorism' in the classroom," he explained, referring to a set of theories about the management of factory employees introduced by Frederick Taylor in the early 1900s. "Primitive utilitarianism" is another term he used when we met some months later to discuss these management techniques with other teachers from the school. His reservations were, however, not apparent in the classroom. Within the terms of what he had been asked to do, he had, indeed, become a master of control. It is one of the few classrooms I had visited up to that time in which almost nothing even hinting at spontaneous emotion in the children or the teacher surfaced while I was there.

The teacher gave the "zero noise" salute again when someone whispered to another child at his table. "In two minutes you will have a chance to talk and share this with your partner." Communication between children in the class was not prohibited but was afforded time slots and, remarkably enough, was formalized in an expression that I found included in a memo that was posted on the wall beside the door: "An opportunity . . . to engage in Accountable Talk."[2] . . .

In speaking of the drill-based program in effect at P.S. 65, Mr. Endicott told me he tended to be sympathetic to the school administrators, more so at least than the other teachers I had talked with seemed to be. He said he believed his principal had little choice about the implementation of this program, which had been mandated for all elementary schools in New York City that had had rock-bottom academic records over a long period of time. "This puts me into a dilemma," he went on, "because I love the kids at P.S. 65." And even while, he said, "I know that my teaching SFA is a charade . . . if I don't do it I won't be permitted to teach these children."

Mr. Endicott, like all but two of the new recruits at P.S. 65—there were about fifteen in all—was a white person, as were the principal and most of the administrators at the school. As a result, most of these neophyte instructors had had little or no prior contact with the children of an inner-city neighborhood; but, like the others I met, and despite the distancing between the children and their teachers that resulted from the scripted method of instruction, he had developed close attachments to his students and did not want to abandon them. At the same time, the class- and race-specific implementation of this program obviously troubled him. "There's an expression now," he said. "'The rich get richer, and the poor get SFA.'" He said he was still trying to figure out his "professional ethics" on the problem that this posed for him.

White children made up "only about one percent" of students in the New York City schools in which this scripted teaching system was imposed,[3] according to the *New York Times*, which also said that "the prepackaged lessons" were intended "to ensure that all teachers—even novices or the most inept"—would be able to teach reading. As seemingly pragmatic and hardheaded as such arguments may be, they are desperation strategies that come out of the acceptance of inequity. If we did not have a deeply segregated system in which more experienced instructors teach the children of the privileged and the least experienced are sent to teach the children of minorities, these practices would not be needed and could not be so convincingly defended. They are confections of apartheid, and no matter by what arguments of urgency or practicality they have been justified, they cannot fail to further deepen the divisions of society.

There is no misery index for the children of apartheid education. There ought to be; we measure almost everything else that happens to them in their schools. Do kids who go to schools like these enjoy the days they spend in them? Is school, for most of them, a happy place to be? You do not find the answers to these questions in reports about achievement levels, scientific methods of accountability, or structural revisions in the modes of governance. Documents like these don't speak of happiness. You have to go back to the schools themselves to find an answer to these questions. You have to sit down in the little chairs in first and second grade, or on the reading rug with kindergarten kids, and listen to the things they actually say to one another and the dialogue between them and their teachers. You have to go down to the basement with the children when it's time for lunch and to the playground with them, if they have a playground, when it's time for recess, if they still have recess at their school. You have to walk into the children's bathrooms in these buildings. You have to do what children do and breathe the air the children breathe. I don't think that there is any other way to find out what the lives that children lead in school are really like.

High school students, when I first meet them, are often more reluctant than the younger children to open up and express their personal concerns; but hesitation on the part of students did not prove to be a problem when I visited a tenth-grade class at Fremont High School in Los Angeles. The students were told that I was a writer, and they took no time in getting down to matters that were on their minds.

"Can we talk about the bathrooms?" asked a soft-spoken student named Mireya.

In almost any classroom there are certain students who, by the force of their directness or the unusual sophistication of their way of speaking, tend to capture your attention from the start. Mireya later spoke insightfully about some of the serious academic problems that were common in the school, but her observations on the physical and personal embarrassments she and her schoolmates had to undergo cut to the heart of questions of essential dignity that kids in squalid schools like this one have to deal with all over the nation.

Fremont High School, as court papers filed in a lawsuit against the state of California document, has fifteen fewer bathrooms than the law requires. Of the limited number of bathrooms that are working in the school, "only one or two . . . are open and unlocked for girls to use." Long lines of girls are "waiting to use the bathrooms," which are generally "unclean" and "lack basic supplies," including toilet paper. Some of the classrooms, as court papers also document, "do not have air conditioning," so that students, who attend school on a three-track schedule that runs year-round, "become red-faced and unable to concentrate" during "the extreme heat of summer." The school's maintenance records report that rats were found in eleven classrooms. Rat droppings were found "in the bins and drawers" of the high school's kitchen, and school records note that "hamburger buns" were being "eaten off [the] bread-delivery rack."

No matter how many tawdry details like these I've read in legal briefs or depositions through the years, I'm always shocked again to learn how often these unsanitary physical conditions are permitted to continue in the schools that serve our poorest students—even after they have been vividly described in the media. But hearing of these conditions in Mireya's words was even more unsettling, in part because this student seemed so fragile and because the need even to speak of these indignities in front of me and all the other students was an additional indignity.

"It humiliates you," said Mireya, who went on to make the interesting statement that "the school provides solutions that don't actually work," and this idea was taken up by several other students in describing course requirements within the school. A tall black student, for example, told me that she hoped to be a social worker or a doctor but was programmed into "Sewing Class" this year. She also had to take another course, called "Life Skills," which she told me was a very basic course—"a retarded class," to use her words—that "teaches things like the six continents," which she said she'd learned in elementary school.

When I asked her why she had to take these courses, she replied that she'd been told they were required, which as I later learned was not exactly so. What was required was that high school students take two courses in an area of study called "The Technical Arts," and which the Los Angeles Board of Education terms "Applied Technology." At schools that served the middle class or upper-middle class, this requirement was likely to be met by courses that had academic substance and, perhaps, some relevance to college preparation. At Beverly Hills High School, for example, the technical-arts requirement could be fulfilled by taking subjects like residential architecture, the designing of commercial structures, broadcast journalism, advanced computer graphics, a sophisticated course in furniture design, carving and sculpture, or an honors course in engineering research and design. At Fremont High, in contrast, this requirement was far more often met by courses that were basically vocational and also obviously keyed to low-paying levels of employment.

Mireya, for example, who had plans to go to college, told me that she had to take a sewing class last year and now was told she'd been assigned to take a class in hairdressing as well. When I asked her teacher why Mireya could not skip these subjects and enroll in classes that would help her to pursue her college aspirations, she replied, "It isn't a question of what students want. It's what the school may have available. If all the other elective classes that a student wants to take are full, she has to take one of these classes if she wants to graduate."

A very small girl named Obie, who had big blue-tinted glasses tilted up across her hair, interrupted then to tell me with a kind of wild gusto that she'd taken hairdressing *twice*! When I expressed surprise that this was possible, she said there were two levels of hairdressing offered here at Fremont High. "One is in hairstyling," she said. "The other is in braiding."

Mireya stared hard at this student for a moment and then suddenly began to cry. "I don't *want* to take hairdressing. I did not need sewing either. I knew how to sew. My mother is a seamstress in a factory. I'm trying to go to college. I don't need to sew to go to college. My mother sews. I hoped for something else."

"What would you rather take?" I asked.

"I wanted to take an AP class," she answered.

Mireya's sudden tears elicited a strong reaction from one of the boys who had been silent up till now: a thin, dark-eyed student named Fortino, who had long hair down to his shoulders. He suddenly turned directly to Mireya and spoke into the silence that followed her last words.

"Listen to me," he said. "The owners of the sewing factories need laborers. Correct?"

"I guess they do," Mireya said.

"It's not going to be their own kids. Right?"

"Why not?" another student said.

"So they can grow beyond, themselves," Mireya answered quietly. "But we remain the same."

"You're ghetto," said Fortino, "so we send you to the factory." He sat low in his desk chair, leaning on one elbow, his voice and dark eyes loaded with a cynical intelligence. "You're ghetto—so you sew!"

"There are higher positions than these," said a student named Samantha.

"You're ghetto," said Fortino unrelentingly. "So sew!"

———————

Admittedly, the economic needs of a society are bound to be reflected to some rational degree within the policies and purposes of public schools. But, even so, there must be *something* more to life as it is lived by six-year-olds or ten-year-olds, or by teenagers, for that matter, than concerns about "successful global competition." Childhood is not merely basic training for utilitarian adulthood. It should have some claims upon our mercy, not for its future value to the economic interests of competitive societies but for its present value as a perishable piece of life itself.

Very few people who are not involved with inner-city schools have any real idea of the extremes to which the mercantile distortion of the purposes and character of education have been taken or how unabashedly proponents of these practices are willing to defend them. The head of a Chicago school, for instance, who was criticized by some for emphasizing rote instruction that, his critics said, was turning children into "robots," found no reason to dispute the charge. "Did you ever stop to think that these robots will never burglarize your home?" he asked, and "will never snatch your pocketbooks. . . . These robots are going to be producing taxes."

Corporate leaders, when they speak of education, sometimes pay lipservice to the notion of "good critical and analytic skills," but it is reasonable to ask whether they have in mind the critical analysis of *their* priorities. In principle, perhaps some do; but, if so, this is not a principle that seems to have been honored widely in the schools I have been visiting. In all the various business-driven inner-city classrooms I have observed in the past five years, plastered as they are with corporation brand names and managerial vocabularies, I have yet to see the two words "labor unions." Is this an oversight? How is that possible? Teachers and principals themselves, who are almost always members of a union, seem to be so beaten down that they rarely even question this omission.

It is not at all unusual these days to come into an urban school in which the principal prefers to call himself or herself "building CEO" or "building manager." In some of the same schools teachers are described as "classroom managers."[4] I have never been in a suburban district in which principals were asked to view themselves or teachers in this way. These terminologies remind us of how wide the distance has become between two very separate worlds of education.

———————

It has been more than a decade now since drill-based literacy methods like Success For All began to proliferate in our urban schools. It has been three and a half years since the systems of assessment that determine the effectiveness of these and similar practices were codified in the federal legislation, No Child Left Behind, that President Bush signed into law in 2002. Since the enactment of this bill, the number of standardized exams children must take has more than doubled. It will probably increase again after the year 2006, when standardized tests, which are now required in grades three through eight, may be required in Head Start programs and, as President Bush has now proposed, in ninth, tenth, and eleventh grades as well.

The elements of strict accountability, in short, are solidly in place; and in many states where the present federal policies are simply reinforcements of accountability requirements that were established long before the passage of the federal law, the same regimen has been in place since 1995 or even earlier. The "tests-and-standards" partisans have had things very much their way for an extended period of time, and those who were convinced that they had ascertained "what works" in schools that serve minorities and children of the poor have had ample opportunity to prove that they were right.

What, then, it is reasonable to ask, are the results?

The achievement gap between black and white children, which narrowed for three decades up until the late years of the 1980s—the period in which school segregation steadily decreased—started to widen once more in the early 1990s when the federal courts began the process of resegregation by dismantling the mandates of the *Brown* decision. From that point on, the gap continued to widen or remained essentially unchanged; and while recently there has been a modest narrowing of the gap in reading scores for fourth-grade children, the gap in secondary school remains as wide as ever.

The media inevitably celebrate the periodic upticks that a set of scores may seem to indicate in one year or another in achievement levels of black and Hispanic children in their elementary schools. But if these upticks were not merely temporary "testing gains" achieved by test-prep regimens and were instead authentic education gains, they would carry over into middle school and high school. Children who know how to read—and read with comprehension—do not suddenly become nonreaders and hopelessly disabled writers when they enter secondary school. False gains evaporate; real gains endure. Yet hundreds of thousands of the inner-city children who have made what many districts claim to be dramatic gains in elementary school, and whose principals and teachers have adjusted almost every aspect of their school days and school calendars, forfeiting recess, canceling or cutting back on all the so-called frills (art, music, even social sciences) in order to comply with state demands—those students, now in secondary school, are sitting in subject-matter classes where they cannot comprehend the texts and cannot set down their ideas in the kind of sentences expected of most fourth- and fifth-grade students in the suburbs. Students in this painful situation, not surprisingly, tend to be most likely to drop out of school.

In 48 percent of high schools in the nation's 100 largest districts, which are those in which the highest concentrations of black and Hispanic students tend to be enrolled, less than half the entering ninth-graders graduate in four years. Nationwide, from 1993 to 2002, the number of high schools graduating less than half their ninth-grade class in four years has increased by 75 percent. In the 94 percent of districts in New York State where white children make up the majority, nearly 80 percent of students graduate from high school in four years. In the 6 percent of districts where black and Hispanic students make up the majority, only 40 percent do so. There are 120 high schools in New York, enrolling nearly 200,000 minority students, where less than 60 percent of entering ninth-graders even make it to twelfth grade.

The promulgation of new and expanded inventories of "what works," no matter the enthusiasm with which they're elaborated, is not going to change this. The use of hortatory slogans chanted by the students in our segregated schools is not going to change this. Desperate historical revisionism that romanticizes the segregation of an older order (this is a common theme of many separatists today) is not going to change this. Skinnerian instructional approaches, which decapitate a child's capability for critical reflection, are not going to change this. Posters about "global competition" will certainly not change this. Turning six-year-olds into examination soldiers and denying eight-year-olds their time for play at recess will not change this.

"I went to Washington to challenge the soft bigotry of low expectations," said President Bush in his campaign for reelection in September 2004. "It's working. It's making a difference." Here we have one of those deadly lies that by sheer repetition is at length accepted by surprisingly large numbers of Americans. But it is not the truth; and it is not an innocent misstatement of the facts. It is a devious appeasement of the heartache of the parents of the black and brown and poor, and if it is not forcefully resisted it will lead us further in a very dangerous direction.

Whether the issue is inequity alone or deepening resegregation or the labyrinthine intertwining of the two, it is well past the time for us to start the work that it will take to change this. If it takes people marching in the streets and other forms of adamant disruption of the governing civilities, if it takes more than litigation, more than legislation, and much more than resolutions introduced by members of Congress, these are prices we should be prepared to pay. "We do not have the things you have," Alliyah told me when she wrote to ask if I would come and visit her school in the South Bronx. "Can you help us?" America owes that little girl and millions like her a more honorable answer than they have received.

ENDNOTES

[1]The names of children mentioned in this article have been changed to protect their privacy.

[2]Since that day at P.S. 65, I have visited nine other schools in six different cities where the same Skinnerian curriculum is used. The signs on the walls, the silent signals, the curious salute, the

same insistent naming of all cognitive particulars, became familiar as I went from one school to the next.

[3]SFA has since been discontinued in the New York City public schools, though it is still being used in 1,300 U.S. schools, serving as many as 650,000 children. Similar scripted systems are used in schools (overwhelmingly minority in population) serving several million children.

[4]A school I visited three years ago in Columbus, Ohio, was littered with "Help Wanted" signs. Starting in kindergarten, children in the school were being asked to think about the jobs that they might choose when they grew up. In one classroom there was a poster that displayed the names of several retail stores: J. C. Penney, Wal-Mart, Kmart, Sears, and a few others. "It's like working in a store," a classroom aide explained. "The children are learning to pretend they're cashiers." At another school in the same district, children were encouraged to apply for jobs in their classrooms. Among the job positions open to the children in this school, there was an "Absence Manager" and a "Behavior Chart Manager," a "Form Collector Manager," a "Paper Passer Outer Manager," a "Paper Collecting Manager," a "Paper Returning Manager," an "Exit Ticket Manager," even a "Learning Manager," a "Reading Corner Manager," and a "Score Keeper Manager." I asked the principal if there was a special reason why those two words "management" and "manager" kept popping up throughout the school. "We want every child to be working as a manager while he or she is in this school," the principal explained. "We want to make them understand that, in this country, companies will give you opportunities to work, to prove yourself, no matter what you've done." I wasn't sure what she meant by "no matter what you've done," and asked her if she could explain it. "Even if you have a felony arrest," she said, "we want you to understand that you can be a manager someday."

52

BAD BOYS
Public Schools in the Making
of Black Masculinity

ANN ARNETT FERGUSON

The previous selection illustrates how schools socially produce and reproduce race and social class distinctions in the United States. In so doing, schools are an important agent of *social reproduction*—they socially reproduce social inequalities that maintain social stratification. Schools also produce and reproduce gender distinctions found in society. The selection that follows examines the social reproduction of race and gender in American public schools. In particular, this excerpt, from Ann Arnett Ferguson's 2000 book, *Bad Boys: Public Schools in the Making of Black Masculinity*, examines the effects gender and racial stereotyping has on African American school boys. Ferguson, an associate professor of African American studies and women's studies at Smith College, explores why African American boys are more often labeled as troublemakers than other gender or racial-ethnic groups of children.

S oon after I began fieldwork at Rosa Parks Elementary School, one of the adults, an African American man, pointed to a black boy who walked by us in the hallway.[1] "That one has a jail-cell with his name on it," he told me. We were looking at a ten-year-old, barely four feet tall, whose frail body was shrouded in baggy pants and a hooded sweatshirt. The boy, Lamar, passed with the careful tread of someone who was in no hurry to get where he was going. He was on his way to the Punishing Room of the school. As he glanced quickly toward and then away from us, the image of the figure of Tupac Shakur on the poster advertising the movie *Juice* flashed into my mind. I suppose it was the combination of the hooded sweatshirt, the guarded expression in his eyes, and what my companion had just said that reminded me of the face on the film poster that stared at me from billboards and sidings all over town.

I was shocked that judgment and sentence had been passed on this child so matter-of-factly by a member of the school staff. But by the end of the school year, I had begun to suspect that a prison cell might indeed have a place in Lamar's future. What I observed at Rosa Parks during more than three years of fieldwork in the school, heard from the boy himself, from his teachers, from his mother, made it clear that just as children were tracked into futures as doctors, scientists, engineers, word processors, and fast-food workers, there were also tracks for some children, predominantly African American and male, that led to prison. This [reading] tells the story of the making of these bad boys, not by members of the criminal justice system on street corners, or in shopping malls, or video arcades, but in and by school, through punishment. It is an account of the power of institutions to create, shape, and regulate social identities.

Unfortunately, Lamar's journey is not an isolated event, but traces a disturbing pattern of African American male footsteps out of classrooms, down hallways, and into disciplinary spaces throughout the school day in contemporary America. Though African American boys made up only one-quarter of the student body at Rosa Parks, they accounted for nearly half the number of students sent to the Punishing Room for major and minor misdeeds in 1991–92. Three-quarters of those suspended that year were boys, and, of those, four-fifths were African American.[2] In the course of my study it became clear that school labeling practices and the exercise of rules operated as part of a hidden curriculum to marginalize and isolate black male youth in disciplinary spaces and brand them as criminally inclined.

But trouble is not only a site of regulation and stigmatization. Under certain conditions it can also be a powerful occasion for identification and recognition. This study investigates this aspect of punishment through an exploration of the meaning of school rules and the interpretation of trouble from the youth's perspective. What does it mean to hear adults say that you are bound for jail and to understand that the future predicted for you is "doing time" inside prison walls? What does school trouble mean under such deleterious circumstances? How does a ten-year-old black boy fashion a sense of self within this context? Children like Lamar are not just innocent victims of arbitrary acts; like other kids, he probably talks out of turn, argues with teachers, uses profanities, brings contraband to school. However, I will argue, the meaning and consequences of these acts for young black males like himself are different, highly charged with racial and gender significance with scarring effects on adult life chances.

The pattern of punishment that emerges from the Rosa Parks data is not unique. Recent studies in Michigan, Minnesota, California, and Ohio reveal a similar pattern.[3] In the public schools of Oakland, California, for example, suspensions disproportionately involved African American males, while in Michigan schools, where corporal punishment is still permitted, blacks were more than five times more likely to be hit by school adults than were whites. In the Cincinnati schools, black students were twice as likely to end up in the in-house suspension room—popularly known as the "dungeon"—and an overwhelming proportion of them were male.[4] In an ominous parallel to Cincinnati's dungeon, disciplinary space at Rosa Parks is designated the "Jailhouse." . . .

Dreams

This [reading] began with an anecdote about the school's vice principal identifying a small boy as someone who had a jail-cell with his name on it. I started with this story to illustrate how school personnel made predictive decisions about a child's future based on a whole ensemble of negative assumptions about African American males and their life-chances. The kids, however, imagined their future in a more positive light. They neither saw themselves as being "on the fast track to prison," as predicted by school personnel, nor did they see themselves as working at low-level service jobs as adults. The boys, in fact, had a decidedly optimistic view about their future.

This scenario, at such variance with that of the administrator's, became clear to me in my final semester at Rosa Parks, when the sixth-graders wrote an essay on the jobs they would like to have as adults. As I scanned these written accounts of students' dreams, I became conscious of a striking pattern. The overwhelming majority of the boys aspired to be professional athletes—playing basketball, baseball, or football—when they grew up. The reasons they gave for this choice were remarkably similar: the sport was something they were good at; it was work they would enjoy doing; and they would make a lot of money.[5] They acknowledged it would be extremely difficult to have such a career, but, they argued, if you worked hard and had the talent, you could make it.

These youthful essays confirmed what the boys had told me in interviews about the adult occupations they imagined for themselves. While a few had mentioned other options such as becoming a stand-up comedian, a Supreme Court justice, or a rap musician, almost all expressed the desire to play on an NBA or NFL team. This was not just an empty fantasy. Most of the boys with whom I had contact in my research were actively and diligently involved in after-school sports, not just as play, but in the serious business of preparing themselves for adult careers. This dream was supported in tangible ways by parents who boasted about their sons' prowess, found time to take them to practice, and cheered their teams on at games. I had assumed initially that these after-school sports activities were primarily a way of parents keeping kids busy to guard against their getting into drugs and sex. However, after talking to parents and kids I realized that what I observed was not just about keeping boys out of trouble but was preparation for future careers.

The occupational dreams of these boys are not at all unique. A survey by Northeastern University's Center for the Study of Sport in Society found that two-thirds of African American males between the ages of thirteen and eighteen believe they can earn a living playing professional sports.[6] Nor is this national pattern for black youth really surprising. For African American males, disengagement from the school's agenda for approval and success is a psychic survival mechanism; so imagining a future occupation for which schooling seems irrelevant is eminently rational. A career as a professional athlete represents the possibility of attaining success in terms of the dominant society via a path that makes schooling seem immaterial, while at the same time affirming central aspects of identification.

I have argued that the boys distance themselves from the school's agenda to avoid capitulating to its strategies for fashioning a self for upward mobility—strategies requiring black youth to distance themselves from family and neighborhood, to reject the language, the style of social interaction, the connections in which identities are grounded. From the highly idealized viewpoint of youth, a career in sports does not appear to require these strategic detachments. Their heroes—players like Michael Jordan, Scottie Pippen, Dennis Rodman, Rickey Henderson, to name just a few—have achieved the highest reaches of success without disguising or eradicating their Blackness.

But these are only dreams, for the chances of getting drafted by professional teams are slim to nonexistent. The probability has been calculated as somewhere in the region of one in ten thousand that a youth will end up in pro football or basketball.[7] Based on these facts, a plethora of popular and scholarly literature, as well as fiction and documentary films, have underscored how unrealistic such ambitions are, making the point that few youths who pour their hearts, energy, and schooling into sports will actually make it to the professional teams where the glory lies and the money is made.[8] They point out this discouraging scenario in order to persuade young black males to rechannel their energies and ambitions into conventional school learning that allows for more "realistic" career options.

Yet, in reality, for these youth efforts to attain high-status occupations through academic channels are just as likely to fail, given the conditions of their schooling and the unequal distribution of resources across school systems.[9] Children attending inner-city public schools are more likely to end up in dead-end, minimum-wage, service sector jobs because they do not have the quality of education available in the suburban public or elite private schools. Today's dreams will be transformed into tomorrow's nightmares.

Nightmares

While I rejected the labeling practices of the school vice principal, in my opening [paragraph], I also reluctantly admitted that by the end of the school year I, too, had come to suspect that a prison cell might have a place in the future of many Rosa Parks students. In contrast to the vice principal, this foreboding was not by any means rooted in a conclusion I had come to about individual children's proclivity for a life of crime, nor was it grounded in any evidence that, as some labeling theories hold, individuals stigmatized as deviant come to internalize this identity and adopt delinquent behaviors at rates higher than other youth. Rather, it emanated from my increased awareness of the way that racial bias in institutions external to school, such as the media and criminal justice system, mirrored and converged with that of the educational system. This convergence intensifies and weights the odds heavily in favor of a young black male ending up in jail. School seems to feed into the prison system, but what exactly is the connection between the two? What are the practical links between the punishing rooms, jailhouses, and dungeons of educational institutions and the cells of local, state, and federal prison systems? There are both long-term causal links as well as visible, immediate connections.

There are serious, long-term effects of being labeled a Troublemaker that substantially increase one's chances of ending up in jail. In the daily experience of being so named, regulated, and surveilled, access to the full resources of the school are increasingly denied as the boys are isolated in nonacademic spaces in school or banished to lounging at home or loitering on the streets. Time in the school dungeon means time lost from classroom learning; suspension, at school or at home, has a direct and lasting negative effect on the continuing growth of a child. When removal from classroom life begins at an early age, it is even more devastating, as human possibilities are stunted at a crucial formative period of life. Each year the gap in skills grows wider and more handicapping, while the overall process of disidentification that I have described encourages those who have problems to leave school rather than resolve them in an educational setting.

There is a direct relationship between dropping out of school and doing time in jail: the majority of black inmates in local, state, and federal penal systems are high school dropouts.[10] Therefore, if we want to begin to break the ties between school and jail, we must first create educational systems that foster kids' identification with school and encourage them not to abandon it.

One significant but relatively small step that could be taken to foster this attachment would be to reduce the painful, inhospitable climate of school for African American children through the validation and affirmation of Black English, the language form that many of the children bring from home/ neighborhood. As I pointed out earlier, the denigration of this form and the assumptions made about the academic potential of speakers of Ebonics pose severe dilemmas of identification for black students—especially for males. The legitimation of Black English in the world of the school would not only enrich the curriculum but would undoubtedly provide valuable lessons to all students about sociolinguistics and the contexts in which standard and nonstandard forms are appropriate. The necessary prerequisite for this inclusion would be a mandatory program for teachers and school administrators to educate them about the nature and history of Ebonics. This was of course the very change called for by the Oakland School Board in 1996. However, it is clear from the controversy that ensued and the highly racialized and obfuscatory nature of the national media's coverage of the Oakland Resolution that there is serious opposition to any innovations that appear to challenge the supremacy of English.[11]

There is also an immediate, ongoing connection between school and jail. Schools mirror and reinforce the practices and ideological systems of other institutions in the society. The racial bias in the punishing systems of the school reflects the practices of the criminal justice system. Black youth are caught up in the net of the juvenile justice system at a rate of two to four times that of white youth.[12] Does this mean that African American boys are more prone to criminal activity than white boys? There is evidence that this is not the case. A study by Huizinga and Elliot demonstrates that the contrast in incarceration statistics is the result of a different *institutional response* to the race of the youth rather than the difference in actual behavior. Drawing on a representative sample of youth between the ages of eleven and seventeen, they compare the delinquent acts individual youth admit to committing in annual self-report interviews with actual police records of delinquency in the areas in which the boys live. Based on the self-reports, they conclude that there were few, if any, differences in the number or type of delinquent acts perpetrated by the two racial groups. What they did find, however, was that there was a substantially and significantly higher risk that the minority youth would be apprehended and charged for these acts by police than the whites who reported committing the same kind of offenses. They conclude that "minorities appear to be at greater risk for being charged with more serious offenses than whites involved in comparable levels of delinquent behavior, a factor which may eventually result in higher incarceration rates among minorities."[13]

Images of black male criminality and the demonization of black children play a significant role in framing actions and events in the justice system in a way that is similar to how these images are used in school to interpret the behavior of individual miscreants. In both settings, the images result in differential treatment based on race. Jerome G. Miller, who has directed juvenile justice detention systems in Massachusetts and Illinois, describes how this works:

> I learned very early on that when we got a black youth, virtually everything—from arrest summaries, to family history, to rap sheets, to psychiatric exams, to "waiver" hearings as to whether or not he would be tried as an adult, to final sentencing—was skewed. If a middle-class white youth was sent to us as "dangerous," he was more likely actually to be so than the black teenager given the same label. The white teenager was more likely to have been afforded competent legal counsel and appropriate psychiatric and psychological testing, tried in a variety of privately funded options, and dealt with more sensitively and individually at every stage of the juvenile justice processing. For him to be labeled "dangerous," he had to have done something very serious indeed. By contrast, the black teenager was more likely to be dealt with as a stereotype from the moment the handcuffs were first put on—easily and quickly relegated to the "more dangerous" end of the "violent-nonviolent" spectrum, albeit accompanied by an official record meant to validate each of a biased series of decisions.[14]

Miller indicates that racial disparities are most obvious at the very earliest and the latest stages of processing of youth through the juvenile justice system, and African American male youth are more likely to be apprehended and caught up in the system in the very beginning. They are also more likely "to be waived to adult court, and to be adjudicated delinquent. If removed from their homes by the court, they were less likely to be placed in the better-staffed and better-run private-group home facilities and more likely to be sent into state reform schools."[15]

Given the poisonous mix of stereotyping and profiling of black males, their chances of ending up in the penal system as a juvenile is extremely high. Even if a boy manages to avoid getting caught within the juvenile justice system through luck or the constant vigilance of parents, his chances of being arrested and jailed are staggeringly high as an adult. A 1995 report by the Sentencing Project finds that nearly one in three African Americans in his twenties is in prison or jail, on probation or parole, on any given day.[16]

The school experience of African American boys is simultaneously replicated in the penal system through processes of surveillance, policing, charges, and penalties. The kids recognize this; the names they give to disciplinary spaces are not just coincidence. They are referencing the chilling parallels between the two.

A systematic racial bias is exercised in the regulation, control, and discipline of children in the United States today. African American males are apprehended and punished for misbehavior and delinquent acts that are overlooked in other children. The punishment that is meted out is usually more severe than that for other children. This racism that systematically extinguishes the potential and constrains the world of possibilities for black males would be brutal enough if it were restricted to school, but it is replicated in other disciplinary systems of the society, the most obvious parallel being the juvenile justice system.

Open Endings

Whenever I give a talk about my research, I am inevitably asked what ideas or recommendations I have for addressing the conditions that I describe. What do I think should be done, listeners want to know? The first few times this happened I felt resentful partly because I knew my colleagues who did research on subjects other than schooling were rarely asked to come up with policy recommendations to address the problems they had uncovered. This request for solutions is made on the assumption that schools, unlike the family and workplace, are basically sound albeit with flaws that need adjusting.

My hesitation to propose solutions comes from a conviction that minor inputs, temporary interventions, individual prescriptions into schools are vastly inadequate to remedy an institution that is fundamentally flawed and whose goal for urban black children seems to be the creation of "a citizenry which will simply obey the rules of society." I stand convinced that a restructuring of the entire educational system is what is urgently required if we are to produce the thoughtful, actively questioning citizens that Baldwin describes in the epigraph to this chapter. To make the point, however, that small programs at Rosa Parks school such as PALS [Partners at Learning Skills]—always underfunded, always dependent on grants of "soft" money that required big promises of quick fixes—served always too few and would inevitably disappear entirely or be co-opted by the institution, was so disheartening, so paralyzing that I am forced to rethink my reply. Is it all or nothing? Can we eradicate forms of institutional racism in school without eliminating racism in the society at large? Are the alternatives either quick hopeless fixes or paralysis because small changes cannot make a difference in the long run? How can the proliferation of local initiatives that spring up, in hope and with enthusiasm, be sustained without taking on institutional goals and attitudes? How can emergent forms appear alongside and out of the old? Most important of all, will attention be paid to the counterdiscourse of the Troublemakers themselves?

When I asked the kids, Schoolboys and Troublemakers, how they thought schooling might be improved, they looked at me blankly. I think they shared my sense of despair. The responses that I wrung out of them seemed trivial, even frivolous. It was all about play, about recreation: a longer recess, bigger play areas, playgrounds with grass not asphalt—and so on. The list that I had dreamed up was the opposite of frivolous. It was all about curriculum: smaller classes, Saturday tutoring, year-round school, antiracist training for student teachers, mutual respect between adults and youth. One thing I am convinced of is that more punitive measures, tighter discipline, greater surveillance, more prisons—the very path that our society seems to be determined to pursue—is not the approach to take. Perhaps, allowing ourselves to imagine the possibilities—what could, should, and must be—is an indispensable first step.

ENDNOTES

[1] This research was assisted by an award from the Social Science Research Council through funding provided by the Rockefeller Foundation. The names of the city, school, and individuals in this ethnography are fictitious in order to preserve the anonymity of participants.

[2] Punishment resulted in suspension 20 percent of the time. Records show that in 1991–92, 250 students, or almost half of the children at Rosa Parks School, were sent to the Punishing Room by adults for breaking school rules, for a total of 1,252 journeys. This figure is based on my count of referral forms kept on file in the Punishing Room. However, it by no means represents the total number of students referred by teachers for discipline. I observed a number of instances where children came into the Punishing Room but the problem was settled by the student specialist on the spot and no paperwork was generated. This seemed especially likely to occur when the adult referring the child had written an informal note rather than on the official referral form, when a parent did not have to be called, or when the infraction was judged by the student specialist to be insignificant. So it is likely that a much larger number of children were sent to the Punishing Room over the year but no record was made as a result of the visit.

[3] "Survey: Schools Suspend Blacks More," *Detroit Free Press*, December 14, 1988, 4A; Joan Richardson, "Study Puts Michigan 6th in Student Suspensions," *Detroit Free Press*, August 21, 1990, p. 1A; Minnesota Department of Children, Families and Learning, *Student Suspension and Expulsion: Report to the Legislature* (St. Paul: Minnesota Department of Children, Families and Learning, 1996); Commission for Positive Change in the Oakland Public Schools, *Keeping Children in Schools: Sounding the Alarm on Suspensions* (Oakland, CA: The Commission, 1992), p. 1; and John D. Hull, "Do Teachers Punish According to Race?" *Time*, April 4, 1994, pp. 30–31.

[4] In Oakland, while 28 percent of students in the system were African American males, they accounted for 53 percent of the suspensions. See note 3 for racial imbalance in corporal punishment in Michigan schools ("Survey: Schools Suspend Blacks More") and the racial discipline gap in Cincinnati (Hull, "Do Teachers Punish?").

[5] It is interesting to note that the girls in the class all responded in a stereotypical way. The vast majority wanted to have "helping" careers in traditional female occupations: teachers, nurses, psychologists. None of the girls gave money as a reason for their choice.

[6] Survey reported in *U.S. News and World Report*, March 24, 1997, p. 46.

[7] Raymie E. McKerrow and Norinne H. Daly, "The Student Athlete," *National Forum* 71, no. 4 (1990): 44.

[8] For examples see Gary A. Sailes, "The Exploitation of the Black Athlete: Some Alternative Solutions," *Journal of Negro Education* 55, no. 4 (1986); Robert M. Sellers and Gabriel P. Kuperminc, "Goal Discrepancy in African-American Male Student-Athletes' Unrealistic Expectations for Careers in Professional Sports," *Journal of Black Psychology* 23, no. 1 (1997); Alexander Wolf, "Impossible Dream," *Sports Illustrated*, June 2, 1997; and John Hoberman, *Darwin's Athletes: How Sport Has Damaged Black America and Preserved the Myth of Race* (Boston: Houghton Mifflin, 1997).

[9] For a shocking demonstration of the difference between schools, see Jonathan Kozol, *Savage Inequalities: Children in America's Schools* (New York: Crown Publishing, 1991).

[10] United States Department of Justice, Profile of Jail Inmates (Washington, DC: U.S. Government Printing Office, 1980). Two-thirds of the black inmates have less than a twelfth-grade education, while the rate of incarceration drops significantly for those who have twelve or more years of schooling.

[11] For an excellent overview of the debate that ensued over the Oakland School Board's resolution and a discussion of Ebonics, see Theresa Perry and Lisa Delpit, eds., *The Real Ebonics Debate: Power, Language, and the Education of African American Children* (Boston: Beacon Press, 1998).

[12] Jerome G. Miller, *Search and Destroy: African-American Males in the Criminal Justice System* (New York: Cambridge University Press, 1996), p. 73.

[13] David Huizinga and Delbert Elliot, "Juvenile Offenders: Prevalence, Offender Incidence, and Arrest Rates by Race," paper presented at "Race and the Incarceration of Juveniles," Racine, Wisconsin, December 1986, quoted in ibid., p. 72.

[14] Ibid., p. 78.

[15] Ibid., p. 73.

[16] Sentencing Project, *Young Black Americans and the Criminal Justice System: Five Years Later* (Washington, DC: Sentencing Project, 1995). This unprecedented figure reflects an increase from the 1990 Sentencing Project findings that one in four black males in their twenties was under the supervision of the criminal justice system.

THE FAMILY

53

THE DEINSTITUTIONALIZATION OF AMERICAN MARRIAGE

ANDREW J. CHERLIN

This is the first of three readings that examine the social institution of the family. Similar to other social institutions we have investigated, the institution of the family is undergoing tremendous change. These changes are hotly debated in the media and by politicians who argue that the institution of the family is in moral decline. Many sociologists disagree with this debate about family values and instead are studying how the structure and social norms of the family are changing. This excerpt by Andrew J. Cherlin, the Griswold Professor of Public Policy and Sociology at Johns Hopkins University, argues that the institution of marriage is becoming deinstitutionalized, which is causing some instability with the family until new social norms become established.

A quarter century ago, in an article entitled "Remarriage as an Incomplete Institution" (Cherlin 1978), I argued that American society lacked norms about the way that members of stepfamilies should act toward each other. Parents and children in first marriages, in contrast, could rely on well-established norms, such as when it is appropriate to

discipline a child. I predicted that, over time, as remarriage after divorce became common, norms would begin to emerge concerning proper behavior
in stepfamilies—for example, what kind of relationship a stepfather should
have with his stepchildren. In other words, I expected that remarriage
would become institutionalized, that it would become more like first marriage. But just the opposite has happened. Remarriage has not become more
like first marriage; rather, first marriage has become more like remarriage.
Instead of the institutionalization of remarriage, what has occurred over the
past few decades is the deinstitutionalization of marriage. Yes, remarriage is
an incomplete institution, but now, so is first marriage—and for that matter,
cohabitation.

By deinstitutionalization I mean the weakening of the social norms that
define people's behavior in a social institution such as marriage. In times of
social stability, the taken-for-granted nature of norms allows people to go
about their lives without having to question their actions or the actions of
others. But when social change produces situations outside the reach of established norms, individuals can no longer rely on shared understandings of
how to act. Rather, they must negotiate new ways of acting, a process that is
a potential source of conflict and opportunity. On the one hand, the development of new rules is likely to engender disagreement and tension among the
relevant actors. On the other hand, the breakdown of the old rules of a gendered institution such as marriage could lead to the creation of a more egalitarian relationship between wives and husbands.

This perspective, I think, can help us understand the state of contemporary marriage. It may even assist in the risky business of predicting the future
of marriage. To some extent, similar changes in marriage have occurred in
the United States, Canada, and much of Europe, but the American situation
may be distinctive. Consequently, although I include information about
Canadian and European families, I focus mainly on the United States.

The Deinstitutionalization of Marriage

Even as I was writing my 1978 article, the changing division of labor in the
home and the increase in childbearing outside marriage were undermining
the institutionalized basis of marriage. The distinct roles of homemaker and
breadwinner were fading as more married women entered the paid labor
force. Looking into the future, I thought that perhaps an equitable division
of household labor might become institutionalized. But what happened instead was the "stalled revolution," in Hochschild's (1989) well-known
phrase. Men do somewhat more home work than they used to do, but there
is wide variation, and each couple must work out their own arrangement
without clear guidelines. In addition, when I wrote the article, 1 out of 6
births in the United States occurred outside marriage, already a much
higher ratio than at midcentury (U.S. National Center for Health Statistics
1982). Today, the comparable figure is 1 out of 3 (U.S. National Center for

Health Statistics 2003). . . . Marriage is no longer the nearly universal setting for childbearing that it was a half century ago.

Both of these developments—the changing division of labor in the home and the increase in childbearing outside marriage—were well under way when I wrote my 1978 article, as was a steep rise in divorce. Here I discuss two more recent changes in family life, both of which have contributed to the deinstitutionalization of marriage after the 1970s: the growth of cohabitation, which began in the 1970s but was not fully appreciated until it accelerated in the 1980s and 1990s, and same-sex marriage, which emerged as an issue in the 1990s and has come to the fore in the current decade.

The Growth of Cohabitation

In the 1970s, neither I nor most other American researchers foresaw the greatly increased role of cohabitation in the adult life course. We thought that, except among the poor, cohabitation would remain a short-term arrangement among childless young adults who would quickly break up or marry. But it has become a more prevalent and more complex phenomenon. For example, cohabitation has created an additional layer of complexity in stepfamilies. When I wrote my article, nearly all stepfamilies were formed by the remarriage of one or both spouses. Now, about one fourth of all stepfamilies in the United States, and one half of all stepfamilies in Canada, are formed by cohabitation rather than marriage (Bumpass, Raley, and Sweet 1995; Statistics Canada 2002). It is not uncommon, especially among the low-income population, for a woman to have a child outside marriage, end her relationship with that partner, and then begin cohabiting with a different partner. This new union is equivalent in structure to a stepfamily but does not involve marriage. Sometimes the couple later marries, and if neither has been married before, their union creates a first marriage with stepchildren. As a result, we now see an increasing number of stepfamilies that do not involve marriage, and an increasing number of first marriages that involve stepfamilies.

More generally, cohabitation is becoming accepted as an alternative to marriage. . . . A number of indicators suggested that the connection between cohabitation and marriage was weakening. The proportion of cohabiting unions that end in marriage within 3 years dropped from 60% in the 1970s to about 33% in the 1990s (Smock and Gupta), suggesting that fewer cohabiting unions were trial marriages (or that fewer trial marriages were succeeding). In fact, Manning and Smock (2003) reported that among 115 cohabiting working-class and lower middle-class adults who were interviewed in depth, none said that he or she was deciding between marriage and cohabitation at the start of the union. Moreover, only 36% of adults in the 2002 United States General Social Survey disagreed with the statement, "It is alright for a couple to live together without intending to get married" (Davis, Smith, and Marsden 2003). And a growing share of births to unmarried women in the United States (about 40% in the 1990s) were to cohabiting couples (Bumpass and Lu 2000). . . .

To be sure, cohabitation is becoming more institutionalized. In the United States, states and municipalities are moving toward granting cohabiting couples some of the rights and responsibilities that married couples have. . . .

The Emergence of Same-Sex Marriage

The most recent development in the deinstitutionalization of marriage is the movement to legalize same-sex marriage. It became a public issue in the United States in 1993, when the Hawaii Supreme Court ruled that a state law restricting marriage to opposite-sex couples violated the Hawaii state constitution (*Baehr* v. *Lewin* 1993). Subsequently, Hawaii voters passed a state constitutional amendment barring same-sex marriage. In 1996, the United States Congress passed the Defense of Marriage Act, which allowed states to refuse to recognize same-sex marriages licensed in other states. The act's constitutionality has not been tested as of this writing because until recently, no state allowed same-sex marriages. However, in 2003, the Massachusetts Supreme Court struck down a state law limiting marriage to opposite-sex couples, and same-sex marriage became legal in May 2004 (although opponents may eventually succeed in prohibiting it through a state constitutional amendment). . . .

Lesbian and gay couples who choose to marry must actively construct a marital world with almost no institutional support. Lesbians and gay men already use the term "family" to describe their close relationships, but they usually mean something different from the standard marriage-based family. Rather, they often refer to what sociologists have called a "family of choice": one that is formed largely through voluntary ties among individuals who are not biologically or legally related (Weeks, Heaphy, and Donovan 2001; Weston 1991). Now they face the task of integrating marriages into these larger networks of friends and kin. The partners will not even have the option of falling back on the gender-differentiated roles of heterosexual marriage. This is not to say that there will be no division of labor; one study of gay and lesbian couples found that in homes where one partner works longer hours and earns substantially more than the other partner, the one with the less demanding, lower paying job did more housework and more of the work of keeping in touch with family and friends. The author suggests that holding a demanding professional or managerial job may make it difficult for a person to invest fully in sharing the work at home, regardless of gender or sexual orientation (Carrington 1999).

We might expect same-sex couples who have children, or who wish to have children through adoption or donor insemination, to be likely to avail themselves of the option of marriage. (According to the United States Census Bureau [2003b], 33% of women in same-sex partnerships and 22% of men in same-sex partnerships had children living with them in 2000.) Basic issues, such as who would care for the children, would have to be resolved family by family. The obligations of the partners to each other following a marital dissolution have also yet to be worked out. In these and many other ways, gay and lesbian couples who marry in the near future would need to create a marriage-centered kin network through discussion, negotiation, and experiment.

Two Transitions in the Meaning of Marriage

In a larger sense, all of these developments—the changing division of labor, childbearing outside of marriage, cohabitation, and gay marriage—are the result of long-term cultural and material trends that altered the meaning of marriage during the 20th century. The cultural trends included, first, an emphasis on emotional satisfaction and romantic love that intensified early in the century. Then, during the last few decades of the century, an ethic of expressive individualism—which Bellah et al. (1985) describe as the belief that "each person has a unique core of feeling and intuition that should unfold or be expressed if individuality is to be realized" (p. 334)—became more important. On the material side, the trends include the decline of agricultural labor and the corresponding increase in wage labor; the decline in child and adult mortality; rising standards of living; and, in the last half of the 20th century, the movement of married women into the paid workforce.

These developments, along with historical events such as the Depression and World War II, produced two great changes in the meaning of marriage during the 20th century. Ernest Burgess famously labeled the first one as a transition "from an institution to a companionship" (Burgess and Locke 1945). In describing the rise of the companionate marriage, Burgess was referring to the single-earner, breadwinner–homemaker marriage that flourished in the 1950s. Although husbands and wives in the companionate marriage usually adhered to a sharp division of labor, they were supposed to be each other's companions—friends, lovers—to an extent not imagined by the spouses in the institutional marriages of the previous era. The increasing focus on bonds of sentiment within nuclear families constituted an important but limited step in the individualization of family life. Much more so than in the 19th century, the emotional satisfaction of the spouses became an important criterion for marital success. However, through the 1950s, wives and husbands tended to derive satisfaction from their participation in a marriage-based nuclear family (Roussel 1989). That is to say, they based their gratification on playing marital roles well: being good providers, good homemakers, and responsible parents.

During this first change in meaning, marriage remained the only socially acceptable way to have a sexual relationship and to raise children in the United States, Canada, and Europe, with the possible exception of the Nordic countries. In his history of British marriages, Gillis (1985) labeled the period from 1850 to 1960 the "era of mandatory marriage." In the United States, marriage and only marriage was one's ticket of admission to a full family life. Prior to marrying, almost no one cohabited with a partner except among the poor and the avant garde. As recently as the 1950s, premarital cohabitation in the United States was restricted to a small minority (perhaps 5%) of the less educated (Bumpass, Sweet, and Cherlin 1991). . . .

But beginning in the 1960s, marriage's dominance began to diminish, and the second great change in the meaning of marriage occurred. In the United States, the median age at marriage returned to and then exceeded the levels of the early 1900s. In 2000, the median age was 27 for men and 25 for women (U.S. Census Bureau 2003a). Many young adults stayed single into their mid to late 20s, some completing college educations and starting careers. Cohabitation prior to (and after) marriage became much more acceptable Childbearing outside marriage became less stigmatized and more accepted. Birth rates resumed their long-term declines and sunk to all-time lows in most countries. Divorce rates rose to unprecedented levels. Same-sex unions found greater acceptance as well.

During this transition, the companionate marriage lost ground not only as the demographic standard but also as a cultural ideal. It was gradually overtaken by forms of marriage (and nonmarital families) that Burgess had not foreseen, particularly marriages in which both the husband and the wife worked outside the home. Although women continued to do most of the housework and child care, the roles of wives and husbands became more flexible and open to negotiation. And an even more individualistic perspective on the rewards of marriage took root. When people evaluated how satisfied they were with their marriages, they began to think more in terms of the development of their own sense of self and the expression of their feelings, as opposed to the satisfaction they gained through building a family and playing the roles of spouse and parent. The result was a transition from the companionate marriage to what we might call the *individualized marriage*. . . .

During this second change in the meaning of marriage, the role of the law changed significantly as well. This transformation was most apparent in divorce law. In the United States and most other developed countries, legal restrictions on divorce were replaced by statutes that recognized consensual and even unilateral divorce. The transition to "private ordering" (Mnookin and Kornhauser 1979) allowed couples to negotiate the details of their divorce agreements within broad limits. Most European nations experienced similar legal developments (Glendon 1989; Théry 1993). Indeed, French social demographer Louis Roussel (1989) wrote of a "double deinstitutionalization" in behavior and in law: a greater hesitation of young adults to enter into marriage, combined with a loosening of the legal regulation of marriage.

Sociological theorists of late modernity (or postmodernity) such as Anthony Giddens (1991, 1992) in Britain and Ulrich Beck and Elisabeth Beck-Gernsheim in Germany (1995, 2002) also have written about the growing individualization of personal life. Consistent with the idea of dein-stitutionalization, they note the declining power of social norms and laws as regulating mechanisms for family life, and they stress the expanding role of personal choice. They argue that as traditional sources of identity such as class, religion, and community lose influence, one's intimate relationships become central to self-identity. Giddens (1991, 1992) writes of the emergence of the "pure relationship": an intimate partnership entered into for its own sake, which lasts only as long as both partners are satisfied with the rewards (mostly intimacy and love) that they get from it. It is in some ways the logi-cal extension of the increasing individualism and the deinstitutionalization of marriage that occurred in the 20th century. The pure relationship is not tied to an institution such as marriage or to the desire to raise children. Rather, it is "free-floating," independent of social institutions or economic life. Unlike marriage, it is not regulated by law, and its members do not enjoy special legal rights. It exists primarily in the realms of emotion and self-identity.

Although the theorists of late modernity believe that the quest for inti-macy is becoming the central focus of personal life, they do not predict that *marriage* will remain distinctive and important. Marriage, they claim, has be-come a choice rather than a necessity for adults who want intimacy, com-panionship, and children. According to Beck and Beck-Gernsheim (1995), we will see "a huge variety of ways of living together or apart which will con-tinue to exist side by side" (pp. 141–42). Giddens (1992) even argues that marriage has already become "just one life-style among others" (p. 154) although people may not yet realize it because of institutional lag.

The Current Context of Marriage

Overall, research and writing on the changing meaning of marriage suggest that it is now situated in a very different context than in the past. This is true in at least two senses. First, individuals now experience a vast latitude for choice in their personal lives. More forms of marriage and more alternatives to marriage are socially acceptable. Moreover, one may fit marriage into one's life in many ways: One may first live with a partner, or sequentially with several partners, without an explicit consideration of whether a marriage will occur. One may have children with one's eventual spouse or with someone else before marrying. One may, in some jurisdictions, marry someone of the same gender and build a shared marital world with few guidelines to rely on. Within marriage, roles are more flexible and negotiable although women still do more than their share of the household work and childrearing.

The second difference is in the nature of the rewards that people seek through marriage and other close relationships. Individuals aim for personal growth and deeper intimacy through more open communication and mutu-ally shared disclosures about feelings with their partners. They may feel justified in insisting on changes in a relationship that no longer provides them with individualized rewards. In contrast, they are less likely than in the past to focus on the rewards to be found in fulfilling socially valued roles such as the good parent or the loyal and supportive spouse. The result of these changing contexts has been a deinstitutionalization of marriage, in which social norms about family and personal life count for less than they did during the heyday of the companionate marriage, and far less than during the period of the institutional marriage. Instead, personal choice and self-development loom large in people's construction of their marital careers.

Why Do People Still Marry?

There is a puzzle within the story of deinstitutionalization that needs solving. Although fewer Americans are marrying than during the peak years of marriage in the mid-20th century, most—nearly 90%, according to a recent estimate (Goldstein and Kenney 2001)—will eventually marry. A survey of high school seniors conducted annually since 1976 shows no decline in the importance they attach to marriage. The percentage of young women who respond that they expect to marry has stayed constant at roughly 80% (and has increased from 71% to 78% for young men). The percentage who respond that "having a good marriage and family life" is extremely important has also remained constant, at about 80% for young women and 70% for young men (Thornton and Young-DeMarco 2001). What is more, in the 1990s and early 2000s, a strong promarriage movement emerged among gay men and lesbians in the United States, who sought the right to marry with increasing success. Clearly, marriage remains important to many people in the United States. Consequently, I think the interesting question is not why so few people are marrying, but rather, why so *many* people are marrying, or planning to marry, or hoping to marry, when cohabitation and single parenthood are widely acceptable options. . . .

The Gains to Marriage

The dominant theoretical perspectives on marriage in the 20th century do not provide much guidance on the question of why marriage remains so popular. The structural functionalists in social anthropology and sociology in the early- to mid-20th century emphasized the role of marriage in ensuring that a child would have a link to the status of a man, a right to his protection, and a claim to inherit his property (Mair 1971). But as the law began to recognize the rights of children born outside marriage, and as mothers acquired resources by working in the paid workforce, these reasons for marriage became less important.

Nor is evolutionary theory very helpful. Although there may be important evolutionary influences on family behavior, it is unlikely that humans have developed an innate preference for marriage as we know it. The classical account of our evolutionary heritage is that women, whose reproductive capacity is limited by pregnancy and lactation (which delays the return of ovulation), seek stable pair bonds with men, whereas men seek to maximize their fertility by impregnating many women. Rather than being "natural," marriage-centered kinship was described in much early- and mid-20th century anthropological writing as the social invention that solved the problem of the sexually wandering male (Tiger and Fox 1971). Moreover, when dependable male providers are not available, women may prefer a reproductive strategy of relying on a network of female kin and more than one man (Hrdy 1999). In addition, marriages are increasingly being formed well after a child is born, yet evolutionary theory suggests that the impetus to marry should be greatest when newborn children need support and protection. In the 1950s, half of all unmarried pregnant women in the United States married before the birth of their child, whereas in the 1990s, only one-fourth married (U.S. Census Bureau 1999). Finally, evolutionary theory cannot explain the persistence of the formal wedding style in which people are still marrying (see below). Studies of preindustrial societies have found that although many have elaborate ceremonies, others have little or no ceremony (Ember, Ember, and Peregrine 2002; Stephens 1963).

The mid-20th-century specialization model of economist Gary Becker (1965, 1981) also seems less relevant than when it was introduced. Becker assumed that women were relatively more productive at home than men, and that men were relatively more productive (i.e., they could earn higher wages) in the labor market. He argued that women and men could increase their utility by exchanging, through marriage, women's home work for men's labor market work. The specialization model would predict that in the present era women with less labor market potential would be more likely to marry because they would gain the most economically from finding a husband. But several studies show that in recent decades, women in the United States and Canada with less education (and therefore less labor market potential) are *less* likely to marry (Lichter et al. 1992; Oppenheimer, Blossfeld, and Wackerow 1995; Qian and Preston 1993; Sweeney 2002; Turcotte and Goldscheider 1998). This finding suggests that the specialization model may no longer hold. Moreover, the specialization model was developed before cohabitation was widespread, and offers no explanation for why couples would marry rather than cohabit.

From a rational choice perspective, then, what benefits might contemporary marriage offer that would lead cohabiting couples to marry rather than cohabit? I suggest that the major benefit is what we might call *enforceable trust* (Cherlin 2000; Portes and Sensenbrenner 1993). Marriage still requires a public commitment to a long-term, possibly lifelong relationship. This commitment is usually expressed in front of relatives, friends, and religious congregants. Cohabitation, in contrast, requires only a private commitment, which is easier to break. Therefore, marriage, more so than cohabitation, lowers the risk that one's partner will renege on agreements that have been made. In the language of economic theory, marriage lowers the transaction costs of enforcing agreements between the partners (Pollak 1985). It allows individuals to invest in the partnership with less fear of abandonment. For instance, it allows the partners to invest financially in joint long-term purchases such as homes and automobiles. It allows caregivers to make relationship-specific investments (England and Farkas 1986) in the couple's children—investments of time and effort that, unlike strengthening one's job skills, would not be easily portable to another intimate relationship.

Nevertheless, the difference in the amount of enforceable trust that marriage brings, compared with cohabitation, is eroding. Although relatives and friends will view a divorce with disappointment, they will accept it more readily than their counterparts would have two generations ago. As I noted, cohabiting couples are increasingly gaining the rights previously reserved to married couples. It seems likely that over time, the legal differences between cohabitation and marriage will become minimal in the United States, Canada, and many European countries. The advantage of marriage in enhancing trust will then depend on the force of public commitments, both secular and religious, by the partners.

In general, the prevailing theoretical perspectives are of greater value in explaining why marriage has declined than why it persists. With more women working outside the home, the predictions of the specialization model are less relevant. Although the rational choice theorists remind us that marriage still provides enforceable trust, it seems clear that its enforcement power is declining. Recently, evolutionary theorists have argued that women who have difficulty finding men who are reliable providers might choose a reproductive strategy that involves single parenthood and kin networks, a strategy that is consistent with changes that have occurred in low-income families. And although the insights of the theorists of late modernity help us understand the changing meaning of marriage, they predict that marriage will lose its distinctive status, and indeed may already have become just one lifestyle among others. Why, then, are so many people still marrying?

The Symbolic Significance of Marriage

What has happened is that although the practical importance of being married has declined, its symbolic importance has remained high, and may even have increased. Marriage is at once less dominant and more distinctive than it was. It has evolved from a marker of conformity to a marker of prestige. Marriage is a status one builds up to, often by living with a partner beforehand, by attaining steady employment or starting a career, by putting away some savings, and even by having children. Marriage's place in the life course used to come before those investments were made, but now it often comes afterward. It used to be the foundation of adult personal life; now it is sometimes the capstone. It is something to be achieved through one's own efforts rather than something to which one routinely accedes.

How Low-Income Individuals See Marriage

Paradoxically, it is among the lower social strata in the United States, where marriage rates are lowest, that both the persistent preference for marriage and its changing meaning seem clearest. Although marriage is optional and often foregone, it has by no means faded away among the poor and near poor. Instead, it is a much sought-after but elusive goal. They tell observers that they wish to marry, but will do so only when they are sure they can do it successfully: when their partner has demonstrated the ability to hold a decent job and treat them fairly and without abuse, when they have a security deposit or a down payment for a decent apartment or home, and when they have enough in the bank to pay for a nice wedding party for family and friends. Edin and Kefalas [2005], who studied childbearing and intimate relationships among 165 mothers in 8 low- and moderate-income Philadelphia neighborhoods, wrote, "In some sense, marriage is a form of social bragging about the quality of the couple relationship, a powerfully symbolic way of elevating one's relationship above others in the community, particularly in a community where marriage is rare."

Along with several collaborators, I am conducting a study of low-income families in three United States cities. The ethnographic component of that study is directed by Linda Burton of Pennsylvania State University. A 27-year-old mother told one of our ethnographers:

> I was poor all my life and so was Reginald. When I got pregnant, we agreed we would marry some day in the future because we loved each other and wanted to raise our child together. But we would not get married until we could afford to get a house and pay all the utility bills on time. I have this thing about utility bills. Our gas and electric got turned off all the time when we were growing up and we wanted to make sure that would not happen when we got married. That was our biggest worry. . . . We worked together and built up savings and then we got married. It's forever for us. . . .

. . . In sum, the demands low-income women place on men include not just a reliable income, as important as that is, but also a commitment to put family first, provide companionship, be faithful, and avoid abusive behavior.

How Young Adults in General See It

The changing meaning of marriage is not limited to the low-income population. Consider a nationally representative survey of 1,003 adults, ages 20–29, conducted in 2001 on attitudes toward marriage (Whitehead and Popenoe 2001). A majority responded in ways suggestive of the view that marriage is a status that one builds up to. Sixty-two percent agreed with the statement "Living together with someone before marriage is a good way to avoid an eventual divorce," and 82% agreed that "it is extremely important to you to be economically set before you get married." Moreover, most indicated a view of marriage as centered on intimacy and love more than on practical matters such as finances and children. Ninety-four percent of those who had never married agreed that "when you marry, you want your spouse to be your soul mate, first and foremost." In contrast, only 16% agreed that "the main purpose of marriage these days is to have children." And over 80% of the women agreed that it is more important "to have a husband who can communicate about his deepest feelings than to have a husband who makes a good living." The authors of the report conclude, "While marriage is losing much of its broad public and institutional character, it is gaining popularity as a Super-Relationship, an intensely private spiritualized union, combining sexual fidelity, romantic love, emotional intimacy, and togetherness" (p. 13). . . .

Alternative Futures

What do these developments suggest about the future of marriage? Social demographers usually predict a continuation of whatever is happening at the moment, and they are usually correct, but sometimes spectacularly wrong. For example, in the 1930s, every demographic expert in the United States confidently predicted a continuation of the low birth rates of the Depression. Not one forecast the baby boom that overtook them after World War II. No less a scholar than Kingsley Davis (1937) wrote that the future of the family as a social institution was in danger because people were not having enough children to replace themselves. Not a single 1950s or 1960s sociologist predicted the rise of cohabitation. Chastened by this unimpressive record, I will tentatively sketch some future directions.

The first alternative is the reinstitutionalization of marriage, a return to a status akin to its dominant position through the mid-20th century. This would entail a rise in the proportion who ever marry, a rise in the proportion of births born to married couples, and a decline in divorce. It would require a reversal of the individualistic orientation toward family and personal life that has been the major cultural force driving family change over the past several decades. It would probably also require a decrease in women's labor force participation and a return to more gender-typed family roles. I think this alternative is very unlikely—but then again, so was the baby boom.

The second alternative is a continuation of the current situation, in which marriage remains deinstitutionalized but is common and distinctive. It is not just one type of family relationship among many; rather, it is the most prestigious form. People generally desire to be married. But it is an individual choice, and individuals construct marriages through an increasingly long process that often includes cohabitation and childbearing beforehand. It still confers some of its traditional benefits, such as enforceable trust, but it is increasingly a mark of prestige, a display of distinction, an individualistic achievement, a part of what Beck and Beck-Gernsheim (2002) call the "do-it-yourself biography" In this scenario, the proportion of people who ever marry could fall further; in particular, we could see probabilities of marriage among Whites in the United States that are similar to the probabilities shown today by African Americans. Moreover, because of high levels of nonmarital childbearing, cohabitation, and divorce, people will spend a smaller proportion of their adult lives in intact marriages than in the past. Still, marriage would retain its special and highly valued place in the family system.

But I admit to some doubts about whether this alternative will prevail for long in the United States. The privileges and material advantages of marriage, relative to cohabitation, have been declining. The commitment of partners to be trustworthy has been undermined by frequent divorce. If marriage was once a form of cultural capital—one needed to be married to advance one's career, say—that capital has decreased too. What is left, I have argued, is a display of prestige and achievement. But it could be that marriage retains its symbolic aura largely because of its dominant position in social norms until just a half century ago. It could be that this aura is diminishing, like an echo in a canyon. It could be that, despite the efforts of the wedding industry, the need for a highly ritualized ceremony and legalized status will fade. And there is not much else supporting marriage in the early 21st century.

That leads to a third alternative, the fading away of marriage. Here, the argument is that people are still marrying in large numbers because of institutional lag; they have yet to realize that marriage is no longer important. A nonmarital pure relationship, to use Giddens' ideal type, can provide much intimacy and love, can place both partners on an equal footing, and can allow them to develop their independent senses of self. These characteristics are highly valued in late modern societies. However, this alternative also suggests the predominance of fragile relationships that are continually at risk of breaking up because they are held together entirely by the voluntary commitment of each partner. People may still commit morally to a relationship, but they increasingly prefer to commit voluntarily rather than to be obligated to commit by law or social norms. And partners feel free to revoke their commitments at any time.

Therefore, the pure relationship seems most characteristic of a world where commitment does not matter. Consequently, it seems to best fit middle-class, well-educated, childless adults. They have the resources to be independent actors by themselves or in a democratic partnership, and without childbearing responsibilities, they can be free-floating. The pure relationship seems less applicable to couples who face material constraints (Jamieson 1999). In particular when children are present—or when they are anticipated anytime soon—issues of commitment and support come into consideration. Giddens (1992) says very little about children in his book on intimacy, and his brief attempts to incorporate children into the pure relationship are unconvincing. Individuals who are, or think they will be, the primary caregivers of children will prefer commitment and will seek material support from their partners. They may be willing to have children and begin cohabiting without commitment, but the relationship probably will not last without it. They will be wary of purely voluntary commitment if they think they can do better. So only if the advantage of marriage in providing trust and commitment disappears relative to cohabitation—and I must admit that this could happen—might we see cohabitation and marriage on an equal footing.

In sum, I see the current state of marriage and its likely future in these terms: At present, marriage is no longer as dominant as it once was, but it remains important on a symbolic level. It has been transformed from a familial and community institution to an individualized, choice-based achievement. It is a marker of prestige and is still somewhat useful in creating enforceable trust. As for the future, I have sketched three alternatives. The first, a return to a more dominant, institutionalized form of marriage, seems unlikely. In the second, the current situation continues; marriage remains important, but not as dominant, and retains its high symbolic status. In the third, marriage fades into just one of many kinds of interpersonal romantic relationships. I think that Giddens' (1992) statement that marriage has already become merely one of many relationships is not true in the United States so far, but it could become true in the future. It is possible that we are living in a transitional phase in which marriage is gradually losing its uniqueness. If Giddens and other modernity theorists are correct, the third alternative will triumph, and marriage will lose its special place in the family system of the United States. If they are not, the second alternative will continue to hold, and marriage—transformed and deinstitutionalized, but recognizable nevertheless—will remain distinctive.

ENDNOTE

Author's Note: I thank Frank Furstenberg, Joshua Goldstein, Kathleen Kieman, and Céline Le Bourdais for comments on a previous version, and Linda Burton for her collaborative work on the Three-City Study ethnography.

REFERENCES

Baehr v. Lewin. 1993. 74 Haw. 530, 74 Haw. 645, 852 P.2d 44.

Beck, U. and E. Beck-Gernsheim. 1995. *The Normal Chaos of Love.* Cambridge, England: Polity Press.

———. 2002 *Individualization: Institutionalized Individualism and Its Social and Political Consequences.* London: Sage.

Becker, G. S. 1965. "A Theory of the Allocation of Time." *Economic Journal* 75:493–517.

———. 1981. *A Treatise on the Family.* Cambridge, MA: Harvard University Press.

Bellah, R., R. Marsden, W. M. Sullivan, A. Swidler, and S. M. Tipton. 1985. *Habits of the Heart: Individualism and Commitment in America.* Berkeley: University of California Press.

Bumpass, L. L. and H.-H. Lu. 2000. "Trends in Cohabitation and Implications for Children's Family Contexts in the United States." *Population Studies* 54:19–41.

Bumpass, L. L., K. Raley, and J. A. Sweet. 1995. "The Changing Character of Stepfamilies: Implications of Cohabitation and Nonmarital Childbearing." *Demography* 32:1–12.

Bumpass, L. L., J. A. Sweet, and A. J. Cherlin. 1991. "The Role of Cohabitation in Declining Rates of Marriage." *Journal of Marriage and the Family* 53:338–55.

Burgess, E. W. and H. J. Locke. 1945. *The Family: From Institution to Companionship.* New York: American Book.

Carrington, C. 1999. *No Place Like Home: Relationships and Family Life among Lesbians and Gay Men.* Chicago: University of Chicago Press.

Cherlin A. 1978. Remarriage as an Incomplete Institution. *American Journal of Sociology* 84:634–50.

———. 1992. *Marriage, Divorce, Remarriage.* Rev. ed. Cambridge, MA: Harvard University Press.

————. 2000. "Toward a New Home Socioeconomics of Union Formation." Pp. 126–44 in *Ties That Bind: Perspectives on Marriage and Cohabitation*, edited by L. Waite, C. Bachrach, M. Hindin, E. Thomson, and A. Thornton. Hawthorne, NY: Aldine de Gruyter.

Davis, J. A., T. W. Smith, and P. Marsden 2003. *General Social Surveys, 1972–2002. Cumulative Codebook*. Chicago: National Opinion Research Center, University of Chicago.

Davis, K. 1937. "Reproductive Institutions and the Pressure for Population." *Sociological Review* 29:289–306.

Edin, K. J. and M. J. Kefalas. 2005. *Promises I Can Keep: Why Poor Women Put Motherhood Before Marriage*. Berkeley: University of California Press.

Ember, C. R., M. Ember, and P. N. Peregrine. 2002. *Anthropology*. 10th ed. Upper Saddle River, NJ: Prentice-Hall.

England, P. and G. Farkas. 1986. *Households, Employment, and Gender: A Social, Economic, and Demographic View*. New York: Aldine.

Giddens, A. 1991. *Modernity and Self-Identity*. Stanford, CA: Stanford University Press.

————. 1992. *The Transformation of Intimacy*. Stanford, CA: Stanford University Press.

Gillis, J. R. 1985. *For Better or Worse: British Marriages, 1600 to the Present*. Oxford, England: Oxford University Press.

Glendon, M. A. 1989. *Abortion and Divorce in Western Law*. Cambridge, MA: Harvard University Press.

Goldstein, J. R. and C. T. Kenney. 2001. "Marriage Delayed or Marriage Forgone? New Cohort Forecasts of First Marriage for U.S. Women." *American Sociological Review* 66:506–19.

Hochschild, A. 1989. *The Second Shift: Working Parents and the Revolution at Home*. New York: Viking.

Hrdy, S. B. 1999. *Mother Nature: Maternal Instincts and How They Shape the Human Species*. New York: Ballantine Books.

Jamieson, L. 1999. "Intimacy Transformed? A Critical Look at the "Pure Relationship." *Sociology* 33:477–94.

Lichter, D. T., D. K. McLaughlin G. Kephart, and D. J. Landry. 1992. "Race and the Retreat from Marriage: A Shortage of Marriageable Men?" *American Sociological Review* 57:781–99.

Mair, L. 1971. *Marriage*. Middlesex, England: Penguin Books.

Manning, W. and P. J. Smock. 2003, May. "Measuring and Modeling Cohabitation: New Perspectives from Qualitative Data." Paper presented at the annual meeting of the Population Association of America, Minneapolis, MN.

Mnookin, R. H. and L. Kornhauser. 1979. "Bargaining in the Shadow of the Law: The Case of Divorce." *Yale Law Journal* 88:950–97.

Oppenheimer V. K., H.-P. Blossfeld, and A. Wackerow. 1995. "United States of America." Pp. 150–73 in *The New Role of Women: Family Formation in Modern Societies*, edited by H. P. Blossfeld. Boulder, CO: Westview Press.

Pollak, R. A. 1985. "A Transaction Costs Approach to Families and Households." *Journal of Economic Literature* 23:581–608.

Portes, A. and J. Sensenbrenner 1993. "Embeddedness and Immigration: Notes on the Social Determinants of Economic Action." *American Journal of Sociology* 98:1320–50.

Qian, Z. and S. H. Preston. 1993. "Changes in American Marriage, 1972 to 1987: Availability and Forces of Attraction by Age and Education." *American Sociological Review* 58:482–95.

Roussel, L. 1989. *La Famille Incertaine*. Paris: Editions Odile Jacob.

Statistics Canada. 2002. *Changing Conjugal Life in Canada*. No. 89-576-XIE. Ottawa, Ontario: Statistical Reference Centre.

Stephens, William N. 1963. *The Family in Cross-Cultural Perspective*. New York: Holt, Rinehart and Winston.

Sweeney, M. M. 2002. "Two Decades of Family Change: The Shift in Economic Foundations of Marriage." *American Sociological Review* 67:132–47.

Théry, I. 1993. *Le Démariage*. Paris: Editions Odile Jacob.

Thornton, A., and L. Young-DeMarco 2001. "Four Decades of Trends in Attitudes toward Family Issues in the United States: The 1960s through the 1990s." *Journal of Marriage and Family* 63:1009–37.

Tiger, L., and R. Fox. 1971. *The Imperial Animal*. New York: Holt, Rinehart and Winston.

Turcotte, P. and F. Goldscheider. 1998. "Evolution of Factors Influencing First Union Formation in Canada." *Canadian Studies in Population* 25:145–73.

U.S. Census Bureau. 1999. "Trends in Premarital Childbearing: 1930–1994." *Current Population Reports*, No. P23–97. Washington, DC: U.S. Government Printing Office.

————. 2003a. "Estimated Median Age at First Marriage, by Sex: 1890 to Present." Retrieved January 11, 2003 (http://www.census.gov/population/www/socdemo/hh-fam.html).

————. 2003b. "Married-Couple and Unmarried-Partner Households: 2000." *Census 2000 Special Reports*, CENSR-5. Washington, DC: U.S: Government Printing Office.

U.S. National Center for Health Statistics. 1982. *Vital Statistics of the United States, 1978,* vol. 1. *Natality.* Washington, DC: U.S. Government Printing Office.

————. 2003. "Births: Preliminary Data for 2002." Retrieved December 15, 2003 (http://www.cdc.gov/nchs/data/nvsr/nvsr51/nvsr51_11.pdf).

Weeks, J., B., Heaphy, and C. Donovan. 2001. *Same-Sex Intimacies: Families of Choice and Other Life Experiments.* London: Routledge.

Weston, K. 1991. *Families We Choose: Lesbians, Gays, Kinship.* New York: Columbia University Press.

Whitehead, B. D. and D. Popenoe. 2001. "Who Wants to Marry a Soul Mate?" Pp. 6–16 in *The State of Our Unions, 2001.* National Marriage Project Retrieved February 12, 2004 (http://marriage.rutgers.edu/Publications/SOOU/NMPAR2001.pdf).

54

THE MOMMY TAX

ANN CRITTENDEN

In this selection, taken from *The Price of Motherhood: Why the Most Important Job in the World Is Still the Least Valued* (2001), Ann Crittenden observes how motherhood is very costly for women in the United States. Crittenden, a former reporter for the *New York Times,* states that women who decide to take time off from paid work to have and raise children pay a "mommy tax" of literally thousands of dollars every year. The amount of income women are penalized for childbearing varies by age and profession, but the overall amount working mothers are losing is staggering. Crittenden's research reveals that the institution of the family is not only gendered, but it is an institution that suffers because of economic forms of gender discrimination against women and mothers.

In the U.S. we have no way to address women's economic disadvantages except through the concept of gender. We see the problem as discrimination on the basis of gender. But what's really going on is a disadvantaging of mothers *in the workforce.*

—Susan Pederson, Historian

O n April 7, 1999, the Independent Women's Forum, a conservative antifeminist organization, held a news conference at the National Press
Club in Washington, D.C. Displayed in the corner of the room was a
large green "check," made out to feminists, for ninety-eight cents. The point
being made was that American women now make ninety-eight cents to a
man's dollar and have therefore achieved complete equality in the workplace.

The sheer nerve of this little exercise in misinformation was astonishing.
Upon closer examination, it turned out that the women who earn almost as
much as men are a rather narrow group: those who are between the ages of
twenty-seven and thirty-three and who have never had children.[1] The Independent Women's Forum was comparing young childless women to men
and declaring victory for all women, glossing over the real news: that mothers are the most disadvantaged people in the workplace. One could even say
that motherhood is now the single greatest obstacle left in the path to economic equality for women.

For most companies, the ideal worker is "unencumbered," that is, free of
all ties other than those to his job. Anyone who can't devote all his or her energies to paid work is barred from the best jobs and has a permanently lower
lifetime income. Not coincidentally, almost all the people in that category
happen to be mothers.

The reduced earnings of mothers are, in effect, a heavy personal tax
levied on people who care for children, or for any other dependent family
members. This levy, a "mommy tax," is easily greater than $1 million in the
case of a college-educated woman.[2] For working-class women, there is increasing evidence both in the United States and worldwide that mothers' differential responsibility for children, rather than classic sex discrimination, is
the most important factor disposing women to poverty.[3]

"This is the issue that women's and children's advocates should be raising," argues Jane Waldfogel, a professor at Columbia University School of
Social Work. "Women's equality is not about equal access to education or
equal job opportunities anymore—those things are done. The part that's left
is the part that has to do with family responsibilities."[4]

The much-publicized earnings gap between men and women narrowed
dramatically in the 1980s and early 1990s. All a girl had to do was stay
young and unencumbered. The sexual egalitarianism evident in so many
television sit-coms, from *Friends* to *Seinfeld* to *Ally McBeal*, is rooted in economic reality. Young women don't need a man to pay their bills or take
them out, any more than men need a woman to iron their shirts or cook
their dinner. Many childless women under the age of thirty-five firmly believe that all of the feminist battles have been won, and as far as they're
concerned, they're largely right.

But once a woman has a baby, the egalitarian office party is over. I ought
to know.

Million-Dollar Babies

After my son was born in 1982, I decided to leave the *New York Times* in order to have more time to be a mother. I recently calculated what that decision cost me financially.

I had worked full-time for approximately twenty years, eight of those at the *Times*. When I left, I had a yearly salary of roughly $50,000, augmented by speaking fees, freelance income, and journalism awards. Had I not had a child, I probably would have worked at least another fifteen years, maybe taking early retirement to pursue other interests. Under this scenario, I would have earned a pension, which I lost by leaving the paper before I had worked the requisite ten years to become vested. (The law has since changed to allow vesting after five years with one employer.)

My annual income after leaving the paper has averaged roughly $15,000, from part-time freelance writing. Very conservatively, I lost between $600,000 and $700,000, not counting the loss of a pension. Without quite realizing what I was doing, I took what I thought would be a relatively short break, assuming it would be easy to get back into journalism after a few years, or to earn a decent income from books and other projects. I was wrong. As it turned out, I sacrificed more than half of my expected lifetime earnings. And in the boom years of the stock market, that money invested in equities would have multiplied like kudzu. As a conservative estimate, it could have generated $50,000 or $60,000 a year in income for my old age.

At the time, I never sat down and made these economic calculations. I never even thought about money in connection with motherhood, or if I did, I assumed my husband would provide all we needed. And had I been asked to weigh my son's childhood against ten or fifteen more years at the *Times,* I doubt whether the monetary loss would have tipped the scales. But still, this seems a high price to pay for doing the right thing.

The mommy tax I paid is fairly typical for an educated middle-class American woman. Economist Shirley Burggraf has calculated that a husband and wife who earn a combined income of $81,500 per year and who are equally capable will lose $1.35 million if they have a child. Most of that lost income is the wages forgone by the primary parent.[5] In a middle-income family, with one parent earning $30,000 per year as a sales representative and the other averaging $15,000 as a part-time computer consultant, the mommy tax will still be more than $600,000. Again, this seems an unreasonable penalty on the decision to raise a child, a decision that contributes to the general good by adding another productive person to the nation.

In lower-income families, the mommy tax can push a couple over the brink. Martha F. Richie, a former director of the U.S. Census Bureau, told me, "There is anecdotal evidence—no real research—that for a lower-earning married couple the decision to have a child, or a second child, throws them into poverty."[6]

Those who care for elderly relatives also discover that their altruism will be heavily penalized. A small survey of individuals who provided informal, unpaid care for family members found that it cost them an average of $659,139 in lost wages, Social Security, and pension benefits over their lifetimes. The subjects reported having to pass up promotions and training opportunities, use up their sick days and vacations, reduce their workload to part-time, and in many cases even quit their paid jobs altogether. This exorbitant "caring tax" is being paid by an increasing number of people, three-quarters of them women. A 1997 study discovered that one in four families had at least one adult who had provided care for an elderly relative or friend.[7]

The mommy tax is obviously highest for well-educated, high-income individuals and lowest for poorly educated people who have less potential income to lose. All else being equal, the younger the mother, and the more children she has, the higher her tax will be, which explains why women are having fewer children, later in life, almost everywhere.

The tax is highest in the Anglo-Saxon countries, where mothers personally bear almost all the costs of caring, and lowest in France and Scandinavia, where paid maternity leaves and public preschools make it easier for mothers to provide care without sacrificing their income. . . .

Sixty Cents to a Man's Dollar

In the Bible, in Leviticus, God instructs Moses to tell the Israelites that women, for purposes of tithing, are worth thirty shekels while men are worth fifty—a ratio of 60 percent.[8] For fifty years, from about 1930 to 1980, the value of employed women eerily reflected that biblical ratio: The earnings of full-time working women were only 60 percent of men's earnings. In the 1980s, that ratio began to change. By 1993, women working full-time were earning an average of seventy-seven cents for every dollar men earned. (In 1997, the gap widened again, as the median weekly earnings of full-time working women fell to 75 percent of men's earnings.)

But lo and behold, when we look closer, we find the same old sixty cents to a man's dollar. The usual way to measure the gender wage gap is by comparing the hourly earnings of men and women who work full-time year-round. But this compares only the women who work like men with men—a method that neatly excludes most women. As we have seen, only about half of the mothers of children under eighteen have full-time, year-round paying jobs.[9]

To find the real difference between men's and women's earnings, one would have to compare the earnings of all male and female workers, both full- and part-time. And guess what one discovers? The average earnings of *all* female workers in 1999 were 59 percent of men's earnings.[10] Women who work for pay are still stuck at the age-old biblical value put on their labor.

My research turned up other intriguing reflections of the 60 percent ratio: A survey of 1982 graduates of the Stanford Business School found that ten years after graduation, the median income of the full- and part-time employed female M.B.A.s amounted to $81,300, against the men's median income of $139,100. Again, the women's share is 58 percent. Another study, of 1974 graduates of the University of Michigan Law School, revealed that in the late 1980s the women's average earnings were 61 percent of the men's—despite the fact that 96 percent of the women were working, and that the men and women were virtually identical in terms of training. The authors of this study concluded that the women's family responsibilities were "certainly the most important single cause of sex differences in earnings."[11]. . .

The Cost of Being a Mother

A small group of mostly female academic economists has added another twist to the story. Their research reveals that working mothers not only earn less than men, but also less per hour than childless women, even after such differences as education and experience are factored out. The pay gap between mothers and nonmothers under age thirty-five is now larger than the wage gap between young men and women. . . .

> Why do working mothers earn so much less than childless women? Academic researchers have worried over this question like a dog over a bone but haven't turned up a single, definitive answer.[12]

Waldfogel argues that the failure of employers to provide paid maternity leaves is one factor that leads to the family wage gap in the United States. This country is one of only six nations in the world that does not require a paid leave. (The others are Australia, New Zealand, Lesotho, Swaziland, and Papua New Guinea.[13]) With no right to a paid leave, many American mothers who want to stay at home with a new baby simply quit their jobs, and this interruption in employment costs them dearly in terms of lost income. Research in Europe reveals that when paid maternity leaves were mandated, the percentage of women remaining employed rose, and women's wages were higher, unless the leaves lasted more than a few months.[14]

In the United States as well, women who are able to take formal paid maternity leave do not suffer the same setback in their wages as comparably placed women who do not have a right to such leaves. This is a significant benefit to mothers in the five states, including California, New York, and New Jersey, that mandate temporary disability insurance coverage for pregnancy and childbirth.[15]

Paid leaves are so valuable because they don't seem to incur the same penalties that employers impose on even the briefest of unpaid career interruptions. A good example is the experience of the 1974 female graduates of the University of Michigan Law School. During their first fifteen years after law school, these women spent an average of only 3.3 months out of the workplace, compared with virtually no time out for their male classmates. More than one-quarter of the women had worked part-time, for an average of 10.1 months over the fifteen years, compared with virtually no part-time work among the men. While working full-time, the women put in only 10 percent fewer hours than full-time men, again not a dramatic difference.

But the penalties for these slight distinctions between the men's and women's work patterns were strikingly harsh. Fifteen years after graduation, the women's average earnings were not 10 percent lower, or even 20 percent lower, than the men's, but almost 40 percent lower. Fewer than one-fifth of the women in law firms who had worked part-time for more than six months had made partner in their firms, while more than four-fifths of the mothers with little or no part-time work had made partner.[16]

Another survey of almost 200 female M.B.A.s found that those who had taken an average of only 8.8 months out of the job market were less likely to reach upper-middle management and earned 17 percent less than comparable women who had never had a gap in their employment.[17]

Working-class women are also heavily penalized for job interruptions, although these are the very women who allegedly "choose" less demanding occupations that enable them to move in and out of the job market without undue wage penalties. The authors of one study concluded that the negative repercussions of taking a little time out of the labor force were still discernible after twenty years.[18] In blue-collar work, seniority decides who is eligible for better jobs, and who is "bumped" in the event of layoffs. Under current policies, many women lose their seniority forever if they interrupt their employment, as most mothers do. Training programs, required for advancement, often take place after work, excluding the many mothers who can't find child care.[19]

Mandatory overtime is another handicap placed on blue-collar mothers. Some 45 percent of American workers reported in a recent survey that they had to work overtime with little or no notice.[20] In 1994 factory workers put in the highest levels of overtime ever reported by the Bureau of Labor Statistics in its thirty-eight years of tracking the data. Where does that leave a woman who has to be home in time for dinner with the kids? Out of a promotion and maybe out of a job. Increasingly in today's driven workplace, whether she is blue- or white-collar, a woman who goes home when she is supposed to go home is going to endanger her economic well-being.

The fact that many mothers work part-time also explains some of the difference between mothers' and comparable women's hourly pay. (About 65 percent of part-time workers are women, most of whom are mothers.[21] Employers are not required to offer part-time employees equal pay and benefits for equal work. As a result, nonstandard workers earn on average about 40 percent less an hour than full-time workers, and about half of that wage gap persists even for similar workers in similar jobs.

Many bosses privately believe that mothers who work part-time have a "recreational" attitude toward work, as one Maryland businessman assured me. Presumably, this belief makes it easier to justify their exploitation. But the working conditions they face don't sound very much like recreation. A recent survey by Catalyst, a research organization focused on women in business, found that more than half of the people who had switched to part-time jobs and lower pay reported that their workload stayed the same. Ten percent reported an increase in workload after their income had been reduced. Most of these people were mothers.[22]

Another factor in the family wage gap is the disproportionate number of mothers who operate their own small businesses, a route often taken by women who need flexibility during the child-rearing years. Female-owned small businesses have increased twofold over small businesses owned by men in recent years.[23] In 1999, women owned 38 percent of all U.S. businesses, compared with only 5 percent in 1972, a remarkable increase that is frequently cited as evidence of women's economic success. One new mother noted that conversations at play groups "center as much on software and modems as they do on teething and ear infections."[24]

Less frequently mentioned is the fact that many of these women-owned businesses are little more than Mom-minus-Pop operations: one woman trying to earn some money on the side, or keep her career alive, during the years when her children have priority. Forty-five percent of women-owned businesses are home-based. And the more than one-third of businesses owned by women in 1996 generated only 16 percent of the sales of all U.S. businesses in that year.[25]

In 1997, although women were starting new businesses at twice the rate of men, they received only 2 percent of institutional venture capital, a principal source of financing for businesses with serious prospects for growth. Almost one-quarter of female business owners financed their operations the same way that they did their shopping: with their credit cards.[26]

Some researchers have suggested that mothers earn less than childless women because they are less productive. This may be true for some mothers who work at home and are subject to frequent interruptions, or for those who are exhausted from having to do most of the domestic chores, or distracted by creaky child-care arrangements. But the claim that mothers have lower productivity than other workers is controversial and unproven. It is easier to demonstrate that working mothers face the same old problem that has bedeviled women in the workplace for decades: [discrimination]. . . .

How to Lower the Mommy Tax

Until now, narrowing the gender wage gap in the United States has depended almost entirely on what might be called the "be a man" strategy. Women are told to finish school, find a job, acquire skills, develop seniority, get tenure, make partner, and put children off until the very last minute. The longer a woman postpones family responsibilities, and the longer her "preparental" phase lasts, the higher her lifetime earnings will be.

Ambitious women of the baby-boom generation and younger have by and large tried to be a man in this way. A good example is Susan Pedersen, a historian who achieved tenure at Harvard in the mid-1990s. By that time, she was married and in her late thirties, but she had postponed having children until her academic career was secure. Motherhood was something she wanted very much, she commented during an interview, but it posed a serious threat to her professional dreams and had to be delayed.[27]

As Pedersen's success demonstrates, this strategy does work—for the very small number who are able to pull it off. And women who have their children later in life do have higher lifetime earnings and a wider range of opportunities than younger mothers. The advice dished out by writers like Danielle Crittenden—no relation—an antifeminist ideologue who has urged women to marry and have their babies young, ignores this, along with some other hard truths. Crittenden never tells her readers that young parents tend to separate and divorce much more frequently than older couples, leaving young mothers and children vulnerable to poverty. Large numbers of the women who end up on welfare are there because they have done exactly what she recommends: married and had children young and then been left to support them alone.[28]

But trying to be a man has its own risks. Many baby-boomer women postponed families only to discover that when they wanted to become pregnant, it was too late. . . . And millions of women don't feel that being a man is the way they want to live their lives. Increasingly, young women are saying that they don't want to put off children until they almost qualify for membership in AARP.

An alternative strategy is followed in countries like France and Sweden, where the government, private employers, and/or husbands share much more of the costs of raising children. This makes it far easier for women to be mothers and to work. In France, for example, families with two preschool-age children receive about $10,000 worth of annual subsidies, including free health care and housing subsidies and excellent free preschools.[29] As a result, child poverty is unusual, and the pay gap between mothers and others is much smaller in France than in the United States or the United Kingdom.

Whenever Europe is singled out as a model, the usual response is that Americans would never support such generous social policies. But in fact, the United States already does have an extremely generous social welfare state. But unlike the welfare states of western Europe, the American government doesn't protect mothers; it protects soldiers.

Men who postpone or interrupt civilian employment for military service pay a tax on their lifetime earnings that is quite comparable to the mommy tax. White men who were drafted during the Vietnam War, for example, were still earning approximately 15 percent less in the early 1980s than comparable nonveterans.[30] This "warrior wage gap" is strikingly similar to the family wage gap, again indicating that mothers' lower earnings are not entirely attributable to gender discrimination.

But there is unquestionable discrimination in the way the government has responded to the financial sacrifices that soldiers and parents, particularly mothers, make. All Americans are asked to "make it up" to veterans of the military: The damage to a caregiver's pocketbook is unmitigated, while the damage to a veteran's wallet has legitimized a massive relief effort. . . .

The benefits paid to military veterans are so lavish that they are now second only to Social Security in terms of government payments to individuals. And they do an excellent job of reducing the warrior tax. The educational benefits in particular help veterans overcome many of the economic disadvantages they suffer by leaving the workplace for a few years.

A congressional study in the early 1990s concluded that the veterans of World War II who took advantage of the G.I. Bill to earn a college degree enjoyed incomes of up to 10 percent more than they might otherwise have earned. Society was also the beneficiary, for the additional taxes paid by the college-educated veterans during their working lives more than paid for the program.[31]

It hardly needs to be said that there is no G.I. Bill, no health care, no subsidized housing, and no job preferences for mothers. As things now stand, millions of women sacrifice their economic independence and risk economic disaster for the sake of raising a child. This says a lot about family values, the nation's priorities, and free riding.

A third way to reduce the mommy tax would be to expand the antidiscrimination laws to cover parents. Joan Williams, a law professor at American University's Washington College of Law, argues that the design of work around masculine norms can be reconceptualized as discrimination. As an example, Williams suggests that if a woman works full-time, with good job evaluations for a significant period, then switches to part-time because of family responsibilities and is paid less per hour than full-time employees doing similar work, she could claim discrimination under the Equal Pay Act. Williams believes that disparate-action suits could also be filed against employers whose policies (including routine and mandatory overtime, promotion tracks, resistance to part-time work) have a disparate impact on women, producing disproportionate numbers of men in top-level positions.[32]

The essential point is that existing laws, and new laws preventing discrimination against people with caregiving responsibilities, could go a very long way toward improving mothers' lifetime earnings.

The Ultimate Mommy Tax: Childlessness

The cost of children has become so high that many American women are not having children at all. One of the most striking findings of Claudia Goldin's survey of white female college graduates is their high degree of childlessness (28 percent). Now that the baby-boomer generation is middle-aged, it is clear that more than one-quarter of the educated women in that age group will never have children. Indeed, the percentage of all American women who remain childless is also steadily rising, from 8 to 9 percent in the 1950s to 10 percent in 1976 to 17.5 percent in the late 1990s.

Is this rising childlessness by choice? Goldin thinks not. She found that in 1978, while in their twenties, almost half of the college-educated boomers who would remain childless had said that they did want children. Goldin calculated that almost one-fifth of this entire generation (19 percent) of white college graduates was disappointed in not having a child. This is the ultimate price of the "be a man" strategy that has been forced on working women. For women in business, the price is staggering. A recent Catalyst survey of 1,600 M.B.A.s found that only about one-fifth of the women had children, compared with 70 percent of the men.[33]

Educated black women have had, if anything, an even harder time combining children with their careers. Many of the most accomplished black women now in their forties and fifties, including Oprah Winfrey, Anita Hill, Eleanor Holmes Norton (the congressional representative for the District of Columbia), and Alexis Herman, secretary of labor in the Clinton administration, have forgone motherhood. These women apparently discovered that the price of success included the lack of parental obligations. And educated black women face an additional problem—an acute shortage of eligible black men.

Americans have a hard time realizing that such deeply personal choices as when or whether to have a child can be powerfully circumscribed by broader social or economic factors. American women, in particular, are stunningly unaware that their "choices" between a career and a family are much more limited than those of women in many European countries, where policies are much more favorable to mothers and children.

ENDNOTES

[1] This calculation was made by economist June O'Neill, using data from the National Longitudinal Survey of Youth. June O'Neill and Solomon Polachek, "Why the Gender Gap in Wages Narrowed in the 1980s," *Journal of Labor Economics* 11 (1993): 205–28. See also June O'Neill, "The Shrinking Pay Gap," *Wall Street Journal*, October 7, 1994.

[2] The concept of the mommy tax was inspired by development economist Gita Sen, who has described the extra economic burden borne by women as a "reproduction tax."

[3] I don't mean to suggest that old-fashioned sex discrimination, even against women who are able to perform as "ideal" workers, is not still alive and well, as numerous recent complaints, from the brokerage offices of Smith Barney to the machine shops of Mitsubishi, can attest. Simply being female still sentences women in virtually every occupation and at every level to lower earnings than men in similar positions. But overt in-your-face discrimination has thankfully declined steadily in recent decades.

[4] Jane Waldfogel, personal communication, October 1996.

[5] Burggraf assumes that the more flexible parent's earnings average $25,750 a year, versus $55,750 for the primary breadwinner. She then multiplies $30,000 (the difference between what the two parents earn) by 45 (the years in a working lifetime) to get the $1.350 million. *The Feminine Economy and Economic Man*, p. 61.

[6] Martha Ritchie, personal communication, January 1995.

[7] Sara Rimer, "Study Details Sacrifices in Caring for Elderly Kin," *New York Times*, November 27, 1999. The National Alliance for Caregivers estimates that the number of employed people who provide care for elderly family members will grow to between 11 and 15.6 million in the first decade of the twenty-first century.

[8] Amity Shlaes, "What Does Woman Want?" *Women's Quarterly* (summer 1996): 10.

[9] According to June O'Neill, an economist and former head of the Congressional Budget Office, "Full-time year-round workers are not likely to be representative of all workers. Women are less likely to be in this category than men." See June O'Neill and Solomon Polachek, "Why the Gender Gap in Wages Narrowed in the 1980s," *Journal of Labor Economics* 2, no. 1, pt. 1 (1993): 208–9.

[10] U.S. Bureau of the Census, Current Population Reports, *Money Income in the U.S.: 1995,* Washington, D.C., March 2000, P60-209, pp. 46–49.

[11] Robert G. Wood, Mary E. Corcoran, and Paul N. Courant, "Pay Differentials among the Highly-Paid: The Male-Female Earnings Gap in Lawyers' Salaries," *Journal of Labor Economics* 11, no. 3 (1993): 417–41.

[12] See Paula England and Michelle Budig, "The Effects of Motherhood on Wages in Recent Cohorts: Findings from the National Longitudinal Survey of Youth," unpublished paper, 1999.

[13] Elizabeth Olson, "U.N. Surveys Paid Leave for Mothers," *New York Times,* February 16, 1998.

[14] Christopher J. Ruhm, "The Economic Consequences of Parental Leave Mandates: Lessons from Europe," *Quarterly Journal of Economics* CXIII, no. 1 (1998): 285–317. Ruhm found that longer leaves (of nine months or more) were associated with a slight reduction in women's relative wages, but Waldfogel discovered that mothers in Britain who exercised their right to a ten-month paid maternity leave and returned to their original employer had wages no different from those of childless women.

[15] Heidi Hartmann, Institute for Women's Policy Research, personal communication, January 8, 1995. Hartmann's research has shown that fully 11 percent of women who have no paid leave have to go on public assistance during their time with a new baby.

[16] Wood, Corcoran, and Courant, "Pay Differentials," pp. 417–28.

[17] This 1993 study was coauthored by Joy Schneer of Rider University's College of Business Administration and Frieda Reitman, professor emeritus at Pace University's Lubin School of Business.

[18] Joyce Jacobsen and Arthur Levin, "The Effects of Intermittent Labor Force Attachment on Female Earnings," *Monthly Labor Review* 118, no. 9 (September 1995): 18.

[19] For a good discussion of the obstacles to mothers' employment in relatively well-paying blue-collar work, see Williams, *Unbending Gender,* pp. 76–81.

[20] This survey of 1,000 workers was conducted by researchers at the University of Connecticut and Rutgers University, and was reported in the *Wall Street Journal,* May 18, 1999.

[21] A survey of more than 2,000 people in four large corporations found that 75 percent of the professionals working part-time were women who were doing so because of child-care obligations. Only 11 percent of the male managers surveyed expected to work part-time at some point in their careers, compared with 36 percent of women managers. *A New Approach to Flexibility: Managing the Work/Time Equation* (New York: Catalyst, 1997), pp. 25–26.

[22] There is other evidence that many so-called part-timers are increasingly working what used to be considered full-time—thirty-five to forty hours a week—for lower hourly pay than regular full-timers. See Reed Abelson, "Part-Time Work for Some Adds Up to Full-Time Job," *New York Times,* November 2, 1998.

[23] In the five years from 1988 through 1992, the number of women-owned sole proprietorships, partnerships, and similar businesses soared 43 percent, compared with overall growth of 26 percent in such businesses. *Wall Street Journal,* January 29, 1996.

[24] Tracy Thompson, "A War Inside Your Head," *Washington Post Magazine,* February 15, 1998, p. 29.

[25] Information on women-owned businesses provided by the National Foundation for Women Business Owners in Washington, D.C., September 2000.

[26] Noelle Knox, "Women Entrepreneurs Attract New Financing," *New York Times,* July 26, 1998.

[27] Susan Pedersen, personal interview, June 1996.

[28] Being a young mother obviously worked for Crittenden, who was affluent enough to have purchased a $1.3-million home in Washington, D.C., while still in her mid-thirties. But not many mothers enjoy such options.

[29] Barbara Bergmann, personal conversation, January 4, 1999.

[30] Joshua D. Angrist, "Lifetime Earnings and the Vietnam Era Draft Lottery: Evidence from Social Security Administrative Records," *American Economic Review* 80, no. 3 (June 1990): 313–31.

[31] David O'Neill, "Voucher Funding of Training Programs: Evidence from the G.I. Bill," *Journal of Human Resources* 12, no. 4 (fall 1977): 425–45; and Joshua D. Angrist, "The Effects of Veterans' Benefits on Education and Earnings," *Industrial and Labor Relations Review* 46, no. 4 (July 1993): 637–57.

[32] Williams, *Unbending Gender*, pp. 101–10.

[33] The theory that much of the childlessness among educated American women is involuntary was supported by an informal class survey of the graduates of Harvard and Radcliffe class of 1971. Roughly one-fifth of both the men and the women were still childless in 1996, when the class was in its mid- to late forties. But many more women than men said they were childless because of "circumstances."

55

INVISIBLE INEQUALITY
Social Class and Childrearing in Black Families and White Families

ANNETTE LAREAU

In addition to gender inequality, the institution of the family produces and reproduces other forms of social inequality in family life. Numerous sociological studies have investigated the transmission of social class values and norms within families. In this selection, Annette Lareau shows how social class affects parenting styles among both white and black families. Lareau, a professor of sociology at the University of Maryland, observed and interviewed 32 children and most of their parents to learn the types of skills parents transmit to their children. This excerpt is from Lareau's prize-winning ethnography *Unequal Childhoods: Class, Race, and Family Life* (2003).

In recent decades, sociological knowledge about inequality in family life has increased dramatically. Yet, debate persists, especially about the transmission of class advantages to children. Kingston (2000) and others question whether disparate aspects of family life cohere in meaningful patterns. Pointing to a "thin evidentiary base" for claims of social class differences in the interior of family life, Kingston also asserts that "class distinguishes neither distinctive parenting styles or distinctive involvement of kids" in specific behaviors (p. 134).

One problem with many studies is that they are narrowly focused. Researchers look at the influence of parents' education on parent involvement in schooling *or* at children's time spent watching television *or* at time spent visiting relatives. Only a few studies examine more than one dynamic inside the home. Second, much of the empirical work is descriptive. For example, extensive research has been done on time use, including patterns of women's labor force participation, hours parents spend at work, and mothers' and fathers' contributions to childcare. . . .

Third, researchers have not satisfactorily explained how these observed patterns are produced. Put differently, *conceptualizations* of the *social processes* through which families differ are underdeveloped and little is known about how family life transmits advantages to children. Few researchers have attempted to integrate what is known about behaviors and attitudes taught inside the home with the ways in which these practices may provide unequal resources for family members outside the home. . . .

Fourth, little is known about the degree to which children adopt and enact their parents' beliefs. Sociologists of the family have long stressed the importance of a more dynamic model of parent–child interaction, but empirical research has been slow to emerge. . . .

I draw on findings from a small, intensive data set collected using ethnographic methods. I map the connections between parents' resources and their children's daily lives. My first goal, then, is to challenge Kingston's (2000) argument that social class does not distinguish parents' behavior or children's daily lives. I seek to show empirically that social class does indeed create distinctive parenting styles. I demonstrate that parents differ by class in the ways they define their own roles in their children's lives as well as in how they perceive the nature of childhood. The middle-class parents, both white *and* black, tend to conform to a cultural logic of childrearing I call "concerted cultivation." They enroll their children in numerous age-specific organized activities that dominate family life and create enormous labor, particularly for mothers. The parents view these activities as transmitting important life skills to children. Middle-class parents also stress language use and the development of reasoning and employ talking as their preferred form of discipline. This "cultivation" approach results in a wider range of experiences for children but also creates a frenetic pace for parents, a cult of individualism within the family, and an emphasis on children's performance.

The childrearing strategies of white and black working-class and poor parents emphasize the "accomplishment of natural growth." These parents believe that as long as they provide love, food, and safety, their children will grow and thrive. They do not focus on developing their children's special talents. Compared to the middle-class children, working-class and poor children participate in few organized activities and have more free time and deeper, richer ties within their extended families. Working-class and poor parents issue many more directives to their children and, in some households, place more emphasis on physical discipline than do the middle-class parents. These findings extend Kohn and Schooler's (1983) observation of class differences in parents' values, showing that differences also exist in the *behavior* of parents *and* children.

Quantitative studies of children's activities offer valuable empirical evidence but only limited ideas about how to conceptualize the mechanisms through which social advantage is transmitted. Thus, my second goal is to offer "conceptual umbrellas" useful for making comparisons across race and class and for assessing the role of social structural location in shaping daily life.

Last, I trace the connections between the class position of family members—including children—and the uneven outcomes of their experiences outside the home as they interact with professionals in dominant institutions. The pattern of concerted cultivation encourages an *emerging sense of entitlement* in children. All parents and children are not equally assertive, but the pattern of questioning and intervening among the white and black middle-class parents contrasts sharply with the definitions of how to be helpful and effective observed among the white and black working-class and poor adults. The pattern of the accomplishment of natural growth encourages an *emerging sense of constraint.* Adults as well as children in these social classes tend to be deferential and outwardly accepting in their interactions with professionals such as doctors and educators. At the same time, however, compared to their middle-class counterparts, white and black working-class and poor family members are more distrustful of professionals. These are differences with potential long-term consequences. In an historical moment when the dominant society privileges active, informed, assertive clients of health and educational services, the strategies employed by children and parents are not equally effective across classes. In sum, differences in family life lie not only in the advantages parents obtain for their children, but also in the skills they transmit to children for negotiating their own life paths.

Methodology

Study Participants

This study is based on interviews and observations of children, aged 8 to 10, and their families. The data were collected over time in three research phases. Phase one involved observations in two third-grade classrooms in a public school in the midwestern community of "Lawrenceville."[1] . . .

Phase two took place at two sites in a northeastern metropolitan area. One school, "Lower Richmond," although located in a predominantly white, working-class urban neighborhood, drew about half of its students from a nearby all-black housing project. I observed one third-grade class at Lower Richmond about twice a week for almost six months. The second site, "Swan," was located in a suburban neighborhood about 45 minutes from the city center. It was 90 percent white; most of the remaining 10 percent were middle-class children.[2] . . . A team of research assistants and I interviewed the parents and guardians. . . . Thus, the total number of children who participated in the study was 88 (32 from the Midwest and 56 from the Northeast). . . .

Phase three, the most intensive research phase of the study, involved home observations of 12 children and their families in the Northeast who had been previously interviewed. Some themes, such as language use and families' social connections, surfaced mainly during this phase. . . .

Concerted Cultivation and Natural Growth

The interviews and observations suggested that crucial aspects of family life *cohered*. Within the concerted cultivation and accomplishment of natural growth approaches, three key dimensions may be distinguished: the organization of daily life, the use of language, and social connections. . . . These dimensions do not capture all important parts of family life, but they do incorporate core aspects of childrearing. Moreover, our field observations revealed that behaviors and activities related to these dimensions dominated the rhythms of family life. Conceptually, the organization of daily life and the use of language are crucial dimensions. Both must be present for the family to be described as engaging in one childrearing approach rather than the other. Social connections are significant but less conceptually essential.

All three aspects of childrearing were intricately woven into the families' daily routines, but rarely remarked upon. As part of everyday practice, they were invisible to parents and children. Analytically, however, they are useful means for comparing and contrasting ways in which social class differences shape the character of family life. I now examine two families in terms of these three key dimensions. I "control" for race and gender and contrast the lives of two black boys—one from an (upper) middle-class family and one from a family on public assistance. I could have focused on almost any of the other 12 children, but this pair seemed optimal, given the limited number of studies reporting on black middle-class families, as well as the aspect of my argument that suggests that race is less important than class in shaping childrearing patterns.

Developing Alexander Williams

Alexander Williams and his parents live in a predominantly black middle-class neighborhood. Their six-bedroom house is worth about $150,000. Alexander is an only child. Both parents grew up in small towns in the South, and both are from large families. His father, a tall, handsome man, is a very successful trial lawyer who earns about $125,000 annually in a small firm specializing in medical malpractice cases. Two weeks each month, he works very long hours (from about 5:30 A.M. until midnight) preparing for trials. The other two weeks, his workday ends around 6:00 P.M. He rarely travels out of town. Alexander's mother, Christina, is a positive, bubbly woman with freckles and long, black, wavy hair. A high-level manager in a major corporation, she has a corner office, a personal secretary, and responsibilities for other offices across the nation. She tries to limit her travel, but at least once a month she takes an overnight trip.

Alexander is a charming, inquisitive boy with a winsome smile. Ms. Williams is pleased that Alexander seems interested in so many things:

> *Alexander is a joy. He's a gift to me. He's a very energetic, very curious, loving, caring person, that, um . . . is outgoing and who, uh, really loves to be with people. And who loves to explore, and loves to read and . . . just do a lot of fun things.*

The private school Alexander attends has an on-site after-school program. There, he participates in several activities and receives guitar lessons and photography instruction.

Organization of Daily Life Alexander is busy with activities during the week and on weekends (Table 1). His mother describes their Saturday morning routine. The day starts early with a private piano lesson for Alexander downtown, a 20-minute drive from the house:

> *It's an 8:15 class. But for me, it was a tradeoff. I am very adamant about Saturday morning TV. I don't know what it contributes. So . . . it was um . . . either stay at home and fight on a Saturday morning [laughs] or go do something constructive. . . . Now Saturday mornings are pretty booked up. You know, the piano lesson, and then straight to choir for a couple of hours. So, he has a very full schedule.*

TABLE 1   Participation in Activities Outside of School: Boys

Boy's Name/ Race/Class	Activities Organized by Adults	Informal Activities
Middle Class		
Alexander Williams (black)	Soccer team	Restricted television
	Baseball team	Plays outside occasionally
	Community choir	with two other boys
	Church choir	Visits friends from school
	Sunday school	
	Piano (Suzuki)	
	School plays	
	Guitar (through school)	
Poor		
Harold McAllister (black)	Bible study in neighbor's house (occasionally)	Visits relatives
		Plays ball with neighborhood kids
	Bible camp (1 week)	Watches television
		Watches videos

Ms. Williams' vehement opposition to television is based on her view of what Alexander needs to grow and thrive. She objects to TV's passivity and feels it is her obligation to help her son cultivate his talents.

Sometimes Alexander complains that "my mother signs me up for everything!" Generally, however, he likes his activities. He says they make him feel "special," and without them life would be "boring." His sense of time is thoroughly entwined with his activities: He feels disoriented when his schedule is not full. This unease is clear in the following field-note excerpt. The family is driving home from a Back-to-School night. The next morning, Ms. Williams will leave for a work-related day trip and will not return until late at night. Alexander is grumpy because he has nothing planned for the next day. He wants to have a friend over, but his mother rebuffs him. Whining, he wonders what he will do. His mother, speaking tersely, says:

> *You have piano and guitar. You'll have some free time.* [Pause] *I think you'll survive for one night.* [Alexander does not respond but seems mad. It is quiet for the rest of the trip home.]

Alexander's parents believe his activities provide a wide range of benefits important for his development. In discussing Alexander's piano lessons, Mr. Williams notes that as a Suzuki student,[3] Alexander is already able to read music. Speculating about more diffuse benefits of Alexander's involvement with piano, he says:

> *I don't see how any kid's adolescence and adulthood could not but be enhanced by an awareness of who Beethoven was. And is that Bach or Mozart? I don't know the difference between the two! I don't know Baroque from Classical—but he does. How can that not be a benefit in later life? I'm convinced that this rich experience will make him a better person, a better citizen, a better husband, a better father—certainly a better student.*

Ms. Williams sees music as building her son's "confidence" and his "poise." In interviews and casual conversation, she stresses "exposure." She believes it is her responsibility to broaden Alexander's worldview. Childhood activities provide a learning ground for important life skills:

> *Sports provide great opportunities to learn how to be competitive. Learn how to accept defeat, you know. Learn how to accept winning, you know, in a gracious way. Also it gives him the opportunity to learn leadership skills and how to be a team player. . . . Sports really provides a lot of really great opportunities.*

Alexander's schedule is constantly shifting; some activities wind down and others start up. Because the schedules of sports practices and games are issued no sooner than the start of the new season, advance planning is rarely possible. Given the sheer number of Alexander's activities, events inevitably overlap. Some activities, though short-lived, are extremely time consuming. Alexander's school play, for example, requires rehearsals three nights the week before the opening. In addition, in choosing activities, the Williamses have an added concern—the group's racial balance. Ms. Williams prefers that Alexander not be the only black child at events. Typically, one or two other black boys are involved, but the groups are predominantly white and the activities take place in predominantly white residential neighborhoods. Alexander is, however, part of his church's youth choir and Sunday School, activities in which all participants are black.

Many activities involve competition. Alex must audition for his solo performance in the school play, for example. Similarly, parents and children alike understand that participation on "A," "B," or "All-Star" sports teams signal different skill levels. Like other middle-class children in the study, Alexander seems to enjoy public performance. According to a field note, after his solo at a musical production in front of over 200 people, he appeared "contained, pleased, aware of the attention he's receiving."

Alexander's commitments do not consume *all* his free time. Still, his life is defined by a series of deadlines and schedules interwoven with a series of activities that are organized and controlled by adults rather than children. Neither he nor his parents see this as troublesome.

Language Use   Like other middle-class families, the Williamses often engage in conversation that promotes reasoning and negotiation. An excerpt from a field note (describing an exchange between Alexander and his mother during a car ride home after summer camp) shows the kind of pointed questions middle-class parents ask children. Ms. Williams is not just eliciting information. She is also giving Alexander the opportunity to develop and practice verbal skills, including how to summarize, clarify, and amplify information:

> *As she drives, [Ms. Williams] asks Alex, "So, how was your day?"*
>
> Alex: *"Okay. I had hot dogs today, but they were burned! They were all black!"*
>
> Mom: *"Oh, great. You shouldn't have eaten any."*
>
> Alex: *"They weren't all black, only half were. The rest were regular."*
>
> Mom: *"Oh, okay. What was that game you were playing this morning?. . .*
>
> Alex: *"It was [called] 'Whatcha doin?'"*
>
> Mom: *"How do you play?"*
>
> *Alexander explains the game elaborately—fieldworker doesn't quite follow. Mom asks Alex questions throughout his explanation, saying, "Oh, I see," when he answers. She asks him about another game she saw them play; he again explains. . . . She continues to prompt and encourage him with small giggles in the back of her throat as he elaborates. . . .*

Not all middle-class parents are as attentive to their children's needs as this mother, and none are *always* interested in negotiating. But a general pattern of reasoning and accommodating is common.

Social Connections   Mr. and Ms. Williams consider themselves very close to their extended families. Because the Williamses' aging parents live in the South, visiting requires a plane trip. Ms. Williams takes Alexander with her to see his grandparents twice a year. She speaks on the phone with her parents at least once a week and also calls her siblings several times a week. Mr. Williams talks with his mother regularly by phone (he has less contact with his stepfather). With pride, he also mentions his niece, whose Ivy League education he is helping to finance.

Interactions with cousins are not normally a part of Alexander's leisure time. . . . Nor does he often play with neighborhood children. The huge homes on the Williamses' street are occupied mainly by couples without children. Most of Alexander's playmates come from his classroom or his organized activities. Because most of his school events, church life, and assorted activities are organized by the age (and sometimes gender) of the participants, Alexander interacts almost exclusively with children his own age, usually boys. Adult-organized activities thus define the context of his social life.

Mr. and Ms. Williams are aware that they allocate a sizable portion of time to Alexander's activities. What they stress, however, is the time they *hold back.* They mention activities the family has chosen *not* to take on (such as traveling soccer).

Summary   Overall, Alexander's parents engaged in concerted cultivation. They fostered their son's growth through involvement in music, church, athletics, and academics. They talked with him at length, seeking his opinions and encouraging his ideas. Their approach involved considerable direct expenses (e.g., the cost of lessons and equipment) and large indirect expenses (e.g., the cost of taking time off from work, driving to practices, and forgoing adult leisure activities). Although Mr. and Ms. Williams acknowledged the importance of extended family, Alexander spent relatively little time with relatives. His social interactions occurred almost exclusively with children his own age and with adults. Alexander's many activities significantly shaped the organization of daily life in the family. Both parents' leisure time was tailored to their son's commitments. Mr. and Ms. Williams felt that the strategies they cultivated with Alexander would result in his having the best possible chance at a happy and productive life. They couldn't imagine themselves not investing large amounts of time and energy in their son's life. But, as I explain in the next section, which focuses on a black boy from a poor family, other parents held a different view.

Supporting the Natural Growth of Harold McAllister

Harold McAllister, a large, stocky boy with a big smile, is from a poor black family. He lives with his mother and his 8-year-old sister, Alexis, in a large apartment. Two cousins often stay overnight. Harold's 16-year-old sister and 18-year-old brother usually live with their grandmother, but sometimes they stay at the McAllisters' home. Ms. McAllister, a high school graduate, relies on public assistance. Hank, Harold and Alexis' father, is a mechanic. He and Ms. McAllister have never married. He visits regularly, sometimes weekly, stopping by after work to watch television or nap. Harold (but not Alexis) sometimes travels across town by bus to spend the weekend with Hank.

The McAllisters' apartment is in a public housing project near a busy street. The complex consists of rows of two- and three-story brick units. The buildings, blocky and brown, have small yards enclosed by concrete and wood fences. Large floodlights are mounted on the corners of the buildings, and wide concrete sidewalks cut through the spaces between units. The ground is bare in many places; paper wrappers and glass litter the area.

Inside the apartment, life is humorous and lively, with family members and kin sharing in the daily routines. Ms. McAllister discussed, disdainfully, mothers who are on drugs or who abuse alcohol and do not "look after" their children. Indeed, the previous year Ms. McAllister called Child Protective Services to report her twin sister, a cocaine addict, because she was neglecting her children. Ms. McAllister is actively involved in her twin's daughters' lives. Her two nephews also frequently stay with her. Overall, she sees herself as a capable mother who takes care of her children and her extended family.

Organization of Daily Life   Much of Harold's life and the lives of his family members revolve around home. Project residents often sit outside in lawn chairs or on front stoops, drinking beer, talking, and watching children play. During summer, windows are frequently left open, allowing breezes to waft through the units and providing vantage points from which residents can survey the neighborhood. A large deciduous tree in front of the McAllisters' apartment unit provides welcome shade in the summer's heat.

Harold loves sports. He is particularly fond of basketball, but he also enjoys football, and he follows televised professional sports closely. Most afternoons, he is either inside watching television or outside playing ball. He tosses a football with cousins and boys from the neighboring units and organizes pick-up basketball games. Sometimes he and his friends use a rusty, bare hoop hanging from a telephone pole in the housing project; other times, they string up an old, blue plastic crate as a makeshift hoop. One obstacle to playing sports, however, is a shortage of equipment. Balls are costly to replace, especially given the rate at which they disappear—theft of children's play equipment, including balls and bicycles, is an ongoing problem. During a field observation, Harold asks his mother if she knows where the ball is. She replies with some vehemence, "They stole the blue and yellow ball, and they stole the green ball, and they stole the other ball."

Hunting for balls is a routine part of Harold's leisure time. One June day, with the temperature and humidity in the high 80s, Harold and his cousin Tyrice (and a fieldworker) wander around the housing project for about an hour, trying to find a basketball:

> *We head to the other side of the complex. On the way . . . we passed four guys sitting on the step. Their ages were 9 to 13 years. They had a radio blaring. Two were working intently on fixing a flat bike tire. The other two were dribbling a basketball.*

Harold: *"Yo! What's up, ya'll."*
Group: *"What's up, Har." "What's up? "Yo."*

They continued to work on the tire and dribble the ball. As we walked down the hill, Harold asked, "Yo, could I use your ball?"

The guy responded, looking up from the tire, "Naw, man. Ya'll might lose it."

Harold, Tyrice, and the fieldworker walk to another part of the complex, heading for a makeshift basketball court where they hope to find a game in progress:

No such luck. Harold enters an apartment directly in front of the makeshift court. The door was open. . . . Harold came back. "No ball. I guess I gotta go back."

The pace of life for Harold and his friends ebbs and flows with the children's interests and family obligations. The day of the basketball search, for example, after spending time listening to music and looking at baseball cards, the children join a water fight Tyrice instigates. It is a lively game, filled with laughter and with efforts to get the adults next door wet (against their wishes). When the game winds down, the kids ask their mother for money, receive it, and then walk to a store to buy chips and soda. They chat with another young boy and then amble back to the apartment, eating as they walk. Another afternoon, almost two weeks later, the children—Harold, two of his cousins, and two children from the neighborhood—and the fieldworker play basketball on a makeshift court in the street (using the fieldworker's ball). As Harold bounces the ball, neighborhood children of all ages wander through the space.

Thus, Harold's life is more free-flowing and more child-directed than is Alexander Williams'. The pace of any given day is not so much planned as emergent, reflecting child-based interests and activities. Parents intervene in specific areas, such as personal grooming, meals, and occasional chores, but they do not continuously direct and monitor their children's leisure activities. Moreover, the leisure activities Harold and other working-class and poor children pursue require them to develop a repertoire of skills for dealing with much older and much younger children as well as with neighbors and relatives.

Language Use Life in the working-class and poor families in the study flows smoothly without extended verbal discussions. The amount of talking varies, but overall, it is considerably less than occurs in the middle-class homes.[4] Ms. McAllister jokes with the children and discusses what is on television. But she does not appear to cultivate conversation by asking the children questions or by drawing them out. Often she is brief and direct in her remarks. For instance, she coordinates the use of the apartment's only bathroom by using one-word directives. She sends the children (there are almost always at least four children home at once) to wash up by pointing to a child, saying one word, "bathroom," and handing him or her a washcloth. Wordlessly, the designated child gets up and goes to the bathroom to take a shower.

Similarly, although Ms. McAllister will listen to the children's complaints about school, she does not draw them out on these issues or seek to determine details, as Ms. Williams would. For instance, at the start of the new school year, when I ask Harold about his teacher, he tells me she is "mean" and that "she lies." Ms. McAllister, washing dishes, listens to her son, but she does not encourage Harold to support his opinion about his new teacher with more examples, nor does she mention any concerns of her own. Instead, she asks about last year's teacher, "What was the name of that man teacher?" Harold says, "Mr. Lindsey?" She says, "No, the other one." He says, "Mr. Terrene." Ms. McAllister smiles and says, "Yeah. I liked him." Unlike Alexander's mother, she seems content with a brief exchange of information.

Social Connections Children, especially boys, frequently play outside. The number of potential playmates in Harold's world is vastly higher than the number in Alexander's neighborhood. When a fieldworker stops to count heads, she finds 40 children of elementary school age residing in the nearby rows of apartments. With so many children nearby, Harold could choose to play only with others his own age. In fact, though, he often hangs out with older and younger children and with his cousins (who are close to his age).

The McAllister family, like other poor and working-class families, is involved in a web of extended kin. As noted earlier, Harold's older siblings and his two male cousins often spend the night at the McAllister home. Celebrations such as birthdays involve relatives almost exclusively. Party guests are not, as in middle-class families, friends from school or from extracurricular activities. Birthdays are celebrated enthusiastically, with cake and special food to mark the occasion; presents, however, are not offered. Similarly, Christmas at Harold's house featured a tree and special food but no presents. At these and other family events, the older children voluntarily look after the younger ones: Harold plays with his 16-month-old niece, and his cousins carry around the younger babies.

The importance of family ties—and the contingent nature of life in the McAllisters' world—is clear in the response Alexis offers when asked what she would do if she were given a million dollars:

> Oh, boy! I'd buy my brother, my sister, my uncle, my aunt, my nieces and my nephews, and my grandpop, and my grandmon, and my mom, and my dad, and my friends, not my friends, but mostly my best friend—I'd buy them all clothes . . . and sneakers. And I'd buy some food, and I'd buy my mom some food, and I'd get my brothers and my sisters gifts for their birthdays.

Summary In a setting where everyone, including the children, was acutely aware of the lack of money, the McAllister family made do. Ms. McAllister rightfully saw herself as a very capable mother. She was a strong, positive influence in the lives of the children she looked after. Still, the contrast with Ms. Williams is striking. Ms. McAllister did not seem to think that Harold's opinions needed to be cultivated and developed. She, like most parents in the working-class and poor families, drew strong and clear boundaries between adults and children. Adults gave directions to children. Children were given freedom to play informally unless they were needed for chores. Extended family networks were deemed important and trustworthy.

The Intersection of Race and Class in Family Life

I expected race to powerfully shape children's daily schedules, but this was not evident (also see Conley 1999; Pattillo-McCoy 1999). This is not to say that race is unimportant. Black parents were particularly concerned with monitoring their children's lives outside the home for signs of racial problems.[5] Black middle-class fathers, especially, were likely to stress the importance of their sons understanding "what it means to be a black man in this society" (J. Hochschild 1995). Mr. Williams, in summarizing how he and his wife orient Alexander, said:

> [We try to] teach him that race unfortunately is the most important aspect of our national life. I mean people look at other people and they see a color first. But that isn't going to define who he is. He will do his best. He will succeed, despite racism. And I think he lives his life that way.

Alexander's parents were acutely aware of the potential significance of race in his life. Both were adamant, however, that race should not be used as "an excuse" for not striving to succeed. Mr. Williams put it this way:

> I discuss how race impacts on my life as an attorney, and I discuss how race will impact on his life. The one teaching that he takes away from this is that he is never to use discrimination as an excuse for not doing his best.

Thus far, few incidents of overt racism had occurred in Alexander's life, as his mother noted:

> Those situations have been far and few between. . . . I mean, I can count them on my fingers.

Still, Ms. Williams recounted with obvious pain an incident at a birthday party Alexander had attended as a preschooler. The grandparents of the birthday child repeatedly asked, "Who is that boy?" and exclaimed, "He's so dark!" Such experiences fueled the Williams's resolve always to be "cautious":

> We've never been, uh, parents who drop off their kid anywhere. We've always gone with him. And even now, I go in and—to school in the morning—and check [in]. . . . The school environment, we've watched very closely.

Alexander's parents were not equally optimistic about the chances for racial equality in this country. Ms. Williams felt strongly that, especially while Alexander was young, his father should not voice his pessimism. Mr. Williams complained that this meant he had to "watch" what he said to Alexander about race relations. Still, both parents agreed about the need to be vigilant regarding potential racial problems in Alexander's life. Other black parents reported experiencing racial prejudice and expressed a similar commitment to vigilance.

Issues surrounding the prospect of growing up black and male in this so-ciety were threaded through Alexander's life in ways that had no equivalent among his middle-class, white male peers. Still, in fourth grade there were no signs of racial experiences having "taken hold" the way that they might as Alexander ages. . . . The research assistants and I saw no striking differences in the ways in which white parents and black parents in the working-class and poor homes socialized their children. . . .

Impact of Childrearing Strategies on Interactions with Institutions

Social scientists sometimes emphasize the importance of reshaping parent-ing practices to improve children's chances of success. Explicitly and implic-itly, the literature exhorts parents to comply with the views of professionals (Bronfenbrenner 1966; Epstein 2001; Heimer and Staffen 1998). Such calls for compliance do not, however, reconcile professionals' judgments regarding the intrinsic value of current childrearing standards with the evidence of the historical record, which shows regular shifts in such standards over time (Aries 1962; Wrigley 1989; Zelizer 1985). Nor are the stratified, and limited, possibilities for success in the broader society examined.

I now follow the families out of their homes and into encounters with representatives of dominant institutions—institutions that are directed by middle-class professionals. Again, I focus on Alexander Williams and Harold McAllister. Across all social classes, parents and children interacted with teachers and school officials, healthcare professionals, and assorted govern-ment officials. Although they often addressed similar problems (e.g., learn-ing disabilities, asthma, traffic violations), they typically did not achieve similar resolutions. The pattern of concerted cultivation fostered an *emerging sense of entitlement* in the life of Alexander Williams and other middle-class children. By contrast, the commitment to nurturing children's natural growth fostered an *emerging sense of constraint* in the life of Harold McAllister and other working-class or poor children.

Both parents and children drew on the resources associated with these two childrearing approaches during their interactions with officials. Middle-class parents and children often customized these interactions; working-class and poor parents were more likely to have a "generic" rela-tionship. When faced with problems, middle-class parents also appeared better equipped to exert influence over other adults compared with working-class and poor parents. Nor did middle-class parents or children display the intimidation or confusion we witnessed among many working-class and poor families when they faced a problem in their children's school experience.

Emerging Signs of Entitlement

Alexander Williams' mother, like many middle-class mothers, explicitly teaches her son to be an informed, assertive client in interactions with professionals. For example, as she drives Alexander to a routine doctor's appointment, she coaches him in the art of communicating effectively in healthcare settings:

> *Alexander asks if he needs to get any shots today at the doctor's. Ms. Williams says he'll need to ask the doctor. . . . As we enter Park Lane, Mom says quietly to Alex: "Alexander, you should be thinking of questions you might want to ask the doctor. You can ask him anything you want. Don't be shy. You can ask anything."*

> *Alex thinks for a minute, then: "I have some bumps under my arms from my deodorant."*
> Mom: *"Really? You mean from your new deodorant?"*
> Alex: *"Yes."*
> Mom: *"Well, you should ask the doctor."*

Alexander learns that he has the right to speak up (e.g., "don't be shy") and that he should prepare for an encounter with a person in a position of authority by gathering his thoughts in advance. . . .

Middle-class parents and children were also very assertive in situations at the public elementary school most of the middle-class children in the study attended. There were numerous conflicts during the year over matters small and large. For example, parents complained to one another and to the teachers about the amount of homework the children were assigned. A black middle-class mother whose daughters had not tested into the school's gifted program negotiated with officials to have the girls' (higher) results from a private testing company accepted instead. The parents of a fourth-grade boy drew the school superintendent into a battle over religious lyrics in a song scheduled to be sung as part of the holiday program. The superintendent consulted the district lawyer and ultimately "counseled" the principal to be more sensitive, and the song was dropped.

Children, too, asserted themselves at school. Examples include requesting that the classroom's blinds be lowered so the sun wasn't in their eyes, badgering the teacher for permission to retake a math test for a higher grade, and demanding to know why no cupcake had been saved when an absence prevented attendance at a classroom party. In these encounters, children were not simply complying with adults' requests or asking for a repeat of an earlier experience. They were displaying an emerging sense of entitlement by urging adults to permit a customized accommodation of institutional processes to suit their preferences.

Of course, some children (and parents) were more forceful than others in their dealings with teachers, and some were more successful than others. Melanie Handlon's mother, for example, took a very "hands-on" approach to her daughter's learning problems, coaching Melanie through her homework day after day. Instead of improved grades, however, the only result was a deteriorating home environment marked by tension and tears.

Emerging Signs of Constraint

The interactions the research assistants and I observed between professionals and working-class and poor parents frequently seemed cautious and constrained. This unease is evident, for example, during a physical Harold McAllister has before going to Bible camp. Harold's mother, normally boisterous and talkative at home, is quiet. Unlike Ms. Williams, she seems wary of supplying the doctor with accurate information:

> Doctor: *"Does he eat something each day—either fish, meat, or egg?"*
> Mom, response is low and muffled: *"Yes."*
> Doctor, attempting to make eye contact but mom stares intently at paper: *"A yellow vegetable?"*
> Mom, still no eye contact, looking at the floor: *"Yeah."*
> Doctor: *"A green vegetable?"* Mom, looking at the doctor: *"Not all the time."* [Fieldworker has not seen any of the children eat a green or yellow vegetable since visits began.]
> Doctor: *"No. Fruit or juice?"*
> Mom, low voice, little or no eye contact, looks at the doctor's scribbles on the paper he is filling out: *"Ummh humn."*
> Doctor: *"Does he drink milk every day?"*
> Mom, abruptly, in considerably louder voice: *"Yeah."*
> Doctor: *"Cereal, bread, rice, potato, anything like that?"*
> Mom, shakes her head: *"Yes, definitely."* [Looks at doctor.]

Ms. McAllister's knowledge of developmental events in Harold's life is uneven. She is not sure when he learned to walk and cannot recall the name of his previous doctor. And when the doctor asks, "When was the last time he had a tetanus shot?" she counters, gruffly, "What's a tetanus shot?" . . .

Still, neither Harold nor his mother seemed as comfortable as Alexander had been. Alexander was used to extensive conversation at home; with the doctor, he was at ease initiating questions. Harold, who was used to responding to directives at home, primarily answered questions from the - doctor, rather than posing his own. Alexander, encouraged by his mother, was assertive and confident with the doctor. Harold was reserved. Absorbing his mother's apparent need to conceal the truth about the range of foods he ate, he appeared cautious, displaying an emerging sense of constraint.

We observed a similar pattern in school interactions. Overall, the working-class and poor adults had much more distance or separation from the school than their middle-class counterparts. Ms. McAllister, for example, could be quite assertive in some settings (e.g., at the start of family observations, she visited the local drug dealer, warning him not to "mess with" the black male fieldworker). But throughout the fourth-grade parent-teacher conference, she kept her winter jacket zipped up, sat hunched over in her chair, and spoke in barely audible tones. She was stunned when the teacher said that Harold did not do homework. Sounding dumbfounded, she said, "He does it at home." The teacher denied it and continued talking. Ms. McAllister made no further comments and did not probe for more information, except about a letter the teacher said he had mailed home and that she had not received. The conference ended, having yielded Ms. McAllister few insights into Harold's educational experience.[6]

Other working-class and poor parents also appeared baffled, intimidated, and subdued in parent-teacher conferences. . . . Working-class and poor children seemed aware of their parents' frustration and witnessed their powerlessness. Billy Yanelli [a working-class boy], for example, asserted in an interview that his mother "hate[d]" school officials.

At times, these parents encouraged their children to resist school officials' authority. The Yanellis told Billy to "beat up" a boy who was bothering him. Wendy Driver's mother advised her to punch a male classmate who pestered her and pulled her ponytail. Ms. Driver's boyfriend added, "Hit him when the teacher isn't looking."

In classroom observations, working-class and poor children could be quite lively and energetic, but we did not observe them try to customize their environments. They tended to react to adults' offers or, at times, to plead with educators to repeat previous experiences, such as reading a particular story, watching a movie, or going to the computer room. Compared to middle-class classroom interactions, the boundaries between adults and children seemed firmer and clearer. Although the children often resisted and tested school rules, they did not seem to be seeking to get educators to accommodate their own *individual* preferences.

Overall, then, the behavior of working-class and poor parents cannot be explained as a manifestation of their temperaments or of overall passivity; parents were quite energetic in intervening in their children's lives in other spheres. Rather, working-class and poor parents generally appeared to depend on the school (Lareau 2000), even as they were dubious of the trustworthiness of the professionals. This suspicion of professionals in dominant institutions is, at least in some instances, a reasonable response.[7] The unequal level of trust, as well as differences in the amount and quality of information divulged, can yield unequal *profits* during an historical moment when professionals applaud assertiveness and reject passivity as an inappropriate parenting strategy (Epstein 2001). Middle-class children and parents often (but not always) accrued advantages or profits from their efforts. Alexander Williams succeeded in having the doctor take his medical concerns seriously. Ms. Marshall's children ended up in the gifted program, even though they did not technically qualify. Middle-class children expect institutions to be responsive to *them* and to accommodate their individual needs. By contrast, when Wendy Driver is told to hit the boy who is pestering her (when the teacher isn't looking) or Billy Yanelli is told to physically defend himself, despite school rules, they are not learning how to make bureaucratic institutions work to their advantage. Instead, they are being given lessons in frustration and powerlessness.

Why Does Social Class Matter?

Parents' economic resources helped create the observed class differences in childrearing practices. Enrollment fees that middle-class parents dismissed as "negligible" were formidable expenses for less affluent families. Parents also paid for clothing, equipment, hotel stays, fast-food meals, summer camps, and fundraisers. In 1994, the Tallingers [a middle-class family] estimated the cost of Garrett's activities at $4,000 annually, and that figure was not unusually high.[8] Moreover, families needed reliable private transportation and flexible work schedules to get children to and from events. These resources were disproportionately concentrated in middle-class families.

Differences in educational resources also are important. Middle-class parents' superior levels of education gave them larger vocabularies that facilitated concerted cultivation, particularly in institutional interventions. Poor and working-class parents were not familiar with key terms professionals used, such as "tetanus shot." Furthermore, middle-class parents' educational backgrounds gave them confidence when criticizing educational professionals and intervening in school matters. Working-class and poor parents viewed educators as their social superiors.

Kohn and Schooler (1983) showed that parents' occupations, especially the complexity of their work, influence their childrearing beliefs. We found that parents' work mattered, but also saw signs that the experience of adulthood itself influenced conceptions of childhood. Middle-class parents often were preoccupied with the pleasures and challenges of their work lives.[9] They tended to view childhood as a dual opportunity: a chance for play and for developing talents and skills of value later in life. Mr. Tallinger noted that playing soccer taught Garrett to be "hard nosed" and "competitive," valuable workplace skills. Ms. Williams mentioned the value of Alexander learning to work with others by playing on a sports team. Middle-class parents, aware of the "declining fortunes" of the middle class, worried about their own economic futures and those of their children (Newman 1993). This uncertainty increased their commitment to helping their children develop broad skills to enhance their future possibilities.

Working-class and poor parents' conceptions of adulthood and childhood also appeared to be closely connected to their lived experiences. For the working class, it was the deadening quality of work and the press of economic shortages that defined their experience of adulthood and influenced their vision of childhood. It was dependence on public assistance and severe economic shortages that most shaped poor parents' views. Families in both classes had many worries about basic issues: food shortages, limited access to healthcare, physical safety, unreliable transportation, insufficient clothing. Thinking back over their childhoods, these parents remembered hardship but also recalled times without the anxieties they now faced. Many appeared to want their own youngsters to concentrate on being happy and relaxed, keeping the burdens of life at bay until they were older.

Thus, childrearing strategies are influenced by more than parents' education. It is the interweaving of life experiences and resources, including parents' economic resources, occupational conditions, and educational backgrounds, that appears to be most important in leading middle-class parents to engage in concerted cultivation and working-class and poor parents to engage in the accomplishment of natural growth. Still, the structural location of families did not fully determine their childrearing practices. The agency of actors and the indeterminacy of social life are inevitable.

In addition to economic and social resources, are there other significant factors? If the poor and working-class families' resources were transformed overnight so that they equaled those of the middle-class families, would their cultural logic of childrearing shift as well? Or are there cultural attitudes and beliefs that are substantially independent of economic and social resources that are influencing parents' practices here? The size and scope of this study preclude a definitive answer. Some poor and working-class parents embraced principles of concerted cultivation: They wished (but could not afford) to enroll their children in organized activities (e.g., piano lessons, voice lessons), they believed listening to their children was important, and they were committed to being involved in their children's schooling. Still, even when parents across all of the classes seemed committed to similar principles, their motivations differed. For example, many working-class and poor parents who wanted more activities for their children were seeking a safe haven for them. Their goal was to provide protection from harm rather than to cultivate the child's talents per se.

Some parents explicitly criticized children's schedules that involved many activities. During the parent interviews, we described the real-life activities of two children (using data from the 12 families we were observing). One schedule resembled Alexander Williams': restricted television, required reading, and many organized activities, including piano lessons (for analytical purposes, we said that, unlike Alexander, this child disliked his piano lessons but was not allowed to quit). Summing up the attitude of the working-class and poor parents who rejected this kind of schedule,[10] one white, poor mother complained:

> I think he wants more. I think he doesn't enjoy doing what he's doing half of the time [light laughter]. I think his parents are too strict. And he's not a child.

Even parents who believed this more regimented approach would pay off "job-wise" when the child was an adult still expressed serious reservations: "I think he is a sad kid" or "He must be dead-dog tired."

Thus, working-class and poor parents varied in their beliefs. Some longed for a schedule of organized activities for their children and others did not; some believed in reasoning with children and playing an active role in schooling and others did not. Fully untangling the effects of material and cultural resources on parents' and children's choices is a challenge for future research. . . .

ENDNOTES

[1] All names of people and places are pseudonyms. The Lawrenceville school was in a white suburban neighborhood in a university community a few hours from a metropolitan area. The student population was about half white and half black; the (disproportionately poor) black children were bused from other neighborhoods.

[2] Over three-quarters of the students at Lower Richmond qualified for free lunch; by contrast, Swan did not have a free lunch program.

[3] The Suzuki method is labor intensive. Students are required to listen to music about one hour per day. Also, both child and parent(s) are expected to practice daily and to attend every lesson together.

[4] Hart and Risley (1995) reported a similar difference in speech patterns. In their sample, by about age three, children of professionals had larger vocabularies and spoke more utterances per hour than the *parents* of similarly aged children on welfare.

[5] This section focuses primarily on the concerns of black parents. Whites, of course, also benefited from race relations, notably in the scattering of poor white families in working-class neighborhoods rather than being concentrated in dense settings with other poor families (Massey and Denton 1993).

[6] Middle-class parents sometimes appeared slightly anxious during parent–teacher conferences, but overall, they spoke more and asked educators more questions than did working-class and poor parents.

[7] The higher levels of institutional reports of child neglect, child abuse, and other family difficulties among poor families may reflect this group's greater vulnerability to institutional intervention (e.g., see L. Gordon 1989).

[8] In 2002, a single sport could cost as much as $5,000 annually. Yearly league fees for ice hockey run to $2,700; equipment costs are high as well (Halbfinger 2002).

[9] Middle-class adults do not live problem-free lives, but compared with the working class and poor, they have more varied occupational experiences and greater access to jobs with higher economic returns.

[10] Many middle-class parents remarked that forcing a child to take piano lessons was wrong. Nevertheless, they continued to stress the importance of "exposure."

REFERENCES

Aries, Philippe. 1962. *Centuries of Childhood: A Social History of the Family.* Translated by R. Baldick. London: Cape.

Bronfenbrenner, Urie. 1966. "Socialization and Social Class through Time and Space." Pp. 362–77 in *Class, Status and Power,* edited by R. Bendix and S. M. Lipset. New York: Free Press.

Conley, Dalton, 1999. *Being Black, Living in the Red: Race, Wealth, and Social Policy in America.* Berkeley: University of California Press.

Epstein, Joyce. 2001. *Schools, Family, and Community Partnerships.* Boulder, CO: Westview.

Gordon, Linda. 1989. *Heroes of Their Own Lives: The Politics and History of Family Violence.* New York: Penguin.

Halbfinger, David M. 2002. "A Hockey Parent's Life: Time, Money, and Yes, Frustration." *New York Times,* January 12, p. 29.

Hart, Betty and Todd Risley. 1995. *Meaningful Differences in the Everyday Experience of Young American Children.* Baltimore, MD: Paul Brooks.

Heimer, Carol A. and Lisa Staffen. 1998. *For the Sake of the Children: The Social Organization of Responsibility in the Hospital and at Home.* Chicago: University of Chicago Press.

Hochschild, Jennifer L. 1995. *Facing Up to the American Dream.* Princeton, NJ: Princeton University Press.

Kingston, Paul. 2000. *The Classless Society.* Stanford, CA: Stanford University Press.

Kohn, Melvin and Carmi Schooler, eds. 1983. *Work and Personality: An Inquiry into the Impact of Social Stratification.* Norwood, NJ: Ablex.

Lareau, Annette. 2000. *Home Advantage: Social Class and Parental Intervention in Elementary Education*. 2d ed. Lanham, MD: Rowman and Littlefield.

———. 2002. "Doing Multi-Person, Multi-Site 'Ethnographic' Work: A Reflective, Critical Essay." Department of Sociology, Temple University, Philadelphia, PA. Unpublished manuscript.

Massey, Douglas and Nancy Denton. 1993. *American Apartheid*. Cambridge, MA: Harvard University Press.

Newman, Kathleen. 1993. *Declining Fortunes: The Withering of the American Dream*. New York: Basic Books.

Pattillo-McCoy, Mary. 1999. *Black Picket Fences: Privilege and Peril among the Black Middle-Class*. Chicago: University of Chicago Press.

Wrigley, Julia. 1989. "Do Young Children Need Intellectual Stimulation? Experts' Advice to Parents, 1900–1985." *History of Education* 29:41–75.

Zelizer, Viviana. 1985. *Pricing the Priceless Child: The Changing Social Value of Children*. New York: Basic Books.

PART VIII

Social Change

56

SOCIAL PROGRESS AND SOCIAL PROBLEMS
Toward a Sociology of Gloom

JOEL BEST

In this reading, the first of five to focus on social change, Joel Best addresses what he calls the *sociology of gloom*. Best, a professor of sociology at the University of Delaware, argues that even though social progress has characterized most of the twentieth century, sociologists tend to focus on social problems instead. What explains this paradox? In fact, according to Best, four paradoxes help us to understand why social progress raises concerns about social problems among sociologists. This selection was originally given as the Presidential Address delivered at the Midwest Sociological Society meetings in Chicago in April, 2000.

We now can look back on all of the twentieth century. Although it is unfashionable to say so, it was a century of considerable social progress in the United States. A newborn male's life expectancy at the turn of the century was 46 years, whereas a male infant born in the year 2000 can expect to live to be 73 years old. Similarly, female life expectancy rose even more—from 48 to 80 years, and nonwhites' life expectancies increased much more than whites' (USBC 1975:55; 1999:93). Levels of education also climbed: in 1900, only about 6 percent of 17-year-olds graduated from high school; in the late 1990s, the figure was around 85 percent (USBC 1975:379; 1999:186). At the beginning of the century, the right to vote was limited to those over age 20; in most states, women could not vote, and in large sections of the former Confederacy, African Americans were effectively blocked from the polls. Today, the franchise is generally available to all citizens over age 17. And the standard of living has risen to roughly seven times its 1900 level: what were then luxury services are now basic utilities; electricity, indoor plumbing, and telephones became virtually ubiquitous. Appliances that would have seemed fantastic in 1900 have become generally affordable; 98 percent of U.S. households have color television sets.

Joel Best, "Social Progress and Social Problems: Toward a Sociology of Gloom" from the *Sociological Quarterly* 42, no. 1 (2001): 1–12. Copyright © 2001. Reprinted with the permission of Blackwell.

Life expectancy, level of education, the right to vote, and the standard of living might be considered basic, bedrock social indicators.[1] Each showed dramatic improvement in the twentieth-century United States. It is very difficult to look at the historical record and not conclude that, at least in this country, the past century was one of great progress.

Yet we usually avoid talking this way. Surveys suggest that most contemporary Americans are reasonably satisfied with their own lives. For years, the General Social Survey has asked people whether they're happy, and the proportion reporting that they are either "very happy" or "pretty happy" has hovered near 90 percent. Still, we are suspicious of what's happening in the larger society: surveys find that Americans tend to be fairly satisfied with their local schools but critical of U.S. education in general; they like their congressional representative but view Congress as a sinkhole; they are generally pleased with the way their own lives are going but worry about the direction the country's headed.[2] Progress, as I've suggested, has become an awkward, unfashionable idea. It was not always so. Characterizing social thought at the end of the nineteenth century, Hillel Schwartz (1996:127, 135) remarks: "at century's end a truly imprudent hyperbole of progress was making the rounds"; there was "intense anticipation of the 20th century." In contrast, the five-hundredth anniversary of Columbus's first voyage produced, not a general celebration of progress, but regretful commentaries about imperialism, racism, genocide, and ecological devastation. The arrival of the year 2000 was celebrated—but a tone of foreboding ran through many commentaries. How did a century of progress lead to so much gloom?

Sociologists seem to take particular care to avoid mentioning progress. We are skeptical about the general "idea of progress . . . that mankind has advanced in the past . . ., is now advancing, and will continue to advance in the foreseeable future" (Nisbet 1980:4).[3] Not only are we uncomfortable with progress as a grand theory of human history, but we worry that progress involves making judgments that violate the principle of cultural relativism. So let me hedge a bit. I am not offering some sort of whiggish interpretation, nor suggesting that progress is something that happens every day in every way. My argument is only that the United States experienced marked social progress during the twentieth century. I concede that, in saying this, I am making judgments—that better health, more education, more people with the opportunity to vote, and a higher standard of living are net improvements—but I suspect that most sociologists share those values.

The real reservation that our profession has toward talking about progress is that it is unseemly, and might encourage complacency and obscure social problems—particularly problems of inequality. The opening paragraphs of a couple of recent social problems textbooks illustrate our discomfort. One asks, "Has the United States turned the corner? Are we in a new era where social problems are diminishing?" It offers some statistics (e.g., "Almost 37 million U.S. residents live below the poverty level"; "On an average day 135,000 children take guns to school") and then concludes, "In short, our problems are worsening" (Eitzen and Baca Zinn 2000:1). Another text concedes that we now enjoy "a level of comfort and security thought impossible by our ancestors" but warns, "there is a dark side to all this promise. . . . One can understand, then, how life in today's world might be thought of as 'the best of times . . . the worst of times'" (Sullivan 2000:3–4).

Obviously, I do not wish to imply that we live in a perfect world devoid of suffering and injustice. Nonetheless, I think our contemporary discomfort with the idea of social progress reveals some interesting things about sociology, American culture more generally, and the production of social problems. I am going to organize my comments around what I see as four paradoxical relationships between social progress and social problems.

The Paradox of Perfectionism

The ideal of social perfectibility runs through American history. The Puritans envisioned creating a community of saints. The Founders sought to devise, not just a new form of government, but an ideal form. And the nineteenth century's great national growth spurt—driven by massive immigration, westward expansion, and industrialization—kept the country's institutional framework in flux, as Americans kept reinventing what the United States would be. Great impulses toward social reform—the Second Great Awakening, the antebellum reform movements for temperance, abolitionism, and women's rights, and later the Progressive Era—reappear throughout that century, as do attempts to establish separate, ideal communities, such as the Mormon Zion and many smaller utopian experiments. The theme was perfectibility: the belief that principled, committed people could create an ideal society.[4]

Sociologists unconsciously buy into this perfectionist ideal when we speak of social "problems."[5] Problems, as every arithmetic student learns, have correct solutions. We do not talk about social "conditions" (which might suggest things unchanging and unchangeable) nor about social "issues" (which might imply that debate will continue unresolved). The term was originally singular; nineteenth-century thinkers identified *the* social problem as the unequal distribution of wealth, and they had no shortage of solutions: "Reform pamphlets, Liberal religious tracts, political manifestoes, literary assessments, and social science texts would define a singular 'social problem' in light of theories Darwinist, Spencerian, eugenicist, or millenarian—each looking ahead to thoroughgoing change" (Schwartz 1997:280). By the beginning of the twentieth century, social problems had become plural, and the implication that these problems could be solved one by one was generally understood. Even today, policy makers continue to characterize social problems as solvable in the short run; they prefer to define social problems as emergencies (Lipsky and Smith 1989), or declare (what are meant to be quick, decisive) wars on social problems (Best 1999), rather than promoting social policies that offer the prospect of long-term, incremental improvements.

Like all beliefs, the ideal of social perfectibility has consequences. Most obviously: *Although perfectionism must be grounded in optimism, it fosters pessimism.* We can call this the *paradox of perfectionism.* A belief in perfectibility is, by definition, optimistic, but in the real world our efforts inevitably fall short of perfection, and this failure promotes and justifies pessimism.

The problem is that perfection is a high standard—unreasonably high if you're talking about social arrangements. Social life is messy, never perfect. Moreover, the values against which we might measure social perfection are contradictory: Americans value both freedom and justice; but a perfectly free society is not likely to be particularly just, nor is a perfectly just society likely to be particularly free. Certainly by some standard—and probably by any standard—social arrangements inevitably fall short of perfection.

The good news for those of us in the social-problems analysis game is that this means we're never going to run out of material. The proportion of Americans living in poverty may be less than half of what it was at mid-century, but we continue to have poverty—and inequality, and crime, and so on. If our goal is a perfect society that has eradicated all social problems, then we will always fall short. The very imperfectibility of society ensures that we will continue to perceive social problems. Moreover, it is often possible to convince ourselves that those problems are getting worse.

The Paradox of Proportion

We talk as though successful social policies will produce a problem-free society. As I've just explained, perfect success is not a realistic goal. However, to the degree that social policies are successful, we find ourselves noticing and worrying about previously overlooked problems. This is the *paradox of proportion: Solving big problems makes formerly small problems seem larger.* That is, as once-prominent problems shrink, smaller problems seem relatively more important, and it becomes easier to demand attention for those smaller problems. The threshold for attracting notice and arousing public concern is lowered.

We may see this most clearly with fatal diseases. One hundred years ago, many of the leading causes of death were infectious diseases: influenza/pneumonia, tuberculosis, diphtheria, typhoid/typhoid fever, and measles all ranked among the ten most common causes of death in 1900 (USBC 1975:58). Today, most of those formerly devastating threats have been brought under something approaching complete control through the advent of vaccinations and antibiotics. Controlling infectious diseases has had a complicated set of effects: because these diseases often killed children, life expectancies have increased; more people now reach older ages; and therefore more people die from diseases of old age (particularly heart disease and cancer). In addition, the reduction and near elimination of formerly devastating diseases means that we now can turn our attention to other, less common but still lethal threats, such as diabetes and breast cancer. Formerly overshadowed by rampant infectious illnesses, these once comparatively minor diseases now attract concentrated attention. In other words, the bar has been lowered; it is now easier for a disease to be recognized as a major health problem. (Note, too, that claims calling attention to formerly ignored problems can complain about this history of neglect as evidence of callous indifference.)

Illiteracy offers a second example. At the end of the nineteenth century, census takers defined illiteracy as an inability to read or write more than one's own name. By that standard, about 10 percent of the population was illiterate. Today, illiteracy has been redefined as "functional illiteracy"— meaning an inability to read at a particular grade level, complete a job application, or fill out an income tax form. By this standard, an estimated sixty million (or more!) adult Americans—most of whom can read some things— qualify as illiterate (Kozol 1985). The justification for redefining illiteracy, of course, is that an increasing proportion of jobs requires more sophisticated reading skills; once again, progress has turned what was formerly not considered problematic into something that is now regarded as troubling.

The same process characterizes claims about equality. Following a century of tremendous progress toward racial and gender equality (remember that, in 1900, lynching had just begun to decline from its historical peak and was still widespread, and few women had the right to vote), we have become increasingly sophisticated at identifying evidence of ever subtler forms of racism, sexism, and other varieties of systematic inequality. Again, I am not challenging the legitimacy of these claims; rather, I am pointing out that social progress, by reducing the most egregious social inequalities, makes it possible to focus social concern on other, less severe phenomena that once might have gone unremarked. Not infrequently, advocates describe these newly identified problems as widespread, severe, consequential, and so on. The paradox of proportion means that relatively smaller problems loom larger than they once did.

The Paradox of Proliferation

Our third paradox, the *paradox of proliferation*, is that *social progress encourages the recognition of a larger number of problems.* In part, this is an artifact of the lower thresholds for identifying social problems that I've already discussed. We can at least suspect that there are many, many social conditions that could be constructed as social problems, if only the standard of harm required to identify a problem is low enough (one thinks of talk show episodes devoted to discrimination people believe they experience because they are too good-looking). But there are additional organizational and institutional arrangements that seem to encourage the proliferation of problems.

A central theme in twentieth-century social progress was increasing attention to rights (Schudson 1998). The rights of an extraordinary array of groups—women, ethnic minorities, the elderly, the young, the disabled, and so on—increasingly came (and continue) to be articulated, acknowledged, and affirmed. Members of different groups are ever more likely to recognize their common interests and proclaim—to themselves and to the larger society—their rights. Moreover, this is becoming easier to do. As a society, we have become accustomed to these claims and readier to entertain them as understandable and legitimate, and our validation of today's claims fosters further claims tomorrow.

Moreover, there is every reason to suspect that there are now more venues or arenas (Hilgartner and Bosk 1988) where people can construct social problems and that these increased opportunities are themselves a product of social progress. Consider television. Even twenty years ago, less than a fifth of Americans had cable television, and satellite reception systems were not available (USBC 1999:581). This meant that most Americans could see the three major networks and maybe PBS and an independent station or two. Most television stations did not broadcast during the late night or early morning hours. Today, most Americans receive cable and/or satellite television signals that offer access to dozens, even hundreds of stations, many broadcasting 24 hours a day. There has been an astonishing increase in the hours that need to be filled with programming, and this has created, among other consequences, far more televised forums for talking about social problems: there are multiple channels devoted to news and current affairs, as well as all manner of talk shows, reality-based cops-and-robbers series, and *20/20*-style magazine-format programs.[6] And, of course, the expansion of television broadcasting cannot compare to the invention of the Internet—an essentially infinite forum that gives anyone with a computer and a modem a platform for addressing everyone else so equipped. The Net offers an almost endless arena for making social problems claims.

Since the 1960s, knowledge about how to promote social problems to the press, the public, and policy makers has disseminated widely. As late as the early 1960s, many commentators dismissed activists and demonstrators as "true believers," "kooks," and "little old ladies in tennis shoes." Sociologists treated social movements as peculiar phenomena and concentrated on explaining why some—presumably troubled—people felt the need to join movements (e.g., Toch 1965). The 1960s, which produced highly visible campaigns—particularly the civil rights, student, and anti-war movements—that many social scientists approved of and even considered heroic, led to more appreciative sociological interpretations. At the same time, the rhetoric, tactics, organizational forms, and personnel of visible movements spread to new causes. The civil rights movement was a direct inspiration for the student and antiwar movements, and by the end of the decade, it was no longer possible to trace the lines of influence, as new causes—women's liberation, gay rights, prisoners' rights, and so on—proliferated. By 1980, Candy Lightner, a suburban real estate agent with no experience as an activist, understood that she could respond to her daughter being killed by a drunk driver by starting what would become a successful, international social movement organization—Mothers Against Drunk Driving (Weed 1993). In turn, Lightner's success inspired other movements, including several started by parents who lost children to other causes and began their own campaigns to call attention to those problems.

The growing numbers of arenas and people with the skills to create and promote social problems reflect an increasingly fragmented public sphere. Again, the good old days of broadcast television offer a comparison. When there were only three major networks, each network expected to capture roughly a third of the viewers at any given time. But, as people have more viewing options, each network's share of the audience has shrunk. Commercial television networks (like magazines) depend upon advertisers and, since the 1950s, advertisers have been spending increasing portions of their budgets on media that target demographically specific audiences. As a consequence, what at the end of the World War II were called the "mass media"—meaning that they had huge, undifferentiated audiences—have basically vanished: network radio, *Life* and the other general-interest weekly magazines with huge circulations, and network television's variety shows all reached vast, heterogeneous audiences, and all are now gone. A visit to the newsstand or a glance at the television listings reveals that mass media have been replaced by targeted media—magazines and television networks aimed at relatively homogeneous audiences—women, Hispanics, young adults, conservative Protestants, wrestling fans, computer owners, and so on. There are now more media outlets, but they are largely aimed at narrowly focused, homogeneous audiences.[7] . . .

Fragmented media aimed at homogeneous audiences attract a less critical reception for prospective social problems claims. To the degree that a homogeneous audience shares moral assumptions, it is easier to devise rhetoric that portrays social problems in terms convincing to that audience. Consider the broad array of claims promoted by feminists who identify the many ways that societal arrangements work to women's disadvantage. Their claims reach largely sympathetic audiences, where they are unlikely to encounter much resistance. And this is no exception: we have many homogeneous networks of arenas, claimants, and audiences.[8] Often, these networks counter criticism of—even questions about—their claims with indignant disdain. Ad hominem attacks on the critics' motives limit the impact of skepticism or critiques, just as warnings that a backlash threatens to undo whatever gains have been made serve to rally solidarity within the network. The result is less a marketplace of competing ideas than a shopping mall of ideological boutiques, each willing to cater to walk-ins, but each still counting on the business of committed, repeat customers from its homogeneous target market.

Increasingly, then, our world is one in which more social problems claims flourish in more, parallel arenas. On occasion, rather different constructions of the same problem, each aimed at a distinctive audience, can merge, sometimes forming peculiar alliances. For example, advocates of traditional moral values—particularly religious and political conservatives—have long denounced pornography for its moral shortcomings, while some feminists oppose pornography as a cause of rape and a method of objectifying women. Although their rationales are very different, the two groups have been able to make common cause in anti-pornography campaigns. But more often, problems simmer within particular arenas. Environmentalists, for instance, exchange countless claims with one another about particular forms of pollution, resource depletion, and so on, yet many of these problems fail to gain much attention from the general public.

At the same time, the expanded media arenas (remember all those television channels) have a constant appetite for new claims. What Anthony Downs (1972) called the "issue-attention cycle" shapes media coverage. News—the very word speaks to the importance of novelty—requires constant refreshing. This is true even in the most visible, most influential venues; the major newspapers, the network news shows, and the major news-weeklies generate an unending demand for new material, or at least new angles on familiar material. Bad driving may not be new, but a well-choreographed campaign to promote "road rage" can gain widespread public recognition, even as the rate of traffic fatalities continues its decades-long decline (Best and Furedi 2001). This means that well-packaged claims that begin in small, homogeneous arenas can get picked up and spread—to a major talk show, to a network's magazine-style program, or to coverage in a prominent newspaper or newsmagazine—for their moment in the national spotlight. In turn, the continual parade of new problems promotes our sense of proliferation, of a society in crisis.

The Paradox of Paranoia

Thus far, I've argued that social progress encourages us to become pessimistic about social problems, to identify and worry about many, sometimes relatively small problems. But this description fails to convey the intensity of contemporary social problems rhetoric, the gloomy sense that things are seriously wrong and getting worse. Social progress has reduced the risks of social life—remember those improvements in life expectancy and standard of living. In response, we seem to worry more, not that we might slide back to where we were, but worse, that we're on the verge of collective catastrophe. This is the *paradox of paranoia: Social progress fosters fears of social collapse.* As we begin a new century, we confront a remarkable array of apocalyptic scenarios in which life as we know it might end through nuclear war, nuclear winter, global warming, overpopulation, overpollution, resource depletion, epidemic disease, ethnic conflict, globalization, economic collapse, famine, genetic engineering, nanotechnology, or robotics[9]—fortunately we at least weathered the Y2K crisis.

These extraordinarily diverse doomsday scenarios share an important quality—all derive from unintended, ironic, potentially catastrophic consequences of social progress. (About the only civilization-ending natural threat to attract recent interest has been the possibility of Earth colliding with a giant asteroid.) Instead, we worry that we will destroy ourselves with the products or by-products of improved technology (nuclear war, nuclear winter, global warming, overpollution, resource depletion, genetic engineering, nanotechnology, robotics), with improvements in health that make us more vulnerable to terrible threats (overpopulation, famine), or with greater integration among societies that creates new possibilities for disaster (nuclear war, ethnic conflict, epidemic disease, globalization, economic collapse, terrorism). Things may have been improving, but we are suspicious. We fear that there will be a terrible reckoning—perhaps in the very near future. If social progress has led to the emergence of large, intertwined systems of institutions, and if we now depend upon those institutional systems, then we must fear institutional collapse.

The same process operates below the global level. Consider attitudes toward education. Until fairly recently, a large share of Americans weren't terribly well educated. A boy who, say, really disliked algebra and diagraming sentences was likely to leave school and start working on the farm or the factory floor; those jobs, while not particularly prestigious, offered incomes that often made it possible to marry and launch a family. Today, there is the fear that leaving school early condemns one to a life of permanent poverty. We now believe societal well-being requires keeping even marginal students in school, so we find ourselves worrying about "schools that fail to teach" (and about medicine that fails to heal, economies that do not guarantee prosperity, and so on). Progress not only makes us conscious of new problems, but those problems seem potentially catastrophic. Again, perfectionism fosters pessimism: our higher expectations for institutions inspire greater fears about possible institutional failures.

A parallel process seems to drive individual behavior. Probably the single greatest medical advance in human history involved keeping sewage and drinking water separate. The creation of effective municipal water supply and sewage systems was one of the great accomplishments of the nineteenth century, although those systems were obviously imperfect. During the course of the twentieth century, we raised our standards for acceptable drinking water (that is, we have lowered the bar for identifying water as problematic, and we have become more sophisticated about identifying contaminants), we have devised more effective methods for treating water to ensure its quality, and we have created increasingly elaborate systems for testing the water supply to monitor its safety (Barzilay, Weinberg, and Eley 1999). The water supply in this country has never been more closely regulated and, quite possibly, has never been better. And the result? A growing proportion of people—worried about the quality of publicly available water—is buying drinking water in little plastic bottles and carrying it with them. What's going on?

These new suspicions about technology, risk, and the future extend to sociology. The German sociologist Ulrich Beck (1992:183) declares that we live in a "risk society" where "the sources of danger are no longer ignorance but knowledge; not a deficient but a perfected mastery over nature." Science, he says, "has become the protector of a global contamination of people and nature" (p. 70). A familiar list of atrocity tales forms the foundation that justifies this suspicion of scientific authority: What about the Tuskegee syphilis experiments? What about Chernobyl? What about Bhopal? We speculate that

AIDS was spawned in germ warfare labs or in a batch of polio vaccine that went bad, that genetically engineered frankenfoods will cause terrible, irreparable harm.

The result is fear of conspiracies, cover-ups, or—at a minimum—catastrophes of unintended consequences. Confronted with debates between activists and epidemiologists, many citizens—and many sociologists—seem to presume that there is something sinister about medicine's failure to substantiate claims about toxic breast implants or Gulf War syndrome (Angell 1996). But is the issue whether some women with breast implants feel ill and are convinced that their symptoms are caused by the implants? Or, rather, is it whether women with breast implants are more likely to feel ill than women without implants? The notion that empirical questions are best judged by adopting scientific methodologies is lost in many contemporary sociological analyses in which ideology seems to trump evidence. It is important to understand the limitations of positivism and to recognize that all knowledge is socially constructed, but this does not require us to assume that all constructions are equally valid (Best 2000). There is something wonderfully comic about manifestos, composed on computers and circulated over the Internet, that pretend to doubt scientific progress.

In a pessimistic age, sociological writing has few heroes, but activists are exceptions. The courage and fortitude of the civil rights movement has induced a sort of halo effect: social activists—well, not the pro-lifers or the New Right, but progressive activists—become the heroes in stories we tell about brave individuals challenging and changing massive social institutions in order to ward off terrible threats. In these stories, our social problems are frightening precisely because we cannot count on existing institutions to work properly. Social progress is an illusion. Things only seem to be getting better; in reality, we are being set up for terrible disasters. Who wouldn't be paranoid?

Discussion

I am arguing, then, that the contemporary spirit of pessimism, the unfashionableness of the idea of social progress, the sense that our collective glass is half empty and probably leaking is, at least in part, a product of the way we construct social problems. In some peculiar ways, it is progress that produces our pessimism. Successful social policies take time, and they usually diminish—but fail to eradicate—social problems, and we are quick to judge partial success as failure. Moreover, as our largest problems get smaller, smaller problems seem relatively larger, and the number of identifiable, now defined-as-pressing problems seems to swell. At the same time, changes in institutions—particularly the media—create more arenas within which social problems can be promoted and compete for public attention, as well as more people with the skills required to construct social problems. Further, our growing ability to recognize and control risks spawns the fear that we actually confront terrible threats that are unrecognized and impossible to control. It is a mark of how far we've come in a century—from a world of deadly infectious childhood diseases and lynchings—that we can now focus our attention on such newly visible problems as the possibilities that cellular phones cause brain tumors or that glass ceilings block female executives' advancement to the very top rungs in Fortune 500 corporations.

My point—and I trust this is obvious—is not that we have no problems, that the problems we have are unimportant, or that they are not worthy of attention and remedy. But, like the fabled glass of water that is either half-full or half-empty, we can describe our social problems in different terms. We could tell a story of progress, of a society gradually—albeit not constantly, consistently, or universally—becoming more egalitarian and more livable—healthier, wealthier, and, if not wiser, at least better educated. Or we could choose to emphasize stories of decay, dissolution, and the danger of impending disaster. In the short run, it is this frightening language that commands attention. Its adherents justify such rhetoric as moral because fear promises to counter complacency and motivate efforts toward further progress. This may be true in the short run. But it is less clear what the long-term consequences of this approach might be.

Pronouncing social progress as trivial and social policies as ineffective may not be the best way to encourage commitment to new policies and further progress. In particular, liberal activists and social scientists whose rhetoric denies that there has been social progress should not be surprised when conservatives use lack of progress (i.e., claims that "nothing works" or that social programs have actually made things worse) as a justification for opposing new social policies. Pessimism and paranoia seem at least as likely to foster disillusionment and despair, as they are to inspire any sort of enthusiasm for further reform. Sociologists need to acknowledge social progress and to stop fearing that that acknowledgment will somehow make things worse.

ENDNOTES

Author's Note: This essay benefited from comments by Robert Broadhead, Russell Dynes, Gary Alan Fine, James Orcutt, Rhys Williams, and Richard Wilsnack.

[1]While these four indicators strike me as particularly significant, I do not mean to imply that every social indicator shows similar improvement. Perhaps the most disturbing current trend is the growth in income inequality over the last three decades (although it should be noted that income inequality declined somewhat during most of the twentieth century) (Morris and Western 1999).

[2]Hibbing and Theiss-Morse (1995:117) report that in their research "about two-thirds of the respondents approved of their own member [of Congress], whereas less that one-fourth approved of congressional membership.". . .

[3]Scholars have traced the histories of progress and decline as ideas (Nisbet 1980; Herman 1997). They argue that a confident belief in progress provided vital cultural support for the rise of science, democracy, and other key institutions in Western civilization, and they worry that contemporary intellectuals no longer believe in the progress of the Western tradition. . . .

[4]Rhys Williams points out that, alternatively, one can argue that pessimism characterizes American intellectual history, that the Puritans envisioned the community of saints, not as a human achievement, but as those chosen by God, that the Founders sought to devise a government that could constrain evil impulses, and so on. Intellectual historians have identified both optimistic and pessimistic strains in American thought. Aaron (1951) offers the classic optimistic, perfectionist interpretation.

[5]Russell Dynes notes that early American sociology was intertwined with reform efforts, and that a perfectionist ideal has deep roots in our discipline.

[6]One important reason for the proliferation of talk shows and reality television programs is that they are relatively inexpensive to produce, making them relatively profitable (Fishman 1998).

[7]Early critiques of mass culture worried about the inevitable homogenization and degradation of the audience (Gans 1974). It took decades to recognize that the mass audience was relatively unattractive to advertisers, and that the magazines with the largest circulations and the television shows with the highest ratings were often less profitable venues for advertising than media with smaller, more homogeneous audiences. Analysts now worry less about homogenization and more about cultural fragmentation (Turow 1997).

[8]The paradoxes of proportion and proliferation reinforce one another. Within a homogeneous arena, problems that disproportionately affect the network's members can loom large, even when they command little attention in the broader society.

[9]The latter two threats are just beginning to attract attention: "Our most powerful 21st-century technologies—genetic engineering, nanotechnology, and robotics (GNR for short)—carry a hidden risk of huge dimensions. . . . Nanotechnology poses the threat of a 'gray goo,' . . . engineered from materials foreign to the environment, which would outcompete the existing biosphere. . . . [A] global disaster could occur in weeks. . . . If we use technology to create robotic intelligences that are superior to ours, they might come to view us as expendable" (Joy 2000).

REFERENCES

Aaron, Daniel. 1951. *Men of Good Hope: A Story of American Progressives.* New York: Oxford University Press.

Angell, Marcia. 1996. *Science on Trial: The Clash of Medical Evidence and the Law in the Breast Implant Case.* New York: Norton.

Barzilay, Joshua I., Winkler G. Weinberg, and J. William Eley. 1999. *The Water We Drink: Water Quality and Its Effects on Health.* New Brunswick, NJ: Rutgers University Press.

Beck, Ulrich. 1992. *The Risk Society.* London: Sage.

Best, Joel. 1999. *Random Violence: How We Talk about New Crimes and New Victims.* Berkeley: University of California Press.

———. 2000. "The Apparently Innocuous 'Just,' the Law of Levity, and the Social Problems of Social Construction." *Perspectives on Social Problems* 12:3–4.

Best, Joel and Frank Furedi. 2001. "The Evolution of Road Rage in Britain and the United States." Pp. 107–27 in *How Claims Spread: Crossnational Diffusion of Social Problems*, edited by Joel Best. Hawthorne, NY: Aldine de Gruyter.

Downs, Anthony. 1972. "Up and Down with Ecology—The 'Issue-Attention Cycle.'" *Public Interest* 28:38–50.

Eitzen, D. Stanley and Maxine Baca Zinn. 2000. *Social Problems.* 8th ed. Boston: Allyn and Bacon.

Fishman, Mark. 1998. "Ratings and Reality: The Persistence of the Reality Crime Genre." Pp. 59–75 in *Entertaining Crime: Television Reality Programs*, edited by Mark Fishman and Gray Cavender. Hawthorne, NY: Aldine de Gruyter.

Gans, Herbert J. 1974. *Popular Culture and High Culture.* New York: Basic Books.

Herman, Arthur. 1997. *The Idea of Decline in Western History.* New York: Free Press.

Hibbing, John R. and Elizabeth Theiss-Morse. 1995. *Congress as Public Enemy.* New York: Cambridge University Press.

Hilgartner, Stephen and Charles L. Bosk. 1988. "The Rise and Fall of Social Problems: A Public Arenas Model." *American Journal of Sociology* 94:53–78.

Joy, Bill. 2000. "Doomsday Scenarios Turn Technology into Threat." *News Journal* (Wilmington, Delaware), April 24, p. A7.

Kozol, Jonathan. 1985. *Illiterate America.* Garden City, NY: Anchor Press.

Lipsky, Michael and Steven Smith. 1989. "When Social Problems Are Treated as Emergencies." *Social Service Review* 63:5–25.

Morris, Martina and Bruce Western. 1999. "Inequality in Earnings at the Close of the Twentieth Century." *Annual Review of Sociology* 25:623–57.

Nisbet, Robert. 1980. *History of the Idea of Progress*. New York: Basic Books.

Schudson, Michael. 1998. *The Good Citizen: A History of American Civic Life*. New York: Free Press.

Schwartz, Hillel. 1996. *Century's End: An Orientation Manual toward the Year 2000*. New York: Currency Doubleday.

———. 1997. "On the Origin of the Phrase 'Social Problems.'" *Social Problems* 44:276–96.

Sullivan, Thomas J. 2000. *Introduction to Social Problems*. 5th ed. Boston: Allyn and Bacon.

Toch, Hans. 1965. *The Social Psychology of Social Movements*. Indianapolis: Bobbs-Merrill.

Turow, Joseph. 1997. *Breaking Up America: Advertisers and the New Media World*. Chicago: University of Chicago Press.

U.S. Bureau of the Census (USBC). 1975. *Historical Statistics of the United States: Colonial Times to 1970*. Washington, DC: GPO.

———. 1999. *Statistical Abstract of the United States: 1999*. 119th ed. Washington, DC: GPO.

Weed, Frank J. 1993. "The MADD Queen: Charisma and the Founder of Mothers Against Drunk Driving." *Leadership Quarterly* 4:329–46.

57

THE McDONALDIZATION OF SOCIETY

GEORGE RITZER

This second reading focuses on one theory of social change called the *McDonaldization of Society*. George Ritzer, a Distinguished University Professor of Sociology at the University of Maryland, argues that societies are being transformed by this process of McDonaldization, in which the principles of the fast-food restaurant have come to influence other aspects of the social structure, such as the family, politics, education, travel, and leisure. After reviewing the dimensions of McDonaldization, Ritzer also summarizes the advantages and disadvantages of this widespread social change.

Ray Kroc, the genius behind the franchising of McDonald's restaurants, was a man with big ideas and grand ambitions. But even Kroc could not have anticipated the astounding impact of his creation. McDonald's is the basis of one of the most influential developments in contemporary society. Its reverberations extend far beyond its point of origin in the United States and in the fast-food business. It has influenced a wide range of undertakings, indeed the way of life, of a significant portion of the world. And that impact is likely to expand at an accelerating rate.[1]

George Ritzer, "The McDonaldization of Society" from *Journal of American Culture* 6, no. 1 (1983): 100–107. Reprinted with the permission of Blackwell.

However, this is not a [reading] about McDonald's, or even about the fast-food business, although both will be discussed frequently throughout these pages. Rather, McDonald's serves here as the major example, the paradigm, of a wide-ranging process I call *McDonaldization*[2]—that is,

> *the process by which the principles of the fast-food restaurant are coming to dominate more and more sectors of American society as well as of the rest of the world.*[3]

As you will see, McDonaldization affects not only the restaurant business but also education, work, health care, travel, leisure, dieting, politics, the family, and virtually every other aspect of society. McDonaldization has shown every sign of being an inexorable process, sweeping through seemingly impervious institutions and regions of the world.

The success of McDonald's itself is apparent: In 1998, its total sales reached $36 billion, with operating income of $3.1 billion.[4] The average U.S. outlet has sales of approximately $1.6 million in a year. McDonald's, which first began franchising in 1955, had 24,800 restaurants throughout the world by the end of 1998. Martin Plimmer, a British commentator, archly notes: "There are McDonald's everywhere. There's one near you, and there's one being built right now even nearer to you. Soon, if McDonald's goes on expanding at its present rate, there might even be one in your house. You could find Ronald McDonald's boots under your bed. And maybe his red wig, too."[5]

McDonald's and McDonaldization have had their most obvious influence on the restaurant industry and, more generally, on franchises of all types:

1. According to one estimate, there are now about 1.5 million franchised outlets in the United States, accounting for about a third of all retail sales. Franchises are growing at a rate of 6% a year.[6] Over 60% of McDonald's restaurants are franchises.[7]

2. Sales in fast-food restaurants in the United States rose to $116 billion by the end of 1998.[8] In 1994, for the first time, sales in so-called quick-service restaurants exceeded those in traditional full-service restaurants, and the gap between them grew to more than $10 billion in 1998.[9]

3. The McDonald's model has been adopted not only by other budget-minded hamburger franchises, such as Burger King and Wendy's, but also by a wide array of other low-priced fast-food businesses . . . [such as Pizza Hut, Taco Bell, KFC, and Subway].

4. Starbucks, a relative newcomer to the fast-food industry, has achieved dramatic success of its own. A local Seattle business as late as 1987, Starbucks had over 1,668 company-owned shops (there are no franchises) by 1998, more than triple the number of shops in 1994. Starbucks planned on having two hundred shops in Asia by the year 2000 and five hundred shops in Europe by 2003.[10]

5. Perhaps we should not be surprised that the McDonald's model has been extended to "casual dining"—that is, more "upscale," higher-priced restaurants with fuller menus (for example, Outback Steakhouse, Fuddrucker's, Chili's, The Olive Garden, and Red Lobster). Morton's is an

even more upscale, high-priced chain of steakhouses that has overtly modeled itself after McDonald's: "Despite the fawning service and the huge wine list, a meal at Morton's conforms to the same dictates of uniformity, cost control and portion regulation that have enabled American fast-food chains to rule the world."[11] . . .

6. Other types of business are increasingly adapting the principles of the fast-food industry to their needs. Said the vice chairman of Toys 'R Us, "We want to be thought of as a sort of McDonald's of toys."[12] . . . Other chains with similar ambitions include Jiffy Lube, AAMCO Transmissions, Midas Muffler & Brake Shops, Hair Plus, H&R Block, Pearle Vision Centers, Kampgrounds of America (KOA), Kinder Care, Jenny Craig, Home Depot, Barnes & Noble, Petstuff, and Wal-Mart.

7. McDonald's has been a resounding success in the international arena. Just about half of McDonald's restaurants are outside the United States (in the mid-1980s, only 25% of McDonald's were outside the United States). The vast majority of the 1,750 new restaurants opened in 1998 were overseas (in the United States, restaurants grew by less than one hundred). Well over half of McDonald's profits come from its overseas operations. McDonald's restaurants are now found in 115 nations around the world. . . .

8. Many highly McDonaldized firms outside of the fast-food industry have also had success globally. In addition to its thousands of stores in the United States, Blockbuster now has just over 2,000 sites in twenty-six other countries. Although Wal-Mart opened its first international store (in Mexico) only in 1991, it now operates about 600 stores overseas (compared with just over 2,800 in the United States, including supercenters and Sam's Club).[13]

9. Other nations have developed their own variants of this American institution. Canada has a chain of coffee shops, Tim Hortons. . . . Paris, a city whose love for fine cuisine might lead you to think it would prove immune to fast food, has a large number of fast-food croissanteries; the revered French bread has also been McDonaldized.[14] India has a chain of fast-food restaurants, Nirula's, that sells mutton burgers (about 80% of Indians are Hindus, who eat no beef) as well as local Indian cuisine.[15] . . .

10. And now McDonaldization is coming full circle. Other countries with their own McDonaldized institutions have begun to export them to the United States. The Body Shop, an ecologically sensitive British cosmetics chain, had over fifteen hundred shops in forty-seven nations in 1998,[16] of which three hundred were in the United States. Furthermore, American firms are now opening copies of this British chain, such as Bath and Body Works.[17]

McDonald's As a Global Icon

McDonald's has come to occupy a central place in American popular culture, not just the business world.[18] A new McDonald's opening in a small town can be an important social event. Said one Maryland high school student at such an opening, "Nothing this exciting ever happens in Dale City.[19] Even big-city newspapers avidly cover developments in the fast-food business. . . .

Two other indices of the significance of McDonald's (and, implicitly, McDonaldization) are worth mentioning. The first is the annual "Big Mac Index" (part of "burgernomics") published by a prestigious magazine, *The Economist*. It indicates the purchasing power of various currencies around the world based on the local price (in dollars) of the Big Mac. The Big Mac is used because it is a uniform commodity sold in many (115) different nations. In the 1998 survey, a Big Mac in the United States cost $2.56; in Indonesia and Malaysia it cost $1.16; in Switzerland it cost $3.87.[20] This measure indicates, at least roughly, where the cost of living is high or low, as well as which currencies are undervalued (Indonesia and Malaysia) and which are overvalued (Switzerland). Although *The Economist* is calculating the Big Mac Index tongue-in-cheek, at least in part, the index represents the ubiquity and importance of McDonald's around the world.

The second indicator of McDonald's global significance is the idea developed by Thomas J. Friedman that "no two countries that both have a McDonald's have ever fought a war since they each got McDonald's." Friedman calls this the "Golden Arches Theory of Conflict Prevention."[21] Another half-serious idea, it implies that the path to world peace lies through the continued international expansion of McDonald's. Unfortunately, it was proved wrong by the NATO bombing of Yugoslavia in 1999, which had eleven McDonald's as of 1997.

To many people throughout the world, McDonald's has become a sacred institution. At the opening of the McDonald's in Moscow, a worker spoke of it "as if it were the Cathedral in Chartres . . . a place to experience 'celestial joy.'"[22] Kowinski argues that shopping malls, which almost always encompass fast-food restaurants, are the modern "cathedrals of consumption" to which people go to practice their "consumer religion."[23] Similarly, a visit to another central element of McDonaldized society, Walt Disney World, has been described as "the middle-class hajj, the compulsory visit to the sunbaked holy city."[24]

McDonald's has achieved its exalted position because virtually all Americans, and many others, have passed through its golden arches on innumerable occasions. Furthermore, most of us have been bombarded by commercials extolling McDonald's virtues, commercials tailored to a variety of audiences and that change as the chain introduces new foods, new contests, and new product tie-ins. These ever-present commercials, combined with the fact that people cannot drive very far without having a McDonald's pop into view, have embedded McDonald's deeply in popular consciousness. A poll of school-age children showed that 96% of them could identify Ronald McDonald, second only to Santa Claus in name recognition.[25] . . .

The Dimensions of McDonaldization

Why has the McDonald's model proven so irresistible? Eating fast food at McDonald's has certainly become a "sign"[26] that, among other things, one is in tune with the contemporary lifestyle. There is also a kind of magic or enchantment associated with such foods and their settings. However, what will be focused on here are the four alluring dimensions that lie at the heart of the success of this model and, more generally, of McDonaldization. In short, McDonald's has succeeded because it offers consumers, workers, and managers efficiency, calculability, predictability, and control.[27]

Efficiency

One important element of McDonald's success is *efficiency,* or the optimum method for getting from one point to another. For consumers, McDonald's offers the best available way to get from being hungry to being full. In a society where both parents are likely to work or where a single parent is struggling to keep up, efficiently satisfying hunger is very attractive. In a society where people rush, from one spot to another, usually by car, the efficiency of a fast-food meal, perhaps even a drive-through meal, often proves impossible to resist.

The fast-food model offers, or at least appears to offer, an efficient method for satisfying many other needs, as well. Woody Allen's orgasmatron offered an efficient method for getting people from quiescence to sexual gratification. Other institutions fashioned on the McDonald's model offer similar efficiency in losing weight, lubricating cars, getting new glasses or contacts, or completing income tax forms.

Like their customers, workers in McDonaldized systems function efficiently following the steps in a predesigned process. They are trained to work this way by managers, who watch over them closely to make sure that they do. Organizational rules and regulations also help ensure highly efficient work.

Calculability

Calculability is an emphasis on the quantitative aspects of products sold (portion size, cost) and services offered (the time it takes to get the product). In McDonaldized systems, quantity has become equivalent to quality; a lot of something, or the quick delivery of it, means it must be good. As two observers of contemporary American culture put it, "As a culture, we tend to believe deeply that in general 'bigger is better.'"[28] Thus, people order the Quarter Pounder, the Big Mac, the large fries. More recent lures are the "double this" (for instance, Burger King's "Double Whopper with Cheese") and the "triple that." People can quantify these things and feel that they are getting a lot of food for what appears to be a nominal sum of money. This calculation does not take into account an important point, however: The high profits of fast-food chains indicates that the owners, not the consumers, get the best deal.

People also tend to calculate how much time it will take to drive to McDonald's, be served the food, eat it, and return home; then, they compare that interval to the time required to prepare food at home. They often conclude, rightly or wrongly, that a trip to the fast-food restaurant will take less time than eating at home. This sort of calculation particularly supports home delivery franchises such as Domino's, as well as other chains that emphasize time saving. A notable example of time saving in another sort of chain is Lens Crafters, which promises people, "Glasses fast, glasses in one hour."

Some McDonaldized institutions combine the emphases on time and money. Domino's promises pizza delivery in half an hour, or the pizza is free. Pizza Hut will serve a personal pan pizza in five minutes, or it, too, will be free.

Workers in McDonaldized systems also tend to emphasize the quantitative rather than the qualitative aspects of their work. Since the quality of the work is allowed to vary little, workers focus on things such as how quickly tasks can be accomplished. In a situation analogous to that of the customer, workers are expected to do a lot of work, very quickly, for low pay.

Predictability

McDonald's also offers *predictability,* the assurance that products and services will be the same over time and in all locales. The Egg McMuffin in New York will be, for all intents and purposes, identical to those in Chicago and Los Angeles. Also, those eaten next week or next year will be identical to those eaten today. Customers take great comfort in knowing that McDonald's offers no surprises. People know that the next Egg McMuffin they eat will not be awful, although it will not be exceptionally delicious, either. The success of the McDonald's model suggests that many people have come to prefer a world in which there are few surprises. "This is strange," notes a British observer, "considering [McDonald's is] the product of a culture which honours individualism above all."[29]

The workers in McDonaldized systems also behave in predictable ways. They follow corporate rules as well as the dictates of their managers. In many cases, what they do, and even what they say, is highly predictable. McDonaldized organizations often have scripts that employees are supposed to memorize and follow whenever the occasion arises. This scripted behavior helps create highly predictable interactions between workers and customers. While customers do not follow scripts, they tend to develop simple recipes for dealing with the employees of McDonaldized systems.[30] As Robin Leidner argues,

> McDonald's pioneered the routinization of interactive service work and remains an exemplar of extreme standardization. Innovation is not discouraged . . . at least among managers and franchisees. Ironically, though, "the object is to look for new, innovative ways to create an experience that is exactly the same no matter what McDonald's you walk into, no matter where it is in the world."[31]

Control through Nonhuman Technology

The fourth element in McDonald's success, *control,* is exerted over the people who enter the world of McDonald's. Lines, limited menus, few options, and uncomfortable seats all lead diners to do what management wishes them to do—eat quickly and leave. Furthermore, the drive-through (in some cases, walk-through) window leads diners to leave before they eat. In the Domino's model, customers never enter in the first place.

The people who work in McDonaldized organizations are also controlled to a high degree, usually more blatantly and directly than customers. They are trained to do a limited number of things in precisely the way they are told to do them. The technologies used and the way the organization is set up reinforce this control. Managers and inspectors make sure that workers toe the line.

McDonald's also controls employees by threatening to use, and ultimately using, technology to replace human workers. No matter how well they are programmed and controlled, workers can foul up the system's operation. A slow worker can make the preparation and delivery of a Big Mac inefficient. A worker who refuses to follow the rules might leave the pickles or special sauce off a hamburger, thereby making for unpredictability. And a distracted worker can put too few fries in the box, making an order of large fries seem skimpy. For these and other reasons, McDonald's and other fast-food restaurants have felt compelled to steadily replace human beings with machines, such as the soft drink dispenser that shuts itself off when the glass is full, the french fry machine that rings and lifts the basket out of the oil when the fries are crisp, the preprogrammed cash register that eliminates the need for the cashier to calculate prices and amounts, and perhaps at some future time, the robot capable of making hamburgers. Technology that increases control over workers helps McDonaldized systems assure customers that their products and service will be consistent.

The Advantages of McDonaldization

This discussion of four fundamental characteristics of McDonaldization makes it clear that McDonald's has succeeded so phenomenally for good, solid reasons. Many knowledgeable people such as the economic columnist, Robert Samuelson, strongly support McDonald's business model. Samuelson confesses to "openly worship[ing] McDonald's," and he thinks of it as "the greatest restaurant chain in history."[32] In addition, McDonald's offers many praiseworthy programs that benefit society, such as its Ronald McDonald Houses, which permit parents to stay with children undergoing treatment for serious medical problems; job-training programs for teenagers; programs to help keep its employees in school; efforts to hire and train the handicapped; the McMasters program, aimed at hiring senior citizens; and an enviable record of hiring and promoting minorities.[33]

The process of McDonaldization also moved ahead dramatically undoubtedly because it has led to positive change.[34] Here are a few specific examples:

- ▾ A wider range of goods and services is available to a much larger portion of the population than ever before.

▼ Availability of goods and services depends far less than before on time or geographic location; people can do things, such as obtain money at the grocery store or a bank balance in the middle of the night, that were impossible before.

▼ People are able to get what they want or need almost instantaneously and get it far more conveniently.

▼ Goods and services are of a far more uniform quality; at least some people get better goods and services than before McDonaldization.

▼ Far more economical alternatives to high-priced, customized goods and services are widely available; therefore, people can afford things they could not previously afford.

▼ Fast, efficient goods and services are available to a population that is working longer hours and has fewer hours to spare.

▼ In a rapidly changing, unfamiliar, and seemingly hostile world, the comparatively stable, familiar, and safe environment of a McDonaldized system offers comfort.

▼ Because of quantification, consumers can more easily compare competing products.

▼ Certain products (for example, diet programs) are safer in a carefully regulated and controlled system.

▼ People are more likely to be treated similarly, no matter what their race, gender, or social class.

▼ Organizational and technological innovations are more quickly and easily diffused through networks of identical operators.

▼ The most popular products of one culture are more easily diffused to others.

A Critique of McDonaldization: The Irrationality of Rationality

Though McDonaldization offers powerful advantages, it has a downside. Efficiency, predictability, calculability, and control through nonhuman technology can be thought of as the basic components of a rational system.[35] However, rational systems inevitably spawn irrationalities. The downside of McDonaldization will be dealt with most systematically under the heading of the irrationality of rationality; in fact, paradoxically, the irrationality of rationality can be thought of as the fifth dimension of McDonaldization. The basic idea here is that rational systems inevitably spawn irrational consequences. Another way of saying this is that rational systems serve to deny human reason; rational systems are often unreasonable.

For example, McDonaldization has produced a wide array of adverse effects on the environment. One is a side effect of the need to grow uniform potatoes from which to create predictable french fries. The huge farms of the Pacific Northwest that now produce such potatoes rely on the extensive use of chemicals. In addition, the need to produce a perfect fry means that much of the potato is wasted, with the remnants either fed to cattle or used for fertilizer. The underground water supply in the area is now showing high levels of nitrates, which may be traceable to the fertilizer and animal wastes.[36] Many other ecological problems are associated with the McDonaldization of the fast-food industry: the forests felled to produce paper wrappings, the damage caused by polystyrene and other packaging materials, the enormous amount of food needed to produce feed cattle, and so on.

Another unreasonable effect is that fast-food restaurants are often dehumanizing settings in which to eat or work. Customers lining up for a burger or waiting in the drive-through line and workers preparing the food often feel as though they are part of an assembly line. Hardly amenable to eating, assembly lines have been shown to be inhuman settings in which to work.

Such criticisms can be extended to all facets of the McDonaldizing world. For example, at the opening of Euro Disney, a French politician said that it will "bombard France with uprooted creations that are to culture what fast food is to gastronomy."[37]

As you have seen, McDonaldization offers many advantages. However, [there are] great costs and enormous risks of McDonaldization. McDonald's and other purveyors of the fast-food model spend billions of dollars each year outlining the benefits of their system. However, critics of the system have few outlets for their ideas. For example, no one is offering commercials between Saturday-morning cartoons warning children of the dangers associated with fast-food restaurants. . . .

It is more valid to critique McDonaldization from the perspective of the future.[38] Unfettered by the constraints of McDonaldized systems, but using the technological advances made possible by them, people would have the potential to be far more thoughtful, skillful, creative, and well-rounded than they are now. In short, if the world were less McDonaldized, people would be better able to live up to their human potential.

We must therefore look at McDonaldization as both "enabling" and "constraining."[39] McDonaldized systems enable us to do many things that we were not able to do in the past. However, these systems also keep us from doing things we otherwise would do. McDonaldization is a "double-edged" phenomenon. We must not lose sight of that fact. . . .

ENDNOTES

[1] For a similar but narrower viewpoint to the one expressed here, see Benjamin R. Barber, "Jihad vs. McWorld," *The Atlantic Monthly,* March 1992, pp. 53–63; *Jihad vs. McWorld* (New York: Times Books, 1995). For a more popular discussion of a similar conflict, see Thomas L. Friedman, *The Lexus and the Olive Tree: Understanding Globalization* (New York: Farrar Straus & Giroux, 1999).

[2] Since . . . 1993, the term *McDonaldization* has, at least to some degree, become part of the academic and public lexicon.

[3] Alan Bryman has recently suggested the term *Disneyization,* which he defines in a parallel manner: "the process by which *the principles* of Disney theme parks are coming to dominate more and more sectors of American society as well as the rest of the world" (p. 26). See Alan Bryman, "The Disneyization of Society," *Sociological Review* 47 (February, 1999): 25–47.

[4] McDonald's, *The Annual* (Oak Brook, IL: 1999).

[5] Martin Plimmer, "This Demi-Paradise: Martin Plimmer Finds Food in the Fast Lane Is Not to His Taste," *Independent* (London), January 3, 1998, p. 46.

[6] Scott Shane and Chester Spell, "Factors for New Franchise Success," *Sloan Management Review* 39 (March 22, 1998): 43ff; Paul Gruchow, "Unchaining America: Communities Are Finding Ways to Keep Independent Entrpreneurs in Business," *Utne Reader*, January-February 1995, pp. 17–18.

[7] McDonald's, *The Annual* (Oak Brook, IL: 1999).

[8] Richard L. Papiernik, "On Site Foodservice Firms Carve out Significant Growth," *Nation's Restaurant News*, October 5, 1998, p. 6.

[9] Richard L. Papiernik, "On Site Foodservice Firms Carve out Significant Growth," *Nation's Restaurant News*, October 5, 1998, p. 6; Mark Albright, "INSIDE JOB: Fast-Food Chains Serve a Captive Audience," *St. Petersburg Times*, January 15, 1995, p. 1H.

[10] Starbucks press releases on the Internet; Lorraine Mirabella, "Trouble Brews for Starbucks as Its Stock Slides 12 Percent," *Baltimore Sun*, August 1, 1998, p. 10c; Margaret Webb Pressler, "The Brain behind the Beans," *Washington Post*, October 5, 1997, pp. H01ff; Alex Witchell, "By Way of Canarsie, One Large Hot Cup of Business Strategy," *New York Times*, December 14, 1994, p. C8.

[11] Glenn Collins, "A Big Mac Strategy at Porterhouse Prices," *New York Times*, August 13, 1996, p. D1.

[12] Timothy Egan, "Big Chains Are Joining Manhattan's Toy Wars," *New York Times*, December 8, 1990, p. 29.

[13] Sources for this information are company press releases on the Internet.

[14] Eric Margolis, "Fast Food: France Fights Back," *Toronto Sun*, January 16, 1997, p. 12.

[15] Valerie Reitman, "India Anticipates the Arrival of the Beefless Big Mac," *Wall Street Journal*, October 20, 1993, pp. Bl, B3.

[16] The Body Shop Website: http://www.bodyshop.com.

[17] Philip Elmer-Dewitt, "Anita the Agitator," *Time*, January 25, 1993, pp. 52ff; Eben Shapiro, "The Sincerest Form of Rivalry," *New York Times*, October 19, 1991, pp. 35, 46; Bath and Body Works Website: http://www.bbwhome.com.

[18] Marshall Fishwick (ed.), *Ronald Revisited: The World of Ronald McDonald* (Bowling Green, OH: Bowling Green University Press, 1983).

[19] John F. Harris, "McMilestone Restaurant Opens Doors in Dale City," *Washington Post*, April 7, 1988, p. D1.

[20] *The Economist*, "Big MacCurrencies," April 11, 1998, p. 58.

[21] Thomas Friedman, "A Manifesto for the Fast World," *New York Times Magazine*, March 28, 1999, p. 84.

[22] Bill Keller, "Of Famous Arches, Beeg Meks and Rubles," *New York Times*, January 28, 1990, sec. 1, pp. 1, 12.

[23] William Severini Kowinski, *The Malling of America: An Inside Look at the Great Consumer Paradise* (New York: William Marrow, 1985), p. 218.

[24] Bob Garfield, "How I Spent (and Spent and Spent) My Disney Vacation," *Washington Post*, July 7, 1991, p. B5. See also Margaret J. King, "Empires of Popular Culture: McDonald's and Disney," in Marshall Fishwick (ed.), *Ronald Revisited: The World of Ronald McDonald* (Bowling Green, OH: Bowling Green University Press, 1983), pp. 106–19.

[25] Steven Greenhouse, "The Rise and Rise of McDonald's," *New York Times*, June 8, 1986, sec. 3, p. 1.

[26] Arthur Asa Berger, *Signs in Contemporary Culture: An Introduction to Semiotics*, 2d ed. (Salem, WI: Sheffield, 1999).

[27] Max Weber, *Economy and Society* (Totowa, NJ: Bedminster, 1921/1968); Stephen Kalberg, "Max Weber's Types of Rationality: Cornerstones for the Analysis of Rationalization Processes in History," *American Journal of Sociology* 85 (1980): 1145–79.

[28] Ian Mitroff and Warren Bennis, *The Unreality Industry: The Deliberate Manufacturing of Falsehood and What It Is Doing to Our Lives* (New York: Birch Lande, 1989) p. 142.

[29] Martin Plimmer, "This Demi-Paradise: Martin Plimmer Finds Food in the Fast Lane Is Not to His Taste," *Independent* (London), January 3, 1998, p. 46.

[30] The idea of recipes comes from the work of Alfred Schutz. See, for example, *The Phenomenology of the Social World* (Evanston, IL: Northwestern University Press, 1932/1967).

[31] Robin Leidner, *Fast Food, Fast Talk: Service Work and the Routinization of Everyday Life* (Berkeley: University of California Press, 1993), p. 82.

[32] Robert J. Samuelson, "In Praise of McDonald's," *Washington Post*, November 1, 1989, p. A25.

[33] Edwin M. Reingold, "America's Hamburger Helper," June 29, 1992, pp. 66–67.

[34] I would like to thank my colleague, Stan Presser, for suggesting that I enumerate the kinds of advantages listed on these pages.

[35] It should be pointed out that the words *rational, rationality,* and *rationalization* are being used differently here and throughout [my research] than they are ordinarily employed. . . .

[36] Timothy Egan, "In Land of French Fry, Study Finds Problems," *New York Times*, February 7, 1994, p. A10.

[37] Alan Riding, "Only the French Elite Scorn Mickey's Debut," *New York Times*, April 13, 1992, p. A13.

[38] In this sense, this resembles Marx's critique of capitalism. Marx was not animated by a romanticization of precapitalist society but, rather, by the desire to produce a truly human (communist) society on the base provided by capitalism. Despite this specific affinity to Marxist theory, this [work] is, as you will see, premised far more on the theories of Max Weber.

[39] These concepts are associated with the work of the social theorist Anthony Giddens. See, for example, *The Constitution of Society* (Berkeley: University of California Press, 1984).

58

THE ATROPHY OF SOCIAL LIFE

D. STANLEY EITZEN

The first reading in this section, by Joel Best (Reading 56), described several of the positive changes that have happened in the twentieth century, yet sociologists focus on social problems more than on social progress. This selection, by D. Stanley Eitzen, a professor emeritus of sociology at Colorado State University, examines how some types of social progress have led to a decrease in social interaction. Eitzen describes several social trends and the implications they have had for society and for increasing social isolation.

Harvard political scientist Robert Putnam has written a provocative book entitled *Bowling Alone*, in which he argues that we Americans are becoming increasingly disengaged from each other. That is, we are less likely than Americans of a generation or two ago to belong to voluntary associations such as the Rotary Club, to play bridge on a regular basis, to participate in a bowling league, to belong to the P.T.A., or to vote. In short,

Putnam maintains that in the past 50 years or so social life has changed dramatically throughout the United States as various social trends isolate us more and more from each other. The effect, he suggests, is that the bonds of civic cement are disintegrating as we become increasingly separated from each other, from our communities and from society. Consequently, the social glue that once held communities together and gave meaning to individual lives is now brittle, as people have become more and more isolated.

I am a sociologist. We sociologists focus on things social the most fundamental of which is social interaction. This is the basic building block of intimate relationships, small groups, formal organizations, communities, and societies. I am concerned and I believe we should all be concerned by some disturbing trends in our society that hinder or even eliminate social interaction, and that indicate a growing isolation as individuals become increasingly separated from their neighbors, their co-workers, and even their family members.

Moving Away

Ours is a mobile society. We move, on average about every five years. We change jobs (14 percent of workers in a typical year leave their jobs voluntarily) or we lose jobs involuntarily (a recent survey indicated that 36 percent of Americans answered "yes" to the question "Has anyone in your immediate family lost a job in the last three years?"). It's important to note here that the bond between workers and employers is badly frayed as employees are no longer loyal to their employers and employers are clearly not loyal to their employees as they downsize locally and outsource their jobs and operations to low-wage economies.

We are also moving away from intimate relationships. With 1.25 million divorces occurring annually in the U.S., 2.5 million move away from their spouses. Immigration has the same consequence, creating transnational families, where families are separated with some members living in the U.S. and one or more members back home in another country.

When we move out of relationships or to new geographical areas, or to new kinds of work, we leave behind our relationships with former neighbors, co-workers, and friends. If we anticipate moving, we act like temporary residents, not making the effort to join local organizations, to become acquainted with our neighbors, and invest our time and money to improve the community.

Living Alone

In 1930, 2 percent of the U.S. population lived alone. In 2000, some 10 percent (27.2 million) of the nation's 105 million households were occupied by single people without children, roommates, or other people. People are living longer and the elderly, especially older women, are most likely to live alone.

Divorce, by definition, initiates living alone, with 2.5 million former spouses annually moving into separate living arrangements. Another source for living alone is the phenomenon of commuter marriage—an arrangement where wives and husbands maintain separate households as a way of solving the dilemmas of dual-career marriages.

Technology and Isolation

Modern technology often encourages isolation. Consider the isolating consequences of air conditioning, certainly a welcome and necessary technology in many places. Before air conditioning, people spent leisure time outside increasing the likelihood of interaction with neighbors and friends. Now they are inside their homes with doors and windows shut enjoying the cool air, but isolating themselves from their neighbors. Television, too, along with VCRs, DVDs, and video games entice us to stay in our homes more and more.

Before refrigerators, shopping was done every day. This meant that people would see the same shop proprietors and their fellow shoppers daily. This created a daily rhythm, a set of interactions, and the sharing of information, gossip, and mutual concerns. Thus, refrigerators, while reducing the spoilage of food and the necessity of going to the store every day, changed interaction patterns.

Because of computers and telecommunications there is a growing trend for workers to work at home. At last count, 28 million Americans worked out of their homes, using computers or telephones instead of face-to-face interaction. While home-based work allows flexibility and independence not found in most jobs, these workers are separated from the rich social networks that often give rise to numerous friendships and make working life enjoyable or at least tolerable.

With the new communications technology, you don't even have to go to a funeral to pay your respects. A new company is now broadcasting funerals on the Internet and you can even sign an electronic guest book and e-mail condolences to the family. Similarly, one can take college courses without attending classes, just using the Internet to communicate with their instructors. Missing, of course, is the face-to-face interaction with fellow students and professors.

Paradoxically, the current communications revolution increases interaction while reducing intimacy. Curt Suplee, science and technology writer for the *Washington Post,* says that we have seen tenfold increases in "communication" by electronic means, and tenfold reductions in person-to-person contact. The more time people spend online, the less they can spare for real-life relationships with family and friends. In effect, as we are increasingly alone before a computer screen, we risk what former U.S. Secretary State Warren Christopher has called "social malnutrition." John L. Locke, a professor of communications, makes a convincing argument in his book, *The De-Voicing of Society,* that e-mail, voice mail, fax machines, beepers, and Internet chat rooms are robbing us of ordinary social talking. Talking, he says, like the grooming of apes and monkeys, is the way we build and maintain social relationships. In his view, it is only through intimate conversation that we can know others well enough to trust them and work with them harmoniously. Most face-to-face communication is nonverbal. Phone communication reduces the nonverbal clues, and e-mail eliminates them entirely. So the new information technologies only create the illusion of communication and intimacy. The result, according to Locke, is that we are becoming an autistic society, communicating messages electronically but without really connecting. In short, these incredible communication devices that combine to network us in so many dazzling ways also separate us increasingly from intimate relationships. Sometimes we even use the technology to avoid the live interaction for whatever reason. Jeffrey Kagan, a telecom industry analyst, sums up the problem: "We are becoming a society that finds it easier, and even preferable to hide behind our computer screens and chat with a raceless, nameless stream of words from across the country or across the globe rather than deal with people face to face and all the complexities, good and bad, of the human relationship."

Geography and Isolation

There is a strong pattern of social homogeneity by place. Cities are arranged into neighborhoods by social class and race. This occurs because of choice, economic means, and the discriminatory behaviors by neighbors, Realtors, and lending institutions. Among multiracial societies, only South Africa exceeds our rate of segregation—a problem that concentrates poverty, social disorder, and dysfunctional schools as well as diminishing social cohesion. The degree of racial-ethnic segregation by neighborhood is higher now than in 1990. A Harvard University study found that about 2.3 million African American and Latino children attend "apartheid" schools, where virtually all students are minorities. Similarly, some neighborhoods are segregated by age. Some retirement communities, for example, limit their inhabitants to persons over 55 and those without minor children. Some 6 million households are in neighborhoods that have controlled-entry systems with guards and electric gates. These gated communities wall the residents off physically and socially from "others." Regarding this exclusiveness, sociologist Philip Slater said that we need heterogeneous neighborhoods: "A community that does not have old people and children, white-collar and blue-collar, eccentric and conventional, and so on, is not a community at all, but [a] kind of truncated and deformed monstrosity. . . ."

Even in non-gated communities, we isolate ourselves. One in three Americans has never spent an evening with a neighbor. The affluent often belong to exclusive clubs and send their children to private schools. Two million children are home schooled, which isolates them from their peers. Some people exercise on motorized treadmills and use other home exercise equipment instead of running through their neighborhoods or working out with others.

The suburbs are especially isolating. Rather than walking to the corner grocery or nearby shop and visiting with the clerks and their neighbors, suburbanites drive somewhere away from their immediate neighborhood to shop among strangers. Or they may not leave their home at all, working, shopping, banking, and paying their bills by computer. For suburban teenagers and children almost everything is away—practice fields, music lessons, friends, jobs, schools, and the malls. Thus, a disconnect from those nearby. Suburban neighborhoods in particular are devoid of meeting places. The lack of community and common meeting places in our cities and especially in the suburbs compounds the isolation of those who have experienced a divorce or the death of a spouse.

Isolation within Families

An especially disturbing trend is the separation of family members from each other. Many spouses are either absent or too self-absorbed to pay very much attention to their children or each other. A recent cover story in *Newsweek* noted that many dual-income couples no longer or rarely have sex because they are too exhausted and too stressed. On average, parents today spend 22 fewer hours a week with their children than parents did in the 1960s. Part of this is because both parents are working outside the home. But it also results from children being overscheduled with outside-the-home activities. These children have little time for play with other children and their activities replace parent–child interaction. To amplify the last point, American children spend more than half of their waking hours in supervised, child-centered environments. This causes economist Ellen Frank to ask: "What happens to parents, to children, and to the rest of us when children arc stored out of sight?"

Although living in the same house, parents and children may tune each other out emotionally, or by using earphones, or by engaging in other solitary activities. A survey by the Kaiser Family Foundation found that the average child spends five and one-half hours a day alone watching television, on the Internet, playing video games, or reading. Some 30 percent of children under 3 have a television in their bedroom. Some older children even have their own rooms equipped with a telephone, television, VCR, microwave, refrigerator, and computer, which while convenient, isolates them from other family members. Many families rarely eat together in an actual sit-down meal. Family members are often too busy and too involved with their individual schedules to spend quality time together as a family. These homes may be full of people but they are really empty.

The Architecture of Isolation

Another contemporary trend—the increased number of megahouses in the suburbs—results in what we might call the architecture of isolation. These huge houses, built, ironically, at the very time that family size is declining, tend to isolate their inhabitants from outsiders and from other family members. They provide all of the necessities for comfort and recreation, thus glorifying the private sphere over public places. Moreover, the number and size of the rooms encourage each family member to have their own space rather than shared spaces. Thus, the inverse correlation between house size and family interaction.

Contemporary house and landscape design focuses interaction in the backyard, surrounded by privacy fences, some of which make our homes and lots to resemble medieval fortresses. Back yards are inviting with grass and flowerbeds, barbeque pits, swimming pools, jungle gyms, and trampolines. The front of the house no longer has a porch. In the past, families spent time on the porch, relaxing and visiting with neighbors. The front yard, too, is less inviting than the back, often with rock instead of grass. It is important to note that the more affluent we are, the more likely our homes and consumer goods promote social isolation.

Consumerism and Isolation

Sociologist George Ritzer in his recent book, *The Globalization of Nothing*, argues that the social world, particularly in the realm of consumption, is increasingly characterized by "nothing," which he defines as a social form that is generally centrally conceived and controlled and comparatively devoid of distinctive substance. The "something" that is lost is more than likely, an indigenous custom or product, a local store, a familiar gathering place, or simply personalized interaction. Corporations provide standardized, mass-produced products for us to consume and become like other consumers in what we wear, what we eat, and what we desire. We purchase goods in chain stores and restaurants (Dillard's, McDonalds) that are efficient but devoid of distinctive content. A mall in one part of the world may be structured much the same in another location. We bank at ATMs anywhere in the world, but without social interaction. The same is true with shopping on the Internet.

Increasingly, Ritzer says, adults go through their daily routines without sharing stories, gossip, and analyses of events with friends on a regular basis at work, at a coffee shop, neighborhood tavern, or at the local grain elevator. These places of conversation with friends have been replaced by huge stores (Wal-Mart, Home Depot) where we don't know the clerks and other shoppers. The locally owned café has been replaced by chain restaurants. In the process we lose the intimacy of local stores, cafés, and hardware stores, which give their steady customers sense of community and the comfort of meaningful connections with others. Sociologist Philip Slater said that "community life exists when one can go daily to a given location at a given time and see many of the people one knows."

Implications for Society

There are several important implications of increasing social isolation for society. First, the disengaged do not participate in elections, leaving a minority to elect our leaders as occurred in the 2000 presidential election when George Bush was elected with 24 percent of the votes of those eligible. This means that the voices of outsiders will be faint, if heard at all, while the voices of the affluent and their money arc heard all the more. All of these consequences support the conservative agenda, as sociologist Paul Starr notes: "These trends could hardly please anyone who cares about the republic, but they have been particularly disturbing to liberals. The most intense periods of liberal reform during the past century—the Progressive era, the New Deal, and the 1960s—were all times when the public was actively engaged, and new forms of civic action and participation emerged. Reforms in that tradition are unlikely to succeed again without the same heightened public arousal, which not only elects candidates but also forces them to pay attention once they are in office."

Second, the breakdown in social connections shows up in everyday sociability, with pernicious effects for social relations as people are less and less civil in schools, at work, in traffic, and in public places.

Third, when people focus only on themselves and people like themselves, they insulate themselves from "others" and from their problems. Thus, we favor dismantling the welfare state and safety net for the less fortunate. We oppose, for example, equity in school funding, allowing rich districts to have superior schools while the disadvantaged have inferior schools. We allow this unraveling of community bonds at our peril, as the walls become thicker between the "haves" and the "have-nots," crime will increase and hostility and fear will reign.

Implications for Individuals

As for individuals, the consequences of this accelerating social isolation are dire. More and more Americans are lonely, bitter, alienated, anomic, and disconnected. This situation is conducive to alcohol and drug abuse, depression, anxiety, and violence. The lonely and disaffected are ripe candidates for membership in cults, gangs, and militias where they find a sense of belonging and a cause to believe in, but in the process they may become more paranoid and, perhaps, even become willing terrorists or mass murderers as were the two alienated adolescents who perpetrated the massacre at Columbine High School in a Denver suburb. At a less extreme level, the alienated will disengage further from society by shunning voluntary associations, by home schooling their children, and by voting against higher taxes for the public good. In short, they will become increasingly self-absorbed, caring only about themselves and ignoring the needs of their neighbors and communities. This translates into the substitution of accumulating things rather than cultivating relationships. In this regard, we should take seriously the admonition by David Wann, the coauthor of *Afluenza: The All-Consuming Epidemic*, who says "We need to acknowledge—as individuals and as a culture—that the best things in life really aren't things. The best things are people. . . ."

What to Do?

I am not a Luddite. I appreciate the wonders of technology. I welcome change. There are good reasons to move and to change careers and to live in nice houses. But we must recognize the unintended consequences of societal trends that deprive us of our shared humanity. Once we have identified the downside of these trends and our complicity in them, what can we do to reverse their negative effects? I don't have all the answers, but I believe that a few structural changes will help to reduce their negative consequences. As a start, we need to rethink urban design. We must reverse urban sprawl, increasing urban density so that people live near their work, near their neighbors, and within walking distance of stores and recreation. Second, as a society we need to invest in the infrastructure that facilitates public activities such as neighborhood schools, walking and biking trails, parks, the arts, libraries, and community recreation centers. Third, communities need to provide activities that bring people together such as public concerts, fairs, recreational sports for people of all ages, and art festivals. And, fourth, since U.S. society is becoming more diverse, we need to break down the structural barriers that isolate us from "others." We need to affirm affirmative action in legislation and deed, eliminate predatory lending practices and other forms of discrimination, and improve our schools so that equality of educational opportunity actually occurs rather than the present arrangement whereby school systems are rigged in favor of the already privileged. You will note that these proposals are opposite from current policy at the community, state, and federal levels, resulting in a descending spiral toward social atomization. We allow this to occur at our own peril.

At a personal level, we need to recognize what is happening to us and our families and work to counteract these isolating trends. Each of us can think of changes in our lives that will enhance human connections. To those changes, may I suggest the following: Engage in public activities. Have meaningful face-to-face conversations with friends on a regular basis. Get to know your neighbors, co-workers, and the people, who provide services for you. Join with others who share a common interest. Work to improve your community. Become an activist, joining with others to bring about social change. And, most of all, we need to moderate our celebration of individualism and our tendency toward self-absorption and develop instead a moral obligation to others, to our neighbors (broadly defined) and their children, to those unlike us as well as those similar to us, and to future generations. If not, then our humanity is compromised and our quality of life diminished.

SUGGESTED FURTHER READINGS

Kane, Hal. 2001. *Triumph of the Mundane: The Unseen Trends That Shape Our Lives and Environment.* Washington, DC: Island Press.

Locke, John L. 1998. *The De-Voicing of Society: Why We Don't Talk to Each Other.* New York: Simon and Schuster.

Oldenburg, Ray. 1997. *The Great Good Place: Cafes, Coffee Shops, Community Centers, Beauty Parlors, General Stores, Bars, Hangouts, and How They Get You through the Day.* New York: Marlowe.

Putnam, Robert D. 2000. *Bowling Alone: The Collapse and Revival of American Community.* New York: Simon and Schuster.

Ritzer, George. 2004. *The Globalization of Nothing.* Thousand Oaks. CA: Pine Forge Press.

Slater, Philip. 1970. *The Pursuit, of Loneliness: American Culture at the Breaking Point.* Boston: Beacon Press.

59

GLOBALIZATION AND SOCIAL MOVEMENTS

JEREMY BRECHER • TIM COSTELLO • BRENDAN SMITH

In this selection we turn our attention to how society can be improved. One important vehicle for social change is *social movements*. The article that follows is by Jeremy Brecher, the author of ten books on labor and social movements; Tim Costello, director of the Massachusetts Campaign on Contingent Work; and Brendan Smith, a journalist and former policy analyst. In it, they examine the potential of social movements to challenge and change the social inequality inherent in global capitalism. They outline several successful worldwide movements of resistance, which they characterize as *globalization from below*, before articulating how social movements can be a powerful force for social change.

It is often said that globalization is inevitable and that there is no alternative. But, in fact, the new global regime is highly vulnerable. It violates the interests of the great majority of the world's people. It lacks political

---

legitimacy. It is riven with divisions and conflicting interests. It has the normal crisis-prone character of capitalist systems, but few of the compensatory non-market institutions that helped stabilize pre-globalization economies. And it has few means to control its own tendency to destroy the natural environment on which it—and its species—depend. These are the reasons that, as the *Financial Times* wrote, the world had swung "from the triumph of global capitalism to its crisis in less than a decade."[1]

Globalization from Below

Just as the corporate and political elites are reaching across national borders to further their agendas, people at the grassroots are connecting their struggles around the world to impose their needs and interests on the global economy. Globalization from above is generating a worldwide movement of resistance: globalization from below.[2]

Throughout the 20th century, nationally based social movements have placed limits on the downsides of capitalism. Workers and communities won national economic regulation and protections ranging from environmental laws to labor unions and from public investment to progressive taxation.

Globalization outflanked both national movements and national economies. It caused a historic break in the institutions, traditions, and movements that had opposed unfettered capitalism since its inception. Not only Communism, but also social democracy, economic nationalism, trade unionism, and democratic government itself were rolled back by the neoliberal tide—and often found their own foundations crumbling from within in the face of forces they could not understand or control.

Nonetheless, the real problems of a system of unrestrained capitalism did not disappear. Globalization only intensified them. And so the impulses that had generated these counter-movements in the first place began to stir.

Like globalization from above, these counter-movements began from many diverse starting points, ranging from local campaigns against runaway plants to union organizing in poor countries, and from protection of indigenous peoples to resistance to corporate-engineered food. Their participants have come to the issues of globalization by way of many different itineraries. For example:

▼ Acid rain and global warming do not respect national borders. They have forced environmentalists around the world to recognize global ecological interdependence.[3] At the same time, environmentalists became increasingly conscious that the actions of global corporations and of institutions such as the World Bank destroyed local environments— symbolized by the destruction of the Amazon rain forest and India's Narmada Valley. While some argued that globalizing capitalism would actually promote environmentalism in the third world, environmentalists discovered that it was instead creating an environmental race to the bottom as countries lowered environmental standards to attract corporations. The WTO's anti-environmental rules—symbolized by its decision condemning a U.S. law for the protection of sea turtles—brought the environmental movement into direct confrontation with this central institution of globalization.

▼ In the 1970s, the world's poorer countries formed the G-77 and initiated a North-South Dialogue with the rich countries to formulate a New International Economic Order. When the rich countries withdrew from this effort in the 1980s and began instead to promote neoliberal policies coordinated through the IMF, World Bank, and WTO, most third world governments went along with their plans, albeit in many cases reluctantly. But networks of third world NGOs continued to develop an alternative agenda and to press it both on their own countries and on international institutions. Third world governments have recently begun to follow their lead. As the rich countries prepared their agenda for the 1999 Seattle WTO extravaganza, poor-country governments began to question whether they had benefited from globalization. Encouraged by the global citizens' movement to halt any new round of WTO negotiations, third world delegations for the first time refused to go along with the rich countries' proposals until their own concerns were addressed, helping to bring the meeting down in shambles. Early in 2000, the G-77 held its first ever head-of-state-level meeting and proposed an alternative program that included debt relief, increased aid, access to technology, and a shift in economic decision making from the World Bank and IMF to the UN.[4]

▼ People in rich countries have a long history of compassionate assistance for poor countries—sometimes in alliance with religious proselytizing and colonialism. With the development of the third world debt crisis in the 1980s, however, many people of conscience in the first world became deeply concerned about the effect of crushing debts on third world people and began to demand cancellation of their debt. Many then went on to address the broader question of the devastating "structural adjustment" policies being imposed on the debtor countries by the IMF, World Bank, and rich countries.

▼ When negotiations started in 1986 for what became the WTO, critics argued that U.S. and other first world proposals would benefit agribusiness and transnational commodity traders, but would drive millions of small farmers in both the North and South off their farms. Advocates for small farmers around the world began holding regular counter-meetings at the negotiations and developed a global network to oppose the proposals. They provided much of the core for international opposition to the emerging WTO. What has been described as "the first really global demonstration," in December 1990, brought farmers from Europe, Japan, North America, Korea, Africa, and Latin America to Brussels—helping force the negotiations into deadlock.[5] Since then, small farmers have been at the forefront of opposition to WTO agricultural policies, efforts to turn seeds into private property, and genetically engineered organisms (GEOs).

▾ From World War II until the 1960s, the labor movement in the United States was a strong supporter of economic liberalization, both as an expression of its alliance with U.S. international policy and as a means to secure expanding markets for U.S.-made products. Faced with a massive loss of jobs in auto, steel, garment, and other industries in the 1970s, the labor movement increasingly campaigned for tariffs and other barriers to imports designed to "save American jobs." Over the 1990s, globalization made such economic nationalist strategies less and less credible. Organized labor increasingly moved toward demanding reform of the global economy as a whole, symbolized by demands for labor rights and environmental standards in international trade agreements to protect all the world's workers and communities from the race to the bottom. Its participation in the Seattle WTO protests represented a new page in U.S. labor history and was followed by the announcement of a long-term "Campaign for Global Fairness."

▾ The burgeoning identity-based movements of the late 20th century found that many identities did not respect national borders. The women's movement slogan "sisterhood is powerful" evolved into a consciousness that "sisterhood is global." A growing awareness of the global oppression of women led to a struggle to define women's rights as internationally protected human rights. Events surrounding the UN's 1995 Beijing women's conference brought large numbers of women in the United States to an awareness of the impact of IMF and World Bank–imposed structural adjustment austerity programs on women in poor countries, and their similarity to the implications of welfare reform for poor women in the United States. The fact that the great majority of those exploited in overseas factories were young women led to a growing concern about the global sweatshop.

▾ From the 1960s on, consumer movements in many countries had enshrined a wide range of protections in national laws and had developed effective legal techniques for imposing a degree of accountability on corporations. Consumer organizations—notably Ralph Nader's Public Citizen—discovered that trade agreements like NAFTA and the WTO were overriding high national standards for such things as food and product safety. They also realized that both neoliberal ideology and competition among countries for investment were tending to lower consumer protection standards all over the world. New consumer issues, such as the right of governments to regulate genetically engineered food, have steadily increased consumer concern over globalization.

▾ African American communities in the U.S. have been concerned with conditions in Africa from the mid-19th century to the struggle against

South African apartheid. But the 1990s saw two specific concerns that brought attention to the global economy. The first was the devastation wreaked on African countries by international debt and the brutal structural adjustment conditionalities the IMF and World Bank imposed on African countries in exchange for helping them roll over their debts. The other was the struggle over the African trade bill (known to its critics as the "NAFTA for Africa" bill) that ostensibly opened U.S. markets to African exports but in fact imposed more stringent structural adjustment–type conditions while doing little to provide desperately needed debt relief. Many African American leaders, including a wide swath of black clergy, became involved in the Jubilee 2000 debt relief campaign and the fight against the "NAFTA for Africa" bill and for an alternative proposed by Rep. Jesse Jackson, Jr.

▾ Groups in Europe, Japan, and the U.S. that had been involved in support for development and popular movements in third world countries found those countries increasingly used as production platforms by global corporations. They began calling attention to the growth of sweatshops and pressuring companies like the Gap and Nike to establish acceptable labor and human rights conditions in their factories around the world. Their efforts gradually grew into an anti-sweatshop movement with strong labor and religious support and tens of thousands of active participants. In the U.S., college students took up the anti-sweatshop cause on hundreds of campuses, ultimately holding sit-ins on many campuses to force their colleges to ban the use of college logos on products not produced under acceptable labor conditions.

Many other people are following their own itineraries toward globalization from below. Some, such as activists in the human rights movement seeking to protect rights of people globally, or public health advocates trying to control tobacco companies and provide AIDS treatment for poor countries, are just as globalized as those described above. Some, such as activists in the immigrant networks spreading out around the world, are in some ways even more global and are challenging globalization from above by their very way of life. Some, like the tens of millions who have participated in nationally organized mass and general strikes and upheavals, are resisting the effects of globalization from above, even if (so far) they are doing so in a national framework.[6] Far more numerous still are the billions of people who are being adversely affected by globalization from above, but who have not yet found their own way to respond. Ultimately, their itineraries may be the most important of all.

Confluence

From diverse origins and through varied itineraries, these movements now find themselves starting to converge. Many of their participants are recognizing their commonalties and beginning to envision themselves as constructing a common movement.

This convergence is occurring because globalization is creating common interests that transcend both national and interest-group boundaries. As author and activist Vandana Shiva wrote in the wake of the Battle of Seattle,

> When labour joins hands with environmentalists, when farmers from the North and farmers from the South make a common commitment to say "no" to genetically engineered crops, they are not acting as special interests. They are defending the common interests and common rights of all people, everywhere. The divide and rule policy, which has attempted to pit consumers against farmers, the North against the South, labour against environmentalist has failed.[7]

Much of the convergence is negative: [D]ifferent groups find themselves facing the same global corporations, international institutions, and market-driven race to the bottom. But there is also a growing positive convergence around common values of democracy, environmental protection, community, economic justice, equality, and human solidarity.

Participants in this convergence have varied goals, but its unifying goal is to bring about sufficient democratic control over states, markets, and corporations to permit people and the planet to survive and begin to shape a viable future. This is a necessary condition for participants' diverse other goals.

Is this confluence a movement, or is it just a collection of separate movements? Perhaps it can most aptly be described as a movement in the early stages of construction. Within each of its components there are some people who see themselves as part of a global, multi-issue movement and others who do not. Those who do are often networked with their counterparts in other movements and other countries. Their numbers are increasing rapidly and they are playing a growing role within their movements and organizations. They are developing a shared vision. And they see themselves as constructing a common movement. It is this emerging movement that we refer to as globalization from below.

Globalization from below is certainly a movement with contradictions. Its participants have many conflicting interests. It includes many groups that previously defined themselves in part via negative reference to each other. It includes both rigidly institutionalized and wildly unstructured elements.

Globalization from below is developing in ways that help it cope with this diversity. It has embraced diversity as one of its central values, and asserts that cooperation need not presuppose uniformity. Its structure tends to be a network of networks, facilitating cooperation without demanding organizational centralization.

Older orientations toward charitable "us helping them" on the one hand, and narrow self-interest on the other, are still present; but there is also a new recognition of common interests in the face of globalization. Solidarity based on mutuality and common interest increasingly forms the basis for the relationships among different parts of the movement.

The movement is generally multi-issue, and even when participants focus on particular issues, they reflect a broader perspective. As Howard Zinn wrote of the Seattle WTO protests,

> In one crucial way it was a turning point in the history of movements of the recent decades—a departure from the single-issue focus of the Seabrook occupation of 1977, the nuclear-freeze gathering in Central Park in 1982, the great Washington events of the Million-Man March, [and] the Stand for Children [march].[8]

Globalization from below has now established itself as a global opposition, representing the interests of people and the environment worldwide. It has demonstrated that, even when governments around the world are dominated by corporate interests, the world's people can act to pursue their common interests.

Globalization from below grew both out of previous movements and out of their breakdown. There is much to be learned from the historical heritage of centuries of struggle to restrain or replace capitalism, and today's activists often draw on past values and practices in shaping their own. But it would be a mistake to simply treat this new movement as an extension of those that went before—or to attach it to their remnants.[9]

Globalization in all its facets presents new problems that the old movements failed to address. That is part of why they declined so radically. It also presents new opportunities that will be lost if the new wine is simply poured back into the old bottles. Besides, the historic break provides an invaluable opportunity to escape the dead hand of the past and to reground the movement to restrain global capital in the actual needs and conditions of people today.[10]

Globalization from below is now a permanent feature of the globalization epoch. Even if its current expressions were to fail, the movement would rise again, because it is rooted in a deep social reality: the need to control the forces of global capital. . . .

The Power of Social Movements (and Its Secret)

The supporters of globalization from above control most of the world's governments. They control the global corporations and most of the world's wealth. They have a grip on the minds of people all over the world. It seems inconceivable that they can be effectively challenged.

Yet social movements have overcome equal or even greater concentrations of wealth and power in the past. Colonized peoples from North America to India, and Africa to Vietnam, have thrown out imperial powers with many times their wealth and firepower. The abolitionist movement eliminated slavery in most of the world and the civil rights movement eliminated legal segregation in the United States. In recent decades, mass movements have brought down powerful dictatorships from Poland to the

Philippines. A coordinated domestic and global movement abolished South African apartheid. To understand how social movements are able to overcome what seem to be overwhelming forces, we need to take a deeper look at the processes underlying such successes.

How Social Movements Arise

Normally, most people follow life strategies based on adapting to the power relations of their world, not on trying to change them. They do so for a varying mix of reasons, including

- ▾ Belief that existing relations are good and right.
- ▾ Belief that changing them is impossible.
- ▾ Fear that changing them would lead to something worse.
- ▾ An ability to meet their own needs and aspirations within existing power relations.
- ▾ Belief that existing power relations can and will change for the better.
- ▾ Identification with the dominant groups or with a larger whole—for example, a religion or nation.
- ▾ Fear of sanctions for violation of social rules or the will of the powerful.[11]

Most institutions and societies have elaborate systems for assuring sufficient consent or acquiescence to allow their key institutions to function. These means of maintaining a preponderance of power—often referred to as "hegemeny"—range from education to media, and from elections to violent repression.[12]

Over time, problems with existing social relationships may accumulate, initiating a process of change. These problems usually affect particular social groups—for example, particular communities, nations, classes, racial, ethnic and gender groups, religious and political groupings, and the like. The process may start with some people internally questioning or rejecting some aspects of the status quo. It becomes a social process as people discover that others are having similar experiences, identifying the same problems, asking the same questions, and being tempted to make the same rejections. Then people begin to identify with those others and to interact with them. This turns what might have been an individual and isolating process into a social one.[13]

Seeing that other people share similar experiences, perceptions, and feelings opens a new set of possibilities. Perhaps collectively we can act in ways that have impacts isolated individuals could never dream of having alone. And if we feel this way, perhaps others do, too.

This group formation process constructs new solidarities. Once a consciousness of the need for solidarity develops, it becomes impossible to say whether participants' motives are altruistic or selfish, because the interest of the individual and the collective interest are no longer in conflict; they are perceived as one.[14]

This process occurs not only in individuals, but also in groups, organizations, and constituencies. Thus form social movements.[15]

Why Social Movements Can Be Powerful

The fact that people develop common aspirations doesn't mean that they can realize them. Why are social movements able to change society? The power of existing social relations is based on the active cooperation of some people and the consent and or acquiescence of others. It is the activity of people— going to work, paying taxes, buying products, obeying government officials, staying off private property—that continually re-creates the power of the powerful.

Bertolt Brecht dramatized this truth in his poem "German War Primer":

> General, your tank is a strong vehicle.
> It breaks down a forest and crushes a hundred people.
> But it has one fault: it needs a driver.[16]

This dependence gives people a potential power over society—but one that can be realized only if they are prepared to reverse their acquiescence.[17] The old American labor song "Solidarity Forever" captures the tie between the rejection of acquiescence and the development of collective power:

> They have taken untold millions
> that they never toiled to earn
> But without our brain and muscle
> not a single wheel can turn.
> We can break their haughty power,
> gain our freedom when we learn
> That the union makes us strong.[18]

Social movements can be understood as the collective withdrawal of consent to established institutions.[19] The movement against globalization from above can be understood as the withdrawal of consent from such globalization.

Ideally, democracy provides institutionalized means for all to participate equally in shaping social outcomes. But in the rather common situation in which most people have little effective power over established institutions, even those that claim to be democratic, people can still exercise power through the withdrawal of consent. Indeed, it is a central means through which democratization can be imposed.

Withdrawal of consent can take many forms, such as strikes, boycotts, and civil disobedience. Gene Sharp's *The Methods of Nonviolent Action* lists no fewer than 198 such methods, and no doubt a few have been invented since it was written.[20] Specific social relations create particular forms of consent and its withdrawal. For example, WTO trade rules prohibit city and state selective purchasing laws like the Massachusetts ban on purchases from companies that invest in Burma—making such laws a form of withdrawal of consent from the WTO, in effect an act of governmental civil disobedience.[21] (Several foreign governments threatened to bring charges against the Massachusetts Burma law in the WTO before it was declared unconstitutional by the U.S. Supreme Court in June 2000.)

The World Bank depends on raising funds in the bond market, so critics of the World Bank have organized a campaign against purchase of World Bank bonds, modeled on the successful campaign against investment in apartheid South Africa. Concerted refusal of impoverished debtor countries to continue paying on their debts—for example, through a so-called debtors' cartel—would constitute a powerful form of withdrawal of consent from today's global debt bondage.

Just the threat of withdrawal of consent can be an exercise of power. Ruling groups can be forced to make concessions if the alternative is the undermining of their ultimate power sources.[22] The movement for globalization from below has demonstrated that power repeatedly. For example, the World Bank ended funding for India's Narmada Dam when 900 organizations in 37 countries pledged a campaign to defund the Bank unless it canceled its support. And Monsanto found that global concern about genetically engineered organisms so threatened its interests that it agreed to accept the Cartagena Protocol to the Convention on Biological Diversity, allowing GEOs to be regulated.[23]

At any given time, there is a balance of power among social actors.[24] Except in extreme situations like slavery or military occupation, unequal power is reflected not in an unlimited power of one actor over the other. Rather, it is embedded in the set of rules and practices that are mutually accepted, even though they benefit one far more than the other. When the balance of power is changed, subordinate groups can force change in these rules and practices.

The power of the people is a secret that is repeatedly forgotten, to be rediscovered every time a new social movement arises. The ultimate source of power is not the command of those at the top, but the acquiescence of those at the bottom. This reality is hidden behind the machinations of politicians, business leaders, and politics as usual. The latent power of the people is forgotten both because those in power have every reason to suppress its knowledge and because it seems to conflict with everyday experience in normal times. But when the people rediscover it, power structures tremble.

Linking the Nooks and Crannies

New movements often first appear in small, scattered pockets among those who are unprotected, discriminated against, or less subject to the mechanisms of hegemony. They reflect the specific experiences and traditions of the social groups among which they arise. In periods of rapid social change, such movements are likely to develop in many such milieus and to appear very different from each other as a result. In the case of globalization from below, for example, we have seen significant mobilizations by French chefs concerned about preservation of local food traditions, Indian farmers concerned about corporate control of seeds, and American university students concerned about school clothing made in foreign sweatshops. Even if in theory people ultimately have power through withdrawal of consent, how can such disparate groups ever form a force that can exercise that power?

One common model for social change is the formation of a political party that aims to take over the state, whether by reform or by revolution. This model has always been problematic, since it implied the perpetuation of centralized social control, albeit control exercised in the interest of a different group.[25] However, it faces further difficulties in the era of globalization.

Reform and revolution depend on solving problems by means of state power, however acquired. But globalization has outflanked governments at local and national levels, leaving them largely at the mercy of global markets, corporations, and institutions. Dozens of parties in every part of the world have come to power with pledges to overcome the negative effects of globalization, only to submit in a matter of months to the doctrines of neoliberalism and the "discipline of the market." Nor is there a global state to be taken over.[26]

Fortunately, taking state power is far from the only or even the most important means of large-scale social change. An alternative pathway is examined by historical sociologist Michael Mann in *The Sources of Social Power*.[27] The characteristic way that new solutions to social problems emerge, Mann maintains, is neither through revolution nor reform. Rather, new solutions develop in what he calls "interstitial locations"—nooks and crannies in and around the dominant institutions. Those who were initially marginal then link together in ways that allow them to outflank those institutions and force a reorganization of the status quo.

At certain points, people see existing power institutions as blocking goals that could be attained by cooperation that transcends existing institutions. So people develop new networks that outrun them. Such movements create subversive "invisible connections" across state boundaries and the established channels between them (Mann 1986:522). These interstitial networks translate human goals into organizational means.

If such networks link groups with disparate traditions and experiences, they require the construction of what are variously referred to as shared worldviews, paradigms, visions, frames, or ideologies. Such belief systems unite seemingly disparate human beings by claiming that they have meaningful common properties:

> An ideology will emerge as a powerful, autonomous movement when it can put together in a single explanation and organization a number of aspects of existence that have hitherto been marginal, interstitial to the dominant institutions of power. (Mann 1986:21)

The emerging belief system becomes a guide for efforts to transform the world. It defines common values and norms, providing the basis for a common program. When a network draws together people and practices from many formerly marginal social spaces and makes it possible for them to act together, it establishes an independent source of power. Ultimately, new power networks may become strong enough to reorganize the dominant institutional configuration.

The rise of labor and socialist movements in the 19th century and of feminist and environmental movements in the 20th century in many ways fits this model of emergence at the margins, linking, and outflanking.[28] So, ironically, does the emergence of globalization from above. . . .

Self-organization in marginal locations and changing the rules of dominant institutions are intimately linked. The rising European bourgeoisie both created their own market institutions and fought to restructure the political system in ways that would allow markets to develop more freely. Labor movements both organized unions and forced governments to protect labor rights, which in turn made it easier to organize unions.

Over time, movements are likely to receive at least partial support from two other sources. Some institutions, often ones that represent similar constituencies and that themselves originated in earlier social movements but have become rigidified, develop a role of at least ambiguous support. And sectors of the dominant elites support reforms and encourage social movements for a variety of reasons, including the need to gain support for system-reforming initiatives and a desire to win popular backing in intra-elite conflicts.

Social movements may lack the obvious paraphernalia of power: armies, wealth, palaces, temples, and bureaucracies. But by linking from the nooks and crannies, developing a common vision and program, and withdrawing their consent from existing institutions, they can impose norms on states, classes, armies, and other power actors.

The Lilliput Strategy

How do these broad principles of social movement–based change apply to globalization from below? In fact, they describe the very means by which it is being constructed. We call this the Lilliput Strategy, after the tiny Lilliputians in Jonathan Swift's fable *Gulliver's Travels* who captured Gulliver, many times their size, by tying him up with hundreds of threads.

In response to globalization from above, movements are emerging all over the world in social locations that are marginal to the dominant power centers. These are linking up by means of networks that cut across national borders. They are beginning to develop a sense of solidarity, a common belief system, and a common program. They are utilizing these networks to impose new norms on corporations, governments, and international institutions.

The movement for globalization from below is, in fact, becoming an independent power. It was able, for example, to halt negotiations for the Multilateral Agreement on Investment (MAI), to block the proposed "Millennium Round" of the WTO, and to force the adoption of a treaty on genetically engineered products. Its basic strategy is to say to power holders, "Unless you accede to operating within these norms, you will face threats (from us and from others) that will block your objectives and undermine your power."

The threat to established institutions may be specific and targeted withdrawals of support. For example, student anti-sweatshop protestors have made clear that their campuses will be subject to sit-ins and other forms of disruption until their universities agree to ban the use of school logos on products made in sweatshops. Or, to take a very different example, in the midst of the Battle of Seattle, President Bill Clinton, fearing loss of electoral support from the labor movement, endorsed the use of sanctions to enforce international labor rights.[29] The threat may, alternatively, be a more general social breakdown, often expressed as fear of "social unrest."[30]

The slogan "fix it or nix it," which the movement has often applied to the WTO, IMF, and World Bank, embodies such a threat. It implies that the movement (and the people of the world) will block the globalization process unless power holders conform to appropriate global norms. This process constitutes neither revolution nor conventional "within the system" and "by the rules" reform. Rather, it constitutes a shift in the balance of power.

As the movement grows in power, it can force the modification of institutions or the creation of new ones that embody and/or impose these norms as enforceable rules.[31] For example, the treaties on climate change and on genetic engineering force new practices on corporations, governments, and international institutions that implement norms propounded by the environmental and consumer movements. Student anti-sweatshop activists force their universities to join an organization that bans university logos on products made under conditions that violate specified rules regarding labor conditions. The world criminal court, endorsed by many countries under pressure of the global human rights movement, but resisted by the United States, would enforce norms articulated at the Nuremberg war crimes tribunal.

These new rules in turn create growing space for people to address problems that the previous power configuration made insoluble. Global protection of human rights makes it easier for people to organize locally to address social and environmental problems. Global restrictions on fossil fuels that cause global warming, such as a carbon tax, would make it easier for people to develop renewable energy sources locally.

While the media have focused on global extravaganzas like the Battle of Seattle, these are only the tip of the globalization from below iceberg. The Lilliput Strategy primarily involves the building of solidarity among people at the grassroots. For example:

▼ Under heavy pressure from the World Bank, the Bolivian government sold off the public water system of its third largest city, Cochabamba, to a subsidiary of the San Francisco–based Bechtel Corporation, which promptly doubled the price of water for people's homes. Early in 2000, the people of Cochabamba rebelled, shutting down the city with general strikes and blockades. The government declared a state of siege and a young protester was shot and killed. Word spread all over the world from the remote Bolivian highlands via the Internet. Hundreds of e-mail messages poured into Bechtel from all over the world demanding that it leave Cochabamba. In the midst of local and global protests, the Bolivian government, which had said that Bechtel must not leave, suddenly reversed itself and signed an accord accepting every demand of the protestors. Meanwhile, a local protest leader was smuggled out of hiding to Washington, D.C., where he addressed the April 16 rally against the IMF and World Bank.[32]

▼ When the Japanese-owned Bridgestone/Firestone (B/F) demanded 12-hour shifts and a 30 percent wage cut for new workers in its American factories, workers struck. B/F fired them all and replaced them with 2,300 strikebreakers. American workers appealed to Bridgestone/Firestone workers around the world for help. Unions around the world organized "Days of Outrage" protests against B/F. In Argentina, a two-hour "general assembly" of all workers at the gates of the B/F plant halted production while 2,000 workers heard American B/F workers describe the company's conduct. In Brazil, Bridgestone workers staged one-hour work stoppages, then "worked like turtles"—the Brazilian phrase for a slow-down. Unions in Belgium, France, Italy, and Spain met with local Bridgestone managements to demand a settlement. U.S. B/F workers went to Japan and met with Japanese unions, many of whom called for the immediate reinstatement of U.S. workers. Five hundred Japanese unionists marched through the streets of Tokyo, supporting B/F workers from the U.S. In the wake of the worldwide campaign, Bridgestone/Firestone unexpectedly agreed to rehire its locked out American workers.[33]

▼ In April 2000, AIDS activists, unions, and religious groups were poised to begin a lawsuit and picketing campaign denouncing the Pfizer Corporation as an AIDS profiteer for the high price it charges for AIDS drugs in Africa. Pfizer suddenly announced that it would supply the drug fluconazole, used to control AIDS side effects, for free to any South African with AIDS who could not afford it. A few weeks later, U.S., British, Swiss, and German drug companies announced that they would cut prices on the principal AIDS drugs, anti-retrovirals, by 85 to 90 percent. Meanwhile, when South Africa tried to pass a law allowing it to ignore drug patents in health emergencies, the Clinton administration lobbied hard against it and put South Africa on a watch list that is the first step toward trade sanctions. But then, according to the *New York Times*, the Philadelphia branch of Act Up, the gay advocacy group, decided

> to take South Africa's cause and start heckling Vice President Al Gore, who was in the midst of his primary campaign for the presidency. The banners saying that Mr. Gore was letting Africans die to please American pharmaceutical companies left his campaign chagrined. After media and campaign staff looked into the matter, the administration did an about face and accepted African governments' circumvention of AIDS drug patents.[34] . . .

How Movements Go Wrong

It is nowhere guaranteed that any particular social movement will succeed in using its potential power to realize the hopes and aspirations of its participants or to solve the problems that moved them to action in the first place. There are plenty of pitfalls along the way.

Schism: From Catholic and Protestant Christians to Sunni and Shiite Muslims, from Communists and socialists to separatists and integrationists, social movements are notorious for their tendency to split. They can often turn into warring factions whose antagonisms are focused primarily on each other. Splits often occur over concrete issues but then perpetuate themselves even when the original issues are no longer salient.

Repression: Movements can be eliminated, or at least driven underground, by legal and extra-legal repression.

Fading out: The concerns that originally drew people into a movement may recede due to changed conditions. An economic upswing or the opening of new lands has often quieted farmer movements. Or constant frustration may simply lead to discouragement and withdrawal.

Leadership domination: In a mild form, the movement evolves into an institution in which initiative and control pass to a bureaucratized leadership and staff, while the members dutifully pay their dues and act only when told to do so by their leaders. In a more virulent form, leaders establish a tyrannical control over members.[35]

Isolation: Movements may become so focused on their own internal life that they are increasingly irrelevant to the experience and concerns of those who are not already members. Such a movement may last a long time as a sect but be largely irrelevant to anyone except its own members.

Cooptation: A movement may gain substantial benefits for its constituency, its members, or its leaders, but do so in such a way that it ceases to be an independent force and instead comes under the control of sections of the elite.

Leadership sell-out: Less subtly, leaders can simply be bought with money, perks, flattery, opportunities for career advancement, or other enticements.

Sectarian disruption: Movements often fall prey to sects that attempt either to capture or to destroy them. Such sects may emerge from within the movement itself or may invade it from without. . . .

To succeed, globalization from below must avoid these pitfalls; promote movement formation in diverse social locations; establish effective linkages; develop a sense of solidarity, a common worldview, and a shared program; and utilize the power that lies hidden in the withdrawal of consent.

ENDNOTES

[1] "Das Kapital Revisited," *Financial Times*, August 31, 1998, p. 14.

[2] As far as we have been able to determine, the terms "globalization from above" and "globalization from below" were coined by Richard Falk and first appeared in print in Jeremy Brecher, John Brown Childs, and Jill Cutler (eds.), *Global Visions: Beyond the New World Order* (Boston: South End Press, 1993). . . . For movements in the early 1990s responding specifically to economic globalization, see Chapter 5 of Jeremy Brecher and Tim Costello, *Global Village or Global Pillage: Economic Reconstruction from the Bottom Up (Cambridge, MA: South End Press, 1994).* See also Richard Falk, *Predatory Globalization: A Critique* (Malden, MA: Blackwell, 1999), especially Chapter 8.

[3] Jeremy Brecher, "The Opening Shot of the Second Ecological Revolution," *Chicago Tribune*, August 16, 1988.

[4] "Poor Countries Draft Proposal on Poverty," *New York Times*, April 12, 2000. The G-77 currently has 133 member nations.

[5] Mark Ritchie, quoted in *Global Village or Global Pillage*, p. 97.

[6] According to labor journalist Kim Moody, "In the last couple of years there have been at least two dozen political general strikes in Europe, Latin America, Asia, and North America. This phenomenon began in 1994. There have been more political mass strikes in the last two or three years than at any time in the 20th century." Kim Moody, "Workers in a Lean World," a speech to the Brecht Forum in New York, New York, November 14, 1997. Broadcast on Alternative Radio (tape and transcript available from http://www.alternativeradio.org).

[7] Vandana Shiva, "The Historic Significance of Seattle," December 10, 1999, MAI-NOT Listserve, Public Citizen Global Trade Watch.

[8] Howard Zinn, "A Flash of the Possible," *The Progressive* 61:1 (January 2000). Available online at http://secure.progressive.org/zinn00l.htm.

[9] For a portrayal of current struggles as a continuation of historical working-class struggles, see Boris Kargarlitsky's recent trilogy *Recasting Marxism, Including New Realism, New Barbarism: Socialist Theory in the Era of Globalization* (London: Pluto Press, 1999), *The Twilight of Globalization: Property, State and Capitalism* (London: Pluto Press, 1999), and *The Return of Radicalism: Reshaping the Left Institutions* (London: Pluto Press, 2000).

[10] It is often pointed out that globalization is creating a capitalism that in significant ways resembles the capitalism that preceded World War I. It could also be observed that globalization from below in some ways resembles the international socialist movement before World War I. Globalization provides an opportunity to reevaluate some of the key features of the post-1914 left, such as its relationship to nationalism and the nation-state; the schisms between social democracy, Communism, and anarchism; and the development of organizational forms adapted to the effort to secure state power via reform or revolution.

[11] For fuller discussion of this subject, with extensive references, see Gene Sharp, *The Politics of Nonviolent Action: Part One: Power and Struggle* (Boston: Porter Sargent, 1973), "Why Do Men Obey?" pp. 16–24.

[12] The analysis of "hegemony" is generally associated with the work of Antonio Gramsci. See Antonio Gramsci, *The Modern Prince and Other Writings* (New York: International Publishers, 1959).

[13] E. P. Thompson describes this process of group formation for the specific case of class: "Class happens when some men, as a result of common experiences (inherited or shared), feel and articulate the identity of their interests as between themselves, and as against other men whose interests are different from (and usually opposed to) theirs." E. P. Thompson, *The Making of the English Working Class* (New York: Vintage, 1996), p. 9.

[14] Solidarity can take a number of forms. . . . See Peter Waterman, *Globalization, Social Movements, and the New Internationalisms* (London: Mansell, 1999). The process of constructing solidarity is illustrated with numerous labor history examples in Jeremy Brecher, *Strike! Revised and Updated Edition* (Cambridge: South End Press Classics, 1999) and analyzed on p. 284.

[15] This highly schematic formulation is based primarily on the study and observation of social movements, combined with theories drawn from many sources, for example, Jean-Paul Sartre, *Critique de la Raison Dialectique [Critique of Dialectical Reason]* (Paris: Gallimard, 1960), and Francesco Alberoni, *Movement and Institution* (New York: Columbia University Press, 1984).

[16] Bertolt Brecht, *Deutsche Kriegsfibel* ["German War Primer"], in *Gesammilte Werke* (Berlin: Suhrkamp, 1967), vol. 4, p. 638. The translation by Martin Esslin originally appeared in Jeremy Brecher and Tim Costello, *Common Sense for Hard Times* (New York: Two Continents/Institute for Policy Studies, 1976), p. 240.

[17] In the "acquiescent state," people's relation to each other is mediated via the market or common relations to authority. The process of movement creation and group formation to some degree replaces these with direct relations. Sartre analyzes this as the transition from the "series" to the "group" (*Critique de la Raison Dialectique*). Op cit.

[18] Written by Ralph Chaplin.

[19] Gene Sharp, who analyzes hundreds of historical examples of nonviolent action in the three volumes of his *Politics of Nonviolent Action* (Boston: Porter Sargent, 1973), concludes that the base of nonviolent action is "the belief that the exercise of power depends on the consent of the ruled who, by withdrawing that consent, can control and even destroy the power of their opponent" (*Part One: Power and Struggle*, p. 4). Sharp emphasizes that nonviolent struggle requires indirect strategies that undermine the opponent strength rather than annihilate the opponent. . . .

[20] Sharp, *Part Two: The Methods of Nonviolent Action* (Boston: Porter Sargent, 1973). See also *Part Three: The Dynamics of Nonviolent Action* (Boston: Porter Sargent, 1973).

[21] In constitutional terms, this would be described as a form of nullification.

[22] Of course, an irrational ruler may not be deterred from acting to repress a nonviolent movement by the fact that doing so may undermine his or her own power. But given an irrational ruler, violence is no more guaranteed to be an effective deterrent than nonviolence.

[23] "United States negotiators gave in to a demand from Europe and most of the rest of the world for what is known as the 'precautionary principle'. . . . Even Greenpeace, an avowed critic of the technology, issued a statement calling the protocol a 'historic step towards protecting the environment and consumers from the dangers of genetic engineering.'" *St. Louis Post-Dispatch*, January 30, 2000. . . . "This protocol is a campaign victory in that it acknowledges that GMOs [genetically modified organisms] are not the same as other crops and products and they require that special measures be taken," said Miriam Mayer of the Malaysia-based Third World Network. . . . The U.S. State Department declined to specify whether the biotechnology company Monsanto had been consulted over the past few days. A State Department source said: "We understand there is no major problem so far as the company is concerned." *The Observer,* January 30, 2000.

[24] As Gramsci put it, "The fact of hegemony undoubtedly presupposes that the interests and strivings of the groups over which the hegemony will be exercised are taken account of, that a certain balance of compromises be formed, that, in other words, the leading group makes some sacrifices" *(Modern Prince,* p. 154).

[25] This critique has long been elaborated in the anarchist and libertarian socialist traditions, and has more recently been developed by the New Left of the 1960s, the Green movement, and the Mexican Zapatistas.

[26] . . . This is not to argue that states are no longer of significance, or that political parties and contests for government power have not played an important role in the past and might not today or in the future. Rather, it is to deny that social movements can or should be reduced to such a strategy.

[27] Michael Mann, *The Sources of Social Power: Volume 1* (Cambridge: Cambridge University Press, 1986), chapter 1, "Societies as Organized Power Networks."

[28] Over time, the labor and socialist movements of course became increasingly focused on national governments and increasingly contained within national frameworks.

[29] This threat, strongly resented by many third world governments, contributed to the deadlocking of the WTO negotiations.

[30] For example, provoking such general social unrest was an articulated objective of many U.S. opponents of the Vietnam War after other means of halting it had failed and public opinion had swung against it without visible effect on policy.

[31] For a similar perspective on how social movements make change through imposing norms, with recent examples and proposals for the future, see Richard Falk, "Humane Governance for the World: Reviving the Quest," in Jan Nederveen Pieterse (ed.), *Global Futures: Shaping Globalization* (United Kingdom: Zed Books, 2000), pp. 23ff. See also *On Humane Governance, Toward a New Global Politics* (University Park: Pennsylvania State University Press, 1995).

[32] "Bolivian Water Plan Dropped after Protests Turn into Melees," *New York Times*, April 11, 2000. For further information on the Cochabamba water struggle, prepared by Jim Schultz, a Cochabamba resident who played a major role in mobilizing global support for the struggle, visit http://www.americas.org.

[33] *ICEM Info 3* (1996) and *ICEM Info 4* (1996); see also Labor Notes, October 1994, July 1996, and December 1996.

[34] Donald G. McNeil, Jr., "As Devastating Epidemics Increase, Nations Take on Drug Companies," *New York Times,* July 9, 2000, and *Toronto Star,* May 12, 2000.

[35] Two classic explorations of this dynamic are Robert Michels, *Political Parties: A Sociological Study of the Oligarchical Tendencies of Modern Democracy* (Glencoe, IL: Free Press, 1949), and Sidney Webb and Beatrice Webb, *The History of Trade Unionism,* 2d. ed. (London: Longmans, Green, 1902). . . .

REFERENCE

Mann, Michael. 1986. *The Sources of Social Power, Volume 1.* Cambridge: Cambridge University Press.

60

WHAT CAN WE DO?
Becoming Part of the Solution

ALLAN G. JOHNSON

This last reading is by Allan G. Johnson, a sociologist at the Hartford College for Women of the University of Hartford. Johnson studies the dynamics of privilege, power, and oppression. He is especially interested in understanding how and why systems of privilege are created and maintained in society. In this selection, adapted from *Privilege, Power, and Difference* (2001), Johnson outlines how every individual can be involved in creating solutions to social problems caused by social inequality. He suggests we learn new strategies to effectively become aware of how each of us is privileged and contributes to the oppression of others based on that privilege. With that awareness comes the ability to better affect social change.

The challenge we face is to change patterns of exclusion, rejection, privilege, harassment, discrimination, and violence that are everywhere in this society and have existed for hundreds (or, in the case of gender, thousands) of years. We have to begin by thinking about the trouble and the challenge in new and more productive ways. . . . Here is a summary of the tools we have to start with.

Large numbers of people have sat on the sidelines and seen themselves as neither part of the problem nor the solution. Beyond this shared trait, however, they are far from homogeneous. Everyone is aware of the whites, hetrosexuals, and men who intentionally act out in oppressive ways. But there is less attention to the millions of people who know inequities exist and want to be part of the solution. Their silence and invisibility allow the trouble to continue. Removing what silences them and stands in their way can tap an enormous potential of energy for change.

The problem of privilege and oppression is deep and wide, and to work with it we have to be able to see it clearly so that we can talk about it in useful ways. To do that, we have to reclaim some difficult language that names what's going on, language that has been so misused and maligned that it generates more heat than light. We can't just stop using words like *racism*, *sexism*, and *privilege*, however, because these are tools that focus our awareness on the problem and all the forms it takes. Once we can see and talk about what's going on, we can analyze how it works as a system. We can identify points of leverage where change can begin.

Reclaiming the language takes us directly to the core reality that the problem is privilege and the power that maintains it. Privilege exists when one group has something that is systematically denied to others not because of who they are or what they've done or not done, but because of the social category they belong to.

Privilege is a feature of social systems, not individuals. People have or don't have privilege depending on the system they're in and the social categories other people put them in. To say, then, that I have race privilege says less about me personally than it does about the society we all live in and how it is organized to assign privilege on the basis of a socially defined set of racial categories that change historically and often overlap. The challenge facing me as an individual has more to do with how I participate in society as a recipient of race privilege and how those choices oppose or support the system itself.

In dealing with the problem of privilege, we have to get used to being surrounded by paradox. Very often those who have privilege don't know it, for example, which is a key aspect of privilege. Also paradoxical is the fact that privilege doesn't necessarily lead to a "good life," which can prompt people in privileged groups to deny resentfully that they even have it. But privilege doesn't equate with being happy. It involves having what others don't have and the struggle to hang on to it at their expense, neither of which is a recipe for joy, personal fulfillment, or spiritual contentment. . . .

To be an effective part of the solution, we have to realize that privilege and oppression are not a thing of the past. It's happening right now. It isn't just a collection of wounds inflicted long ago that now need to be healed. The wounding goes on as I write these words and as you read them, and unless people work to change the system that promotes it, personal healing by itself cannot be the answer. Healing wounds is no more a solution to the oppression that causes the wounding than military hospitals are a solution to war. Healing is a necessary process, but it isn't enough. . . .

Since privilege is rooted primarily in systems—such as families, schools, and workplaces—change isn't simply a matter of changing people. People, of course, will have to change in order for systems to change, but the most important point is that changing people isn't enough. The solution also has to include entire systems, such as capitalism, whose paths of least resistance shape how we feel, think, and behave as individuals, how we see ourselves and one another.

As they work for change, it's easy for members of privileged groups to lose sight of the reality of privilege and its consequences and the truth that the trouble around privilege is their trouble as much as anyone else's. This happens in large part because systems of privilege provide endless ways of seeing and thinking about the world that make privilege invisible. These include denying and minimizing the trouble; blaming the victim; calling the trouble something else; assuming everyone prefers things the way they are;

mistaking intentions with consequences; attributing the trouble to others and not their own participation in social systems that produce it; and balancing the trouble with troubles of their own. The more aware people can be of how these behaviors limit their effectiveness, the more they can contribute to change both in themselves and the systems where they work and live.

With these tools in hand, we can begin to think about how to make ourselves part of the solution to the problem of privilege and oppression. . . .

STUBBORN OUNCES
(To One Who Doubts the Worth of Doing Anything
if You Can't Do Everything)

> You say the little efforts that I make
> will do no good; they will never prevail
> to tip the hovering scale
> where Justice hangs in balance.
> > > > I don't think
> I ever thought they would.
> But I am prejudiced beyond debate
> In favor of my right to choose which side
> shall feel the stubborn ounces of my weight.[1]

Stubborn Ounces: What Can We Do?

There are no easy answers to the question of what can we do about the problem of privilege. There is no twelve-step program, no neat set of instructions. Most important, there is no way around or over it: the only way out is through it. We won't end oppression by pretending it isn't there or that we don't have to deal with it.

Some people complain that those who work for social change are being "divisive" when they draw attention to gender or race or social class and the oppressive systems organized around them. But when members of dominant groups mark differences by excluding or discriminating against subordinate groups and treating them as "other," they aren't accused of being divisive. Usually it's only when someone calls attention to how differences are used for oppressive purposes that the charge of divisiveness comes up.

In a sense, it *is* divisive to say that oppression and privilege exist, but only insofar as it points to divisions that already exist and to the perception that the status quo is normal and unremarkable. Oppression promotes the worst kind of divisiveness because it cuts us off from one another and, by silencing us about the truth, cuts us off from ourselves as well. Not only must we participate in oppression by living in an oppressive society, we also must act as though oppression didn't exist, denying the reality of our own experience and its consequences for people's lives, including our own.

What does it mean to go out by going through? What can we do that will make a difference? I don't have the answers, but I do have some suggestions.

Acknowledge That the Trouble Exists

A key to the continued existence of every oppressive system is unawareness, because oppression contradicts so many basic human values that it invariably arouses opposition when people know about it. The Soviet Union and its East European satellites, for example, were riddled with contradictions so widely known among their people that the oppressive regimes fell apart with an ease and speed that astonished the world. An awareness of oppression compels people to speak out, to break the silence that continued oppression depends on.

This is why most oppressive cultures mask the reality of oppression by denying its existence, trivializing it, calling it something else, blaming it on those most victimized by it, or diverting attention from it. Instead of treating oppression as a serious problem, we go to war or get embroiled in controversial "issues" such as capital gains tax cuts or "family values" or immigrant workers. There would be far more active opposition to racism, for example, if white people lived with an ongoing awareness of how it actually affects the everyday lives of those it oppresses as "not white." As we have seen, however, the vast majority of white people *don't* do this.

It's one thing to become aware and quite another to stay that way. The greatest challenge when we first become aware of a critical perspective on the world is simply to hang on to it. Every system's paths of least resistance invariably lead away from critical awareness of how the system works. In some ways, it's harder and more important to pay attention to systems of privilege than it is to people's behavior and the paths of least resistance that shape it. . . .

Pay Attention

Understanding how privilege and oppression operate and how you participate in them is where the work for change begins. It's easy to have opinions, but it takes work to know what you're talking about. The simplest way to begin is by reading, and making reading about privilege part of your life. Unless you have the luxury of a personal teacher, you can't understand this issue without reading, just as you'd need to read about a foreign country before you traveled there for the first time, or about a car before you tried to work under the hood. Many people assume they already know what they need to know because it's part of everyday life. But they're usually wrong. Just as the last thing a fish would discover is water, the last thing people discover is society itself and something as pervasive as the dynamics of privilege.

We also have to be open to the idea that what we think we know is, if not wrong, so deeply shaped by systems of privilege that it misses most of the truth. This is why activists talk with one another and spend time reading one another's writing: seeing things clearly is tricky. This is also why people who are critical of the status quo are so often self-critical as well: they know how complex and elusive the truth really is and what a challenge it is to work toward it. People working for change are often accused of being orthodox and rigid, but in practice they are typically among the most self-critical people around. . . .

Little Risks: Do Something

The more you pay attention to privilege and oppression, the more you'll see opportunities to do something about them. You don't have to mount an expedition to find those opportunities; they're all over the place, beginning in yourself. As I became aware of how male privilege encourages me to control conversations, for example, I also realized how easily men dominate group meetings by controlling the agenda and interrupting, without women's objecting to it. This pattern is especially striking in groups that are mostly female but in which most of the talking nonetheless comes from a few men. I would find myself sitting in meetings and suddenly the preponderance of male voices would jump out at me, an unmistakable sign of male privilege, in full bloom.

As I've seen what's going on, I've had to decide what to do about this little path of least resistance and my relation to it that leads me to follow it so readily. With some effort, I've tried out new ways of listening more and talking less. At times my methods have felt contrived and artificial, such as telling myself to shut up for a while or even counting slowly to ten (or more) to give others a chance to step into the space afforded by silence. With time and practice, new paths have become easier to follow and I spend less time monitoring myself. But awareness is never automatic or permanent, for paths of least resistance will be there to choose or not as long as male privilege exists.

As you become more aware, questions will arise about what goes on at work, in the media, in families, in communities, in religious institutions, in government, on the street, and at school—in short, just about everywhere. The questions don't come all at once (for which we can be grateful), although they sometimes come in a rush that can feel overwhelming. If you remind yourself that it isn't up to you to do it all, however, you can see plenty of situations in which you can make a difference, sometimes in surprisingly simple ways. Consider the following possibilities:

Make noise, be seen. Stand up, volunteer, speak out, write letters, sign petitions, show up. Every oppressive system feeds on silence. Don't collude in silence. Breaking the silence is especially important for dominant groups, because it undermines the assumption of solidarity that dominance depends on. If this feels too risky, you can practice being aware of how silence reflects your investment in solidarity with other dominant-group members. This can be a place to begin working on how you participate in making privilege and oppression happen: "Today I said nothing, colluded in silence, and this is how I benefited from it. Maybe tomorrow I can try something different."

Find little ways to withdraw support from paths of least resistance and people's choices to follow them, starting with yourself. It can be as simple as not laughing at a racist or heterosexist joke or saying you don't think it's funny, or writing a letter to your senator or representative or the editor of your newspaper, objecting to an instance of sexism in the media. When my local newspaper ran an article whose headline referred to sexual harassment as "earthy behavior," for example, I wrote a letter pointing out that harassment isn't "earthy."

The key to withdrawing support is to interrupt the flow of business as usual. We can subvert the assumption that we're all going along with the status quo by simply not going along. When we do this, we stop the flow, if only for a moment, but in that moment other people can notice and start to think and question. It's a perfect time to suggest the possibility of alternatives, such as humor that isn't at someone else's expense, or of ways to think about discrimination, harassment, and violence that do justice to the reality of what's going on and how it affects people. . . .

Dare to make people feel uncomfortable, beginning with yourself. At the next local school board meeting, for example, you can ask why principals and other administrators are almost always white and male (unless your system is an exception that proves the rule), while the teachers they supervise are mostly women and people of color. Or look at the names and mascots used by local sports teams and see if they exploit the heritage and identity of Native Americans; if that's the case, ask principals and coaches and owners about it.[2] Consider asking similar kinds of questions about privilege and difference in your place of worship, workplace, and local government. . . .

Some will say it isn't "nice" to make people uncomfortable, but oppressive systems do a lot more than make people feel uncomfortable, and there isn't anything "nice" about allowing that to continue unchallenged. Besides, discomfort is an unavoidable part of any meaningful process of education. We can't grow without being willing to challenge our assumptions and take ourselves to the edge of our competencies, where we're bound to feel uncomfortable. If we can't tolerate ambiguity, uncertainty, and discomfort, then we'll never get beneath superficial appearances or learn or change anything of much value, including ourselves.

And if history is any guide, discomfort—to put it mildly—is also an unavoidable part of changing systems of privilege. As sociologist William Gamson noted in his study of social movements, "the meek don't make it."[3] To succeed, movements must be willing to disrupt business as usual and make those in power as uncomfortable as possible. Women didn't win the right to vote, for example, by reasoning with men and showing them the merits of their position. To even get men's attention, they had to take to the streets in large numbers at considerable risk to themselves. At the very least they had to be willing to suffer ridicule and ostracism, but it often got worse than that. In England, for example, suffragettes were jailed and, when they went on hunger strikes, were force fed through tubes run down their throats. The modern women's movement has had to depend no less on the willingness of women to put themselves on the line in order to make men so uncomfortable that they've had to pay attention and, eventually, to act.

It has been no different with the civil rights movement. Under the leadership of men like Martin Luther King, the movement was dedicated to the principle of nonviolence. As with the movement for women's suffrage, however, they could get white people's attention only through mass demonstrations and marches. Whites typically responded with violence and intimidation.[4] As Douglas McAdam showed in his study of that period, the Federal government intervened and enacted civil rights legislation only when white violence against civil rights demonstrators became so extreme that the government was compelled to act.[5] . . .

Openly choose and model alternative paths. As we identify paths of least resistance, we can identify alternatives and then follow them openly so that other people can see what we're doing. Paths of least resistance become more visible when people choose alternatives, just as rules become more visible when someone breaks them. Modeling new paths creates tension in a system, which moves toward resolution. We don't have to convince anyone of anything. As Gandhi put it, the work begins with us as we try to be the change we want to see happen in the world. If you think this has no effect, watch how people react to the slightest departures from established paths and how much effort they expend trying to ignore or explain away or challenge those who choose alternative paths.

Actively promote change in how systems are organized around privilege. The possibilities here are almost endless, because social life is complicated and privilege is everywhere. You can, for example,

Speak out for equality in the workplace.

Promote diversity awareness and training.

Support equal pay and promotion.

Oppose the devaluing of women and people of color and the work they do, from dead-end jobs to glass ceilings.

Support the well-being of mothers and children and defend women's right to control their bodies and their lives.

Object to the punitive dismantling of welfare and attempts to limit women's access to reproductive health services.

Speak out against violence and harassment wherever they occur, whether at home, at work, or on the street.

Support government and private services for women who are victimized by male violence. Volunteer at the local rape crisis center or battered-women's shelter. Join and support groups that intervene with and counsel violent men.

Call for and support clear and effective anti-harassment policies in workplaces, unions, schools, professional associations, religious institutions, and political parties, as well as public spaces such as parks, sidewalks, and malls.

Object to theaters and video stores that carry violent pornography. This doesn't require a debate about censorship—just the exercise of freedom of

speech to articulate pornography's role in the oppression of women and to express how its opponents feel about it.

Ask questions about how work, education, religion, and family are shaped by core values and principles that support race privilege, gender privilege, and other forms of privilege. You might accept women's entry into combat branches of the military or the upper reaches of corporate power as "progress," for example. But you could also raise questions about what happens to people and societies when political and economic institutions are organized around control, domination, "power over," and, by extension, competition and the use of violence. Is it progress to allow selected women to share control with men over oppressive systems?

Support the right of women and men to love whomever they choose. Raise awareness of homophobia and heterosexism. For example, ask school officials and teachers about what's happening to gay and lesbian students in local schools. If they don't know, ask them to find out, since it's a safe bet these students are being harassed, suppressed, and oppressed by others at one of the most vulnerable stages of life. When sexual orientation is discussed, whether in the media or among friends, raise questions about its relation to patriarchy. Remember that it isn't necessary to have answers to questions in order to ask them.

Pay attention to how different forms of oppression interact with one another. There has been a great deal of struggle within women's movements, for example, about the relationship between gender oppression and other forms of oppression, especially those based on race and social class. White middle- and upper-middle-class feminists have been criticized for pursuing their own agenda to the detriment of women who aren't privileged by class or race. Raising concerns about glass ceilings that keep women out of top corporate and professional positions, for example, does little to help working- or lower-class women. There has also been debate over whether some forms of oppression are more important to attack first or produce more oppressive consequences than other forms.

One way out of this conflict is to realize that patriarchy isn't problematic just because it emphasizes *male* dominance, but because it promotes dominance and control as ends in themselves. In that sense, all forms of oppression draw support from common roots, and whatever we do that calls attention to those roots undermines *all* forms of oppression. If working against patriarchy is seen simply as enabling some women to get a bigger piece of the pie, then some women probably will "succeed" at the expense of others who are disadvantaged by race, class, ethnicity, and other characteristics. One could make the same argument about movements for racial justice: If it just means enabling well-placed blacks to get ahead, then it won't end racial oppression for the vast majority. But if we identify the core problem as *any* society organized around principles of domination and privilege, then changing *that* requires us to pay attention to all the forms of oppression those principles promote. Whether we begin with race or gender or ethnicity or class or the capitalist system, if we name the problem correctly we'll wind up going in the same general direction.

Work with other people. This is one of the most important principles of participating in social change. From expanding consciousness to taking risks, being in the company of people who support what you're trying to do makes all the difference in the world. For starters, you can read and talk about books and issues and just plain hang out with other people who want to understand and do something about privilege and oppression. The roots of the modern women's movement were in consciousness-raising groups where women did little more than talk about themselves and try to figure out how they were shaped by a patriarchal society. It may not have looked like much at the time, but it laid the foundation for huge social change. . . .

It is especially important to form alliances across difference—for men to ally with women, whites with people of color, heterosexuals with lesbians and gay men. What does this mean? As Paul Kivel [author of *Uprooting Racism* (1996)] argues, one of the keys to being a good ally is a willingness to listen—for whites to listen to people of color, for example—and to give credence to what people say about their own experience.[6] This isn't easy to do, of course, since whites, heterosexuals, and men may not like what they hear about their privilege from those who are most damaged by it. It is difficult to hear anger about privilege and oppression and not take it personally, but that is what allies have to be willing to do. It's also difficult for members of privileged groups to realize how mistrusted they are by subordinate groups and to not take that personally as well. . . .

Don't keep it to yourself. A corollary of looking for company is not to restrict your focus to the tight little circle of your own life. It isn't enough to work out private solutions to social problems like oppression and keep them to yourself. It isn't enough to clean up your own act and then walk away, to find ways to avoid the worst consequences of oppression and privilege at home and inside yourself and think that's taking responsibility. Privilege and oppression aren't a personal problem that can be solved through personal solutions. At some point, taking responsibility means acting in a larger context, even if that means letting just one other person know what you're doing. It makes sense to start with yourself, but it's equally important not to end with yourself.

A good way to convert personal change into something larger is to join an organization dedicated to changing the systems that produce privilege and oppression. Most college and university campuses, for example, have student organizations that focus on issues of gender, race, and sexual orientation. There are also national organizations working for change, often through local and statewide branches. Consider, for example, the National Organization for Women (NOW), the National Association for the Advancement of Colored People (NAACP), the National Conference for Community and Justice (formerly the National Conference of Christians and Jews), the National Gay and Lesbian Task Force, the Southern Poverty Law Center, the

National Organization of Men Against Sexism, the Feminist Majority, the National Abortion Rights Action League, the Southern Christian Leadership Conference, and the National Urban League. . . .

Don't let other people set the standard for you. Start where you are and work from there. Make lists of all the things you could actually imagine *doing*—from reading another book about inequality to suggesting policy changes at work to protesting against capitalism to raising questions about who cleans the bathroom at home—and rank them from the most risky to the least. Start with the least risky and set reasonable goals ("What small risk for change will I take *today*?"). As you get more experienced at taking risks, you can move up your list. You can commit yourself to whatever the next steps are for you, the tolerable risks, the contributions that offer some way—however small it might seem—to help balance the scales. As long as you do something, it counts.

In the end, taking responsibility doesn't have to involve guilt and blame, letting someone off the hook, or being on the hook yourself. It simply means acknowledging an obligation to make a contribution to finding a way out of the trouble we're all in, and to find constructive ways to act on that obligation. You don't have to do anything dramatic or earth-shaking to help change happen. As powerful as oppressive systems are, they cannot stand the strain of lots of people doing something about it, beginning with the simplest act of naming the system out loud.

What's in It for Me?

It's risky to promote change. You risk being seen as odd, being excluded or punished for asking questions and setting examples that make people uncomfortable or threaten privilege. We've all adapted in one way or another to life in a society organized around competition, privilege, and difference. Paths of least resistance may perpetuate oppression, but they also have the advantage of being familiar and predictable and therefore can seem preferable to untried alternatives and the unknown. There are inner risks—of feeling lost, confused, and scared—along with outer risks of being rejected or worse. Obviously, then, working for change isn't a path of least resistance, which raises the question of why anyone should follow Gandhi's advice and do it anyway.

It's an easier question to answer for subordinate groups than it is for dominants, which helps explain why the former have done most of the work for change. Those on the losing end have much to gain by striving to undo the system that oppresses them, not only for themselves in the short run, but for the sake of future generations. The answer comes less easily for those in dominant groups, but they don't have to look very far to see that they have much to gain—especially in the long run—that more than balances what they stand to lose.[7]

When whites, heterosexuals, and men join the movement against privilege and oppression, they can begin to undo the costs of participating in an oppressive system as the dominant group. Few men, for example, realize how much they deaden themselves in order to support (if only by their silence) a system that privileges them at women's expense, that values maleness by devaluing femaleness, that makes women invisible in order to make men appear larger than life. Most men don't realize the impoverishment to their emotional and spiritual lives, the price they pay in personal authenticity and integrity, how they compromise their humanity, how they limit the connections they can have with other people, how they distort their sexuality to live up to core patriarchal values of control. They don't realize how much they have to live a lie in order to interact on a daily basis with their mothers, wives, sisters, daughters, women friends and co-workers—all members of the group male privilege oppresses. So the first thing men can do is claim a sense of aliveness and realness that doesn't depend on superiority and control, and a connection to themselves and the world—which they may not even realize was missing until they begin to feel its return.

In similar ways, most whites don't realize how much energy it takes to defend against their continuing vulnerability to guilt and blame and to avoid seeing how much trouble the world is in and the central role they play in it. When whites do nothing about racial privilege and oppression, they put themselves on the defensive, in the no-safe-place-to-hide position of every dominator class. But when white people make a commitment to participate in change, to be more than part of the problem, they free themselves to live in the world without feeling open to guilt simply for being white.

In perhaps more subtle ways, homophobia and heterosexism take a toll on heterosexuals. The persecution of lesbians, for example, is a powerful weapon of sexism that encourages women to silence themselves, to disavow feminism, and tolerate male privilege for fear that if they speak out, they'll be labeled as lesbians and ostracized.[8] In similar ways, the fear of being called gay is enough to make men conform to masculine stereotypes that don't reflect who they really are and to go along with an oppressive gender system they may not believe in. And because homosexuals all come from families, parents and siblings may also pay a huge emotional price for the effects of prejudice, discrimination, and persecution directed at their loved ones.

With greater authenticity and aliveness comes the opportunity to go beyond the state of arrested development, the perpetual adolescence that privilege promotes in dominant groups, to move away from unhealthy dependencies on the subordination and undervalued labor of others and toward healthy interdependencies free of oppressive cultural baggage.

When people join together to end any form of oppression, they act with courage to take responsibility to do the right thing, and this empowers them in ways that can extend to every corner of their lives. Whenever we act with courage, a halo effect makes that same courage available to us in other times and places. When we step into our legacies and take responsibility for them, we can see how easily fear keeps us from acting for change in ourselves and in the systems we participate in. As we do the work, we build a growing store of experience to draw on in figuring out how to act with courage again and again. As our inner and outer lives become less bound by the strictures of fear and compromise, we can claim a deeper meaning for our lives than we've known before.

The human capacity to choose how to participate in the world empowers all of us to pass along something different from what's been passed to us. With each strand of the knot of privilege that we help to work loose and unravel, we don't act simply for ourselves, we join a process of creative resistance to oppression that's been unfolding for thousands of years. We become part of the long tradition of people who have dared to make a difference—to look at things as they are, to imagine something better, and to plant seeds of change in themselves, in others, and in the world.

ENDNOTES

[1] Bonaro W. Overstreet, *Hands Laid Upon the Wind* (New York: Norton, 1955), p. 15.

[2] For more on this, see Ward Churchill, "Crimes against Humanity," *Z Magazine* 6 (March 1993): 43–47. Reprinted in Margaret L. Andersen and Patricia Hill Collins (eds.), *Race, Class, and Gender*, 3d ed. (Belmont, CA: Wadsworth, 1998), pp. 413–20.

[3] William A. Gamson, "Violence and Political Power: The Meek Don't Make It," *Psychology Today* 8 (July 1974): 35–41.

[4] For more on this, see the excellent PBS documentary of the civil rights movement, *Eyes on the Prize.*

[5] Doug McAdam, *Political Process and the Development of Black Insurgency 1930–1970* (Chicago: University of Chicago Press, 1982).

[6] See Kivel, *Uprooting Racism: How White People Can Work for Racial Justice* (Philadelphia: New Society Publishers, 1996), part 3, "Being Allies."

[7] A lot of what follows came out of a brainstorming session with my friend and colleague Jane Tuohy as we worked out the design for a gender workshop.

[8] See Suzanne Pharr, *Homophobia: A Weapon of Sexism* (Inverness, CA: Chardon Press, 1988).